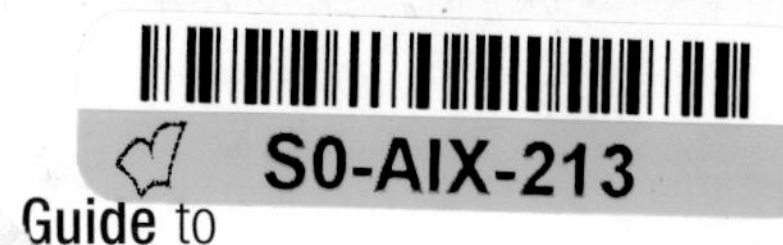

T Guide to

Japan

written and researched by

Simon Richmond and Jan Dodd

with additional contributions from

Sophie Branscombe, Robert Goss, Jean Snow and Martin Zatko

www.roughguides.com

LABI
AKIHABARA
パソコン館
5F
企業・法人
専用窓口
4F
パソコン
サプライ
3F
デスクトップ
パソコン
2F
ノート
パソコン
1F
モバイル
パソコン
B1F
デジタル
カメラ
LABI
AKIHABAR
パソコン館
現金値引して安心価格保証 + さらにポイント進呈
TVゲーム・ソフト&ハードetc.
トキワムセン

Contents

Regional cuisines colour section following p.216

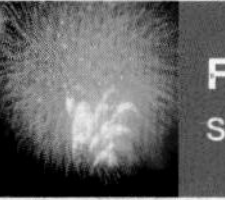

Festival fun colour section following p.536

Manga & anime colour section following p.680

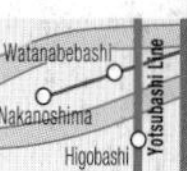

Colour maps following p.872

◀◀ Floating *torii* at Itsukushima-jinja, Miyajima ◀ Commuters in Akihabara, Tokyo

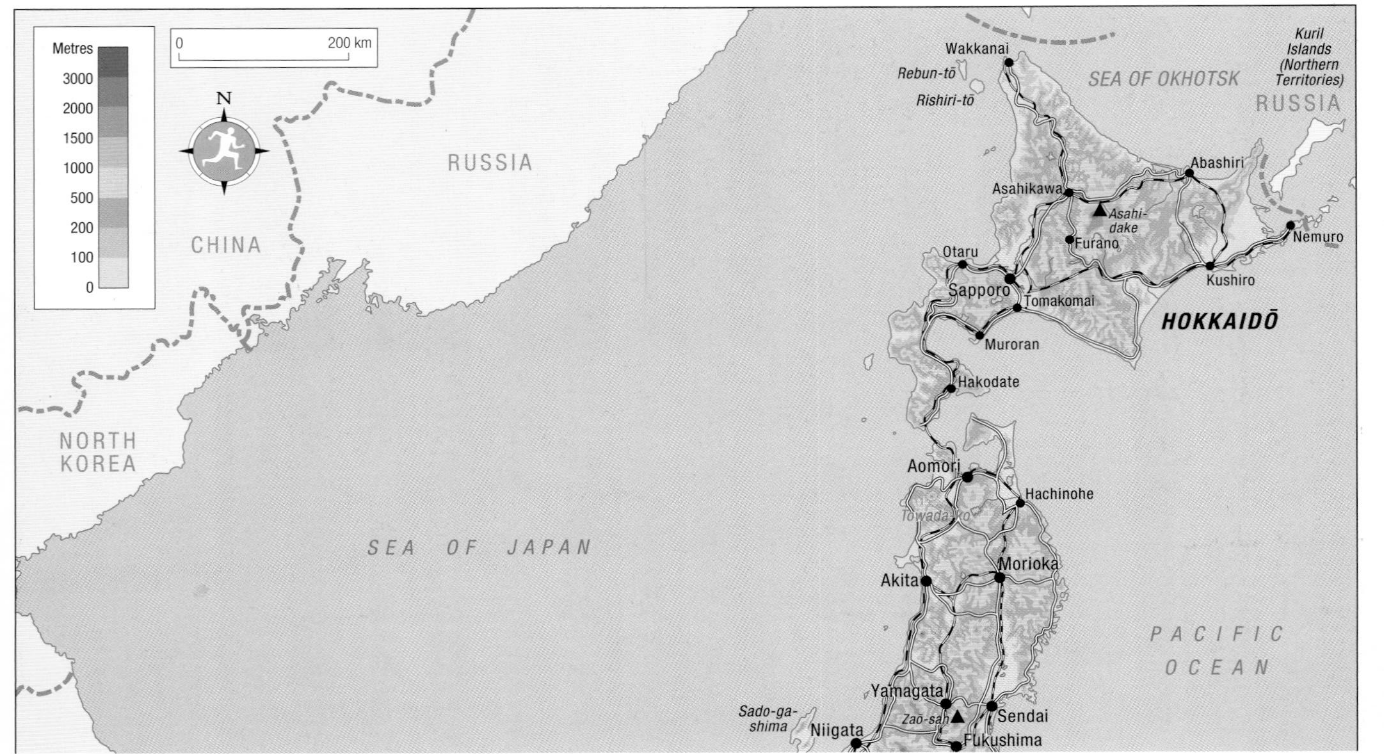
Metres
3000
2000
1500
1000
500
200
100
0
0
200 km
N
RUSSIA
CHINA
NORTH KOREA
SEA OF JAPAN
SEA OF OKHOTSK
Kuril Islands (Northern Territories)
RUSSIA
PACIFIC OCEAN
HOKKAIDŌ
Wakkanai
Rebun-tō
Rishiri-tō
Abashiri
Asahikawa
Asahi-dake
Furano
Nemuro
Kushiro
Otaru
Sapporo
Tomakomai
Muroran
Hakodate
Aomori
Hachinohe
Towada-ko
Morioka
Akita
Yamagata
Zaō-san
Sendai
Sado-ga-shima
Niigata
Fukushima

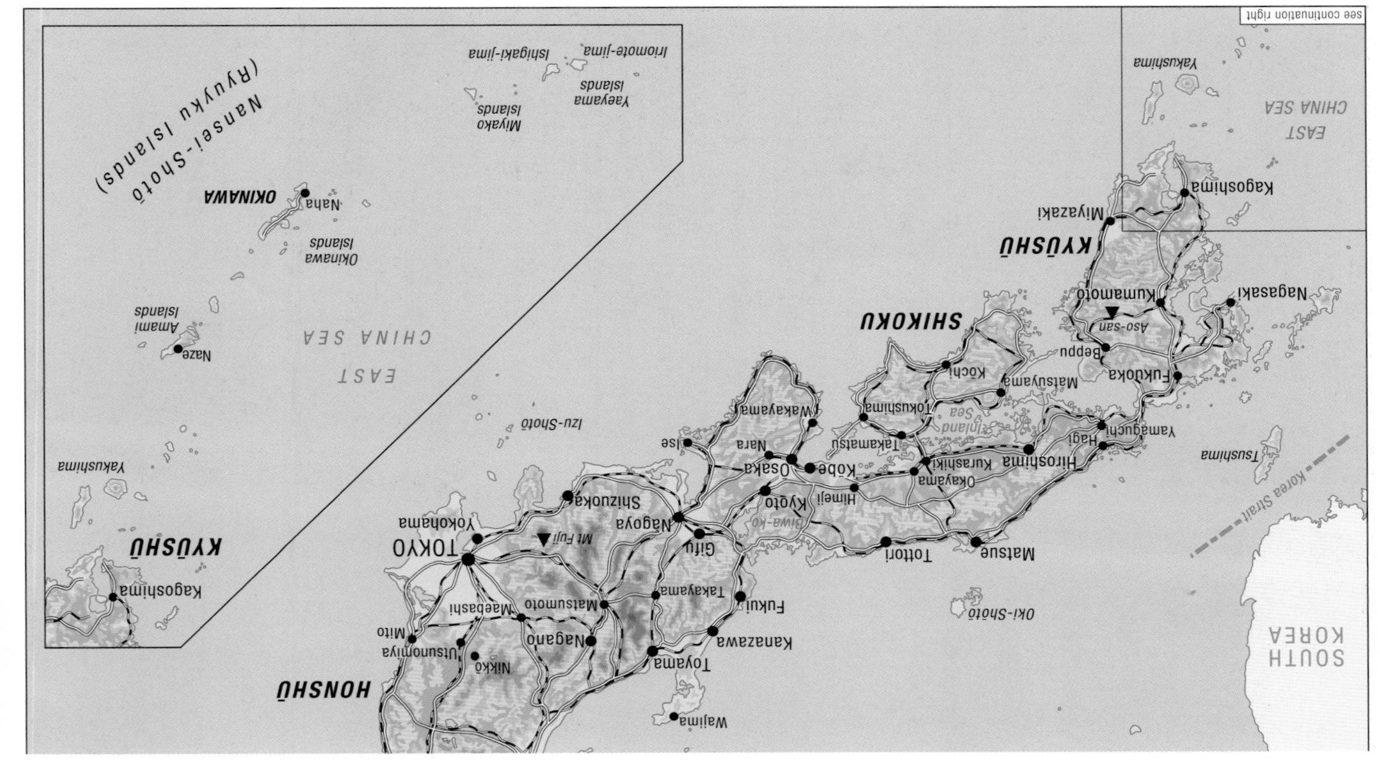
SOUTH KOREA
Korea Strait
Tsushima
Oki-Shōtō
HONSHŪ
Wajima
Kanazawa
Toyama
Fukui
Takayama
Gifu
Nagano
Matsumoto
Nikkō
Utsunomiya
Mito
Maebashi
TOKYO
Yokohama
Mt Fuji
Shizuoka
Nagoya
Ise
Kyoto
Biwa-ko
Osaka
Nara
Wakayama
Kōbe
Himeji
Tottori
Matsue
Okayama
Kurashiki
Hiroshima
Hagi
Yamaguchi
Takamatsu
Tokushima
Inland Sea
SHIKOKU
Kōchi
Matsuyama
KYŪSHŪ
Fukuoka
Beppu
Aso-san
Kumamoto
Nagasaki
Miyazaki
Kagoshima
Yakushima
EAST CHINA SEA
Izu-Shotō
EAST CHINA SEA
KYŪSHŪ
Kagoshima
Yakushima
Naze
Amami Islands
Okinawa Islands
OKINAWA
Naha
Nansei-Shotō
(Ryukyu Islands)
Miyako Islands
Ishigaki-jima
Yaeyama Islands
Iriomote-jima
see continuation right

Introduction to Japan

Anyone who's ever eaten sushi, read manga, or sipped sake may feel they know something about this slinky archipelago of some 6800 volcanic islands. And yet, from the moment of arrival in Japan, it's almost as if you've touched down on another planet. Prepare to be pleasantly disorientated as you negotiate this fascinating land where ancient gods, customs and craftsmanship are mixed up with cutting edge modern technology, futuristic fashions and up-to-the-second style.

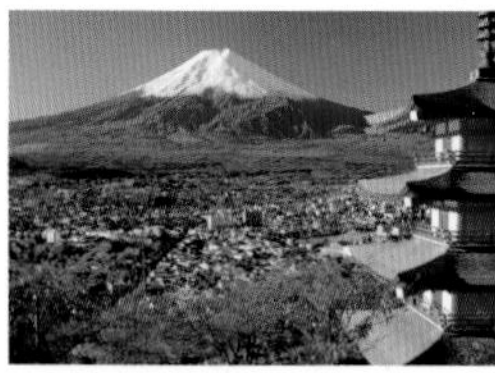

High-speed trains whisk you from one end of the country to another with awe-inspiring punctuality. In the suburbs of a sprawling metropolis, you can catch sight of a farmer tending his paddy field, then turn the corner and find yourself next to a neon-festooned (video) games parlour. One day you could be picking through fashions in a boutique designed by an award-winning architect, the next relaxing in an outdoor hot-spring pool, watching cherry blossom or snowflakes fall, depending on the season.

Few other countries have, in the space of a few generations, experienced so much or made such an impact. Industrialized at lightning speed in the late nineteenth century, Japan shed its feudal trappings to become the most powerful and outwardly aggressive country in Asia in a matter of decades. After defeat in World War II, it transformed itself from atom-bomb victim to economic giant, the envy of the world. Having weathered a decade-long recession from the mid-1990s, Japan is now relishing its "soft power" as the world's pre-eminent purveyor of pop culture, with the visual mediums of anime and manga leading the way.

In the **cities** you'll first be struck by the mass of people. These hyperactive metropolises are the place to catch the latest trend, the hippest fashions and must-have gadgets before they hit the rest of the world. It's not all about modernity, however: Tokyo, Kyoto, Ōsaka and Kanazawa, for example, also provide the best opportunities to view traditional performance arts, such as kabuki and nō plays, as well as a wealth of Japanese visual arts in major museums. **Outside the cities** there's a vast range of travel options, from the UNESCO World Heritage-listed Shiretoko National Park in Hokkaidō to the balmy subtropical islands of Okinawa, and you'll seldom have

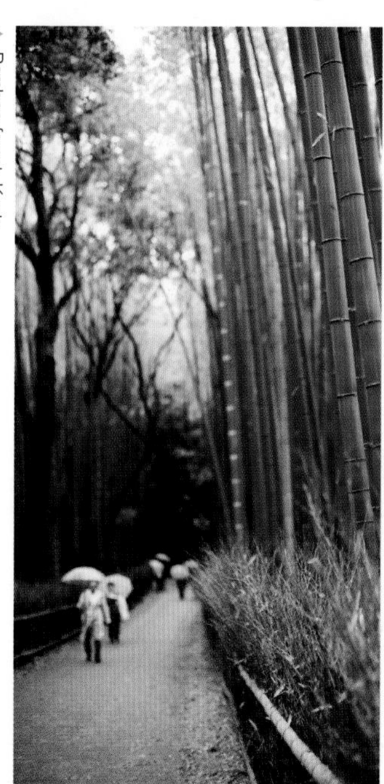

▶ Bamboo forest, Kyoto

Fact file

• Japan is made up of around 6800 **islands**, the main five being (in descending order of size) Honshū, Hokkaidō, Kyūshū, Shikoku and Okinawa. Travelling from Sōya Misaki, Japan's northernmost point, to Hateruma-jima, the southernmost island in Okinawa, you'll cover over 3000km.

• Despite many Japanese telling you what a small country they live in, Japan is in fact twice the size of the UK. This sense of smallness lays in the fact that much of the country is covered by densely forested mountains; some 127.5 million people are thus squished into the flat quarter of Japan's land surface, making the southern coastal plain of Honshū from Tokyo down to Ōsaka one of the most densely populated areas in the world.

• Among this population Japanese predominate, making this one of the world's most **ethnically homogeneous** societies. The most significant non-Japanese group living in the country are Koreans, numbering around 900,000. Indigenous people such as the Ainu account for no more than 100,000 people. Japan is also a rapidly ageing society, with a very low birth rate and long life expectancy.

• Though not the **economic powerhouse** it once was, Japan's economy is the third largest in the world after that of the US and China. Manufacture of electronics, machine tools and automobiles continue to be the main industries. Price deflation has been persistent for the past two decades as the nation has staggered from one economic crisis to another.

• **Emperor Akihito** is the head of state. It's a ceremonial position but one that is still greatly respected.

to go far to catch sight of a lofty castle, ancient temple or shrine, or locals celebrating at a colourful street festival.

In common with all developed countries, Japan is not a cheap place to travel in or to, but there's no reason why it should be wildly expensive either. Some of the most atmospheric and traditionally Japanese places to stay and eat are often those that are the best value. There's been significant price-cutting in some areas in recent years, particularly airline tickets, which now rival the famed bargain rail passes as a means to get to far-flung corners of the country.

It's not all perfect, however. The Japanese are experts at focusing on detail (the exquisite wrapping of gifts and the tantalizing presentation of food are just two examples) but often miss the broader picture. Rampant development and sometimes appalling pollution are difficult to square with a country also renowned for cleanliness and appreciation of nature. Part of the problem is that natural cataclysms, such as earthquakes and typhoons, regularly hit Japan,

A more eco-friendly Japan – again

In his fascinating book *Just Enough: Lessons in Living Green from Traditional Japan* (ⓦwww.justenoughjapan.com), Azby Brown documents how, in the mid-nineteenth century, the country was "conservation-minded, waste-free, well-housed and well-fed, and economically robust".

Today Japan's government is rediscovering the virtues of such sustainable living. At the United Nations Summit on Climate Change in 2009, Japan announced its medium-term goal of **reducing greenhouse gas emissions** by 25 percent from the 1990 level by 2020. Then, in April 2010, Tokyo launched a mandatory scheme to cut carbon dioxide emissions from large office buildings and factories.

Citizens are also striving to live life in a healthier, more organic and sustainable way. There's **Mottanai** (ⓦmottainai.info/english/who.html), a project to promote a self-sustaining society through reducing waste, reusing finite resources and recycling, while the town of Ogawa, in Saitama prefecture north of Tokyo, has become a model of organic agriculture: food waste is recycled into liquid fertilizer and methane gas and organic food products such as sake, soy sauce and dried noodles have been developed.

The blog **Tokyo Green Space** (ⓦtokyogreenspace.wordpress.com) highlights bright eco ideas practiced in the capital. Some of these, such as the **Ginza Bee Project** (ⓦgin-pachi.jp), where 300,000 bees make honey from nectar collected in nearby parks, and the minuscule **Ginza Farm** (ⓦwww.iknowledge.jp/ginza_farm), recall what life was like two centuries ago when Tokyo was called Edo.

For an insight into Japan's forward-thinking sustainable technologies and ideas, there's the annual **Eco-Products fair** (ⓦeco-pro.com/eco2009/english/index.html). It's also worth visiting **Greenz.jp** (ⓦgreenz.jp/en) to find out about Green Drinks, a monthly get-together of eco-aware people in Tokyo, or dropping by **Ecozzeria** (ⓦwww.ecozzeria.jp), an environmental strategy centre in Tokyo's Shin-Marunouchi Building.

▲ Shinkansen streaking through downtown Tokyo

so few people expect things to last for long anyway. There's no denying either the pernicious impact of mass tourism, with ranks of gift shops, ugly hotels and crowds often ruining potentially idyllic spots.

And yet, time and again, Japan redeems itself with unexpectedly beautiful landscapes, charmingly courteous people, and its tangible sense of history and cherished traditions. Few will be able to resist the chance to get to grips with its mysterious yet tantalising culture that blurs the traditional boundaries between East and West – Japan is unique, neither wholly one nor the other.

Where to go

Two weeks is the minimum needed to skim the surface of what Japan can offer. The capital, Tokyo, and the former imperial city and thriving cultural centre of Kyoto, will be top of most visitors' itineraries, and deservedly so, but you could avoid the cities entirely and head to the mountains or smaller islands to discover an alternative side of the country, away from the most heavily beaten tourist tracks.

It would be easy enough to spend two weeks just in **Tokyo**. The metropolis is home to some of the world's most ambitious architecture, stylish shops and internationally celebrated restaurants and bars – as well as glimpses of traditional Japan at scores of temples, shrines and imperial gardens. Consider

Loving the machine

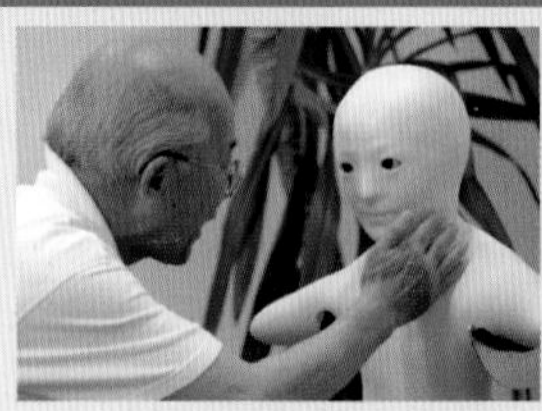

The thirtieth anniversary in 2009 of Mobile Suit Gundam, a hit anime franchise, served as the opportunity to construct an 18m tall, 35-tonne replica of one of its key robot characters on Tokyo's Odaiba. During the two months RX-78-2 Gundam was on display it drew 4.15 million visitors. Crowds are also flocking to see another giant anime robot statue – Tetsujin 28 – built to commemorate Kōbe's recovery from its 1995 earthquake (see p.517). And it's difficult to turn a corner without seeing an image of Tezuka Osamu's Astro Boy (see p.805), perhaps the most famous anime robot of all; his latest role is the official ambassador for Japan's bid for the 2022 World Cup.

Japan's love of humanistic robots goes back several centuries to the Edo era when much smaller *karakuri ningyo* (mechanized automata and puppets) were crafted to serve tea, or to decorate the portable shrines used in festivals: you can still see such dolls in action today on the floats used in festivals in Takayama (p.363) and Furukawa (p.368) among other places. These are the roots of a culture that continues to see robots as entertainment, life assistants and even friends. One robot called I-Fairy has officiated at a wedding while another, the robot seal Paro (Ⓦwww.parorobots.com) is being used for therapy in hospitals and elderly care homes.

This is just the tip of the coming robotic iceberg. As Timothy Hornyak points out in his fascinating book *Loving the Machine* (Ⓦwww.lovingthemachine.com), "more and more intelligent machines are expected to start working in Japanese society in areas such as healthcare as its population ages rapidly and its workforce shrinks."

also taking in a couple of the city's surrounding attractions, in particular the historic towns of **Nikkō**, home to the amazing Tōshō-gū shrine complex, and **Kamakura**, with its giant Buddha statue and tranquil woodland walks.

Northern Honshū sees surprisingly few overseas visitors, but its sleepy villages and relaxed cities deserve to be better known. The Golden Hall of **Hiraizumi** more than justifies the journey, and can be easily combined with the islet-sprinkled **Matsushima Bay** or rural **Tōno**. The region is also known for its vibrant **summer festivals**, notably those at Sendai, Aomori, Hirosaki and Akita, and for its sacred mountains, including **Dewa-sanzan**, home to a sect of ascetic mountain priests, and the eerie, remote wastelands of **Osore-zan**.

Further north, across the Tsugaru Straits, **Hokkaidō** is Japan's final frontier, with many national parks including the outstanding **Daisetsu-zan National Park**, offering excellent hiking trails over mountain peaks and through soaring rock gorges. The lovely far northern islands of **Rebun-tō** and **Rishiri-tō** are ideal summer escapes. Hokkaidō's most historic city is **Hakodate**, with its late nineteenth-century wooden houses and churches built by expat traders, while its modern capital, **Sapporo**, is home to the raging nightlife centre of Suskino and the original Sapporo Brewery. Winter is a fantastic time to visit and catch Sapporo's amazing Snow Festival and go skiing at some of Japan's top resorts including **Niseko**.

Skiing, mountaineering and soaking in hot springs are part of the culture of **Central Honshū**, an area dominated by the magnificent Japan Alps. Both the old castle town of **Matsumoto**, and **Nagano**, with its atmospheric temple of pilgrimage, Zenkō-ji, can be used as a starting point for exploring the region. Highlights include the tiny mountain resort of **Kamikōchi** and the immaculately preserved Edo-era villages of **Tsumago** and **Magome**, linked by a short hike along the remains of a 300-year-old stone-paved road. **Takayama** deservedly draws many visitors to its handsome streets lined with merchant houses and temples, built by generations of skilled carpenters. In the remote neighbouring valleys you'll find the rare thatched houses of **Ogimachi**, **Suganuma** and **Ainokura**, remnants of a fast-disappearing rural Japan.

On the Sea of Japan coast, the historic city of **Kanazawa** is home to Kenroku-en, one of Japan's best gardens, and the stunning 21st Century Museum of Contemporary Art, Kanazawa. **Nagoya**, on the heavily industrialized southern coast, is a more manageable city than Tokyo or Ōsaka, and has much to recommend it, including the fine Tokugawa Art Museum and many great places to eat. The efficient new airport nearby also makes the city a good alternative entry point. From Nagoya it's a short hop to the pretty castle towns of **Inuyama** and **Gifu**, which holds summer displays of the ancient skill of *ukai*, or cormorant fishing.

▲ Japanese macaques sleeping in an onsen, Nagano

▲ Passengers on the metro

South of the Japan Alps, the **Kansai** plains are scattered with ancient temples, shrines and the remnants of imperial cities. **Kyoto**, custodian of Japan's traditional culture, is home to its most refined cuisine, classy ryokan, glorious gardens, and magnificent temples and palaces. Nearby **Nara** is a more manageable size but no slouch when it comes to venerable monuments, notably the great bronze Buddha of Tōdai-ji and Hōryū-ji's unrivalled collection of early Japanese statuary. The surrounding region contains a number of still-thriving religious foundations, such as the highly atmospheric temples of **Hiei-zan** and **Kōya-san**, the revered Shinto shrine **Ise-jingū**, and the beautiful countryside pilgrimage routes of the UNESCO World Heritage-listed Kumano region.

Not all of Kansai is so rarefied, though. The slightly unconventional metropolis of **Ōsaka** has an easy-going atmosphere and boisterous nightlife, plus several interesting sights. Further west, the port of **Kōbe** offers a gentler cosmopolitan atmosphere, while **Himeji** is home to Japan's most fabulous castle, as well as some impressive modern gardens and buildings.

For obvious reasons **Hiroshima** is the most visited location in **Western Honshū**. On the way there, pause at **Okayama** to stroll around one of Japan's top three gardens, Kōraku-en, and the appealingly preserved Edo-era town of **Kurashiki**. The beauty of the Inland Sea, dotted with thousands of islands, is best appreciated from the idyllic fishing village of **Tomonoura**, the port of **Onomichi** and the relaxed islands of **Nao-shima**, **Ikuchi-jima** and **Miya-jima**.

Crossing to the San-in coast, the castle town of **Hagi** retains some handsome samurai houses and atmospheric temples, only surpassed by even more enchanting **Tsuwano**, further inland. One of Japan's most venerable shrines, **Izumo Taisha**, lies roughly midway along the coast, near the lake- and seaside city of **Matsue**, home to the region's only original castle.

Location for Japan's most famous pilgrimage, a walking tour around 88 Buddhist temples, **Shikoku** also offers dramatic scenery in the **Iya valley** and along its rugged coastline. Its largest city, Matsuyama, has an imperious castle and the splendidly ornate Dōgo Onsen Honkan – one of Japan's best hot springs. There's also the lovely garden Ritsurin-kōen in **Takamatsu** and the ancient Shinto shrine at **Kotohira**.

The southernmost of Japan's four main islands, **Kyūshū** is probably best known for **Nagasaki**, an attractive and cosmopolitan city that has overcome its terrible war-time history. Hikers and onsen enthusiasts should head up into the central highlands, where **Aso-san**'s smouldering peak dominates the world's largest volcanic crater, or to the more southerly meadows of **Ebino Kōgen**. So much hot water gushes out of the ground in **Beppu**, on the east coast, that it's known as Japan's hot-spring capital. **Fukuoka**, on the other hand, takes pride in its innovative modern architecture and an exceptionally lively entertainment district.

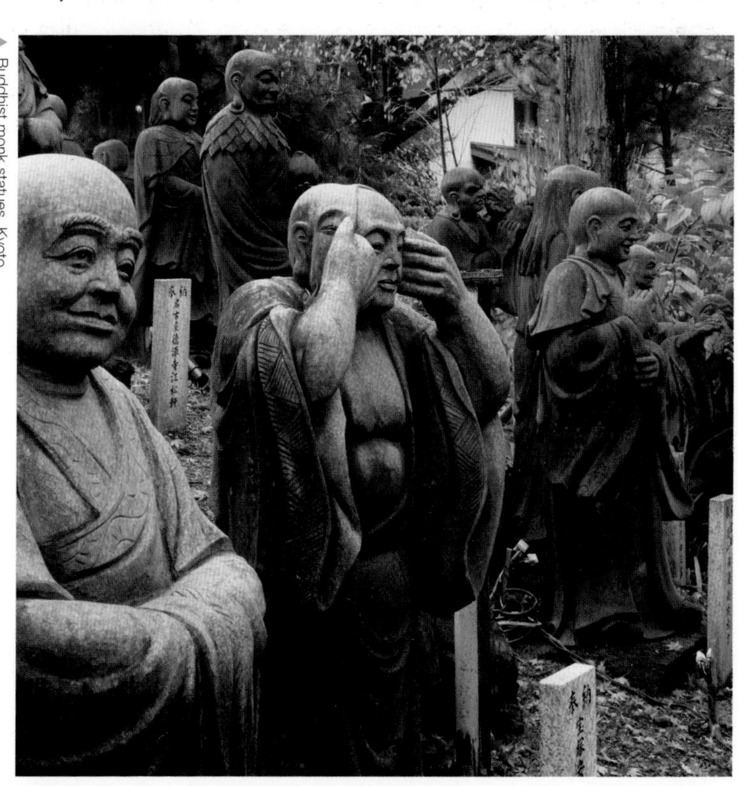

▲ Buddhist monk statues, Kyoto

Okinawa comprises more than a hundred islands stretching in a great arc from southern Kyūshū to within sight of Taiwan. An independent kingdom until the early seventeenth century, traces of the island's distinctive, separate culture still survive. The beautifully reconstructed former royal palace dominates the capital city, **Naha**, but the best of the region lies on its remoter islands. This is where you'll find Japan's most stunning white-sand beaches and its best diving, particularly around the subtropical islands of **Ishigaki** and **Iriomote**.

When to go

Average temperature and weather patterns vary enormously across Japan. The main influences on Honshū's climate are the mountains and surrounding warm seas, which bring plenty of rain and snow. **Winter** weather differs greatly, however, between the western Sea of Japan and the Pacific coasts, the former suffering cold winds and heavy snow while the latter tends towards dry, clear winter days. Regular heavy snowfalls in the mountains provide ideal conditions for skiers.

Despite frequent showers, **spring** is one of the most pleasant times to visit Japan, when the weather reports chart the steady progress of the cherry blossom from warm Kyūshū in March to colder Hokkaidō around May. A rainy season (*tsuyu*) during June ushers in the swamp-like heat of

▲ Sushi restaurant

summer; if you don't like tropical conditions, head for the cooler hills or the northern reaches of the country. A bout of typhoons and more rain in September precede **autumn**, which lasts from October to late November; this is Japan's most spectacular season, when the maple trees explode into a range of brilliant colours.

▲ Fuji TV headquarters, Tokyo

Also worth bearing in mind when planning your visit are Japan's **national holidays**. During such periods, including the days around New Year, the "Golden Week" break of April 29 to May 5 and the Obon holiday of mid-August, the nation is on the move, making it difficult to secure last-minute transport and hotel bookings. Avoid travelling during these dates, or make your arrangements well in advance.

Average daily temperatures and monthly rainfall

	Jan	Feb	Mar	Apr	May	Jun	Jul	Aug	Sep	Oct	Nov	Dec
Akita												
Max/Min °C	2/-5	3/-5	6/-2	13/4	18/8	23/14	26/18	28/19	24/15	18/8	11/3	4/-2
rainfall mm	142	104	104	105	112	127	198	188	211	188	191	178
Kōchi												
Max/Min °C	12/4	12/4	15/7	19/12	22/17	24/19	28/24	29/25	28/22	23/17	19/12	14/7
rainfall mm	64	142	160	188	244	323	257	213	323	279	175	107
Nagasaki												
Max/Min °C	9/2	10/2	14/5	19/10	23/14	26/18	29/23	31/23	27/20	22/14	17/9	12/4
rainfall mm	71	84	125	185	170	312	257	175	249	114	94	81
Sapporo												
Max/Min °C	2/-10	2/-10	6/-7	13/-1	18/3	21/10	24/16	26/18	22/12	17/6	11/-1	5/-6
rainfall mm	25	43	61	84	102	160	188	155	160	147	56	38
Tokyo												
Max/Min °C	10/1	10/1	13/4	18/10	23/15	25/18	29/22	31/24	27/20	21/14	17/8	12/3
rainfall mm	110	155	228	254	244	305	254	203	279	228	162	96

29 things not to miss

It's impossible to see everything Japan has to offer in one trip – and we don't suggest you try. What follows is a selective taste of the country's highlights: stunning traditional and contemporary architecture, dramatic landscapes, fabulous festivals and tempting food. They're arranged in five colour-coded categories, in no particular order, to help you find the very best things to see, do, eat and experience. All highlights have a page reference to take you straight into the guide, where you can find out more.

01 **Kyoto** Page **403** • The capital of Japan for a thousand years, endowed with an almost overwhelming legacy of temples, palaces and gardens, and also home to the country's richest traditional culture and most refined cuisine.

02 Skiing Page **62** • Hit the slopes and enjoy the perfect powder snow at Niseko in Hokkaidō or the great runs and charming atmosphere of Nagano's Nozawa Onsen.

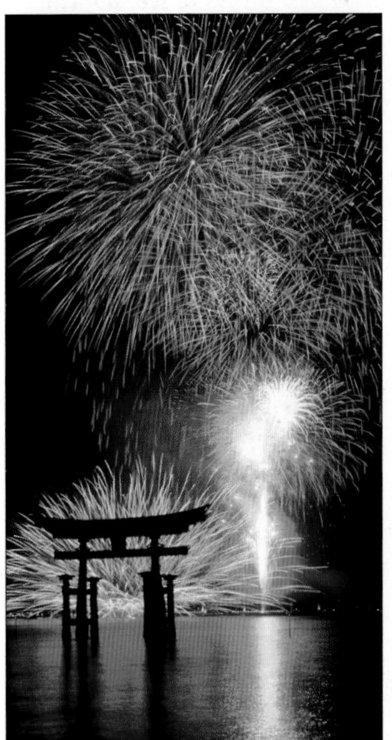

03 Fireworks Page **59** • Spectacular displays are held every July and August across the country, including at the famous torii at Miya-jima in Western Honshū.

04 Tsukiji Page **135** • This hyperactive Tokyo fish and produce market is the place to go for an early breakfast and the freshest sashimi and sushi in the country.

05 Yuki Matsuri Page **289** • Gawp at mammoth snow and ice sculptures in Sapporo, Hokkaidō, every February.

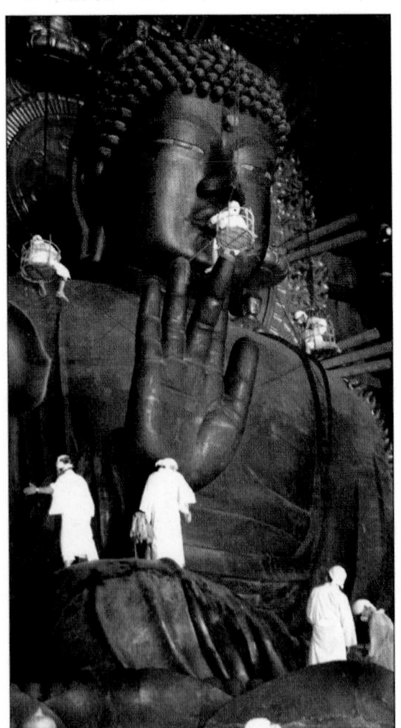

06 Nara Page **463** • The ancient former capital is home to the monumental bronze Buddha of Tōdai-ji and fine collections of religious art.

07 Naoshima Page **605** • One of the best places to experience the beauty of the Inland Sea is this tranquil island, with its amazing contemporary art museums, public sculptures and installations.

08 Hiroshima Page **549** • Pay your respects to the A-bomb's victims at the Peace Memorial Park and Museum in the city of Hiroshima, impressively reborn from the ashes of World War II.

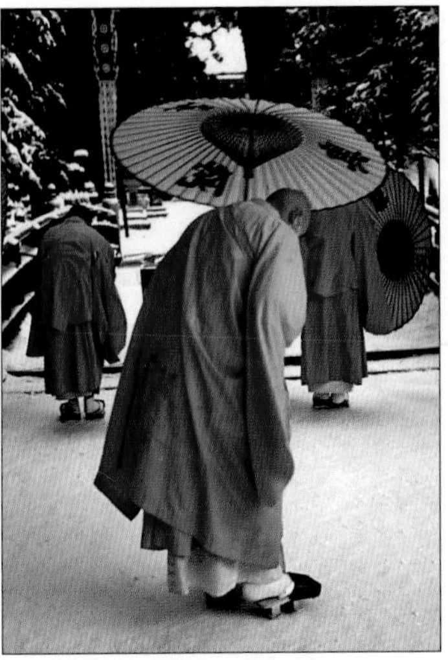

09 Koya-san Page **498** • Mingle with monks and pilgrims on one of Japan's holiest mountains, home to over a hundred monasteries.

10 Kabuki Page **160** • Tokyo's National Theatre or Shimbashi Embujo are among the places where you can enjoy this most dramatic of traditional Japanese performing arts.

11 The Kiso Valley Page **360** • The three-hour hike from Tsumago to Magome in Nagano takes you through gorgeous countryside between two lovingly preserved Edo-era "post towns".

12 Earth Celebration Page **280** • Vibrant international world music festival, hosted by the drumming group Kodō on the lovely island of Sado-ga-shima.

13 Kaiseki-ryōri Page **50** • Indulge yourself with a meal of kaiseki-ryōri, Japan's haute cuisine, comprising a selection of beautifully prepared morsels made from the finest seasonal ingredients.

14 Yakushima Page **720** • Commune with thousand-year-old cedar trees in Kirishima-Yaku National Park, a UNESCO World Heritage Site.

15 Climb Mount Fuji Page **85** • Make the tough but rewarding hike up Japan's tallest peak, a long-dormant volcano of classic symmetrical beauty.

16 Stay at a ryokan Page **44** • Treat yourself to a night of luxury in a ryokan, a traditional Japanese inn, where you enter a world of understated elegance and meticulous service.

17 Awa Odori Page **614** • Dance the night away at the country's biggest Obon bash, held in Tokushima, Shikoku.

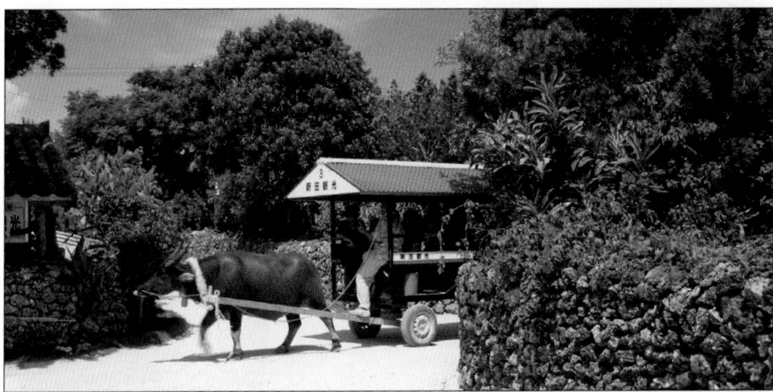

18 Taketomi-jima, Okinawa Page **759** • Unwind on this tiny island graced with a charming village of buildings roofed with terracotta tiles and surrounded by beautiful flower gardens.

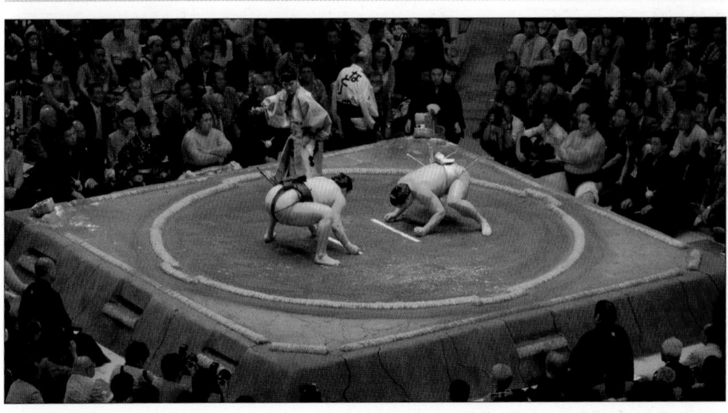

19 Sumo Page **60** • Visit a major sumo tournament and see the titanic, ritualized clashes of Japan's sporting giants.

20 Nikkō Page **172** • Set amid splendid mountains north of Tokyo, this pilgrim town is home to the fabulously over-the-top Tosho-gū shrine, one of Japan's most sumptuous buildings.

21 Kamikōchi Page **356** • The busy but beautiful mountain village of Kamikōchi preserves a Shangri-la atmosphere and serves as the gateway to the magnificent Northern Alps.

22 Kumano Kodō Page **503** • Wander the ancient pilgrimage route of the "Land of the Gods", discover sacred mountain sites, and soak in the healing waters of isolated hot springs.

23 Onsen Page **641** • Take a dip at a top onsen resort town, such as Dōgo, with its magnificent bathhouse, or experience the exquisite warmth of a rotemburo (outdoor bath) as the snow falls.

24 Sake breweries Page **53** • Drop by venerable sake breweries in Obuse or Takayama to discover the amazing varieties of this ancient Japanese alcoholic beverage made from rice.

25 Himeji Page **521** • Relive the days of the samurai at Himeji-jō, the premier example of a feudal-era fortress.

26 Golden Gai Page **126** • Stroll through Tokyo's Kabukichō, the neon-soaked district of love hotels, host clubs and *fuzoku* (sex industry) businesses, to this atmospheric warren of tiny, atmospheric bars.

27 Roppongi Art Night Page **110** • A dawn to dusk celebration of contemporary art in Tokyo's Roppongi Art Triangle, with thrilling street performances at the end of March.

28 Kenroku-en Page **377** • Nature has been tamed and primped to its most beautiful at Kanazawa's star attraction, one of the country's top traditional gardens.

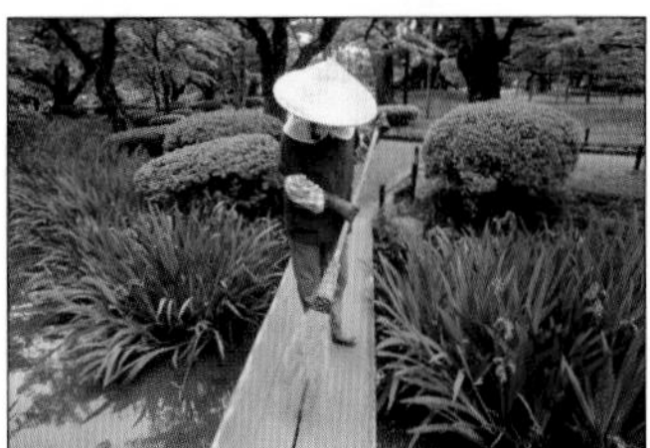

29 Ogimachi Page **370** • Quaint village filled with distinctive *gasshō-zukuri* houses, whose steep-sided thatched roofs are said to recall two hands joined in prayer.

Basics

Basics

Getting there

Tokyo's Narita International Airport (see p.91), Ōsaka's Kansai International Airport (see p.483) and Centrair (p.385) near Nagoya are the main international flight gateways, with Tokyo's Haneda Airport (see p.91) also set to offer more international connections over the next few years.

Airfares are highest around the Golden Week holiday period at the beginning of May, and the Obon festival in mid-August, as well as at Christmas and New Year, when seats are at a premium. Prices drop during the "shoulder" seasons – April to June and September to October – with the best deals in the low season, January to March and November to December (excluding Christmas and New Year).

Flights from the UK and Ireland

ANA, British Airways, Japan Airlines and Virgin fly nonstop **from London** to Tokyo, taking about twelve hours. Return fares start from around £500. However, you can find occasional special deals for as low as £400, so it pays to shop around. There are no direct flights **from Dublin**; if you fly via London, expect to pay in the region of €800.

Flights from the US and Canada

A number of airlines fly nonstop from the US and Canada to Tokyo, Ōsaka and Nagoya, including Air Canada, ANA, American Airlines, Continental, Japan Airlines and United with connections from virtually every US regional airport. Flying time is around fifteen hours from New York, thirteen hours from Chicago and ten hours from Los Angeles. Low season return fares to Tokyo start at around US$1000 from Chicago or New York; US$800 from Los Angeles; and Can$1200 from Vancouver.

Flights from Australia, New Zealand and South Africa

Qantas, Japan Airlines and Air New Zealand operate **nonstop** flights to Tokyo from Australia and New Zealand. Flying time is around ten hours from Australia and twelve hours from New Zealand. **Return fares** from Australia to Tokyo kick off at around Aus$1300 with one stopover, or Aus$1500 for a nonstop flight. From New Zealand prices start at roughly NZ$1700, though the most direct routings will cost at least NZ$2000.

Flying **from South Africa**, you'll be routed through Southeast Asia or the Middle East. Promotional fares can be as cheap as R8000, though you're more likely to be paying in the region of R10,000 and above.

Train and ferry

Adventurous travellers can take advantage of a number of alternative routes to Japan from Europe and Asia via **train and ferry**. There are three long-distance train journeys – the Trans-Siberian, Trans-Mongolian and Trans-Manchurian – all of which will put you on the right side of Asia for a hop across to Japan. The shortest ferry route is on the hydrofoil between Busan in South Korea and Fukuoka (Hakata port) on Japan's southern island of Kyūshū.

The Trans-Siberian train and ferries from Russia

The classic overland adventure route to or from Japan is via the **Trans-Siberian** train, a seven-night journey from Moscow to Vladivostok on Russia's far eastern coast. The cost of a one-way ticket in a four-berth sleeper compartment between Moscow and Vladivostok is around £360/US$520/A$620, on top of which you'll need to factor in costs for visas, hotels etc along the way. It's far from impossible to buy tickets yourself once in Russia, but to avoid some of the inevitable hassles, and for convenience, using an agent is recommended: some are suggested below. The same agents can arrange tickets on the **Trans-Manchurian** train, which heads from Moscow down through northern China and terminates in Beijing, and the **Trans-Mongolian**, which runs from Moscow via Mongolia to Beijing. You can then take a train to Shanghai and pick up a ferry to Japan (see below).

Vladivostok Air (ⓦwww.vladivostokavia.ru) offers connections from Vladivostok to Fukuoka, Nagoya, Narita and Toyama. Business Intour Service in Vladivostok (ⓦwww.bisintour.com) handles bookings on the fairly regular **ferries** that run to the Japanese port of Fushiki, near Toyama (see p.372). This takes 42 hours and the cheapest ticket is around US$1420/¥129,000 including a basic berth and all meals.

For those planning to return by this route to Europe from Japan, start by arranging your **visa** at the Russian Embassy in Tokyo (2-1-1 Azabudai, Minato-ku, Tokyo 106; ⓣ03/3583-5982) or the consulate (1-2-2 Nishimidorigaoka, Toyonaka-shi, Ōsaka; ⓣ06/6848-3452).

The shortest journey from Russia to Japan is on the ferry service (May–Oct) from **Korsakov** on the Siberian island of Sakhalin to Wakkanai in Hokkaidō; see p.321 for details.

Trans-Siberian tour agents

GW Travel UK ⓣ0161/928-9410, ⓦwww.gwtravel.co.uk.
Mir Corporation US ⓣ206/624-7289, ⓦwww.mircorp.com.
MO Tourist CIS Russian Centre Japan ⓣ03/5296-5783, ⓦwww.mo-tourist.co.jp.
Monkey Business China ⓣ8610/6591 6519, ⓦwww.monkeyshrine.com.
Russian Experience UK ⓣ0845/521 2910, ⓦwww.trans-siberian.co.uk.
Sundowners Australia ⓣ03/9672 5300, ⓦwww.sundownerstravel.com.
Travel Directors Australia ⓣ08/9242 4200, ⓦwww.traveldirectors.com.au.
White Nights US ⓣ1800/490 5008, ⓦwww.wnights.com.

Ferries from China and South Korea

Both the Shanghai Ferry Company (ⓣ06/6243-6345, ⓦwww.shanghai-ferry.co.jp) and Japan–China International Ferry Co (ⓣ06/6536-6541, ⓦwww.shinganjin.com) ply the **Shanghai–Ōsaka** route (48hr; from ¥20,000). Conditions on board are good, the berths are clean and comfortable, and facilities include swimming pools, restaurants and even discos. China Express Line ferries (ⓣ078/321-5791, ⓦwww.celkobe.co.jp.) sail weekly between **Tianjin and Kōbe** (51hr; from ¥22,000). Orient Ferry (ⓣ0832/32-6615, ⓦwww.orientferry.co.jp) has services between **Qingdao and Shimonoseki** (40hr; ¥19,000).

There are daily ferry and hydrofoil services from Busan in South Korea to Fukuoka (p.653) and Shimonoseki (p.567).

Airlines, agents and operators

Contact details for airlines in the listings below are given selectively, reflecting the territories from which they offer flights to Japan.

Airlines

Air Canada ⓦwww.aircanada.ca.
Air France ⓦwww.airfrance.com.
Air New Zealand ⓦwww.airnewzealand.com.
All Nippon Airways (ANA) ⓦwww.ana.co.jp.
American Airlines ⓦwww.aa.com.
British Airways ⓦwww.britishairways.com.
Cathay Pacific ⓦwww.cathaypacific.com.
Continental Airlines ⓦwww.continental.com.
Delta ⓦwww.delta.com.
Japan Airlines (JAL) ⓦwww.jal.com.
KLM Royal Dutch Airlines ⓦwww.klm.com.
Korean Airlines ⓦwww.koreanair.com.
Lufthansa ⓦwww.lufthansa.com.
Malaysia Airlines ⓦwww.malaysiaairlines.com.
Northwest Airlines ⓦwww.nwa.com.
Qantas ⓦwww.qantas.com.au.
Singapore Airlines ⓦwww.singaporeair.com.
Thai Airways International ⓦwww.thaiair.com.
United Airlines ⓦwww.united.com.
Virgin Atlantic ⓦwww.virgin-atlantic.com.

Agents and operators

Artisans of Leisure US ⓣ1-800/214-8144, ⓦwww.artisansofleisure.com. Luxury private tours including ones focused on food, art and gardens.
AWL Pitt Australia ⓣ02/9264 7384, ⓦwww.japanpackage.com.au. Sydney-based agent offering a variety of Japan packages, and Japan Rail passes.

Six steps to a better kind of travel

At Rough Guides we are passionately committed to travel. We feel strongly that only through travelling do we truly come to understand the world we live in and the people we share it with – plus tourism has brought a great deal of **benefit** to developing economies around the world over the last few decades. But the extraordinary growth in tourism has also damaged some places irreparably, and of course **climate change** is exacerbated by most forms of transport, especially flying. This means that now more than ever it's important to **travel thoughtfully** and **responsibly**, with respect for the cultures you're visiting – not only to derive the most benefit from your trip but also to preserve the best bits of the planet for everyone to enjoy. At Rough Guides we feel there are six main areas in which you can make a difference:

- Consider what you're contributing to the **local economy**, and how much the services you use do the same, whether it's through employing local workers and guides or sourcing locally grown produce and local services.
- Consider the **environment** on holiday as well as at home. Water is scarce in many developing destinations, and the biodiversity of local flora and fauna can be adversely affected by tourism. Try to patronize businesses that take account of this.
- Travel with a purpose, not just to tick off experiences. Consider **spending longer** in a place, and getting to know it and its people.
- Give thought to how often you **fly**. Try to avoid short hops by air and more harmful night flights.
- Consider **alternatives to flying**, travelling instead by bus, train, boat and even by bike or on foot where possible.
- Make your trips "**climate neutral**" via a reputable carbon offset scheme. All Rough Guide flights are offset, and every year we donate money to a variety of charities devoted to combating the effects of climate change.

AWL Travel UK ⓣ020/7222 1144, ⓦwww.awlt.com. UK-based Japan specialist.

Baumann Travel US ⓣ914/419-8470, ⓦwww.baumanntravel.com. Arts and cultural tours, covering themes such as Japanese gardens and cuisine.

Deep Powder Tours Australia ⓣ02/9525 9774, ⓦwww.deeppowdertours.com. Ski trips to Niseko, and other Japanese resorts.

Elite Orient Tours US & Canada ⓣ1-800/668-8100 or 416/977-3026, ⓦwww.elitetours.com. Canada-based company specialising in Japan.

Hike Japan Japan ⓣ03/5226 1169, ⓦwww.hikejapan.com. Small-group hiking tours. Itineraries include some unusual destinations such as the volcanoes of Kyūshū and the island Yakushima.

HIS Travel Japan Australia ⓣ02/9267 3333, New Zealand ⓣ09/336 1336; ⓦwww.traveljapan.com.au. Flights, packages and customized itineraries are available from this long-established specialist.

IACE Travel US ⓣ1-866/735-4223, ⓦwww.iace-asia.com. US-based Japan specialist with many packages and themed tours to Tokyo.

Inside Japan UK ⓣ0117/314 4620, ⓦwww.insidejapantours.com. Great range of well-designed small-group, self-guided and fully tailored trips, ranging from Tokyo stopovers to climbing Mount Fuji.

Into Japan UK ⓣ01865/841 443, ⓦwww.intojapan.co.uk. Upmarket tailor-made and special-interest tours. Options at the time of writing included a fifteen-day kabuki tour.

Jalpak/Jaltour US ⓣ1-800/221-1081, ⓦwww.jalpak.com; UK ⓣ020-7389-8341, ⓦwww.jaltour.co.uk. Japan Airlines' tour arm sells a range of holiday packages.

Japan Adventures Japan ⓣ090-8275-5012, ⓦwww.japan-adventures.com. Specializes in hiking and mountain climbing trips in Hokkaidō and the Okutama national park area west of Tokyo.

Japan Journeys UK ⓣ020/7766 5267, ⓦwww.japanjourneys.co.uk. Tokyo options include an anime and manga-themed tour.

Japan Package Tours Australia ⓣ03/9909 7212, ⓦwww.japanpackagetours.com.au. Fully escorted and self-guided tours, tailor-made itineraries, accommodation packages and rail passes.

Japan Travel Bureau (JTB) US ⓣ1-877/798-9808, ⓦwww.jtbusa.com; Canada ⓣ416/367 5824, ⓦwww.jtbi.ca; Australia ⓣ1300/739 330,

Ⓦwww.japantravel.com.au. As well as the usual options, they handle Sunrise Tours (see p.32) taking in the capital and surrounding region.
Japan Travel Centre UK Ⓣ020/7611 0150, Ⓦwww.japantravel.co.uk. Offers flights, accommodation packages, Japan Rail passes and guided tours.
Journeys East US Ⓣ1-800/527-2612, Ⓦwww.journeyseast.com. Small-group cultural tours focusing on art and architecture.
Kintetsu International Express US Ⓣ1-800/422-348, Ⓦwww.japanforyou.com. A good variety of trips on offer, covering everything from architecture to onsen.
Magical Japan UK Ⓣ0161/440 7332, Ⓦwww.magicaljapan.co.uk. Their guided tours all offer at least three days in and around Tokyo; customized packages possible.
Mitsui Travel Australia Ⓣ02/9262 2720, Ⓦwww.mitsuitravel.com.au. Options include a three-night onsen tour to Tokyo and Hakone.
Oka Tours Japan Ⓣ0422/266644, Ⓦwww.okatours.com. Cycling tours, both moderate and challenging in terms of terrain covered, on Sado Island, Niigata and the Izu peninsula.
Oxalis Holidays UK Ⓣ020/7099 6147, Ⓦwww.oxalis-adventures.com. Broad range of escorted small-group tours, many including Tokyo.
Price Travel Services Australia Ⓣ1800/221 707 or 02/9247 3086, Ⓦwww.pricetravelservices.com.au. Experienced Australia-based agent.
Travel Japan by H.I.S. Australia Ⓣ02/9267 0333, New Zealand Ⓣ09/336 1336; Ⓦwww.traveljapan.com.au. Provides everything from flights to Tokyo to packages and customized itineraries.
ViaJapan! UK Ⓣ020/7484 3328, Ⓦwww.viajapan.co.uk. UK-based arm of major Japanese travel company H.I.S., offering flights, packages and rail passes.
Wright Way Travel US Ⓣ708/848-1976, Ⓦwww.wrightwaytravel.org. An annual tour to Japan focused around the work and legacy of architect Frank Lloyd Wright.

Getting around

The time of year is an important factor to consider when arranging your transport around Japan. Peak travelling seasons are the few days either side of New Year, the Golden Week holidays of late April and early May, and the mid-August Obon holiday (see pp.57–59 for further details of public holidays). During these times the whole of Japan can seem on the move, with trains, planes and ferries packed to the gills and roads clogged with traffic. Book well in advance and be prepared to pay higher fares on flights, as all discounts are suspended during peak periods.

Domestic **travel agencies**, such as JTB, can book all types of transport and are also useful sources for checking travel schedules. The staff in these agencies have access to the *jikokuhyō* timetable, an incredible source of information, updated monthly, on virtually every form of public transport in Japan. There's always a *jikokuhyō* available for consultation at stations, and most hotels have a copy too. If you're going to travel around Japan a lot, get hold of a JR English timetable for all the Shinkansen and many major express train services, available from JNTO offices in Japan and abroad and at major train stations. Also incredibly useful is the **Hyperdia Timetable** (Ⓦwww.hyperdia.com), an online resource maintained by Hitachi Information Systems, which will provide a whole range of travel options, including transfers by air, bus, train and ferry between almost any two points in Japan.

By rail

The vast majority of services on Japan's brilliant rail network are operated by the six regional **JR (Japan Railways)** companies: JR Hokkaidō (Ⓦwww2.jrhokkaido.co.jp/global/index.html), JR East (Ⓦwww.jreast.co.jp), JR Central (Ⓦenglish.jr-central.co.jp), JR West (Ⓦwww.westjr.co.jp), JR Shikoku

Eating and drinking on trains and at stations

On long-distance trains there'll almost always be a **trolley**, laden with overpriced drinks and snacks, being pushed down the aisle. You're generally better off both financially and in culinary terms packing your own picnic for the train, but useful fallbacks are the station **noodle stands** and the **ekiben**, a contraction of *eki* (station) and bentō (boxed meal). At the station noodle stalls you can get warming bowls of freshly made hot noodles, usually soba or the thicker udon, for under ¥500. *Ekiben*, often featuring local speciality foods, are sold both on and off the trains and come in a wide range of permutations. If you have time, pop into a convenience or department store close to the station for a more keenly priced selection of bentō.

(Ⓦwww.jr-shikoku.co.jp) and JR Kyūshū (Ⓦwww.jrkyushu.co.jp). JR is run as a single company as far as buying tickets is concerned. Smaller rail companies, including Hankyū, Kintetsu, Meitetsu, Odakyū and Tōbu, are based in the major cities and surrounding areas, but in the vast majority of Japan it's JR services that you'll be using.

Individual **tickets** can be pricey, especially for the fastest trains, but many discount tickets and **rail passes** are available to cut the cost. If you plan to travel extensively by train, the various Japan Rail Passes provide the best overall deal (see p.34), while the discount tour packages by the Japan Travel Bureau's Sunrise Tours arm (see box, p.32) are also excellent value. If you have lots of time, and are travelling during the main student holiday periods, the **Seishun Jūhachi-kippu** (see p.35) is also an excellent buy.

Shinkansen

For many visitors, riding the **Shinkansen** (新幹線) or **Bullet Train** (so-called because of the smooth, rounded design of the earliest locomotives) is an eagerly anticipated part of a trip to Japan. You'll barely notice the speed of these smooth-running trains, which on the top-of-the-range *E5* series can reach 320kph. They are also frighteningly punctual – two seconds late on the platform and you'll be waving goodbye to the back end of the train – and reliable: only the severest weather conditions or earthquakes stop the Shinkansen.

There are six main Shinkansen lines. The busiest route is the **Tōkaidō-Sanyō** line, which runs south from Tokyo through Nagoya, Kyoto, Ōsaka and Hiroshima, terminating at Hakata Station in Fukuoka (the Tōkaidō line runs from Tokyo to Shin-Ōsaka Station, while the Sanyō line continues from there to Fukuoka).

The **Tōhoku line** is the main northern route, passing through Sendai and terminating at Shin-Aomori. This line will extend through the Seikan Tunnel to Hakodate by 2015. The **Akita line** runs from Tokyo to Akita on the north coast, while the **Yamagata line** to Shinjō, in the middle of the Tōhoku region, splits off west from the Tōhoku line at Fukushima.

The **Jōetsu line** heads north from Tokyo, tunnelling through the mountains to Niigata along the Sea of Japan coast, with the **Nagano line** (also known as the Hokuriku line) branching off west at Takasaki to end at Nagano. There are plans to extend this line from Nagano to Kanazawa by 2014. The **Kyūshū line** connects Kagoshima with Hakata.

To travel by Shinkansen you'll pay a hefty **surcharge** on top of the basic fare for a regular train. Three types of Shinkansen services are available: the *Kodama* (こだま), which stops at all stations; the *Hikari* (ひかり), which stops only at major stations; and the *Nozomi* (のぞみ; available on the Tōkaidō–Sanyō line only), the fastest service, for which you'll have to pay an extra fee (and which you're not allowed to take if you're travelling on most types of rail pass). If you're travelling from Tokyo to Fukuoka, the *Nozomi* shaves an hour off the six-hour journey on the *Hikari*, but for shorter hops to Nagoya, Kyoto or Ōsaka the time saved isn't generally worth the extra expense.

Japan mileage chart

	Aomori	Fukuoka	Hiroshima	Kagoshima	Kanazawa	Kōbe	Kōchi	Kyoto	Matsue	Matsuyama
Aomori										
Fukuoka	1746									
Hiroshima	1463	283								
Kagoshima	2067	321	604							
Kanazawa	798	948	665	1269						
Kōbe	1151	595	312	916	353					
Kōchi	1436	618	335	939	638	285				
Kyoto	1066	680	397	1001	268	85	370			
Matsue	1380	409	185	730	582	313	439	343		
Matsuyama	1449	631	348	952	651	298	121	383	452	
Miyazaki	2019	407	556	142	1221	868	891	953	682	904
Morioka	213	1664	1381	1985	716	1069	1354	984	1298	1367
Nagano	695	1084	801	1405	263	489	774	404	747	787
Nagasaki	1920	174	457	314	1122	769	792	854	583	805
Nagoya	957	822	539	1143	272	227	512	142	485	525
Niigata	481	1265	982	1586	317	670	955	585	899	968
Ōsaka	1117	629	346	950	319	34	319	51	347	332
Sapporo	283	2029	1746	2350	1081	1434	1719	1349	1663	1732
Sendai	398	1578	1295	1899	635	983	1268	898	1217	1281
Tokushima	1245	557	274	878	447	94	224	179	378	238
Tokyo	771	1205	922	1526	492	610	895	525	868	908
Tottori	1253	536	309	857	455	186	312	216	127	325
Yokohama	807	1169	886	1490	528	574	859	489	832	872

On the train there are announcements and electronic signs in English telling you which stations are coming up. Get to the door in good time before the train arrives, as you'll generally only have a few seconds in which to disembark before the train shoots off again.

Other trains

Aside from the Shinkansen, the fastest services are **limited express** (*tokkyū*; 特急) trains, so-called because they make a limited number of stops. Like Shinkansen, you have to pay a surcharge to travel on *tokkyū* and there are separate classes of reserved and non-reserved seats (see box, p.34). Less common are the **express**, or *kyūkō* (急行), trains, which also only stop at larger stations but carry a lower surcharge. The **rapid**, or *kaisoku* (快速), trains are slower still, making more stops than a *kyūkō*, but with no surcharge. **Ordinary**, or *futsū* (普通), trains are local services stopping at all stations and usually limited to routes under 100km.

Sunrise Tours

There are several great-value deals only available to overseas visitors on tourist visas offered by Sunrise Tours, a division of the Japan Travel Bureau. For example, for ¥19,400, Sunrise offers a two-day, one-night unaccompanied trip to Kyoto from Tokyo with reserved seats on the Shinkansen and a night's accommodation at a reasonable tourist hotel in Kyoto – for slightly more you can upgrade the hotel and go on the faster *Nozomi* trains. This is cheaper than the cost of a return Shinkansen ticket to Kyoto alone. The package is also flexible: you can stay longer than one night in Kyoto and return on any train you like (on a pre-specified day) as long as you cancel your return seat reservation and take your chances in the unreserved section of the train (see box, p.34). There are Shinkansen tours starting in Ōsaka, Kyoto and Nagoya, too; for the latest details see ⓦwww.jtbgmt.com/sunrisetour.

	Miyazaki	Morioka	Nagano	Nagasaki	Nagoya	Niigata	Ōsaka	Sapporo	Sendai	Tokushima	Tokyo	Tottori
Miyazaki												
Morioka	1937											
Nagano	1357	613										
Nagasaki	436	1838	1258									
Nagoya	1095	875	262	996								
Niigata	1538	399	214	143	476							
Ōsaka	902	1035	455	803	193	636						
Sapporo	2302	496	978	2203	1240	764	1400					
Sendai	1851	185	497	1752	756	318	949	681				
Tokushima	830	1163	583	731	321	764	128	1528	1077			
Tokyo	1478	558	229	1379	383	353	576	1054	373	704		
Tottori	809	1171	620	710	3358	772	220	1536	1090	251	741	
Yokohama	1442	594	265	1343	347	389	540	1090	409	668	36	705

The above categories of train and surcharges apply to all JR services, and to some, but not all, private rail routes. To further confuse matters, you may find that if you're travelling on a JR train on one of the more remote branch lines, you may be charged an additional fare due to part of the old JR network having been sold off to another operating company.

There are only a handful of overnight **sleeper trains** – the main services are from Tokyo and Ōsaka to Aomori and Sapporo; if you have a Japan Rail Pass and want a berth for the night, you'll have to pay the berth charge (couchette cabin sleeping four to six: ¥6000–10,000; private double or single room: ¥6000–38,000 depending on the class of cabin), plus the surcharge for the express or limited express service. A few overnight trains have reclining seats, which JR Pass holders can use without paying a surcharge. Reservations are necessary.

There are several **SL (steam locomotive)** services across the country, which run from spring through to autumn, mainly on weekends and holidays. These leisurely trains, with lovingly restored engines and carriages, have proved a huge hit with tourists and you'd be well advised to book in advance. Among the more popular routes are the Senmō line between Kushiro and Shibecha, along with the SL Fuyu-no-Shitsugen-go service in winter (p.332); the Yamaguchi line between Ogōri and Tsuwano in Western Honshū (p.576); and the Mōka line from Shimodate to Motegi via Mashiko in Tochigi-ken (see p.179).

Left luggage

You'll usually only find left-luggage offices at the largest train stations in big cities, though all train stations, many subway stations, department stores and shopping centres have coin lockers where you can stash your bags. These come in a range of sizes, charging from ¥300 to ¥600 for a day's storage.

Train classes and reservations

On Shinkansen trains and JR *tokkyū* (limited express) and *kyūkō* (express) services, there's a choice of ordinary, or *futsū-sha* (普通車), carriages or more expensive first-class **Green Car**, or *guriin-sha* (グリーン車), carriages where seats are two abreast either side of the aisle (as opposed to three). There may be a choice between smoking, or *kitsuen* (喫煙), and non-smoking, or *kin'en* (禁煙), cars; all JR East Shinkansen services are entirely non-smoking. On *Nozomi* Shinkansen it's also possible to buy standing-only tickets for a small discount.

Each train also has both reserved, or *shitei-seki* (指定席), and unreserved, or *jiyū-seki* (自由席), sections. Seat reservations cost between ¥300 and ¥500, depending on the season; they are free if you have a rail pass. You cannot sit in the reserved section of a train without a reservation, even if it's empty and the unreserved section full, although you can buy a reservation ticket from the train conductor.

If you don't have a reservation, aim to get to the station with thirty minutes to spare, locate your platform and stand in line at the marked section for the unreserved carriages; ask the platform attendants for *jiyū-seki*, and they'll point the way. If you have a reservation, platform signs will also direct you where to stand, so that you're beside the right door when the train pulls in.

Buying tickets

JR tickets can be bought at any JR station and at many travel agencies. At major city stations there will be a fare map in English beside the vending machine. Otherwise, if you're buying your ticket from the ticket counter, it's a good idea to have written down on a piece of paper the date and time you wish to travel, your destination, the number of tickets you want and whether you'll need smoking or non-smoking seats. A fall-back is to buy the minimum fare ticket from the vending machine, and pay any surcharges on or when leaving the train.

To make **advance reservations** for *tokkyū* and Shinkansen trains, or to buy special types of tickets, you'll generally need to go to the green window, or *midori-no-madog-uchi*, sales counters, marked by a green logo. In order to swap your exchange voucher for a Japan Rail Pass, you'll have to go to a designated ticket office; they're listed in the booklet you'll receive with your rail pass voucher and on the rail pass website.

Japan Rail passes

If you plan to make just one long-distance train journey, such as Tokyo to Kyoto one way, a **Japan Rail Pass** (Ⓦwww.japanrailpass.net) will not be good value. In all other cases it will be and you should invest in one before you arrive, since the full Japan Rail Pass can only be bought *outside* Japan (other types of passes can bought inside the country though). For unfettered flexibility, the comprehensive Japan Rail Pass is the way to go, while regional Japan Rail Passes are good deals if they fit with your travel itinerary. All the prices quoted below are for ordinary rail passes (green car passes cost more) and note that you will have to be travelling on a tourist visa to buy any of these passes.

The traditional **Japan Rail Pass** allows travel on virtually all JR services throughout Japan, including buses and ferries, and is valid for seven (¥28,300), fourteen (¥45,100) or 21 (¥57,700) consecutive days. The major service for which it is not valid is the *Nozomi* Shinkansen; if you're caught on one of these, even unwittingly, you'll be liable for the full fare for the trip. As with all JR tickets, children aged between 6 and 11 inclusive pay half-price, while those under 6 travel free.

The **JR East Pass** (Ⓦwww.jreast.co.jp/e/eastpass/top.html) covers all JR East services, including the Shinkansen. This pass is particularly good value if you're aged between 12 and 25. For five days' consecutive use, the price is ¥20,000 (¥16,000 for 12- to 25-year-olds), while a ten-day pass is ¥32,000 (¥25,000 for 12- to 25-year-olds). Even better value is the flexible four-day pass (¥20,000/¥16,000), which is valid for any four days within a month from the date

Travel information service

JR East Infoline (daily 10am–6pm; ⓣ050-2016-1603) is an information service in English, Chinese and Korean dealing with all train enquiries nationwide. Train bookings cannot be made on this service but they will be able to tell you about the fastest route between any two points on the system and where to make a seat reservation.

when the pass is issued. **JR-West** offers a couple of local travel passes (see p.480) while both **JR Hokkaidō and JR Kyūshū** (see p.285 and p.651) offer a pass for their respective networks.

If you buy any of these passes abroad, the cost in your own currency will depend on the exchange rate at the time of purchase – you might be able to save a little money by **shopping around** between agents offering the pass, because they don't all use the same exchange rate. You'll be given an exchange voucher which must be swapped for a pass in Japan **within three months**. Once issued, the dates on the pass cannot be changed. Exchanges can only be made at designated JR stations; you'll be issued with a list of locations when you buy your pass. Again, note that passes can only be issued if you're travelling on a **temporary visitor visa**; JR staff are very strict about this and you'll be asked to show your passport when you present your exchange voucher for the pass or when you buy a pass directly in Japan. Also, note that if you lose your pass it will not be replaced, so take good care of it.

Rail Pass holders can get a discount, typically around ten percent, at all JR Group Hotels; check the list in the information booklet provided when you buy your pass.

Other discount tickets

The **Seishun Jūhachi-kippu** (青春１８きっぷ; ⓦwww.jreast.co.jp/e/pass/seishun18.html) is available to everyone regardless of age, but only valid during school vacations. These are roughly March 1 to April 10 (sold Feb 20–March 31), July 20 to September 10 (sold July 1–Aug 31) and December 10 to January 20 (sold Dec 1–Jan 10). For ¥11,500 you get five day-tickets that can be used to travel anywhere in Japan as long as you take only the slow *futsū* and *kaisoku* trains. The tickets can also be split and used individually by different people. If you're not in a hurry, this ticket can be the biggest bargain on the whole of Japan's rail system, allowing you, for example, to use one of the day tickets (value ¥2300) to travel from Tokyo to Nagasaki (total journey time 23hr 36min). The tickets are also handy for touring a local area in a day, since you can get on and off trains as many times as you wish within 24 hours.

Kaisūken (回数券) are usually four or more one-way tickets to the same destination. These work out substantially cheaper than buying the tickets individually (so are good for groups travelling to the same destintation). Among other places they are available on the limited express services from Tokyo to Matsumoto and Nagano-ken.

Furii kippu (フリー切符) excursion-type tickets are available for various areas of Japan, usually with unlimited use of local transport for a specified period of time. The

Discount ticket shops

In most big cities, usually in shopping areas near stations, you can find **discount ticket shops**, or *kinken shoppu* (金券ショップ), which sell, among other things, cheap airline and Shinkansen tickets. These shops buy up discount group tickets and sell them on individually, usually at around twenty percent cheaper than the regular prices. These are legitimate operations, but you'll need to be able to read and speak some Japanese to be sure you've got the ticket you need, and there may be some days when travel isn't allowed. With the Shinkansen tickets you can't make seat reservations at a discount shop, so you'll need to go to a JR ticket office to arrange these.

Hakone Furii Pass (see p.189), offered by the Odakyū railway company, covering routes from Tokyo to the lakeland area of Hakone, is particularly good value. If you plan to travel in one area, it's always worth asking the JR East Infoline (see box, p.35) or the tourist information offices if there are any other special tickets that could be of use.

By air

The big two domestic airlines are All Nippon Airways (ANA; Ⓦwww.ana.co.jp) and Japan Airlines (JAL; Ⓦwww.jal.co.jp). Both carriers offer substantial discounts for advance bookings with an extra discount if the booking is made entirely online. Other local airlines include: **Skymark** (Ⓦwww.skymark.co.jp), with cut-price routes between Tokyo and Fukuoka, Kōbe, Naha and Sapporo and Kōbe-Naha; **Air Do** (Ⓦwww.airdo.jp) for discount services on routes from Tokyo to destinations in Hokkaidō; **Skynet Asia Airways** (Ⓦwww.skynetasia.co.jp) for flights between Tokyo and Kyūshū, including Kumamoto, Miyazaki and Nagasaki; **IBEX Airlines** (Ⓦwww.ibexair.co.jp/english/index.html) for flights from Ōsaka's Itami airport to Sendai, Fukushima, Oita and a few other destinations; and **Starflyer** (Ⓦwww.starflyer.jp) for Tokyo–Ōsaka–Kita-Kyūshū flights. The busiest routes apart, there remains little competition as far as prices and quality of service are concerned.

If you're not using a rail pass (see p.34), discounted plane fares are well worth considering. For example, to travel by train to Sapporo from Tokyo costs ¥22,780 and takes the better part of a day, compared with a discounted plane fare which can fall to as low as ¥9000 from Tokyo to Shin-Chitose airport, near Sapporo, a journey of ninety minutes. Discounts are generally not available during the peak travelling seasons.

Both JAL and ANA offer **discount flight passes** to overseas visitors, which are definitely worth considering if you plan to make several plane trips. JAL has the **oneworld Yokoso** and the **Welcome to Japan** passes (Ⓦwww.jal.co.jp/yokosojapan). The former, only available to those using oneworld carriers to fly into Japan (including JAL, BA and Qantas), allows you to make up to five flights at ¥10,000 per sector; the latter, available to anyone regardless of which airline used, allows two flights for ¥26,000, three for ¥39,000, four for ¥52,000 and five for ¥65,000. ANA offers the similar **Star Alliance Japan Airpass** (Ⓦhttp://tinyurl.com/2wwmf7u), with up to five flights available on each pass at ¥11,550 per flight; and the **Visit Japan** fare with up to five flights available from ¥13,000 per flight (with a minimum of two flights). These fares are excellent value if you plan to visit far-flung destinations, such as the islands of Okinawa, where standard one-way fares from Tokyo cost over ¥30,000. These tickets are not available during peak travelling seasons such as July and August and the New Year and Golden Week holidays.

By bus

Japan has a comprehensive system of long-distance **buses**, or *chōkyori basu* (長距離バス), including night buses (*yakō basu*) between major cities. Fares are always cheaper than the fastest trains, but the buses are usually slower and can get caught up in traffic, even on the expressways, Japan's fastest roads, especially during peak travel

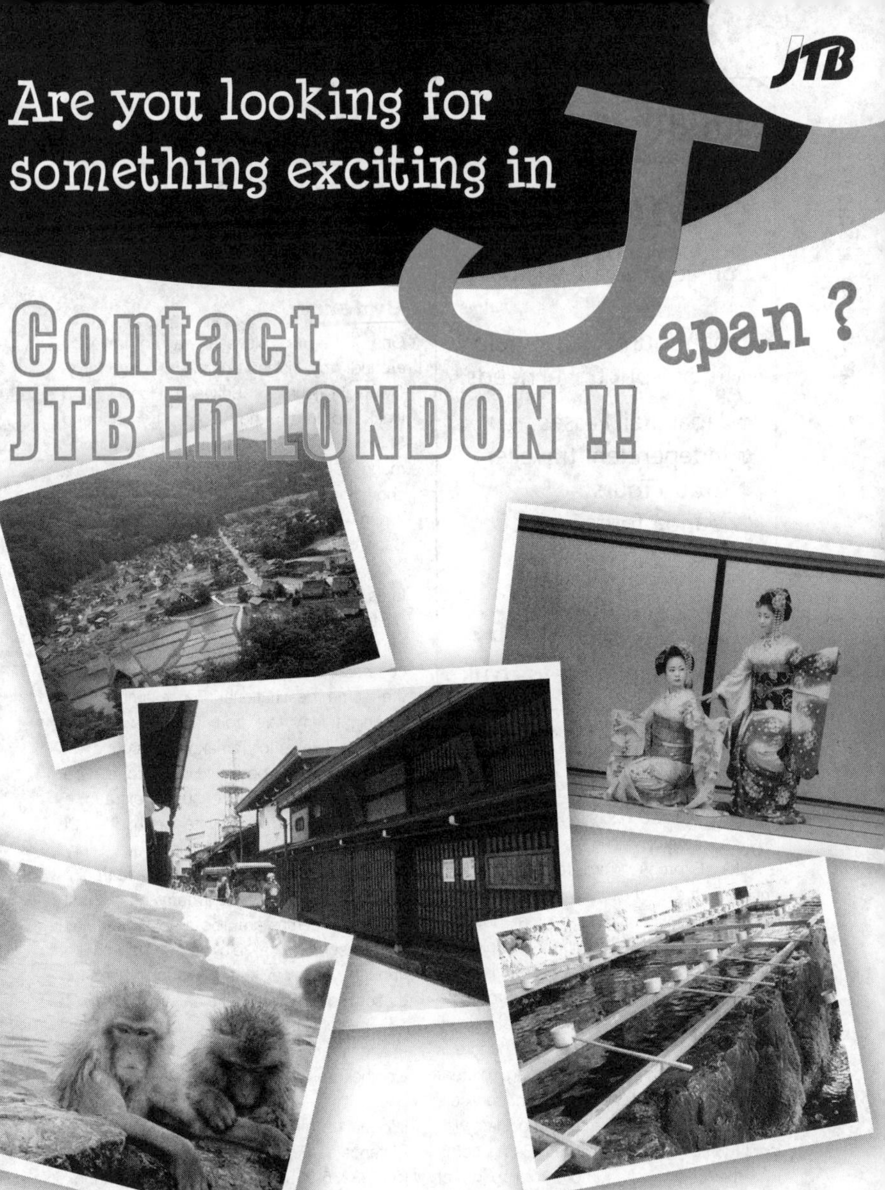
JTB
Are you looking for something exciting in Japan?
Contact JTB in LONDON !!

periods. Most bus journeys start and finish next to or near the main train station. For journeys over two hours, there is usually at least one rest stop during the journey.

Willer Express (Ⓦwillerexpress.com) is one of the largest long-distance bus operators and offers some great deals. A seven-hour overnight service from Tokyo to Kyoto, for example, can cost as little as ¥3500 compared to ¥12,710 (non-reserved seat) on the Shinkansen which takes two hours and forty minutes. There are hundreds of small bus companies operating different routes, so for full details of current services, timetables and costs make enquiries with local tourist information offices. Buses come into their own in the more rural parts of Japan where there are few or no trains. With a handful of exceptions (mentioned in the Guide), you don't need to book tickets on such services but can pay on the bus. JR runs a number of buses, some of which are covered by the various rail passes. Other private bus companies may also offer bus passes to certain regions; again check with local tourist offices for any deals.

By ferry

One of the most pleasant ways of travelling around this island nation is by **ferry**. Overnight journeys between Honshū and Hokkaidō in the north, and Kyūshū and Shikoku in the south, are highly recommended. If you can't spare the time, try a short hop, say to one of the islands of the Inland Sea, or from Niigata to Sado-ga-shima.

On the **overnight ferries** the cheapest fares, which entitle you to a sleeping space on the floor of a large room with up to a hundred other passengers, can be a bargain compared with train and plane fares to the same destinations. For example, the overnight ferry fare from Ōarai, two hours north of Tokyo, to Tomakomai, around an hour south of Sapporo on Hokkaidō, can be as low as ¥8500. Even if you pay extra for a bed in a shared or private berth, it's still cheaper than the train and you'll have a very comfortable cruise as part of the bargain; see Ⓦwww.sunflower.co.jp/ferry/index.shtml for details. Ferries are also an excellent way of transporting a bicycle or motorbike (though you'll pay a small supplement for these) and many also take cars.

Ferry **schedules** are subject to seasonal changes and also vary according to the weather, so for current details of times and prices it's best to consult the local tourist information office. Contact the Japan Long Distance Ferry Service Association (Ⓣ03/3265-9685, Ⓦwww.jlc-ferry.jp/index.html) for more information; there are links on

Cable cars and ropeways

It's worth noting a linguistic distinction that applies to the transport at several of Japan's mountain resorts. What is known in the West as a cable car (a capsule suspended from a cable going up a mountain) is called a **ropeway** in Japan, while the term "**cable car**" means a funicular or rack-and-pinion railway.

the website to the sites of major long-distance ferry services; tickets can be booked on some sites.

By car

While it would be foolhardy to rent a car to get around Japan's big cities, **driving** is often the best way to tour the country's less populated and off-the-beaten-track areas. Japanese roads are of a very high standard, with the vast majority of signs on main routes being in *rōmaji* as well as Japanese script. Although you'll have to pay tolls to travel on the expressways (reckon on around ¥30 per kilometre), many other perfectly good roads are free and regular petrol averages around ¥105 a litre. For a group of people, renting a car to tour a rural area over a couple of days can work out much better value than taking buses. It's often possible to rent cars for less than a day, too, for short trips.

There are **car rental** counters at all the major airports and train stations. The main Japanese companies include Mazda Rent-a-car (ⓦwww.mazda-rentacar.co.jp); Nippon Rent-a-car ⓣ03/3485-7196, ⓦwww.nipponrentacar.co.jp); Nissan Rent-a-car (ⓣ0120-00-4123, ⓦwww.nissan-rentacar.com); and Toyota Rent-a-car (ⓣ0800-7000-815, ⓦrent.toyota.co.jp). Budget, Hertz and National also have rental operations across Japan (although not as widely spread). For local car rental firms' contact numbers, see the Listings sections in the relevant city accounts. Rates, which vary little between companies and usually include unlimited mileage, start from around ¥6500 for the first 24 hours for the smallest type of car (a subcompact Minica, seating four people), plus ¥1000 insurance. During the peak seasons of Golden Week, Obon and New Year, rates for all cars tend to increase.

Most cars come with a **GPS** (Global Positioning Satellite) navigation system. It's sometimes possible to get an English-language version CD to work with the GPS – ask for this when you book. Input the telephone number for a location (say the number of the hotel you're staying at or a museum you want to visit) and the GPS system will plot the course for you.

Since you're unlikely to want to drive in any of the cities, the best rental **deals** are often through **Eki Rent-a-Car** (ⓣ03/3358-2130, ⓦwww.ekiren.co.jp), which gives a discounted rate by combining the rental with a train ticket to the most convenient station for the area you wish to explore. Eki-Rent-a-Car's offices are close to stations, as are often those of other major car rental firms.

To rent a car you must have an **international driver's licence** based on the 1949 Geneva Convention (some international licences such as those issued in France, Germany and Switzerland are not valid), as well as your national licence. Officially, if you have a French, German or Swiss licence (regular or international) you are supposed to get an official Japanese translation of the licence – contact your local Japanese embassy for further info. You may get lucky and find a car rental firm that doesn't know or ignores this rule, but don't count on it. If you've been in Japan for more than six months you'll need to apply for a Japanese licence.

Driving is on the left, the same as in Britain, Ireland, Australia and most of Southeast Asia, and international traffic signals are used. The bilingual *Japan Road Atlas* (¥2890) published by Shōbunsha includes many helpful notes, such as the dates when some roads close during winter. If you're a member of an automobile association at home, the chances are that you'll qualify for reciprocal rights with the Japan Auto Federation (ⓦwww.jaf.or.jp), which publishes the English-language *Rules of the Road* book, detailing Japan's driving code.

The top **speed limit** in Japan is 80kph, which applies only on expressways, though drivers frequently exceed this and are rarely stopped by police. In cities, the limit is 40kph. There are always car parks close to main train stations; at some your vehicle will be loaded onto a rotating conveyor belt and whisked off to its parking spot. Reckon on ¥500 per hour for a central city car park and ¥300 per hour elsewhere. If you manage to locate a parking meter, take great care not to overstay the time paid for (usually around ¥300/hour); some have mechanisms to trap cars, which will only be released once the fine has been paid directly into the meter (typically ¥10,000–15,000). In rural areas, parking is not so much of a problem and is rarely charged.

Japanese addresses

Japanese **addresses** are described by a hierarchy of areas, rather than numbers running consecutively along named roads. A typical address starts with the largest administrative district, the *ken* (prefecture), accompanied by a seven-digit postcode – for example, Nagasaki-ken 850-0072. The four exceptions are Tokyo-*to* (metropolis), Kyoto-*fu* and Ōsaka-*fu* (urban prefectures), and Hokkaidō – all independent administrative areas at the same level as the *ken*, also followed by a seven-digit code. Next comes the *shi* (city) or, in the country, the *gun* (county) or *mura* (village). The largest cities are then subdivided into *ku* (wards), followed by *chō* (districts), then *chōme* (local neighbourhoods), blocks and, finally, individual buildings.

If a building has a name and/or holds several different businesses or homes on different floors you'll find the floor number generally listed according to the US fashion with the first floor (1F) being the ground floor and the second floor (2F) being the first floor above ground. B1F, B2F and so on, stands for the floors below ground level, Some addresses, where the block is entirely taken up by one building, will only have two numerals. If an address has four numerals, the first one is for a separate business within a certain part of the building.

Japanese addresses are written in reverse order from the Western system. However, when written in English, they usually follow the Western order; this is the system we adopt in the guide. For example, the address 2F Maru Bldg, 2-12-7 Kitano-chō, Chūō-ku, Kōbe-shi identifies the second floor of the Maru Building which is building number 7, somewhere on block 12 of number 2 *chōme* in Kitano district, in Chūō ward of Kōbe city. Buildings may bear a small metal tag with their number (eg 2-12-7, or just 12-7), while lampposts often have a bigger plaque with the district name in *kanji* and the block reference (eg 2-12). Note that the same address can also be written 12-7 Kitano-chō 2-chōme, Chūō-ku.

Though the system's not too difficult in theory, actually **locating an address** on the ground can be frustrating. The consolation is that even Japanese people find it tough. The best strategy is to have the address written down, preferably in Japanese, and then get to the nearest train or bus station. Once in the neighbourhood, start asking; local police boxes (*kōban*) are a good bet and have detailed maps of their own areas. If all else fails, don't be afraid to phone – often someone will come to meet you.

If you've drunk any **alcohol** at all, even the smallest amount, don't drive – it's illegal and if you're stopped by the police and breathalyzed you'll be in big trouble.

By bike

Although you're unlikely to want to **cycle** around the often traffic-clogged streets of Japan's main cities, a bike is a great way to get from A to B in the smaller towns and countryside, allowing you to see plenty en route. Cycle touring is a very popular activity with students over the long summer vacation. Hokkaidō, in particular, is a cyclist's dream, with excellent roads through often stunning scenery and a network of basic but ultra-cheap cyclists' accommodation.

In many places you can **rent bikes** from outlets beside or near the train station; some towns even have free bikes – enquire at the tourist office. Youth hostels often rent out bikes, too, usually at the most competitive rates. You can buy a brand-new bike in Japan for under ¥20,000 but you wouldn't want to use it for anything more than getting around town; for sturdy touring and mountain bikes, hunt out a specialist bike shop or bring your own. Although repair shops can be found nationwide, for foreign models it's best to bring essential spare parts with you. And despite Japan's low crime rate, a small but significant section of the Japanese public treats bikes as common property; if you don't want to lose it, make sure your bike is well chained whenever you leave it.

If you plan to take your bike on a train or bus, ensure you have a bike bag in which to parcel it up; on trains you're also supposed to pay a special **bike transport supplement** of ¥270 (ask for a *temawarihin kippu*), though ticket inspectors may not always check.

If you're planning a serious cycling tour, an excellent investment is *Cycling Japan* by Brian Harrell, a handy practical guide detailing many touring routes around the country. There's also useful cycling information on the following sites: Ⓦwww.japancycling.org, kancycling.com and www.outdoorjapan.com. If you're up for a two-month pedal from Hokkaidō to Kyūshū, see the website for Bicycling for Everyone's Earth (BEE; Ⓦwww.beejapan.org).

Hitching

There's always a risk associated with **hitching**. That said, Japan is one of the safest and easiest places in the world to hitch a ride, and in some rural areas it's just about the only way of getting around without your own transport. It's also a fantastic way to meet locals, who are often only too happy to go kilometres out of their way to give you a lift just for the novelty value (impecunious students apart, hitching is very rare in Japan), or the opportunity it provides to practise English or another foreign language.

As long as you don't look too scruffy you'll seldom be waiting long for a ride. It's a good idea to write your intended destination in large *kanji* characters on a piece of card to hold up. Carry a stock of small gifts you can leave as a thank you; postcards, sweets and small cuddly toys are usually popular. Will Ferguson's *A Hitchhiker's Guide to Japan* and his entertaining travel narrative *Hokkaidō Highway Blues* (see p.815) are useful reference books.

Accommodation

It's wise to reserve at least your first few nights' accommodation before arrival, especially at the cheaper hostels and minshuku (family-run B&B-style inns) in Tokyo and Kyoto, where budget places are scarce. If you do arrive without a reservation, make use of the free accommodation booking services in Narita and Kansai International airports (see p.91 and p.483).

Once in Japan, book one or two days ahead to ensure you can stay where you like. Outside the peak season, however, you'll rarely be stuck for accommodation. Around major **train stations** there's usually a clutch of business hotels and a **tourist information desk** – most will make a booking for you.

Most large- and medium-sized hotels in big cities have English-speaking receptionists who'll take a booking over the phone. The cheaper and more rural the place, however, the more likely you are to have to speak in Japanese, or a mix of Japanese and English. Don't be put off: armed with the right phrases (see Language, p.815), and speaking slowly and clearly, you should be able to make yourself understood – many of the terms you'll need are actually English words pronounced in a Japanese way. If you're having difficulty, the staff at your current accommodation may be able to help. Booking online is an option, with the advantage that you'll often get a slightly lower room rate; major chains and those places that receive a lot of foreign guests generally have an English-language page.

Almost without exception, **security** is not a problem, though it's never sensible to leave valuables lying around in your room. In

Japanese script

To help you find your way around, we've included **Japanese script** for all place names, and for sights, hotels, restaurants, cafés, bars and shops where there is no prominent English sign. Where the English name for a point of interest is very different from its Japanese name, we've also provided the *rōmaji*, so that you can easily pronounce the Japanese.

hostels it's advisable to use lockers, if provided, or leave important items at the reception desk. Standards of **service** and **cleanliness** vary according to the type of establishment, but are usually more than adequate. Check-in is generally between 4pm and 7pm, and check-out by 10am.

While credit cards are becoming more widely accepted, in many cases **payment** is still expected in cash. In hostels and many cheaper business hotels you'll be expected to pay when you check in. While all hotel rates must include five percent consumption tax, there are a couple of other taxes to look out for. Most top-end hotels add a service charge of ten to fifteen percent, while in Tokyo the Metropolitan Government levies a tax of ¥100 per person per night in rooms that cost over ¥10,000 per person per night (or ¥200 if the room costs over ¥15,000); check to make sure if these are included in the published room rate. In hot-spring resorts, there's a small **onsen tax** (usually ¥150), though again this may already be included in the rates. And it's always worth asking when booking if there are any deals, usually referred to as "plans", such as special weekend rates at business hotels. **Tipping** is not necessary, nor expected, in Japan. The only exception is at high-class Japanese ryokan, where it's good form to leave ¥2000 for the room attendant – put the money in an envelope and hand it over discreetly at the end of your stay.

Online accommodation resources

There are a number of general booking and information sites, the best of which are listed below. More links can be found at Ⓦhttp://tinyurl.com/3y3wpxc.

Ikyu Ⓦikyu.com. Japanese-only site offering heavily discounted rooms at nearly one thousand top-class hotels and ryokan.

Japan Hotel Association Ⓦwww.j-hotel.or.jp. Covering most major cities, though the hotels tend to be part of big, expensive chains. Lots of information provided.

Japan Hotel Net Ⓦwww.japanhotel.net. Offering a good range of accommodation nationwide, with a special section on ski resorts. Lots of information, including photos.

JAPANiCAN Ⓦwww.japanican.com. Good deals on around four thousand hotels, ryokan and tours across the country.

Japan Ryokan Association Ⓦwww.ryokan.or.jp. Around 1300 ryokan and hotels offering Japanese-style accommodation, many of them with onsen baths. Links take you to the relevant homepage and there's plenty of background information about staying in ryokan.

Japan Ryokan & Hotel Association Ⓦwww.nikkanren.or.jp. Well-organized site covering everything from business hotels to minshuku. It gives the basic information, including room rates, access and facilities, plus a link to the home site where available.

Japanese Guest Houses Ⓦwww.japaneseguesthouses.com. Over 550 ryokan – from humble to grand – across the country. Also offer cultural tours in Kyoto.

Japanese Inn Group Ⓦwww.japaneseinngroup.com. A long-established association of about eighty good-value ryokan and minshuku.

The Ryokan Collection Ⓦwww.ryokancollection.com. Book one of 23 top ryokan in six locations across Japan.

Travel Rakuten Ⓦtravel.rakuten.co.jp/en. Pick of the local booking sights with great discounts on published rates and the broadest selection of properties.

Welcome Inn Group Ⓦwww.itcj.jp. Covers a wide range of mostly Japanese-style accommodation, as well as hotels, pensions and youth hostels. Their main office is at the Tokyo TIC (see p.92).

Hotels

Most Western-style **hotel** rooms have en-suite bathrooms, TV, phone, high-speed internet access and air conditioning as standard. Don't expect a lot of character, however, especially among the older and cheaper business hotels, although things are slowly beginning to improve and even relatively inexpensive chains are now smartening up their act. **Rates** for a double or twin room range from an average of ¥30,000 at a top-flight hotel, to ¥15,000–20,000 for a smartish establishment, which will usually have a restaurant and room service. At the lowest level, a room in a basic hotel with minimal amenities will cost ¥5000–10,000. Charges are almost always on a per-room basis and usually exclude meals, though breakfast may occasionally be included. **Single room** rates usually range from just over half to three-quarters the price of a double. Most hotels offer non-smoking rooms and some have "ladies' floors".

Business hotels

Modest **business hotels** constitute the bulk of the middle and lower price brackets. Primarily designed for those travelling on business and usually clustered around train stations, they are perfect if all you want is a place to crash out, though at the cheapest places you may find just a box with tiny beds, a desk and a chair crammed into the smallest possible space. While the majority of rooms are single, most places have a few twins, doubles or "semi-doubles" – a large single bed which takes two at a squeeze. Squeeze is also the operative word for the aptly named "unit baths", which business hotels specialize in; these moulded plastic units contain a shower, bathtub, toilet and washbasin but leave little room for manoeuvre. That said, some business hotels are relatively smart and there are a number of reliable chains including *Tōyoko Inn* (Ⓦwww.toyoko-inn.com), which has scores of hotels across the country, offering a simple breakfast and free internet connections in their room rates. More upmarket are *Washington Hotels* (Ⓦwh-rsv.com/english) and the *Solare* group (Ⓦwww.solarehotels.com), which encompasses *Chisun* business hotels and the smarter *Loisir* and *Solare Collection* chains.

Capsule hotels

Catering mainly for commuters – often in various states of inebriation – who have missed their last train home are **capsule hotels**; you'll find them mostly near major stations. Inside are rows of coffin-like tubes, roughly 2m by 1m, containing a mattress, bedding, phone, alarm and TV built into the plastic surrounds. The "door" consists of a flimsy curtain, which won't keep out the loudest snores, and they are definitely not designed for claustrophobics. However, they're relatively cheap (averaging around ¥4000 per night) and fun to try at least once, though the majority are for men only. You can't stay in the hotel during the day – not that you'd want to – but you can leave luggage in their lockers. Check-in usually starts around 4pm and often involves buying a ticket from a vending machine in the lobby. Rates generally include a *yukata* (cotton dressing gown), towel and toothbrush set. Kyoto and Ōsaka offer a couple of stylish modern takes on the capsule hotel that are worth trying (see pp.412–413 and p.487).

Love hotels

Love hotels – where you can rent rooms by the hour – are another quintessential Japanese experience. Generally located in entertainment districts, they are immediately

Accommodation price codes

Accommodation in this book has been graded according to the following **price codes**, which refer to the cheapest double or twin room available, including taxes. In the case of hostels providing **dormitory accommodation**, we've given the price per person. Note that rates may increase during peak holiday periods, in particular around Christmas and New Year, the Golden Week (April 29–May 5) and Obon (the week around Aug 15).

❶ ¥3000 and under	❹ ¥7001–10,000	❼ ¥20,001–30,000
❷ ¥3001–5000	❺ ¥10,001–15,000	❽ ¥30,001–40,000
❸ ¥5001–7000	❻ ¥15,001–20,000	❾ ¥40,001 and over

recognizable from the sign outside quoting prices for "rest" or "stay", and many sport ornate exteriors. Some can be quite sophisticated: the main market is young people or married couples taking a break from crowded apartments. All kinds of tastes can be indulged at love hotels, with rotating beds in mirror-lined rooms now decidedly passé in comparison with some of the fantasy creations on offer. Some rooms even come equipped with video cameras so you can take home a souvenir DVD of your stay. You usually choose your room from a back-lit display indicating those still available, and then negotiate with a cashier lurking behind a tiny window (eye-to-eye contact is avoided to preserve privacy). Though "rest" rates are high (from about ¥5000 for 2hr), the price of an overnight stay can cost the same as a business hotel (roughly ¥8000–10,000), although you usually can't check in until around 10pm. To learn more about love hotels buy the photo book *Love Hotels* by Ed Jacob (Ⓦwww.quirkyjapan.or.tv/lovehotelbookintro.htm).

Japanese-style accommodation

A night in a traditional Japanese inn, or **ryokan**, is one of the highlights of a visit to Japan. The best charge five-star hotel rates, but there are plenty where you can enjoy the full experience at affordable prices. Cheaper are **minshuku**, family-run guesthouses, and the larger government-owned **kokuminshukusha** (people's lodges) located in national parks and resort areas. In addition, some temples and shrines offer simple accommodation, or you can arrange to stay with a Japanese family through the **homestay** programme.

It's advisable to **reserve** at least a day ahead and essential if you want to eat in. Though a few don't take foreigners, mainly through fear of language problems and cultural faux pas, you'll find plenty that do listed in the guide chapters. JNTO also publishes useful lists of ryokan and distributes brochures of the Welcome Inn Group and Japanese Inn Group (see online accommodation resources, p.42), both of which specialize in inexpensive, foreigner-friendly accommodation.

Ryokan

Rooms in a typical **ryokan** are generally furnished with just a low table and floor cushions sitting on pale green rice-straw matting (tatami) and a hanging scroll – nowadays alongside a TV and phone – decorating the alcove (*tokonoma*) on one wall. Though you'll increasingly find a toilet and washbasin in the room, baths are generally communal. The rules of ryokan etiquette (see box, p.45) may seem daunting, but overall these are great places to stay.

Room rates vary according to the season, the grade of room, the quality of meal you opt for and the number of people in a room; prices almost always include breakfast and an evening meal. Rates are usually quoted per person and calculated on the basis of two people sharing. One person staying in a room will pay slightly more than the advertised per-person price; three people sharing a room, slightly less. On average, a night in a basic ryokan will cost between ¥8000 and ¥10,000 per head, while a more classy establishment, perhaps with meals served in the room, will cost up to ¥20,000. Top-rank ryokan with exquisite meals and the most attentive service imaginable can cost upwards of ¥50,000 per person.

At cheaper ryokan it's possible to ask for a room without **meals**, though this is frowned on at the more traditional places and, anyway, the delicious multicourse meals are often very good value. If you find miso soup, cold fish and rice a bit hard to tackle in the morning, you might want to opt for a Western breakfast, if available.

Minshuku and kokuminshukusha

There's a fine line between the cheapest ryokan and a **minshuku**. In general, minshuku are smaller and less formal than ryokan: more like staying in a private home, with varying degrees of comfort and cleanliness. All rooms will be Japanese-style, with communal bathrooms and dining areas. A night in a minshuku will cost from around ¥4500 per person excluding meals, or from ¥6000 with two meals; rates are calculated in the same way as for ryokan.

In country areas and popular resorts, you'll also find homely guesthouses called

Staying in Japanese-style accommodation

Whenever you're staying in Japanese-style accommodation, you'll be expected to check in early – between 3pm and 6pm – and to follow local custom from the moment you arrive.

Just inside the front door, there's usually a row of **slippers** for you to change into, but remember to slip them off when walking on the tatami (see p.65 for more on footwear). The **bedding** is stored behind sliding doors in your room during the day and only laid out in the evening. In top-class ryokan this is done for you, but elsewhere be prepared to tackle your own. There'll be a mattress (which goes straight on the tatami) with a sheet to put over it, a soft quilt to sleep under and a pillow stuffed with rice husks.

Most places provide a **yukata**, a loose cotton robe tied with a belt, and a short jacket (*tanzen*) in cold weather. The *yukata* can be worn in bed, during meals, when going to the bathroom and even outside – in resort areas many Japanese holidaymakers take an evening stroll in their *yukata* and wooden sandals (*geta*; also supplied by the ryokan). Wrap the left side of the *yukata* over the right; the opposite is used to dress the dead.

The traditional Japanese **bath** (*furo*) has its own set of rules (see p.66). It's customary to bathe in the evenings. In ryokan there are usually separate bathrooms for men (男) and women (女), but elsewhere there will either be designated times for males and females, or you'll simply have to wait until it's vacant – it's perfectly acceptable for couples and families to bathe together, though there's not usually a lot of space.

Evening **meals** tend to be early, at 6pm or 7pm. Smarter ryokan generally serve meals in your room, while communal dining is the norm in cheaper places. **At night** the doors are locked pretty early, so check before going out – they may let you have a key.

pensions – a word borrowed from the French. Though the accommodation and meals are Western-style, these are really minshuku in disguise. They're family-run – generally by young couples escaping city life – and specialize in hearty home cooking. Rates average around ¥8000 per head, including dinner and breakfast.

In the national parks, onsen resorts and other popular tourist spots, minshuku and pensions are supplemented by large, government-run **kokuminshukusha**, which cater to family groups and tour parties. They're often quite isolated and difficult to get to without your own transport. The average cost of a night's accommodation is around ¥8000 per person, including two meals.

Temples and shrines

A few Buddhist **temples** and Shinto **shrines** take in regular guests for a small fee, and some belong to the Japanese Inn Group (see p.42) or the Japan Youth Hostels association (see opposite). By far the best places to experience temple life are at the Buddhist retreat of Kōya-san (p.500) and in Kyoto's temple lodges (see p.415).

Though the accommodation is inevitably basic, the food can be superb, especially in temple lodgings (*shukubō*), where the monks serve up delicious vegetarian cuisine (*shōjin ryōri*). In many temples you'll also be welcome to attend the early-morning prayer ceremonies. Prices vary between ¥4000 and ¥10,000 per person, with no meals or perhaps just breakfast at lower rates.

Youth hostels

Japan has over three hundred **youth hostels** spread throughout the country, offering cheap accommodation. Once you've included meals, however, a night at a hostel may work out only slightly less expensive than staying at a minshuku, or a night at a business hotel such at Tōyoko Inn. The majority of hostels are well run, clean and welcoming. The best are housed in

Homestay programmes & WWOOF

Homestay **programmes** are a wonderful way of getting to know Japan – contact any of the local tourism associations and international exchange foundations listed in this book to see if any programmes are operating in the area you plan to visit. It's also possible to arrange to stay at one of nearly 400 so organic farms and other rural properties around Japan through **WWOOF** (Willing Workers on Organic Farms; ⓦwww.wwoof.org). Bed and board is provided for free in return for work on the farm; see Living in Japan, p.75, for more details. This is a great way to really experience how country folk live away from the big cities and the beaten tourist path. To get a list of host farms you have to take out an annual membership, though a few examples are posted on the Japanese site (ⓦwww.wwoofjapan.com).

wonderful old farmhouses or temples, often in great locations; you'll also find hostels in most big cities. In general, you can stay up to six nights in any one hostel, though longer stays are possible if they're not booked up. The main drawbacks are an evening curfew and, at some hostels, a raft of regulations.

The average **price** of hostel accommodation ranges from around ¥3000 per person for a dorm bed up to ¥5500 for a private room, with optional meals costing around ¥600 for breakfast and ¥1000 for dinner. Rates at some hostels increase during peak holiday periods, while most charge an additional ¥600 per night to non-members (see below).

Youth hostels are either run by the government or by Japan Youth Hostels (JYH; ⓦwww.jyh.or.jp), which is affiliated to Hostelling International (HI; ⓦwww.hihostels.com), or they may be privately owned. **Membership** cards are not required at government hostels, but all JYH and many private hostels ask for a current Youth Hostel card. Non-members have to buy a "welcome stamp" (¥600) each time they stay at a JYH or private hostel; six stamps within a twelve-month period entitles you to the Hostelling International card. JNTO offices abroad and around Japan stock a free **map** that gives contact details of all JYH hostels.

It's essential to make **reservations** well in advance for the big-city hostels and during school vacations: namely, New Year, March, around Golden Week (late April to mid-May), and in July and August. At other times, it's a good idea to book ahead, since hostels in prime tourist spots are always busy, and some close for a day or two off-season (others for the whole winter). If you want an evening meal, you also need to let them know a day in advance. Hostel accommodation normally consists of either dormitory bunks or shared Japanese-style tatami rooms, with communal bathrooms and dining areas. An increasing number also have private or family rooms, but these tend to fill up quickly. **Bedding** is provided. The majority of hostels have **laundry** facilities and a few offer internet access, for which there is usually a small charge.

Though hostel **meals** vary in quality, they are often pretty good value. Dinner will generally be Japanese-style, while breakfast frequently includes bread, jam and coffee, sometimes as part of a buffet. Some hostels have a basic kitchen. Note that one or two hostels don't provide evening meals and there may not be any restaurants close by, so ask when you book.

Check-in is generally between 3pm and 8pm (by 6.30pm if you're having the evening meal), and you have to vacate the building during the day (usually by 10am). In the evening, most hostels lock up around 11pm – while in many loudspeakers announce when it's time to bath, eat, turn the lights out and get up; there's even an approved way to fold hostel blankets. Some people find this boarding-school atmosphere totally off-putting, but you'll come across plenty of hostels with a more laidback attitude. You won't be expected to do any chores, beyond clearing the table after meals and taking your sheets down to reception when you leave.

Camping and mountain huts

There are thousands of **campsites** (*kyampu-jō*) scattered throughout Japan, with prices ranging from nothing up to ¥5000 or more to pitch a tent. In some places you'll also pay an entry fee of a few hundred yen per person, plus charges for water and cooking gas. In general, facilities are pretty basic compared with American or European sites; many have no hot water, for example, and the camp shop may stock nothing but pot-noodles. Most sites only open during the summer months, when they're packed out with students and school parties.

JNTO publishes lists of selected campsites, or ask at local tourist offices. If you haven't got your own tent, you can often hire everything on-site or rent simple cabins from around ¥2500 – check before you get there. The best sites are in national parks and can be both time-consuming and costly to get to unless you have your own transport. Sleeping rough in national parks is banned, but elsewhere in the countryside **camping wild** is tolerated. However, it's advisable to choose an inconspicuous spot – don't put your tent up till dusk, and leave early in the morning.

In the main hiking areas, you'll find a good network of **mountain huts** (*yama-goya*). These range from basic shelters to much fancier places with wardens and meals. Huts get pretty crowded in summer and during student holidays; count on at least ¥5000 per head, including two meals. Many places will also provide a picnic lunch. You can get information about mountain huts from local tourist offices.

Long-term accommodation

There's plenty of long-term **rental accommodation** available in Japan, making it a relatively easy and affordable country in which to set up home.

Newcomers who arrive without a job, or are not on some sort of expat package that includes accommodation, usually start off in what's known as a **gaijin house (foreigner house)**. Located in Tokyo, Kyoto and other cities with large foreign populations, these are shared apartments with a communal kitchen and bathroom, ranging from total fleapits to the almost luxurious. They're usually rented by the month, though if there's space, weekly or even nightly rates may be available. You'll find *gaijin* houses advertised in the English-language press, or simply ask around. Monthly rates for a shared apartment in Tokyo start at ¥30,000–40,000 per person if you share a room and ¥50,000–60,000 for your own room. A deposit may also be required.

The alternative is a private apartment. These are usually rented out by real estate companies, though you'll also find places advertised in the media. Unfortunately, some prejudiced landlords may simply refuse to rent to non-Japanese. Some rental agencies specialize in dealing with foreigners, or you could ask a Japanese friend or colleague to act as an intermediary. When you've found a place, be prepared to pay a deposit of one to two months' rent in addition to the first month's rent, key money (usually one or two months' non-refundable rent when you move in) and a month's rent in commission to the agent. You may also be asked to provide information about your financial situation and find someone – generally a Japanese national – to act as a guarantor. The basic monthly rental in Tokyo starts at ¥50,000–60,000 per month for a one-room box, and upwards of ¥100,000 for somewhere more comfortable with a separate kitchen and bathroom.

Food and drink

One of the great pleasures of a trip to Japan is exploring the full and exotic range of Japanese food and drink. While dishes such as sushi and tempura are common the world over these days, there are hundreds of other types of local cuisine that will be new and delicious discoveries – see the *Regional cuisines* colour section for a few ideas. Many Japanese recipes embody a subtlety of flavour and mixture of texture rarely found in other cuisines, and the presentation is often so exquisite that it feels an insult to the chef to eat what has been so painstakingly crafted.

Picking at delicate morsels with chopsticks is only one small part of the dining experience. It's far more common to find Japanese tucking into robust and cheap dishes such as hearty bowls of **ramen noodles** or the comforting concoction **karē raisu** (curry rice) as well as burgers and fried chicken from ubiquitous Western-style fast-food outlets. All the major cities have an extensive range of restaurants serving Western and other Asian dishes, with Tokyo, Kyoto and Ōsaka in particular being major destinations for foodies. In addition, each region has its own distinctive culinary traditions.

Eating out needn't cost the earth. Lunch is always the best-value meal of the day, seldom costing more than ¥2000. If you fuel up earlier in the day, a cheap bowl of noodles for dinner could carry you through the night.

Meals

Breakfast is generally served from around 7am to 9am at most hotels, ryokan and minshuku. At the top end and mid-range places you'll generally have a choice between a Western-style breakfast or a traditional meal consisting of miso soup, grilled fish, pickles and rice; at the cheaper minshuku and ryokan only a Japanese-style meal will be available. Western-style breakfasts, when available, sometimes resemble what you might eat at home, but most commonly involve wedges of thick white tasteless bread, and some form of eggs and salad. Most cafés also have a "morning-service" menu which means *kōhii* and *tōsuto* (coffee and toast).

Restaurants generally open for **lunch** around 11.30am and finish serving at 2pm. Lacklustre sandwiches are best passed over in favour of a full meal at a restaurant; set menus (called *teishoku*) are always on offer and usually cost around ¥1000 for a couple of courses, plus a drink.

Teishoku are sometimes available at night, when you may also come across **course menus**, which involve a series of courses and are priced according to the number of courses and quality of ingredients used. At any time of day you can snack in stand-up noodle bars – often found around train stations – and from revolving conveyor belts at cheap sushi shops.

Dinner, the main meal of the day, is typically served from 6pm to around 9pm. The major cities are about the only option for late-night dining. In a traditional Japanese meal (see pp.50–53 for a description of the main dishes) you'll usually be served all your courses at the same time, but at more formal places rice and soup are always served last. You are most likely to finish your meal with a piece of seasonal **fruit**, such as melon, orange, persimmon or *nashi* (a crisp type of pear), or an ice cream (if it's green, it will be flavoured with *macha* tea).

At **tea ceremonies** (see box, p.55), small, intensely sweet *wagashi* are served – these prettily decorated sweetmeats are usually made of pounded rice, red azuki beans or chestnuts. *Wagashi* can also be bought from specialist shops and department stores and make lovely gifts.

Where to eat and drink

A *shokudō* is a kind of canteen that serves a range of traditional and generally inexpensive dishes. Usually found near train and subway stations and in busy shopping districts, *shokudō* can be identified by the displays of plastic meals in their windows. Other restaurants (*resutoran*) usually serve just one type of food, for example sushi and sashimi (*sushi-ya*), or *yakitori* (*yakitori-ya*), or specialize in a particular style of cooking, such as *kaiseki* (haute cuisine) or *tepanyaki*, where food is prepared on a steel griddle, either by yourself or a chef.

All over Japan, but particularly in city suburbs, you'll find bright and breezy **family restaurants**, such as *Royal Host* and *Jonathan's*, American-style operations specifically geared to family dining and serving Western and Japanese dishes – the food can be on the bland side, but is invariably keenly priced. They also have menus illustrated with photographs to make ordering easy. If you can't decide what to eat, head for the restaurant floors of major **department stores**, where you'll find a collection of Japanese and Western operations, often outlets of reputable local restaurants. Many will have plastic food displays in their front windows and daily special menus.

Western and other ethnic food restaurants proliferate in the cities, and it's seldom a problem finding popular **foreign cuisines** such as Italian (*Itaria-ryōri*), French (*Furansu-ryōri*), Korean (*Kankoku-ryōri*), Chinese (*Chūgokū* or *Chūka-ryōri*) or Thai (*Tai-ryōri*) food. However, the recipes are often adapted to suit Japanese tastes, which can mean less spicy dishes than you may be used to.

Coffee shops (*kissaten*) are something of an institution in Japan, often designed to act as a lounge or business meeting place for patrons starved of space at home or the office. Others have weird designs or specialize in certain things, such as jazz or comic books. In such places a speciality coffee or tea will usually set you back ¥500 or more. There are also plenty of cheap and cheerful operations like *Doutor* and *Starbucks*, serving drinks and snacks at reasonable prices; search these places out for a cheap breakfast or a quick bite.

The best-value and liveliest places to **drink** are the **izakaya** pub-type restaurants, which also serve an extensive menu of mainly small dishes. Traditional *izakaya* are rather rustic-looking, although in the cities you'll come across more modern, trendy operations aimed at the youth market. One type of traditional *izakaya* is the *robatayaki*, which serves charcoal-grilled food. Most *izakaya* open around 6pm and shut down around midnight if not later. From mid-June to late August, outdoor **beer gardens** – some attached to existing restaurants and *izakayas*, other stand-alone operations – flourish across Japan's main cities and towns; look out for the fairy lights on the roofs of buildings, or in street-level gardens and plazas.

Regular bars, or **nomiya**, often consist of little more than a short counter and a table, and are run by a *mama-san* if female, or *papa-san* or master if male. Prices at most *nomiya* tend to be high and, although you're less likely to be ripped off if you speak some Japanese, it's no guarantee. All such bars operate a **bottle keep** system for regulars to stash a bottle of drink with their name on it

Bentō: the Japanese packed lunch

Every day millions of Japanese trot off to school or work with a bentō stashed in their satchel or briefcase. Bentō are boxed lunches which are either made at home or bought from shops all over Japan. Traditional bentō include rice, pickles, grilled fish or meat and vegetables. There are thousands of permutations depending on the season and the location in Japan (see box on railway food, p.31), with some of the best being available from department stores – there's always a model or picture to show you what's inside the box. At their most elaborate, in classy restaurants, bentō come in beautiful multilayered lacquered boxes, each compartment containing some exquisite culinary creation. Among housewives it's become something of a competitive sport and art form to create fun designs out of the bentō ingredients for their children's lunch. Empty bentō boxes in a huge range of designs are sold in the household section of department stores and make lovely souvenirs.

Kaiseki-ryōri: Japanese haute cuisine

Japan's finest style of cooking, *kaiseki-ryōri*, comprises a series of small, carefully balanced and expertly presented dishes. Described by renowned Kyoto chef Murata Yoshihiro as "eating the seasons", this style of cooking began as an accompaniment to the tea ceremony and still retains the meticulous design of that elegant ritual. At the best *kaiseki-ryōri* restaurants the atmosphere of the room in which the meal is served is just as important as the food, which will invariably reflect the best of the season's produce; you'll sit on tatami, a scroll decorated with calligraphy will hang in the *tokonoma* (alcove) and a waitress in kimono will serve each course on beautiful china and lacquerware. For such a sublime experience you should expect to pay ¥10,000 or more for dinner, although a lunchtime *kaiseki* bentō (see box, p.149) is a more affordable option, typically costing around ¥5000.

behind the bar. It's generally best to go to such bars with a regular, since they tend to operate like mini-clubs, with non-regulars being given the cold shoulder. *Nomiya* stay open to the early hours, provided there are customers. A variation on the *nomiya* is the *tachinomiya* or standing bar which are usually cheaper and more casual. Some specialize in selling premium wines or sake, and they often serve good food alongside the drinks.

Some bars also have cover charges (for which you'll usually get some small snack with your drink), although there's plenty of choice among those that don't, so always check before buying your drink. Bars specializing in **karaoke** aren't difficult to spot; if you decide to join in, there's usually a small fee to pay and at least a couple of songs with English lyrics to choose from.

Ordering and etiquette

On walking into most restaurants in Japan you'll be greeted by the word *Irasshaimase* ("welcome"). Indicate with your fingers how many places are needed. After being seated you'll be handed an *oshibori*, a damp, folded hand towel, usually steaming hot, but sometimes offered refreshingly cold in summer. A chilled glass of water (*mizu*) will also usually be brought automatically.

To help you decipher the menu there's a basic glossary of essential words and phrases on p.831; for more detail, try *Japanese: A Rough Guide Phrasebook*, or the comprehensive *What's What in Japanese Restaurants* by Robb Satterwhite. It's always worth asking if an English menu is available (*eigo no menyū ga arimasu-ka*). If a restaurant has a plastic food window display, get up from your seat and use it to point to your waiter or waitress what you want. If all else fails, look round at what your fellow diners are eating and point out what you fancy. Remember that the *teishoku* (set meal) or *kōsu* (course) meals offer the best value. The word *Baikingu* (written in katakana and standing for "Viking") means a help-yourself buffet.

Don't stick **chopsticks** (*hashi*) upright in your rice – this is an allusion to death. If you're taking food from a shared plate, turn the chopsticks round and use the other end to pick up the food. Also, never cross your chopsticks when you put them on the table or use them to point at things. When it comes to eating soupy noodles, it's considered good form to slurp them up noisily; it's also fine to bring the bowl to your lips and drink directly from it.

When you want the **bill**, say *okanjō kudasai*; the usual form is to pay at the till on the way out, not to leave the money on the table. There's no need to leave a tip, but it's polite to say *gochisō-sama deshita* ("That was delicious!") to the waiter or chef. Only the most upmarket Western restaurants and top hotels will add a service charge (typically ten percent).

Sushi, sashimi and seafood

Many non-Japanese falsely assume that all **sushi** is fish, but the name actually refers to the way the rice is prepared with vinegar, and you can also get sushi dishes with egg or vegetables. Fish and seafood are, of course, essential and traditional elements of Japanese cuisine, and range from the seaweed used in *miso-shiru* (soup) to the slices of tuna, salmon and squid laid across the slabs of sushi rice. Slices of raw fish and seafood on their own are called **sashimi**.

In a traditional **sushi-ya** each plate is freshly made by a team of chefs working in full view of the customers. If you're not sure of the different types to order, point at the trays on show in the glass chiller cabinets at the counter, or go for the *nigiri-zushi mori-awase*, six or seven different types of fish and seafood on fingers of sushi rice. Other types of sushi include *maki-zushi*, rolled in a sheet of crisp seaweed, and *chirashi-zushi*, a layer of rice topped with fish, vegetables and cooked egg.

While a meal at a reputable *sushi-ya* averages ¥5000 (or much more at a high-class joint), at **kaiten-zushi** shops, where you choose whatever sushi dish you want from the continually replenished conveyor belt, the bill will rarely stretch beyond ¥3000 per person. In *kaiten-zushi*, plates are colour-coded according to how much they cost, and are totted up at the end for the total cost of the meal. If you can't see what you want, you can ask the chefs to make it for you. Green tea is free, and you can usually order beer or sake.

To try **fugu**, or blowfish, go to a specialist fish restaurant, which can be easily identified by the picture or model of a balloon-like fish outside. *Fugu*'s reputation derives from its potentially fatally poisonous nature rather than its bland, rubbery taste. The actual risk of dropping dead at the counter is virtually nil – at least from *fugu* poisoning – and you're more likely to keel over at the bill, which (cheaper, farmed *fugu* apart) will be in the ¥10,000 per-person bracket. *Fugu* is often served as part of a set course menu including raw slivers of fish (sashimi) and a stew made from other parts of the fish served with rice.

A more affordable and tasty seafood speciality is **unagi**, or eel, typically basted with a thick sauce of soy and sake, sizzled over charcoal and served on a bed of rice. This dish is particularly popular in summer, when it's believed to provide strength in the face of sweltering heat.

Noodles

The three main types of **noodle** are soba, udon and ramen. **Soba** are thin noodles made of brown buckwheat flour. If the noodles are green, they've been made with green tea powder.

There are two main styles of serving soba: hot and cold. *Kake-soba* is served in a clear hot broth, often with added ingredients such as tofu, vegetables and chicken. Cold noodles piled on a bamboo screen bed, with a cold sauce for dipping (which can be flavoured with chopped spring onions, seaweed flakes and *wasabi* – grated green horseradish paste) is called *zaru-soba* or *mori-soba*. In more traditional restaurants you'll also be served a flask of the hot water (*soba-yu*) to cook the noodles, which is added to the dipping sauce to make a soup drink once you've finished the soba.

In most soba restaurants, **udon** will also be on the menu. These chunkier noodles are made with plain wheat flour and are served in the same hot or cold styles as soba. In **yakisoba** and **yakiudon** dishes the noodles are fried, often in a thick soy sauce, along with seaweed flakes, meat and vegetables.

Ramen, or yellow wheat-flour noodles, were originally imported from China but have now become part and parcel of Japanese cuisine. They're usually served in big bowls in a steaming oily soup, which typically comes in three varieties: *miso* (flavoured with fermented bean paste), *shio* (a salty soup) or *shōyu* (a broth made with soy sauce). The dish is often finished off with a range of garnishes, including seaweed, bamboo shoots, pink and white swirls of fish paste, and pork slices. You can usually spice it up with condiments such as minced garlic or a red pepper mixture at your table. Wherever you eat ramen, you can also usually get **gyōza**, fried half-moon-shaped dumplings filled with pork or seafood, to accompany them.

Rice dishes

A traditional meal isn't considered finished until a bowl of rice has been eaten. This Japanese staple also forms the basis of both the alcoholic drink sake and **mochi**, a chewy dough made from pounded glutinous rice, usually prepared and eaten during festivals such as New Year.

Rice is an integral part of several cheap snack-type dishes. **Onigiri** are palm-sized triangles of rice with a filling of soy, tuna, salmon roe, or sour *umeboshi* (pickled plum), all wrapped up in a sheet of crisp *nori* (seaweed). They can be bought at convenience stores for around ¥150 each and are ingeniously packaged so that the *nori* stays crisp until the *onigiri* is unwrapped. **Donburi** is a bowl of rice with various toppings, such as chicken and egg (*oyako-don*, literally "parent and child"), strips of stewed beef (*gyū-don*) or *katsu-don*, which come with a *tonkatsu* (see below) pork cutlet.

A perennially popular Japanese comfort food is **curry rice** (*karē raisu* in *rōmaji*). Only mildly spicy, this bears little relation to the Indian dish: what goes into the sludgy brown sauce that makes up the curry is a mystery, and you'll probably search in vain for evidence of any beef or chicken in the so-called *biifu karē* and *chikin karē*. The better concoctions are very tasty and invariably cheap.

Meat dishes

Meat is an uncommon part of traditional Japanese cuisine, but in the last century dishes using beef, pork and chicken have become a major part of the national diet. Burger outlets are ubiquitous, and expensive steak restaurants, serving up dishes like **sukiyaki** (thin beef slices cooked in a soy, sugar and sake broth) and **shabu-shabu** (beef and vegetable slices cooked at the table in a light broth and dipped in various sauces), are popular treats.

Like *sukiyaki* and *shabu-shabu*, **nabe** (the name refers to the cooking pot) stews are prepared at the table over a gas or charcoal burner by diners who throw a range of raw ingredients (meat or fish along with vegetables) into the pot to cook. As things cook they're fished out, and the last thing to be immersed is usually some type of noodle. *Chanko-nabe* is the famous chuck-it-all-in stew used to beef up sumo wrestlers.

Other popular meat dishes include: **tonkatsu**, breadcrumb-covered slabs of pork, crisply fried and usually served on a bed of shredded cabbage with a brown, semi-sweet sauce; and **yakitori**, delicious skewers of grilled chicken (and sometimes other meats and vegetables). At the cheapest *yakitori-ya*, you'll pay for each skewer individually, typically around ¥100 or less a stick. **Kushiage** is a combination of *tonkatsu* and *yakitori* dishes, where skewers of meat, seafood and vegetables are coated in breadcrumbs and deep-fried.

Vegetarian dishes

Despite being the home of macrobiotic cooking, **vegetarianism** isn't a widely practised or fully understood concept in Japan. You might ask for a vegetarian (*saishoku*) dish in a restaurant and still be served something with meat or fish in it. If you're a committed vegetarian, things to watch out for include *dashi* stock, which contains *bonito* (dried tuna), and omelettes, which may contain chicken stock. To get a truly vegetarian meal you will have to be patient and be prepared to spell out exactly what you do and do not eat when you order. **Vege-Navi** (vege-navi.jp) lists many vegetarian, vegan and macrobiotic options across the country.

If you're willing to turn a blind eye to occasionally eating meat, fish or animal fats by mistake, then tuck in because Japan has bequeathed some marvellous vegetarian foods to the world. Top of the list is **tofu**, compacted cakes of soya-bean curd, which comes in two main varieties, *momengoshi-dōfu* (cotton tofu), so-called because of its fluffy texture, and the smoother, more fragile *kinugoshi-dōfu* (silk tofu). Buddhist cuisine, *shōjin-ryōri*, concocts whole menus based around different types of tofu dishes; although they can be expensive, it's worth searching out the specialist restaurants serving this type of food, particularly in major temple cities, such as Kyoto, Nara and Nagano. Note, though, that the most popular tofu dish you'll come across in restaurants – *hiya yakko*, a small slab of chilled tofu topped with grated ginger, spring onions and soy sauce – is usually sprinkled with *bonito* flakes.

Miso (fermented bean paste) is another crucial ingredient of Japanese cooking, used in virtually every meal, if only in the soup *miso-shiru*. It often serves as a flavouring in vegetable dishes and comes in two main varieties, the light *shiro-miso* and the darker, stronger-tasting *aka-miso*.

One question all foreigners in Japan are asked is "can you eat **nattō**?". This sticky, stringy fermented bean paste has a strong taste, pungent aroma and unfamiliar texture, which can be off-putting to Western palates. It's worth trying at least once, though, and is usually served in little tubs at breakfast, to be mixed with mustard and soy sauce and eaten with rice.

Other Japanese dishes

Said to have been introduced to Japan in the sixteenth century by Portuguese traders, **tempura** are lightly battered pieces of seafood and vegetables. Tempura are dipped in a bowl of light sauce (*ten-tsuyu*) mixed with grated *daikon* radish and sometimes ginger. At specialist tempura restaurants, you'll generally order the *teishoku* set meal, which includes whole prawns, squid, aubergines, mushrooms and the aromatic leaf *shiso*.

Oden is a warming dish, usually served in winter but available at other times too – it tastes much more delicious than it looks. Large chunks of food, usually on skewers, are simmered in a thin broth, and often served from portable carts (*yatai*) on street corners or in convenience stores from beside the till. The main ingredients are blocks of tofu, *daikon* (a giant radish), *konnyaku* (a hard jelly made from a root vegetable), *konbu* (seaweed), hard-boiled eggs and fish cakes. All are best eaten with a smear of fiery English-style mustard.

Japan's equivalent of the pizza is **okonomiyaki**, a fun, cheap meal that you can often assemble yourself. A pancake batter is used to bind shredded cabbage and other vegetables with either seafood or meat. If it's a DIY restaurant, you'll mix the individual ingredients and cook them on a griddle in the middle of the table. Otherwise, you can sit at the kitchen counter watching the chefs at work. Once cooked, *okonomiyaki* is coated in a sweet brown sauce and/or mayonnaise and dusted off with dried seaweed and flakes of bonito fish, which twist and curl in the rising heat. At most *okonomiyaki* restaurants you can also get fried noodles (*yakisoba*). In addition, *okonomiyaki*, along with its near-cousin **takoyaki** (battered balls of octopus), are often served from *yatai* carts at street festivals.

Authentic Western restaurants are now commonplace across Japan, but there is also a hybrid style of cooking known as **yōshoku** ("Western food") that developed during the Meiji era at the turn of the twentieth century. Often served in *shokudō*, *yōshoku* dishes include omelettes with rice (*omu-raisu*), deep-fried potato croquettes (*korokke*) and hamburger steaks (*hanbāgu*) doused in a thick sauce. The contemporary version of *yōshoku* is **mukokuseki** or "no-nationality" cuisine, a mishmash of world cooking styles usually found in *izakaya*.

Drinks

The Japanese are enthusiastic social drinkers. It's not uncommon to see totally inebriated people slumped in the street, though on the whole drunkenness rarely leads to violence.

If you want a **non-alcoholic** drink, you'll never be far from a coffee shop (*kissaten*) or a *jidō hambaiki* (vending machine), where you can get a vast range of canned drinks, both hot and cold; note canned tea and coffee is often very sweet. Soft drinks from machines typically cost ¥110 and hot drinks are identified by a red stripe under the display. Vending machines selling beer, sake and other alcoholic drinks shut down at 11pm, the same time as liquor stores. A few 24-hour convenience stores may sell alcohol after this time; look for the *kanji* for sake (酒) outside.

Sake

Legend has it that the ancient deities brewed **sake** (also known as *nihonshu*) – Japan's most famous alcoholic beverage – from the first rice of the new year. Although often referred to as rice wine, the drink, which comes in thousands of different brands, is actually brewed so is more closely related to beer (which long ago surpassed sake as Japan's most popular alcoholic drink).

Made either in sweet (*amakuchi*) or dry (*karakuchi*) varieties, sake is graded as *tokkyū* (superior), *ikkyū* (first) and *nikyū* (second), although this is mainly for tax purposes; if you're after the best quality,

Drinking etiquette

If you're out **drinking** with Japanese friends, always pour your colleagues' drinks, but never your own; they'll take care of that. In fact, you'll find your glass being topped up after every couple of sips. The usual way to make a **toast** in Japanese is "*kampai*".

In many bars you'll be served a small snack or a plate of nuts (*otōshi*) with your first drink, whether you've asked for it or not; this typically accounts for a cover charge being added to the bill. It's fine to get blinding drunk and misbehave with your colleagues at night, but it's very bad form to talk about it in the cold light of day.

connoisseurs recommend going for *ginjō-zukuri* (or *ginjō-zō*), the most expensive and rare of the *junmai-shu* pure rice sake. Some types of sake are cloudier and less refined than others, and there's also the very sweet, milky *amazaké*, often served at temple festivals and at shrines over New Year.

In restaurants and *izakaya* you'll be served sake in a small flask (*tokkuri*) so you can pour your own serving or share it with someone else. You will also be given the choice of drinking your sake warm (*atsukan*) or cold (*reishu*). The latter is usually the preferred way to enable you to taste the wine's complex flavours properly; never drink premium sake warm. When served cold, sake is sometimes presented and drunk out of a small wooden box (*masu*) with a smidgen of salt on the rim to counter the slightly sweet taste. Glasses are traditionally filled right to the brim and are sometimes placed on a saucer or in a *masu* to catch any overflow; they're generally small servings because, with an alcohol content of fifteen percent or more, sake is a strong drink – and it goes to your head even more quickly if drunk warm. For more on sake, check out ⓦwww.sake-world.com and also see the box on regional sake in the *Regional cuisines* colour section.

Beer

American brewer William Copeland set up Japan's first brewery in Yokohama in 1870 to serve **beer** to fellow expats streaming into the country in the wake of the Meiji Restoration. Back then the Japanese had to be bribed to drink it, but these days they need no such encouragement, knocking back a whopping 6.11 billion litres of beer and "beer-like beverages" (see below) a year. Copeland's brewery eventually became Kirin, one of the nation's big-four brewers along with Asahi, Sapporo and Suntory. All turn out a range of lagers and ale-type beers (often called black beer), as well as half-and-half concoctions. There are also low-malt beers called *happoshu*, and no-malt varieties called *dai-san-no-biiru*, which have proved very popular of late because of their lower price (the higher the malt content, the higher the government tax), even if they generally taste insipid.

Standard-size cans of beer cost around ¥200 from a shop or vending machine, while bottles (*bin-biiru*) served in restaurants and bars usually start at ¥500. Draught beer (*nama-biiru*) is often available and, in beer halls, will be served in a *jokki* (mug-like glass), which comes in three different sizes: *dai* (big), *chū* (medium) and *shō* (small).

Microbrew craft beers from around Japan (sometimes called *ji-biiru* – "regional beer") are becoming more popular and many have way more character than found in the products of the big four. For more information on the craft beer scene there's the bilingual free magazine *The Japan Beer Times* (ⓦJapanbeertimes.com) and the blog *Beer in Japan* (ⓦbeerinjapan.com).

Other alcoholic drinks

Generally with a higher alcohol content and cheaper than sake is **shōchū**, a distilled white spirit made from rice, barley or potato. You can get an idea of its potency, anything from 25 to 50 percent proof, by its nickname: white lightning. *Shōchū* is typically mixed with a soft drink into a *sawā* (as in lemon-sour) or a *chūhai* highball cocktail, although premium brands can be enjoyed on their own or with ice. There's something of a *shōchū* boom currently going on in Japan and the best brands are very drinkable and served like sake (see p.715 for more on *shōchū*). The cheap stuff, however, can give you a wicked hangover.

The Japanese love **whisky**, with the top brewers producing several respectable brands, often served with water and ice and called *mizu-wari*. In contrast, Japanese **wine** (*wain*), often very sweet, is a less successful product, at least to Western palates. Imported wines, however, are widely sold – not only are they becoming cheaper but there is now a better choice and higher quality available in both shops and restaurants.

Tea, coffee and soft drinks

Unless you're in a specialist *kissaten*, most of the time when you order coffee in Japan you'll get a blend (*burendo*), a medium-strength drink that is generally served black and comes in a choice of hot (*hotto*) or iced (*aisu*). If you want milk, ask for *miruku-kōhii* (milky coffee) or *kafe-ōre* (café au lait).

You can also get regular **black tea** in all coffee shops, served either with milk, lemon or iced. If you want the slightly bitter Japanese **green tea**, *ocha* ("honourable tea"), you'll usually have to go to a traditional teahouse. Green teas, which are always served in small cups and drunk plain, are graded according to their quality. *Bancha*, the cheapest, is for everyday drinking and, in its roasted form, is used to make the smoky *hōjicha*, or mixed with popped brown rice for the nutty *genmaicha*. Medium-grade *sencha* is served in upmarket restaurants or to favoured guests, while top-ranking, slightly sweet *gyokuro* (dewdrop) is reserved for special occasions. Other types of tea you may come across are *ūron-cha*, a refreshing Chinese-style tea, and *mugicha*, made from roasted barley.

As well as the international brand-name **soft drinks** and fruit juices, there are many other soft drinks unique to Japan. You'll probably want to try *Pocari Sweat*, *Post Water* or *Calpis* for the name on the can alone.

The way of tea

Tea was introduced to Japan from China in the ninth century and was popularized by Zen Buddhist monks, who appreciated its caffeine kick during their long meditation sessions. Gradually tea-drinking developed into a formal ritual known as *cha-no-yu*, or the "way of tea", whose purpose is to heighten the senses within a contemplative atmosphere. The most important aspect of the **tea ceremony** is the etiquette with which it is performed. Central to this is the selfless manner in which the host serves the tea and the humble manner in which the guests accept it.

The spirit of *wabi*, sometimes described as "rustic simplicity", pervades the Japanese tea ceremony. The traditional teahouse is positioned in a suitably understated garden, and naturalness is emphasized in all aspects of its architecture: in the unpainted wooden surfaces, the thatched roof, tatami-covered floors and the sliding-screen doors (*fusuma*) which open directly onto the garden. Colour and ostentation are avoided. Instead, the alcove, or *tokonoma*, becomes the focal point for a single object of adornment, a simple flower arrangement or a seasonal hanging scroll.

The utensils themselves also contribute to the mood of refined ritual. The roughcast tea bowls are admired for the accidental effects produced by the firing of the pottery, while the water containers, tea caddies and bamboo ladles and whisks are prized for their rustic simplicity. The guiding light behind it all was the great tea-master Sen no Rikyū (1521–91), whose "worship of the imperfect" has had an indelible influence on Japanese aesthetics.

Having set the tone with the choice of implements and ornamentation, the host whisks powdered green tea (*macha*) into a thick, frothy brew and present it to each guest in turn. They take the bowl in both hands, turn it clockwise (so the decoration on the front of the bowl is facing away) and drink it down in three slow sips. It's then customary to admire the bowl while nibbling on a dainty sweetmeat (*wagashi*), which counteracts the tea's bitter taste.

The media

If you can read Japanese there are scores of daily newspapers and hundreds of magazines covering almost every subject. In the big cities, English newspapers and magazines are readily available, while on TV and radio there are some programmes presented in English or with an alternative English soundtrack, such as the main news bulletins on NHK. Throughout this guide we list websites wherever useful (some will be in Japanese only).

Newspapers and magazines

Japan's top paper, the *Yomiuri Shimbun*, sells over fourteen million copies daily (combining its morning and evening editions), making it the most widely read newspaper in the world. Lagging behind by about two million copies a day is the *Asahi Shimbun,* seen as the intellectual's paper, with the other three national dailies, the *Mainichi Shimbun*, the right-wing *Sankei Shimbun* and the business paper the *Nihon Keizai Shimbun*, also selling respectable numbers.

The English-language daily **newspaper** you'll most commonly find on newsstands is *The Japan Times* (Ⓦwww.japantimes.co.jp). It has comprehensive coverage of national and international news, as well as occasionally interesting features, some culled from the world's media. Other English newspapers include *The International Herald Tribune* (Ⓦwww.asahi.com/english), published in conjunction with the English-language version of the major Japanese newspaper *Asahi Shimbun*; the *Daily Yomiuri* (Ⓦwww.yomiuri.co.jp/dy/); and the Japan edition of the *Financial Times*.

The free weekly Tokyo listings **magazine** *Metropolis* (Ⓦmetropolis.co.jp) is packed with interesting features, reviews, and listings of film, music and other events. *Japanzine* (Ⓦwww.seekjapan.jp), a free monthly published in Nagoya but also available in Kyoto, Ōsaka and Tokyo, is worth searching out. The twice-yearly publication *KIE* (Kateigaho International Edition; ¥1260; Ⓦint.kateigaho.com) is a gorgeous glossy magazine which covers cultural matters, with many travel features and in-depth profiles of areas of Tokyo and other parts of Japan. Other widely available English-language **magazines** include *Time* and *Newsweek*.

Bookstores such as Kinokuniya and Maruzen stock extensive ranges of imported and local magazines. If you're studying Japanese, or even just trying to pick up a bit of the language during your vacation, the bilingual magazine *Hiragana Times* is good. *Pia* and the Walker series (*Tokyo Walker*, *Kansai Walker*) are the best Japanese listings magazines.

Radio

You can listen to FM **radio** in Japan the regular way (though you'll need a radio built for the local market, as the 76–90 MHz FM spectrum here is unique to Japan) or via the internet, where you're likely to hear more interesting music on stations such as **Samurai FM** (Ⓦwww.samurai.fm), which links up DJs in London and Tokyo. There's also **Radio Japan Online** (Ⓦwww.nhk.or.jp/nhkworld/english/radio/program/index.html), which streams programmes in 18 languages from Japan's national broadcaster.

Pop music stations in Tokyo and the Kantō area include **Inter FM** (76.1MHz; Ⓦwww.interfm.co.jp), **J-WAVE** (81.3MHz; Ⓦwww.j-wave.co.jp/bnj/), **FM Yokohama** (84.1MHz; Ⓦwww.fmyokohama.co.jp), **Tokyo FM** (80.0MHz; Ⓦwww.tfm.co.jp), and **Bay FM** (78.0MHz; Ⓦwww.bayfm.co.jp/info/index.html).

Television

The state broadcaster, NHK (Ⓦwww.nhk.or.jp), has two non-digital TV channels (NHK and NHK Educational). Many TV sets can access a bilingual soundtrack, and thus it's possible to tune into English-language commentary for NHK's nightly 7pm news; films and imported TV shows on both NHK and the commercial channels are also sometimes broadcast with an alternative English soundtrack. The other main channels are Nihon TV (Ⓦwww.ntv.co.jp), TBS (Ⓦwww.tbs.co.jp), Fuji TV (Ⓦwww.fujitv.co.jp), TV Asahi (Ⓦwww.tv-asahi.co.jp) and TV Tokyo (Ⓦwww.tv-tokyo.co.jp). **Digital**, **satellite** and **cable** channels available in all top-end hotels include BBC World, CNN and MTV.

Festivals

Don't miss attending a festival (matsuri) if one happens during your visit – it will be a highlight of your stay in Japan. The more important events are listed below. See the *Festival fun* colour section for an introduction to Japanese festivals and pp.78–79 for a complete list of public holidays.

In recent years, several **non-Japanese festivals** have caught on, with a few adaptations for local tastes. Women give men gifts of chocolate on **Valentine's Day** (February 14), while on **White Day** (March 14) men get their turn to give their loved ones more chocolates (white, of course). **Christmas** is celebrated in Japan as an almost totally commercial event. Christmas Eve, rather than New Year, is *the* time to party and a big occasion for romance – you'll be hard-pressed to find a table at any fancy restaurant or a room in the top hotels.

Major festivals and public holidays

Note: if any of the following public holidays fall on a Sunday, then the following Monday is also a holiday.

January

Ganjitsu (or Gantan) **January 1.** On the first day of the year everyone heads for the shrines and temples to pray for good fortune. Public holiday.

Yamayaki January 15. The slopes of Wakakusa-yama, Nara, are set alight during a grass-burning ceremony.

Seijin-no-hi (Adults' Day) **Second Monday in January.** 20-year-olds celebrate their entry into adulthood by visiting their local shrine. Many women dress in sumptuous kimono. Public holiday.

February

Setsubun February 3 or 4. On the last day of winter by the lunar calendar, people scatter lucky beans round their homes and at shrines or temples to drive out evil and welcome in the year's good luck. In Nara, the event is marked by a huge lantern festival on February 3.

Yuki Matsuri February 5–11. Sapporo's famous snow festival features giant snow sculptures.

March

Hina Matsuri (Doll Festival) **March 3.** Families with young girls display beautiful dolls (*hina ningyō*) representing the emperor, empress and their courtiers dressed in ancient costume. Department stores, hotels and museums often put on special displays at this time.

Dates in Japan

According to the Japanese system of numbering years, which starts afresh with each change of emperor, 2011 is the 22nd year of Heisei – Heisei being the official name of Emperor Akihito's reign.

Cherry-blossom festivals Late March to early May. With the arrival of spring in late March, a pink tide of cherry blossom washes north from Kyūshū, travels up Honshū during the month of April and peters out in Hokkaidō in early May. There are cherry-blossom festivals, and the sake flows at blossom-viewing parties.

April

Hana Matsuri April 8. The Buddha's birthday is celebrated at all temples with parades or quieter celebrations, during which a small statue of Buddha is sprinkled with sweet tea.

Takayama Matsuri April 14–15. Parade of ornate festival floats (*yatai*), some carrying mechanical marionettes.

May

Kodomo-no-hi (Children's Day) May 5. The original Boys' Day now includes all children as families fly carp banners, symbolizing strength and perseverance, outside their homes. Public holiday.

Aoi Matsuri (Hollyhock Festival) May 15. Costume parade through the streets of Kyoto, with ceremonies to ward off storms and earthquakes.

Kanda Matsuri Mid-May. One of Tokyo's top three *matsuri*, taking place in odd-numbered years at Kanda Myōjin, during which people in Heian-period costume escort eighty gilded *mikoshi* through the streets.

Tōshō-gū Grand Matsuri May 17. Nikkō's most important festival, featuring a parade of over a thousand costumed participants and horseback archery to commemorate the burial of Shogun Tokugawa Ieyasu in 1617. There's a smaller-scale repeat performance on October 17.

Sanja Matsuri Third weekend in May. Tokyo's most boisterous festival takes place in Asakusa. Over a hundred *mikoshi* are jostled through the streets, accompanied by lion dancers, geisha and musicians.

June

Otaue June 14. Ceremonial planting of rice seedlings according to time-honoured techniques at Ōsaka's Sumiyoshi Taisha shrine, accompanied by dance and song performances.

Sannō Matsuri Mid-June. In even-numbered years the last of Tokyo's big three *matsuri* (after Kanda and Sanja) takes place, focusing on colourful processions of *mikoshi* through Akasaka.

July

Hakata Yamagasa July 1–15. Fukuoka's main festival culminates in a 5km race, with participants carrying or pulling heavy *mikoshi*, while spectators douse them with water.

Tanabata Matsuri (Star Festival) July 7. According to legend, the only day in the year when the astral lovers, Vega and Altair, can meet across the Milky Way. Poems and prayers are hung on bamboo poles outside houses.

Gion Matsuri July 17. Kyoto's month-long festival focuses around a parade of huge floats hung with rich silks and paper lanterns.

Music festivals

Late July and August in Japan is the time for **rock and popular music festivals**. One of the best is the **Earth Celebration** on Sado-ga-shima (see box, p.280), where the famed Kodo drummers collaborate with guests from the world music scene. If you want to catch up on the latest in Japanese rock and pop then schedule your visit to coincide with the most established event, as far as foreign bands is concerned, **Fuji Rock** (Ⓦwww.fujirockfestival.com). This huge three-day event hosts a wide range of top-name acts covering musical genres from dance and electronica to jazz and blues on multiple stages. It takes place at Naeba Ski Resort in Niigata prefecture, easily accessible from Tokyo via Shinkansen. It's possible to visit for a day, camp or stay in the hotels that in winter cater to the ski crowd.

Attracting an audience of well over 100,000 and simpler to get to is **Summer Sonic** (Ⓦwww.summersonic.com), a two-day event held in Chiba, just across the Edo-gawa River from Tokyo. This festival showcases a good mix of both local and overseas bands and has both indoor and outdoor performances.

Rock in Japan (Ⓦrijfes.jp), focusing on domestic bands, is usually held in August at Hitachi Seaside Park, north of Tokyo in Ibaraki-ken (accessible from Ueno Station). More general in its scope is the **Tokyo Summer Music Festival** (Ⓦwww.arion-edo.org/tsf), held throughout July around the city, which encompasses classical and world-music performances.

Hanabi Taikai Last Saturday in July. The most spectacular of Japan's many summer firework displays takes place in Tokyo, on the Sumida River near Asakusa. Some cities also hold displays in early August.

August

Nebuta and Neputa Matsuri August 1–7. Aomori and Hirosaki hold competing summer festivals, with parades of illuminated paper-covered figures.
Tanabata Matsuri August 6–8. Sendai's famous Star Festival is held a month after everyone else, so the lovers get another chance.
Obon (Festival of Souls) August 13–15, or July 13–15 in some areas. Families gather around the ancestral graves to welcome back the spirits of the dead and honour them with special *Bon-odori* dances on the final night.
Awa Odori August 12–15. The most famous *Bon odori* takes place in Tokushima, when up to eighty thousand dancers take to the streets.

September

Yabusame September 16. Spectacular displays of horseback archery (*yabusame*) by riders in samurai armour at Tsurugaoka Hachimangū shrine in Kamakura.

October

Okunchi Matsuri October 7–9. Shinto rites mingle with Chinese- and European-inspired festivities to create Nagasaki's premier celebration, incorporating dragon dances and floats in the shape of Chinese and Dutch ships.
Kawagoe Grand Matsuri October 14–15. One of the liveliest festivals in the Tokyo area, involving some 25 ornate floats and hundreds of costumed revellers.
Jidai Matsuri October 22. Kyoto's famous, if rather sedate, costume parade vies with the more exciting Kurama Matsuri, a night-time fire festival which takes place in a village near Kyoto.

November

Shichi-go-san (Seven-five-three) November 15. Children of the appropriate ages don traditional garb to visit their local shrine.

December

Ōmisoka December 31. Just before midnight on the last day of the year, temple bells ring out 108 times (the number of human frailties according to Buddhist thinking), while people all over the country gather at major shrines to honour the gods with the first shrine visit of the year.

Sports and outdoor activities

Big believers in team spirit, the Japanese embrace many sports with almost religious fervour. Baseball is actually more popular than the home-grown sumo, and hot on the heels of both sports is soccer. Martial arts, such as aikido, judo and karate, all traditionally associated with Japan, have a much lower profile than you might expect. Tokyo, with its many dōjō (practise halls), is the best place in the country in which to view or learn these ancient sports. Tokyo's TICs (see p.92) have a full list of dōjō that allow visitors to watch practise sessions for free.

Popular **outdoor activities** include **skiing**, **hiking** and **mountain climbing**. The Tokyo-based **International Adventurers Club** (IAC; ⓦwww.iac-tokyo.org) and **Outdoor Club Japan** (ⓦoutdoorclubjapan.com), and the **International Outdoor Club** (IOC; ⓦwww.iockansai.com) in the Kansai region provide informal opportunities to explore the countryside in the company of like-minded people. The bilingual bimonthly magazine *Outdoor Japan* (ⓦwww.outdoorjapan.com) is also a mine of useful information.

Baseball

Baseball first came to Japan in the 1870s, but it wasn't until 1934 that the first professional teams were formed. Now Japan is *yakyū* (baseball) crazy, and if you're in the country from April to the end of October during the baseball season, think about watching a professional match. Even if you're not a fan, the buzzing atmosphere and audience enthusiasm can be infectious.

In addition to the two professional leagues, **Central** and **Pacific**, each with six teams, there's the equally (if not more) popular **All-Japan High School Baseball Championship**. You might be able to catch one of the local play-offs before the main tournament, which is held each summer at Kōshien Stadium near Ōsaka.

In the professional leagues, the teams are sponsored by big businesses, a fact immediately apparent from their names, such as the Yakult (a food company) Swallows and Yomiuri (a newspaper conglomerate) Giants. The victors from the Central and Pacific leagues go on to battle it out for the supreme title in the seven-match Japan Series every autumn. **Tickets** for all games are available from the stadia or at advance ticket booths. They start at ¥1500 and go on sale on the Friday two weeks prior to a game. For more information on Japan's pro-baseball leagues, check out the official professional league site Ⓦwww.npb.or.jp, and the fan-site Baseball Guru Ⓦbaseballguru.com/bbjp1.html.

Sumo

There's something fascinating about Japan's national sport **sumo**, even though the titanic clashes between the enormous, near-naked wrestlers can be blindingly brief. The age-old pomp and ceremony that surrounds sumo – from the design of the *dohyō* (the ring in which bouts take place) to the wrestler's slicked-back topknot – give the sport a gravitas completely absent from Western wrestling. The sport's aura is enhanced by the majestic size of the wrestlers themselves: the average weight is 136kg, but they can be much larger – Konishiki, one of the sumo stars of the 1990s, for example, weighed 272kg.

At the start of a bout, the two *rikishi* (wrestlers) wade into the ring, wearing only *mawashi* aprons, which are essentially giant jockstraps. Salt is tossed to purify the ring, and then the *rikishi* hunker down and indulge in the time-honoured ritual of psyching each

A short history of sumo

Accounts of sumo bouts (*basho*) are related in Japan's oldest annals of history dating back around 2000 years when it was a Shinto rite connected with praying for a good harvest. By the Edo period, sumo had developed into a spectator sport, and really hit its stride in the post-World War II period when *basho* started to be televised. The old religious trappings remain, though: the *gyōji* (referee) wears robes similar to those of a Shinto priest and above the *dohyō* hangs a thatched roof like those found at shrines.

Sumo players are ranked according to the number of wins they have had, the top-ranking wrestler being called the *yokozuna*, and the next rank down *ōzeki*. In a neat reversal of Japan's appropriation of baseball and export of professional players to the US league, several of sumo's most revered stars of recent years were born abroad, including Konishiki (aka the "dump truck") and Akebono, who both hail from Hawaii, Musashimaru from American Samoa and Asashoryu, the first Mongolian-born fighter to reach the rank of *yokozuna*.

Even though he is one of the most successful *yokuzuna* ever, Asashoryu battled with sumo's strict code of conduct throughout his career and was forced into early retirement in 2010 after punching a man outside a Tokyo nightclub. This and other un-sumo-like behaviour, such as wrestlers being found in possession of pot and being involved in illegal gambling, has tarnished the sport, the popularity of which has plummeted over recent years, particularly among young Japanese. The sport's saviour may just be its current crop of overseas stars such as the Estonian-born *ōzeki* Baruto and the Bulgarian Kotooshu who was the first European-born wrestler to win the Emperor's Cup in 2008. Tall and relatively light for a sumo player, the *ōzeki* has been dubbed the David Beckham of sumo.

The annual sumo tournaments

The must-see **annual sumo tournaments** are held at the following locations, always starting on the Sunday closest to the tenth of the month and lasting for two weeks: Kokugikan Hall in **Tokyo** (Jan, May & Sept); Ōsaka Furitsu Taiiku Kaikan in **Ōsaka** (March); Aichi-ken Taiiku-kan in **Nagoya** (July); and the Fukuoka Kokusai Centre, **Fukuoka** (Nov).

Despite sumo's declining popularity, it's still difficult to book the prime ringside **seats** (around ¥45,000 for four seats in a tatami mat block) but quite feasible to bag reserved seats in the balconies (starting around ¥3200 for a Western-style seat). The cheapest unreserved seats (¥2800) go on sale on the door on the day of the tournament at 9am. To be assured of a ticket you'll need to line up well before that, especially towards the end of a *basho*. Matches start at 10am for the lower-ranked wrestlers and at this time of day it's OK to sneak into any vacant ringside seats to watch the action close up; when the rightful owners turn up, just return to your own seat. The sumo superstars come on around 4pm and tournaments finish at around 6pm.

Full details in English about ticket sales can be found on the sumo association's website (Ⓦwww.sumo.or.jp). If you can't get a ticket, note that NHK televises each *basho* daily from 3.30pm, and you can tune in to FEN on 810 KHz for a simultaneous English commentary.

other out with menacing stares. When ready, each *rikishi* attempts to throw his opponent to the ground or out of the ring using one or more of 82 legitimate techniques. The first to touch the ground with any part of his body other than his feet, or to step out of the *dohyō*, loses.

Despite their formidable girth, top *rikishi* enjoy the media status of supermodels, their social calendars being documented obsessively by the media. When not fighting in tournaments, groups of *rikishi* live and train together at their *heya* (stables), the youngest wrestlers acting pretty much as the menial slaves of their older, more experienced, colleagues. If you make an advance appointment, it's possible to visit some *heya* to observe the early-morning practise sessions; contact the Tokyo TICs (see p.92) for details. For all you could want to know and more on the current scene, plus how to buy tickets, check out the official website of sumo's governing body, Nihon Sumo Kyōkai, at Ⓦwww.sumo.or.jp.

Soccer

Soccer was introduced to Japan in 1873 by an Englishman, Lieutenant Commander Douglas of the Royal Navy, but it wasn't until Japan's first professional soccer league, the **J-League** (Ⓦwww.j-league.or.jp), was launched in 1993 that the sport captured the public's imagination. Following on from the success of the 2002 World Cup, hosted jointly by Japan and Korea, the sport is now a huge crowd puller. Japan is also pitching to be the host for the 2022 World Cup (Ⓦwww.dream-2022.jp).

Games are played between March and October, with a break in August. Sixteen clubs play in the top J1 league, twelve in the J2, and all participate in the JL Yamazaki Nabisco Cup. There is a host of other cups and contests including the JOMO Cup, in which fans pick their dream teams from among all the J-League players.

Aikido

Half-sport, half-religion, **aikido** translates as "the way of harmonious spirit" and blends elements of judo, karate and kendo into a form of non-body-contact self-defence. It's one of the newer martial arts, having only been created in Japan in the twentieth century, and, as a rule, is performed without weapons. For a painfully enlightening and humorous take on the rigours of aikido training, read Robert Twigger's *Angry White Pyjamas* (see p.813).

To find out more about the sport, head to the **International Aikido Federation**, 17-18 Wakamatsuchō, Shinjuku-ku (合気会; Ⓣ03/3203-9236, Ⓦwww.aikikai.or.jp).

Judo

Probably the martial art most closely associated with Japan, **judo** is a self-defence technique that developed out of the Edo-era fighting schools of Jūjutsu. All judo activities in Japan are controlled by the **All-Japan Judo Federation**, at the Kōdōkan Dōjō, 1-16-30 Kasuga, Bunkyō-ku (講道館; ⓣ03/3818-4172, ⓦwww.judo.or.jp), reached from either Kasuga or Kōrakuen subway stations in Tokyo. The *dōjō* holds classes most evenings (Mon–Fri 5–8pm, Sat 5–7.30pm), and there's also a hostel here where you can stay if you have an introduction from an authorized judo body or an approved Japanese sponsor. Judo is also taught at the **Nippon Budōkan Budō Gakuen**, 2-3 Kitanomaru-kōen, Chiyoda-ku (日本武道館; ⓣ03/3216-5143, ⓦwww.nipponbudokan.or.jp), near Kudanshita subway station in Tokyo.

Karate

Karate has its roots in China and was only introduced into Japan via the southern islands of Okinawa in 1922. Since then the sport has developed many different styles, several with governing bodies and federations based in Tokyo. The **Japan Karate Association**, 2-23-15 Koraku, Bunkyō-ku (日本空手協会; ⓣ03/5800-3091, ⓦwww.jka.or.jp), is the world's largest karate association teaching the Shokotan tradition. You can apply to train or watch classes here, but it's best to call or email first. The closest subway stations are Iidabashi and Kōrakuen.

The umbrella organization, **Japan Karatedō Federation**, 6F, 2 Nippon Zaidan Building, 1-11-2 Toranomon, Minato-ku, Tokyo (ⓣ03/3503-6640, ⓦwww.karatedo.co.jp), can advise on the main styles of karate and the best place to see practise sessions or take lessons. The closest subway station is Toranomon.

Kendo

Meaning "the way of the sword", **kendo** is Japanese fencing using either a long bamboo weapon, the *shinai*, or a lethal metal *katana* blade. This martial art has the longest pedigree in Japan, dating from the Muromachi period (1392–1573). It developed as a sport during the Edo period and is now watched over by the **All-Japan Kendo Federation**, Nippon Budōkan, 2-3 Kitanomaru-kōen, Chiyoda-ku, Tokyo (全日本剣道連盟; ⓣ03/3211-5804, ⓦwww.kendo.or.jp), near Kudanshita subway station. Practise sessions are not generally open to the public, but you might be fortunate enough to catch the All-Japan Championships held in Tokyo each autumn at the Budōkan.

Skiing and snowboarding

Japan is a **ski and snowboard paradise**; even on the shortest trip to the country it's easy to arrange a day-trip to the slopes since many major resorts on Honshū are within a couple of hours' train ride of Tokyo, Nagoya or Ōsaka. Serious skiers will want to head to the northern island of Hokkaidō, which has some of the country's best ski resorts.

The **cost** of a ski trip needn't be too expensive. Lift passes are typically ¥4000 per day, or less if you ski for several days in a row; equipment rental averages around ¥4000 for the skis, boots and poles per day, while accommodation at a family-run minshuku compares favourably to that of many European and American resorts.

Transport to the slopes is fast and efficient; at one resort (Gala Yuzawa in Niigata; ⓦwww.galaresort.jp) you can step straight off the Shinkansen onto the ski lifts. Ski maps and signs are often in English, and you're sure to find some English-speakers and, at the major resorts, *gaijin* staff, if you run into difficulties.

Top resorts can get very crowded, especially at weekends and holidays; if you don't want to ski in rush-hour conditions, plan your trip for midweek. In addition, the runs are, on the whole, much shorter than in Europe and the US. Compensating factors, however, are fast ski lifts, beautiful scenery – especially in the Japan Alps – and the opportunity to soak in onsen hot springs at night.

Recommended for beginners is either **Gala Yuzawa** (ⓦwww.galaresort.jp/winter) or **Naeba** (ⓦwww.princehotels.co.jp/ski/naeba-e/index.html), both reached in under two hours from Tokyo by Shinkansen. **Nozawa Onsen** (p.348) also has good beginners' runs, but its off-the-beaten-track location makes it a better bet for more experienced skiers. **Appi Kōgen** and **Zaō** in northern Honshū (p.225) and **Hakuba** in Nagano (p.349) are considered the Holy Trinity of Japanese ski resorts. **Shiga Kōgen** (see p.351) is another mammoth resort in Nagano. If you're after the best powder-snow skiing without the crowds, head north to Hokkaidō, to the world-class resorts of **Furano** (see p.318) and **Niseko** (see p.301). There are also many slopes easily accessible on a day-trip from Sapporo (see box, p.295).

All the major travel agents offer **ski packages**, which are worth considering. Hakuba-based **Ski Japan Holiday** (Ⓦwww.japanspecialists.com) and Niseko-based **SkiJapan.com** (Ⓦwww.skijapan.com) both have plenty of experience setting up deals for the expat community. **Youth hostels** near ski areas also often have excellent-value packages, including accommodation, meals and lift passes, and can arrange competitive equipment rental.

The most current and comprehensive English-language guide to Japan's ski resorts is *Snow-search Japan* (Ⓦwww.wsg-media.com) with details of over seventy resorts.

Mountaineering and hiking

Until the twentieth century, few Japanese would have considered climbing one of their often sacred mountains for anything other than religious reasons. These days, prime highland beauty spots such as Kamikōchi are very popular with day **hikers** and serious **mountaineers**, so much so that they risk being overrun. In addition, there are scores of national parks and other protected areas (see p.797), and exploring these and other picturesque parts of the countryside on foot is one of the great pleasures of a trip to Japan. Nevertheless, bear in mind that those areas close to cities can get very busy at weekends and holidays. If you can, go midweek or out of season when the trails are less crowded.

Hiking trails, especially in the national parks, are well marked. Campsites and mountain huts open during the climbing season, which runs from June to the end of August. The efficient train network means that even from sprawling conurbations like Tokyo you can be in beautiful countryside in just over an hour. Top hiking destinations from the capital include the lakes, mountains and rugged coastline of the Fuji-Hakone-Izu National Park (see p.185) to the southwest and Nikkō (see p.172) to the north. Also west of the capital is the Chichibu-Tama National Park and the sacred mountain Takao-san, particularly lovely when the leaves change colour each autumn. The website Ⓦwww.outdoorjapan.com has useful ideas and information if you plan to go hiking or camping in Japan.

Rafting, canoeing and kayaking

All the snow that gets dumped on Japan's mountains in winter eventually melts, swelling the country's numerous rivers. Although the vast majority of these have been tamed by dams and concrete walls along the riverbanks, there are stretches that provide the ideal conditions for **whitewater rafting**, **canoeing** and **kayaking**. Prime spots for these activities are Minakami in Gunma-ken (p.179), Hakuba in Nagano-ken (p.349), the Iya Valley (p.619) and Shimanto-gawa (p.627), both in Shikoku, and Niseko (p.301) in Hokkaidō. A reputable firm to contact to find out more is Canyons (Ⓦwww.canyons.jp).

Golf

One of Japan's premier pro-golfing events is the **Japan Open Golf Championship** (Ⓦwww.jga.or.jp), held in October with a total prize fund of ¥200 million. If you fancy a round yourself, there are details of 2349 eighteen-hole or more courses at **Golf in Japan** (Ⓦwww.golf-in-japan.com). Course fees vary widely from ¥3000 at the cheapest places to over ¥40,000 for a round at the most exclusive links.

Beaches, surfing and diving

Given that Japan is an archipelago, you'd be forgiven for thinking that it would be blessed with some pleasant beaches. The truth is that industrialization has blighted much of the coastline and that many of the country's beaches are covered with litter and/or polluted. The best **beaches** are those furthest away from the main island of Honshū, which means those on the islands of Okinawa, or the Izu and Ogasawara islands south of Tokyo.

Incredibly, Japan's market for surf goods is the world's largest, and when the surfers aren't hauling their boards off to Hawaii and Australia, they can be found braving the waves at various home locations. Top spots include the southern coasts of Shikoku and Kyūshū (see box, p.704). Closer to Tokyo, pros head for the rocky east Kujūkuri coast of the Chiba peninsula, while the beaches around Shōnan, near Kamakura, are fine for perfecting your style and hanging out with the trendiest surfers. A useful website is Ⓦwww.japansurf.com.

The best places to head for **diving** are Okinawa (see p.730), around the island of Sado-ga-shima, near Niigata (see p.275), and off the Izu Peninsula, close to Tokyo (see p.220). Walruses may fancy braving ice-diving in the frozen far northern reaches of Hokkaidō (see p.327). Check out Ⓦwww.divejapan.com for more information.

Culture and etiquette

Japan is famous for its complex web of social conventions and rules of behaviour. Fortunately, allowances are made for befuddled foreigners, but it will be greatly appreciated – and even draw gasps of astonishment – if you show a grasp of the basic principles. The two main danger areas are to do with footwear and bathing, which, if you get them wrong, can cause great offence. For tips on eating and drinking etiquette, see p.50 and p.54.

Some general pointers

Japan is a strictly hierarchical society where men generally take precedence over women, so ladies shouldn't expect doors to be held open or seats vacated. **Sexual discrimination** is widespread, and foreign women working in Japan can find the predominantly male business culture hard going.

Pushing and shoving on crowded trains or buses is not uncommon. Never respond by getting angry or showing **aggression**, as this is considered a complete loss of face. By the same token, don't make your **opinions** known too forcefully or contradict people outright; it's more polite to say "maybe" than a direct "no".

The meaning of "yes" and "no" can in themselves be a problem, particularly when **asking questions**. For example, if you say "Don't you like it?", a positive answer means "Yes, I agree with you, I don't like it", and "No" means "No, I don't agree with you, I *do* like it". To avoid confusion, try not to ask negative questions – stick to "Do you like it?" And if someone seems to be giving vague answers, don't push too hard unless it's important. There's a good chance they don't want to offend you by disagreeing or revealing a problem.

Blowing your nose in public is considered rude – just keep sniffing until you find somewhere private. Finally, you'll be excused for not **sitting** on your knees, Japanese-style, on tatami mats. It's agony for people who aren't used to it, and many young Japanese now find it uncomfortable. If you're wearing trousers, sitting cross-legged is fine; otherwise, tuck your legs to one side.

Meetings and greetings

Some visitors to Japan complain that it's difficult to meet local people, and it's certainly true that many Japanese are shy of foreigners, mainly through a fear of being unable to communicate. A few words of Japanese will help enormously, and there are various opportunities for fairly formal contact, such as through the Goodwill Guides (see p.80). Otherwise, try popping into a local bar, a *yakitori* joint or suchlike; the chances are someone emboldened by alcohol will strike up a conversation.

Whenever Japanese meet, express thanks or say goodbye, there's a flurry of **bowing**. The precise depth of the bow and the length of time it's held for depend on the relative status of the two individuals. Foreigners aren't expected to bow, but it's terribly infectious and you'll soon find yourself bobbing with the best of them. The usual compromise is a slight nod or a quick half-bow. Japanese more familiar with Western customs might offer you a hand to shake, in which case treat it gently – they won't be expecting a firm grip.

Japanese **names** are traditionally written with the family name first, followed by a given name, which is the practice used throughout this book (except where the Western version has become famous, such as Issey Miyake). When dealing with foreigners, however, they may well write their name the other way round. Check if you're not sure because, when **addressing people**, it's normal to use the family name plus *-san;* for example, Suzuki-san. *San* is an honorific term applied to others, so you do not use it when introducing yourself or your family. As a foreigner, you can choose whichever of your names you feel comfortable with; inevitably they'll tack a *-san* on the end. You'll also often hear *-chan* or *-kun* as a form of address; these are diminutives reserved for very good friends, young children and pets. The suffix *-sama* is the most polite form of address.

Japanese people tend to **dress** smartly, especially in Tokyo. Tourists don't have to go overboard, but will be better received if they look neat and tidy, while for anyone hoping to do business, a snappy suit is *de rigueur*. It's also important to be **punctual** for social and business appointments.

Business meetings invariably go on much longer than you'd expect, and rarely result in decisions. They are partly for building up the all-important feeling of trust between the two parties (as is the after-hours entertainment in a restaurant or karaoke bar). An essential part of any business meeting is the swapping of *meishi* (**name cards**). Always carry a copious supply, since you'll be expected to exchange a card with everyone present. It's useful to have them printed in Japanese as well as English. *Meishi* are offered with both hands, held so that the recipient can read the writing. It's polite to read the card and then place it on the table beside you, face up. Never write on a *meishi*, at least not in the owner's presence, and never shove it in a pocket – put it in your wallet or somewhere suitably respectful.

Hospitality, gifts and tips

Entertaining, whether it's business or purely social, usually takes place in bars and restaurants. The host generally orders and, if it's a Japanese-style meal, will keep passing you different things to try. You'll also find your glass continually topped up. It's polite to return the gesture but if you don't drink, or don't want any more, leave it full.

It's a rare honour to be invited to someone's home in Japan, and if this happens you should always take a **gift**, which should always be wrapped, using plenty of fancy paper and ribbon if possible. Most shops gift-wrap purchases automatically and anything swathed in paper from a big department store has extra cachet.

Japanese people love giving gifts, and you should never refuse one if offered, though it's good manners to protest at their generosity first. Again it's polite to give and receive with both hands, and to belittle your humble donation while giving profuse thanks for the gift you receive. However, it's not the custom to open gifts in front of the donor, thus avoiding potential embarrassment.

Tipping is not expected in Japan. If someone's been particularly helpful, the best approach is to give a small present, or offer some money discreetly in an envelope.

Shoes and slippers

It's customary to change into **slippers** when entering a Japanese home or a ryokan, and not uncommon in traditional restaurants, temples and, occasionally, in museums and art galleries. If you come across a slightly raised floor and a row of slippers, then use them; leave your shoes either on the lower floor (the *genkan*) or on the shelves (sometimes lockers) provided. Also try not to step on the *genkan* with bare or stockinged feet. Once inside, remove your slippers before stepping onto tatami, the rice-straw flooring, and remember to change into the special **toilet slippers** kept inside the bathroom when you go to the toilet.

Toilets

Although you'll still come across traditional Japanese squat-style **toilets** (*toire* or *otearai*; トイレ／お手洗い), Western sit-down toilets are becoming the norm. Look out for nifty enhancements such as a heated seat and those that flush automatically as you walk away. Another handy device plays the sound of flushing water to cover embarrassing noises.

Hi-tech toilets, with a control panel to one side, are very common. Finding the flush button can be a challenge – in the process you may hit the temperature control, hot-air dryer or, worst of all, the bidet nozzle, resulting in a long metal arm extending out of the toilet bowl and spraying you with warm water.

There are lots of public lavatories on the street or at train and subway stations; department stores and big shops also have bathroom facilities for general use. Note that public toilets rarely provide paper.

Bathing

Taking a traditional Japanese **bath**, whether in an onsen, a *sentō* or a ryokan, is a ritual that's definitely worth mastering. Key points to remember are that everyone uses the same water, that the bathtub is only for soaking and to never pull out the plug. It's therefore essential to wash and rinse the soap off thoroughly – showers and bowls are provided, as well as soap and shampoo in most cases – before stepping into the bath. Ryokan and the more upmarket public bathhouses provide small towels (bring your own or buy one on the door if using a cheaper *sentō*), though no one minds full nudity. Baths are typically **segregated**, so memorize the *kanji* for male (男) and female (女).

Shopping

Even if you're not an inveterate shopper, cruising Japan's gargantuan department stores or rummaging around its vibrant discount outlets is an integral part of local life that shouldn't be missed. Japan also has some of the most enticing souvenirs in the world, from lacquered chopsticks and delicate handmade paper to the latest electronic gadgets.

All prices are fixed, except in flea markets and some discount electrical stores where bargaining is acceptable. Though it's always worth asking, surprisingly few shops take **credit cards** and fewer still accept cards issued abroad, so make sure you have plenty of cash.

In general, shop **opening hours** are from 10am or 11am to 7pm or 8pm. Most shops close one day a week, not always on Sunday, and smaller places tend to shut on public holidays. If you need anything **after hours**, you'll find late-opening convenience stores in even the smallest towns, and stores that are open 24 hours in most towns and cities, often near the train station.

Arts and crafts

Many of Japan's **arts** and **crafts** date back thousands of years and have been handed down from generation to generation (see p.783 for more on the arts). Though the best can be phenomenally expensive, there are plenty of items at more manageable prices that make wonderful **souvenirs**. Most department stores have at least a small crafts section, but it's far more enjoyable to trawl Japan's specialist shops. Kyoto is renowned for its traditional crafts, and in Tokyo you'll find a number of artisans still plying their trade, while most regions have a vibrant local crafts industry turning out products for the tourists.

Some of Japan's most beautiful traditional products stem from **folk crafts** (*mingei*), ranging from elegant, inexpensive **bambooware** to **woodcarvings**, **toys**, **masks**, **kites** and a whole host of delightful **dolls** (*ningyō*). Peg-shaped *kokeshi* dolls from northern Honshū are among the most appealing, with their bright colours and sweet, simple faces. Look out, too, for the rotund, round-eyed *daruma* dolls, made of papier-mâché, and fine, clay *Hakata-ningyō* dolls from northern Kyūshū.

Ceramics

Japan's most famous craft is its **ceramics** (*tōjiki*). Of several distinct regional styles, *Imari-ware* (from Arita in Kyūshū) is best known for its colourful, ornate designs, while the iron-brown unglazed *Bizen-ware* (from near Okayama, see p.538) and Mashiko's simple folk-pottery (see p.179) are satisfyingly rustic. Other famous names include *Satsuma-yaki* (from Kagoshima), *Kasama-yaki* (from Ibaraki), Kanazawa's highly elaborate *Kutani-yaki* and Kyoto's *Kyō-yaki*. Any decent department store will stock a full range of styles, or you can visit local showrooms. Traditional tea bowls, sake sets and vases are popular souvenirs.

Lacquerware

Originally devised as a means of making everyday utensils more durable, **lacquerware** (*shikki* or *urushi*) has developed over the centuries into a unique art form. Items such as trays, tables, boxes, chopsticks and bowls are typically covered with reddish-brown or black lacquer and either left plain or decorated with paintings, carvings, sprinkled with eggshell or given a dusting of gold or silver leaf. Though top-quality lacquer can be hugely expensive, you'll still find very beautiful pieces at reasonable prices. Lacquer needs a humid atmosphere, especially the cheaper pieces which are made on a base of low-quality wood that cracks in dry conditions, though inexpensive plastic bases won't be affected. Wajima (see p.382) is one of the most famous places for lacquerware in Japan.

Paper products and woodblock prints

Traditional Japanese **paper** (*washi*), made from mulberry or other natural fibres, is fashioned into any number of tempting souvenirs. You can buy purses, boxes, fans, oiled umbrellas, lampshades and toys all made from paper, as well as wonderful stationery.

Original **woodblock prints**, *ukiyo-e*, by world-famous artists such as Utamaro, Hokusai and Hiroshige, have long been collectors' items fetching thousands of pounds. However, you can buy copies of

Duty-free shopping

Foreigners can buy **duty-free** items (that is, without the five percent consumption tax – see box, p.70), but only in certain tourist shops and the larger department stores. Perishable goods, such as food, drinks, tobacco, cosmetics and film, are exempt from the scheme, and most stores only offer duty-free if the total bill exceeds ¥10,000. The shop will either give you a duty-free price immediately or, in department stores in particular, you pay the full price first and then apply for a refund at their "tax-exemption" counter. The shop will attach a copy of the customs document (*wariin*) to your passport, to be removed by customs officers when you leave Japan. Note, however, that you can often find the same goods elsewhere at a better price, including tax, so shop around first.

Antique and flea markets

The regular outdoor **antique** and **flea markets** of Tokyo and Kyoto, usually held at shrines and temples (see individual city accounts for details), are great fun to attend. You need to get there early for the best deals, but you're likely to find some gorgeous secondhand kimono, satin-smooth lacquerware or rustic pottery, among a good deal of tat. Flea markets are great also for stocking up on inexpensive clothes and household items.

these "pictures of the floating world", often depicting Mount Fuji, willowy geisha or lusty heroes of the kabuki stage, at tourist shops for more modest sums. Alternatively, some art shops specialize in originals, both modern and antique.

Textiles, metalwork and pearls

Japan has a long history of making attractive **textiles**, particularly the silks used in kimono (see box, p.69). Other interesting uses of textiles include **noren**, a split curtain hanging in the entrance to a restaurant or bar; cotton **tenugui** (small hand towels), decorated with cute designs; and the **furoshiki**, a square, versatile wrapping cloth that comes in a variety of sizes.

While the chunky **iron kettles** from Morioka in northern Honshū are rather unwieldy mementos, the area also produces delicate *fūrin*, or **wind chimes**, in a variety of designs. **Damascene** is also more portable, though a bit fussy for some tastes. This metal inlay-work, with gold and silver threads on black steel, was originally used to fix the family crest on sword hilts and helmets, though nowadays you can buy all sorts of jewellery and trinket boxes decorated with birds, flowers and other intricate designs.

Pearls, however, are undoubtedly Japan's most famous jewellery item, ever since Mikimoto Kōkichi first succeeded in growing cultured pearls in Toba in 1893. Toba (see p.510) is still the centre of production, though you'll find specialist shops in all major cities, selling pearls at fairly competitive prices.

Food and drink

Edible souvenirs include various types of **rice-crackers** (*sembei*), both sweet and savoury, vacuum-packed bags of **pickles** (*tsukemono*), and Japanese **sweets** (*okashi*) such as the eye-catching *wagashi*. Made of sweet, red-bean paste in various colours and designs, *wagashi* are the traditional accompaniment to the tea ceremony. **Tea** itself (*ocha*) comes in a variety of grades, often in attractive canisters, while **sake** (see p.53), premium *shōchū* or Japanese whiskey are other great gift options, and often come in interesting-shaped bottles with beautiful labels.

Books and music

Imported foreign-language **books** are expensive and only available in major cities. However, some locally produced English-language books are cheaper here than at home, if you can find them at all outside Japan. The best bookstores are Kinokuniya, Tower Books (part of Tower Records), Maruzen, Yūrindō and Junkudō, all of which stock imported newspapers and magazines as well as a variable selection of foreign-language books. Most top-class hotels have a small bookstore with a range of titles on Japan and a limited choice of imported fiction and journals.

Imported **CDs and records** are a lot easier to get hold of, alongside a mammoth local output of pop and rock. Major record stores such as Tower Records and HMV have a tremendous selection. Imported CDs typically cost under ¥2000, while CDs of foreign artists produced for the Japanese market, with translated lyrics and extra tracks, generally start in the region of ¥2300.

Department stores

Japan's most prestigious **department stores** are Isetan, Mitsukoshi and Takashimaya, followed by the more workaday Seibu, Tōbu and Matsuzakaya. All of these big names have branches throughout Japan, and sell almost everything, from fashion, crafts and household items to stationery and toys. One floor is usually devoted to restaurants, while bigger stores may also have an art gallery, travel bureau, ticket agent and a currency-exchange desk, as well as English-speaking staff and a duty-free service. Seasonal sales, particularly those at New Year and early July, can offer great bargains.

Electrical and electronic goods

Japan is a well-known producer of high-quality and innovative **electrical** and **electronic goods**. New designs are tested on the local market before going into export production, so this is the best place to check out the latest technological advances. The majority of hi-tech goods are sold in discount stores, where prices may be up to forty percent cheaper than at a conventional store. Akihabara, in Tokyo, is the country's foremost area for electronic goods, but in every major city you can buy audio equipment, computers, software and any number of ingenious gadgets at competitive prices.

Similarly, Japanese **cameras** and other photographic equipment are among the best in the world. Shinjuku, in Tokyo, is the main centre, where you can pick up the latest models and find discontinued and second-hand cameras at decent prices.

Before buying anything, compare prices – many shops are open to bargaining – and make sure the items come with the appropriate voltage switch (Japanese power supply is 100V). It's also important to check that whatever you buy will be compatible with equipment you have at home, if necessary. For English-language instructions, after-sales service and guarantees,

The comeback of the kimono

In Japan **kimono** are still worn by both sexes on special occasions, such as weddings and festival visits to a shrine. But as the demand for high-class kimono, such as those made by the craftspeople of Kyoto, declines – a result of the falling birth rate and Japan's ageing population – the one bright spot for the industry is the trend to adapt old kimono to new uses. Increasing numbers of fashion-conscious young women have taken to wearing a kimono like a coat over Western clothes or coordinating it with coloured rather than white *tabi* (traditional split-toed socks). At the same time, fashion designers are turning to kimono fabrics and styles for contemporary creations.

Few visitors to Japan fail to be impressed by the beauty and variety of kimono available, and every department store has a corner devoted to ready-made or tailored kimono. Ready-made versions can easily cost ¥100,000, while ¥1 million for the best made-to-measure kimono is not uncommon. Much more affordable secondhand or antique kimono can be found in tourist shops, flea markets or in the kimono sales held by department stores, usually in spring and autumn. Prices can start as low as ¥1000, but you'll pay more for the sumptuous, highly decorated wedding kimono (they make striking wall hangings), as well as the most beautifully patterned **obi**, the broad, silk sash worn with a kimono. A cheaper, more practical alternative is the light cotton **yukata**, popular with both sexes as dressing gowns; you'll find them in all department stores and many speciality stores, along with **happi coats** – the loose jackets that just cover the upper body. To complete the outfit, you could pick up a pair of **zōri**, traditional straw **sandals**, or their wooden counterpart, **geta**.

If you want to try the full kimono look, you'll find that most of the big hotels have a studio where you can dress up and have your photo taken (typically around ¥10,000–15,000), while some guesthouses also offer the opportunity. The most popular place to don kimono is, of course, Kyoto (see p.403). Men can get in on the act, too, dressing up in what is called "samurai" style (around ¥5000), though the male kimono is much less florid in design than the female version, and is usually in muted colours such as black, greys and browns.

stick to export models, which you'll find mostly in the stores' duty-free sections, but bear in mind they may not be any cheaper than you would pay at home.

Contemporary fashion

Top Japanese labels such as Issey Miyake, Yohji Yamamoto, Comme des Garçons and Evisu jeans are worn by fashionistas around the world, but there are also plenty of up-and-coming designers and streetwear labels to discover in Japan. The epicentre of chic is Tokyo's Omotesandō and the surrounding Aoyama and Harajuku areas. If you want to check out the latest designers and labels, such as Jun Takahashi, Tsumori Chisato and Yanagawa Arashi, then head to the boutiques here and in trendy Daikan'yama and Naka-Meguro, or hit town during Tokyo Fashion Week (Ⓦwww.jfw.jp) held twice a year. Kyoto also has an interesting fashion scene (see p.444).

Finding clothes that fit is becoming easier as young Japanese are, on average, substantially bigger-built than their parents, and foreign chains tend to carry larger sizes. **Shoes**, however, are more of a problem. While stores stock larger sizes nowadays, the range is still pretty limited – your best bet is to try a large department store.

Travel essentials

Costs

Despite its reputation as being an outrageously expensive country, prices in Japan have dropped or at least stabilized in recent years, and with a little planning it is a manageable destination even for those on the absolute minimum **daily budget** (¥8000–10,000). By the time you've added in some transport costs, a few entry tickets, meals in classier restaurants and one or two nights in a ryokan or business hotel, at least ¥15,000 per day is more realistic.

If you plan to travel around the country, it's a good idea to buy a **Japan Rail Pass** (see p.39) before departure, though it's also worth investigating special deals on internal flights. Within the country, all sorts of discount fares and excursion tickets are available, while overnight ferries and buses are an economical way of getting around; see p.36 for more details.

Holders of the **International Student Identity Card** (ISIC; Ⓦwww.isiccard.com) are eligible for discounts on some transport and admission fees, as are children. If you're planning to stay several nights in youth hostels, it's worth buying a **Hostelling International card** (Ⓦwww.hihostels.com) which qualifies you for a reduction of ¥600 on the rates (see p.146).

It's also worth checking JNTO's website (Ⓦwww.jnto.go.jp) for further tips on how to save money. **Welcome Card** schemes, for example, operate in some areas of the country, which entitle you to discounts at certain museums, sights, shops, restaurants

Consumption tax

A **consumption tax** (*shōhizei*) of five percent is levied on virtually all goods and services in Japan, including restaurant meals and accommodation. This is supposed to be included in the advertised price, though you'll occasionally come across hotels that haven't quite got round to it yet; double-check to be on the safe side.

and transport services. At the time of writing, there were ten Welcome Card schemes in operation, including the Tokai area (see p.387) and the Tokyo museum pass (see p.93).

Crime and personal safety

Japan boasts one of the lowest crime rates in the world. Nonetheless, it always pays to be careful in crowds and to keep money and important documents stowed in an inside pocket or money belt, or in your hotel safe.

The presence of **police boxes** (*kōban*) in every neighbourhood helps discourage petty crime, and the local police seem to spend the majority of their time dealing with stolen bikes (bicycle theft is rife) and helping people find addresses. This benevolent image is misleading, however, as the Japanese police are notorious for forcing confessions and holding suspects for weeks without access to a lawyer. Amnesty International have consistently criticized Japan for its treatment of illegal immigrants and other foreigners held in jail.

It's best to carry your **passport** or ID at all times; the police have the right to arrest anyone who fails to do so. In practice, however, they rarely stop foreigners. If you're found without your ID, the usual procedure is to escort you back to your hotel or apartment to collect it. Anyone found **taking drugs** will be treated less leniently; if you're lucky, you'll simply be fined and deported, rather than sent to prison.

The generally low status of women in Japan is reflected in the amount of **groping** that goes on in crowded commuter trains – there are even pornographic films and comics aimed at gropers. If you do have the misfortune to be groped, the best solution is to grab the offending hand, yank it high in the air and embarrass the guy as much as possible. More violent **sexual abuse** is rare, though harassment, stalking and rape are seriously under-reported. Women should exercise the same caution about being alone with a man as they would anywhere. Violent crimes against women do occur, as the murders of Lucie Blackman, who worked as a hostess in a Tokyo club, in 2000, and of English-language teacher Lindsay Ann Hawker in 2007 sadly prove.

In **emergencies**, phone ⓣ110 for the police or ⓣ119 for an ambulance or fire engine. You can call these numbers free from any public phone by pressing the red button before dialling. If possible, ask someone to call for you, since few police speak English, though Tokyo Metropolitan Police do run an English-language hotline on ⓣ03/3501-0110 (Mon–Fri 8.30am–5.15pm). Two other useful options are Tokyo English Language Lifeline (TELL; ⓣ03/5774-0992, ⓦwww.telljp.com; daily 9am–11pm) and Japan Helpline (ⓣ0570/000-911, ⓦwww.jhelp.com; 24hr).

Each prefecture also has a Foreign Advisory Service, with a variety of foreign-language speakers who can be contacted as a last resort (see individual city Listings sections for details).

Earthquakes

Japan is home to one-tenth of the world's active volcanoes and the site of one-tenth of its major earthquakes (over magnitude 7 on the Richter scale). At least one quake is recorded every day somewhere in the country, though fortunately the vast majority consist of minor tremors that you probably won't even notice. The most recent major quake occurred at Kōbe in January 1995, when more than six thousand people died, many of them in fires that raged through the old wooden houses, though most of the newer structures – built since the 1980s, when tighter regulations were introduced – survived.

There's a sequence of major quakes in Tokyo every seventy-odd years. The last one was in 1923 so the next "Big One" has been expected for at least a decade. Tokyo is equipped with some of the world's most sophisticated sensors, and architects employ mind-boggling techniques to try to ensure the city's new high-rises remain upright.

Nevertheless, earthquakes are notoriously difficult to predict and it's worth taking note of a few basic **safety procedures** (see box, p.72). Aftershocks may go on for a long time, and can topple structures that are already weakened. Note that most casualties are

Earthquake safety procedures

If you do have the misfortune to experience more than a minor rumble, follow the safety procedures listed below:

- Extinguish any fires and turn off electrical appliances.
- Open any doors leading out of the room you're in, as they often get jammed shut, blocking your exit.
- Stay away from windows because of splintering glass. If you have time, draw the curtains to contain the glass.
- Don't rush outside (many people are injured by falling masonry), but get under something solid, such as a ground-floor doorway, or a desk.
- If you are outside when the quake hits, head for the nearest park or other open space.
- If the earthquake occurs at night, make sure you've got a torch (all hotels, ryokan, etc provide flashlights in the rooms).
- When the tremors have died down, go to the nearest open space, taking your documents and other valuables with you. It's also a good idea to take a cushion or pillow to protect your head against falling glass.
- Eventually, make your way to the designated neighbourhood emergency centre and get in touch with your embassy.

caused by fire and traffic accidents, rather than collapsing buildings.

Electricity

The electrical current is 100v, 50Hz AC in Japan east of Mt Fuji, including Tokyo, and 100v, 60Hz AC in western Japan including Nagoya, Kyoto and Ōsaka. Japanese plugs have either two flat pins or, less commonly, three pins (two flat and one rounded, earth pin). If you are coming from North America or Canada, the voltage difference should cause no problems with computers, digital cameras, cell phones and the like, most of which can handle between 100V and 240V. Larger appliances such as hair dryers, curling irons and travel kettles should work, but not quite as efficiently, in which case you may need a converter. And, while Japanese plugs look identical to North American plugs, there are subtle differences, so you may also need an adaptor.

Entry requirements

All visitors must have a passport valid for the duration of their stay. Citizens of Ireland, the UK and certain other European countries can stay for up to ninety days without a visa, providing they are visiting Japan for tourism or business purposes. This stay can be extended for another three months (see below). Citizens of Australia, Canada, New Zealand and the US can also stay for up to ninety days without a visa, though this is not extendable and you are required to be in possession of a return air ticket. Anyone from these countries wishing to stay longer will have to leave Japan and then re-enter.

Citizens of certain other countries must apply for a **visa** in advance in their own country. Visas are usually free, though in certain circumstances you may be charged a fee of around ¥3000 for a single-entry visa. The rules on visas change from time to time, so check first with the nearest Japanese embassy or consulate, or on the Japanese Ministry of Foreign Affairs website Ⓦwww.mofa.go.jp.

To get a **visa extension** you'll need to fill in two copies of an "Application for Extension of Stay", available from immigration bureaus (see individual city Listings for details). These must be returned along with passport photos, a letter explaining your reasons for wanting to extend your stay, and a fee of ¥4000. In addition, you may be asked to show proof of sufficient funds to support your stay, and a valid onward ticket out of the country. If you're not a national of one of the few countries with six-month reciprocal visa exemptions (these include Ireland and the UK), expect a thorough grilling from the immigration officials. An easier option – and the only alternative available to nationals of those countries who are not eligible for an extension – is a short trip out of the country, say to South Korea or Hong Kong, though you'll still have to run the gauntlet of immigration officials on your return.

Citizens of the UK, Ireland, Canada, Australia, New Zealand, South Korea, France, Germany, Denmark, Taiwan and Hong Kong aged between 18 and 30 can apply for a **working holiday visa**, which grants a stay of up to one year and entitles the holder to take paid employment as long as your stay is "primarily deemed to be a holiday" – full details of the scheme can be found at ⓦhttp://tinyurl.com/c2zwhx.

British nationals are also eligible for the **volunteer visa scheme**, which allows holders to undertake voluntary work for charitable organizations in Japan for up to one year. Your application must include a letter from the host organization confirming details of the voluntary work to be undertaken and the treatment the volunteer will receive (pocket money and board and lodging are allowed, but formal remuneration is not). You must also be able to show evidence of sufficient funds for your stay in Japan.

Foreigners staying in Japan for more than ninety days must obtain **alien registration status** before the period is up; apply at the local government office for the area where you are staying. The alien registration card (often referred to as a *gaijin* card) includes your photograph and must be carried at all times. In addition, if you're on any sort of working visa and you leave Japan temporarily, you must get a **re-entry visa** before you leave if you wish to continue working on your return. Re-entry visas are available from local immigration bureaus.

Japanese embassies and consulates

You'll find a full list of **embassies and consulates** on ⓦwww.mofa.go.jp/about.

Australia 112 Empire Circuit, Yarralumla, Canberra (ⓣ02/6273 3244, ⓦwww.au.emb-japan.go.jp); 17th Floor, Comalco Place, 12 Creek St, Brisbane (ⓣ07/3221 5188, ⓦwww.brisbane.au.emb-japan.go.jp); Level 15, Cairns Corporate Tower, 15 Lake St, Cairns (ⓣ07/4051-5177); 45F Melbourne Central Tower, 360 Elizabeth St, Melbourne (ⓣ03/9639 3244); 21F The Forrest Centre, 221 St George's Terrace, Perth (ⓣ08/9480 1800); Level 34, Colonial Centre, 52 Martin Place, Sydney (ⓣ02/9231 3455).

Canada 255 Sussex Drive, Ottawa (ⓣ613/241-8541, ⓦwww.ca.emb-japan.go.jp); 2300 Trans Canada Tower, 450-1st Street SW, Calgary (ⓣ403/294-0782); 600 Rue de la Gauchetière West, Suite 2120, Montreal (ⓣ514/866-3429); Suite 3300, Royal Trust Tower, 77 King St West, Toronto (ⓣ416/363-7038); 900-1177 West Hastings St, Vancouver (ⓣ604/684-5868).

China 7 Ri Tan Rd, Jian Guo Men Wai, Beijing (ⓣ010/6532-2361, ⓦwww.cn.emb-japan.go.jp); 37F Metropolitan Tower, 68 Zourong Rd, Central District, Chongqing (ⓣ023/6373-3585); Garden Tower, 368 Huanshi Dong Lu, Guangzhou (ⓣ020/8334-3009); 46–47F One Exchange Square, 8 Connaught Place, Central, Hong Kong (ⓣ2522-1184, ⓦwww.hk.emb-japan.go.jp); 8 Wan Shan Rd, Shanghai (ⓣ021/5257-4766).

Ireland Nutley Building, Merrion Centre, Nutley Lane, Dublin (ⓣ01/202 8300, ⓦwww.ie.emb-japan.go.jp).

New Zealand Level 18, Majestic Centre, 100 Willis St, Wellington (ⓣ04/473-1540, ⓦwww.nz.emb-japan.go.jp); Level 12, ASB Bank Centre, 135 Albert St, Auckland (ⓣ09/303-4106); Level 5, Forsyth Barr House, 764 Colombo St, Christchurch (ⓣ03/366-5680).

South Africa 259 Baines St, Groenkloof, Pretoria (ⓣ012/452-1500, ⓦwww.japan.org.za); 2100 Main Tower, Standard Bank Center, Heerengracht, Cape Town (ⓣ021/425-1693).

South Korea 18-11 Junghak-dong, Jongno-gu, Seoul (ⓣ02/2170-5200, ⓦwww.kr.emb-japan.go.jp); 1147-11, Choryang-3-dong, Dong-ku, Busan (ⓣ051/465-5101).

UK 101–104 Piccadilly, London (ⓣ020/7465-6500, ⓦwww.uk.emb-japan.go.jp); 2 Melville Crescent, Edinburgh (ⓣ0131/225-4777, ⓦwww.edinburgh.uk.emb-japan.go.jp).

US 2520 Massachusetts Ave NW, Washington DC (ⓣ202/238-6700, ⓦwww.us.emb-japan.go.jp); One Alliance Center, Suite 1600, 3500 Lenox Rd, Atlanta (ⓣ404/240-4300); Federal Reserve Plaza, 14th Floor, 600 Atlantic Ave, Boston (ⓣ617/973-9774); Olympia Centre, Suite 1100, 737 North Michigan Ave, Chicago (ⓣ312/280-0400); 1225 17th Street, Suite 3000, Denver (ⓣ303/534-1151); 1742 Nuuanu Ave, Honolulu (ⓣ808/543-3111); 2 Houston Center, 909 Fannin, Suite 3000, Houston (ⓣ713/652-2977); 350 South Grand Ave, Suite 1700, Los Angeles (ⓣ213/617-6700); Brickell

Bay View Centre, Suite 3200, 80 SW 8th St, Miami (Ⓣ305/530-9090); 299 Park Ave, New York (Ⓣ212/371-8222); 50 Fremont St, Suite 2300, San Francisco (Ⓣ415/777-3533); 601 Union St, Suite 500, Seattle (Ⓣ206/682-9107).

Gay and lesbian travellers

Homosexual travellers should encounter few problems in Japan – it's highly unlikely for eyebrows to be raised if a same-sex couple check into the same room, for example. There are no laws against homosexual activity, though it can hardly be said Japan is an out and proud gay-supporting nation. Marriage remains an almost essential step on the career ladder at many corporations, and such expectations keep many Japanese gays in the closet, often leading double lives, and outside the main cities the gay scene is all but invisible. This said, in recent times homosexuality and other alternative forms of sexuality have become more acceptable and there are a few openly gay public figures (although mainly media celebrities).

Useful online English sources of information on the city's gay life include Fridae (Ⓦwww.fridae.com); GayNet Japan (Ⓦwww.gnj.or.jp); Out Japan (Ⓦwww.outjapan.com); Utopia (Ⓦwww.utopia-asia.com/tipsjapn.htm); and the tri-lingual lesbian-focused Tokyo Wrestling (Ⓦwww.tokyowrestling.com).

Health

Japan has high standards of health and hygiene, and there are no significant diseases worth worrying about. There are no immunizations or health certificates needed to enter the country.

Medical treatment and drugs are of a high quality, but can be expensive – if possible you should bring any medicines you might need with you, especially prescription drugs. Also bring a copy of your prescription and make sure you know what the generic name of the drug is, rather than its brand name. Some common drugs widely available throughout the US and Europe are generally not available in Japan. The contraceptive pill is available, but only on prescription.

Although mosquitoes buzz across Japan in the warmer months, **malaria** is not endemic, so there's no need to take any tablets. It's a good idea to pack mosquito repellent, however, and to burn coils in your room at night, or to use a plug-in repellent.

Tap **water** is safe to drink throughout Japan, but you should avoid drinking directly from streams or rivers. It's also not a good idea to walk barefoot through flooded paddy fields, due to the danger of water-borne parasites. Food-wise, you should have no fears about eating raw seafood or sea fish, including the notorious *fugu* (globe fish). However, raw meat and river fish are best avoided.

In the case of an **emergency**, the first port of call should be to ask your hotel to phone for a doctor or ambulance. You could also head for, or call, the nearest tourist information office or international centre (in major cities only), which should be able to provide a list of local doctors and hospitals with English-speaking staff. Alternatively, you could call the toll-free 24-hour Japan Helpline (Ⓣ0570/000-911, Ⓦwww.jhelp.com) or, in a last resort, contact the Prefecture's Foreign Advisory Service (see "Emergencies" in individual city listings in the Guide).

If you need to call an **ambulance** on your own, dial Ⓣ119 and speak slowly when you're asked to give an address. Ambulance staff are not trained paramedics, but will take you to the nearest appropriate hospital. Unless you're dangerously ill when you go to hospital, you'll have to wait your turn in a clinic before you see a doctor, and you'll need to be persistent if you want to get full details of your condition: some doctors are notorious for withholding information from patients.

For minor ailments and advice you can go to a **pharmacy**, which you'll find in most shopping areas. There are also numerous smaller private **clinics**, where you'll pay in the region of ¥10,000 to see a doctor. You could also try **Asian medical remedies**, such as acupuncture (*hari*) and pressure point massage (*shiatsu*), though it's worth trying to get a personal recommendation to find a reputable practitioner.

Insurance

It's essential to take out a good **travel insurance** policy, particularly one with comprehensive medical coverage, due to the high cost of hospital treatment in Japan.

Rough Guides travel insurance

Rough Guides has teamed up with WorldNomads.com to offer great **travel insurance** deals. Policies are available to residents of over 150 countries, with cover for a wide range of **adventure sports**, 24hr emergency assistance, high levels of medical and evacuation cover and a stream of **travel safety information**. Roughguides.com users can take advantage of their policies online 24/7, from anywhere in the world – even if you're already travelling. And since plans often change when you're on the road, you can extend your policy and even claim online. Roughguides.com users who buy travel insurance with WorldNomads.com can also leave a positive footprint and donate to a community development project. For more information go to ⓦ**www.roughguides.com/shop**.

Internet

Cybercafés can be found across Japan – often as part of a 24-hour computer-game and *manga* centre (see box, p.150). Free access is sometimes available (usually in cultural exchange centres, or regular cafés looking to boost business); otherwise, expect to pay around ¥200–400 per hour. Cybercafés come and go fairly swiftly, although the copyshop Kinko's is pretty reliable, and has branches (some 24hr) across Japan; check ⓦwww.kinkos.co.jp to find the one nearest you. Also see the Listings sections of town and city accounts in the Guide for internet availability.

Many **hotels** offer broadband and/or wi-fi access in every room, often free or for a small daily fee (typically ¥1000). Others may provide at least one terminal for guests travelling without their own computer, generally also for free.

Laundry

All hotels provide either a laundry service or, at the lower end, coin-operated machines. These typically cost ¥100–300 for a wash (powder ¥30–50) and ¥100 for ten minutes in the drier. You'll also find coin-operated laundries (*koin randorii*) in nearly all Japanese neighbourhoods, often open long hours. Virtually all Japanese washing machines use cold water.

Living in Japan

Overall **employment opportunities** for foreigners have shrunk since the Japanese economy took a nosedive in the early 1990s, though finding employment is far from impossible, especially if you have the right qualifications (a degree is essential) and appropriate visa. In fact, the number of well-qualified, Japanese-speaking *gaijin* in the country employed in specialist jobs has increased over the last decade.

Working holiday visas, for which you don't need a job in advance, are available to citizens of a handful of countries – see p.73 for more details. All other foreigners must have sponsorship papers from a prospective employer in place before applying for a work visa, which need not be obtained in your home country (but must be applied for outside of Japan). A few employers may be willing to hire you before the proper papers are sorted out, but you shouldn't rely on this, and if you arrive without a job make sure you have plenty of funds to live on until you find one. Anyone staying in Japan more than ninety days must also apply for alien registration status (see p.73). For tips on finding long-term **accommodation**, see p.47.

The most common job available to foreigners is **teaching English**. Some of the smaller schools are far from professional operations (and even the biggies get lots of complaints), so before signing any contract it's a good idea to talk to other teachers and, if possible, attend a class and find out what will be expected of you. If you have a professional teaching qualification, plus experience, or if you also speak another language such as French or Italian, your chances of getting one of the better jobs will be higher.

Another option is to get a place on the government-run **Japan Exchange and Teaching Programme** (JET; ⓦwww.jetprogramme.org), aimed at improving foreign-language teaching in schools and promoting international understanding. The scheme is open to graduates aged under 40, preferably holding some sort of language-teaching qualification. Benefits include a generous salary, help with accommodation, return air travel to Japan and paid holidays. Applying for the JET programme is a lengthy process for which you need to be well prepared. Application forms for the following year's quota are available from late September, the deadline for submission being early December. Interviews are held in January and February, with decisions made in March. After health checks and orientation meetings, JETs head off to their posts in late July on year-long contracts, which can be renewed for up to two more years by mutual consent.

A much more limited job option for *gaijin* is **rewriting** or **editing** English **translations** of Japanese text for technical documents, manuals, magazines and so on. For such jobs, it's a great help if you know at least a little Japanese. These days there are also good opportunities for *gaijin* with **ski instructor** or **adventure sports** experience to work on the ski slopes, particularly in resorts such as Niseko, Furano and Hakuba which target overseas visitors. Other options include **modelling**, for which it will be an asset to have a professional portfolio of photographs, and **bar work** and **hostessing**, with the usual warnings about the dangers inherent in this type of work. Whatever work you're looking for – or if you're doing any sort of business in Japan – a smart set of clothes will give you an advantage, as will following other general rules of social etiquette (see p.64).

Employment resources

Apart from the websites listed below, the main places to look for job adverts are the free weekly magazines *Metropolis* and *Tokyo Notice Board* (see p.56).

GaijinPot ⓦ www.gaijinpot.com. Classifieds focused on English-language teaching.

Japan Association for Working Holiday Makers ⓦ www.jawhm.or.jp. Job referrals for people on working holiday visas.

Jobs in Japan ⓦ www.jobsinjapan.com. Broad range of classified ads.

Work in Japan ⓦ www.daijob.com/wij. Japan's largest bilingual jobs website.

WWOOF (Willing Workers on Organic Farms) ⓦ www.wwoofjapan.com. Opportunities to work and live on organic farms across Japan, plus a few hotels and resorts.

Studying Japanese language and culture

There are all sorts of opportunities to study Japanese language and culture. In order to get a **student** or **cultural visa**, you'll need various documents from the institution where you plan to study and proof that you have sufficient funds to support yourself, among other things. Full-time courses are expensive, but once you have your visa you may be allowed to undertake a minimal amount of paid work.

Japan's Ministry of Education, Culture, Sports, Science and Technology (MEXT; ⓦ www.mext.go.jp) offers various **scholarships** to foreign students wishing to further their knowledge of Japanese or Japanese studies, undertake an undergraduate degree, or become a research student at a Japanese university. You'll find further information on the informative Study in Japan website (ⓦ www.studyjapan.go.jp), run by the Ministry of Foreign Affairs, or by contacting your nearest Japanese embassy or consulate.

Tokyo, Ōsaka, Kyoto and other major cities have numerous **Japanese language schools** offering intensive and part-time courses. Among the most established are Berlitz (ⓦ www.berlitz.co.jp), with branches nationwide, and Tokyo Kogakuin Japanese Language School (5-30-16 Sendagaya, Shibuya-ku; ⓣ 03/3352-3851, ⓦ www.technos-jpschool.ac.jp). The monthly bilingual magazine *Hiragana Times* (ⓦ *www.hiraganatimes.com*) and the listings magazines *Metropolis* and *Tokyo Journal* also carry adverts for schools, or check out the Association for the Promotion of Japanese Language Education (2F Ishiyama Building, 1-58-1 Yoyogi, Shinjuku-ku; ⓣ 03/4304-7815, ⓦ www.nisshinkyo.org), whose website lists accredited institutions.

Mail

Japan's **mail** service is highly efficient and fast, with post offices (*yūbin-kyoku*) all over the country, easily identified by their red-and-white signs – a T with a parallel bar across the top, the same symbol that you'll find on the red letterboxes. All post can be addressed in Western script (*rōmaji*) provided it's clearly printed.

In urban post offices there are separate counters, with English signs, for postal and banking services; in central post offices you can also exchange money at rates comparable to those in banks. If you need to send bulkier items or **parcels** back home, all post offices sell reasonably priced special envelopes and boxes for packaging. The maximum weight for an overseas parcel is 30kg (less for some destinations). A good compromise between expensive air mail and slow sea mail is Surface Air Lifted (SAL) mail, which takes around three weeks to reach most destinations, and costs somewhere between the two. For English-language information about postal services, including postal fees, see the Post Office website Ⓦwww.post.japanpost.jp.

Central **post offices** generally open Monday to Friday 9am to 7pm, Saturday 9am to 5pm and Sunday 9am to 12.30pm, with most other branches opening Monday to Friday 9am to 5pm only. A few larger branches may also open on a Saturday from 9am to 3pm, and may operate after-hours services for parcels and express mail. Major post offices that are open daily 24 hours can be found in Shinjuku (see map, pp.124–125) and Shibuya (see map, p.129) among other city areas. For sending parcels and baggage around Japan, take advantage of the excellent, inexpensive *takuhaibin* (or *takkyūbin*, as it's more commonly known) or **courier delivery services**, which can be arranged at most convenience stores, hotels and some youth hostels. These services – which typically cost under ¥2000 – are especially handy if you want to send luggage (usually up to 20kg) on to places where you'll be staying later in your journey or to the airport to be picked up prior to your departure.

Maps

The Japan National Tourist Organization publishes four tourist **maps** covering Tokyo, Kansai, Kyoto and the whole country. These are available free at JNTO offices abroad and at the TICs in Japan, and are fine for most purposes. Tourist offices in other areas usually provide local maps. If you need anything more detailed, most bookshops sell maps, though you'll only find English-language maps in the big cities. By far the most useful are the **bilingual maps** published by Kodansha or Shōbunsha, which are available from specialist shops outside Japan. Kodansha's *Tokyo City Atlas* is a must for anyone spending more than a few days in the city, while Shōbunsha's bilingual *Japan Road Atlas* is a little dated but still the best available map for exploring by car. If you're **hiking**, the best maps are those in the *Yama-to-kōgen* series, also published by Shōbunsha but in Japanese only.

Note that **maps on signboards** in Japan, such as a map of footpaths in a national park, are usually oriented the way you are facing. So, if you're facing southeast, for example, as you look at the map, the top will be southeast and the bottom northwest.

Money

The **Japanese currency** is the **yen** (¥; *en* in Japanese). Notes are available in denominations of ¥1000, ¥2000, ¥5000 and ¥10,000, while coins come in values of ¥1, ¥5, ¥10, ¥50, ¥100 and ¥500. Apart from the ¥5 piece, a copper-coloured coin with a hole in the centre, all other notes and coins indicate their value in Western numerals For current **exchange rates** see Ⓦwww.xe.com.

Though **credit and debit cards** are becoming more widely accepted, Japan remains very much a cash society. The most useful cards to carry are Visa and American Express, followed closely by MasterCard, then Diners Club; you should be able to use these in hotels, restaurants, shops and travel agencies accustomed to serving foreigners. However, many retailers only accept locally issued cards.

Credit card emergency numbers

If you lose a credit or debit card, call the following toll-free numbers, available 24 hours:

American Express Ⓣ0120-779 656
MasterCard Ⓣ00531/11-3886
Visa International Ⓣ00531/11-1555

ATMs

The simplest way of obtaining cash in Japan is by making an **ATM** withdrawal on a credit or debit card. Both the **post office** and Seven Bank (whose machines are located in **7-Eleven** stores) operate ATMs which accept foreign-issued cards. Post office machines accept Visa, PLUS, MasterCard, Maestro, Cirrus and American Express, with instructions provided in English; 7-Eleven ATMs accept all of these, too, except overseas-issued MasterCard brand cash cards and credit cards (including Cirrus and Maestro cards). Withdrawal limits will depend on the card issuer and your credit limit. If the machine doesn't allow you to withdraw money in the first instance, try again with a smaller amount.

Seven Bank ATMs are often accessible 24 hours. You'll also find post office ATMs not only in post offices, but also in stations, department stores and the like throughout the main cities – they're identified with a sticker saying "International ATM Service". Their ATMs have more restricted hours than the Seven Bank machines, but the ones in major post offices can be accessed at weekends and after the counters have closed, though none is open round the clock. You can also try **Citibank** (ⓦwww.citibank.co.jp), which operates a number of ATMs in Tokyo, Sapporo, Nagoya, Ōsaka, Kyoto and Fukuoka. Most are accessible outside normal banking hours, and some are open 24 hours. If you're having problems, pick up the phone beside the ATM and ask to speak to someone in English.

Changing money

You can change cash and travellers' cheques at the exchange counters, or *ryōgae-jo* (両替所) of main **post offices** and certain **banks**. The post office handles cash and travellers' cheques in six major currencies, including American, Canadian and Australian dollars, sterling and euros; the most widely accepted brands of cheque are American Express, Visa, Thomas Cook and MasterCard. There's little variation in rates between banks and the post office and there are no commission fees. Post office exchange counters have slightly longer opening hours (generally Mon–Fri 9am–4pm); banks open Monday to Friday from 9am to 3pm, but some don't open their exchange desks until 10.30am or 11am. Big **department stores** often have an exchange desk, which can be useful at other times, though most only handle dollars or a limited range of currencies and might charge a small fee. **Hotels** are only supposed to change money for guests, but some might be persuaded to help in an emergency. Remember to take your passport along in case it's needed, and allow plenty of time, since even a simple transaction can take twenty minutes or more. Finally, when changing money, ask for a few ¥10,000 notes to be broken into lower denominations; these come in handy for ticket machines and small purchases.

Opening hours and public holidays

Business hours are generally Monday to Friday 9am to 5pm, though private companies often close much later in the evening and may also open on Saturday mornings. Department stores and bigger

Public holidays

If one of the holidays listed below falls on a Sunday, then the following Monday is also a holiday.

New Year's Day Jan 1
Coming of Age Day Second Mon in Jan
National Foundation Day Feb 11
Spring Equinox March 20/21
Showa Day April 29
Constitution Memorial Day May 3
Greenery Day May 4
Children's Day May 5
Marine Day Third Mon in July
Respect the Aged Day Third Mon in Sept
Autumn Equinox Sept 23/24
Health and Sports Day Second Mon in Oct
Culture Day Nov 3
Labour Thanksgiving Day Nov 23
Emperor's Birthday Dec 23

shops tend to open around 10am and shut at 7pm or 8pm. Local shops, however, will generally stay open later, while many convenience stores are open 24 hours. Most shops take one day off a week, not necessarily on a Sunday.

The majority of **museums** close on a Monday, but stay open on Sundays and national holidays (closing the following day instead); last entry is normally thirty minutes before closing. However, during the New Year festival (January 1–3), Golden Week (April 29–May 5) and Obon (the week around August 15), almost everything shuts down. Around these periods all transport and accommodation is booked out weeks in advance, and all major tourist spots get overrun.

Phones

You're rarely far from a payphone in Japan, but only at certain ones – usually grey or metallic silver and bronze colour, with a sign in English – can you make **international calls**. These phones can be difficult to find; try a major hotel or international centre.

The vast majority of payphones take both coins (¥10 and ¥100) and **phonecards** (*terefon kādo*; テレフォンカード). The latter come in ¥500 (50-unit) and ¥1000 (105-unit) versions and can be bought in department and convenience stores and at station kiosks. Virtually every tourist attraction sells specially decorated phonecards, though you'll pay a premium for these, with a ¥1000 card only giving ¥500 worth of calls.

Payphones don't give change, but do return unused coins, so for local calls use ¥10 rather than ¥100 coins. For international calls, it's best to use a phonecard and to call between 7pm and 8am Monday to Friday, or at any time at weekends or holidays, when rates are cheaper. Alternatively, use a **prepaid calling card**, such as KDDI's Super World card (ⓦhttp://tinyurl.com/29b969u), Primus (ⓦwww.primustel.co.jp), or Brastel (ⓦwww.brastel.com); all are available at convenience stores.

Everywhere in Japan has an **area code**, which can be omitted if the call is a local one. Area codes are given for all telephone numbers throughout this Guide. Toll-free numbers begin with either ⓣ0120 or 0088; in a few cases you may come across codes such as 0570, which are non-geographical and should always be included with the main number wherever you're calling from. Numbers starting with 080 or 090 are to mobile phones. For operator assistance for overseas calls, dial ⓣ0051.

Mobile phones

Practically everyone in Japan seems to have a **mobile phone**, or *keitai-denwa*, sometimes shortened to *keitai* (携帯電話), many of which include features such as GPS navigation and the ability to use the device like a prepaid travel card on trains, subways and in shops. If a mobile phone has a camera (practically all do), they can also read **QR codes**, which feature a square black-and-white pattern. Increasingly seen on advertisements and in shops, these codes usually have links to a website or email address that the phone can access, or might contain an address, telephone numbers and map of a particular place.

The only foreign phones that reliably work in Japan are some **3G models** – contact your mobile phone service provider before leaving your home country to check on the current situation. If your phone isn't compatible with Japan's transmission technology, the solution for short-term visitors is to **rent** a Japan-compatible mobile phone (buying a prepaid phone in Japan generally requires you to show proof of local residency). Phones can be rented at the major international airports, in Tokyo, or online. Options include **GoMobile** (ⓦwww.gomobile.co.jp), who will deliver your phone to a nominated address in Japan such as your hotel, and **PuPuRu** (ⓦwww.pupuru.com/en) who also rent out data cards for internet access on your laptop. Other mobile phone operators include industry-biggie **DoCoMo** (ⓦwww.nttdocomo.co.jp) and **Softbank** (ⓦwww.softbank.jp/en), both of which have rental booths at Narita Airport (3G handsets should work with either of these networks).

Phoning abroad from Japan

The main companies in Japan offering **international phone calls** are KDDI (ⓣ001), Softbank Telecom (ⓣ0041), Cable & Wireless IDC (ⓣ0061) and NTT (ⓣ0033). If

Phoning Japan from abroad

To **call Japan** from abroad, dial your international access code (UK and Ireland ⓣ00; US ⓣ011; Canada ⓣ011; Australia ⓣ0011; New Zealand ⓣ00), plus the country code (ⓣ81), then the area code minus the initial zero, then the number.

you want to call abroad from Japan from any type of phone, choose a company (there's little difference between them all as far as rates are concerned) and dial the relevant access code, then the country code (UK ⓣ44; Ireland ⓣ353; US and Canada ⓣ01; Australia ⓣ61; New Zealand ⓣ64; South Africa ⓣ27), then the area code minus the initial zero, then the number.

For operator assistance for overseas calls, dial ⓣ0051. You can make international operator-assisted calls by calling ⓣ0051 via KDDI.

Smoking

Smoking is banned on nearly all public transport and in most public buildings, shops, offices, restaurants, bars, cafés, cinemas and the like, though in some cases smoking is allowed in designated areas. An increasing number of cities, including Tokyo, Ōsaka and Kyoto, are also clamping down on smoking in the street. Again, you can light up in designated areas – look for the smoke-swathed huddle around the pavement ashtrays. Fines for smoking where it's prohibited typically start at ¥2000, though at the moment you are more likely to get away with a warning.

Time

The whole of Japan is nine hours ahead of Greenwich Mean Time, so at noon in London it's 9pm in Tokyo. Japan is fourteen hours ahead of Eastern Standard Time in the US. There is no daylight saving, so during British Summer Time, for example, the difference drops to eight hours.

Tourist information

The **Japan National Tourism Organization** (JNTO; ⓦwww.jnto.go.jp) maintains a number of overseas offices (see opposite). Within Japan, JNTO operates **Tourist Information Centres** (TIC), all of which have English-speaking staff, in central Tokyo (see p.92), Tokyo's Narita airport (see p.91) and Kansai International airport (see p.483). Though staff will help sort out routes and timetables, they can't make travel reservations, nor usually sell tickets to theatres, cinemas and so on; instead, they'll direct you to the nearest appropriate outlet.

There is a network of government-run **tourist information offices** (観光案内所; *kankō annaijo*), many with English-speaking staff, in all major towns and cities and in the prime tourist destinations; you'll find a full list on the JNTO website. These offices are usually located in or close to the main train station or in the city centre, and are indicated by a sign with a red question mark in a white circle against a black background and the word "information". In practice, the amount of English information available – whether written or spoken – is a bit hit and miss, but staff should be able to assist with local maps, hotel reservations and simple queries. There are also ordinary local tourist information offices: practically every town (and many villages) has these, though there's only a slim chance of getting English-language assistance.

Another useful source of English-language information is the **Goodwill Guides**, groups of volunteer guides mostly in central and western Japan who offer their services free – although you're expected to pay for their transport, entry tickets and any meals you have together. Their language abilities vary, but they do provide a great opportunity to learn more about Japanese culture and to visit local restaurants, shops and so forth with a Japanese-speaker. Again, you'll find the groups listed on the JNTO website. Otherwise, tourist information offices can usually provide contact details of local groups and may be willing to help with arrangements; try to give at least two days' notice.

JNTO offices abroad

Australia Suite 1, Level 4, 56 Clarence St, Sydney (ⓣ02/9279 2177, ⓦwww.jnto.org.au).

Canada 481 University Ave, Suite 306, Toronto (Ⓣ416/366-7140, Ⓦwww.ilovejapan.ca).
UK 5th Floor, 12/13 Nicholas Lane, London (Ⓣ020/7398-5670, Ⓦwww.seejapan.co.uk).
US 11 West 42nd St, 19th Floor, New York (Ⓣ212/757-5640, Ⓦwww.japantravelinfo.com); 340 E. 2nd St, Little Tokyo Plaza, Suite 302, Los Angeles (Ⓣ213/623-1952).

Travelling with children

With high standards of health, hygiene and safety, and lots of interesting things to do, Japan is a great place to travel with children. At museums and other sights, school-age kids usually get reduced rates, which may be up to half the adult price. Children under age 6 ride free on trains, subways and buses, while those aged 6 to 11 pay half fare.

It's a good idea to bring a lightweight, easily collapsible **pushchair**. You'll find yourself walking long distances in cities and, while many subway and train stations now have lifts, there are still plenty of stairs.

Finding **hotels** offering **family rooms** that fit more than three people is tough: international chain hotels are your best bet. A great alternative is a Japanese-style ryokan or minshuku where you can share a big tatami room. Only at the more upmarket Western-style hotels will you be able to arrange **babysitting**.

All the products you need – such as **nappies** and **baby food** – are easily available in shops and department stores, though not necessarily imported varieties. If you need a particular brand, it would be wise to bring it with you. Although **breast-feeding** in public is generally accepted, it's best to be as discreat as possible. Most Japanese women who breastfeed use the private rooms provided in department stores, public buildings and in many shops, or find a quiet corner.

Although it's rather dated, Kodansha's *Japan for Kids* still contains a lot of useful general information; it's also worth checking out Ⓦwww.tokyowithkids.com.

Travellers with disabilities

Disability has always been something of an uncomfortable topic in Japan, with disabled people generally hidden from public view. In recent years, however, there has been a certain shift in public opinion, particularly in the wake of the bestseller *No One's Perfect* by Ototake Hirotada, the upbeat, forthright autobiography of a 23-year-old student born without arms or legs.

The government is spearheading a drive to provide more accessible hotels and other facilities (referred to as "barrier-free" in Japan). Most train and subway **stations** now have an extra-wide manned ticket gate and an increasing number have escalators or lifts. Some **trains**, such as the Narita Express from Narita International airport into Tokyo, have spaces for wheelchair users, but you should reserve well in advance. For travelling short distances, **taxis** are an obvious solution, though none is specially adapted and few drivers will offer passengers help getting in or out of the car.

New **hotels** are required to provide accessible facilities and several older ones are making them available, too. Your best bet is one of the international chains or modern Western-style business hotels, which are most likely to provide fully adapted rooms, ramps and lifts; check ahead to ensure the facilities meet your requirements. Similarly, most modern shopping complexes, museums and other public buildings are equipped with ramps, wide doors and accessible toilets.

But while things are improving, Japan is not an easy place to get around for anyone using a wheelchair, or for those who find it difficult to negotiate stairs or walk long distances. In cities, the sheer crush of people can also be a problem at times. Although it's usually possible to organize assistance at stations, you'll need a Japanese-speaker to phone ahead and make the arrangements. For further information and help, contact the Japanese Red Cross Language Service Volunteers (c/o Volunteers Division, Japanese Red Cross Society, 1-1-3 Shiba Daimon, Minato-ku, Tokyo 105-8521). You'll find useful, if slightly outdated, information on their website, Ⓦaccessible.jp.org.

Guide

Guide

1

Tokyo

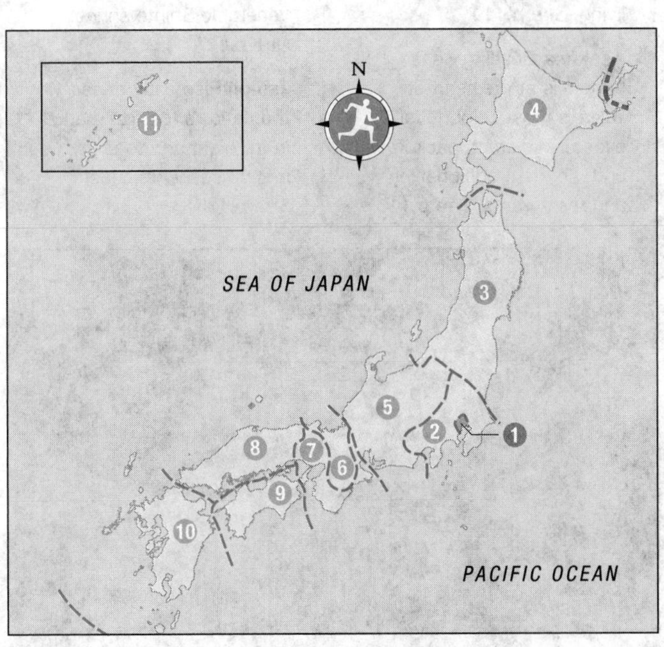

CHAPTER 1 Highlights

* **Akihabara** This nonstop "electric town" is a must-see for manga and anime fans and has a great new arts centre. See p.107
* **Roppongi** The hedonists' playground has evolved into a forum for major art exhibitions and sophisticated urban living. See p.110
* **Asakusa** Bustling Sensō-ji temple is at the heart of Tokyo's most colourful and evocative district, packed with craft shops, traditional inns and restaurants. See p.113
* **Shinjuku** Tokyo in a microcosm, from the tiny bars of Golden Gai to the Gotham-City-like Tokyo Metropolitan Government Building. See p.123
* **Meiji-jingū** Escape the urban clamour amid the verdant grounds of the city's most venerable Shinto shrine. See p.127
* **Tsukiji** Rise early to see the nation's top fish market in full flight and to enjoy a fresh sushi breakfast. See p.135

▲ Neon Arch, Shinjuku

1

Tokyo

A fuel-injected adrenaline rush into a neon-bright future, **TOKYO** (東京) is a mercurial metropolis flashing by in a blur of conflicting images. Obsessed with the latest trends and fashions, the world's largest city – the heart of which is home to at least **eight million people** – is also fiercely proud of its heritage. Lively neighbourhood festivals are held virtually every day of the year, and people regularly visit their local shrine or temple and scrupulously observe the passing seasons in manicured gardens.

Caught up in an untidy web of overhead cables, plagued by seemingly incessant noise, its freeways often clogged with bumper-to-bumper traffic, this concrete-and-steel conurbation may seem the stereotypical urban nightmare. Yet back from the frenetic main roads are tranquil backstreets, where dinky wooden houses are fronted by neatly clipped bonsai trees; wander beyond the hi-tech emporia, and you'll discover charming fragments of the old city such as temples and shrines wreathed in wisps of smoking incense.

The fact is that centuries-long experience of organizing itself to cope with the daily demands of millions of inhabitants has made Tokyo something of a **model metropolitan environment**. Trains run on time and to practically every corner of the city, crime is hardly worth worrying about, and shops and vending machines provide everything you could need (and many things you never thought you did), 24 hours a day.

With so much going on, first-time visitors should be prepared for a massive assault on the senses – just walking the streets of this hyperactive city can be an energizing experience. It need not be an expensive one, either. You'll be pleasantly surprised by how **affordable** many things are. Cheap-and-cheerful *izakaya* – bars that serve food – and casual cafés serving noodles and rice dishes are plentiful, the metro is a bargain, and tickets for a sumo tournament or a kabuki play can be bought for the price of a few drinks.

Browsing the shops and marvelling at the passing parade is mesmerising – the next best thing to having a ringside seat at the hippest of fashion shows. The city's great wealth and relative lack of planning restrictions have given architects almost unparalleled freedom to realize their wildest dreams. Likewise, in Tokyo's uber-chic bars, restaurants and clubs you'll see today what the rest of the world will get tomorrow. You may not figure out exactly what makes it tick – and you're sure to get a little lost while trying – but the conclusion is inescapable: Tokyo is a fun, seductive and addictive experience.

Some history

The city's founding date is usually given as 1457, when minor lord Ōta Dōkan built his castle on a bluff overlooking the Sumida-gawa and the bay. However, a

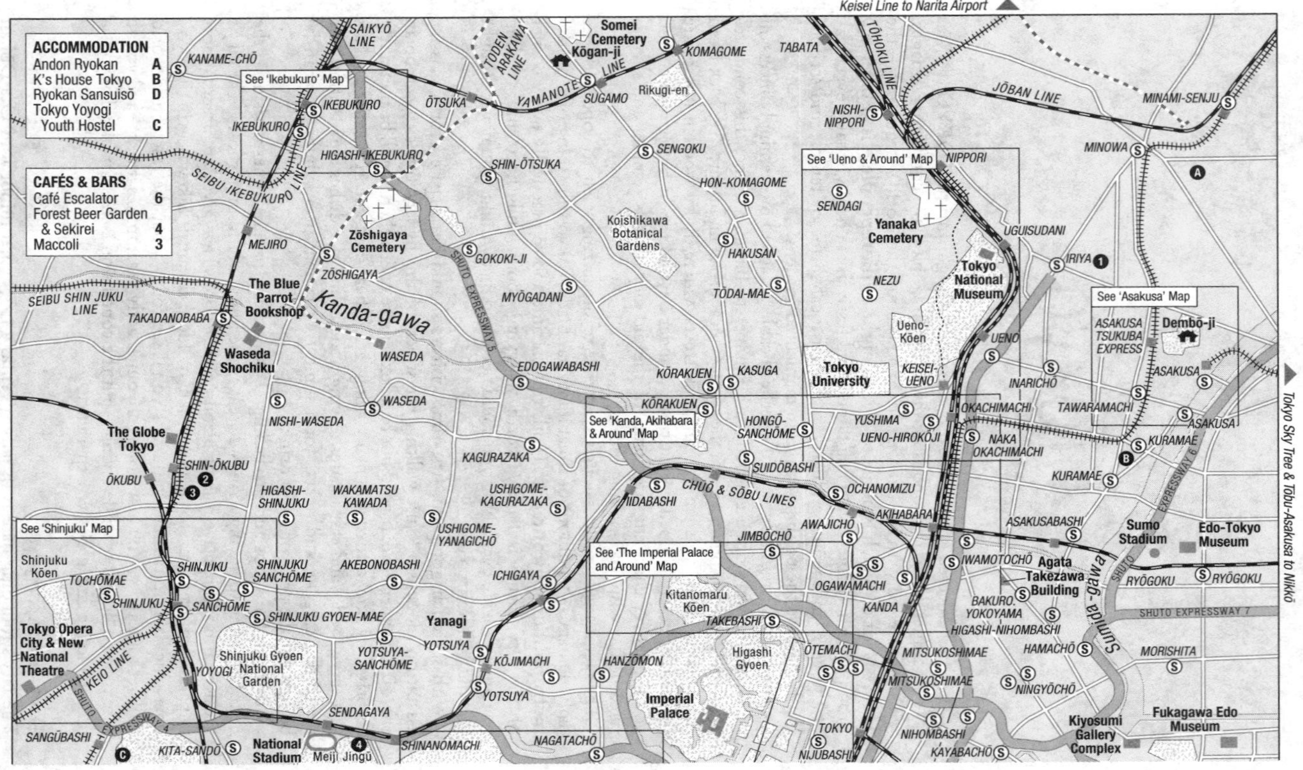
ACCOMMODATION
Andon Ryokan A
K's House Tokyo B
Ryokan Sansuisō D
Tokyo Yoyogi Youth Hostel C
CAFÉS & BARS
Café Escalator 6
Forest Beer Garden & Sekirei 4
Maccoli 3
Keisei Line to Narita Airport
Tokyo Sky Tree & Tōbu-Asakusa to Nikkō
See 'Ikebukuro' Map
See 'Ueno & Around' Map
See 'Asakusa' Map
See 'Kanda, Akihabara & Around' Map
See 'The Imperial Palace and Around' Map
See 'Shinjuku' Map
SAIKYŌ LINE
KANAME-CHŌ
IKEBUKURO
HIGASHI-IKEBUKURO
SEIBU IKEBUKURO LINE
ŌTSUKA
TODEN ARAKAWA LINE
YAMANOTE LINE
SUGAMO
Somei Cemetery
Kōgan-ji
KOMAGOME
Rikugi-en
TABATA
TŌHOKU LINE
NISHI-NIPPORI
JŌBAN LINE
MINAMI-SENJU
MINOWA
SHIN-ŌTSUKA
SENGOKU
HON-KOMAGOME
NIPPORI
SENDAGI
Yanaka Cemetery
UGUISUDANI
IRIYA
Koishikawa Botanical Gardens
HAKUSAN
MEJIRO
Zōshigaya Cemetery
GOKOKI-JI
ZŌSHIGAYA
SHUTO EXPRESSWAY 5
MYŌGADANI
TŌDAI-MAE
NEZU
Tokyo National Museum
SEIBU SHIN JUKU LINE
TAKADANOBABA
The Blue Parrot Bookshop
Kanda-gawa
WASEDA
Waseda Shochiku
Ueno-Kōen
UENO
Tokyo University
KEISEI-UENO
EDOGAWABASHI
KŌRAKUEN
KASUGA
ASAKUSA TSUKUBA EXPRESS
Dembō-ji
ASAKUSA
INARICHŌ
NISHI-WASEDA
OKACHIMACHI
YUSHIMA
TAWARAMACHI
HONGŌ-SANCHŌME
UENO-HIROKŌJI
NAKA OKACHIMACHI
KURAMAE
The Globe Tokyo
SHIN-ŌKUBU
ŌKUBU
KAGURAZAKA
SUIDŌBASHI
HIGASHI-SHINJUKU
WAKAMATSU KAWADA
USHIGOME-KAGURAZAKA
CHŪŌ & SŌBU LINES
OCHANOMIZU
IIDABASHI
AKIHABARA
AWAJICHŌ
ASAKUSABASHI
Sumo Stadium
Edo-Tokyo Museum
USHIGOME-YANAGICHŌ
JIMBŌCHŌ
Shinjuku Kōen
TOCHŌMAE
SHINJUKU
SHINJUKU SANCHŌME
AKEBONOBASHI
ICHIGAYA
IWAMOTOCHŌ
Agata Takezawa Building
RYŌGOKU
SHUTO
Sumida-gawa
SANCHŌME
SHINJUKU GYOEN-MAE
Kitanomaru Kōen
OGAWAMACHI
KANDA
BAKURO-YOKOYAMA
SHUTO EXPRESSWAY 7
Yanagi
TAKEBASHI
HIGASHI-NIHOMBASHI
Tokyo Opera City & New National Theatre
YOTSUYA
YOTSUYA-SANCHŌME
Shinjuku Gyoen National Garden
Higashi Gyoen
ŌTEMACHI
MITSUKOSHIMAE
HAMACHŌ
MORISHITA
KEIO LINE
YOYOGI
KŌJIMACHI
HANZŌMON
NINGYŌCHŌ
SHUTO EXPRESSWAY 4
SENDAGAYA
Imperial Palace
SANGŪBASHI
KITA-SANDŌ
National Stadium
Meiji Jingū
SHINANOMACHI
NAGATACHŌ
TOKYO
NIJUBASHI
NIHOMBASHI
KAYABACHŌ
Kiyosumi Gallery Complex
Fukagawa Edo Museum

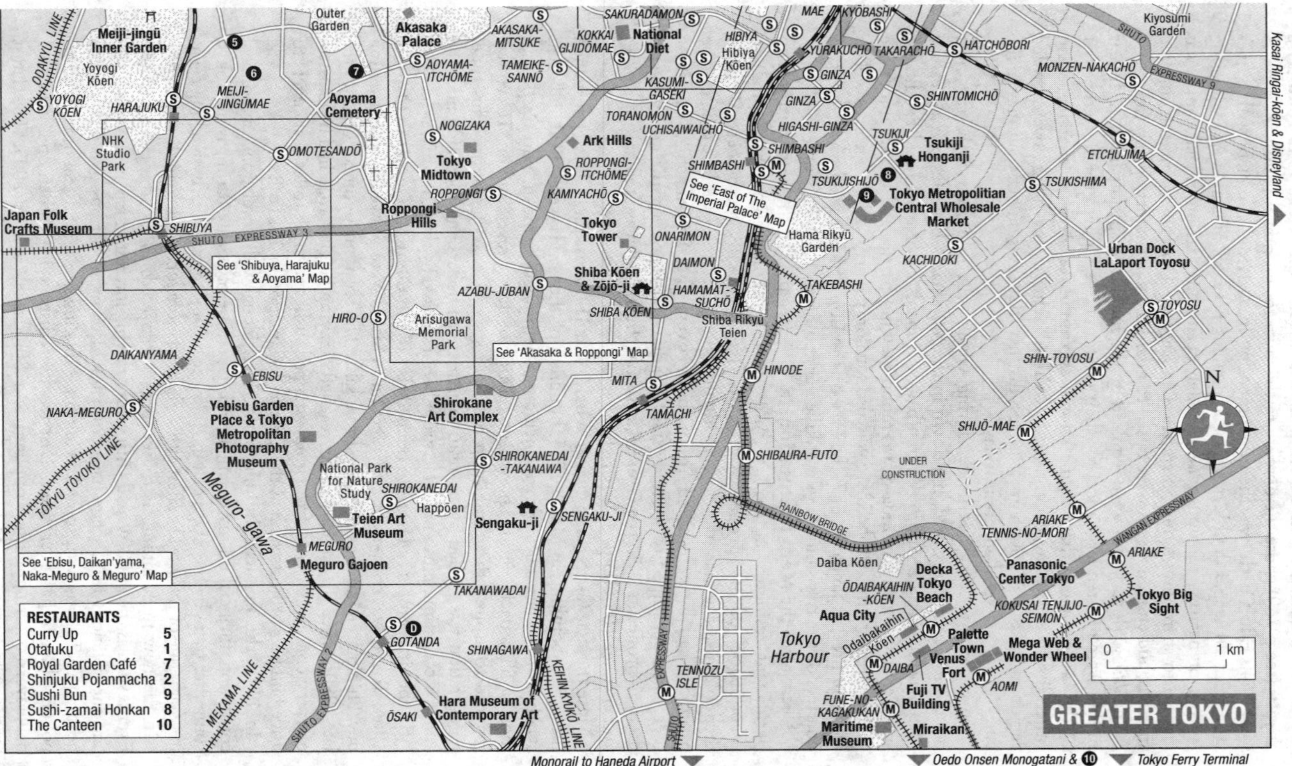
GREATER TOKYO
RESTAURANTS
Curry Up 5
Otafuku 1
Royal Garden Café 7
Shinjuku Pojanmacha 2
Sushi Bun 9
Sushi-zamai Honkan 8
The Canteen 10
Kasai Ringai-kōen & Disneyland
Monorail to Haneda Airport
Oedo Onsen Monogatani & 10
Tokyo Ferry Terminal
See 'Shibuya, Harajuku & Aoyama' Map
See 'Akasaka & Roppongi' Map
See 'East of The Imperial Palace' Map
See 'Ebisu, Daikan'yama, Naka-Meguro & Meguro' Map
0
1 km
N
Meiji-jingū Inner Garden
Yoyogi Kōen
NHK Studio Park
Outer Garden
Akasaka Palace
Aoyama Cemetery
Tokyo Midtown
Roppongi Hills
Ark Hills
Tokyo Tower
Shiba Kōen & Zōjō-ji
National Diet
Hibiya Kōen
Tsukiji Honganji
Tokyo Metropolitan Central Wholesale Market
Hama Rikyū Garden
Shiba Rikyū Teien
Kiyosumi Garden
Urban Dock LaLaport Toyosu
Japan Folk Crafts Museum
Arisugawa Memorial Park
Shirokane Art Complex
Yebisu Garden Place & Tokyo Metropolitan Photography Museum
National Park for Nature Study
Happōen
Teien Art Museum
Sengaku-ji
Meguro Gajoen
Meguro-gawa
Hara Museum of Contemporary Art
Tokyo Harbour
Daiba Kōen
Decka Tokyo Beach
Aqua City
Odaibakaihin Kōen
Palette Town
Venus Fort
Fuji TV Building
Mega Web & Wonder Wheel
Panasonic Center Tokyo
Tokyo Big Sight
Maritime Museum
Miraikan
UNDER CONSTRUCTION
RAINBOW BRIDGE
ODAKYŪ LINE
TŌKYŪ TŌYOKO LINE
MEKAMA LINE
KEIHIN KYŪKŌ LINE
SHUTO EXPRESSWAY 3
SHUTO EXPRESSWAY 2
SHUTO EXPRESSWAY 1
SHUTO EXPRESSWAY 9
WANGAN EXPRESSWAY
YOYOGI KŌEN
HARAJUKU
MEIJI-JINGŪMAE
OMOTESANDŌ
NOGIZAKA
AOYAMA-ITCHŌME
AKASAKA-MITSUKE
TAMEIKE-SANNŌ
KOKKAI GIJIDŌMAE
SAKURADAMON
KASUMI-GASEKI
TORANOMON
UCHISAIWAICHŌ
HIBIYA
YŪRAKUCHŌ
MAE
KYŌBASHI
TAKARACHŌ
HATCHŌBORI
MONZEN-NAKACHŌ
GINZA
HIGASHI-GINZA
SHINTOMICHŌ
TSUKIJI
TSUKIJISHIJŌ
SHIMBASHI
ETCHUJIMA
TSUKISHIMA
KACHIDOKI
TOYOSU
SHIN-TOYOSU
SHIJŌ-MAE
ARIAKE
TENNIS-NO-MORI
KOKUSAI TENJIJO-SEIMON
ŌDAIBAKAIHIN-KŌEN
DAIBA
AOMI
FUNE-NO-KAGAKUKAN
ROPPONGI
ROPPONGI-ITCHŌME
KAMIYACHŌ
ONARIMON
DAIMON
HAMAMATSUCHŌ
SHIBA KŌEN
TAKEBASHI
HINODE
SHIBAURA-FUTO
AZABU-JŪBAN
HIRO-O
SHIBUYA
DAIKANYAMA
EBISU
NAKA-MEGURO
MITA
TAMACHI
SHIROKANEDAI-TAKANAWA
SHIROKANEDAI
SENGAKU-JI
MEGURO
TAKANAWADAI
GOTANDA
SHINAGAWA
ŌSAKI
TENNŌZU ISLE

far more significant event occurred in 1590, when the feudal lord **Tokugawa Ieyasu** (see p.769) chose the obscure castle-town for his power base.

By 1640 **Edo Castle** was the most imposing in all Japan, complete with a five-storey central keep, a double moat and a spiralling network of canals. A bewildering warren of narrow, tortuous lanes, sudden dead ends and unbridged canals was created to snare unwelcome intruders. Drainage work began on the surrounding marshes, and embankments were raised to guard the nascent city against floods.

The *daimyō* (lords) who were required by the shogun to spend part of each year in Edo were granted large plots for their estates on the higher ground to the west of the castle, an area that became known as **Yamanote**. Artisans, merchants and other lower classes were confined to **Shitamachi**, a low-lying, overcrowded region to the east. Though growing less distinct, this division between the "high" and "low" city is still apparent today.

During two centuries of peace, during which time Edo grew to be the most populous city in the world, life down in the Shitamachi buzzed with a wealthy merchant class and a vigorous, often bawdy, subculture of geisha and kabuki, of summer days on the Sumida-gawa, moon-viewing parties and picnics under the spring blossom. Inevitably, there was also squalor, poverty and violence, as well as frequent fires; in January 1657, the **Fire of the Long Sleeves** laid waste to three-quarters of the city's buildings and killed an estimated 100,000 people.

A year after the **Meiji Restoration**, in 1868 (see p.771), the emperor took up permanent residence in the city, now renamed **Tokyo** (Eastern Capital) in recognition of its proper status. As Japan quickly embraced Western technologies, the face of Tokyo gradually changed: the castle lost much of its grounds, canals were filled in or built over, and Shitamachi's wealthier merchants decamped to more desirable Yamanote. However, the city was still disaster-prone: in 1923 the **Great Kantō Earthquake** devastated half of Tokyo and another 100,000 people perished.

More trauma was to come during **World War II**. In just three days of sustained incendiary bombing in March 1945, hundreds of thousands were killed and great swathes of the city burnt down, including Meiji-jingū, Sensō-ji, Edo Castle and most of Shitamachi. From a prewar population of nearly seven million, Tokyo was reduced to around three million people in a state of near-starvation. This time, regeneration was fuelled by an influx of American dollars and food aid under the Allied Occupation, plus a manufacturing boom sparked by the Korean War in 1950.

By the time Emperor Hirohito opened the Tokyo **Olympic Games** in October 1964, Tokyo was truly back on its feet and visitors were wowed by the stunning new Shinkansen trains running west to Ōsaka. The economy boomed well into the late 1980s, when Tokyo land prices reached dizzying heights, matched by excesses of every conceivable sort, from gold-wrapped sushi and mink toilet-seat covers to huge building projects such as the Odaiba reclamation in Tokyo Bay.

In 1991, **the financial bubble** burst. This, along with revelations of political corruption, financial mismanagement and the release of deadly Sarin gas on Tokyo commuter trains by the AUM cult in 1995 (see p.776) – a particularly shocking event in what is one of the world's safest cities – led to a more sober Tokyo in the late 1990s.

In the new millennium, as the economy recovered, so did the city's vitality. Events such as the **2002 World Cup**, plus growing interest in Japanese pop culture and the delicious food scene have contributed to more curious overseas visitors heading to Tokyo, with some staying on – making the capital feel more cosmopolitan than it has ever been. District after district has undergone structural makeovers, starting with Roppongi and Shiodome back in 2003. The latest megadevelopment is at Oshiage east of the Sumida-gawa where the **Tokyo Sky Tree** (see p.116), set to be completed in 2012, is already Japan's tallest structure.

Arrival, information and orientation

If you're **arriving** in Tokyo from abroad, you'll touch down at Narita International Airport or Haneda Airport. If you're coming to the capital from elsewhere in Japan, more likely you'll arrive at one of the main train stations (Tokyo, Ueno, Shinagawa or Shinjuku) or the long-distance bus terminals, mainly at Tokyo and Shinjuku stations.

By plane

Narita International Airport (新東京国際空港; ⓣ0476/34-8000, ⓦwww.narita-airport.jp), better known as **Narita** (成田), is around 66km east of the city centre. There are two terminals, both of which have **tourist information** and **Welcome Inn Reservation Centres** for accommodation bookings. If you have a Japan Rail Pass exchange order (see p.35), you can arrange to use your pass either immediately or at a later date at the JR travel agencies in the basement.

Located on a spit of land jutting into Tokyo Bay 20km south of the Imperial Palace, **Haneda Airport** (羽田空港; ⓣ03/5757-8111, ⓦwww.tokyo-airport-Building.co.jp) is where most domestic flights and a few international services touch down. The opening of a third terminal and a fourth runway at the end of 2010 has seen more international routes offered from the airport.

Transport between the city and airports

The fastest way into Tokyo **from Narita** is on the **New Skyliner** (36–44min; ¥2400) express train operated by Keisei (ⓦwww.keisei.co.jp), who also offer the cheapest connection into town in the form of the *tokkyū* (limited express) service, which costs ¥1000 to Ueno (every 30min; 1hr 11min). Both trains stop at Nippori where it's easy to transfer to the Yamanote or the Keihin Tōhoku lines.

JR's **Narita Express** (**N'EX**; ⓦwww.jreast.co.jp/e/nex) runs to several city stations. The cheapest fare is ¥2940 to Tokyo Station (every 30min; 1hr), and there are also direct services to Shinjuku (hourly; 1hr 20min) for ¥3110. N'EX services to Ikebukuro (¥3110) and Yokohama (¥4180) via Shinagawa are much less frequent.

If you have a non-Japanese passport, JR offers a great **discount package**: for ¥3500 you can get a ticket on the N'EX to any Tokyo stations it serves, or Yokohama, plus a Suica card (see p.94) to the value of ¥2000 (comprising a ¥500 deposit plus ¥1500 of train and subway travel). This makes travelling on the N'EX a much better deal than the JR *kaisoku* (rapid) trains which chug slowly into Tokyo Station (hourly; 1hr 20min) for ¥1280.

Airport Limousine buses (ⓣ03/3665-7220, ⓦwww.limousinebus.co.jp) are prone to traffic delays, but can be useful if you're weighed down by luggage and staying at or near a major hotel. Tickets are sold in each of the arrival lobbies; the buses depart directly outside (check which platform you need) and stop at many major hotels and train stations around the city. Journeys to central Tokyo cost around ¥3000 and take at least ninety minutes. Once you factor in the cost of a taxi from one of the train stations to your hotel, these buses can be a good deal. The ¥3100 **Limousine & Metro Pass** combines a one-way bus trip from Narita to central Tokyo and a one-day metro pass valid on nine of Tokyo's thirteen subway lines. **Taxis** to the city centre cost at least ¥20,000, and are no faster than going by bus.

From Haneda Airport, it's a twenty-minute monorail journey to Hamamatsuchō Station on the Yamanote line (daily 5.20am–11.15pm; every 5–10min; ¥460). Alternatively you can board a Keihin Kūkō-line train to Shinagawa or Sengakuji and connect directly with other rail and subway lines. A taxi from Haneda to central Tokyo costs ¥6000; a limousine bus to Tokyo Station is ¥900.

There are frequent direct bus (1hr 20min; ¥3000) and train (1hr 10min; ¥1580) connections between Narita and Haneda.

By train and bus

Most Shinkansen **trains** pull into **Tokyo Station** (東京駅), close to the Imperial Palace, or **Shinagawa Station** (品川駅), around 6km southwest. A few Shinkansen from the north go only as far as **Ueno Station** (上野駅), some 4km northeast of the Imperial Palace. All three stations are on the Yamanote line and are connected to several subway lines. Other long-distance JR services stop at Tokyo and Ueno stations, Shinjuku Station on Tokyo's west side and Ikebukuro Station in the city's northwest corner.

Non-JR trains terminate at different stations: the Tōkyū Tōyoko line from Yokohama ends at Shibuya Station (渋谷駅); the Tōbu Nikkō line runs from Nikkō to Asakusa Station (浅草駅), east of Ueno; and the Odakyū line from Hakone finishes at Shinjuku Station (新宿駅), which is also the terminus for the Seibu Shinjuku line from Kawagoe. All these stations have subway connections and (apart from Asakusa) are on the Yamanote rail line.

Long-distance buses pull in at several major stations around the city. The main overnight services from Kyoto and Ōsaka arrive beside the eastern Yaesu exit of Tokyo Station; other buses arrive at Ikebukuro, Shibuya, Shinagawa and Shinjuku.

By boat

Long-distance **ferries** from Tokushima (p.612), Kita-Kyūshū and the Okinawan islands arrive at **Tokyo Ferry Terminal** (東京フェリーターミナル) at Ariake, on the man-made island of Odaiba (see p.137) in Tokyo Bay. For details see **Ocean Tokyu Ferry** (Ⓣ03/5148 0109, Ⓦwww.otf.jp) and **Maruei Ferry/A Lione** (Ⓣ03/5643 6170, Ⓦwww.aline-ferry.com). Buses run from the port to Shin-Kiba Station, from which you can catch a subway train or the overland JR Keiyō line. A taxi to central Tokyo costs around ¥2000.

Information

The official online sources for Tokyo information are the excellent websites of the **Tokyo Convention and Visitors Bureau** (Ⓦwww.tcvb.or.jp) and the **Tokyo Metropolitan Government** (Ⓦwww.tourism.metro.tokyo.jp). There are several **tourist information centres** (TICs) in the city, the best being the **Tokyo Tourist Information Centre** at 1F Tokyo Metropolitan Government No. 1 Building, 2-8-1 Nishi-Shinjuku, Tochō-mae Station (daily 9.30am–6.30pm; Ⓣ03/5321-3077). It also has small branches at Haneda Airport (daily 9am–10pm; Ⓣ03/5757-9345) and in the Kesei line station at Ueno (daily 9.30am–6.30pm; Ⓣ03/3836-3471).

JNTO's main office (daily 9am–5pm; Ⓣ03/3201-3331) is on the tenth floor of Tokyo Kotsu Kaikan, immediately east of Yūrakuchō Station. Other information sources are the **Asakusa Culture and Sightseeing Centre** (daily 9.30am–8pm; Ⓣ03/3842-5566) across from Kaminari-mon; and the **Odakyū Sightseeing Service Centre** (daily 8am–6pm; Ⓣ03/5321-7887, Ⓦwww.odakyu.jp/english), on the ground floor on the west side of Shinjuku Station.

Decent free **maps** of the city are available from any of the TICs. Kodansha's bilingual *Tokyo City Atlas* (¥2100), available at the city's major bookstores, is more detailed and, importantly, includes *chōme* and block numbers to help pin down addresses (see box, p.40). Bilingual maps on public noticeboards outside the main exits to most subway and train stations are handy for getting your immediate bearings.

The best **English-language magazine** is the free weekly *Metropolis* (Ⓦmetropolis.co.jp). There's also the *Weekender* (Ⓦweekenderjapan.com), which caters to the

The GRUTT Pass

One of the best deals on offer in Tokyo is the **Grutt Pass**. For ¥2000 you get a ticket booklet which allows free or discounted entry to seventy attractions, including all major museums. Valid for two months after first being used, the ticket can be bought at participating venues and the Tokyo Metropolitan Government tourist information centre in Shinjuku (see opposite), among other outlets; for more details see ⓦwww.museum.or.jp/grutto.

expat and diplomatic scene. The quarterly *Tokyo Journal* (¥600; ⓦwww.tokyo.to) carries the occasional interesting feature. You'll find these publications at TICs, larger hotels, foreign-language bookstores and places frequented by *gaijin*.

Orientation

Tokyo is a vast place, spreading from the mountains in the north and west to tropical islands some 1300km to the south, but as a visitor you're unlikely to stray beyond its most central municipalities, or wards (*ku* in Japanese). A useful reference point is the **Yamanote line**, an elongated overland train loop that encloses the city centre and connects most places of interest to visitors.

The city is split into five chunks in this chapter: **central Tokyo** (p.100) including the Imperial Palace, Ginza, Marunouchi, Kanda, Akihabara, Akasaka and Roppongi; **eastern Tokyo** (p.113) covering Ryōgoku, Oshiage and Asakusa; **northern Tokyo** (p.116) including Ueno, Yanaka and Ikebukuro; **southern and western Tokyo** (p.123) covering Shinjuku, Harajuku, Aoyama, Shibuya, Ebisu, Daikan'yama, Meguro and Shinagawa; and **bayside Tokyo** (p.135) including Tsukiji and Odaiba.

City transport

Getting around Tokyo is easy thanks to the city's super-efficient **trains and subways**. However, to really see the city, walking and cycling (see p.96) are the best ways to explore. Tokyo also has a couple of monorails, one tram line, and many buses, too.

The subway

Its colourful map may look daunting, but Tokyo's **subway** is relatively easy to negotiate. The simple colour coding on trains and maps, as well as clear signposts (many in English), directional arrows and alpha-numeric codes for all central subway stations, make this by far the most *gaijin*-friendly form of transport. Avoid travelling at rush hour (7.30–9am & 5.30–7.30pm), and you'll have a much less crowded journey.

There are two systems, the nine-line **Tokyo Metro** (ⓦwww.tokyometro.jp) and the four-line **Toei** (ⓦwww.kotsu.metro.tokyo.jp). The systems share some stations, but unless you buy a special ticket from the vending machines that specifies your route from one system to the other, or you have a pass (see box, p.94), you cannot switch mid-journey between the two sets of lines without paying extra at the ticket barrier. Subways have connecting passageways to overland train lines, such as the Yamanote. A **colour map** of the subway system appears at the back of the book.

Tokyo transport passes

If you're on a **short visit** and making minimal use of the metro or trains, buy **kaisūken**, carnet-type tickets. These come in three types: regular *kaisūken*, which give you eleven tickets of a specific value for the price of ten (thus eleven ¥160 tickets will cost you ¥1600); off-peak *kaisūken*, which give you twelve tickets for the price of ten, but can only be used from 10am to 4pm on weekdays; and Saturday/Sunday and public holiday *kaisūken*, tickets which give you fourteen tickets for the price of ten. There are special buttons labelled in Japanese on the automated ticket machines at the stations, or you can buy them at a ticket office.

If you need to ride the metro and trains a lot in the space of a day, you'll find both Tokyo Metro and Toei have day tickets for use exclusively on their own subway systems (¥710 and ¥700 respectively), the Toei pass also covering the city's buses and one tram line. However, it's far more convenient to get a one-day **economy pass** covering both systems for ¥1000. For day-use of the city's subways, JR trains and buses, there's the **Tokyo Free Ticket** (¥1580), but you'd really have to be tearing all over town to get your money's worth.

Although they don't save you any money, the most convenient way to travel is to use a **PASMO** (Ⓦwww.pasmo.co.jp) or a JR **Suica** stored-value card. Both can be used on all subways, many buses and both JR and private trains in the wider Tokyo area. Tap the pass on the electronic sensor as you go through the ticket barriers or board the bus and the appropriate fare will be deducted. The card can be recharged at ticket machines and ticket offices. To get either card, you have to spend a minimum of ¥2000, of which ¥500 is a deposit, which will be returned to you, plus any remaining value (minus a small processing fee) when you cash in the card before leaving Tokyo.

You'll generally pay for your **ticket** at the vending machines beside the electronic ticket gates. There are no ticket sales windows other than at major stations. Most trips across central Tokyo cost no more than ¥190, but if in doubt, buy the cheapest ticket (¥160) and sort out the difference with the gatekeeper at the other end.

Trains run from around 5am to just after midnight daily, and during peak daytime hours as frequently as every five minutes (and at least every fifteen minutes at other times). Leaving a station can be complicated by the number of exits, but there are maps close to the ticket barriers and on the platforms indicating where the exits emerge, and strips of yellow tiles on the floor mark the routes to the ticket barriers.

Trains

JR East trains (Ⓦwww.jreast.co.jp) are another handy way of getting around the city. The main lines you'll find useful are the circular **Yamanote** (coloured lime green on the transport map); the **Chūō line** (deep orange), which starts at Tokyo Station and runs west to Shinjuku and the suburbs beyond; the **Sōbu line** (yellow) from Chiba in the east to Mitaka in the west, which runs parallel to the Chūō line in the centre of Tokyo; and the **Keihin Tōhoku line** (blue) from Ōmiya in the north, through Tokyo Station, to Yokohama and beyond. It's fine to transfer between JR lines on the same ticket, but you'll have to buy a new ticket if you transfer to a subway line, unless you have a PASMO or Suica card (see above).

The lowest fare on JR lines is ¥130. Like the subways, JR offers prepaid cards and *kaisūken* (carnet) deals on tickets. One of the handiest is the **Suica** (see above). Also a good deal is the one-day **Tokunai Pass** (¥730), which gives unlimited travel within the Tokyo Metropolitan District Area.

Buses

Once you've got a feel for the city, **buses** can be a good way of cutting across the few areas not served by a subway or train line. Only a small number of the buses or routes are labelled in English. The final destination is on the front of the bus, along with the route number. You pay on entry, by dropping the flat rate (usually ¥200) into the fare box by the driver (there's a machine in the box for changing

Tokyo tours and classes

For a quick overview of Tokyo there are the usual **bus tours**, but if these are not your cup of tea, and you still fancy having a guide on hand, there are also various **walking** or **cycling** tours, as well as culinary and culture classes. See p.96 for details of sightseeing ferries.

Bus tours

Established operations such as **Hato Bus Tours** (Ⓦwww.hatobus.com), **Japan Grey Line** (Ⓦwww.jgl.co.jp/inbound) and **Sunrise Tours** (Ⓦwww.jtbgmt.com/sunrisetour), have a wide variety of tours to choose from ranging from half-day jaunts around the central sights (¥5000) to visits out to Kamakura, Nikkō and Hakone (from ¥14,000).

Sky Bus Ⓣ03/3215-0008, Ⓦwww.skybus.jp. Offers four routes, most in open-top double-decker buses: choose from a route around the Imperial Palace grounds and through Ginza and Marunouchi (¥1500; 50min); from Tokyo Tower to the Rainbow Bridge (¥1700; 1hr); or an Odaiba night course (¥2000; 2hr). Their Omotesandō–Shibuya course is in a trolley-style bus (¥1200; 1hr 10min).

Cooking/craft/photography tours and classes

Alfie Goodrich Photography Lesson Ⓣ090-9971-7805, Ⓦwww.alfiegoodrich.com. Tokyo is a photographer's dream and in the hands of this professional camera guy you can learn how to shoot it to its best advantage. Group/one-to-one lessons start at ¥2000/5000 and can take place at a mutually agreed spot in central Tokyo.

A Taste of Culture Ⓣ03/5716-5751, Ⓦwww.tasteofculture.com. Food writer Elizabeth Andoh leads highly popular trips around Japanese markets helping you to identify Japanese products and runs cooking classes. You'll need to book well in advance.

HIS Experience Japan Ⓦhisexperience.jp. Try your hand at calligraphy, *taiko* drumming, wielding a samurai sword, learning to make sushi or soba, or one of the many other cultural experiences offered by local tour company HIS. Rates range from ¥5000 to ¥30,000 depending on the tour; small-group and customized options are available.

Walking tours

Otaku2 Akiba Tour Ⓦwww.otaku2.com. Anime and manga scholar Patrick Galbraith (narrator of the Tokyo Realtime Akihabara tour, see below) or one of his equally knowledgeable colleagues, leads a two-and-a-half-hour tour of Akihabara on Sundays including a visit to a maid café (¥3000).

Tokyo Realtime Ⓦwww.tokyorealtime.com. These excellent self-guided audio-tours are a fine option for independent types. The sixty-minute walks cover Kabukichō and Akihabara and can be downloaded online (US$5.99) or bought in local bookshops (¥1200; see p.164).

Tokyo Tour Guide Services Ⓦwww.tourism.metro.tokyo.jp/english/guideservice/index.html. Ten walking tours – a few free, most for a fee – accompanied by volunteer guides under the auspices of Tokyo Metropolitan Government. Tours last about three hours, departing Monday to Friday at 1pm from the tourist information centre in the Metropolitan Government Building in Shinjuku (see p.92). Reserve in advance online.

Tokyo by bike

Avoid the busy main roads and Tokyo can be a joy to **cycle**. Rental operations include **Tokyo Rent A Bike** (Ⓦwww.tokyorentabike.com; ¥900/day) and **Cool Bike** (Ⓦwww.coolbike.jp; ¥2000/day if you pick it up from Iidabashi Station or ¥2500 if delivered to your hotel). The cheapest option is **Sumida Park bicycle park**, underground beside the bridge in Asakusa (daily 6am–8pm; ¥200 for 24hr, ¥500 for 7 days; Ⓣ03/5246-1305), but they only have a limited number of bikes available. Other rental outfits are listed on Ⓦcycle-tokyo.cycling.jp, as well as lots of useful information about cycling in the city. Also check out the interactive cycle map at Ⓦx2tokyo.jp/X2TOKYO/map.html, designed by a collective of ten influential Tokyo bikers whose goal is to make "Tokyo a stylish bicycle city". Guided cycling tours are also offered by **Tokyo Great Cycling Tour** (Ⓣ03/4590-2995, Ⓦwww.tokyocycling.jp; ¥10,000 including lunch) on Tuesday, Thursday, Saturday and Sunday. Reservations required.

notes). The Transport Bureau of Tokyo Metropolitan Government issues a useful English pamphlet and map of all the bus routes; pick one up from one of the tourist information centres (see p.92).

Ferries

The Tokyo Cruise Ship Company (Ⓣ0120-977311, Ⓦwww.suijobus.co.jp) runs several **ferry** services, known as *suijō basu* (water buses), in and around Tokyo Bay. They can be a great-value way to cruise Tokyo's waterfront. The most popular is the double-decker service plying the 35-minute route (daily 10am–6.30pm; every 40min; ¥760) between the Sumida-gawa River Cruise stations at Asakusa, northeast of the city centre, and Hinode Sanbashi, on Tokyo Bay. The river and bayside views of the city are reason enough for hopping aboard, especially if you want to visit Asakusa and the gardens at Hama Rikyū on the same day, and then walk into Ginza. The ferries stop at the gardens en route, and you can buy a combination ticket for the ferry and park entrance for around ¥1020.

For a few extra hundred yen you can travel on **Himiko**, a space-age ferry (4 daily between Asakusa and Odaiba via Hinode), designed by Matsumoto Leiji, a famous manga artist. From Thursday to Saturday between 8 and 11pm the ferry changes its name to **Jicoo** (Ⓣ0120-049490, Ⓦwww.jicoofloatingbar.com) and morphs into a floating bar shuttling from Hinode, under the Rainbow Bridge, to Odaiba and back.

Hinode Sanbashi (close by Hinode Station on the Yurikamome monorail or a 10min walk from Hamamatsuchō Station on the Yamanote line) is also the jumping-off point for several good daily **cruises** around Tokyo Bay, and for ferries to various points around the island of Odaiba, or across to Kasai Rinkai-kōen on the east side of the bay.

Taxis

For short hops around the centre of Tokyo, **taxis** are often the best option, though heavy traffic can slow them down. The basic rate is ¥710 for the first 2km, after which the meter racks up ¥80 every 274m, plus a time charge when the taxi is moving at less than 10km per hour. Between 11pm and 5am, rates are about twenty percent higher.

When flagging down a taxi, a red light next to the driver means the cab is free; green means it's occupied. There are designated stands in the busiest parts of town, but be prepared for long queues after the trains stop at night, especially in areas such as Roppongi and Shinjuku.

Accommodation

The choice of accommodation in Tokyo ranges from no-expense-spared **luxury hotels** to atmospheric **ryokan** and budget **hostels** charging around ¥2000 a night. Central Tokyo (comprising Ginza, Nihombashi, Akasaka and Roppongi) is largely the domain of expensive, world-class establishments and upmarket business hotels. For cheaper rooms, there's a greater choice in Shinagawa, Shibuya and Shinjuku to the south and east, and Asakusa, Ueno and Ikebukuro in the north. Wherever you stay, remember that trains stop running around midnight; if you're a night animal, opt for somewhere near one of the entertainment districts to avoid costly taxi journeys.

Whatever your budget, it's wise to **reserve** your first few nights' accommodation before arrival. Welcome Inn Reservation Centre desks (Ⓦwww.itcj.jp; daily 8am–8pm) in both terminals of Narita Airport (see p.91) and in JNTO's TIC (see p.92; daily 9am–noon & 1–5pm; Ⓣ03/3286-6611) can assist on arrival.

In addition to the standard hotel **taxes** (see p.42) there's an extra charge of ¥100 per person per night on rooms costing over ¥10,000 per night, and ¥200 for those costing ¥15,000 or above. For more extensive accommodation listings and information about long-term accommodation in the city, see the *Rough Guide to Tokyo*.

Akasaka and Roppongi

The following hotels are marked on the map on p.111.

Asia Center of Japan ホテルアジア会館 8-10-32 Akasaka, Minato-ku Ⓣ03/3402-6111, Ⓦwww.asiacenter.or.jp. A long-established place with a solid reputation. Rooms are small and unflashy but have everything you need. Book online for discounts. Aoyama-itchōme or Nogizaka stations. ❺

The b roppongi 3-9-8 Roppongi, Minato-ku Ⓣ03/5412-0451, Ⓦwww.ishinhotels.com. A boutique-style business hotel that won't break the bank or offend the eyes, although uninspiring plastic-unit bathrooms are present throughout. A light breakfast is included in the rates. There are other equally appealing *b*'s in Akasaka (Ⓣ03/3586-0811) and Ikebukuro (Ⓣ03/3980 1911). Roppongi Station. ❺

Chisun Grand Akasaka 6-3-17 Akasaka, Minato-ku Ⓣ03/5572-7788, Ⓦwww.solarehotels.com. The flagship of the good-value Chisun chain is a real step up in quality from similar business hotel operations. The appealing rooms, split over two wings and decorated in warm browns and reds, include spacious bathrooms. Akasaka Station. ❻

Grand Hyatt Tokyo 6-10-3 Roppongi, Minato-ku Ⓣ03/4333-1234, Ⓦtokyo.grand.hyatt.jp. The spacious rooms at this glamorous hotel are made more appealing with wood fittings and natural-coloured fabrics. The restaurants and bars are all very chic. Roppongi Station. ❾

Hotel Ōkura 2-10-4 Toranomon, Minato-ku Ⓣ03/3582-0111, Ⓦwww.okura.com/tokyo. A Tokyo classic with its 1950s lobby and beguiling garden view. The contemporary floor rooms bring the design more up to date, but really it's the retro ambience of the public areas that's the sell here. Kamiyachō Station. ❾

Capsule hotels

Tokyo's **capsule hotels** (see p.43) can come in handy if you miss your last train home. The marjority are for men only; those listed below accept both men and women. Other capsule hotels, usually for men only, can be found near the stations in Shinjuku, Shibuya, Ebisu and Ueno. An alternative crash pad is a manga café (see p.150).

Capsule Inn Akihabara 6-9 Akihabara, Taitō-ku Ⓣ03/3251-0841, Ⓦwww.capsuleinn.com. There are 29 capsules for women at this 140-bed place that's handy for *otaku* central. ¥4000. Akihabara Station, see map, p.108.

Capsule Hotel Riverside カプセルホテルリバーサイド 2-20-4 Kaminarimon Ⓣ03/3844-1155, Ⓦwww.asakusa-capsule.jp. English-speaking staff, an instruction leaflet in English and 21 capsules for women on a separate floor. ¥3000. Asakusa Station, see map, p.114.

Villa Fontaine Roppongi 1-6-2 Roppongi, Minato-ku ⓣ03/3560-1110, ⓦwww.hvf.jp/eng. Stylish business hotel with pleasantly decorated rooms that are larger than average. Rates, which include a buffet breakfast, are discounted online, especially at weekends. Across the road, their Roppongi annexe is also good, and they have other nice, conveniently located branches in Shiodome and Kabukichō. Roppongi-itchōme Station. 5

Asakusa and around

The following hotels are marked on the map on p.114 (except *Andon Ryokan* and *K's House Tokyo*, which are marked on the map on pp.88–89).

Andon Ryokan 2-34-10 Nihonzutsumi, Taitō-ku ⓣ03/3873-8611, ⓦwww.andon.co.jp. Housed in an ultra-modern building, this designer ryokan glows invitingly like a lantern at night. The tatami rooms share bathrooms and are tiny, but come equipped with DVD players, and there's also free internet access, super-friendly English-speaking staff, and a jacuzzi spa you can book for private dips. Minowa Station. 3

Asakusa View Hotel 3-17-1 Nishi-Asakusa, Taitō-ku ⓣ03/3847-1111, ⓦwww.viewhotels.co.jp/asakusa. At Asakusa's grandest hotel the rooms are less memorable than the sparkling public areas, but are reasonably spacious and you'll get some terrific views from the higher floors, plus all the facilities and restaurant choices that you'd expect from a higher-end hotel. Asakusa (Tsukuba Express rail) or Tawaramachi stations. 8

K's House Tokyo 3-20-10 Kuramae, Taitō-ku ⓣ03/5833-0555, ⓦwww.kshouse.jp. Just south of Asakusa, this spick-and-span hostel gets lots of accolades for its facilities and location. There are bunk-bed dorms and private rooms with TV and internet access, plenty of showers and toilets, plus an attractive lounge area with a well-equipped kitchen, and a roof terrace. Kuramae Station. 2

Ryokan Shigetsu 旅館指月 1-31-11 Asakusa, Taitō-ku ⓣ03/3843-2345, ⓦwww.shigetsu.com. This smart little ryokan is a haven of kimono-clad receptionists and tinkling *shamisen* music. There's a choice of small Western- or Japanese-style rooms, all en suite. On the top floor is an authentic wooden Japanese bath, with views over temple roofs. Asakusa Station. 5–6

Sakura Hostel 2-24-2 Asakusa, Taitō-ku ⓣ03/3847-8111, ⓦwww.sakura-hostel.co.jp. A friendly, well-run hostel a couple of minutes' walk northwest of Sensō-ji. Dorms cost ¥2940 per person and there are also private rooms. Each floor has its own shower and toilet area and there's a good kitchen and TV lounge. Asakusa Tsukuba Express or Asakusa subway stations. 3

Sukeroku-no-yado Sadachiyo 助六の宿貞千代 2-20-1 Asakusa, Taitō-ku ⓣ03/3842-6431, ⓦwww.sadachiyo.co.jp. Step back into Edo-era Asakusa in this delightful old inn. The elegant tatami rooms are all en suite, though you can also use the traditional Japanese-style baths. Meals are available and they can also arrange performances of traditional arts, including geisha dances. Asakusa (Tsukuba Express Railway) or Tawaramachi stations. 6

Ginza and around

The following hotels are marked on the map on p.104.

Four Seasons Hotel Tokyo at Marunouchi Pacific Century Place Marunouchi, 1-11-1 Marunouchi, Chiyoda-ku ⓣ03/5222-7222, ⓦwww.fourseasons.com. Chic interior design and superb service are part of the deal at this luxury hotel in a very handy location beside Tokyo Station. Facilities include a spa, fitness centre and French restaurant. Tokyo Station. 9

Ginza Yoshimizu 3-11-3 Ginza, Chūō-ku ⓣ03/3248-4432, ⓦwww.yoshimizu.com. Look for the bamboo shoots that point out this discreet and very appealing inn. Inside, modern and traditional Japanese styles blend seamlessly to create an attractive and soothing retreat. Only natural products are used in the tatami rooms, some of which are en suite, while the meals are all organic. Rates include breakfast. Higashi-Ginza Station. 7

Marunouchi Hotel 1-6-3 Marunouchi, Chiyoda-ku ⓣ03/3217-1111, ⓦwww.marunouchi-hotel.co.jp. This moderately priced hotel packs a surprisingly classy punch, with its atrium lobby, choice of restaurants and cheerful, well-furbished rooms. Tokyo and Ōtemachi stations. 8

Mitsui Garden Hotel 8-13-1 Ginza, Chūō-ku ⓣ03/3543-1131, ⓦwww.gardenhotels.co.jp. Mitsui's impressive flagship hotel stands out from the crowd with its chic style courtesy of Italian designer Piero Rissoni. Rooms are decorated in earthy tones but it's the bird's-eye views of the city and bay that grab the attention. Shinbashi Station. 7

Ikebukuro

The following hotels are marked on the map on p.122.

Kimi Ryokan 2-36-8 Ikebukuro, Toshima-ku ⓣ03/3971-3766, ⓦwww.kimi-ryokan.jp. This is a great-value institution on Tokyo's budget scene and a good place to meet fellow travellers, with friendly English-speaking staff and a kitchen area – be sure to book well ahead. It's a bit tricky to find, in the backstreets of west Ikebukuro, and note that there's a 1am curfew. Ikebukuro Station. ❷

Metropolitan 1-6-1 Nishi-Ikebukuro, Toshima-ku ⓣ03/3980-1111, ⓦwww.metropolitan.jp. Ikebukuro's plushest hotel offers all the facilities you'd expect, including several restaurants and limousine bus connections to Narita Airport. The rooms are comfortable and well priced. Ikebukuro Station. ❼

North of the Imperial Palace

The following hotels are marked on the map on pp.88–89.

Hōmeikan Daimachi Bekkan 鳳明館台町別館 5-12-9 Hongō, Bunkyō-ku ⓣ03/3811-1187, ⓦwww.homeikan.com. Of the three ryokan under the Hōmeikan name, it's the Daimachi Bekkan that's the real looker, with its ancient carpentry and traditional design. There are no en-suite bathrooms, but all rooms have tatami mats and some look out on an exquisite little Japanese garden. Hongō San-chōme or Kasuga stations. ❹

Tokyo International Youth Hostel 18F, Central Plaza, 1-1 Kaguragashi, Shinjuku-ku ⓣ03/3235-1107, ⓦwww.tokyo-ih.jp. Bunk down (for ¥3860 per night) at this smart hostel located high above Iidabashi Station – it's one of the rare hostels that offers terrific views of the city. Reception is open 3–10pm and there's an 11pm curfew. Exit B2b from the subway brings you straight up into the lift lobby. Iidabashi Station.

Shibuya and Aoyama

Cerulean Tower Tōkyū Hotel 26-1 Sakuragaoka-chō, Shibuya-ku ⓣ03/3476-3000, ⓦwww.ceruleantower-hotel.com; see map, pp.132–133. Shibuya's ritziest digs; some rooms have bathrooms with a glittering view of the city, and there's a pool and gym (free to guests on the executive floor, otherwise ¥2000), several restaurants, a jazz club and even a nō theatre in the basement. Shibuya Station. ❾

Floracion 4-17-58 Minami-Aoyama, Minato-ku ⓣ03/3403-1541, ⓦwww.floracion-aoyama.com; see map, p.129. In a quiet residential area, but handy for Omotesandō, with small, acceptable Western-style rooms. Their Japanese-style ones offer more space and better value. Omotesandō Station. ❼

Fukudaya 福田屋 4-5-9 Aobadai, Meguro-ku ⓣ03/3467-5833, ⓦwww.fukudaya.com; see map, pp.132–133. Ageing-with-grace ryokan that's handy for trendy Aobadai and Naka-Meguro. Western-style rooms are available, too, all with attached toilet but the baths are shared. The manager is friendly and speaks English. Shinsen Station, or take bus in direction of Ikejiri Ōhashi from Shibuya Station. ❺

Granbell Hotel, Shibuya 15-17 Sakuragaoka-cho, Shibuya-ku ⓣ03/5457-2681, ⓦwww.granbellhotel.jp; see map, pp.132–133. Curtains with Ray Lichtenstein-style prints, kettles and TVs from the trendy Japanese electronics range Plus Minus Zero, and a cool palette of greys and crisp whites give this new boutique hotel a hip atmosphere. A newer set of rooms offers nature-themed decoration. There's an equally groovy Granbell in Akasaka (ⓣ03/5575-7130, ⓦwww.granbellhotel.jp/akasaka). Shibuya Station. ❼

Tōkyū Stay Aoyama 2-27-18 Minami-Aoyama, Shibuya-ku ⓣ03/3497-0109 ⓦwww.tokyustay.co.jp; see map, p.129. Designed for long-staying guests, but also open to short-stay visitors, this high-rise hotel and apartment complex scores for facilities, location and slick decor. There's a women-only floor, wonderful views, and rates include breakfast. ❼

Shinjuku

The following hotels are marked on the map on pp.124–125.

Kadoya Hotel 1-23-1 Nishi-Shinjuku, Shinjuku-ku ⓣ03/3346-2561, ⓦwww.kadoya-hotel.co.jp. This efficient business hotel is a little charmer, and the single rooms are a bargain for such a handy location. A major plus is the lively *Izekaya Hatago* in the basement. Shinjuku Station. ❺

Park Hyatt Tokyo 3-7-1-2 Nishi-Shinjuku, Shinjuku-ku ⓣ03/5322-1234, ⓦwww.parkhyatttokyo.com. The pick of Nishi-Shinjuku's luxury hotels, this is the epitome of sophistication and holds up very well to newer rivals elsewhere in the city. All rooms, plus the restaurants and spa, pool and fitness centre, occupying the pinnacles of Tange Kenzō's tower, have breathtaking views. Tochōmae Station. 9

Shinjuku Astina Hotel Tokyo 1-2-9 Kabukichō, Shinjuku-ku ⓣ03/3200-0220, ⓦwww.bw-shinjuku.com. This appealing new hotel is proof that Kabukichō is on the up. The executive-floor rooms are particularly plush with more space and a soothing cream, wood and pale grey colour scheme. Rates include breakfast. Shinjuku Station. 7

Tokyo Yoyogi Youth Hostel 3-1 Kamizonochō, Shibuya-ku ⓣ03/3467-9163, ⓦwww.jyh.or.jp/english/kanto/yoyogi/index.html. Part of the Olympic Youth Centre and located on the ground floor of the curved building at the top of the hill and towards the rear of the complex, this hostel offers small but comfortable, modern single rooms only (¥3000), with shared bathrooms. Guests must be out between 9am and 4pm, and although there's a 10pm curfew the doors are not closed so you can return later if you choose. Sangūbashi Station.

Ueno and around

The following hotels are marked on the map on p.118.

Ryokan Katsutarō 旅館勝太郎 4-16-8 Ikenohata, Taitō-ku ⓣ03/3821-9808, ⓦwww.katsutaro.com. Handily located within walking distance of Ueno Park, this homely place has just seven slightly faded tatami rooms, plus coin laundry and internet access. They also run a newer annexe in Yanaka. A good alternative if *Sawanoya* (see below) is full. Nezu Station. 3

Sawanoya Ryokan 2-3-11 Yanaka, Taitō-ku ⓣ03/3822-2251, ⓦwww.sawanoya.com. This welcoming family-run inn is a real home from home. Though nothing fancy, it offers good-value tatami rooms; only two are en suite, but the two great Japanese-style baths more than compensate. Facilities also include free internet access, bike hire (¥200 per day), coin laundry and complimentary tea and coffee. Nezu Station. 3

Suigetsu Hotel Ohgaisō 水月ホテル鴎外荘 3-3-21 Ikenohata, Taitō-ku ⓣ03/3822-4611, ⓦwww.ohgai.co.jp. One of very few mid-range hotels with a Japanese flavour, this is built around the Meiji-period house and traditional garden of novelist Mori Ōgai. The three wings contain a mix of Western-style and tatami rooms (the latter are more expensive but pack more atmosphere). Rates can be with or without meals. Nezu Station. 5–7

Central Tokyo

A vast chunk of **central Tokyo** is occupied by the **Imperial Palace** or *Kōkyo* (皇居), home to the emperor and his family, and the city's geographical and spiritual heart. The surrounding public gardens provide a gentle introduction to the city, with a glance back to its origins as a castle town.

East of the palace, the city really gets into its stride. The districts of **Marunouchi**, **Ginza** and **Nihombashi** form the heart of downtown Tokyo, with the city's most chic shopping street, its financial centre and major train station, plus enough bars and restaurants to last a lifetime. The best approach is simply to wander, but there are several specific sights, notably a clutch of **art museums** and the **Tokyo International Forum**, with its soaring glass atrium.

Northeast of the palace is lively **Akihabara**, crammed with cut-price electronic goodies and multistorey manga stores, while to southwest are **Akasaka** and **Roppongi**. In the former you'll find **Hie-jinja**, one of Tokyo's most historic shrines, while in the latter an "Art Triangle" has been formed by the **National Art Center Tokyo**, the **Suntory Museum of Art** in the huge **Tokyo Midtown** complex and the **Mori Art Museum** in the equally enormous **Roppongi Hills** development. **Tokyo Tower** remains the area's retro landmark and nearby is the venerable temple **Zōjō-ji**.

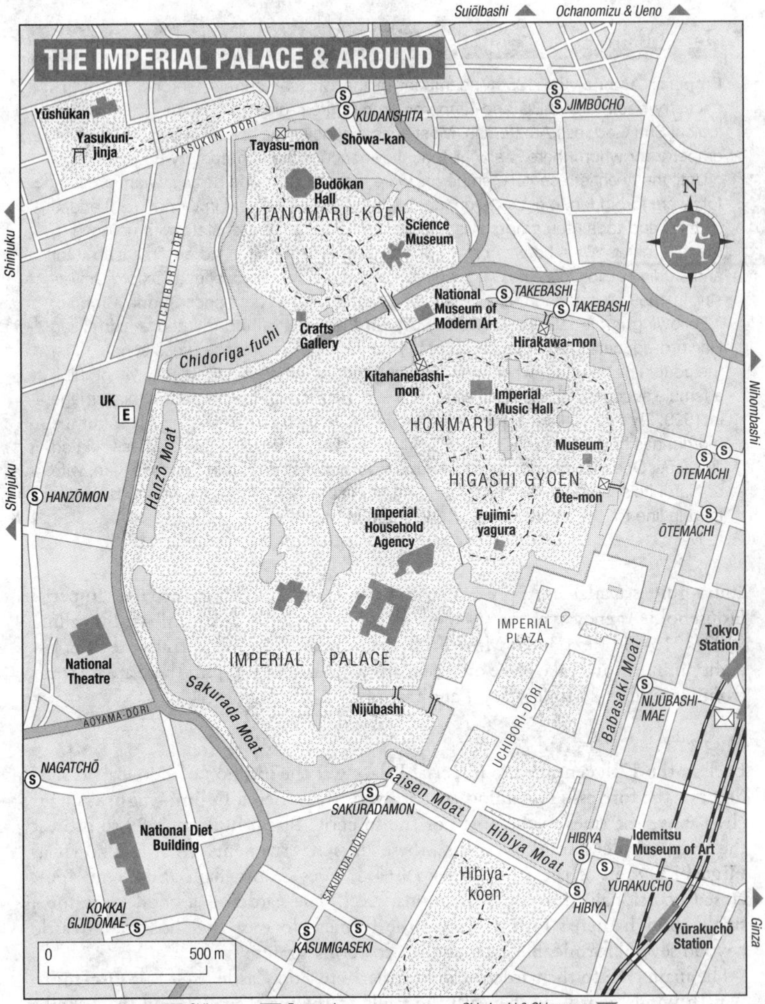

THE IMPERIAL PALACE & AROUND

The Imperial Palace and around

Huge and windswept, the **Imperial Plaza** forms a protective island in front of the modern Royal Palace. Follow the groups of local tourists straggling across the broad avenues to view one of the palace's most photogenic corners, **Nijūbashi**, where two bridges span the moat and a jaunty little watchtower perches on its grey stone pedestal beyond. Though this double bridge is a late nineteenth-century embellishment, the tower dates back to the seventeenth century and is one of the castle's few original structures.

Twice a year (on Dec 23, the emperor's birthday, and on Jan 2) thousands of well-wishers file across Nijūbashi to greet the royal family. Apart from these two days, the general public is only admitted to the palace grounds on pre-arranged **official tours**, conducted in Japanese but with English-language brochures and

Descendants of the Sun Goddess

Emperor Akihito, the 125th incumbent of the Chrysanthemum Throne, traces his ancestry back to 660 BC and Emperor Jimmu, great-great-grandson of the mythological Sun Goddess Amaterasu. Most scholars, however, acknowledge that the first emperor for whom there is any historical evidence is the fifth-century Emperor Ojin.

Until the twentieth century, emperors were regarded as living deities whom ordinary folk were forbidden to set eyes on, or even hear. Japan's defeat in World War II ended all that, and today the emperor is a symbolic figure, a head of state with no governmental power. While he was crown prince, **Emperor Akihito** had an American tutor and studied at Tokyo's elite Gakushūin University, followed by a stint at Oxford University. In 1959 he broke further with tradition by marrying a commoner, **Shōda Michiko**.

Following in his father's footsteps, **Crown Prince Naruhito** married a high-flying Harvard-educated diplomat Owada Masako in 1993. The intense press scrutiny that the couple came under when they failed to produce a male heir (current laws prohibit a female succession) has been sited as one of reasons for the princess's miscarriage in 1999. Two years later the crown princess gave birth to a baby girl, **Aiko**, but the mother has barely been seen in public since, suffering from a variety of stress-related illnesses. One piece of good news for the royal succession is that Princess Kiko, wife of Naruhito's younger brother, gave birth to Hisahito in 2006 – the young prince is third in line for the throne after his uncle and father.

audio-guides available. Apply online up to two months in advance via the Imperial Household Agency website (Ⓦwww.kunaicho.go.jp/eindex.html) or by calling Ⓣ03/3213-1111 ext 3485 (Mon–Fri 8.45am–noon & 1–5pm). Tours are free, last eighty minutes and take place on weekdays at 10am and 1.30pm; there are no tours from December 28 to January 4 and from July 21 to August 31.

Higashi Gyoen

Back in the 17th century the Imperial Palace was the location of Edo Castle. The finest of the fortress's remaining watchtowers, three-tiered **Fujimi-yagura**, stands clear above the trees to the north of the Imperial Plaza. Built in 1659 to protect the main citadel's southern flank, these days it ornaments what is known as **Higashi Gyoen** or the East Garden (東御苑; Tues–Thurs, Sat & Sun 9am–4pm; closed occasionally for court functions; free). The garden is a good place for a stroll, though there's little to evoke the former glory of the shogunate's castle beyond several formidable gates and the towering granite walls.

The main gate to the garden – and formerly to Edo Castle itself – is **Ōte-mon**. A path winds gently up, beneath the walls of the main citadel, and then climbs more steeply towards **Shiomizaka**, the "Tide-Viewing Slope", from where it was once possible to gaze out over Edo Bay. You emerge on a flat grassy area, empty apart from the stone foundations of **Honmaru** (the "inner citadel"), with fine views from the top, and a scattering of modern edifices, among them the pretty, mosaic-clad **Imperial Music Hall**.

Kitanomaru-kōen

The northern citadel of Edo Castle is now occupied by **Kitanomaru-kōen** (北の丸公園), another park with a couple of interesting museums. Immediately to the right as you emerge from the Higashi Gyoen through the Kitahanebashi-mon gate, is the **National Museum of Modern Art** or *Kokuritsu Kindai Bijutsukan* (国立近代美術館; Tues–Sun 10am–5pm, Fri until 8pm; ¥420, or ¥800 including the Crafts Gallery; Ⓣ03/5777-8600). Its excellent collection showcases Japanese art since 1900, including Kawai Gyokudo's magnificent screen painting *Parting*

Spring and works by Kishida Ryusei, Fujita Tsuguharu and postwar artists such as Yoshihara Jiro.

A short walk away on the west side of Kitanomaru-kōen, the **Crafts Gallery** or *Kōgeikan* (工芸館; Tues–Sun 10am–5pm, Fri until 8pm; ¥420; ⓣ03/5777-8600) exhibits a selection of top-quality traditional Japanese crafts, many by modern masters. Erected in 1910 as the headquarters of the Imperial Guards, this neo-Gothic red-brick pile is one of very few Tokyo buildings dating from before the Great Earthquake of 1923.

At the north end of the park is the **Budōkan hall**, built in 1964 to host Olympic judo events. The design, with its graceful, curving roof and gold topknot, pays homage to a famous octagonal hall in Nara's Hōryū-ji temple, though the shape is also supposedly inspired by that of Mount Fuji. Today the huge arena is used for sports meetings, graduation ceremonies and rock concerts.

Yasukuni-jinja

Across the road from Kitanomaru-kōen, a monumental *torii*, claimed to be Japan's tallest, marks the entrance to **Yasukuni-jinja** (靖国神社; ⓦwww.yasukuni.or.jp). This shrine, whose name means "for the repose of the country", was founded in 1869 to worship supporters of the emperor killed in the run-up to the Meiji Restoration. Since then it has expanded to include the legions sacrificed in subsequent wars, in total nearly 2.5 million souls, of whom some two million died in the Pacific War alone; the parting words of kamikaze pilots were "see you at Yasukuni".

Not surprisingly, all sorts of controversy revolve around Yasukuni-jinja. Its foundation was part of a Shinto revival promoting the new emperor (see p.771) and so it became a natural focus for the increasingly aggressive nationalism that ultimately took Japan to war in 1941. Then, in 1978, General Tōjō and a number of other Class A war criminals were enshrined here, to be honoured along with all the other military dead. Subsequent visits made to Yasukuni by politicians on the anniversary of Japan's defeat in World War II (August 15) continue to cause protests both at home and abroad.

For many ordinary Japanese, however, Yasukuni is simply a place to remember family and friends who died in the last, troubled century. Its surprisingly unassuming inner shrine stands at the end of a long avenue lined with cherry and ginkgo trees, and through a simple wooden gate. The architecture is classic Shinto styling, solid and unadorned except for two gold imperial chrysanthemums embossed on the main doors.

To the right of the inner shrine you'll find the fascinating **Yūshūkan** (daily 9am–5pm; ¥800; ⓣ03/3261-8326), a military museum established in 1882. The displays are well presented, with plentiful information in English, but the controversy is as much what is left out as what is included. Events such as the Nanking Massacre ("Incident" in Japanese) and other atrocities by Japanese troops are glossed over, while the Pacific War is presented as a war of liberation, freeing the peoples of Southeast Asia from Western colonialism. The most moving displays are the ranks of faded photographs and the "bride dolls" donated by the families of young soldiers who died before they were married. You exit through a hall full of military hardware, including a replica of the gliders used by kamikaze pilots on their suicide missions, its nose elongated to carry a 1200kg bomb, while a spine-chilling, black *kaiten* (manned torpedo) lours to one side.

Hibiya

South of the palace grounds is pleasant **Hibiya-kōen** (日比谷公園), Tokyo's first European-style park, constructed in 1903, while up the road is the **Imperial**

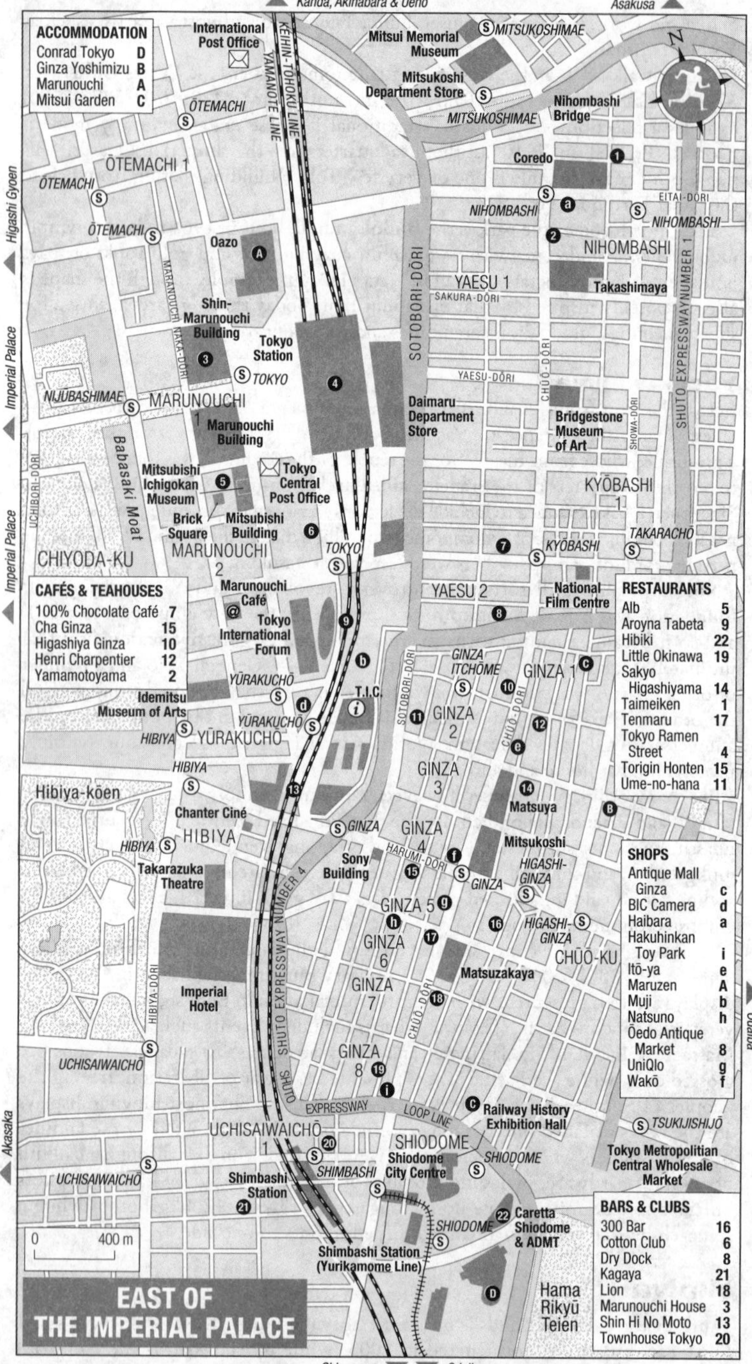
EAST OF THE IMPERIAL PALACE
ACCOMMODATION
Conrad Tokyo D
Ginza Yoshimizu B
Marunouchi A
Mitsui Garden C
CAFÉS & TEAHOUSES
100% Chocolate Café 7
Cha Ginza 15
Higashiya Ginza 10
Henri Charpentier 12
Yamamotoyama 2
RESTAURANTS
Alb 5
Aroyna Tabeta 9
Hibiki 22
Little Okinawa 19
Sakyo Higashiyama 14
Taimeiken 1
Tenmaru 17
Tokyo Ramen Street 4
Torigin Honten 15
Ume-no-hana 11
SHOPS
Antique Mall Ginza c
BIC Camera d
Haibara a
Hakuhinkan Toy Park i
Itō-ya e
Maruzen A
Muji b
Natsuno h
Ōedo Antique Market 8
UniQlo g
Wakō f
BARS & CLUBS
300 Bar 16
Cotton Club 6
Dry Dock 8
Kagaya 21
Lion 18
Marunouchi House 3
Shin Hi No Moto 13
Townhouse Tokyo 20
Kanda, Akihabara & Ueno
Asakusa
Higashi Gyoen
Imperial Palace
Imperial Palace
Akasaka
Odaiba
Shinagawa
Odaiba
0 400 m
International Post Office
Mitsui Memorial Museum
Mitsukoshi Department Store
MITSUKOSHIMAE
Nihombashi Bridge
Coredo
ŌTEMACHI 1
ŌTEMACHI
NIHOMBASHI
EITAI-DŌRI
Oazo
YAESU 1
SAKURA-DŌRI
Takashimaya
Shin-Marunouchi Building
Tokyo Station
TOKYO
SOTOBORI-DŌRI
YAESU-DŌRI
CHŪŌ-DŌRI
SHUTO EXPRESSWAY NUMBER 1
NIJŪBASHIMAE
MARUNOUCHI 1
Marunouchi Building
Daimaru Department Store
Bridgestone Museum of Art
SHOWA-DŌRI
Babasaki Moat
UCHIBORI-DŌRI
Mitsubishi Ichigokan Museum
Tokyo Central Post Office
KYŌBASHI 1
Brick Square
Mitsubishi Building
TAKARACHŌ
KYŌBASHI
CHIYODA-KU
MARUNOUCHI 2
Marunouchi Café
YAESU 2
National Film Centre
Tokyo International Forum
YŪRAKUCHŌ
T.I.C.
GINZA ITCHŌME
GINZA 1
Idemitsu Museum of Arts
HIBIYA
GINZA 2
GINZA 3
Hibiya-kōen
Chanter Ciné
Matsuya
GINZA
GINZA 4
Mitsukoshi
HIBIYA
Sony Building
HARUMI-DŌRI
HIGASHI-GINZA
Takarazuka Theatre
GINZA 5
SHUTO EXPRESSWAY NUMBER 4
GINZA 6
Matsuzakaya
CHŪŌ-KU
HIBIYA-DŌRI
Imperial Hotel
GINZA 7
GINZA 8
UCHISAIWAICHŌ
SHUTO EXPRESSWAY LOOP LINE
Railway History Exhibition Hall
TSUKIJISHIJŌ
UCHISAIWAICHŌ 1
SHIODOME
Shiodome City Centre
Tokyo Metropolitan Central Wholesale Market
SHIMBASHI
Shimbashi Station
Caretta Shiodome & ADMT
Shimbashi Station (Yurikamome Line)
Hama Rikyū Teien
KEIHIN-TŌHOKU LINE
YAMANOTE LINE
MARUNOUCHI NAKA-DŌRI

Hotel, which first opened in 1890. The original building was subsequently replaced by an Art Deco, Aztec-palace creation by American architect Frank Lloyd Wright, a stunning building which famously withstood both the Great Kantō Earthquake (which struck the city on Sept 1, 1923, the day after the hotel's formal opening) and World War II. Wright's building was replaced by the current looming tower in the late 1960s. Today, just a hint of Wright's style exists in the *Old Imperial Bar*, incorporating some of the original brickwork; Wright's original facade and main lobby have been reconstructed in Meiji Mura (see p.395).

Yūrakuchō and Marunouchi

East of the Imperial Palace and west of Ginza is **YŪRAKUCHŌ** (有楽町), home to the **Tokyo International Forum** (東京国際フォーラム), a stunning creation by American architect Rafael Viñoly, which hosts concerts and conventions, plus the Ōedo Antique Market (see p.164). The boat-shaped main hall consists of a 60m-high atrium sheathed in 2600 sheets of earthquake-resistant glass, with a ceiling ribbed like a ship's hull.

Immediately north and west of the International Forum, the business-focused **MARUNOUCHI** (丸の内) district has lately been transformed from a dull stretch of offices to a dynamic, tourist friendly location. A major programme of construction and development – including the restoration of Tokyo Station's original handsome red-brick structure, scheduled to be completed in 2013 – has added swish shopping plazas, restaurants and cafés to the area. A recent addition is the **Mitsubishi Ichigokan Museum** (Wed–Fri 10am–8pm, Tues, Sat & Sun 10am–6pm; price depends on the exhibition; ⓣ03/5777-8600), focusing on nineteenth-century European art, and housed in a meticulous reconstruction of British architect Josiah Conder's original red-brick office block, erected on the same site in 1894, only to be demolished in 1968. The museum forms part of **Marunouchi Brick Square**, where shops and restaurants overlook a lovely landscaped garden.

Two blocks south of here, above the **Imperial Theatre**, the **Idemitsu Museum of Arts** (出光美術館; Tues–Thurs, Sat & Sun 10am–5pm, Fri 10am–7pm; ¥1000; ⓣ03/5777-8600) houses a magnificent collection of mostly Japanese art, though only a tiny proportion is on show at any one time.

Ginza

GINZA (銀座), the "place where silver is minted", took its name after Shogun Tokugawa Ieyasu started making coins here in the early 1600s. It was a happy association – Ginza's Chūō-dōri grew to become Tokyo's most stylish shopping street. Though some of its shine has faded and cutting-edge fashion has moved elsewhere, Ginza still retains much of its elegance and its undoubted snob appeal. Here you'll find the greatest concentration of exclusive shops, art galleries and restaurants in the city, as well as branches of most major department stores.

The unusually regular pattern of streets here is due to British architect Thomas Waters, who was given the task of creating a less combustible city after a fire in 1872 destroyed virtually all of old, wooden Ginza. His **"Bricktown"**, as it soon became known, proved an instant local tourist attraction, with its rows of two-storey brick houses, tree-lined avenues, gaslights and brick pavements. Most of the first businesses here dealt in foreign goods, and in no time Ginza had become the centre of all that was modern, Western and, therefore, fashionable. In the 1930s the height of sophistication was simply to stroll around Ginza, and the practice still continues, particularly on Sunday afternoons, when Chūō-dōri becomes a pedestrian promenade.

Tokyo's art beat

There are hundreds of small **commercial galleries** in Tokyo – stepping into them you may just discover the next Murakami Takeshi or Yayoi Kusama. **Ginza** has long been the bastion of the gallery scene, though the majority are pretty conservative in what they show. Good picks here include **Ginza Graphic Gallery** (7-7-2 Ginza, Chūō-ku; ⓣ03/3571-5206, ⓦwww.dnp.co.jp/gallery/ggg), **Shiseidō Gallery** (B1F 8-8-3 Ginza, Chūō-ku; ⓣ03/3572-3901, ⓦwww.shiseido.co.jp/gallery) and **Tokyo Gallery + BTAP** (7F 8-10-5 Ginza, Chūō-ku; ⓣ03/3571-1808, ⓦwww.tokyo-gallery.com).

There's an interesting trend for old office buildings and warehouses in less trafficked areas to be used as display spaces. Across the Sumida-gawa near Kiyosu-bashi, seven diverse galleries have gathered in the **Kiyosumi Gallery Complex** (1-3-2 Kiyosumi, Kōtō-ku; Kiyosumi-Shirakawa Station), while there are three in the **Shirokane Art Complex** (3-1-15 Shirokane Minato-ku; Shirokane-Takanawa Station) east of Hiro-o. More central is the **Agata-Takezawa Building** (1-2-11 Higashi-Kanda, Chiyoda-ku; Bakurochō Station), the hub of an up-and-coming arty neighbourbhood. Anchored by the respected Taro Nasu Gallery (ⓦwww.taronasugallery.com), you'll find here other exhibition spaces and an interesting bunch of arts, crafts and fashion tenants.

April's **Art Fair Tokyo** (ⓦwww.artfairtokyo.com) brings together around one hundred galleries with a strong focus on contemporary work. Exhibitions listings and interesting features on the Tokyo art scene can be found at **Tokyo Art Beat** (ⓦwww.tokyoartbeat.com).

Approaching from the west, Ginza begins at the Sukiyabashi crossing, where Sotobori-dōri and Harumi-dōri intersect. The **Sony Building** (daily 11am–7pm; free; ⓣ03/3573-2563), occupying the crossing's southeast corner, is primarily of interest for techno-freaks, with four of its eleven storeys showcasing the latest Sony gadgets. Continuing east along Harumi-dōri, you'll reach the intersection with Chūō-dōri known as **Ginza Yon-chōme crossing**, which marks the heart of Ginza. A number of venerable emporia cluster round the junction. **Wakō**, now an exclusive department store, started life over a century ago as the stall of a young, enterprising watchmaker who developed a line called Seikō (meaning "precision"); its clock tower, built in 1894, is one of Ginza's most enduring landmarks.

Nihombashi

North of Ginza, **NIHOMBASHI** (日本橋) was once the heart of Edo's teeming Shitamachi (see p.87), growing from a cluster of riverside markets in the early seventeenth century to become the city's chief financial district. The earlier warehouses and moneylenders have evolved into the banks, brokers and trading companies that line the streets today.

Since 1603, the centre of Nihombashi, and effectively of all Japan, was an arched red-lacquer-coated **bridge** that marked the start of the Tōkaidō, the great road running between Edo and Kyoto. Distances from Tokyo are still measured from a bronze marker at the halfway point of the present stone bridge, erected in 1911. Even though the Shuto Expressway passes right over it, it's still worth swinging by here to see the bronze dragons and wrought-iron lamps that decorate the bridge.

A little further north on Chūō-dōri, past the main branch of **Mitsukoshi department store** (see p.161), is the **Mitsui Memorial Museum** (三井記念美術館; Tues–Sun 10am–5pm; ¥1000; ⓣ03/5777-8600), where a superb collection spanning three hundred years of Japanese and Asian art is on display alongside a replica of the Jo'an teahouse, held to be one of the finest examples of teahouse architecture.

Crossing back over Nihombashi and heading south along Chūō-dōri, a row of cheerful red awnings on the left-hand side side announces another of Tokyo's grand old stores, **Takashimaya** (see p.161). Further south, at the junction of Chūō-dōri and Yaesu-dōri, is the **Bridgestone Museum of Art** (ブリヂストン美術館; Tues–Sat 10am–8pm, Sun 10am–6pm; ¥800; ⓣ03/5777-8600). This superb collection focuses on the Impressionists and continues through all the great names of early twentieth-century European art, plus a highly rated sampler of Meiji-era Japanese paintings in Western style. It's not an extensive display, but offers a chance to enjoy works by artists such as Renoir, Picasso and Van Gogh in what is often an almost deserted gallery.

Kanda

Northwest of Nihombashi is **KANDA** (神田), where two great shrines lie on the north bank of the Kanda-gawa River and are within easy reach of both the JR and Marunouchi subway line stations at Ochanomizu. Half hidden among woods is **Yushima Seidō** (湯島聖堂; daily: May–Oct 9.30am–5pm; Nov–April 9.30am–4pm; free), dedicated to the Chinese sage Confucius. The Seidō ("Sacred Hall") was founded in 1632 as an academy for the study of the ancient classics at a time when the Tokugawa were promoting Confucianism as the State's ethical foundation. Today, the quiet compound contains an eighteenth-century wooden gate and, at the top of broad steps, the imposing, black-lacquered Taisen-den, or "Hall of Accomplishments", where the shrine to Confucius is located; look up to see panther-like guardians poised on the roof tiles.

Follow the road round to the north of Yushima Seidō to find the entrance to **Kanda Myōjin** (9am–4.30pm; free), one of the city's oldest shrines and host to one of its top three festivals, the **Kanda Matsuri** (see p.158). Founded in 730 AD, the shrine originally stood in front of Edo Castle, where it was dedicated to the gods of farming and fishing (Daikoku and Ebisu). Later, the tenth-century rebel Taira no Masakado – who was beheaded after declaring himself emperor – was also enshrined here. When Shogun Tokugawa Ieyasu was strengthening the castle's fortifications in 1616, he took the opportunity to move the shrine, but mollified Masakado's supporters by declaring him a guardian deity of the city.

Akihabara

Some 500m southeast of Kanda Myōjin, a blaze of adverts and a cacophony of competing audio systems announce **Akihabara** (秋葉原). Akiba, as it's popularly known, is Tokyo's foremost discount shopping area for electrical and electronic goods of all kinds, hence it's also known as the city's "Electric Town". These days it's also "the" destination for anime and manga fans (see *Manga & anime* colour section) and the spawning ground for the decidedly surreal "maids' cafés".

Inside the **Akihabara Crossfield** complex is the **Tokyo Anime Center** (daily 11am–7pm; free; ⓣ03/5298-1188), which has small displays on recent anime but is really little more than a glorified shop selling anime-related goods.

Today's electronic stores are direct descendants of a postwar black market in radios and radio parts that took place beneath the train tracks around Akihabara Station. You can recapture some of the atmosphere in the narrow passages under the tracks just west of the station in the tiny stalls of **Tōkyō Radio Depāto** (東京ラジオデパート) – four floors stuffed with plugs, wires, boards and tools for making or repairing audio-visual equipment.

Contemporary art is also starting to find its way into Akiba. On a side street off Chūō-dōri, you'll find the landscaped entrance to a new art complex, **3331 Arts Chiyoda** (check website for opening hours; mostly free; ⓣ03/6803-2441,

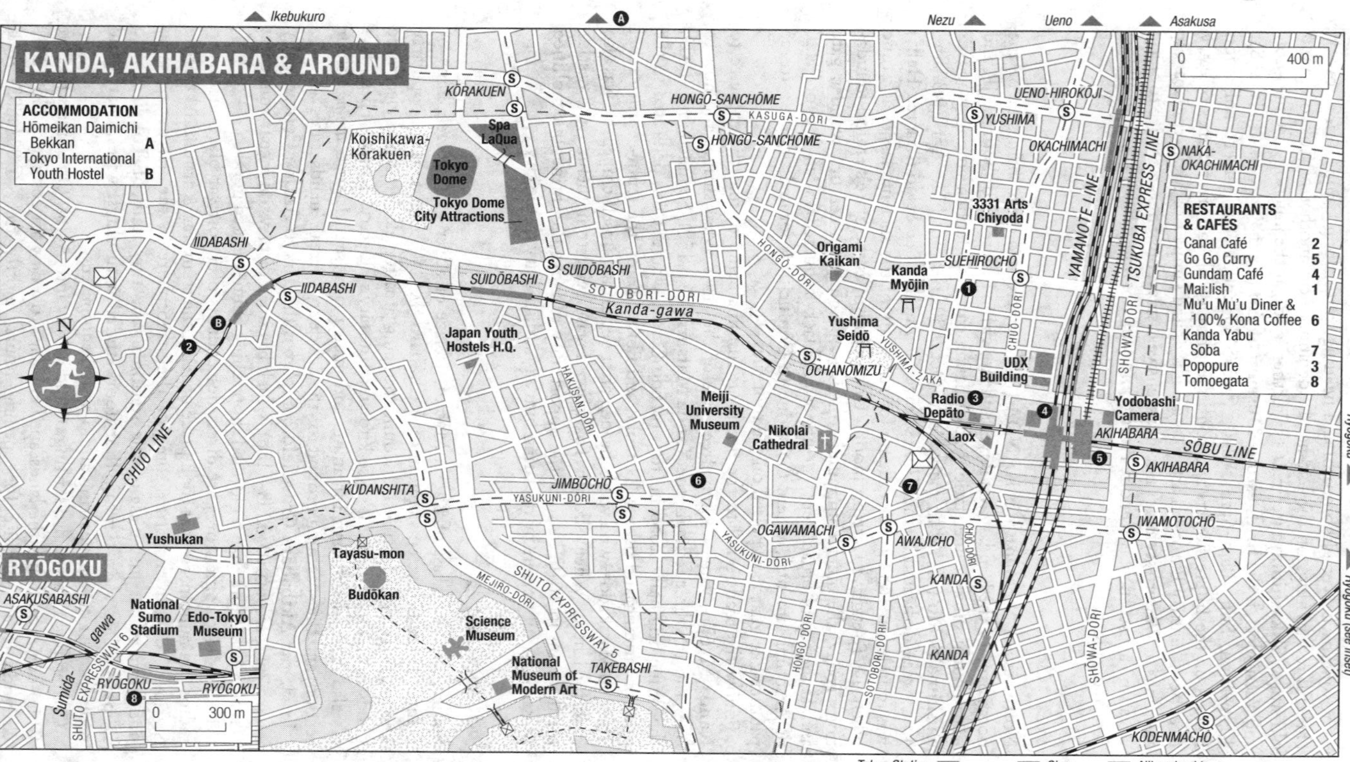

KANDA, AKIHABARA & AROUND
ACCOMMODATION
Hōmeikan Daimichi Bekkan A
Tokyo International Youth Hostel B
RESTAURANTS & CAFÉS
Canal Café 2
Go Go Curry 5
Gundam Café 4
Mai:lish 1
Mu'u Mu'u Diner & 100% Kona Coffee 6
Kanda Yabu Soba 7
Popopure 3
Tomoegata 8
0 400 m
Ikebukuro
Nezu
Ueno
Asakusa
Shinjuku
Ryōgoku
Ryōgoku (see inset)
Tokyo Station
Ginza
Nihombashi
KŌRAKUEN
HONGŌ-SANCHŌME
KASUGA-DŌRI
UENO-HIROKŌJI
YUSHIMA
OKACHIMACHI
NAKA-OKACHIMACHI
YAMANOTE LINE
TSUKUBA EXPRESS LINE
Spa LaQua
Koishikawa-Kōrakuen
Tokyo Dome
Tokyo Dome City Attractions
3331 Arts Chiyoda
IIDABASHI
SUIDŌBASHI
SOTOBORI-DŌRI
Kanda-gawa
HONGŌ-DŌRI
Origami Kaikan
Kanda Myōjin
SUEHIROCHŌ
CHŪŌ-DŌRI
SHŌWA-DŌRI
Japan Youth Hostels H.Q.
Yushima Seidō
YUSHIMA-ZAKA
OCHANOMIZU
UDX Building
Radio Depāto
Yodobashi Camera
AKIHABARA
SŌBU LINE
Laox
Meiji University Museum
Nikolai Cathedral
CHŪŌ LINE
HAKUSAN-DŌRI
KUDANSHITA
JIMBŌCHŌ
YASUKUNI-DŌRI
OGAWAMACHI
AWAJICHO
IWAMOTOCHŌ
KANDA
Yushukan
Tayasu-mon
Budōkan
MEJIRO-DŌRI
SHUTO EXPRESSWAY 5
Science Museum
National Museum of Modern Art
TAKEBASHI
KODENMACHŌ
RYŌGOKU
ASAKUSABASHI
National Sumo Stadium
Edo-Tokyo Museum
Sumida-gawa
SHUTO EXPRESSWAY 6
0 300 m

Ⓦwww.3331.jp). Based inside a renovated junior high school, the centre hosts close to twenty galleries, with a revolving mix of exhibitions, interactive installations, and workshops.

Suidōbashi

From Akihabara you can take the Sōbu line west to **SUIDŌBASHI** (水道橋), where the stadium, shopping centres and amusement-park thrill rides of **Tokyo Dome City** (Ⓦwww.tokyo-dome.co.jp) punctuate the skyline. The centrepiece is the plump, white-roofed **Tokyo Dome** (東京ドーム), popularly known as the "Big Egg", Tokyo's major baseball venue and home ground of the Yomiuri Giants (see p.167).

Immediately to the west of Tokyo Dome is **Koishikawa-Kōrakuen** (小石川後楽園; daily 9am–5pm; ¥300), a fine example of an early seventeenth-century **stroll-garden**. Zhu Shun Shui, a refugee scholar from Ming China, advised on the design, so Chinese as well as Japanese landscapes feature, the most obvious being the Full-Moon Bridge, echoing ancient stone bridges of western China, and Seiko Lake, modelled on Hangzhou's West Lake. The main entrance gate lies in the garden's southwest corner, midway between Suidōbashi and Iidabashi stations.

Tokyo's public baths and onsen

Until just a few decades ago, when people began installing bathrooms at home, life in Tokyo's residential neighbourhoods focused round the *sentō*, the public bath. Though you no longer find them every few blocks, a surprising number of bathhouses survive; we've listed a couple below.

The *sentō* are overshadowed by two enormous **onsen** (hot spring) complexes: Spa LaQua in Suidōbashi and Ōedo Onsen Monogatari in Odaiba. Both are much more expensive than a traditional *sentō*, and offer extensive bathing facilities, a range of places to eat and relaxation areas with very comfortable reclining chairs. For tips on bathing etiquette, see p.66.

Asakusa Kannon Onsen 浅草観音温泉 2-7-26 Asakusa, Taitō-ku ⓣ03/3844-4141; see map, p.114. This big, old, ivy-covered *sentō* right next to Sensō-ji uses real onsen water. The clientele ranges from *yakuza* to grannies – very Asakusa. Daily except Wed 6.30am–6pm; ¥700. Asakusa Station.

Jakotsu-yu 蛇骨湯 1-11-11 Asakusa, Taitō-ku ⓣ03/3841-8641, Ⓦwww.jakotsuyu.co.jp; see map, p.114. Traditional neighbourhood *sentō* down a back alley just south of Rox department store. It's fed with "black", mineral-rich hot-spring water and one bath is designed to give you a mild but stimulating electric shock. Daily except Tues 1pm–midnight; ¥450. Asakusa (Tsukuba Express line) or Tawaramachi stations.

Ōedo Onsen Monogatari 大江戸温泉物語 2-57 Omi, Koto-ku ⓣ03/5500-1126, Ⓦwww.ooedoonsen.jp; see map, pp.88–89. More of a theme park than a bathhouse, this giant Odaiba onsen has outdoor footbaths, though you'll have to pay extra for the one in which tiny fish nibble the dead skin from your feet, and for the hot-sand bath and the range of massages. In the large dining and relaxation area street performers keep the atmosphere jolly. There are free shuttle buses from Shinagawa and Tokyo stations. Mon–Fri ¥2000, or ¥1500 after 6pm, Sat & Sun ¥2200/1700. Telecom Centre Station (Yurikamome monorail).

Spa LaQua 6F, 1-1-1 Kasuga, Bunkyō-ku ⓣ03/5800-9999, Ⓦwww.laqua.jp; see map, p.108. A luxurious bathing complex using real onsen water. It's also a great place to pass the time if you miss the last train home. Daily 11am–9am; Mon–Fri ¥2565, Sat & Sun ¥2880; ¥1890 surcharge midnight–6am. Access to the Healing Baden set of special therapeutic saunas (11am–11pm) costs ¥525 extra. Suidōbashi Station.

Akasaka

Once an agricultural area where plants that produce a red dye were farmed (hence the locality's name, which means "red slope"), **AKASAKA** (赤坂) developed as a high-class entertainment district in the late nineteenth century for the modern breed of politicians and bureaucrats working in nearby Nagatachō. The area still has its fair share of exclusive establishments, and their presence, along with the TBS Broadcasting Centre and some of Tokyo's top hotels, lends Akasaka a certain cachet.

At the southern end of Akasaka's main thoroughfare, Sotobori-dōri, stands a huge stone *torii* gate, beyond which is a picturesque avenue of red *torii* leading up the hill to **Hie-jinja** (日枝神社), a Shinto shrine dedicated to the god Ōyamakui-no-kami, who is believed to protect against evil. Hie-jinja hosts one of Tokyo's most important festivals, the **Sannō Matsuri** (see p.158).

Heading north from the shrine along Sotobori-dōri and across Benkei-bashi, the bridge that spans what was once the outer moat of the shogun's castle, you'll soon reach the **New Ōtani** hotel. Within its grounds is a beautiful traditional Japanese **garden** (free), originally designed for the *daimyō* Katō Kiyomasa, lord of Kumamoto in Kyūshū, over four hundred years ago.

Roppongi

One of Tokyo's top nightlife destinations, **ROPPONGI** (六本木) has expanded its all-round charms with daytime attractions including major art galleries and the mammoth shopping, residential and office developments Roppongi Hills and Tokyo Midtown. In particular, Suntory Museum of Art, the National Arts Center, Tokyo, and Mori Art Museum form points on the so-called "Art Triangle Roppongi".

Tokyo Midtown

A block northwest of the main Roppongi crossing along Gaien-Higashi-dōri, **Tokyo Midtown** covers a site of nearly seventy thousand square metres, and includes the small picturesque park Hinokichō-koen, and the 248m **Midtown Tower**, home to the *Ritz Carlton* hotel. Strongly influenced by traditional Japanese architecture and art, Midtown's design is a lot more streamlined and subtle than its nearby rival Roppongi Hills.

On the west side of the complex is the traditional and highly stylish **Suntory Museum of Art** (サントリー美術館; Mon & Sun 10am–6pm, Wed–Sat 10am–8pm; entrance fee varies with exhibition; ⓣ03/3470-1073). The museum hosts changing exhibitions from its beautiful collection of ceramics, lacquerware, paintings and textiles. There's also a traditional tea ceremony room (Thurs 11.30am–5.30pm; ¥1000), with the actual ceremony performed at 1pm and 3pm.

Two giant triangular planes of steel, concrete and glass peeking out of a lawn to the rear of the main Midtown complex are part of the fascinating **21_21 Design Site** (daily 11am–8.30pm; ¥1000; ⓣ03/3475-2121), a collaboration between architect Andō Tadao and fashion designer Issey Miyake. More of a forum to discuss and display design in general than a museum, the main gallery is buried one floor into the ground to provide an elevated, airy space in which to view exhibitions on a single theme.

National Art Center, Tokyo

A couple of minutes' walk west of Tokyo Midtown is the visually stunning **National Art Center Tokyo** (NACT; 国立新美術館; daily except Tues 10am–6pm; entrance fee varies with exhibition; ⓣ03/6812-9900). A billowing wave of pale green glass ripples across the facade of the Kurokawa Kisha-designed building which, at 48,000 square metres, is Japan's largest gallery. The bulk of the

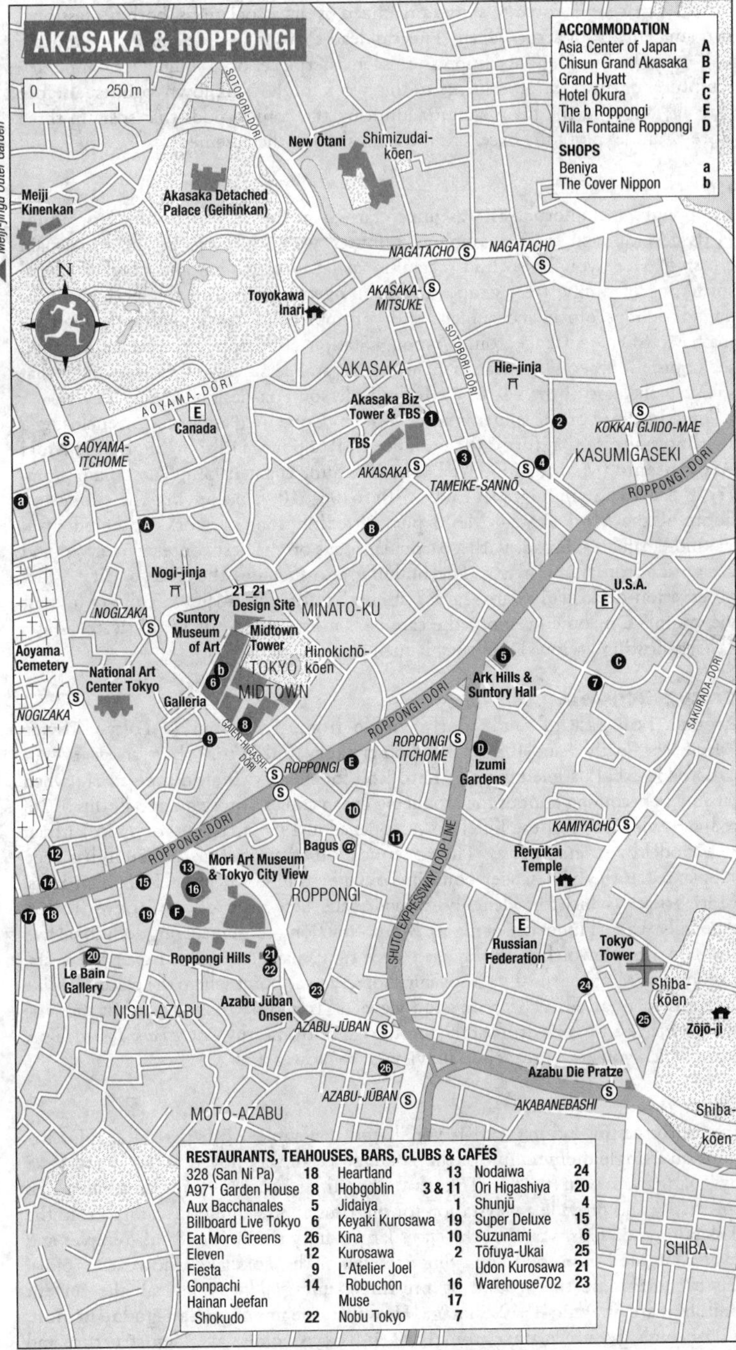
AKASAKA & ROPPONGI
0 250 m
ACCOMMODATION
Asia Center of Japan A
Chisun Grand Akasaka B
Grand Hyatt F
Hotel Ōkura C
The b Roppongi E
Villa Fontaine Roppongi D
SHOPS
Beniya a
The Cover Nippon b
Meiji-jingū Outer Garden
Meiji Kinenkan
Akasaka Detached Palace (Geihinkan)
SOTOBORI-DŌRI
New Ōtani
Shimizudai-kōen
NAGATACHO
NAGATACHO
Toyokawa Inari
AKASAKA-MITSUKE
AKASAKA
Hie-jinja
AOYAMA-DŌRI
Canada
Akasaka Biz Tower & TBS
TBS
AKASAKA
TAMEIKE-SANNŌ
KOKKAI GIJIDO-MAE
KASUMIGASEKI
AOYAMA-ITCHOME
ROPPONGI-DŌRI
Nogi-jinja
21_21 Design Site
MINATO-KU
U.S.A.
NOGIZAKA
Suntory Museum of Art
Midtown Tower
Hinokichō-kōen
TOKYO MIDTOWN
Aoyama Cemetery
National Art Center Tokyo
Galleria
NOGIZAKA
Ark Hills & Suntory Hall
SAKURADA-DŌRI
GAIEN-HIGASHI-DŌRI
ROPPONGI
ROPPONGI ITCHOME
Izumi Gardens
KAMIYACHŌ
Bagus @
Mori Art Museum & Tokyo City View
ROPPONGI
SHUTO EXPRESSWAY LOOP LINE
Reiyūkai Temple
Russian Federation
Tokyo Tower
Roppongi Hills
Le Bain Gallery
NISHI-AZABU
Azabu Jūban Onsen
AZABU-JŪBAN
Shiba-kōen
Zōjō-ji
Azabu Die Pratze
AKABANEBASHI
AZABU-JŪBAN
MOTO-AZABU
Shiba-kōen
SHIBA
RESTAURANTS, TEAHOUSES, BARS, CLUBS & CAFÉS
328 (San Ni Pa) 18
A971 Garden House 8
Aux Bacchanales 5
Billboard Live Tokyo 6
Eat More Greens 26
Eleven 12
Fiesta 9
Gonpachi 14
Hainan Jeefan Shokudo 22
Heartland 13
Hobgoblin 3 & 11
Jidaiya 1
Keyaki Kurosawa 19
Kina 10
Kurosawa 2
L'Atelier Joel Robuchon 16
Muse 17
Nobu Tokyo 7
Nodaiwa 24
Ori Higashiya 20
Shunjū 4
Super Deluxe 15
Suzunami 6
Tōfuya-Ukai 25
Udon Kurosawa 21
Warehouse702 23

NACT's space is devoted to shows organized by art associations, both professional and amateur, from across Japan. This can lead to a very eclectic mix: one minute you may be viewing an Impressionist masterpiece or a huge contemporary sculpture or installation, the next the work of an unknown painter. Before leaving, linger in the main atrium, admiring the conical pods that soar up three storeys, and explore the excellent museum shop in the basement.

Roppongi Hills

Roppongi's metamorphosis was jump-started by the success of the **Roppongi Hills** development that's a couple of minutes' walk southwest of the area's main crossing. Here you'll also find a traditional Japanese garden and pond, a liberal sprinkling of funky street sculptures and an open-air arena for free performances, amid the shops, offices and residences. If you approach Roppongi Hills through the main Metro Hat entrance from Roppongi Station, at the top of the escalators you'll see Louise Bourgeois' **Maman**, a giant bronze, stainless steel and marble spider that squats at the base of the 54-storey, Kohn Pederson Fox-designed **Mori Tower**.

Directly ahead of the spider is the "Museum Cone", a glass structure enclosing a swirling staircase that forms the entrance to Roppongi Hills' highlight, the **Mori Art Museum** (MAM; Mon, Wed, Thurs & Sun, 10am–10pm, Tues 10am–5pm, Fri & Sat 10am–midnight; ¥1500; ⓣ03/6406-6100), occupying the prime top floors of the Mori Tower. MAM puts on exhibitions of works gathered from around Japan and abroad, with a particular focus on the best contemporary art and design, and on Asian artists. The building also includes the **Tokyo City View** observation deck (daily 9am–1am, last entry midnight; ¥1500), Tokyo's highest viewpoint. On some evenings the café here morphs into the sophisticated *Mado Lounge*, hosting various DJ events, launch parties and the like.

Tokyo Tower

Around 1km east of, and clearly visible from, Roppongi is **Tokyo Tower** (東京タワー; daily 9am–10pm; main observatory ¥820, top observatory ¥1420; ⓣ03/3433-5111), something of a retro icon for the city. Built during an era when Japan was becoming famous for producing cheap copies of foreign goods, this 333m red-and-white copy of the Eiffel Tower, opened in 1958, manages to top its Parisian role model by several metres. The uppermost observation deck, at 250m, has been supplanted as the highest viewpoint in Tokyo by the roof deck of Roppongi Hills' Mori Tower (which, incidentally, provides the best view of the Tokyo Tower, especially when illuminated at night). More attractions, most incurring additional fees and none really worth seeing in their own right, have been added over the years, including a gaggle of the usual souvenir shops – to the point where the place feels like an amusement arcade. There are good views of Tokyo Bay from here, but the wise will save their cash for a drink at the rooftop bar of the nearby *Prince Park Tower Tokyo*, from which you get a great close-up view of the tower itself.

Zōjō-ji

In nearby **Shiba-kōen** (芝公園) you'll find venerable **Zōjō-ji** (増上寺). Dating from 1393, the family temple of the Tokugawa clan was moved to this site in 1598 by Tokugawa Ieyasu (the first Tokugawa shogun) in order to protect southeast Edo spiritually and provide a waystation for pilgrims approaching the capital from the Tōkaidō road. This was once the city's largest holy site, with 48 sub-temples and over a hundred other buildings. Since the fall of the Tokugawa, however, Zōjō-ji has been razed to the ground by fire three times, and virtually all the current buildings are of a mid-1970s vintage. However, the imposing **San-gadatsu-mon**, a 21m-high gateway dating from 1612, is Tokyo's oldest wooden structure and classed as an Important Cultural Property. Ahead lies the **Taiden** (Great Main Hall), while to the right are ranks of *jizō* statues, capped with red bonnets and decorated with plastic flowers and colourful windmills that twirl in the breeze.

Eastern Tokyo

Until recently the prime attraction for visitors east across the Sumida-gawa was **Ryōgoku**, home to the capital's sumo stadium and the engaging **Edo-Tokyo Museum**, covering the city's history from the seventeenth century to the present day. Looming over both these is the soaring **Tokyo Sky Tree** telecommunications tower, a mega construction project that is drawing attention to the previously untouristed residential and industrial area of **Oshiage**.

This part of Tokyo, the core of the Shitamachi area (see p.90), is the capital at its most traditional. Nowhere is this more obvious than among the craftshops and neighbourhood restaurants and ryokan of **Asakusa** and in the constant festival atmosphere around its magnificent temple, **Sensō-ji**.

Ryōgoku

East across the Sumida-gawa and best accessed by the Sōbu-line train, **RYŌGOKU** (両国) becomes thronged with sumo fans three times a year when the basho occur (see p.61 for details) at the **National Sumo Stadium** (国技館). If you're not fortunate to be in Tokyo during these times, it's still possible to visit the stadium, which is immediately outside Ryōgoku Station's west exit, and view the one-room historical **museum** (Mon–Fri 10am–4.30pm; closed during tournaments; free) there – though it is really for die-hard fans only. Simply wandering the narrow streets immediately south of the train tracks, which until recently housed many of the major "stables" where wrestlers lived and trained, is interesting even though rising land prices have forced most of them out. Nevertheless, there's still a good chance of crossing paths with some junior wrestlers, in their *yukata* and wooden *geta* with slicked-back hair, popping out to a store or for a quick snack of *chanko-nabe* (a bulk-building meat and vegetable stew). If you're feeling peckish yourself, one of the best places to sample the stew is *Tomoegata* restaurant (see p.144).

You'll need plenty of stamina for the extensive **Edo-Tokyo Museum** (江戸東京博物館; Tues–Fri & Sun 9.30am–5.30pm, Sat 9.30am–7.30pm; ¥600; ⓣ03/3626-9974), housed in a colossal building behind the Sumo Stadium; the ticket lasts a whole day, so you can come and go. The museum tells the history of Tokyo from the days of the Tokugawa shogunate to postwar reconstruction, using life-sized replicas, models and holograms, as well as more conventional screen paintings, ancient maps and documents, with plenty of information in English, including a free audio guide. The museum's display about life in Edo's Shitamachi, with its pleasure quarters, festivals and vibrant popular culture, is particularly good.

Asakusa

ASAKUSA (浅草) is best known as the site of Tokyo's most venerable Buddhist temple, **Sensō-ji**, whose towering worship hall is filled with a continual throng of petitioners and holiday-makers. Stalls before the temple cater to the crowds, peddling trinkets and keepsakes as they have done for centuries; old-fashioned craftshops display exquisite hair combs, paper fans and calligraphy brushes; and all around is the inevitable array of restaurants, drinking places and fast-food stands. It's the infectious carnival atmosphere that makes Asakusa so appealing. The

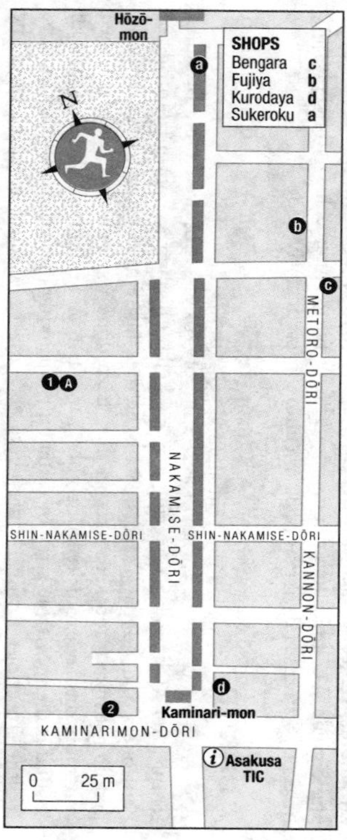

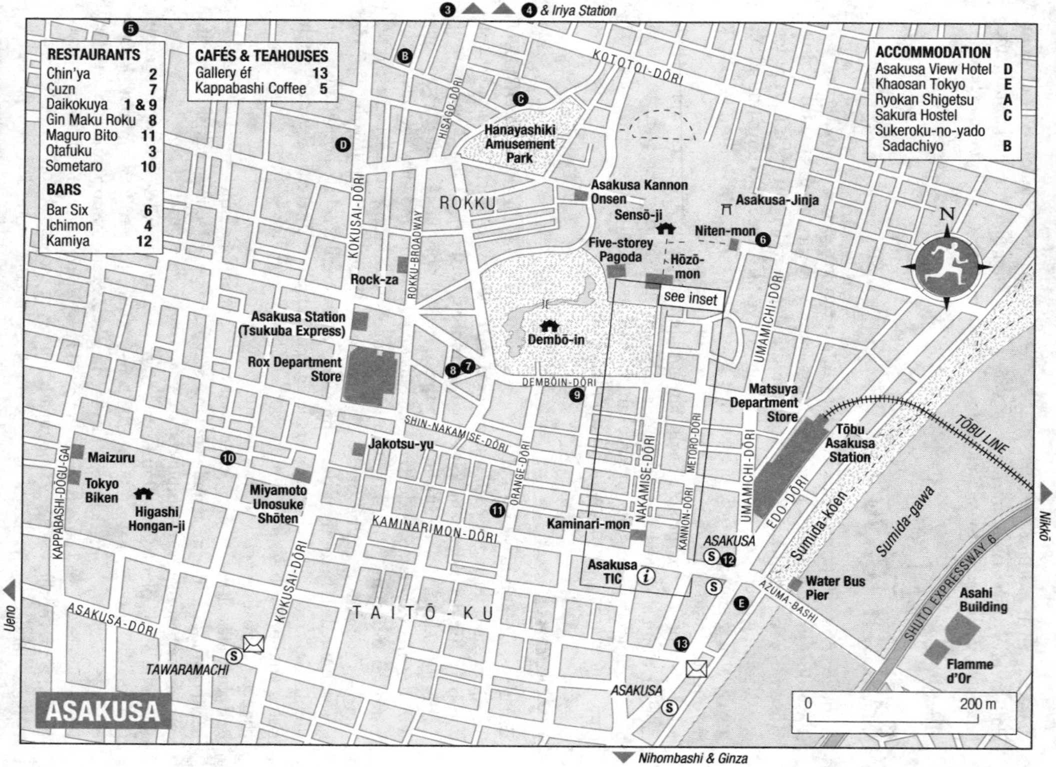

ASAKUSA

RESTAURANTS
Chin'ya 2
Cuzn 7
Daikokuya 1 & 9
Gin Maku Roku 8
Maguro Bito 11
Otafuku 3
Sometaro 10

BARS
Bar Six 6
Ichimon 4
Kamiya 12

CAFÉS & TEAHOUSES
Gallery éf 13
Kappabashi Coffee 5

ACCOMMODATION
Asakusa View Hotel D
Khaosan Tokyo E
Ryokan Shigetsu A
Sakura Hostel C
Sukeroku-no-yado Sadachiyo B

3 & 4 & Iriya Station
KOTOTOI-DŌRI
HISAGO-DŌRI
Hanayashiki Amusement Park
ROKKU
KOKUSAI-DŌRI
ROKKU-BROADWAY
Rock-za
Asakusa Kannon Onsen
Asakusa-Jinja
Sensō-ji
Niten-mon
Five-storey Pagoda
Hōzō-mon
see inset
Dembō-in
UMAMICHI-DŌRI
N
Asakusa Station (Tsukuba Express)
Rox Department Store
DEMBŌIN-DŌRI
Matsuya Department Store
TŌBU LINE
Tōbu Asakusa Station
SHIN-NAKAMISE-DŌRI
Jakotsu-yu
ORANGE-DŌRI
METORO-DŌRI
NAKAMISE-DŌRI
KANNON-DŌRI
UMAMICHI-DŌRI
EDO-DŌRI
Sumida-kōen
Sumida-gawa
Nikkō
Maizuru
Tokyo Biken
Higashi Hongan-ji
KAPPABASHI-DŌGU-GAI
Miyamoto Unosuke Shōten
KAMINARIMON-DŌRI
Kaminari-mon
ASAKUSA
Asakusa TIC
Water Bus Pier
AZUMA-BASHI
SHUTO EXPRESSWAY 6
Asahi Building
Flamme d'Or
Ueno
ASAKUSA-DŌRI
KOKUSAI-DŌRI
TAITŌ-KU
TAWARAMACHI
ASAKUSA
0 200 m
Nihombashi & Ginza

biggest festival here is the Sanja Matsuri (see p.158), but there are numerous smaller celebrations; ask at the **information centre** (daily 9.30am–8pm; English language assistance daily 10am–5pm; ⓣ03/3842-5566) in front of Sensō-ji's main gate if there's anything on.

Though you can easily reach Asakusa by subway, a more pleasant way of getting here – or away – is **by river** (see p.96 for details). The ferry terminal is under Azuma-bashi, opposite Philippe Starck's eye-catching **Flamme d'Or Building**. There are downriver departures roughly every thirty to forty minutes (daily 10am–6.30pm; ¥720 to Hama Rikyū Teien, ¥760 to Hinode Pier); note that 3.40pm is usually the last departure that stops at Hama-Rikyū Onshi Teien (see p.136).

Sensō-ji

The great **Kaminari-mon**, or "Thunder Gate", named after its two vigorous guardian gods of thunder and wind (Raijin and Fūjin), marks the southern entrance to **Sensō-ji** (浅草寺). This magnificent temple, also known as Asakusa Kannon, was founded in the mid-seventh century to enshrine a tiny golden image of Kannon, the goddess of mercy, which, legend has it, was ensnared in the nets of two local fishermen.

There's a great sense of atmosphere as you approach the main hall with its sweeping, tiled roofs from **Nakamise-dōri**, a colourful parade of small shops selling all manner of souvenirs. The double-storeyed treasure gate, **Hōzō-mon,** stands astride the entrance to the main temple complex; the treasures, fourteenth-century Chinese sutras, are locked away on the upper floor. Its two protective gods – *Niō*, the traditional guardians of Buddhist temples – are even more imposing than those at Kaminari-mon. Beyond, the crowd clustered around a large, bronze incense bowl waft the pungent smoke – breath of the gods – over themselves for its supposed curative powers before approaching the temple's inner sanctum where the little Kannon is a *hibutsu*, a hidden image considered too holy to be on view. Three times a day (6.30am, 10am & 2pm) drums echo through the hall into the courtyard as priests chant sutras beneath the altar's gilded canopy.

Like many Buddhist temples, Sensō-ji accommodates Shinto shrines in its grounds, the most important being **Asakusa-jinja** (浅草神社), dedicated to the two fishermen brothers who netted the Kannon image, and their overlord. More popularly known as Sanja-sama, "Shrine of the Three Guardians", this is the focus of the tumultuous **Sanja Matsuri**, Tokyo's biggest festival (see p.152).

Amuse Museum and around

Sensō-ji's eastern entrance is guarded by the attractively aged **Niten-mon**, dating from 1618. Just outside the gate to the left is the excellent **Amuse Museum** (galleries Tues–Sun 10am–6pm; ¥1000; ⓣ03/5806-1181), a six-storey complex with several engaging exhibition spaces mostly taken up by a rotating showcase of pieces from private collector Tanaka Chuzaburo's more than thirty items from Japan's cultural past. The permanent collection of traditional patched clothing (*boro*) looks more like the interior of a trendy boutique than an exhibition space, and the building's rooftop terrace offers fantastic views of Sensō-ji and the Tokyo Sky Tree, which is worth the visit alone.

East of the museum, a narrow strip of park, **Sumida-kōen** (隅田公園), beside the Sumida-gawa provides the stage for one of the city's great summer firework displays (*hanabi taikai*), held on the last Saturday of July.

West of Sensō-ji

When kabuki and bunraku were banished from central Edo in the 1840s, they settled in the area known as **Rokku** (Block 6), between Sensō-ji and today's

Kokusai-dōri. Over the next century almost every fad and fashion in Japanese popular entertainment started life here, from cinema to cabaret and striptease. Today a handful of the old venues survive, most famously **Rock-za**, with its daily strip-show. It's a lively area to explore and there are many fun places to drink (see p.151).

The wide avenue of Kokusai-dōri forms the western boundary of Rokku. Near its southerly junction with Kaminarimon-dōri, just south from the Rox department store, **Miyamoto Unosuke Shōten** (宮本卯之助商店; daily except Tues 9am–6pm; ⓣ03/3874-4131) is an Aladdin's cave of traditional Japanese percussion instruments and festival paraphernalia: masks, shortened kimono-style *happi* coats, flutes, cymbals and all kinds of *mikoshi* (portable Shinto shrine). The shop has specialized in drums since 1861, resulting in an impressive collection from around the world that now fills the fourth-floor **Drum Museum** (Wed–Sun 10am–5pm; ¥300; ⓣ03/3842-5622). A red dot on the label of an instrument indicates those not to be touched; blue dots mean you can tap lightly, just with your hands; and the rest have the appropriate drumsticks ready and waiting.

Continuing westwards from the Drum Museum brings you after a few blocks to Kappabashi-dōgu-gai. Locally known as **Kappabashi** (かっぱ橋), or "Kitchenware Town", this is where you'll find everything you could need to equip a professional kitchen. You don't have to be a bulk-buyer, however, and this is a great place to pick up unusual souvenirs, such as the plastic food displayed outside restaurants to tempt the customer. The best examples are absolutely realistic; try Maizuru (まいづる; daily 9am–6pm; ⓣ03/3843-1686) or Tokyo Biken (東京美研; Mon–Sat 9am–5.30pm, Sun 11am–5pm; ⓣ03/3842-5551). Note that many shops along here close on Sunday.

Tokyo Sky Tree

Clearly visible across the Sumida-gawa from Asakusa, and within walking distance, is the city's sleek new digital communications tower, **Tokyo Sky Tree** (ⓦwww.tokyo-skytree.jp). Triangular shaped at its base, and tapering up to 634m, making it Japan's tallest structure, the Sky Tree takes over the functional role of the dated, lower Tokyo Tower. Shaping up to be the city's defining twenty-first century landmark, the tower's design incorporates time-honoured architectural techniques used for constructing five-story pagodas, hopefully making it resistant to both earth tremors and strong winds.

Accessible from both Oshiage (押上) and Narihira-bashi (業平橋) stations, the complex – scheduled to open in spring 2012 – will not only offer the city's highest observatory (at 450m) but also an aquarium and planetarium at the base, and the inevitable restaurants and shopping opportunities. It's worth visiting even before this – as a steady stream of visitors is already doing – to photograph the structure close up and to drop by the **information plaza** (ⓣ03/6658-8012; Tues–Sun 10am–5pm) by Narahira-bashi that has display models and images showing what it will all look like once completed. The area surrounding the tower is also quaint, offering up – for now – a less touristy Shitamachi experience than over in Asakusa.

Northern Tokyo

Two subway stops or a short walk west of Kappabashi is **Ueno**, best known for its park and museums, including the flagship **Tokyo National Museum**, offering a comprehensive romp through Japanese art history. The Yamanote line loops west from Ueno past **Rikugi-en**, a serene classical garden, before rattling into

Ikebukuro, worth exploring for its two huge department stores, discount shops and cosmopolitan vibe.

Ueno

Most people visit **UENO** (上野) for its park, **Ueno Kōen**, which is home to a host of good museums, including the prestigious **Tokyo National Museum**, plus a few relics from Kan'ei-ji, a vast temple complex that once occupied this hilltop. But Ueno also has proletarian, Shitamachi roots, and much of its eastern district has a rough-and-ready feel, which is best experienced in the market area of Ameyokochō (see box below).

Ueno Kōen

Cut through with wide avenues where families come to feed the pigeons at weekends, **Ueno Kōen** (上野公園) is where all Tokyo seems to flock during the spring cherry-blossom season. From Ueno Station there are two routes into the park: "Park Exit" takes you to the main, east gate where you'll find an **information desk** (daily 9am–5pm); while the "Shinobazu Exit" brings you out closer to the southern entrance, above Keisei-Ueno Station. If you take the southerly option, at the top of the steps leading up to the park from the street you'll find a bronze statue of **Saigo Takamori**, out walking his dog. Despite his casual appearance, this is the "Great Saigo", leader of the Restoration army, who helped bring Emperor Meiji to power but then committed ritual suicide in 1877 after his ill-fated Satsuma Rebellion (see p.771).

As you follow the main path northwards, the red-lacquered **Kiyomizu Kannon-dō** comes into view on the left. Built out over the hillside, this temple is a smaller, less impressive version of Kyoto's Kiyomizu-dera (see p.425), but has the rare distinction of being one of Kan'ei-ji's few existing remnants, dating from 1631.

The temple faces westwards over a broad avenue lined with ancient cherry trees towards **Shinobazu Pond**. Once an inlet of Tokyo Bay, the pond is now a wildlife protection area and hosts a permanent colony of wild black cormorants as well as temporary populations of migrating waterfowl. A causeway leads out across its reeds and lotus beds to a small, leafy island occupied by an octagonal-roofed temple, **Benten-dō**, dedicated to the goddess of good fortune, water and music (among other things). The inside ceiling sports a snarling dragon.

From here you can head back into the park on the tree-lined avenue that marks the approach to Tokugawa Ieyasu's shrine, **Tōshō-gū** (東照宮). Ieyasu died in 1616 and is buried in Nikkō (see p.172), but this was his main shrine in Tokyo,

Ameyokochō

The bustling **market** area south of Ueno Station, **Ameyokochō** (アメ横丁), extends nearly half a kilometre along the west side of the elevated JR train lines down to Okachimachi Station. The name is an abbreviation of "Ameya Yokochō", or "Candy Sellers' Alley", dating from the immediate postwar days when sweets were a luxury and the hundreds of stalls here mostly peddled sweet potatoes coated in sugar syrup (*daigakuimo*). Since rationing was in force, black-marketeers joined the candy sellers, dealing in rice and other foodstuffs, household goods and personal possessions. Later, American imports also found their way from army stores onto the streets here, especially during the early 1950s during the Korean War, which is when the market was legalized. Today, Ameyokochō still retains a flavour of those early days: gruff men with sandpaper voices shout out their wares; stalls specializing in everything from bulk tea to jewellery and fish line the street; and there's a clutch of *yakitori* bars under the arches.

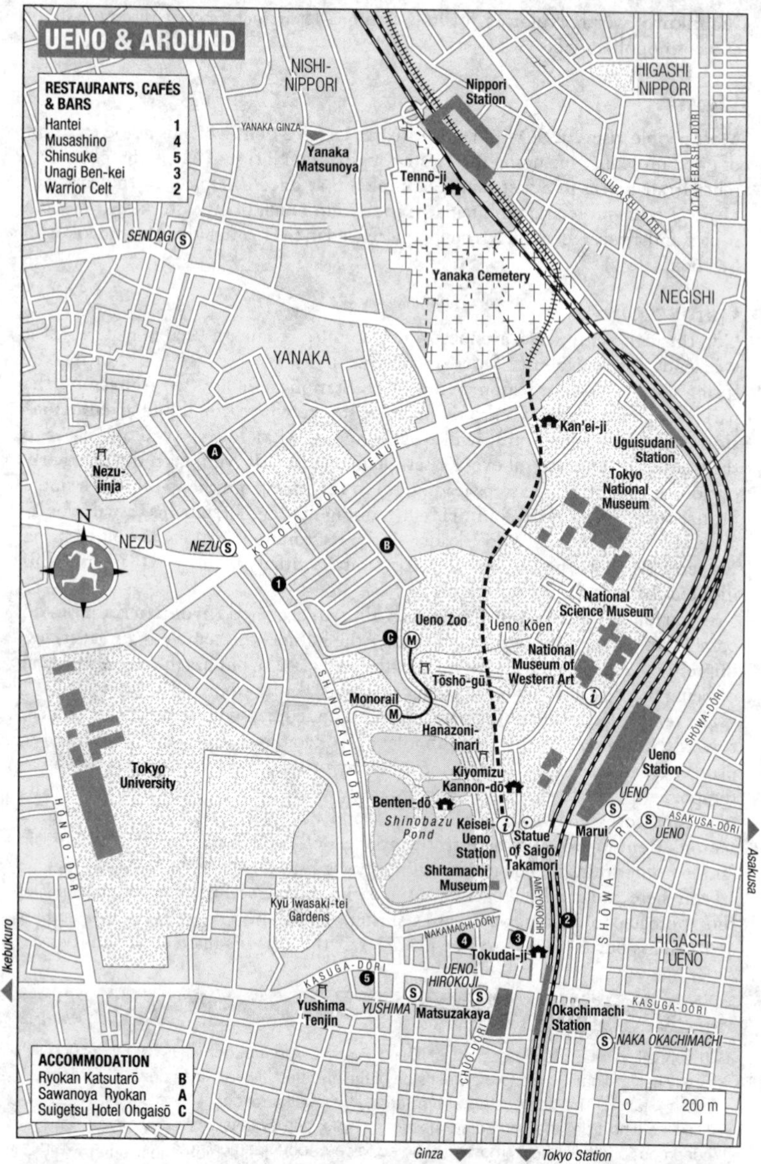

founded in 1627 and rebuilt on a grander scale in 1651. For once it's possible to penetrate beyond the screened entrance and enclosing walls to take a closer look inside (daily 9am–sunset; ¥200).

The seventeenth-century, five-storey pagoda rising above the trees to the north of Tōshō-gū is actually marooned inside **Ueno Zoo** (上野動物園; Tues–Sun 9.30am–5pm; ¥600; ⓣ03/3828-5171). Considering this zoo is over a century old, it's less depressing than might be feared and is a good place to entertain kids.

Tokyo National Museum

Dominating the northern reaches of Ueno Park is the **Tokyo National Museum** (*Tokyo Kokuritsu Hakubutsukan*; 東京国立博物館; April–Sept Tues–Thurs 9.30am–5pm, Fri 9.30am–8pm, Sat & Sun 9.30am–6pm; Oct–March Tues–Sun 9.30am–5pm, Oct–Dec Fri till 8pm; ¥600; ⓣ03/5405-8686), containing the world's largest collection of Japanese art, plus an extensive collection of Oriental antiquities. Though the newer galleries are a great improvement, backed up by an unusual amount of information in English, the museum style tends towards old-fashioned reverential dryness. Nevertheless, among such a vast collection there's something to excite everyone's imagination. Displays are rotated every few months from a collection of 110,000 pieces, and the special exhibitions are usually also worth seeing if you can stand the crowds.

It's best to start with the **Hon-kan**, the central building, which presents the sweep of Japanese art, from Jōmon-period pottery (pre-fourth century BC) to early twentieth-century painting, via theatrical costume for kabuki, nō and bunraku, colourful Buddhist mandalas, *ukiyo-e* prints, exquisite lacquerware and even seventeenth-century Christian art from southern Japan.

A passage in the building's northwest corner leads to the **Heisei-kan**, where you'll find the splendid Japanese Archeology Gallery containing important recent finds. Highlights are the chunky, flame-shaped Jōmon pots and a collection of super-heated Sue stoneware, made using a technique introduced from Korea in the fifth century.

In the southwest corner of the compound lurks the **Hōryū-ji Hōmotsu-kan** containing a selection of priceless treasures donated over the centuries to Nara's Hōryū-ji temple (see p.472). The most eye-catching display comprises 48 gilt-bronze Buddhist statues in various poses, each an island of light in the inky darkness, while there's also an eighth-century inkstand, water container and other items said to have been used by Prince Shōtoku (see p.767) when annotating the lotus sutra.

The museum's final gallery is the **Tōyō-kan**, on the opposite side of the compound, housing a delightful hotchpotch of Oriental antiquities where Javanese textiles and nineteenth-century Indian prints rub shoulders with Egyptian mummies and a wonderful collection of Southeast Asian bronze Buddhas.

Other museums

In the park's northeast corner, the **National Science Museum** (国立科学博物館; Tues–Thurs, Sat & Sun 9am–5pm, Fri 9am–8pm; ¥600; ⓣ03/3822-0111) offers lots of videos and interactive displays, though sadly nothing's labelled in English – make sure you pick up an audio guide by the ticket desk (¥300). Displays over six floors cover natural history as well as science and technology. In the "exploration space" on the second floor, pendulums, magnets, mirrors and hand-powered generators provide entertainment for the mainly school-age audience.

Yanasen

North of Ueno, **Nezu** (根津) and **Yanaka** (谷中) are two of Tokyo's most charmingly old-fashioned neighbourhoods and a world away from the usual hustle and bustle of the city. Along with neighbouring **Sendagi** (千駄木) they form an area referred to as **Yanasen** where you can experience a slower and more relaxed side of Tokyo. Strewn with small temples, craft shops, galleries and cafés, it's a great area to wander and make your own discoveries, but highlights include the historic and tranquil shrine **Nezu-jinja** (根津神社), picturesque and historic **Yanaka Cemetery** (谷中霊園) and the old-style shopping street of **Yanaka Ginza**.

South of here is the **National Museum of Western Art** (国立西洋美術館; Tues–Sun 9.30am–5pm, Fri till 8pm; ⓣ03/3828-5131), with Rodin statues on the forecourt. The main building was designed by Le Corbusier in 1959 to house the mostly French Impressionist paintings left to the nation by shipping magnate Matsukata Kōjirō. Since then, works by Rubens, Tintoretto, Max Ernst and Jackson Pollock have broadened the scope of this impressive collection.

At the southern end of the park, the **Shitamachi Museum** (下町風俗資料館; Tues–Sun 9.30am–4.30pm; ¥300; ⓣ03/3823-7451) occupies a partly traditional-style building beside Shinobazu Pond. A reconstructed merchant's shop-house and a 1920s tenement row, complete with sweet shop and coppersmith's workroom, fill the ground floor. The upper floor is devoted to rotating exhibitions focusing on articles of daily life. All the museum's exhibits have been donated by local residents; take your shoes off to explore the shop interiors and you can handle most items.

Kyū Iwasaki-tei Gardens

The west side of central Ueno is dominated by seedy love hotels and dubious bars. A short walk past Yushima Station, however, is a remnant of a much more genteel past. The **Kyū Iwasaki-tei Gardens** (旧岩崎邸庭園; daily 9am–5pm; ¥400; ⓣ03/3823-8340) date from 1896 and surround an elegant **house**, designed by British architect Josiah Conder, that combines a Western-style two-storey mansion with a traditional single-storey Japanese residence. The wooden Jacobean and Moorish-style arabesque interiors of the Western-style mansion are in fantastic condition – in stark contrast to the severely faded screen paintings of the Japanese rooms. The lack of furniture in both houses makes them a little lifeless, but it's nonetheless an impressive artefact in a city where such buildings are increasingly rare. You can take tea in the Japanese section (¥500) or sit outside and admire the gardens, which also combine Eastern and Western influences.

Rikugi-en

Five minutes' walk south of Komagome Station on the Yamanote line, **Rikugi-en** (六義園; daily 9am–5pm; ¥300) is Tokyo's best surviving example of a classical, Edo-period stroll-garden, designed in the early 18th century by high-ranking feudal lord **Yanagisawa Yoshiyasu**. Both a perfectionist and a literary scholar, Yanagisawa took seven years to create this celebrated garden – with its 88 allusions to famous scenes, real or imaginary, from ancient Japanese poetry – and then

Tokyo's last tramline

Tokyo once had an extensive tram network, of which only the 12km **Toden Arakawa line** (都電荒川線) remains, running north from Waseda to Minowa-bashi. The most interesting section is the short stretch from **Kōshinzuka Station**, a fifteen-minute walk northwest of Sugamo Station, from where the line heads southwest towards Higashi-Ikebukuro, rocking and rolling along narrow streets and through Tokyo back yards. Most of the original tramlines were private enterprises – the Arakawa line was built purely to take people to the spring blossoms in Asukayama Park – and have gradually been replaced with subways. Now the last of the *chin chin densha* ("ding ding trains"), as they're known from the sound of their bells, the Arakawa line, will probably survive for its nostalgia value if nothing else. Tickets cost ¥160, however far you travel; you pay as you enter. Station signs and announcements are in English.

named it Rikugi-en, "garden of the six principles of poetry", in reference to the rules for composing *waka* (poems of 31 syllables).

Few of the 88 landscapes have survived – the guide map issued at the entrance identifies a mere eighteen. Nevertheless, Rikugi-en still retains its rhythm and beauty, beginning as you enter with an ancient, spreading cherry tree, then slowly unfolding along paths that meander past secluded arbours and around the indented shoreline of an islet-speckled lake. In contrast, there are also areas of more natural woodland and a hillock from which to admire the whole scene.

Ikebukuro

Northern Tokyo's main commercial hub is **IKEBUKURO** (池袋). Cheap accommodation and good transport links have attracted an increasing number of expatriates, typically Chinese and Taiwanese, but including a broad sweep of other nationalities, to settle around here, which lends Ikebukuro a faintly cosmopolitan air. Either side of the hectic station (around one million passengers pass through each day), the massive department stores Tōbu and Seibu square off against each other.

Nishi-Ikebukuro

On Ikebukuro's west side, on the ground floor of the glass-fronted Metropolitan Plaza, is the excellent **Japan Traditional Crafts Centre** (全国伝統的工芸品センター; daily 11am–7pm; free; ⓣ03/5954-6066). Charged with promoting "authentic" crafts, the centre showcases a large and continually changing selection of handmade items from all over Japan.

Walking past the nearby Metropolitan Art Space and continuing west through an area of lanes rich in restaurants and bars, you'll shortly arrive at the main entrance to picturesque **Rikkyō University** (立教大学), founded as St Paul's School in 1874 by an American Episcopalian missionary. Through the gateway, the old university courtyard has an incongruous Ivy League touch in its vine-covered halls, white windows and grassy quadrangle.

Back towards the station is the equally distinctive **Myonichi-kan**, or "House of Tomorrow" (明日館; Tues–Sun 10am–4pm, closed occasionally during functions; ¥400, or ¥600 including Japanese tea and sweets; ⓣ03/3971-7535). This old school, designed by Frank Lloyd Wright and his assistant Endo Arata, is best appreciated from inside, where you get the full effect of the clean, bold lines, echoed in the hexagonal chairs, light fittings and other original furnishings. To find the school, walk south from the Metropolitan Art Space for about five minutes, looking out for the signs as you go.

Higashi-Ikebukuro

On the east side of Ikebukuro Station, the **Seibu** department store rules. While the group has been retrenching in recent years, Seibu has a history of innovation and spotting new trends, and so it remains a popular shopping destination. Apart from the main store, there are also branches of Parco, Loft and Wave, Seibu offshoots specializing in fashion, household goods and music respectively.

Heading further east, you can't miss the monstrous **Sunshine 60** building. An underground passage at the end of Sunshine 60-Dori leads into the sixty-storey tower, just one of four buildings comprising the **Sunshine City** complex of shops, offices, exhibition space, a hotel and various cultural centres – though compared to the city's newer developments, it all looks rather dowdy. There's an **observatory** (10am–9.30pm; ¥620) on the top floor, but the best thing to do, if you have kids, is visit the wacky indoor theme park **Namco Namjatown** (daily 10am–10pm; entry ¥300, day/night passport ¥3900/2500).

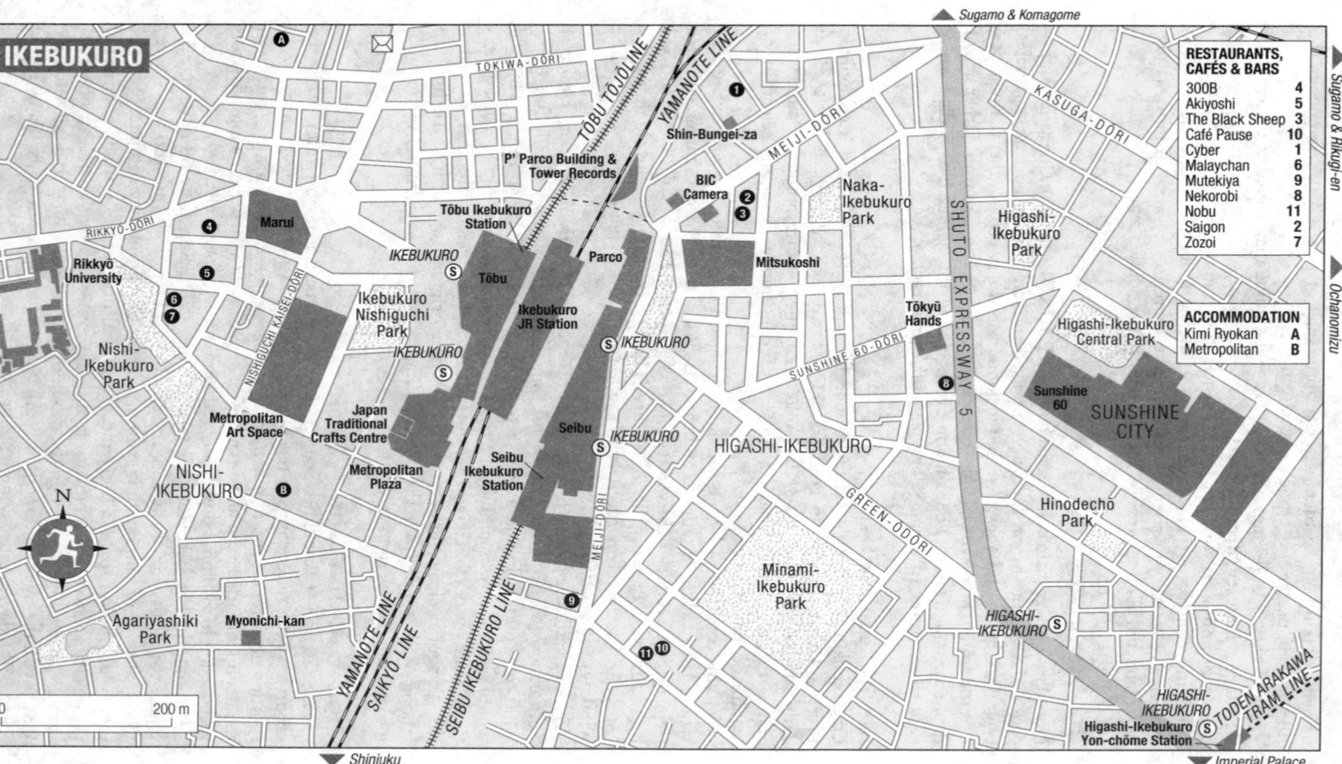
IKEBUKURO
RESTAURANTS, CAFÉS & BARS
300B 4
Akiyoshi 5
The Black Sheep 3
Café Pause 10
Cyber 1
Malaychan 6
Mutekiya 9
Nekorobi 8
Nobu 11
Saigon 2
Zozoi 7
ACCOMMODATION
Kimi Ryokan A
Metropolitan B
Sugamo & Komagome
Sugamo & Rikugi-en
Ochanomizu
Imperial Palace
Shinjuku
TOKIWA-DŌRI
TŌBU TŌJŌLINE
YAMANOTE LINE
Shin-Bungei-za
MEIJI-DŌRI
KASUGA-DŌRI
P' Parco Building & Tower Records
BIC Camera
Naka-Ikebukuro Park
Higashi-Ikebukuro Park
SHUTO EXPRESSWAY 5
Marui
RIKKYŌ-DŌRI
Tōbu Ikebukuro Station
IKEBUKURO
Tōbu
Parco
Mitsukoshi
Rikkyō University
Ikebukuro Nishiguchi Park
Ikebukuro JR Station
Tōkyū Hands
Higashi-Ikebukuro Central Park
NISHIGUCHI KAISEI-DŌRI
Nishi-Ikebukuro Park
SUNSHINE 60-DŌRI
Sunshine 60
SUNSHINE CITY
Metropolitan Art Space
Japan Traditional Crafts Centre
Seibu
HIGASHI-IKEBUKURO
Seibu Ikebukuro Station
Metropolitan Plaza
NISHI-IKEBUKURO
GREEN-ŌDORI
Hinodechō Park
N
Minami-Ikebukuro Park
Agariyashiki Park
Myonichi-kan
YAMANOTE LINE
SAIKYŌ LINE
SEIBU IKEBUKURO LINE
HIGASHI-IKEBUKURO
TODEN ARAKAWA TRAM LINE
Higashi-Ikebukuro Yon-chōme Station
0 200 m

Southern and western Tokyo

Tokyo's **southern and western districts** are where you'll find the city's younger, hipper areas. **Shinjuku** – with its skyscrapers, department stores and red-light district – buzzes with life, and includes one of the city's most beautiful parks, **Shinjuku Gyoen**. A short train ride west will bring you to a couple of charming museums where you can learn more about **anime** (see *Manga & anime* colour section).

Immediately south of Shinjuku, **Aoyama** and **Harajuku** offer a collective showcase of contemporary Tokyo fashion and style, as well as the verdant grounds of the city's most venerable shrine, **Meiji-jingū**. The transport hub of **Shibuya**, further south, is another youth-orientated commercial enclave, as is nearby **Daikan'yama**.

Further south, **Ebisu** is home to the excellent **Tokyo Metropolitan Museum of Photography**, while neighbouring **Meguro** has the tranquil **National Park for Nature Study** and **Happōen** traditional garden and teahouse. East of here is the temple **Sengaku-ji**, a key location in one of the city's bloodiest true-life samurai sagas, and the transport and hotel hub of **Shinagawa**.

Shinjuku

Some 4km due west of the Imperial Palace, **SHINJUKU** (新宿) is the modern heart of Tokyo. From the love hotels and hostess bars of Kabukichō to shop-till-you-drop department stores and hi-tech towers, the district offers a tantalising microcosm of the city.

Vast **Shinjuku Station**, a messy combination of three train terminals and connecting subway lines, splits the area into two. There's also the separate **Seibu Shinjuku Station**, northeast of the JR station. At least two million commuters are fed into these stations every day and spun out of sixty exits. If you get lost here (it's easily done), head immediately for street level and get your bearings from the skyscrapers to the west.

West of the station, **Nishi-Shinjuku** (西新宿) is dominated by skyscrapers. The one to aim for is the monumental **Tokyo Metropolitan Government Building** or TMGB (東京都庁), a 400,000-square-metre complex from which the city is administered, designed by Tange Kenzō. The complex – which includes twin 48-storey towers, an adjacent tower block, the Metropolitan Assembly Hall (where the city's councillors meet) and a sweeping, statue-lined and colonnaded plaza – feels like Gotham City. On the ground floor of the No. 1 Tower you'll find the excellent **Tokyo Tourist Information Centre** (see p.92); free tours (Mon–Fri 10am–3pm) of the complex depart from here. Both the towers have observation rooms on their 45th floors (Mon–Fri 9.30am–10pm, Sat & Sun 9.30am–7pm; free); the southern one is preferable as it has a café. It's worth timing your visit for dusk, so you can see the multicoloured lights of Shinjuku spark into action as the setting sun turns the sky a deep photochemical orange.

Of the area's other towers, the most visually striking is the new **Mode Gakuen Cocoon Tower**. This dazzling fifty-storey cross-hatched structure, close to Shinjuku Station, houses a fashion and computer studies college.

Still on the station's west side, squashed up against the tracks running north from the Odakyū department store, is **Omoide Yokochō** (思い出横丁), meaning "memories alley". It's also known as Shomben Yokochō (Piss Alley), a reference to the time when patrons of the area's many cramped *yakitori* joints and bars had to relieve themselves in the street for lack of other facilities. Don't be put off; there are toilets these days and the alley remains a cheap and atmospheric place to eat and drink. Enjoy it while you can, as there's talk of redeveloping the area. A pedestrian

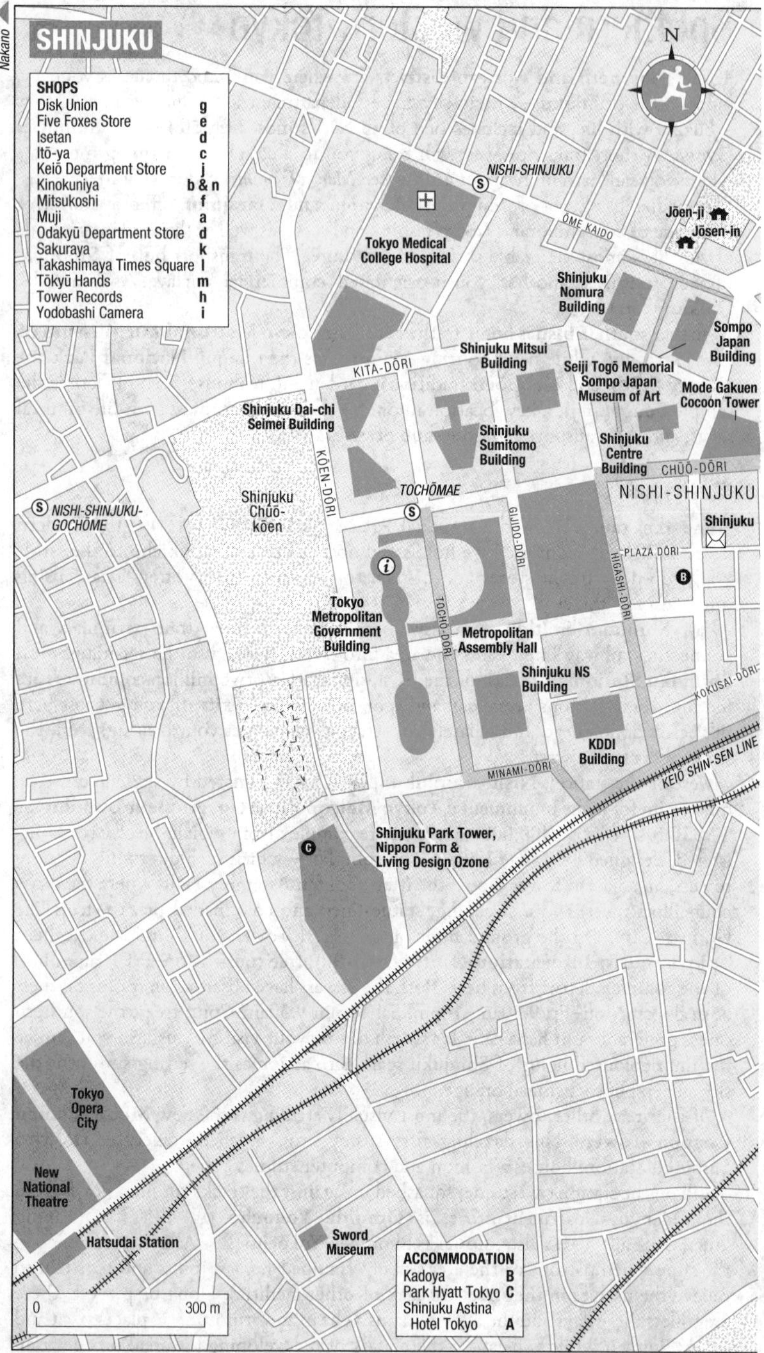
SHINJUKU
Nakano
SHOPS
Disk Union g
Five Foxes Store e
Isetan d
Itō-ya c
Keiō Department Store j
Kinokuniya b & n
Mitsukoshi f
Muji a
Odakyū Department Store d
Sakuraya k
Takashimaya Times Square l
Tōkyū Hands m
Tower Records h
Yodobashi Camera i
N
NISHI-SHINJUKU
ŌME KAIDO
Jōen-ji
Jōsen-in
Tokyo Medical College Hospital
Shinjuku Nomura Building
Sompo Japan Building
Shinjuku Mitsui Building
Seiji Togō Memorial Sompo Japan Museum of Art
Mode Gakuen Cocoon Tower
KITA-DŌRI
Shinjuku Dai-chi Seimei Building
Shinjuku Sumitomo Building
Shinjuku Centre Building
CHŪŌ-DŌRI
KŌEN-DŌRI
TOCHŌMAE
NISHI-SHINJUKU
Shinjuku Chūō-kōen
NISHI-SHINJUKU-GOCHŌME
GIJIDŌ-DŌRI
Shinjuku
PLAZA DŌRI
HIGASHI-DŌRI
B
Tokyo Metropolitan Government Building
TOCHŌ-DŌRI
Metropolitan Assembly Hall
Shinjuku NS Building
KOKUSAI-DŌRI
KDDI Building
MINAMI-DŌRI
KEIŌ SHIN-SEN LINE
C
Shinjuku Park Tower, Nippon Form & Living Design Ozone
Tokyo Opera City
New National Theatre
Hatsudai Station
Sword Museum
ACCOMMODATION
Kadoya B
Park Hyatt Tokyo C
Shinjuku Astina Hotel Tokyo A
0
300 m

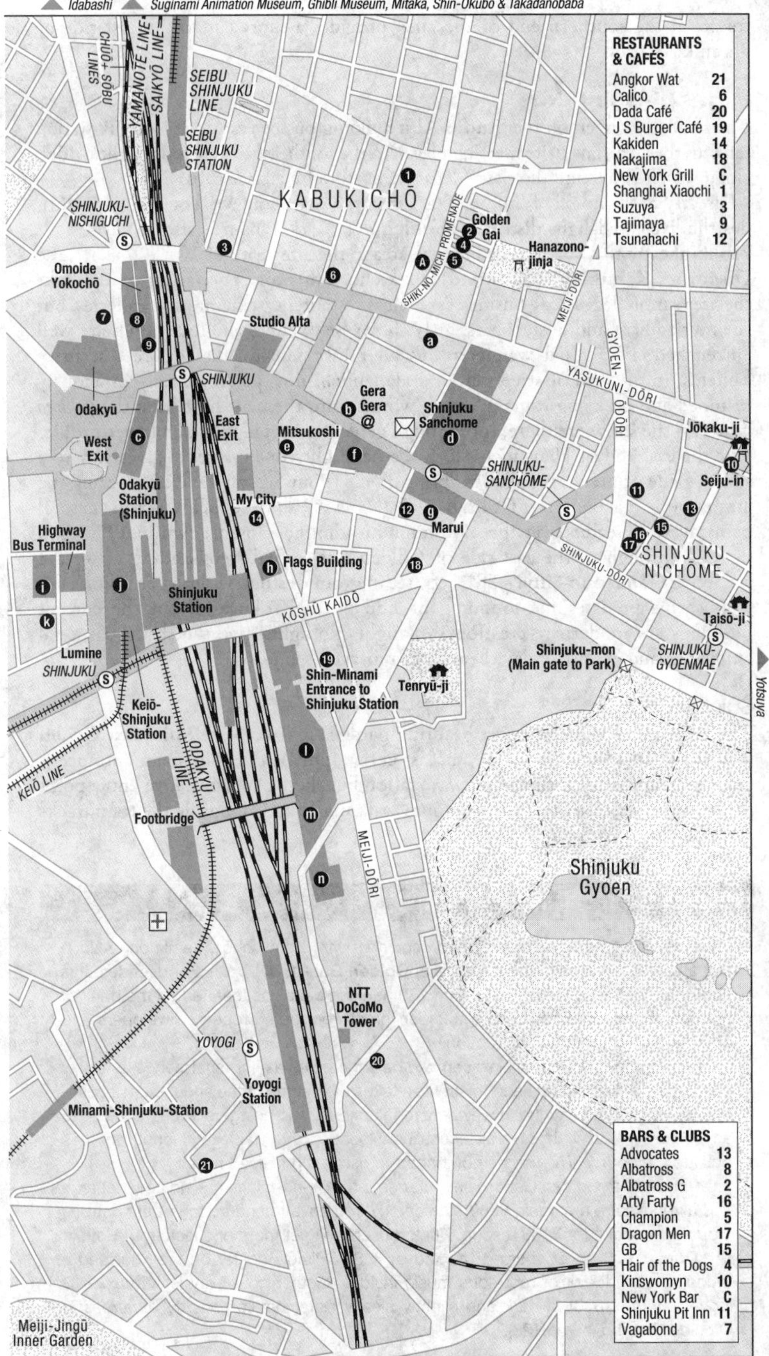

Idabashi
Suginami Animation Museum, Ghibli Museum, Mitaka, Shin-Ōkubo & Takadanobaba
RESTAURANTS & CAFÉS
Angkor Wat 21
Calico 6
Dada Café 20
J S Burger Café 19
Kakiden 14
Nakajima 18
New York Grill C
Shanghai Xiaochi 1
Suzuya 3
Tajimaya 9
Tsunahachi 12
BARS & CLUBS
Advocates 13
Albatross 8
Albatross G 2
Arty Farty 16
Champion 5
Dragon Men 17
GB 15
Hair of the Dogs 4
Kinswomyn 10
New York Bar C
Shinjuku Pit Inn 11
Vagabond 7
KABUKICHŌ
SEIBU SHINJUKU LINE
SEIBU SHINJUKU STATION
CHŪŌ + SŌBU LINES
YAMANOTE LINE
SAIKYŌ LINE
SHINJUKU-NISHIGUCHI
Omoide Yokochō
Golden Gai
Hanazono-jinja
SHIKI-NO-MICHI PROMENADE
MEIJI-DŌRI
GYOEN-ŌDŌRI
YASUKUNI-DŌRI
Studio Alta
SHINJUKU
Odakyū
West Exit
East Exit
Gera Gera @
Mitsukoshi
Shinjuku Sanchome
SHINJUKU-SANCHŌME
Jōkaku-ji
Seiju-in
Odakyū Station (Shinjuku)
My City
Marui
SHINJUKU NICHŌME
SHINJUKU-DŌRI
Highway Bus Terminal
Flags Building
Shinjuku Station
KŌSHU KAIDŌ
Taisō-ji
SHINJUKU-GYOENMAE
Shinjuku-mon (Main gate to Park)
Yotsuya
Lumine
SHINJUKU
Shin-Minami Entrance to Shinjuku Station
Tenryū-ji
Keiō-Shinjuku Station
KEIŌ LINE
ODAKYŪ LINE
Footbridge
MEIJI-DŌRI
Shinjuku Gyoen
NTT DoCoMo Tower
YOYOGI
Yoyogi Station
Minami-Shinjuku-Station
Meiji-Jingū Inner Garden
Harajuku

tunnel at the southern end of the alley provides a short cut to the east side of Shinjuku Station.

Higashi-Shinjuku

The huge TV screen on the **Studio Alta** building on the east side of the JR station remains the area's favourite meeting place. To the southeast of here is **Shinjuku-dōri**, along which you'll find the classy department store Isetan (see p.161).

Directly to the north of Studio Alta, across the wide boulevard of Yasukuni-dōri, lies the lively red-light district **Kabukichō** (歌舞伎町), named after a never built kabuki theatre that was planned for the area in the aftermath of World War II. The **Discovery Kabukichō** (Ⓦ www.d-kabukicho.com) project was set up to highlight the area's more legitimate businesses, such as restaurants, cinemas and galleries, but the myriad host and hostess bars, girly shows, sex venues and love hotels are well entrenched. For casual wanderers it's all pretty safe thanks to street security cameras. In the grid of streets around Hanamichi-dōri you'll see self-consciously primped and preening touts who fish women into the male host bars; the *yakuza* who run the show are there, too, though generally keeping a much lower profile.

At the east end of Hanamichi-dōri, the neon glitz unexpectedly gives way to a slinky glade of greenery called Shiki-no-michi (Four Seasons lane). Bordering the atmospheric bar quarter **Golden Gai** (ゴールデン街; see below), this natural pathway was created over the old Shinjuku tramline, closed down in 1970. Nip directly through to the east side of Golden Gai to find steps leading up to the attractive **Hanazono-jinja** (花園神社), set in grounds studded with vermilion *torii*. This shrine predates the founding of Edo by the Tokugawa, but the current buildings are modern re-creations. At night spotlights give the shrine a special ambience, and every Sunday there's a flea market (see p.164).

Shinjuku Gyoen

The largest and arguably most beautiful gardens in Tokyo are **Shinjuku Gyoen** (新宿御苑; Tues–Sun 9am–4.30pm, last entry 4pm; ¥200). The main entrance is close by Shinjuku-gyoenmae subway station but there's an alternative entry point through the western gate, a five-minute walk under and alongside the train tracks from Sendagaya Station.

Golden Gai renaissance

Intellectuals and artists have rubbed shoulders with Kabukichō's demimonde since just after World War II in the tiny bars of **Golden Gai** (ゴールデン街). For decades, this hugely atmospheric warren of around 150 drinking dens has teetered on the brink of oblivion, the cinderblock buildings under threat from both property developers and from their own shoddy construction.

Recently, though, Golden Gai seems to be undergoing a mini-renaissance as a new generation of bar masters and mistresses takes over some of the shoebox establishments. Most bars continue to welcome regulars only (and charge exorbitant prices to anyone else), but with several places now posting their table and drink charges outside the door, *gaijin* visitors don't need to risk being fleeced rotten.

Champion, at Golden Gai's main entrance off Shiki-no-michi, has no cover charge and all drinks are a bargain ¥500. The catch? You have to endure tone-deaf patrons crooning karaoke for ¥100 a song. Punk rockers will get more of a kick from **Hair of the Dogs** (¥800 cover charge), marked by a Sex Pistols poster on the door and a thudding soundtrack of rebellious music inside. Another possibility is **Albatross G** (cover charge ¥300), a dark and slightly sleazy sister bar to the arty *Albatross* in Omoide Okochō (see p.123).

The grounds, which once held the mansion of Lord Naitō, the *daimyō* of Tsuruga on the coast of the Sea of Japan, were opened to the public after World War II. Apart from spaciousness, the gardens' most notable feature is the variety of design. The southern half is traditionally Japanese, with winding paths, stone lanterns, artificial hills, and islands in ponds linked by zigzag bridges, and is home to *Rakuutei*, a pleasant **teahouse** (10am–4pm; ¥700). At the northern end of the park are formal, French-style gardens, with neat rows of tall birch trees and hedge-lined flowerbeds. Clipped, broad lawns dominate the middle of the park, modelled on English landscape design.

West of Shinjuku: animation museums

Returning to Shinjuku Station, take the JR Chūō line six stops west to **Ogikubo** (荻窪), the closest station to Suginami, an area long associated with the anime industry, with several production houses and many key artists resident. It's also home to the engaging **Suginami Animation Museum** (杉並アニメーションミュージアム; Tues–Sun 10am–5.30pm; free), which can be reached by a five-minute bus journey from either platform 0 or 1 outside Ogikubo Station. The museum offers colourful displays tracing the history of animation in Japan, interactive computer games allowing you to create your own animations, a small theatre screening anime, and a library packed with manga and DVDs (some with English subtitles).

Three stops further west along the Chūō line is **Mitaka** (三鷹), near where you'll find the wonderful **Ghibli Museum** (三鷹の森ジブリ美術館; daily except Tues 10am–6pm; ¥1000, reductions for children; ⓣ0570/055-777, ⓦwww.ghibli-museum.jp), located at the southwest corner of leafy Inokashira Park. The museum celebrates the work of the Ghibli animation studio, responsible for some of Japan's most popular films (see p.805). Beautifully designed throughout, the museum gives visitors an insight not only into Ghibli's films but also the animator's art in general. There's also a small cinema where original short animated features, exclusive to the museum, are screened.

In order to keep the museum free of crowds, only 2400 **tickets** are available daily; all must be purchased in advance and are for a specified time. The museum's website lists details in English of how to apply for tickets overseas. In Japan, you'll have first to make a reservation by phone (ⓣ0570/084-633), then go to a Lawson convenience store within three days to pick up your ticket; you'll need to specify the date and time (10am, noon, 2pm or 4pm) you would like to visit when you reserve. Given the massive popularity of Ghibli's films, the museum can be booked out for weeks at a time, particularly during school holidays and over weekends.

Meiji-jingū

Covering parts of both Aoyama and Harajuku, the areas immediately south of Shinjuku, is **Meiji-jingū** (明治神宮), Tokyo's premier Shinto shrine. A memorial to Emperor Meiji, who died in 1912, and his empress Shōken, who died in 1914, the shrine is split into two sections, the main one being the **Inner Garden**, beside Harajuku Station. Of less importance is the **Outer Garden**, between Sendagaya and Shinanomachi stations, which contains the Meiji Memorial Picture Gallery and several sporting arenas, including the National Stadium and Jingū Baseball Stadium.

Meiji-jingū is the focus of several **festivals** during the year, the most important of which is **Hatsu-mōde** (meaning "first visit of the year to a shrine"), held on January 1 when some three million descend on the shrine. Apart from the festivals, Meiji-jingū is best visited midweek, when its calm serenity can be appreciated minus the crowds.

The Inner Garden

The most impressive way to approach the **Inner Garden** is through the southern gate next to Jingū-bashi, the bridge across from Harajuku's mock-Tudor station building. From the gateway, a wide gravel path runs through densely forested grounds to the 12m-high **Ō-torii**, the largest Myōjin-style gate in Japan, made from 1500-year-old cypress pine trees from Taiwan.

To the left of the Ō-torii is the entrance to the **Jingū Naien** (神宮内苑; daily 8.30am–5pm; ¥500), a traditional garden – said to have been designed by the emperor Meiji for his wife – which is at its most beautiful (and most crowded) in June, when over one hundred varieties of **irises**, the empress's favourite flowers, pepper the lush greenery with their purple and white blooms.

Returning to the garden's entrance, the gravel path turns right and passes through a second wooden *torii*, **Kita-mon** (north gate), leading to the impressive **honden** (central hall). With their Japanese cypress wood and green copper roofs, the buildings are a fine example of how Shinto architecture can blend seamlessly with nature. There are exits from the courtyard on its eastern and western flanks; follow either of the paths northwards through the woods to arrive at the pleasant grassy slopes and pond before the main **Treasure House**. Don't bother going in – the contents of the museum are no more thrilling than the lumpen grey concrete building that houses them.

Harajuku

As well as the wooded grounds of Meiji-jingū, **HARAJUKU** (原宿) is also blessed with Tokyo's largest park, **Yoyogi-kōen**. Once an imperial army training ground, the park was dubbed "Washington Heights" after World War II, when it was used to house US military personnel. In 1964 the land was used for the Olympic athletes' village, after which it became Yoyogi-kōen. Two of the stadia, built for the Olympics, remain the area's most famous architectural features. The ship-like steel suspension roof of Tange Kenzō's **Yoyogi National Stadium** was a structural engineering marvel at the time and is still used for sporting events and concerts. The smaller stadium, which looks like the sharp end of a giant swirling seashell, is used for basketball.

Omotesandō and around

Harajuku's most elegant boulevard, **Omotesandō** (表参道), leads from the entrance to Meiji-jingū and is lined with *zelkova* trees and an impressive collection of modern architecture. On either side are dense networks of streets, packed with funky little shops, restaurants and bars. One of the most famous roads is **Takeshita-dōri** (竹下通り), whose hungry mouth gobbles up teenage fashion victims as they swarm out of the north exit of Harajuku Station and spits them out the other end on Meiji-dōri minus their cash. The shops sell every kind of tat imaginable and provide a window on Japanese teen fashion. On weekends the crush of bodies on the street is akin to that on the trains at rush hour.

Back towards the crossing of Meiji-dori with Omotesandō, look out for Laforet, a trendy boutique complex, behind which is the excellent **Ōta Memorial Museum of Art** or *Ōta Kinen Bijutsukan* (太田記念美術館; Tues–Sun 10.30am–5pm; fee varies with exhibition; Ⓣ03/3403-0880). The small galleries on two floors feature *ukiyo-e* paintings and prints from the private collection of the late Ōta Seizō, an insurance tycoon. The art displayed, which changes every month or two, comes from a collection of twelve thousand pieces, including masterpieces by Utamaro, Hokusai and Hiroshige.

In complete contrast is the **Design Festa Gallery** (デザイン・フェスタ・ギャラリー; daily 11am–8pm; free; Ⓣ03/3479-1442), an anything-goes contemporary art

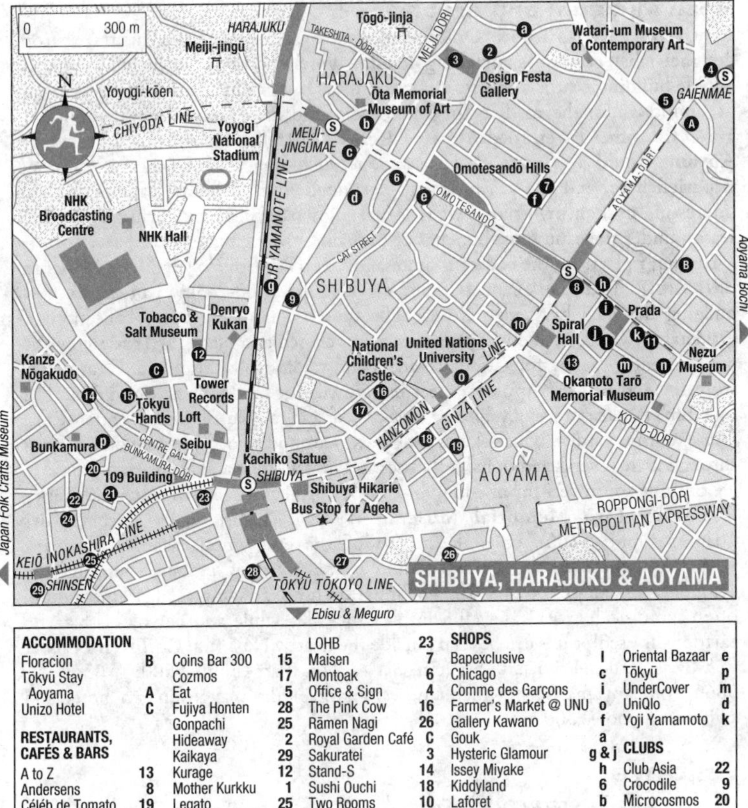

space jutting out of the boutique-clogged backstreets of Harajuku like some bargain-basement Pompidou Centre. The gallery is an offshoot of Design Festa, Japan's biggest art and design event (Ⓦ www.designfesta.com). Day-Glo paintings, graffiti, mad scaffolding and traffic cones swarm over the building's front like some alien metal creeper. Inside the art is eclectic, ranging from sculpture to video installations – even the toilet is plastered from floor to ceiling with artworks. There's also a good *okonomiyaki* café and bar here. To find the gallery, take the street directly opposite the eastern Meiji-dōri end of Takeshita-dōri, then turn north at the second junction on your left.

Midway along the northern flank of Omotesandō is the Andō Tadao-designed **Omotesandō Hills**, a glitzy complex of upmarket designer shops, restaurants and residences. At the southeastern corner Andō re-created part of the Dojunkai Aoyama Apartments, in homage to the much-loved housing block that once stood on the site. In their later years, the crumbling apartments were occupied by artists and small boutiques, and many felt that something of the district's bohemian spirit had been lost when they were destroyed to make way for Omotesandō Hills. The hip Harajuku style, however, is still very much in evidence along nearby **Cat Street** – this curvy pathway that shadows the course of the old Shibuya river and provides a pleasant walking route is lined with one-off fashion shops and quirky emporia.

Nezu Museum and around

As it crosses Aoyama-dōri, Omotesandō narrows and becomes lined with top designer-label boutiques including **Prada**, which occupies an incredible glass-bubble building that is a tourist attraction in its own right. At the far eastern end of Omotesandō, the road to the left leads round into Tokyo's most important graveyard, officially entitled **Aoyama Reien** (青山霊園), but generally known as **Aoyama Bochi**. Everyone who was anyone, including Hachikō the faithful dog, is buried here, and the graves, many decorated with elaborate calligraphy, are interesting in their own right. Many locals enjoy partying here during the *hanami* season under the candyfloss bunches of pink cherry blossoms.

Turning right from the end of Omotesandō, you'll hit the lovely **Nezu Museum** (根津美術館; Tues–Sun 10am–4.30pm; ¥1000; ⓣ03/3400-2536) in an elegant new building designed by Kengo Kuma. The museum houses a classy collection of Oriental artworks, including the *Irises* screens, classed as a National Treasure by the government's Agency for Cultural Affairs and traditionally displayed for a month from the end of each April – expect big crowds for this popular exhibition. The museum's best feature, enjoyable any time of year and fully justifying the entrance fee, is its extensive garden, which slopes gently away around an ornamental pond. Dotted through it are several traditional teahouses and mossy stone and bronze sculptures.

Continue southwest for one long block and turn right again to reach the quirky **Okamoto Tarō Memorial Museum** (岡本太郎記念館; daily except Tues 10am–5.30pm; ¥600), once the studio of the eponymous avant-garde artist (1911–96) whose most famous creation is the *Tower of the Sun* sculpture, the symbol of Ōsaka's Expo in 1970. The museum houses examples of his intriguing, often whimsical, work, as well as a pleasant café, while another of his bizarre, cartoon-like sculptures can be seen outside the nearby **National Children's Castle** (こどもの城; Tues–Fri 12.30–5.30pm, Sat & Sun 10am–5pm; ¥500; ⓣ03/3797-5666), on Aoyama-dōri, which houses a large kids' playground, a hotel and swimming pool (¥300 extra).

Shibuya

It's hard to beat **SHIBUYA** (渋谷), birthplace of a million-and-one consumer crazes, as a mind-blowing introduction to contemporary Tokyo. Here teens and 20-somethings throng **Centre Gai** (センター街), the shopping precinct that splits the district's rival department store groups: **Tōkyū** (which owns the prime station site, the Mark City complex and the Bunkamura arts hall) and **Seibu** (whose outlets include the fashionable, youth-oriented Loft and Parco stores). Although there are a few interesting museums in the area – most particularly the **Japan Folk Crafts Museum** – Shibuya is primarily an after-dark destination.

A perch from which to view the crowds of people swarming across Shibuya Crossing is from the bridge corridor linking the JR station with Shibuya Mark City complex. This space has been put to excellent use as the gallery for Okamoto Tarō's fourteen panel painting *Myth of Tomorrow* (*Asu no Shinwa*), a 30m-long mural depicting the moment the atomic bomb exploded in Hiroshima. Originally created in the late 1960s for a luxury hotel in Mexico and lost for decades, this powerful work seldom seems to stop the rushing commuters in their tracks.

East of Shibuya station is the 34-storey **Shibuya Hikarie**, due to open in 2012. This complex of offices, shops, restaurants and cultural facilities will also have a two-thousand-seat theatre with a lobby providing a sweeping view of the skyline. Immediately west of the crossing, the **109 Building**, packed with fashion stores, stands at the apex of Bunkamura-dōri and Dōgenzaka **Dōgenzaka** (道玄坂), the latter is one of Tokyo's most famous love-hotel districts.

Quirky Tokyo museums

Beyond the antique ceramics, painted scrolls and other objets d'art displayed in the city's more traditional museums, Tokyo has several institutions devoted to some unlikely subjects. The following are a few of our favourites:

Meguro Parasitological Museum, near Meguro Station (目黒寄生虫館; Tues–Sun 10am–5pm; free; ⓣ03/3716-1264; see map, pp.132–133). Learn all about the dangers of creepy-crawlies in uncooked food; specimens here include record-breaking tapeworms (one is 8.8m long) pickled in jars, along with some gruesome photographs of past victims.

Meiji University Museum near Ochanomizu Station (明治大学博物館; daily 10am–5pm; closed Aug 10–16 & Dec 26–Jan 7; free; ⓣ03/3296-4448; see map, p.108). The "military fork" and delightfully named "sleeve entangler" used by Edo-era law enforcers are some of the less horrific exhibits in this museum's "criminal zone". The hard stuff includes spine-chilling instruments of torture and capital punishment, alongside woodblock prints illustrating how they were used.

Tobacco and Salt Museum, near Shibuya Station (たばこと塩の博物館; Tues–Sun 10am–5.30pm; ¥100; ⓣ03/3476-2041; see map, p.129). Covers the two products that were once government monopolies. Includes two thousand different packs of cigarettes from around the world.

Denryokukan (TEPCO 電力館; daily except Wed 10am–6pm; free; ⓣ03/3477-1191; see map, p.129)). The English brochure says "Let's make friends with electricity" and TEPCO, Tokyo's power company, goes out of its way to convince you that this is possible. Magical Square on the fifth floor and the Energy World displays on the sixth will provide maximum distraction for inquisitive kids.

Just two stops from Shibuya on the Keiō Inokashira line to Komaba-Tōdaimae Station lies the excellent **Japan Folk Crafts Museum** or *Mingeikan* (民芸館; Tues–Sun 10am–5pm; ¥1000; ⓣ03/3467-4527), a must-see for lovers of hand-crafted pottery, textiles and lacquerware. The gift shop is a fine source of souvenirs. Opposite the museum stands a nineteenth-century **nagayamon** (long gate house), brought here from Tochigi-ken by the museum's founder, Yanagi Sōetsu (see p.787).

Ebisu, Daikan'yama and Naka-Meguro

Named after the Shinto god of good fortune, **EBISU** (恵比寿) is home to hundreds of buzzing bars and many stylish restaurants. Connected to the station by a long moving walkway is **Yebisu Garden Place** (恵比寿ガーデンプレイス), a huge shopping, office and entertainment complex built on the site of the nineteenth-century brewery that was once the source of the area's fortunes. The best reason for coming here is to visit the **Tokyo Metropolitan Museum of Photography** or *Tōkyō-to Shashin Bijutsukan* (東京都写真美術館; Tues–Sun 10am–6pm, Thurs & Fri until 8pm; admission charges vary; ⓣ03/3280-0031), on the west side of the complex. Wonderful photographs by major Japanese and Western photographers are displayed in regularly changing exhibitions, along with study rooms and an experimental photography and imaging room. Afterwards, head for the 38th and 39th floors of the adjacent **Yebisu Tower**; you don't need to eat or drink here to enjoy the spectacular free views of the city.

A ten-minute stroll west along Komazawa-dōri from Ebisu Station, or one stop from Shibuya on the Tōku Tōyoko line, is **DAIKAN'YAMA** (代官山), home to some of the city's classiest homes, shops and watering holes. The village-like area's laid-back vibe is a refreshing break from the frenzy of nearby Shibuya. Close to

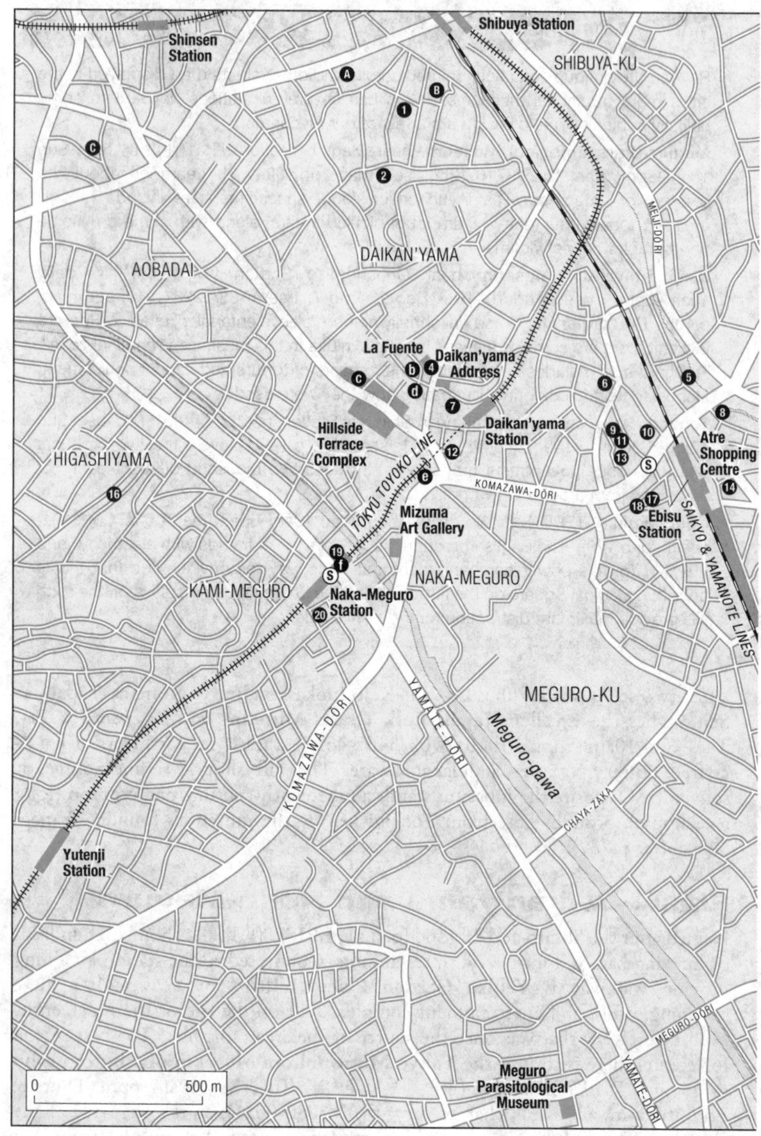

the station are the smart **Daikan'yama Address** and **La Fuente** complexes where you'll find more fashionable boutiques and ritzy restaurants and cafés.

Immediately to the southwest is bohemian **NAKA-MEGURO** (中目黒). Liberally sprinkled with eclectic boutiques and small cafés and bars, the district hugs the banks of the Meguro-gawa, a particularly lovely spot to head during cherry-blossom season and in the height of summer, when the waterway provides some natural air conditioning.

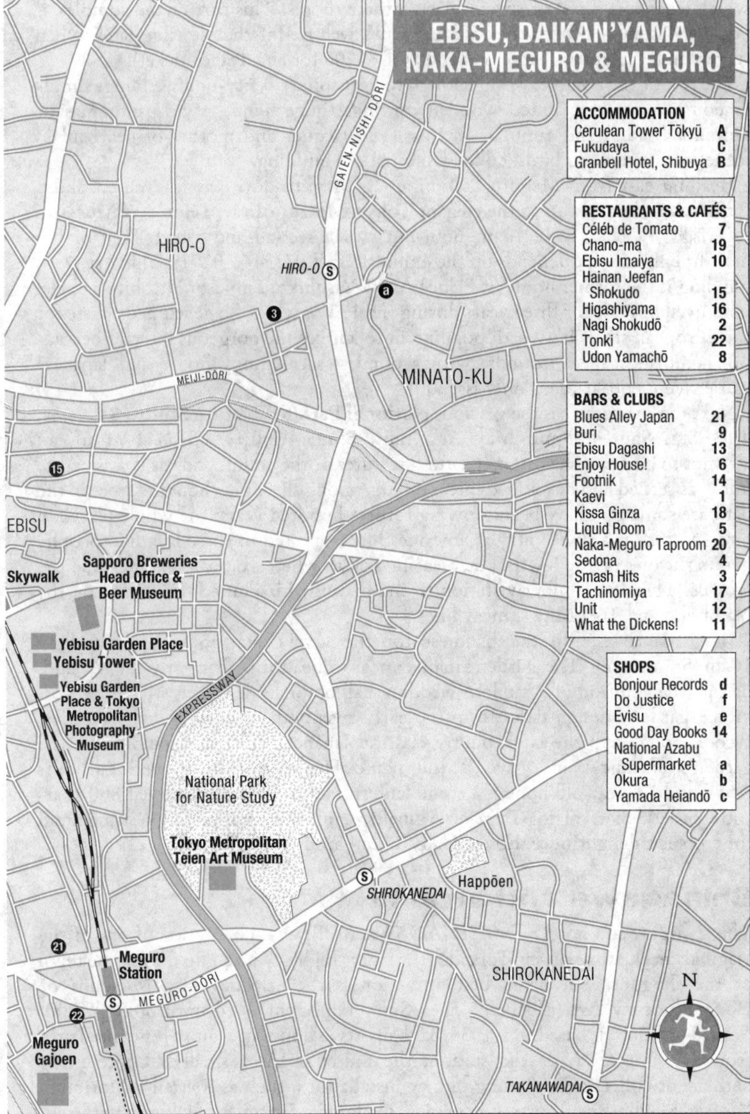

Meguro and around

South of Ebisu, **MEGURO** (目黒) offers some off-the-beaten-path sightseeing options. From Meguro Station, follow the road southwest downhill, towards the mammoth wedding hall, hotel and restaurant complex of **Meguro Gajoen** (目黒雅叙園; ⓣ03/5434-3920, ⓦwww.megurogajoen.co.jp). The current building replaced the original wedding hall, built in 1931 and known as Ryūgū-jō (Fairytale Dragon Palace). All that remains of that is the *hyakudan kaidan* ("100-step stairway") which leads to a series of spectacularly ornate rooms. This part of the complex is not always open – check the wedding hall's website for the viewing dates, when there will be an entry charge of ¥1500 (or ¥1200 for an advance ticket).

The rest of the complex – big enough to host some twenty-odd weddings simultaneously – sports painted wooden carvings (huge *ukiyo-e*-style panoramas of kimonoed ladies and samurai warriors) and lacquer and mother-of-pearl inlaid scenes of flowers and birds, culled from the old building.

Heading east from Meguro Station along Meguro-dōri, past the raised Shuto Expressway, brings you to the elegant **Tokyo Metropolitan Teien Art Museum** (東京都庭園美術館; daily 10am–6pm but closed second and fourth Wed of the month; entrance fee depends on the exhibition; ⓣ03/3443-0201). This Art Deco building is the former home of Prince Asaka Yasuhiko, Emperor Hirohito's uncle, who lived in Paris for three years during the 1920s, where he developed a taste for the European style. It's worth popping in to admire the gorgeous interior decoration and landscaped grounds, with a pond, tea-ceremony house and Japanese gardens (entry to gardens only is ¥200).

Next to the grounds is the spacious **National Park for Nature Study** (自然教育園; Tues–Sun 9am–4.30pm, May–Aug until 5pm; ¥300; ⓣ03/3441-7176), an attempt to preserve the original natural features of the countryside as it was before Edo was settled and developed into Tokyo. Among the eight thousand trees in the park are some that have been growing for five hundred years; the whole place is a bird-spotter's paradise. Entry at any one time is limited to three hundred people, making it one of the few public areas in Tokyo where you can really escape the crowds. The closest subway station to the park is **Shirokanedai** (白金台), on the Namboku and Toei Mita subway lines.

Shirokanedai is also the handiest for the lovely **Happōen** (八芳園; daily 10am–5pm; free). The garden's name means "beautiful from any angle" and, despite the addition of a modern wedding hall on one side, this is still true. Most of the garden's design dates from the early twentieth century, when a business tycoon bought up the land, built a classical Japanese villa (still standing by the garden's entrance) and gave it the name Happōen. The garden harbours two-hundred-year-old bonsai, a stone lantern said to have been carved 800 years ago by the Heike warrior Taira-no Munekiyo, and a central pond. Nestling amid the trees is a delightful **teahouse** (daily 11am–5pm; ¥800 for tea).

Shinagawa and around

The transport and hotel hub **SHINAGAWA** (品川) was the location of one of the original checkpoints on the Tōkaidō, the major highway into Edo during the reign of the shoguns. The area's best attraction is the eclectic **Hara Museum of Contemporary Art** (原美術館; Tues–Sun 11am–5pm, Wed until 8pm; ¥1000; ⓣ03/3445-0651). Based in a 1938 Bauhaus-style house in a quiet residential area around 800m south of the station, the museum has a small but interesting permanent collection including quirky installations, such as *Rondo* by Morimura Yasumasa, whose self-portrait occupies the downstairs toilet. The building itself, designed by Watanabe Jin, the architect responsible for Ueno's Tokyo National Museum and Wakō in Ginza, is worth a look, as are the tranquil sculpture gardens overlooked by the museum's pleasant café.

Sengaku-ji (泉岳寺), the famous temple that houses the graves of **Asano Takumi** and his **47 rōnin** (see box opposite), is around 1km north of Shinagawa; the closest station is Sengaku-ji on the Toei Asakusa line. Most of the temple was destroyed during the war and has since been rebuilt, but a striking gate dating from 1836 and decorated with a metalwork dragon remains. The statue and grave of **Oishi Kuranosuke**, the avenging leader of the 47 *rōnin*, are in the temple grounds.

The 47 rōnin

Celebrated in kabuki and *bunraku* plays, as well as on film, *Chūshingura* is a true story of honour, revenge and loyalty. In 1701, a young *daimyō*, Asano Takumi, became embroiled in a fatal argument in the shogun's court with his teacher and fellow lord Kira Yoshinaka. Asano had lost face in his performance of court rituals and, blaming his mentor for his lax tuition, drew his sword within the castle walls and attacked Kira. Although Kira survived, the shogun, on hearing of this breach of etiquette, ordered Asano to commit *seppuku*, the traditional form of suicide, which he did.

Their lord having been disgraced, Asano's loyal retainers, the **rōnin** – or masterless samurai – vowed revenge. On December 14, 1702, the 47 *rōnin*, lead by **Oishi Kuranosuke**, stormed Kira's villa, cut off his head and paraded it through Edo in triumph before placing it on Asano's grave in Sengaku-ji. The shogun ordered the *rōnin*'s deaths, but instead all 47 committed *seppuku* on February 14, 1703, including Oishi's 15-year-old son. They were buried with Asano in Sengaku-ji, and today their graves are still wreathed in the smoke from the bundles of incense placed by their gravestones.

A **museum** (daily 9am–4pm; ¥200) to the left of the main building contains the personal belongings of the *rōnin* and their master Asano, as well as a receipt for the severed head of Kira.

Bayside Tokyo

Several of the city's prime attractions are to be found around Tokyo Bay. The teeming fish market of **Tsukiji** provides a rowdy early-morning antidote to the serenity of the nearby traditional gardens, **Hama Rikyū Teien**. Across the Rainbow Bridge lies the modern waterfront suburb of **Odaiba**, built on vast islands of reclaimed land and home to **Miraikan**, Tokyo's best science museum, as well as huge shopping malls and the Big Site convention centre.

On the north side of the bay, **Kasai Rinkai-kōen** is a good place to catch the sea breeze and has a fine **aquarium**. From the park, the Cinderella spires of **Tokyo Disneyland** are clearly visible to the west. Though you probably won't have time to visit both in one day, these places are at adjacent stops on the JR Keiyō line from Tokyo Station. Coming from Odaiba, you can pick up the Keiyō line at Shin-Kiba Station.

Tsukiji

A dawn visit to the vast **Tokyo Metropolitan Central Wholesale Market** (東京都中央卸売市場; Mon–Sat 4am–noon but check the website for occasional holidays; Ⓦwww.tsukiji-market.or.jp/tukiji_e.htm), more popularly known as **TSUKIJI** (築地), is one of Tokyo's undisputed highlights. The closest subway station is Tsukiji-Shijō (築地市場), although Tsukiji is also convenient.

The site on which the market is located dates back to 1657, when Tokugawa Ieyasu had the debris from the Furisode (Long Sleeves) Fire shovelled into the marshes at the edge of Ginza, thus creating "reclaimed land" – which is what **Tsukiji** means. The market relocated to this area from Nihombashi following the 1923 earthquake, the current complex starting operations in 1935. It's likely that it will move again, probably around 2014 (see box, p.136).

Tsukiji's main action is centred on its **jōnai-shijō** (main market) lying closest to the water in the crescent-shaped hangar. The headline **tuna auctions** happen between 5am and 6.15am, and viewing, when allowed, is from within a

Tsukiji Troubles

Generating ¥1.7 billion in sales daily, Tsukiji is undoubtedly big business, but during recent years the market's volume of trade has been dropping (down some seventy thousand tonnes between 2002 and 2007), along with the number of wholesalers and middlemen who work there.

Uppermost on merchants' minds is Tokyo government's plan to shift the market to Toyosu, 2km across the bay. The site was previously used by Tokyo Gas, and the highly toxic ground must be thoroughly cleaned up before any construction starts on the new complex where tourists are likely to be kept at arm's length from the action, restricted to walkways overlooking the wholesale fish section. This will help solve the problems caused in recent years by increasingly large groups of tourists disrupting the key tuna auctions. On a couple of occasions the authorities have had to put a temporary ban on visitor attendance at the auctions. Rules now stipulate a maximum of 140 visitors, split into two groups with separate viewing times in a cordoned-off area; registration for a place starts at 4.30am.

cordoned-off area accommodating around seventy people (see box above). It's well worth getting up early to witness sales of these rock-solid frozen fish, looking like steel torpedoes, all labelled with yellow stickers indicating their weight and country of origin. Depending on the quality, each tuna sells for between ¥600,000 and ¥1 million.

There are plenty of other things to see later in the day, including auctions for other seafood, meat, fruit and vegetables. From around 6am, restaurateurs and food retailers pick their way through the day's catch, which is put on sale at 1600 different wholesalers' stalls. Afterwards, head to one of the area's plentiful sushi stalls and noodle bars servicing the sixty thousand people who pass through here each day. One good choice, in one of the rows of sushi stalls directly opposite the market's fish section, is *Sushi Bun* (see p.146).

Before leaving the area, weave your way through the **jōgai-shijō** (outer market), a dense grid of streets immediately to the northeast, heaving with fishmongers, grocers, pottery merchants and kitchenware sellers – there's activity here later into the day when the main market is winding down. Closer to Tsukiji subway station is **Tsukiji Hongan-ji** (築地本願寺), one of the largest and most Indian-looking of Tokyo's Buddhist temples. Pop inside to see the intricately carved golden altar and cavernous interior, with room for a thousand worshippers.

Hama Rikyū Onshi Teien

Less than a ten-minute walk southeast of the bustling market is the serene traditional garden of **Hama Rikyū Onshi Teien** (浜離宮庭園; Tues–Sun 9am–4.30pm; ¥300). This beautifully designed park once belonged to the shogunate, who hunted ducks here. These days the ducks, protected inside the garden's nature reserve, are no longer used for target practice and only have to watch out for the large number of cats that wander the twisting pathways. There are three ponds, the largest spanned by a trellis-covered bridge that leads to a floating teahouse, *Nakajima-no-Chaya* (¥500 for tea). One of the best times of year to come here is in early spring, when lilac wisteria hangs in fluffy bunches from trellises around the central pond. From the Tokyo Bay side of the garden, you'll get a view across to the Rainbow Bridge, and can see the floodgate which regulates how much sea water flows in and out of this pond with the tides. By far the nicest way of approaching the gardens is to take a ferry from Asakusa, down the Sumida-gawa (see p.96 for details).

Odaiba

ODAIBA (お台場) is an island of reclaimed land in Tokyo Bay. The name means "cannon emplacements", referring to the defences set up in the bay by the shogun in 1853 to protect the city from Commodore Perry's threatening Black Ships (see p.770). The remains of the two cannon emplacements are now dwarfed by the huge landfill site – Rinkai Fukutoshin, of which Odaiba is a part – on which the Metropolitan Government set about constructing a twenty-first-century city in 1988. The subsequent economic slump and spiralling development costs slowed the project down and, when the Rainbow Bridge linking Odaiba to the city opened in 1993, the area was still a series of empty lots. Odaiba has since slightly filled out and is most appreciated by locals for its seaside location and sense of space – so rare in Tokyo. At night, the illuminated Rainbow Bridge, giant technicolour Ferris wheel and twinkling towers of the Tokyo skyline make Odaiba a romantic date location.

Panasonic Centre Tokyo

Less than a minute's walk from Ariake monorail station is **Panasonic Centre Tokyo** (Tues–Sun 10am–6pm; free; ⓣ03/3599-2600), the electronics group's showcase where you can try out the latest Nintendo games on a large-screen plasma display or high-resolution projector, as well as check out the company's technologies of tomorrow. The centre includes the fun "digital network museum" **Risupia** (¥500), at which you're issued with an electronic tag upon entering the hi-tech display hall; as you learn about science and mathematics from the computer games and simulations within, the tag keeps track of how well you're doing.

Tokyo Big Sight and Palette Town

Outside of Kokusai Tenjijō Seimon station, you can't fail to see the Tokyo International Exhibition Centre, better known as the **Tokyo Big Sight** (東京ビッグサイト; ⓣ03/5530-1111, ⓦwww.bigsight.jp). With an entrance composed of four huge inverted pyramids, this is one of Japan's largest venues for business fairs and exhibitions; in front stands a 15.5m sculpture of a saw, sticking out of the ground as if left behind by some absent-minded giant. Check their website for details of events.

Aomi Station is the stop for **Palette Town** (パレットタウン), a vast shopping and entertainment complex. On the east side, **Mega Web** (daily 11am–9pm; free; ⓣ03/3599-0808) is a design showcase for Toyota's range of cars. Give them a call to sign up for various activities, such as designing your own auto using CAD technology, taking a virtual-reality drive (¥500) or a spin in an electric vehicle

Getting to and from Odaiba

The simplest way of reaching Odaiba is to hop on the **Yurikamome monorail** (ⓦwww.yurikamome.co.jp), which starts at Shimbashi Station and arcs up to the Rainbow Bridge on a splendid circular line, stopping at all the area's major sites before terminating at Toyosu. A one-day ticket for the monorail (¥800) is a good idea if you intend to see all of the island – walking across Odaiba can be a long slog. In addition, trains on the Rinkai line, linked with the JR Saikyo line and the Yūrakuchōsubway line, run to the central Tokyo-Teleport Station on Odaiba. **Buses** from Shinagawa Station, southwest of the bay, cross the Rainbow Bridge and run as far as the Maritime Museum, stopping at Odaiba Kaihin-kōen on the way. There is also a variety of bus services (some free) to the Ōedo Onsen Monogatari. Finally, **ferries** shuttle from the pier at Hinode (日の出) to either Ariake pier on Odaiba or the Maritime Museum via Harumi and Odaiba Kaihin-kōen – the journey costs just ¥520 and doubles as a Tokyo Bay cruise.

(¥200), or even selecting a Toyota model and taking it for a test drive (¥300). Just behind the showroom are some more hi-tech diversions, the best of which is the **Wonder Wheel** (daily 10am–10pm; ¥900), a 115m-diameter candy-coloured Ferris wheel, which takes sixteen minutes to make a full circuit.

The west side of Palette Town is dominated by **Venus Fort** (daily 11am–9pm) one of Tokyo's most original shopping and factory outlet malls. It's partly designed as a mock Italian city, complete with piazza, fountains and Roman-style statues – even the ceiling is painted and lit to resemble a perfect Mediterranean sky from dawn to dusk.

Miraikan and around

West of Palette Town is Tokyo's best science museum, the **National Museum of Emerging Science and Innovation,** also known as the **Miraikan** (日本科学未来館; daily except Tues 10am–5pm; ¥600; ⓣ03/3570-9151). Here you can learn about the latest in robot technology, superconductivity (including maglev trains), space exploration and much more, as well as check out the weather around the world by looking up at a giant sphere covered with one million light-emitting diodes and showing the globe as it appears from space that day. All displays have English explanations and there are also plenty of English-speaking volunteer guides on hand. Directly south of here is the onsen complex, **Ōedo Onsen Monogatari** (see p.109); both can be accessed from the Telecom Center station on the monorail.

From Miraikan it's a short walk north to the excellent **Museum of Maritime Science** (船の科学館; Mon–Fri 10am–5pm, Sat & Sun 10am–6pm; ¥700; ⓣ03/5550-1111), housed in a concrete reproduction of a sixty-thousand-tonne cruise ship. The exhibits include many detailed model boats and the engines of a giant ship. Docked outside are a couple of real boats: the *Sōya*, which undertook scientific missions to the South Pole, and the *Yōtei Marine*, a ferry refitted as an exhibition space. Within the museum grounds you'll also find a couple of lighthouses, submarines, a flying boat and the opportunity to practise canoeing (April–Oct; ¥600).

Odaiba beach and the Rainbow Bridge

Odaiba's man-made **beach** begins as you turn the corner of the island and the Rainbow Bridge comes into view, as well as an unexpected scale copy of the Statue of Liberty. Fronting the beach are a couple of linked shopping malls, **Aqua City** and **Decks Tokyo Beach**, while on the other side of the monorail is Tange Kenzō's futuristic **Fuji TV Building** with a huge metal sphere suspended in its middle – it looks like it's been made from a giant Meccano set. You can pay to head up to the twenty-fifth-floor **viewing platform** (Tues–Sun 10am–8pm; ¥500) or save the cash for a drink in the *Sky Lounge* at the top of the neighbouring *Grand Pacific Le Daiba* hotel where the view is thrown in for free.

From the Sunset Beach row of restaurants beside the Decks Mall, you can walk across onto one of the shogun's gun emplacement islands, now a public park, or continue walking across the **Rainbow Bridge**. This 918m-long single-span suspension bridge has two levels, the lower for the waterfront road and the monorail, and the upper for the Metropolitan Expressway. On both sides is a pedestrian promenade linking the **observation rooms** (daily: April–Oct 10am–9pm; Jan–March & Nov–Dec 10am–6pm; ¥300) in the anchorages at either end of the bridge. The walk along the bridge takes about forty minutes and, weather permitting, provides magnificent views across the bay. One minute's walk from the exit from the shoreside observation room is Shibaura Futō Station (芝浦ふ頭), where you can board the monorail.

Tokyo for kids

Tokyo is a fantastic city for kids. For starters, there's a whole swathe of **museums**, the best ones being Miraikan (see opposite), the National Science Museum (see p.119) and Edo-Tokyo Museum (see p.113). For animal lovers, there's the fabulous aquarium at Kasai Rinkai-kōen (see below) and Ueno **zoo** (see p.118).

The city also boasts Tokyo Disneyland, of course (see below), and the thrill of the rides at Tokyo Dome (see p.109) as well as the wonderful Ghibli Museum (see p.127), based on the popular anime films produced by the Ghibli studio. If your children are six or under, the National Children's Castle (see p.130) will keep them occupied for many an hour.

See p.165 for a list of **shops** featuring the latest hit toys and Japanese crazes. For older, tech-savvy kids, the electronic emporia of Akihabara will be a must (see p.107).

Kasai Rinkai-kōen

Another way to enjoy Tokyo Bay is to head out to **Kasai Rinkai-kōen** (葛西臨海公園; open 24hr; free). This park, a favourite weekend spot for many families, is around 7km east of Odaiba. Bird enthusiasts also come to ogle waterbirds and waders in the well-designed bird sanctuary. The park's biggest draw is its large, well-stocked aquarium, the **Tokyo Sea Life Park** (Tues–Sun 9.30am–5pm, last entry 4pm; ¥700). One of the nicest ways back to central Tokyo from here is to hop on a **ferry** for the 55-minute ride (¥800) via Ariake to Hinode Sanbashi near Hamamatsuchō. Boats leave hourly from the park's western pier; see p.96 for further details.

Tokyo Disney Resort

The big daddy of Tokyo's theme parks, **Tokyo Disney Resort** (東京ディズニーリゾート; ☎0570-008-632) comprises two separate but adjacent attractions: **Tokyo Disneyland**, a close copy of the Californian original, and **DisneySea Park**, a water- and world-travel-themed area.

You'll need to devote a day to each park to get your money's worth. A one-day "**passport**" for either costs ¥5800, a two-day passport to both parks is ¥10,000, and there are also a couple of discount passports available for Disneyland only, if you enter later in the day. The resort is generally open from 8am or 9am to 10pm, but hours may vary and the park is occasionally closed for special events, so it's best to call to check times beforehand. Expect long queues.

The gates to Disneyland sit right in front of **Maihama Station** (on the JR Keiyō line, 15min from Tokyo Station), which is served by direct buses from Shinjuku and Yokohama, as well as Narita and Handa airports.

Eating

When it comes to **gastronomic experiences**, few places can compare to Tokyo. The number, range and quality of restaurants are breathtaking, with practically any world cuisine you can think of available alongside all the usual (and many unusual) Japanese dishes.

There's no need to panic about **prices**. Even Michelin-starred restaurants offer good-value set-meal specials, particularly for lunch. There's an abundance of fast-food options (see p.140) and cafés (see p.146) offering light meals. Many of the pubs (*izakaya*) and live music venues listed on pp.150–154 and pp.156–157 serve fine food, too.

Fast-food city

Tokyo's **fast food** options include the usual Western suspects as well as local chains such as *Yoshinoya* (Ⓦwww.yoshinoya.com) serving reasonably tasty *gyūdon* (stewed strips of beef on rice), and *Tenya* (Ⓦwww.tenya.com) for tempura and rice dishes. *Sekai-no-Yamachan* (Ⓦwww.yamachan.co.jp) is a chain *izakaya* hailing from Nagoya serving spicy chicken wings (*tebasaki*) with four branches in Shinjuku and more elsewhere in the capital. ¥500 gets you a plate of five chicken wings, so tasty it's guaranteed you'll order more. A huge hit of recent years has been *Soup Stock Tokyo* (Ⓦwww.soup-stock-tokyo.com), serving a great selection of hearty broths.

Convenience stores such as 7-Eleven, AM/PM and Lawson sell snacks and meals round the clock, which can be heated up in the shop's microwave. For more upmarket goodies, make your way to the basement food halls of the major department stores.

One of the easiest options is to head to the restaurant floors of **department stores** and **shopping malls**. They harbour a wide choice of cuisines under one roof, often with plastic food displays in the windows and lots of daily specials.

For up-to-date **information** on Tokyo's restaurant scene, check out the free weekly magazine *Metropolis*, the excellent Tokyo Food Page (Ⓦwww.bento.com), Gourmet Navigator (Ⓦwww.gnavi.co.jp) and Eatpia (Ⓦwww.eatpia.com).

Akasaka

The following restaurants are marked on the map on p.111.

Aux Bacchanales 2F Ark Mori Building, 1-12-32 Akasaka, Minato-ku Ⓣ03/3582-2225, Ⓦwww.auxbacchanales.com. Tucked away in the Ark Hills complex, this is one of Tokyo's most authentic Parisian-style brasseries – their steak frites is the real thing – and it's a pleasant spot to hang out sipping coffee or red wine. Roppongi-itchōme Station. A meal will cost around ¥2500. Daily 10am–midnight.

Jidaiya 時代屋 3-14-3 Akasaka, Minato-ku Ⓣ03/3588-0489, Ⓦtokyo-jidaiya.jp. Charming farmhouse-style place in the heart of Akasaka, all dark wood, tatami and traditional ornaments. There's an English menu to help you select between the wide range of dishes, including a wild boar stew for ¥4000 and a *kaiseki*-style course for ¥8000. Lunch is a great deal at under ¥1000. Akasaka Station. Mon–Fri 11.30am–2.30pm & 5pm–4am, Sat & Sun 5–11pm.

Kurosawa 黒澤 2-7-9 Nagatachō, Chiyoda-ku Ⓣ03/3580-9638, Ⓦ9638.net/eng/index.html. Quality soba and pork dishes are the speciality of this atmospheric restaurant, whose design was inspired by Akira Kurosawa's films. They also have a couple of other equally good restaurants *Udon Kurosawa* (饂飩くろさわ; 6-11-16 Roppongi, Minato-ku Ⓣ03/3403-9638), and *Keyaki Kurosawa* (欅くろさわ; 3-2-15 Nishi-Azabu, Minato-ku Ⓣ03/5775-9638) both near Roppongi Hills. Tameike-sannō Station. Mon–Fri 11.30am–3pm, 5–10pm, Sat noon–9pm.

Shunjū 春秋 27F San'nō Park Tower, 2-11-1 Nagatachō, Chiyoda-ku Ⓣ03/3592-5288, Ⓦwww.shunju.com. Shunjū offers stylish interior design and food made from the freshest seasonal ingredients. The buffet lunch is good (although the place gets busy with office workers), while in the evening set menus kick off at ¥6000 (plus twenty percent in service and taxes). Branches include *Shunjū Tsugihagi* (Ⓣ03/3595-0511) opposite the *Imperial Hotel*. Tameike-sannō Station. Mon–Sat 11.30am–2.30pm & 5–11pm.

Asakusa

The following restaurants are marked on the map on p.114.

Chin'ya ちんや 1-3-4 Asakusa, Taitō-ku Ⓣ03/3841-0010, Ⓦwww.chinya.co.jp. Founded in 1880, this famous, traditional *shabu-shabu* and *sukiyaki* (both variations on hot-pot meals with thinly sliced beef cooked in a broth with vegetables and dipping sauces) restaurant offers basic menus from ¥3200. The place occupies seven floors, with cheaper, more casual dining in the basement (from ¥2600). Asakusa Station. Daily except Tues noon–9pm.

Daikokuya 大黒家 1-38-10 Asakusa, Taitō-ku ⓣ03/3844-1111, ⓦwww.tempura.co.jp. There's always a lunchtime queue at this Meiji-era tempura restaurant in an attractive old building opposite Dembō-in garden. The speciality is *tendon*, a satisfying bowl of shrimp, fish and prawn fritters on a bed of rice (from ¥1470). Asakusa Station. Open 11.30am–8.30pm; closing days vary.

Maguro Bito まぐろ人 1-5-9 Asakusa, Taitō-ku ⓣ03/3844-8736. Highly popular *kaiten-zushi* shop where the quality of fish and other ingredients is excellent. Be prepared to wait, though the queue moves fairly quickly. Electronically price-coded plates range from ¥130 to ¥400. Asakusa Station. Daily 11am–10pm.

Otafuku 大多福 1-6-2 Senzoku, Taitō-ku ⓣ03/3871-2521, ⓦwww.otafuku.ne.jp. Customers have been coming to this charming restaurant for over eighty years to sample its delicious selection of around forty different types of *oden* (¥110–530/dish). Wash it all down with a glass of pine-scented *taruzake* (sake aged in wooden barrels). Iriya Station. Tues–Sun 5–11pm.

Sometarō 染太郎 2-2-2 Nishi-Asakusa, Taitō-ku ⓣ03/3844-9502. Homely restaurant specializing in *okonomiyaki*, cheap and filling savoury pancakes cooked on a hotplate. One good-sized bowl costs from ¥400, depending on the ingredients, or you can opt for an "introductory set" of three varieties for ¥1575 (enough to feed two). Tawaramachi Station. Tues–Sun noon–10pm.

Waentei-Kikko 和えん亭 吉幸 2-2-13 Asakusa, Taito-ku, ⓣ03/5828-8833, ⓦwww.waentei-kikko.com. A rare chance to see an excellent live performance of the shamisen (a Japanese banjo) in a delightful wooden house transported to Asakusa from Takayama. The lunch bentō is beautifully presented *kaiseki*-style food for ¥2500 (dinner starts at ¥6825). Asakusa Station. Daily except Wed 11.30am–1.30pm, 5–9.30pm.

Ebisu, Hiro-o, Meguro and Naka-Meguro

The following restaurants are marked on the map on pp.132–133.

Chano-ma 6F Nakameguro Kangyō Building, 1-22-4 Kami-Meguro, Meguro-ku ⓣ03/3792-9898. Slip off your shoes and relax on the huge, padded, bed-like platform, overlooking the river and train tracks. They serve some very tasty rustic-style Japanese dishes, as well as a great selection of teas and flavoured lattes. Set lunches are under ¥1000. Naka-Meguro Station. Mon–Thurs & Sun noon–2am, Fri & Sat noon–4am.

Ebisu Imaiya えびす今井屋 1-7-11 Ebisu-Nishi, Shibuya-ku ⓣ03/5456-0255, ⓦwww.imaiya.co.jp. Serves top-quality *yakitori* as well as a choice selection of sake. Downstairs it's casual and lively; for more privacy and service from kimonoed waitresses, book a private room upstairs. Expect to pay ¥3000–5000 per person. Ebisu Station; take the road opposite with Mizuho bank on the corner, and you'll find the restaurant on the right-hand side. Mon–Thurs & Sun 5pm–1am, Fri & Sat 5pm–3am.

Higashiyama 東山 1-21-25 Higashiyama, Meguro-ku ⓣ03/5720-1300, ⓦwww.higashiyama-tokyo.jp. An elegant hillside restaurant and bar that's the epitome of Tokyo cool. The course menu is a great deal at ¥6000 and they have a fine selection of sake and *sochu* to match. The same company is behind the equally stylish and appealing *Higashiya* teahouse (see p.148). Naka-Meguro Station. Mon–Sat 6pm–midnight.

Rāmen mania

Soba and udon noodles have their fans – with preferred places to slurp these being *Kurosawa* (see opposite), *Udon Yamachō* (see p.142) and *Yabu Soba* (see p.144) – but it's the Chinese-style yellow noodle **rāmen** that Tokyoites really go crazy over. Noodles in a soup flavoured with miso (fermented soya bean paste), salt or *shōyu* (a broth made with soy sauce) are standard rāmen dishes but *tsukemen* (rāmen served dry with broth for dipping) has become especially popular of late. It's not unusual for long queues to form outside popular rāmen stalls (such as *Mutekiya*, see p.143, or *Rāmen Nagi*, see p.145), and there are scores of blogs devoted to the quest for the best bowl, such as ⓦwww.ramenadventures.com, and www.ramentokyo.com. **Tokyo Rāmen Street** (B1F First Avenue, Tokyo Station ⓣ03/3210-0077, ⓦwww.tokyoeki-1bangai.co.jp/en; daily 11am–10.30pm), inside Tokyo Station, and **Rāmen Kokugikan** (ラーメン国技館, 5F Aqua City, 1-7-1 Daiba, Minato-ku; daily 11am–11pm), on Odaiba, both comprise several rāmen stalls in one location, which – if you have the appetite – makes it simple to do a taste comparison between the various styles to find your favourite.

Tonki とんき 1-1-2 Shimo-Meguro, Meguro-ku ⓣ03/3491-9928. Tokyo's most famous *tonkatsu* (breaded pork cutlets) restaurant, where a seemingly telepathic team makes order of chaos. There's no reservations so you'll most likely find yourself queuing up outside waiting for a seat. A meal will cost around ¥2000 per person. Meguro Station. Daily except Tues 4–10.45pm.

Udon Yamachō うどん山長 1-1-5 Ebisu, Minato-ku ⓣ03/3443-1701. Tucked away beside the stream flowing east of Ebisu station, this simply decorated place serves up delicious gourmet udon noodles at wooden tables under paper lanterns. There are plenty of excellent side dishes if you want to make a full meal of it. Ebisu Station. Daily 11.30am–3.30pm & 5pm–4.30am.

Ginza, Marunouchi and around

The adventurous will want to sample the numerous *yakitori* joints nestling under the railway tracks between Yūrakuchō and Shimbashi stations. All the following are marked on the map on p.104.

A16 Brick Square, 2-6-1 Marunouchi, Chiyoda-ku ⓣ03/3212-5215, ⓦwww.giraud.co.jp/a16. California-style Italian food, served at indoor and outdoor tables facing the lovely garden at Brick Square – a great place to relax over a glass of wine and a crisp slice of pizza in between browsing Marunouchi's boutiques. Tokyo Station. Mon–Sat 11am–11pm, Sun until 10pm.

Aroyna Tabeta あろいなたべた 3-7-11 Marunouchi, Chiyoda-ku ⓣ03/5219-6099, ⓦwww.tabeta.com. Note the big ¥630 sign – that's the price you'll pay for all the tasty and authentically spicy food, including set meals, at this basic Thai place under the tracks between Yūrakuchō and Shimbashi stations. Yūrakuchō Station. Daily 11am–11pm.

Dhaba India 2-7-9 Yaesu, Chūō-ku ⓣ03/3272-7160. Give your taste buds a workout at this bustling, nicely decorated South Indian restaurant. Specialities include crisy dosa and a delicious sweet-and-sour fish curry, plus a wide selection of set meals, all reasonably priced around ¥2000. Kyōbashi Station. Mon–Fri 11.15am–3pm & 5–11pm, Sat & Sun noon–3pm & 5–10pm.

Little Okinawa 8-7-10 Ginza, Chūō-ku ⓣ03/3572-2930 ⓦwww.little-okinawa.co.jp. The welcome at this cosy Okinawan restaurant is as warm as it would be in the southern islands. Try Ryūkyū dishes such as *champuru* (Okinawan-style stir-fry, around ¥850) and the strong tipple *awamori*. Bookings recommended. Shimbashi Station. Mon–Fri 5pm–3am, Sat & Sun 4pm–midnight.

Sakyo Higashiyama 左京ひがしやま B1F Oak Ginza, 3-7-2 Ginza Chūō-ku ⓣ03/3535-3577. Refined *kyō-ryori* (Kyoto-style cuisine) is served at this rustic bamboo and wood-decorated basement space with an open kitchen. The lunch set for ¥2100 includes six delicious, seasonal courses. Ginza Station. Mon–Sat 11am–2pm & 5.30–9pm.

Taimeiken 1-12-10 Nihombashi, Chūō-ku ⓣ03/3271-2464 ⓦwww.taimeiken.co.jp. Tokyoites swoon at the nostalgia of one of Tokyo's original Western-style restaurants. The cafeteria downstairs serves the same large portions of curry rice, *omu-rice, tonkatsu* and noodles as upstairs in the more formal restaurant, but at lower prices. Nihombashi Station. Mon–Sat 11am–9pm.

Tenmaru 天〇 6-9-2 Ginza, Chūō-ku ⓣ03/3289-1010. Consistently good tempura restaurant in a basement just off Chūō-dōri. Expect to spend at least ¥2000 a head. Limited English menu available. Ginza Station. Mon–Fri 11.30am–3pm & 5–9.20pm, Sat & Sun 11.30am–9.30pm.

Torigin Honten 鳥ぎん本店 B1, 5-5-7 Ginza, Chūō-ku ⓣ03/3571-3333, ⓦwww.torigin-ginza.co.jp. Bright, popular restaurant serving *yakitori* and *kamameshi* (kettle-cooked rice with a choice of toppings), tucked down an alley two blocks east of Ginza's Sony Building. The *kamameshi* or a weekday lunch set both cost around ¥800. Ginza Station. Daily 11.30am–10pm.

Harajuku and Aoyama

The following restaurants are marked on the map on p.129.

A to Z Minami Aoyama 5-8-3 ⓣ03/5464 0281. Enter the offbeat world of artist Yoshitomo Nara in this impressive café – part art installation, part kindergarten for the art-school set. The food includes tasty salads, noodle and rice dishes (under ¥1000) – all the kind of things a Japanese mum might cook up. Omotesandō Station. Daily 11.30am–11.30pm.

Curry Up 2-35-9-105 Jingūmae, Shibuya-ku ⓣ03/5775-5446, ⓦcurryup.jp; see map, pp.88–89. Punning name aside, there's not much to dislike about this stylish new curry canteen where they keep the menu simple and the food hot and spicy. Try the butter chicken (from ¥800 for a small portion). Meiji-jingūmae Station. Mon–Fri 11.30am–3pm, 5–8.30pm, Sat & Sun 11.30am–7.30pm.

Eat 2-12-27 Kita-Aoyama, Minato-ku ⓣ03/6459-2432. The burger made of top-quality Kobe beef is a headliner at this fab little diner, but they also do an equally delicious lamb version and classy renditions of American faves such as seafood gumbo and burritos for under ¥2000 per person. Gaienmae Station. Mon–Sat 11.30am–3.30pm, 6–10.30pm, Sun 11.30am–3pm.

Maisen まい泉 4-8-5 Jingūmae, Shibuya-ku ⓣ03/3470-0071. In a converted bathhouse, this long-running *tonkatsu* restaurant serves up great-value set meals. The former bathroom is the restaurant's smoking section. Omotesandō Station. Daily 11am–10pm.

Mother Kurkku 2-18-21 Jingūmae, Shibuya-ku ⓣ03/5414-0581, ⓦwww.kurkku.jp. Kurkku is Finnish for "cucumber", not many of which are in evidence at this ecologically sound operation including a shop, library and charming roof garden. This is the more relaxed and cheaper of the two restaurants in the stylish complex, where organic pork dishes are a speciality and are usually served grilled with a healthy selection of organic vegetables. Meiji-jingūmae Station. Daily 11am–midnight, Fri & Sat until 4am.

Royal Garden Café 2-1-19 Kita Aoyama, Minato-ku ⓣ03/5414 6170, ⓦwww.royal-gardencafe.com; see map, pp.88–89. With its spacious reclaimed-wood interior, bakery and wrap-around terrace sheltered by leafy trees, this organic food café at the entrance to Meiji-jingu outer garden strikes all the right notes. There's another branch in Shibuya at the *Unizo* hotel. Daily 11am–11pm.

Sakuratei さくら亭 3-20-1 Jingūmae, Shibuya-ku ⓣ03/3479-0039. Funky cook-your-own *okonomiyaki*, *monjayaki* (a Tokyo variation on the batter pancake, more loose in texture like scrambled egg) and *yakisoba* joint behind the weird and wonderful Design Festa gallery (see p.128). From 11.30am to 3pm you can eat as much as you like within 90min for ¥980, and it's just as good value at night. Meiji-jingūmae Station. Daily 11.30am–11pm.

Two Rooms 5F AO Building, 3-11-7 Kita-Aoyama, Minato-ku ⓣ03/3498-0002, ⓦwww.tworooms.jp. A sophisticated formal restaurant and a relaxed bar with a spacious outdoor terrace that provides one of the best views in Tokyo. Enjoy European-style food using top-quality Japanese ingredients, enhanced by polite service. On Sunday there's a brunch for ¥2950. Lunch sets start at ¥1850, dinner tasting menus at ¥7500. Omotesandō Station. Restaurant 11.30am–2.30pm, 6–10pm, bar 11.30am–2am, until 10pm Sun.

Ikebukuro

The following restaurants are marked on the map on p.122.

Akiyoshi 秋吉 3-30-4 Nishi-Ikebukuro, Toshima-ku ⓣ03/3982-0601, ⓦwww.akiyoshi.co.jp. Unusually large but typically inexpensive *yakitori* bar with a good atmosphere and a helpful picture menu. You might have to queue at peak times for the tables, but there's generally space at the counter. Ikebukuro Station. Daily 5pm–midnight.

Malaychan 3-22-6 Nishi-Ikebukuro, Toshima-ku ⓣ03/5391-7638, ⓦwww.malaychan.jp. Unpretentious Malay restaurant dishing up decent food, from grilled fish on banana leaf and *mee goreng* to winter steam boats (the Malay equivalent of *suki-yaki*). Weekday lunch menus start at ¥840, and in general you'll eat well for around ¥2000. Ikebukuro Station. Mon 5–11pm, Tues–Sat 11am–2.30pm & 5–11pm, Sun 11am–11pm.

Mutekiya 無敵家 1-7-1 Minami-Ikebukuro, Toshima-ku ⓣ03/3982-7565, ⓦwww.mutekiya.com. Rāmen fans should head straight to this joint, where the queue moves fairly quickly. While you wait you can decide on the size of your helping, its flavour and whether you want extra toppings and so forth – it's all delicious. Ikebukuro Station. Daily 10.30am–4am.

Nobu 2-14-3 Minami-Ikebukuro, Toshima-ku ⓣ03/5396-2697. Cozy little Italian restaurant and wine bar, with the must-eat dish being the *tonkatsu* spaghetti, made up of a piece of fried pork on spaghetti topped with a spicy tomato sauce – it's only on the lunch menu, but you can ask for it at night. Ikebukuro Station. Tues–Sun 11.30am–3pm & 6pm–midnight.

Kanda, Akihabara and Ryōgoku

The following restaurants are marked on the map on p.108.

Go Go Curry ゴーゴーカレー 1-16-1 Kanda-Sakumachō, Chiyoda-ku ⓣ03/5256-5525, ⓦwww.gogocurry.com. No doubt about it, the official meal of Akihabara regulars is *tonkatsu* curry (fried pork on rice with curry sauce), and one of the heartiest is at the growing *Go Go Curry* chain – the *honten* (main branch) is of course in Akihabara. Akihabara Station. Daily 11am–10pm.

Kanda Yabu Soba かんだやぶそば 2-10 Kanda-Awajichō, Chiyoda-ku ⓣ03/3251-0287. Since 1880, soba connoisseurs have been coming here to slurp their noodles and to listen to the cheerful waiting staff's distinctive singsong cries. You might have to wait at busy times, but it doesn't take long, and there's an attractive garden to admire. Prices start at around ¥630. Awajichō Station. Daily 11.30am–8pm.

Tomoegata 巴潟 2-17-6 Ryōgoku, Sumida-ku ⓣ03/3632-5600, ⓦwww.tomoegata.com. In the heart of sumo territory, this is one of the best places to sample the wrestlers' body-building stew, *chanko-nabe*. For around ¥3000 you can have the full-blown meal cooked at your table, though most people will find the smaller, ready-made version (¥840; lunch only) more than enough. Ryōgoku Station. Daily 11.30am–2pm & 5–11pm.

Roppongi, Nishi-Azabu and Azabu-Juban

The following restaurants are marked on the map on p.111.

Gonpachi 権八 1-13-11 Nishi-Azabu, Minato-ku ⓣ03/5771-0170, ⓦwww.gonpachi.jp. A faux-Edo-period storehouse is the home of this atmospheric Japanese restaurant. Take your pick between soba and grilled items on the ground and second floors, while on the third floor there's sushi. The whole place has a wonderful samurai drama atmosphere. Also branches in Ginza, Odaiba and Shibuya-ku (ⓣ03/5784-2011; see map, p.129). A meal costs around ¥4000. Roppongi Station. Daily 11.30am–5pm.

Hainan Jeefan Shokudo 海南鶏飯食堂 6-11-16 Roppongi, Minato-ku ⓣ03/5474 3200, ⓦwww.route9g.com. Serving Singaporean street-food favourites with most dishes under ¥2000. The portions aren't huge but it's all tasty and nicely presented. There's an equally good branch in Ebisu (ⓣ03/3447-3615; see map, p.132). Roppongi Station. Mon–Fri 11.30am–2pm & 6pm–midnight, Sat & Sun 11.30am–3pm & 6–11pm; closed 3rd Mon of month.

L'Atelier de Joël Robuchon 2F Roppongi Hills Hillside, 6-10-1 Roppongi, Minato-ku ⓣ03/5772-7500, ⓦwww.joel-robuchon.com. The French masterchef has six Tokyo outposts, including a café in Takashimya. This one offers delicious *degustation* menus, which start at ¥2950 for lunch, and ¥4800 for dinner. There's a no-bookings policy, so you may have to wait at the long counter before getting a seat, where you can watch the chefs creating mini-masterpieces in the open kitchen. Roppongi Station. Daily 11.30am–2.30pm & 6–10pm.

Nobu Tokyo Toranomon Towers Office, 4-1-28 Toranomon, Minato-ku ⓣ03/5733-0070, ⓦwww.nobutokyo.com. The famous black-cod dinner (Robert de Niro's favourite) is a good deal at ¥3500 at Nobu Matsuhisa's Tokyo operation. For something a bit different, try *tiradito*, the chef's South American twist on sashimi. Kamiyachō Station. Mon–Fri 11.30am–2pm, daily 6–10.30pm.

Nodaiwa 野田岩 1-5-4 Higashi-Azabu, Minato-ku ⓣ03/3583-785, ⓦwww.nodaiwa.com. Kimono-clad waitresses shuffle around this 160-year-old *kura* (storehouse), converted into one of Tokyo's best eel restaurants. If busy, they may guide you to the annexe (*bekkan*) around the corner, which has almost an identical interior. Around ¥5000 for a meal. Kamiyachō Station. Mon–Sat 11am–1.30pm & 5–8pm.

Suzunami 鈴波 B1F Galleria, Tokyo Midtown, 9-7-4 Akasaka, Minato-ku ⓣ03/5413-0335, ⓦwww.suzunami.co.jp. This restaurant, specializing in silver cod marinated in sake, is a good choice out of the many in Midtown. Their filling set meals, which start at around ¥1000, are great value and all are rounded off with a glass of plum wine. Roppongi Station. Daily 11am–10pm.

Tōfuya-Ukai とうふ屋うかい 4-4-13 Shiba-kōen, Minato-ku ⓣ03/3436-1028, ⓦwww.ukai.co.jp. This stunning re-creation of an Edo-era mansion (incorporating huge beams from an old sake brewery) serves unforgettable tofu-based *kaiseki*-style cuisine. Book well ahead, especially for dinner (at least a month in advance). Lunches start at ¥5500, dinner from ¥8400. Akebanebashi Station. Daily 11am–8pm.

Shibuya

The following restaurants are marked on the map on p.129.

Céléb de Tomato 2-2-2 Shibuya, Shibuya-ku ⓣ03/5766 3005, ⓦwww.celeb-de-tomato.com. There's a craze in Tokyo for tomato-based cuisine, and this mini-chain, with branches also in Akasaka, Daiken'yama and near Omotesandō, is a great place to catch the bug. They display the ruby and yellow fruits like polished jewels and make lovely dishes and drinks from them, including a lip-smacking range of freshly squeezed juices – ideal for a gourmet bloody mary. Shibuya Station. Daily 11am–9pm.

Kaikaya 開花屋 23-7 Maruyama-chō, Shibuya-ku ⓣ03/3770-0878, ⓦwww.kaikaya.com. A convivial, smokey *izakaya*, specializing in fish and plastered with snaps of carousing customers. There's an English menu and the friendly staff are happy to advise on what to order; expect the bill to be about ¥4000. Shinsen Station. Daily 11.30am–2pm & 6–11.30pm.

Kurage 1-19-8 Jin'nan, Shibuya-ku ⓣ03/3463-3323, ⓦwww.jellyfish.bz/shop/tokyo/kurage/kurage.html. Artists and art lovers hang out at this appealingly trendy café after visiting the exhibitions at the adjoining gallery of Tokyo Wonder Site. The deli lunch costs ¥840 for rice, soup and a choice of three tasty Japanese dishes. The photo menu helps with ordering. Shibuya Station. Daily 10am–11.30pm.

Nagi Shokudō なぎ食堂 15-10-103 Uguisandanichō, Shibuya-ku ⓣ050-1043-7751, ⓦnagi-shokudo.jugem.jp. Vegan café that has built a strong following for its supremely tasty food (curries and the like, with most dishes under ¥1000) – so good that even meat eaters approve. Part of the appeal is that they display quirky art and sell hip zines and indie CDs as well as offering a good selection of alcohol. Shibuya Station. Mon–Sat noon–4pm, 6–10.30pm.

Rāmen Nagiラーメン凪 1-3-1 Higashi, Shibuya-ku ⓣ03/3499-0390, ⓦn-nagi.com/index.php. At this crazy busy gourmet rāmen joint, the waiter will give you a choice of how soft or hard you'd like their superb noodles cooked; they're then served in a rich pork broth and topped with delicious pork slices and a heap of chopped scallions. There's also a branch in Shinjuku's Golden Gai – perfect for late-night cravings since it's open until 4am (2am on Sunday). Shibuya Station. Mon–Sat 11.30am–4pm, 5pm–3am, Sun noon–9pm.

Sushi Ouchi 2-8-4 Shibuya, Shibuya-ku, ⓣ03/3407-3543. Few Tokyo *sushi-ya* ensure they use the best organic produce and fish caught only from the wild. This one does, and the pleasant surprise is that it's very affordable – you can eat well for under ¥3000. The interior creates a warm, farmhouse feel. Shibuya Station. Mon–Sat noon–1.30pm, 5.30–9.30pm.

Shinjuku and around

All the following restaurants are marked on the map on pp.124–125.

Angkor Wat アンコールワット 1-38-13 Yoyogi, Shibuya-ku ⓣ03/3370-3019. Tokyo's best Cambodian restaurant. There are set meals, but you can also tell the waiters your budget and let them bring you a suitable selection of dishes (allow ¥2000 per head). The sweet spicy salads, soups and vegetable rolls are all excellent. It's a 5min walk west of Yoyogi Station; look for the pottery elephant outside the entrance on a side street. Yoyogi Station. Mon–Fri 11am–2pm & 5–11pm, Sat & Sun 5–11pm.

J.S. Burgers Café 3F 4-1-7 Shinjuku, Shinjuku-ku ⓣ03/5367-0185, ⓦjsb-cafe.jp. A fab range of home-made chunky burgers, hot dogs and sandwiches is served at this retro-styled café atop the Journal Standard boutique. Lunch deals (¥880–980) include the self-serve salad bar. There's another branch in Shibuya. Shinjuku Station. Mon–Sat 11.30am–10pm, Sat & Sun 11am–9pm.

Nakajima 中島 3-32-5 Shinjuku, Shinjuku-ku ⓣ03/3356-7962, ⓦshinjuku-nakajima.com. At lunch all the delicious dishes served here are made with sardines – they're a bargain at around ¥1000 per course meal. At night, you can sample the chef's Kansai *kapo* style of cooking (similar to *kaiseki ryōri*, see p.50) which has earned him a Michelin star. Shinjuku Station. Mon–Sat 11.30am–1.45pm, 5.30–8.30pm.

Shanghai Xiaochi 上海小吃 1-3-10 Kabukichō, Shinjuku-ku ⓣ03/3232-5909, ⓦshanghai-xiaochi.com. Don't be scared of entering this dingy alley to find this Chinese restaurant presided over by the ebullient Reiko. The authentic dishes here, such as clams in soy sauce with *age-pan* (fried bread), really hit the spot. Shinjuku Station. Mon–Sat 6pm–5am, Sun until 2am.

Shinjuku Pojanmacha 新宿ポジャンマチャ 1-2-3 Hyakunin-chō, Shinjuku-ku ⓣ03/3200-8683, ⓦwww.s-pocha.com; see map, pp.88–89. Also known simply as "Pocha", this rustic *yakiniku* (grilled meat) restaurant is painted with colourful cartoon scenes of Korean life. It serves the rice beer *makgeolli* the traditional way in big wooden bowls with a ladle. If you like the drink, also check out the bar Maccoli (see p.154) further down the same street. Shin-Okubo Station. Mon–Thurs noon–midnight, Fri–Sun until 3am.

Suzuya Kabukichō Ichibangai-iriguchi, Shinjuku-ku ⓣ03/3209-4408, ⓦwww.toncya-suzuya.co.jp.

Little appears to have changed at this famous *tonkatsu* restaurant since it opened just after World War II. Their twist on the breaded pork cutlet dish (from ¥1200) is to serve it *ochazuke* style – you poor green tea over the meat and rice to make a kind of savoury porridge. Shinjuku Station.

 **Tsunahachi** つな八 3-31-8 Shinjuku, Shinjuku-ku ⓣ03/3352-1012. The main branch of the famous tempura restaurant almost always has a queue, though you're likely to get seated quickly if you settle for the upstairs rooms away from the frying action, or the non-smoking section. Everything is freshly made, and even the ¥1300 set menu (including soup, rice and pickles) will fill you up. Shinjuku Station. Daily 11.15am–10pm.

Tsukiji and Odaiba

The following restaurants are marked on the map on pp.88–89.

The Canteen 1F The Soho, 2-7-4 Aomi, Koto-ku ⓣ03/5530-0261. Cosy up in the booths and flip through the glossy mags while enjoying Japanese home cooking at this hip office complex on the Odaiba waterfront. Fune-no-Kagakukan station. Mon–Fri 9am–10pm, Sat 10am–6pm.

Sushi Bun 鮨文 5 Tsukiji, Chūō-ku ⓣ03/3541-3860, ⓦwww.sushibun.com. One of the most *gaijin*-friendly options among the rows of sushi stalls within Tsukiji fish market, with an English menu and sets starting from ¥2100. You won't regret spending ¥3675 for their top-quality ten-piece selection, which includes creamy *uni* (sea urchin). ⓦwww.tsukijigourmet.or.jp gives full details of the market's other sushi stall. Tsukijishijō Station. Mon–Sat 6am–2.30pm, but closed during occasional market holidays.

Sushi-zanmai Honkan すしざんまい本館 4-11-9 Tsukiji Chūō-ku ⓣ03/3541-1117, ⓦwww.kiyomura.co.jp. This is the main branch of a popular chain of sushi restaurants run by Kimura Kiyoshi, the self-proclaimed "King of Tuna". It's the best *kaiten-zushi* operation in the area and is open around the clock. A meal is likely to cost ¥2500 per person. Tsukiji Station. Daily 24 hours.

Ueno and around

All the following restaurants are marked on the map on p.118.

Hantei はん亭 2-12-15 Nezu, Bunkyō-ku ⓣ03/3828-1440, ⓦwww.hantei.co.jp. Stylish dining in a beautiful, three-storey wooden house. There's only one dish, *kushiage* – deep-fried skewers of crunchy seafood, meat and vegetables with special dipping sauces – served in combination plates, six at a time: ¥2900 for the first plate (plus two appetizers), ¥1400 thereafter, until you say stop. Nezu Station. Tues–Sat noon–2.30pm & 5–10pm, Sun noon–2.30pm & 4–9.30pm.

Musashino 2-8-11 Ueno, Bunkyō-ku ⓣ03/3831-1672. Ueno is famed for its *tonkatsu*, worth trying at this traditional restaurant behind bamboo screens and pot plants, where prices for a big thick slab that melts in the mouth are reasonable. Choose between standard *rōsu* (loin cutlet) or fillet, at around ¥1500 including soup, rice and pickles. They also serve fried prawns (*ebi-fry*). Ueno-Hirokōji Station. Daily 11.30am–9pm.

Unagi Ben-kei 鰻弁慶 4-5-10 Ueno, Bunkyō-ku ⓣ03/3831-2283. Eel (*unagi*) is the order of the day at this informal, traditional restaurant on three floors. Try their *unagi donburi* lunchtime set for a taster (¥1400; Mon–Fri). They also do well-priced *sukiyaki* meals (¥1700 for lunch), as well as *shabu-shabu*, tempura and sashimi. English menu available. Ueno Station. Daily 11.30am–9.50pm, closed third Mon of month.

Cafés and teahouses

You can hardly walk a block of central Tokyo without passing a chain **café** – as often as not a *Starbucks*, although local operations, such as *Doutor* and *Tully's*, are also pretty common. For all the convenience and keen prices of these operations, don't miss sampling at least one of the many other individual cafés, sometimes called **kissaten**, where the emphasis is on service and creating an interesting, relaxing space, often using quirky decor and unusual music. Many of the cafés listed below are good places for snacks and light meals, and some offer alcohol, too, making them an alternative to bars.

Teahouses are becoming more popular as the health benefits of tea are promoted. The *Imperial* (ⓣ03/3504-1111, see map, p.104), *New Ōtani* (ⓣ03/3265-1111, see map, p.111) and *Ōkura* hotels (see p.111), all have traditional rooms in which tea ceremonies are regularly held; expect to pay around ¥1000. Better is the tea ceremony at *Andon Ryokan* (see p.98; guests/non-guests ¥500/1000) where the whole process is properly explained in English and you get to practise making tea yourself. There are also teahouses with pretty settings in Hama Rikyū Onshi Teien (p.136), Shinjuku Gyoen (p.126) and Happōen (p.134).

Asakusa

The following are marked on the map on p.114.

Gallery éf 2-19-18 Kaminarimon, Taitō-ku ⓣ03/3841-0442, ⓦwww.gallery-ef.com. This café-bar is one of Asakusa's trendiest hangouts, with decent lunch sets for around ¥900. To the rear is a *kura* (traditional storehouse) that provides an intimate venue for an eclectic mix of exhibitions, concerts and performance art. Asakusa Station. Daily except Tues: café and gallery 11am–7pm, bar 6pm–midnight.

Kappabashi Coffee 3-25-11 Nishi-Asakusa, Taitō-ku ⓣ03/5828-0308. Chunky wooden furniture offset against white walls lends an unexpectedly sophisticated air to this café at the north end of Kappabashi-dōgu-gai, serving a big choice of coffees, teas, infusions and juices, as well as cakes and light meals. Iriya station. Daily 10am–7pm.

Nagaya Sabō 長屋茶房 1-6-5 Bunka, Sumida-ku ⓣ03/3611-1821, ⓦwww.tenshinan.jp/café. Hand-roasted and ground beans are used for the coffee at this charming café and traditional teahouse in the neighbourhood of the Tokyo Sky Tree (see p.116). Try their silky smooth cheesecake flavoured with a hint of sake. Oshiage Station. Daily except Thurs noon–7pm.

Ebisu and Daikan'yama

See map on pp.132–133.

Kissa Ginza 1-3-9 Ebisu-Minami, Shibuya-ku ⓣ03/3710-7320, ⓦwww15.ocn.ne.jp/~ginza. Retro cool 1960s style *kissaten* by day, groovy DJ bar complete with glitter ball by night. Ebisu Station. Daily 10am–late.

Sedona La Fuente Daikan'yama, 11-1 Sarugaku-chō, Shibuya-ku ⓣ03/6416-3838, ⓦwww.sedona-daikanyama.com. Enjoy hanging with hipsters at this spacious café/bar combined with a boutique selling both new and used clothes. Lunch is a great deal at ¥680. Daikan'yama Station. Daily 11.30am–11pm.

Purr-fect cafés

The latest hit in Tokyo's polymorphous *kissaten* culture is **cat cafés**, offering quality time with well-groomed pedigree felines. Particularly popular among young women and dating couples, they are relaxing places, offering the pleasures of pet ownership without the commitment. A great example is **Calico** (キャリコ; 6F, 1-16-2 Kabukichō, Shinjuku-ku; ⓣ03/6457-6387, ⓦcafecalico.com, daily 11am–6.30am; see map, pp.124–125; Shinjuku Station) where ¥600 gets you thirty minutes of quality cat time. There are English instructions on the house rules, and inexpensive drinks and food starting at ¥150 for a coffee and ¥300 for a dubious-looking but delicious-tasting fondant chocolate biscuit. Another option is **Nekorobi** (ねころび; 3F Tact TO Bldg, 1-28-1 Higashi-Ikebukuro, Toshima-ku; ⓣ03/6228-0646, www.nekorobi.jp; daily 11am–11pm; see map, p.122; Ikebukuro Station), where you have to spend at least ¥1000 per visit, including drinks.

Ginza and around

The following appear on the map on p.104.

100% Chocolate Café 2-4-16 Kyōbashi, Chūō-ku ⓣ03/3237-3184, ⓦwww.choco-cafe.jp. Indulge your inner chocoholic at this café with 56 varieties to choose from. A mug of their hot chocolate should satisfy the most hardcore addict, or try the chocolate fondue (served with pretzels and café au lait). The decor takes up the theme, from the "chocolate library" lining one wall to the chocolate-bar ceiling. Kyōbashi Station; Mon–Fri 8am–8pm, Sat & Sun 11am–7pm.

Cha Ginza 5-5-6 Ginza, Chiyoda-ku ⓣ03/3571-1211, ⓦwww.uogashi-meicha.co.jp. This teahouse run by a tea wholesaler offers a modern take on the business of sipping *sencha*. Two cups of the refreshing green stuff plus a traditional sweet will cost you ¥500. The rooftop area, where they serve *macha*, is the place to hang out with those Tokyo ladies who make shopping a career. Ginza Station. Tues–Sun 11am–7pm.

Henri Charpentier 2-8-20 Ginza, Chūō-ku ⓣ03/3562-2721, ⓦwww.henri-charpentier.com. Discover the ultimate in Tokyo patisseries on the ground floor and a *salon de thé* below. Here you can enjoy crêpe suzette flambéed at your table, as well as a range of gold-flecked chocolate morsels and seasonal specialities, to go with a choice of coffees, teas and infusions. Don't leave before checking out the toilets – if you can find them. Ginza-Itchōme Station. Daily 11am–9pm.

Higashiya Ginza 2F Pola Ginza, 1-7-7 Ginza, Chūō-ku ⓣ03/3538-3230, ⓦwww.higashiya.com. Ginza Station. Tearoom and shop known for its relaxing atmosphere and delicious assortments of seasonal Japanese sweets. Another branch, *Ori Higashiya*, is located inside the Le Bain shopping complex in Nishi-Azabu (see map, p.111). Daily 11am–9pm.

Harajuku and Aoyama

Unless mentioned otherwise, the following appear on the map on p.129.

Andersens 5-1-26 Aoyama, Minato-ku ⓣ03/3407-3333. This outpost of Hiroshima's famed Swedish-style bakery has an excellent range of pastries and sandwiches and a reasonably priced sit-down café – a good option for breakfast and lunch. Omotesandō Station. Daily 7am–10pm.

Café Escalator 3F Houei Bldg, 2-31-3 Jingūmae, Shibuya-ku ⓣ03-5775-1315, ⓦshop.escalator.co.jp/café; see map, pp.88–89. Could this be the perfect Tokyo café-bar? The home-baked goods, light meals and craft beer selection set it apart, as does the attached record store selling a wonderful collection of indie LPs, CDs and cassette tapes (remember them?) from around the world. Harajuku or Meiji-Jingūmae Station. Mon–Fri noon–10pm, Sat & Sun 1–7pm.

Hideaway 202 3-20-1 Jingumae, Shibuya-ku ⓣ03-5410 2343, ⓦwww.treehouse.jp/hideaway. A cool travellers' vibe pervades this café-bar tucked away in a quiet corner of Harajuku near Design Festa. There's a tree growing through it and you can climb up to their treehouse to enjoy drinks or the tasty curries. Harajuku or Meiji-Jingūmae Station. Daily except Wed 11am–10pm.

Yoku Moku ヨックモック 5-3-3 Minami-Aoyama, Minato-ku ⓣ03/5485-3330, ⓦwww.yokumoku.co.jp. Hushed café with courtyard tables, in tune with the elegant sensibilities of the designer boutiques of Omotesandō. There's also a shop selling nicely packaged cakes, chocolates and confectionery, including its famous wafer-thin rolled biscuits. Omotesandō Station. Daily 10am–7pm.

Ikebukuro

The following appear on the map on p.122.

Café Pause 2-14-12 Minami-Ikebukuro, Toshima-ku ⓣ03/5950-6117, ⓦwww.geocities.jp/cafe_pause_ikebukuro. Hip gallery café in the backstreets east of the station, hosting regular exhibitions, parties and events, including monthly get-togethers for local designers and artists. It's also a relaxed place for a quiet coffee. Ikebukuro Station. Mon–Sat noon–11pm, Sun noon–10pm.

Zozoi 3-22-6 Nishi-Ikebukuro, Toshima-ku ⓣ03/5396-6676. Sheepskin-covered stools and a statue of a Beefeater are part of the eclectic decor at this amiable café offering home-made cakes and biscuits, with a pleasant view onto the park. Ikebukuro Station. Mon–Sat noon–10pm, Sun noon–9.30pm.

Kanda, Akihabara and around

The following are marked on the map on p.108.

Gundam Café 1-1 Kanda-Hanaokacho, Chiyoda-ku ⓣ03/3251-0078, ⓦwww.g-café.jp. Set up as something out of the incredibly popular anime series *Mobile Suit Gundam*, with a futuristic sci-fi interior and costumed staff to match. During the day, it operates as a café, then as a bar from 5pm. Mon–Fri 10am–10pm, Sat 8.30am–11pm, Sun 8.30am–9.20pm.

Mai:lish 2F FH Kowa Square, 3-6-2 Soto-Kanda, Chiyoda-ku ⓣ03/5289-7310, ⓦwww.mailish.jp. Akiba is packed with all kinds of maid cafés where the cosplaying (the act of donning costumes) staff will treat you like a prince (or princess). Some are nice, some decidedly naughty and other just plain bizarre. This long-running one offers a relaxed atmosphere, and is a good example of what the maid café experience is all about. Suehirochō Station. Daily 11am–10pm.

Mu'u Mu'u Diner & 100% Kona Coffee 3-14-3 Kanda-Ogawamachi, Chiyoda-ku ⓣ03/3518-6787. Swap the dusty books of Jimbōchō for a sunny Hawaiian vibe at this café-restaurant, decked out with surfboards and hibiscus garlands. Besides Hawaiian Kona coffee, it also serves Kona beer as well as meals. Jimbōchō Station. Daily 11am–11pm.

Popopure 2F 1-8-10 Soto-Kanda, Chiyoda-ku ⓣ03/3252-8599, ⓦwww.popopure.com. A maid café where you'll find a few non-Japanese, English-speaking maids – a rarity – and where, for ¥1500, you can voice an anime character, and then get it dubbed on a DVD. Daily 11am–9pm.

Roppongi and Azabu-Jūban

The following appear on the map on p.111.

Eat More Greens 2-2-5 Azabu-Jūban, Minato-ku ⓣ03/3798-3191, ⓦwww.eatmoregreens.jp. Taking its inspiration from urban US vegetarian cafés and bakeries is this appealing place, featuring good organic food, random wood furniture and a street-side terrace. Mon–Fri 11am–11pm, Sat & Sun 9am–11pm.

Kina 貴奈 3-13-12 Roppongi, Minato-ku ⓣ03/3478-1678, ⓦwww.kina-roppongi.com. A great survivor of the 1970s Roppongi scene is this spectacular *kissaten*. The fab retro lamps and comfy sofas have to be seen to be believed. Apart from coffee, they do a great tea and traditional Japanese sweet set for ¥800. Roppongi Station. Mon–Fri noon–11pm, Sat noon–9pm.

Shibuya

The following appear on the map on p.129.

Lion ライオン 2-19-13 Dōgenzaka, Shibuya-ku ⓣ03/3461-6858, ⓦlion.main.jp. Not the place for animated conversations, this *Addams* Family-style institution amid the love hotels of Dōgenzaka is where salarymen and pensioners come to appreciate classical music with their coffee. Seats are arranged to face a pair of enormous speakers. Shibuya Station. Daily 11am–10.30pm.

LOHB 4F Likes Bldg, 2-3-1 Dōgenzaka, Shibuya-ku ⓣ03/3464 1919 ⓦwww.sunroyalgroup.co.jp. The acronym stands for Likes Oriental Health and Beauty, which is meaningless – all you need to know is that this café-bar provides a first-class view across the mesmerizing Shibuya crossing. Shibuya Station. Daily 11.30am–midnight.

Shinjuku and around

Unless otherwise stated, see map on pp.124–125.

Dada Café 5-23-10 Yoyogi, Shibuya-ku ⓣ03/3350-2245, ⓦwww.religare.biz. In an artfully renovated old Japanese house tucked off the main street, this delightful café/bar and gallery is a quiet refuge for drinks or a simple meal. Yoyogi Station. Mon–Thurs 11.30am–10pm, Fri & Sat until 10.30pm.

Tajimaya 但馬屋 Omoide Yokochō, Shinjuku-ku ⓣ03/3342-0881, ⓦwww.shinjuku.or.jp/tajimaya. Appearing way too gentile for this ragged set of dining and drinking alleys is this elegant café serving quality drinks and cakes on a pretty assortment of china. Shinjuku Station. Daily 10am–10.30pm.

Nightlife and entertainment

Tokyo's **nightlife** and **entertainment** options run the gamut from grand theatres and multiplex cinemas to broom-cupboard bars and live music venues (known as "live houses"). The distinction between restaurants, bars and clubs in the city's *sakariba* ("lively places"), such as Ginza, Shibuya or Shinjuku, is hazy, with many places offering a range of entertainment depending on the evening or customers' spirits.

On the cultural side, you can sample all of Japan's major **performing arts**, from stately **nō**, the oldest in its theatrical repertoire, to **Butō**, the country's unique contribution to contemporary dance. If you only have the energy, or budget, for one cultural experience, save it for **kabuki** (see p.788). Information about these and other performances is available in the English-language press and from the TICs (see p.92). Tickets are available from theatres and ticket agencies (see p.167).

Bars and izakaya

Tokyo is a drinkers' paradise with a vast range of bars and *izakaya* (gastro-pubs) serving practically any brand of booze from around the world as well as local tipples such as sake, *shōchū* (a vodka-like spirit) and award-winning Japanese whiskey. The recent poor economy has also put downward pressure on prices – you'll find many no-frills *izakaya* touting how cheap their drinks and food are. **Opening hours** are generally daily from 5pm to around midnight Sunday to Thursday, extended until 4am on Friday and Saturday; the reviews give specific hours where they depart from the norm.

Roppongi easily has Tokyo's greatest concentration of **foreigner-friendly gaijin bars**, but note that many are closed on Sunday. If there's live music anywhere you'll often pay for it through higher drinks prices or a cover charge. Some regular bars also have cover charges (and *izakaya* almost always do, though you'll usually get a small snack served with your first drink), but there's plenty of choice among those that don't, so always check the deal before buying your drink.

For **bars with a view**, towering major hotels such as the *New Ōtani*, the *Park Hyatt* and the *Cerulean Tower Tōkyū Hotel* are hard to beat, though you'll need to dress up not to feel out of place amid the gold-card crowd.

Manga cafés

If you're into computer games, manga or anime, then dropping by one of Tokyo's many **manga cafés** is a great way to pass some time. These places, open 24 hours, also act as cybercafés and unofficial crash-pads for those who have missed their last trains home. One of the best is **Gera Gera** (Ⓦwww.geragera.co.jp), with its main branch in Shinjuku (B1 Remina Building, 3-17-4 Shinjuku, Shinjuku-ku; Ⓣ03/3350-5692). Pay ¥280 for 30 minutes (then ¥80/10min) Monday to Thursday and slightly more Friday to Sunday; consume all the soft drinks you want for an extra ¥180. They also have package rates (three hours in the day or five hours at night for ¥1080) and comfy double-seat sofas – good if you fancy chilling out while watching a film. **Bagus** (Ⓦwww.bagus-comic.com) is another major chain, which also has English-language DVDs; you can find branches in Shibuya (6F, 28-6 Udagawa-chō, Shibuya-ku), in the same building as HMV Records, and Roppongi (12F, Roi Building, 5-5-1 Roppongi). Rates start at ¥420 for the first hour and then ¥100 for every extra 15 minute. From 11pm to 8am you can park yourself here for six hours for ¥1260, drinks included.

Asakusa and Ueno

The following places are marked on the maps on p.114 and p.118.

Bar Six 2-34-3 Asakusa, Taitō-ku ⓣ03/5806-1181, ⓦwww.amusemuseum.com. Sophisticated watering hole on the sixth floor of the Amuse Museum complex (see p.115) offering an amazing view of Asakusa, and especially Sensō-ji, which is illuminated at night. A stand-up outdoor terrace also surrounds the bar. Asakusa Station.

Cuzn 1-41-8 Asakusa, Taitō-ku ⓣ03/3842-3223, ⓦwww.cuzn.jp. Tucked away on a quiet street behind the Rox department store, this friendly, rustic bar has a comfy sofa area, free internet access and sometimes shows international football matches on its big screen. The food's not bad, either. Asakusa Station.

Gin Maku Roku 銀幕ロック 2F 1-41-5 Asakusa ⓣ03/5828-6969. An intimate, backstreet bar full of colourful characters and festooned with homely bric-a-brac. A stage is squeezed in for the occasional live gig (around ¥1000), which could feature anything from rockabilly to Balkan gypsy music. Asakusa (Tsukuba Express railway) or Tawaramachi stations.

Kamiya 1-1-1 Asakusa, Taitō-ku ⓣ03/3841-5400. Established in 1880, this was Tokyo's first Western-style bar. It's famous for its *Denki Bran* ("electric brandy" – a mix of gin, wine, Curaçao and brandy), invented in 1883. It's a potent tipple, though they also make a "weaker" version at fifteen percent alcohol. The ground floor is the liveliest and most informal; pay for your first round of food and drinks at the cash desk as you enter. Closed Tues. Asakusa Station.

Shinsuke 3-31-5 Yushima, Bunkyo-ku ⓣ03/3832-0469. Bookings are essential for this venerable *izakaya* where they only serve one good brand of sake in sweet or dry versions, hot or cold. The sashimi is excellent as are their famous sardine rissoles (*iwashi no ganseki*). Yushima Station. Mon–Sat 5–9.30pm.

The Warrior Celt 3F, Ito Building, 6-9-22 Ueno ⓣ03/3836-8588, ⓦwww.warriorcelt.jp. Things can get pretty raucous at this good-time bar in the thick of Ueno. What awaits you there are a fine range of beers, a nightly happy hour (5–7pm), live bands and, last but not least, ladies' night on Thurs (cocktails ¥500). Ueno Station.

Ebisu

The following places are marked on the map on pp.132–133.

Buri 1-14-1 Ebisu-nishi, Shibuya-ku ⓣ03/3496-7744, ⓦwww.buri-group.com. Chilled one-cup sake is the speciality at this trendy *tachnomiya* (standing only bar) that's one of the best in town. They serve a good range of *yakitori* and other tasty nibbles. Ebisu Station.

Ebisu Dagashi Bar えびす駄菓子バー 1-13-7 Ebisu-Nishi, Shibuya-ku ⓣ03/5458-5150,

Karaoke bars and boxes

Legend has it that **karaoke**, literally translated as "empty orchestra", was invented by an Ōsaka record store manager in the early 1970s. Today the mainstay of this ¥1 trillion business is the **karaoke box**, a building packed with comfy booths kitted out with a karaoke system. Rental of these boxes is by the hour and they have proved particularly popular with youngsters, women and families.

If you fancy flexing your vocal cords, branches of the major karaoke box operator **Karaoke-kan** (カラオケ館; ⓦwww.karaokekan.jp) are liberally peppered across the capital: rooms 601 and 602 in their 30-8 Udagawachō branch in Shibuya (see map, p.129) were featured in the film *Lost in Translation*. An hour of karaoke here costs from ¥1000 with drinks and snacks extra. Catering to foreigners are **Fiesta** (3F Crest Roppongi Building, 7-9-3 Roppongi, Minato-ku; ⓣ03/5410-3008, ⓦwww.fiesta-roppongi.com; ¥3500 including three drinks; Roppongi Station; see map, p.111; Mon 7pm–midnight, Tues–Sat until 5am) and the long-running **Smash Hits** (B1F M2 Hiro-o Building, 5-2-26 Hiro-o, Shibuya-ku; ⓣ03/3444-0432, ⓦwww.smashhits.jp; ¥3000 including two drinks; Hiro-o Station; see map, pp.132–133; Mon–Sat 7pm–3am), both of which offer thousands of songs in English as well as several other languages.

Ⓦ www.dagashi-bar.com. Sweet-toothed customers will be in heaven at this fun *izakaya* festooned with baskets of all-you-can-eat sweets that patrons can dip into for free. Check the website for details of other Tokyo branches. Ebisu Station.

Enjoy House! 2F Daikan'yama Techno Building, 2-9-9 Ebisu-Nishi, Shibuya-ku Ⓣ 03/5489-1591. The unique look here is zebra prints, low velour sofas, red lace curtains and tons of shiny disco balls. It gets busy at weekends, with a suitably young and attitude-free crowd. Ebisu Station.

Footnik 1F Asahi Building, 1-11-2 Ebisu, Shibuya-ku Ⓣ 03/5795-0144, Ⓦ www.footnik.net. A bar devoted to football that has a game or two on the big screen every night, and reasonable food. For popular matches you'll have to pay an entry charge. Ebisu Station.

What the Dickens! 4F Roob 6 Building, 1-13-3 Ebisu-Nishi, Shibuya-ku Ⓣ 03/3780-2099. This old English pub, complete with beams and candle-lit nooks, has draught Guinness and Bass pale ale, plus live music nightly. The food – a range of hearty pies served with potatoes, veggies and bread – promises to warm the cockles of a homesick heart. Ebisu Station.

Ginza and around

The following places are marked on the map on p.104.

300 Bar B1F Fazenda Building, 5-9-11 Ginza, Chūō-ku Ⓣ 03/3572-6300, Ⓦ www.300bar.com. The bargain-basement face of Ginza is this unusually large standing-only bar, where all food and drinks are ¥315. Though you have to buy two food/drink tickets to enter, it's still cheap by Tokyo standards. Ginza Station.

Dry Dock 3-25-10 Shimbashi, Minato-ku Ⓣ 03/5777-4755, Ⓦ www.shimbashi-dry-dock.com. Cosy craft-beer bar with a nautical theme, nestling beneath the train tracks. It's no smoking inside and patrons often spill outside as they enjoy the regularly changing menu of Japanese and overseas microbrews. No food is served on Saturday. Shimbashi Station. Mon–Fri 5pm–midnight, Sat until 10pm.

Kagaya B1F Hanasada Building, 2-15-12 Shinbashi, Minato-ku Ⓣ 03/3591-2347, Ⓦ www1.ocn.ne.jp/~kagayayy/main.html. English-speaking Mark runs this simple basement bar as if he's hosting an 8-year-old's birthday party with alcohol. Around ¥3000 will get you plenty of drink, food and side-splittingly silly games. Phone ahead to check it's open and make a reservation. Shinbashi Station. Closed Sun.

Lion 7-9-20 Ginza, Chūō-ku Ⓣ 03/3571-2590. Opened in 1934, this beer hall, flagship of the Sapporo chain, is a rather baronial place with its dark tiles and mock wood-panelling. There are sausages, sauerkraut and other German snacks on offer alongside international pub fare, and a restaurant upstairs. You'll find other branches scattered around Tokyo. Ginza Station.

Marunouchi House 7F Shin-Marunouchi Bldg, 1-5-1 Marunouchi, Chiyoda-ku Ⓦ www.marunouchi-house.com. The best thing about the funky open-plan space here, which comprises seven different restaurants and bars, is that you can take your drinks out on to the broad, wrap-around terrace for great views of Tokyo Station and towards the Imperial Palace. Check out *Limelight*, a homage to Japan's local neighbourhood "snack" bars (cover charge at night). Tokyo Station. Daily 11pm–4am (until 11pm Sun & hols).

Shin Hi No Moto 新日の基 1-chōme Yūrakuchō, Chiyoda-ku Ⓣ 03/3214-8012. A lively, English-owned *izakaya* under the tracks just south of Yūrakuchō Station. It's one of the few places to try the excellent Sapporo Red Star beer, or cheap, strong *shōchū* (grain liquor). The seafood and vegetables come fresh from Tsukiji. Reservations are recommended, especially at weeekends. Yūrakuchō or Hibiya stations.

Harajuku, Aoyama and Shibuya

The following places are marked on the map on p.129.

Coins Bar 300 B1 Noa Shibuya Building, 36-2 Udagawa-chō, Shibuya-ku Ⓣ 03/3463-3039. No need to ask about the prices at this spacious, stylish basement bar: it's ¥315 for any drink or plate of food. A top choice if you're on a budget. Shibuya Station.

CoZmo's Café & Bar 1-6-3 Shibuya, Shibuya-ku Ⓣ 03/3407-5166, Ⓦ www.cozmoscafe.com. Taking its lead from *The Pink Cow* around the corner, this appealing café-bar hosts an interesting series of events, detailed on their website. Shibuya Station. Closed Mon.

Fujiya Honten 富士屋本点 2-3 Sakuragaoka-chō, Shibuya-ku Ⓣ 03/3461-2128. No frills, good-value standing bar with some fifty different bottles of wines on offer from as little as ¥1600, and a dozen by the glass at ¥400. Shibuya Station.

Summer Beer Gardens

Helping to mitigate Tokyo's sticky summers are the **outdoor beer gardens** that sprout up around the city from late May through to early September, typically on the roofs of department stores such as Tobu in Ikebukuro, or in street-level gardens and plazas.

A couple of the best beer gardens can be found in Meiji-Jingū's Outer Garden close to Shinanomachi Station. **Forest Beer Garden** (ⓣ03/5411-3715; Mon–Fri 5–9pm, Sat & Sun noon–9pm; see map, pp.88–89) fronts the Meiji Kinenkan wedding hall and offers an all-you-can-eat-and-drink deal (*tabi/nomi-hodai*) for men/women ¥4000/3800. Inside the Meiji Kinenkan itself is **Sekirei** (ⓣ03/3746-7723, ⓦwww.meijikinenkan.gr.jp; Mon–Sat 4.30–10.30pm, Sun 5.30–10.30pm), overlooking a floodlit garden where classical Japanese dance (*Nihon Buyō*) is performed nightly at around 8pm.

Among the roof-top options, a standout is **Kudan Kaikan** (九段会館; 1-6-5 Kudan-minami, Chiyoda-ku; ⓣ03/3261-5521, ⓦwww.kudankaikan.or.jp; Kudanshita Station. Mon–Fri 5–10pm, Sat & Sun 5–9pm; see map, p.101), which also has *tabi/nomi-hodai* deals for ¥4000 and great views towards the Imperial Palace.

Harajuku Taproom 2F 1-20-13 Jingūmae, Shibuya-ku ⓣ03/6438 0450, ⓦbairdbeer.com. Just off Takeshita-dori is this real ale nirvana serving beers from Baird Brewing Company in Numazu. The interior feels like a woodsy country pub. There's also a Naka-Meguro Taproom (ⓣ03/5768-3025; see map, p.132–133). Harajuku Station. Mon–Fri 5pm–midnight, Sat & Sun noon–midnight.

Legato 15F E-Space Tower, 3-6 Maruyama-cho, Shibuya-ku ⓣ03/5784-2121. A fancy Italian restaurant with a bar offering a jaw-dropping floor-to-ceiling view over Shibuya from fifteen floors up. Shibuya Station. Mon–Fri 11.30am–2pm, daily 5.30pm–4am.

Montoak 6-1-9 Jingūmae, Shibuya-ku ⓣ03/5468-5928, ⓦwww.montoak.com. Snooty but stylish café-bar, with a glass facade facing onto Harajuku's famous shopping street. DJs create a suitable loungey vibe, and there's sometimes live music at weekends. Meiji-Jingūmae Station. Daily 10am–11pm.

The Pink Cow Villa Moderna, 1-3-18 Shibuya, Shibuya-ku ⓣ03/3406-5597, ⓦwww.thepinkcow.com. There's always something interesting going on – book readings, comedy improv, art classes – at this funky haven for local artists and writers, run by the friendly Tracey. It stocks a good range of imported wines and serves tasty Tex-Mex style food. Shibuya Station.

Stand-S 37-16 Udagawachō, Shibuya-ku ⓣ03-5452-0277, ⓦstand-s.blogspot.com. Going for the bar-meets-Swedish sauna look in a big pine-clad way is this groovy *tachinomiya* with a DJ and curious drink options such as Mojito Beer (tastier than it sounds). Shibuya Station. Daily 6pm–midnight.

Ikebukuro

The following places are marked on the map on p.122.

300B 2F 3-29-4 Nishi-Ikebukuro ⓣ03/3986-3005. This big *izakaya*, popular with a young crowd for its cheap prices and good food, is a good option if you're in the area and are looking to unwind. Ikebukuro Station.

The Black Sheep B1, 1-7-12 Higashi-Ikebukuro, Toshima-ku ⓣ03/3987-2289. Lively, friendly bar behind BIC Camera, with a choice of seven beers on tap and great fish and chips. On Wednesdays there's a special deal on draught pale ale and weekends feature live music. Ikebukuro Station.

Roppongi and around

The following are marked on the map on p.111.

A971 Café Tokyo Midtown, 9-7-3 Akasaka, Minato-ku ⓣ03/5413-7340, ⓦwww.a971.com. This relaxed café-bar and restaurant at the front of the Midtown complex, with mid-twentieth-century modernist furnishings, has proved itself a popular hangout. Roppongi Station. Mon–Thurs 10am–2am, Fri & Sat until 5am, Sun until midnight.

Heartland 1F Roppongi Hills West Walk, 6-10-1 Roppongi, Minato-ku ⓣ03/5772-7600, ⓦwww.heartland.jp. It's often standing room only at this trendy but friendly bar in the northwest corner of Roppongi Hills. Sink one of their trademark green bottled beers and watch arty videos on the panoramic plasma screen behind the bar.

Hobgoblin Aoba Roppongi Building, 3-16-33 Roppongi, Minato-ku ⓣ03/3568-1280, ⓦwww.hobgoblin.jp. British microbrewery Wychwood serves its fine ales at this spacious bar that's a Roppongi classic – which means you'll be part of a very boozy, noisy crowd of *gaijin* at weekends and on nights when there are major sports matches on the big-screen TVs. Its real strength is the very comforting English pub-style food, including pies and fish and chips. See the website for details of branches in Shibuya and Akasaka. Roppongi Station.

Shinjuku

The following places are marked on the map on pp.124–125. Also see p.126 for recommended bars in Golden Gai and p.156 for gay-friendly bars in Shinjuku Nichōme.

Albatross アルバトロス 1-2-11 Nishi-Shinjuku, Shinjuku-ku ⓣ03/3342-5758. Groovy *nomiya* (with a tiny art gallery upstairs) set amid the pint-sized bars and *yakitori* joints of Omoide Yokochō. They're welcoming of foreigners and, with a cover charge of ¥300 and drinks at ¥500, you're not going to get stung. A highlight is the rooftop seating area with splendid views of the area. Shinjuku Station.

Maccoli Bar 1-5-24 Hyakunin-chō, Shinjuku-ku ⓣ03/6380-3487, ⓦwww.hongmi.jp. Makgeolli (also spelled maccoli) is a Korean rice beer that tastes like drinking yoghurt with a mild alcoholic kick. It's a drink with a growing following in Japan and you can sample it straight or mixed with various fruits at this friendly and stylish bar tucked away in Koreatown. Shin-Okubo Station.

Vagabond 1-4-20 Nishi-Shinjuku, Shinjuku-ku ⓣ03/3348-9109. A local institution, with jazz pianists who tinkle the ivories every night and colourful art plastered on the walls. There's a ¥500 cover charge. Also has a downstairs bar, without live music. Shinjuku Station.

Clubs

A few **clubs** seem to weather the vagaries of fashion, but generally the ever-eclectic Tokyo scene seems to be moving away from major events in big spaces to more intimate nights in smaller bars where a DJ may have a particular following. Consult the media before heading out to see what's on; most major clubs post their schedule on their websites. **iFlyer** (ⓦwww.iflyer.jp) provides a good overview of the scene, and you'll also find discounts on **cover charges** here, which is typically ¥2500–3000 including your first drink. Most clubs don't really get going until after 11pm, especially at weekends, and the majority stay open until around 4am.

Ageha Studio Coast, 2-2-10 Shin-kiba, Kōtō-ku ⓣ03/5534-2525, ⓦwww.ageha.com; see map, pp.88–89. Giant warehouse space housing an ultra-cool mega-club with several dance areas, an outdoor pool, a body-shaking sound system and a roster of high-profile events. It's way across Tokyo Bay, but there's a free shuttle bus here from the east side of Shibuya Station – check the website for details and turn up at least half an hour before you want to depart to get a ticket to board the bus. Shin-Kiba Station.

Club Asia 1-8 Maruyamachō, Shibuya-ku ⓣ03/5458-2551, ⓦwww.clubasia.co.jp; see map, p.129. Another mainstay of the clubbing scene, with the emphasis on techno and trance nights. It's in the heart of the Dōgenzaka love-hotel district and is a popular place for one-off events such as gigs by visiting DJs. Shibuya Station.

Eleven 1-10-11 Nishi-Azabu, Minato-ku ⓣ03/5775-6206, ⓦwww.go-to-eleven.com; see map, p.111.Once the home of famed club *Yellow*, this basement space has been reborn as the practically identical *Eleven*, offering mainly techno and house on Friday and Saturdays. Check their schedule for openings on other nights which vary. Roppongi Station.

Microcosmos 2-23-12 Dōgenzaka, Shibuya-ku ⓣ03/5784-5496, ⓦwww.microcosmos-tokyo.com. see map, p.129. A good example of a new breed of Tokyo club, this chic café by day morphs into an appealing dance space at night with a relaxed vibe. Shibuya Station.

Muse 1-13-3 Nishi-Azabu, Minato-ku ⓣ03/5467-1188, ⓦwww.muse-web.com; see map, p.111. A pick-up joint, but an imaginatively designed one,

PechaKucha nights

What started as an idea for an event to help bring people to a new "creative art" venue called *SuperDeluxe* (see below) has gone viral to become a worldwide phenomenon in over three hundred cities. Co-created by Tokyo-based architects Astrid Klein and Mark Dytham (KDa), the idea was to come up with a presentation format – twenty images shown for twenty seconds each – that would help keep things going at a fast pace. *PechaKucha* nights (the name is taken from the Japanese for "chit chat") ended up being the perfect platform for Tokyo's young and upcoming creators who, before then, would never have had a place to share their works in front of an audience that numbers in the hundreds. Presentation topics are eclectic, so expect surprises, and you'll find a fun crowd made up of the city's "creative class"; for details of when they're on see ⓦwww.pecha-kucha.org.

spread across three floors, with lots of interesting little rooms to explore or canoodle in. There's also a groovy dance area at the back, which gets packed at weekends. Roppongi Station.

328 (San Ni Pa) 3-24-20 Nishi-Azabu, Minato-ku ⓣ03/3401-4968, ⓦwww.3-2-8.jp; see map, p.111. An eternal fixture of the Tokyo club scene is this basement DJ bar; the entrance is next to the police box at Nishi-Azabu crossing. Tends to be more laidback than other late-night Roppongi options, but can still get packed out at weekends. Roppongi Station.

Super Deluxe B1, 3-1-25 Nishi-Azabu, Minato-ku ⓣ03/5412-0515, ⓦwww.super-deluxe.com; see map, p.111. Billing itself as a place for "thinking, drinking people" *Super Deluxe* hosts a brilliant range of arty events – anything from live music performances and CD launches to the monthly *PechaKucha* nights (see above), a showcase for Tokyo's creative community. Roppongi Station.

Unit Za-House Building, 1-34-17 Ebisu-Nishi, Shibuya-ku ⓣ03/5459-8630, ⓦwww.unit-tokyo.com; see map, pp.132–133. DJ events are mixed with concerts by an interesting selection of artists and bands at this cool three-floor club, café and lounge bar. Ebisu or Daikan'yama stations.

Warehouse702 B1F Fukuo Building, 1-4-5 Azabu-Juban, Minato-ku ⓣ03/6230-0343, ⓦwww.warehouse702.com; see map, p.111. The latest incarnation for this spacious basement space that switches names every couple of years. The gay-friendly night, *The Ring*, is held here as well as a range of other club nights. Azabu-Jūban Station.

Womb 2-16 Maruyama-chō, Shibuya-ku ⓣ03/5459-0039, ⓦwww.womb.co.jp; see map, p.129. A mega-club with a spacious dance floor, enormous glitter ball and a pleasant chill-out space. Top DJs work the decks, and at big events it can get very crowded. Shibuya Station.

Gay bars and clubs

The **Shinjuku-Ni-chōme** (新宿二丁目) area is the epicentre of Tokyo's gay world and is packed with hundreds of small bars and clubs; this is as cruisey as it gets for Japan and can be a fun, relaxed place for people of any sexual persuasion to hang out. Even so, compared with London, San Francisco or Sydney, Tokyo's scene is a low-key affair. Dates for your diary include the **Tokyo Gay and Lesbian Parade** (ⓦparade.tokyo-pride.org), which has been known to attract three thousand marchers and many more spectators, but has yet to establish itself as an annual event; and the hugely popular **Nichōme Matsuri** (penultimate weekend in August), with drag shows and dancing in the street. The annual **Tokyo International Lesbian and Gay Video and Film Festival** (ⓦwww.tokyo-lgff.org), usually held in late July, is also a permanent fixture of Tokyo's gay calendar, showing films from around the world with English subtitles.

Apart from the venues listed below, most of which are in Nichōme (the closest subway station is Shinjuku-Sanchōme), there are several gay and lesbian events held at clubs around the city, including *Ageha* and *Warehouse* – see the club listings opposite. Unless otherwise mentioned, these bars are marked on the Shinjuku map on pp.124–125.

Advocates Café アドボケイツカフェ Seventh Tenka Building, 2-18-1 Shinjuku, Shinjuku-ku ⓣ03/3358-3988, ⓦwww. advocates -cafe.com. It's a rare night out in Nichōme that doesn't include drinks here. The bar itself is barely big enough for ten people, which is why scores of patrons hang out on the street corner outside, creating a block party atmosphere.

Arty Farty アーティファーティ 2F Dai 33 Kyutei Building, 2-11-7 Shinjuku, Shinjuku-ku ⓣ03/5362-9720, ⓦwww.arty-farty.net. As the night draws on, this bar with a small dancefloor becomes packed with an up-for-fun crowd. The music is generally handbag house and disco. They also have a newer annexe around the corner at 2-14-11 Shinjuku.

Chestnut & Squirrel 3F Dai-ishi Building, 3-7-5 Shibuya, Shibuya-ku ⓣ090/9834-4842 ⓦ2d-k.oops.jp/cs/cs.html; see map, p.129. Friendly lesbian bar night, with a mixed crowd of Japanese and *gaijin*. Cunningly, the name translates into Japanese as *kuri-to-risu* (clitoris, geddit?). There's also the lesbian bar *Liam* here Tues, Fri & Sun, when there's a ¥1000 cover charge including one drink. Shibuya Station. Wed 7pm–midnight.

Dragon Menドラゴン 2-11-4 Shinjuku, Shinjuku-ku ⓣ03/3341-0606. Good music and strong drinks served by tattooed *gaijin* waiters clad only in underpants account for the popularity of this huge (by Nichōme standards) bar.

GB B1 Business Hotel T Building, 2-12-3 Shinjuku, Shinjuku-ku ⓣ03/3352-8972. Only for the boys, this smoky basement bar is a long-standing pick-up joint for Japanese and foreigners. The initials stand for *Ginger Bar*, after Hollywood icon *Ginger Rogers*. Women are only allowed in at Halloween.

Kaevi 4F Yoshino Bldg, 17-10 Sakuragaoka-chō, Shibuya-ku ⓣ090/3462-9200, ⓦkeivi.com; see map, pp.132–133. This friendly bar is worth a look if only to enjoy its extraordinary decor that includes deer antlers, fairy lights, Japanese dolls and tropical fish. There's a map on the wall (and on their website) detailing other gay and lesbian bars in the area. Shibuya Station.

Kinswomyn キンズウイメン 3F Dai-ichi Tenka Building, 2-15-10 Shinjuku, Shinjuku-ku ⓣ03/3354-8720. Tokyo's top women-only bar, which has a more relaxed ambience (and lower prices) than many of Nichōme's other lesbian haunts. Drinks are ¥700 and there's no cover charge. Shinjuku-Sanchōme Station.

Townhouse Tokyo タウンハウス東京 6F Koruteire Ginza Building, 1-11-5 Shimbashi, Minato-ku ⓣ03/3289-8558, ⓦwww13.ocn.ne.jp/~t_h_tky; see map, p.104. Spacious men-only bar, welcoming to *gaijin*. Be prepared for a spot of karaoke with the salaryman clientele, the sweetener being that all drinks are ¥500. Shimbashi Station. Mon–Fri 6pm–2am, Sat 4pm–midnight.

Live music, film and cultural events

As far as the **performing arts** are concerned, there's always plenty going on in Tokyo. If you don't understand Japanese, colourful extravaganzas like **Takarazuka** or the more traditional **kabuki** are the easiest to enjoy, but even the notoriously difficult **nō** or **Butō** are worth seeing once. Tokyo may not seem the obvious place to seek out a classical concert or Shakespeare play, but major international **orchestras** and **theatre** groups often pass through on their tours, and the city now boasts several top-class performance halls.

Live music

Tokyo has a wide range of **live-music venues** offering everything from mellow jazz to hard rock and indie pop. "Live houses" are little more than a pub with a small stage, but the city also has several prestigious venues, such as the Tokyo Dome (affectionately known as the "Big Egg"), where big international acts play when they're in town. Check the websites listed below for performance schedules.

Grab any chance you have to see a concert of **traditional Japanese music**, played on instruments such as the *shakuhachi* (flute), the *shamisen* (a kind of lute that is laid on the ground) and the *taiko* (drum). Top groups to watch out for include Kodō (see p.280), the theatrical drumming ensemble that occasionally plays Tokyo venues. Live *shamisen* playing can be enjoyed at the restaurant *Waentei-Kikko* in Asakusa (see p.141).

Billboard Live Tokyo 4F Garden Terrace, Tokyo Midtown 9-7-4 Akasaka, Minato-ku ⓣ03/3405-1133, ⓦwww.billboard-live.com; see map, p.111. A relatively intimate space at which everyone on the three levels gets a great view of the stage, on which mainstream pop, rock and lounge music artists play. Roppongi Station.

Blue Note 6-3-16 Minami-Aoyama, Minato-ku ⓣ03/5485-0088, ⓦwww.bluenote.co.jp; see map, p.129. Tokyo's premier jazz venue, part of the international chain, attracts world-class performers. Entry for shows at 7pm and 9pm is from ¥6000 (including one drink), depending on the acts. Omotesandō Station. Closed Sun.

Blues Alley Japan B1 Hotel Wing International Meguro, 1-3-14 Meguro, Meguro-ku ⓣ03/5496-4381, ⓦwww.bluesalley.co.jp; see map, pp.132–133. This offshoot of the Washington DC blues and jazz club occupies a small basement space near the station. Admission charges depend on the act. Meguro Station.

Club Citta 4-1-26 Ogawachō, Kawasaki ⓣ044/246-8888, ⓦclubcitta.co.jp. A major live-music venue, in Kawasaki around 20min from central Tokyo, hosting a variety of local and international rock bands. It's part of an entertainment and shopping complex called La Cittadella. Kawasaki Station.

Club Quattro 5F Quattro Building, 32-13 Udagawa-chō, Shibuya-ku ⓣ03/3477-8750, ⓦwww.club-quattro.com; see map, p.129. Intimate rock-music venue which tends to showcase up-and-coming bands and artists, though it also plays host to well-known local and international acts. Shibuya Station.

Crocodile 6-18-8 Jingūmae, Shibuya-ku ⓣ03/3499-5205; see map, p.129. You'll find everything from samba to blues and reggae, as well as monthly stand-up comedy nights, at this long-running basement space on Meiji-dōri, between Harajuku and Shibuya. Cover charge ¥2000–3000. Meiji-jingūmae or Shibuya stations.

Cyber B1, 1-43-14 Higashi-Ikebukuro ⓣ03/3985-5844, ⓦwww.ikebukuro-cyber.com; see map, p.122. Dark, throbbing rock dive among the soaplands and love hotels north of Ikebukuro Station. The bands are variable. Concerts start as early as 4.30pm. Entry ¥2000 and up. Ikebukuro Station.

JZ Brat 2F *Cerulean Tower Tōkyū Hotel*, 26-1 Sakuragaoka-chō, Shibuya-ku ⓣ03/5728-0168, ⓦwww.jzbrat.com; see map, pp.132–133. Swanky jazz club in Shibuya's top hotel, with a spacious contemporary design and a respectable line-up of artists. Sets at 7.30pm and 9.30pm. Music charge from ¥3000. Shibuya Station.

Liquid Room 3-16-6 Higashi, Shibuya-ku ⓣ03/5464-0800, ⓦwww.liquidroom.net; see map, pp.132–133. A live music venue with some DJ events, usually held in their *Liquid Loft* space. Also on the premises is the *Time Out* café-bar. Ebisu Station.

Shinjuku Pit Inn B1F Accord Shinjuku Building, 2-12-4 Shinjuku, Shinjuku-ku ⓣ03/3354-2024, ⓦwww.pit-inn.com see map, pp.124–125. Serious, long-standing jazz club which has been the launch platform for many top Japanese performers and which also attracts overseas acts. Daytime shows are 2.30pm–5pm (¥1300); evening sessions kick off at 8pm (¥3000). Shinjuku Station.

Classical music, opera and ballet

Tokyo is well served with **Western classical music** venues and there are usually one or two concerts every week, either by one of Tokyo's several resident symphony orchestras or by a visiting group, as well as occasional performances of **opera** and **ballet**.

Major performance halls include Tokyo Opera City (ⓣ03/5353-9999, ⓦwww.operacity.jp) and the New National Theatre (see p.159), both in Shinjuku, and Yūrakuchō's Tokyo International Forum (ⓣ03/5221-9000, ⓦwww.t-i-forum.or.jp). Among the older auditoria, Suntory Hall (ⓣ03/3505-1001, ⓦwww.suntory.co.jp/suntoryhall), in Akasaka's Ark Hills, NHK Hall (ⓣ03/3465-1751), south of Meiji-kōen, the Orchard Hall (ⓣ03/3477-9111, ⓦwww.bunkamura.co.jp), in Shibuya's Bunkamura, and Tokyo Bunka Kaikan (ⓣ03/3828-2111, ⓦwww.t-bunka.jp) in Ueno are the main venues. Tickets are available from the relevant box office or a ticket agency (see p.167). A limited number of cheap seats (sometimes half-price) often go on sale on the day of the performance – be prepared to queue if you want these.

Cinema

Average ticket prices are around ¥1800 (¥2500 for *shitei-seki* – reserved seats), but you can cut the cost by buying discount tickets in advance from a **ticket agency**,

Major Tokyo festivals

Whenever you visit Tokyo, the chances are there'll be a **festival** (*matsuri*) taking place somewhere in the city. The tourist information centres can provide comprehensive lists of events in and around Tokyo, or check in the English press for what's on. Below is a review of the city's biggest festivals (see pp.57–59 for more about nationwide celebrations). Note that dates may change, so be sure to double-check before setting out.

January 1: Ganjitsu (or Gantan) The first shrine visit of the year (*hatsu-mōde*) draws the crowds to Meiji-jingū, Hie-jinja, Kanda Myōjin and other city shrines. Performances of traditional dance and music take place at Yasukuni-jinja. National holiday.

January 6: Dezomeshiki At Tokyo Big Sight in Odaiba, firemen in Edo-period costume pull off dazzling stunts atop long bamboo ladders.

Second Monday in January: Momoteshiki Archery contest and other ancient rituals at Meiji-jingū to celebrate "Coming-of-Age Day". A good time to spot colourful kimono, here and at other shrines.

Febuary 3 or 4: Setsubun The last day of winter is celebrated with a bean-scattering ceremony to drive away evil. The liveliest festivities take place at Sensō-ji, Kanda Myōjin, Zōjō-ji and Hie-jinja.

Early April: Hanami Cherry-blossom-viewing parties get into their stride. The best displays are at Chidorigafuchi Park and nearby Yasukuni-jinja, Aoyoma Cemetery, Ueno-kōen and Sumida-kōen.

Mid-May: Kanda Matsuri One of Tokyo's top three festivals, taking place in odd-numbered years at Kanda Myōjin, during which people in Heian-period costume escort eighty gilded *mikoshi* through the streets.

Third weekend in May: Sanja Matsuri Tokyo's most rumbustious annual bash, when over one hundred *mikoshi* are jostled through the streets of Asakusa, accompanied by lion dancers, geisha and musicians.

Mid-June: Sannō Matsuri In even-numbered years the last of the big three festivals (after Kanda and Sanja) takes place, focusing on colourful processions of *mikoshi* through Akasaka.

Early July: Yasukuni Matsuri The four-night summer festival at Tokyo's most controversial shrine is well worth attending for its jovial parades, *Obon* dances and festoons of lanterns.

Late July and August: Hanabi Taikai The summer skies explode with thousands of fireworks, harking back to traditional "river-opening" ceremonies. The Sumida-gawa display is the most spectacular (view it from riverboats or Asakusa's Sumida-kōen on the last Sat in July), but those in Edogawa, Tamagawa, Arakawa and Harumi come close.

Mid-August: Fukagawa Matsuri Every three years Tomioka Hachiman-gū, a shrine in Fukugawa, east across the Sumida-gawa from central Tokyo, hosts the city's wettest festival, when spectators throw buckets of water over a hundred *mikoshi* being carried through the streets. The next will take place in 2011.

Mid-November: Tori-no-ichi Fairs selling *kumade*, bamboo rakes decorated with lucky charms, are held at shrines on "rooster days", according to the zodiacal calendar. The main fair is at Ōtori-jinja (Iriya Station).

November 15: Shichi-go-san Children aged 3, 5 and 7 don traditional garb to visit the shrines, particularly Meiji-jingū, Hie-jinja and Yasukuni-jinja.

Late November: Tokyo International Film Festival (Ⓦwww.tiff-jp.net) One of the world's top competitive film festivals, with a focus on Japanese and Asian releases. The main venues for the week-long festival are the cinemas in Roppongi Hills and Shibuya's Bunkamura, though screenings take place at halls and cinemas throughout the city.

December 17–19: Hagoita-ichi The build-up to New Year begins with a battledore fair outside Asakusa's Sensō-ji temple.

such as Ticket Saison and Pia (see p.167). On "Cinema Day", generally the first Wednesday of the month, tickets at all cinemas cost only ¥1000. Hollywood blockbusters predominate, and fims are generally subtitled in Japanese, not dubbed. Listings are published every Friday in *The Japan Times* and *Metropolis*, which also has reviews as well as maps locating all the major cinemas.

Major releases are shown at multiplexes such as Mediage, Aqua City Odaiba (Ⓣ03/5531-7878, Ⓦwww.cinema-mediage.com); and Toho Cinemas Roppongi Hills (Ⓣ03/5775-6090, Ⓦwww.tohotheater.jp), which has all-night screenings every weekend and shows Japanese and foreign art-house films, often with English subtitles.

For **art-house and independent** releases, head for Iwanami Hall (Ⓣ03/3262-5252, Ⓦwww.iwanami-hall.com) in Jimbochō, Uplink (Ⓣ03/6825-5502, Ⓦwww.uplink.co.jp) or Cinema Rise (Ⓣ03/3464-0052, Ⓦwww.cinemarise.com) in Shibuya. Shin-Bungei-za (Ⓣ03/3971-9422, Ⓦwww.shin-bungeiza.com), in Ikebukuro, offers a revolving schedule of double bills, as does Waseda Shochiku (Ⓣ03/3200-8968, Ⓦwww.wasedashochiku.co.jp) in Takadanobaba.

To see Japanese films with English subtitles, the main place to head is the National Film Centre (Ⓣ03/3272-8600, Ⓦwww.momat.go.jp), near Kyōbashi Subway Station, a real treasure-trove for film lovers, with a gallery showing film-related exhibitions and two small cinemas showing old films from their vast archive of mostly Japanese classics. Cinemart (Ⓣ03/5413-7711, Ⓦwww.cinemart.co.jp) in Roppongi has a Global Recognition Series (Ⓦwww.gr-movie.jp) screening Japanese films that have gained kudos at overseas festivals with English subtitles. The biggest of the city's several **film festivals** is the **Tokyo International Film Festival** (see opposite for details).

Contemporary dance

The highly expressive dance form **butō** (or butoh; see p.789) shouldn't be missed if you're interested in modern dance. Among the more active venues are Azabu Die Pratze (Ⓣ03/5545-1385, Ⓦwww.geocities.jp/kagurara2000) near Tokyo Tower, Plan B (Ⓣ03/3384-2051, Ⓦwww.i10x.com/planb), near Nakano-Fujimichō Station, and Kochūten (Ⓣ0422/21-4984, Ⓦwww.dairakudakan.com), the studio of legendary butō troupe Dairakudakan near Kichijoji Station.

Contemporary theatre

One of the most entertaining popular theatrical experiences you can have in Tokyo is **Takarazuka** (see p.496), the all-singing, all-dancing, all-female revue staged at the Takarazuka Theatre (Ⓣ03/5251-2001, Ⓦkageki.hankyu.co.jp), just north of the *Imperial Hotel*.

The most accessible of Tokyo's **avant-garde theatres** include Tiny Alice (Ⓣ03/3354-7307, Ⓦwww.tinyalice.net), near Shinjuku-Sanchōme Station; Setagaya Public Theatre (Ⓣ03/5432-1526, Ⓦwww.setagaya-ac.or.jp/sept), near Sangenjaya Station; and Theater Cocoon (Ⓣ03/3477-9999, Ⓦwww.bunkamura.co.jp) in Shibuya's Bunkamura arts centre. All are known for hosting collaborative works featuring Japanese and international groups.

Overseas theatre companies often appear at the Tokyo Globe (Ⓣ03/3366-4020, Ⓦwww.tglobe.net) or Shinjuku's New National Theatre (Ⓣ03/5352-9999, Ⓦwww.nntt.jac.go.jp), though seats sell out months in advance for the bigger names. Easier to come by are tickets for the expat theatre group **Tokyo International Players** (Ⓦwww.tokyoplayers.org). Their website lists their productions, mounted four or five times a year. The city's major theatre event **Festival/Tokyo** (Ⓦfestival-tokyo.jp), held annually October to December, also showcases a diverse range of productions with performances both from Japanese and international troupes.

Au revoir Kabuki-za

In May 2010 **Kabuki-za**, Tokyo's oldest and largest theatre devoted to kabuki, was destroyed to make way for a new tower block and a more modern stage and performance hall. A kabuki theatre has stood on this Ginza site since 1889; its last guise was a 1950s restoration of the florid 1924 version of the building (the original burned down in 1921). Until the new theatre reopens in 2013, regular performances of kabuki will take place at Shinbashi Enbujō (see below).

Traditional theatre

While Kabuki-za is being rebuilt (see above), Tokyo's main venue for **kabuki** performances is **Shimbashi Enbujō** (新橋演舞場; ⓣ03/3541-2600, ⓦwww.shochiku.co.jp/play/enbujyo) in Ginza. The other main venue for kabuki is **Kokuritsu Gekijō** (ⓣ03/3230-3000, ⓦwww.ntj.jac.go.jp), the national theatre west of the Imperial Palace near Hanzōmon Station, which holds a varied programme of traditional theatre and music. There are also performances here three or four times a year of **bunraku** (see p.788). English-language programmes and earphones are available, and tickets start at ¥1500 for kabuki and ¥4500 for *bunraku*.

There are several schools of **nō** (see p.787) in Tokyo, each with their own theatre, including the **National Nō Theatre** (ⓣ03/3230-3000, ⓦwww.ntj.jac.go.jp), five minutes' walk from Sendagaya Station, and Shibuya's **Kanze Nō-gakudō** (ⓣ03/3469-5241, ⓦwww.kanze.com). Also in Shibuya, the Cerulean Tower Nō Theatre (ⓣ03/3477-6412, ⓦwww.ceruleantower.com), in the basement of the *Cerulean Tower* hotel (see p.99), hosts nō performances.

Shopping

Cruising the boutiques and fashion malls while toting a couple of designer-label carrier bags is such a part of Tokyo life that it's hard not to get caught up in the general enthusiasm. There are shops to suit every taste and budget, from funky **fashion boutiques** and swanky **department stores** to some great **crafts shops** and wonderfully quirky **souvenir** and **novelty stores**. Antique and bargain hunters shouldn't miss out on a visit to one of the city's **flea markets**, which if nothing else can turn up some unusual curios.

In general, store **opening hours** are from 10am or 11am to 7pm or 8pm. Most shops close one day a week, not always on Sunday, and smaller places often shut on public holidays. Though it's always worth asking, few shops take **credit cards** and fewer still accept cards issued abroad, so make sure you have plenty of cash. More information can be found online at ⓦwww.tokyo-bazaar.com.

Ginza remains the preserve of the city's conservative elegance, and is still regarded as Tokyo's traditional shopping centre. **Shinjuku** has long put up a strong challenge, with an abundance of department stores and malls offering everything under one roof. Young and funky, **Shibuya** and **Harajuku** are probably the most enjoyable places to shop: even if you don't want to buy, the passing fashion parade doesn't get much better. The haute couture boutiques along **Omotesandō** and in nearby **Aoyama** provide a more rarefied shopping experience, while, of the northern districts, **Asakusa** figures highly for its plethora of small, traditional crafts shops. **Akihabara** has long been known as "electric town" thanks to its myriad hi-tech emporia, but is also now the go-to location for manga and anime. **Ueno** is famous for the lively Ameyoko-chō market. Also worth a look are the shopping malls out at **Odaiba**, such as Decks Tokyo Beach, with its retro 1960s-style arcade, and Venus Fort, a mall devoted to the tastes of young women, as well as the huge mall Urban Dock LaLaport Toyosu.

Department stores

Although they're not as popular as they once were, Tokyo's massive **department stores** are likely to have almost anything you're looking for. They're also more likely to have English-speaking staff and a duty-free service than smaller shops, though prices tend to be slightly above average. Seasonal sales can offer great bargains. Unless otherwise mentioned, they are open daily 10am to 8pm.

Isetan 3-14-1 Shinjuku, Shinjuku-ku ⓣ03/3352-1111, ⓦwww.isetan.co.jp; see map, pp.124–125. One of the city's best department stores, with an emphasis on well-designed local goods and a reputation for promoting up-and-coming fashion designers. Their daily opening ceremony, with staff bowing as you walk through the store, is worth attending. Shinjuku-Sanchōme Station.

Matsuzakaya 3-29-5 Ueno, Taitō-ku ⓣ03/3832-1111, ⓦwww.matsuzakaya.co.jp/ueno; see map, p.118. Three-hundred-year-old store based with its main branch in Ueno and another in Ginza (6-10-1 Ginza, Chūō-ku ⓣ03/3572-1111; Ginza Station; see map, p.104). Ueno-Hirokōji Station.

Mitsukoshi 1-4-1 Nihombashi-Muromachi, Chūō-ku ⓣ03/3241-3311, ⓦwww.mitsukoshi.co.jp; see map, p.104. Tokyo's most prestigious and oldest department store is elegant, spacious and renowned for its high-quality merchandise. Designer boutiques and more contemporary fashions are concentrated in the southerly *shin-kan* ("new building"). Another major branch is at 4-6-16 Ginza, Chūō-ku (ⓣ03/3562-1111; Ginza Station; see map, p.104). Mitsukoshimae Station.

Muji B1-2F Shinjuku Piccadilly, 3-15-15 Shinjuku, Shinjuku-ku ⓣ03-5367-2710; see map, pp.124–125; one of the newest and biggest branches of this Internationally famous "no-brand" houseware, life style and fashion chain company offering a wide range of their goods induding classy Muji Labo fashon range, which you'll also find at their store in Tokyo Midtown.

Seibu 1-28-1 Minami-Ikebukuro, Toshima-ku ⓣ03/3981-0111, ⓦwww.seibu.jp; see map, p.122. Sprawling department store with a reputation for innovation, especially in its homeware store Loft and funky fashion offshoot Parco, whose racks and shelves groan with the latest must-have items. There's also a cluster of Seibu, Loft and Parco stores in Shibuya. Ikebukuro Station. Mon–Sat 10am–9pm, Sun 10am–8pm.

Takashimaya 2-4-1 Nihombashi, Chūō-ku ⓣ03/3211-4111, ⓦwww.takashimaya.co.jp; see map, p.104. Like Mitsukoshi, Takashimaya has a long and illustrious past, a great food hall and stocks a very broad range of goods, though it appeals to decidedly conservative tastes. There's a huge branch in Shinjuku at Takashimaya Times Square (5-24-2 Sendagaya, Shibuya-ku ⓣ03/5361-1111; see map, pp.124–125). Nihombashi Station.

Tōbu 1-1-25 Nishi-Ikebukuro, Toshima-ku ⓣ03/3981-2211, ⓦwww.tobu-dept.jp; see map, p.122. One of Japan's largest and most confusing department stores, Tōbu is mainly of interest for its excellent basement food halls so large they occupy two floors. Ikebukuro Station.

Tōkyū 2-24-1 Dōgenzaka, Shibuya-ku ⓣ03/3477-3111, ⓦwww.tokyu-dept.co.jp; see map, p.129. Top dog in the Shibuya department store stakes, the main store specializes in designer fashions and interior goods, while the branch at the station has a good food floor. Shibuya Station.

Tokyo's wholesale districts

Tokyo's **wholesale districts** can be fun to poke around. Best known to visitors are the fish and fresh produce market **Tsukiji** (p.135) and the "Kitchenware Town" **Kappabashi** (p.116). Other ones to search out include the area around **Edo-dōri**, north of Asakusabashi Station, which specializes in traditional Japanese dolls. Further north along Edo-dōri, the area called **Kuramae** is "Toy Town", where shops sell fireworks, fancy goods and decorations, as well as cheap plastic toys. **Bakurochō** and **Yokoyamachō** are the textile districts where you'll also find shops selling cheap clothes.

Tōkyū Hands 12-10 Udagawachō, Shibuya-ku ⓣ03/5489-5111, ⓦwww.tokyu-hands.co.jp; see map, p.129. If you've got a craft hobby, home project or are an outdoors type, this brilliant shop is sure to stock what you need and many items you never even knew you needed until now. It's also a great place to look for quirky souvenirs. Branches also in Ikebukuro (see map, p.122) and at Takashimaya Times Square (see map, pp.124–125). Shibuya Station.

Fashion

The best of Tokyo's **boutiques** and **fashion stores** rate among some of the most exciting in the world, with a sense of interior design more akin to chic art galleries or trendy clubs than mere peddlers of clothes. The city's epicentre of clothing chic is **Omotesandō**, where the roll call of brands – Gucci, Louis Vuitton, Armani, Chanel, Issey Miyaki and Yohji Yamamoto – reads like a who's who of fashion. **Daikan'yama**, **Naka-Meguro** and **Shimo-Kitazawa** are also worth browsing around – the fashion shops in the last two areas are slightly cheaper and less precious. Unless otherwise mentioned, stores are open daily 11am to 8pm.

Bapexclusive 5-5-8 Minami-Aoyama, Minato-ku ⓣ03/3407-2145, ⓦwww.bape.com; see map, p.129. The hip streetwear brand has a string of boutiques all over Aoyama and Harajuku, of which this is the main showroom. Also check out the super-cute Bape Kids store (3-29-11 Jingūmae) with its playpool filled with multicoloured rubber bananas. One of their T-shirts will set you back at least ¥6000. Omotesandō Station.

Comme des Garçons 5-2-1 Minami-Aoyama, Minato-ku ⓣ03/3406-3951; see map, p.129. More like an art gallery than a clothes shop, this beautiful store offers a suitable setting for high fashion for men and women by renowned designer Rei Kawakubo. Omotesandō Station.

Evisu 1-1-5 Kami-Meguro, Meguro-ku ⓣ03/3710-1999, ⓦwww.evisu.com; see map, pp.132–133. Main branch of the ultra-trendy Japanese jeans designer. Stock up here on shirts, T-shirts, sweaters and a full range of accessories. Ebisu Station. Daily noon–8pm.

Five Foxes' Store 3-26-6 Shinjuku, Shinjuku-ku ⓣ03/5367-5551; see map, pp.124–125. Stylish showcase for Comme ça de Mode, a bright and affordable unisex clothing brand. Shinjuku Station. Mon–Sat 11am–11pm, Sun 11am–8pm.

Hysteric Glamour 5-5-3 Minami-Aoyama, Minato-ku ⓣ03/6419-3899, ⓦwww.hystericglamour.jp; see map, p.129. The premier outlet for this fun, retro-kitsch Americana label that is one of Japan's leading youth brands. They also have a shop at 6-23-2 Jingūmae (Meiji-Jingūmae). Omotesandō Station.

Laforet 1-11-6 Jingūmae, Shibuya-ku ⓣ03/3475-0411, ⓦwww.laforet.ne.jp/index.html; see map, p.129. This pioneering "fashion building" is packed with boutiques catering to the fickle tastes of Harajuku's teenage shopping mavens. Wander through and catch the *zeitgeist*. Meiji-jingūmae Station.

Okura おくら 20-11 Sarugaku-chō, Shibuya-ku ⓣ03/3461-8511, ⓦwww.hrm.co.jp/okura/index.html; see map, p.132–133. Youthful boutique specializing in indigo-dyed traditional and contemporary Japanese fashions, from jeans and T-shirts to kimono and *tabi* socks. Daikan'yama Station.

Kimono fashion

Bargain pre-loved kimono are best found at flea markets (see p.164) and shops such as **Oriental Bazaar** (p.163) and **Chicago** (6-31-21 Jingumae, Shibuya-ku; ⓣ03/3409-5017; see map, p.129). **Gallery Kawano** (ギャラリー 川野; 102 Flats-Omotesandō, 4-4-9 Jingūmae, Shibuya-ku; ⓣ03/3470-3305; see map, p.129) has a very good selection of antique kimono alongside more affordable secondhand ones.

Designers are starting to use kimono fabrics to create more modern fashions either for a full garment (ie shirts and ties) or for patchwork detail on jeans, bags and T-shirts. Among the places to check out such creations are **Do Justice** (1-23-1 Kami-Meguro, Meguro-ku ⓣ03/5724-3223, ⓦwww.dojustice.jp; see map, pp.132–133); **Gouk** (B1F, 3-27-23 Jingūmae, Shibuya-ku ⓣ03/3408-7256, ⓦwww.gouk.jp; see map, p.129); and **Momo** (6-1-6-107 Minami-Aoyama, Minato-ku ⓣ03/3406-4738, ⓦwww.aoyama-momo.net; see map.129).

Sou Sou 2F From-1st Bldg, 5-3-10 Minami-Aoyama, Minato-ku ⓣ03/3407-7877, ⓦwww.sousou.co.jp; see map, p.129. Named after the Japanese saying *sō sō*, meaning "I agree with you", this range of modern design shoes and clothes based on traditional forms, such as split toe *tabi*, is eminently agreeable. There's an outlet also in Venus Fort (see p.138). Omotesandō Station.

Tsumori Chisato 4-21-25 Minami-Aoyama, Minato-ku ⓣ03/3423-5170; see map, p.129. Girlish streetwear that captures the Harajuku look but with better tailoring, materials and attention to detail. Omotesandō Station.

UnderCover 5-3 Minami-Aoyama, Minato-ku ⓣ03/3407-1232; see map, p.129. Jun Takahashi's UnderCover brand of clothing isn't so underground any more, but remains youthful and eclectic. Omotesandō Station. Daily 10am–8.30pm.

Uniqlo 5-7-7 Ginza, Chūō-ku ⓣ03/3569-6781, ⓦwww.uniqlo.co.jp; see map, p.104. Proving inexpensive can still be cool is this successful local brand. This is their flagship Tokyo store, while their Harajuku branch (6-10-8 Jingūmae, Shibuya-ku ⓣ03/5468-7313; see map, p.129) specializes in T-shirts. There are other branches in all Tokyo's main shopping centres. Ginza Station. Daily 11am–9pm.

Arts and crafts

The largest concentration of traditional **arts and crafts** shops is in Asakusa, though a few beautiful Edo-era shops still survive in the thick of Ginza and Nihombashi. Also worth checking out are the shops attached to major **museums**; in particular, head to the Japan Folk Crafts Museum (see p.131) near Shibuya for the best of traditional souvenirs; and Roppongi Hills' MAM (see p.112) and the NACT (see p.110) for great contemporary design goods. Listed below are a few of the more interesting places to head for.

Bengara べんがら 1-35-6 Asakusa, Taitō-ku ⓣ03/3841-6613, ⓦwww.bengara.com; see map, p.114. The best place to look for *noren*, the split curtain that can be seen hanging outside every traditional shop or restaurant. Asakusa Station. Daily 10am–6pm; closed third Sun of month.

Beniya べにや民芸店 42-7-1 Minami-Aoyama, Minato-ku ⓣ03/5875-3261, ⓦbeniya.m78.com; see map, pp.88–89. Stocks one of Tokyo's best ranges of folk crafts (*mingei*) from around the country. They also stage craft exhibitions – check their website for details. Aoyama Itchōme Station. Thurs–Tues 10am–7pm.

The Cover Nippon 3F Galleria, Tokyo Midtown, 9-7-3 Akasaka, Minato-ku ⓣ03/5413-0658, ⓦwww.thecovernippon.jp; see map, p.111. A fantastic selection of Japanese design goods made by small, quality manufacturers – everything from beer and honey to cotton fabric, furniture and lacquerware. Roppongi Station. Daily 11am–9pm.

Fujiya ふじ屋 2-2-15 Asakusa, Taitō-ku ⓣ03/3841-2283; see map, p.114. Hand-printed cotton towels (*tenugui*) designed by octogenarian Kawakami Keiji and his son. Some Fujiya towels are collectors' items. Asakusa Station. Daily except Wed 10am–6pm.

Haibara はいばら 2-7-6 Nihombashi, Chūō-ku ⓣ03/3272-3801, ⓦwww.haibara.co.jp; see map, p.104. This lovely old shop has been selling traditional *washi* paper – and everything made from it – since 1806. Nihombashi Station. Mon–Fri 10am–6.30pm, Sat 9.30am–5pm.

Itō-ya 2-7-15 Ginza, Chūō-ku ⓣ03/3561-8311, ⓦwww.ito-ya.co.jp; see map, p.104. This fabulous stationery store is a treasure-trove full of packable souvenirs, such as traditional *washi* paper, calligraphy brushes, inks and so on. Other branches in Shibuya, Shinjuku and Ikebukuro, among other locations. Ginza Station. Wed–Sat 10.30am–8pm, Sun–Tues 10.30am–7pm.

Kurodaya 黒田屋 1-2-5 Asakusa, Taitō-ku ⓣ03/3844-7511; see map, p.114. Established in 1856, Kurodaya specializes in wood-block prints and items made of traditional *washi* paper. Asakusa Station. Tues–Sun 11am–7pm.

Musubi むす美 2-31-8 Jingumae, Shibuya-ku ⓣ03/5414-5678, ⓦwww.kyoto-musubi.com; see map, pp.88–89. Pick up the beautifully printed fabric *furoshiki* here to use instead of wrapping paper for gifts – they're great gifts in themselves. Meiji-jingūmae Station. Thurs–Tues 11am–7pm.

Natsuno 夏野 6-7-4 Ginza, Chūō-ku ⓣ03/3569-0952, ⓦwww.e-ohashi.com; see map, p.104. An incredible collection of over a thousand types of chopstick, plus chopstick rests and rice bowls. Prices range from ¥200 up to ¥60,000 or more. They have another store just off Omotesandō (4-2-17 Jingūmae, Shibuya-ku ⓣ03/3403-6033); and a branch in the Galleria at Tokyo Midtown. Ginza Station. Mon–Sat 10am–8pm, Sun 10am–7pm.

Oriental Bazaar 5-9-13 Jingū-mae, Shibuya-ku ⓣ03/3400-3933; see map, p.129. Popular, one-stop souvenir emporium, selling everything from secondhand kimono to origami paper, all at reasonable prices. Meiji-jingūmae Station. Daily except Thurs 10am–7pm.

Yamada Heiandō 山田平安堂 2F Hillside Terrace,

18-12 Sarugaku-chō, Shibuya-ku ⓣ03/3464-5541, ⓦwww.heiando.com; see map, pp.132–133. For lacquerware of the quality found on tables no less distinguished than those of the Imperial Household and Japan's embassies. Designs are both traditional and contemporary and include several affordable pieces. Daikan'yama Station. Mon–Sat 10.30am–7pm, Sun 10.30am–6.30pm.

Antique and flea markets

There's at least one **flea market** in Tokyo every weekend – arrive early to snag any bargains. Among the regular markets, one of the best is **Ōedo Antique Market** (ⓦwww.antique-market.jp) at the Tokyo International Forum (see p.105) on the first and third Sundays of the month, weather permitting. A smaller market springs into life at Hanazono-jinja (see p.126) every Sunday.

Alternatively, try the more upmarket, covered **antique halls**, such as **Antique Mall Ginza** (アンティークモール銀座; 1-3-1 Ginza, Chūō-ku; ⓦwww.antiques-jp.com; daily except Wed 11am–7pm). Among a good deal of tat, you'll come across original *ukiyo-e*, magnificent painted screens, or samurai armour – but don't expect any particular bargains.

About five times a year (usually in Feb/March, May, June, Sept & Dec) the major **Heiwajima Antiques Fair** is held over three days at the Ryūtsū Centre (ⓣ03/3980-8228) – you'll find it one stop on the monorail from Hamamatshuchō to Haneda. If you're in town, it's well worth the journey. The TICs (see p.92) can give you the current schedule for this and all the other markets and fairs around Tokyo.

Books

Tokyo is the best place in Japan to buy **books** and **magazines** in English and a few other languages. The widest selection can be found in Shinjuku's seven-storey Kinokuniya store (5-24-2 Sendagaya, Shinjuku-ku; ⓣ03/5361-3301, ⓦwww.kinokuniya.com) and at Tower Records (1-22-14 Jinnan, Shibuya-ku; ⓣ03/3496-3661, ⓦwww.towerrecords.jp/store/store03.html) in Shibuya, where the prices tend to be cheaper. Maruzen (1-6-4 Marunouchi, Chiyoda-ku; ⓣ03/3273-3313) near Tokyo Station stocks a wide range of imported and locally produced books, with a strong showing in art and design.The best selections of **secondhand books** are at the excellent Good Day Books (1-11-2 Ebisu, Shibuya-ku; ⓣ03/5421-0957, ⓦwww.gooddaybooks.com) and The Blue Parrot Bookshop (3rd floor Obayashi Building, 2-14-10 Takadanobaba, Shinjuku-ku; ⓣ03/3202-3671, ⓦwww.blueparrottokyo.com).

Music

In an age of digital downloads, Tokyo bucks the trend by sustaining many **CDs and record shops**. Foreign outlets including HMV and Shibuya's Tower Records (see above) offer some of the best prices for imported CDs (typically under ¥2000), while locally pressed CDs generally start in the region of ¥2300. Shibuya has the city's highest concentration of recorded music shops: head to the Udagawachō district near Tōkyū Hands to find scores of outlets specializing in hip-hop, house and techno. The music stores of Shimo-Kitazawa are another good place to root around.

Bonjour Records (24-1 Sarugaku-cho, Shibuya-ku; ⓣ03/5458-6020, ⓦwww.bonjour.co.jp; see map, pp.132–133) is Tokyo's trendiest CD store. For **secondhand records** and CDs, Disk Union (ⓦwww.diskunion.co.jp) and Recofan (ⓦwww.recofan.co.jp) are two names to look out for. Both have branches in Shibuya and Shinjuku, among other places.

Electrical goods and cameras

Akihabara boasts Tokyo's biggest concentration of stores selling **electrical** and **electronic goods**. Anything you can plug in, log onto or interact with is available

Fabulous farmers' markets

Tokyo's **farmers' markets** are great places to buy fresh organic produce and unique edible gifts from across Japan. The main one, hosting about forty different vendors, is **Farmers' Market @ UNU** (ⓦwww.farmersmarkets.jp; Sat & Sun 10am–4pm; see map, p.129), held in front of the United Nation's University on Aoyama-dōri. Different vendors turn up each day, and once a month on Saturdays they also host a night market where you can sample organic beers, coffee and eats. **Earthday Market** (ⓦwww.earthdaymarket.com) is held on a Sunday towards the end of the month in Yoyogi Park. For details of other markets, see ⓦwww.marche-japon.org.

from a bewildering array of stores split into several outlets, with multiple floors selling overlapping product ranges. Of the big stores, **Laox** (1-2-9 Soto-Kanda, Chiyoda-ku; ⓣ03/3253-7111, ⓦwww.laox.co.jp; see map, p.108) is probably the best place to start: they have a well-established duty-free section with English-speaking staff, and nine stores where you can buy everything from pocket calculators to plasma-screen TVs. You'll also find plenty of discount stores in Shinjuku, Ikebukuro and Shibuya.

Shinjuku is Tokyo's prime area for **cameras** and photographic equipment. **Yodobashi Camera** (1-1-1 Nishi-Shinjuku, Shinjuku-ku; ⓣ03/3346-1010, ⓦwww.yodobashi.co.jp; see map, pp.124–125) claims to be the world's largest camera shop and offers decent reductions and stocks. There's another huge branch in Akihabara, selling a broader range of electrical goodies. Ikebukuro also has a solid reputation for new and secondhand deals at reasonable prices. The market here is dominated by **BIC Camera** (ⓦwww.biccamera.com), which is renowned for its cheap prices and has outlets all over Tokyo, including its flagship store in Yūrakuchō (1-11-1 Yūrakuchō, Chiyoda-ku; ⓣ03/5221-1111; see map, p.104), selling practically any electronic goods you could want. See p.69 for general pointers about buying electrical goods and cameras in Japan.

Toys, games, anime and manga

The land that gave the world Donkey Kong, Super Mario Brothers, the Tamigotchi and Hello Kitty is forever throwing up new must-have **toys, games** and **novelties**. Step into one of Tokyo's major toy stores, such as **Kiddyland** (6-1-9 Jingūmae, Shibuya-ku; ⓣ03/3409-3431, ⓦwww.kiddyland.co.jp; see map, p.129) or **Hakuhinkan**, at 8-8-11 Ginza, Chūō-ku (ⓣ03/3571-8008, ⓦwww.hakuhinkan.co.jp. see map, p.104), and you'll find the range quite amazing. For more traditional toys and novelties, head for the nostalgia-filled stalls of Asakusa.

Anime and manga fans will want to take the opportunity to stock up on memorabilia. The best place to head is Akihabara where **Radio Kaikan** (ラジオ会館; 1-15-16 Soto-Kanda, Taitō-ku; see map, p.108) is nirvana for otaku. Akiba has a branch of **Mandarake** (ⓦwww.mandarake.co.jp), although you'll find the main outlet of this retailer of all things anime and manga, including rarities, in Nakano Broadway shopping centre west of Shinjuku.

Listings

Banks and exchange The bigger branches of Tokyo-Mitsubishi UFJ (ⓦwww.bk.mufg.jp) and SMBC (Sumitomo Mitsubishi Banking Corporation; ⓦwww.smbcgroup.com) are your best bets for changing cash or travellers' cheques. If you need money outside banking hours (see p.78), the major department stores often have exchange desks, though most only handle dollars or a limited range of currencies and might charge a small fee. In addition to the ATMs run by the post office and those in 7-Eleven stores, Citibank (ⓦwww.citibank.co.jp) ATMs in Tokyo are accessible outside normal banking hours, and some are open 24 hours.

Embassies Australia, 2-1-14 Mita, Minato-ku (ⓣ03/5232-4111, ⓦwww.australia.or.jp); Canada, 7-3-38 Akasaka, Minato-ku (ⓣ03/5412-6200, ⓦwww.canadainternational.gc.ca); China, 3-4-33 Moto-Azabu, Minato-ku (ⓣ03/3403-3380, ⓦwww.china-embassy.or.jp); Ireland, 2-10-7 Kōjimachi, Chiyoda-ku (ⓣ03/3263-0695, ⓦwww.irishembassy.jp); New Zealand, 20-40 Kamiyamachō, Shibuya-ku (ⓣ03/3467-2271, ⓦwww.nzembassy.com/japan); Russian Federation, 2-1-1 Azabudai, Minato-ku (ⓣ03/3583-4224, ⓦtokyo.rusembassy.org); South Africa, 2-7-9 Hirakawachō, Chiyoda-ku (ⓣ03/3265-3366); South Korea 1-2-5 Minami-Azabu, Minato-ku (ⓣ03/3452-7611); UK, 1 Ichibanchō, Chiyoda-ku (ⓣ03/5211-1100, ⓦukinjapan.fco.gov.uk/en); US, 1-10-5 Akasaka, Minato-ku (ⓣ03/3224-5000, ⓦtokyo.usembassy.gov).

Emergencies The Tokyo Metropolitan Police has an English-language hotline on ⓣ03/3501-0110 (Mon–Fri 8.30am–5.15pm). Japan Helpline (ⓣ0570/000-911, ⓦwww.jhelp.com/en/jhlp.html) provides 24hr advice in English. Tokyo English Life Line (ⓣ03/5774-0992, ⓦwww.teljp.com) provides telephone counselling (daily 9am–11pm). Numbers for the emergency services are listed in Basics on p.71.

Hospitals and clinics To find an English-speaking doctor and the hospital or clinic best suited to your needs, phone the Tokyo Medical Information Service (ⓣ03/5285-8181, ⓦwww.himawari.metro.tokyo.jp; Mon–Fri 9am–8pm); they can also provide emergency medical translation services over the phone. Two major hospitals with English-speaking doctors are St Luke's International Hospital (9-1 Akashichō, Chūō-ku ⓣ03/3541-5151, ⓦwww.luke.or.jp) and Tokyo Adventist Hospital (3-17-3 Amanuma, Suginami-ku ⓣ03/3392-6151, ⓦwww.tokyoeisei.com); their reception desks are open Monday to Friday 8.30–11am for non-emergency cases. Among several private clinics with English-speaking staff, try Tokyo Medical and Surgical Clinic (32 Shiba-kōen Building, 3-4-30 Shiba-kōen, Minato-ku ⓣ03/3436-3028, ⓦwww.tmsc.jp; by appointment only Mon–Fri 8.30am–5.30pm, Sat 8.30am–noon).

Immigration To renew visas, apply to the Tokyo Regional Immigration Bureau (5-5-30 Konan, Minato-ku ⓣ03/5796-7112, ⓦwww.immi-moj.go.jp; Mon–Fri 9am–noon & 1–4pm). To reach it, take the Konan exit from Shinagawa Station and then bus #99 from bus stop 8. Go early in the day since the process takes forever.

Internet access Cybercafés can be found across Tokyo often as part of a 24-hour computer-game and manga café (see p.150). Connection charges are around ¥200–400 per hour. There's also internet access at branches of Kinko's throughout Tokyo; call their toll-free number ⓣ0120-001966 or check ⓦwww.kinkos.co.jp to find the one nearest you. Most hotels offer broadband access (via cable, wi-fi or both) in every room, often for free or for a daily fee (typically ¥1000). Others may provide at least one terminal for guests travelling without their own computer, generally for free, though a nominal rate may apply at budget hotels and hostels.

The following places offer free or cheap (for the cost of a cup of coffee) internet connections: Marunouchi Café (Mon–Fri 8am–9pm, Sat & Sun 11am–8pm), 1F, Shin Tokyo Building, 3-3-1 Marunouchi, Chiyoda-ku; Apple Ginza Store, 3-5-12 Ginza, Chūō-ku (daily 10am–9pm); and Wired Cafes (ⓦwww.cafecompany.co.jp/ourcafe/wiredcafe.html) with branches in Aoyama Itchōme, Harajuku, Nihombashi, Shibuya and Shinjuku among other places. Marunouchi Café allows you to plug in your own computer if you have one. Note that you will need your passport or other ID to use the computers at some of these establishments.

Left luggage Most hotels will keep luggage for a few days. If not, the baggage room (daily 8am–8pm) at Tokyo Station takes bags for up to fifteen days at a daily rate of ¥410 for the first five days and ¥820 per day thereafter. At the time of writing, the baggage room was located at the far southeastern end of the station, beyond the Highway Bus stops, but it may be moved once the redevelopment of the station is complete. Note that coin-operated lockers (¥300–800 depending on the size) can only be used for a maximum of three days.

Lost property If you've lost something, try the local police box (*kōban*). Alternatively, ask your hotel to help call the following offices to reclaim lost property: taxis ⓣ03/3648-0300; JR ⓣ03/3231-1880; Tokyo Metro ⓣ03/3834-5577; Toei bus and subway ⓣ03/3812-2011. If all else fails, contact the Metropolitan Police Lost and Found Office on ⓣ03/3501-0110.

Pharmacies The American Pharmacy in the Marunouchi Building (2-4-1 Marunouchi, Chiyoda-ku; Mon–Fri 9am–9pm, Sat 10am–9pm, Sun 10am–8pm; ⓣ03/5220-7716) has English-speaking pharmacists and a good range of drugs and general medical supplies. Alternatively, try the National Azabu Pharmacy (ⓣ03/3442-3495), above the National Azabu supermarket (nearest subway station Hiro-o). Major hotels usually stock a limited array of common medicines.

Post offices Until 2013, Tokyo's Central Post Office is closed for reconstruction as part of the major redevelopment of the west side of Tokyo Station. Major post offices that are open daily 24 hours can be found in Shinjuku (see map, pp.124–125) and Shibuya (see map, p.129) among other city areas.

Sports The Yomiuri Giants play at Tokyo Dome (1-3 Koraku, Bunkyō-ku; ⓣ03/5800-9999, ⓦwww.tokyo-dome.co.jp/e/dome) near Suidōbashi Station, while the Yakult Swallows are based at Jingū Stadium (13 Kasumigaoka, Shinjuku-ku ⓣ03/3404-8999) near Gaienmae Station. Tickets start from aournd ¥1500. If you're keen to see some martial arts action, the TICs (see p.92) can provide a list of *dōjō* that allow visitors to watch practice sessions for free. Football fans can watch FC Tokyo (ⓦwww.fctokyo.co.jp) or Tokyo Verdi 1969 (ⓦwww.verdy.co.jp) play at the Ajinomoto Stadium (376-3 Nishimachi, Chōfu ⓣ0424/40-0555, ⓦwww.ajinomotostadium.com), near Tobitakyu Station on the Keiō Line from Shinjuku.

For tickets to a tournament at the National Sumo Stadium (see p.113), go to a ticket agency (see below) or queue up early – before 8am – outside the stadium box office for one of the unreserved tickets sold on the day (¥2100); note that tickets are particularly hard to come by on the first and last days. Dates of tournaments, as well as other useful information, are posted on the Nihon Sumō Kyōkai website (ⓦwww.sumo.or.jp).

Taxis Major taxi firms include Hinomaru Limousine (ⓣ03/3212-0505, ⓦwww.hinomaru.co.jp); and Nippon Kōtsū (ⓣ03/3799-9220, ⓦwww.nihon-kotsu.co.jp/en).

Ticket agencies To buy tickets for theatre performances, concerts and sporting events, use one of the major advance ticket agencies: Ticket Pia (ⓦt.pia.co.jp), branches of which can be found in all main city areas; Lawson (ⓦl-tike.com), which has thousands of convenience stores across the city; or CN Playguide (ⓦwww.cnplayguide.com). Major events sell out quickly; don't expect to be able to buy tickets at the venue door.

Travel details

Trains

Asakusa Station to: Nikkō (14 daily; 1hr 55min).

Shibuya Station to: Yokohama (every 5min; 30min).

Shinjuku Station to: Hakone (hourly; 1hr 30min); Kamakura (every 10–20min; 1hr); Matsumoto (18 daily; 2hr 37min); Nikkō (daily; 1hr 55min); Shimoda (daily; 2hr 45min); Yokohama (every 20–30min; 30min).

Tokyo Station to: Fukuoka (Hakata Station; 2 hourly; 5hr); Hiroshima (hourly; 4–5hr); Kamakura (every 10–20min; 1hr); Karuizawa (hourly; 1hr 20min); Kyoto (every 15–30min; 2hr 15min–3hr 40min); Morioka (3 hourly; 2hr 20min–3hr 30min); Nagano (every 30min–1hr; 1hr 40min–2hr); Nagoya (every 15–30min; 1hr 40min–3hr); Niigata (1–3 hourly; 2hr–2hr 20min); Okayama (every 30min–1hr; 3hr 15min–4hr); Sendai (every 10–15min; 1hr 40min–2hr 20min); Shimoda (hourly; 2hr 40min–3hr); Shin-Kōbe (every 30min–1hr; 3hr 15min); Shin-Ōsaka (every 15–30 min; 2hr 30min–4hr 10min); Yokohama (every 5–10min; 40min).

Buses

Ikebukuro Station to: Ise (3 daily; 8hr); Kanazawa (4 daily; 7hr 30min); Nagano (4 daily; 4hr 10min); Niigata (hourly; 5hr 30min); Ōsaka (daily; 8hr); Toyama (3 daily; 6hr 50min).

Shibuya Station to: Himeji (daily; 9hr); Kōbe (daily; 8hr 40min).

Shinagawa Station to: Hirosaki (daily; 9hr 15min); Imabari (1 daily; 12hr 10min); Kurashiki (1 daily; 11hr); Tokushima (daily; 9hr 20min).

Shinjuku Station to: Akita (daily; 8hr 30min); Fuji Yoshida (14 daily; 1hr 50min); Fukuoka (daily; 14hr 20min); Hakone-Tōgendai (14 daily; 2hr 11min); Kawaguchi-ko (14 daily; 1hr 45min); Kurashiki (2 daily; 11hr); Matsumoto (16 daily; 3hr 10min); Nagano (4 daily; 3hr 40min); Nagoya (2 daily; 7hr 10min); Okayama (2 daily; 10hr 30min); Ōsaka (4 daily; 7hr 40min); Sendai (8 daily; 5hr 30min–6hr 30min); Takayama (2 daily; 5hr 30min).

Tokyo Station to: Aomori (2 daily; 9hr 30min); Fukui (daily; 8hr); Hiroshima (daily; 12hr); Kōbe (daily; 8hr 45min); Kōchi (daily; 11hr 35min); Kyoto (hourly; 8hr); Matsuyama (2 daily; 11hr 55min); Morioka (2 daily; 7hr 30min); Nagoya (16 daily; 5hr 20min); Nara (daily; 9hr 30min); Ōsaka (hourly; 8hr 20min); Sendai (daily; 5hr 30min); Shimonoseki (2 daily; 14hr 20min); Takamatsu (daily; 10hr 15min); Yamagata (4 daily; 5hr 30min–8hr).

Ferries

Takeshiba Ferry Terminal to: Ōshima jetfoil (3–5 daily; 1hr 45min–2hr); ferry (3 weekly; 8hr).

Tokyo Ferry Terminal to: Kita-Kyūshū (daily; 35hr); Naha (June–Sept 5 weekly; 3 days); Tokushima (daily; 18hr 40min).

Flights

Haneda to: Akita (7 daily; 1hr); Asahikawa (13 daily; 1hr 35min); Fukuoka (2–4 hourly; 1hr 45min–2hr); Hakodate (9 daily; 1hr 15min); Hiroshima (14 daily; 1hr 25min); Kagoshima (hourly; 1hr 50min); Kansai International (19 daily; 1hr 15min); Kōchi (8 daily; 1hr 50min); Komatsu (for Kanazawa) (11 daily; 1hr); Kumamoto (hourly; 1hr 50min); Kushiro (5 daily; 1hr 35min); Matsuyama (11 daily; 1hr 15min); Memanbetsu (7 daily; 1hr 40min); Miyazaki (hourly; 1hr 45min); Nagasaki (16 daily; 1hr 55min); Noto (2 daily; 1hr); Ōita (11 daily; 1hr 30min); Okayama (4 daily; 1hr 20min); Okinawa (Naha) (1–4 hourly; 2hr 30min); Ōsaka (Itami) (1–2 hourly; 1hr); Ōshima (daily; 30min); Sapporo (Chitose) (every 30min; 1hr 30min); Takamatsu (10 daily; 1hr 10min); Tokushima (6 daily; 1hr 15min); Toyama (6 daily; 1hr); Wakkanai (2 daily; 1hr 45min); Yamagata (daily; 55min).

Narita to: Nagoya Centrair (4 daily; 1hr).

2

Around Tokyo

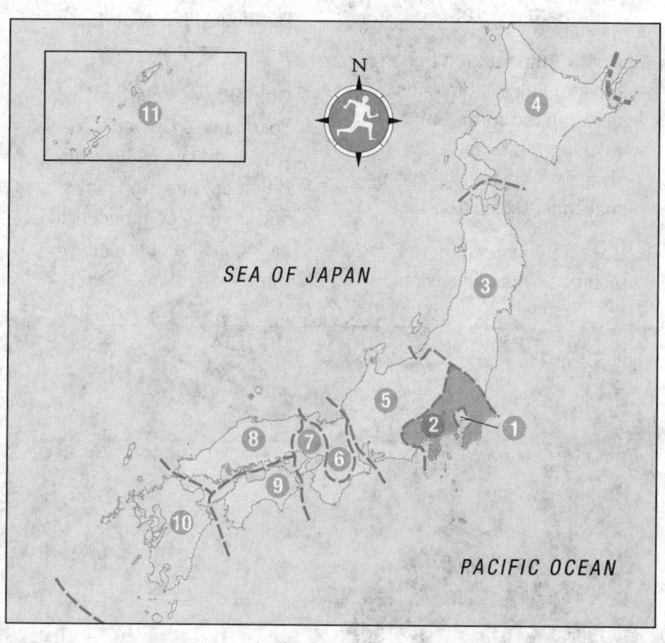

CHAPTER 2

Highlights

* **Nikkō** The dazzling shrine Tōshō-gū is the star turn of this cosy mountain town, surrounded by a beautiful national park and lakes. See p.172
* **Kawagoe** Explore kura-lined streets and old temples and shrines of this historic town that preserves a little slice of old Edo. See p.182
* **Mount Fuji** You don't need to climb Fuji to admire its snowcapped form, but reaching the summit is a rewarding, once-in-a-lifetime challenge. See p.185
* **Hakone** This premier onsen resort has many traditional ryokan, a funicular and ropeway ride, plus a lovely lake which you can sail across in a seventeenth-century-style galleon. See p.189
* **Kamakura** Japan's ancient seaside capital offers woodland walks between peaceful temples and bustling shrines, plus a giant bronze Buddha with a secretive smile. See p.203
* **Chinatown, Yokohama** Yokohama's Chinatown – the largest in Japan – is a blast of bright colours, pungent smells and frenetic commercial life, all focused around the lively Kantei-byō shrine. See p.217

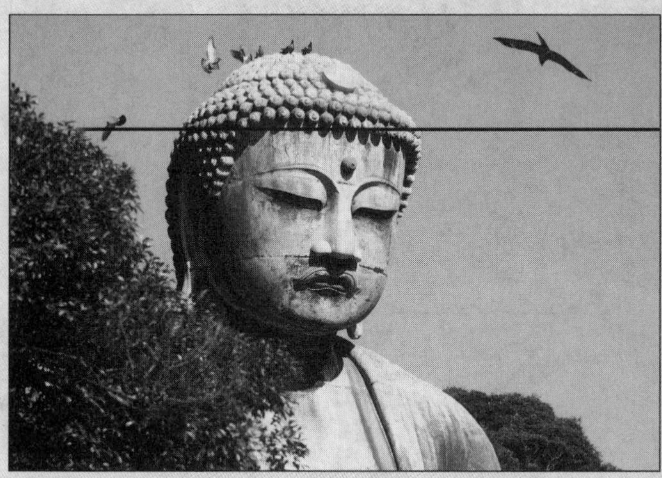

▲ Kamakura's giant bronze Daibutsu

2

Around Tokyo

Tokyo is hemmed into its coastal location on the Kantō plain by a ring of mountains and volcanoes, featuring temples, parks and several bustling towns and cities. It doesn't take long to get out of the capital – two hours at most – and it's well worth the effort. The single best reason for venturing out lies to the north, at **Nikkō**, where the incredible shrine complex of **Tōshō-gū**, built to deify the Tokugawa shogun, offers a riotous feast for the senses. The surrounding mountains are beautiful throughout the year and hold some fantastic walking country. Also make time to visit the spectacular waterfalls nearby, up at the lakes by Chūzenji.

The temple complex of **Naritasan Shinshō-ji**, with its lovely pagoda, extensive gardens, woods and ornamental ponds, is the highlight of the pilgrim town of **Narita**, some 60km northeast of Tokyo. Heading 40km further in the same direction will bring you to **Mito**, home to Kairaku-en, one of Japan's top three traditional landscaped gardens.

Some 40km north of Tokyo is **Kawagoe**, a great place to wander through nostalgic nineteenth-century streetscapes, poke around ancient temples and shrines, and indulge in some serious souvenir shopping. Sacred **Mount Takao**, just an hour west of the capital, provides a more verdant escape for the casual walker and is the starting point for serious hikes northwest to the **Chichibu-Tama National Park**.

Looming to the west of Tokyo is Japan's most famous landmark, the venerable **Mount Fuji**, where you can either make the tough ascent up the volcano or simply relax in the surrounding countryside. Nearby, the inviting landscapes of the Fuji-Hakone-Izu National Park, particularly around **Hakone** and south through **Izu Hantō**, warrant a couple of days' exploration. Off the coast here, **Ōshima** pokes its smouldering head out of the ocean, its laidback way of life providing a beguiling excursion for those on a more leisurely schedule.

Closer to Tokyo, **Kamakura** is one of Japan's major historical sights, home to several imposing Zen temples and the country's second-largest bronze Buddha, the magnificent **Daibutsu**. There are also hiking trails through the surrounding hills, and an enjoyable train ride further along the coast to the sacred island of Enoshima. Just north of Kamakura you're back into the urban sprawl where Tokyo merges with **Yokohama**, Japan's second-largest and most cosmopolitan city.

Nikkō and around

If you make one trip from Tokyo, it should be to the pilgrim town of **NIKKŌ** (日光), 128km north of the capital, where the World Heritage-listed **Tōshō-gū** shrine complex sits amid mountains crisscrossed by outstanding hiking trails within the Nikkō National Park. Tōshō-gū attracts masses of Japanese tourists year-round, who tramp dutifully around the shrine and the surrounding holy buildings. After you've done the same, it's worth investigating the far less crowded

Nikkō Tōshō-gū Museum of Art, and the **Nikkō Tamozawa Imperial-villa Memorial Park**, then crossing the Daiya-gawa to explore the dramatically named **Ganman-ga-fuchi abyss**, which is in fact a tranquil riverside walk. The most beautiful parts of the national park are around **Chūzenji-ko lake**, some 17km from Nikkō.

With a very early start it's possible to see both Tōshō-gū and Chūzenji-ko in a long day-trip from Tokyo, but to get the most out of the journey it's best to stay overnight; cramming both places into one day during the peak summer and autumn seasons is impossible.

Some history

Although Nikkō has been a holy place in both the Buddhist and Shinto religions for over a thousand years, its fortunes only took off with the death of **Tokugawa Ieyasu** in 1616. In his will, the shogun requested that a shrine be built here in his honour. However, the complex, completed in 1617, was deemed not nearly impressive enough by Ieyasu's grandson, **Tokugawa Iemitsu**, who ordered work to begin on the elaborate decorative mausoleum seen today.

Iemitsu's dazzling vision had an underlying purpose. The shogun wanted to stop rival lords amassing money of their own, so he ordered the *daimyō* to supply the materials for the shrine, and to pay the thousands of craftsmen. The mausoleum, Tōshō-gū, was completed in 1634 and the jury has been out on its over-the-top design ever since. Whatever you make of it, Tōshō-gū – along with the slightly more restrained Taiyūin-byō mausoleum of Iemitsu – is entirely successful at conveying the immense power and wealth of the Tokugawa dynasty.

Despite its popularity as a tourist destination today, barely a century ago Nikkō, in the wake of the Meiji Restoration, was running to seed. It was foreign diplomats and businesspeople who began to favour it as a highland retreat from the heat of the Tokyo summer in the 1870s.

Arrival and information

The simplest way of reaching Nikkō is to take a Tōbu-Nikkō from Asakusa in Tokyo. An alternative access point for this line is Kita-Senju Station on both the Hibiya and Chiyoda subway lines. Kaisoku (rapid) trains make the journey in around two hours and twenty minutes and cost ¥1320 one-way. The "Spacia" tokkyū (limited express) takes just under two hours, and costs ¥2740. On some trains you'll need to change at Shimo-Imaichi. Tōbu also run one early-morning direct train to Nikkō from Shinjuku and Ikebukuro, but the Nikkō Pass (see below) isn't valid for travel on it. You can also reach Nikkō on JR trains but the fares are higher, so travelling with JR only makes sense if you have a rail pass from them. The fastest route (around 2hr total) is by Shinkansen from either Tokyo or Ueno to Utsunomiya (宇都宮), where you change to the JR Nikkō line for a local train to the JR Nikkō terminus, a minute's walk east of the Tōbu station.

Tōbu Nikkō Station, resembling a giant Swiss chalet, and the JR Nikkō Station, a historic wooden building designed by Frank Lloyd Wright, are side by side, at the foot of the town, next to a small plaza surrounded by gift shops; the main road in the western corner runs up to Tōshō-gū. Inside both stations there are luggage lockers and, at Tōbu, an **information** desk (daily 8.30am–5pm; ⓣ0288/53-4511), where you can find maps and leaflets on the area. Buses up to the lake and on to Yumoto run at fairly frequent intervals from the train stations between 6am and 6pm. If you haven't bought a Tōbu pass, it's still possible to save money on transport by buying a two-day bus pass at either train station. Unlimited return trips to Chūzenji cost ¥2000, while to Yumoto it's ¥3000.

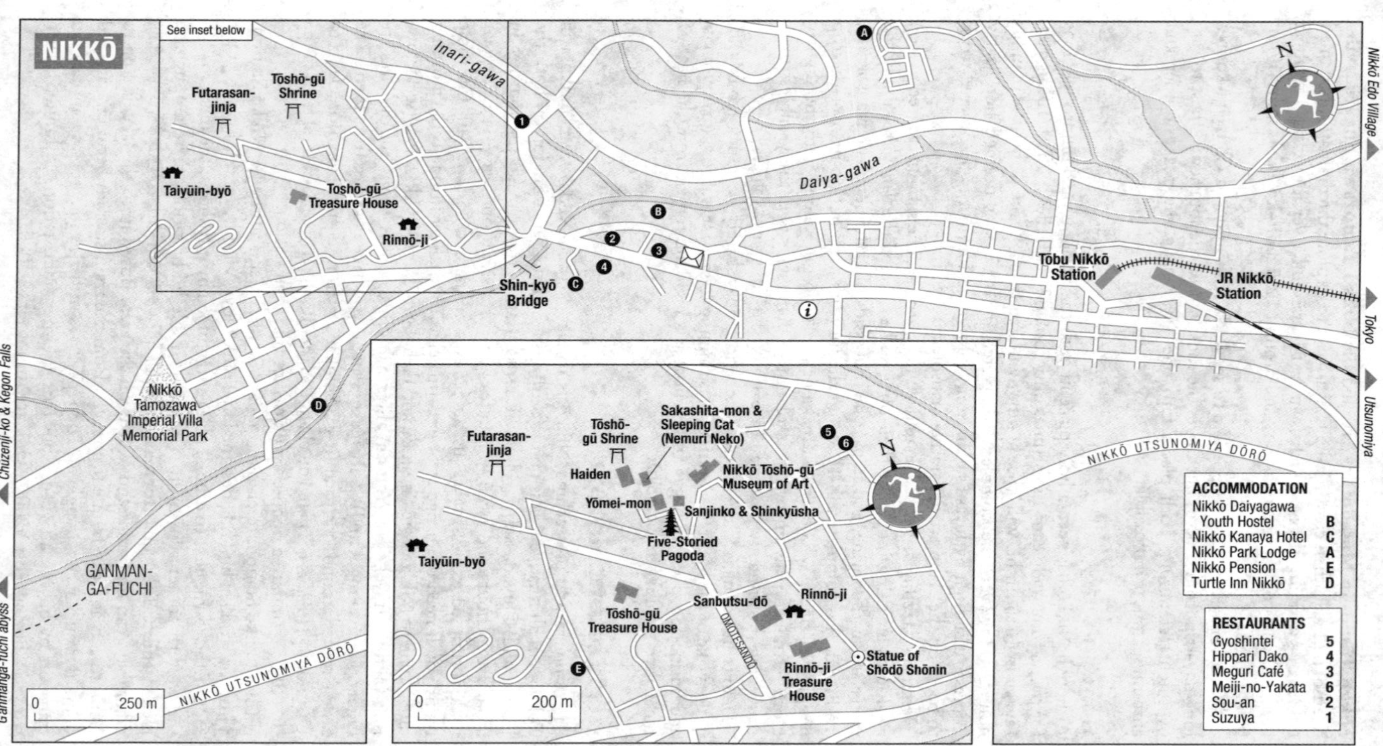
NIKKŌ
See inset below
Inari-gawa
Futarasan-jinja
Tōshō-gū Shrine
Taiyūin-byō
Toshō-gū Treasure House
Rinnō-ji
Shin-kyō Bridge
Daiya-gawa
Tōbu Nikkō Station
JR Nikkō Station
Nikkō Edo Village
Tokyo
Utsunomiya
Chūzenji-ko & Kegon Falls
Ganmanga-fuchi abyss
Nikkō Tamozawa Imperial Villa Memorial Park
GANMAN-GA-FUCHI
NIKKŌ UTSUNOMIYA DŌRO
0 250 m
Futarasan-jinja
Tōshō-gū Shrine
Sakashita-mon & Sleeping Cat (Nemuri Neko)
Haiden
Nikkō Tōshō-gū Museum of Art
Yōmei-mon
Sanjinko & Shinkyūsha
Five-Storied Pagoda
Taiyūin-byō
Sanbutsu-dō
Rinnō-ji
OMOTESANDŌ
Tōshō-gū Treasure House
Rinnō-ji Treasure House
Statue of Shōdō Shōnin
0 200 m
ACCOMMODATION
Nikkō Daiyagawa Youth Hostel B
Nikkō Kanaya Hotel C
Nikkō Park Lodge A
Nikkō Pension E
Turtle Inn Nikkō D
RESTAURANTS
Gyoshintei 5
Hippari Dako 4
Meguri Café 3
Meiji-no-Yakata 6
Sou-an 2
Suzuya 1

The main **tourist office** is the Nikkō Kyōdo Centre (daily 9am–5pm; ⓣ0288/54-2496, ⓦwww.nikko-jp.org), on the main road from the station to the Tōshō-gū complex. If you're planning on walking in the area, you can pick up the free *Tourist Guide of Nikkō*, which shows you all the hiking trails found within Nikko National Park.

Internet access (¥50/15min) is also available at the centre, and at the restaurants *Asian Garden* and *Hippari Dako* (see p.178). The main post office, on the approach road to Tōshō-gū, has an ATM (Mon–Thurs 8.45am–6pm, Friday 8.45am–7pm, Sat & Sun 9am–5pm) which accepts foreign-issued cards, as do the ones in the post offices opposite Tōbu Station and up at Chūzenji; otherwise, it's nearly impossible to use credit cards in the town.

City transport

Tōbu offers various travel passes covering the return trip from Tokyo and transport around the Nikkō area. These tickets, which can only be bought at Tōbu stations, include the fare from Asakusa to Nikkō (express train surcharges for the Spacia still apply), unlimited use of local buses, and discounts on entrance charges at many of the area's attractions, including the cable cars and boat trips at Chūzenji-ko. It's not worth buying the pass if you only intend to visit Tōshō-gū, but if you're planning a trip out to Chūzenji-ko, the most useful ticket is the two-day All Nikkō Pass (¥4400). For further details of all the passes and train times, see ⓦwww.tobu.co.jp/foreign.

Accommodation

There's plenty of **accommodation** covering all categories in Nikkō and the surrounding area. However, in peak holiday seasons and autumn, advance reservations are essential. Rates at virtually all places are slightly higher in August, October to early November, and during major holidays.

Nikkō Daiyagawa Youth Hostel 日光大谷川ユースホステル 1075 Naka-Hatsuishi-machi ⓣ0288/54-1974, ⓦwww.jyh.or.jp. English signposts on the main road to Tōshō-gū point the way down a narrow back path to this cosy hostel, facing the river. Run by a very hospitable family, it gets rave reviews. Dorm beds ¥2730.

Nikkō Kanaya Hotel 1300 Kami-Hatsuishi-machi ⓣ0288/54-0001, ⓦwww.kanayahotel.co.jp. This charming heritage property, practically a museum piece, remains Nikkō's top Western-style hotel, harking back to the glamorous days of early twentieth-century travel. There are some cheaper rooms with en-suite shower or just a toilet (the hotel has a communal bath), but for the full effect, splash out on the deluxe grade. 5–7

Nikkō Park Lodge 2828-5 Tokorono, ⓣ0288/53-1201, ⓦwww.nikkoparklodge.com. A great hostel in a lovely spot high up on the north bank of the river, with a second location in front of Tōbu Nikkō Station. Vegan dinners are available. Dorm beds ¥2990; doubles from ¥8000. 2

Nikkō Pension 日光ペンション 10-9 Nishi-sandō ⓣ0288/53-3636, ⓦwww.nikko-pension.jp. Eccentric decorations enliven this small Western-style hotel close by Tōshō-gū. The rooms are comfy and excellent value, and there's also French-influenced cooking and an onsen. 5

Turtle Inn Nikkō 2-16 Takumi-chō ⓣ0288/53-3168, ⓦwww.turtle-nikko.com. Popular pension run by an English-speaking family in a quiet location next to the Daiya-gawa. There are small, plain tatami rooms with common bathrooms, and en-suite Western-style rooms. They also run *Hotori-an*, a modern annexe located near the path to the Ganman-ga-fuchi abyss. Add ¥1050 for breakfast, or ¥2100 for the evening meal. 5

The Town

First impressions of Nikkō as you come out of either train station aren't great – the uphill approach to the shrine is lined with tatty shops and houses. However, the walk along the town's main street takes no more than fifteen minutes.

Temple and shrine ticket information

You can **save money** if you buy the right ticket for Nikkō's main temples and shrines. If you intend to see Rinnō-ji, Tōshō-gū and Futarasan-jinja, buy the ¥1000 *nisha-ichiji* combination ticket, which includes entrance to the Taiyūin-byō and the roaring dragon hall (*Honji-dō*) in Tōshō-gū, but not the area of Tōshō-gū containing the sleeping cat carving and Ieyasu's tomb (these last two can be tacked onto the combination ticket for an additional ¥520). The combination ticket can be bought from booths beside the Sanbutsu-dō hall in Rinnō-ji and outside the Omote-mon gate to Tōshō-gū.

At the top of the main street is one of the town's most famous landmarks, the red-lacquered **Shin-kyō bridge** (神橋; daily: April–Sept 8am–5pm, Oct to mid-Nov 8am–4pm, mid-Nov to March 9am–4pm; ¥500; ⓦwww.shinkyo.net). Legend has it that when the Buddhist priest Shōdō Shōnin visited Nikkō in the eighth century he was helped across the Daiya-gawa at this very spot by the timely appearance of two snakes, who formed a bridge and then vanished. The original arched wooden structure first went up in 1636, but has been reconstructed many times since. Unless you must have a close-up shot of the bridge, there's little need to pay the entrance fee, as the structure is clearly visible from the road.

Take the left-hand path uphill across from the bridge and you'll emerge in front of the main compound of **Rinnō-ji** (輪王寺; April–Oct 8am–5pm; Nov–March 8am–4pm; ¥400), a Tendai Buddhist temple founded in 766 by Shōdō Shōnin; his statue stands on a rock at the entrance. The large, red-painted hall, **Sanbutsu-dō**, houses three giant gilded statues: the thousand-handed Kannon, the Amida Buddha and the fearsome horse-headed Kannon. It's worth paying to view these awe-inspiring figures from directly beneath their lotus-flower perches (entry is included in the combination ticket, which you can buy at the booth outside). Rinnō-ji's **Treasure House** (Hōmotsuden; 宝物殿; ¥300), opposite the Sanbutsu-dō, has some interesting items on display, but its nicest feature is the attached Shōyō-en, an elegant garden with a path around a small pond.

Tōshō-gū

Broad, tree-lined Omotesandō leads up to the main entrance to **Tōshō-gū** (東照宮; daily: April–Oct 8am–5pm; Nov–March 8am–4pm), just to the west of Rinnō-ji. You'll pass under a giant stone *torii* gate (one of the few remaining features of the original 1617 shrine), while on the left is an impressive red and green five-storey pagoda, an 1819 reconstruction of a 1650 original, which burned down. Ahead is the Omote-mon gate, the entrance to the main shrine precincts, where you'll need to hand over a section of your combination ticket or Tōshō-gū and sleeping cat-only ticket (¥1300), either of which can be bought from the booth in front of the gate.

Inside the precincts, turn left to reach the **Three Sacred Storehouses** (*Sanjinko*) on the right and the **Sacred Stables** (*Shinkyūsha*) on the left, where you'll spot Tōshō-gū's most famous painted woodcarvings – the "hear no evil, see no evil, speak no evil" **monkeys**, which represent the three major principles of Tendai Buddhism. The route leads to the steps up to the dazzling **Yōmei-mon** (Sun Blaze Gate), with wildly ornate carvings, gilt and intricate decoration. A belfry and drum tower stand alone in front of the gate. Behind the drum tower is the **Honji-dō**. This small hall is part of Rinnō-ji temple and contains a ceiling painting of a "roaring dragon"; a priest will demonstrate how to make the dragon roar by standing beneath its head and clapping to create an echo.

It's better to see the roaring dragon rather than fork out ¥520 for the less impressive **sleeping cat** (*nemuri neko*) beyond the Yōmei-mon. You'd easily miss this minute carving, just above the Sakashita-mon gate to the right of the inner precinct, if it wasn't for the gawping crowd. Two hundred stone steps lead uphill from the gate to the surprisingly unostentatious **tomb of Ieyasu**, amid a glade of pines, and about the only corner of the shrine where tourists are generally absent.

Directly in front of the Yōmei-mon is the serene white and gold gate of **Kara-mon**, beyond which is the **Haiden**, or hall of worship. The side entrance to the hall is to the right of the gate; you'll need to remove your shoes and stop taking photographs. Inside, you can walk down into the Honden, the shrine's central hall, still decorated with its beautiful original paintwork.

Nikkō Tōshō-gū Museum of Art and around

Before rushing off, check out the **Nikkō Tōshō-gū Museum of Art** (日光東照宮美術館; daily: April–Oct 8am–5pm; Nov–March 8am–4pm; ¥800), at the back of the shrine complex, to the left as you walk out of the Omote-mon gate. This traditional, impressively simple wooden mansion dates from 1928 and is the former head office of the shrine. Inside, the sliding doors and screens were decorated by the top Japanese painters of the day and together constitute one of the most beautiful collections of this type of art that you'll see in Japan.

Not far east of here are the grounds of **Meiji-no-Yakata** (明治の館), the early twentieth-century holiday home of the American trade representative F.W. Horne. The various houses amid the trees are now fancy restaurants (see p.179), but it's worth wandering around even if you don't eat here to take in the pretty gardens and sylvan setting.

Futarasan-jinja and Taiyūin-byō

A trip around Tōshō-gū is likely to quench your appetite for sightseeing, but it's worth pressing on to some of the other temples and shrines in the surrounding woods. On leaving the main shrine, take the path next to Tōshō-gū's pagoda, and head west to the **Futarasan-jinja** (二荒山神社; daily: April–Oct 8am–4.30pm, Nov–March 9am–3.30pm), whose simple red colour scheme comes as a relief to the senses. This shrine, originally established by the priest Shōdō Shōnin in 782, is the main one dedicated to the deity of Nantai-san, the volcano whose eruption created nearby Chūzenji-ko. There are some good paintings of animals and birds on votive plaques in the shrine's main hall, while the attached garden (¥200) offers a quiet retreat, with a small teahouse serving *macha* green tea and sweets for ¥350. You can also inspect the *bakemono tōrō*, a "phantom lantern" made of bronze in 1292 and said to be possessed by demons.

Just beyond Futarasan-jinja, and bypassed by the tourist mêlée, is the charming **Taiyūin-Reibyō** (大猷院霊廟; ¥550), which contains the mausoleum of the third shogun, Tokugawa Iemitsu, who died in 1651. This complex – part of Rinnō-ji

Grand Festival

Every year, on May 18, the Grand Festival re-stages the spectacular **burial of Ieyasu** at Tōshō-gū, with a cast of over one thousand costumed priests and warriors taking part in a colourful procession through the shrine grounds, topped off with horseback archery. It's well worth attending, as is its smaller-scale cousin (also called the Grand Festival) on October 17, which doesn't have the archery and only lasts half a day, and the "Light Up Nikkō" event (end of Oct, beginning of Nov), during which the major temple buildings are illuminated at night to great effect.

and hidden away on a hillside, surrounded by lofty pines – was deliberately designed to be less ostentatious than Tōshō-gū. Look out for the green god of wind and the red god of thunder in the alcoves behind the Niten-mon gate, and the beautiful Kara-mon (Chinese-style gate) and fence surrounding the gold and black lacquer inner precincts.

Nikkō Tamozawa Imperial Villa Memorial Park and around

In stark contrast to Nikkō's temples and shrines is the Zen-like simplicity of the beautifully restored **Nikkō Tamozawa Imperial Villa** (日光田母沢御用邸記念公園; 9am–4.30pm; closed Tues; ¥500). A ten-minute walk west of the Shin-kyō bridge along the main road, this 106-room residence, surrounded by manicured gardens (including a 400-year-old weeping cherry tree), combines buildings of widely different heritage, some parts dating back to 1632. Three emperors have lived in it, including Akihito, who was evacuated here during World War II. As you stroll the corridors, take time to appreciate the intricate details and the gorgeous screen paintings.

Another tranquil escape is close at hand. From the villa, take the road heading south down to the Daiya-gawa; five minutes' walk west along the river is the Ganman-bashi, a small bridge across from which begins the riverside pathway through the **Ganman-ga-fuchi abyss** (含満ヶ淵). Part of this walk, along the attractive and rocky river valley, is lined by the *Narabi-jizō*, some fifty decaying stone statues of Jizō, the Buddhist saint of travellers and children.

Chūzenji-ko

Ten kilometres west of Nikkō lies **CHŪZENJI-KO** (中禅寺湖) and the dramatic **Kegon Falls** (華厳の滝) that flow from it. Frequent local buses (¥1100 each way) usually take less than an hour to get here, running east from the train stations in Nikkō along Route 120 and up the twisting, one-way road to reach Chūzenji, the lakeside resort, though travelling times can easily be doubled – or even tripled – during *kōyō* in mid-October, the prime time for viewing the changing autumn leaves, when it's bumper-to-bumper traffic.

Both the lake and waterfalls were created thousands of years ago, when nearby **Mount Nantai** (男体山; 2486m) erupted, its lava plugging the valley. Walking west along the shore for around 1km will bring you to the second **Futarasan-jinja** (二荒山神社) of the Nikkō area. This colourful shrine, which once bore the name now adopted by the town, has a pretty view of the lake, but is nothing extraordinary. There's also a third Futarasan-jinja, on the summit of the sacred volcano of Nantai-san, which is owned by the shrine. To reach it you'll have to pay ¥500 and hike up the 2484m peak; it takes around four hours and should only be attempted in good weather.

Eating

Nikkō's speciality is *yuba-ryōri* – milky, thin strips of tofu, usually rolled into tubes and cooked in various stews. You're likely to be served this at your hotel, ryokan or minshuku, the best place to **eat** if you stay overnight, since most restaurants shut around 8pm.

Gyoshintei 堯心亭 ⓣ0288/53-3751. Sample exquisitely prepared *shōjin-ryōri* vegetarian food (bentō ¥3230, course menu from ¥4050) in a traditional tatami room served by kimono-clad waitresses. It's part of the Meiji-no-Yakata complex (see p.177). Open 11.30am–7pm; closed Thurs.

Hippari Dako ひっぱり凧 Classic *yakitori* and noodle café popular with tourists, as the written recommendations and *meishi* that plaster the walls testify. The menu has plenty of vegetarian options, plus beer and sake.

Meguri Cafe 廻 ☎0288/25-3122. A bit past the post office is this cool vegan café run by a husband-wife team, with meals that use vegetables grown in their own garden, as well as local organic produce – even the yummy desserts are made without eggs or any dairy products. Try to get there for lunch (until 2pm), a set meal on Mon–Wed (¥1050) or vegetable ramen on other days (¥945). Daily 11.30am–6pm.

Meiji-no-Yakata 明治の館 ☎0288/53-3751. The dishes, such as curry rice, are simple, but the charming stone villa, once a Meiji-era holiday home, is a nostalgic treat. It's nice to enjoy coffee and cakes on their terrace, while behind the main house, *Yūan san Bō* serves more upmarket set courses. Daily 11am–7.30pm.

Sou-an 草庵 ☎0288/53-0534. The shop by sweets maker Nisshodo – specializing in *yokan*, a Japanese sweet primarily made of azuki red beans – includes this lovely café and garden. A drink and dessert set is ¥800. Daily 9am–6pm.

Suzuya 鈴家 ☎0288/53-6117. Just before you cross over the bridge up the slope from the Kosugi Hōan Museum of Art. This stand-alone restaurant is a good place to sample *yuba-ryōri*; the set lunch costs ¥1400 and includes tempura, rice, noodles and rolled tofu. Daily 11am–3pm.

Mashiko

Some 30km south of Nikkō, the village of **MASHIKO** (益子) is home to a major pottery museum, numerous pottery shops and over three hundred working kilns spread out around the surrounding paddy fields. **Mashiko-yaki**, the distinctive country-style earthenware pottery, has been made in this area since the Nara period (710–84), although the village only achieved nationwide fame in the 1930s, when the potter and "living national treasure" Hamada Shōji (1894–1978) built a kiln here and promoted Mashiko-yaki pottery throughout Japan. Hamada's former residence has since been restored and relocated – along with his traditional-style kiln – to the impressive **Tōgei Messe** complex (陶芸メッセ; Feb–Dec 9.30am–5pm; Nov–Jan 9.30am–4pm; closed Mon; ¥600; ☎0285/72-7555). The building contains a pottery studio and a **museum** featuring works by Hamada and Bernard Leach, the renowned English potter who lived in the village for a short time.

The easiest way to get to Mashiko is by **Shinkansen** (50min; ¥4290) from Tokyo to Utsunomiya (宇都宮駅), where you transfer to a **bus** (1hr; ¥1100) that leaves from stop 14, to the left of Miyano-hashi, the bridge on the west side of the station.

Minakami and adventure sports

The sprawling township of **MINAKAMI** (水上), buried deep in the mountains of Gunma-ken, about 65km west of Nikkō, has become one of the hottest spots in Japan for adventure sports. No fewer than ten whitewater rafting companies, including **Canyons** (☎0278/72-2811, ⓦwww.canyons.jp), offer trips down the Tone-gawa. Other activities include paragliding, canyoning, abseiling, rock-climbing and a wide variety of treks, including the ascent to the summit of **Tanigawa-dake** (谷川岳; 1977m). To relax after all this, head to **Takaragawa onsen** (宝川温泉; daily 9am–5pm; ¥1500 before 4pm, ¥1000 after 4pm; ⓦwww.takaragawa.com), famous for its mixed-sex bathing (though it also has separated baths) and its four huge rotemburo.

To reach Minakami, take the Shinkansen to **Jōmō-Kōgen** (上毛高原) from where the town is a twenty-minute bus ride. The **tourist office** (daily 9am–5.15pm; ☎0278/72-2611) is opposite the station. **Places to stay** include the Canyons-run *Alpine Lodge* (see above; ④), offering private rooms and tatami dorms plus a lively bar, and *Shyōbun* (尚文; ☎278/72-2466; ⑨), a beautifully designed ryokan in contemporary rustic style.

Mito

Around 100km northeast of Tokyo, **MITO** (水戸) was once home to the Mito clan, one of the three main families of the Tokugawa Shogunate (see p.160) – although you'd hardly guess the town's former importance from its nondescript central district, dominated by an inelegant train and bus terminal complex. Most of the town's worthwhile sights were the work of Mito's ninth lord, **Nariaki Tokugawa**, who in 1841 created the sprawling **Kairakuen** (偕楽園; March to late Sept 6am–7pm; Oct to late Feb 7am–6pm; free), now officially classified as one of the nation's top three gardens. The garden's name means "to share pleasure", and it's justly famous for its three thousand fragrant plum trees which blossom in February and March, attracting crowds of visitors, though the garden is lovely in all seasons.

Arrival and information

Mito is on the Jōban line between Tokyo and Hitachi. Frequent express **trains** depart from Ueno Station (65min; ¥7020 return), or you can take a local train (2hrs; ¥2600 return). Mito's **tourist office** (daily 9am–6pm; Ⓣ029/221-6456, Ⓦwww.mitokoumon.com) is on your right as you exit the turnstiles at the station.

The Town

Kairakuen lies several kilometres outside the town centre. Coming into Mito on the train from Tokyo, you'll pass right through it. The station in the park, is usually only open during the peak plum blossom season on weekends. To reach the gardens from Mito Station, take a bus (15min; ¥230 one-way) from stand 4 or 6 outside the north exit to the terminal below the park: steep stairs lead up the hill to the main gates.

At the centre of the main section of plum tree plantings stands **Kōbuntei** (好文亭; daily 9am–4pm; ¥190), a replica of the original two-storey house that was used by Mito clan members as a retreat and a venue for poetry readings; it's decorated with beautifully painted screens and the second-floor observation room affords sweeping views of the garden and nearby Lake Senba. From here it's a brisk twenty-minute walk across the train lines to the **Tokugawa Museum** (徳川博物館; Wed–Fri 10am–4.30pm, Sat & Sun 10am–5pm; ¥630–1050; Ⓦwww.tokugawa.gr.jp), housing artefacts once owned by various Tokugawa feudal lords and their families, with a focus on clan family portraits and samurai armour and weaponry.

Returning to Mito Station, take the first right on the left-hand side of the Livin' department store and walk uphill, bearing right, for a couple of minutes until you reach the well-preserved **Kōdōkan** (弘道館; daily 9am–4pm; ¥190), the Mito clan's school of calligraphy and swordsmanship. The visual displays, paintings and artefacts offer an insight into the lives of those who were privileged enough to receive the rigorous academic training provided here. Some eight hundred apricot trees also blossom here in late February and March.

Eating

Mito is known for the quality of its *nattō* and its coarse "old style" ramen served in a plainer soup unsullied by Korean culinary influences. The tourist office has a map showing the best-known ramen places. For something a bit fancier, try the great-value ramen set lunch at *Fukurokuju* on the ninth floor of *Hotel Season*; for ¥1000, you get a bowl of noodles, side dish, salad and desert and coffee or tea, plus a great view across the lake to Kairakuen. The hotel is around five minutes' walk from the south exit of Mito Station on the banks of the Sakura-gawa. The *Kairakuen Rest House* (偕楽園レストハウス), at the east gate of the garden, offers a variety of inexpensive meals featuring mucus-like fermented soya beans.

Narita

Ten million people annually make the pilgrimage to the enormous temple complex of **Naritasan Shinshō-ji** (成田山新勝寺) in **NARITA** (成田), 60km northeast of Tokyo. Even if you don't have to kill time between connecting flights at the nearby international airport (see p.91), it's well worth visiting this thousand-year-old temple, which is an important landmark in the Shingon sect of Buddhism. It's such a vast place that as long as you're not here on one of the main festival days (New Year, and Setsubun on Feb 3 or 4), it doesn't feel crowded.

Arrival and information

Narita is connected both to Tokyo (1hr) and the airport (7min) by JR and Keisei trains which arrive at separate stations about one minute's walk from each other and around fifteen minutes' walk from the temple.

There's a **tourist information** desk next to the JR station and at the **Narita Tourist Pavilion** (Jan–May & Oct–Dec 9am–5pm; June–Sept 10am–6pm; closed Mon; Ⓦwww.nrtk.jp), on Omotesandō, where internet access is available.

Accommodation

Azure Guesthouse Ⓣ0476/91-5708, Ⓦwww.azure-guesthouse.com. A friendly place with English-speaking staff and good facilities, around 10min walk southwest of the train stations. Dorm beds ¥3000, private room ❹

Kirinoya Ryokan 桐之家旅館 Ⓣ0476/22-0724, Ⓦwww.naritakanko.jp/kirinoya. Five minutes east of the main entrance to Naritasan Shinshō-ji, this spotless if somewhat worn establishment has tatami- and Western-style rooms, and is crammed full with heirlooms, including gold-plated suits of armour, swords and muskets. Breakfast (¥525–735) and dinner (¥1050–1365) available. ❹

Ohgiya Ryokan 扇屋旅館 Ⓣ0476/22-1161, Ⓦwww.naritakanko.jp/ohgiya. A 10min walk from the station towards the temple, with rooms overlooking a lovely garden with a carp pond. ❺

The Town

The temple's ornate Niō-mon gate is at the end of the shopping street, Omotesandō, lined with souvenir stalls and *unagi* (eel) restaurants – the town is famous for them. The colourful three-storey pagoda in front of the Great Main Hall dates from the eighteenth century and is decorated with fearsome gilded dragon heads snarling from under brightly painted rafters. Behind the main hall, the temple's pretty gardens include a calligraphy museum, small forests and ornamental ponds.

If you have more time, head to the impressive **National Museum of Japanese History** (国立歴史民族博物館; 9.30am–5pm, last entry 4.30pm; closed Mon; ¥420; Ⓦwww.rekihaku.ac.jp), in **Sakura** (佐倉), four stops south of Narita on the Keisei line. It houses a great collection of Japanese arts and crafts, including Jōmon-period pottery figurines (which look as though they could be Picasso sculptures) and detailed models of temples, towns and settlements through the ages.

Eating and drinking

Restaurants are abundant, particularly along Omotesandō. Opposite the Tourist Pavilion, try *Kikuya* (daily 10am–9pm), serving reasonably priced *unagi* in classy surroundings. *The Barge Inn* (daily 10am–2pm & 4pm–2am), also on Omotesandō, is a lively British-style pub popular with local expats and visiting flight crews.

Kawagoe and around

Saitama-ken is home to the interesting old castle town of **KAWAGOE** (川越), just 40km north of Tokyo. Although it doesn't look promising on arrival, Kawagoe's compact area of sights, around 1km north of the main station, is aptly described as a "Little Edo", and once you've browsed the many traditional craft shops and paused to sample the town's culinary delights, you'll probably find the day has flown by.

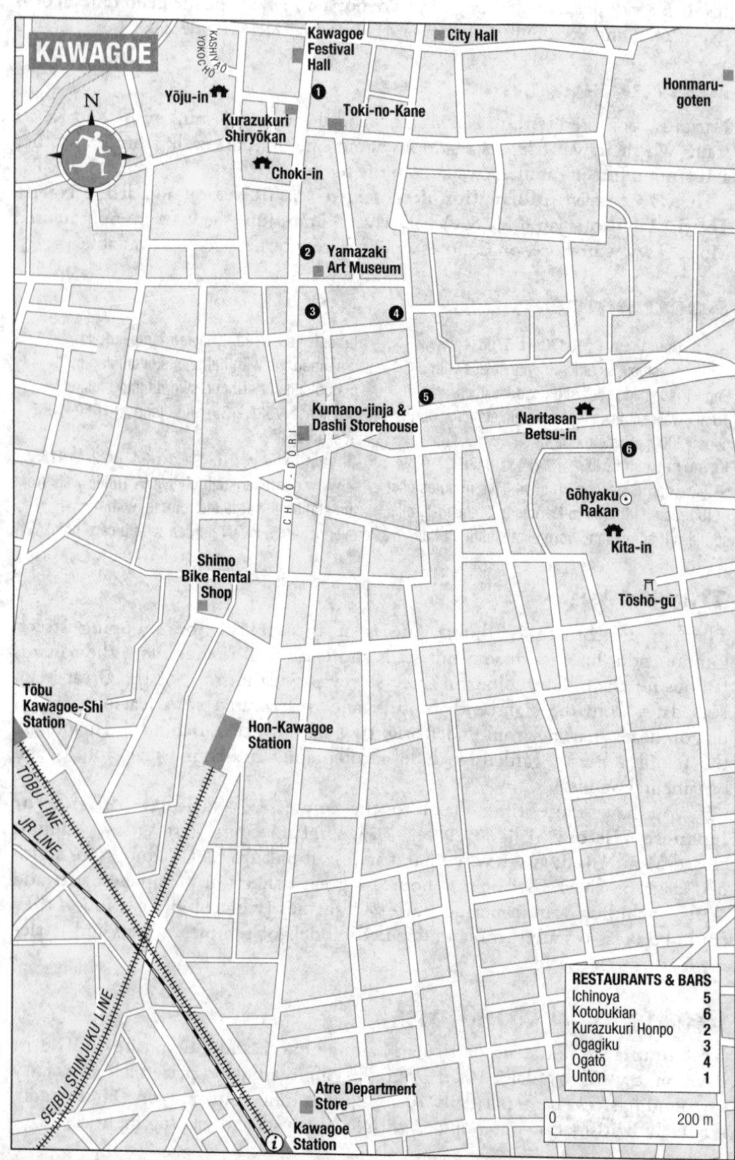

This would certainly be the case on the third Saturday and Sunday of October, when Kawagoe's grand *matsuri* is held, one of the most lively festivals in the Tokyo area, involving some 25 ornate floats (called *dashi*) and hundreds of costumed celebrants.

Kawagoe's fortunes owe everything to its strategic position on the Shingashi River and Kawagoe-kaidō, the ancient highway to the capital. If you wanted to get goods to Tokyo – then called Edo – they more than likely had to go via Kawagoe, and the town's merchants prospered as a result, accumulating the cash to build fireproof **kurazukuri**, the black, two-storey shophouses for which the town is now famous. At one time there were over two hundred of these houses, but their earthen walls didn't prove quite so effective against fire as hoped (nor were they much use in the face of Japan's headlong rush to modernization). Even so, some thirty remain, with sixteen prime examples clustered together along Chūō-dōri, around 1km north of the JR and Tōbu stations.

Arrival and information

Of the three **train lines** to Kawagoe, the fastest is the express on the Tōbu line from Ikebukuro (32min; ¥450); you can get off either at Kawagoe Station (which is also on the slower JR Saikyō line) or at Tōbu Kawagoe-shi, which is marginally closer to Chūō-dōri. Seibu Shinjuku-line trains run from Shinjuku to Hon-Kawagoe Station (43min; ¥480), which is the most convenient for the *kurazukuri*.

The staff at the **tourist office** (daily 9am–4.30pm; Ⓣ049/222-5556, Ⓦwww.koedo.or.jp) at Kawagoe Station may speak some English and can provide you with a map of the town and an English pamphlet on the sights. Immediately northwest of the main square, in front of the Seibu line terminus, is the Shimo bicycle store (daily 10am–7pm), where you can rent **bicycles** (¥700/day) – handy if you plan to see all of Kawagoe's somewhat scattered sights.

The Town

Along Chūō-dōri, around 200m before the main enclave of *kurazukuri*, you'll pass a small shrine, **Kumano-jinja** (熊野神社), beside which is a tall storehouse containing a magnificent *dashi* float. At the next major crossroads, on the right-hand side is the old Kameya *okashi* (sweet) shop, warehouse and factory. These buildings now house the **Yamazaki Art Museum** (山崎美術館; daily except Wed 9.30am–5pm; closed last two days of the month; ¥500; Ⓣ049/224-7114), dedicated to the works of Meiji-era artist Gaho Hashimoto. Some of his elegant screen paintings hang in the main gallery, while there are artistic examples of the sugary confections once made here in the converted *kura* (storehouses); entry includes a cup of tea and *okashi*.

Continuing up Chūō-dōri, you'll pass several craft shops, as well as the **Kurazukuri Shiryōkan** (蔵造り資料館; 9am–4.30pm; closed Mon; ¥100; Ⓣ049/222-5399), a museum housed inside an old tobacco wholesaler's, one of the

Railway Museum

The **Railway Museum** (Tetsudō Hakubutsukan; 鉄道博物館; daily except Tues 10am–6pm; ¥1000; Ⓦwww.railway-museum.jp) in Ōmiya (大宮) is sure to thrill many a trainspotter's heart. Some 36 different pieces of rolling stock, including beautifully detailed antique carriages and late nineteenth-century steam trains, tell the story of the development of Japan's railways from 1872. Ōmiya Station is most easily accessed from Ueno in Tokyo; from here the museum can be reached by a regular rail service to Tetsudo Hakubutsukan Station.

first *kurazukuri* to be rebuilt after the great fire of 1893. Just north of here is the **Kawagoe Festival Hall** (川越まつり会館; ¥500), which houses two magnificent *dashi* floats along with videos of past festivals and various displays; there are no English descriptions.

Opposite the Kurazukuri Shiryōkan, just off Chūō-dōri, you won't miss the **Toki-no-Kane** (時の鐘), the wooden bell tower (rebuilt in 1894) that was used to raise the alarm when fires broke out. An electric motor now powers the bell, which is rung four times daily. Returning to Chūō-dōri and taking the first street off to the west will bring you to **Yōju-in** (養寿院), another handsomely wrought temple with pleasant grounds. Just north of here is the **Kashiya Yokochō** (菓子屋横町), or confectioners' alley, a picturesque pedestrian street still lined with several colourful sweet and toy shops.

Kita-in

Kawagoe's other major highlight, around 500m east of Hon-Kawagoe station, is **Kita-in** (喜多院), the main temple complex of the Tendai Buddhist sect. There's been a temple on these grounds since 830, and it gained fame when the first Tōkugawa shogun, Ieyasu, declared the head priest Tenkai Sōjō a "living Buddha". Such was the reverence in which the priests here were held that, when the temple burnt down in 1638, the third shogun, Iemitsu, donated a secondary palace from Edo Castle (on the site of Tokyo's present-day Imperial Palace) as a replacement building. This was dismantled and moved here piece by piece, and is now the only remaining structure from Edo Castle which survives anywhere.

You have to pay an entry fee to view the palace part of the temple (daily 9am–4.30pm; ¥400; ⓦ049/222-0859), but it's well worth it. The room with a painted floral ceiling is believed to be where Iemitsu was born. Serene gardens surround the palace and a covered wooden bridge leads across into the temple's inner sanctum, decorated with a dazzling golden chandelier. The entry fee also includes access to the **Gohyaku Rakan**, a remarkable grove of stone statues. Although the name translates as "500 Rakans", there are actually 540 of these enigmatic dwarf disciples of Buddha, and no two are alike. Should you know your Chinese birth sign, it's fun to search the ranks for it, as twelve of the statues include the zodiac symbols of animals and mythical beasts. Kita-in also has its own mini **Tōshō-gū**, which, like its famous cousin in Nikkō, enshrines the spirit of Tokugawa Ieyasu and is decorated with bright colours and elaborate carvings.

Mount Takao

An hour west of Shinjuku, **Mount Takao** (高尾山; 600m), also referred to as Takao-san, is a particularly pleasant place for a quick escape from Tokyo, and a starting point for longer trails into the mountains in the **Chichibu-Tama National Park** (秩父多摩国立公園). The Keiō line from Shinjuku provides the simplest and cheapest way of reaching the terminus of Takao-san-guchi (1hr; ¥370). After a hike up or a ride on the cable car or chairlifts, you'll get to **Yakuo-in** (薬王院; ⓦwww.takaosan.or.jp/index.html), a temple founded in the eighth century and notable for the ornate polychromatic carvings which decorate its main hall. It hosts the spectacular **Hiwatarisai** fire ritual on the second Sunday in March back in Takao-san-guchi, where you can watch priests and pilgrims march across hot coals – and even follow them yourself.

At the base of the mountain you'll find the delightful *Ukai Toriyama* (うかい鳥山; Mon–Fri 11am–9.30pm, Sat 11am–8pm, Sun 11am–7pm; ⓣ042/661-0739, ⓦwww.ukai.co.jp/toriyama), a traditional restaurant specializing in charcoal-broiled chicken and Hida beef. The food is served by kimono-clad waitresses in small tatami rooms, with set menus starting at ¥4730.

Eating

Local gourmands flock to Kawagoe for **eel**, most famously sampled at the venerable *Ichinoya* (いちのや; 1-18-10 Matsue-chō), where there are two floors of tatami rooms in which to scoff set courses of broiled eel. Less pricey, but just as tasty, are the *unagi* restaurants *Ogatō* (小川藤) and *Ogagiku* (小川菊), both a short walk southeast of the *kurazukuri*. The area is also known for its *satsumaimo* (sweet potato) dishes; sample some at the confectionery shop and café *Kurazukuri Honpo* (くらづくり本舗) on Chūō-dōri. *Kotobukian* (寿庵; closed Wed), beside Kita-in, is good for soba. For udon, try the popular *Unton* (うんとん), behind the soy-sauce store Kinbue on Chūō-dōri, opposite the Kawagoe Festival Hall.

Fuji Five Lakes

The best reason for heading 100km west from Tokyo towards the area known as **FUJI FIVE LAKES** is to climb Mount Fuji (富士山), Japan's most sacred volcano and, at 3776m, its highest mountain. Fuji-san, as it's respectfully known by the Japanese, has long been worshipped for its latent power (it last erupted in 1707) and near-perfect symmetry; it is most beautiful from October to May, when the summit is crowned with snow. The climbing season is basically July and August;

Climbing Mount Fuji

"A wise man climbs Fuji once. A fool climbs it twice", says the Japanese proverb. Don't let the sight of children and grannies trudging up lull you into a false sense of security: this is a tough climb. There are several routes up the volcano, with the ascent divided into sections known as stations. Most people take a bus to the Kawaguchi-ko fifth station (*go-gōme*), about halfway up the volcano, where a Swiss-chalet-style gift shop marks the end of the road. The traditional hike, though, begins at Fuji-Yoshida; walking from here to the fifth station takes around five hours, and it's another six hours before you reach the summit. Many choose to climb at night to reach the summit by dawn; during climbing season, the lights of climbers' torches resemble a line of fireflies trailing up the volcanic scree.

Essential items to carry include at least one litre of water and some food, a torch and batteries, a raincoat and extra clothes; however hot it might be at the start of the climb, the closer you get to the summit the colder it becomes, with temperatures dropping to well below freezing, and sudden rain and lightning strikes are not uncommon. You can rest en route at any of seventeen huts, most of which provide dorm accommodation from around ¥5000 per night (add ¥1000 on weekends) for just a bed (no need for a sleeping bag), with an option to add meals for ¥1000 each; it's essential to book in advance during peak season (August). The huts also sell snacks and stamina-building dishes, such as curry rice. For a full list of the huts and contact numbers, go to the Fuji-Yoshida city website (see "Arrival and information", p.187), which also has lots of information on climbing the mountain. Once you've summited, it will take around an hour to make a circuit of the crater. If you're too tired, just take part in the time-honoured tradition of making a phone call or mailing a letter from the post office.

Mount Fuji's official climbing season runs from July 1 to the end of August; during this period all the facilities on the mountain, including huts and phones at the summit, are open. For more details, pick up a free copy of the *Mount Fuji Climber's Guide Map*, available at the local tourist office (see p.187) or from the website above. You can climb outside these dates, but don't expect all, or indeed any, of the facilities to be in operation, and be prepared for snow and extreme cold towards the summit.

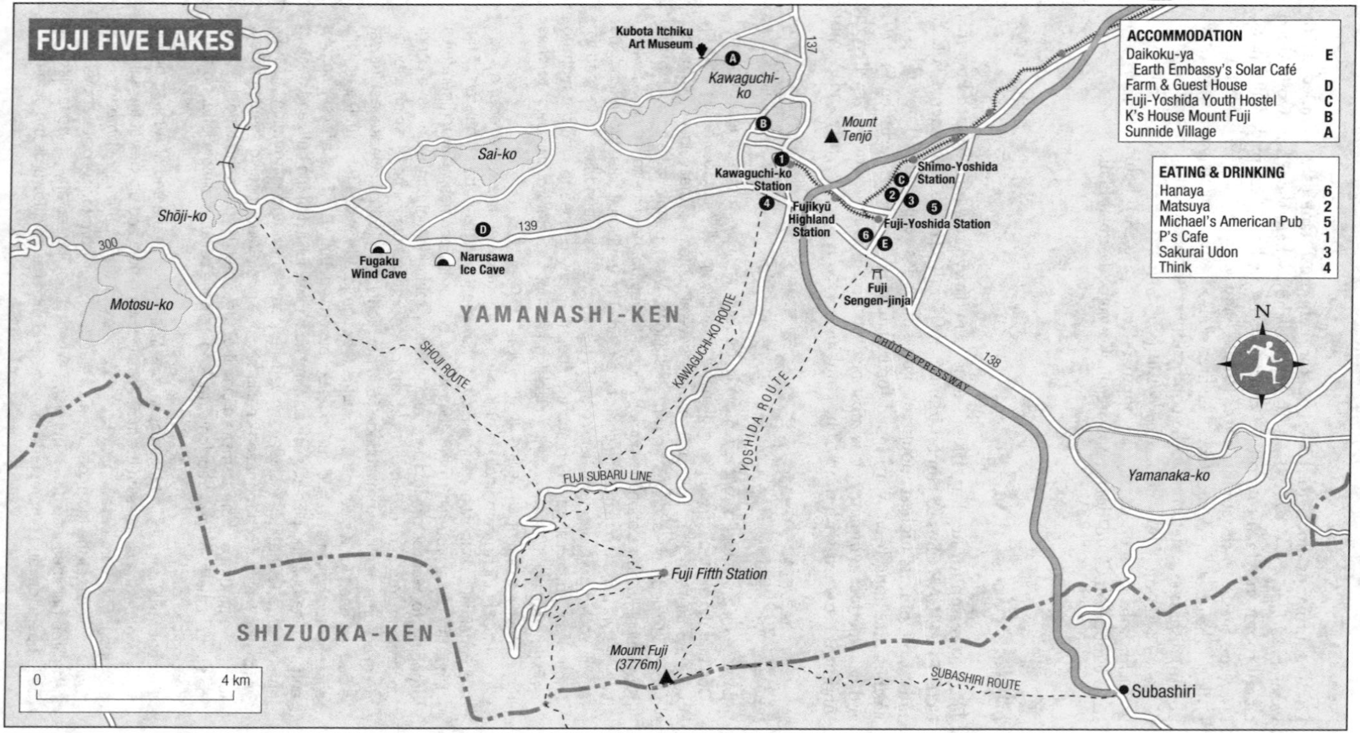

FUJI FIVE LAKES

ACCOMMODATION

Daikoku-ya	E
Earth Embassy's Solar Café	
Farm & Guest House	D
Fuji-Yoshida Youth Hostel	C
K's House Mount Fuji	B
Sunnide Village	A

EATING & DRINKING

Hanaya	6
Matsuya	2
Michael's American Pub	5
P's Cafe	1
Sakurai Udon	3
Think	4

Ōtsuki
Kubota Itchiku Art Museum
Kawaguchi-ko
137
Mount Tenjō
Shimo-Yoshida Station
Kawaguchi-ko Station
Fujikyū Highland Station
Fuji-Yoshida Station
Fuji Sengen-jinja
Sai-ko
Shōji-ko
139
300
Fugaku Wind Cave
Narusawa Ice Cave
Motosu-ko
YAMANASHI-KEN
KAWAGUCHI-KO ROUTE
YOSHIDA ROUTE
SHOJI ROUTE
CHŪŌ EXPRESSWAY
138
N
Yamanaka-ko
FUJI SUBARU LINE
Fuji Fifth Station
SHIZUOKA-KEN
Mount Fuji (3776m)
SUBASHIRI ROUTE
Subashiri
0 4 km

even if you don't fancy the rather daunting ascent, just getting up close to Japan's most famous national symbol is a memorable experience. Apart from Fuji-san, the single most interesting sight is the wonderfully atmospheric shrine **Fuji Sengen-jinja**, in the area's transport hub of **Fuji-Yoshida**.

During the summer, the **five lakes** in the area are packed with urbanites fleeing the city. **Kawaguchi-ko** is not only a popular starting point for climbing Mount Fuji, but also features a kimono museum and the easily climbable Mount Tenjō, which has outstanding views of Fuji-san and the surrounding lakes. The smallest of the other four lakes, horseshoe-shaped **Shōji-ko** (精進湖), 2km west of Kawaguchi-ko, is by far the prettiest. The largest lake, **Yamanaka-ko** (山中湖), southeast of Fuji-Yoshida, is just as developed as Kawaguchi-ko and has fewer attractions, while **Motosu-ko** (本栖湖) and **Sai-ko** (西湖) – the best for swimming and camping – are fine, but not so extraordinary that they're worth the trouble of visiting if you're on a short trip.

Arrival and information

The easiest way to reach the Fuji Five Lakes area is to take the **bus** (¥1700; 1hr 45min in good traffic) from the Shinjuku bus terminal in Tokyo, on the west side of the train station; during the climbing season there are frequent services, including at least three a day that run directly to the fifth station on Mount Fuji. The **train** journey from Shinjuku Station involves transferring from the JR Chūō line to the Fuji Kyūkō line at Ōtsuki, from where a local train chugs first to Fuji-Yoshida and then on to Kawaguchi-ko. On Sundays and public holidays, an early-morning train from Shinjuku does the trip in just over two hours (¥2390). A comprehensive system of **buses** will help you get around once you've arrived at either Fuji-Yoshida or Kawaguchi-ko. Also see the box on p.189 for details of useful travel passes to the area.

English-language **information** is available from the Fuji-Yoshida Tourist Information Service (daily 9am–5pm; ⓣ0555/22-7000, ⓦwww.city.fujiyoshida.yamanashi.jp), to the left as you exit Fuji-Yoshida Station, and at Kawaguchi-ko Tourist Information Centre (daily 8.30am–5.30pm; ⓣ0555/72-6700), outside Kawaguchi-ko Station.

Accommodation

Fuji-Yoshida and Kawaguchi-ko have plenty of good **places to stay**, including youth hostels and hotels. Fuji climbers could consider overnighting in one of the mountain huts (see p.185), but the claustrophobic should stick to the roomier accommodation at the base of the mountain. There are also several campsites around the lakes.

Daikoku-ya 大国屋 Honchō-dōri, Fuji-Yoshida ⓣ0555/22-3778. This original pilgrims' inn on the main road still takes guests in its very traditional and beautifully decorated tatami rooms (owner prefers guests who can speak some Japanese). Rate includes two meals. Closed Oct–April. ❹

Earth Embassy's Solar Café Farm & Guest House Narusawa-mura 8529-74, on Rte 139 towards Shoji-ko, 300m past the Koyodai-iriguchi bus stop ⓣ0555/85-3329, ⓦwww.earthembassy.org. Rustic organic café and farm run by volunteers who give cooking and farming workshops. There's no running hot water, but the local onsen is a 15min walk and ¥1200. Reservations are essential as it sometimes closes in winter. The last bus here from Kawaguchi-ko Station is around 5.30pm. Tatami rooms ¥3000/person, treehouse ¥2000/person, or ¥1500 with your own tent.

Fuji-Yoshida Youth Hostel 富士吉田ユースホステル 2-339 Shimo Yoshida Hon-chō, Fuji-Yoshida-shi ⓣ0555/22-0533, ⓦwww.jyh.or.jp. Small, appealing hostel with tatami rooms in a family home, a 20min walk from Fuji-Yoshida Station, less from Shimo-Yoshida, the preceding station. English is spoken and meals are available. Closed in January. Dorm beds ¥3885.

K's House Mount Fuji 6713-108 Funatsu, Kawaguchi-ko-machi ⓣ0555/83-5556, ⓦwww.kshouse.jp/fuji-e. This hostel gives you a choice of either bunk-bed dorms or private tatami-style rooms, some en suite, and includes a well-equipped kitchen, comfy lounge, internet access, laundry and bike rental. They'll even pick up from the station for free (8am–7.30pm). Dorm beds ¥2500, private rooms from ¥3400/person for two. ❸

Sunnide Village Kawaguchi-ko ⓣ0555/76-6004, ⓦwww.sunnide.com. An attractive complex of hotel and holiday cottages, with spectacular views across the lake towards Mount Fuji. They have lovely public baths too. It's on the north side of the lake, towards the Itchiku Kubota Art Museum. ❹

Fuji-Yoshida

FUJI-YOSHIDA (富士吉田), some 100km west of Tokyo, lies so close to Mount Fuji that when the dormant volcano eventually blows her top the local residents will be toast. For the time being, however, this small, friendly town acts as an efficient transport hub for the area, as well as the traditional departure point for journeys up the volcano, with frequent buses leaving for Fuji-san's fifth station (see box, p.185) from outside the train station.

The volcano aside, the town's main attraction is its Shinto shrine. To reach it, head southwest from the station uphill along the main street, Honchō-dōri, which will take you past several ornate **pilgrims' inns** (*oshi-no-ie*). These old lodging houses, where pilgrims used to stay before climbing Mount Fuji, are set back from the road, their entrances marked by narrow stone pillars; some still operate as minshuku today.

Where the road hits a junction, turn left and after a couple of hundred metres you'll see a giant *torii* and a broad gravel pathway lined with stone lanterns leading to **Fuji Sengen-jinja** (富士浅間神社), a large, colourful shrine set in a small patch of forest. Sengen shrines, dedicated to the worship of volcanoes, encircle Fuji, and this is the most important, dating right back to 788. The beautiful main shrine (*honden*) was built in 1615. Look around the back for the jolly, brightly painted wooden carvings of the deities Ebisu the fisherman and Daikoku, the god of wealth, good humour and happiness, who appears content to let a rat nibble at the bales of rice he squats upon.

Kawaguchi-ko and around

At first glance, there doesn't seem to be a whole lot to commend the shabby lakeside resort of **KAWAGUCHI-KO** (河口湖), a couple of kilometres west of Fuji-Yoshida. With its cruise boats and crass souvenir shops, this is the tourist hub of the area and is often choked with traffic during the holiday season. However, the fabulous view of Mount Fuji and lake Kawaguchi-ko from the top of **Tenjō-zan** (天上山) makes a trip here worth the effort. You can either take a three-minute cable-car ride up to the lookout (daily: March, April 1–15 & Oct 16–Nov 30 9am–5.10pm; Apr 16–Oct 15 9am–5.20pm; Dec–Feb 9am–4.40pm; ¥700 return) or get some exercise by hiking up, which takes around 45 minutes. Kawaguchi-ko's other highlight is the **Itchiku Kubota Art Museum** (久保田一竹美術館; Dec–March 10am–4.30pm; closed Wed; Apr–Nov daily 9.30am–5.30pm; ¥1300), on the northern shore of the lake. Housed in a Gaudí-esque-style building, the museum holds the work of Kubota Itchiku, who has refined the traditional *tsujigahana* textile-patterning technique and applied it to kimono. Inside the pyramid-shaped building are pieces from the artist's *Symphony of Light* series, a continuous mountain landscape through the seasons, formed when the kimono are placed side by side. The museum is some 4km west of the town and can be reached by bus from both Fuji-Yoshida and Kawaguchi-ko.

Eating and drinking

Fuji-Yoshida is renowned for its thick handmade *teuchi* udon noodles, topped with shredded cabbage and carrot. It's prepared and served in local homes at lunchtime only; the tourist office can provide a Japanese list and map of the best places. One of the easiest to locate is the convivial *Hanaya* (花屋), towards the top of Honchō-dōri, but it's also worth searching out *Sakurai Udon* (桜井うどん; closed Sun) downhill from the train station, just off Honchō-dōri to the right when you reach the watch shop. Both serve just three types of dishes: *yumori*, noodles in a soup; *zaru*, cold noodles; and *sara*, warm noodles dipped in hot soup. Also down this way is the cute café *Matsuya* (まつや; 10am–7pm; closed Mon), where you can access the **internet**.

If you're staying overnight in Fuji-Yoshida, a warm welcome is guaranteed at *Michael's American Pub* (daily except Thurs 6pm–2am, lunch 11.30am–4pm except Sat; ⓣ0555/24-3917, ⓦwww.mfi.or.jp/michael), while over in Kawaguchi-ko *Think* (daily except Tues 11am–2am; ⓣ0555/73-1551) is a great café, restaurant and bar rolled into one. *P's Café* in Kawaguchi-ko Station is a pleasant internet café (daily 7am–8pm), where the house speciality is udon topped with horsemeat.

Hakone

South of Mount Fuji and 90km west of Tokyo is the lakeland, mountain and onsen area known as **HAKONE** (箱根), always busy at weekends and holidays. Most visitors follow the well-established day-trip route, which is good fun and combines rides on several trains or buses, a funicular, a cable car and a sightseeing ship, styled as a seventeenth-century galleon, across the **lake**, Ashino-ko. However, the scenery is so pretty, and there's so much else to do – such as seeing great art at the Hakone Open-Air Museum and the Pola Museum of Art, not to mention soaking in numerous onsen – that an overnight stay is encouraged. Weather permitting, you'll also get great views of nearby Mount Fuji.

The traditional day-trip itinerary, described below, runs anticlockwise from **Hakone-Yumoto**, gateway to the **Fuji-Hakone-Izu National Park**, then over

Hakone Freepasses & Fuji Hakone Pass

If you plan to follow the traditional Hakone route, invest in either the two-or three-day Hakone Freepass (¥5000/5500 from Shinjuku). Both cover a return journey on the Odakyū line from Shinjuku to Odawara, and unlimited use of the Hakone-Tozan line, Hakone-Tozan funicular railway, cable car, boat across the lake and most local buses. Besides saving you money on the total cost of all these trips, the passes give discounts at many of Hakone's attractions. The same passes from Odawara or Gotemba cost ¥3900/4400; there's also a ¥2000 one-day ticket from here that doesn't cover the cable car or the boat. For ¥870 extra one way, you can take the more comfortable "Romance Car" which goes directly from Shinjuku through to Hakone-Yumoto in ninety minutes.

If you're going directly from Hakone to the neighbouring Fuji Five Lakes area (or vice versa) then the three-day Fuji Hakone Pass (¥7200) is the way to go. This offers the same deal as a Hakone Freepass and covers a one-way express bus trip to or from Kawaguchi-ko, plus bus connections between the lakeland area and Hakone. For full details of all passes check ⓦwww.odakyu.jp/English, or visit the Odakyū Sightseeing Service Centre (daily 8am–6pm; ⓣ03/5321-7887) at the west exit of Shinjuku Station, where you'll find English-speaking staff and make reservations for tours and hotels.

HAKONE

ACCOMMODATION	
Fuji Hakone Guest House	A
Fujiya Hotel	C
Hakone Lake Villa Youth Hostel	E
Hyatt Regency Hakone Resort & Spa	B
Moto-Hakone Guest House	F
The Prince Hakone	D

Mount Sōun, across the length of **Ashino-ko** to **Moto-Hakone**, and back to the start. Approaching Hakone from the west, you can follow a similar route clockwise from Hakone-machi, on the southern shore of Ashino-ko, to Hakone-Yumoto.

Arrival and information

Most people visit Hakone aboard the Odakyū-line **train** from Shinjuku, using one of the company's excellent-value travel passes (see p.189). Alternatively, you can take the Odakyū express **bus** (¥1950) from Shinjuku bus terminal, which will get you to Ashino-ko in a couple of hours. If you're using a JR rail pass (see p.34), the fastest route is to take a Shinkansen to **Odawara** (小田原), from where you should transfer to an Odakyū train or bus into the national park area. It's also possible to visit from the Fuji Five Lakes area, in which case you'll enter Hakone through **Sengokuhara** to the north, passing through the major town of **Gotemba**.

You can pick up a map of the area and plenty of other **information** at the very friendly Hakone tourist office (daily 9am–5.45pm; ⓣ0460/85-5700; ⓦwww.hakone.or.jp), across the street from Hakone-Yumoto Station, in the buildings at the bus terminal.

Accommodation

With excellent transportation links you can **stay** pretty much anywhere in the national park and get everywhere else easily. There's a good range of budget options and some top-grade ryokan that are a real treat as well as the *Fujiya Hotel*, certainly one for heritage buffs.

Fuji-Hakone Guest House 富士箱根ゲストハウス 912 Sengokuhara ⓣ0460/84-6577, ⓦhakone.syuriken.jp/hakone. This convivial guesthouse, run by the friendly, English-speaking Takahashi-san and his family, has tatami rooms and onsen water piped into a communal bath. ❺

Fujiya Hotel 富士屋ホテル Miyanoshita ⓣ0460/82-2211, ⓦwww.fujiyahotel.co.jp. The first Western-style hotel in Japan, the *Fujiya* is a living monument to a more glamorous era of travel, boasting lots of Japanese touches, including traditional gardens and decorative gables like those you find in temples. The plush 1950s-style decor is retro-chic and the rooms are good value, especially Sun–Fri, when foreign guests qualify for a cheaper rate. ❼

Hakone Lake Villa Youth Hostel Moto-Hakone ⓣ0460/83-1610, ⓦwww.jyh.or.jp. In a secluded spot, surrounded by woods above Ashino-ko's eastern shore, this pleasant hostel has tatami and Western-style dorms, a lounge with a large outdoor deck, a bath filled with onsen water and good-value meals. Dorm beds ¥3000.

Hyatt Regency Hakone Resort & Spa Gōra ⓣ0460/82-2000, ⓦwww.hakone.regency.hyatt.com. This slickly designed hotel is a treat, offering some of the most spacious rooms in Hakone and elegant facilities. It's also where you'll find Hakone's largest spa, which features eight treatment rooms and two onsen baths. ❽

Moto-Hakone Guest House Moto-Hakone ⓣ0460/83-7880, ⓦhakone.syuriken.jp/hakone. A short bus ride (get off at Ashinokoen-mae) or stiff 10min walk uphill from the village takes you here, where the reward for the journey is spotless Japanese-style rooms. Singles ¥5250, breakfast is an extra ¥840/person. ❺

The Prince Hakone Moto-Hakone ⓣ0460/83-1111, ⓦwww.princehotels.com/en/the_prince_hakone. The renovated Prince is at a prime location on the Komaga-take side of Ashino-ko with a multitude of facilities, including access to a rotemburo with a view of the lake. ❼

Hakone-Yumoto

HAKONE-YUMOTO (箱根湯元), the small town nestling in the valley at the gateway to the national park, is marred by scores of concrete-block hotels and *bessō*, vacation villas for company workers – not to mention the usual cacophony of souvenir shops. It does, however, have some good **onsen** which are ideal for unwinding after a day's sightseeing around the park. Up the hill from the station is the **Kappa Tengoku Notemburo** (かっぱ天国野天風呂; daily 10am–10pm; ¥750; Ⓦ www.kappa1059.co.jp), a small, traditional outdoor onsen, which can get crowded. More stylish is **Tenzan Notemburo** (天山野天風呂; daily 9am–11pm; ¥1200), a luxurious public onsen complex at Oku-Yumoto, 2km southwest of town. A free shuttle bus runs to the baths from the bridge just north of Hakone-Yumoto Station.

Miyanoshita and around

Rising up into the mountains, the Hakone-Tozan switchback railway zigzags for nearly 9km alongside a ravine from Hakone-Yumoto to the village of Gōra. There are small traditional inns and temples at several of the stations along the way, but the single best place to alight is the village onsen resort of **MIYANOSHITA** (宮ノ下). Interesting antique and craft shops are dotted along its main road, and there are several hiking routes up 804m **Mount Sengen** on the eastern flank of the railway – one path begins just beside the station. At the top you'll get a great view of the gorge below. Back down in Miyanoshita is the historic *Fujiya* hotel (see p.191), which opened for business in 1878 and is well worth a look.

Travelling two more stops on the Hakone-Tozan railway brings you to **Chōkoku-no-Mori**, where you should alight if you want to visit the nearby **Hakone Open-Air Museum** (彫刻の森美術館; daily 9am–5pm; ¥1600; Ⓦ www.hakone-oam.or.jp). This worthwhile museum is packed with sculptures, ranging from works by Rodin and Giacometti to Michelangelo reproductions and bizarre modern formations scattered across the landscaped grounds, which have lovely views across the mountains to the sea. You can rest between galleries at several restaurants or cafés, and there's also a traditional Japanese teahouse here.

Gōra and Ōwakudani

The Hakone-Tozan railway terminates at **GŌRA** (強羅), another possible place to stay overnight or have lunch. Continuing west on the day-trip route, you'll transfer to a **funicular tram** (¥410), which takes ten minutes to cover the short but steep distance to **Sōunzan**, the start of the **cable car** (¥1330 one-way) across Mount Sōun.

The **cable car** takes thirty minutes to reach the Tōgendai terminal beside Ashino-ko, stopping at a couple of points along the way. If the weather is fine, you should get a good glimpse of Mount Fuji in the distance as you pop over the hill at the first stop, **ŌWAKUDANI** (大涌谷; Ⓦ www.owakudani.com). This is the site of a constantly bubbling and steaming valley formed by a volcanic eruption three thousand years ago. You can hike up the valley through the lava formations to the bubbling pools where eggs are boiled until they are black, then scoffed religiously by every tourist.

Pola Museum of Art and Sengokuhara

If volcanic activity and a cable car isn't your thing, once you get to Gōra you can transfer to the bus bound for the splendid **Pola Museum of Art** (ポーラ美術館; daily 9am–5pm; ¥1800; Ⓦ www.polamuseum.or.jp). This diverse and eclectic collection of Western art and glasswork (predominantly French Impressionists and Ecole de Paris artists) includes some outstanding pieces by the likes of Renoir, Monet, Picasso, Van Gogh, Cézanne and Gallé; there's also a fine selection of Japanese paintings and ceramics. Everything is displayed in modern galleries in a stunning building that blends beautifully with the surrounding forest, with an on-site café and restaurant.

Continuing north on the same bus, you soon reach the pleasant village of **SENGOKUHARA** (仙石原), another possible place to stay the night. Several museums here aim to cater to the rarefied tastes of Japanese women. Perhaps the most interesting – and certainly the most beautifully situated – of these is the **Lalique Museum Hakone** (箱根ラリック美術館; daily 9am–5pm; ¥1500; Ⓣ0406/84-2225, Ⓦwww.lalique-museum.com), dedicated to the delicate glass pieces of the French artist René Lalique. From opposite the museum a reasonably frequent **bus** heads south towards the Tōgendai cable-car terminus.

Ashino-ko to Moto-Hakone

From **Tōgendai** (桃原台), a shoreline trail winds along the western side of **Ashino-ko** (芦ノ湖) to the small resort of Hakone-machi some 8km south, taking around three hours to cover. The western lakeshore, forming part of the Prince empire of hotels and resorts, is not covered by the Hakone Free Pass (see p.189) and so is somewhat marginalized – and all the more peaceful for it. However, most visitors hop straight from the cable car on to one of the colourful sightseeing ships (¥970; Ⓦwww.hakone-kankosen.co.jp), modelled after the seventeenth-century man o' war *The Sovereign of the Seas*, that regularly sail the length of the lake in around thirty minutes. Boats also run from Tōgendai to the *Prince* hotel resort at **Hakone-en**, midway down the east side of the lake, where there's a cable car (¥1050) up the 1357m **Komaga-take** (駒ヶ岳), from where there's a fabulous view.

A cluster of upmarket hotels and ryokan can be found at **Hakone-machi**, where the sightseeing boats dock. This is also the location of the **Hakone Barrier** (箱根関所; daily 9am–5pm, Dec–Feb 9am–4.30pm; ¥500; Ⓦwww.hakonesekisyo.jp) through which all traffic on the **Tōkaidō**, the ancient road linking Kyoto and Edo, once had to pass. What stands here today is a reproduction, enlivened by waxwork displays which provide the historical background. There's nothing much to keep you here, though; instead, stroll north of the barrier around the wooded promontory, past the bland reconstruction of the Emperor Meiji's Hakone Detached Palace, and take in the views of the lake.

Part of the Tōkaidō, shaded by 420 lofty cryptomeria trees planted in 1618, and now designated "Natural Treasures", runs for around 1km beside the road leading from the Hakone Barrier to the lakeside **MOTO-HAKONE** (元箱根) tourist village. The prettiest spot around here is the vermilion *torii* gate, standing in the water just north of Moto-Hakone – a scene celebrated in many an *ukiyo-e* print and modern postcard. The gate belongs to the **Hakone Gongen** (箱根権現) and is the best thing about this small Shinto shrine, set back in the trees, where samurai once came to pray. From either Hakone-machi or Moto-Hakone you can take a **bus** back to Hakone-Yumoto or Odawara (see p.190).

Eating and drinking

Hakone-Yumoto is stacked with good places **to eat**. *Yama Soba*, on the main road between the station and the tourist office, serves up soba sets from ¥1100. *Chikuzen*, across the road, is the best of the town's udon restaurants. There are also three good-value restaurants at the *Tenzan Notemburo* onsen complex, serving rice, *shabu-shabu* and *yakiniku* dishes.

In Miyanoshita, the *Fujiya Hotel*'s *Orchid Lounge* is great for afternoon tea, while its ornate French restaurant is an excellent, if pricey, choice for lunch or dinner. The *Picot Bakery* (ピコット; daily 8.30am–7pm; Ⓣ0460/82-5541) on the main road outside the *Fujiya* is a good place to pick up bread and cakes for breakfast or lunch.

A long-time favourite is *Gyōza Centre* (11.30am–3pm & 5–8pm; closed Thurs), on the main road between Gōra and the Hakone Open-Air Museum. This two-floor **restaurant** usually has a long queue of customers waiting to sample the thirteen types of delicious home-made *gyōza*, including ones stuffed with prawns (*ebi*) and fermented beans (*nattō*). A set meal with rice and soup costs around ¥1150.

Lys, the café-restaurant at the Lalique Museum Hakone in Sengokuhara (see p.193), has a wonderful setting with a view of the mountains and garden seating in summer; lunch here costs around ¥2000.

Izu Hantō

Formed by Mount Fuji's ancient lava flows, **Izu Hantō** protrudes like an arrowhead into the ocean southwest of Tokyo, a mountainous spine whose tortured coastline features some superb scenery and a couple of decent beaches. It takes at least two days to make a complete circuit of this region, taking in some intriguing historical sights and stopping at a few of the peninsula's estimated 2300 hot springs.

Direct train services from Tokyo run down Izu's more developed east coast, passing through **Atami**, with its stylish art museum, to the harbour town of **Shimoda**, a good base for exploring southern Izu and one of the places Commodore Perry parked his "Black Ships" in 1854, as well as the site of Japan's first American consulate. Over on west Izu, **Dōgashima** is another famous beauty spot, with a crop of picturesque islands set in clear, tropical-blue water. The only settlement of any size in central Izu is **Shuzenji**, whose nearby **onsen** resort has long been associated with novelists such as Kawabata and Natsume Sōseki (see p.816).

Izu's mild climate makes it a possible excursion even in winter, though it's close enough to Tokyo to be crowded at weekends, and is best avoided during the summer holidays. If you haven't got a JR pass and want to explore the whole peninsula, check out the various discount tickets available, of which the most useful is the four-day "Izu Free Q Kippu" (¥13,190), which covers the Shinkansen from Tokyo as well as local transport by train and bus. Renting a car is a good idea, as public transport is slow and only really covers the main coastal settlements; you'll find rental companies in Atami (Toyota Rent-a-Car; ⓣ0557/81-0100), Shimoda and Shuzenji (see p.196 & p.202 for details).

Atami

Situated on the Shinkansen line between Tokyo and Ōsaka, the hot-spring resort of **ATAMI** (熱海) serves as the eastern gateway to Izu, and one of the jumping-off points for Ōshima (see p.220). The main reason to come here is to visit the outstanding **MOA Museum of Art** (MOA美術館; 9.30am–4.30pm; closed Thurs; ¥1600; ⓦwww.moaart.or.jp), carved into a hillside above the town. Though it takes a bit of effort to get to, the museum's remarkable architecture and collection of mostly ancient Oriental art easily justify a visit. You can buy slightly reduced tickets (¥1300) at the **tourist information** desk (daily: April–Sept 9am–5.30pm; Oct–March 9am–5pm; ⓣ0557/85-2222) inside Atami Station before hopping on a bus from the station concourse up to the museum (5min; ¥160). Buses drop you outside the museum's lower entrance, from where you ride four escalators that cut through the rock to the main exhibition halls. Each room contains just a few pieces, of which the most famous – only put on show in February of each year – is a dramatic folding screen entitled *Red and White Plum*

Will Adams

In 1600 a Dutch ship washed up on east Kyūshū. It was the lone survivor of five vessels that had set sail from Europe two years previously; three-quarters of the crew had perished from starvation and the remaining 24 were close to death.

One of those rescued was the navigator, an Englishman called **Will Adams** (1564–1620). He was summoned by Tokugawa Ieyasu, the future shogun, who quizzed Adams about European affairs, religion and various scientific matters. Ieyasu liked what he heard and made Adams his personal adviser on mathematics, navigation and armaments. Adams, known locally as Anjin ("pilot"), later served as the shogun's interpreter and as a diplomat, brokering trade treaties with both Holland and Britain. In return he was granted **samurai status**, the first and last foreigner to be so honoured, along with a Japanese wife and an estate near Yokosuka on the Miura Peninsula.

Adams' main task, however, was to oversee the construction of Japan's first Western-style sailing ships. In 1605 he set up a shipyard at **Itō**, on the east coast of Izu, where he built at least two ocean-going vessels over the next five years. His fascinating life story is told in Giles Milton's *Samurai William* and also forms the basis for James Clavell's novel, *Shogun*. Each August Itō's Anjin Matsuri celebrates Adams.

Blossoms by the innovative Ogata Kōrin (1658–1716). The most eye-catching exhibit is a full-size replica of a golden tearoom, lined with gold leaf and equipped with utensils made of gold, and built in 1586. The museum's well-tended gardens contain teahouses serving *macha* and sweet cakes (¥630).

Shimoda

At Atami trains peel off down the east coast of Izu, cutting through craggy headlands and running high above bays ringed with fishing villages or resort hotels. Nearly halfway down the peninsula, **ITŌ** (伊東) port was where Will Adams launched Japan's first Western-style sailing ships (see above), but there's nothing really to stop for until you reach **SHIMODA** (下田). Off season, this small, amiable town, with its attractive scenery and sprinkling of temples and museums, makes a good base for a couple of days' exploring. Its sights revolve around the arrival of Commodore Perry's so-called Black Ships (*Kurofune*) in 1854, making it one of Japan's first ports to open to foreign trade. The people of Shimoda are immensely proud of their part in Japanese history and you'll find Black Ships everywhere; there's even a **Black Ships Festival** (around the third Friday to Sunday in May), when American and Japanese naval bands parade through the streets, followed by the inevitable fireworks.

Some history

Having signed an initial treaty in Yokohama, which granted America trading rights in Shimoda and Hakodate (on Hokkaidō) and consular representation, Commodore Perry (see p.771) sailed his Black Ships down to Izu. Here, in Shimoda's Ryōsen-ji temple, he concluded a supplementary **Treaty of Friendship** in 1854. Russian, British and Dutch merchants were granted similar rights soon after, and in 1856 **Townsend Harris** arrived in Shimoda as the first American Consul. By now, however, it was obvious Shimoda was too isolated as a trading post and Harris began negotiating for a revised treaty, which was eventually signed (again in Shimoda) in July 1858, with Kanagawa replacing Shimoda as an open port, so the burgeoning foreign community decamped north to Yokohama.

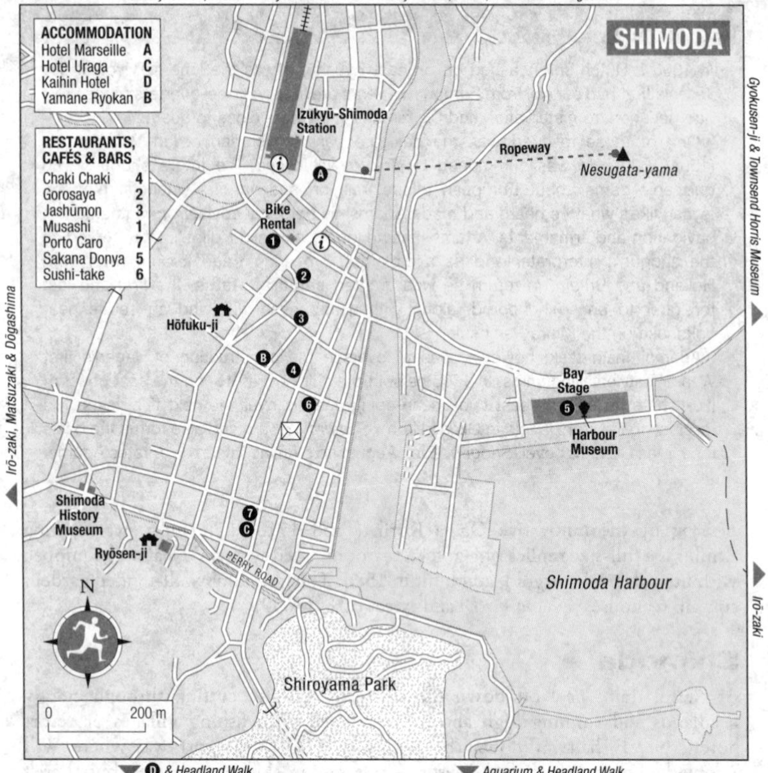

Arrival and information

JR express trains run direct from Tokyo Station to Izukyū-Shimoda Station on the north side of town, several times a day; there's also the daily *Super View Odoriko* service from Ikebukuro and Shinjuku to Shimoda and back, which has extra-wide windows to take in the spectacular coastal views; reservations are essential. Some trains divide at Atami for Shuzenji, so check you're on the right section. JR passes are only valid for the journey as far as Itō; beyond Itō it's a private line down to Shimoda.

There's an **information** desk inside the front exit (daily 9am–5pm; ⓣ0558/22-3200), where you can buy the bilingual *140 Best Izu Shimoda Guidebook* (¥840). The Shimoda Tourist Association (daily 10am–5pm; ⓣ0558/23-5593, ⓦwww.shimoda-city.info) is to the left of the station beside the main crossroads. Both places can help with town maps and accommodation.

Town and regional transport

Local **buses** covering both Shimoda and destinations around the peninsula depart from in front of the train station. You can **rent bikes** at Noguchi Rentacycle (daily 9.30am–6pm; ¥500/hr, ¥2000/day; ⓣ0558/22-1099), one block south of the station. **Car rental** is available from Nippon Rent-a-Car (ⓣ0558/22-5711), Nissan (ⓣ0558/23-4123) and Toyota (ⓣ0558/27-0100), all with outlets close to the station.

If you're exploring the southern area up to Dōgashima and Irō-zaki (see p.201 & p.199), it's worth buying the two-day "Minami Izu Free Pass" (¥2790); you'll make a saving on these two day-trips alone, and their buses also serve Rendaiji. The pass is available from the Tōkai Bus (TB) office (daily 8.30am–5.30pm; ⓣ0558/22-2511) on the other side of the bus terminal from the station, under the *Hotel Marseille*. You can also get to Irō-zaki on one of the tourist boats which depart from Shimoda's tourist wharf during peak season (3 daily: March 25–31; April 29–May 6; July 29–Aug 20; Dec 30–Jan 5; rest of year 3 daily Mon, Sat & Sun; 40min; ¥1530).

Accommodation

Much of the town's accommodation consists of either pricey resort **hotels** on the harbourfront or rather run-down minshuku. However, there are a few appealing options around the station and among the older streets to the south. Other possibilities in the area include Rendaiji's more stylish ryokan and a beach-side hotel at Kisami-Ōhama.

Kaihin Hotel 下田海浜ホテル 3-26-7 Shimoda-shi, a five-minute walk from Perry Rd ⓣ0558/22-2065, ⓦwww.itoenhotel.com/hotel/shimoda. Not the prettiest building, but the location on a quiet bay and the reasonable rates (including two meals) are a plus. Rooms are mostly Japanese-style, with balconies and sea views, and there are two onsen baths, one with sea views, plus a rotemburo. ⑥

Hotel Marseille 3F, 1-1-5 Higashi-Hongo ⓣ0558/23-8000. Modest but well-kept business hotel beside the station with a cheerful French theme. The single rooms (around ¥8000) are small but the doubles and twins are a decent size and nicely decorated. ⑤

Hotel Uraga ホテルウラガ 3-3-10 Shimoda-shi ⓣ0558/23-6600. Clean, bright business hotel in the south part of town. It's worth paying a little extra for the larger, twin rooms (⑥), but all the rooms are comfortable, and the coffee shop serves Japanese and Western breakfasts. Some English spoken. ⑤

Yamane Ryokan やまね旅館 1-19-15 Shimoda-shi ⓣ0558/22-0482. One of the better budget minshuku in central Shimoda. Don't be put off by the slight whiff of cats at the entrance – the simple tatami rooms and communal bathrooms are clean and well kept. ④

The Town: central Shimoda

Central Shimoda lies on the northwestern shore of a well-sheltered harbour, surrounded by steep hills. Most of its sights are in the older, southerly district, where you'll find a number of attractive grey-and-white latticed walls near the original fishing harbour; this style of architecture (known as *namako-kabe*), found throughout Izu, is resistant to fire, earthquakes and corrosive sea air. Your first stop should be **Ryōsen-ji** (了仙寺), where Perry signed the Treaty of Friendship, though this small but elaborate temple, founded in 1635, is less interesting than its attached **museum** (daily 8.30am–5pm; ¥500; ⓦwww.izu.co.jp/~ryosenji). It is full of fascinating historical documents and wood-block prints, many of them original, from the 1850s. Delightful portraits of Perry and his devilish crew, penned by Japanese artists, contrast with the European view of Japan – embellished with Chinese touches – from contemporary editions of the *Illustrated London News* and other European journals. Many exhibits relate to the tragic Saito Okichi, the servant of Consul Harris, who earned the nickname of Tōjin ("foreigner's concubine"), while a second room contains a somewhat incongruous display of sex in religious art, including some beautiful pieces from India, Nepal and Japan's Shinto shrines.

From Ryōsen-ji, **Perry Road** leads east along a small river lined with willows and picturesque old houses, some now converted into cafés and antique shops. Heading back west past Ryōsen-ji, you'll soon come to the **Shimoda History Museum** (下田開国博物館; daily 8.30am–5.30pm; ¥1000), housed in two *namako-kabe* buildings on opposite sides of the street. Alongside more caricatures of big-nosed foreigners, Harris and Okichi are again much in evidence, and the museum also includes plenty of information, much of it in English, about local life, including the area's distinctive architecture and festivals.

Heading north again, the last sight in central Shimoda is **Okichi's grave**. When Okichi died in 1890, none of her family came forward to claim her body, so it was left to a local priest to bring her back to the family temple for burial. She now lies behind the otherwise unremarkable **Hōfuku-ji** (宝福寺), where there's another small museum (daily 8am–5pm; ¥300) dedicated to her memory.

The Town: eastern Shimoda

The east side of Shimoda is dominated by the 200m peak of **Nesugata-yama** (寝姿山). On a clear day it's worth taking the ropeway (daily 9am–5pm, departures every 10–15min; ¥1000 return) from beside the train station up to the summit for dramatic views of the harbour and out to the Izu islands on the eastern horizon. Nesugata-yama's south face drops steeply to the harbour, where there's a string of resort hotels and the Bay Stage building, with its **Harbour Museum** (daily except Tues 9am–5pm; ¥500) on the second floor. Here, the story of Shimoda's brief spell in the limelight is enlivened by holograms re-enacting the 1854 arrival of Perry, as well as that of a Russian Admiral who pitched up here the same year. From the tourist wharf outside you can take a short twenty-minute **harbour cruise** (daily 9.10am–3.30pm, every 30min; ¥920) on a replica Black Ship – more a paddle steamer – or set off on longer excursions to Irō-zaki (see opposite).

If time allows, follow the promenade round to the far, eastern, side of the bay to **Gyokusen-ji** (玉泉寺), where Townsend Harris established Japan's first American consulate in 1856 – he lived and worked there for about fifteen months, accompanied by his Dutch interpreter, Chinese servants and, possibly, Okichi. On entering the **Townsend Harris Museum** (daily 8am–5pm; ¥300), to the right of the temple, you're greeted by a startling, life-size model of Harris, complete with splendid handlebar moustache, relaxing in his rocking chair in full evening dress while Okichi offers him a glass of milk.

You can then retrace your steps to Perry Road and follow the coast road south around the Shiroyama headland. The pleasant hour-long **walk** takes you past **Shimoda Aquarium** (daily 9am–4.30pm; ¥1900) – not really worth the entry fee – and along a quiet cycle track to the next bay. Turn right when you meet the road to return to Perry Road. You can also climb the hill you've been walking round for good views over the town and harbour. It's particularly spectacular in June, when over a million hydrangea blooms colour the slopes.

Eating and drinking

Shimoda has a number of affordable *izakaya* and sushi **restaurants**, as well as straightforward soba joints. There are a few good **coffee shops** scattered around town and along Perry Road, some of which double as antiques showrooms.

Chaki Chaki 茶気茶気 1-20-10 Shimoda-shi ⓣ0558/27-1331. Shimoda-style is given a contemporary twist in this surprisingly sophisticated café-bar. It also serves tasty light meals along the lines of cajun chicken, pasta and bagels. Lunch sets from around ¥1100. Open noon–2pm & 6–11pm; closed Mon.

Gorosaya ごろさや 1-5-25 Shimoda-shi ⓣ0558/23-5638. Relaxed and popular fish restaurant where it's best to book ahead. Their standard *teishoku* (around ¥1600) includes a choice of sashimi, tempura or broiled fish. Other options include the winter-time *Ikenda-ni-miso* (traditional fisherman's seafood casserole) and Chinese-style seafood dumplings. English menu. Open 11.30am–2pm & 5–9pm; closed Thurs.

Jashūmon 邪宗門 1-11-19 Shimoda-shi ⓣ0558/22-3582. A 180-year-old *namako-kabe* building makes an atmospheric venue for this coffee shop littered with artful knick-knacks. It also serves cakes and a limited range of sandwiches. Open 10am–7pm; closed Wed.

Musashi むさし 1-13-1 Shimoda-shi ⓣ0558/22-0934. Rustic soba restaurant also serving standard rice and noodle dishes, all for ¥1200 or less. In winter, try their *nabe yaki udon*, a flavourful udon hot pot with a choice of toppings. Open 11am–4pm; closed Tues.

Porto Caro 2F, 3-3-7 Shimoda-shi ⓣ0558/22-5514. This cute Mediterranean restaurant turns out pretty authentic-tasting pizza, pasta and paella, among other dishes. The lunchtime deals are good value from around ¥1200; in the evening count on at least ¥2000/person. English menu. Open 11.30am–2pm & 6–10pm; closed Wed.

Sakana Donya 魚どんや 1-1 Soto-gaoka ⓣ0558/25-5151. Bright and breezy *kaitenzushi* joint in the harbourside Bay Stage building. Prices range from ¥130–530/plate. You can also order from the English menu. Daily 11am–3.30pm & 5.30–8pm.

Sushi-take 寿司竹 2-4-6 Shimoda-shi ⓣ0558/22-2026. Choose from the picture menu or counter display at this sushi outlet, or simply opt for one of the well-priced sushi sets (from ¥1500). They also serve *donburi* dishes, including *aji-don*, local horse-mackerel (saurel). Open 11.30am–3pm & 5–11pm; closed Thurs.

Rendaiji Onsen

Set in a narrow valley just west of National Highway 414, this quiet, one-street village consists mostly of exclusive ryokan that tap into the area's abundant supply of hot water. It's these onsen baths that make **RENDAIJI ONSEN** (蓮台寺温泉) worth a visit, though there are also a few meandering back lanes to explore, and you might want to splash out on a night of luxury. Two or three **trains** an hour (3–4min; ¥160) run between Shimoda – roughly 3km to the south – and Rendaiji Station, from where it's a short walk west across the river and highway to the village. Local **buses** are slightly less frequent, but most drop you right on the main street (1–2 hourly; 10min; ¥160).

The most appealing of Rendaiji's **onsen** is the big wooden public bath (¥700) at *Kanaya Ryokan* (金谷旅館; ⓣ0558/22-0325; ❺, or ❽ including two meals), a traditional place with several pools, including a rotemburo, where many of your fellow bathers will be local families. They even have an observatory for stargazing and a tea ceremony room. You'll find the ryokan on the main highway, just north of the village turning; there's a bus stop right outside or it's a couple of minutes' walk to the station. Walking south, you come to the immaculate entrance of *Seiryū-sō* (清流荘; ⓣ0558/22-1361; ❾ including two meals) on the left before the bridge; the baths and spa complex here are for residents only.

Opposite *Seiryū-sō*, a road heads west into Rendaiji proper. Here you'll find the beautiful and welcoming old *Ishibashi Ryokan*, also known as the *Kur Hotel* (石橋旅館; ⓣ0558/22-2222, ⓦwww.kur-ishibashi.com; ❼ including two meals), with several baths (non-guests ¥1050) including a little rotemburo. It's tucked under a small hill on the right as you walk from the highway. Continue past it for a few minutes until you come to a neat bamboo fence belonging to *Rendaiji-sō* (蓮台寺荘; ⓣ0558/22-3501; ❽ including two meals), another elegant ryokan with a good choice of baths (non-guests ¥1000; noon–8pm) and attractive gardens. On the opposite side of the road, up a small lane, *Sakuraya* (さくらや; ⓣ0558/22-1966; ❺, or ❼ including two meals), with simple but spruce tatami rooms, is one of the cheaper options in Rendaiji.

South to Irō-zaki

In summer, Izu's beaches are packed with surfers and sun-worshippers, but out of season they're usually fairly deserted. The major resort is just north of Shimoda, at Shirahama, but there are a couple of smaller, more attractive bays southwest of the town on the bus route to Izu's southern cape, **Irō-zaki**. From Izukyū-Shimoda Station **buses** depart for Irō-zaki roughly every thirty minutes, but check before boarding as some buses skip certain stops. Another scenic way of getting here – or returning to Shimoda – is to take one of the **tourist boats** that ply between Shimoda and Irō-zaki port (see below).

Around 4km southwest of Shimoda, Highway 136 passes through the village of **KISAMI** (吉佐美) where a road forks left across a river towards the coast. **Kisami-Ōhama** (吉佐美大浜), the name of Kisami's sandy bay, is one of south Izu's more attractive beaches – marred slightly by a factory on the far horizon – and a popular surfing spot. Just before you reach the beach, *Ernest House* (ⓣ0558/22-5880, ⓦwww.ernest-house.com; ❺) makes an attractive **place to stay**; its fresh, bright rooms get booked up at weekends and in season, so it's wise to phone ahead. They offer **meals**, including great picnic breakfasts; otherwise the laidback *Café Marley* (Fri–Mon 9am–8pm; ⓣ0558/22-2935), just back from the beach, is also recommended. If you're travelling by bus, ask the driver to drop you on the main road at Ōhama-iriguchi, from where it's a ten-minute walk. A little further along the coast, **YUMIGAHAMA** (弓ヶ浜) is a larger, more developed resort, but has the advantage that the bus takes you all the way down to the wide horseshoe bay, ringed with pines and casuarina.

Continuing round the coast, the road climbs through lush vegetation to emerge in an expanse of car parks that cap the headland. Fortunately, **IRŌ-ZAKI** (石廊崎) improves dramatically as you walk out along the promontory for about 500m, past souvenir shops and a lighthouse, to a minuscule **shrine** balanced on the cliff edge. The views here are superb: on either side the sea has cut deep-blue gashes into the coastline, leaving behind a sprinkling of rocky islets between which colourful **tourist boats** bob and weave. The boats leave from Irō-zaki port – a tiny fishing village sheltering in the northern bay; from the headland it's a pleasant five-minute stroll downhill, or get off the bus at the *Irōzaki-kō iriguchi* stop on the main road, a short walk from the village. Depending on the weather and the season, there are one or two trips per hour around the headland and back (25min; ¥1200). In addition, on certain days boats sail from here back to Shimoda (see p.195).

Matsuzaki

Travelling from Shimoda, the main road cuts across Izu's upland spine to **MATSUZAKI** (松崎) on the west coast. Though spoiled by an ugly high-rise hotel plonked in its midst, this modest town hides some attractive streets of traditional latticework buildings along the riverfront and down by its busy harbour. Along the river a clock tower stands in front of **Nakasetei** (中瀬邸; daily 9am–5pm; ¥100), an old kimono merchant's shop and residence that's worth a quick look.

Matsuzaki is also an onsen resort, but its main attraction is a couple of good-value **accommodation** options. For budget travellers, there's the appealingly aged *Sanyo-sō Youth Hostel* (三余荘 ユースホステル; ⓣ0558/42-0408; ❷), set among rice fields 3km east of town; Shimoda–Matsuzaki buses stop right outside and you can rent bikes to explore the surrounding area. Alternatively, there's *Izu-Matsuzaki-sō* (伊豆まつざき荘; ⓣ0558/42-0450; ❻–❼ including two meals), at the north end of Matsuzaki's rather grey beach, which offers a choice of comfortable Western or Japanese rooms, onsen baths and a roof-top rotemburo.

Both these places serve food, but if you're looking for somewhere to **eat** in Matsuzaki, head south round the bay to the port, where *Mingei Sabō* (民芸茶房; daily 7.30am–8.30pm; ⓣ0558/42-0773) doubles as a fishmonger and folksy restaurant, serving fresh fish *teishoku* from around ¥1100. Back along the beach, behind a small pine grove, *Hamamiya* (浜宮; daily except Wed 11.30am–2.30pm & 5.30–9pm; ⓣ0558/42-1789) is a more upmarket fish place with set meals in the region of ¥1600.

Dōgashima

Just 5km up the road from Matsuzaki, **DŌGASHIMA** (堂ヶ島) is west Izu's prime tourist trap, with hotels, souvenir shops and cafeterias catering to a steady stream of punters. The focus of all this activity is a collection of picturesque limestone outcrops lying serenely offshore. You can admire these islands from various viewpoints around the bay or, better still, from one of the **tour boats** run by Dōgashima Marine (Ⓣ0558/52-0013) which set off from a jetty in front of the main car park to putter round the bay or along the coast. The most popular is a twenty-minute ride in which the highlight is sailing into a cave with a large cavity in its roof (daily every 10–15min; 8.15am–4.30pm; ¥1100); afterwards, walk up onto the hill immediately north of the jetty to watch the boats sail through from above. At weekends and peak holiday seasons, a longer cruise takes you south down the coast to Cape Hagachizaki (3–4 daily; 50min; ¥2200).

The old part of Dōgashima, a traditional fishing village known as **Sawada** (沢田), occupies the bay's south side, and it's the best place for affordable accommodation, but otherwise there's no reason to linger.

With an hour to spare, Dōgashima's **Orchid Resort** (daily 8.30am–5pm; ¥1300), accessed from the central car park, is surprisingly interesting, if a little expensive. This botanical garden grows more than eight thousand orchids, from cosseted miniatures to hardier varieties growing wild in the woods.

Arrival and information

The centre of Dōgashima is a car park which also doubles as the **bus terminal**. The **tourist office** (Sept–July 8.30am–5pm; closed Sun; Aug daily 8.30am–5pm; Ⓣ0558/52-1268) lies across the main road, north of the tourist jetty, and can help with local maps (in Japanese only) and hotel bookings; if they're closed, try the Tōkai Bus office (daily 9am–4pm), opposite. **Onward transport** consists of hourly buses north through Toi to Shuzenji.

Practicalities

Dōgashima is dominated by big, expensive resort **hotels**, most of which have stunning views and luxurious onsen. The pick of the bunch is the elegant *NEW Ginsui* (NEW銀水荘; Ⓣ0558/52-2211; ❽), located on its own beach, 1km north of town. If that's too expensive, head for Sawada fishing village at the southern end of Dōgashima, where you'll find dozens of minshuku, such as the cheerful *Koharu-sō* (小春荘; Ⓣ0558/52-0181; ❹, or ❻ including two meals), one block in from the main road, and *Yasumi-sō* (保海荘; Ⓣ0558/52-0285; ❹, or ❻ including two meals), a spotless place one block further west; both dish up great seafood.

There's no shortage of **places to eat** if you don't mind the cafeteria-style dining rooms of the souvenir shops. For somewhere less hectic – despite its location on the central car park – *Sebama-zushi* (瀬浜寿司; daily except Fri 11am–8pm; Ⓣ0558/52-0124) serves sashimi and sushi sets from around ¥1600 and ¥2000, as well as a few staples such as soba.

Inland to Shuzenji Onsen

Travelling north from Dōgashima the road hugs the coast, climbing over headlands and then zigzagging down to fishing villages squeezed into sheltered bays. At **TOI** (土肥), the largest settlement in west Izu, the main road turns inland, but a few buses continue on up the coast to **HEDA** (戸田), a very picturesque village, with onward bus connections to Shuzenji; these buses are few and far between, so check the timetables before setting off. Both Toi (3 daily; 50min; ¥2500) and Heda (4 daily; 30min; ¥2000) are linked by ferry to Numazu (沼津; White Marine

ⓣ0558/94-3323), while Toi also has regular sailings to Shimizu (清水) on the west coast of Suruga Bay, near Shizuoka (4–7 daily; 1hr; ¥2200; Suruga Bay Ferry ⓣ0543/53-2221); both towns are on the JR Tōkaidō Line.

Beyond Toi, Highway 136 climbs eastward through pine-clad mountains before dropping down into the wide valley of **SHUZENJI** (修善寺). The modern town holds no interest beyond its transport connections, but the original settlement of **SHUZENJI ONSEN** (修善寺温泉), some 3km southeast, has a couple of historical sights that are worth exploring.

Arrival and information

Travelling to Shuzenji from Tokyo, the best option is an *Odoriko-gō* Limited Express **train** direct from Tokyo Station; the trains divide at Atami, so make sure you're in the right carriage. Alternatively, hop on any of the regular JR services to Mishima, from where the private Izu-Hakone Railway runs south to Shuzenji (¥500). **Buses** depart from outside the station to Shuzenji Onsen (every 10–20min; ¥210), dropping you at a terminal east of the village centre, and also to Shimoda, Dōgashima and other destinations around the peninsula. Shuzenji's **tourist information** office (daily 9am–5pm; ⓣ0558/72-2501, ⓦwww.shuzenji.info) is in the city hall, on the main road coming into Shuzenji Onsen, a short walk east of the bus terminus. If you want to **rent a car**, you could try Nissan (ⓣ0558/72-2332) or Toyota (ⓣ0558/74-0100) – both have branches near Shuzenji Station.

Accommodation

It's best to stay in Shuzenji Onsen rather than in Shuzenji itself. Prices for accommodation get cheaper the further away you get from the river.

Fukui 民宿福井 ⓣ0558/72-0558. Of a group of minshuku on the northern hillside, this is one of the few that welcomes non-Japanese speakers; none of the rooms has its own bathroom, but it's got a lovely little rotemburo perched on the hillside. ❹, or with two meals included ❺

Goyōkan 五葉館 ⓣ0558/72-2066, ⓦwww.goyokan.co.jp. A few doors down to the east of *Yukairō Kikuya* (see below) and behind a latticework facade, the lack of en-suite facilities at this comfortable ryokan is compensated for by large onsen baths and the English-speaking owner. ❺, or with two meals included ❻

Hanakomichi 花小道 ⓣ0558/72-1178. A smart, mid-range option in a traditional-style building overlooking the *Tokko-no-yu* onsen from the south. Two meals included. ❼

Shuzenji Youth Hostel 修善寺ユースホステル ⓣ0558/72-1222, ⓦwww.jyh.or.jp. A well-run hostel in the hills above the west side of town. Take a bus bound for "New Town" from Shuzenji Station and get off 15min later at "New Town-guchi" (¥310), from where the hostel is signed a 3min walk uphill. The last bus departs from the station at 6.45pm and there are no restaurants nearby, but the hostel meals are excellent value. Closed the first Mon of each month. ❷

Yukairō Kikuya 湯回廊菊屋 ⓣ0558/72-2000. One of the nicest options hereabouts, this elegant ryokan – patronized most famously by the writer Natsume Sōseki (see p.816) – sits under a high-peaked roof immediatley opposite the bus station. Two meals included. ❾

The Town

Shuzenji Onsen consists of little more than one road and a string of riverside hotels and souvenir shops along a narrow valley. Follow the main street west and you'll soon reach an open area with some pleasant older buildings and a succession of red-lacquered bridges over the tumbling Katsura-gawa. Here, on a rocky outcrop beside the river, Shuzenji's first and most famous **onsen**, *Tokko-no-yu*, is now considered too public to be used for bathing, though you can soak your feet. According to legend, the onsen was "created" in 807 AD by Kōbō Daishi, the founder of Shingon Buddhism (see p.499), when he found a boy washing his ailing father in the river; the priest struck the rock with his *tokko* (the short, metal rod carried by Shingon priests) and out gushed hot water with curative powers. He is also credited with founding the nearby **temple**, **Shūzen-ji** (修善寺), from which the town gets its name. Standing at the top of the steps on the river's north bank, the present temple was rebuilt in 1883 and its now quiet halls belie a violent history.

During the Kamakura period (1185–1333), Shūzen-ji was a favourite place of exile for the shoguns' potential rivals. In 1193 Minamoto Noriyori, the younger brother of Shogun Yoritomo, committed suicide – some say he was murdered – after being banished here on suspicion of treason. A more famous death occurred soon after when **Minamoto Yoriie** was murdered in the bath. Yoriie was the son of Yoritomo and succeeded to the title of Shogun in 1199, aged only 18. Four years later his mother, Hōjō Masako, and grandfather seized power and sent Yoriie packing to Shūzen-ji, where he started planning his revenge. Yet the plot was discovered in 1204 and not long after Yoriie was found dead, supposedly killed by bathing in poisoned water. Opposite the temple office you'll find a small **museum** (daily: April–Sept 8.30am–4.30pm, Oct–March 8.30am–4pm; ¥300) full of temple treasures, including possessions allegedly belonging to Kōbō Daishi and Minamoto Yoriie, and what is said to be Yoriie's death mask, all red and swollen. There's also information, some of it in English, about the many novels and plays inspired by these dramatic events, including Okamoto Kidō's famous modern kabuki play *Shūzenji Monogatari*, written in 1911.

Minamoto Yoriie's unassuming grave lies on the hillside directly across the valley from Shūzen-ji, beside a smaller temple, **Shigetsu-den** (指月殿), which a repentant Hōjō Masako built to appease the soul of her son. Though not a dramatic building, it's the oldest in Shuzenji and has a fine Buddha statue inside accompanied by two guardians.

Returning to the bridge beside *Tokko-no-yu*, the old-style building set back to your right with a watchtower offers a lovely cedarwood **onsen bath**, *Hako-yu* (筥湯; noon–9pm; ¥350). Alternatively, follow the path west along the river, meandering across pretty bridges and through bamboo groves, and 400m later you'll emerge near a modern bathhouse, *Yu-no-sato-mura* (湯の里村; daily 9am–10pm; ¥700 for 1hr, ¥950 no time limit), complete with both rotemburo and sauna. The bathhouse marks the western outskirts of Shuzenji village; turn right and you're back on the main street.

Eating and drinking

For **eating**, you'll find plenty of atmosphere at *Nanaban* (なゝ番; daily except Thurs 10am–4pm; ⓣ0558/72-0007), a rustic soba restaurant on the main road east of Shuzenji Onsen's bus terminal. Though they serve reasonably priced rice and noodle dishes, their speciality is *Zen-dera* soba, in which you dip cold soba in an eye-watering, do-it-yourself sauce of sesame and freshly grated horseradish – it's said to bring you the blessings of Buddha, so is surely a bargain at ¥1260. In the evening, you could try *Okura* (おくら; 11.30am–2pm & 5.30–9pm; closed Mon; ⓣ0558/73-2266), a friendly little *izakaya* on the opposite side of the road, with an English menu and well-priced set meals from around ¥1300.

Kamakura and Enoshima

An hour's train ride south of Tokyo lies the small, relaxed town of **Kamakura**, trapped between the sea and a circle of wooded hills. The town is steeped in history, and many of its 65 temples and 19 shrines date back some eight centuries, when, for a brief and tumultuous period, it was Japan's political and military centre. Its most famous sight is the **Daibutsu**, a glorious bronze Buddha

Kamakura festivals

Kamakura Matsuri take place in early April (second Sun to third or fourth Sun) and mid-September, and include displays of horseback archery and costume parades, though the summer fireworks display (second Tues in Aug) over Sugami Bay is the most spectacular event.

surrounded by trees, but the town's ancient **Zen temples** are equally compelling. Kamakura is also well known for its **spring blossoms** and **autumn colours**, and many temple gardens are famous for a particular flower – Japanese apricot at Zuisen-ji and Tōkei-ji in February, and hydrangea at Meigetsu-in in mid-June. Kamakura's prime sights can be covered on a day-trip from Tokyo, but the town more than justifies a two-day visit, allowing you time to explore the enchanting temples of **east Kamakura**, to follow one of the gentle "hiking courses" up into the hills, or to ride the Enoden line a few kilometres west to tiny **Enoshima** island. In summer, the coast here is a favourite spot for windsurfing.

Some history

In 1185 the warlord **Minamoto Yoritomo** became the first permanent shogun and the effective ruler of Japan. Seven years later he established his military government – known as the Bakufu, or "tent government" – in Kamakura. Over the next century, dozens of grand monuments were built here, notably the great Zen temples founded by monks fleeing Song-dynasty China. Zen Buddhism flourished under the patronage of a warrior class who shared similar ideals of single-minded devotion to duty and rigorous self-discipline.

The Minamoto rule was brief and violent. Almost immediately, Yoritomo turned against his valiant younger brother, Yoshitsune, who had led the clan's armies, and hounded him until Yoshitsune committed ritual suicide (*seppuku*) – a favourite tale of kabuki theatre. Both the second and third Minamoto shoguns were murdered, and in 1219 power passed to the Hōjō clan, who ruled as fairly able regents behind puppet shoguns. Their downfall followed the Mongol invasions in the late thirteenth century, and in 1333 Emperor Go-Daigo wrested power back to Kyoto; as the imperial armies approached Kamakura, the last Hōjō regent and an estimated eight hundred retainers committed *seppuku*. Kamakura remained an important military centre before fading into obscurity in the late fifteenth century. Its temples, however, continued to attract religious pilgrims until Kamakura was "rediscovered" in the last century as a tourist destination and a desirable residential area within commuting distance of Tokyo.

Arrival and information

The easiest way of **getting to Kamakura** is either the JR Yokosuka line from Tokyo Station via Yokohama, or the JR Shōnan-Shinjuku line from Shinjuku via Shibuya and Yokohama (1hr; ¥890); from Tokyo Station, make sure you board a Yokosuka- or Kurihama-bound train to avoid changing at Ōfuna. Trains stop at Kita-Kamakura before pulling into **Kamakura Station** three minutes later. For a two-day outing it's worth considering the Kamakura-Enoshima Free Kippu (¥1970), a discount ticket covering the return trip by JR services from Tokyo, and unlimited travel on the Enoden line and Shōnan monorail (see p.212).

Outside the main, eastern, exit of Kamakura Station, and immediately to the right, there's a small **tourist information** window (daily: April–Sept 9am–5.30pm; Oct–March 9am–5pm; ⓣ0467/23-3050) with English-speaking staff. They hand out free maps with the main sights marked in English, or you can buy a slightly more detailed colour map along with a booklet (¥200) outlining suggested itineraries and the hiking trails; though it's mostly in Japanese, basic details are provided in English.

Town and area transport

Local **buses** depart from the main station concourse. Given the narrow roads and amount of traffic, however, it's usually quicker to use the trains as far as possible and then walk. The only time a bus might come in handy is for the more far-flung restaurants or the eastern sites; in the latter case you want stand 4 for Kamakura-gū and stand 5 for Sugimoto-dera (¥190 minimum fare). To make three or more journeys by bus, you'll save money by buying a Kamakura Free Kippu (¥550), a day-pass available from the JR ticket office. The pass also covers JR trains from Kamakura to Kita-Kamakura and Enoden line services as far as Hase.

A better, but more expensive, option is to rent a **bike** from the outfit outside the station's east exit; turn right as you emerge and it's up the slope on the south side of the square (daily 8.30am–5pm; ⓣ0467/24-2319). Rates are on a sliding scale, from ¥500 for the first hour to ¥1500 for a day on weekdays, and slightly more on weekends and national holidays. You'll need to show a passport and give the name of your hotel.

On the west side of Kamakura Station are ticket machines and platforms for the private **Enoden line** (ⓦwww.enoden.co.jp) to Hase and Enoshima, with trains

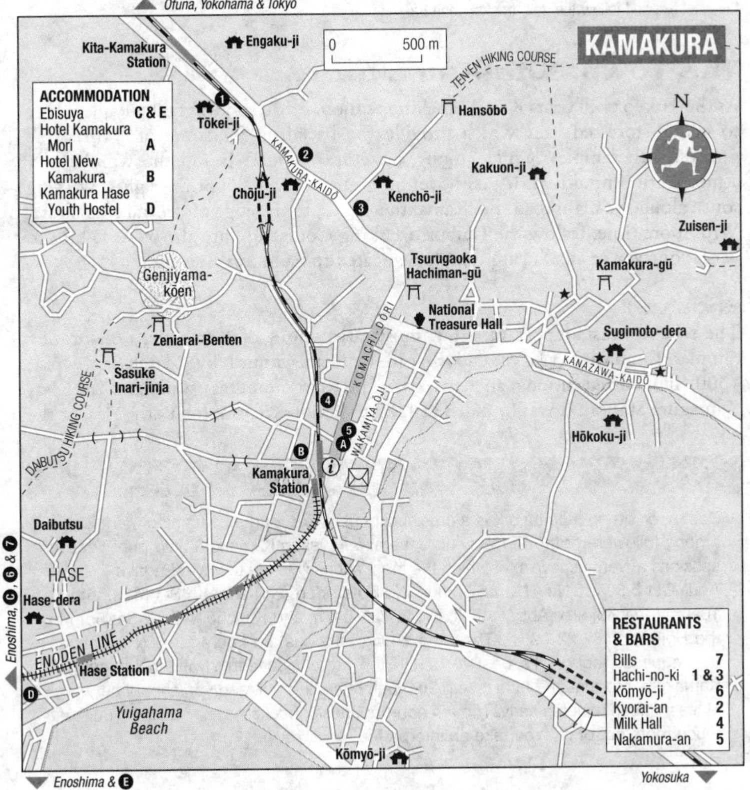

running roughly every twelve minutes from 6am to 11pm. If you plan to hop on and off the Enoden line a lot – for example, going from Kamakura to Hase to Enoshima and back, or on to Fujisawa to pick up a Tokyo-bound train – and haven't got any other form of discount ticket, it's worth investing in the "One Day Free Ticket" (¥580), which entitles you to unlimited travel on the Enoden line.

Accommodation

Central Kamakura offers little budget **accommodation**, but a fair choice of mid-range hotels. Another option is to stay on Enoshima (see p.211) and enjoy the island when the crowds have gone. Many places charge more at weekends and during peak holiday periods, when it's harder to get a room anyway.

Hotel Kamakura Mori ホテル鎌倉 mori 3F, 1-5-21 Komachi ⓣ0467/22-5868, ⓦwww.kamakuramori.net. A short walk up Wakamiya-ōji from the station, the *Mori* offers clean, decent-sized twin or triple rooms with TV and en-suite bathrooms, though it's somewhat expensive. ❻

Hotel New Kamakura 13-2 Onarimachi ⓣ0467/22-2230. The nicest place to stay in Kamakura is this welcoming hotel in an early twentieth-century, Western-style building, a minute's walk north of Kamakura Station – take the west exit and follow the train tracks. Don't be put off by the car park out front. Includes a choice of Western- or Japanese-style rooms. ❹

Kamakura Hase Youth Hostel 鎌倉はせユースホステル 5-11 Sakanoshita ⓣ0467/24-3390, ⓦwww1.kamakuranet.ne.jp/hase_yh. Small hostel with bunk-bed dorms, a 3min walk from Hase Station – follow the tracks heading away from Kamakura. Check in is 4–8pm, with a curfew of 10pm. They also serve breakfast (¥300) and dinner (¥700). HI members ¥3000 per person; non-members ¥4000.

The Town: Kita-Kamakura

As the Tokyo train nears Kita-Kamakura Station, urban sprawl gradually gives way to gentle, forested hills which provide the backdrop for some of Kamakura's greatest Zen temples. Chief among these are **Kenchō-ji** and the wonderfully atmospheric **Engaku-ji**. It takes over an hour to cover the prime sights, walking south along the main road, the Kamakura-kaidō, to the edge of central Kamakura. With more time, follow the Daibutsu Hiking Course up into the western hills to wash your yen at an alluring temple dedicated to **Zeniarai Benten**.

Engaku-ji

The second most important – but most satisfying – of Kamakura's major Zen temples, **Engaku-ji** (円覚寺; daily: April–Oct 8am–5pm; Nov–March 8am–4pm; ¥300) lies buried among ancient cedars just two minutes' walk east of Kita-Kamakura Station. It was founded in 1282 to honour victims (on both sides) of the

Zazen

Zazen, or sitting meditation, is a crucial aspect of Zen Buddhist training, particularly among followers of the Rinzai sect. Several temples in Kamakura hold public *zazen* sessions at various levels, of which the most accessible are those at Engaku-ji (daily: April–Oct 5.30am; Nov–March 6am in the Butsu-den; 2nd and 4th Sun of month at 10am in the Hōjō, or Abbot's hall; ⓣ0467/22-0478) and Kenchō-ji (Fri & Sat 5pm in the Hōjō; ⓣ0467/22-0981). These hour-long sessions are free and no reservations are required, though it's best to check the current schedule with the temple or Kamakura information office (see p.204) before setting out, and you should get there at least fifteen minutes early. Though non-Japanese speakers are welcome, you'll get much more out of it if you take an interpreter.

ultimately unsuccessful Mongolian invasions in 1274 and 1281. The layout follows a traditional Chinese Zen formula – a pond and bridge (now cut off by the train tracks), followed by a succession of somewhat austere buildings – but the encroaching trees and secretive gardens add a gentler touch.

The first building inside the compound is Engaku-ji's two-storey main gate, **San-mon**, a magnificent structure rebuilt in 1783, and beneath which the well-worn flagstones bear witness to generations of pilgrims. Beyond, the modern **Butsu-den** (Buddha Hall) houses the temple's primary Buddha image, haloed in soft light, while behind it the charming **Shari-den** lies tucked off to the left past an oblong pond. This small reliquary, usually closed to visitors, is said to contain a tooth of the Buddha brought here from China in the early thirteenth century. It's also considered Japan's finest example of Song-dynasty Zen architecture, albeit a sixteenth-century replica. The main path continues gently uphill to another pretty thatched building, **Butsunichi-an** (¥100), where regent Hōjō Tokimune was buried in 1284; in fine weather green tea is served in its attractive garden (¥500 including entrance). Finally, tiny **Ōbai-in** enshrines a pale-yellow Kannon statue, but its best attribute is a nicely informal garden with a grove of Japanese apricot.

On the way out, follow signs up a steep flight of steps to the left of San-mon to find Kamakura's biggest bell, **Ōgane**, forged in 1301 and an impressive 2.5m tall. At the adjacent teahouse you can enjoy a cup of *macha* (¥600) while admiring the view across the valley to Tōkei-ji, the next stop.

Tōkei-ji

One minute's walk along the main road from Engaku-ji, **Tōkei-ji** (東慶寺; daily: March–Oct 8.30am–5pm; Nov–Feb 8.30am–4pm; ¥100; ⓦwww.tokeiji.com) was founded as a nunnery in 1285 by the young widow of Hōjō Tokimune. It's an intimate temple, with a pleasing cluster of buildings and a profusion of flowers at almost any time of year: Japanese apricot in February, magnolia and peach in late

Daibutsu Hiking Course

Past **Tōkei-ji** (東慶寺) continuing along the main valley is Jōchi-ji (浄智寺), beside which you'll find steps which mark the start of the **Daibutsu Hiking Course** (大仏ハイキングコース). This meandering ridge-path (2.2km) makes an enjoyable approach to Hase's Great Buddha (see p.211), but in any case it's well worth taking a diversion as far as the captivating cave-shrine dedicated to the goddess **Zeniarai Benten** (銭洗弁天), the "Money-Washing Benten", an incarnation of the goddess of good fortune, music and water. Follow the somewhat erratic signs for Genjiyama-kōen (源氏山公園) along a trail heading southeast through the park, to a road junction where the main trail turns right. Here, you'll pick up signs pointing steeply downhill to where a *torii* and banners mark the shrine entrance. Duck under the tunnel to emerge in a natural amphitheatre filled with a forest of *torii* wreathed in incense and candle-smoke.

If you're following the Daibutsu Hiking Course all the way to Hase, then rather than retracing your steps, take the path heading south under a tunnel of tightly packed *torii*, zigzagging down to the valley bottom. Turn right at a T-junction to find another avenue of vermilion *torii* leading uphill deep into the cryptomeria forest. At the end lies a simple shrine, **Sasuke Inari-jinja** (佐助稲荷神社), dating from before the twelfth century and dedicated to the god of harvests. His messenger is the fox; as you head up the steep path behind, to the left of the shrine buildings, climbing over tangled roots, you'll find fox statues of all shapes and sizes peering out of the surrounding gloom. At the top, turn right and then left at a white signboard to pick up the hiking course for the final 1500m to the Daibutsu (see p.211).

March, followed by peonies and then irises in early June; September is the season for cascades of bush clover.

South to Kenchō-ji

Back at the main road, walk southeast for another five minutes to find the greatest of Kamakura's Zen temples, **Kenchō-ji** (建長寺; daily 8.30am–4.30pm; ¥300; Ⓦwww.kenchoji.com), headquarters of the Rinzai sect and Japan's oldest Zen training monastery. More formal than Engaku-ji and a lot less peaceful, largely because of the neighbouring high school, Kenchō-ji contains several important buildings, most of which have been relocated here from Tokyo and Kyoto to replace those lost since the temple's foundation in 1253. Again, the design of the layout shows a strong Chinese influence; the founding abbot was another Song Chinese émigré, in this case working under the patronage of Hōjō Tokiyori, the devout fifth regent and father of Engaku-ji's Tokumine.

The main complex begins with the towering, copper-roofed **San-mon**, an eighteenth-century reconstruction, to the right of which hangs the original temple **bell**, cast in 1255 and considered one of Japan's most beautiful. Beyond San-mon, a grove of gnarled and twisted juniper trees hides the dainty, nicely dilapidated **Butsu-den**. The main image is, unusually, of Jizō (the guardian deity of children) seated on a lotus throne, his bright, half-closed eyes piercing the gloom. Behind is the **Hattō**, or lecture hall, one of Japan's largest wooden Buddhist buildings. The curvaceous Chinese-style gate, **Kara-mon**, and the **Hōjō** hall beyond are much more attractive structures. Walk round the latter's balcony to find a **pond-garden** generally attributed to a thirteenth-century monk, making it Japan's oldest-surviving Zen garden, though it's been spruced up considerably.

Behind the Hōjō, a path heads the up steep steps past **Hansōbō**, a shrine guarded by statues of long-nosed, mythical *tengu*. This is the start of the **Ten'en Hiking Course** (天園ハイキングコース). It takes roughly one and a half hours to complete the five-kilometre trail from Kenchō-ji, which loops round the town's northeast outskirts to Zuisen-ji (see opposite); for a shorter walk (2.5km), you can cut down earlier to Kamakura-gū (see opposite).

From Kenchō-ji it's only another five minutes through the tunnel and downhill to the side entrance of Tsurugaoka Hachiman-gū (see below).

The Town: Central Kamakura

Modern Kamakura revolves around its central train station and a couple of touristy streets leading to the town's **most important shrine**, Tsurugaoka Hachiman-gū. The traditional approach to this grand edifice lies along Wakamiya-ōji, which runs straight from the sea to the shrine entrance. Shops here peddle a motley collection of souvenirs and crafts, the most famous of which is *kamakura-bori*, an 800-year-old method of laying lacquer over carved wood. More popular, however, is *hato*, a pigeon-shaped French-style biscuit first made by Toshimaya bakers a century ago. You can buy them all over town, but walk up Wakamiya-ōji to find their main shop (daily except Wed 9am–7pm; Ⓣ0467/25-0810), with telltale ironwork pigeons on the outside, halfway along. Shadowing Wakamiya-ōji to the west is **Komachi-dōri**, a narrow, pedestrian-only shopping street, packed with more souvenir shops, restaurants and, increasingly, trendy boutiques.

Tsurugaoka Hachiman-gū

A majestic, vermilion-lacquered *torii* marks the front entrance to **Tsurugaoka Hachiman-gū** (鶴岡八幡宮; daily 6am–8.30pm), the Minamoto clan's guardian shrine since 1063. Hachiman-gū, as it's popularly known, was moved to its present site in 1191, since when it has witnessed some of the more unsavoury episodes of

Kamakura history. Most of the present buildings date from the early nineteenth century, and their striking red paintwork, combined with the parade of souvenir stalls and the constant bustle of people, creates a festive atmosphere in sharp contrast to that of Kamakura's more secluded Zen temples.

Three humpback bridges lead into the shrine compound between two connected ponds known as **Genpei-ike**. These were designed by Minamoto Yoritomo's wife, Hōjō Masako, and are full of heavy, complicated symbolism, anticipating the longed-for victory of her husband's clan over their bitter enemies, the Taira; strangely, the bloodthirsty Masako was of Taira stock. The **Mai-den**, an open-sided stage at the end of a broad avenue, was the scene of another unhappy event in 1186, when Yoritomo forced his brother's mistress, Shizuka, to dance for the assembled samurai. Yoritomo wanted his popular brother, Yoshitsune, killed and was holding Shizuka prisoner in the hope of discovering his whereabouts; instead, she made a defiant declaration of love and only narrowly escaped death herself, though her newborn son was murdered soon after. Her bravery is commemorated with classical dances and nō plays during the shrine **festival** (Sept 14–16), which also features demonstrations of horseback archery on the final day.

Beyond the Mai-den, a long flight of steps leads up beside a knobbly, ancient ginkgo tree, reputedly 1000 years old and scene of the third shogun's murder by his vengeful nephew, to the **main shrine**. It's an attractive collection of buildings set among trees, though, as with all Shinto shrines, you can only peer in. Appropriately, the principal deity, Hachiman, is the God of War.

The **Hōmotsu-den** (daily 8.30am–4.30pm; ¥200), in a corridor immediately left of the shrine, contains a missable exhibition of shrine treasures. Instead, head back down the steps and turn left to find the beautifully restrained, black-lacquered **Shirahata-jinja**, dedicated to the first and third Kamakura shoguns, then take the path south to the modern **Kamakura National Treasure Hall** (鎌倉国宝館; 9am–4.30pm; closed Mon; ¥400; English leaflet ¥250). This one-room museum is noted for its collection of Kamakura- and Muromachi-period art (1192–1573), mostly gathered from local Zen temples. Unfortunately, only a few of the priceless pieces are on display at any one time.

The Town: East Kamakura

The eastern side of Kamakura contains a scattering of less-visited shrines and temples, including two of the town's most enchanting corners. Though it's possible to cover the area on foot in a half-day (less if you hop on a bus for the return journey), by far the best way to explore these scattered locations is to rent a bicycle (see p.205 for information on buses and bikes).

If you're starting from Hachiman-gū, you can work your way eastwards through a quiet suburban area north of the main highway, the Kanazawa-kaidō, until you find signs indicating an optional left turn for **Kamakura-gū** (鎌倉宮). Mainly of interest for its history and torchlight nō dramas in early October, this was founded by Emperor Meiji in 1869 to encourage support for his new imperial regime. The shrine is dedicated to Prince Morinaga, a forgotten fourteenth-century hero who was held for nine months in a Kamakura cave before being executed. The small cave and a desultory treasure house (daily 9am–4pm; ¥300) lie to the rear of the classically styled shrine, but don't really justify the entry fee.

A road heading north from Kamakura-gū marks the beginning – or end – of the short cut to the Ten'en Hiking Course (see opposite), though the main trail starts 900m further east, near **Zuisen-ji** (瑞泉寺; daily: 9am–4.30pm; ¥200). The temple's fourteenth-century Zen garden, to the rear of the main building, is rather dilapidated, but the quiet, wooded location and luxuriant gardens in front of the temple make it an attractive spot.

From here you have to drop south and join the main road for the last short stretch to one of Kamakura's oldest temples, **Sugimoto-dera** (杉本寺; daily 8am–4.30pm; ¥200), at the top of a steep, foot-worn staircase lined with fluttering white flags. Standing in a woodland clearing, the small, thatched temple, founded in 734, exudes a real sense of history. Inside its smoke-blackened hall, spattered with pilgrims' prayer stickers, you can slip off your shoes and take a look behind the altar at the three wooden statues of Jūichimen Kannon, the eleven-faced Goddess of Mercy. The images were carved at different times by famous monks, but all three are at least 1000 years old.

Just a couple of minutes further east along Kanazawa-kaidō, turn right over a small bridge to reach the entrance to **Hōkoku-ji** (報国寺; daily 9am–4pm; ¥200 for access to the Bamboo Garden), or Take-dera, the "Bamboo Temple". The well-tended gardens and simple wooden buildings are attractive in themselves, but the temple is best known for a grove of evergreen bamboo protected by the encircling cliffs.

To **return** to central Kamakura, you can catch a bus for the 2km ride from opposite Sugimoto-dera. Alternatively, take the small lane to the left in front of Hōkoku-ji and follow it west through an attractive residential area, which cuts off at least a chunk of the highway.

Hase-dera and the Daibutsu

The west side of Kamakura, an area known as **Hase** (長谷), is home to the town's most famous sight, the **Daibutsu** (Great Buddha), cast in bronze nearly 750 years ago. On the way, it's worth visiting **Hase-dera** to see an image of Kannon, the Goddess of Mercy, which is said to be Japan's largest wooden statue. Both these sights are within walking distance of Hase Station, three stops from Kamakura Station (¥190) on the private Enoden line.

Hase-dera (長谷寺; daily: March–Sept 8am–5pm; Oct–Feb 8am–4.30pm; ¥300; Ⓦwww.hasedera.jp) stands high on the hillside a few minutes' walk north of Hase Station, with good views of Kamakura and across Yuigahama beach to the Miura peninsula beyond. Though the temple's present layout dates from the mid-thirteenth century, according to legend it was founded in 736, when a wooden eleven-faced Kannon was washed ashore nearby. The statue is supposedly one of a pair carved from a single camphor tree in 721 by a monk in the original Hase, near Nara; he placed one Kannon in a local temple and pushed the other out to sea.

Nowadays the **Kamakura Kannon** – just over 9m tall and gleaming with gold leaf (a fourteenth-century embellishment) – resides in an attractive, chocolate-brown and cream building at the top of the temple steps. This central hall is flanked by two smaller buildings: the right hall houses a large Amidha Buddha carved in 1189 for Minamoto Yoritomo's 42nd birthday to ward off the bad luck traditionally associated with that age; the one on the left shelters a copy of an early fifteenth-century statue of Daikoku-ten, the cheerful God of Wealth. The real one is in the small **treasure hall** (Wed–Mon 9am–4pm) immediately behind, alongside the original temple bell, cast in 1264. The next building along is the Sutra Repository, where a revolving drum contains a complete set of Buddhist scriptures – one turn of the wheel is equivalent to reading the whole lot. Ranks of Jizō statues are a common sight in Hase-dera, some clutching sweets or "windmills" and wrapped in tiny woollen mufflers; these sad little figures commemorate stillborn or aborted children. Finally, a cave in the far northern corner of the complex contains statues of the goddess Benten and her sixteen children, or disciples, though it can't compete with the atmospheric setting of the Zeniarai Benten cave-shrine (see p.207).

The Daibutsu

From Hase-dera, turn left at the main road and follow the crowds north for a few hundred metres to find the **Daibutsu** (大仏; daily: April–Sept 7am–6pm; Oct–March 7am–5.30pm; ¥200), in the grounds of Kōtoku-in temple. After all the hype, the Great Buddha can seem a little disappointing, but as you approach, and his serene, rather aloof face comes into view, the magic begins to take hold. He sits on a stone pedestal, a broad-shouldered figure lost in deep meditation, with his head slightly bowed, his face and robes streaked grey-green by centuries of sun, wind and rain. The 13m-tall image represents Amida Nyorai, the future Buddha who receives souls into the Western Paradise, and was built under the orders of Minamoto Yoritomo to rival the larger Nara Buddha, near Kyoto. Completed in 1252, the statue is constructed of bronze plates bolted together around a hollow frame – you can climb inside for ¥20 (daily 8am–4.30pm) – and evidence suggests that, at some time, it was covered in gold leaf. Amazingly, it has withstood fires, typhoons, tidal waves and even the Great Earthquake of 1923.

Eating and drinking

Kamakura is famous for its beautifully presented Buddhist vegetarian cuisine, known as **shōjin ryōri**, though there's plenty more casual dining on offer at local restaurants. For a picnic, Kinokuniya has a good food hall on the west side of Kamakura Station, or try Union Store on Wakamiya-ōji. In summer, funky wooden bars line the beaches from Kamakura to Enoshima.

Hachi-no-ki Honten 鉢の木本店 7 Yamanouchi ⓣ0467/22-8719; two other branches side by side, opposite Tōkei-ji ⓣ0467/23-3722(3723). Reservations are recommended for this famous *shōjin ryōri* restaurant beside the entrance to Kenchō-ji. Prices start at around ¥2000. Tues–Fri 11.30am–2.30pm, Sat & Sun 11am–3pm; main Kita-Kamakura branch 11am–2.30pm & 5–7pm, closed Wed.

Kōmyō-ji 光明寺 6-1-19 Zaimokuza ⓣ0467/22-0603. Enjoy the full *shōjin ryōri* experience in this temple set in beautiful gardens on the coast in southern Kamakura. Prices start at ¥4000 for a minimum of two people. Reservations required at least a day in advance. Open for lunch only.

Kyorai-an 去来庵 157 Yamanouchi ⓣ0467/24-9835. Specializing in beef stew prepared in a demi-glace sauce, the restaurant itself is inside a traditional Showa-era house. The set meal with toast or rice, salad and coffee is the best value (¥2600). Open 11am–3pm and weekends until 5pm; closed Fri.

Milk Hall ミルクホール 2-3-8 Komachi ⓣ0467/22-1179, ⓦwww.milkhall.co.jp. Relaxed, jazz-playing coffee house-cum-antique shop buried in the backstreets west of Komachi-dōri. Best for a coffee and cake, or an evening beer, rather than as a place to eat. Occasional live music. Daily 11am–10.30pm.

Nakamura-an なかむら庵 1-7-6 Komachi ⓣ0467/25-3500. A homely restaurant that has them queuing up outside at weekends for the handmade soba. To find it, walk up Wakamiya-ōji and take the first left after the Union Store. Dishes start at ¥700. Open 11am–4.30pm; closed Tues.

Enoshima

Tied to the mainland by a 600m-long bridge, the tiny, sacred island of **Enoshima** (江の島) has a few sights – some shrines, a botanical garden and a couple of missable caves – but its prime attraction is as a pleasant place to walk, away from motor traffic.

Enoshima is 25 minutes west of Kamakura Station on the Enoden line (¥250). You can pick up an English-language map of the island at the small **tourist office** (daily 10am–5pm; ⓣ0466/26-9544, ⓦwww.fujisawa-kanko.jp), on the left as you come off the bridge.

The Island

From Enoshima Station it's roughly fifteen minutes' walk southwest to the island, via a bridge constructed over the original sand spit. Enoshima's eastern side shelters a

Enoshima to Tokyo

There are three options if you're heading directly back **to central Tokyo** from Enoshima. The most straightforward is the Odakyū-Enoshima line direct to Shinjuku, though note that weekday services are few and far between. The trains depart from Katase-Enoshima Station (片瀬江ノ島駅); from the island causeway, turn left across the river to find the station with its distinctive Chinese-style facade. A pleasant alternative is to take the Shōnan monorail to Ōfuna, on the main JR lines to central Tokyo via Yokohama; Shōnan-Enoshima Station (湘南江ノ島駅) is located just north of the Enoden line station. The last option is to hop on the Enoden line west to its terminal in Fujisawa, where you have to change stations for JR services to central Tokyo.

yacht harbour and car parks, but otherwise the knuckle of rock – less than 1km from end to end – is largely covered with woods and a network of well-marked paths. From here, walk straight ahead under the bronze *torii* and uphill past restaurants and souvenir shops to where the steps begin; though the climb's easy enough, there are three escalators tunnelled through the hillside (¥350, or pay for each separately).

Enoshima is mostly famous for a naked **statue of Benten**, sitting in an octagonal hall halfway up the hill (daily 9am–4.30pm; ¥150), and although ranked among Japan's top three Benten images, it's a little hard to see what all the fuss is about. Continuing round the hill, you'll pass several other shrine buildings belonging to **Enoshima-jinja**, founded in the thirteenth century and dedicated to the guardian of sailors and fisherfolk, before emerging beside a nicely laid-out **botanical garden**, known as the Samuel Cocking Park (April–June, Sept & Oct Mon–Fri 9am–6pm, Sat & Sun 9am–8pm; July & Aug daily 9am–8pm; Nov–March Mon–Fri 9am–5pm, Sat & Sun 9am–8pm; ¥200).

Practicalities

It's possible to **stay** on Enoshima at the *Ebisuya* (恵比寿屋; 1-4-16 Enoshima Ⓣ0466/22-4105, Ⓦwww.ebisuyaryokan.jp; ❺ including two meals), a good-value ryokan. Just under the bronze *torii* and down an alley on the left, it offers well-maintained Western and tatami rooms, plus traditional baths and excellent meals.

If you're looking for somewhere to **eat**, get out at Shichirigahama Station (七里ヶ浜駅) on the Enoden line for chef Bill Granger's first **Bills restaurant** to open outside Australia (1-1-1 Shichirigahama; Mon 8am–5pm, Tues–Thurs 8am–10pm, Fri–Sat 8am–11pm; Ⓣ0467/33-1778, Ⓦwww.bills-jp.net). You'll want to go for the popular breakfasts, which are served until 3pm on weekends. Another branch is located in Yokohama, inside the Akarenga (see p.219).

Yokohama and around

On its southern borders Tokyo merges with **YOKOHAMA** (横浜), Japan's second most populous city (home to 3.6 million people) and a major international port. Yokohama feels far more spacious and airy than the capital, thanks to its open harbour frontage and generally low-rise skyline, and though it can't claim any outstanding sights, the place has enough of interest to justify a day's outing from Tokyo. Locals are proud of their city's international heritage, and there's definitely a cosmopolitan flavour to the place, with its scattering of Western-style buildings, Chinese temples and world cuisines, and its sizeable foreign community. It might seem strange to come all this way to look at nineteenth-century European-style architecture, but the upmarket suburb of **Yamate** is one of the city's highlights, an area of handsome residences, church spires and bijou teashops. Yamate's "exotic" attractions still draw Japanese tourists in large numbers, as do the vibrant alleys and speciality restaurants of nearby **Chinatown**. There's a clutch of assorted **museums** along the seafront, and north to where **Kannai** boasts a few grand old Western edifices, in complete contrast to the **Minato Mirai 21** development's hi-tech skyscrapers in the distance.

Some history

When Commodore Perry sailed his "Black Ships" into Tokyo Bay in 1853, Yokohama was a mere fishing village of some eighty houses on the distant shore. But it was this harbour, well out of harm's way as far as the Japanese were concerned, that the shogun designated one of the five **treaty ports** open to foreign trade in 1858. At first foreign merchants were limited to a small compound in today's Kannai – allegedly for their protection from anti-foreign sentiment – but eventually they moved up onto the more favourable southern hills.

From the early 1860s until the first decades of the twentieth century, Yokohama flourished on the back of raw silk exports, a trade dominated by British merchants. During this period the city provided the main conduit for new ideas and inventions into Japan: the first bakery, photographers, ice-cream shop, brewery and – perhaps most importantly – the first railway line, which linked today's Sakuragichō with Shimbashi in central Tokyo in 1872. Yokohama was soon established as Japan's major international port and held pole position until the **Great Earthquake** levelled the city in 1923, killing more than 40,000 people. It was eventually rebuilt, only to be devastated again in air raids at the end of World War II. By this time Kōbe in western Japan was in the ascendancy and, though Yokohama still figures among the world's largest ports, it never regained its hold over Japanese trade.

Arrival

On the northwest side of town, **Yokohama Station** functions as the city's main transport hub, offering train, subway, bus and even ferry connections, and featuring several gargantuan department stores. The best way to get to Yokohama **from central Tokyo** is on a Tōkyū-Tōyoko-line **train** from Shibuya Station (every 5min; 30min; ¥260), which calls at Yokohama Station before heading off underground to Minato Mirai and terminating at the Motomachi-Chūkagai Station. If you're coming from Tokyo Station, you can choose from the Tōkaidō or Yokosuka lines (both every 5–10min; 30min; ¥450), or the Keihin-Tōhoku line (every 5–10min; 40min; ¥450). All three are JR lines; the first two terminate at Yokohama Station, while the latter continues to Sakuragichō, Kannai and Ishikawachō. From Shinjuku, JR's Shōnan-Shinjuku line brings you into Yokohama Station (every 20–30min; 30min; ¥540).

Arriving straight **from Narita Airport**, services on JR's **Narita Express** (N'EX) depart roughly every hour for Yokohama Station and take ninety minutes (¥4180), but not all N'EX trains go to Yokohama and some divide at Tokyo Station, so check before you get on. Otherwise, get on the cheaper rapid train (JR, "Airport Narita"), which takes two hours to reach Yokohama Station (¥1890). From **Haneda Airport**, the choice is a Keihin-Kyūkō line train (40min; ¥470) to Yokohama Station or a limousine bus (30min; ¥560), which drops you at **YCAT** (Yokohama City Air Terminal), just east of Yokohama Station; in both cases, services depart roughly every ten minutes.

Shinkansen trains from Kyoto, Ōsaka and points south pause briefly at **Shin-Yokohama**, 5km north of the centre. From here there's a subway link to the main Yokohama Station (¥230), Sakuragichō and Kannai, but it's cheaper and usually quicker to get the first passing JR Yokohama-line train and change at

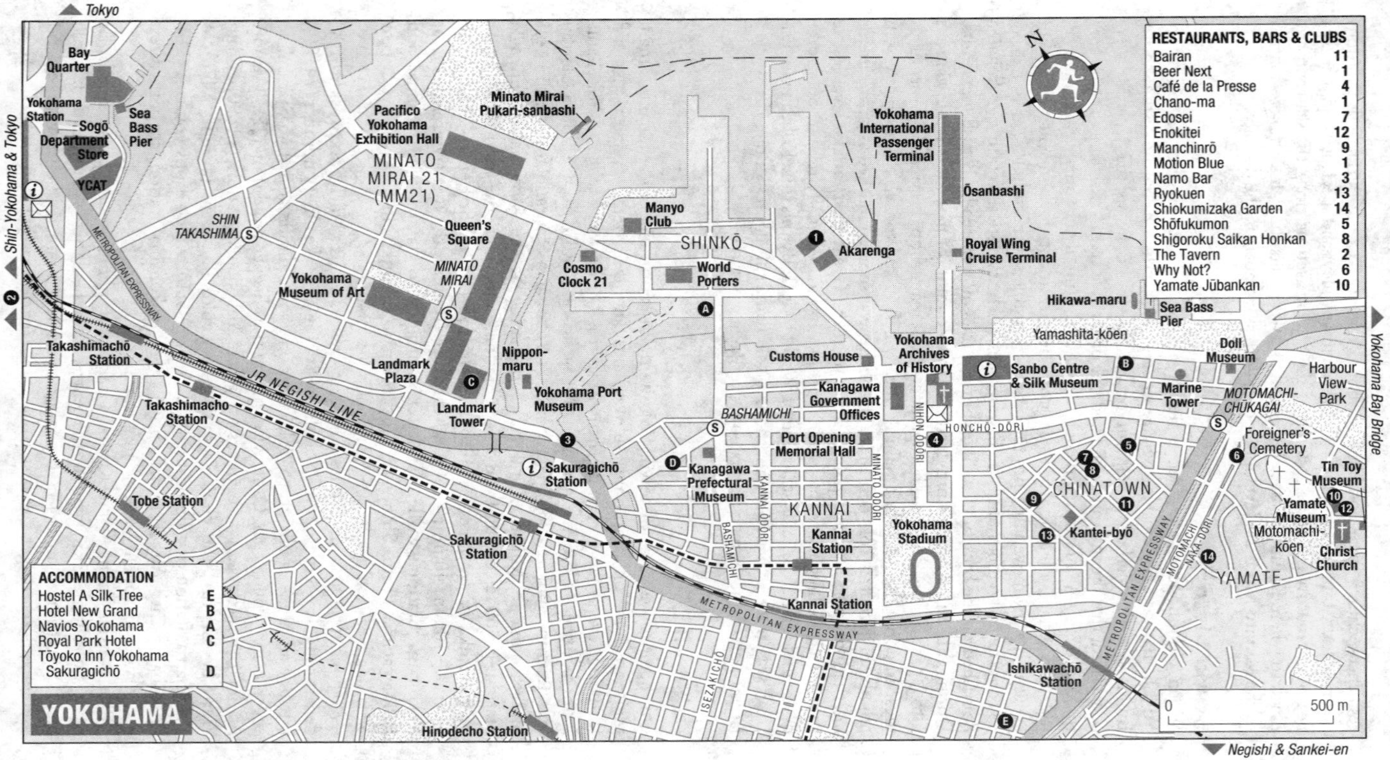

YOKOHAMA
RESTAURANTS, BARS & CLUBS
Bairan 11
Beer Next 1
Café de la Presse 4
Chano-ma 1
Edosei 7
Enokitei 12
Manchinrō 9
Motion Blue 1
Namo Bar 3
Ryokuen 13
Shiokumizaka Garden 14
Shōfukumon 5
Shigoroku Saikan Honkan 8
The Tavern 2
Why Not? 6
Yamate Jūbankan 10
ACCOMMODATION
Hostel A Silk Tree E
Hotel New Grand B
Navios Yokohama A
Royal Park Hotel C
Tōyoko Inn Yokohama Sakuragichō D
Tokyo
Shin-Yokohama & Tokyo
Yokohama Bay Bridge
Negishi & Sankei-en
Bay Quarter
Yokohama Station
Sogō Department Store
Sea Bass Pier
YCAT
Pacifico Yokohama Exhibition Hall
Minato Mirai Pukari-sanbashi
MINATO MIRAI 21 (MM21)
SHIN TAKASHIMA
Queen's Square
MINATO MIRAI
Yokohama Museum of Art
Manyo Club
SHINKŌ
Cosmo Clock 21
World Porters
Akarenga
Yokohama International Passenger Terminal
Ōsanbashi
Royal Wing Cruise Terminal
Hikawa-maru
Sea Bass Pier
Yamashita-kōen
Takashimachō Station
Takashimacho Station
JR NEGISHI LINE
METROPOLITAN EXPRESSWAY
Landmark Plaza
Landmark Tower
Nippon-maru
Yokohama Port Museum
Customs House
Yokohama Archives of History
Sanbo Centre & Silk Museum
Doll Museum
Harbour View Park
Marine Tower
MOTOMACHI-CHŪKAGAI
Kanagawa Government Offices
BASHAMICHI
NIHON ŌDŌRI
HONCHŌ-DŌRI
Port Opening Memorial Hall
MINATO ŌDŌRI
Sakuragichō Station
Kanagawa Prefectural Museum
KANNAI ŌDŌRI
KANNAI
Yokohama Stadium
Kannai Station
Kannai Station
CHINATOWN
Kantei-byō
Foreigner's Cemetery
Tin Toy Museum
Yamate Museum
Motomachi-kōen
Christ Church
MOTOMACHI NAKA-DŌRI
YAMATE
Tobe Station
Sakuragichō Station
Ishikawachō Station
ISEZAKICHŌ
Hinodecho Station
0 500 m

Higashi-Kanagawa Station onto the Keihin-Tōhoku line (¥160). **Ferries** from Tokyo and Ōshima call at the Ōsanbashi pier, a short walk from the city centre.

Information

Yokohama's plethora of **tourist offices**, with English-speaking staff, puts Tokyo's to shame. The most useful is the one immediately outside **Sakuragichō Station**'s east entrance (April–Nov & Jan–Feb daily 9am–6pm; Dec & March 9am–7pm; ⓣ045/211-0111). Other options include the office in the harbour-front **Sanbo Centre** east of Kannai Station (Mon–Fri 9am–5pm; ⓣ045/641-4759) and the booth in the underground concourse of **Yokohama Station** (daily 9am–7pm; ⓣ045/441-7300); all provide free **city maps** and brochures, and can help with hotel reservations. The Yokohama Convention and Visitors Bureau (ⓦwww.welcome.city.yokohama.jp/eng/tourism), the Kanagawa Prefectural Tourist Association (ⓦwww.kanagawa-kankou.or.jp) and the city's homepage, ⓦwww.city.yokohama.jp/en, are all good online resources.

City transport

Getting around central Yokohama is best done on either the Tōkyū-Tōyoko line or the JR Negishi line (the local name for Keihin-Tōhoku trains); trains on both lines run every five minutes, with a minimum fare of ¥180. A single **subway** line connects Kannai and stations north to Shin-Yokohama, on the Shinkansen line, but services only run every five to fifteen minutes and the minimum fare is ¥200.

Another good option is the "Akai Kutsu" **sightseeing bus**, a retro-style red bus that runs from outside Sakuragichō Station's east exit via Minato Mirai, Akarenga complex, Chinatown and Yamashita-kōen to Harbour View Park, then loops back via Ōsanbashi pier. Services run every half-hour on weekdays and every twenty minutes at weekends from 10am to 6pm (May–Oct until 7pm). Individual tickets cost ¥100, but you'll probably be better off buying a day-pass (¥300), available from tourist offices or on the bus.

Perhaps the most enjoyable way of getting about the city is on the *Sea Bass* **ferries** (ⓦwww.yokohama-cruising.jp) that shuttle between Yokohama Station (from a pier in the Bay Quarter shopping complex) and southerly Yamashita-kōen, with some services stopping at Minato Mirai and Akarenga on route. There are departures every fifteen minutes (roughly 10am–7.30pm, or 8pm March–Nov), with one-way tickets costing ¥700 to Yamashita-kōen, ¥400 to Minato Mirai and ¥580 to Akarenga.

Accommodation

Yokohama's luxury **hotels**, all located in the Minato Mirai 21 district, are a tourist attraction in their own right. You'll need a reservation at the weekend (when premium rates also usually apply), though weekdays shouldn't be a problem. Lower down the scale, there are a few reasonable business hotels scattered round the city centre and some welcome new budget options.

Yokohama sightseeing cruises

From Yamashita-kōen you can also join the *Marine Shuttle* or *Marine Rouge* for a variety of **sightseeing cruises** round the harbour (from ¥1000 for 40min; ⓦwww.yokohama-cruising.jp); the *Marine Rouge* also offers lunch and dinner cruises (¥2520 plus ¥5500–11,000 for food). In addition, the bigger and more luxurious *Royal Wing* cruise ship (ⓣ045/662-6125, ⓦwww.royalwing.co.jp) runs lunch, tea and dinner cruises from Ōsanbashi pier (¥2000–2400 plus food options starting at ¥2100).

Hostel A Silk Tree 8F 3-9-4 Matsukage-chō, Naka-ku ⓣ045/719-1541. Spotlessly clean hostel in a tenement block 3min walk from Ishikawachō Station. Two can squeeze in the basic, tatami-mat boxes, and facilities include a kitchen corner, internet access, coin-operated showers (on the ground floor; ¥200), laundry and bike rental (¥300/day). Singles ¥3000, doubles ¥4500. ❶

Hotel New Grand 10 Yamashitachō, Naka-ku ⓣ045/681-1841, ⓦwww.hotel-newgrand.co.jp. Built in the late 1920s in European style, the main building retains some of its original elegance – many rooms in the newer tower offer bay views. ❽

Navios Yokohama 2-1-1 Shinkō, Naka-ku ⓣ045/633-6000, ⓦwww.navios-yokohama.com. One of the best-value options in Yokohama; ask for a room facing the Landmark for terrific night-time views. Facilities include free internet access. ❻

Royal Park Hotel 2-2-1-3 Minato Mirai, Nishi-ku ⓣ045/221-1111, ⓦwww.yrph.com. Occupying the 52nd to 67th floors of the Landmark Tower, spectacular views are guaranteed. The rooms are fairly spacious and come with good-sized bathrooms. As well as a fitness club and swimming pool (¥2100–5250), facilities include a tea-ceremony room (¥1500) and the *Sirius Sky Lounge*. ❾

Tōyoko Inn Yokohama Sakuragichō 東横イン横浜桜木町 6-55 Hon-chō, Naka-ku ⓣ045/671-1045. One of several Yokohama branches of this Japan-wide chain of budget business hotels, with good-value rooms, free internet access and breakfast. ❸

The City

Yokohama retains a few European-style buildings from its days as a treaty port, some of which lie scattered around **Kannai**, the traditional city centre. For a more evocative atmosphere, climb up to **Yamate** (also known as "the Bluff"), while **Chinatown**, back down on the levels, makes for a lively contrast, with its hordes of colourful trinket shops and bustling restaurants. From here it's a short stroll to the harbour-front **Marine Tower** and a couple of nearby museums, or a train ride north to where the aptly named **Landmark Tower**, Japan's tallest building, pinpoints the futuristic **Minato Mirai 21** (MM21) development. Among its gleaming hotels, shopping malls and conference centres, notable sights include a modern art museum and an incongruous four-masted barque, the **Nippon-maru**.

Motomachi and Yamate

Southeast of central Yokohama, just before the land rises to Yamate hill, **Motomachi** (元町) is a chic shopping street from prewar days which used to serve the city's expatriate community. The narrow, semi-pedestrianized lane still exudes a faint retro flavour with its European facades, though the small boutiques and family stores are gradually giving way to the regular national and international chains. Nowadays, you'll get more of the old Motomachi feel in the two streets to either side, particularly Naka-dōri (仲通り), to the south, with its funky cafés and galleries.

At the northeast end of Motomachi, a wooded promontory marks the beginning of the Yamate (山手) district. Take any of the paths heading uphill through **Harbour View Park** to find a lookout point where the British and French barracks once stood – the panoramic view of the harbour and its graceful Bay Bridge is particularly beautiful at night. Turning inland and walking through the park will bring you to the **Yokohama Foreign General Cemetery** (Gaikokujin Bochi; 外国人墓地; March–Dec Sat & Sun noon–4pm; ¥200) on the western hillside. Over 4500 people from more than forty countries are buried here, the vast majority either British or American.

If you head south along the cemetery's eastern perimeter, you'll pass a handsome row of houses, including the turreted Yamate Jūbankan – now a French restaurant (see p.220) – and, next door to it, the **Yamate Museum** (daily 11am–4pm; ¥200; ⓣ045/622-1188), housed in a 1909 buliding. Just beyond, the square tower of **Christ Church**, founded in 1862 but rebuilt most recently in 1947, adds a village-green touch to the neighbourhood, which is still the most popular residential district for Yokohama's wealthy expatriates.

Regional cuisines

***Itadakimasu* and *oishii* – Japanese for "bon appétit" and "delicious" – are words that you'll utter frequently on any culinary tour of Japan. Alongside myriad local variations of staples such as noodles, sushi and seafood, and drinks such as sake and shōchū, there are unexpected surprises such as candied crickets, pickled pigs' ears, wafer-thin slices of raw horsemeat and a barbecued lamb dish named after a Mongolian warrior (see p.296) to be discovered between the cold climes of Hokkaidō and the sunny shores of Okinawa.**

Businessmen eating ramen ▲

Somen noodle-making ▼

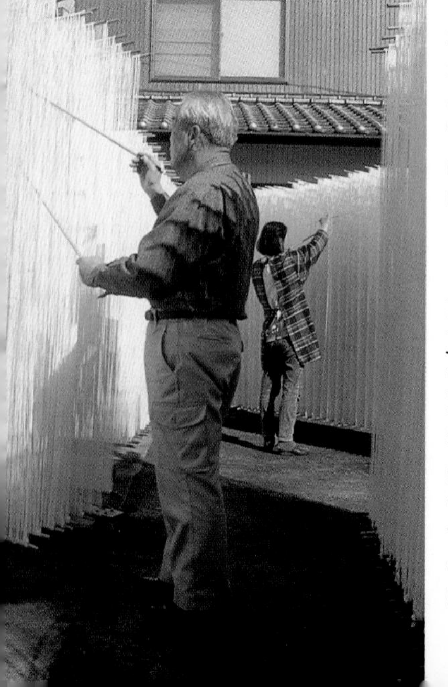

Oodles of noodles

That staple of Japanese cuisine – noodles – can be enjoyed in a multiplicity of dishes. **Asahikawa** (see p.314) excels at making thinner than usual rāmen (yellow wheat noodles) in a *shōyu* (soy sauce) based soup, while Sapporo's recipe favours a soup enriched with a slab of butter and kernels of corn. Down south in **Fukuoka** (p.654), Hakata-rāmen is made with a thick pork broth, the best of which takes days to prepare.

Aficionados of soba (buckwheat noodles) swear the best are made in Nagano-ken (see p.338) where they are called **shinshū soba**, after the old Japanese name for the region. Competitive types will want to sample *wanko-soba* in Morioka (p.248) – small bowls of thin, flat soba consumed in eating contests, while in Tōno (see p.243) rough, handmade *hitsuko soba* – eaten with a mix of chicken, raw egg, onion and mushroom – can be enjoyed at a more leisurely pace.

Wheat is used to make **sanuki-udon** in Kagawa-ken on Shikoku, a thicker noodle served in the stew-like *shippoku-udon*, which is packed with vegetables. The thinner wheat noodles of this region, **somen**, are especially good in Shōdoshima (see p.603) and Matsuyama (see p.636).

Marine delights

Head to **Shikoku** to sample some of Japan's best fish dishes. In Kōchi (see p.621) try *katsuo-no-tataki*, **bonito** that has been lightly seared and left raw inside before it is sliced and served like sashimi with grated radish. Afterwards, compliment the chef with a cry of *makkoto umaizeyo*, which means "Very tasty!" in the local dialect. If you visit either Uwajima (p.630) or Tokushima (p.612), dig into the delicacy *taimeshi* (grilled red sea bream served on rice).

In **Hokkaido**, sample the island's excellent salmon in *Ishikari-nabe*, a red-miso-flavoured hotpot of salmon and shellfish, daikon, leeks, Chinese cabbage and tofu; the salmon is also used in *ruibe*, a freeze-dried method of preparation that was perfected centuries ago by the island's native Ainu population. Also renowned here is crab; to try the sweetest – long-legged, snow and king – head to Wakkanai (p.320), the Shiretoko peninsula (p.327), Kushiro (p.332) and Hakodate (p.307) – the last two have wonderful seafood markets.

Speciality meats

Kōbe beef is a favourite of chefs around the world for its melt-in-the-mouth texture and superb flavour. But other areas of Japan also produce top-grade beef, including Matsuzaka in Mie-ken and **Hida beef** from Gifu-ken. One of the best places to enjoy cuts of this meat is in Takayama (see p.363), where it is often served in conjunction with a portion of the delicious (and spectacular looking) *hōba miso* – spicy miso paste, mixed with vegetables, roasted over a charcoal brazier atop a large magnolia leaf.

Nagoya (p.384) is renowned for its succulent **chicken**, called *kochin* – the best way to enjoy it is at the city's *yakitori* bars or as *tebasaki*, spicy deep-fried chicken wings that are the perfect partner to an icy glass of beer. While in town, you should also try the delicious eel dish, *hitsumabushi* (see p.392), another local speciality. In Kyūshū, *shishi nabe* (wild boar stew) is a popular winter dish around Miyazaki, while Kumamoto (see p.681) is known for *basashi* (**horsemeat sashimi**), served with ginger or garlic, that's also a speciality of Matsumoto in Nagano-ken (see p.352).

▲ Fresh crab on ice, Hakodate

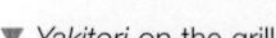

▼ *Yakitori* on the grill

Mongolian mutton barbecue ▲

Okinawa food market ▲

Shōchū bottle and cup ▼

Ryūkyū cuisine

Practically every part of the pig, from the head to the trotters (*tibichi*), is used in Okinawan **Ryūkyū cuisine**. The blood is sautéed with vegetables for *chii-irichii*, while the stomach and intestines go into *nakami* soup. Some believe eating plenty of pork is the secret to longevity: the islands have Japan's highest percentage of centenarians, 28 per every 100,000 people.

Goat stew (*yagijiru*) is a rustic dish popular in the Miyako Islands, and if you're feeling adventurous you could try goat sashimi or *irabū-jiru* (sea snake stew). Okinawa also produces many different types of **tofu**, including the delicious, silky-smooth *jimamedōfu*, made from peanuts, though the island's most famous dish is **champurū**, a vegetable stir fry that is often made with sponge gourd (*nābera*), bitter melon (*gōya*), wheat gluten (*fu*) and wheat noodle (*somen*).

Regional tipples

Thousands of **sake** breweries – identified by a ball of cedar leaves hanging over the shop door – make *ji-zaké* (regional sake). Good ones that are open to visitors can be found in Asahikawa (p.314), Kotohira (p.611), Obuse (p.347) and Takayama (p.367).

Kagoshima (p.715) is Japan's biggest producer of **shōchū**, a potent vodka-like liquor traditionally distilled from grain, although its speciality is sweet potato *shōchū*. In Kōchi (p.621) *shōchū* is made from chestnuts, and across Japan there are many other types, the ingredient imparting a distinct flavour to each.

Like wine, Okinawa's pungent rice liquor *awamori* improves with age. It's a very palatable beverage, but should be drunk with care; the strongest versions (called *hanazake*) have an alcohol content of up to sixty percent.

Just behind the church, the **Tin Toy Museum** (ブリキのおもちゃ博物館; Mon–Fri 9.30am–6pm, Sat & Sun 9.30am–7pm; ¥200) houses a wonderful collection of 13,000 tin toys from the 1890s to the 1960s; in a separate shop next door, you can buy a huge variety of Christmas decorations and stocking fillers at any time of year.

Chinatown and down to the harbour

From Yamate, drop down through Motomachi-kōen and cross Motomachi shopping street to find one of the several colourful entrance gates to **Chinatown** (中華街). Founded in 1863, Yokohama's Chinatown is the largest in Japan: its streets contain roughly two hundred restaurants and over three hundred shops, while some eighteen million tourists pass through its narrow byways every year to browse stores peddling Chinese herbs or cooking utensils, groceries and garish souvenirs. Few leave without tasting what's on offer, from steaming savoury dumplings to a full-blown meal in one of the famous speciality restaurants (see p.219).

The focus of community life is **Kantei-byō** (関帝廟; daily 9am–7pm; free), a shrine dedicated to Guan Yu, a former general and guardian deity of Chinatown. The building is a bit cramped, but impressive nonetheless, with a colourful ornamental gateway and writhing dragons wherever you look. It's ¥500 to enter and see the red-faced, long-haired Guan Yu, but not really worth it. The best times to visit are during the major festivities surrounding Chinese New Year (Jan or Feb), Guan Yu's birthday (the 24th day of the sixth lunar month; June or July) and Chinese National Day (Oct 1).

From the eastern edge of Chinatown it's a short hop down to the harbour – aim for the pink-grey **Marine Tower** (Ⓦwww.marinetower.jp). This 106m-high tower, built in 1961 to celebrate the port's centenary, is supposedly the world's tallest lighthouse, though it's better to save your money for the Landmark Tower's much higher observation deck (see p.218). In front of the tower, **Yamashita-kōen** (Sun–Thurs 10am–7pm, Fri & Sat 10am–10pm) is a pleasant seafront park – more grass than trees – created as a memorial to victims of the Great Earthquake. Here you can pick up a *Sea Bass* ferry or take a harbour cruise (see p.215) from the pier beside the **Hikawa-maru**. This retired passenger liner, also known as the *Queen of the Pacific*, was built in 1930 for the NYK line Yokohama–Seattle service, though it was commandeered as a hospital ship during World War II. It now serves as a museum (日本郵船氷川丸; Tues–Sun 10am–5pm; ¥200, or ¥500 for a combination ticket with the nearby NYK Maritime Museum; Ⓣ045/641-4362, Ⓦwww.nyk.com/rekishi).

At the south end of Yamashita-kōen, the **Doll Museum** (Ningyō no Ie; 人形の家; daily 10am–6.30pm, closed third Mon of month; ¥500; Ⓦwww.museum.or.jp/yokohama-doll-museum) offers a diverting display of dolls from around the world. The vast collection ranges from American "blue-eyed friendship dolls", sent to Japan in the 1920s at a time of increasing tension between the two countries, to Japanese folk and classical dolls.

Yokohama's rapid growth in the late nineteenth century was underpinned by a flourishing export trade in raw silk. You can learn all about the practical aspects of silk production at the **Silk Museum** (シルク博物館; 9am–4.30pm; closed Mon; ¥500; Ⓦwww.silkmuseum.or.jp), in the Sanbo Centre at the north end of Yamashita-kōen. Opposite the museum, the **Ōsanbashi** (大さん橋) pier is where cruise ships pull up to berth at Yokohama's International Passenger Terminal. Originally dating from the late nineteenth century, the pier was rebuilt in 2002 to a beautifully fluid, low-slung design inspired by ocean waves.

Kannai

Continuing north from the Silk Museum across a leafy square, you come to a modern, windowless building which houses the **Yokohama Archives of History**

(横浜開港資料館; 9.30am–5pm; closed Mon; ¥200; Ⓦwww.kaikou.city.yokohama.jp). The museum details the opening of Yokohama (and Japan) to the outside world after 1853 through an impressive collection of photos, artefacts and documents, including contemporary newspaper reports from London, helped by an unusual amount of English translation.

You're now in the thick of Yokohama's administrative district, where several European-style facades still survive. Kanagawa government offices occupy the next block north, while the biscuit-coloured **Customs House**, opposite, is a more attractive structure, topped by a distinguished, copper-clad dome. A road north of here leads to Shinkō island (see opposite), but for now follow the road heading inland, Minato Ōdōri, to find the graceful **Port Opening Memorial Hall**; erected in 1918, this red-brick neo-Renaissance building now serves as public function rooms. In front of the hall, turn north again, onto Honchō-dōri, to reach the last and most ornate of Yokohama's European-style facades, with Neoclassical flourishes. The building was completed in 1904 as the headquarters of a Yokohama bank, and then later converted into the **Kanagawa Prefectural Museum of Cultural History** (神奈川県立歴史博物館; 9.30am–5pm; closed Mon; ¥300; Ⓣ045/201-0926, Ⓦch.kanagawa-museum.jp). Though much of the material is devoted to Yokohama, including woodblock prints of the Black Ships and big-nosed, red-haired foreigners, exhibits also cover Kamakura's Zen temples and local folk culture. Although short on information in English, enthusiastic English-speaking guides are on hand to answer questions.

Minato Mirai 21 (MM21)

In a bid to beat Tokyo at its own game, Yokohama boasts Japan's tallest building and is creating a mini-city of apartment blocks, offices, recreational and cultural facilities: **Minato Mirai 21** (みなとみらい21; Ⓦwww.minatomirai21.com), or **MM21**, a growing development that will eventually occupy over two square kilometres of reclaimed land and disused dockyards.

MM21 can be accessed from either Minato Mirai Station on the Tōkyū-Tōyoko line or Sakuragichō train and subway station, from where a covered moving walkway whisks you towards the awesome, 296m-tall **Landmark Tower** (Ⓦwww.yokohama-landmark.jp). The **Sky Garden observation deck** (Sun–Fri 10am–9pm, Sat 10am–10pm; ¥1000) is on the 69th floor, and on clear days, when Fuji is flaunting its beauty, superb views more than justify the entry fee. You can also enjoy a coffee for about the same price in the opulent *Sirius Sky Lounge* on the seventieth floor of the *Royal Park Hotel*, or splash out on an early-evening cocktail as the city lights flicker on; after 5pm there's an additional live music charge of ¥1050–2100.

A water-filled dock in front of Landmark Tower is now home to the sleek **Nippon-maru** training sail ship, part of the enjoyable **Yokohama Port Museum** (横浜みなと博物館; 10am–5pm; closed Mon; ¥600; Ⓦwww.nippon-maru.or.jp). The *Nippon-maru* was built in 1930 and saw service up until 1984, during which time she sailed the equivalent of 45 times round the world; when her pristine white sails are hoisted (around ten times a year), it's clear why she's more familiarly known as the *Swan of the Pacific*. You can explore the entire vessel, with plenty of English labelling throughout, and alternating Japanese and English commentary over the loudspeakers.

North of the Landmark Tower is the splendid **Yokohama Museum of Art** (横浜美術館; daily except Thurs 10am–6pm; ¥500; varying prices for special exhibitions; Ⓣ045/221-0300, Ⓦwww.yaf.or.jp/yma), in which mostly twentieth-century Japanese and Western art is set off to fine effect by designer Tange Kenzō's cool, grey space, which grabs your attention as much as the exhibits.

Shinkō island

Between MM21 and Ōsanbashi is **Shinkō** island, which was reclaimed about a hundred years ago as part of Yokohama's then state-of-the-art port facilities. The slowly revolving **Cosmo Clock 21** (Mon–Fri 11am–9pm; Sat & Sun 11am–10pm; occasionally closed on Thurs; ¥700) here is one of the world's largest Ferris wheels, with a diameter of 112m; one circuit takes around fifteen minutes, allowing plenty of time to take in the view, which is particularly spectacular at night.

Cosmo Clock's changing colours provide a night-time spectacle in their own right, and one of the best places from which to admire them is the rooftop of the **Manyo Club** (万葉倶楽部; daily 10am–9am; ¥2620, plus ¥1680 after 3am; ⓣ045/663-4126), a spa complex in the next block east. Spread over five floors, it offers a variety of hot-spring baths – the water is trucked in from Atami onsen down the coast – in addition to massages and treatments, restaurants and relaxation rooms. Its best feature, though, is the circular rooftop footbath. Get a spot facing west for a grandstand view over MM21.

On the other side of Shinkō island, two handsome red-brick warehouses dating from 1911 now form the attractive **Akarenga** (赤レンガ) shopping, dining and entertainment complex. Live music concerts and other events often take place in summer and at weekends in the plaza, which transforms into a skating rink in winter.

Eating

One of Yokohama's highlights is sampling the enormous variety of restaurants and snack-food outlets cramming the streets of **Chinatown**. In Yamate and Motomachi, European cuisine predominates, while the restaurants in the new developments of MM21 cater to every taste and budget. Besides the establishments listed below, there are shopping malls such as Landmark Plaza, Queen's Square, Cross Gate and Shinkō island's World Porters, all of which make happy culinary hunting grounds. In fine weather, the casual little eating places on the ground floor of Akarenga are a good option, if only because you can take your food to the tables outside.

Chinatown

Bairan 梅蘭 133-10 Yamashita-chō ⓣ045/651-6695. Small, unpretentious restaurant tucked in the backstreets and known for its Bairan *yakisoba*, stir-fried noodles served like a sort of pancake, crispy on the outside and with a juicy pork or beef stuffing (¥900 and ¥1260, respectively) – one serving is big enough for two. Mon–Fri 11.30am–3pm & 5–10pm, Sat & Sun 11am–10pm.

Edosei 江戸清 192 Yamashita-chō ⓣ045/681-3133. Mega-size steamed dumplings are the speciality here, stuffed with interesting ingredients including black bean and walnut, onion and seafood, and shrimp and chilli, as well as the usual barbecued pork. Mon–Fri 9am–8pm, Sat & Sun 9am–9pm. Prices vary, but one dumpling can be as much as ¥500.

Manchinrō 萬珍樓 153 Yamashita-chō ⓣ045/681-4004, ⓦwww.manchinro.com. This famous restaurant has been serving tasty Cantonese cuisine since 1892. Though prices are on the high side, the portions are generous. Noodle and fried-rice dishes start at around ¥1100, lunch sets at ¥2500, and evening course menus at ¥5000. The branch behind serves a full range of dim sum. Daily 11am–10pm.

Ryokuen 緑苑 220 Yamashita-chō ⓣ045/651-5651. Simple, stylish Chinese teashop with some thirty types of tea on the menu, from ¥800 for a pot serving up to six small cups. Open 11.30am–6.30pm; closed Thurs.

Shōfukumon 招福門 81-3 Yamashita-chō ⓣ045/664-4141. Multistorey restaurant offering all-you-can-eat dim sum deals for ¥2625, plus fried rice and soup. Mon–Fri 11.30am–10pm, Sat & Sun 11am–10pm.

Suro Saikan Honkan 四五六菜館本館 190 Yamashita-chō ⓣ045/681-3456. Decorated with gorgeous mosaics, this place is popular for its reliable Shanghai cuisine. Weekday lunch sets start at under ¥700, course menus from around ¥3500, lunch or dinner. Mon–Fri 11.30am–10pm, Sat 11am–11pm, Sun 11am–10pm.

The rest of the city

Café de la Presse 2F Media Centre Building, 11 Nihon-dōri ⓣ045/222-3348. Viennese-style café in the corner of one of Yokohama's grand old buildings, with a smarter restaurant attached. The speciality is macaroons, though they also serve cakes, sandwiches and light meals (set lunch ¥1100). Open 10am–9pm; closed Mon.

Chano-ma 3F Akarenga 2, 1-1-2 Shinkō, Naka-ku ⓣ045/650-8228. Sit back with a cocktail and nibble modern Japanese dishes at this large, relaxed restaurant-cum-tearoom with a very contemporary vibe. Lunch sets from ¥1000. Mon–Thurs & Sun 11am–11pm, Fri & Sat 11am–5am.

Enokitei えの木てい 89-6 Yamate-chō ⓣ045/623-2288. Set in a venerable Yamate home, this cute English-style café serves dainty sandwiches and home-made cakes. Tues–Fri 11am–7pm.

Shiokumizaka Garden 汐汲坂ガーデン3-145 Motomachi, Naka-ku ⓣ045/641-5310. A café-restaurant with a slightly bohemian air, it serves nicely presented dishes with an Italian twist, plus a big range of scrumptious home-made cakes. Set lunches from ¥1260; around ¥2500 at night. Mon 11am–6pm, Tues–Thurs & Sun 11am–10pm, Fri & Sat 11am–10.30pm.

Yamate Jūbankan 山手十番館 247 Yamate-chō ⓣ045/621-4466. Pleasant French restaurant in a pretty clapboard house opposite the Foreigners' Cemetery. Although the upstairs is on the formal side (set lunches from ¥3500), the more casual ground floor includes sandwiches and *croques* (¥800), or a more filling lunch platter (¥2000). In July and August they run a popular beer garden. Daily 11am–9pm.

Bars and nightlife

Though it's generally less boisterous than Tokyo, Yokohama has no shortage of lively drinking holes. The west side of Yokohama Station comprises the main **nightlife** area, but the area around Chinatown and across to Kannai Station also has a sprinkling of bars.

Beer Next 3F Akarenga 2, 1-1-2 Shinkō, Naka-ku ⓣ045/226-1961. Stylish beer hall and restaurant with its refreshing own-brew, Spring Valley beer (¥550). They also have Guinness on tap. Daily 11am–11pm.

Motion Blue 3F Akarenga 2, 1-1-2 Shinkō, Naka-ku ⓣ045/226-1919. This cool jazz club attracts top acts – for which you'll pay top prices. There's no charge, though, to park yourself at the attached *Bar Tune*'s long counter and soak up the ambience. Also hosts several free performances each month. Mon–Fri 5pm–midnight, Sat & Sun 11am–1.30pm & 5pm–midnight.

Namo Bar 2F Cross Gate, 1-1-67 Sakuragi-chō, Naka-ku ⓣ045/210-9201. Sleek, modern *izakaya* offering over three hundred types of *shōchū* (distilled liquor) and around forty plum wines. The food menu features Nagoya-style cuisine. Daily 11am–2pm & 5pm–4am.

The Tavern B1F 2-14 Minami Saiwai-chō ⓣ045/322-9727, ⓦwww.the-tavern.com. This British-style pub is popular with local expats, and serves the sort of bar food that will appeal to homesick Brits, including an all-you-can-eat Sunday roast lunch (¥1500). Turn left out of Yokohama Station, behind Takashimaya department store, to find it opposite the Daiei store. Mon & Tues 6pm–midnight, Wed & Thurs 6pm–1am, Fri 6pm–5am, Sat 5pm–5am, Sun noon–midnight.

Why Not? B1 1-31 Motomachi, Naka-ku ⓣ045/663-2955, ⓦwww.clubwhynot.com. Spacious basement bar-cum-dance club with DJs on Friday and Saturday nights (entry ¥1000–2000). The rest of the week it's a regular bar. All-night happy hour on Tuesdays. Open 6pm–2am; closed Mon.

Izu-Ōshima

Some 110km south of Tokyo **IZU-ŌSHIMA** (伊豆大島), or simply Ōshima, is the nearest and largest, at 52km in circumference, of the **Izu-Shotō**, a chain of seven volcanic islands stretching over 300km of ocean. While the others are now dormant, Ōshima's **Mihara-yama** (764m) has the dubious distinction of being the world's third most active volcano after Italy's Stromboli and Kilauea in Hawaii. It's probably better known, however, as the location for the *Godzilla* films (see p.803), for which the barren lava fields provide a fittingly apocalyptic backdrop. Mihara-yama's most recent major eruption took place in 1986, when the island was

Getting to Izu-Ōshima

The best way of **getting to Ōshima** is on one of the jetfoils (2 daily; 1hr 45min–2hr 10min; ¥6940) operated by Tokai Kisen (ⓣ03/5472-9999, ⓦwww.tokaikisen.co.jp) that depart **from Tokyo**'s Takeshiba pier, two stops from Shimbashi on the Yurikamome monorail. The same company also runs a ferry service (1 daily July & Aug; 1 daily except Tues Sept–June; 4hr 20min–8hr; from ¥4270). Outward sailings leave from Takeshiba pier at 10pm or 11pm, arriving in Ōshima early the next morning, while the return boat departs early afternoon, getting back to Tokyo the same evening; times vary, so check locally for the current schedule. These ferries also call at **Yokohama**'s Ōsanbashi pier on Friday and Saturday on the outward journey and on Saturday and Sunday on the return leg; fares from Yokohama start at ¥4140. Other options include jetfoils **from Atami** (2–3 daily; 45min; ¥4430), also operated by Tokai Kisen. ANA has a daily morning **flight** to Ōshima from Haneda airport (30min; from ¥13,100), though by the time you've included travelling to the airport and check-in time, the jetfoils are just as quick.

evacuated, but fortunately for much of the time it simply steams away. Ōshima's other main draw is its forests of **camellia**, particularly in early spring when the blossoms of an estimated three million trees colour the lower slopes a dusky red, an event celebrated with a month-long **festival** (Feb–March) of folk dances and other events. Try if possible to come midweek – spring and autumn are best – and stay at least one night, to experience the slow pace of island life.

Arrival and information

Arriving **by sea**, ferries bring you in to Motomachi, on the west side of the island, while jetfoils either dock here or at the tiny port of **Okata** (岡田), 7km away on the more sheltered north coast, depending on the weather. If you're travelling by jetfoil, remember to check which port it's leaving from for the return journey, either by going to the port terminal in Motomachi or phoning Tokai Kisen (ⓣ04992/2-5522). Ōshima **airport** is about 4km north of Motomachi.

The **tourist office** (daily 8.30am–5pm; ⓣ04992/2-2177, ⓦwww.izu-oshima.or.jp) lies across the road from Motomachi ferry terminal. They provide maps, bus timetables and a wealth of other information, though very little in English. You can also pick up basic maps at the bus ticket office in Okata.

Island transport

By far the best way of **getting around** the island is with your own transport. There are a number of **car rental** outfits, including Nissan Rent-a-Car (ⓣ04992/2-2693) and Toyota (ⓣ04992/2-1611), as well as local company Ōshima Rent-a-Car Association (ⓣ04992/2-1043). Rates start at around ¥5000 for the smallest car for up to six hours, and the car will be delivered to the port if you book in advance.

You can rent **motorbikes** from Tōma garage (当馬; 2hr ¥3000, 1 day ¥6000; ⓣ04992/2-1515) on the main road in Motomachi near the post office, and **mountain bikes** (2hr ¥1000, 1 day from ¥1800) from Marukyu (丸久; ⓣ04992/2-3317), on the road heading east from Motomachi port, or from Ranburu (らんぶる; ⓣ04992/2-3398), beside *Pension Minamoto* (see p.222). The most popular route is to cycle round the island (44km), which takes five to six hours and is best tackled anticlockwise to reduce the number of climbs.

Otherwise, it's perfectly possible to get around by **bus**. There are at least nine services daily on the main route running north from Motomachi to Okata (20min; ¥350) and Ōshima Park (35min; ¥540). These buses stop on the road by the entrance to the airport (10min; ¥210), but there's also one bus a day to the airport terminal at 8.45am (8min; ¥250). The second main route takes you south from Motomachi to Habu (9–11 daily; 35min; ¥660) on the island's southeastern tip, while other routes head up Mihara-yama (see opposite). If you anticipate using the bus a lot, you could consider buying a one-day "free ticket" for ¥2000; you can only use this for travel between 10am and 4pm. Although there are designated bus stops, you can flag down a passing bus anywhere. A **taxi** from Motomachi to Okata will cost around ¥3000 and around ¥1500 to the airport; call Ōshima Kankō Jidōsha on ⓣ04992/2-1051.

Motomachi

Ōshima's main town, **MOTOMACHI** (元町), is generally a sleepy little place which only springs into action when a ferry docks. It is, however, the hub of island life, where you'll find most of the facilities, and it makes a good base for exploring the island, as well as boasting a couple of moderately interesting sights of its own. On the town's southern outskirts, about 600m from the port, the rather grand **Museum of Volcanoes**, or *Kazan Hakubutsukan* (火山博物館; daily 9am–5pm; ¥500; ⓣ04992/2-4103), was built after the 1986 eruption partly to lure tourists back to the island.

Back in the centre, it's worth dropping by the **camellia-oil factory**, Takata Seiyu-jō (高田製油所; daily 10am–5pm, closes occasionally; free; ⓣ04992/2-1125), in a backstreet just north of *Hotel Akamon* (see below), to see if the presses are in action. The factory uses traditional methods to dry, steam and press the nuts to produce the pure, golden oil which can be used for everything from cooking to hair care. Nothing is wasted: the remaining pressed cake is burnt in local pottery kilns and the ash used in the glaze.

After that, the only thing to do is wallow in one of Motomachi's **onsen** baths. The nicest is **Hama-no-yu** (浜の湯; daily: July & Aug 11am–7pm; Sept–June 1–7pm; ¥400), a big public rotemburo on the cliff edge 300m north of the ferry terminal; you'll need a swimming costume. It's the perfect spot for watching the sun go down – particularly on clear days when Mount Fuji's silhouette adds a poetic touch. The other option is the glitzy new **Gojinka Onsen** complex (御神火温泉; daily 9am–9pm, closed 2nd Thurs & Fri of month, also occasionally in Feb, March & Aug; ¥1000; ⓣ04992/2-0909), a couple of minutes further up the same road, with regular onsen baths, a sauna and an onsen swimming pool. On days when the overnight ferry arrives, they open at 6.30am.

Accommodation

One of the smartest **places to stay** in central Motomachi is the *Hotel Akamon* (ホテル赤門; ⓣ04992/2-1213; ❼ including two meals), with a choice of tatami or Western-style rooms (the latter in separate chalet-style cottages), an attractive rotemburo and onsen bath, and excellent seafood meals. To find it, walk up the road heading inland (east) from the ferry terminal, then take the first left where you'll see its distinctive red gates at the end of the lane. On the same lane is the equally welcoming *Pension Minamoto* (ペンションみなもと; ⓣ04992/2-1002; ❺, or ❻ including two meals), with simpler Japanese and Western-style rooms – none en suite – and good food. On the town's northern outskirts, about ten minutes' walk from the port, *Subaru Pension* (すばるペンション; ⓣ04992/2-1142, ⓔCYF02002@nifty.ne.jp; ❺, or ❼ including two meals) has an English-speaking owner, a choice of room styles and good meals.

Eating

In the evening you're best off eating in your hotel, but Motomachi does have a reasonable choice of **restaurants** in among the ramen and soba joints. Among a row of little places opposite the port, *Otomodachi* (おともだち; daily 7am–3pm & 5–10pm; ⓣ04992/2-0061) is a reliable bet serving a broad range of reasonably priced set meals (dishes from ¥700). Moving up a notch, *Sushikō* (寿し光; 11am–2pm & 5–11pm; ⓣ04992/2-0888), upstairs in a modern building, just south of the ferry terminal and on the left, has sushi and sashimi sets from ¥1000, as well as pizzas, salads, *donburi* and the like. *Umisachi* (魚味幸; Mon–Sat 5–11pm; ⓣ04992/2-2942), a friendly *izakaya* on the east side of town, is also worth seeking out: from the port walk east up to the main north–south road, go straight across at the traffic lights and you'll find it on the left where the road makes a right-hand bend.

Mihara-yama and the rest of the island

From Motomachi the road climbs steeply up the mostly grassy slopes of **Mihara-yama** (三原山), affording good views over Motomachi and the island's west coast and, if you're lucky, northwest across Izu Hantō to Mount Fuji. At the top, a clutch of souvenir shops sits on the rim of a much older crater, from where you get your first sight of the smouldering new summit, its flanks streaked with black ribbons left by the 1986 lava flows. A path leads 2.2km across the floor of the old crater, where grasses are gradually recolonizing the black, volcanic soils, and up to the new summit, from where you can peek down into the new crater's sulphurous pit. You can then continue for another 2.5km round the rim and either return to the car park or walk down the northern slopes to rejoin the road 3km further down, but still 500m above sea level, near the *Oshima Onsen Hotel* (大島温泉ホテル; ⓣ04992/2-1673; ❼ including two meals). The hotel itself is rather dilapidated and overpriced, but its rotemburo (daily 1–9pm; ¥800) offers a great view of the volcano. Another option is to walk all the way down to the coast from the volcano; a popular trail heads northeast to bring you out near Ōshima-kōen (see below) in a couple of hours.

If you want to **eat** before setting off on these walks, drop by the *Gojinka Chaya* (御神火茶屋; daily 9am–4pm; ⓣ04992/2-2161), a rustic little restaurant-cum-teashop right on the crater rim where the path begins, which serves limited set meals, as well as drinks and ices in summer.

Mihara-yama can be reached **by bus** from both Motomachi (5 daily; 25min; ¥860) and Ōshima-kōen (2 daily; 25min; ¥840); buses on both routes also call at the hotel on the way down.

The east coast

Next stop is down among the camellias on the east coast. The flower of the camellia, or *tsubaki* as the tree is known locally, is the symbol of the island, and you can see why if you're here in spring (Jan–March) when the blossoms are at their peak. Though the native species grows wild, dozens of different varieties put on a show in **Tsubaki-en botanical garden** (椿園; daily 8.30am–5pm; free; ⓣ04992/2-9111), part of the larger **Ōshima-kōen** (大島公園; ⓦwww12.ocn.ne.jp/~umihuru) municipal park. Outside the flowering season, when the garden is closed, you get some idea of what all the fuss is about in the one-room **museum** (daily 8.30am–4.30pm; free) across the road from the garden.

The road south of Ōshima-kōen and all the way round to Motomachi takes you along through the most beautiful and least populated part of the island. On the southeast tip, **HABU-MINATO** (波浮港), sitting on perfect horseshoe-shaped bay – an ancient, flooded caldera – makes a pleasant place to stop. It's hard to imagine now that in the early twentieth century this one-street village, with its row of old wooden fishermen's houses, was one of Japan's most important fishing ports.

Continuing westwards, about 8km from Habu, you can't miss one of the island's more unusual sights. When they were building the road in 1953, workmen uncovered a perfect, 1km-long **geological cross section** through the rock strata, **Chisō-setsu-danmen** (地層切断面). The successive layers reveal at least one hundred volcanic eruptions stretching back over 15,000 years. Locals call it the *baumkuchen* – German layer cake. From here it's another 7km back to Motomachi.

Travel details

Trains

The trains between the major cities listed below are the fastest, direct services. There are also frequent slower services, run by JR and several private companies, covering the same destinations. It is usually possible, especially on long-distance routes, to get there faster by changing between services.

Atami to: Kyoto (16 daily; 2hr–3hr 40min); Shimoda (every 30min; 1hr–1hr 25min); Tokyo (at least every 10min; 35min–2hr 10min).

Enoshima to: Tokyo (Shinjuku Station) (4–7 daily; 1hr).

Kamakura to: Enoshima (every 10–15min; 25min); Tokyo (every 10–20min; 1hr).

Kawagoe to: Tokyo (Ikebukuro Station) (every 20min; 32min).

Mito to: Tokyo (Ueno Station) (14 daily; 65min).

Narita to: Tokyo (Ueno Station) (every 30min; 1hr).

Nikkō to: Tokyo (Asakusa Station) (every hour; 2hr 20min); (Shinjuku Station) (daily, 2hr 30min).

Shimoda to: Rendaiji (every 20–30min; 3–4min); Tokyo (hourly; 2hr 40min–3hr).

Shuzenji to: Mishima (every 10–15min; 30–40min); Tokyo (2 daily; 2hr 10min).

Takao to: Tokyo (Shinjuku) (every 30min; 1hr).

Yokohama to: Kamakura (every 10–20min; 25min); Tokyo (every 5–10min; 40min); Tokyo (Shibuya Station) (every 5min; 30min); Tokyo (Shinjuku Station) (every 20–30min; 30min).

Buses

The buses listed below are mainly long-distance services – often travelling overnight – between the major cities, and local services where there is no alternative means of transport. For shorter journeys, however, trains are almost invariably quicker and often no more expensive.

Dōgashima to: Matsuzaki (every 15–20min; 6–10min); Shuzenji (1–2 hourly; 1hr 30min); Toi (1–2 hourly; 40min).

Heda to: Shuzenji (7 daily; 50min); Toi (5 daily; 30min).

Kawaguchi-ko to: Tokyo, Shinjuku (ever hour; 1hr 45min).

Shimoda to: Dōgashima (1–2 hourly; 1hr–1hr 40min); Irō-zaki (1–2 hourly; 40min); Matsuzaki (1–2 hourly; 50min–1hr 30min); Shuzenji (1 daily; 2hr).

Toi to: Shuzenji (1–2 hourly; 50min).

Yokohama to: Hirosaki (1 daily; 9hr 45min); Hiroshima (1 daily; 12hr); Kyoto (2 daily; 6hr 30min–9hr); Nagoya (1 daily; 6hr 30min); Nara (1 daily; 8hr); Ōsaka (3 daily; 7hr 15min–8hr).

Ferries and jetfoils

Atamai to: Ōshima (jetfoil: 2–3 daily; 45min).

Heda to: Numazu (5 daily; 30min).

Ōshima to: Atami (2–3 daily; 45min); Tokyo (jetfoil: 2–3 daily; 1hr 45min–2hr 10min; ferry: 1 daily July & Aug; 1 daily except Tues Sept–June; 4hr 20min–5hr); Yokohama (Sat & Sun 1 daily; 3hr 30min).

Toi to: Numazu (3–4 daily; 50min); Shimizu (4–7 daily; 1hr).

Tokyo to: Ōshima (jeftoil: 2–3 daily; 1hr 45min–2hr 10min; ferry: 1 daily July & Aug; 1 daily except Tues Sept–June; 8hr).

Yokohama to: Ōshima (Fri & Sat 1 daily; 6hr 30min).

Flights

Tokyo to Ōshima: (1 daily; 30min).

Northern Honshū

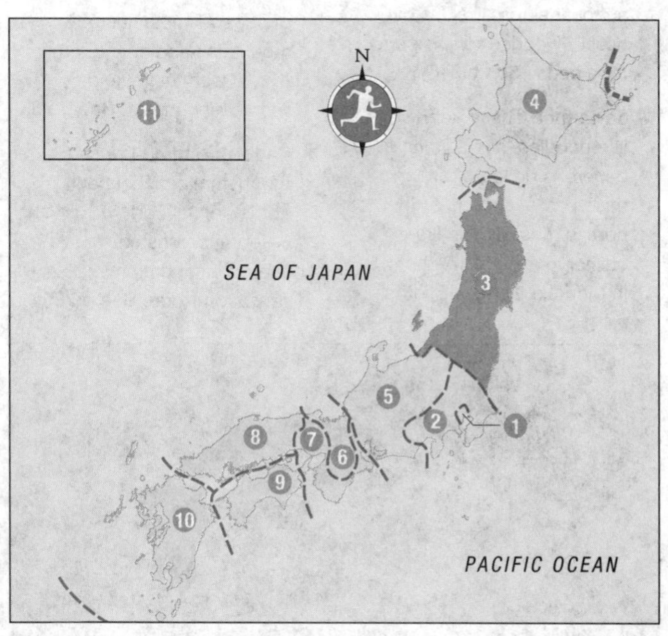

CHAPTER 3

Highlights

✱ **Kinkazan** Roam the steeply wooded slopes of this island with its views, framed by wind-whipped pines, of Matsushima Bay and Oshika Hantō. See p.239

✱ **Cycling in the Tōno valley** Mostly flat, this valley, with its evocative landscape of rice paddies and traditional houses, surrounded on all sides by heavily wooded hills, is perfect for a pedal. See p.243

✱ **Ja-ja men** These udon-like noodles, served with a generous dollop of brown miso paste, are one of the north's most distinctive culinary flavours. Try them in Morioka along with other regional specialities. See p.250

✱ **Kakunodate** Discover the samurai heritage of this appealing town, including streets of gloriously preserved grand houses with extensive, impeccably maintained gardens. See p.265

✱ **Dewa-sanzan** Visit one of Japan's most sacred mountains and spend a day or two with the legendary *yamabushi* priests. See p.268

✱ **Sado-ga-shima** Dance to the rhythmic global beat at the annual Earth Celebration hosted by international drumming sensation Kodo. See p.280

▲ Kinkasan Island

3

Northern Honshū

When the famous poet Matsuo Bashō set out on his travels along the "narrow road to the deep north" in 1689, he commented, somewhat despondently, "I might as well be going to the ends of the earth." Even today, many urban Japanese regard the harsh, mountainous provinces of **NORTHERN HONSHŪ** as irredeemably backward. Not that it's all thatched farmhouses and timeless agricultural vistas, but certainly rural traditions have survived here longer than in most other parts of the country. However, it doesn't take long to discover the region's huge array of **festivals**; nor do you have to delve much deeper to find the rich heritage of folk tales and evidence of ancient religious practices that give parts of northern Honshū a deliciously mysterious tang.

Northern Honshū, or **Tōhoku** as much of the area is known, was the last part of Japan's main island to be brought under central control. As such, it boasts more in the way of military sights – ruined castles, samurai towns and aristocratic tombs – than great temples or religious foundations. The one glorious exception is north of **Sendai** at the seemingly insignificant town **Hiraizumi**, whose opulent Golden Hall (Konjiki-dō) is a highlight of any tour of the region. By way of contrast, the archetypal north-country town lies not far away at **Tōno**, often referred to as the birthplace of Japanese folklore, where goblin-like *kappa* inhabit local rivers and fairy children scamper through old farmhouses. Much of this is now heavily commercialized, but it's still worth exploring Tōno's more secretive shrines, with their references to primitive cults. Darker forces are also at work much further north where souls in purgatory haunt **Osore-zan**'s volcanic wasteland on the hammer-head Shimokita Hantō. In summer, pilgrims come here to consult blind mediums, while over on the west coast the holy mountain of **Dewa-sanzan** is home to *yamabushi*, ascetic priests endowed with mystical powers.

Northern Tōhoku Welcome Card

If you're spending any time in Akita-ken, Aomori-ken or Iwate-ken, make sure you get a **Tōhoku Welcome Card**. This free card, valid for a year, provides discounts of up to fifty percent (though mostly ten to twenty percent) on hotels, restaurants, museums, car rental and other facilities in the three prefectures. Eligibility is restricted to overseas visitors staying in Japan for a year or less. The cards are available from the Tokyo TIC (see p.92) and local tourist offices, or online at ⓦwww.northern-tohoku.gr.jp/welcome; you'll need to take along your passport. The card comes with a useful booklet in English outlining all the participating organizations and businesses.

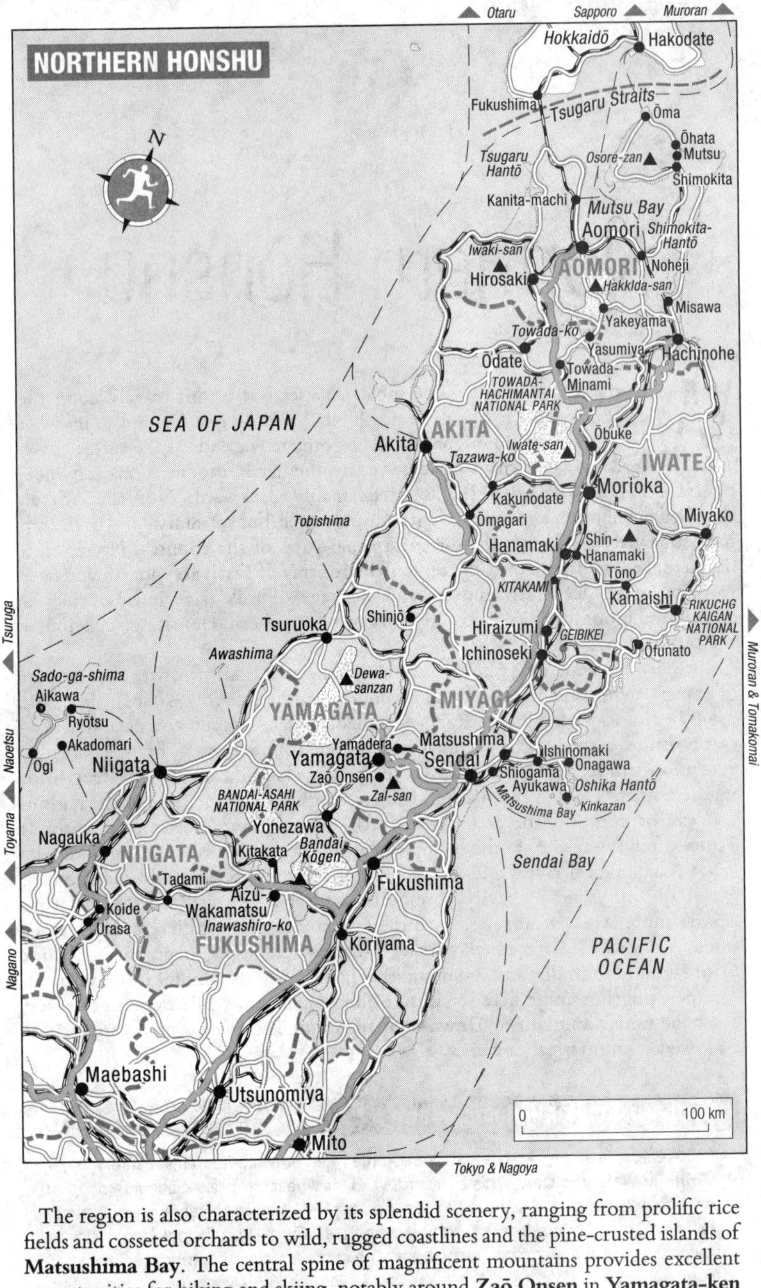

The region is also characterized by its splendid scenery, ranging from prolific rice fields and cosseted orchards to wild, rugged coastlines and the pine-crusted islands of **Matsushima Bay**. The central spine of magnificent mountains provides excellent opportunities for hiking and skiing, notably around **Zaō Onsen** in **Yamagata-ken** and the more northerly **Towada-Hachimantai** area. Both are noted for their flora and fauna, including black bears in remoter districts, while **Towada-ko** itself is a massive crater lake accessed via the picturesque **Oirase valley**. The World

Heritage-listed **Shirakami-Sanchi** mountains, on the border between Aomori and Akita prefectures, are equally beautiful, and remote enough to remain undeveloped. In **Sado-ga-shima**, a large island lying off Niigata, dramatic mountain and coastal scenery provides the backdrop for a surprisingly rich culture – a legacy of its isolation and the infamous characters once exiled to the island.

JR offers a variety of **special rail tickets** covering the Tōhoku region (see p.34 for details). Although there are good **transport** links between the main cities (including a recently extended Shinkansen service to Aomori), you'll need to allow plenty of time to explore the more remote corners of northern Honshū – this is one place where car rental is definitely worth considering. Public buses can be sporadic at the best of times, with many services stopping completely in winter, when **heavy snowfalls** close the mountain roads. In general, the **best time to visit** is either spring or autumn, before it gets too busy and while the scenery is at its finest, though the uplands also provide welcome relief from summer's sweltering heat. Note, however, that early August sees thousands of people flocking to Tōhoku's big four **festivals** in Sendai, Aomori, Hirosaki and Akita. If you're travelling at this time, make sure you've got your transport and accommodation sorted out well in advance. Apart from ski resorts, many tourist facilities outside the major cities shut down from early November to late April.

Yamagata and around

Few tourists make it to **YAMAGATA** (山形), a large, workaday city ringed by high mountains, and those that do are usually just passing through. Apart from a couple of engaging museums, Yamagata's prime attraction is as a base for visiting nearby **Yamadera**'s atmospheric temples, and **Zaō Onsen**, which provides excellent opportunities for summer hiking and winter skiing, and is known for its beguiling "snow monsters" – fir trees engulfed in wind-sculpted ice and snow. In early August (5–7), the city turns out for its major festival, the **Hanagasa Matsuri**, during which *yukata*-clad women wearing flowery hats perform a slow, graceful dance, making this otherwise unexciting city a worthwhile stop.

Arrival, information and accommodation

Yamagata is a stop on a spur of the Tōhoku Shinkansen from Tokyo to Fukushima and is along the very scenic Senzan line from Sendai (80min; ¥1100). There are several places to get tourist information, but the best is the main **tourist office** (daily 9am–5.30pm; ⓣ0236/47-2266) in the **station**, immediately to the right as you exit the turnstiles. The office has helpful English-speaking staff and plentiful English-language information. Limousine buses (45min; ¥740) run between the **airport** and central Yamagata, stopping outside the station and at the central **bus terminal** in the Yamakō Building (山交ビル), behind Ekimae-dōri's Yamazawa department store. All long-distance buses use this terminal, while most city buses depart from outside the station's east exit.

The city is fairly easy to navigate on foot, but you can also pick up (and drop off) a free **rental bike** at seven locations around the city, including the tourist office at the station, where you can get full details of the bike rental system. Alternatively, a circular bus runs every ten minutes between the station and major sights (daily 9.30am–6.30pm; ¥100 flat fare). For **car rental**, there are several companies clustered around the Kajō Central Building; try Eki Rent-a-Car (ⓣ0236/46-6322) or Toyota (ⓣ0236/25-0100). If you need to **change money**, there are branches of Yamagata Bank and 77 Bank close to the station on Ekimae-dōri.

Accommodation

Yamagata has a reasonable choice of **accommodation** within easy walking distance of the train station. However, for more atmospheric lodging, stay in nearby Zaō Onsen (see opposite) or Yamadera (see p.232).

Castle ホテルキャッスル 4-2-7 Tōka-machi ⓣ0236/31-3311, ⓦwww.hotelcastle.co.jp. About 7min walk from the station on Ekimae-dōri, this large hotel has a range of well-sized, contemporary Western-style rooms. ⑥

Metropolitan ホテルメトロポリタン 1-1-1 Kasumi-chō ⓣ023/28-1111, ⓦwww.metro-yamagata.jp. Smart, modern hotel conveniently located above the station; if you're travelling on a JR rail pass you can enjoy substantial discounts. ⑥

Sole Inn ソーレイン 4-2-7 Tōka-machi ⓣ023/642-2111, ⓕ642-2114. Well placed on Ekimae-dōri, directly across from the *Metropolitan*. Rates for the small but spick and span rooms include a light breakfast and free internet access in the lobby. ③

Yamashiroya Ryokan 山城屋旅館 1-1 Sawai-machi ⓣ023/622-3007, ⓔinfo@e-yamashiroya.jp. Located in the backstreets just to the north of the station, with basic but perfectly adequate tatami rooms. ④

The City

Central Yamagata occupies a grid of streets lying northeast of the train station. Its southern boundary is Ekimae-dōri, a broad avenue leading straight from the station as far as the *Hotel Castle*, from where the main shopping street, Nanokamachi-dōri, strikes north to the former **Prefectural Office** (文翔館), about twenty minutes' walk from the station. This imposing, European-style building of stone and ornate stucco dominates the north end of Nanokamachi-dōri. Originally built in 1911, the interior (daily 9am–4.30pm; closed first and third Mon each month; free) has been magnificently restored, particularly the third floor with its parquet-floored dining room and elegant Assembly Hall.

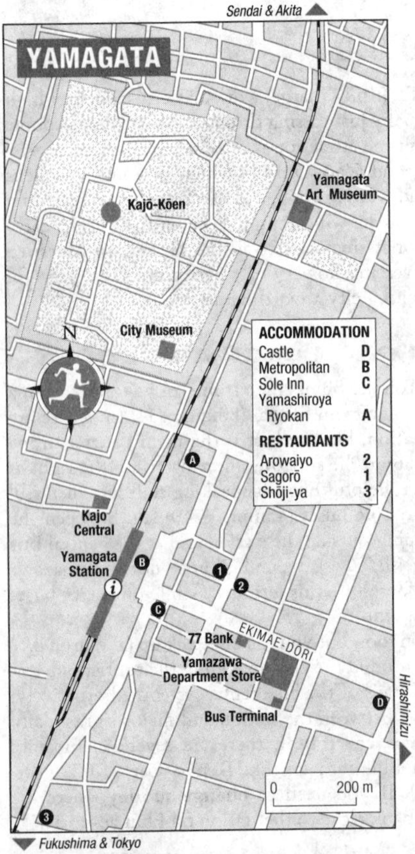

From the Prefectural Office, head west to the **Yamagata Art Museum** (Tues–Sun 10am–4.30pm; ¥500, though some exhibitions may cost more) beside the castle walls. This modern museum boasts a small collection of major European names, such as Picasso, Chagall, Renoir and Monet, but unless there's a special exhibition of interest it's not really worth the entrance fee. Instead, cross the train tracks to enter **Kajō-kōen** (霞城公園) by its beautifully restored East Gate, the only remnant of the former castle. The **City Museum**, or *Kyōdokan* (郷土館; Tues–Sun 9am–4.30pm;

YAMAGATA

ACCOMMODATION	
Castle	D
Metropolitan	B
Sole Inn	C
Yamashiroya Ryokan	A
RESTAURANTS	
Arowaiyo	2
Sagorō	1
Shōji-ya	3

¥200), occupies a delightful, multicoloured clapboard building in the park's southeast corner. Erected in 1878, this museum originally served as the town's main hospital, and its exhibits include a fearsome array of early medical equipment and anatomical drawings, including a guide to pregnancy rendered as woodblock prints.

On the city's southeastern outskirts, the pretty little pottery village of **Hirashimizu** (平清水) has a surprisingly rural atmosphere. There's just one main street and a small river running down from the hills, which provides local potters with their distinctive, speckled clay. If you explore a little, you'll find several family **potteries** with showrooms (daily 9am–5/6pm), such as Shichiemon-gama (七右衛門窯; ⓣ023/642-7777), which offers visitors the chance to throw a pot or two (daily 9am–3pm; ¥800–2000). To reach Hirashimizu, take a bus from Yamagata Station (hourly; 15min; ¥460).

Eating

Yamagata's **speciality foods** include marbled Yonezawa beef, similar to the more famous Matsuzaka variety, and *imoni*, a warming winter stew of taro, meat, onions and *konnyaku* (a jelly-like food made from the root of the devil's tongue plant) served in a slightly sweet sauce. To try the local beef, head for *Arowaiyo* (アロワイヨ; 2-5-2 Kasumichō; daily 5pm–midnight), a casual restaurant with steak sets from ¥2800, and a popular expat hangout. It's on Ōtemon-dōri, to the north of Ekimae-dōri (take the second left as you walk away from the station). The same stretch of street has plenty of other good bars and restaurants, including *Sagoro* (佐五郎; 1-6-10 Kasumichō; ⓣ0236/31-3560), a *sukiyaki* and *shabu-shabu* restaurant where set menus start from ¥4200; it's directly across from *Arowaiyo*. Heading south (right) from the station for about 400m, along the street that runs beside the train tracks, you'll find Yamagata's oldest soba restaurant, *Shōji-ya* (庄司屋; 14-28 Sawaimachi). Here you can try handmade soba in all its various forms (¥750–1500), and you might even be able to see the chefs rolling your noodles in the attached workshop.

Zaō Onsen

Roughly 20km southeast of Yamagata city, **ZAŌ ONSEN** (蔵王温泉) is the main focus of activity in the Zaō quasi-national park, an attractive region of volcanoes, crater lakes and hot springs. In winter (Dec to late March), the resort offers some of Japan's best **skiing**, with a dozen or so runs to choose from, as well as night skiing and onsen baths to soak away the aches and pains. Non-skiers can enjoy the cable-car ride over **Juhyō Kōgen**, where a thick covering of snow and hoarfrost transforms the plateau's fir trees into giant "snow monsters" (*juhyō*).

Head southeast from the bus station for ten minutes and you will reach the **Zaō Sanroku Ropeway** (蔵王山麓ロープウェイ; every 10min; daily 8.15am–5pm; ¥1400 return), which whisks you up to Juhyō Kōgen. The *juhyō* are at their best in February, though you can see photos of them at other times of year in the **Juhyō Museum** (daily 9am–4pm; free), located in the ropeway terminal building. A second ropeway (8.30am–4.45pm; ¥1100 extra) continues up from here to Zaō Jizō Sanchō Station at 1661m. This top station lies between Sampō Kōjin-san (1703m) and Jizō-san (1736m), just two of the peaks that make up the ragged profile of **Zaō-san**. In the summer hiking season (May–Oct) you can follow the right-hand (southeasterly) path over Jizō-san and Kumano-dake (1841m) for spectacular views and a fairly rugged hour's walk to the desolate, chemical-blue **Okama crater lake** (お釜).

There are a number of ski runs in the area, and a shuttle bus (mid-Dec to late-March; ¥100) moves skiers and snowboarders between them. Consult the *Skier's Guide* maps, available at the tourist office, for the difficulty level of each run (green is beginner, red is intermediate and black is advanced). There is a variety of passes available for day and night skiing, with prices ranging from ¥4200 to ¥11,500. Passes include access to all 38 chairlifts; the use of the ropeways and cable cars costs extra.

To recover after skiing, the area has plenty of public baths where you can have a good, long soak. The unforgettable *Dai-rotemburo* (大露天風呂; mid-April to Oct daily 9am–sunset; ¥450), overflowing with steamy sulphur-laden water, is large enough to ease the aching muscles of more than two hundred visitors at once.

Practicalities

Buses run approximately every hour from Yamagata Station to the Zaō Onsen bus terminal (40min; ¥980), at the bottom of the village, and one bus goes all the way to Okama lake at 9.30am (May–Oct; 90min; ¥3980 return), leaving Okama at 1pm – the only return journey to Yamagata Station. During the peak ski season, highway buses run between Zao Onsen and Sendai (mid-Dec to late March; leaving Sendai at 8am and 10am, and returning at 3pm and 4.30pm; 1hr 40min; ¥1500 one way).

To the right of the bus terminal you'll find the **tourist office** (daily 9am–6pm ⓣ0236/94-9328) where there are some English maps and pamphlets available. The *Skier's Guide*, although in Japanese, is particularly useful for its map of the runs.

For **accommodation**, the reasonable and comfortable *Lodge Chitoseya* (ロッジちとせや; ⓣ0236/94-9145, ⓦwww.lodge-chitoseya.com; ❹, with meals ❺), located after the first bridge on the road to the far right of the station, has a youth hostel atmosphere. The more high-end *Takamiya* (高見屋; ⓣ0236/94-9333, ⓦwww.zao.co.jp/takamiya; ❽–❾ including meals) offers an authentic ryokan experience with lavish *kaiseki* meals and a choice of baths, all of which are small but full of character – especially at night. It's perched on the hill directly north of the bus station, to the right of the *torii*.

Yamadera

The temple complex of Risshaku-ji, or **YAMADERA** (山寺) as it's more popularly known, is one of Tōhoku's most holy places. It was founded in 860 AD by a Zen priest of the Tendai sect and reached its peak in the Kamakura period (1185–1333). Today around forty temple buildings still stand scattered among the ancient cedars on a steep, rocky hillside. The temple lies close to Yamadera Station, which is on the JR Senzan line between Yamagata and Sendai.

From the station, cross the river and follow the road right, past shops selling walking sticks, snacks and souvenirs, to where you can see the temple roofs on the slopes of Hōju-san. Ignore the first two flights of steps to your left and take the third staircase up to the temple's main hall, **Kompon Chūdō**. This impressive building, dating from 1356, shelters a flame brought from Enryaku-ji, the centre of Tendai Buddhism near Kyoto (see p.455), 1100 years ago and which has supposedly been burning ever since – as you peer inside, it's the hanging lantern on the left-hand side. Walking back west along the hillside, you pass a small shrine and a solemn statue of Bashō who, travelling before the days of coach parties, penned a characteristically pithy ode to Yamadera: "In the utter silence of a temple, a cicada's voice alone penetrates the rocks." He sits across from the modern **Hihōkan** (mid-April to Dec daily 8am–4.30pm; ¥200), which houses a fine collection of temple treasures.

A few steps further on, **San-mon** marks the entrance to the mountain (daily 6am–6pm; ¥300), from where over 1100 steps meander past moss-covered *Jizō* statues, lanterns and prayer wheels, and squeeze between looming rocks carved with prayers and pitted with caves. It takes about forty minutes to reach the highest temple, **Okuno-in**, where breathless pilgrims tie prayer papers around a mammoth lantern and light small bunches of incense sticks. Before setting off downhill, don't miss the views over Yamadera from the terrace of **Godai-dō**, perched on the cliff-face just beyond the distinctive red **Nōkyō-dō** pavilion.

Yamadera village consists mainly of expensive ryokan and souvenir shops; some of the latter have steaming vats of *konnyaku* balls boiling outside which make for a good warming snack on a cold day (¥100/skewer). Trains run hourly to both Yamagata (¥230) and Sendai (¥820); however, if you need **accommodation**, *Yamadera Pension* (山寺ペンション; ⓣ0236/95-2134; ❻ including meals) is the most attractive option. It's in a half-timbered building right in front of the station, with a decent **restaurant** downstairs that specializes in handmade soba.

Sendai

The largest city in the Tōhoku region, **SENDAI** (仙台) is a sprawling but pleasant place, with broad, tree-lined avenues and a lively downtown district. Though often just regarded as a staging post on the way to Matsushima Bay (see p.236), the city's **castle ruins**, with their local history museum, and the ornate mausoleum of Sendai's revered founder, the *daimyō* **Daté Masamune**, are worth a brief stop. During the **Tanabata Matsuri** (Star Festival; Aug 6–8), the city centre is awash with thousands of bamboo poles festooned with colourful paper tassels, poems and prayers, celebrating the only day in the year – weather permitting – when the two astral lovers, Vega the weaver and Altair the cowherd, can meet.

Arrival, information and getting around

The majority of visitors to Sendai arrive at the main JR **station** on the east side of town; local and long-distance **buses** stop on the station's west side. The city also has an international **airport**, with flights from Seoul, Beijing, Guam, Shanghai and Taipei, as well as domestic services; limousine buses (40min; ¥910) and trains (25min; ¥630) on the airport line run from the airport to Sendai Station. **Ferries** from Nagoya and Hokkaidō (Tomakomai) dock at Sendai Port, northwest of the city, which is served by local buses (40min; ¥490).

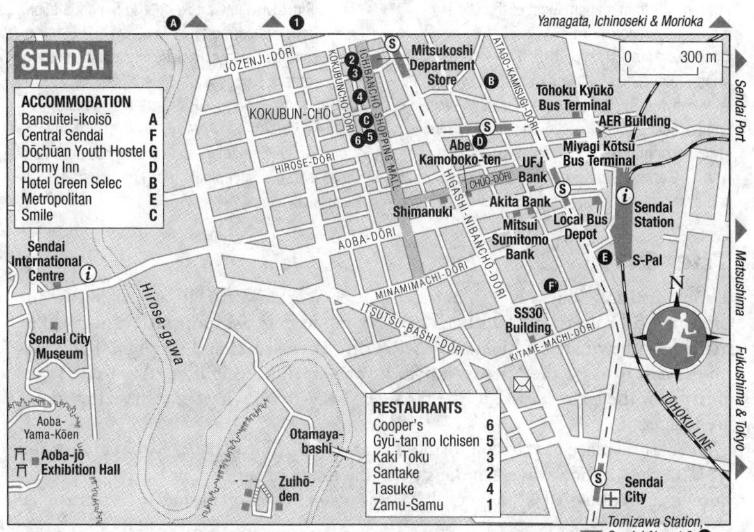

Sendai's main **tourist office** (daily 8.30am–8pm; ⓣ022/222-4069) is located on the station's second floor; the English-speaking staff can help with city maps and hotel bookings.

The best way of **getting around** Sendai is by the **local bus**, Loople Sendai, which stops at most of the city's sights – ask the tourist office for a route map. The flat fare is ¥250, payable to the driver as you exit, or there's a one-day pass (¥600). If you are heading beyond the city centre, you could also try the Marugoto Pass (¥2600), sold at View Plaza and JTB, which includes two days of unlimited travel on inner-city buses (including Loople) and subways, plus the JR lines that service Yamadera, Matsushima and Sendai Airport. Sendai has one **subway line**, running north–south, which is particularly useful for *Dōchūan Youth Hostel*. To reach the subway from Sendai's JR station, follow the signs through the basement of the Seibu store.

Accommodation

Sendai has plenty of mid-range and expensive business **hotels** within walking distance of the station, but is less well equipped with budget accommodation.

Bansuitei-ikoisō 晩翠亭いこい荘 5-6 Kimachi-dōri, Aoba-ku ⓣ022/222-7885, ⓦwww.ikoisouryokan.co.jp. An excellent ryokan just outside the downtown area but easily accessible by bus from bus stop #29 (get off at the last stop, follow the narrow street across the road for one block and take a left), and the subway (get off at Kita-yonbanchō and walk west for three blocks, taking a left after the *kōban*). Rooms are impeccably clean and nicely decorated. Substantial discounts are offered for online bookings. ❹

Central Sendai ホテルセントラル仙台 4-2-6 Chūō, Aoba-ku ⓣ022/711-4111, ⓦwww.hotel-central.co.jp. The highlight of this quintessential business hotel is the location – less than 5min from the JR train station. Most of the flowery rooms are singles, from ¥7140. ❺

Dōchūan Youth Hostel 道中庵ユースホステル 31 Onoda-Kitayashiki, Taihaku-ku ⓣ022/247-0511, ⓦwww.jyh.or.jp. The best of three youth hostels in Sendai, built among trees in traditional farmhouse style. Accommodation is in small tatami dormitories with a TV and washbasin; there's also a cedar bath and excellent food – the English-speaking warden grows his own rice and vegetables. The only downside is the hostel's out-of-the-way location: it's 15min by subway from central Sendai to Tomizawa Station (¥290), then a 10min walk due east. ❸

Dormy Inn ドーミーイン 2-10-17 Chūō, Aoba-ku ⓣ022/715-7077, ⓕ715-7078. About 5min from the station, near Hirose-dōri subway station, this budget business hotel has a range of boxy but adequate en-suite rooms. Singles from Y6000. ❹. A similar choice, right across the street, is the Hotel Green Selec (ホテルグリーンセレク 2-9-14 Hon-chō; ⓣ022/221-3311; ❹).

Metropolitan ホテルメトロポリタン 1-1-1 Chūō, Aoba-ku ⓣ022/268-2525, ⓦwww.s-metro.stbl.co.jp. Big, swish hotel next door to Sendai Station, with a range of comfortable Western- and Japanese-style rooms. Facilities include a choice of restaurants, a bar, gym and indoor pool. ❼

Smile スマイルホテル 3F, 4-3-22 Ichiban-chō, Aoba-ku ⓣ022/261-7711, ⓦwww.smile-hotels.com. Simple, but smart and modern business hotel on Ichiban-chō shopping street. Free internet access. ❺

The City

Though central Sendai had to be rebuilt after World War II, its streets follow the original grid pattern laid out by Daté Masamune in the seventeenth century. The main downtown area, a high-rise district of offices, banks and shopping malls, lies on the east bank of the **Hirose-gawa**. Its principal thoroughfare, Aoba-dōri, runs west from the train station to the far side of the river, where the city's few sights are located.

The natural place to start exploring is the wooded hilltop park, **Aobayama-kōen** (青葉山公園), which was once the site of the magnificent Sendai Castle, popularly known as **Aoba-jō** (青葉城). Only a few stretches of wall and a reconstructed gateway remain, but the site is impeccable, protected by the river to the east and a deep ravine on its south side. Buses run from Sendai Station (bus stop #9) to Aobajōshi-mae, a twenty-minute journey, from where it's a short walk to the **statue of Masamune** astride his horse, surveying the city below. Missing one eye since childhood, Masamune was a fearsome warrior, nicknamed the "One-Eyed Dragon". He had been granted the fiefdom in return for helping bring Tokugawa Ieyasu to power in 1603, and his Daté clan continued to rule Sendai for the next 270 years. Their castle was constructed in highly ornate Momoyama style, with painted ceilings and huge rooms divided by glorious screens, more like a luxurious palace than a fortress. Though the exhibition hall is a bit gimmicky, you can get an idea of its former glory in the small **Aoba-jō Exhibition Hall** (青葉城資料展示館; daily 9am–4/5pm; ¥700), located above the park's souvenir shops, where a short computer-generated film takes you "inside" the castle; the red seats are equipped with foreign-language headphone sets.

Ten minutes' walk down the north side of the hill brings you to the more interesting **Sendai City Museum** (仙台市博物館; Tues–Sun 9am–4.15pm; ¥400, extra for special exhibitions). This modern, well-laid-out installation traces the city's history from the early Stone Age to the present day, though the main emphasis is on the glory days under Masamune and his successors. On the second floor you'll find displays of his armour, with the distinctive crescent moon on the helmet, his sword and various portraits – always with two eyes.

When Daté Masamune died in 1636, aged 70, he was buried in the **Zuihō-den** (瑞鳳殿) on a wooded hillside just along the river from Aoba-jō. Eventually his two successors joined him, and their three **mausoleums** (daily 9am–4/4.30pm; ¥550) now stand at the top of broad, stone steps. The opulent, Momoyama-style mausoleums, with polychrome carvings glittering against the plain dark wood and overhanging eaves, are fairly recent reconstructions from a five-year project during which the graves were opened. You can see the treasures they unearthed, as well as a fascinating video of the excavations, in a one-room **museum** beside the Zuihō-den. Though the mausoleums are only a short distance from Aoba-jō as the crow flies, it takes a good twenty minutes to walk here; by bus, you first have to go back to Sendai Station and then out again (bus stop #11) to the Otamaya-bashi stop.

Eating and drinking

Sendai's **speciality foods** include *gyū-tan* (grilled, smoked or salted calf's tongue) and, in winter (Dec–March), oysters from Matsushima Bay. *Sasa-kamaboko*, a leaf-shaped cake of rather rubbery white-fish paste, is a popular local snack, which you can sample in *Abe Kamaboko-ten*, a famous shop in the Chūō-dōri shopping mall. Chūō-dōri and the connecting Ichiban-chō arcades are good places to look for **restaurants and cafés**, while S-Pal, at the south end of Sendai Station, also has a decent selection. **Kokubun-chō**, just west of the Ichiban-chō shopping mall, is Sendai's main entertainment district.

Cooper's 1F, 2-1-3 Kokubun-chō. Although not quite the "Gastro-pub with Modern British Foods" they claim to be, this pub-cum-restaurant has a big menu of pasta, pizza, steak and various snack foods. The emphasis is really on the beer selection; and they even have Guinness-flavoured ice cream. Mon–Sat 5–11pm, Sun 5–9pm.

Gyū-tan no Ichisen 牛タンの一仙 4-3-3, Ichiban-chō. A good alternative if *Tasuke* (see p.236) is closed, this no-frills basement *gyū-tan* restaurant, just off the Ichiban-chō arcade, has all sorts of tongue dishes (from ¥1000), including stew. Daily 11am–midnight.

Kaki Toku かき徳 2F, 4-9-1 Ichiban-chō. Elegant oyster and seafood restaurant with a choice of tables or tatami seating. Set menus cost ¥3500–6300, though there are plenty of cheaper options, including rice and tempura dishes from ¥800. Daily 11.30am–2.30pm & 5–10pm.

Santake さん竹 4-9-24 Ichiban-chō. Casual soba shop opposite Mitsukoshi department store on the Ichiban-chō arcade. Individual dishes from ¥750, or ¥1000 plus for a set meal. English menu available. Tues–Sun 11am–8pm.
Tasuke 太助 4-4-13, Ichiban-chō. One of Sendai's best-known *gyū-tan* restaurants, where you can eat tongue in all its forms. Wed–Mon 11.30am–10pm.

Zamu-Samu ザムサム 2F, 17-19 Nittsu-chō. In an ideal location for guests at *Bansuitei-ikoisō*, this tasty Indian buffet (¥880) brings in the crowds at lunch time (11.30am–3pm); the evening menu is more refined, with a wide range of curries and vegetarian/non-vegetarian thalis starting at ¥2100.

Listings

Banks and exchange There are branches of major foreign exchange banks, such as Akita, Mitsubishi Sumitomo Bank and UFJ, at the east end of Aoba-dōri, near Sendai Station.
Buses Long-distance JR buses (ⓣ022/256-6646) for Niigata and Tokyo (Shinjuku) leave from the east side of Sendai Station. Express buses go to Kyoto, Ōsaka, Nagoya and destinations around Tōhoku from the Miyagi Kōtsū (ⓣ022/261-5333) bus terminal at the west end of Hirose-dōri, as does the JR bus to Akita. On the opposite side of the road, buses from Tōhoku Kyūkō (ⓣ022/262-7031) leave for Tokyo Station.
Car rental There are several car rental places outside the east exit of Sendai Station, including Eki Rent-a-Car (ⓣ022/292-6501), Mazda (ⓣ022/293-1021) and Nippon (ⓣ022/297-1919).
Emergencies The main police station is at 3-79 Itsutsubashi Aoba-ku (ⓣ022/222-7171). In an absolute emergency, contact the English Hotline on ⓣ022/224-1919. For other emergency numbers, see p.71.
Hospitals Sendai City Hospital, 3-1 Shimizu-kōji (ⓣ022/266-7111), has a 24hr emergency clinic; otherwise, ring the English Hotline (daily 9am–8pm; ⓣ022/224-1919) for advice on clinics with English-speaking doctors.
Internet Net-U (5F, AER Building, ⓣ022/724-1200), near the west exit of the station, offers 30min internet access free of charge from 10am–8pm daily. The Sendai International Centre (daily 9am–8pm; ⓣ022/265-2450; ⓦwww.sira.or.jp), out near the castle, also offers free internet access.
Post office Sendai Central Post Office, 1-7 Kitame-machi, Aoba-ku, has a 24hr service for stamps and international mail (Mon–Sat).
Shopping The main shopping streets are the covered malls of Chūō-dōri and Ichiban-chō. For traditional crafts, try Shimanuki, towards the west end of Chūō-dōri, which sells a good range of *kokeshi* dolls, wooden toys, *ittōbori* carved birds, fabrics, ironware and lacquer goods. Maruzen is the best place in town for foreign-language books and magazines; you'll find it on the first floor of the AER Building.
Taxis Kankō (ⓣ022/252-1385) and Nikkō (ⓣ022/241-4181).

Matsushima Bay

The jumble of wooded islands dotting **Matsushima Bay**, a short train ride northeast of Sendai, is officially designated one of Japan's top three scenic areas, along with Miyajima and Amanohashidate. Roughly 12km by 14km, the bay contains over 260 islands of every conceivable shape and size, many supposedly taking on familiar shapes such as tortoises, whales, or even human profiles, and each with scraggy fringes of contorted pine trees protruding out of the white rock faces. In between, the shallower parts of the bay have been used for farming oysters for around three hundred years.

Bashō, travelling through in 1689, commented that "much praise had already been lavished upon the wonders of the islands of Matsushima", but many visitors today find the bay slightly disappointing. Nevertheless, a **boat trip** among the islands makes an enjoyable outing, though it's best to avoid weekends and holidays when hordes of sightseers descend on the area. **Matsushima town** has a couple of less-frequented picturesque spots, and a venerable temple, **Zuigan-ji**, with an impressive collection of art treasures. Most people visit Matsushima on a day-trip from Sendai, but there are some reasonable accommodation options in the area that are worth considering if you're heading on up the coast to Kinkazan (see p.239).

Touring the bay

The fastest approach to Matsushima town is the JR Senseki line from the basement of Sendai Station to **Matsushima Kaigan** station (松島海岸; 30–40min; ¥400). A more scenic route is via **SHIOGAMA** (塩釜), from where you can travel on across the bay by boat; take the JR Senseki line to Hon-shiogama (本塩釜; 20–30min; ¥320). Shiogama Station's **tourist information office** (daily 10am–4pm) can give you timetables and point you to the **Marine Gate ferry pier** (マリンゲート), ten minutes' walk to the east; turn right outside the station and right again under the train tracks, and you'll see the terminal building straight ahead. The Marine Gate pier is the departure point for both local **ferries** serving the inhabited islands and **tourist boats**, which take a leisurely trip through Matsushima Bay before dropping you in Matsushima town. In high season (late April to Nov) boats run every thirty minutes (8.30am–4pm; 50min; ¥1400, or ¥2200 for the upper deck), and there's also the option of a longer voyage into the northern reaches of the bay (daily; by group reservation only; 60min). From December to March, there are sailings every hour only on the shorter course.

It's also possible to take a cruise round the bay **from Matsushima** tourist pier (roughly every hour; April–Oct 9am–4pm; Nov–March 9am–3pm; 50min; ¥1400), though they tend to be more crowded than the boats from Shiogama.

Matsushima

The modern town of **MATSUSHIMA** (松島) is little more than a strip of resort hotels and souvenir shops, but its origins go back to 828 AD, when a Zen priest called Jikaku Daishi Enrin founded the temple of **Zuigan-ji** (瑞巌寺; daily: April–Sept 8am–5pm; Oct–March 8am–3.30/4.30pm; ¥700), set back from the bay. The entrance to the temple is marked by a suitably grand grove of four-hundred-year-old cedar trees halfway between (and a five-minute walk from) the central tourist pier, where boats from Shiogama dock, and the train station (Matsushima-kaigan). Zuigan-ji has been rebuilt many times since its foundation, but retains a compelling sense of history. Though deceptively plain from the outside, the buildings bear the unmistakeable stamp of Daté Masamune, the first lord of Sendai, who oversaw Zuigan-ji's reconstruction in the early seventeenth century. He employed the best craftsmen and the highest-quality materials to create a splendid monument of intricately carved doors and transoms, wood-panelled ceilings and gilded screens lavishly painted with hawks, chrysanthemums, peacocks and pines. What would ordinarily be the highlight of a visit to the temple, the main building, is off limits to visitors until 2016 while it undergoes a renovation. However, you can still get a taste for Masamune's style with a walk around the neighbouring guard-house and the modern **Seiryū-den** (both included in the ticket). Alongside the normal array of temple treasures, this museum has statues of a squinting Masamune, in full armour and in an uncompromising mood, alongside his angelic-looking wife and eldest daughter. This statue of Masamune is a rarity in that it shows his missing right eye.

In front of Zuigan-ji, just north of the ferry pier, two tiny islands are threaded together with arched vermilion bridges. No one knows why the bridges were built with precarious gaps between the planks, but one suggestion is that it kept women (who were forbidden) from crossing and sullying the sacred ground, because of their awkward traditional shoes and kimono. The object of their curiosity was the **Godai-dō** (五大堂), a picturesque pavilion built by order of Masamune in the early

1600s. It houses statues of five Buddhist deities, which can only be viewed every 33 years – the next is 2039. Meanwhile, you'll have to make do with the charming carvings of the twelve animals of the zodiac decorating the eaves.

There are a couple of larger, less-frequented islands along the seafront, of which **Oshima** (雄島), five minutes' walk south, is the more interesting. Once a retreat for Buddhist priests, the island's soft rock is pocked with caves, tablets and monuments; from its east side you get attractive views of Matsushima Bay. The second island, **Fukuura-jima** (福浦島; daily 8am–5pm; ¥200), lies north of Godai-dō across a 252m-long bridge. A natural botanical garden, it's home to more than 250 native plant species, and makes a good picnic spot.

The hills around Matsushima town provide plenty of opportunities for panoramic views of the bay. Of the four main lookout points, southerly **Sōkanzan** (双観山) is reckoned to offer the best all-round views, including both Shiogama and Matsushima itself; take a taxi (¥2500 return fare) to avoid the thirty-minute climb on a busy road. Alternatively, **Saigyō Modoshi-no-matsu** (西行戻しの松) is a more pleasant, fifteen-minute scramble west of the station.

Practicalities

A good first stop if you arrive by train is the **tourist office** outside Matsushima Kaigan Station (Mon–Fri 9.30am–4.30pm, Sat & Sun 9am–5pm; Ⓣ022/354-2263, Ⓦwww.matsushima-kanko.com), which has English-speaking staff and English-language material on the area.

While Matsushima is a very easy day-trip from Sendai (see train details on p.234), the area also has a number of smart but expensive **hotels**; prices are more reasonable on weekdays and in winter (Dec to early April). Right on the waterfront, the modern *Century Hotel* (センチュリーホテル; Ⓣ022/354-4111, Ⓦwww.centuryhotel.co.jp; ❻) has a choice of Western or tatami en-suite rooms, plus seafront balconies at the higher end and a huge onsen bath with picture windows over the bay. Alternatively, *Resort Inn Matsushima* (リゾートイン松島; Ⓣ022/355-0888, Ⓔinfo@resort-inn.jp; ❹) is a bright hotel with modern en-suite rooms. To reach it, turn right from the station and follow the road leading under the tracks and up the hill about 700m.

Most of Matsushima's **restaurants** lining the main road cater to tourists, but there are a couple of attractive alternatives. *Santori Chaya* (さんとり茶屋; Thurs–Tues 11.30am–3pm & 5.30–10pm), a small, simple place on the seafront north of the Godai-dō, serves a range of reasonable *teishoku* (traditional set menu) as well as sashimi, sushi and rice dishes; head upstairs for sea views over the kitchen roof. For a snack or light lunch, try the thatched *Donjiki Chaya* (どんじき茶屋), surrounded by gardens in the woods south of Zuigan-ji, which offers soba, *dango* (rice dumplings) and drinks. You'll also find a number of smaller places along the road between the station and the main street which serve reasonably priced seafood dishes.

Oshika Hantō

North of Sendai, Honshū's coastal plain gives way to a fractured shoreline of deep bays and knobbly peninsulas. The first of these is the **Oshika Hantō**, a rugged spine on the eastern edge of Sendai Bay, whose broken tip forms the tiny island of **Kinkazan**. This has been a sacred place since ancient times, but its prime attractions these days are its isolation and the hiking trails through forests inhabited by semi-wild deer and monkeys. The main gateway to the area is **Ishinomaki**, from where buses run down the peninsula to **Ayukawa**, a former whaling port with a moderately interesting museum and connecting ferries to Kinkazan. Many tourist facilities close in winter (Nov–March), so check the schedules first at the information offices in Sendai or Matsushima and ask them to help with booking accommodation.

Connections at Ishinomaki can be quite poor, with waits of up to an hour for an onward bus or train. If you have time to kill and an interest in manga, you might want to visit the entertaining **Mangattan Museum** (March–Nov daily but closed every third Tues, 9am–6pm; Dec–Feb daily except Tues 9am–5pm; ¥800), housed in a flying saucer-style building across the river from the main shopping strip. From the street in front of the station, take a left at the second traffic lights and follow the road until the bridge.

Kinkazan

The first inhabitants of **KINKAZAN** (金華山; "Mountain of the Gold Flowers"), a conical island lying 1km off the tip of Oshika Hantō, were gold prospectors. Though the seams were exhausted long ago, Kinkazan is still associated with wealth and good fortune, and its prime sight, the shrine of **Koganeyama-jinja**, is dedicated to the twin gods of prosperity, Ebisu and Daikoku. The shrine stands in a clearing, cropped by hungry deer, on the west slope of Kinkazan, fifteen minutes' walk from the ferry pier – turn left from the pier and follow the road steeply uphill. From behind the shrine buildings a rough path leads on a stiff 2km hike up Kinkazan (445m), where the effort is rewarded with truly magnificent views along the peninsula and west towards distant Matsushima.

Various other **hiking trails** are indicated on the small green map you'll be given on the ferry to Kinkazan, which you can also pick up from Ayukawa tourist office (see p.240). However, the paths themselves are poorly signed and may well be overgrown, so check the route before setting out. Additionally, the northern part of the island has been deemed too dangerous for hiking – the maps indicate the areas that are off limits. Remember also to take plenty of food and water. If you do get lost, head down to the rough track that circumnavigates the island; the whole place is less than 25km around, so you can't go too far wrong.

Practicalities

The best way of getting to Kinkazan is to take the JR Senseki line from Sendai (or Matsushima) to **Ishinomaki** (石巻) and then hop on a bus for the scenic ride south to **Ayukawa** (1hr 25min; ¥1460). Buses depart seven times a day (only three times on weekends and holidays) from bus stop #2 outside Ishinomaki Station, where there's also a small **tourist office** (daily 9am–5.30/6pm; ⓣ0225/93-6448); **car rental** is available through Eki Rent-a-Car (ⓣ0225/93-1665). There are hourly **ferries** from Ayukawa to Kinkazan from late April to early November (9.30am–2pm; 30min; ¥900), and two boats per day during the rest of the year (10.30am & 1.30pm).

The most atmospheric **accommodation** on Kinkazan is the pilgrims' lodge at Koganeyama-jinja (黄金山神社; ⓣ0225/45-2301, ⓔkinkasan@cocoa.ocn.ne.jp; dorm beds ¥9000 per person, including two meals), where you can attend the shrine's early-morning prayer sessions.. The only other choices are two fairly rundown minshuku a few hundred metres down the dirt road leading away from the right of the ferry pier: *Ambe Ryokan* (安部旅館; ⓣ0225/45-3081; closed Nov–May; ❺, including two meals) and *Shiokaze* (潮風; ⓣ0225/45-2666 daytime; ❺, including two meals). Note that it's essential to book ahead and that there are no **restaurants** on the island, so bring something along to eat for lunch.

Ayukawa

The sleepy town of **AYUKAWA** (鮎川), on the southwest tip of Oshika Hantō, makes an alternative base for Kinkazan. A thriving port until commercial **whaling** was banned in 1987, Ayukawa's only sight is a smart whaling museum beside the ferry pier. Despite the moratorium, Japan still hunts whales for "scientific purposes" and the residents of Ayukawa continue to receive whale-meat rations. You can even eat whale (*kujira*) in local restaurants and buy whale products in the souvenir shops.

The well-designed **Oshika Whale Land** museum (おしかホエールランド; daily 9am–4/5pm, closed Tues Dec–March; ¥700) pushes a more conservationist line while also tracing the history of Ayukawa's whaling fleet. The first exhibition hall takes you through the stylized ribcage of a whale, accompanied by recordings of their eerie underwater chatter. There are various films and interactive displays concerning the life of whales, many aimed at children, though you might want to miss the section full of pickled organs and embryos.

The museum, Kinkazan **ferry pier** and **bus terminal** are all grouped together at the south end of Ayukawa. You can buy ferry tickets in an office next to the bus stop (daily 8am–4.30/5pm; ⓣ0225/45-2181), while the **tourist office** (daily 8.30am–5pm; ⓣ0225/45-3456) is a few doors further north. Staff here can provide maps and help with bookings for accommodation in both Ayukawa and Kinkazan.

For **accommodation** in Ayukawa, the minshuku *Minami-sō* (南荘; ⓣ&ⓕ0225/45-2501; ❺), close to the ferry pier, is the most likely place to be open all year. It's in a grey iron building on the hill above the pier but, despite appearances, is perfectly adequate and turns out pretty good food. A smarter option is *Atami-sō* (あたみ荘; ⓣ&ⓕ0225/45-2227; ❺), on the main road coming into town, or the more refined *Ojika Ryokan* (おじか旅館; ⓣ0225/45-3068; ❺), in the backstreets two minutes' walk north of the pier.

Ayukawa is short on places to eat, especially at night, so it's best to book dinner and breakfast at your hotel. For lunch, however, you'll find several **restaurants** along the road behind the tourist office selling fresh seafood, as well as a few places serving soba and other standard dishes near Whale Land.

Hiraizumi and around

For a brief period in the eleventh century the temples of **Hiraizumi**, around 120km north of Sendai and now a quiet backwater, rivalled even Kyoto in their magnificence. Though the majority of monasteries and palaces have since been lost, the gloriously extravagant **Konjiki-dō** and the other treasures of **Chūson-ji** temple bear witness to the area's former wealth and level of artistic accomplishment. Hiraizumi also boasts one of Japan's best-preserved Heian-period gardens at **Mōtsū-ji**, while a boat ride along the nearby Satetsu-gawa, between the towering cliffs of **Geibikei gorge**, provides a scenic contrast.

Travelling north to Hiraizumi by **train** – whether on the Tōhoku Shinkansen or the Tōhoku main line – it's necessary to change at **ICHINOSEKI** (一関), a small town 8km further south. From Ichinoseki you can either hop on the next stopping train or pick up one of the more frequent local buses, which depart from outside the station, though note that the last Hiraizumi bus leaves at around 7pm (6.30pm Sun). Ichinoseki is also the terminal for Geibikei trains, and you might find it more convenient to visit the gorge before travelling on to Hiraizumi. In Ichinoseki it's worth visiting the useful **information office** (daily 9am–5pm; ⓣ0191/23-2350), right outside the gate to the platform as you exit Ichinoseki Station, for English-language maps and brochures. There are also a couple of **car rental** outlets nearby: Eki Rent-a-Car (ⓣ0191/21-5570) and Toyota (ⓣ0191/23-2100); and several reasonable business **hotels**, notably the *Toyoko Inn* (東横イン; ⓣ0191/31-1045,

Ⓦwww.toyoko-inn.com; ❹) and the *Hotel Sunroute* (ホテルサンルート; Ⓣ0191/26-4311, Ⓦwww.sunroute.jp; ❹).

Hiraizumi

Nowadays it's hard to imagine **HIRAIZUMI** (平泉) as the resplendent capital of the **Fujiwara** clan, who chose this spot on the banks of the Kitakami-gawa for their "paradise on earth". At first sight it's a rather dozy little town on a busy main road, but the low western hills conceal one of the most important sights in northern Honshū, the gilded **Konjiki-dō**, which has somehow survived war, fire and natural decay for nearly nine hundred years. You can easily cover this and the nearby gardens of **Mōtsū-ji** in a day, staying either in Hiraizumi or Ichinoseki, or even as a half-day stopover while travelling between Sendai and Morioka.

In the early twelfth century, Fujiwara Kiyohira, the clan's first lord, began building a vast complex of Buddhist temples and palaces, lavishly decorated with gold from the local mines, in what is now Hiraizumi. Eventually, the Fujiwara's wealth and military might started to worry the southern warlord **Minamoto Yoritomo** (see p.768), who was in the throes of establishing the Kamakura shogunate. Yoritomo's valiant brother, **Yoshitsune**, had previously trained with the warrior monks of Hiraizumi, so when Yoritomo turned against him (see p.768), Yoshitsune fled north. Though at first he was protected by the Fujiwara, they soon betrayed him on the promise of a sizeable reward, and in 1189 Yoshitsune committed suicide (although according to one legend he escaped to Mongolia, where he resurfaced as Genghis Khan). Meanwhile, Yoritomo attacked the Fujiwara, destroying their temples and leaving the town to crumble into ruin. Bashō, passing through Hiraizumi five hundred years after Yoshitsune's death, caught the mood in one of his famous haiku: "The summer grass, 'tis all that's left of ancient warriors' dreams."

The flight of Yoshitsune to Hiraizumi is commemorated with a costume parade during the town's main spring **festival** (May 1–5), which also features open-air nō performances at Chūson-ji. Other important events include an ancient **sacred dance**, Ennen-no-Mai, held by torchlight at Mōtsū-ji on January 20, May 5 and during the autumn festival (Nov 1–3).

Arrival, information and accommodation

There is a **tourist office** (daily 8.30am–4.30pm; Ⓣ0191/46-2110) in the small building to the right as you exit the station, which has maps in English and helpful English-speaking staff. Buses for **Mōtsū-ji** and **Chūson-ji** (both ¥140), as well as Ichinoseki (¥310), depart from in front of the tourist office, and you can **rent bikes** (April–Nov daily 8am–5pm; ¥1000 per day; unavailable when it rains) from *Swallow Tours* beside the information office. Despite its small size, Hiraizumi has both a **post office** and foreign exchange **bank**, both located in the backstreets to the west of the station.

Accommodation options in Hiraizumi are fairly limited. One possibility is the clean and comfortable *Shirayama Ryokan* (志羅山旅館; Ⓣ0191/46-2883, Ⓕ46-3914; ❻ including meals), located in the side streets west of the station. You'll need to call ahead to let them know when you plan to arrive. Another option is to camp at the *Kinkei Sanroku Campground* (Ⓣ0191/46-2869), 500m north of Mōtsū-ji; the accommodation here also includes simple shared bungalows for ¥1000 per person.

Chūson-ji

The Fujiwara's first building projects concentrated on **Chūson-ji** (中尊寺; daily: April–Oct 8am–5pm; Nov–March 8.30am–4.30pm; ¥800 including Konjiki-dō,

Kyōzō and the Sankōzō), which had been founded by a Tendai priest from Kyoto in the mid-ninth century. Of the temple's forty original buildings, only two remain: Konjiki-dō (the Golden Hall) and the nearby sutra repository, Kyōzō. They sit on a forested hilltop, alongside a number of more recent structures, on the main bus route north from Ichinoseki and Hiraizumi stations (20min and 5min respectively).

From the main road, a broad avenue leads uphill past minor temples sheltering under towering cryptomeria trees, until you reach the first building of any size, the Hon-dō, at the top on the right-hand side. A few minutes further on, set back on the left, a concrete hall shelters Chūson-ji's greatest treasure. The **Konjiki-dō** (金色堂) is tiny – only 5.5 square metres – and protected behind plate glass, but it's still an extraordinary sight. The whole structure, bar the roof tiles, gleams with thick gold leaf, while the altar inside is smothered in mother-of-pearl inlay and delicate, gilded copper friezes set against dark, burnished lacquer. The altar's central image is of Amida Nyorai, flanked by a host of Buddhas, Bodhisattvas and guardian kings, all swathed in gold. This extravagant gesture of faith and power took fifteen years to complete and was unveiled in 1124; later, the mummified bodies of the four Fujiwara lords were buried under its altar.

Behind the Konjiki-dō, the second of Chūson-ji's original buildings, the **Kyōzō**, is not nearly so dramatic. This small, plain hall, erected in 1108, used to house more than five thousand Buddhist sutras written in gold or silver characters on rich, indigo paper. The hall next door to the **Kyōzō** was built in 1288 to shelter the Konjiki-dō – and now houses an eclectic collection of oil paintings – while, across the way, there's a much more recent nō stage where outdoor performances are held in summer by firelight (Aug 14), and during Hiraizumi's two major festivals in spring and autumn. Finally, the road beside the entrance to the Konjiki-dō leads to the modern **Sankōzō** (讃衡蔵), a museum containing what remains of Chūson-ji's treasures. The most valuable items are a statue of the Senju Kannon (Thousand-Armed Goddess of Mercy), a number of sutra scrolls and a unique collection of lacy metalwork decorations (*kalavinkas*), which originally hung in the Konjiki-dō.

Mōtsū-ji

Hiraizumi's other main sight, the Heian-period gardens of **Mōtsū-ji** (毛越寺; daily April–Oct 8am–5pm; Nov–March 8.30am–4.30pm; ¥500), lies eight minutes' walk west from Hiraizumi Station. In the twelfth century the Fujiwara added to this temple, originally founded in 850, until it was the largest in northern Honshū. Nothing remains now save a few foundation stones and Japan's best-preserved Heian garden, the **Jōdo-teien**. The garden's main feature is a large lake, speckled with symbolic "islands", in the midst of velvet lawns. There are a few simple buildings among the trees and ancient foundation stones, but otherwise the garden is simply a pleasant place to stroll. You'll find flowers in bloom in almost every season, including cherry blossom, lotus, bush clover and azaleas, but the most spectacular display is in late June, when thirty thousand irises burst into colour. As you leave the temple gate, pop into the small **museum** on the left, which is most of interest for its photos of Mōtsū-ji's colourful festivals, including the sacred Ennen-no-Mai dance (see p.241), and a poetry-writing contest in Heian-period dress, which takes place on the last Sunday in May.

Eating

There are a couple of small **restaurants** lining the road from the station to Mōtsū-ji temple, including *Seoul Shokudō* (ソウル食堂; Tues–Sun evenings only), a *yakiniku* (Korean barbecue) restaurant that has set meals, an English menu and a good range of vegetarian choices. Just before *Seoul Shokudō*, on the same side of the road, is the much more refined *Gokusui-tei* (曲水亭; Wed–Mon noon–3pm & 5–9pm), which serves traditional Japanese meals. On the north side of the station, just before the crossroads, *Izumiya* (泉屋; daily 9am–5.30pm) offers good-value *soba teishoku* from ¥530. You'll also find several similar restaurants, albeit with slightly inflated prices, near Chūson-ji. If you fancy a picnic, head for the small supermarket on the road to Mōtsū-ji.

Around Hiraizumi

The Hiraizumi area boasts two river **gorges** with confusingly similar names. **Geibikei** (猊鼻渓), as opposed to Gembikei, is the more impressive of the two, a narrow defile best viewed by boat, some 20km east of Hiraizumi. Unless you've got your own transport, however, the easiest way to get there is by bus (bus stop #7; ¥620; 45min) or train (JR Ōfunato line to Geibikei Station; 30min) from Ichinoseki Station. It's an attractive ride either way, marred at the end by a huge cement works. From the bus stop, turn left at the main road and then take the first right; from the train station, turn right and walk along the lane for five minutes, then follow the road under the tracks to find the boat dock.

Though not cheap, the Geibikei **boat trip** (hourly 8.30/9am–3/4.30pm; 90min; ¥1500; Ⓣ0191/47-2341) is a lot of fun. Despite poling fairly sizeable wooden punts upstream for 2km, the boatmen still find breath to regale their passengers with local legends, details of the passing flora and endless statistics about the gorge. It's all in Japanese, of course, but the general mirth is infectious.

The Tōno valley

The town of **Tōno** is set in a bowl of low mountains in the heart of one of Japan's poorest regions, surrounded by the flat **Tōno valley**. The people of Tōno and the farmers of the valley take pride in their living legacy of farming and folk traditions, embodied by the district's **magariya** – large, L-shaped farmhouses – and a number of museums devoted to the old ways. But the area is perhaps most famous for its wealth of **folk tales**, known as *Tōno Monogatari* (see box, p.245); there are references to these legends throughout the valley, alongside ancient shrines, rock carvings and traces of primitive cults, which help give Tōno its slightly mysterious undercurrent.

To make the most of the Tōno valley you really need your own transport – head to Tōno to **hire cars** or **bikes** (see p.244). There are also some **local buses** that run from outside the station, but the only really useful routes are those heading northeast to Denshō-en and Furusato-mura (see p.247). These buses also stop near *Tōno Youth Hostel* (see p.244).

If you plan to spend the day cycling around the valley, you can stock up on **picnic** supplies at the Topia shopping mall, a block from the station. The ground floor of the mall has a well-stocked supermarket as well as a small farmers' market selling very fresh and cheap fruit and vegetables, complete with biographical notes and photographs of the farmers (and their families) who brought the produce to market.

Tōno

TŌNO (遠野) itself is a small town set among flat rice-lands, with orchards and pine forests cloaking the surrounding hills. Although it's mainly a place to make use of for its hotels, banks and other facilities, there are a couple of museums to see before

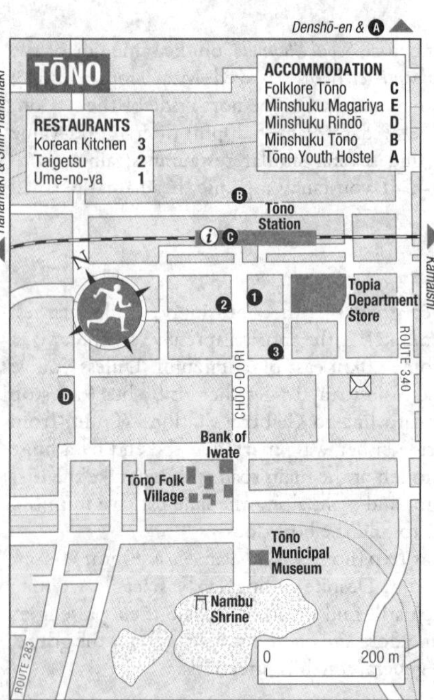

you set off round the valley. Allow a couple of days to do the area justice.

Arrival, information and getting around

Travelling to Tōno by **train**, you can enjoy an attractive journey east on the JR Kamaishi line from Hanamaki, or Shin-Hanamaki for the Shinkansen. Tōno's **tourist office** (daily 8.30am–5.30pm; ⓣ0198/62-1333, ⓦwww.tonojikan.jp) is on the right as you exit the station. Though the staff don't speak much English, they have English-language maps and brochures, and a larger-scale Japanese map which is useful for navigating around the valley. The attached shop stocks copies of *The Legends of Tōno* (see box opposite; ¥2100); you might also find it at the Municipal Museum or Denshō-en (see p.247).

There's a **car rental** place inside the station, Tōno Kankō Rent-a-Car (ⓣ0198/62-1375), and a Mitsubishi Rent-a-Car (ⓣ0198/62-3154) nearby where vehicles can be hired in three- or six-hour increments (from around ¥4000). However, most people opt to cycle; you can **rent bikes** from the information office and other outlets on the station concourse (¥500/2hr; up to ¥1000/day), or from *Tōno Youth Hostel* (see below) for ¥800. Tōno maps show three recommended cycling routes (also possible by car), of around four hours each, which cover the main sights – they're reasonably well signposted, though not always in English.

Accommodation

Tōno has a decent selection of **accommodation** within walking distance of the station. If you want more atmosphere, however, you can stay in a real *magariya* farmhouse on the west side of town, while Tōno's excellent youth hostel is located about 4km northeast.

Folklore Tōno フォルクローロ遠野 5-7 Shinkoku-chō ⓣ0198/62-0700, ⓕ62-0800. A small JR-owned hotel inside the station building, with Western-style rooms. Rates include a simple breakfast. ❺

Minshuku Magariya 民宿曲り屋 30-58-3 Niisato, Ayaori-chō ⓣ0198/62-4564. This traditional farmhouse is located 3km southwest of the station (around ¥900 by taxi). The ten rooms are all Japanese-style, with shared facilities, and excellent meals are served round a big open hearth. On the downside, it's a little inconvenient to get to, no one speaks English and they don't accept anyone aged under 16. Rates include two meals. ❻

Minshuku Rindō 民宿りんどう 2-34 Daiku-chō ⓣ0198/62-5726, ⓔrindou@crocus.ocn.ne.jp. Simple, homely minshuku on an attractive street roughly 5min walk west from the station. The owner speaks a little English and rooms are offered with or without meals. ❹–❺

Minshuku Tōno 民宿とおの 2-17 Zaimoku-chō ⓣ0198/62-4395, ⓦwww.minshuku-tono.com. Small, friendly minshuku with an English-speaking owner, on the north side of the railway tracks. Two meals included in the rates. ❻

Tōno Youth Hostel 遠野ユースホステル 13-39-5 Tsuchibuchi-chō ⓣ0198/62-8736,

ⓦwww.jyh.or.jp. Delightful modern hostel with dorms, family rooms and excellent-value meals. It's set among rice fields about 15min walk from the Denshō-en or Ashiarai-gawa bus stops (see p.247). The genial manager speaks a little English and can advise on local cycling routes; bike rental is available. ❸

The Town

From Tōno Station it's an eight-minute walk straight across town and over the river to the **Tōno Municipal Museum** (遠野市立博物館; daily 9am–5pm; closed last day of the month; ¥310, or ¥520 combined entrance with Tōno Folk Village) at the back of a red-brick building which doubles as the library. This entertaining museum gives a good overview of Tōno's festivals, crafts and agricultural traditions.

Walking back towards the station, turn left just across the river for **Tōno Folk Village** (とおの昔話村; daily 9am–5pm; ¥310, or ¥520 combined entrance with Tōno Municipal Museum). The "village" consists of several buildings, including the ryokan where Yanagita Kunio (see box below) stayed while researching his legends, and an old storehouse containing more dramatizations of the stories.

Eating

Local **speciality foods** include *hitsuko soba*, small bowls of rough, handmade noodles eaten with a mix of chicken, raw egg, onion and mushrooms, and the regional dish, *nambu hitssumi* (or *suiton*), a soup laced with seasonal vegetables and dumplings. You can try these, along with other specialities, at many of the area's minshuku.

For a coffee or quick **snack**, walk down the main road from the station to the well-priced *Taigetsu* (待月; daily 10am–11pm), which serves good cake and coffee along with staples such as cheese toast, curry rice and ramen dishes. On the opposite side of the road, *Ume-no-ya* (うめのや; daily except Tues 11.30am–8pm) is another simple place, offering good portions of curry rice, *ebi*-fry (fried prawns), omelettes from ¥500 and set meals from ¥950. If you want a break from Japanese

The legends of Tōno

When the far-sighted folklorist **Yanagita Kunio** visited Tōno in 1909, he found a world still populated with the shadowy figures of demons and other usually malevolent spirits which the farmers strove to placate using ancient rituals. The following year he published **Tōno Monogatari** (published in English as *The Legends of Tōno*), the first book to tap the rich oral traditions of rural Japan. The 118 tales were told to him by Kyōseki Sasaki (or Kizen), the educated son of a Tōno peasant, to whom goblins, ghosts and gods were part of everyday life.

People in Tōno still talk about **Zashiki Warashi**, a mischievous child spirit (either male or female) who can be heard running at night and is said to bring prosperity to the household. Another popular tale tells of a farmer's beautiful daughter who fell in love with their horse. When the farmer heard that his child had married the horse, he hanged it from a mulberry tree, but his grieving daughter was whisked off to heaven clinging to her lover.

Probably the most popular character from the legends, however, is the *kappa*, an ugly water creature which, while not being unique to Tōno, seems to exist here in large numbers. You'll find *kappa* images everywhere in town – on postboxes, outside the station; even the police box is *kappa*-esque. The traditional *kappa* has long skinny limbs, webbed hands and feet, a sharp beak, and a hollow on the top of his head that must be kept full of water. He's usually green, sometimes with a red face, and his main pastime seems to be pulling young children into ponds and rivers. Should you happen to meet a real *kappa*, remember to bow – on returning your bow, the water will run out of the hollow on his head and he'll have to hurry off to replenish it.

flavours, try *Korean Kitchen* (daily except Tues 11.30am–2pm & 5.30–10/11pm), on the same street as the post office. It has lunches from ¥880, including barbecued meat sets and noodles, as well as the usual range of meaty and spicy *yakiniku* pleasures at night. The **folk village** restaurants (same opening times as the village) are a good place to try local delicacies such as *ayu* (river fish) and *jingisukan* (barbecued lamb).

West of Tōno

West of Tōno the main valley narrows, funnelling the road and railway along beside the Sarugaishi-gawa. The wooded southern hillside hides some unusual shrines and an appealing group of Buddha images, which makes one of the best short trips out of Tōno. Further up the valley, an imposing *magariya* farmhouse attracts a lot of attention, but if you are short on time it's better to save your energy for more accessible examples on the east side of town.

Heading out of Tōno on the south side of the river (on the old Route 283) for 2.5km, look out for a stone staircase on the left. At the bottom of the steps, past the house, you'll find a tree festooned with red and white ribbons and, behind it, **Unedori-jinja** (卯子酉神社). This tiny shrine is dedicated to the god in charge of matrimonial affairs; if you want to get married, tie a red ribbon onto the tree with your left hand. Having wowed the god with your skill, go back and climb the stone steps, cross a lane and follow the path into a narrow, wooded valley filled with mossy stones. Keep looking closely at these stones: at first you won't see anything, but gradually faint outlines appear, then full faces and rounded bodies, until you're seeing little figures everywhere. Known as the **Gohyaku Rakan** (五百羅漢), there are supposedly five hundred of these Buddhist "disciples", which were carved by a local monk in the late eighteenth century to commemorate victims of a terrible famine in 1754.

Before heading back down to the main road, turn right (east) along the lane and continue for 700m until you come to a *torii* on the right and a steep path leading up through the pine woods. At the top of a short, stiff climb there's a larger shrine building (usually locked) and two small shrines with a collection of phallic and female symbols made of stone or wood. Though rather dilapidated nowadays, this is one of the few remaining shrines dedicated to **Konsei-sama**, the local God of Fertility, and an interesting vestige of an ancient cult.

The thatch-roofed **Chiba Magariya** (千葉家の曲り家; daily: April–Oct 8.30am–5pm; Nov–March 9am–4pm; ¥350) stands high above the valley some 11km west of Tōno, north of the main valley up a steep side road. Once housing the Chiba family, fifteen labourers and twenty horses, this two-hundred-year-old farmhouse was selected for restoration as an important example of a *magariya*, an L-shaped building with the stables in the shorter wing. If you do venture out this way, take a look at the **Tsuzuki Stone** (続石), 500m before the farmhouse and set back in the woods. Though it's said to be natural, the enormous, rounded boulder balanced on a smaller stone looks like a dolmen.

Northeast of Tōno

The broad valley northeast of Tōno is home to a number of somewhat touristy "folk villages" aimed at preserving the old crafts. The best one to visit is **Furusato-mura**, though the smaller **Denshō-en** and **Sui-kōen** are slightly more accessible. Other sights to aim for include a *kappa* pool, an old watermill and a temple housing Japan's tallest Kannon statue. However, the area's chief highlight is its scenery – rice fields and rolling hills dotted with the occasional thatched farmhouse. The best way to explore is to hire a bike and follow the country lanes.

Denshō-en and Jōken-ji

The main road northeast of Tōno (Route 340) leads past **Denshō-en** (伝承園; daily 9am–5pm, last entry 4pm; ¥310), about 5km out of town. This village museum contains various buildings relocated from around Tōno, including a waterwheel, storehouses and a *magariya*, where local folk demonstrate weaving, rope-making and other crafts. Inside the *magariya*, follow the narrow corridor at the back to reach a small shrine room filled with brightly dressed dolls. These are images of **Oshira-sama**, an agricultural deity worshipped throughout northern Honshū. They're stick-like figures, their faces either drawn on or simply carved, and are made from mulberry – according to legend, Tōno's original Oshira-sama came from the same tree on which the horse-husband died (see box, p.245). The deities, often used by blind mediums, are also supposed to predict the future – hence all the prayer papers tied around the shrine. Denshō-en is one of the few places in the area that it's feasible to reach by local bus. Services depart every hour or so from Tōno Station and drop you either at the village or 100m further back at the Ashiarai-gawa stop (15–20min; ¥290).

A short distance east along the main road from Denshō-en, a signposted right turn leads to **Jōken-ji** (常堅寺). Founded in 1490, the temple is mainly of interest for its statue of **Obinzuru-sama**, a little figure in a cloak and hat with a very shiny anatomy – the deity is supposed to cure illnesses if rubbed in the appropriate place. Behind the temple there's a **kappa pool**, home to a particularly helpful *kappa* credited with dousing a fire in Jōken-ji. An eccentric local has built a small shrine to himself beside the pool and may well regale you with incomprehensible but good-natured stories.

Fukusen-ji and Furusato-mura

Just before Denshō-en, a road branches north, following the main valley for another 2km to **Fukusen-ji** (福泉寺; April–Nov daily 8am–5pm; ¥300). This fairly modern temple, founded in 1912, is famous for its 17m-tall image of **Kannon**, the Goddess of Mercy. The slender, gilded statue with a blue hairdo is carved from a single tree trunk and took the craftsman twelve years to make. It stands in an attractive temple at the top of the hill, where the artist's tools and photos of the huge tree being brought to Tōno by train are also on display.

Continue on this road another 3km and you'll reach **Furusato-mura** (ふるさと村; daily 9am–5pm, last entry 4pm; ¥520). The biggest and most attractive of Tōno's folk museums, Furusato-mura resembles a working village, with its own rice fields, vegetable plots and duck ponds. There are five refurbished *magariya* on the hillside from the eighteenth and nineteenth centuries, where pensioners sit beside smoking hearths, busily making souvenirs such as straw slippers, wooden *kappa* and bamboo baskets – if you want to have a go, the old folk do a number of different workshops, including ones to make a straw horse or a bamboo dragonfly, as well as soba making and *mochi* pounding (¥600–1000). You can also buy their handiwork in the museum shop, where there's also a small **restaurant** with some good-value lunch sets. Some Denshō-en buses continue up the valley to Furusato-mura, though they're fairly sporadic (every 1–2hr; 25min; ¥500).

If you want to return to town after Fukusen-ji, follow the road back towards Denshō-en for about one minute and take the Tōno-Towa Bicycle Path indicated by the happy *kappa* on the sign to the right. This 8km-long path winds through rice fields and along streams and is pleasantly traffic-free until the path meets up with Route 396 for the last 2km.

East of Denshō-en: Sui-kōen

The most beautiful part of the Tōno valley lies **east of Denshō-en**, though to appreciate it you'll have to get off onto the side roads. One attractive ride takes you out to an old watermill and then loops back past the third folk village. To find the turning, follow Route 340 for 3km east from Denshō-en and then fork right immediately after crossing a red-lacquered bridge. The lane climbs gently uphill, past a number of old farms to a small, thatched **watermill** (山口の水車). On the way you pass the **house of Kyōseki Sasaki** (see box, p.245), opposite which there's a path signed to **Dan-no-hana** (ダンノハナ). In the not-so-distant past, old people were sent to places called Dan-no-hana to die; however, in this case the old folk got bored waiting, so they came down to work the fields during the day and returned to their hill at night.

Heading back down to the main road, look out on the left for a turning signed to Denderano (デンデラ野). Follow this lane west for nearly 2km and you'll come to the last of the folk-villages, **Takamuro Sui-kōen** (水光園; daily 10am–4pm, closed every fourth Mon; ¥310), with a *magariya*, a *kappa* pool and displays of antique farm implements. From here you can drop down to the main road, or continue west along country lanes.

Morioka and around

A former castle town on the confluence of three rivers, the small, congenial city of **MORIOKA** (盛岡) has no outstanding sights, but the combination of an attractive setting, good range of accommodation and interesting local cuisine makes it a good overnight stop on the journey through northern Honshū. With a couple of hours to spare, you could also take a wander around the castle ruins and some of

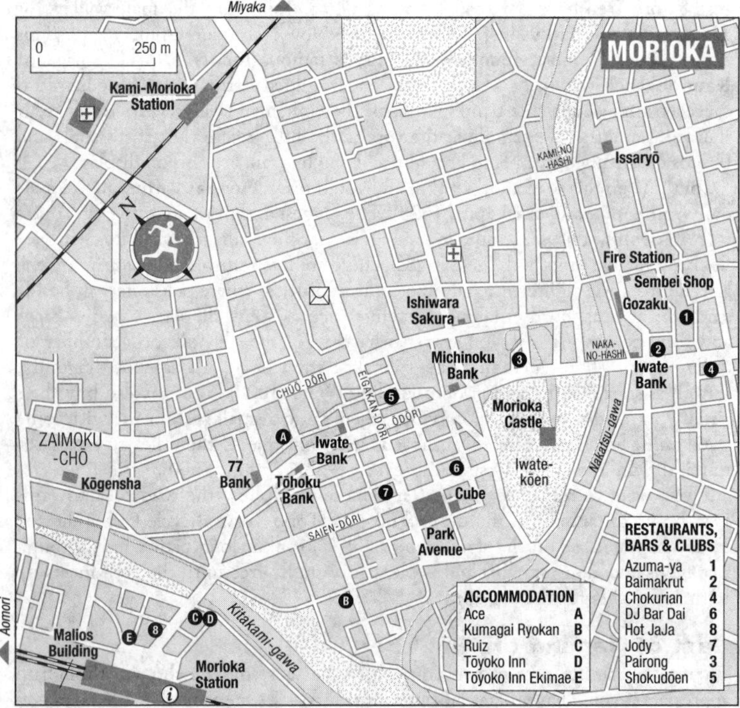

the older neighbourhoods. Additionally, Morioka is one of the main access points for hikes around the nearby **Hachimantai plateau**.

The city has two major summer festivals. At the end of the rice-planting season the **Chagu-Chagu Umakko** (second Saturday in June) features a 15km procession of richly caparisoned horses, ending at the city's Hachiman-gū shrine. Then, in early August (1–3), thousands of dancers parade through town during the **Sansa Odori**, accompanied by flutes and drums and followed by a general knees-up.

Arrival and information

Local and long-distance **buses** depart from the east side of Morioka Station (note that many bus services only operate from late April to late November), with services running to Tokyo, the Hachimantai plateau and Towada-ko. Both the Akita and Tōhoku Shinkansen pass through Morioka station.

Central Morioka can easily be covered **on foot**, but another option is to **rent a bike**. Sasaki Bicycles (Ⓣ019/624-2692; ¥200/hr, ¥1000/day), by *Hotel Ruiz*, is one of several bicycle rental places. There is also an "100-yen" **loop bus** that runs between the station and various central locations.

Morioka's **Northern Tōhoku information centre** (daily 9am–5.30pm; Ⓣ019/625-2090) is located on the train station's second floor, near the southern entrance to the Shinkansen tracks. The helpful English-speaking staff can provide maps and information about the region, and there's also a JR information desk in the same office.

Accommodation

Ace ホテルエース Ⓣ019/654-3811, Ⓕ654-3815. Just north of Ōdōri, this is a good choice if you want to stay in the downtown area. The rooms are comfortable, although it's worth paying a little extra to stay in the new wing. ④

Kumagai Ryokan 熊ヶ井旅館 Ⓣ019/651-3020, Ⓦkumagairyokan.com. South of Saien-dōri and about 8min walk from the station in a lane leading off the side street right after the Christian centre. With a welcoming English-speaking owner, attractive Japanese-style rooms and well-priced meals, this ryokan is the best option in town. ④

Ruiz ホテルルイズ Ⓣ019/625-2611, Ⓕ625-3381. Located near the station, just before the Kitagami-kawa, this standard mid-range business hotel has a choice of Western- or Japanese-style rooms and a number of unexciting in-house restaurants. ④

Tōyoko Inn Morioka Ekimae 東横イン盛岡駅前 Ⓣ019/625-1045, Ⓦwww.toyoko-inn.com. Opposite the station, this branch of the *Tōyoko Inn* chain has smart and clean rooms, and rates include a light Japanese breakfast. Also has free internet access. There is a second *Tōyoko Inn* next to *Hotel Ruiz*. ④

The City

From the station, located on the far west side of town, it takes about twenty minutes to walk along Saien-dōri, one of Morioka's two major shopping streets, straight to **Morioka castle**. Once the seat of the Nambu lords, it took 36 years to complete (1597–1633), only for it to be destroyed in the battles of the Meiji Restoration. If you turn right in front of the castle park, **Iwate-kōen** (岩手公園), and walk down to the Nakatsu-gawa, you can pick up a pleasant riverside path to the east of the old walls. Alternatively, head east along **Ōdōri**, the city's foremost shopping street, and cross the river via the **Naka-no-hashi** bridge (中ノ橋).

Immediately over the river, you can't miss the ornate red-brick and grey-slate facade of **Iwate Bank**, which dates from 1911. Turn left beside the bank and you'll come to a row of traditional Meiji-era buildings known as **Gozaku** (ござ九), whose centrepiece is a shop selling brushes, straw and wicker goods. Stores opposite specialize in the region's most famous **crafts** – heavy iron kettles and eye-catching cotton textiles dyed with intricate patterns – while appetizing odours greet you at the top of the street, where a *sembei* shop turns out local-style rice crackers sprinkled with sesame seeds or nuts; walk round the side and you can see the bakers hard at work.

Continue north to the next T-junction where you'll find an old blackened **kura** (traditional storehouse) on your right. Turn left to reach the renowned seventeenth-century bridge, **Kami-no-hashi** (上ノ橋), although you'd be forgiven for missing the bridge's most important feature: the eighteen bronze, bulb-shaped topknots forged in the early 1600s which ornament the railings.

Heading south from Kami-no-hashi, back on the other side of the river, the next major avenue is Chūō-dōri, lined with civic offices. About 400m west of the river, a three-hundred-year-old cherry tree bulges out of a 15m-wide fissure in a rounded granite boulder. Known as the **Ishiwari Sakura**, or "rock-splitting cherry" (石割桜), no one knows whether the tree really split the rock, but it's a startling sight. If you follow Chūō-dōri west to the Kitakami-gawa, you'll reach a small neighbourhood known as **Zaimoku-chō**, whose main feature is a traditional shopping street running parallel to the river. Among smart modern boutiques there are a number of craftshops, notably **Kōgensha** (光原社; daily 10am–6pm), with two outlets on opposite sides of the street; they sell a good range of modern and more traditional ironware, paper and bamboo designs.

Eating, drinking and entertainment

By far the highlight of a visit to Morioka is its cuisine, the city's most famous speciality being **wanko-soba**, named after the small bowls that the thin, flat buckwheat noodles are served in. They're often eaten as a contest, during which diners don an apron and shovel down as many bowls as possible while a waitress relentlessly dishes up more; to stop, you have to get the top on to your emptied bowl – easier said than done. Another rather odd Morioka concoction, **reimen**, is originally a summer dish, though you can easily find it year-round in Morioka and other parts of the country. This consists of a large bowl of cold, semi-transparent, slightly chewy egg noodles eaten with Korean *kimchi* (spicy pickled vegetables) and a variety of garnishes that might include boiled egg, sesame seeds and slices of apple or cold meat.

The final local speciality is another unusual noodle dish; **ja-ja men**, a bowl of thick, white noodles (a bit like udon) that comes with a few slices of cucumber, red pickles and a slab of brown miso paste. You'll find *ja-ja men* in many of the city's noodle shops; mix up the miso paste and noodles once you are served and, if you're still hungry when you've finished, crack open and beat up one of the raw eggs on the table and hand it to your server, who will pour broth over it: the result is a bowl of soup, called *chii tantan*, designed to cleanse the palate. A little bland eaten straight, most locals mix either grated ginger or miso paste (found in small pots on the table) with it to give it a bit more body and flavour.

Restaurants

Azuma-ya 東家 1-8-3 Nakanohashi-dōri. Across the street from the Nakachan department store, this is a good place to head to for *wanko-soba* if *Chokurian* (see opposite) is full; *wanko* course menus start at ¥2625. Daily 11am–8pm.

Baimakrut 1-4-22 Nakanohashi-dōri. Against a backdrop of unrelenting Thai pop music, the Thai chef at this welcoming restaurant whips up great curries at lunch (set menus from ¥840) and all sorts of Thai goodies at night. Daily 11.30am–2.30pm & 6–11pm.

Chokurian 直利庵 1-12-13 Nakanohashi-dōri. Opened in 1884, this is the best-known restaurant in town for *wanko-soba*. Expect to pay ¥2625–5200, although they also serve reasonably priced standard noodle dishes in an adjoining room. Daily except Wed 11am–8pm.

Hot JaJa ホットジャジャ 9-5 Ekimae-dōri. If you can't get into *Pairong* (see opposite), head to this *ja-ja men* place near the station. The noodles are good, and they also serve the good local Baeren

Beer, which is inspired by German brewing traditions. *Ja-ja men* starts from ¥450, with sets from ¥750. Daily 10am–11.30pm.

Pairong 白龍 5-15 Uchimaru. Just off Ōdōri, across from Iwate-kōen; walk under the big *torii* and look on the left side. One of the most popular places for *ja-ja men*, with huge but cheap portions. The portions are so filling that the staff advise new customers to try the regular (*futsū*, ¥500) size first; the egg soup costs another ¥50. Expect queues during peak lunch and dinner hours. Mon–Sat 11.30am–9pm.

Shokudōen 食道苑 1-8-2 Ōdōri. Nestled in the backstreets of Morioka's drinking area, here you can try *reimen*, served to your required level of spiciness, as well *yakiniku* dishes, for as little as ¥850. Daily 11.30am–midnight, closed first and third Tues of month.

Clubs and bars

Morioka has a surprisingly bustling **club scene**. *DJ Bar Dai* (Tues–Sun 10pm until late; Ⓦwww.djbardai.com) in the basement of the Toishita Building on Saien-dōri is the place to go for deep funk and hip-hop, with the cream of the region's DJs taking turns on the decks. For more traditional funk, R&B and soul, head over to *Jody* (daily 7.30pm–3am). This intimate **bar** is located in the basement of the Vent Vert Building on Eigakan-dōri, which runs north to Ōdōri. Drinks start from ¥700, and there is a ¥1000 table charge.

Listings

Banks Iwate Bank, Tōhoku Bank, Michinoku Bank and 77 Bank all have branches with foreign-exchange desks on Ōdōri. Iwate Bank also has a branch outside the train station.

Car rental Nippon Rent-a-Car (Ⓣ019/635-6605), Nissan (Ⓣ019/654-5825), Toyota (Ⓣ019/622-0100) and Eki Rent-a-Car (Ⓣ019/624-5212) all have offices in or near the station.

Hospitals The two main central hospitals are Iwate Medical University Hospital, 19-1 Uchi-maru (Ⓣ019/651-5111), and the Prefectural Hospital, 1-4-1 Ueda (Ⓣ019/653-1151).

Internet access There is free internet access at the Iwate International Association, 5F AIINA (Ⓣ019/654-8900, Ⓦiwate-ia.or.jp). Located next to Malios at the East-West Passage of Morioka Station, this is the local forum for international exchange; they can also offer help and advice to any foreigner in difficulties.

Post office The Central Post Office, Morioka Chūō Yūbin-kyoku, Morioka-shi, just north of Chūō-dōri, has the best hours. There's also a more convenient sub-post office in the blocks in front of the station.

Shopping Nambu ironware, dyed cotton textiles and plain wooden *kokeshi* dolls are the representative crafts of this region. A recommended craft shop is Kōgensha (see opposite), but you'll also find local souvenirs on the station's first floor and in Park Avenue, Morioka's main department store on Saien-dōri. Or try the more modern Cube II, next door.

Taxi Call the station's central booking office on Ⓣ019/622-5240 (daily 9am–5am).

Around Morioka

Tōhoku's highest peak, **Iwate-san** (岩手山; 2041m), dominates Morioka's northern horizon and marks the eastern edge of the **Hachimantai plateau**, a beautiful area for hiking among marshes and pine forests. At present the volcanic peak is off limits, but you can spend a day walking around the plateau to the north of Iwate-san, from where it's an easy stroll to the less daunting summit of **Hachimantai** (八幡平; 1613m). From the Hachimantai Chōjō bus stop, a well-marked path leads to the summit (40min), across Hachiman-numa marshes. Afterwards you can follow a variety of tracks wandering across the plateau with views south to the barren slopes of Iwate-san.

There are a couple of infrequent bus routes from Morioka to Hachimantai Chōjō, taking between two, and two and half hours (one way around ¥1300). The timetables, however, change annually and services are limited to summer months. Contact the tourist office in Morioka station (see p.249) for full details.

Aomori and around

Honshū's most northerly city, **AOMORI** (青森), sits at the bottom of Mutsu Bay, sheltered by the two claws of the Tsugaru and Shimokita peninsulas. It's a small and rather characterless city, though it comes to life during the **Nebuta Matsuri** (Aug 2–7), one of Japan's biggest and rowdiest festivals, which features giant illuminated floats and energetic dancing. It takes less than a day to cover Aomori's main sights, of which the most appealing is a park displaying *nebuta* floats.

Southwest of Aomori, the small town of **Hirosaki** has a number of interesting historical sights clustered around its once magnificent castle that can be covered on a day-trip. You could also explore the **Shimokita Hantō**, the axe-head peninsula peering over Aomori from the east, which is dominated by the sacred **Osore-zan**, an eerie wasteland where souls hover between life and death.

Arrival, information and city transport

Aomori Station lies on the west side of the city centre, just inland from the Bay Bridge and **Aomori passenger terminal**, where **ferries** from Wakinosawa (on the Shimokita Hantō) dock. Arriving by boat from Hokkaidō's Hakodate port, you'll pull up at a wharf further west, from where it's a twenty-minute bus ride into the centre (¥300). **Long-distance buses** terminate at Aomori Station, as do limousine buses from the **airport** (40min; ¥680). The recently extended Tohoku Shinkansen from Tokyo, which passes through Sendai, Ichinoseki, Morioka and Hachinohe, arrives at Shin-Aomori Station, five minutes by JR Ōu line from Aomori Station.

There are several places where you can get information, but the most useful **tourist office** is the City Tourism Office (daily 8.30am–7pm; ⓣ0177/23-4670), located next to the JR Bus terminal to the left-hand side of the station exit, which has English-speaking staff.

Most of central Aomori is manageable on foot, but you'll need **local buses** to reach the southern sights. Both the green Shiei buses and the less frequent blue-and-white JR buses run out to Nebuta-no-sato from Aomori Station; rail passes are valid on these JR services.

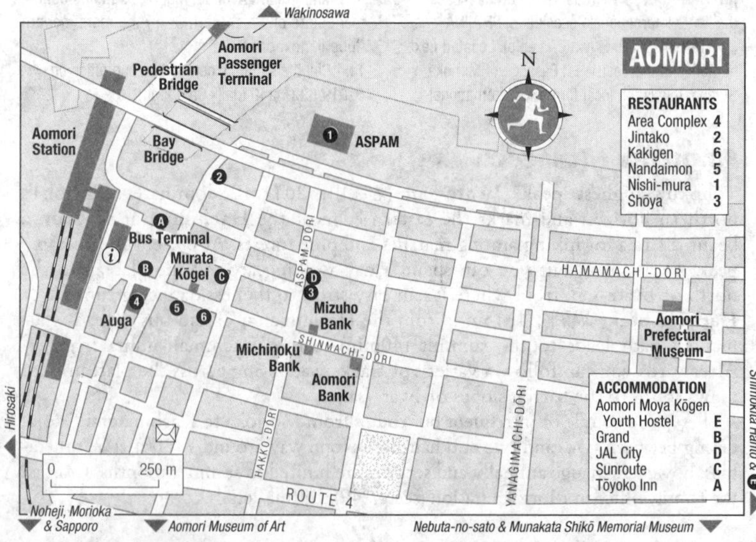

Accommodation

It's a good idea to book **accommodation** in advance in Aomori at any time of year, but this is essential during the Nebuta Matsuri (Aug 2–7). Though there's a decent range of chain business hotels in the city centre, it's short on budget places and ryokan.

Aomori Moya Kōgen Youth Hostel 青森雲谷高原ユースホステル 9-5 Aza Yamabuki ōaza Moya ⓣ017/764-2888, ⓦwww.jyh.or.jp. Relaxed youth hostel nestled at the foot of the Moya plateau, a 40min bus ride from Aomori train station. You can't beat the clean shared tatami rooms, herbal tea and Guinness, although it gets a little cramped when busy. There's also an onsen next door. Take the bus outside the JR Aomori Station going towards Moya Hills or the *Hotel Villa City Moya* (last bus 6.30pm) and get off at the Moya Kōgen stop; the hostel is one minute's walk down to the right. ¥2500–4000 per person, plus ¥200 heating fee Nov–early April.

Grand Hotel グランドホテル 1-1-23 Shin-machi ⓣ0120-23-1011, ⓔinfo2@agh.co.jp. This old-fashioned hotel on the main street is slightly dated but offers a range of comfortable, well-furnished rooms, some with sea views. ❺

JAL City ホテルJALシティ 2-4-12 Yasukata ⓣ0177/32-2580, ⓦaomori.jalcity.co.jp. The smart rooms at this popular hotel are well priced, and there's a decent in-house restaurant. It's about six minutes' walk east from the station. ❻

Sunroute ホテルサンルート 1-9-8 Shin-machi ⓣ0177/75-2321, ⓔpost@sunroute-aomori.com. Good business hotel with largish, en-suite Western-style rooms and a choice of restaurants. ❺

Tōyoko Inn 東横イン 1-3-5 Yasukata ⓣ0177/35-1045, ⓦwww.toyoko-inn.co.jp. Modern business hotel in a great spot facing the station. Rooms are clean and bright and come with free internet access. A light Japanese breakfast is included in the rate. ❹

The City

The harbour-front **ASPAM** (Aomori Prefectural Centre for Tourism and Industry) building – a greyish glass pyramid about ten minutes' walk northeast of the station – is a good place to start exploring the city. There's usually a video of the Nebuta Matsuri festival playing in the entrance hall, while you can also catch a twenty-minute panoramic slide show of the region including its festivals and scenery on the second floor (hourly 10am–5pm; ¥600). It's not really worth forking out for the thirteenth-floor observation lounge (daily 9am–10pm; ¥400, or ¥800 with the slide show at the Panorama Theatre), but take a look at the second floor, where they occasionally have demonstrations of local crafts.

Roughly fifteen minutes' walk southeast of ASPAM, the **Aomori Prefectural Museum** (青森県立郷土館; Tues–Sun: May–Oct 9.30am–6pm; Nov–April 9am–5pm; March–Dec ¥310; Jan & Feb ¥250) takes a look at the region's history, culture and natural environment. Archeological digs have revealed evidence of human occupation in the area since at least 3000 BC, and the museum kicks off with Jōmon-period earthenware pots, replica thatched huts and the beautiful, insect-eyed *dogū* figurines whose ritualistic purpose is still unclear. The most immediately interesting displays, however, are in the top-floor gallery devoted to local folk culture, where vine-woven baskets and rice-straw raincoats rub shoulders with fertility dolls and the distinctive agricultural deity Oshira-sama (see p.247).

From here you can return to Aomori Station along Aomori's main shopping street, **Shinmachi-dōri**, with its banks, craft shops and department stores. At the west end, in front of the station, is the **Auga Building** (アウガ), which has a good old-fashioned **food market** in the basement floor (Mon–Sat 5am–6.30pm). A large proportion of the stalls are loaded with iridescent fish, hairy crabs, scallops and squids, but among them you'll find neat pyramids of Aomori's other staple product: juicy, oversized apples.

Out of the centre

The city's remaining sights are all in the southern suburbs, of which by far the most popular is the exhibition of festival floats at **Nebuta-no-sato** (ねぶたの里; daily: April–Nov 9am–5pm; Dec–March 10am–5pm; April–Nov ¥630, Dec–March ¥420). JR and Shiei buses (1–2 hourly; 30min; ¥450) drop you on the main road, from where it's a short walk to the entrance. One of Japan's great summer festivals, the Nebuta Matsuri, is named after the gigantic bamboo-framed paper lanterns (*nebuta*) which take the form of kabuki actors, samurai or even sumo wrestlers in dramatic poses. The features are painted by well-known local artists, and the lanterns – lit nowadays by electricity rather than candles – are mounted on wheeled carts and paraded through the night-time streets of Aomori. According to the most popular local legend, the lanterns originated in 800 AD, when local rebels were lured out of hiding by an imaginative general who had his men construct an eye-catching lantern and play festive music. Among the displays, you can see several of today's magnificent *nebuta* in a darkened hall on the hillside to the left as you walk through the park, alongside photos of early festivals and of construction techniques.

One of Aomori's most famous citizens, a woodblock artist inspired by Van Gogh, is honoured in the **Munakata Shikō Memorial Museum** (棟方志功記念館; Tues–Sun 9.30am–5pm; ¥500). The small museum shows rotating exhibitions of Shikō's bold, almost abstract, scenes of local festivals and Aomori people. Though best known for his black-and-white prints, Shikō also dabbled in oils, painted screens and calligraphy. To reach the museum, take a bus from Aomori Station bound for Koyanagi and get off at the Munakata Shikō Kinenkan-dōri-mae stop (15min; ¥190), from where it's a four-minute walk west to the museum, in front of the NTT building.

Another trip worth making is to the **Aomori Museum of Art** (青森県立美術館; June–Sept 9am–6pm; Oct–May 9.30am–5pm; closed every second and fourth Monday; ¥500; temporary exhibits cost extra). The stark white rectangular building seems an extension of the snowy landscape that surrounds it for much of the year, and is itself a marvel to admire. Inside is a selection of works commissioned by Hirosaki-born artist Yoshimoto Nara, famous for his sculptures of big white dogs, a few pieces by Munakata Shikō, a chilling photography exhibit from the Vietnam War and three enormous murals by Marc Chagall. Take a bus from Aomori Station bound for the Menkyo Center and get off at Kenritsu-bijutsukan-mae bus stop, right in front of the museum (20min; ¥330).

Eating, drinking and entertainment

Seafood, apples and apple products fill Aomori's food halls and souvenir shops. Among the more appetizing **speciality foods**, *hotate kai-yaki*, fresh scallops from Mutsu Bay grilled in their shells and served with a dash of miso sauce, and *jappa-jiru*, a winter cod-fish stew, are both worth a try.

Area Complex エリアコンプレックス B1 Auga Bldg ☎0177/21-4499. This collection of small stalls and restaurants, attached to the market in the basement of Auga building, is a great place to sample the local seafood. They have sushi, sashimi, grilled scallops and seafood *donburi*, and you can also get ramen and standard *teishoku* sets here. Daily 10am–9pm.

Jintako 甚太古 1-6 Yasukata ☎0177/22-7727. Cosy restaurant, with dinner concerts in the evenings by some of Aomori's famous *shamisen* (traditional stringed instrument) players. Reservations are essential. ¥5000 or ¥6000 for the concert and a set menu featuring a variety of regional dishes. Daily 6–11pm (last orders 9.30pm), closed first and third Sun of the month.

Kakigen 柿源 Shin-machi 1-chōme. Small, casual restaurant specializing in *hotate* and other seafood, though also serving *tonkatsu*, *donburi* and noodle dishes at reasonable prices (from ¥600). Look for its moss-green *noren* (hanging curtain) just east of the *Hotel Sunroute* on Shinmachi-dōri. Daily 10.30am–8.30pm.

Nandaimon 南大門 Shin-machi 1-chōme. This cheap and cheerful Chinese-Korean eatery serves good-value *yakiniku*, grilled *hotate* and other seafood. Lunch sets start at ¥725. English menu available. Daily 11am–midnight.

Nishi-mura 西村 10F ASPAM ⓣ0177/34-5353. Choose from a broad range of inexpensive local cuisine including *hotate* and *jappa-jiru* (winter cod-fish stew), or set meals from ¥1260. Reservations recommended in the summer. Daily 10.30am–9.30pm (Sun till 8pm).

Shōya 庄や 2F, 2-4-12 Yasukata, attached to *Hotel JAL City*. Lively and sometimes rowdy branch of a nationwide *izakaya* chain. There is a picture menu with small dishes of grilled fish, sashimi, omelettes and other snacks meant for sharing (from ¥400). A second branch is situated next to the bus terminal. Daily 11.30am–11pm.

Listings

Airport information ⓣ0177/73-2135, ⓦwww.aomori-airport.co.jp.

Banks Dai-ichi Kangyō, Michinoku and Aomori banks are all located on Shinmachi-dōri, around the junction with ASPAM-dōri.

Bicycle rental You can rent fixed-gear bikes (May–Oct 10am–5pm) for ¥300 a day from the bicycle parking lot to the left of the station. You'll need to show photo ID.

Buses Limousine buses to Aomori airport (13 daily; ¥680; 40min) leave from the main bus terminal by the station, as do long-distance buses for Tokyo, Sendai and Morioka.

Car rental Eki Rent-a-Car (ⓣ0177/22-3930), Toyota (ⓣ0177/34-0100) and Nippon (ⓣ0177/22-2369) all have branches near the station.

Emergencies The main police station is at 2-15 Yasukata Aomori-shi (ⓣ0177/23-0110). For other emergency numbers, see p.71.

Ferries Higashi-Nihon Ferry Co. (ⓣ0177/82-3631) operates daily ferries to Hokkaidō (Hakodate) from the car ferry wharf (accessible by bus from Aomori station; 20min; ¥300). Passenger ferries for the coast of Shimokita Hantō (Shimokita Kisen; ⓣ0177/22-4545) leave from the passenger terminal beside Bay Bridge.

Hospital Aomori City Hospital, 1-14-20 Katsuda (ⓣ0177/34-2171).

Internet access The I-plaza (daily 10am–9pm), on the fourth floor of the Auga building, offers an hour's free internet access.

Post office Aomori Central Post Office is located on the west side of town, at 1-7-24 Tsutsumi-machi.

Shopping Apart from ASPAM's souvenir and craft shops, browse the shops along Shinmachi-dōri, where Murata Kōgei (むらた工芸; daily at least 10am–6pm) stocks a good range of local kites, embroidery, lacquerware, brightly painted horses and Tsugaru *kokeshi* dolls.

Taxis Aomori Taxi (ⓣ0177/38-6000); and Miyago Kankō Taxi (ⓣ0177/43-0385).

Shimokita Hantō

The **Shimokita Hantō** protrudes into the ocean northeast of Aomori like a great axe-head. Its jagged blade is covered with low, forested peaks, of which the most notorious is **Osore-zan**, the "terrible mountain" where spirits of the dead are believed to linger on their way to a Buddhist paradise. Despite its growing commercialization, Osore-zan's bleak crater lake, surrounded by a sulphurous desert where pathetic statues huddle against the bitter winds, is a compelling, slightly spine-tingling place.

Osore-zan

The main focus of **Osore-zan** (恐山), an extinct volcano consisting of several peaks, lies about halfway up its eastern slopes, where **Osorezan-Bodaiji** (May–Oct daily 6am–6pm; ¥500) sits on the shore of a silvery crater lake. Though the temple was founded in the ninth century, Osore-zan was already revered in ancient folk religion as a place where dead souls gather, and it's easy to see why – the desolate volcanic landscape, with its yellow- and red-stained soil, multicoloured pools and bubbling, malodorous streams, makes for an unearthly scene. The temple also receives a steady trickle of non-spectral visitors, while during the summer **festival** (July 20–24) people arrive in force to contact their ancestors or the recently deceased, through the mediation of *itako*, usually blind, elderly women who turn a profitable trade. During the open season (May–Oct) four **buses** a day run up to the temple from Mutsu (see below; 4 daily; 40min; ¥1500 return); the last bus leaves Osore-zan at 5.30pm (3.50pm in Oct). From Mutsu, the road to Osorezan-Bodaiji winds through pine forests, past a succession of stone monuments and a spring where it's customary to stop for a sip of purifying water. At the top you emerge by a large lake beside which a small humped bridge represents the journey souls make between this world and the next; it's said that those who led an evil life find it impossible to cross over. After a quick look round the temple, take any path leading over the hummock towards the lake's barren foreshore. The little heaps of stones all around are said to be the work of children who died before their parents. They have to wait here, building stupas, which demons gleefully knock over during the night – most people add a pebble or two in passing. Sad little statues, touchingly wrapped in towels and bibs, add an even more melancholy note to the scene. Many have offerings piled in front of them: bunches of flowers, furry toys – faded and rain-sodden by the end of summer – and plastic windmills whispering to each other in the wind.

Bodaiji temple offers decent **accommodation** (Ⓣ0175/22-3826, Ⓕ22-3402; ❼ including meals), though you'll need to book in advance. For most visitors, however, it's something of a relief to be heading back down to Mutsu, leaving Osore-zan to its wandering souls.

Mutsu

A workaday town on the southern edge of Shimokita Hantō, **MUTSU** (むつ) is the main base for Osore-zan. The easiest **access** route is via JR train from Noheji station (野辺地), on the main Tōhoku line, to Shimokita Station in Mutsu's southern suburbs. **Local buses** to Osore-zan stop at Shimokita Station (下北駅) on their way to the central Mutsu bus terminal, so you can go up to the mountain straight off the JR train and get off in the centre of Mutsu on the way back down if you plan to stay the night. Alternatively, blue-and-white JR buses (for which rail passes are valid) run from Ōminato Station, the last stop on the local JR line, to the JR bus terminal, which is confusingly called Tanabu Station (田名部駅), on the east side of Mutsu town centre.

Mutsu's **tourist office** (daily 10am–5pm; Ⓣ0175/22-0909) is in the ground-floor lobby of Masakari Plaza (まさかりプラザ), a pink building immediately northwest of the JR bus terminal. Staff can provide English-language maps and bus timetables. One of the nicest **places to stay** in Mutsu is the *Murai Ryokan* (むら井旅館; Ⓣ0175/22-4755, Ⓕ23-4572; ❺–❻ with meals, ❹ without), just in front of Masakari Plaza. None of the tatami rooms is en suite, but everything's extremely clean and the food is excellent value. A good alternative is the *Hotel New Green* (ホテルニューグリーン; Ⓣ0175/22-6121, Ⓕ22-5180; ❹–❺), with a choice of Western- or Japanese-style rooms. It's about five minutes' walk from the JR bus terminal; follow the road straight ahead (west) past the private bus terminal and Matsukiya department store, then left at the T-junction.

For **food**, the smart *Nankō* (楠こう; Ⓣ0175/22-7377; daily 11.30am–9.30pm), located down the side street on the left just before the *Hotel New Green*, has good deals on *teishoku* (from ¥1200), but seafood, steaks and stews are also available (from ¥1000). Alternatively, the second-floor restaurant in the Masakari Plaza serves a decent range of Japanese-style set meals for around ¥1100, and noodle dishes for as little as ¥450.

Hirosaki

Behind its modern facade, **HIROSAKI** (弘前), former seat of the Tsugaru clan, still retains a few reminders of its feudal past. Most of its sights lie around **Hirosaki-kōen**,

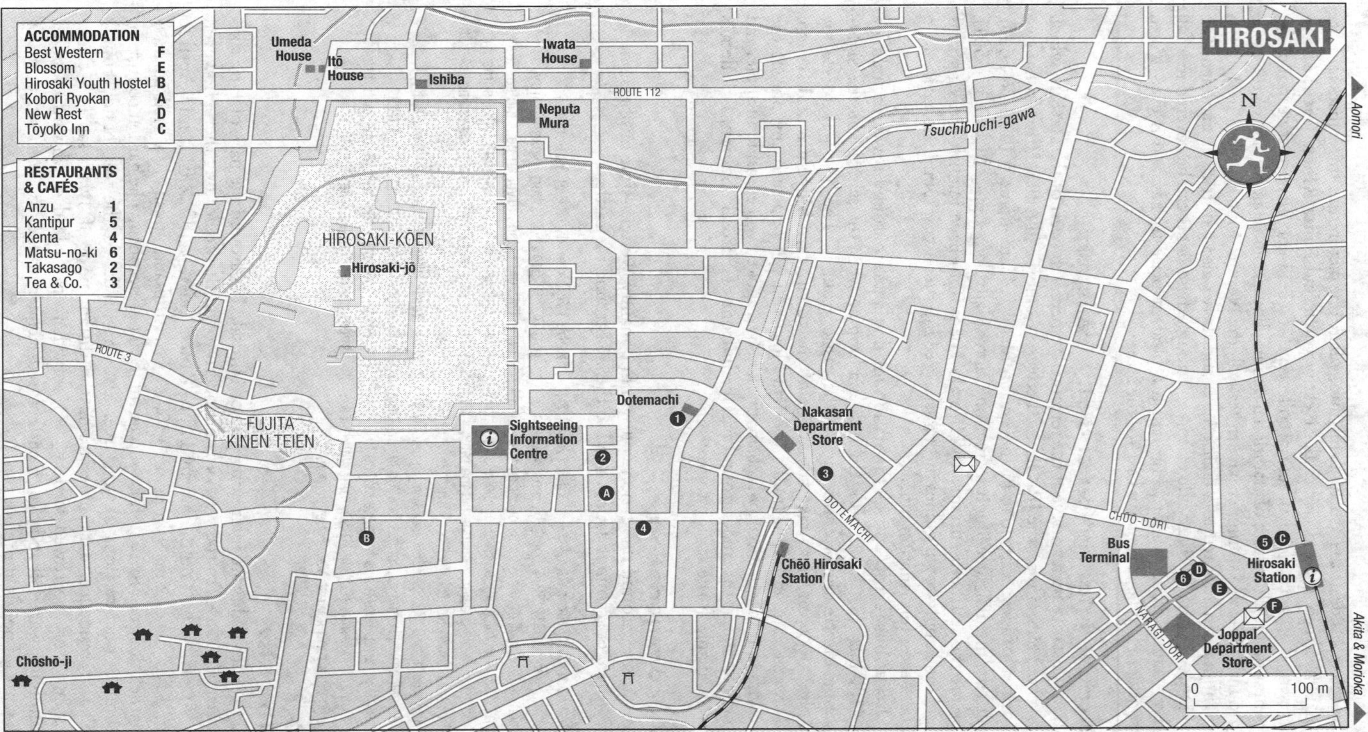

HIROSAKI
ACCOMMODATION
Best Western F
Blossom E
Hirosaki Youth Hostel B
Kobori Ryokan A
New Rest D
Tōyoko Inn C
RESTAURANTS & CAFÉS
Anzu 1
Kantipur 5
Kenta 4
Matsu-no-ki 6
Takasago 2
Tea & Co. 3
Aomori
Akita & Morioka
N
0
100 m
Umeda House
Itō House
Ishiba
Iwata House
ROUTE 112
Neputa Mura
Tsuchibuchi-gawa
HIROSAKI-KŌEN
Hirosaki-jō
ROUTE 3
FUJITA KINEN TEIEN
Sightseeing Information Centre
Dotemachi
Nakasan Department Store
DOTEMACHI
CHŪO-DŌRI
Chēō Hirosaki Station
Bus Terminal
Hirosaki Station
NARAGI-DŌRI
Joppal Department Store
Chōshō-ji

on the west side of the Tsuchibuchi-gawa, where one picturesque turret marks the site of Hirosaki-jō, the old city castle. Nearby you'll find **Fujita Kinen Teien**, a well-preserved Japanese garden, and a collection of Meiji-era Western-style buildings, contrasting with a street of traditional samurai houses on the north side of the castle grounds. Hirosaki's summer lantern festival, the **Neputa Matsuri** (Aug 1–7), has its own museum attached to a craft centre, and there's also a district of dignified **Zen temples** out on the west side of town. Though these sights can be covered in a full day's outing from Aomori, Hirosaki is a pleasant place to stay and is even worth considering as an alternative base for the area.

Arrival, information and city transport

Long-distance **buses** arrive at the terminal immediately west of the **station**, which is served by trains on the JR Ōu line between Aomori and Akita. Hirosaki has two **tourist offices**: a big one in the station (daily 8.45am–6pm; ⓣ0172/26-3600), plus the main Sightseeing Information Centre (daily 9am–6pm; ⓣ0172/37-5501), beside the southern entrance to Hirosaki-kōen. Both have English-speaking staff and can supply town guides in English. Free internet access (30min) is available in the station information office.

Local buses stop outside the station for destinations around town, including a "¥100 bus" (flat ¥100 fare) which does a loop between the station and the Sightseeing Information Centre outside the castle grounds. The best way to see the sights, however, is to take advantage of the town's **free bicycle rental** system. Between 9am and 4pm (mid May–late Nov) you can pop into any one of the town's four bike stations, which are marked by a spoked wheel inside an apple, and include one in the underground passage in front of Hirosaki Station. Full details are available at the station tourist office.

Accommodation

In the area around the station you will find mainly Western-style business hotels. For budget accommodation, head to the area around the castle.

Blossom Hotel Hirosaki ブロッサムホテル弘前 7-3 Ekimaechō ⓣ0712/32-4151, ⓔblossom@aioros.ocn.ne.jp. Smallish and brightly decorated hotel that has discounts for women travelling alone and families. Simple breakfast included in the rates. ④

Hirosaki Youth Hostel 弘前ユースホステル 11 Mori-machi ⓣ0172/33-7066, ⓦwww.jyh.or.jp. Old but welcoming hostel in a prime location for exploring the castle area. Take a bus from the station to Daigaku Byōin-mae (20min; ¥100), from where it's a 5min walk further west. ¥3045 per person.

Kobori Ryokan 小掘旅館 89 Hon-chō ⓣ0172/32-5111, ⓔkobori_ryokan@hiroyado.com. This old wooden ryokan near the castle offers a choice of smart tatami rooms, some with bath, as well as two Western-style rooms. ⑥ with meals, ⑤ without.

New Rest Hotel ホテルニューレスト 14-2 Ekimae-chō ⓣ0172/33-5300, ⓕ33-2327. Basic business hotel near the train station, with bright, simple rooms. Singles from ¥3500. ④

The City

The older and more interesting part of Hirosaki lies around the park of Hirosaki-kōen (弘前公園), to the west of the modern town. Before heading there, however, it's worth exploring the nearby **Fujita Kinen Teien** (藤田記念庭園; mid-April to mid-Nov Tues–Sun 9am–5pm; ¥300), a beautiful and unusually varied Japanese garden designed in 1919 for a successful local businessman. The garden consists of three distinct sections flowing over a steep hillside. At the top, beside Fujita's elegant residence, dark pines frame the distant peak of Iwaki-san – a classic example of "borrowed scenery" – from where paths lead downward, beside a tumbling waterfall and over a perfect, red-lacquer bridge, to another flat area of lawns and ponds at the bottom.

Back at the main park gates, the modern **Sightseeing Information Centre** houses an information desk (see opposite), crafts displays and a **float pavilion** in the hall behind. These floats, which mostly carry tableaux depicting historical scenes, originated in the late seventeenth century when merchants would parade them round the streets as part of a local shrine festival – an English pamphlet is available. Beyond the float pavilion, two colourful Western-style buildings stand out against the sleek concrete and steel. The **Former City Library** (daily 9am–5pm; free) and **Missionaries' House** (daily 9am–6pm; free) both date from the early 1900s and are nicely preserved.

Ōte-mon, the main entrance to **Hirosaki-kōen**, lies across the road from the Sightseeing Centre. It takes ten minutes to walk from this gate, zigzagging between moats and walls, to reach the inner keep of **Hirosaki-jō** (弘前城), where a tiny, three-storey tower (April to mid-Nov daily 9am–5pm; ¥300) guards the southern approach. There's nothing left of the original castle, constructed by the Tsugaru lords in 1611, but the tower was rebuilt in 1810 using traditional techniques and now houses a collection of armour and swords. In late April the little white turret, floodlit and framed in pink blossom, is the focus of a **cherry-blossom festival** (April 23–May 5), as the park's five thousand trees signal the end of the harsh northern winter.

Leaving the park by its northern gate (Kita-mon), you emerge opposite the old **Ishiba** shop (daily 9am–5pm, though there are irregular closures each month; ¥100), which was built 250 years ago to sell rice baskets and other household goods to the Tsugaru lords. Since the family (now selling sake) still lives here, you can only get a glimpse of the warehouse behind. However, there are several more houses you can visit from this era in a smart residential street behind the Ishiba shop. At the west end of the street, the **Itō House** (伊藤家) was once the home of the *daimyō*'s official doctor, while the next-door **Umeda House** was the residence of a minor samurai, as was the **Iwata House** (岩田家), 500m further east.

Neputa Mura (ねぷた村; daily: Apr–Nov 9am–5pm; Dec–March 9am–4pm; ¥500), a museum focusing on Hirosaki's lantern festival, lies at the northeast corner of Hirosaki-kōen. The **Neputa Matsuri** (Aug 1–7) is similar in style to Aomori's Nebuta festival (see p.252), but in this case the giant lanterns are fan-shaped and painted with scenes from ancient Chinese scrolls or with the faces of scowling samurai. Like the festival itself, the museum gets off to a rousing start with a demonstration of energetic drumming (you can try it yourself afterwards), after which you'll see a collection of impressive floats, followed by a display of local crafts – this is a good place to pick up souvenirs, such as ingenious spinning tops, cotton embroideries or stylish black-and-white Tsugaru pottery.

Hirosaki's final sight is a "temple town", around fifteen minutes' walk southwest of the castle park or twenty minutes by bus from the station – take bus #3 for Shigemori (¥200) and get off at the Chōshō-ji Iriguchi stop. In the seventeenth century around thirty temples were relocated to this spot, of which the most interesting is **Chōshō-ji** (長勝寺; daily: April–Oct 9am–4.30pm; Jan–March, Nov & Dec by appointment only; ⓣ0172/32-0813; ¥300). It stands at the end of a tree-lined road through a large, two-storey gate, dating from 1629, which barely contains the two guardian gods peering out of the gloom. Inside, go to the wooden sliding doors of the building to the right, ring the bell on the post inside, and someone will show you into the **main sanctuary** and the mortuary rooms behind. Chōshō-ji was the family temple and burial place of the Tsugaru clan; in 1954, excavations revealed the mummified body of Prince Tsugutomi, son of the eleventh lord, who had died about a century before – his death was variously blamed on assassination, poisoning or eating peaches with imported sugar. During the cherry-blossom festival (see p.58) the mummy is on display, but usually you'll have to make do with a photo in the mortuary room behind the main altar, where it's rather overshadowed by a life-like statue of Tsugaru Tamenobu, the founder of the clan.

Eating and entertainment

Like Aomori, Hirosaki has a fine tradition of folk **music**, played on the *Tsugaru jamisen*, which has a thicker neck than the ordinary *shamisen* stringed instrument and is struck harder. You can hear dinner concerts at *Anzu* (see below) and many other places in town.

Anzu 杏 1-44 Oyakata-machi ⓣ0172/32-6684. Opposite the Asahi bowling alley, on a side street at the west end of Dotemachi, this cosy restaurant has two evening *jamisen* concerts at 7.30pm and 9.30pm – reservations are recommended. Set meals range from ¥3000 to ¥6000. Mon–Sat 5–11pm.

Kantipur カンティプル Ekimae-chō ⓣ0172/55-0371. Friendly Indian restaurant serving a range of good curries and other Indian dishes, such as naan and tandoori, plus Thai curries. Set lunch menus from ¥750, or expect to pay around ¥2000 per person for dinner. It's on the ground floor of the same building as the *Toyoko Inn*, just to the right as you exit the station. Daily 11am–3pm & 5pm–midnight.

Kenta けん太 3 Okeya-chō ⓣ0172/35-9614. Cheap and popular *izakaya* that specializes in grilled food such as *yakitori*; prices for individual dishes start at ¥550. Fills up quickly on the weekends – if you can't get a seat here, there's another branch around the corner. Daily 5pm–2am.

Matsu-no-ki 松ノ木 Ekimae-chō ⓣ0172/34-2521. This small *izakaya*, with aged wood interiors and retro posters, is across the pedestrian mall from *Blossom Hotel*. It does a range of *teishoku* lunches (from ¥850) and has dinner sets from ¥2100 including one beer. Daily 11.30am–2.30pm & 5pm–midnight.

Takasago 高砂 1-2 Oyakata-machi. Inexpensive soba restaurant in an attractive old wooden house southeast of the castle grounds. The limited menu includes tempura soba, *zaru* soba and curry soba. Prices start at ¥650. Tues–Sun 11am–6pm.

Tea & Co Dotemachi ⓣ0172/39-1717. Relaxed coffee shop inside a store across the river from the Nakasan department store, with a great range of teas and coffees and some luscious home-made cakes. Daily 10am–8pm.

South to Towada-ko

Japan's third-largest lake, **Towada-ko** (十和田湖), fills a 300m-deep volcanic crater in the northern portion of the Towada-Hachimantai National Park. The steep-sided, crystal-clear lake rates as one of northern Honshū's top tourist attractions, but for many visitors the real highlight is the approach over high passes and along deep, wooded valleys. Though there are four main access roads, the most attractive route is south from Aomori via the Hakkōda mountains, Sukayu Onsen and the picturesque **Oirase valley**. For this last stretch it's the done thing to walk the final few kilometres beside the tumbling Oirase-gawa, and then hop on a cruise boat across to the lake's main tourist centre, **Yasumiya**.

Many roads around Towada-ko are closed in winter, and public **buses** only operate from April to November. During the season, however, there are regular services to the lake from Aomori, Morioka, Hachinohe, Hirosaki and (to the south) Towada-minami, a station on the line between Ōdate and Morioka. It's best to buy tickets in advance on all these routes. Tickets can be bought at any JR green ticket window; Japan rail passes (not Japan East rail passes) are valid, but you still should book in advance.

Hakkōda-san and the Oirase valley

Leaving the dreary outskirts of Aomori behind, Route 103 climbs steeply onto the Kayano plateau and round the flanks of **Hakkōda-san**. Every winter, cold, wet winds dump snow up to 8m deep over these mountains, transforming the fir trees into "snow monsters" (see p.231) and maintaining a flourishing ski industry. In summer, however, this beautiful spot offers excellent walking among Hakkōda-san's old volcanic peaks, of which the tallest is Ōdake (1584m). To ease the climb you can whisk to the top of nearby Tamoyachi-dake (1326m) on the **Hakkōda Ropeway** (八甲田ロープウェイ; daily 9am–3.40/4.20pm; return ¥1800) and then walk down to **Sukayu Onsen** (酸ヶ湯温泉), both of which are stops on the bus route from Aomori to Towada-ko. The most famous of several onsen resorts in the area, Sukayu consists of just one **ryokan** (Ⓣ0177/38-6400, Ⓕ38-6677; ❻ including two meals), which has a "thousand-person" cedar-wood bath (7am–6pm; ¥600). Sukayu's healing waters have been popular since the late seventeenth century and this is one of very few onsen left in Japan which is not segregated.

South of Sukayu the road crosses another pass and then starts descending through pretty, deciduous woodlands – spectacular in autumn – to **YAKEYAMA** (焼山) village, where you'll find the secluded *Oirase Youth Hostel* (おいらせユースホステル; Ⓣ0176/74-2031, Ⓦwww.jyh.or.jp; dorm beds ¥3360 per person; closed mid-Nov to mid-April). Yakeyama also marks the start of the **Oirase valley** walk, but it's better to join the path 5km further down the road at **ISHIGEDO** (石ヶ戸). From here it takes less than three hours to walk the 9km to Towada-ko following a well-trodden path running gently upstream, marred slightly by the fairly busy main road which you have to join for short stretches. But for the most part you're walking beside the Oirase-gawa as it tumbles among ferns and moss-covered rocks through a narrow, tree-filled valley punctuated by ice-white waterfalls. You emerge at lakeside **NENOKUCHI** (子ノ口), where you can either pick up a passing bus or take a scenic cruise across Towada-ko to Yasumiya (see below for details).

Towada-ko

Two knobbly peninsulas break the regular outline of **Towada-ko**, a massive crater lake trapped in a rim of pine-forested hills within the Towada-Hachimantai National Park. The westerly protuberance shelters the lake's only major settlement, **YASUMIYA** (休屋), which is also known somewhat confusingly as Towada-ko. Roughly 44km in circumference, the lake is famous for its spectacularly clear water, with visibility down to 17m, best appreciated from one of several **boat trips** that run from early April to the end of January, though sailings are fairly limited in winter. The most interesting route is from Yasumiya to Nenokuchi (April to early Nov; hourly; 50min; ¥1400); there's also a limited service that starts and finishes at Yasumiya from December to late March (4 daily; 1hr; ¥1100). Alternatively, you can hire bicycles (¥630 for two hours) at Yasumiya and drop them off at Nenokuchi (or vice versa). Once you've navigated the lake, the only other thing to do in Towada-ko is pay a visit to the famous statue of the **Maidens by the Lake** (おとめの像), which stands on the shore fifteen minutes' walk north of central Yasumiya. The two identical bronze women, roughcast and naked, seem to be circling each other with hands almost touching. They were created in 1953 by the poet and sculptor Takamura Kōtarō, then 70 years old, and are said to be of his wife, a native of Tōhoku, who suffered from schizophrenia and died tragically young.

About 20km east of Towada-ko along Route 454, the town of **SHINGŌ** is home to **Kirisuto No Haka** (Christ's Grave), a grave with a huge wooden cross which was built here in 1935 to commemorate an unusual local myth. The story goes that Jesus came to Japan as a 21-year-old and learned from a great master, before returning to Judea to spread the wonders of "sacred Japan". It was these revolutionary teachings that lead Jesus to the Cross, though that's where the tale takes another odd twist; it was actually Jesus's brother who was crucified at

Cavalry, while Christ himself escaped to Shingō, where he married, had several children and lived until the ripe old age of 106. A small **museum** (daily except Wed 9am–5pm; ¥200) displays mysterious scripture which apparently proves the story's legitimacy, though it doesn't give too many details about the man who discovered it, Banzan Toya, the nationalist historian who created the tale in the 1930s at a time when Japan was funnelling substantial manpower and money into attempts to prove Japanese racial superiority; other historians of the day managed to discover Moses' grave in Ishikawa-ken and uncover the fantastic tale of Moses receiving the Ten Commandments and Star of David directly from the Emperor of Japan.

Not to be outdone, Toya had more discoveries up his sleeve. Just a few minutes' walk west from Christ's Grave lie the **Ooishigami Pyramids**. According to other ancient writings "discovered" by Toya, the Japanese built pyramids tens of thousands of years before the Egyptians and Mexicans. Both pyramids look a lot like little more than a bunch of huge boulders, although the top of the second pyramid is a great spot for a packed lunch. The grave and pyramids are a short, well-signposted walk west of the town centre.

Practicalities

Though the small town of Yasumiya consists almost entirely of hotels and souvenir shops, its shady lakeside setting makes it a pleasant overnight stop. The town centre is dominated by two **bus terminals** opposite each other on a T-junction just inland from the boat pier; the more northerly one serves JR buses only. The **information office** (daily 8am–5pm; ⓣ0176/75-2425), in a separate building immediately right (north) of the JR bus terminal, has town maps and can help with **accommodation**. It's advisable to book rooms in advance from July through to October, when people come for the autumn leaves. The lakeside *Towada-ko Grand Hotel* (十和田湖グランドホテル; ⓣ0176/75-1111, ⓦwww.itoenhotel.com/hotel/towada; ❺), to the south of the ferry pier, offers a choice of Western or tatami rooms and rates include three meals. Among a number of minshuku near the centre of Yasumiya, try the *Sansō Kuriyama* (山荘くりやま; ⓣ&ⓕ0176/75-2932; ❺ including meals) or the older *Shunzan-sō* (春山荘; ⓣ0176/75-2607; ❹–❺ including meals); both are a few minutes' walk inland from the pier. In summer, the patches of flat land around Towada-ko fill with tents; the closest **campsite** to Yasumiya is 3km southwest at *Oide Camp-jō* (生出キャンプ場; ⓣ0176/75-2368; late April–Oct).

Moving on from Yasumiya, buses to Towada-minami and Aomori leave from the JR bus terminal; other services to Hirosaki and Hachimantai use the Towada-ko terminal, opposite. If you're heading to Akita, take a bus south to Towada-minami (十和田南) and then a local train to **Ōdate** (大館) on the main JR line between Aomori and Akita.

Akita and around

One of the few large cities on the northwest coast of Japan, modern **AKITA** (秋田) is an important port and industrial centre with access to some of the country's few domestic oil reserves. Though it was founded in the eighth century, almost nothing of the old city remains and Akita's few central sites – three contrasting museums – can easily be covered on foot in half a day. With its airport and Shinkansen services, however, Akita makes a convenient base for the region. The small town of **Kakunodate**, a short train ride to the east, has a preserved street of two-hundred-year-old samurai houses, while you can soak in luxury at

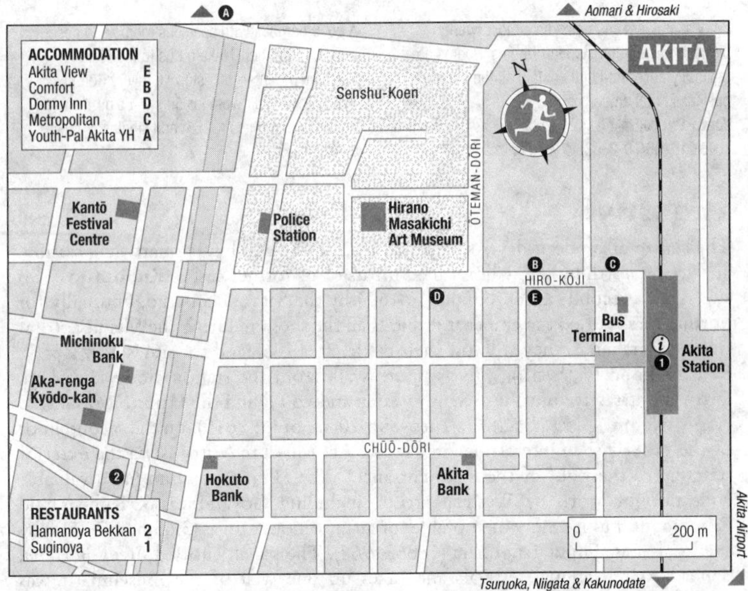

Nyūtō Onsen, a group of hot springs at the end of the Sendatsu-gawa valley, 10km northeast of Japan's deepest lake, **Tazawa-ko**.

The city of Akita is also home to the last of the great Tōhoku summer festivals, the **Kantō Matsuri** (Aug 3–6) – though it's a pleasantly low-key affair compared to events in Sendai (p.233) and Aomori (p.252). During the festival, men parade through the streets balancing tall bamboo poles strung with paper lanterns, which they transfer from their hip to head, hand or shoulder while somehow managing to keep the swaying, top-heavy structure upright.

Arrival and information

Most visitors to Akita arrive at the JR **station**, located on the east side of town, though the city also has its own **airport** some forty minutes to the south, reached by limousine bus (¥900). The city's **tourist office** (daily 9am–6/7pm; ⓣ0188/32-7941) is directly across from the main JR ticket gates and stocks English-language maps and other printed information.

Accommodation

Akita has plenty of mid-range and high-end business hotels around the station, and also offers a good variety of budget accommodation.

Akita View 秋田ビューホテル 6-1-2 Naka-dōri ⓣ0188/32-1111, ⓦwww.akitaviewhotel.co.jp. Opposite *Comfort Hotel*, this place has clean, spacious rooms as well as a range of restaurants and even a pool in the fitness centre. ❻

Comfort コンフォートホテル 3-23 Senshukubota-machi ⓣ0188/25-5611, ⓦwww.choice-hotels.jp. Well-placed modern business hotel with bright rooms just a 2min walk from Akita Station. All rates include a light buffet breakfast. ❹

Dormy Inn ドーミーイン 2-3-1 Naka-dōri ⓣ0188/35-6777, ⓕ35-8777. This swanky business hotel has contemporary monochrome interiors, spacious singles and a good range of facilities. Also has a nice public bath on the 11th floor and free internet access. ❹

Metropolitan ホテルメトロポリタン 7-2-1 Naka-dōri ⓣ0188/31-2222, ⓦwww.jrhotelgroup.com. Immediately outside the station, this classy hotel is part of the JR East collection, which means

JR pass holders can enjoy an almost twenty percent discount on standard rooms. Rooms are tastefully decorated and contain all the usual business hotel amenities. ❼

Youth-Pal Akita YH ユースパルあきた 3-1 Kamiya-shiki ⓣ0188/80-2303, ⓔyouthpal@tkcnet.ne.jp. A good bargain, with spacious rooms and decent meals. To get here, take a bus to the Akita Seishonen Center (bus stop #6; every 30min; ¥160), then walk west for 5min– it's on the right. Dorm rooms (¥3255) and singles are also available. ❸

The City

The centre of modern-day Akita is bounded to the east by its smart train station, and to the north by the willow-lined moats of its former castle, **Kubota-jō**. This was Akita's second castle, founded in 1604 by the Satake clan who, unusually for northerners, backed the emperor rather than the shogun during the Meiji Restoration. Nevertheless, they still lost their castle after 1868 and the site is now a park, **Senshū-kōen** (千秋公園), a five-minute walk from the station along Hiro-kōji. Cross the attractive moat into Senshū-kōen and you'll find the **Hirano Masakichi Art Museum** (平野政吉美術館; Tues–Sun 10am–5pm; ¥610), on the second floor of the otherwise uninteresting Prefectural Art Museum (entry is via the exterior stairway to the right of the main entrance). The Hirano museum has a valuable collection of work by Western artists, including Goya, Picasso, Rubens and Rembrandt, but it's more memorable for an enormous canvas (3.65m by 20.5m) by the local artist Fujita Tsuguhara (1886–1968). The panel, entitled *Events in Akita*, depicts Akita's annual festivals and takes up one wall of the museum. It was completed in an incredible fifteen days in 1937, after which the wall of Tsuguhara's studio had to be knocked down to get it out.

You can learn more about local celebrations at the **Kantō Festival Centre**, or *Neburi-Nagashi-kan* (ねぶり流し館; daily 9.30am–4.30pm; ¥100, or ¥250 with Aka-renga Kyōdo-kan – see below), located to the west of Senshū-kōen and across a small river. There are videos of recent Kantō Matsuri and sample *kantō* to try out. The *kantō* is a bamboo pole, up to 10m tall and weighing perhaps 60kg, to which dozens of paper lanterns are attached on crossbars. During the festival as many as two hundred poles are carried through the streets in celebration of the coming harvest, as teams of men and young boys show their skill in balancing and manipulating the hefty poles.

Leaving the Festival Centre, turn right and head south down this street for about 500m to the unmistakeable, red-and-white-brick **Aka-renga Kyōdo-kan** (赤れんが郷土館; daily 9.30am–4.30pm; ¥200). This Western-style building was erected in 1912 as the headquarters of Akita Bank, and its well-preserved banking hall and offices are worth a quick look. A modern extension behind houses a series of woodcuts by Katsuhira Tokushi, a self-taught local artist who won recognition for his appealingly bold, colourful portrayals of local farmers and scenes of rural life.

Eating and drinking

The region's most famous **speciality food** is *kiritampo*, a substantial stew of chicken, mushrooms, onions, glass noodles, seasonal vegetables and the key ingredient, *mochi* (rice cakes), made of pounded, newly harvested rice and shaped round a cedar-wood stick before grilling over a charcoal fire. *Shottsuru* is more of an acquired taste – a strong-tasting stew made with a broth of fermented, salted fish. The most famous **restaurant** at which to sample these and other local dishes is *Hamanoya Bekkan*, 4-2-11 Ōmachi (濱乃家別館; ⓣ0188/62-6611; daily 11.30am–10pm), located in Akita's main bar and restaurant area, one block southeast of the Aka-renga Kyōdo-kan museum, in an amazingly well-preserved old house. Prices aren't too outrageous, but reservations are advisable on weekend evenings in the main restaurant. The station and surrounding streets also provide a whole variety of eating choices, including *Suginoya*, 3F Topica Building, 7-1-2 Naka-dōri (杉のや; daily 10am–9pm), which is less refined than *Hamanoya* but has a helpful window display and serves a wider range of foods at cheaper prices, including *kiritampo*, *shottsuru* and set meals from ¥1300.

Listings

Airport information ⓣ0188/86-3366, ⓦwww.akita-airport.com.
Banks and exchange For foreign exchange, try Akita Bank or Hokuto Bank on Chūō-dōri, running parallel to Hiro-koji two blocks further south, or the Michinoku Bank near the Akarenga-kan.
Buses Long-distance buses to Tokyo and Sendai stop outside Akita Station.
Car rental Eki Rent-a-Car (ⓣ0188/33-9308), Nissan Rent-a-Car (ⓣ0188/24-4123) and Toyota Rentals (ⓣ0188/33-0100) are all located near Akita's JR station.
Emergencies The main police station is at 1-9 Meitoku-ch, Senshū Akita-shi (ⓣ0188/35-1111). In an absolute emergency contact the Akita International Association on ⓣ0188/64-1181. For other emergency numbers, see p.71.
Ferry Shin-nihonkai Ferry (ⓣ0188/80-2600) sails five times a week to Tomakomai (11hr 20min), the main port on Hokkaidō and a gateway to Sapporo.
Hospitals The biggest central hospital is the Red Cross Hospital, 222-1 Kamikitade Saruta-nawashirusawa (ⓣ0188/29-5000).
Post office The central post office is located at 5 Hodōno Teppo-machi, Akita-shi.

Kakunodate

While Akita City has lost nearly all of its historical relics, nearby **KAKUNODATE** (角館) still has the air of a feudal town, with its strictly delineated samurai and merchants' quarters. Kakunodate was established as a military outpost in 1620 by the lords of Akita, with a castle on a hill to the north, a samurai town of around eighty residences, and 350 merchants' homes in a cramped district to the south. This basic layout and a handful of the samurai houses have survived the years, as have several hundred of the weeping cherry trees brought from Kyoto three centuries ago. It's still an atmospheric place, and although you can visit on a day trip from either Akita or Morioka, it merits an overnight stay.

Arrival and information

Kakunodate is best reached by train from either Akita or Morioka. The **station** lies on the southeast side of town, where you will also find the **tourist office** (daily 9am–5.30/6pm; ⓣ0187/54-2700) in a *kura*-style building to the right as you exit the station. You can get English-language maps and other printed information here, and they also have **bike rental** (¥300/hr).

Accommodation

Folklore Kakunodate フォルクローロ角館 ⓣ0187/53-2070, ⓦhotel.eki-net.com. Located right beside the station, this is your best bet if you want a simple, modern Western-style room. Rates include a basic breakfast. ❺
Ishikawa Ryokan 石川旅館 ⓣ0187/54-2030, ⓕ54-2031. Comfortable tatami rooms, some en suite, with two meals included in the rates. To get here from the station take a left one block before the post office. ❼
Takahashi Ryokan 高橋旅館 ⓣ&ⓕ0187/53-2659. Just north of the post office, rates at this simple but comfy ryokan include two meals. ❻
Tamachi Bukeyashiki Hotel 田町武家屋敷ホテル ⓣ0187/52-1700, ⓕ52-1701. Housed in a stunning Meiji-style building, this traditional inn provides equally attractive and luxurious tatami rooms. There are also smart Western-style rooms available. It's four blocks south of Inaho (see p.266). ❼ with breakfast, ❽ with two meals.

The Town

Pick up a town map from the tourist information centre (see p.265) before setting off for the samurai quarter, roughly fifteen minutes' walk northwest. You can't miss the division between the packed streets of the commercial town – now mostly modern and rather run-down – and the wide avenues where the samurai lived in their spacious mansions among neatly fenced gardens. The most interesting of the samurai houses is the **Aoyagi-ke** (青柳家; daily: April–Nov 9am–5pm; Dec–March 9am–4pm; ¥500), a large, thatched house towards the northern end of the samurai quarter, which is easily identified by an unusually grand entrance gate. Aoyagi-ke was built in 1890 and occupied until 1985; it now contains an odd mix of galleries, including samurai armour, agricultural implements, memorabilia from the Sino-Japanese and Pacific wars, and a wonderful display of antique gramophones and cameras.

A little further up the same street, the impressive **Ishiguro-ke** (石黒家; daily 9am–5pm; ¥300) is one of the oldest of Kakunodate's samurai houses. Built in 1809 for the *daimyō*'s financial adviser, its main features are two large fireproof warehouses (*kura*) used for storing rice, miso and other valuables. At the top end of the street, inside a sterile, green concrete exterior, the **Hirafuku Memorial Art Museum** (平福記念美術館; daily: April–Nov 9am–4.30pm; Dec–March 9am–4pm; ¥300, or ¥510 with the Denshōkan) houses a small but decent collection of traditional Japanese art. Heading south again, the **Denshōkan** (伝承館; same times and price) occupies a more attractive red-brick building. This museum of Satake-clan treasures also doubles as a training school for *kaba-zaiku*, the local craft in which boxes, tables and tea caddies are coated with a thin veneer of cherry bark. Developed in the late eighteenth century to supplement the income of impoverished samurai, *kaba-zaiku* is now Kakunodate's trademark souvenir. If you prefer your bark still on the trees, turn right outside the Denshōkan, where there's a 2km tunnel of cherry trees along the Hinokinai-gawa embankment.

Eating and drinking

In the samurai quarter, the Aoyagi-ke (see above) has a decent **restaurant** (daily, same times) serving *inaniwa udon*; long, slippery noodles in a thin soup of mushrooms, onion and bamboo shoots. Alternatively, try the noodles at *Kosendō* (古泉洞; daily 9am–4.30pm), set in an old schoolhouse that's also in the samurai quarter. In the centre of town, *Inaho* (食堂いなほ; daily except Thurs 11am–4pm & 6–8pm) and the more casual *Murasaki* (むら咲; daily 11am–2pm & 5–10pm, closed two irregular days each month) offer daily set menus at reasonable prices; they're both down a side street to the north of the main station road, at the block before the Akita Bank – *Inaho* is upstairs in the corner building, while *Murasaki* is further down, around the bend in the street. The hundred-year-old *Hyakusui-en* (百穂苑; daily 11am–3pm, dinner with reservation only; ⓣ0187/55-5715; courses range from ¥2100 to ¥9870) is popular for its hearty meals and traditional interiors, which include sunken *irori* fireplaces. The restaurant is twenty minutes' walk from the station in the old merchants' quarter: you'll find it in a brown *kura* between the Hirafuku Memorial Art Museum and the river.

Nyūtō Onsen

Northeast of Tazawa-ko, on the southeastern fringes of the Towada Hachimantai National Park, are numerous ski resorts and a hot-spring area, **Nyūtō Onsen** (乳頭温泉). This is made up of seven different onsen and adjoining ryokan, the most famous and quaint being the **Tsurunoyu Onsen** (鶴の湯温泉; ⓣ0187/46-2139, ⓦwww.tsurunoyu.com; ⑥ with two meals; bath only ¥500), a 350-year-old establishment housing eight separate baths and three rotemburo, each fed by a different source; the basic tatami rooms come with a small *irori* or fire pit. There are more spacious rooms at *Tsurunoyu*'s slightly less traditional sister property, the *Yamanoyado Inn* (山の宿; ⓣ0187/46-2100; ❼), a little further back down the road. It's a fifteen-minute walk from Nyūtō Onsen to **Ganiba Onsen** (蟹場温泉; ⓣ0187/46-2021; ❼ with two meals), whose rotemburo (open to non-guests; daily 9am–4.30pm; ¥500) nestles quietly next to a small brook and forest – an ideal place to get rid of travelling stress – while the well-kept tatami rooms look out onto the surrounding woods, with some adjoining the wraparound veranda.

The nearest train station for Nyūtō Onsen is Tazawako, 20km northeast of Kakunodate on the Shinkansen line between Morioka (40min; ¥1780) and Akita (1hr; ¥3080). From the station, take a bus going towards the Tazawa Kōgen Ski-jō (every 70–90min; 50min) and get off at the Tazawa Kōgen Onsen bus stop. Call *Tsurunoyu* or *Ganiba Onsen* beforehand, and someone will pick you up at the Tazawa Kōgen Onsen bus stop.

Dewa-sanzan and around

Pilgrims have been trekking up the slopes of **Dewa-sanzan** (出羽三山; also known as Dewa-san), one of Japan's most sacred mountains, for more than a thousand years. It's an arduous rather than difficult climb, taking in ancient cedar woods, alpine meadows and three intriguing shrines where *yamabushi* (mountain ascetics) continue to practise their secret rites. It's best to visit Dewa-san in summer (July to late Sept), when all three shrines are open, but at any time of year you'll find white-clothed pilgrims climbing the well-worn steps to the outer shrine on the summit of **Haguro-san**. From here the path follows the ridge to **Gassan** (月山), the highest peak, before finally descending to the outer shrine, **Yudono-jinja**, an ochre-coloured rock washed by a hot spring. Though it's possible to complete the circuit in a long day, it's more enjoyable to spread it over two or three days and spend a couple of nights in the *shukubō* (temple lodgings) scattered over the mountain or in the village of **Haguro-machi**, the traditional start of the pilgrimage. Alternatively, **Tsuruoka** town, a short bus ride to the northwest, provides a convenient base and has a few moderately interesting historical sights of its own.

Tsuruoka

A former castle-town with a handful of attractive, willow-lined streets in its old centre, **TSURUOKA** (鶴岡) is mainly useful as a staging post on the pilgrimage to Dewa-san. Its few sights are located in and around **Tsuruoka-kōen**, the town's park and site of the castle, and include an eclectic local museum and an unusual Edo-period school for samurai.

The old centre of Tsuruoka lies on the banks of the Uchi-gawa, some 2km southwest of the station, which is surrounded by business hotels, department stores and bus terminals. It takes about twenty minutes to walk from the station, partly along the river, to reach Tsuruoka-kōen, and Tsuruoka's prime sight, the **Chidō Hakubutsukan** (致道博物館; daily 9am–4.30pm; ¥700). Once a retirement home for lords of the ruling Sakai clan, the compound now contains a number of striking buildings, beginning with the **Nishitagawa District Office**, built in 1881 in Western style. The **Goinden**, the lords' residence, was constructed only two decades earlier but to a classic Japanese design, and now houses a few Sakai family heirlooms as well as a beautiful collection of bamboo fishing rods made by trainee samurai. Local folk culture is well represented in a massive thatched farmhouse and in a modern building packed with old fishing tackle, sake barrels, lacquerware and huge wooden mortars.

Walking back along the south side of Tsuruoka-kōen, you'll pass another beautifully preserved Western-style building, the **Taishōkan**, built in 1915 as an assembly hall, but now housing a missable museum of local luminaries. The **Chidō-kan** (致道館; Tues–Sun 9am–4.30pm; free), a little further along on the right-hand side, is however worth a quick stop. This Confucian school was founded in 1805 by the ninth Sakai lord, who wanted to restore order among his restless clan and educate young samurai. Inside there are still a few of the original buildings, including a shrine to Confucius and the main auditorium, where you can see the old textbooks and printing blocks as well as some marvellous photos of the school when it was still in use (it closed in 1873). As you head back to the station from here, look out for the virginal white, wooden **Catholic church** (daily 8am–6pm; free), built by French missionaries in 1903; it houses a black Madonna and child as well as several faded stained-glass windows.

Practicalities

Tsuruoka's **train station** is located on the northeast side of town, while the Shōkō Mall **bus centre** lies a few minutes' walk west along the tracks under the *Dai-ichi Hotel* (第一ホテル). Most buses also stop outside the station, including limousine buses serving the local **Shōnai Airport** (40min; ¥760). However, note that some long-distance buses start from outside the *Dai-ichi Hotel*. The town's **information office** (daily March–Oct 9.30–5.30pm, Nov–Feb 10am–5pm; Ⓣ0235/25-7678, Ⓦwww.city.tsuruoka.yamagata.jp) is to the right as you exit the station building; you can pick up a **bicycle** for the day free of charge here. **Car rental** is available at Eki Rent-a-Car (Ⓣ0235/24-2670; daily 8.30–6.30pm), next to the information office.

For somewhere convenient to **stay** near the station, the *Washington Hotel* (ワシントンホテル; Ⓣ0235/25-0111, Ⓦwww.wh-rsv.com; ⑤), right opposite, has cheerful rooms, though it fills up quickly with business travellers midweek. Alternatively, the friendly *Narakan* (奈良館; Ⓣ0235/22-1202, Ⓕ24-3548; ④) has good-value tatami rooms and meals available on request; go left from the station for five minutes, then turn right at *Hotel Alpha One* and walk five more minutes until the first set of traffic lights, where it's just on the left. Further away, the *Tsuruoka Youth Hostel* (鶴岡ユースホステル; Ⓣ0235/73-3205, Ⓦwww.jyh.or.jp; dorm beds ¥2625 per person) is a fifteen-minute walk from Sanze Station, three stops out of town on the local line. It's off the beaten track, but if you fancy some macrobiotic vegetarian food, 1950s jazz and a day off from your travels, it makes for a welcoming rest. Ask for directions to the hostel (and a map) at the tourist office in Tsuruoka before you set out, as it can be hard to find.

In Tsuruoka proper, there's a decent udon **restaurant**, *Sanmai-an* (三昧庵), beside the Chidō Hakubutsukan. Between the Catholic church and Tsuruoka-kōen, the bright and modern *Pizzeria Gozaya* (daily except Tues 11.30am–2pm & 6pm–late, closed Thurs night) does good pizzas and other Italian dishes, with prices starting from ¥1000. You'll also find several well-priced places serving staples, such as soba, udon and *izakaya* fare, just outside the station.

Dewa-sanzan

A lumpy extinct volcano with three peaks, **Dewa-sanzan** faces the Sea of Japan across the famously prolific rice fields of the Shōnai plain. Many people take the road up its first peak, **Haguro-san** (羽黒山; 414m), but it's well worth slogging up the 2446 stone steps from the bus stop, among venerable cedars, to reach the impressive, thatch-roofed **Gosaiden**, which enshrines the deities of each of the three mountains. Dewa-san's middle shrine perches atop **Gas-san** (1984m), with spectacular views in clear weather, though otherwise it's the least interesting of the three mountains. If time is short, you might want to skip round by road to **Yudono-jinja**, on the third peak, visiting a couple of rather grisly mummified monks en route.

Today Dewa-san and its three shrines fall under the Shinto banner, but the mountain was originally home to one of the colourful offshoots of Esoteric Buddhism, later unified as **Shugendō**. The worship of Dewa-san dates from the seventh century, when an imperial prince fled to this area following the death of his father. In a vision, a three-legged crow led him to Haguro-san (Black Wing Mountain), where he lived to the ripe old age of 90, developing his unique blend of Shinto, Buddhism and ancient folk religion. Later the **yamabushi**, the sect's itinerant mountain priests (literally "the ones who sleep in the mountains"), became famous for their mystic powers and their extreme asceticism – one route to enlightenment consisted of living in caves off a diet of nuts and wild garlic. Though once fairly widespread, the sect dwindled after the mid-nineteenth century, when Shinto reclaimed Japanese mountains for its own. Nevertheless, you'll still find a flourishing community of *yamabushi* around Dewa-san, kitted out in their natty checked jackets, white knickerbockers and tiny, black pillbox hats. They also carry a huge conch-shell horn, the haunting cry of which summons the gods.

The best time to see *yamabushi* in action is during the area's various **festivals**. The biggest annual bash is the Hassaku Matsuri (Aug 24–31), when pilgrims take part in a fire festival on Haguro-san to ensure a bountiful harvest. At New Year, Haguro-san is also the venue for a festival of purification, known as the Shōreisai, which combines fire and acrobatic dancing with ascetic rituals.

Practicalities

There are various ways of tackling Dewa-san, depending on the time of year and how much walking you want to do. The recommended **route**, described on p.269, involves climbing Haguro-san on the first day and then continuing via Gas-san to Yudono-jinja on the second. From there you can either head straight back to Tsuruoka or spend the night in a *shukubō* and visit the Ōami temples the next day. However, note that Gassan-jinja (July to mid-Sept) and Yudono-jinja (May–early Nov) are only open in summer; the path itself stays open longer, depending on the weather.

Two **bus services** run from Tsuruoka: one via Haguro-machi to the Haguro-sanchō stop at the top of Haguro-san, with onward services to Gas-san Hachigōme (see p.270) from July to September; the second operates between May and early November, looping round from Tsuruoka to Yudono-jinja. These services are few and far between, so make sure you pick up a map and timetable at Tsuruoka's **information centre** (see opposite for details), where they can also help book accommodation. In Haguro-machi, the **Haguro Centre** (羽黒センター; 24hr; ⓣ0235/62-2260) is primarily a **taxi** service, but they also stock some English-language information and can assist in finding accommodation.

If possible, try to spend at least one night at a **shukubō** (temple lodging) while visiting Dewa-san. There are over thirty in Haguro-machi's Tōge district, including a number of traditional thatch-roofed inns, each run by a *yamabushi*; you may well be invited to attend a prayer service, involving a lot of conch-blowing and a ritual fire. Prices don't vary much (typically ¥7000–7500/person, with meals) and they all serve the exquisitely prepared *shōjin-ryōri* (Buddhist vegetarian cuisine) favoured by *yamabushi*. In Haguro-machi, *Sankō-in* (三光院; ⓣ0235/62-2302; ❺) is a lovely old thatched place near the Haguro Centre, or try the nearby, and also thatched, *Ōrimbō* (桜林坊; ⓣ0235/62-2322; ❺). If you have problems booking directly, the Haguro Town Office (ⓣ0235/62-2111) may be able to assist.

There are also a couple of useful *shukubō* on Haguro-san itself and near Yudono-jinja. In Haguro-san, *Saikan* (斎館; ⓣ0235/62-2357, ⓕ62-2352; ❺ including meals) is an impressive old building with great views over the Shōnai plain, while the newer *Sanrōjo* (参籠所; ⓣ0235/54-6131, ⓕ54-6134; ❺ including meals; May–early Nov only) occupies a wonderful setting beside the Yudono-jinja bus terminal. Both these places also serve excellent vegetarian lunches to non-residents (from ¥1500; reservations recommended). If you'd like to try your hand at being a *yamabushi*, there are several two- and three-day taster courses available in which you get to stand under waterfalls, leap over fires and take part in a pilgrimage. Prices start from around ¥25,000; contact the Tsuruoka tourist office for information (see p.268).

Haguro-san

Regular buses from Tsuruoka (8–15 daily; 40min; ¥680) serve the village of **HAGURO-MACHI** (羽黒町) at the beginning of the mountain trail; get off at the Haguro Centre stop, just where the road kinks left to the start of the path up the mountain. Before heading off along the track, **Ideha Bunka Kinenkan** (いでは文化記念館; daily except Tues 9/9.30am–4/4.30pm; ¥400), a little further along the main road, is worth a look if you're interested in the *yamabushi*. This surprisingly hi-tech museum contains examples of *yamabushi* clothes and foodstuffs, as well as holograms of various rituals.

A weather-beaten, red-lacquered gate marks the start of the **Haguro-san trail** (1.7km; roughly 1hr), which consists of three long staircases built by a monk in the early seventeenth century. The first stretch is a deceptively gentle amble beside a river, where pilgrims purify themselves, among stately cedar trees. After passing a magnificent five-storey pagoda, last rebuilt in the fourteenth century, it's uphill all the way, past a little **teashop** (late April to early Nov daily 8.30am–5pm) with superb views, until a large red *torii* indicates you've made it. If you're staying at *Saikan* (see above), it's on the left at the end of a mossy path just before you duck under the *torii*.

The shrine compound contains a collection of unmistakeably Buddhist buildings. At the centre stands a monumental vermilion hall, the **Gosaiden**, where the mountain's three deities are enshrined behind gilded doors under an immaculate thatch. In front of the hall, the lily-covered **Kagami-ike** is said to mirror the spirits of the gods. However, it's better known for its treasure-trove of over five hundred antique polished-metal hand mirrors; in the days before women were allowed onto Dewa-san, their male relatives would consign one of their mirrors into the pond. The best of these are now on display in the shrine **museum** (mid-April to late Nov daily 8.30am–4/4.30pm; ¥300). There's also a useful relief map of Dewa-san here.

Follow the paved road exiting the compound's south side and you'll find the Haguro-sanchō bus stop among restaurants and souvenir shops. Buses depart from here for Tsuruoka (6–12 daily; 50min; ¥990) via Haguro-machi (15min; ¥530), and also to Gas-san Hachigōme (see below); alternatively, it's a forty-minute walk further south – take the footpath rather than the road – to the Kyūka-mura stop beside Gas-san Visitor Centre, where you can also pick up buses to Gas-san (see below).

Gas-san and Yudono-jinja

It's a long 20km hike along the ridge from Haguro-san to **Gas-san**, so it really is worth taking a bus as far as the "Eighth Station", Gas-san Hachigōme. In summer (July–Sept) there are buses from Tsuruoka (4 daily; 1hr 30min) via Haguro-machi, Kyūka-mura and Haguro-sanchō. Even from the Eighth Station it takes over two hours to cover the final 5km along the ridge to Gas-san (1900m), though it's a beautiful walk across the marshy Mida-ga-hara meadows, renowned for their profusion of rare alpine plants in late June.

The final few metres are a bit of a scramble onto the rocky peak, where **Gassan-jinja** (July to mid-Sept daily 6am–5pm; ¥500) huddles behind stout stone walls. There's not a lot to the shrine, but you need to be purified before venturing inside; bow your head while a priest waves his paper wand over you and chants a quick prayer; then rub the paper cut-out person (which he gives you) over your head and shoulders before placing it in the water.

From Gas-san, the trail drops more steeply to **Yudonosan-jinja** (湯殿山神社; May to early Nov daily 8am–5pm; ¥500), located in a narrow valley on the mountain's west flank (9km). For the final descent you have to negotiate a series of iron ladders strapped to the valley side where the path has been washed away. Once at the river it's only a short walk to the inner sanctum of Dewa-san, which occupies another walled area. Inside, take off your shoes and socks before receiving another purification, and then enter the second compound. Having bowed to the steaming orange boulder, you can then haul yourself over it using ropes to reach another little shrine on the far side. It's then just a ten-minute trot down the road to the Yudono-san (湯殿山) bus stop, where the *Sanrōjo shukubō* (see opposite) occupies a black-and-white building beside the *torii*.

If you're arriving at Yudono-san by road, you can catch a shuttle bus by the *torii* up to Yudono-jinja (5min; ¥100), or it's a steepish, twenty-minute walk. From May to early November you can get here by local bus from Tsuruoka (3 daily; 1hr 20min; ¥1480).

Dainichibō and Chūren-ji

On the way back to Tsuruoka from Yudono-jinja, the hamlet of **ŌAMI** (大網) is worth a stop for its two "living Buddhas", the naturally mummified bodies of ascetic Buddhist monks who starved themselves to death. The mummies, or *miira*, are on display in two competing temples on either side of Ōami, each less than ten minutes' walk from where the bus drops you next to the village store; all buses from Yudono-san to Tsuruoka stop at Ōami (27min; ¥780).

Dainichibō (大日坊; daily 8am–5pm; ¥500) is the more accessible of the two temples on the east side of the village; from the bus stop, follow red signs of a little bowing monk to take a left in front of the post office and past a school; you'll see the temple's colourful flags after about ten minutes. The temple was supposedly founded in 807 AD by Kōbō Daishi (see p.499) – after a brief purification ceremony and introductory talk, the head priest will show you the hard-working saint's staff, a handprint of Tokugawa Ieyasu and other temple treasures, before taking you to the mummy. The tiny figure sits slumped on an altar, dressed in rich, red brocades from which his hands and skull protrude, sheathed in a dark, glossy, parchment-thin layer of skin. He's said to have died in 1782 at the age of 96, which is quite extraordinary when you learn that he lived on a diet of nuts, seeds and water. As the end drew closer, the monk took himself off to a cave to meditate and eventually stopped eating all together. Finally he was buried alive with a breathing straw until he expired completely. Apparently this road to enlightenment was not uncommon prior to the nineteenth century, when the practice was banned.

Though it's a bit further to walk (2km), **Chūren-ji** (注連寺; daily 8am–5pm; ¥500) is slightly less commercialized and more atmospheric. To reach the temple, head north from the bus stop on a country road. There are signs at every junction except one, where you need to take the left fork past a graveyard. Again, you receive a short talk and a purification ceremony before entering the side hall, where the *miira* rests in a glass case.

Niigata

Most visitors to **NIIGATA** (新潟), the largest port-city on the Sea of Japan coast, are either on their way to Sado-ga-shima (see p.275) or making use of the ferry and air connections to Korea, China and Russia. It's a likeable but unexciting city, sitting on the banks of Shinano-gawa, with few specific sights beyond a well-presented local history museum. In 1964 a tidal wave devastated much of east Niigata, though the area on the west side of the river retains some attractive streets of older houses.

Arrival, information and city transport

Limousine buses run between the city's **airport** and Niigata Station (2–3 hourly; 30min; ¥400), while ferries dock at one of three **ferry terminals** on the east bank of the Shinano-gawa. All three terminals are linked by local bus (15–30min; ¥200) to Niigata Station; alternatively, a taxi will cost around ¥1200. Most **express buses** use the Bandai City Bus Centre, about 500m northwest of Niigata Station, though some also stop outside the station. **Local buses** depart from the station terminal and may stop outside Bandai City depending on the route.

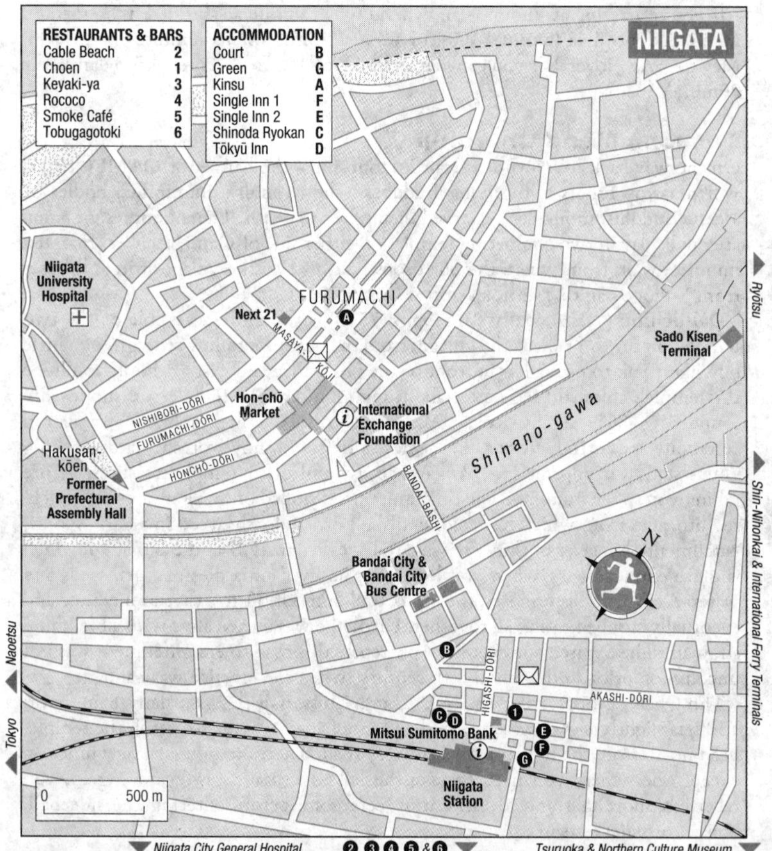

Within the central district there's a flat fare of ¥200, which you pay on exit; on most buses you need to take a ticket as you enter. Another good way to get around is to use the city's great **bike rental** system; you can get and drop off bikes at a number of locations around the city, including the station (from ¥100 for 3hr). Full details are available at the **tourist office** (daily 9am–6pm; ⓣ025/241-7914) outside the station's central (Bandai) exit. You can also get English-language maps and information here, and the staff can help with hotel reservations and ferry tickets to Sado.

Accommodation

Niigata has no shortage of chain hotels around the station; most are business hotels offering clean and comfortable rooms for reasonable prices. There are also quite a few more traditional options scattered around the city.

Court こーとホテル 2-3-35 Benten ⓣ025/247-0505, ⓔinnniigata.info@courthotels.co.jp. Smart, mid-range business hotel located halfway between the station and Bandai City. ⑤

Green グリーンホテル 1-4-9 Hanazono ⓣ025/246-0341, ⓕ246-0345. Cramped but clean budget business hotel to the right as you exit Niigata Station. Rooms in the new building are slightly better, though prices in the old wing can get as low as ¥4200 for a single. Nearby, there are two *Single Inn* business hotels offering very similar accommodation for marginally more (singles ¥4380). ④

Kinsu THE HOTEL 金寿 1429-8 Higashibori-dōri ⓣ025/229-1695, ⓕ229-1393. A good choice downtown, in an interesting area of old streets surrounded by decent restaurants and bars. The rooms are simple, but clean. ④

Shinoda Ryokan 篠田旅館 1-2-8 Benten ⓣ025/245-5501, ⓕ244-0902. A nice old ryokan just past the *Tōkyū Inn*. Only the more expensive rooms have their own bathroom. ⑥ including two meals.

Tōkyū Inn 東急イン, 1-2-4 Benten ⓣ025/243-0109, ⓦwww.tokyuhotelsjapan.com. This big hotel opposite the station has a range of good-sized en-suite rooms, and free internet access. ⑤

The City

On the southwestern edge of the city centre, the pleasant park of **Hakusan-kōen** (白山公園) contains a shrine to the God of Marriage and various stone monuments, including one to the happiness of pine trees. There are also a couple of manicured lily-pad covered ponds around which wisteria trellises bloom into life in late spring. The gingerbread building next to the park is the **Former Prefectural Assembly Hall** (Tues–Sun 9am–4.30pm; free). This was built in 1883, and local representatives continued to meet in this impressive hall until 1932 – sepia photos show Japan's new democracy in action. In the northwest corner of the park, **Enkikan** (燕喜館; daily 9am–5pm, closed every first and third Mon), a Meiji-era teahouse transplanted from Kyoto with pristine tatami rooms overlooking a peaceful garden, provides great atmosphere for a rest; tea (¥300) is served in the room of your choice. If you're staying near the station, you can reach Hakusan-kōen by taking a bus bound for Irefune-chō from in front of Niigata Station (15min; ¥200); this drops you right next to the assembly hall.

From the assembly hall, either get back on a passing Irefune-chō or Furumachi bus, or walk northwest along Nishibori-dōri for 1km to reach the landmark **Next 21** building; head up to the nineteenth-floor observation lounge (daily 8am–11.30pm) for a free view of the city. Despite competition from Bandai City, this area, known as **Furumachi** (古町), remains Niigata's foremost shopping district, though you'll still find some older buildings hidden away in the backstreets. Another relic of the past is the **Hon-chō Market** (本町市場; daily 10am–5pm; closed three days a month, usually on Sun), spread over a few streets to the south of Masaya-kōji. This fresh-produce market is a great place to look for cheap places to eat and to try out your bargaining skills.

The fertile plains around Niigata supported a number of wealthy landowners who lived in considerable luxury until the Land Reform Act of 1946 forced them to sell all rice land above 7.5 acres per household. One such was the Itō family, whose superb mansion is now the centrepiece of the **Northern Cultural Museum** (北方文化博物館; daily 9am–4.30/5pm; ¥800). The huge house was erected in 1887 and comprises sixty rooms containing family heirlooms, but the classic garden steals the show – viewed from inside, it forms a magnificent frieze along one side of the principal guest room. The museum is located in Yokogoshi village, 12km southeast of the city centre, and can be reached by express bus from Bandai City or the Eki-mae terminal by Niigata Station (10 daily; ¥490 one way); the last bus back leaves at around 5pm.

Eating and drinking

Niigata is famous for its fresh fish and fragrant rice, which means excellent sushi. Glutinous rice is used to make *sasa-dango*, a sweet snack of bean paste and rice wrapped in bamboo leaves, while in winter, *noppe* combines taro, ginkgo nuts, salmon roe and vegetables in a colourful stew that is commonly served as a side dish. Niigata-ken's most famous product, however, is its sake. You can sample it at many of the numerous **restaurants** and **bars** in the streets near the station and around Furumachi.

Cable Beach 1-2-15 Komeyama. Intimate Italian restaurant on the quiet side of Niigata Station. Follow the main road outside the south exit; it's down a side street just beyond *Keyaki-ya* (see opposite). Closed Tues.

Choen 張園 1-6-2 Higashi-ōdōri ⓣ025/241-7620. Cheap and cheerful Chinese restaurant serving good-value lunch sets from ¥700. You'll eat well for ¥2000 at night. They have a second shop in Furumachi, in the backstreets just behind *Hotel Kinso*. Daily 11am–3pm & 5–11pm.

Keyaki-ya 欅屋 1-1-2 Komeyama. Lively *izakaya* facing the south side of the station, with lots of snack foods and small meat dishes on the menu (from ¥700) and crowds of enthusiastic 20-somethings filling the two floors of funky booths and long tables.

Rococo 3-1-15 Komeyama. Extremely popular restaurant with eclectic furnishings

Echigo-Tsumari

Every three years the mountainous, rural and relatively unspoilt Echigo-Tsumari region of Niigata-ken hosts a spectacular international art festival, the **Echigo-Tsumari Art Triennial**, from mid-July to early September (the next will be in 2012). Artists from all over the world are invited to exhibit their work, with previous standouts being Cai Guo Quiang from China, who reconstructed an old Chinese climbing kiln, and Rina Banerjee, who, inspired by the Taj Mahal, converted a school gymnasium into a giant birdcage. For more details check out ⓦwww.echigo-tsumari.jp.

Even if you're not in Japan during the festival, a visit to this region is still a rewarding journey. The main places to head for are **Tokamachi**, **Matsudai** and **Matsunoyama**, all of which have fascinating permanent exhibition facilities built for the past triennials and plenty of sculptures and other artworks sited in paddy fields and on hillsides. The best way to get around is to hire a car, although during the festival there are also free bikes available at all the main sites. Otherwise you can travel here by local train from either Echigo-Yuzawa on the Niigata Shinkansen route or Saigata on the Joetsu line.

By the far the most memorable lodging experience is spending a night in one of the art pieces. Serbian Marina Abramovic's *Dream House* (夢の家; ⓣ025/596-3134, ⓦwww.tsumari-artfield.com/dreamhouse; ❺–❻ with meals), a refurbished century-old farmhouse, is one great option, while the architectural genius *House of Light* (光の館; ⓣ025/761-1090, ⓦwww11.ocn.ne.jp/~jthikari; Tokamachi-shi; ❼), designed by James Turrell for the purpose of meditation, stuns with its retractable roof and slick, modern interior. Both are short taxi rides from Tokamachi Station and are open from April to December.

that match the randomness of the menu, where spring rolls and pad Thai mingle with spicy cheese pizza and chicken wings (dishes from ¥350). Also has cheap but delicious cakes. It's on the block after *Cable Beach* (see opposite) as you walk away from the station. 11am–12.30am.

Smoke Café 1-18-4 Sasaguchi ⓣ025/246-0250, ⓦwww.smokecafe.jp. This friendly, trendy bar specializes in international beers, including Guinness and Bass Pale Ale (pints from ¥800), and also does good pizza and pasta. It's just south of the station, on the second floor of a modern two-storey building in the backstreets immediately behind the *Chisun Hotel* and a large Bic Camera home electronics store. Daily 11.30am–2pm & 6pm–3am (Fri & Sat till 4am).

Tobugagotoku 1-18-4 Sasaguchi ⓣ025/244-0899. From the same company that runs *Smoke Café* next door is this atmospheric *izakaya* specializing in regional dishes from places as far afield as Kochi and Kagoshima. The dark, natural decor gives off an old European ambience that matches the Euro-inspired local microbrewed beer. They also serve local sake. Daily 5pm–1am.

Listings

Airport information ⓣ025/275-2633, ⓦwww.niigata-airport.gr.jp.

Banks and exchange You'll find foreign exchange banks near the station on Akashi-dōri and along Masaya-kōji on the west side of the river.

Bookshops Kinokuniya, on the sixth floor of the LoveLa department store in the Bandai City complex, has Niigata's best selection of foreign-language books.

Car rental Try Eki Rent-a-Car ⓣ025/245-4292; Nippon ⓣ025/245-3221; Nissan ⓣ025/243-5523.

Ferries Sado Kisen (ⓣ025/245-1234) operates ferries and jetfoil services to Ryōtsu (Sado) from the Sado Kisen Terminal, reached by local bus from Niigata Station (15min). Ferries to Otaru (Hokkaidō) are run by Shin-Nihonkai Ferry (ⓣ025/273-2171) and leave from the Shin-Nihonkai Ferry Terminal; take a bus from the station for Rinkō Nichōme and get off at the Suehiro-bashi stop (20min).

Hospitals The largest central hospital is Niigata University Hospital, 1-754 Asahimachi-dōri (ⓣ025/227-2478).

Post office Niigata Central Post Office, 2-6-26 Higashi-ōdōri, is located a few minutes' walk north of the station.

Taxis Fuji ⓣ025/244-5166; Hato ⓣ025/287-1121; Miyakō ⓣ025/222-0611.

Sado-ga-shima

For centuries, the rugged, S-shaped island of **Sado-ga-shima** (佐渡島) was a place of exile for criminals and political undesirables; though even today it has a unique atmosphere born of its isolation and a distinct cultural heritage that encompasses haunting folk songs, nō theatre and puppetry, as well as the more recently established Kodô drummers. It's a deceptively large island, consisting of two parallel mountain chains linked by a fertile central plain that shelters most of Sado's historical relics. These include several important **temples**, such as Kompon-ji, founded by the exiled Buddhist monk Nichiren, and a couple of bizarre, hi-tech **museums** where robots perform nō plays and narrate local history. The Edo-period gold mines of **Aikawa**, on Sado's northwest coast, make another interesting excursion, but the island's greatest attractions are really its scenery and glimpses of an older Japan.

Sado also has a packed calendar of **festivals** from April to November. Many of these involve *okesa* folk songs and the devil-drumming known as *ondeko* (or *oni-daiko*), both of which are performed nightly during the tourist season in Ogi and Aikawa. Throughout June, nō groups perform in shrines around the central plain, while the island's biggest event nowadays is the Kodô drummers' international Earth Celebration, held in Ogi (see box, p.280).

Some history

Since before the twelfth century, Sado was viewed as a suitably remote place for exiling undesirables. The most illustrious exile was the ex-emperor Juntoku

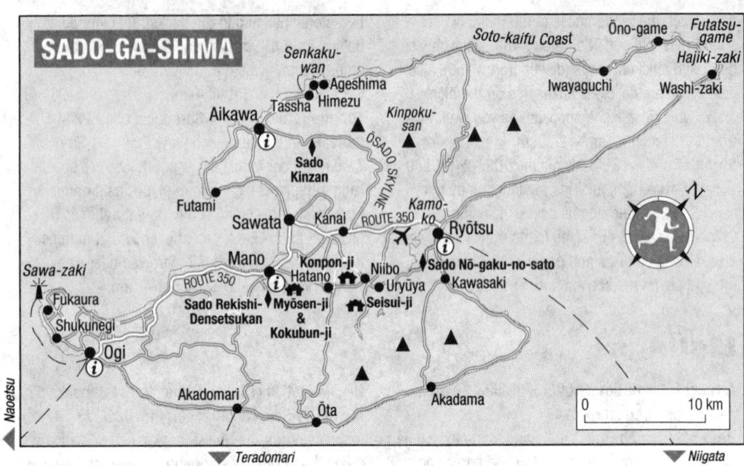

(reigned 1211–21), who tried to wrest power back from Kamakura and spent the last twenty years of his life on Sado. A few decades later, Nichiren, the founder of the eponymous Buddhist sect (see p.781), found himself on the island for a couple of years; he wasted no time in erecting temples and converting the local populace. Then there was Zeami, a famous actor and playwright credited with formalizing nō theatre, who died here in 1443 after eight years in exile.

In 1601, rich seams of gold and silver were discovered in the mountains above Aikawa. From then on, criminals were sent to work in the mines, supplemented by "homeless" workers from Edo (Tokyo), who dug some 400km of tunnels down to 600m below sea level – all by hand. In 1896 Mitsubishi took the mines over from the imperial household and today they're owned by the Sado Gold Mining Co., which continued to extract small quantities of gold up until 1989.

Island practicalities

The main gateway to Sado is **Ryōtsu** town, on the east coast, which is best reached by ferry from Niigata. Sado Kisen (Niigata Ⓣ025/245-1234, Ryōtsu Ⓣ0259/27-5614) operates car **ferries** (5–7 daily; 2hr 30min; from ¥2320) and jet-foil services (5–12 daily; 1hr; ¥6220 one way, or ¥11,250 five-day return ticket) from Niigata's Sado Kisen Terminal (see p.272). Reservations are required for the jetfoil and recommended for all crossings in the summer season. Sado Kisen ferries also operate between **Naoetsu port**, south of Niigata (20min by bus from Naoetsu Station), and **Ogi** on the island's south coast (1–4 daily; 2hr 40min; ¥2530). There's also a ferry service from Teradomari to **Akadomari** (赤泊) on the island's southeast coast (1–3 daily, closed Jan 23–Feb 6; 1hr; from ¥2760).

You'll find maps, bus timetables and other **information** at each of the ferry terminals, though it's worth arriving in Ryōtsu to make the most of their well-provisioned tourist office and English-speaking staff before heading into the wilds. While here be sure to pick up a copy of the excellent annually updated English tourist map published by MIJ International (Ⓦwww.mijintl.com).

As long as you allow plenty of time (around three days), it's possible to get around most of the island by **bus**, although in winter some services only operate at weekends, while others stop completely. Even at the best of times, a number of routes have only two or three buses per day, so make sure you carry a copy of the island's bus timetable (available in English from the tourist office). If you're visiting over a weekend, take advantage of the ¥2000 ticket which covers all transport over two consecutive weekend days (including national holidays).

By far the most flexible option for exploring Sado, however, is to **rent a car**; you'll find Sado Kisen Rent-a-Car (ⓣ0259/27-5195; from ¥5775/day) at all three ferry terminals. Nakao Cycle (ⓣ0259/23-5195) in Ryōtsu's main shopping street rents out bikes for ¥1500 per day. You can also **rent bikes** in Mano, Ogi and at some youth hostels (see individual accounts for details).

Ryōtsu and around

Sitting on a huge horseshoe bay with the mountains of Sado rising behind, **RYŌTSU** (両津) is an appealing little place and makes a good base for a night. The town revolves around its modern ferry pier (両津埠頭) and bus terminal, at the south end, while there's still a flavour of the original fishing community in the older backstreets to the north, among the rickety wooden houses with their coiled nets and fishy odours. Much of the town occupies a thin strip of land between the sea and a large saltwater lake, **Kamo-ko**, which is now used for oyster farming.

The **Sado Nō-gaku-no-sato** museum (佐渡能楽の里; daily 8.30am–5pm; ¥800), on the south shore of Kamo-ko lake, celebrates Sado's long association with nō. There's nothing in English, but the masks and costumes are enjoyable, as is the short performance by remarkably life-like robots, who are admirably suited to nō's studied movements. To reach the museum, take a bus on the Minami-sen route (line 2) for Sawata and get off after ten minutes at the Nō-gaku-no-sato-mae stop.

Practicalities

The main Sado-ga-shima **tourist office** (daily 8.30am–5.30/6pm; ⓣ0259/23-3300, ⓦwww.ryotsu.sado.jp) is located in a row of shops opposite the ferry terminal building. Buses depart from the bus terminal under the ferry building, where you'll also find car rental agencies and taxis. There's a **post office** on the north side of the channel leading from the lake, near the middle bridge, and foreign-exchange **banks** further along this high street.

Though Ryōtsu has plenty of resort **hotels**, there's little in the way of more affordable accommodation. Your best bet is the friendly *Sado Seaside Hotel* (佐渡シーサイドホテル; ⓣ0259/27-7211, ⓦwww2u.biglobe.ne.jp/~sado; ❺; including two meals ❻), which offers rather worn tatami rooms – some en suite – but a warm welcome, free internet, good food and an onsen bath. The hotel is located on a pebbly strip of beach at the very southern end of Ryōtsu, 1.6km from the pier; if you phone from Niigata, they'll meet you off the ferry. In the centre of Ryōtsu, about ten minutes' walk north from the pier, the *Kagetsu Hotel* (花月ホテル; ⓣ0259/27-3131, ⓦwww5.ocn.ne.jp/~kagetsu; ❺; with meals ❻–❼) is a much smarter place, with elegant tatami rooms and a garden running down to the lake. Alternatively, try the larger *Yoshidaya* (吉田家; ⓣ0259/27-2151, ⓔyoshidah@jeans.ocn.ne.jp; ❼) nearby.

For something to **eat**, friendly *Tōkyō-an* (東京庵), on the main street two blocks north of the river, specializes in handmade soba, while *Tenkuni* (天国) dishes up moderately priced (around ¥1000) sashimi, tempura and *donburi* dishes at lunch time – it's south of the river on the main road, then down the right fork between a school and a temple.

Central Sado

Sado's **central plain** is the most heavily populated part of the island and home to a number of impressive temples, some dating back to the eighth century. Two routes cross this plain linking Ryōtsu to towns on the west coast: the main highway cuts southwest from Kamo-ko to Sado airport and on to **Sawata**, served by buses on the Hon-sen route (line 1), while the quieter, southerly route takes you through **Niibo** (新穂), **Hatano** (畑野) and **Mano** (真野) along the Minami-sen bus route (line 2). The majority of historical sites lie scattered across this southern district – for many of them you'll need your own transport or be prepared to walk a fair distance. One solution is to **rent a bike** (see p.277).

Sado's most accessible and important temple, **Kompon-ji** (根本寺; daily 9am–4.30pm; ¥300), is located a few kilometres south of Niibo village; buses from Ryōtsu run here fairly regularly during the day. Kompon-ji marks the spot where the exiled Nichiren lived in 1271, though the temple itself was founded some years later. If you can get there before the coach parties, it's a pleasant stroll round the mossy garden with its thatched temple buildings filled with elaborate gilded canopies, presided over by a statue of Nichiren in his characteristic monk's robes.

On the eastern outskirts of **MANO** (真野), **Myōsen-ji** (妙宣寺) was founded by one of Nichiren's first disciples and includes a graceful five-storey pagoda. Nearby **Kokubun-ji** (国分寺) dates from 741 AD, though the temple's present buildings were erected in the late seventeenth century. If you follow this side road south, skirting round the back of Mano town, you come to a simple shrine dedicated to Emperor Juntoku. He's actually buried about 800m further up the valley, but the next-door **Sado Rekishi-Densetsukan** (佐渡歴史伝説館; daily 8am–5/5.30pm; ¥700) is more interesting. This museum is similar in style to Ryōtsu's Sado Nō-gaku-no-sato (see p.277), though in this case the robots and holograms represent Juntoku, Nichiren and other characters from local history or folk tales. The museum lies about thirty minutes' walk southeast from central Mano and about ten minutes from the nearest bus stop, Mano goryō-iriguchi, on the route from Sawata south to Ogi (line 4).

A few kilometres north along the coast from Mano, **SAWATA** (佐和田) serves as Sado's main administrative centre. Sawata is not the most alluring of places, but if you happen to be passing through around lunchtime, pop along to the **Silver Village** resort, on the town's northern outskirts, to catch the fifteen-minute display of *bun'ya*, a form of seventeenth-century puppetry performed by a couple of master puppeteers (April–Nov daily at noon, 12.45pm & 1.30pm; ¥750).

Practicalities

Sawata's bus terminal is located on the north side of town, not far from the *Silver Village*. You can **rent bikes** at *Silver Village* (シルバービレッジ佐渡; daily 9am–6pm; ¥2000 per day), or in Mano's **tourist office** (May–Oct daily 8.30am–5.30pm; Dec–April Mon–Fri 8.30am–5.30pm; ⓣ0259/55-3589) for only ¥1100 a day; the office is located a few doors south of the main junction between Route 350 and the Niibo road.

One of the nicest **places to stay** in central Sado is the homely *Green Village Patio House*, 750-4 Uryūya (グリーンヴィレッジパティオハウス; ⓣ0259/22-2719, ⓕ22-3302; dorm beds ¥3360 per person), to the east of Niibo village – ask the bus driver to let you off at the turning. As well as good-value meals, laundry facilities and free internet access, they have bikes for rent and can suggest cycling routes. Alternatively, *Silver Village* (ⓣ0259/52-3961, ⓔsilver2@e-sadonet.tv; ❺, ❻ with meals) in Sawata has comfortable Western-style en-suite rooms with sea views.

Ogi and around

Sado's second port is tiny **OGI** (小木), situated near the island's southern tip. This sleepy fishing town is best known for its tub boats, which now bob around in the harbour for tourists, and the annual Earth Celebration hosted by the locally based Kodô drummers (see box, p.280), during which the village's population almost doubles. But the area's principal attraction is its picturesque indented coastline to the west of town. You can take boat trips round the headland or cycle over the top to **Shukunegi**, a traditional fishing village huddled behind a wooden palisade.

The **tub boats**, or *tarai-bune*, were originally used for collecting seaweed, abalone and other shellfish from the rocky coves. Today they're made of fibreglass, but still resemble the cutaway wooden barrels from which they were traditionally made. If you fancy a shot at rowing one of these awkward vessels, go to the small jetty west of the ferry pier, where the women will take you out for a ten-minute spin round the harbour (daily 8.20am–5pm; ¥450 per person). The jetty is also the departure point for **sightseeing boats** (April–Nov, 6–18 daily; 40min; ¥1400 return trip) which sail along the coast past caves and dainty islets as far as Sawa-zaki lighthouse.

Buses run west along the coast as far as Sawasaki (line 11; 5 daily; 25min), but the ideal way to explore the **headland** is to rent a bicycle (see p.277). After a tough uphill pedal out of Ogi on the road to Shukunegi, turn right towards a concrete *jizō* standing above the trees. From here continue another 300m along this sideroad and you'll find a short flight of steps leading up to the **Iwaya cave** (岩屋) – the old trees and tiny, crumbling temple surrounded by *jizō* statues make a good place to catch your breath. Further along the Shukunegi road, next to a still-functioning boatyard, the **Sadokoku Ogi Folk Culture Museum** (March–Oct daily 8.30am–5pm; Dec–Feb Mon–Fri 8.30am–5pm; ¥500) is worth a brief stop. It contains a delightful, dusty jumble of old photos, paper-cuts, tofu presses, straw raincoats and other remnants of local life. Behind, in a newer building, there's a relief map of the area and beautiful examples of the ingenious traps used by Ogi fisherfolk.

From here the road drops down steeply to **SHUKUNEGI** (宿根木) fishing village, a registered national historic site tucked in a fold of the hills beside a little harbour full of jagged black rocks. The village itself is hardly visible behind its high wooden fence – protection against the fierce winds – where its old wooden houses, two of which are open to the public in summer (¥400 each), are all jumbled together with odd-shaped corners and narrow, stone-flagged alleys.

Practicalities

Ogi is split in two by a small headland, with the original fishing harbour to the west and the **ferry terminal** on its east side. **Local buses** use the station behind Ogi **post office**, just inland from the tourist-boat pier. The town's **tourist office** (Mon–Sat 8.30am–5.15/6pm; Ⓣ0259/86-3200) occupies the ground floor of the Marine Plaza building, one block west of the post office, where you can get maps, book accommodation and arrange car and bike rental. This building is also used for evening performances of *okesa odori* folk singing (April–Oct; ¥500).

It's a good idea to book **accommodation** well ahead in summer, but during the rest of the year you shouldn't have any problem. The cheapest option is the basic *Ogi Sakuma-sō Youth Hostel* (小木佐久間荘ユースホステル; Ⓣ0259/86-2565; Ⓦwww.jyh.or.jp; dorm beds from ¥3000 per person), located a good twenty minutes' walk uphill from the ferry; take the road heading west for Shukunegi, then turn right beside the Shell fuel station. For something more central, the popular seafront *Minshuku Sakaya* (民宿さかや; Ⓣ0259/86-2535, Ⓕ86-2145; ❺ including meals) offers clean tatami rooms and tasty food. It's about five minutes' walk east of the ferry terminal – unfortunately its sea views are blocked by the harbour wall. The more traditional *Gonzaya Ryokan* (ごんざや旅館; Ⓣ0259/86-3161, Ⓕ86-3162; ❻–❼) offers the option of rooms with en-suite facilities and without meals, and is located inland from the local bus terminal. Finally, a classier option – despite its shabby outward appearances – is the *Hotel New Kihachiya* (ホテルニュー喜八屋; Ⓣ0259/86-3131, Ⓕ86-3141; ❼), which has Western and tatami rooms, some with harbour views.

For **food**, try *Sakae-zushi* (栄寿司) in the block behind the Marine Plaza, where they serve sea-fresh sushi and sashimi at reasonable prices. Alternatively, head for

Children of the drum

In the early 1970s a group of musicians came to the seclusion of Sado-ga-shima to pursue their study of traditional *taiko* drumming and to experiment with its potent music. A decade later the **Kodô Drummers** unleashed their primal rhythms on the world, since when they have continued to stun audiences with their electrifying performances. The name Kodô can mean both "heartbeat" and "children" – despite its crashing sound, the beat of their trademark giant *Ōdaiko* is said to resemble the heart heard from inside the womb.

The drummers are now based in Kodô village, a few kilometres north of Ogi, where they have set up the **Kodô Cultural Foundation**. Apart from a two-year apprenticeship programme, the drummers hold occasional workshops (*Kodō juku*) which are open to anyone with basic knowledge of Japanese. Each year, usually the third week of August, they also host the three-day **Earth Celebration** arts festival when percussionists from all over the world and a friendly multinational audience of several thousand stir up the sleepy air of Ogi. Details of Kodô scheduled tours and the next Earth Celebration are posted on their website (@www.kodo.or.jp).

Shichiemon (七右衛門), at the top of the shopping street curving behind the western harbour, which dishes up just one variety of delicious, handmade soba (¥480; lunchtime only; closed 1st and 15th of every month).

North Sado

Sado's northern promontory contains the island's highest mountains and some of its best coastal scenery. **Aikawa**, the only settlement of any size in this area, was once a lively mining town whose gold and silver ores filled the shoguns' coffers. The mines are no longer working, but a section of tunnel has been converted into a museum, **Sado Kinzan**, where yet more computerized robots show how things were done in olden times. North of Aikawa there's the rather overrated **Senkaku-wan**, a small stretch of picturesque cliffs; it's better to head on up the wild **Soto-kaifu** coast to Hajiki-zaki on the island's northern tip. Not surprisingly, this area isn't well served by public transport, particularly in winter when snow blocks the mountain passes; to explore this part of the island you really need to rent a car or be prepared to do a lot of cycling.

Aikawa

After gold and silver were discovered in 1601, the population of **AIKAWA** (相川) rocketed from a hamlet of just ten families to 100,000 people, including many who were convict labourers. Now a mere tenth of that size, there's nothing specific to see in Aikawa beyond the mine museum a few kilometres out of town. Nevertheless, it's not an unattractive place for an overnight stay once you get off the main road and delve among the temples, shrines and wooden houses pressed up against the hillside.

The road from Sawata enters Aikawa from the southeast beside the *Sado Royal Hotel Manchō* and then turns north along the seafront, past the bus terminal and skirts round the main town centre. Just beyond the municipal playing fields, at the north end of Aikawa, a right turn leads up a steep narrow valley to the old gold mines of **Sado Kinzan** (佐渡金山; Jan–March, Nov & Dec 8.30am–5pm; April–Oct 8am–5.30pm; ¥800). The Sōdayū tunnel, one of the mine's richest veins, is now a museum showing working conditions during the Edo period, complete with sound effects and life-size mechanical models, followed by a small exhibition with equally imaginative dioramas of the miners at work. If you don't have your own transportation, you can reach Sado Kinzan by local bus from Aikawa (4 daily; 10min).

Practicalities

Aikawa's **tourist office** (daily 8.30am–5.15/6pm; Ⓣ0259/74-2220) is located outside the bus terminal's seaward side. If you're looking for somewhere to **stay** in Aikawa, head straight for *Dōyū Ryokan* (道遊旅館; Ⓣ0259/74-3381, Ⓕ74-3783; ❺), on a quiet street one block inland from the bus terminal. Onsen addicts should walk south along the seafront to the large and luxurious *Hotel Ōsado* (ホテル大佐渡; Ⓣ0259/74-3300, Ⓦwww.oosado.com; ❻–❼), which offers both Japanese and Western-style rooms, to indulge in its glorious rotemburo. The best place to look for somewhere to **eat** is in the main shopping street north of *Dōyū Ryokan*.

The northern cape

Five kilometres north of Aikawa, the road skirts round the edge of a bay where jagged cliffs crumble away into clusters of little islands. You get a pretty good view of the bay of **Senkaku-wan** from the road itself or from the observatory in Ageshima-yūen (揚島遊園; daily 8am–5.30pm; ¥500), a park on the bay's north side. If you want to get closer, a variety of **tour boats** regularly set sail during the summer season (April–Nov) from **Tassha** village (達者), 2km further south; expect to pay around ¥800 for a thirty-minute trip in either a glass-bottomed "shark" boat or ordinary sightseeing (*yūransen*) boats. Tassha and Ageshima-yūen are both stops on the Kaifu-sen bus route (line 3) from Aikawa to Iwayaguchi, with services roughly every hour. On the hilltop near Ageshima-yūen, there's a good **youth hostel**, the *Sado Belle Mer* (佐渡ベルメールユースホステル; Ⓣ0259/75-2011, Ⓦwww.jyh.or.jp; ❹, ❺ including meals, and the government-run *Kokuminshukusha Senkaku-sō* (国民宿舎尖閣荘; Ⓣ0259/75-2226, Ⓦwww.senkakusou.com; ❺ including meals). They're both a few minutes' walk from the Himezu bus stop.

Continuing north, the settlements gradually peter out and the scenery becomes wilder as you approach **Ōno-game**, a 167m rock rising up from the ocean. From here a pretty coastal pathway leads around to the island of **Futatsu-game**, linked to the mainland by a thin strip of black-sand beach; along the path is an intriguing cave, **Sai-no-Kawara**, housing hundreds of *jizō* statues. In summer this area is popular for swimming and camping, but it's worth doing at any time of year for the journey alone, especially if you return to Ryōtsu down the east coast, where you're treated to further precariously twisting roads clinging to the base of the mountains as they plummet into the sea.

Travel details

Trains

Akita to: Aomori (3 daily; 2hr 30min); Kakunodate (17 daily; 50min); Morioka (hourly; 1hr 30min); Niigata (3 daily; 3hr 40min); Tokyo (hourly; 4hr–4hr 30min); Tsuruoka (15 daily; 2hr).

Aomori to: Akita (3 daily; 2hr 25min); Hakodate (hourly; 2hr); Hirosaki (hourly; 30min–1hr); Morioka (hourly; 1hr 45min); Noheji (1–2 hourly; 30–45min); Sendai (hourly; 2hr 30min).

Hiraizumi to: Hanamaki (hourly; 45min); Kitakami (hourly; 30min); Morioka (hourly; 1hr 20min); Sendai (hourly; 45min–1hr).

Ichinoseki to: Geibikei (11 daily; 30min); Hiraizumi (hourly; 8min); Kogota (hourly; 50min); Morioka (hourly; 40min); Sendai (every 30min; 30min); Shin-Hanamaki (every 30min; 25min).

Ishinomaki to: Kogota (11 daily; 45min); Sendai (every 30min; 55min–1hr 20min).

Matsushima-kaigan to: Hon-Shiogama (every 30min; 10min); Ishinomaki (every 30min; 30–45min); Sendai (every 30min; 30–40min).

Morioka to: Akita (hourly; 1hr 30min); Aomori (hourly; 1hr 45min); Hanamaki (every 30min; 20–35min); Kakunodate (hourly; 50min); Kitakami (every 30min; 50min); Noheji (hourly; 1hr 15min); Sendai (every 30min; 45min); Shin-Hanamaki (every 30min; 12min); Tazawako (15 daily; 40min); Tokyo (every 30min; 2hr 20min–3hr 30min); Towada-minami (7 daily; 2hr).

Niigata to: Kanazawa (5 daily; 3hr 40min); Nagano (1–2 hourly; 2hr 15min, with one transfer); Tokyo (1–2 hourly; 2hr); Tsuruoka (7 daily; 1hr 55min).
Noheji to: Aomori (1–2 hourly; 30–45min); Morioka (hourly; 1hr 15min); Shimokita (9 daily; 45min–1hr).
Sendai to: Hon-Shiogama (every 30min; 20–30min); Matsushima-kaigan (every 30min; 30–40min); Ichinoseki (hourly; 30min); Ishinomaki (every 30min; 55min–1hr 20min); Morioka (hourly; 45min); Tokyo (every 20min; 1hr 35min–2hr 30min); Yamadera (hourly; 50min–1hr 5min).
Tōno to: Hanamaki (12 daily; 55min–1hr 10min); Morioka (3 daily; 1hr 25min); Shin-Hanamaki (12 daily; 45min–1hr).
Towada-minami to: Morioka (7 daily; 2hr); Ōdate (9 daily; 30–40min).
Tsuruoka to: Akita (7 daily; 2hr); Niigata (7 daily; 1hr 50min).
Yamagata to: Sendai (hourly; 1hr 15min–1hr 30min); Tokyo (hourly; 2hr 50min); Yamadera (hourly; 20min).

Buses

Akita to: Sendai (10 daily; 3hr 50min); Tokyo (daily; 8hr 30min).
Aomori to: Morioka (4 daily; 3hr 15min); Sendai (6 daily; 4hr 50min); Tokyo (daily; 9hr 30min–10hr); Towada-ko (April–Oct, 6–8 daily; 3hr 15min).
Hirosaki to: Morioka (hourly; 2hr 15min); Sendai (9 daily; 4hr 20min); Tokyo (daily; 10hr); Towada-ko (late April to late Oct, 3 daily; 3hr 15min–4hr); Yokohama (daily; 11hr).
Ichinoseki to: Chōson-ji (every 15–20min; 25min); Geibikei (9–11 daily; 30–40min); Hiraizumi (every 15–20min; 20min).
Ishinomaki to: Ayukawa (7 daily; 1hr 30min); Tokyo (Shinjuku) (daily; 7hr 10min).
Morioka to: Aomori (4 daily; 3hr 15min); Hirosaki (hourly; 2hr 15min); Sendai (hourly; 2hr 40min); Tokyo (2 daily; 7hr 30min).
Niigata to: Kanazawa (2 daily; 4hr 40min); Kyoto (daily; 8hr 10min); Nagano (4 daily; 3hr 15min); Ōsaka (daily; 9hr 20min); Sendai (8 daily; 4hr 5min); Tokyo (Ikebukuro) (16 daily; 5hr 20min); Yamagata (2 daily; 3hr 40min).
Ryōtsu to: Aikawa (1–2 hourly; 1hr); Mano (1–2 hourly; 45min); Sawata (1–2 hourly; 45min).
Sawata to: Aikawa (1–2 hourly; 20min); Ogi (9 daily; 1hr).
Sendai to: Akita (10 daily; 3hr 50min); Aomori (6 daily; 4hr 50min); Hirosaki (9 daily; 4hr 20min); Morioka (hourly; 2hr 40min); Nagoya (daily; 10hr 30min); Niigata (8 daily; 4hr); Ōsaka (daily; 12hr 20min); Tokyo (daily; 6hr 30min); Tokyo (Shinjuku) (3 daily; 5hr 30min); Tsuruoka (10 daily; 2hr 20min); Yamagata (every 30min; 1hr 10min).
Towada-ko to: Aomori (April–Oct, 6–8 daily; 3hr 15min); Hirosaki (late April to late Oct, 3 daily; 3hr 15min–4hr); Hachimantai (late April to Nov, daily; 2hr 30min); Ōdate (April to early Nov, daily; 1hr 30min); Towada-minami (April to early Nov, 4 daily; 1hr).
Tsuruoka to: Sendai (7 daily; 2hr 35min); Tokyo (2 daily; 8–9hr); Yamagata (11 daily; 2hr).
Yamagata to: Niigata (2 daily; 3hr 40min); Sendai (every 30min; 1hr 10min); Tokyo (4 daily; 6hr 20min–8hr 30min); Tsuruoka (9 daily; 1hr 50min).

Ferries

Akita to: Tomakomai (Hokkaidō) (5 weekly; 11hr 20min).
Aomori to: Hakodate (8 daily; 4hr).
Kinkazan to: Ayukawa (3–10 daily; 25min).
Niigata to: Otaru (Hokkaidō) (1–2 daily; 18hr); Ryōtsu (10–19 daily; 1hr–2hr 30min).
Ogi to: Naoetsu (1–4 daily; 2hr 40min).
Sendai to: Nagoya (3 weekly; 21hr); Tomakomai (Hokkaidō) (6 weekly; 15hr).

Flights

From Northern Honshū there are a number of international connections, mainly to Russia, Korea and China.
Akita to: Nagoya (4 daily; 1hr 10min); Ōsaka (Itami) (2 daily; 1hr 20min); Sapporo (3 daily; 55min); Tokyo (8 daily; 1hr); Haneda (Tokyo) (9 daily; 1hr 10min).
Aomori to: Nagoya (2 daily; 1hr 25min); Ōsaka (Itami) (2 daily; 1hr 35min); Sapporo (2 daily; 45min); Seoul (South Korea) (4 weekly; 2hr 50min); Tokyo (6 daily; 1hr 15min).
Niigata to: Fukuoka (daily; 1hr 45min); Guam (2 weekly; 4hr 45min); Harbin (4 weekly; 2hr 30min); Khabarovsk, Russia (weekly; 1hr 55min); Nagoya (4 daily; 55min); Ōsaka (Itami) (10 daily; 1hr 10min); Sapporo (3 daily; 1hr 10min); Seoul, South Korea (2 daily; 2hr); Shanghai, China (2 weekly; 4hr); Vladivostok, Russia (weekly; 1hr 20min).
Sendai to: Beijing, China (6 weekly; 5–7hr); Fukuoka (5 daily; 2hr); Dalian (2 weekly; 3hr 10min); Guam (2 weekly; 3hr 45min); Hiroshima (daily; 1hr 35min); Nagoya (6 daily; 1hr 10min); Naha (Okinawa) (daily; 2hr 55min); Narita (2 daily; 1hr 10min); Ōsaka (Itami) (14 daily; 1hr 20min); Sapporo (11 daily; 1hr 10min); Seoul, South Korea (daily; 2hr 30min); Shanghai, China (3 weekly; 3hr 30min); Taipei, Taiwan (2 weekly; 3hr 40min).
Tsuruoka (Shōnai) to: Tokyo (4 daily; 1hr).
Yamagata to: Nagoya (daily; 1hr 5min); Ōsaka (Itami) (3 daily; 1hr 20min); Sapporo (daily; 1hr 5min); Tokyo (daily; 1hr).

Hokkaidō

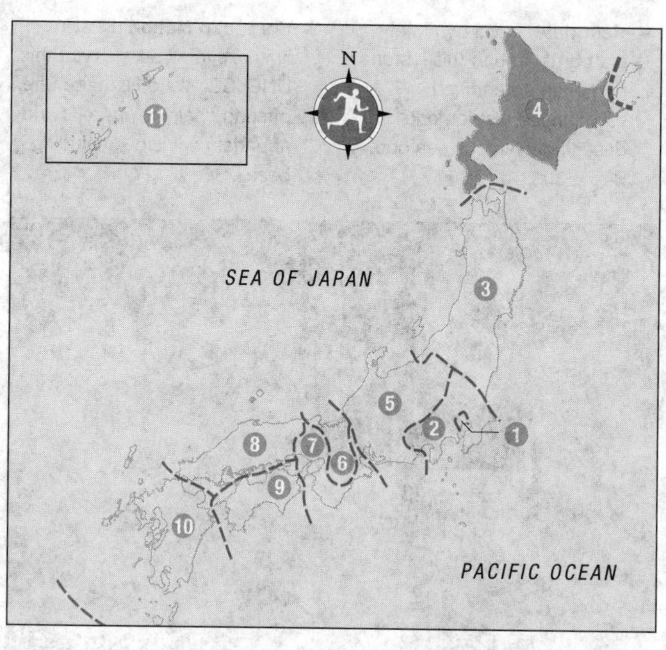

CHAPTER 4 Highlights

* **Sapporo** Hokkaidō's fun capital has historic brick buildings, a park designed by Isamu Noguchi, and freshly brewed beer. See p.288

* **Niseko** Superb powder snow, great scenery and chic accommodation and dining add up to Japan's best ski resort. See p.301

* **Hakodate** Travel by rickety old trams around this historic port, with a gentrified harbourside district, and deservedly famous seafood. See p.303

* **Daisetsu-zan National Park** Home to Asahi-dake, Hokkaidō's highest mountain, the spectacular Sōunkyō Gorge and relaxing onsen. See p.316

* **Rishiri-tō and Rebun-tō** These beautiful, far northern islands are sprinkled with wild flowers and perfect for hiking. See p.322

* **Shiretoko National Park** Nature's in all her glory at this UNESCO World Heritage Site, offering challenging treks and abundant wildlife – including bears. See p.327

▲ The view from one of Hakodate's cable cars

Hokkaidō

An unspoiled frontier, an escape from industrialized Japan and a chance to connect with nature – although this vision of **HOKKAIDŌ** (北海道) is rose-tinted, Japan's main northern island certainly has an untamed and remote quality. Over seventy percent of it is covered by forest, and wildlife is ubiquitous, both in and out of the enormous national parks, where you'll also find snow-covered slopes, active volcanoes and bubbling onsen. This is Japan's second-largest island, yet a mere five percent of the population lives here. Even so, cities such as the stylish capital **Sapporo** and historically important **Hakodate** are just as sophisticated and packed with facilities as their southern cousins.

Only colonized by the Japanese in the last 150 years, Hokkaidō is devoid of ancient temples, shrines and monuments over 200 years old. What it does have is a fascinating cultural history, defined by its dwindling **Ainu** population (see p.288). Spring through autumn are the ideal times to explore the island's six major national parks and countryside. Apart from those highlighted opposite, **Shikotsu-Tōya National Park** has two beautiful lakes and a volcano that only started sprouting in 1943, while the countryside around **Furano** bursts in colour with fields of lavender and other flowers. Come winter Hokkaidō takes on a special quality; you can ski at some of Japan's best – and least crowded – ski resorts or view many snow and ice festivals, of which Sapporo's giant **Yuki Matsuri** is the most famous.

Arrival and information

Hokkaidō's main **gateway** is New Chitose airport, 40km south of Sapporo, where you can pick up connecting flights to other places on the island. The Shinkansen line is currently being extended to Hakodate, with likely completion around 2015. For now, the fastest way from Tokyo by **train** is by Shinkansen to Shin-Aomori and then limited express to Hakodate. There are also nightly direct sleeper trains from Tokyo to Sapporo, via Hakodate, and several a week from Ōsaka; if you're using a rail pass, you'll need to pay a supplement for these. Also consider the overnight **ferry** services from Honshū. MOL (Ⓦwww.sunflower.co.jp) offers a service from Tokyo to Sapporo and other places in Hokkaido via the ports of Oarai and Tomakomai, with bus connections to and from the ports at either end, for ¥9900; see the website for details.

Frequent trains and buses make **getting around** most of Hokkaidō easy. The **Hokkaidō Rail Pass** (Ⓦwww2.jrhokkaido.co.jp/global), costing from ¥15,000 for a three-day ticket, is well worth considering. However, to reach more remote corners of the island hiring a car is best. Cycling is also very popular. Useful websites for general and driving information include Ⓦwww.visit-hokkaido.jp/en and Ⓦnorthern-road.jp/navi/eng/index.htm.

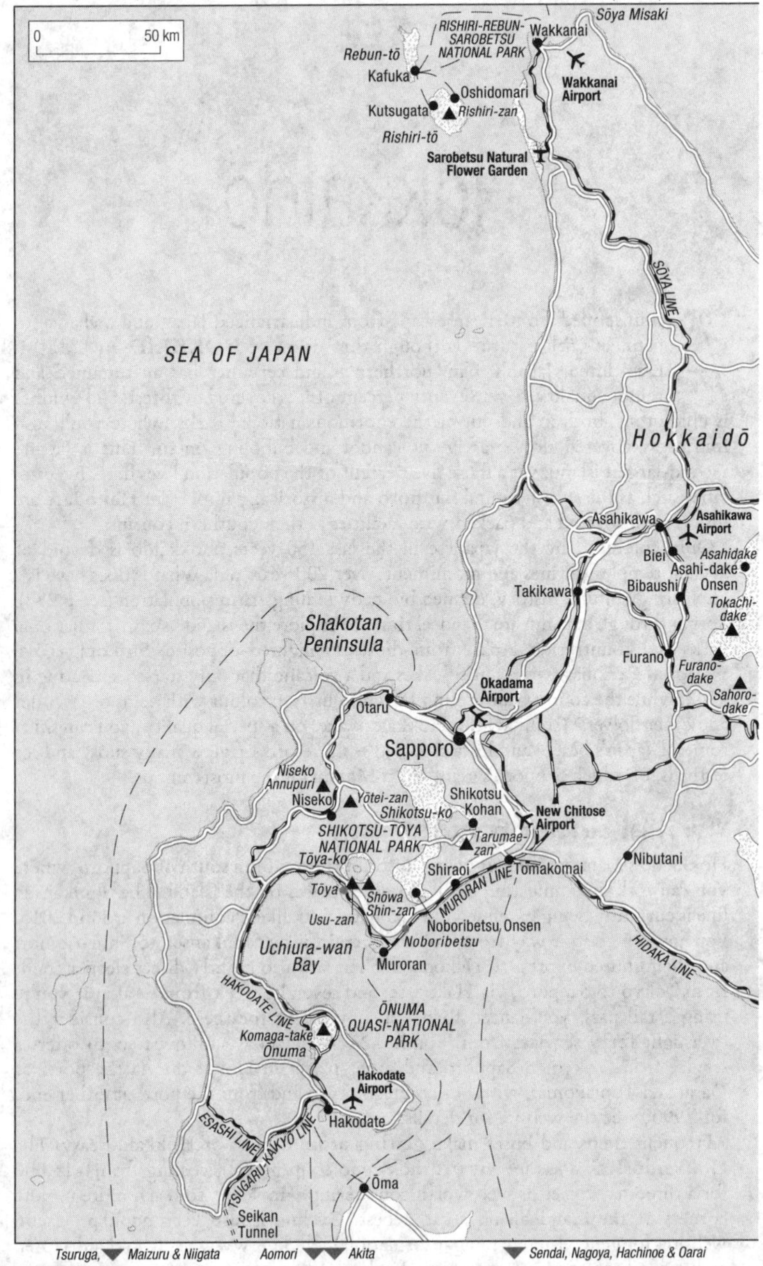
Korsakov (Sakhalin)
Sōya Misaki
0 50 km
RISHIRI-REBUN-SAROBETSU NATIONAL PARK
Wakkanai
Rebun-tō
Kafuka
Wakkanai Airport
Oshidomari
Kutsugata
Rishiri-zan
Rishiri-tō
Sarobetsu Natural Flower Garden
SŌYA LINE
SEA OF JAPAN
Hokkaidō
Asahikawa
Asahikawa Airport
Biei
Asahidake
Asahi-dake Onsen
Bibaushi
Takikawa
Tokachi-dake
Shakotan Peninsula
Furano
Furano-dake
Okadama Airport
Sahoro-dake
Otaru
Sapporo
Niseko Annupuri
Niseko
Yōtei-zan
Shikotsu Kohan
Shikotsu-ko
New Chitose Airport
SHIKOTSU-TŌYA NATIONAL PARK
Tarumae-zan
Tōya-ko
Nibutani
Shiraoi
Tomakomai
Tōya
Shōwa Shin-zan
MURORAN LINE
Usu-zan
Noboribetsu Onsen
Noboribetsu
Uchiura-wan Bay
Muroran
HIDAKA LINE
HAKODATE LINE
ŌNUMA QUASI-NATIONAL PARK
Komaga-take
Ōnuma
Hakodate Airport
Hakodate
ESASHI LINE
TSUGARU-KAIKYO LINE
Ōma
Seikan Tunnel
Tsuruga, Maizuru & Niigata
Aomori
Akita
Sendai, Nagoya, Hachinoe & Oarai

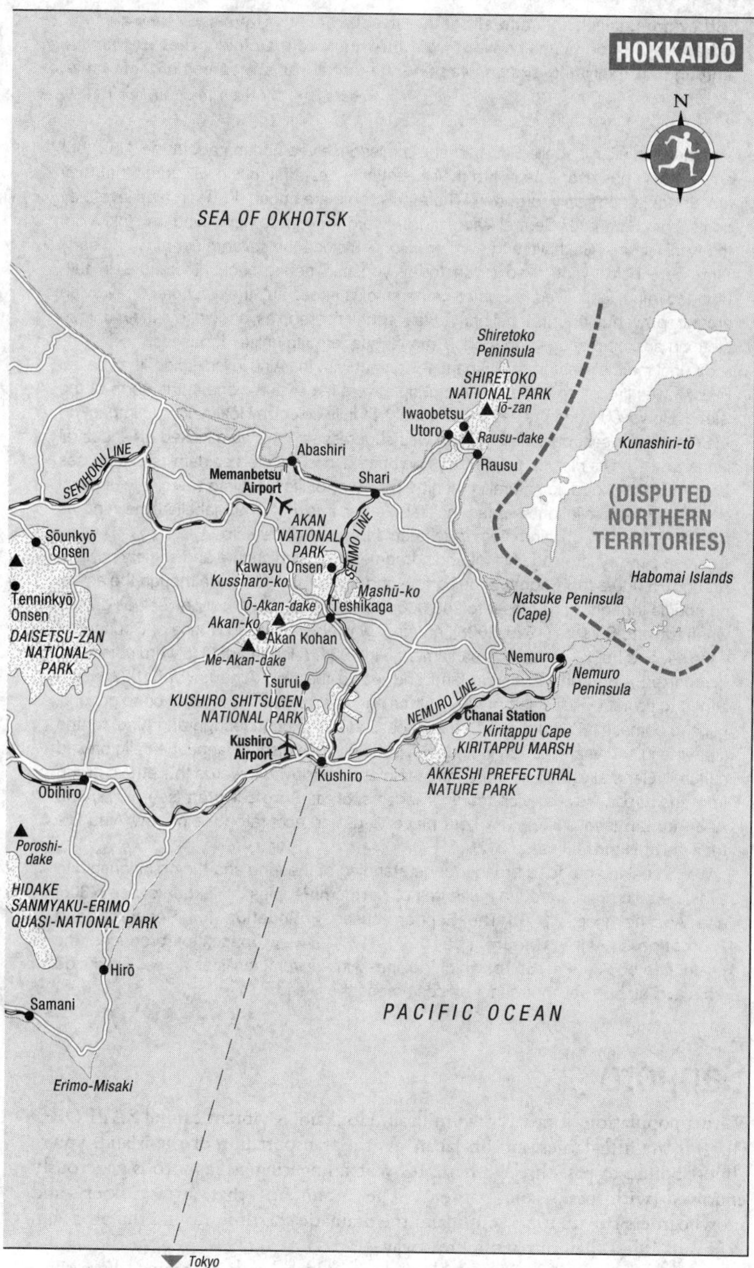
HOKKAIDŌ
N
SEA OF OKHOTSK
Shiretoko Peninsula
SHIRETOKO NATIONAL PARK
Iō-zan
Iwaobetsu
Utoro
Rausu-dake
Rausu
Kunashiri-tō
Abashiri
SEKIHOKU LINE
Memanbetsu Airport
Shari
(DISPUTED NORTHERN TERRITORIES)
AKAN NATIONAL PARK
SENMO LINE
Sōunkyō Onsen
Kawayu Onsen
Kussharo-ko
Mashū-ko
Habomai Islands
Tenninkyō Onsen
Ō-Akan-dake
Teshikaga
Natsuke Peninsula (Cape)
Akan-ko
Akan Kohan
DAISETSU-ZAN NATIONAL PARK
Me-Akan-dake
Nemuro
Nemuro Peninsula
Tsurui
KUSHIRO SHITSUGEN NATIONAL PARK
NEMURO LINE
Chanai Station
Kiritappu Cape
KIRITAPPU MARSH
Kushiro Airport
Kushiro
AKKESHI PREFECTURAL NATURE PARK
Obihiro
Poroshi-dake
HIDAKE SANMYAKU-ERIMO QUASI-NATIONAL PARK
Hirō
Samani
PACIFIC OCEAN
Erimo-Misaki
Tokyo

The Ainu

...they are uncivilizable and altogether irreclaimable savages, yet they are attractive ...I hope I shall never forget the music of their low sweet voices, the soft light of their mild, brown eyes and the wonderful sweetness of their smile.

Isabella Bird, *Unbeaten Tracks in Japan*, 1880.

Victorian traveller Isabella Bird had some misconceived notions about the **Ainu**, but anyone who has ever listened to their hauntingly beautiful music will agree that they are a people not easily forgotten. The Ainu's roots are uncertain – some believe they come from Siberia or Central Asia, and they are thought to have lived on Hokkaidō, the Kuril Islands, Sakhalin and northern Honshū since the seventh century. The early Ainu were hairy, wide-eyed (even today you can notice such differences in full-blooded Ainu) and lived a hunter-gatherer existence, but their culture – revolving around powerful **animist** beliefs – was sophisticated, as shown by their unique clothing and epic songs and stories in a language quite unlike Japanese.

Up until the Meiji restoration Japanese contact with the Ainu in Hokkaidō, then called Ezochi, was limited to trade and the people were largely left alone in the north of the island. However, when the Japanese sought to fully colonize Hokkaidō, the impact on the Ainu was disastrous. Their culture was suppressed, they were kicked off ancestral lands, saw forests cleared where they had hunted, and suffered epidemics of diseases from which they had no natural immunity. Their way of life went into seemingly terminal decline and assimilation seemed inevitable after a law of 1899 labelled the Ainu as former aborigines, obliging them to take on Japanese citizenship.

Over a century later, against all odds, fragments of Ainu culture and society remain. Around 25,000 people admit to being full- and part-blooded Ainu (although the actual number is thought to be closer to 200,000). A tiny piece of political power was gained when Kayano Shigeru (1926–2006), an Ainu, was elected to the House of Councillors – the second house of Japan's parliament – in 1994. A landmark legal verdict in 1997 recognized Ainu rights over the land and led to the New Ainu Law of 1997 which aimed to protect what is left of Ainu culture and ensure that it is passed on to generations to come. In 2008 Japan's Diet also passed a resolution recognizing Ainu, for the first time in 140 years, as "an indigenous people with a distinct language, religion and culture". Generally, there is more interest in and sensitivity towards this ethnic group from the Japanese who visit tourist villages such as **Poroto Kotan** (see p.312) and **Akan-kohan** (see p.330). The best place to get an accurate idea of how Ainu live today is at **Nibutani** (see p.312).

Worth seeking out for a broader understanding of the Ainu and their relationship to similar ethnic groups are the museums of Northern Peoples in Hakodate (see p.306) and Abashiri (see p.326). The Sapporo-based **Foundation for Research and Promotion of Ainu Culture** (ⓣ011/271-4171, ⓦwww.frpac.or.jp) produces the useful free booklet *Payean ro*, which outlines Ainu cultural facilities across Hokkaidō – it's available at several tourist offices across the island.

Sapporo

With a population of nearly two million, Hokkaidō's vibrant capital **SAPPORO** (札幌) is the fifth-largest city in Japan. As the transport hub of the island, you're almost bound to pass through here. It's worth lingering as Sapporo is generously endowed with parks and gardens. The mountains that attract skiers and snowboarders rise up to its south, and the dramatic coastline around the Shakotan Peninsula is less than thirty minutes away.

Sapporo is also synonymous with its beer, which has been brewed here since 1891; a visit to the handsome, late nineteenth-century **Sapporo Brewery** is a must, as is a stroll through the grounds and museums of the **Botanical Gardens**, which date from the same era. After dark, the bars and restaurants of **Susukino** (pronounced "suskino") spark to life and you'd be hard pressed to find a livelier nightlife district outside of Tokyo or Ōsaka.

Pleasantly cool temperatures tempt many visitors to Sapporo's **Summer Festival** (usually July 21–Aug 20), which features outdoor beer gardens and other events in **Ōdōri-kōen**, the swathe of parkland that cuts through the city centre. This park is also the focus of activity during the fabulous **Yuki Matsuri**, a snow festival held every February (see below).

Sapporo's name comes from the Ainu word for the area, *Sari-poro-betsu*, meaning "a river which runs along a plain filled with reeds". The city's easy-to-follow grid-plan layout was designed in the 1870s by a team of European and American experts engaged by the government to advise on Hokkaidō's development. Statues of these advisers can be found around Sapporo; the most famous (overlooking the city from atop Hitsujigaoka hill in the south) is the one of the American **Dr William S. Clark**, who set up Hokkaidō University and whose invocation to his students – "Boys, be ambitious!" – has been adopted as the city's motto.

Arrival and information

New Chitose airport (新千歳空港; ⓣ0123/23-0111, ⓦwww.new-chitose-airport.jp) is 40km southeast of Sapporo. From here, the fastest way to Sapporo is on the frequent JR train (35min; ¥1040); the bus is cheaper (¥1000) but takes at least twice as long to arrive at the same point. There are also a few flights from Tokyo and Sendai to **Okadama airport** (札幌丘珠空港; ⓣ011/781-4161, ⓦwww.okadama-airport.co.jp), 8km northeast of Sapporo, but it's mainly for services within Hokkaidō; a regular bus (30min; ¥400) runs from here to opposite the JR Sapporo station; the same journey by taxi costs around ¥3000.

Arriving by **train**, you'll pull in at busy JR Sapporo Station, six blocks north of **Ōdōri-kōen**, the **park** that bisects Sapporo from east to west. Long-distance **buses** terminate at Chūō Bus Terminal just northeast of Ōdōri-kōen and Sapporo Station Bus Terminal on the south side of the train station beneath the Esta

The Yuki Matsuri and other snow festivals

Sapporo's famous snow festival, the **Yuki Matsuri** (ⓦwww.snowfes.com), has its origins in the winter of 1950, when six small snow statues were created by high-school children in Ōdōri-kōen, the city's main park. The idea caught on and by 1955 the Self Defence Force (the Japanese military) was pitching in to help build gigantic snow sculptures, which included intricately detailed copies of world landmarks such as the Taj Mahal.

Running from around February 5–11 and spread across three sites (Ōdōri-kōen, Susukino and Sapporo Tsudome), the festival now includes an international **snow sculpture** competition and many other events, such as snowboard jumping and nightly music performances in the park. Arrive one week in advance and you'll be able to see the statues being made, as well as take part in the construction, since at least one giant statue in Ōdōri-kōen is a community effort – all you need do is turn up and offer your services. **Book** transport and accommodation well ahead of time: with two million visitors flooding into Sapporo during the *matsuri*, finding last-minute options for both can be a challenge.

If you don't make it to Sapporo's snow festival, there are several others around Hokkaidō that take place in January and February, including at Abashiri (see p.325), Asahikawa (see p.314), Otaru (see p.298), Shikotsu-ko (see p.313), and Sōunkyō (see p.317).

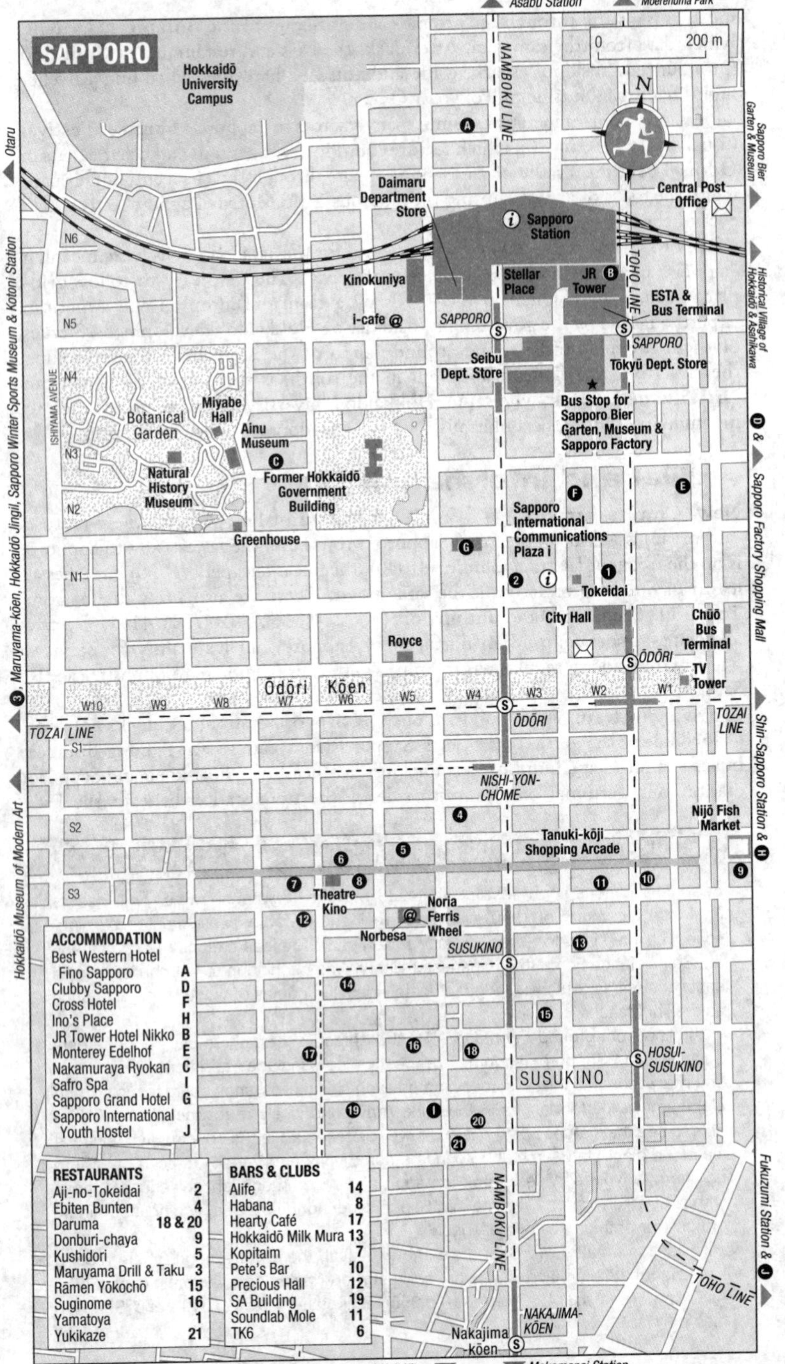
SAPPORO
Asabu Station
Sakaemachi Station & Moerenuma Park
0 200 m
N
Hokkaidō University Campus
NAMBOKU LINE
Otaru
Sapporo Bier Garten & Museum
Daimaru Department Store
Central Post Office
Sapporo Station
N6
Kinokuniya
Stellar Place
JR Tower
TOHO LINE
Historical Village of Hokkaidō & Asahikawa
ESTA & Bus Terminal
i-cafe
SAPPORO
N5
Seibu Dept. Store
Tōkyū Dept. Store
N4
ISHIYAMA AVENUE
Botanical Garden
Miyabe Hall
Ainu Museum
Bus Stop for Sapporo Bier Garten, Museum & Sapporo Factory
D &
N3
Natural History Museum
Former Hokkaidō Government Building
Sapporo Factory Shopping Mall
N2
Sapporo International Communications Plaza i
Greenhouse
N1
Tokeidai
City Hall
Chūō Bus Terminal
Royce
ŌDŌRI
TV Tower
3, Maruyama-kōen, Hokkaidō Jingū, Sapporo Winter Sports Museum & Kotoni Station
W10 W9 W8 W7 Ōdōri Kōen W6 W5 W4 W3 W2 W1
TOZAI LINE
S1
NISHI-YON-CHŌME
Shin-Sapporo Station & H
S2
Nijō Fish Market
Tanuki-kōji Shopping Arcade
Hokkaidō Museum of Modern Art
S3
Theatre Kino
Noria Ferris Wheel
Norbesa
SUSUKINO
HOSUI-SUSUKINO
ACCOMMODATION
Best Western Hotel Fino Sapporo A
Clubby Sapporo D
Cross Hotel F
Ino's Place H
JR Tower Hotel Nikko B
Monterey Edelhof E
Nakamuraya Ryokan C
Safro Spa I
Sapporo Grand Hotel G
Sapporo International Youth Hostel J
RESTAURANTS
Aji-no-Tokeidai 2
Ebiten Bunten 4
Daruma 18 & 20
Donburi-chaya 9
Kushidori 5
Maruyama Drill & Taku 3
Rāmen Yōkochō 15
Suginome 16
Yamatoya 1
Yukikaze 21
BARS & CLUBS
Alife 14
Habana 8
Hearty Café 17
Hokkaidō Milk Mura 13
Kopitaim 7
Pete's Bar 10
Precious Hall 12
SA Building 19
Soundlab Mole 11
TK6 6
Fukuzumi Station & J
NAKAJIMA-KŌEN
Nakajima-kōen
Sapporo Concert Hall Kitara
Makomanai Station

Sapporo addresses

Finding your way around central Sapporo is easy compared to many other Japanese cities because every address has a precise location within the city's **grid plan**. The city blocks are named and numbered according to the compass points, the apex being the **TV Tower** in Ōdōri-kōen. Sapporo Station, for example, is six blocks north of the TV Tower and three blocks west, so its address is Kita 6 (North Six), Nishi 3 (West Three), while **Nijō Fish Market** is Minami 3 (South Three), Higashi 1-2 (West One-Two).

shopping complex. The closest **ferry** port to Sapporo is Otaru (see p.298), 40km to the northwest.

Sapporo has several excellent tourist information facilities, all staffed by English speakers. Start your visit at the **Hokkaidō-Sapporo Food and Tourism Information Centre** (daily 8.30am–8pm; ⓣ011/213-5088, ⓦwww.welcome.city.sapporo.jp), inside Sapporo Station. You can sort out train tickets and rail passes here, as well as access the internet and do some food souvenir shopping. More leaflets, along with English books, magazines, free internet access and a jobs and events noticeboard, are available at the **Sapporo International Communications Plaza "i"** (Mon–Sat 9am–5.30pm; ⓣ011/211-3678, ⓦwww.plaza-sapporo.or.jp), on the 3rd floor of the MN Building, opposite the **Tokeidai**, the city's famous clock tower. Also look out for the monthly free magazine *Sapporo Source* (ⓦwww.sapporosource.com), available at the tourist offices, many hotels and bars around town.

City transport

Most of Sapporo's sights are within easy **walking** distance of each other, but the efficient network of subways and buses can be useful if you get tired. There are three **subway** lines: the green **Namboku line** and the blue **Tōhō line** run from north to south through Sapporo Station, while the orange **Tozai line** intersects them both, running east to west under Ōdōri-kōen. The lowest fare is ¥200, which covers all the stops in the city centre between Sapporo Station in the north and Nakajima-kōen in the south, and Maruyama-kōen in the west and Higashi Sapporo in the east. There's also a purple **tram** line, which for a flat fare of ¥170 runs from Nishi-Yon-Chōme, just south of Ōdōri-kōen, out to Mount Moiwa, south of the city, and back to Susukino. **Buses** depart from in front of the Esta building next to Sapporo Station or nearby; fares start at ¥200.

There are all-day **passes** for the subway (¥800) or a combined all-day pass covering the subway, tram and the city routes of the JR, Jotetsu and Chūō bus lines for ¥1000 (¥500 on Sat, Sun and holidays). For long-term visitors the "Withyou" travel card, which gives ten percent extra travel for free and is valid on all types of transport, is useful. Public transport stops running at around 11.30pm, after which you can hail one of the many **taxis** that roam Sapporo's streets. Call the Taxi Association (ⓣ011/892-6000; Japanese only) to book one.

Accommodation

Even though Sapporo has plenty of **accommodation**, many places get booked up well in advance of the summer season and the snow festival in February. There can be great bargains to be had at the upmarket hotels in winter, when rates are slashed. The bulk of the hotels are clustered around Sapporo Station, but if it's nightlife you're after then you are better off staying in Susukino. If you can't find a room in town, consider staying at nearby Otaru (see p.298).

Best Western Hotel Fino Sapporo Kita 8, Nishi 4-15 ⓣ011/729-4055, ⓦwww.bwjapan.co.jp/finosapporo. The stylish design in a natural palette of colours helps this business hotel stand out from the crowd around the station. Bathrooms include massage showers and there's a pleasant café next to the lobby where the buffet breakfast is served. ❻

Hotel Clubby Sapporo Kita 2, Higashi 3 ⓣ011/242-1111. This smart hotel is part of the Sapporo Factory redevelopment. Leather and wood fittings lend an old-fashioned air to the lobby and restaurant, but the rooms are modern, spacious and elegantly decorated. ❼

Cross Hotel 2-23 Kita, Nishi 2 ⓣ011/272-0010, ⓦwww.crosshotel.com. The city's best boutique-style hotel offers rooms in three appealing decorative styles (natural, urban and hip), a relaxing rooftop pool and bath and a cool lounge bar. ❼

Ino's Place 4-6-5 3jo, Higashi-Sapporo, Shiroishi-ku ⓣ011/832-1828, ⓦwww.inos-place.com. Few – if any – hostels have a juggling shop but there's one at this cosy, welcoming place run by the wonderfully friendly Eiji and Miwa (who both speak fluent English). Internet access, a well-equipped kitchen and pleasant lounge are other advantages. It's a 5min walk from Shiroishi subway station on the Tozai line – check their website for instructions on how to get there. Dorm beds ¥2900, single ¥3800.

JR Tower Hotel Nikko Sapporo Kita 5, Nishi 2 ⓣ011/251-222, ⓦwww.jrhotels.co.jp. Dazzling views are guaranteed from the smallish rooms and the 35th-floor bar and restaurant of this luxury hotel, which occupies the top dozen floors of the JR Tower atop Sapporo Station. Facilities include a spa on the 22nd floor which has real onsen water pumped in. Rates are reduced by twenty percent if you have a JR rail card. ❼

Hotel Monterey Edelhof Kita 2, Nishi 1 ⓣ011/242-7111, ⓦwww.hotelmonterey.co.jp. Designed to evoke Vienna at the turn of the nineteenth century this upmarket hotel has a quirky charm. There's also a fancy spa on the fourteenth floor (guests/non-guests ¥1515/2725). ❽

Nakamuraya Ryokan 中村屋旅館 Kita 3, Nishi 7 ⓣ011/241-2111, ⓦwww.nakamura-ya.com. This high-quality Japanese inn near the Botanical Garden is a wonderful choice. The tatami rooms are spacious, the maids wear kimono and there's a large communal bath and café in the lobby. ❺

Safro Spa Minami 6, Nishi 5 ⓣ011/531-2233, ⓦwww.safro.org. Amazingly luxurious and excellent-value capsule hotel in the heart of Susukino. Facilities include ornamental baths, a gym and a mini-cinema. There's also a floor of capsules for women. Check-in from 5pm. Add ¥500 to the ¥4100 entry charge on weekends. ❷

Sapporo Grand Hotel Kita 1, Nishi 4 ⓣ011/261-3311, ⓦwww.grand1934.com. Dating back to 1934, the city's first European-style hotel has undergone a successful facelift in recent years. Among the vast range of rooms are some very nicely remodelled ones and there's an unbeatable range of facilities, including a spa and small display area on the hotel and city's history. ❼

Sapporo International Youth Hostel Toyohira 6-5-35 6jo, Toyohira ⓣ011/825-3120, ⓦwww.youthhostel.or.jp/kokusai. Just east of Exit 2 of Gakuen-Mae Station on the Tōhō-line, this large modern hostel has dorm rooms, tatami rooms for families, and twins for married couples. English spoken. Dorm beds ¥3800/person. ❹

The City

Seeing central Sapporo's sights will fill a day – most visitors make a beeline for the **Sapporo Bier Garten and Beer Museum** but also make time to explore the **Botanical Gardens** or the entertaining **Sapporo Winter Sports Museum**. Head out of the city centre to see the **Historical Village of Hokkaidō**, a huge landscaped park featuring more than sixty restored buildings from the island's frontier days. **Moerenuma**, a park designed by the late Japanese-American sculptor Isamu Noguchi, also makes for a pleasant half-day trip.

Botanical Gardens

A ten-minute walk southwest of Sapporo Station is the compact and pretty **Botanical Gardens** (植物園; gardens: May–Sept 9am–4pm; Oct 9am–3.30pm; closed Mon; ¥400; greenhouse only: Nov–April Mon–Fri 10am–3pm, Sat 10am–noon; ¥100), Kita 3, Nishi 8. Immediately to the right as you enter is the small but interesting **Ainu Museum**, known as the "Batchelor Kinenkan" in memory of the Reverend John Batchelor, a British priest and author of *The Ainu* *of Japan*, considered to be the definitive work on Hokkaidō's indigenous people. The museum has a collection of around 2500 Ainu artefacts (though only a fraction is displayed at any time), ranging from clothes made of bird skins from the Kuril islands to a sacred altar for performing the ritual slaughter of a bear cub – there are English-language captions. Following the red-gravel pathway around to the right of the museum leads you to **Miyabe Hall**, with intriguing displays of letters and journals belonging to Professor Miyabe Kingo, the first director of Hokkaidō University, who established the gardens in 1886. Miyabe's descriptions of his travels abroad, written in English and illustrated with photographs, make fascinating reading.

The gardens themselves are very attractive, with a long pond, a greenhouse, a rockery, shaded forest walks and neat flower gardens, including a collection which shows the plants and flowers used by the Ainu in their daily lives. In the centre of it all stands the **Natural History Museum**, housed in a pale green wooden building dating from 1882. Inside you'll find a staggering collection of bizarre stuffed animals, such as snarling wolves and huge sea lions, as well as other curiosities including a dog sled from Sakhalin.

The University and Former Government Building

More attractive late nineteenth-century buildings are dotted throughout the campus of **Hokkaidō University**, at Kita 8, Nishi 7, northwest of Sapporo Station, including the one housing the university's **museum** (10am–4pm; closed Mon; free). Also look out for the Model Barn, a big wooden structure built in 1877.

On your way to or from the gardens, swing by the **Former Hokkaidō Government Building** (赤れんが; daily 8.45am–6pm; free), at Kita 3, Nishi 6. This palatial red-brick building, dating to 1888, is a fine example of the local architecture that fused the late, nineteenth-century European and New World influences flooding into the country with Japanese traditions. Inside, the wood-panelled interiors have been nicely maintained and hung with large-scale historical paintings.

Ōdōri-kōen and around

Five blocks south of Sapporo Station, opposite the Sapporo International Communication Plaza, is the **Tokeidai** (時計台; 8.45am–5pm; closed Mon; ¥200), Kita 1, Nishi 2, a wooden clock tower that's one of the city's key landmarks. You'd be right in thinking that this wood-clad building would look more at home somewhere like Boston, because that's where it was made in 1878; inside is an uninspiring exhibition on the building's history. One block south lies Ōdōri-kōen and the contrasting 147m red steel **Sapporo TV Tower** (Ⓦwww.tv-tower.co.jp, April 9.30am–10pm; May–Oct 9am–10pm; Nov–March 9.30am–9.30pm; ¥700), at Ōdōri Nishi 1. During the snow festival, the viewing platform provides a lovely vista down the park, particularly at night.

The neon-illuminated excess of **Susukino** (すすきの), the largest area of bars, restaurants and nightclubs north of Tokyo, begins on the southern side of Ōdōri-kōen, and is best explored at night. If you're here during the day, you could follow the covered shopping arcade **Tanuki-kōji** to its eastern end where you'll find the lively **Nijō Fish Market** (二条市場), Minami 3, Higashi 1-2, ideal for lunch or a fresh sushi breakfast (see p.296).

Four blocks west of the end of Ōdōri-kōen, the large, white **Hokkaidō Museum of Modern Art** (北海道立近代美術館; 10am–5pm; closed Mon; ¥450 for permanent exhibition), Kita 1, Nishi 17, holds a modest but absorbing collection of paintings and sculptures, some by Japanese artists. The nearest subway station is Nishi Juhatchōme, on the Tozai line.

If you've not yet had your fill of parks, **Nakajima-kōen** (中島公園), Minami 9, Nishi 4, is the third of central Sapporo's large-scale green spots and is worth visiting to see the **Hasso-an**, an early Edo-period teahouse.

Sapporo Bier Garten and Beer Museum

The hugely popular **Sapporo Bier Garten and Beer Museum** (サッポロビール博物館; daily 9am–5.30pm; free) stands just east of the city centre. It was an American adviser to Hokkaidō who noted the hops growing locally and realized that with its abundant winter ice Sapporo was the ideal location for a commercial brewery. When the first brewery opened in 1876, locals didn't touch beer, so for years Sapporo exported to the foreign community in Tokyo, which is where the company's headquarters are now.

Built in 1891, this grand red-brick complex was originally the factory of the Sapporo Sugar Company; it's now Sapporo's smallest brewery since much of the building has been turned over to an exhibition on the brewing process and the history of the company, not to mention several restaurants, pubs and souvenir shops. At the end of the exhibition, while sipping beer samples (one for ¥200, three for ¥400), you can admire a wall coated with a century's worth of colourful ad posters.

Bus #88 runs every 30 minutes directly to the complex (¥200) from behind Tōkyū department store, near Sapporo Station. The bus goes via the **Sapporo Factory**, Kita 2, Higashi 4, the first of Sapporo's breweries in the city, converted in 1993 into a shopping and entertainment complex.

Maruyama-kōen and around

The upscale suburb of Maruyama-kōen is where you'll find the island's principal Shinto shrine **Hokkaidō Jingū** (北海道神宮; Ⓦwww.hokkaidojingu.or.jp) amid a leafy park where 1400 cherry trees break into spectacular blossom each May.

From Maruyama-kōen subway station hop on bus #14 to reach the fun **Sapporo Winter Sports Museum** (daily: May–Oct 9am–6pm; Nov–April 9.30am–5pm; ¥600; Ⓦwww.sapporo-dc.co.jp). Occupying the Ski Jump Stadium at Okurayama (大倉山) built for the 1972 Winter Olympics, the museum's highlight is a ski jump simulator that gives you an idea of what it's like to participate in this daring winter sport. There are also simulations for bobsledding, cross-country skiing and speed skating, among other things – it's all a hoot, and afterwards you can ride the passenger lift (¥500 return) to the top of the ski jump to see the view for real. From the bus stop the museum is about ten minutes' walk uphill; a taxi from Maruyama-kōen station is around ¥1000.

Historical Village of Hokkaidō

One of Hokkaidō's highlights is the **Historical Village of Hokkaidō** (北海道開拓の村; May–Sept 9am–4.30pm; ¥830; Oct–Apr 9.30am–4pm; ¥680; closed Mon; Ⓦwww.kaitaku.or.jp), some 14km east of the city centre. This impressive museum, laid out across a spacious park, gathers together some sixty buildings constructed around Hokkaidō between the mid-nineteenth and early twentieth centuries, as large-scale immigration from Honshū cranked up. Wandering around the village's four main areas, representing town, farm, mountain and fishing communities, will give you a strong impression of what Hokkaidō looked like before prefabricated buildings and concrete expressways became the norm.

The buildings have been restored as beautifully inside as out and spruced up with displays related to their former use, be it a sweet shop, a silkworm house or a woodcutter's shanty. There are guides in some houses (explanations in Japanese only) and written English explanations in all. It's a good idea to wear slip-on shoes,

Winter sports in Sapporo

As you'd expect for the location of the 1972 Winter Olympics, there are several good ski hills within easy reach of Sapporo including **Teine** (Ⓦwww.sapporo-teine.com), **Kokusai** (Ⓦwww.sapporo-kokusai.jp) and **Takino Snow World** (Ⓦwww.takinopark.com) which offers six cross-country ski courses from 5–16km long.

At **Snowmobile Land** (Ⓣ011/661-5355, Ⓦsnowmobileland.jp), you can take a ride on one of the eponymous machines over a 90km course that winds through the forests to viewpoints looking out over the city and, most dramatically, into the base of a quarry. Rates start at ¥7000 for 30 minutes, but if you sign up for the full run (¥13,500) it includes pick up from Sapporo and all protective gear. To reach the course (usually open from Dec through to the end of March), take the subway to Maruyama-kōen, then bus #41 to Fukui Entei-mae, or call ahead to book a place on their free shuttle bus.

as you'll be taking them off a lot to explore the interiors. In summer, you can hop aboard the horse-drawn trolley car (¥270) that plies the main street – in winter this is replaced by a sleigh. Some of the houses are shut from December to April (hence the reduced admission fee), but the village is worth visiting even then for its special atmosphere when blanketed in snow.

To cover the whole site will take you at least half a day; you can bring a picnic or there are a couple of inexpensive **restaurants** and refreshment stops within the village. You can extend your visit by exploring the neighbouring grounds of **Nopporo Forest Park**, created to commemorate Hokkaidō's centennial, which contains the mildly interesting **Historical Museum of Hokkaidō** (9.30am–4.30pm; closed Mon; ¥300) and **Centennial Memorial Tower**, a 100m-tall metal spike which you can ascend for a free view of the city.

Buses run directly to the Historical Village each morning from stop #3 at the south exit of Sapporo Station, taking around an hour. There are more frequent buses from platform 10 at the terminus beneath Shin Sapporo Station, connected to the city centre by both train and subway. A taxi from Shin Sapporo to the park will cost you around ¥1000. Alternatively, take a train from Sapporo Station to Shinrin Kōen Station (¥260) and then a bus from there to the park.

Moerenuma Park

A forty-minute subway and bus ride northwest of the city centre, **Moerenuma Park** (モエレ沼公園; Ⓦwww.sapporo-park.or.jp/moere) is part playground, part sculpture garden, displaying the works of internationally renowned artist **Isamu Noguchi** (see p.601). In the giant glass pyramid, with observation decks and a library/lounge, you can peruse English-language books about the artist, who died shortly after completing the masterplan for the park in 1988. With massed plantings of cherry trees, wide lawns, the spectacular Sea Fountain water sculpture and a shallow pebbled bathing beach, the park is popular with local families, and a convivial spot for a picnic.

To reach it, take the subway to Kanjō-dōri station. From the bus terminal above the station take bus #69 or #79 (¥320) and get off at Moere-kōen-higashiguchi, from where the park is a five-minute walk.

Eating

Sapporo is renowned for its **ramen** – try the version called *batā-kōn*, which is a noodle broth laden with butter and corn. Another local speciality is the lamb *jingisukan* barbecue (see box, p.296).

Meal fit for a Khan

Lamb is an uncommon meat on Japanese menus but not in Sapporo, home of the *jingisukan*, or "Genghis Khan" barbecue. This delicious feast of flame-grilled meat and vegetables gets its name from the convex table grill on which it's cooked, said to resemble the Mongolian-warrior's helmet. All of the restaurants at the **Sapporo Bier Garten** (ⓣ0120-150-550, ⓦwww.sapporo-bier-garten.jp, daily 11.30am–9pm) next to the Sapporo Beer Museum (see p.294) offer the dish, as does the rival beer garden **Kirin Biiru-en** (キリンビール園; Minami 10, Nishi 1 ⓣ011/533-3000). At either you can pig out on as much barbecue and beer as you can within one hundred minutes, for a set price of around ¥3700. You'll be provided with a plastic bib to protect against dribbles from the dipping sauce, but it's still best to dress down, since the smell of sizzled mutton lingers long after you've left. The big beer gardens, packed with tourists, have a boisterous Germanic quality; for a more intimate *jingisukan* experience try *Daruma* (see below).

Other easy options include the many outlets on the restaurant floor of **Stellar Place** above Sapporo Station or those in the upscale shopping centre **Maruyama Class** above Maruyama-kōen station. For the restaurants below, where we've given a telephone number it's advisable to book ahead.

Aji-no-Tokeidai 味の時計台 Kita 1, Nishi 3. A dependable and inexpensive noodle chain, serving large tasty bowls of ramen. You'll be asked whether you want your soup flavoured with miso, *shōyu* (soy sauce) or *shio* (salt).

Daruma だるま Minami 5, Nishi 4. This is the original cosy 15-seater branch of this *jingisukan* joint; it's tucked away on a narrow street in the midst of Susukino; look for the red lantern and scowling bald Genghis on the sign outside. One plate of meat costs ¥735. If full, you could try the larger places at Minami 6, Nishi 4 and Minami 4, Nishi 4. Mon–Thurs 5pm–2.30am, Fri & Sat until 4.30am, Sun until 12.30am.

Donburi-chaya どんぶり茶屋 Nijo Ichiba, Minami 3, Higashi 1-2, within Nijō Fish Market. There's often a queue of people waiting here for the rice bowls topped with a selection of fresh seafood for around ¥1500. The miso soup comes with crab and they also do a *jingisukan* and scallop rice bowl combo. Open 7am–5.30pm; closed Wed.

Ebiten Bunten 蛯天分店 Minami 2, Nishi 4 ⓦwww.ebiten.co.jp. Great-value tempura restaurant, with a stuffed brown bear for decoration. You can get a meal of rice topped by plump batter-covered prawns for under ¥1000.

Kushidori 串鳥 Minami 2, Nishi 5. A row of red lanterns dangles from the front of this busy *yakitori* joint. Sit at the counter to take in the full atmosphere of the place. An English menu eases ordering from a wide range of skewered delights, starting around ¥115 a serving. Daily 5pm–1am.

Maruyama Drill & Taku Kita 1, Nishi 27 ⓣ011/213-7374. A cute café-bar serving an appealing range of inexpensive curry rice dishes as well as gourmet burgers and home-made apple, orange and tomato juice. Downstairs in the same building is the Zen-minimalist *Taku* (ⓣ011/615 2929) where the menu promises a taste of the island's best produce. It's a block west of Maruyama-kōen subway station, behind the bus station. Daily 11am-midnight

Rāmen Yōkochō ラーメン横丁 Minami 5, Nishi 3. Of the scores of ramen joints crammed into a narrow, atmospheric alley in the heart of Susukino, this place is one of the better choices. A huge bowl of freshly cooked noodles costs around ¥1000. Daily around 11am–2am.

Suginome 杉ノ目 Minami 5, Nishi 5 ⓣ011/521-0888. Housed in a historic stone building, this traditionally decorated place is a good spot in which to sample *kaiseki*-style course meals made using local produce from ¥7350. Mon–Sat 5–11pm.

Yamatoya 大和家 Kita 1, Nishi 2 ⓣ011/241-6353. Reasonably priced, unassuming sushi and tempura shop behind the Clock Tower that gets the nod from local foodies. Mon–Fri 11am–10pm, Sat 11am–9.30pm.

Yukikaze 雪風 Minami 7, Nishi 4. There's often a queue of eager customers waiting at this convivial, late-night ramen shop where the noodle dish is made with loving care and better-than-average ingredients. Daily 9pm–4am.

Drinking, nightlife and entertainment

Amid the myriad hostess clubs and sex joints of the neon-drenched party district of **Susukino** there are plenty of reputable bars and restaurants – it's easy to avoid the sleazy places. The covered shopping arcade **Tanuki-kōji** also has a good selection of bars. In the summer, outdoor **beer gardens** sprout across the city including in Odori-kōen.

A popular date spot is the fluorescent multicoloured **Noria Ferris wheel** (daily 11am–3am; ¥600), atop the Norbesa shopping mall at Minami 3, Nishi 5. Major **dance clubs** include *Alife* (Minami 4, Nishi 6; Ⓦalife.jp), *Soundlab Mole* (Minami 3, Nishi 2; Ⓦwww.mole-sapporo.jp) and *Precious Hall* (Minami 4, Nishi 7; Ⓦwww.precioushall.com) – these last two sometimes host gay dance nights. For more on the clubbing scene check Ⓦwww.sapporolife.com/index2.html.

For classical and other popular music concerts there's **Sapporo Concert Hall Kitara** (Ⓣ011/520-2000, Ⓦwww.kitara-sapporo.or.jp), while **Theater Kino** (Minami 2, Nishi 6; Ⓣ011/231-9355) is a two-screen cinema showing mainly art-house films.

Habana Minami 3, Nishi 5. On the 2nd and 3rd floors along Tanuki-kōji shopping arcade, this Cuban-styled café-bar offers spicy chicken and rice entrées and lively Latin American music, plus occasional salsa parties.

Hokkaidō Milk Mura Minami 4, Nishi 3 Ⓣ011/219-6455. Hokkaidō is famous in Japan for the quality of its milk products, and in this quirkily decorated bar many flavours of ice cream are paired with alcohol to make original cocktails.

Kopitaim Minami 3, Nishi 7 Ⓣ011/219-7773. Take an instant holiday from Japan at this fairly authentic Southeast Asian-style café-bar at the far west end of Tanuki-kōji shopping arcade. It's a relaxed place for a drink or light bite to eat.

Pete's Bar Minami 3, Nishi 1 Ⓦwww.petesbar.jp. Offering a similar formula to TK6 (see below), this is another convivial *gaijin* bar with reasonable pub grub and committed regulars. There's live acoustic music on the last Thursday of the month.

TK6 Minami 2, Nishi 6 Ⓦwww.tk6.jp. At the western end of the Tanuki-kōji arcade, this spacious and relaxed *gaijin*-run café-bar serves Aussie meat pies, salads and burgers (around ¥800) with their draught ales.

Listings

Banks Bank of Tokyo Mitsubishi, Ōdōri, Nishi 3, changes all major currencies, as does the Ōdōri post office (one block west), the central post office (see p.298) and Hokkaidō Bank, Minami 1, Nishi 3.

Bookshops Kinokuniya, Kita 5, Nishi 5 (daily 10am–9pm), just west of Sapporo Station, has the best selection of English-language books and magazines.

Car rental Eki Rent-a-Car Ⓣ011/742-8211; Nippon Rent-a-Car Ⓣ011/746-0919; Orix Rent-a-Car Ⓣ011/241-0543.

Consulates Australia, Kita 1, Nishi 3-2 Ⓣ011/242-4381; China, Minami 13, Nishi 23 Ⓣ011/563-6191; South Korea, Kita 2, Nishi 12, Ⓣ011/621-0288; Russia, Minami 14, Nishi 12 Ⓣ011/561-3171; US, Kita 1, Nishi 28 Ⓣ011/641-1115.

Gay and lesbian Sapporo

Next to Tokyo, Sapporo has Japan's most visible gay and lesbian bar scene and even trumps the capital with its **Rainbow March** (Ⓦwww.rainbowmarch.org/english.html), Japan's longest-running lesbian, gay and transgender parade, held every September in Susukino. A relatively spacious bar where *gaijin* should receive a friendly welcome is **Hearty Café** (Minami 6, Nishi 7; Ⓣ011/530-6022); more hit and miss are the twenty-plus tiny gay bars in the **SA Building** (Minami 6, Nishi 6). Although it's slightly dated, the web document **Queer Hokkaidō** (Ⓦwww.hajet.org/lifearticles/Queer_Hokkaido.pdf) is also a useful reference with some recommendations for outside of Sapporo, too.

Emergencies The main police station is at Kita 1, Nishi 5 ⓣ011/242-0110. In an absolute emergency, contact the Foreign Advisory Service on ⓣ011/241-9110. For other emergency numbers, see p.71.
Hospital Sapporo City General Hospital, Kita 11, Nishi 13 ⓣ011/726-2211.
Internet Available at both main tourist offices (see p.291). Alternatively, there are plenty of internet cafés and manga cafés offering facilities; try the *i-café* with branches at Norbesa, Minami 3, Nishi 5, and *Sapporo Century Royal Hotel*, Kita 5, Nishi 5, near Sapporo Station. Rates start at ¥200 for 30min.
Laundry Shirokuma, Minami 8, Nishi 6.
Post office The central post office is at Kita 6, Higashi 1 (Mon–Fri 9am–7pm, Sat 9am–5pm, Sun 9am–12.30pm). There's also a branch in the Paseo shopping centre in the JR Sapporo station complex (Mon–Fri 10am–7pm, Sat & Sun 10am–5pm).
Shopping Sapporo has branches of all of Japan's top department stores, including Mitsukoshi, Seibu, Daimaru and Tōkyū. The covered shopping arcade Tanuki-kōji, stretching for six blocks across Minami 3, is worth exploring, as are the shopping malls Stellar Place (next to Sapporo Station) and Sapporo Factory (particularly good for outdoor clothing and camping gear). Another good outdoor gear shop is ICI Sports (*Ishii Supotsu*), Kita 11, Nishi 15, while for cross-country skis and gear head to Nissen Sports, Minami 3, Nishi 3. A good souvenir is chocolates from the city's top confectioners, Royce – their main shop faces Odori-kōen at Nishi 5.

Otaru

The attractive port of **OTARU** (小樽), some 40km northwest of Sapporo, grew rich at the turn of the nineteenth century on the back of herring fishing and as a base for the modern development of Hokkaidō. Reminders of this wealth remain in the shape of scores of handsome, heritage-listed Meiji-era buildings, many of which have been converted into hotels, restaurants, shops and bars. Parts of town are touristy, but to escape the crowds just hop on a bus to **Shukutsu** to find a couple of the best architectural examples from Otaru's glory days.

Arrival and information

Limited express **trains** (¥620) from Sapporo take 30–45 minutes to reach Otaru JR Station; **buses** and local trains to the city are slower and slightly cheaper. JR Hokkaidō's good-value **Sapporo-Otaru Welcome Pass** (¥1500), available to overseas visitors, includes a return train ticket and a one-day Sapporo subway ticket, which can be used on a separate day. There's also the Otaru Furii Kippu (¥1900) which combines return train travel from Sapporo with a Chūō bus one-day pass (¥750 if bought separately) to get around town.

Ferries (ⓣ0134/22-6191) from Niigata (see p.272) and Maizuru (north of Kyoto) dock at the ferry terminal, some 5km east of the train station. Regular buses run between the ferry terminal and the train station; a taxi will cost around ¥1000.

There's a helpful **tourist office** inside the station (daily 9am–6pm; ⓣ0134/29-1333).

Accommodation

Otaru has plenty of appealing, good-value **hotels**, so if Sapporo is booked up, consider staying here.

Kuramure 蔵群 2-685 Asarigawa Onsen ⓣ0134/51-5151, ⓦwww.kuramure.com. Nestling in a valley bubbling with hot springs, 20min drive from Otaru Chikko Station, this elegant modern ryokan combines contemporary design with traditional architectural touches. Rates include two meals. ⑨

Otaru Furukawa 小樽ふる川 2-15 Ironai ⓣ0134/29-2345, ⓦwww.otaru-furukawa.com. A pleasing mix of a traditional Japanese inn and Western-style hotel, offering great extras such as the opportunity to hire a private bath (¥2100 for 50min) with a view of the Otaru canal. ⑤–⑧

Otaru Guest House 3-9-5 Midori Otaru ⓣ0134/22-4162, ⓦwww.tengu.co.jp. This delightful guesthouse occupies a 1927 building combining Western and Japanese influences. There are three rooms in the main building and one in the attached *kura* (storehouse). Take bus #19 from Otaru Station to Shyōgyō Gakkō-mae. ⑤

Otaru Tenguyama Youth Hostel 2-13-1 Mogami Otaru ⓣ0134/33-7080, ⓦwww.tengu.co.jp. There are great views of Otaru from this pleasant pension-style hostel near the cable car up Tenguyama. Dorm beds ¥3300/person, private rooms ¥3800/person.

Hotel Vibrant 1-3-1 Ironai ⓣ0134/31-3939, ⓦwww.vibrant-otaru.jp. Occupying a former bank, the *Vibrant* offers good-value rooms, with wooden floors. Rates include breakfast served in the soaring ex-banking hall. Singles start at ¥5140. ④

The Town

Otaru's romantic, antique atmosphere is best experienced beside the *Otaru Unga* (小樽運河), the portside canal lined with brick warehouses, particularly the section between Chūō-dōri, the main street heading towards the harbour from the train station, and parallel Nichigin-dōri. **Sakai-machi Hon-dōri**, which shadows the canal to the south, is also worth exploring, particularly for its many cut and blown glass shops (an Otaru speciality); the main one to head to is **Kitaichi Glass Sangokan** (ⓦwww.kitaichiglass.co.jp), or, if you want to try your hand at the craft, **K's Blowing** (ⓦwww.ks-blowing.jp).

On Nichigin-dōri, **The Bank of Japan Otaru Museum** (日本銀行旧小樽支店金融資料館; 9.30am–5pm; closed Mon; free), a stone and brick structure dating

from 1912, was designed by Kingo Tatsuno, the architect of the original Tokyo Station. Look for the striped owl keystones decorating the exterior – the birds are guardian deities of the Ainu. Inside, the 105m-high ceiling of the main banking hall looks as impressive today as it must have to Otaru's citizens back in the early twentieth century.

Facing the canal to the left of Chūō-dōri is a small branch of the **Otaru Museum** (daily 9.30am–5pm; ¥400; ⓦtinyurl.com/2693sw2), which holds an average collection of historical and nature displays in a converted 1893 warehouse. North along the canal, behind Unga Park, the former **Otaru Branch of Nihon Yusen Co** (9.30am–5pm; closed Mon; ¥300), once the offices of one of Japan's major shipping companies, now contains a faithful reproduction of the original interiors.

For a wonderful view of town, ride the cable car up **Tenguyama** (天狗山; daily 9am–9pm; ¥1100), where there's also good skiing in winter (day lift ticket ¥3100). Buses (¥210) run to the cable car from platform #3 outside Otaru Station.

Shukutsu

It's a 20-minute bus ride to **Shukutsu** (祝津), home of the area's best sight: the spectacular traditional Japanese villa **Nishin Goten Kihinkan Villa** (にしん御殿小樽貴賓館; daily April–Dec 9am–5pm, Jan–March 9am–4pm; ¥1000). The Aoyama family, herring tycoons of the early twentieth century, spared little expense when they commissioned this beautiful wooden building, which is surrounded by ornamental gardens and contains exquisite screen paintings, fixtures and antique pieces.

A short walk away in the surrounding area (which is refreshingly free of commercial trappings compared to downtown Otaru), you'll find several other heritage buildings dating from the herring boom era, including stone warehouses and the large-scale fishermen's dormitory **Nishin Goten** (鰊御殿; daily: April–Oct 9am–5pm; Nov 9am–4pm; ¥300) in a prominent hillside position overlooking the small harbour. Bus #11 from Otaru Station heads to Shukutsu. In summer, a great alternative is to hop on the Otaru Aquarium-bound **boats** from Otaru's Pier no. 3.

Eating and drinking

Otaru is renowned for its sushi and sashimi **restaurants**. It also has a **microbrewery**, *Otaru Biiru* (ⓦwww.otarubeer.com; daily 11am–11pm), beside the Otaru Canal, turning out quaffable German-style ales.

Aotsuka 青塚 Shukutsu. Drop by this simple café opposite Shukutsu's harbour for super-fresh, good-value fish dishes around ¥1000. Herring, the fish that made the area's fortunes, are grilled over charcoal outside. Daily 9am–7pm.

Hikari 光 Miyako Arcade. Good for a cup of coffee, cake or light meal at under ¥1000, this hushed café, packed to the rafters with antique glass lamps and china, is a rare treat and generally unmobbed by the tourist throng. Open 11am–6pm; closed Wed.

Kita-no-Aisukuriimu-yasan 北のアイスクリーム屋さん 1-2-18 Ironai. Popular ice-cream parlour offering unique flavours such as squid, sea urchin and *nattō*, alongside more common ones. Daily 10am–7pm.

Sakaiya さかい家 4-4 Sakai-machi. Occupying a handsome 1907 wooden building, this café is a charming place to sample green tea and traditional sweets. Apr–Oct 10am–7pm, Nov–March 10am–6pm.

Uminekoya 海猫屋 2-2-14 Ironai. In an old warehouse covered in ivy, one block back from the canal, this is a cosy, atmospheric place for a drink or a light meal of pasta for under ¥2000. Daily 11am–11pm.

Uomasa 魚真 2-5-11 Inaho ⓣ0134/29-0259. You'll find scores of touristy sushi restaurants on Sakai-machi Hon-dōri, but this unassuming one on a side street closer to Otaru Station is a winner. Their 15-piece sushi set is great value at ¥2500. Mon–Sat noon–2pm & 4–10pm.

Niseko

Around 70km south of Otaru is **NISEKO** (ニセコ), Japan's premier **winter resort**, with awesome amounts of perfect powder snow and top-class, interlinked ski fields. The resort hugs Mount Niseko Annupuri and faces the dormant volcano Mount Yōtei-san (also known as the Ezo Fuji for its resemblance to its more famous southern cousin). The village of **Hirafu** (比羅夫), close to the area's main town of **Kutchan** (倶知安), has seen the brunt of development, much of it through foreign investment and not all of it particularly sympathetic to the magnificent natural surroundings.

During the ski season (Dec–April) the *gaijin* population of Hirafu booms as skiers jet in from as far afield as Melbourne, Hong Kong and London to take advantage of a fantastic range of facilities, including stylish accommodation and dining options. Situated within the Niseko-Shakotan-Otaru Quasi National Park, the area also makes a good **summer base** when it's far less crowded and becomes the focal point for many **adventure sports** including whitewater rafting, mountain biking and kayaking; cyclists should mark September's Niseko Cycle Week (Ⓦwww.nisekocycleweek.com), which includes guided road tours of the area, downhill mountain bike races, technique sessions and night parties, on their calendars.

Arrival and information

Alight from the **train** at **Kutchan** and connect to Hirafu by bus (15min; free). Various return packages offered by JR from either Sapporo or Otaru make things really simple and can be unbeatable deals: for example, train, bus, ski-lift ticket and ski or snowboard rental for ¥5500 for the day – check with tourist information in Sapporo (see p.291) for what's available. Many **buses** run directly to the ski slopes from Sapporo and New Chitose Airport (from around ¥2300 one-way); from the latter there's also the door-to-door **Skybus** (Ⓦnewsb.skybus-jp.com; ¥6000 one-way) service.

In summer, public transport is scaled back and it gets a whole lot trickier (but not impossible) to get here and around without your own car. Also note that some guesthouses and many restaurants and bars are only open during the ski season.

Both Kutchan and Niseko stations have small tourist information booths where you might find English-speaking assistants. There's also a **welcome centre** at the Grand Hirafu Parking Lot no. 1, where the bus from Kutchan terminates. More information is available at Ⓦwww.nisekotourism.com.

Accommodation

Niseko's best selection of **hotels** and **pensions** is clustered at Hirafu. If you're looking for somewhere more peaceful, consider the options at Annupuri, Hanazono and Higashiyama, all of which are nearby. There are also plenty of **self-catering** apartments and chalets; apart from those listed below, try **Hokkaido Tracks** (Ⓣ0136/23-3503, Ⓦwww.hokkaidotracks.com). Unless otherwise mentioned, all rates for the listings below include breakfast.

Hirafu

Grand Papa 163 Yamada Ⓣ0136/23-2244, Ⓦwww.niseko-grandpapa.co.jp. Largish, convivial pension with an alpine theme: they even offer fondue dinners. Japanese culture classes are also held here. Add ¥1000/person for a room with attached bathroom. ❺

J-Sekka 167-3 Aza-Yamada Ⓣ0136/21-6133, Ⓦwww.j-sekka.com. A set of spacious self-catering apartments is attached to this fab restaurant/deli complex (see p.303). The decor successfully mixes Japanese antique rusticity with icy-white smoothness. ❼

Kimamaya by Odin 170-248 Aza-Yamada ⓣ0136/23-2603, ⓦwww.kimamaya.com. French expat Nicolas Gontard has created a charming, modern pension from the bones of an old minshuku, preserving the beams and cosy atmosphere. Meals are taken in the glass-sided *Barn* restaurant next door, which looks spectacular when lit up at night. ⑦

Souiboku 191-29 Aza-Yamada ⓣ0136/21-5020, ⓦwww.suibokuhirafu.com. Imagine the place James Bond would stay in Niseko and you'll get the measure of these deluxe self-catering apartments. Masses of faux fur, Frette linens and light grey walls accented by lovely antique-style pieces and art. ⑧

The Vale Niseko 194-5 Aza-Yamada ⓣ0136/22-0038, ⓦwww.thevaleniseko.com. Ski-in, ski-out self-catering apartments and hotel rooms are available at this well-designed contemporary complex with a lively restaurant/bar, relaxing onsen and tiny lap pool. ⑦

Annupuri, Hanazono and Higashiyama

Black Diamond Lodge 24-3 Higashiyama ⓣ0136/44-1144, ⓦwww.bdlodge.com. One of Niseko's best backpacker lodges, this comfortable place includes breakfast in its rates and has a lively restaurant and bar. They also arrange various ski tours and packages as well as equipment rental and car hire. Dorm beds from ¥4500/person.

Hotel Kanronomori ホテル甘露の森 415 Aza-Niseko ⓣ0136/58-3800, ⓦwww.kanronomori.com. Ten minutes' walk from the Annupuri Kokusai ski lifts, and surrounded by greenery, this appealing 78-room ryokan combines Japanese- and Western-style rooms. There's a large rotemburo and rates include two meals. ⑦

Niseko Annupuri Youth Hostel 479-4 Aza-Niseko ⓣ0136/58-2084, ⓦwww.youthhostel.or.jp. The most convenient youth hostel for the slopes at Annupuri is a charming European-style log-cabin pension with a roaring fire. Dorm beds ¥3250/person.

Niseko Northern Resort Annupuri 480-1 Aza-Niseko ⓣ0136/58-3311, ⓦwww.niseko-northern.com. A good upmarket choice next to the ski lifts offering spacious "Scandinavian chic" rooms with white wood and red brick accents. Fine facilities include a rotemburo and classy bar area. ⑦

Hilton Niseko Village Higashiyama ⓣ0136/44-1111, ⓦwww.hilton.com. There are fantastic views of Mount Yōtei from this tower sporting a glitzy lobby area and an excellent range of food and beverage options – just as well, as there's little else around here. Rooms are fine but lack the pizzazz of other Niseko options. ⑧

Niseko Weiss Hanazono ⓣ0136/23-3311. Discover the quieter side of Niseko resort before Hanazono gets overdeveloped with a stay at this stylish boutique hotel. There are both Japanese- and Western-style rooms, and a great set of onsen baths. ⑥

The resort

Niseko United (ⓦwww.niseko.ne.jp/en) is the umbrella name for three separate ski resorts: **Grand Hirafu/Hanazono**, **Niseko Village** and Niseko **Annupuri**. You can buy individual lift tickets from each of the resorts, but the smartest deal is to go for one of the All Mountain Passes (from ¥4900 for an eight-hour ticket), which is issued as an electronic tag – you'll need to wave it at the barrier by each of the lifts – with a ¥1000 refundable deposit.

If you're looking to ski Niseko's **backcountry**, then hire a guide from either Niseko Adventure Centre (NAC; ⓣ0136/23-2093, ⓦwww.nac-web.com) or Niseko Outdoor Adventure Sports Club (NOASC; ⓣ0136/23-1688, ⓦwww.noasc.com), both in Hirafu; each employs English-speaking guides and also offers snowboarding, telemark skiing and ice climbing in winter and activities such as kayaking and white-water rafting in summer. Other reputable and local ski tour operators include Black Diamond Tours (ⓦwww.blackdiamondtours.com) and Ski Japan (ⓣ0136/22-4611, ⓦwww.skijapan.com). Soaking in an **onsen** is a fine way to wind down after a day on the slopes. Try *Popolo* at *Hotel Niseko Scot* (daily 10am–10pm; ¥800) next to the *Grand Hirafu* ski lifts, or *Yukoro* (ゆころ; daily 2–10pm; ¥600) at the southeastern end of Hirafu village.

Eating and drinking

All of Niseko's hotels and pensions offer meals, but the area has such a good range of **restaurants, cafés** and **bars** that you can easily opt for a room only. Unless mentioned, the places below are only open during the ski season. Where there's a telephone number it's a good idea to book, particularly at weekends.

Ab *Hotel Niseko Scot*, Hirafu. The après-ski bar at the base of Grand Hirafu's slopes packs in an up-for-it crowd in season. They have different theme nights and at weekends DJs help make things more lively. Daily noon–10pm.

Abucha 1 Hirafu ⓣ0136/22-5620. At the main intersection in the village, this popular bakery, café and bar is a good option for breakfast or lunch away from the slopes. It can get busy in the evenings when a good range of standard Japanese dishes, including *nabe* stews (around ¥2500), is offered. *Abucha 2* is found in the Souiboku complex (see opposite) but it doesn't have the same atmosphere. Open year-round daily 7am–4pm & 6pm–2am.

Bang-Bang Hirafu ⓣ0136/22-4292, ⓦniseko.or.jp/bangbang. Set back from the main drag, this convivial restaurant specializes in local fish dishes and *yakitori* (over 30 different types from ¥160–450). It's one of the few places where you're likely to be surrounded by more Japanese than *gaijin*. The owner speaks excellent English. In addition to the ski season, it's also open between Aug and mid-Oct. Open 5.30–11.30pm; closed Wed.

Gentem Hirafu ⓣ0136/23-3154. How's this for cultural fusion – a Mongolian yurt in a Japanese ski village serving vaguely Southeast Asian dishes (around ¥2000/meal including a ¥400 cover charge). It's a fun, unusual atmosphere, and, if you make a booking – which is advisable – they will pick you up and drop you back to your lodgings after. It's located just off the main road midway between Hirafu and Higashiyama. Daily 6–11.30pm.

Graubünden Hirafu ⓣ0136/22-3371. This fantastic bakery-café is located on the way out of Hirafu towards Kutchan. They do a scrumptious selection of sandwiches and cakes (all for under ¥1000), with leaf tea served in tea-cosy-covered pots. Jan–March 10am–8pm, April–Dec 10am–7pm; closed Thurs.

Gyu+Bar Hirafu. Downhill from the main intersection on the right, the entrance to this funky DJ bar is through a Coca-Cola vending-machine-turned door. Daily 6pm–1am

J-Sekka Deli & Café ⓣ0136/21-3088, ⓦj-sekka.com. Specialising in the cream of Hokkaidō produce, this relaxed, colourful deli-café is the ideal place for breakfast, coffee or a light meal for under ¥2000. Their restaurant *Sekka Dining*, open every evening in the winter, offers Niseko's best fine-dining experience with delicious items such as meltingly good beef cheeks, super-fresh scallops and amazing desserts concocted by a talented Kiwi chef; expect to pay upwards of ¥6000/person. To cap off the night, there's also the stylish *Maki Lounge* with an open fire for cocktails and other relaxing beverages. Deli & Café open daily Dec–May 7am–10pm & June–Nov 9am–6pm.

Kamimura Hirafu ⓣ0136/21-2288, ⓦwww.kamimura-niseko.com. The full white tablecloth experience from a talented chef who brings out the best from local produce. Set menus, which may include dishes such as a snow crab and avocado salad and roasted wagyu beef with puréed local potato, kick off at ¥6500. Service is excellent, too. Reservations are essential. Daily 5.30–11pm.

Tsubara Tsubara Hirafu ⓣ0136/23-1116. Soup curry is a Hokkaidō speciality and a great place to try it is at this friendly, relaxed bistro where the heat rating runs from a bland 0 to an on-fire 20. It's good value too, with a meal under ¥1500. Daily 11.30am–3pm & 6–9.30pm.

Hakodate and around

If you travel to Hokkaidō by train, the first major city you'll come to after emerging from the Seikan Tunnel is **HAKODATE** (函館), 260km southwest of Sapporo. This attractive **port** was one of the first to open to foreign traders following the Japan–US amity treaty of 1854. Over the next few years, ten countries including Britain, Russia and the US established consulates in Hakodate, with both foreigners and rich Japanese building fancy wooden homes and elaborate churches on the steep hillsides. Many of these late nineteenth- and early twentieth-century buildings have been preserved, particularly in the **Motomachi** area, which is Hakodate's highlight.

Among the city's other draws are the lively fish and fresh produce market **Asa-ichi**; an outstanding exhibition on **Ainu** culture at the Hakodate City

HAKODATE

Hakodate Harbour
Hakodate dokku-mae
Ōnuma Quasi National Park, Seikan Tunnel & Hakodate-ko Port
Goryūkaku, Yunokawa & 6
Yachigashira
Hakodate Station & Bus Station
HAKODATE-EKI-MAE
Asa-ichī
SHIYAKUSHO-MAE
City Hall
UOICHIBA-DŌRI
JŪJIGAI
HORAI-CHŌ
Aka-renga Warehouses
Hakodate City Museum of Northern Peoples
SUEHIRO-CHŌ
MOTOI-ZAKA
Old British Consulate
Museum of Photographic History & Information
Motomachi-kōen
Old Public Hall of Hakodate Ward
Kanemori Yōbutsukan
HACHIMAN - ZAKA
MOTOMACHI
Hakodate-yama
Motomachi Roman Catholic
DAISAN - ZAKA
Russian Orthodox
Episcopal
NIJUKKEN - ZAKA
NAHBU - ZAKA
Cable Car Station
YUCHI - ZAKA
GOKOKUJINJA-ZAKA
Tsugaru-Kaikyō Strait
0 250 m

ACCOMMODATION	
Hakodate Youth Guesthouse	L
Hotel & Spa Resort La Vista	F
Loisir	C
Nagashima	K
Niceday Inn	G
Pension Hakodate-Mura	I
Pension Jyō-Kura	B
Route Inn	A
Tōyoko Inn Hakodate	D & H
Villa Concordia	J
Winning Hotel	E

RESTAURANTS, CAFES & BAR	
Asari	12
Bar Shares Hishii	10
Café Tutu	4
Daimon Yokochō	1
Fudemura	6
Hakodate Bay Bishoku Club	5
Hakodate Beer	2
Hishii	11
Lucky Pierrot	8
Nihombashi	3
Rocket Bar	7
Tonetsu	9

Museum of Northern Peoples; and the night view from the top of **Hakodate-yama**. The **Ōnuma Quasi National Park**, a beautiful lakeland and mountain area with good hiking trails, is an easy day-trip. Try and time your visit for the **Hakodate Port Festival** (Aug 1–5), when 20,000 people parade through town performing the "squid dance", an entertaining jig where hands are flapped and clapped in time to rhythmic drumming.

Arrival and information

Hakodate's **airport** (Ⓣ0138/57-8881) lies 8km north of the city; buses (¥400) take roughly twenty minutes from here to reach the central Hakodate Station, on the eastern side of the harbour, where **trains** also terminate. The **bus station** is in front of the train station. **Ferries** dock at Hakodate-kō Port, some 4km north of Hakodate Station. Catch either bus #101 or #111 to Hakodate Station (¥230 or ¥250, depending on which ferry you alight from); a taxi from the port to the city centre is around ¥2000.

The helpful Hakodate **tourist office** (daily: April–Oct 9am–7pm; Nov–March 9am–5pm; Ⓣ0138/23-5440, Ⓦhttp://bit.ly/d5wFFh) is next to Hakodate Station.

City transport

Hakodate's sights are spread out. There's a good **tram** system with two lines, both starting at the onsen resort of Yunokawa (湯の川) east of the city. Each runs past Goryōkaku and the train station before diverging at the Jūjigai stop in Motomachi. From here, tram #5 heads west to Hakodate Dokku-mae (函館どっく前), while tram #2 continues further south to Yachigashira (谷地頭) on the eastern side of Hakodate-yama. One-day (¥1000) and two-day passes (¥1700) can be bought from the tourist office for unlimited use of both the trams and most city **buses**. These passes, only worth buying if you plan to tour extensively around town, also cover the bus service up Hakodate-yama. The ¥600 all-day **tram** ticket is better value; individual tram trips cost ¥200–250. Trams run between 7am and 10pm.

Accommodation

Hotels are busiest during the summer, when you'll need to book ahead. Prices at most places drop considerably in winter. There are plenty of business hotels near the train station including branches of the reliable chains *Tōyoko Inn*, *Hotel Route Inn* and *Loisir*: all have good deals for online bookings.

Hakodate Youth Guesthouse 17-6 Horai-chō Ⓣ0138/26-7892, Ⓦwww.youthhostel.or.jp. The highlight of this guesthouse with Western-style rooms is its top-floor lounge with a view of Hakodate-yama. Free home-made ice cream is offered every night at 9pm to tempt people back before the 11pm curfew. Take the Yachigashira-bound streetcar to Horai-chō, from where it's a 3min walk. Dorm beds ¥3800–4800.

Hotel & Spa Resort La Vista 12-6 Toyokawa-chō Ⓣ0138/23-6111, Ⓦtinyurl.com/26fa7td. With great views of the harbour and Hakodate-yama, Hakodate's newest luxury hotel offers elegantly designed rooms and a fantastic set of rooftop baths. Rates are very affordable out of season. ❼

Nagashima 長島 18-5 Horai-chō Ⓣ0138/26-2101, Ⓦwww5b.biglobe.ne.jp/~m-naga. Good-value, spotless minshuku near Hakodate-yama, offering mainly tatami rooms, plus a couple of Western-style ones. The shared bathroom has a *hinoki* (a type of pine) tub. Rates include two meals, although they also offer room only for ¥4200/person. ❺

Niceday Inn 9-11 Ōtemachi Ⓣ0138/22-5919. Friendly hostel in a convenient location between the station and Motomachi. All the rooms have two bunk beds and are very small, but if it's quiet you may get one to yourself. The owners speak English and there's free tea and coffee. ❸

Pension Hakodate-Mura 16-12 Suehiro-chō Ⓣ0138/22-8105, Ⓦbb-hakodatemura.com. Appealing B&B just off the waterfront at the start of

Motomachi. Offers both Western- and Japanese-style rooms, with most sharing a common bathroom. Breakfast included. ❺

Pension Jyō-Kura じょう蔵 9-8 Ōmachi ⓣ0138/27-6453, ⓦwww11.plala.or.jp/j-kura. Cutesy pension with a facade styled like a *kura* (storehouse). There's a homely common area where breakfast is served (¥800) and a choice of Western- or Japanese-style rooms. ❹

Villa Concordia 3-5 Suehiro-chō ⓣ0138/24-5300. Super spacious, design-conscious suites – each with a kitchen and spectacular views of Hakodate-yama – are offered at this new boutique property, which also has a beauty spa. ❾

Winning Hotel 22-11 Suehiro-chō ⓣ0138/26-1111, ⓦwww.hotel-winning.jp. In a modern but Art Deco-styled building facing the harbour, the rooms here are pleasantly decorated, large, and some have lovely views. ❺–❼

The City

Lording it over Hakodate is the 334m **Hakodate-yama** (函館山). On a clear day the view from the summit is spectacular, but best of all is the night-time panorama, when the twinkling lights of the port and the boats fishing for squid just off the coast create a magical scene – though be prepared to share it with hordes of tourists. The energetic can climb to the summit along various trails (May–Oct), but most people opt for the **cable car** (函館山ロープウェイ; daily: May–Oct 10am–10pm; Nov–April 10am–9pm; ¥640 one way, ¥1160 return), a seven-minute uphill walk from the Jūjigai tram stop. There's also a direct bus from Hakodate Station (end April to mid-Oct 1.15–9pm; 30min; ¥360). The serpentine road up the mountain is closed to private vehicles between 5pm and 10pm.

Motomachi

Heading downhill from the mountain, you'll find yourself in **Motomachi** (元町), with its Western-style, late nineteenth-century architecture; combined with the steeply raked streets, it's easy when you're here to see why Hakodate is known as the San Francisco of Japan. The best thing to do is simply wander about, stopping to explore some of the churches, which are free (few of the other buildings merit their entrance charges). The most striking is the white **Russian Orthodox Church** of 1919, seven minutes uphill from Jūjigai tram stop, complete with green copper-clad onion domes and spires. Inside, there's an impressive icon-festooned carved-wood altarpiece, and piped Russian choral music adds to the atmosphere. Nearby, the **Episcopal Church**, with its unusual modern architecture, is more interesting from the outside than in, while, slightly downhill, the Gothic-style **Motomachi Roman Catholic Church** is worth a look for its decoration, which is based on the Stations of the Cross.

Walking west for a couple of hundred metres across the hillside streets will bring you to the extraordinary **Old Public Hall of Hakodate Ward** (daily 9am–5pm, April–Oct until 7pm; ¥300), a sky-blue and lemon confection with pillars, verandas and fancy wrought-iron and plaster decoration. This replacement was completed in 1910 after a fire destroyed the original hall. In front of the hall is small Motomachi Park, beneath which is the **Old British Consulate**, from where the Empire's affairs in Hokkaidō were looked after from 1859 to 1934. The cream-and-blue building now houses a ho-hum museum, the twee *Victorian Rose Tea Restaurant* and a giftshop.

Far more interesting is the **Hakodate City Museum of Northern Peoples** (北方民族資料館; daily 9am–5pm, April–Oct until 7pm; ¥300), in an old bank down Motoi-zaka, which leads away from the consulate. The museum's superb collection of artefacts relating to the **Ainu** and other races across Eastern Siberia and the Alaskan islands has clear, English captioning and is well worth the entrance fee. Some of the clothes on display are amazing – look out for the Chinese silk robe embroidered with dragons, an example of the types of items traded between China, the islanders of Sakhalin and the Ainu.

Across the street is one more building worth a look before leaving Motomachi – the handsome **Kanemori Yōbutsukan** (金森洋物館; Tues–Sun April–Oct 9am–4.30pm; Nov–March 9am–4pm; ¥100), a former haberdashery shop dating from 1880 which has been faithfully restored to something of its original condition and is now a branch of the local history museum. Upstairs you'll see some interesting photos and a diorama of turn-of-the-century Hakodate.

Goryōkaku

The remains of **Goryōkaku** (五稜郭), a late nineteenth-century Western-style fort, lie some 3km northeast of the station and around ten minutes' walk north of the Goryōkaku-kōen-mae tram stop. The star-shaped fort was built to protect Hokkaidō against attack from Russia. In the event, however, it was used by Tokugawa Yoshinobu's naval forces in a last-ditch battle to uphold the shogun against the emperor in the short-lived civil war that ushered in the Meiji Restoration of 1869. The Emperor's victory is celebrated each year in mid-May with a period costume parade.

What's left of the fort today – a leafy park planted with 1600 cherry trees, the moat and outer walls – looks best ninety metres up from the inelegant **viewing tower** (daily: April 21–Oct 20 8am–7pm; Oct 21–April 20 9am–6pm; ¥840; ⓦwww.goryokaku-tower.co.jp) by the main entrance. On weekend evenings from late July to mid-August, open-air plays about Hakodate's history are performed enthusiastically by five hundred amateurs; check with the tourist office for details.

Eating and drinking

The best places to feast on fresh seafood are the sushi and *donburi* restaurants scattered around the morning market near Hakodate Station (see below). **Local specialities** include crab (*kani*), squid (*ika*) and ramen noodles in a salty soup topped with seafood.

For something a little unusual, head to the hamburger and curry chain *Lucky Pierrot*, where the menu includes a variety of original burgers; there are ten branches in the city, including just west of the Jūjigai tram stop and next to the Aka-renga brick warehouses.

Goryōkaku is the city's main **drinking** area although you'll also find several bars around the converted warehouses in Motomachi. Unless mentioned, expect bars to be open daily from 5pm to at least midnight.

Asari 阿佐利 10-11 Horai-chō ⓣ0138/23-0421. The old wooden building and tatami-floor dining rooms of this restaurant are just part of the pleasure – the rest is in the quality of the *sukiyaki*, their speciality dish, using meat fresh from the butchers downstairs. Lunch (11.30am–1.30pm) is a bargain at ¥1200–1400; set menus at other times start at ¥2300. Open 11.30am–8pm; closed Wed.

Asa-ichi

No visit to Hakodate is complete without dropping by the atmospheric **Asa-ichi** (朝市; ⓦwww.hakodate-asaichi.com; daily Jan–April 6am–noon, May–Dec 5am–noon), the morning market immediately to the west of the train station. Even if you arrive at the relatively late hour of 9am, there's still plenty to see at the hundreds of tightly packed stalls in this waterside location. Old ladies in headscarves squat amid piles of vegetables and flowers in the central hall, and huge, alien-like red crabs, squid, sea urchin and musk melons are the local specialities. Sample the seafood atop a bowl of ramen or rice before leaving: **Aji-no-ichiban** (味の一番; daily 7am–2pm), at the back of the market, is a good choice – they serve a *donburi* topped with creamy sea urchin, salmon roe and fresh crab for ¥1700, as well as delicious, freshly squeezed melon juice (May–Oct).

Café Tutu 13-5 Suehiro-chō. Trendy café-bar to the rear of one of the renovated brick warehouses. It's a nice place to relax over gourmet coffee and cake and flick through magazines. Daily 11.30am–11pm; closed Thurs from Nov–April.
Daimon Yokochō 大門横丁. Take your pick from some 26 *yatai* (stalls) serving everything from *oden* and sushi to ramen and *yakitori*. It's an atmospheric place and a good spot to drop by for a beer and small plate of food. Daily 5pm–midnight.
Fudemura ふでむら 36-1 Goryōkaku-chō. Very hospitable soba noodle restaurant on the way to the viewing tower. They also make desserts and cakes using buckwheat. The set meal with charcoal-grilled crab is a steal at ¥1000. Daily 11am–9pm.
Hakodate Bay Bishoku Club 函館ベイ美食倶楽部 12-7 Toyakawa-chō. Adjoining the converted brick warehouses by the waterfront is this attractive complex of seven restaurants around a free outdoor foot spa. Take your pick between seafood *donburi* (around ¥2500) at *Kikuyo*, Hakodate-style *shio* (salt) ramen (¥700) at *Ajisai*, soup curry at *Megumi* (¥1000) or a *jingisukan* lamb barbecue at *Mei Mei Tei* (¥2000).
Hakodate Beer 12-12 Toyokawamachi. This cavernous brewery pub/restaurant serves the local *ji-biiru*. Sample four of their brews for ¥1200. Sometimes there's live music. Daily 11am–10pm.
Hishii ひし伊 9-4 Horai-chō. Near the Horai-chō tram stop, this elegant ivy-draped 1920s wooden building houses a serene teashop and antique kimono shop. There's a tatami area on the second floor. Daily 10am–10pm. They also run the nearby *Bar Shares Hishii* at 27-1 Motomachi; Mon–Sat 7.30pm–2am.
Nihombashi 日本橋 7-9 Motomachi. Good-value Japanese restaurant serving huge set meals and bowls of noodles in a relaxing atmosphere amid the old houses of Motomachi. Daily 11.30am–6pm.
Rocket Bar Suehiro-chō. Elvis croons and Big Boy grins at this all American café-bar that doubles up as a vintage clothes store. Find it opposite the Jūjigai tram stop. Open 11.30am–10pm; closed Wed.
Tonetsu とん悦 22-2 Horai-chō. Convivial *tonkatsu* restaurant with tatami seating and a good range of reasonably priced set meals from ¥1000, including free coffee. Open 11.30am–9pm; closed Tues.

Listings

Banks There's an ATM in the post office upstairs at Hakodate Station and several banks nearby that can change cash and travellers' cheques (Mon–Fri 9am–2.30pm only).
Car rental Eki Rent-a-Car (ⓣ0138/22-7864), next to Hakodate Station.
Hospital Hakodate City Hospital, 1-10-1 Minato-chō ⓣ0138/43-2000.
Internet HotWeb Café, 18-1 TMO Building, Wakamatsu-chō (10am–8pm; closed Tues; ¥400/hour including one soft drink), is on the main road leading from Hakodate Station, one block beyond the Wako department store. I-Café, 2nd floor, Pabot Bldg, 9-3 Yanagawa-chō, is open 24hr and charges ¥300/hour.
Laundry *Aqua Garden Hotel*, 19-13 Ōtemachi, 5min walk south of the station, has a coin laundry and is open 7am–midnight.
Police The main police station is on the western side of Goryōkaku-kōen. For emergency numbers, see p.83.
Post office The central post office, 1-6 Shinkawa-chō, is a 10min walk east of Hakodate Station, near the Shinkawa-chō tram stop. Mon–Fri 9am–7pm, Sat & Sun 9am–5pm.

Ōnuma Quasi National Park

Just 29km north of the city, the serene **Ōnuma Quasi National Park** (大沼国定公園) can easily be visited in a day but is worth considering as an overnight stop. Of the park's three **lakes**, the largest and most beautiful is **Ōnuma**, carpeted with water lilies and containing more than one hundred tiny islands, many linked by humpback bridges. The view from the lake towards the 1133m jagged peak of the dormant volcano of **Komaga-take** (駒ヶ岳) is rightly considered to be one of the most breathtaking in Japan.

Ōnuma is popular with tour groups, but they are usually herded into sightseeing boats, leaving the walking paths around the lake and islands quiet for strolls. **Cycling** is another good way of exploring; bikes can be rented (around ¥500/hr or ¥1500/day) from numerous shops around the station. **Hikers** can also tackle the **volcano**, which has two main routes, both taking around two and a half hours to complete.

Practicalities

Local **trains** from Hakodate to Ōnuma-kōen Station take 50 minutes (¥530), while limited express trains take 20 minutes (¥1130). There are also three daily **buses** (1hr, one-way/return ¥710/1270). Information is available from **Ōnuma International Communication Plaza** (Ⓦwww.onuma-guide.com; daily 8.30am–5.30pm) next to the train station.

Accommodation options including a **campsite** on the eastern shore of Ōnuma Lake, around 6km from Ōnuma-kōen Station. The friendly *Ōnuma Kōen Youth Hostel* (Ⓣ0138/67-4126, Ⓦwww.youthhostel.or.jp; dorm beds ¥3960/person), three minutes' walk from Ikedaen Station, offers bunk-bed dorms, good breakfasts and dinners and activities such as canoeing, cross-country skiing and ice fishing, depending on the season. The upmarket choice is the Western-style *Crawford Inn Ōnuma* (クロフォード・イン大沼; Ⓦcrawford.jp/en/index.html; ❼) next to Ōnuma-kōen Station, and named after Prof. Joseph Crawford who introduced the railways to Hokkaidō.

Shikotsu-Tōya National Park and around

Follow the coastal road or rail line around Uchiura-wan from Hakodate and you'll reach the eastern side of the **SHIKOTSU-TŌYA NATIONAL PARK** (支笏洞爺国立公園), one of Hokkaidō's prettiest lakeland and mountain areas, but also the most developed, thanks to its proximity to Sapporo, some 80km to the north. Both the park's two main caldera lakes – **Tōya-ko** to the east and **Shikotsu-ko** to the west – have gorgeous locations, are active volcanoes and are surrounded by excellent hiking trails. Between the two lakes lies **Noboribetsu Onsen**, Hokkaidō's largest hot-spring resort, worth visiting to soak up the otherworldly landscape of bubbling and steaming **Jigokudani** (Hell Valley).

Birth of a volcano

On December 28, 1943, severe earthquakes began shaking the area around Usu-zan and continued to do so until September 1945. In the intervening period a new lava dome rose out of the ground, sometimes at the rate of 1.5m a day. By the time it had stopped growing, Shōwa Shin-zan, the "new mountain" named after the reigning emperor, stood 405m above sea level. The wartime authorities were desperate to hush up this extraordinary event for fear that the fledgling mountain would serve as a beacon for US bomber planes.

Fortunately, Shōwa Shin-zan's daily growth was carefully documented by local postmaster and amateur volcanologist **Mimatsu Masao**. After the war, Mimatsu bought the land on which the mountain stood, declaring, "I purchased the volcano to continue my research uninterrupted. I did not buy it to make money. Nor did I buy it for tourists to gawk at." His efforts were rewarded in 1958 when Shōwa Shin-zan was made a Special Natural Treasure by the government.

Nevertheless, Mimatsu never turned away tourists – but nor did he charge them admission, a practice still upheld. The **Mimatsu Masao Memorial Hall** (三松正夫記念館; daily 8am–5pm; ¥300), tucked behind the ghastly row of giftshops at the base of the volcano, contains an interesting collection of exhibits on the history of the fledgling volcano.

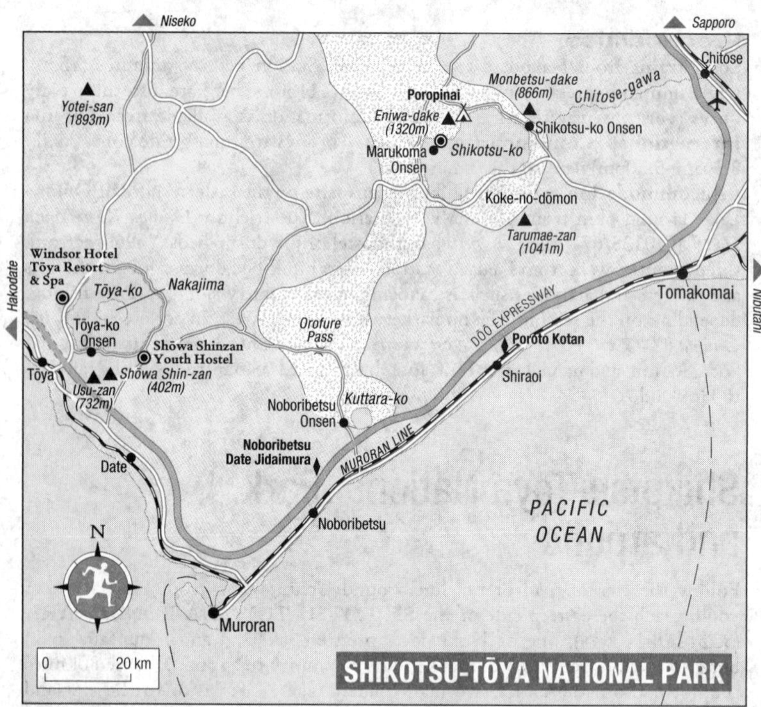

Tōya-ko

The beautiful caldera lake of **Tōya-ko** (洞爺湖) is punctuated dead centre by the conical island of **Nakajima**. Its southern shore is home to the tired-looking resort **Tōya-ko Onsen** (洞爺湖温泉), where you'll find most accommodation and local transport connections. Between April 28 and October 31 spectacular fireworks (nightly 8.45–9.05pm) illuminate the lake. Pretty as the location is, the best reason for visiting Tōya-ko is to see the nearby active volcano **Usu-zan** (有珠山), around 2km south, and its steaming "parasite volcano" **Shōwa Shin-zan** (昭和新山; see p.309).

Arrival and information

Trains run to Tōya Station, on the coast, from where you can get a bus (20min; ¥320) up the hill to Tōya-ko Onsen. There are also seven daily **buses** to Tōya-ko Onsen from Sapporo (2hr 50min; one-way/return ¥2700/4790). Buses pull in at the Dōnan bus station, two minutes' walk from the shore of Tōya-ko. From April to October, four buses (15min, ¥330) daily run from the same station to Shōwa Shin-zan. The **tourist office** (daily 9am–5pm; Ⓣ0142/75-2446, Ⓦwww.laketoya.com) is above the bus station.

The lake and around

Usu-zan remains frighteningly active; the last eruption, on March 31, 2000, coated Tōya-ko Onsen with volcanic dust and forced a three-month evacuation. The area damaged by the eruptions – known as the **Konpira Promenade** (daily April 20–Nov 10; free) – is nerve-shreddingly close to town. In front of it, in the newly built **Visitors' Centre and Volcanic Science Museum** (Ⓦwww.toyako-vc.jp; daily

9am–5pm; ¥600) you can watch a film – with seat-trembling sound effects – about that eruption and other explosions on the mountain. You can also walk or take a three-minute bus ride (¥160) to the **Nishiyama Promenade** (daily April 20–Nov 10; free), an 800m walkway across the recent break in the earth's crust.

To look directly into the beast, ride the **cable car** (有珠山ロープウェイ; Ⓦwww.usuzan.com; daily: Apr–Oct 8am–5pm; Nov–March 9am–4pm; ¥1450 return) to a viewing platform 300m from the crater, which also provides stunning vistas over Shōwa Shin-zan, Tōya-ko and out to sea. The rope-way station is at the end of the row of tourist shops by Shōwa Shin-zan.

The best way to enjoy the positive side of volcanic activity is to take an **onsen** dip. Most of the lakeside hotels allow day visitors – try the *Tōya Sun Palace* (daily 10am–3pm; ¥800), featuring two floors with more than twenty different soaking pools, some with lake views, and a large swimming pool with artificial waves and a water slide, for which you'll need your bathing costume. There are also nice rooftop baths (daily 1–5pm) at the *Toya-kohantei* (洞爺湖畔亭; daily 11am–8pm; ¥700), which is closer to the bus station.

For a cruise on the lake, hop aboard the kitsch castle-styled **ferry** *Espoir* (daily: April–Nov 8am–4.30pm sailings every 30min; Nov–April 9am–4pm sailings every hour; ¥1320). Only the summer cruises stop at Nakajima, where you can see Ezo deer grazing in the forests. Animal lovers can also arrange a day's horseriding at **Lake Toya Ranch** (Ⓣ0142/73-2455, Ⓦwww.dioce.co.jp/toya) on the west side of the lake.

Practicalities

Tōya-ko Onsen has plenty of resort-style **hotels**, which usually include two meals in their rates and offer substantial discounts outside the busy summer season. *Toyakohantei* (洞爺湖畔亭; Ⓣ0142/75-2211, Ⓦwww.noguchi-k.co.jp/kohan; ⑦) is a good upmarket option, although if it's unfettered luxury you're after, head to the west side of the lake to the stylish *Windsor Hotel Tōya Resort & Spa* (Ⓦwww.windsor-hotels.co.jp; ⑨). The *Shōwa Shinzan Youth Hostel* (Ⓣ0142/75-2283, Ⓦwww.youthhostel.or.jp; ¥3300/person), at the turn-off to Shōwa Shin-zan and a ten-minute bus or taxi ride (¥1300) from Tōya-ko Onsen, has bunk-bed dorms, shared tatami rooms, its own onsen and rents bikes (¥1000/day).

Back in Tōya-ko Onsen, the restaurant *Wakaseimo Hompo* (わかせいも本舗; daily 11am–7pm), with lake views, is a good place for lunch; afterwards, sample their various baked goods for dessert or takeaway presents.

Noboribetsu Onsen

East around the coast from Tōya-ko, and nestling amid lush green mountain slopes ripped through by a bubbling cauldron of volcanic activity, is **NOBORIBETSU ONSEN** (登別温泉). Hokkaidō's top hot-spring resort may be peppered with lumpen hotel buildings and tacky souvenir shops, but its dramatic landscape is definitely worth seeing and there's ample opportunity for some serious onsen relaxation.

Arrival and information

Trains run to Noboribetsu Station from where the resort is a thirteen-minute bus ride (¥330). There are also direct **buses** to Noboribetsu Onsen from Sapporo's New Chitose airport, and the nearby ports of Tomakomai to the north and Muroran to the south. At the resort's bus terminal you'll find one of Noboribetsu's trio of **tourist offices** (daily 9am–6pm; Ⓣ0143/84-3311, Ⓦwww.noboribetsu-spa.jp).

The resort

A ten-minute walk from the bus station up Gokuraku-dōri, Noboribetsu's main street, will bring you to a roadside **shrine** guarded by two brightly painted statues of demons. This is the entrance to **Jigokudani** (地獄谷; Hell Valley), a steaming, lunar-like valley created by an ancient volcanic eruption. It takes less than an hour to explore the area, wandering along wooden pathways through a landscape of rusty red rocks, streaked green and white by mineral deposits, ending up at **Oyu-numa**, a malevolent-looking hot-water lake. Along the way you can soothe your feet in a natural foot bath.

All the hotels draw water from Jigokudani (ten thousand tonnes are pumped out daily), and many have built elaborate **baths** so that guests can enjoy the water's therapeutic benefits. The tourist offices provide a list of the baths open to the public, the most ostentatious of which are those at the **Dai-ichi Takimoto-kan** (第一滝本館; daily 9am–4pm ¥2000; 4–8pm ¥1500). The main bathing hall has a sweeping view across Jigokudani and there's also a swimming pool (for which you'll need a costume). Also worth checking out are the baths at the **Noboribetsu Grand Hotel** (Tues, Wed & Fri–Sun 12.30–4pm, Mon & Thurs 2.30–4pm; daily 6–7.30pm; ¥1500).

If you have more time, skip the village's deplorable bear park in favour of the whacky Edo-era theme park **Noboribetsu Date Jidaimura** (登別伊達時代村; April–Oct daily 9am–5pm; Nov–March 10am–4pm, closed Wed; ¥2900; Ⓦwww.edo-trip.jp) where you can watched costumed theatre shows and ninja performances.

Practicalities

Rates at all of the onsen's **hotels** typically include two meals. Five minutes' walk downhill from the bus station the modest-sized, modern ryokan *Kashoutei Hanaya* (花鐘亭はなや; Ⓣ0143/84-2521, Ⓦwww.kashoutei-hanaya.co.jp; ⑦) is an excellent choice, with delicious meals, Japanese-style rooms and a lovely rotemburo. A masterclass in contemporary chic is *Bōrō Noguchi Noboribetsu* (望楼NOGUCHI登別; Ⓣ0143/84-3939, Ⓦwww.bourou.com; ⑨), featuring Western-style suites, each with their own private spa bath. It's also worth checking internet deals for the more traditional *Dai-ichi Takimoto-kan* (Ⓣ0143/84-3322, Ⓦwww.takimotokan.co.jp; ⑦).

Poroto Kotan and Nibutani

The re-created Ainu village of Poroto Kotan (ポロトコタン; daily 8.45am–5pm; ¥750, Ⓦwww.ainu-museum.or.jp) is in the southern coastal town of Shiraoi, on the train line between Sapporo and Hakodate, a few stops northeast of Noboribetsu. It's a very touristy experience but you can see traditionally dressed Ainu men and women perform the ritual dance, *Iyomante Rimse*, and listen to the haunting music of the *mukkur*, a mouth harp made of bamboo and thread.

For a more accurate idea of how Ainu live today, head to **Nibutani** (二風谷), some 50km due east of the port of Tomakomai on Route 237 – the only place in Japan where they form a majority of the community. A fascinating personal collection of Ainu artefacts is on display in the charming **Kayano Shigeru Ainu Memorial Museum** (April–Nov daily 9am–5pm; Dec–March by appointment only; Ⓣ01457/2-3215; ¥400, or ¥700 with the Nibutani Ainu Culture Museum). The **Nibutani Ainu Culture Museum** (daily 9am–4.30pm; ¥400 or ¥700 with the Kayano Shigeru Ainu Memorial Museum), on the opposite side of the village main road, is also worth a look. To reach Nibutani take a **train** south from Tomakomai to Tomikawa Station (富川), from where buses run to the village.

For **eating**, *Soba Dokorofukan* (そば処福庵; daily 11.30am–2pm & 6–10pm) serves buckwheat noodles and set meals (under ¥1000), while *Ajino Daiō* (味の大王; daily 9am–2pm) offers spicy *jigokudani ramen* (¥800); both are on Gokuraku-dōri.

Shikotsu-ko

Tourist development around the beautiful lake of **SHIKOTSU-KO** (支笏湖) is remarkably low-key, despite this being the closest part of the park to Sapporo. At 363m, this is Japan's second-deepest lake (after Tazawa-ko in Akita-ken), and its blue waters never freeze over. All buses stop at the tiny village of **SHIKOTSU-KO ONSEN** (支笏湖温泉), nestled in the woods beside the mouth of the Chitose-gawa on the east side of the lake, and mercifully free of the multistorey hotels present at Tōya-ko.

Arrival and information

Daily buses run to Shikotsu-ko Onsen from New Chitose airport (1hr; ¥1020 one-way). If you're coming from Sapporo it's better to take a train to Chitose (the town not the airport) to pick up the same bus (¥900). From June to October there are four direct buses daily from Sapporo (1hr 30min; ¥1330). **Getting around** the lake is best with your own transport, as there are no local buses. You can rent a bike from the youth hostel in Shikotsu-ko Onsen for ¥1800 a day (or ¥1200 if you're staying at the hostel).

The **visitor centre** (April–Nov daily 9am–5.30pm; Dec–March 9.30am–4.30pm; closed Tues; ⓣ0123/25-2404), next to the bus terminal, has displays in Japanese on the area's nature and geology, and puts on a good slide show of the lake through the seasons – you can also pick up a free area map here.

Accommodation

Most of the area's **ryokan and hotels** are a moment's walk from the bus terminal. The large *Shikotsu-ko Youth Hostel* (支笏湖ユースホステル; ⓣ0123/25-2311, ⓦwww.youthhostel.or.jp; ¥2900/person) has reasonable bunk-bed and tatami rooms and friendly management. A cosier budget option is *Log Bear* (ログベアー; ⓣ0123/25-2738, ⓦweb.mac/logbear; ❺), a charming log cabin and café amid the tourist shops next to the bus terminal. The owner speaks English and it's ¥5000 per person for bed and breakfast; all rooms have shared bathrooms. The ★ *Shikotsuko Daiichi Hoteru Suizantei* (支笏湖第一寶亭留翠山亭; ⓣ0123/25-2323; ❼–❽ including two meals) is a gorgeous contemporary-styled ryokan where the most expensive rooms have their own private onsen baths; day visitors can sample the baths from noon to 3pm (¥1200).

For **camping**, *Poropinai* (ポロピナイ; ⓣ0123/25-2755; ¥300/night), at the northern end of the lake, has the most attractive location and is a good spot for swimming. Further around the lake is the plush ryokan *Marukoma Onsen* (丸駒温泉; ⓣ0123/25-2341; ❼ including two meals), with wonderful rotemburo (open to non-residents 10am–3pm; ¥1000) and stunning views across Shikotsu-ko to Tarumae-zan.

The lake and around

There are the usual boat rides on the lake (30min; ¥1100), as well as a gentle, self-guided **nature walk**, lasting about two hours, over the old red-painted railway bridge across the Chitose-gawa and along the lakeshore to the campsite at **Morappu** (モラップ), 7km south. Just behind the centre is where the **Chitose-Shikotsu-ko Ice Festival** is held from the end of January to the third week of February – it's well worth coming to see the ice sculptures and caves which are particularly dramatic when illuminated at night.

Hiking routes

One of the easiest trails starts at the northern end of the village and leads up **Monbestu-dake** (紋別岳; 866m), which takes around one hour and twenty minutes to climb. The hike up **Eniwa-dake** (恵庭岳; 1319m), on the north side of the lake above the *Poropinai* campsite, is more challenging and takes at least two and a half hours; staff at the visitors' centre advise only climbing to the Miharashi-dai, beneath the 1319.7m summit, because the trail to the top can be dangerous. After this climb, you could unwind beside the lake at the foot of the mountain in the lovely rotemburo at **Marukoma Onsen** (see p.313).

Most people, however, opt to climb **Tarumae-zan** (樽前山), an active volcano (the last eruption was in 1951) south of the lake. The hike begins at the seventh "station", three-quarters of the way up the volcano at the end of a dirt road; the easiest way of reaching the start is to hitch a ride from Shikotsu-ko. The walk from the seventh station up to the summit (1041m) shouldn't take more than an hour. At the top, the pungent aroma from the steaming crater discourages lingering. Following the northwest trail down from Tarumae-zan towards the lake leads, after a couple of hours, to the moss-covered gorge of **Koke-no-dōmon** (苔の洞門); sadly, erosion at this site means that you'll only be able to view the soft green velvet rock walls from a distance. From here it's a 14km hike back to Shikotsu-ko Onsen.

Central Hokkaidō

Daisetsu-zan, Japan's largest national park, which features the island's highest mountain, **Asahi-dake** (2290m), and the spectacular **Sōunkyō gorge**, dominates central Hokkaidō. The fields around the picturesque village of **Bibaushi**, southwest of the national park, are best viewed in summer, when lavender, sunflowers and other blooms create a multicoloured patchwork. Further south is **Furano**, one of Japan's top ski resorts and location of World Cup skiing competitions. **Asahikawa**, Hokkaidō's second-largest city, is the area's transport hub and offers a few sights of note as well as lively nightlife.

Asahikawa

Mainly a place for business, **ASAHIKAWA** (旭川), 136km northeast of Sapporo, straddles the confluence of the Ishikari, Biei, Chubetsu and Ushibetsu rivers and is surrounded by mountains. It's the access point for the Daisetsu-zan National Park (see p.316), some 40km east, and worth considering as a base for park activities or, in winter, the various nearby ski slopes, including Furano (see p.318).

Asahikawa's **Winter Festival**, held over five days in the second week of February, is as spectacular as Sapporo's Yuki Matsuri (see p.289). The giant stage for the festival's opening and closing events holds the world record for the largest snow sculpture. The festival's many other snow and ice sculptures are displayed in Tokiwa-kōen and along pedestrianized Showa-dōri among other places.

Arrival and information

Asahikawa **airport** (ⓣ0166/83-3939, ⓦwww.aapb.co.jp) is 18km to the east of the city, towards Biei (see p.318); regular buses head into town from here (30min; ¥570). **Trains** arrive at the JR station, at the southern end of Heiwa-dōri, the city's main shopping street.

There's a helpful **tourist office** (daily: July–Sept 8.30am–7pm; Jan–June & Oct–Dec 10am–5.30pm; ⓣ0166/22-6704, ⓦwww.asahikawa-daisetsuzan.info) inside the station to the right as you exit the ticket barrier. Tourist information is also available from the international department in the Third Asahikawa Government Office, 10-chōme, 6-jo-dōri (Mon–Fri 9am–5pm), where they also have free **internet** access. Alternatively, to get online try *Comic Buster Compa 3.7* (daily 11am–3am; ¥500/hr), six blocks north of the station along Heiwa-dōri and to the left. There's an **ATM** within the JR station and at the Central Post Office, next to the *Loisir Hotel Asahikawa* (see below).

Accommodation

There are many **hotels** within easy walking distance of the station, including the *Asahikawa Terminal Hotel* (旭川ターミナルホテル; ⓣ0166/24-0111, ⓦwww.asahikawa.th.com; ❺), which is right outside and offers good online discounts. The classy *Loisir Hotel Asahikawa* (ロワジールホテル旭川; ⓣ0166/25-8811, ⓦwww.solarehotels.com; ❻), at 6-chōme, 7-jo-dōri, has free internet access in rooms and a spa/gym in the basement.

The City

Asahikawa's main tourist attractions are spread out and getting to them by public transport involves shuttling from the city centre on a variety of buses, all leaving from around the JR Station. Most locals will recommend that you visit **Asahiyama Zoo** (旭山動物園; April–Oct 9.30am–5.15pm; May–March 10.30am–3.30pm; ¥800; ⓦwww5.city.asahikawa.hokkaido.jp/asahiyamazoo), a twenty-minute bus ride east of the city centre (leave from stop 5; ¥400). The penguins, polar bears, seals, amur leopards and others that live here are cute and appear well cared for at what, thanks to skilful marketing, is Japan's most popular zoo.

West of the city centre is a trio of museums that comprise the **Hokkaidō Folk Arts and Crafts Village** (北海道伝統美術工芸村; ⓣ0166/62-8811, ⓦwww.yukaraori.co.jp; ¥1200 for all three). The most interesting of the three is the **International Dyeing and Weaving Art Museum** (daily April–Oct 9am–5.30pm, Nov 9am–5pm; Dec 9am–5pm closed Mon; closed Jan–March; ¥550), which exhibits a diverse collection of handwoven fabrics from around the world, from sixteenth-century Belgian tapestries to beautiful kimono. The **Yukara Ori Folk Craft Museum** (daily April–Oct 9am–5.30pm, Nov 9am–5pm; Dec–March 9am–5pm; closed Mon; ¥450) displays the colourful local style of textile and you can watch weavers at work. Least appealing is the kitsch **Snow Crystals Museum** (daily April–Oct 9am–5.30pm, Nov 9am–5pm; Dec–March 9am–5pm; closed Mon; ¥650); the displays on the myriad shapes of snow crystals are pretty but dwarfed by the castle-like complex with turrets, an ice corridor and a two-hundred-seat concert hall with a sky-painted ceiling. Buses to the complex leave from platforms 6, 7, 11 and 13.

Asahikawa was once a major Ainu settlement. There's a modest collection of Ainu-related artefacts on display at the **Kawamura Kaneto Ainu Memorial Hall**

Asahikawa's sake breweries

The pure waters flowing off Daisetsu-zan are one reason that Asahikawa has long had a flourishing sake industry. To sample some of the local product, head to the **Takasago Sake Brewery** (高砂酒造; Mon–Sat 9am–5.30pm, Sun 9am–5pm; ⓦwww.takasago-sake.co.jp), set in a traditional wooden building around ten minutes' walk east of Asahikawa Station. They've been making sake here since 1899 and from late January to early March they have a tradition of building an ice dome in which some of their sakes are fermented. If you have more time, head 6km north of the city centre to the **Otokoyama Sake Brewery and Museum** (酒造り資料館; daily 9am–5pm; ⓦwww.otokoyama.com), where you can also taste the award-winning rice wines for free. Buses #67, #70, #71 and #667 from platform 18 in front of the JR station will get you here.

(川村カ子トアイヌ記念館; July–Aug 8am–6pm; Sept–June 9am–5pm; ⓣ0166/51-2461; ¥500), which celebrates the Ainu chief Kaneto who worked as a surveyor with Hokkaidō's railways. Occasionally Ainu dance performances and events take place – call ahead to check. Buses #24 and #23 run to the hall from platform 14. The **Ainu Kotan Matsuri**, an Ainu festival, is held each September, beside the Ishikari-gawa around 10km south of Asahikawa.

Eating and drinking

There are plenty of places to **eat** around Heiwa-dōri and, one block west, the **Sanroku** entertainment district, where you'll find lively *izakaya* and sushi bars. Asahikawa is renowned for its shōyu-style ramen: sample it at *Aji-no-Daiō* (味の大王), 8 chōme, 1-jo-dōri, or *Hachiya*, 7 chōme, 5-jo-dōri, both on the atmospheric alleyway Furariito (ふらりーと). Tasty Italian-style bistro food made with organic local ingredients is served up at *Nacon* (ⓣ0166/25-1900; Fri & Sat noon–3pm, Mon–Sat 6pm–1am; around ¥3000), 7 chōme, 5-jo-dōri, a cute basement space opposite Furariito alley.

Asahikawa has a couple of *gaijin* **bars** but they're lacklustre; instead, sample the local beer at *Taisetsu Ji Beer* (大雪地ビール館; daily 11.30am–10pm), a couple of blocks east of the JR station along Miyashita-dōri. There's also the stylish *Machibar* (daily 11am–11pm), 8 chōme, 2-jo-dōri, on Heiwa-dōri.

Daisetsu-zan National Park

The 2309-square-kilometre **Daisetsu-zan National Park** (大雪山国立公園) offers a spectacular range of gorges, hot springs and mountains – including **Asahi-dake**, the island's tallest peak – crisscrossed by hiking trails which could keep you happily occupied for days. Tourism in the park is generally low-key, especially at the wooded and remote **Asahidake Onsen**. **Sōunkyō Onsen**, on the northeast edge of the park, hosts the bulk of tourists, though a tasteful redevelopment has made it much more attractive than most hot-spring resorts. The highlight here is the **gorge**, a 20km corridor of jagged cliffs, 150m high in places. In July, the mountain slopes are covered with alpine flowers, while September and October see the landscape painted in vivid autumnal colours; these are the best months for hiking. During the winter, both Asahi-dake and **Kuro-dake** in Sōunkyō are popular skiing spots, enjoying the longest ski season in Japan (usually Oct–June).

Asahidake Onsen

Quiet and uncommercialized **ASAHIDAKE ONSEN** (旭岳温泉) is little more than a handful of hotels and pensions dotted along a road that snakes up to the cable-car station, from where hikers in the summer and skiers in the winter are whisked to within striking distance of the 2291m summit of **Asahi-dake** (旭岳). The area's remoteness means that it remains a delightful and relatively little-visited destination. Cross-country skiers in particular will appreciate the kilometres of groomed trails, some of the best in Japan, which wind through beautiful forests of white birch and Hokkaidō spruce.

Arrival and information

There are between two and four **buses** daily from Asahikawa Station (platform 4) to Asahidake Onsen (1hr 45min; ¥1320), all stopping at Tenninkyō Onsen en route; check with the tourist office at Asahikawa Station for the timetable.

Near the cable car, the **tourist office** (daily: June–Oct 9am–5pm; Nov–May 10am–4pm) has nature displays (all in Japanese), information on weather conditions on the mountain and hiking maps.

Accommodation and eating

The park's **campsite** (ⓣ0166/97-2544; ¥500/person) is open from June 10 to September 30; tent and camping equipment rental is available. All other **places to stay** have rates based on bed, breakfast and dinner.

Daisetsuzan Shirakaba-sō Hotel and Youth Hostel 大雪山白樺荘 ⓣ0166/97-2246, ⓦpark19.wakwak.com/~shirakaba. There's both hotel and hostel-style lodgings at this lovely wooden building, opposite the campsite bus stop and next to a running stream; the attached log house has a convivial communal lounge and there's a rotemburo (¥500 for non-guests). Evening meals are excellent and the hostel staff can provide all you need to climb Asahi-dake, including a bell to warn off bears. Dorm bed ¥5530/person. ⑤

Lodge Nutapu-Kaushipe ロッジヌタプカウシペ ⓣ&ⓕ0166/97-2150. Next to the youth hostel and equally appealing is this attractive wooden cabin with six comfortable, Japanese-style rooms – all non-smoking. They also run a noodle café. ⑤

La Vista Daisetsuzan, ラビスタ大雪山 ⓣ0166/97-2323; ⓦtinyurl.com/25erlmn. In the style of a large alpine chalet, the onsen's newest hotel offers pleasant, spacious accommodation, lovely views and nicely designed onsen baths. ⑦

Hotel Beamonte ホテルベアモンテ ⓣ0166/97-2321. These upmarket but unremarkable lodgings, opposite the visitor centre, offer mainly Western-style rooms. In its favour are the nicely designed onsen baths, including rotemburo, and small gym. ⑥

Asahi-dake and around

The **cable car** (ⓦhttp://wakasaresort.com; June 15–Oct 10 one way/return ¥1500/2800; Oct 11–June 14 ¥1000/1800) takes about fifteen minutes to reach the top station, worth visiting for its ethereal landscape of steaming pools and rocky outcrops even if you're not planning to hike to the top of Asahi-dake. Check the website for running times as they vary greatly by month, with the service closed from November 11 to December 10.

Asahi-dake's peak is an arduous ninety-minute to two-hour slog over slippery volcanic rock from the cable-car station, but the view from the summit is fantastic. From here you can hike across to Sōunkyō (see below). There's also a good two-hour walk, mainly downhill and through forests, from the campsite in Asahidake Onsen to **Tenninkyō Onsen** (天人峡温泉), where a gaggle of tourist hotels stands at the mouth of a dramatic gorge which terminates in two spectacular **waterfalls**. From the main car park at Tenninkyō Onsen you can catch the bus to Asahikawa (¥1180) or back to Asahidake Onsen (¥730).

Sōunkyō Onsen

On the northeastern edge of Daisetsu-zan, 70km east of Asahikawa, is **SŌUNKYŌ ONSEN** (層雲峡温泉), the park's main resort and ideal base for viewing the astonishing **Sōunkyō gorge**, its jagged rock walls carved out by the Ishikari-gawa. Rent a **bike** from the *Northern Lodge* (¥1000; see p.318) and follow the riverside route for 8km to Ōbako. About 3km east of the resort, pause to view the **Ginga and Ryusei waterfalls**. A twenty-minute climb up the opposite hill will lead to a viewpoint from where you'll get a fabulous view of the two cascades of white water tumbling down the cliffs. Continuing along the cycling and walking path, you'll eventually arrive at **Ōbako** ("Big Box"), a touristy spot where visitors line up to be photographed in front of the river that gushes through the narrow gap in the perpendicular cliffs.

The **Sōunkyō visitor centre** (daily June–Sept 8am–6pm; Oct–May 9am–5pm, closed Mon; ⓣ01658/9-4400), with excellent nature displays, sits at the top of the village's main street, which itself is lined with small hotels, shops and a large bathing complex, **Kurodake-no-yu** (黒岳の湯; 10am–9pm; closed Wed; ¥600). From January to the end of March, it's also possible to enjoy the **Hyōbaku Matsuri** (Ice Waterfall Festival; ¥100), a park of giant ice sculptures which are lit spectacularly every night from 5pm to 10pm.

Hiking across the park

You can start the **Daisetsu-zan hike** across the park's central mountain range either from the top of the cable car at Asahidake Onsen (see p.316) or from Sōunkyō Onsen where there's also a **cable car** (Ⓦwww.rinyu.co.jp; one way/return ¥1000/1850), followed by a **chairlift** (one way/return ¥400/600) up to within one hour's hike of the 1984m **Kuro-dake** (Black Mountain); check the website for running times, which vary month by month. From the summit, capped by a small shrine and giving marvellous views of the park, there's a choice of two trails to Asahi-dake – the southern route via Hokkai-dake (2149m) is the more scenic.

By the time you reach Asahi-dake's summit, you'll have spent around six hours walking, so returning on foot to Sōunkyō Onsen the same day is only possible if you set out at the crack of dawn. There are overnight huts on the mountain, but the more comfortable option is to continue down to Asahidake Onsen and rest there for the night. If you don't want to backtrack for your luggage, consider having it sent on by *Takkyūbin* (see p.77). Also make sure you're well prepared for the hike with food, topographical maps, and bells to scare away the odd bear, even though they're not that common to see. For more on what to do should you encounter a bear, see p.329.

Practicalities

The closest **train** station to Sōunkyō Onsen is **Kamikawa** (上川), 20km north; buses (¥800) take thirty minutes from here to reach the resort. Some of the **buses** passing through Kamikawa and on to Sōunkyō originate in Asahikawa (¥1950); see Ⓦwww.dohokubus.com for the schedule. There's a **tourist office** (daily 10am–5.30pm; Ⓣ01658/5-3350, Ⓦwww.sounkyo.net) in the bus terminal building.

The budget **place to stay** is the *Sōunkyō Youth Hostel* (Ⓣ01658/5-3418, Ⓦwww.youthhostel.or.jp/sounkyo; dorm beds ¥2940/person), a ten-minute walk uphill from the bus terminal, near the *Prince Hotel*. The dorms here have bunk beds, meals are served in a rustic lounge area and you can get information – mainly in Japanese – on hiking in the park. Within the village itself, between May and October *Midori* (民宿みどり; Ⓣ01658/5-3315; ❺ including meals) offers basic tatami rooms and a friendly manager who may be found at the souvenir shop downstairs. You can also check to see whether the *gaijin*-owned *Black Mountain Lodge* (Ⓦwww.kurodakelodge.com; ¥3500/person) is taking guests. If you crave a bit more luxury, a good choice is *Northern Lodge* (Ⓣ01658/5-3231, Ⓦwww.h-northernlodge.com; ❹–❺ including two meals), offering both tatami and Western-style rooms.

In the same complex as Kurodake-no-yu are a couple of **restaurants**, including *Beer Grill Canyon*, which serves tasty thin-crust pizza, pasta and creative dishes such as Ezo venison stroganoff (¥1500). Internet access is also available here.

Furano and around

Surrounded by beautiful countryside, **FURANO** (富良野) is famous throughout Japan as the location of a popular soap opera *Kita no Kuni Kara* (*From the Northern Country*), about a Tokyo family adapting to life in Hokkaidō. The landscape evokes Provençal France, with bales of hay lying around and lone poplars etched against the peaks of Daisetsu-zan National Park. The busiest season is June and July, when vast fields of lavender and other flowers bloom, drawing visitors to the gently undulating countryside hereabouts – ideal for walks, cycling and photography; the most scenic farmlands surround the tranquil settlements of **Kamifurano** (上富良野), **Biei** (美瑛) and **Bibaushi** (美馬牛). In winter, Furano is known for its **skiing**.

The local tourism office is working hard to ensure that the Japanese character and charm of the area aren't lost or overlooked by visiting *gaijin*. During the ski season a free cultural performance is held every Saturday night at the restaurant at the Kitanomine gondola station. This includes a presentation of the town's "belly button dance", the highlight of Furano's **Heso Matsuri** (Navel Festival), held every July 28–29 and celebrating the town's position at the centre of Hokkaidō.

Further afield, if you need goals for your perambulations head to Kamifurano where the **Goto Sumio Museum of Art** (後藤純男美術館; daily 9am–5pm; ¥1000; Ⓦwww.gotosumiomuseum.com) contains dreamy landscape paintings from one of Japan's major contemporary artists, or to Furano's wine and cheese factories (see p.320). Furano and the outlying towns in the area can also be used as a base for a hike up the 2077m active volcano of **Tokachi-dake**, some 20km southwest and within the Daisetsu-zan National Park.

Arrival and information

Furano is connected by direct **bus** with Sapporo (around 2hr 30min; ¥2200); if you're coming to ski, ask to be dropped at Kitanomine-iriguchi (the hub of the ski village) rather than getting off in the centre of town. In summer and sometimes in winter there are also direct **trains** from Sapporo, but usually the fastest way is to take a limited express to Takikawa then change to the local train along the Furano line. From Asahikawa, the train takes one hour and fifteen minutes (¥1040), passing through Biei, Bibaushi and Kami-Furano. Regular buses also run from Asahikawa via Furano train station to the *New Furano Prince Hotel*; a taxi here from Furano Station costs around ¥2300.

The **Furano tourist office** (Ⓣ0167/23-3388, Ⓦwww.furanotourism.com; daily 9am–6pm) has operations both next to Furano Station and at the Kitanomine gondola station.

Accommodation

If you've come to ski, it's most convenient to stay in either the *Prince* **hotels** or at Kitanomine village from where you can walk to the lifts. However, Furano town itself isn't too far away and is connected to the slopes by regular buses.

Alpine Backpackers Ⓣ0167/22-1311, Ⓦwww.alpn.co.jp. Five minutes' walk from the Kitanomine ski lifts, this great lodge has bunk-bed dorms or twins, a kitchen, a bakery-café, free internet access and young, enthusiastic staff. They also organize balloon trips year-round, plus adventure sports such as rafting, mountain biking and horseriding in summer. Dorm beds from ¥2700/person. ❸

Bibaushi Liberty Youth Hostel Ⓣ0166/95-2141, Ⓦbit.ly/aVqHRq. Next to the train station, this stylish hostel offers comfy bunk-bed dorms and private rooms; excellent, inexpensive meals are also available. Dorm beds from ¥3780/person for YH members. ❹

Furano Fresh Powder Ⓣ0167/23-4738, Ⓦwww.freshpowder.com. Opposite the Kitanomine ski slopes are these six well-equipped self-catering units, sleeping between four and eight people. There's a five-day minimum rental during ski season. ❾

Pension Hōzuki ほうずき Ⓣ&Ⓕ0166/92-1225. Two kilometres from Biei Station, this lovely

Skiing in Furano

Furano's winter focus is its **ski resort** (Ⓦprincehotels.co.jp/ski/furano; day ticket ¥4200) on the slopes of Mount Kitanomine, a popular option with those seeking to escape the crowded foreigner scene at Niseko (see p.301). The slopes are challenging, but not as varied or as long as Niseko's; to go off-piste, or try backcountry skiing with qualified English-speaking guides, contact **Hokkaidō Powder Guides** (Ⓣ0167/22-5655, Ⓦwww.hokkaidopowderguides.com).

Fertile Furano

It's not just flowers that thrive in Furano's fertile soil. The area is also known for its melons, potatoes, onions, milk and grapes. At **Chateau Furano** (Ⓦwww.furanowine.jp; Sept–May 9am–4.30pm, June–Aug till 6pm; free), around 4km northwest of Furano Station, you can sip from a range of 18 different wines; some of them are fairly palatable. The obvious accompaniment is cheese, and this can be sampled at the **Furano Cheese Factory** (富良野チーズ工房; Ⓦwww.furano.ne.jp/furano-cheese; Apr–Oct 9am–5pm; Nov–Mar till 4pm; free), about 1km east of the *New Furano Prince Hotel*. Apart from selling concoctions such as a brie turned black with squid ink, this fun facility also allows you to practise milking a fake cow (¥100) and sign up for bread, butter-, cheese- and ice cream- making workshops (¥680–850).

guesthouse is surrounded by greenery, with an English-speaking owner and Western-style twin rooms. 6

Natulux Hotel Ⓣ0167/22-1777; Ⓦwww.natulux.com. Next to Furano Station, this tasteful boutique property sports a minimalist design contrasting concrete walls with black or brown wooden fixtures. The English-speaking management are very obliging and guests can use the neighbouring sports complex with swimming pool for free. 6

New Furano Prince Hotel Ⓣ0167/22-1111, Ⓦwww.princehotels.co.jp/newfurano. A few kilometres south of Kitanomine village, this 400-bed oval-shaped tower block is a world unto itself, featuring everything from several restaurants and bars, ski rental and a coin laundry to a sophisticated onsen (guests/non-guests Y750/¥1500) and a cutesy log cabin shopping village. Families will love their Snow Land winter amusement park. In winter there are package deals with meals and ski-lift tickets. The Prince group has a second smaller hotel in Furano that's mainly used by groups. 7

Phytoncide Mori no Kaori フィトンチッド森の香り Ⓣ0167/39-1551, Ⓦwww.woodlandfarm.co.jp. Pronounced "feetonchido" (it means "the fresh smell of the forest"), this is one of Furano's most original accommodation options. The charming owners, who bake their own bread and serve foods grown on their organic farm, have an amazing collection of antique cash registers. Each of the six Western-style rooms has its own bath/toilet, and one is wheelchair-accessible. Rates include two meals. 8

Eating and drinking

You're likely to **eat** in your hotel or pension at night, as meals are generally included in room rates. Still, there are a few places worth visiting, including *Kuma Gera* (くまげら; Ⓣ0167/39-2345; Ⓦwww.furano.ne.jp/kumagera), a lively place in the midst of Furano town where they serve the meat-laden *banzoku nabe* (bandit's stew). In Kitanomine, there's the rustic restaurant/bar/bakery *Yuiga Doxon* (唯我独尊, Ⓣ0167/22-5599) where they make their own very palatable beers, sausages, smoked meats and baked goods.

For a nightcap try *Soh's Bar*, in a log and stone cabin in the forest near the New Furano Hotel, where you can admire the collection of cigarette packets whether you're a "miserable smoker" or not. On the way there you can go gift shopping in the attractive log house complex Ningle Terrace.

Wakkanai

The windswept port of **WAKKANAI** (稚内), 320km from Sapporo, is the gateway to the **Rishiri-Rebun-Sarobetsu National Park** (see p.322) and, in particular, the lovely islands of Rebun-tō and Rishiri-tō. There's little reason to linger in town, but there are a few places of minor interest in the area, if you find yourself killing time waiting for a ferry.

A short stroll from Wakkanai Station is the impressive **North Breakwater Dome**, a 427m-long arched corridor supported by seventy concrete pillars. For a longer walk (around one hour, round-trip), head west of the train station to **Wakkanai-kōen** (稚内公園), a grassy park from where, on a clear day, you can see the island of **Sakhalin**, some 60km northwest; it's now part of Russia but before World War II it was occupied by the Japanese.

Desolate cape **Sōya Misaki** (宗谷岬), 32km east of Wakkanai, is the northernmost point of Japan. A couple of monuments, "The Bell for World Peace" and the "Tower of Prayer", a memorial to the Korean Airlines plane shot down by the Soviet Union just north of the cape, mark this dull spot, served by at least four daily buses from Wakkanai (50min; ¥2430 return).

Some 35km south of Wakkanai lies **Sarobetsu Natural Flower Garden** (サロベツ原生花園), best visited between May and September, when its marshlands become a riot of colourful blooms. To reach the park, take a local train to Toyotomi Station (45min; ¥900), and then catch a bus (15min; ¥430).

Wakkanai is snowbound in winter, but this is also the best time for nature lovers to observe a colony of spotted seals (*azarashi*) basking on the rocks at **Bakkai** (抜海), a fifteen-minute local train ride south of town and then a thirty-minute walk – staff at the tourist information counter (see below) will give you a map if you're interested. Another quirky reason for heading here out of season is to attend the **Japan Cup National Dogsled Races**, held the last weekend of February.

Arrival and information

Wakkanai Station is close by both the **ferry** terminal and the new combined bus terminal and cinema. Inside the station is a helpful **tourist office** (daily May–Sept 10am–6pm; Oct–Jan same hours, closed Sun; Feb–March same hours, closed Wed; Ⓣ0162/24-1216, Ⓦwww.welcome.wakkanai.hokkaido.jp). A bus from Wakkanai's **airport** (Ⓣ0162/27-2121), 10km east of the port, costs ¥590 for the thirty-minute journey, and a taxi ¥3500. There are also direct overnight buses from Sapporo (7hr; ¥6000).

If you're heading on to Rishiri-tō and Rebun-tō, stock up on cash in Wakkanai as there are no foreign exchange facilities on either of the islands. There's an **ATM** that accepts overseas cards at the **post office**, five blocks west of the JR station (ATM hours Mon–Fri 8.45am–7pm, Sat & Sun 9am–5pm).

Practicalities

Wakkanai has plenty of **accommodation**. The most convenient youth hostel (May–Oct) for the port is *Wakkanai Moshiripa* (稚内モシリパユースホステル; Ⓣ0162/24-0180, Ⓦwww.youthhostel.or.jp; dorm beds ¥3360/person), five minutes' walk north from the train station and east of the ferry terminal; guests must check in before 8pm. Better equipped and open year-round is *Wakkanai Youth*

The Russian connection

There's a monument in Wakkanai-kōen to nine female telephone operators who committed suicide in Sakhalin's post office at the end of World War II, rather than be captured by the Russians. Russo-Japanese relations are now much improved and there's steady trade between Wakkanai and its northern neighbour, as witnessed by the many signs in Russian around town. From mid-May to October a **ferry** runs between Wakkanai and the town of **Korsakov** on Sakhalin (5hr 30min; economy class ¥22,500 one way, ¥35,000 return); see Ⓦwww.kaiferry.co.jp for details.

Hostel (稚内ユースホステル; ⓣ0162/23-7162, ⓦwww.youthhostel.or.jp; dorm beds ¥3360/person), a ten-minute walk south from JR Minami Wakkanai Station. Business hotels include *Wakkanai Sun Hotel* (ⓣ0162/22-5311, ⓦwww.sunhotel.co.jp; ⑤), immediately south of the JR station, which has free internet access in its lobby. The most luxurious option is the *ANA Hotel Wakkanai* (ⓣ0162/23-8111, ⓦwww.ana-hotel-wakkanai.co.jp; ⑦), directly in front of the ferry terminal. Prices here drop dramatically in the off season.

Definitely sample some **seafood** while you're in town; particularly convivial is *Takechan* (竹ちゃん; daily 11.30am–2pm & 5–10pm), specializing in sushi and *tako-shabu* (octopus stew; ¥1500). Handy for the station is *Sakita* (咲田), offering tasty lunch set menus for under ¥600, while a fifteen-minute walk south of the JR station is *Wakkanai Fukukō Ichiba* (稚内副港市場), where you can combine a seafood meal at several inexpensive restaurants with a dip in the spacious onsen baths of **Minato no Yu** (港のゆ; daily 10am–10pm; ¥700 plus ¥150 for a towel).

Rishiri-Rebun-Sarobetsu National Park

The two islands that make up the bulk of the **Rishiri-Rebun-Sarobetsu National Park** (利尻礼文サロベツ国立公園) are quite different: slender **Rebun-tō** is low-lying, its gentle hills sprinkled with alpine flowers, while **Rishiri-tō** is a Fuji-like volcano rising from the sea. Offering lovely scenery and mild weather, both islands are exceptionally popular with Japanese tourists from June to September, when accommodation should be booked well in advance. At other times you're likely to have the islands to yourself, although they pretty much close down entirely between November and March. In order to get the most out of a stay here it's worth scheduling a couple of nights on each island.

Rishiri-tō

Most people come to **RISHIRI-TŌ** (利尻島) to hike up of the central 1721m volcano **Rishiri-zan** (利尻山). The island is sometimes called Rishiri-Fuji because its shape is said to resemble the famous southern volcano; in reality it's spikier and a lot less symmetrical. Even if the weather is unpromising, it's still worth making the ascent (which takes ten to twelve hours) to break through the clouds on the upper slopes and be rewarded with panoramic views from the summit, which is crowned with a small shrine.

The most straightforward ascent starts some 3km south of the main port of **Oshidomari** (鴛泊), at the Rishiri Hokuroku campsite. Information and maps for

Getting to the islands

There's a daily flight to **Rishiri-tō** from New Chitose; the **airport** (ⓣ0163/82-1770) is a few kilometres west of Oshidomari. Most visitors, however, come by **ferry** from Wakkanai to Oshidomari (1hr 40min; ¥1980 one way); from May to September there are four services daily, then three daily in October, dropping to two from November through March before increasing to three again in April.

Rebun-tō is only accessible by ferry. From May to September five **ferries** daily go from Wakkanai to Kafuka (1hr 55min; ¥2200), and there are at least a couple each day during the rest of the year. Daily ferries also sail between Kafuka on Rebun-tō and Oshidomari and Kutsugata on Rishiri-tō (40min; ¥780 one-way). Hostels and most minshuku will pick you up from the ferry terminals, if you book in advance. For full details of the ferries go to ⓦwww.heartlandferry.jp.

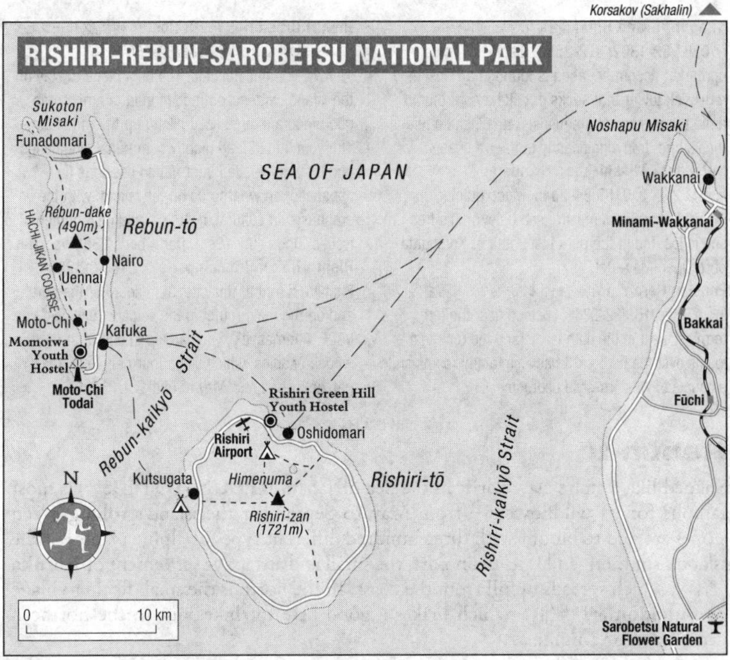

RISHIRI-REBUN-SAROBETSU NATIONAL PARK

the climb are available from the island's tourist office (see below); climbing groups are occasionally organized by staff at the local youth hostel. Around fifteen minutes' climb from the peak of Chōkan-zan (長官山), the eighth station up the volcano, there's a basic hut where you can take shelter en route. Take plenty of water as there's none available on the mountain.

A less strenuous alternative to climbing Rishiri-zan is the three-hour hiking trail which starts at pretty **Himenuma** pond (姫沼) and continues across the slopes of two smaller mountains, Kopon-zan and Pon-zan, to the Rishiri Hokuroku campsite. To get to Himenuma from Oshidomari, follow the coastal road 1km or so west until you reach a junction going up into the hills. The walk to the pond is quite steep – you might be able to hitch a lift – and takes around an hour.

Information and island transport

The **tourist office** (mid-April to mid-Oct daily 8am–5.40pm; ⓣ01638/2-2201, ⓦwww.town.rishiri.hokkaido.jp), inside the ferry terminal at Oshidomari, has maps and English notes on the hikes to Rishiri-zan and Himenuma.

Bicycles are a good way to get around and can be rented from near the ferry terminal and from the youth hostel for around ¥2000 a day. Otherwise, **buses** run in both directions around the island (a circuit which takes 1hr 45min; ¥2200). If you arrive by ferry at Kutsugata on the western side of Rishiri, you'll need to get a bus north to Oshidomari (30min; ¥730).

Accommodation

Island Inn Rishiri アイランド イン リシリ ⓣ0163/84-3002. Located in Kutsugata on the island's west coast, the large, modern Western-style rooms here have views of either the port or the mountains. There's a public bath and rates include two meals. ⑦

Kitaguni Grand Hotel 北国グランドホテル Ⓣ0163/82-1362, Ⓕ2-2556. Rishiri-tō's most upmarket accommodation is found in an unsightly red-brick tower that sticks out like a sore thumb amid the surrounding houses. Rates include two meals and drop significantly in the off season. ⑧

Kutsugata Misaki-kōen campsite 沓形岬公園キャンプ場 Ⓣ0163/84-2345. Much quieter than Rishiri Hokuroku campsite (see below), this free site is located in the park just south of Kutsugata port. Open May–Oct.

Pension Hera-san-no-ie ペンションへらさんの家 Ⓣ&Ⓕ0163/82-2361. Located near the ferry terminal, next to the path leading up the rock that looms over the harbour. It has nice tatami rooms and a couple of Western-style bedrooms. ⑥

Rishiri Green Hill Youth Hostel 利尻グリーンヒルユースホステル Ⓣ0163/82-2507, Ⓦwww.youthhostel.or.jp. The best place to stay on the island, with accommodation in tatami rooms, good food and organized hiking up the mountain. The young staff lead nightly communal singalongs and provide detailed information sessions (in Japanese) on what to do on the island, with the emphasis on cultural, historical and environmental issues. Open June–Sept. Dorm beds ¥3960/person.

Rishiri Hokuroku campsite Ⓣ0163/82-2394. Pitching a tent at this site, 3km south of the port and on the main route up the volcano, will cost you ¥300. Alternatively, you can kip in one of the wooden cabins, which sleep four people (¥3000/person). Open mid-May to mid-Oct.

Rebun-tō

Shaped like a crab's claw adrift in the Sea of Japan, **REBUN-TŌ** (礼文島) is most famous for its wildflowers – from May to September the island's rolling green slopes are said to bloom with three hundred different types of alpine plants. At the island's southern end is its main port, the small and attractive settlement of **Kafuka** (香深), which spreads uphill from the coast. In the north is the small fishing village of **Funadomari** (船泊), which makes a good base for hikes out to the northern cape, Sukoton Misaki.

The whole island is fabulous **hiking** territory. The longest and most popular hike is the 32km (8hr) **Hachi-jikan** down the west coast from Sukoton Misaki (スコトン岬), the island's northernmost point, to Moto-chi (元地) in the south. The cliffs at the end of this hike can be slippery and sometimes dangerous; easier is the **Yo-jikan** (4hr) course, which omits the difficult coastal section of the Hachi-jikan course from Uennai to Moto-chi. The youth hostel (see opposite) arranges walking groups for the two hikes and holds briefings the night before. Stock up on food and drink before you start, as there are no refreshment stops along the way and it's not safe to drink river water on the island.

Information and island transport

Rebun's **tourist office** (May–Sept daily 8am–5.30pm; Ⓣ0163/86-2655), in the ferry terminal at Kafuka, has a good map of the island, marked with the main hiking routes including ones up Rebun-dake and to the Momo-iwa ("Peach-Shaped Rock") on the west coast. Staff can also help with booking accommodation. If time is limited, consider taking one of the three **bus tours** (¥3300–4000), which cover all the scenic highlights and are timed to connect with the ferries; details are available from the tourist office. **Bike rental** is available from several shops near the ferry terminal for ¥500 an hour, or ¥2000 a day.

Accommodation

Field Inn Seikan-sō 星観荘 Ⓣ0163/87-2818. This comfortable minshuku in Funadomari occupies a Scandinavian-sytle wooden cottage with great views. Rooms have bunk beds and rates include two meals. ⑤

Hana Rebun 花れぶん Ⓣ0163/86-1177. Next to the Kafuka ferry terminal, this is the luxury option with appealing traditional-style rooms combining Western and Japanese interior design. The most expensive suites sport outdoor tubs on balconies. Rates include two meals ⑨

Kaidō 海憧 Ⓣ0163/87-2717, Ⓕ87-2183. Larger than the *Field Inn Seikan-sō*, this establishment next to the beach campsite has tatami rooms and some cheaper dorm accommodation ((¥6000/person; under 40s only). Rates include two meals. ⑤

Momo-iwa-sō Youth Hostel 桃岩荘ユースホステル ⓣ0163/86-1421, ⓦwww.youthhostel.or.jp. Occupying a dramatic location on the rocky western coast, south of Moto-chi and 15min drive from Kafuka, this hostel makes a good base for the Hachi-jikan hiking course; it's situated at the end of the walk, but staff can organize transport to the start. It gets packed at the height of the season and the atmosphere becomes akin to a summer camp, featuring lots of singing and dancing from the high-spirited staff. Dorm beds ¥3045/person.

Eastern Hokkaidō

With three major national parks, **eastern Hokkaidō** will be a high priority for those interested in Japan's natural environment. Public transport is sparse, so consider renting a car to get around. **Abashiri** is known throughout Japan for its old maximum-security prison (now a museum), and winter boat tours through the drift ice on the Sea of Okhotsk. Jutting into these inhospitable waters northeast of Abashiri is **Shiretoko National Park**, a UNESCO World Heritage Site and one of Japan's most naturally unspoiled areas. Inland, south of the peninsula, the **Akan National Park** is also stunning, with hot springs and three scenic lakes. More eco-tourist delights await at **Kushiro Shitsugen National Park** and **Kiritappu Marsh** where you can spot regal red-crested cranes among many other fauna and flora.

Abashiri

Bordered by a couple of pretty lakes, the fishing port of **ABASHIRI** (網走), 350km from Sapporo, is best visited in the dead of winter, when snow covers the less appealing modern parts of the town, whooper swans fly in to winter at Lake Tofutsu a few kilometres east of the harbour and drift ice (*ryūhyō*) floats across the Sea of Okhotsk (see p.326).

Arrival and information

Memanbetsu (女満別) **airport** is 20km south of Abashiri and 25 minutes from town by bus (¥880). By **train**, the fastest option is the limited express from Sapporo via Asahikawa (5hr 20min), while **buses** from Sapporo (¥6210; ⓦwww.j-bus.co.jp) take six hours. There's also a plodding local train on the Senmō line from the port of Kushiro (see p.332), 146km south.

Cranes, swans and eagles

Birdwatchers will be thrilled by eastern Hokkaidō. The area is home to three of Japan's top four ornithological spectacles: red-crested white cranes (*tancho-zuru*) in the Kushiro and Kiritappu regions (see p.333); whooper swans, also in the Kushiro region, and near Abashiri and Odaito towards the Notsuke Peninsula; and Steller's sea eagles at Rausu on the Shiretoko Peninsula. The fourth must-see is cranes at Arasaki in Kyūshū. The best months to view all of these are January, February and March.

The **red-crested white cranes**, commonly called *tancho*, are a symbol of Japan and were once found all over the country. However, they became so rare in the twentieth century that they were thought to be almost extinct. Fortunately, the birds – designated a "Special Natural Monument" in 1952 – have survived and their population, living exclusively in eastern Hokkaidō, now numbers around one thousand. Thanks to feeding programmes at several sites around the Kushiro Shitsugen National Park (see p.333), it's possible to see these grand but shy birds; with a 2m wingspan they are the largest in Japan.

Inside the JR station is the helpful **tourist office** (Mon–Sat 9am–5pm; ⓣ0152/44-5849, ⓦwww.city.abashiri.hokkaido.jp). There's free **internet** access at the Ekō Centre (エコーセンター; 9am–7pm; closed Mon), on the north bank of the Abashiri-gawa across the bridge near the *Abashiri Central Hotel*.

Accommodation

There are several **business hotels** near the JR station including branches of the reliable *Hotel Route Inn* and *Tōyoko Inn*.

Abashiri Central Hotel 網走セントラルホテル ⓣ0152/44-5151, ⓦwww.abashirich.com. The town's top choice offers a classy selection of rooms, a good restaurant (serving a buffet lunch for ¥1200) and is convenient for the shopping district. ❺

Abashiri Ryūhyō-no-Oka Youth Hostel 網走流氷の丘ユースホステル ⓣ0152/43-8558, ⓦwww.youthhostel.or.jp. Modern hostel overlooking the Sea of Okhotsk. It's a long, steep walk up here so catch a taxi (around ¥1000). Bicycle rental is available. Dorm beds ¥3100/person.

Auberge Kita-no-dan-dan Auberge 北の暖暖 ⓣ0152/45-5963. Five minutes by taxi from the JR station is this engagingly rustic retreat atop a hill and surrounded by greenery. There's a rotemburo and rates include two European-style meals. ❽

Shimbashi ホテルしんばし ⓣ0152/43-4307, ⓕ45-2091. Directly opposite the JR station is this old-style hotel with decent tatami and Western-style rooms with singles from ¥4500. Its restaurant serves good-value set meals and cheap noodle dishes. ❹

The Town

An excellent vantage point from which to take in Abashiri's coastal location is the summit of **Tento-zan**, directly behind the train station, where you'll also find several enjoyable museums. At the informative **Okhotsk Ryūhyō Museum** (オホーツク流氷館; daily: April–Oct 8am–6pm; Nov–March 9am–4.30pm; ¥520) you can touch huge lumps of ice in a room where the temperature is kept at minus 15°C; coats are provided for warmth. A panoramic film of the drift ice is also screened regularly throughout the day. A five-minute walk downhill from here is the **Hokkaidō Museum of Northern Peoples** (北海道立北方民族博物館; 9.30am–4.30pm; closed Mon; ⓦhoppohm.org; ¥450), with interesting displays on the native peoples of northern Eurasia and America, prompting comparisons between the different cultures. A colour-coded chart at the start of the exhibition will help you identify which artefacts belong to which races; look out for the Inuit cagoules, fascinating garments made of seal intestines.

Most Japanese associate Abashiri with its **maximum-security prison**, featured in a popular series of jail drama films called *Abashiri Bangaichi*. The town's current prison

Viewing the drift ice

Global warming has impacted on the drift ice off the coast of Abashiri and the Shiretoko Peninsula, with both its volume and the season for its sighting – typically February to late March – shrinking. Should the conditions be right, the ideal way to witness this astonishing phenomenon is to hop aboard the *Aurora*, an **ice-breaking sightseeing boat**, for a one-hour tour (Jan 20 to the first Sun in April daily; ⓣ0152/43-6000; ⓦwww.ms-aurora.com; ¥3300), which departs from Abashiri four to six times a day, depending on the month and weather. The boat cracks through the ice sheets, throwing up huge chunks, some more than 1m thick. An alternative is to take the slow-moving sightseeing train **Ryuhyo Norokko-go** (流氷ノロッコ号; ¥810), which chugs along the coast between Abashiri and Shiretoko-Shari twice a day between the end of January and mid-March; if that's not available, there's also the regular *futsu* train that runs into Akan National Park (see p.329). **Gojiraiwa-Kankō** (ⓦhttp://kamuiwakka.jp/driftice) in Utoro (see p.328) offers walking trips across the ice and the chance to get in the frozen water, comfortably attired in a dry suit.

no longer houses high-grade criminals or political undesirables, and the original nineteenth-century penitentiary has been relocated to the foot of Tento-zan and transformed into the jolly **Abashiri Prison Museum** (博物館網走監獄; daily: April–Oct 8am–6pm; Nov–March 9am–5pm; ¥1050; Ⓦwww.kangoku.jp/world). This large, open-air site features waxworks of various detainees (look out for the tattooed *yakuza* in the bathhouse, and Shiratori Yoshie, a famous escapee, crawling across the rafters in the cell block). Check with the tourist office for coupons to get discounted entry to all these museums and about a bus service that runs a circuit around them.

From late January to early March, fun winter activities take place on frozen Abashiri-ko, on the town's western flank. You can take a **snowmobile** for a spin around a 7km course over the lake (daily 9am–4.30pm; ¥3000), or be dragged around the ice sitting inside a raft or astride an inflatable banana. This site, along with the quay at Abashiri Port, is also the location for the town's mini **snow festival**, which takes place in the second week of February each year. Buses run to the lake from outside Abashiri Station. If none of that feels cold enough, then try **diving** beneath the ice (Ⓣ0152/61-5102; ¥30,000 for two dives).

Eating

Abashiri specializes in fresh **seafood** – don't leave town without trying some of its succulent crabs. Reliable and inexpensive is *Sushiyasu* (寿し安; daily 11am–11pm), a couple of blocks behind the *Abashiri Central Hotel*: sushi sets cost as little as ¥900 for lunch and ¥1550 for dinner. You could also sample locally brewed Abashiri Beer and grilled beef at **Yakiniku Abashiri Biirukan** (Yakiniku 網走ビール館; daily 11.30am–3pm & 5–10pm), a five-minute walk from the station towards the port.

Shiretoko National Park

Since 176,000 acres of the Shiretoko Peninsula, including the **SHIRETOKO NATIONAL PARK** (知床国立公園), gained UNESCO World Heritage Site status in 2005, there's been an increasing amount of investment in, as well as visitors to, this magnificent ecosystem 42km east of Abashiri. Even so, by any standards the park, which covers about half the 70km-long peninsula thrusting into the Sea of Okhotsk, remains virtually untouched by signs of human development: there are few roads or tourist facilities and **wildlife** is abundant – you're almost guaranteed to encounter

Hiking in the Shiretoko National Park

The peak of **Rausu-dake** (羅臼岳), the tallest mountain in Shiretoko at 1661m, can be reached in around four-and-a-half hours from the *Iwaobetsu Youth Hostel* (see p.329), passing a natural rotemburo on the way. From the summit there are spectacular views along the whole peninsula, and to the east you should be able to see Kunashiri-tō, one of the disputed Kuril Islands, or "Northern Territories" as they are known in Japan (see p.330). It takes a full day to continue across Rausu-dake to Rausu.

Iō-zan (硫黄山), the active volcano that produces hot water for the Kamuiwakka-no-taki waterfalls, is a more difficult climb. The trail begins beside the Shiretoko Ōhashi, the bridge just beyond the entrance to the falls. A hike to the 1562m summit and back takes at least eight hours and can be combined with a visit to the hot waterfall.

You'll need to be a serious mountaineer to tackle the difficult ridge trail linking Iō-zan and Rausu-dake; bring a topographical map, take precautions against bears (see p.329) and plan to stay one or two nights at the campsites along the way. The **Rusa Field House** (ルサフィールドハウス; Ⓣ0153-89-2722; May–Oct Wed–Sun 9am–5pm, Feb–April same days 10am–6pm), about 10km north along the coast from Rausu, can provide rules and current information to mountaineers and sea kayakers.

wild deer, foxes and even brown bears (see opposite). Peak season is from June to September, the best period for hiking and viewing the five small lakes at Shiretoko Go-ko, most easily reached from the peninsula's main town Utoro (see below). In the winter, drift ice litters the shore, and some 2000 Steller's sea eagles can be observed near **RAUSU** (羅臼; ⓦwww.rausu-shiretoko.com) on the peninsula's southeast coast. This remote fishing village has fewer facilities than Utoro but can still be used as a base for touring the park; it's the only place offering cruises in winter too – try **Hamanasu Kankō** (ⓣ0153-87-3830; from ¥6000/person).

Arrival and information

The gateway to the Shiretoko peninsula is **SHARI** (斜里), where there's a JR station on the Senmō line. From the bus terminal opposite frequent services run to Utoro (50min; ¥1490) and less frequently to Rausu (1hr; ¥1600). Between May and October, services continue up to Iwaobetsu for the youth hostel and as far as Kamuiwakka-no-taki. In the same time period there are services to Rausu (¥2410) via the Shiretoko Pass; note this road is closed to traffic between November and late April. For more details check ⓦwww.sharibus.co.jp. Rausu is also connected by bus with JR Nemuro Station on the Nemuro line.

There's a **tourist office** in the road station on the way into Utoro (8am–7.30pm daily; ⓣ0152/24-2639, ⓦwww.town.shari.hokkaido.jp/sh), or if you're on the other side of the peninsula there's the **Rausu Visitor Center** (羅臼ビジターセンター; ⓣ0153/87-2828; May–Oct 9am–5pm; Nov–April 10am–4pm; closed Mon) about 1km or so out of Rausu, near the Kuma-no-yu hot springs.

Utoro and around

Roads stop halfway up both sides of the peninsula, so the only way you'll get to see the rocky cape, with its unmanned lighthouse and waterfalls plunging over sheer cliffs into the sea, is to take one of the sightseeing boats from **UTORO** (ウトロ); trips on the largest boat, the **Aurora** (ⓣ0152/24-2147, ⓦwww.ms-aurora.com; 1hr 30min course ¥3100; 3hr 45min course ¥6500) run daily between June and September; you'll get closer to the coastline on one of the smaller boats that offer similar cruises for around ¥8000. Near Utoro's tiny harbour are several large rocks, one of which is nicknamed "Godzilla", for reasons that become obvious when you see it.

Coming into town, drop by the excellent **Shiretoko World Heritage Conservation Center** (知床世界遺産センター; ⓦshiretoko-whc.jp; April–Oct Wed–Sun 8.30am–5.30pm; Nov–April same days 9am–4.30pm; free) to learn about the park and its nature. Further up the coast is the older **Shiretoko Shizen Centre** (知床自然センター; daily: April 20–Oct 20 8am–5.40pm; Oct 21–April 19 9am–4pm; ⓦwww.shiretoko.or.jp), which shows a twenty-minute giant-screen film (¥500) throughout the day, with swooping aerial shots of the mountains and rugged coastline. Behind the centre, a few well-marked nature trails lead through forests and heathland to cliffs, down which a waterfall cascades.

Some 9km further north, past the *Iwaobetsu Youth Hostel* (see opposite), lies the **Shiretoko Go-ko** (知床五湖; late April–early Nov, 7.30am–6.30pm), where five jewel-like lakes are linked by wooden walkways and sinuous forest paths. In fine weather some of the lakes reflect the mountains, and a lookout point west of the car park provides a sweeping view across the heathland to the sea. The further you walk around the 2.4km circuit, the more serene the landscape becomes. A bus from Utoro runs to the lakes four times a day – hitching is another option. Allow at least an hour to see all five lakes. Just before the turn-off to the lakes, a dirt road continues up the peninsula. Following this track for about twenty minutes by car, as it rises uphill, will bring you to **Kamuiwakka-no-taki** (カムイワッカの滝), a cascading warm-water

Beware bears

The **brown bear** (*ezo higuma*) is common to wilderness areas of Hokkaidō, with around 200 thought to be living in the Shiretoko-hantō (see p.327). The bears, which can grow to a height of 2m and weigh up to 400kg, can be dangerous if surprised. If you're planning a hiking trip in these parts, it is important to be alert for bears and take appropriate precautions so you don't disturb them. Carrying a bell that jangles as you walk is a good idea as this will warn bears of your approach and hopefully keep them away. It's also vital, if carrying food, that you take great care to keep this away from bears. Don't discard food scraps around where you camp – leave them until you reach a river or stream where they can be washed away. If you do encounter a bear, don't run away – this will be an invitation for them to chase you – and don't make any sudden movements or look them directly in the eyes. Try to remain as still as possible until the bear gets bored and moves on.

river and series of waterfalls, creating three levels of natural rotemburo. To reach the bathing pools you'll have to climb up the river. Bring your bathing costume and rent straw sandals at the start of the climb – they make a world of difference on the dangerously slippery rocks. The topmost pool is the warmest and has the loveliest waterfall. The water is mildly acidic, so be warned that if you have any cuts it's going to sting, and bring a water bottle to rinse off with afterwards.

Accommodation and eating

Utoro has the best range of accommodation, as well as the well-maintained **campsite** *Shiretoko Yaei-jō* (知床野営場; ⓣ0152/24-2722; ¥500/person/night). Unless mentioned otherwise, rates will include two meals. There's also a reasonable selection of **restaurants**: try *Ikkyuya* (一休屋), just north of the bus station, where large bowls of ramen noodles shouldn't cost you more than ¥700.

Accommodation

Iwaobetsu Youth Hostel 知床岩尾別ユースホステル ⓣ0152/24-2311, ⓦwww.youthhostel.or.jp. Nestling in a valley beside the Iwaobetsu-gawa, this hostel is large and well managed, with welcoming staff and good food. Dorm beds ¥2900/person. Closed March 26–April 28 & Nov 26–Dec 23.

Mine-no-yu 峰の湯 ⓣ01538/7-3001. The least shabby of Rausu's three large onsen hotels, the majority of rooms here are Japanese-style but have attached Western-style toilets and baths. ⑦

Minshuku Maruman 民宿マルマン ⓣ01538/7-2479. Probably the best deal in Rausu, but don't expect anything luxurious. Meals included. ⑤

Shiretoko Grand Hotel 知床グランドホテル ⓣ0152/24-2021, ⓔinfo@shiretoko.co.jp. This opulent hotel has both Western- and Japanese-style rooms, as well as a rooftop onsen bath and rotemburo with views across the harbour. ⑦

Yuhi-no-Ataru Ie 夕陽のあたる家 ⓣ0152/24-2764, ⓦwww.yuuhuinoataruie.com. In Utoro, a 15min hike up the second road off to the right after the bus station – take the pedestrian pathway and walk straight ahead until you see a building with a painting of a white-tailed eagle on it. The rooms are pretty good with beds plus a tatami lounge area. ⑦

Akan National Park

Some 50km south of the Shiretoko Peninsula is the densely forested **AKAN NATIONAL PARK** (阿寒国立公園), its 905 square kilometres harbouring three major **lakes** – Mashū-ko, Kussharo-ko and Akan-ko – and the **volcanic peaks** of Me-Akan and Ō-Akan. Patchy public transport makes this a difficult area to tour unless you have your own car or don't mind hitching. Nevertheless, the park is a haven for birdwatchers and walkers and has some pleasant lakeside onsen, while in **Akan Kohan** you can see traditional Ainu dancing, as well as the rare balls of algae known as *marimo*.

The disputed Kuril Islands

A protracted territorial dispute over the **Kuril Islands**, some of which can be seen clearly from the Shiretoko Peninsula, means that technically Japan and Russia are still fighting World War II. A peace accord has yet to be signed because of Russia's continued occupation of these volcanic islands, which are strung across the Sea of Okhotsk between the Kamchatka Peninsula and northeastern Hokkaidō.

Known in Japan as the **Northern Territories**, or *Chishima* (Thousand Islands), and in Russia as the Kurils, only five of the islands are permanently inhabited. Japan demands the return of the four southernmost islands of Kunashiri, Shikotan, Etorofu and the Habomai group, the closest of which is less than 20km off Hokkaidō's coast. The islands themselves are fairly desolate; it is their strategic importance, **rich mineral resources** and the surrounding fishing grounds that make them so desirable.

Arrival and information

Buses run to Akan Kohan (see below) from Asahikawa (2 daily; 5hr; ¥4580) via Sōunkyō (see p.317; 3hr 30min; ¥3260). There are also services from Kushiro (see p.332; 4 daily; 2hr; ¥2650) and, between February and November, Abashiri (daily; 5hr 30min; ¥4100) via Kawayu Onsen (see opposite) and Mashū-ko where it pauses for a 20-minute sightseeing break. You can also pick up this bus from outside JR Mashū Station; check Ⓦ www.akanbus.co.jp for the latest schedule.

There's free internet access and plenty of information on local activities, including hiking trails, at the **tourist office** (daily 9am–6pm; Ⓣ 0154/67-2254, Ⓦ www.lake-akan.com), opposite the *New Akan Hotel Shangrila* about 5 minutes' walk from the bus terminal towards the lake.

Accommodation

There's a decent wooded (and free) **campsite** five minutes' walk beyond the Ainu Kotan village (see below). Good-value minshuku include *Kiri* (桐; Ⓣ 0154/67-2755; ⑤) and *Yamaguchi* (山口; Ⓣ 0154/67-2555; Ⓦ www.tabi-hokkaido.co.jp/~yamaguchi/english; ⑤) where rates include two meals. To see how amazing Ainu carving can be take a peak – or better yet stay – at the beautifully designed *Hinanoza* (鄙の座; Ⓣ 0154/67-3050; Ⓦ www.hinanoza.com; ⑧), the most luxurious of the Tsuruga group's three properties by the lake.

Akan Kohan

The compact onsen resort of **AKAN KOHAN** (阿寒湖畔) on the southern shore of Akan-ko is the most commercialized part of the national park, with no shortage of tacky giftshops down its main street. However, it can be used as a base for hikes up the nearby peaks of **Me-Akan-dake** (雌阿寒岳; 1499m) and **O-Akan-dake** (雄阿寒岳; 1371m). At the western end of town, a ten-minute walk from the bus station, is the **Ainu Kotan** (アイヌコタン), a contrived Ainu "village" which is little more than a short road of giftshops selling identical carved wood figures. Some two hundred Ainu are said to live in the town. Traditional dance and music performances (¥1000) are staged in the thatched *chise* (house) at the top of the shopping parade, and there's a tiny **museum** (daily 10am–10pm; ¥300) in a hut beside the *chise* with some interesting traditional Ainu costumes.

At the eastern end of Akan Kohan is the **Akan Kohan Eco Museum Centre** (阿寒湖畔エコミュージアムセンター; Wed–Mon 9am–5pm; free), where you can find out how the Akan caldera was formed and view *marimo* up close. These velvety green balls of algae are native to Akan-ko, which is one of the few places in the world where you'll find this nationally designated "special natural treasure". Despite their rarity and the fact that it can take two hundred years for the *marimo* to grow to the size of baseballs, it's possible to buy bottled baby *marimo* in all of Akan's giftshops. From the museum, pleasant woodland trails lead to the **Bokke** (ボッケ), a small area of bubbling mud pools beside the lake. Dedicated botanists might want to take the boat trip across the lake to the small island of **Churui-shima** (チュウルイ島), where the **Marimo Exhibition Centre** (April–Nov daily 7.30am–5.30pm; ¥400, or ¥1520 including the return boat trip) has an underwater viewing tank. If you're lucky, you'll see the *marimo* balls bobbing up to the surface of the lake as they photosynthesize – the process which produces the gases that make them float – during the day (they sink back to the lake bed at night). Many of the hotels allow day visitors into their **onsen** baths, usually between 11am and 3pm, for around ¥1500; those at *Akan Yuku-no-sato Tsuruga* are particularly impressive.

Mashū-ko

Some 35km east of Akan-ko, just outside the park boundaries, is the famed lake **MASHŪ-KO** (摩周湖), lying at the bottom of sheer cliffs that keep tourists at bay and the waters pristine. There are three lookout points over the 212m-deep caldera lake, which on rare occasions sparkles a brilliant blue. Usually, though, the view is obscured by swirling mists and thick cloud, creating a mysterious atmosphere which led the Ainu to christen Mashū-ko "The Devil's Lake".

There's only one bus a day from JR Mashū Station in **Teshikaga** (弟子屈) to Mashū-ko (¥540); it pauses at the lookout for twenty minutes before continuing on to Kawayu Onsen (see below). Similarly there's one bus daily from Kawayu Onsen that pauses at Mashū-ko en route to JR Mashū. The large and modern *Mashū-ko Youth Hostel* (摩周湖ユースホステル; ⓣ015/482-3098, ⓦwww.masyuko.jp; dorms ¥3500/person; rooms ❸), halfway to the lake from Teshigaku, runs a number of reasonably priced guided tours of the area. Meals are served next door in the good-value *Great Bear* restaurant.

Kussharo-ko and Kawayu Onsen

West of Mashū-ko is the Akan National Park's largest lake, picturesque **Kussharo-ko** (屈斜路湖), which at eighty square kilometres is the biggest **crater lake** in Japan. It's also said to be the home of Kussie, Japan's answer to the Loch Ness Monster. Whether it has a monster, Kussharo-ko is special because it is fed by onsen water, creating a warm temperature and several natural rotemburo around its edge, such as the piping-hot pools at **Wakoto Hantō** (和琴半島), a mini-promontory on the lake's southern shore. You can hop into another lakeside rotemburo at **Kotan Onsen** (コタン温泉), an easy cycle ride from the *Kussharo-Gen'ya Youth Guesthouse* (see p.332). Kotan Onsen also features the **Museum of Ainu Folklore** (アイヌ民俗資料館; mid-April to Oct daily 9am–5pm; ¥400), in a strikingly modern concrete building, but it's only worth a visit if you've not checked out any of the other collections around Hokkaidō.

A strong whiff of sulphur from the hot springs drifts over the area's main village, **KAWAYU ONSEN** (川湯温泉), 3km from the lake. Here you'll find several hotels and minshuku, free *ashiyu* (foot baths) and the bus terminal. With a good **tourist office** (daily 9am–5pm; ⓣ015/483-2670, ⓦwww.kawayuonsen.com), a post office with an **ATM** (Mon–Fri 8.45am–6pm & Sat 9am–noon) and free **internet** access at the town hall, it also makes for a good base for touring the park.

Plenty of information – virtually all in Japanese – on the park is available at the **Kawayu Eco-Museum Center** (川湯エコミュージアムセンター; daily 9am–6pm). The center can also provide information on the several hiking trails around the village, one of which is wheelchair-accessible, and rent out cross-country skis and snowshoes in winter. Contact **River & Field** (ⓣ080-6648 4288) if you're interested in taking a guided canoe tour of the Kushiro River (from ¥5000/person, minimum two people).

Practicalities

Kawayu Onsen's **train** station is on the Senmō line and is a ten-minute bus journey (¥280) south of the village; buses are timed to meet the trains, with the last bus to the onsen leaving at 6.30pm. In Kawayu Onsen the nicest place to stay is *Hotel Kitafukurou* (ホテルきたふくろう; ⓣ015/483-2960; ❼), with both pleasant Japanese- and Western-style rooms and onsen baths (open to non-guests noon–6pm; ¥600); the rates here include two meals.

There are several campsites beside the lake, including two at Wakoto Hanto. *Kussharo-Gen'ya Youth Guesthouse* (屈斜路原野ユースホステル; ⓣ015/484-2609, ⓦwww.gogogenya.com; ¥3700/person) is in a tent-like wooden building some thirty minutes' walk from the southern shore of Kussharo-ko. The rooms are Western-style and superb Japanese meals are available. You can rent mountain bikes (¥1500/day) or take advantage of the various tours on offer, which include cross-country skiing in winter. In the evening, the staff will also take you to a natural rotemburo beside the lake.

If you're looking for somewhere to **eat** in Kawayu Onsen there's the friendly *San San Go Go* (三三五五; 11.30am–2pm & 6–10pm; closed Mon) on the main shopping street, serving tasty set meals, including fried chicken and *jingisukan* (stir-fried mutton), for around ¥1200. At JR Kawayu Station the cute café *Orchard Grass* (10am–6pm; closed Tues; daily same hours July–Sept) serves excellent curry rice (¥830).

Kushiro

The industrial port of **KUSHIRO** (釧路) is the southern gateway to both the Akan National Park (see p.329) and the Kushiro Shitsugen National Park (see oppsoite). If you have time to kill, you could visit a couple of the town's attractions. A fifteen-minute bus ride southeast from the station is the excellent **Kushiro City Museum** (釧路市立博物館; 9.30am–5pm; closed Mon; ¥400) beside Lake Harutori. The dramatic exterior is designed to represent the outstretched wings of a *tancho* crane; among the natural history exhibits inside is a reconstructed mammoth skeleton, and there's a good collection of Ainu artefacts. Another time-filler is the colourful **MOO** (standing for "Marine Our Oasis"), a redeveloped waterside complex of shops and restaurants, fifteen minutes' walk directly south of the station.

Practicalities

Kushiro **airport** (ⓣ0154/57-8304) is 22km northwest of town and connected with it by regular buses (50min; ¥910). There are several limited express **trains** from Sapporo. In the train station there's a helpful **tourist office** (daily 9am–5.30pm; ⓣ0154/22-8294, ⓦwww.kushiro-kankou.or.jp/english); if you're headed for the Kushiro Shitsugen National Park, ask for the very useful *Kushiro*

SL Fuyu-no-Shitsugen-go

For two months, from around the third week of January, the steam locomotive **SL Fuyu-no-Shitsugen-go** (Winter Wetland Train) runs between Kushiro and Shibecha (標茶) on the Senmō train line just north of the **Kushiro Shitsugen National Park**; a couple of services at the start of the season continue up the line to Kawayu Onsen (see p.331). A party atmosphere is guaranteed in the carriages, which are decorated with toy animals and heated by potbelly stoves, on which you can toast dried fish snacks bought from the buffet car. There's also an observation car, with a guide on hand to point out the wildlife as the service passes through the Kushiro Shitsugen National Park (see opposite). A seat reservation for the service is essential (¥1840); more details can be found at ⓦwww.jrhokkaido.co.jp.

Erimo Misaki

One of the windiest places in Japan, **ERIMO MISAKI** (襟裳岬), 160km southwest of Kushiro, is a dramatic place at any time of the year, but particularly beautiful in summer. Practically at the cape's tip is **Kaze-no-Yakata** (風の館; May–Sept 8am–7pm; Jan–April & Oct–Dec 8.30am–5pm; ¥500), a fascinating "wind" **museum**. A wind tunnel re-creates what it's like to stand in a 25-metre-per-second gale (in case it's not so windy outside) and there are telescopes to watch the colony of seals that bask on the rocks below.

The closest train station is at **Obihiro** (帯広), 115km northwest, from where you'll need to take two buses to reach the cape, the first heading for **Hirō**, where you'll change to the service running to **Samani** (様似) via the cape. There's also a direct bus daily from Sapporo (3hr 45min; ¥3500). Comfortable **accommodation** is available at *Misakisō* (みさき荘; ⓣ01466/3-1316; ⑥ including two meals), a traditional ryokan just below the museum and overlooking the cape.

Wetland Teku-Teku Map. There are several inexpensive business **hotels** close to the station, one of the cheapest being *Ocean* (オーシャン; ⓣ0154/24-4000; ④) with singles for ¥3700. Alternatively, *Kushiro ANA Hotel* (釧路全日空ホテル; ⓣ0154/31-4111, ⓦwww.anahotelkushiro.jp; ⑦), offers upmarket rooms and harbour views.

A great place for **lunch** near the station is *Washō Market* (和商市場; Mon–Sat 8am–6pm), famed for *katedon* – a rice bowl topped with your choice of seafood.

Kushiro Shitsugen National Park

Japan's largest protected wetland, at 45,200 acres, is the **Kushiro Shitsugen National Park** (釧路湿原国立公園). Birdwatchers flock here in winter to see **tancho cranes** (see p.325), but the wetlands are home to many other birds and animals, including deer, grey herons, whooper swans and eagles.

One of the best places to observe the cranes is actually just north of the park, in the fields near the village of **TSURUI** (鶴居), an hour's drive north of Kushiro, at the **Tsurui Itō Japanese Crane Sanctuary** (鶴居・伊藤タンチョウサンクチュアリ; Oct–Mar Thurs–Mon 9am–4.30pm). Half an hour further north of here towards Akan, the **Akan International Crane Centre GRUS** (Nov–March daily 9am–5pm; April–Oct 9am–5pm, closed Mon; ¥400) has breeding facilities and an interesting exhibition hall.

Park practicalities

The park is best toured by **car**, but the Akan Kohan-bound bus from Kushiro Station also passes several of the facilities; get details from Kushiro's tourist office.

There's excellent **accommodation** in Tsurui at *Hickory Wind* (ヒッコリーウィンド; ⓣ0154/64-2956, ⓦwww.summitphotographic.com/hickory1.htm; ⑦ including two meals), which has four comfortable Western-style rooms in a rustic building overlooking the crane sanctuary. Call ahead to be picked up at the airport or Tsurui bus station. At **Tōro**, on the east side of the park, the cosy *Kushiro Shitsugen Tōro Youth Hostel* (釧路湿原とうろユースホステル; ⓣ0154/87-2510, ⓦwww.youthhostel.or.jp; dorm beds ¥3360) is only moments from the train station.

Kiritappu Shitsugen

More wildlife, including Kuril seals and sea otters, may be spotted east from Kushiro in the direction of the Nemuro Peninsula at the **Kiritappu Shitsugen** (Wetland) prefectural park (霧多布湿原), where the town of Hamanaka (浜中) and the Friends of Kiritappu Marsh have built the **Kiritappu Shitsugen Centre**

(霧多布湿原センター; May–Oct daily 9am–5pm; Nov–April 9.30am–4pm; closed Tues Jan–May; ⓦwww.kiritappu.or.jp/center). Kiritappu is a two-hour drive from Kushiro on Route 44; the Shitsugen centre lies ten minutes' drive south of Chanai (茶内) train station on the MG road. If you want **to stay** in Kiritappu, continue east on the MG road to **Biwase Bay** (琵琶瀬湾) and the friendly eco-lodge *Pension Porch* (ペンションポーチ; ⓣ0153/62-2772; ❻).

Travel details

Trains

Abashiri to: Asahikawa (4 daily; 3hr 44min); Kushiro (4 daily; 3hr); Sapporo (4 daily; 5hr 14min).
Asahikawa to: Abashiri (4 daily; 3hr 44min); Furano (11 daily; 1hr 10min); Sapporo (35 daily; 1hr 30min); Wakkanai (3 daily; 3hr 30min).
Hakodate to: Aomori (10 daily; 2hr); Hachinohe (9 daily; 3hr); Ōnuma-kōen (7 daily; 20min); Sapporo (11 daily; 3hr 14min); Tokyo (2 overnight sleeper; 12hr 40min).
Kushiro to: Abashiri (4 daily; 3hr); Sapporo (7 daily; 3hr 35min).
Sapporo to: Abashiri (4 daily; 5hr 15min); Asahikawa (35 daily; 1hr 30min); Hakodate (11 daily; 3hr 15min); Kushiro (7 daily; 3hr 35min); New Chitose airport (55 daily; 40min); Noboribetsu (15 daily; 1hr 10min); Ōsaka (daily; 22hr 15min); Otaru (27 daily; 30min); Tokyo (2 daily; 16hr); Tomakomai (16 daily; 40min); Wakkanai (3 daily; 5hr).
Wakkanai to: Asahikawa (5 daily; 4hr); Sapporo (3 daily; 5hr).

Buses

Abashiri to: Sapporo (9 daily; 6hr); Shari (5 daily; 1hr).
Asahikawa to: Asahidake Onsen (2 daily; 1hr 30min); Furano (5 daily; 1hr 30min); Kushiro (2 daily; 6hr 30min); Sapporo (every 20–40min; 2hr 30min); Sōunkyō Onsen (5 daily; 1hr 45min); Tenninkyō Onsen (2 daily; 1hr); Wakkanai (daily; 4hr 40min).
Hakodate to: Ōnuma-kōen (3 daily; 1hr); Sapporo (6 daily; 5hr 10min).
Kushiro to: Akan (2 daily; 2hr 10min); Asahikawa (2 daily; 6hr 30min); Obihiro (4 daily; 2hr 25min).
Sapporo to: Abashiri (9 daily; 6hr); Furano (11 daily; 3hr); Kushiro (2 daily; 6hr 30min); Niseko (3 daily; 3hr); Noboribetsu (2 daily; 1hr 40min); Tōya-ko (daily; 3hr); Wakkanai (7 daily; 6hr).
Wakkanai to: Asahikawa (daily; 4hr 40min); Sapporo (7 daily; 6hr).

Ferries

Hakodate to: Aomori (9 daily; 3hr 30min; high-speed 2 daily; 1hr 45min); Ōma (2 daily; 1hr 45min).
Muroran to: Aomori (1 daily; 7hr); Niigata (3 weekly; 16hr 30min); Ōma (daily; 3hr).
Otaru to: Maizuru (1 daily; 31hr); Niigata (1 daily except Mon; 19hr).
Tomakomai to: Akita (4 weekly; 11hr 20min); Hachinohe (1 daily; 8hr); Nagoya (3–4 weekly; 38hr 45min); Sendai (1 daily; 14hr 45min); Oarai for Tokyo (1 daily; 30hr).
Wakkanai to: Rebun-tō (2–4 daily; 1hr 40min); Rishiri-tō (2–4 daily; 1hr 45min).

Flights

Asahikawa to: Hakodate (daily; 1hr); Kansai International (2 daily; 2hr); Kushiro (2 daily; 45min); Nagoya (daily; 1hr 50min); Tokyo (7 daily; 1hr 45min).
Hakodate to: Asahikawa (daily; 1hr); Kansai International (2 daily; 1hr 45min); Kushiro (1 daily; 1hr 10min); Nagoya (1 daily; 1hr 20min); Sapporo (7 daily; 40min); Sendai (3 weekly; 1hr); Tokyo (7 daily; 1hr 15min).
Kushiro to: Asahikawa (2 daily; 45min); Hakodate (daily; 1hr 10min); Kansai International (June–Sept daily; 2hr 30min); Nagoya (daily; 2hr); Sapporo (5 daily; 45min); Tokyo (5 daily; 1hr 45min).
Memanbetsu to: Kansai International (daily; 2hr 10min); Nagoya (daily; 2hr); Sapporo (6 daily; 50min); Tokyo (6 daily; 1hr 40min).
Sapporo (New Chitose) to: Fukuoka (5 daily; 2hr 10min); Kansai International (9 daily; 1hr 50min); Nagoya (12 daily; 1hr 30min); Tokyo (46 daily; 1hr 30min). Also international flights to Australia (Cairns), China (Shanghai, Hong Kong), South Korea (Seoul, Busan) and Taiwan (Taipei).
Sapporo (Okadama) to: Hakodate (7 daily; 40min); Kushiro (5 daily; 45min).
Wakkanai to: Sapporo (daily; 50min); Tokyo (daily; 1hr 45min).

Central Honshū

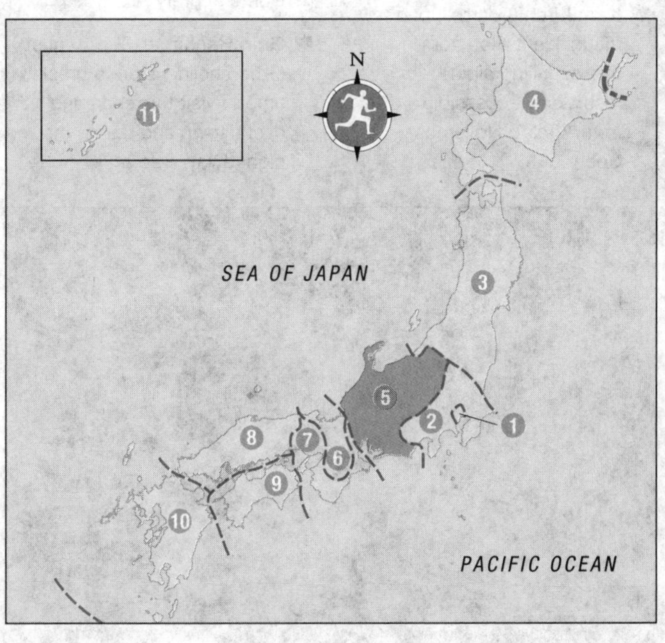

CHAPTER 5

Highlights

* **Obuse** Enjoy gourmet treats, sake, traditional architecture and art in this rural town – a model of sensitive tourist development. See p.346

* **Matsumoto** Survey the mountains surrounding this friendly city from the donjon of Japan's oldest wooden castle. See p.352

* **Kamikōchi** Climb Japan's magnificent Alps from this beguiling alpine resort only accessible from April to November. See p.356

* **Takayama** Famous for its skilled carpenters, whose craftsmanship is evident in the town's attractive merchant houses, shrines and temples. See p.363

* **Kanazawa** Refined city that's home to verdant Kenroku-en and the cutting-edge vision of the 21st Century Museum of Contemporary Art. See p.373

* **Gujō Hachiman** The August O-bon holidays are a great time to visit this charming castle town and dance the night away. See p.397

▲ Matsumoto Castle

5

Central Honshū

Dominated by the magnificent **Japan Alps**, peppered with top onsen and ski resorts, old castle- and temple-towns, and quaint old-fashioned villages in remote valleys, **CENTRAL HONSHŪ** offers a fantastic choice of terrain and travel possibilities. If all you want to do is admire the grand scenery – even for a day – that's easily done thanks to the Shinkansen line that zips from Tokyo to **Nagano**, where you should pause long enough to visit the venerable and atmospheric temple, **Zenkō-ji**.

Apart from the highlights mentioned opposite, other places in the region known locally as Chubu that are worth seeing include the summer resort of **Karuizawa** and the charming village of **Nozawa Onsen**, northeast of Nagano, where you'll find excellent ski slopes and free hot-spring baths. **Hakuba** is another popular skiing and outdoor activities destination, while in the southern half of Nagano-ken it's possible to explore several immaculately preserved post towns along the old Nakasendō route from Kyoto to Tokyo, even hiking for a day between the best of them – **Tsumago** and **Magome**.

On the west side of the Alps, there's the convivial town of **Takayama** and the unusual A-frame thatched houses of the **Shirakawa-gō** and **Gokayama** valleys, where three villages – **Ogimachi**, **Suganuma** and **Ainokura** – have been designated UNESCO World Heritage Sites. This area can also be accessed from the Sea of Japan, where the elegant, historic city of **Kanazawa** is an ideal base. The tranquil fishing villages dotted around the rugged coastline of the **Noto Hantō** peninsula, northeast of Kanazawa, are also worth searching out.

Along the southern Pacific Ocean side of Chubu run the main expressways and train lines that link Tokyo with the Kansai region. Ugly vistas of rampant industrialization bracket these transportation links, yet even here there are places worth stopping to see, including Japan's fourth main city, **Nagoya**, home to the region's main airport. This enjoyable and easily negotiated metropolis can be used as a base for day-trips to the attractive castle town of **Inuyama**, where you can see summertime displays of the ancient skill of *ukai* (cormorant fishing), or to **Meiji Mura**, an impressive outdoor museum of architecture dating from the beginning of the twentieth century.

A couple of train lines cut across from the southern to the northern coasts, but many places in the mountains are only served by buses, which can be infrequent and pricey. Sometimes renting a car will be your best bet, although some of the most scenic routes – such as the **Skyline Drive** across the Alps from Gifu-ken to Nagano-ken – are closed in winter because of deep snow. The mountain resort of Kamikōchi and the Tateyama-Kurobe Alpine route are similarly off limits between November and April.

Nagano

Surrounded by fruit orchards and snowcapped peaks, **NAGANO** (長野), capital of Nagano-ken, had its moment in the international spotlight back in 1998 when it hosted the Winter Olympics. For the Japanese, however, this modern, compact city some 200km northwest of Tokyo has been on the tourist map for centuries.

Every year, millions of pilgrims descend on Nagano to pay homage at **Zenkō-ji** (善光寺), home of a legendary sixth-century image of Buddha.

The temple's popularity is linked to the fact that it has traditionally welcomed believers of all Buddhist sects, has never barred women and is run alternately by an abbot of the Tendai sect and an abbess of the Jōdo sect. Visitors can join the hundreds of daily petitioners searching for the "key to paradise" which lies beneath Zenkō-ji's main temple building (see p.340); find it and you'll have earned eternal salvation.

This temple aside, there's little else special to see in the city itself, although it's a very handy base for trips to surrounding destinations such as Karuizawa (see p.342), Togakushi (p.344), Obuse (p346), Nozawa Onsen (p.348), Hakuba (p.349) and Kanbayashi Onsen (p.351), home to Japan's famed snow monkeys.

Arrival, information and getting around

Nagano's JR station is the terminus for **trains** on the Nagano Shinkansen line from Tokyo, and also the hub for services around the prefecture and up to the Sea of Japan. Long-distance **buses** pull in at the Nagano Bus Terminal on Basu Tāminaru-dōri, west of the JR station.

The excellent **tourist information centre** (daily 9am–6pm; ⓣ026/226-5626) is inside the station's main concourse. Also check out the city website: ⓦwww.city.nagano.nagano.jp; and *Go! Nagano* (ⓦwww.go-nagano.net), the prefecture's official tourism guide.

The best way to **get around** is on foot – walking the 2km up to Zenkō-ji (see p.340) is an especially good way of taking in the city. Alternatively, you can hop on a bus from platform one on the west side of the JR station (¥100) or take the local Nagano Dentetsu, a private railway with its terminus beneath the Midori department store – this is also the line for trains to Obuse (see p.346) and Yudanaka Onsen (see p.351).

Accommodation

Nagano has plenty of **accommodation** with several business hotels clustered close to the station including a branch of Tōyoko Inn. The most atmospheric place to stay is near Zenkō-ji – also handy should you want to get up early to join the morning service there. There are also a few temple lodgings (*shukubō*), open only to genuine Zen Buddhist students; bookings can be made at Zenkō-ji's administrative office on ⓣ026/234-3591.

Kokusai 21 ホテル国際21 576 Agata-machi ⓣ026/234-1111, ⓦwww.kokusai21.co.jp. Battling it out with the *Saihokukan* (see below) as Nagano's top hotel, *Kokusai 21* has a more contemporary look. Rooms are spacious and well appointed, but slightly dull. It has a good selection of restaurants and great views from its sixteenth-floor bar. ❻

Metropolitan Nagano 1346 Minami-Ishido-chō ⓣ026/291-7000, ⓦwww.metro-n.co.jp. Good-value upmarket hotel beside the west exit of the JR station, with high-standard Western-style rooms, a stylish lobby and restaurants. ❻

Saihokukan 528-1 Agata-machi ⓣ026/235-3333, ⓦsaihokukan.com. This venerable hotel has been in business since 1890, although the current building is of a much more modern vintage. There are economy rooms here, but you're better off going for the larger and far more plush regular rooms. ❺–❼

Shimizuya Ryokan 49 Daimon-chō ⓣ026/232-2580, ⓔshimizuya.ryokan@gmail.com. Serviceable, foreigner-friendly ryokan in a very handy location on the approach to Zenkō-ji. All rooms are tatami and bathrooms are shared. For a single person it's ¥4725. ❹

Zenkō-ji Kyōju-in Youth Hostel 善光寺教授院ユースホステル 479 Motoyoshi-chō ⓣ026/232-2768, ⓕ232-2767. Ideal if you're planning an early-morning visit to Zenkō-ji, which is just a minute's walk away. The hostel is housed in an atmospheric old temple building, of which the management are understandably very protective; you'll have to leave your belongings in lockers in the entrance hall before being shown into the large tatami dorms – if it's not busy you might have a whole room to yourself. ¥3960 per person.

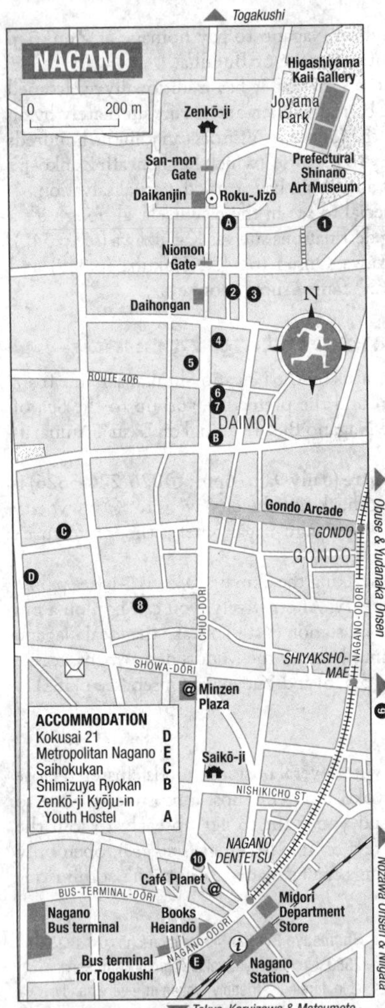

RESTAURANTS & BARS			
The Fujiya Gohonjin	4	Liberty	9
Gomeikan	5	Mankatei	1
Ichiryū Manpei	7	Patio Daimon	6
India Za Supaisu	10	Suyakame Honten	8
Kosugetei	3	Tokugyōbō	2

The City

The traditional way to approach Zenkō-ji is on foot. Head north along Chūō-dōri, west of the JR station, and you'll first pass **Saikō-ji** (西光寺), a small temple tucked away in a quiet courtyard. Also known as Karukaya-san, after the Buddhist saint who founded it in 1199, the main temple building contains two wooden statues of Jizō, the guardian of children, one carved by Karukaya, and the other by his son Ishidō.

Continuing along Chūō-dōri, the road begins to narrow around the area known as **Daimon** (大門), where you'll find many gift shops and restaurants. On the left is the **Daihongan** (大本願), the nunnery and residence of the high priestess of Zenkō-ji, who is usually a member of the imperial family. In the courtyard, look out for the fountain with a statue of Mizuko Jizō, the patron saint of aborted and stillborn babies – little dolls and toys are left as offerings around the base.

Zenkō-ji and around

Passing through the impressive 13.6m-tall gate **Niō-mon** (仁王門) and a short precinct lined with more souvenir stalls and lodgings, you'll see the **Roku-Jizō** on the right, a row of six large metal statues symbolizing the guardians of the six worlds through which Buddhists believe the soul must pass: hell, starvation, beasts, carnage, human beings and heavenly beings. On the left is **Daikanjin** (大勧進), the home of the high priest; the entrance is reached by crossing an attractive arched bridge and there is a pretty garden inside.

At the top of the precinct stands the **San-mon** (山門), the huge, double-storey wooden gateway into Zenkō-ji's central courtyard, a gathering place not only for pilgrims but also pigeons, which have their own elaborate metal coop on the left-hand side. On the same side is the **Kyōzō**, or sutra repository, an elegant wooden building that is only open occasionally. In the centre of the courtyard stands a large metal cauldron decorated with a lion whose mouth exhales the perfumed smoke of incense sticks. A charm for health and good fortune, pilgrims waft the smoke around their bodies before moving on to the vast, imposing main hall, the Hondō, which dates from 1707.

The Ikkō Sanzon Amida Nyorai

Zenkō-ji's most sacred object is the **Ikkō Sanzon Amida Nyorai**, a triad of Amida Buddha images sharing one halo. This golden statue is believed to have been made by Buddha himself in the sixth century BC and is said to have arrived in Japan some 1200 years later as a gift from Korea to the emperor. For a while, the image was kept in a specially built temple near Ōsaka, where it became the focus of a clan feud. The temple was eventually destroyed and the statue dumped in a nearby canal, from where it was later rescued by **Honda Yoshimitsu**, a poor man who was passing by and apparently heard Buddha call. Honda brought the image back to his home in Nagano (then called Shinano). When news of its recovery reached Empress Kōgyoku, she ordered a temple to be built in its honour and called it Zenkō-ji after the Chinese reading of Honda's name. The empress also ordered that the image should never be publicly viewed again, so a copy was made and it is this that is displayed once every six years in the grand **Gokaichō festival**, held from early April to late May. The next festival is in 2016.

If you're at all uncomfortable in the dark, don't enter the **Okaidan**, a pitch-black passage that runs beneath the Hondō's innermost sanctum. This is the resting place of the revered **Ikkō Sanzon Amida Nyorai** (see box above), and pilgrims come down here to grope around in the dark tunnel for the metaphorical "key to paradise" – the closest they will ever get to this sacred object. Buy a ticket (¥500) from one of the machines to the right of Binzuru's statue, and follow the chattering crowds plunging into the darkness. Once you're in, keep your right hand on the wall and chances are you'll find the key (it actually feels more like a door knob) towards the end of the passage.

Back in the light, enter the outer sanctuary of the hall and look straight ahead for the worn-out statue of Binzuru, a physician and fallen follower of Buddha; pilgrims rub the statue in the hope of curing their ailments. Just beyond is the awesome worshipper's hall, a vast space with golden ornaments dangling from the high ceiling, where pilgrims used to bed down on futons for the night.

People traditionally come for the **morning service**, which starts around 5.30am; it's worth making the effort to attend in order to witness Zenkō-ji at its most mystical, with the priests wailing, drums pounding and hundreds of pilgrims joined in fervent prayer. Afterwards, the Ojuzu Chōdai ceremony takes place in the courtyard in front of the Hondō. Pilgrims kneel while the high priest or priestess rustles by in their colourful robes, shaded by a giant red paper umbrella; as they pass, they bless the pilgrims by tapping them on the head with prayer beads.

A couple of minutes east of Zenkō-ji, across Joyama-kōen, is the **Prefectural Shinano Art Museum** (長野県信濃美術館; daily except Wed 9am–4.30pm; ¥500), worth popping into mainly for the modern gallery devoted to the vivid, dreamy landscape paintings of celebrated local artist Higashiyama Kaii (1908–99).

Eating and drinking

You'll find plenty of places to **eat** on or around Chūō-dōri, with handmade soba being a popular local dish. To sample *shōjin ryōri*, the vegetarian cuisine prepared for the monks, head for the area around Zenkō-ji. There are many small **bars** around Gondō, as well as a beer garden in summer on top of the Nagano Dentetsu Building, at the eastern end of the Gondō arcade. A popular *gaijin* bar is *Liberty*, a short walk east of the Shiyakshō-mae stop on the Nagano Dentetsu line, or you could try the funky beer and curry joint *India Za Supaisu* (INDIAザすぱいす) near the stranded London double-decker bus turned hot dog café at the southern end of Chūō-dōri.

The Fujiya Gohonjin 80 Daimon-chō ⓣ026/232-1241. The Meiji-era elegance of this one-time hotel has been spruced up with a snazzy contemporary design to become a very sophisticated Italian restaurant. The food is pretty authentic with *al dente* pasta and rustic meat and fish dishes on the menu. Their café-bar overlooking traditional gardens is a lovely place to relax with a drink. Daily 11.30am–midnight.

Gomeikan 五明館 515 Daimon-chō ⓣ026/232-1221. Decent traditional restaurant, catering mainly to tourists, in an old white building halfway up Chūō-dōri. The lunch special is ¥1400, the bentō box of prepared titbits ¥2500, while full meals cost ¥5000. Daily except Wed, 11am–2.30pm & 5–7.30pm.

Ichiryū Manpei 一粒万平 ⓣ026/234 8255. Lots of fresh, locally produced veggies figure in the wholesome meals prepared here. The lunch-time buffet clocks in at a reasonable ¥1300. Daily except Tues 11.30am–6.30pm.

Kosugetei 小菅亭 ⓣ026/232-2439. Two blocks southeast of the Niomon gate, this cute soba restaurant is decorated with lots of lucky cat statues and old advertisements. The noodles are made on the premises and their tempura *zaru-soba* set for ¥980 is a good deal. Daily: April–Nov 11am–3pm & 5–8pm; Dec–March 11am–3pm.

Mankatei 萬佳亭 Jōyama-kōen ⓣ026/232-2326. Enjoy the fine dishes, including sashimi and delicate noodles, waitresses in kimono and the twinkling cityscape views at this classy restaurant east of Zenkō-ji, on the edge of Joyama-kōen, overlooking the downtown area. Daily 11am–2pm & 5–9pm.

Patio Daimon ぱてぃお大門 On the corner of Chūō-dōri and Route 406, this complex of restaurants and shops is styled like traditional white-walled *kura* (storehouses). Most tastes and budgets are catered for here, from a cheerful café specializing in tofu-based sweets to the private dining room (Fri & Sat only; ¥15,000 per head).

Suyakame Honten すや亀本店 625 Nishi-go-chō ⓣ026/35-4022. Café and shop specializing in miso – they even serve miso ice cream, an acquired taste. From 11.30am to 2.30pm they offer a set menu of rice balls topped with different types of miso sauce (¥410). Daily 10.30am–5pm.

Tokugyōbō 德行坊 448 Motoyoshi ⓣ026/232-0264. This old pilgrim's inn is a good place to sample *shōjin ryōri*. Prices start from ¥3000 per person and reservations are recommended; the owner speaks a little English. Daily noon–1pm & 5–6.30pm.

Listings

Banks and exchange There are several branches of Hachijū Ni ("82") Ginkō around the city offering foreign exchange, including one about 5min walk west of JR Nagano Station.

Bookshop Books Heiandō (daily 10am–7.30pm), opposite the west exit of the station, has a small selection of English books.

Car rental Eki Rent-a-Car (ⓣ026/227-8500), beside the Zenkō-ji exit of the JR station.

Emergencies The main Prefectural Police Office is at 692-2 Habashita (ⓣ026/244-0110). For other emergency numbers, see p.71.

Hospital Nagano's main hospital is Nagano Sekijūji Byōin, 5-22-1 Wakasato ⓣ026/226-4131.

Internet There's free access at the tourist information centre and on the third floor of Minzen Plaza on the corner of Chūō-dōri and Showa-dōri, in the International Exchange Plaza (daily 10am–7pm, except first and third Wed of month). Café Planet is a 24-hour internet and manga café, a few minutes' walk west of the JR station.

Post office The central post office is at 1085-4 Minami-Agata.

Karuizawa and around

At Nagako-ken's eastern edge, on the slopes of Asama-yama, is the ritzy resort of **KARUIZAWA** (軽井沢) where Crown Prince Akihito (now the emperor) met his future wife, Michiko, on the tennis courts in the 1950s, and where John Lennon and Yoko Ono vacationed in the 1960s and 1970s. Decades of such superstar patronage have lent this small town a fashionable reputation, and the place can get very hectic in summer as Tokyoites descend to relax in the cooler mountain air and spend up a storm at the giant outlet mall and tacky tourist-shop strip either side of the main station. It's pretty easy to escape this commercial frenzy and enjoy Karuizawa's natural tranquillity on easy trekking and cycling routes into the forested hills dotted with charming wooden villas and heritage buildings.

Arrival and information

The fastest route to Karuizawa is by **train** on the Shinkansen from either Tokyo or Nagano. Regular train services only go as far as Yokokawa Station, from where you have to travel up to Karuizawa by bus (¥500) from the valley below. There are also direct buses from Ikebukuro in Tokyo, as well as Ōsaka and Kyoto.

Karuizawa's sights are widely scattered, so it's best to pick up the good English map of the area from the friendly assistants at the **tourist information office** (daily 9am–5.30pm; ⓣ0267/42-2491, ⓦkaruizawa-kankokyokai.jp) at the station. The most enjoyable way of exploring is by **bicycle**; you can rent one from the many outlets near the station (around ¥500 a day). Otherwise, frequent **buses** run from in front of Karuizawa Station to Kyū-Karuizawa (¥160) and on to the *Old Mikasa Hotel* (¥270).

Accommodation

Karuizawa is not a cheap place to **stay**, so if you're on a budget, plan on visiting for the day.

APA Hotel Karuizawa-Ekimae ⓣ0267/42-0665, ⓦtinyurl.com/2b7olct. Handily located beside the JR station, this dependable business hotel chain charges reasonable rates (for Karuizawa) for functional rooms. A plus is their restaurant's open-air terrace where you can take breakfast. ❺

Hoshinoya Karuizawa 星のや軽井沢 ⓣ0267/45-6000, ⓦwww.hoshinoya.com/en. Outstandingly beautiful, luxury onsen hotel, which blends with the forest and is 75 percent energy self-sufficient thanks to hydro-power generators. Choose between garden, river and mountainside villas, each equally gorgeous and all sporting cypress wood bathtubs. ❽–❾

Karuizawa Prince Hotel East ⓣ0267/42-1111, ⓦwww.princehotels.co.jp. The best deal of several *Prince* properties located on a sprawling compound south of the station and offering a mammoth shopping plaza, spa and onsen, tennis, golf and, in winter, direct access to a small ski field. Choose between stylish, large hotel rooms or log cabins. ❻–❼

Mampei Hotel 万平ホテル ⓣ0267/42-1234, ⓦwww.mampei.co.jp. The area's grand dame, established in 1894, is where Lennon stayed when he was in town. Surrounded by the forest, it has a quirky, rambling elegance, although the cheapest rooms are dowdy. ❼–❽

Kyū-Karuizawa and Naka-Karuizawa

The scenic part of town begins in **Kyū-Karuizawa** (旧軽井沢), about 1km north of the station. Work your way past the tourists jamming the pedestrianized, tacky shopping street dubbed "Little Ginza", to emerge into a forest. Here you'll find the quaint wooden **Anglican Chapel**, fronted by a bust of the Canadian missionary Alexander Croft Shaw, who helped popularize the area as a retreat. A short walk southeast is the historic *Mampei Hotel* (see above), which has a small museum of its memorabilia (free).

Heading northwest along the main road, Mikasa-dōri, it's a pleasant 2km cycle ride or hike up to the secluded **Old Mikasa Hotel** (旧三笠ホテル; daily 9am–4.30pm; ¥400), an elegant wooden building dating from 1906 that's now a national monument. Follow the road north from here, past the camping ground, to **Kose** (小瀬) where a 10km hike to the scenic Shiraito Falls (白糸の滝) starts, and onwards west to Mine-no-chaya (峰の茶屋) from where you can take a bus back to Karuizawa Station.

A 6km pedal west of Karuizawa is **Naka-Karuizawa** (中軽井沢), another beautiful area for cycling, hiking and relaxing. The main focus is the **Hoshino area** (ⓦwww.hoshino-area.jp) where you'll find the luxury resort hotel *Hoshinoya* (see p.343), an excellent onsen, **Tonbo-no-yu** (トンボの湯; daily 10am–10pm; ¥1200), a forest of chestnut and larch trees where you can take guided nature tours (reservations on (☎0267/45-7777), and a stylish, low-key shopping and dining complex, **Harunire Terrace**. If you don't feel like cycling, a **free bus** runs here from the south side of Karuizawa Station; enquire at the tourist information office (see p.343) about the schedule.

Onioshidashien

Looming ominously over Karuizawa is 2568m **Asama-yama** (浅間山), Japan's highest triple-cratered active volcano, which last erupted in 2004. The closest you can get to the crater is on its north side at **Onioshidashien** (鬼押出し園; mid-March to end Nov daily 8am–5pm; ¥600), 21km from Karuizawa. Onioshidashien was the scene of a cataclysmic eruption on August 5, 1783, when ashes from the blowout were said to have darkened the sky as far as Europe, and a 7km-wide lava flow swept away Kanbara village. When the lava cooled it solidified into an extraordinary landscape of black boulders and bizarre rock shapes, where alpine plants now sprout and across which twisting pathways have been laid. To see the scale of the place, head up to the observation floor in the gift shop and restaurant complex at the entrance. Most of the crowds head for the central temple, **Kannon-dō**, standing on a raised red platform amid the black rocks, but you can easily escape them by continuing past to the quieter area behind.

Regular **buses** run to Onioshidashien from outside Karuizawa Station (50min; ¥1180).

Eating

Restaurants are plentiful; in Kyū-Karuizawa, try *Kawakamian* (川上庵; daily 11am–9pm), a smart place for soba and tempura set meals (around ¥1785). The same dishes can be enjoyed overlooking a babbling river at *Sekireibashi Kawakamian* (せきれい橋川上庵; daily 11am–10pm), their branch in Hoshino's Harunire Terrace (see above), where you'll also find several other appealing dining options. Seven minutes' walk north of Karuizawa Station, *Kastanie* (Sept–July daily except Wed noon–9pm; Aug daily noon–9pm, Fri & Sat till 10pm) offers fine pizzas, grilled meat dishes and excellent coffees, while on the dining strip south of the station, *Torimaru* (とりまる; daily 11am–9pm) is a great place to fill up on inexpensive and tasty *bukkakedon* (fried chicken and various toppings atop a bowl of rice).

Togakushi

The alpine area of **Togakushi** (戸隠), 20km northwest of Nagano, is bounded by the jagged ridge of Togakushi-yama and Mount Iizuna. As well as great scenery, there's a decent museum and a legendary shrine worth visiting. If you come in winter there's also good skiing.

The **Togakushi Minzoku-kan** (戸隠民族館; daily 9am–5pm; ¥500; ☎026/254-2395) is a museum complex of traditional farm buildings, some of which have exhibits on the **Ninja warriors** who once trained here (see box opposite). Within the complex, the Togakure-ryū Ninpō Shiryōkan displays some amazing photographs of the stealthy fighters in action and examples of their lethal weapons. The Ninja House next door is great fun, with a maze of hidden doors and staircases that is fiendishly difficult to find your way out of.

Opposite the museum is the entrance to **Togakushi Okusha** (戸隠奥社), the innermost of the three main sanctuaries of the Togakushi shrine. According to ancient Shinto belief, the mountain was created when the god Ame-no-Tajikarao

Ninja: the shadow warriors

Long before their ancient martial art was nabbed by a bunch of cartoon turtles, the **Ninja** were Japan's most feared warriors, employed by lords as assassins and spies. They practised **Ninjutsu**, "the art of stealth", which emphasized non-confrontational methods of combat. Dressed in black, Ninja moved like fleeting shadows and used a variety of weapons, including *shuriken* (projectile metal stars) and *kusarikama* (a missile with a razor-sharp sickle on one end of a chain), examples of which are displayed in the Togakushi Minzoku-kan (see opposite).

According to legend, Ninjutsu was developed in the twelfth century, when the warrior Togakure Daisuke retreated to the mountain forests of Iga, near Nara, and met Kain Dōshi, a monk on the run from political upheaval in China. Togakure studied Dōshi's fighting ways and it was his descendants who developed them into the **Togakure-ryū school** of Ninjutsu. By the fifteenth century, there were some fifty family-based Ninjutsu schools across Japan, each jealously guarding their techniques.

Although the need for Ninja declined while Japan was under the peaceful rule of the Shogunate, the Tokugawa had their own force of Ninjutsu-trained warriors for protection. One Ninja, Sawamura Yasusuke, even sneaked into the "black ship" of Commodore Perry in 1853 to spy on the foreign barbarians. Today, the Togakure-ryu school of Ninjutsu, emphasizing defence rather than offence, is taught by the 34th master, Hatsumi Masaaki, in Noda, Chiba-ken, just north of Tokyo.

tossed away the rock door of the cave where the Sun Goddess Amaterasu had been hiding (see p.767). The shrine is reached via a 2km-long corridor of soaring cedar trees. The adventurous can continue further along the route up the sharp ridge to the summit; take food, water and warm waterproof clothing as it's a strenuous route, and be sure to log your name in the climbers' book at the start of the trail. Having looked round the inner shrine – a rustic collection of small wooden and stone buildings nestling under the rocks – head back downhill along the pleasant and shaded woodland trails through the Togakushi Ōmine Recreational Forest to the attractive village of **CHŪSHA** (中社), a good base for skiing in winter (for details of the Tokagushi ski area see Ⓦwww.togakushi.com/skimenou). Here you'll find the outer sanctuary of the shrine, the **Hōkōsha** (宝光社), decorated with intricate wooden carvings, along with shops selling all manner of baskets and goods made of woven bamboo strips: the best one (where you can also see a basket weaver at work) is downhill, opposite the Spar grocery store.

Practicalities

Buses (¥2400 return) leave from outside Heiandō Books, opposite Nagano train station, and run along the vertiginous Bird-line Driveway, giving panoramic views of the city as they wind up the mountain around a series of hairpin bends. Stay on the bus through Chūsha, about one hour from Nagano, and get off a couple of stops later when you reach the entrance to the Togakushi Okusha.

Chūsha has a couple of pleasant **accommodation** options, including the excellent-value *Togakushi Kōgen Yokokura Youth Hostel* (戸隠高原横倉ユースホステル; Ⓣ026/254-2030, Ⓕ254-2540; ¥3000 per person), which offers tatami dorms in a partly thatched, 150-year-old pilgrim's lodge, five minutes' walk south of the shrine, near the ski resort. It's run by a hospitable woman who speaks a little English, and there's also a quaint log-cabin café.

Back on the main road, in the thatched farmhouse opposite the Hōkōsha shrine, is *Uzuraya* (うずらや), Chūsha's top **restaurant** for freshly made soba. The excellent

Italian cuisine and home-made desserts at *Yamabōshi* (やまぼうし; ⓣ026/254-2624; daily except Wed 10.30am–8.30pm), on the way to the shrine, are also well worth the journey up here.

Obuse

Famous for its connection with the artist Hokusai and its production of chestnuts, **OBUSE** (小布施), some 20km northeast of Nagano, is one of Japan's most attractive small towns. The streets around the venerable Ichimura estate and brewery in the centre of town have been beautified and many residents take part in an open garden scheme. Pavements have been relaid with blocks of chestnut wood and old buildings have been spruced up and turned into excellent restaurants, bars and a super-stylish hotel. Casually exploring Obuse, surrounded by orchards and vineyards and dotted with traditional houses, temples, small museums and craft galleries, is a wonderful way to pass a day; even better is to stay overnight and use Obuse as a base for trips around the area, including to nearby Yudanaka Onsen (see p.351).

Arrival and information

Obuse is twenty minutes by **train** (¥650 or ¥750 on the limited express) from Nagano on the Nagano–Dentetsu line. Pick up an English **map** of the town at Nagano's tourist information centre (see p.339), or at the **Obuse Guide Centre and Café** (daily 9am–6pm; ⓣ026/247-5050), about five minutes' walk southeast of the station. Free internet access is also available at the Obuse Guide Centre. The best way of **getting around** is to rent a bicycle from one of several places, including the station and the youth hostel (around ¥400 per day). From March to November an hourly **shuttle bus** makes a circuit of the town's sights – an all-day ticket costs ¥300.

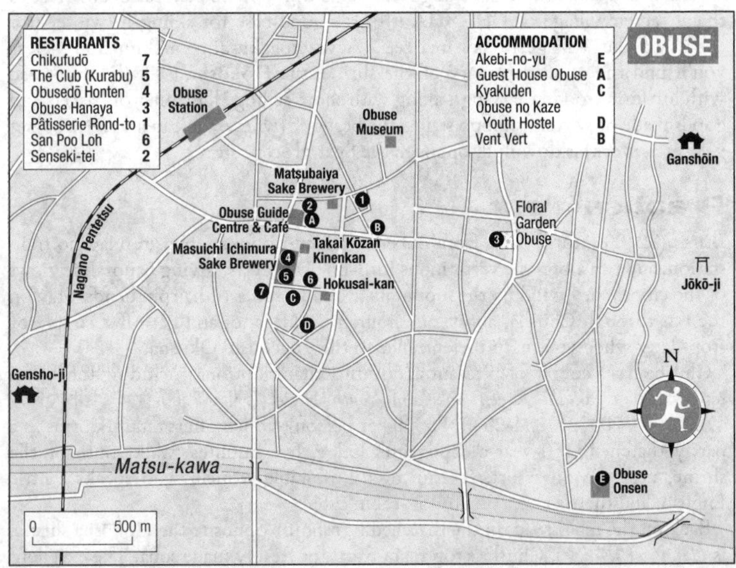

Accommodation

Akebi-no-yu あけびの湯 ⓣ026/247-4800, ⓕ247-4760. This modern ryokan complex's hillside position on the east of town grants the rooms splendid mountain views. Guests also can wallow in the adjoining onsen baths (daily 6–8.30am & 10am–10pm; ¥500 for non-guests). Rates include two meals. 7

Guest House Obuse ⓣ026/247-5050, ⓦwww.ala-obuse.net/gesthouse/index.html. Behind the Obuse Guide Centre & Café, this charming guest-house offers three Western-style rooms and, in a converted *kura*, a two-storey family-style place sleeping up to four for ¥23,100. Add ¥800 per person for breakfast. 6

Kyakuden ⓣ026/247-1111, ⓦwww.kyakuden.com. John Morford, the interior designer of Tokyo's celebrated *Park Hyatt*, is also responsible for the chic contemporary style of this luxe hotel, which incorporates three *kura* transplanted from Nagano city and a central koi-filled pond. Rates include breakfast. 8

Obuse no Kaze Youth Hostel おぶせの風ユースホステル ⓣ026/247-4489, ⓦhomepage2.nifty.com/obusenokaze. A great budget choice, this youth hostel is run by a hospitable family; it is close by the Hokusai-kan, with a choice of Western-style dorms or tatami rooms, as well as private rooms. 2

Vent Vert ヴァンヴェール ⓣ026-247-5512, ⓦwww.obusenoyado.com. Over a cute French brasserie, this small hotel has four nicely designed Western-style rooms with en-suite bathrooms. 5

The Town

The **Hokusai-kan** (北斎館; daily: March–Sept 9am–6pm; Oct–Feb 9am–5pm; ¥500), about ten minutes' walk southeast of the station, is devoted to the master of *ukiyo-e* woodblock prints, **Katsushika Hokusai**. In 1842, the 83-year-old artist was invited to live and work in Obuse by Takai Kōzan, the town's leading merchant and art lover. A special studio, the thatched roofed **Hekiiken**, was built for Hokusai, and it was here that he completed four paintings for the ceilings of two large festival floats and a giant mural of a phoenix for the ceiling of the Ganshōin temple. The beautiful floats, decorated with dragons, seascapes and intricate carvings, are displayed in the museum along with some forty other works, including painted scrolls, delicate watercolours and woodblock prints. The red-roofed **Ganshōin** (岩松院; daily: April–Oct 9am–5pm; Jan–March, Nov & Dec 9.30am–4.30pm; ¥300), housing the beguiling phoenix mural (the Great Ho-o), is a pleasant walk or bicycle ride 1km east, towards the hills.

Near the Hokusai-kan, amid the Masuichi-Ichimura compound, is the **Takai Kōzan Kinenkan** (高井鴻山記念館; daily: March–Sept 9am–6pm; Oct–Feb 9am–5pm; ¥300), the atmospheric home of Hokusai's patron, who was also an accomplished artist and calligrapher. His drawings of ghosts and goblins are meant as ironic comments on the turbulent early Meiji-era years and are quite intriguing, as is the sketch of a giant mammoth. In one of the rooms you can see long banners inscribed with *kanji* characters as well as the 2.5m-long brush used to paint them.

Sake and chestnuts

You can sample the four excellent **sakes** of Masuichi-Ichimura brewery (ⓦwww.masuichi.com), and a few others, at the *teppa* counter in the brewery's shop (daily 9am–7pm; ¥150–320). Try *Hakkin*, the only sake in Japan to be brewed in huge cedar barrels the old-fashioned, labour-intensive way – hence its high price. Around the corner you can also sip some award-winning sake for free at Obuse's other brewery Matsubaya (松葉屋本店; ⓦwww.matsubaya-honten.co.jp).

Mauichi's sister company Obusedō (ⓦwww.obusedo.com) is just one of several **chestnut confectioners** in town battling it out for the public's sweet tooth. Others are Chikufudō (ⓦwww.chikufudo.com) and Kanseidō (ⓦwww.kanseido.co.jp), both of which have restaurants serving meals featuring the sweet nut.

A ¥1000 combination ticket allows entry to both of the previous museums and the delightful **Obuse Museum** (おぶせミュージアム; daily: March–Sept 9am–6pm; Oct–Feb 9am–5pm; ¥500; ⓣ026/247-6111), which includes the Nakajima Chinami Gallery, an exhibition of this highly regarded artist's colourful works. Also on display are five more of the town's traditional festival floats, along with regularly changing art exhibitions.

Look out for a couple of attractive temples as you explore the compact town. **Gensho-ji** (玄照寺), on the west side of Obuse, has an elaborately carved gate dating from 1799 and some very glitzy gilded chandeliers. In stylistic contrast is **Jōkō-ji** (浄光寺) on the east side of town, near Ganshōin. This simple, squat, thatch-roofed structure at the top of a flight of rocky steps seems as old as time.

Eating and drinking

If anything can tempt you to linger in Obuse, it will be its fine selection of **restaurants** and **cafés**, several of which are attached to the Masuichi brewery (see box, p.347).

The Club 蔵部 ⓣ026/247-5300. Masuichi's most animated and convivial space, with an open kitchen where you can watch the chefs at work preparing a good range of local meat and fish dishes to complement their sakes. Dinner with drinks will cost around ¥3500 per person. Daily 11.30am–2.30pm & 5.30–9pm.

Obusedō Honten 小布施堂本店 ⓣ026/247-2027. Behind the confectionery shop of the same name is this Zen-calm restaurant, offering a *kaiseki ryōri*-style menu of local delicacies that changes monthly (from ¥2630). Drinks and chestnut sweets are also available. Daily 10am–5pm.

Obuse Hanaya 花屋 ⓣ026/247-1187. On the east side of town overlooking the Floral Garden is this delightful restaurant and café offering Western-style meals (lunch ¥1000, dinner ¥3000) using fresh local produce. Daily except Thurs 11am–9pm.

Pâtisserie Rond-to Close by the Obuse Museum is this little French-style café, bakery and confectioners. Their pastries, chocolates and home-made ice creams are irresistible. Wed–Mon 9.30am–7pm.

San Poo Loh 傘風楼 ⓣ026/247-1113. The pizzas are excellent at this fine-dining Italian restaurant offering outdoor tables with shady umbrellas and a very stylish interior. If you're staying at *Kyakuden* this is where you'll have breakfast. There's an equally chic cocktail and piano lounge, *Oni Bar*, upstairs (daily 7–11pm). Daily 7.30am–9pm.

Senseki-tei 泉石亭 ⓣ026/247-5166 ⓦwww.kanseido.co.jp. Chestnuts figure large in the wide range of set menus (starting around ¥1000) at this appealing restaurant overlooking an exquisite ornamental garden. Wed–Mon 11am–7.30pm.

Ski resorts and onsen villages

Nagano-ken's mountains are home to several wonderful ski resorts and onsen villages, including the delightful **Nozawa Onsen**, self-proclaimed home of Japanese skiing; **Hakuba**, a valley with seven different ski resorts; and **Shiga Kōgen**, Japan's biggest skiing area, lying within the Jōshinetsu Kōgen National Park, which is also home to **Yudanaka Onsen**, famous for its snow monkeys, which splash about in their very own rotemburo.

Nozawa Onsen

Even though international word is out on how great the skiing is at **NOZAWA ONSEN** (野沢温泉), this village of four thousand people, nestled at the base of Kenashi-yama (1650m), 50km northeast of Nagano, maintains a traditional atmosphere. Dotted along the narrow, twisting streets, you'll find thirteen free bathhouses, all lovingly tended by the locals. Most impressive is **Ōyu bathhouse**, housed in a temple-like wooden building in the centre of the village; each side has two pools, one of which is so hot that it's almost impossible to get into.

Nozawa claims to be the birthplace of Japanese skiing since it was here, in 1930, that Hannes Schneider – an Austrian who popularized the two-pole technique – gave skiing demonstrations to an awestruck audience. One of the resort's most difficult runs is named after Schneider, and photos of the man in action, impeccably dressed in suit and tie, can be seen in the **Japan Museum of Skiing** (daily except Tues 9am–4pm; ¥300), housed in a white, church-like building at the bottom of the Hikage slope.

The **ski resort** (Ⓦ www.nozawaski.com; one-day lift pass ¥4600; open late Nov to early May) is family friendly, has lots of English signs and varied terrain that will put all levels through their paces. Time your visit to coincide with the spectacular **Dōso-jin fire festival**, held every January 15 (see *Festival fun* colour section).

Arrival and information

From Nagano, JR **trains** run to Togari-Nozawa-Onsen on the Iiyama line (1hr; ¥740); Nozawa Onsen is a twenty-minute bus (¥300) or taxi ride (¥3000) from the station. There's also a direct bus from Nagano (1hr 15min; ¥1400); for timetables, check with the Nagano information office or with Nozawa Onsen's **tourist information centre** (daily 7.30am–6pm; Ⓣ 0269/85-3155, Ⓦ www.nozawakanko.jp), opposite the village's central bus terminal, where you can also pick up English brochures and maps.

Accommodation

Unless mentioned, accommodation rates include breakfast and dinner.

Hotel Garni Haus St Anton Ⓣ 0269/85-3597, Ⓦ www.nozawa.com/stanton. A cute little piece of Switzerland transplanted to the heart of the village, near the restaurants and bars. ⑦

Pension Schnee ペンションシュネー Ⓣ 0269/85-2012, Ⓦ www.pensionschnee.com. Pretty Western-style place on the mountainside next to the ski museum and run by a friendly couple who were once Olympic competitors. ⑥

Ryokan Sakaya 旅館さかや Ⓣ 0269/85-3118, Ⓦ www.ryokan-sakaya.co.jp. Elegant ryokan, behind the Ōyu bathhouse, with its own spacious onsen bath and a choice of Western- or Japanese-style rooms. ⑦

Villa Nozawa Ⓣ 0269/85 3272, Ⓦ www.nozawaholidays.com. Savvy foreigner-friendly operation offering several excellent accommodation options around the village, including a self-catering house that sleeps up to eight. Rates include breakfast only. ⑥

Eating and drinking

For a snack, try *onsen manjū*, deliciously plump dumplings with different fillings, best bought from the street vendors whose wooden steam-boxes can be found in the village centre. *Panorama House Buna*, on the slopes, serves a *curry udon* that is worth going up the mountain for even if you don't ski. Towards the foot of the village *Akabitei* (逢華亭) is a great for *okonomiyaki* and *yaki-soba*, while *Yoshimi Shokudō* (良味食堂) is a fine place to sample the local noodles. To cool down after your onsen, slip into the long-running *Stay*, a convivial bar in the centre of town.

Hakuba

Situated in the dramatic northern Japanese Alps, 60km northwest of Nagano, **HAKUBA** (白馬) is one of Japan's top ski destinations, featuring six resorts. The largest and most popular is **HAPPŌ-ONE** (八方尾根; Ⓦ www.hakuba-happo-or.jp), site of the 1998 Nagano Olympics downhill course. The valley is perfect for skiers and snowboarders who prefer a variety of terrain and plenty of après ski fun. Locally based Ski Japan Holidays (Ⓣ 0261/72-6663, Ⓦ www.japanspecialists.com) can arrange ski trips here as well as tours to other attractions in the area.

With two very pretty **lakes** – Aoki and Kizaki – the Hakuba valley also makes a fine base for a whole range of outdoor pursuits in summer. The reliable Evergreen Outdoor Centre (Ⓣ0261/72-5150, Ⓦwww.evergreen-outdoors.com) offers everything from rafting and mountain biking in summer to backcountry ski expeditions and avalanche-awareness courses in the winter.

Arrival and information

There are plenty of buses from Nagano to Hakuba (1hr; ¥1500) as well as four daily direct buses from Shinjuku, Tokyo (4hr 30min; ¥4700), and a direct service from Narita airport (see Ⓦwww.hakubus.com; ¥9800). During winter, check the following website for details about the free bus service from Nagano that is sometimes run by the Hakuba 47 ski area (Ⓦwww.hakuba47.co.jp). The best way to get here by **train** is from Matsumoto (see p.352) along the JR Ōito line; by express it's about an hour's journey. There are also a few direct trains to Shinjuku in Tokyo.

The **tourist information centre** (daily 8.30am–5pm; Ⓣ0261/72-2279, Ⓦvill.hakuba.nagano.jp) is to the left as you exit JR Hakuba Station; you can leave your bags here for ¥300. For current information on the area, go to Ⓦwww.hakubaconnect.com.

Accommodation

New places to **stay** keep appearing every year. In addition to those listed below, check out the chalets and backpacker lodge deals offered by *Snowbeds Travel* (Ⓣ03/9555-4839, Ⓦwww.skijapantravel.com) and the luxury self-catering apartment *Altitude Hakuba* (Ⓦwww.altitudehakuba.com).

Azekura Sanso あぜくら山荘 Ⓣ0261/72-5238, Ⓦwww.azekura.com. Modern log house, in the Happo ski area, offering a rustic but comfortable retreat with its own rotemburo. If you work at the lodge for four hours, your day's lodging and meals will be covered. ❻

Hakuba Alps Backpackers Ⓣ0261/75-4038, Ⓦwww.hakubabackpackers.com. In Kamishiro, two stops down the train line from Hakuba, this relaxed hostel, toped by a windmill, is run by a very friendly Kiwi–Japanese couple. It's a little scruffy but the price and location, close by Goryu ski field, are ideal. Dorm bed ¥3000.

K's House Hakuba Alps Ⓣ0261/75-4445, Ⓦkshouse.jp/hakuba-e. Also in Kamishiro, this appealing budget option replicates the successful formula of the Kyoto and Tokyo hostel operation. Dorm beds are only ¥2800 and it's only a short walk from Goryu.

Phoenix Hotel Ⓣ0261/72-4060, Ⓦphoenixhotel.jp. Next to the *Hakuba Tōkyu Hotel* is this elegant boutique-style hotel and chalet operation. It's surprisingly reasonably priced – especially if you go for the rooms which share showers (there's also an onsen bath). Note the hotel only operates during the ski season, but the chalets are open year-round. ❹

Powderhouse Ⓣ0261/75-3343, Ⓦwww.powderhouse.jp. Sleek boutique-style lodge close to the *Hakuba 47* resort. This Aussie-run place has only six rooms, which are all large and comfortable. There are several tennis courts, only open during the summer. Rates include breakfast and transportation from Nagano; a five-course dinner is available for ¥5000. ❼

Eating and drinking

Places to **eat** and **bars** are scattered along the valley – the night shuttle-bus services (mid-Dec to early March; ¥200) make it easy to get to most of them from wherever you're staying. For après ski **drinks**, the Echoland strip between Hakuba Ski Jumping Stadium and *Hakuba 47* remains popular; a recommended bar here is the reggae-suffused *Master Braster*. Over in Kamishiro there's usually some party on at the ever-popular *Tracks Bar*, while *Bradbury's Bar* in the *Aqua Alpine Hotel* oozes sophistication with its white baby grand piano and comfy lounge. In Wadano try the English-style bar *The Pub* and the wine bar *Vendimia*, both next to the *Moninoki Hotel*.

Gravity Worx ⓣ0261/72-5434. In a big log cabin, a minute's walk right of Hakuba Station, this long-running café-bar is run by welcoming English-speaking staff and serves excellent home-made pizza, pasta, salads and desserts. Daily 10am–8pm; closed Tues out of ski season.

Mangetsu-do 満月堂 ⓣ0261/75-1707. On the Echoland strip this cool *izakaya* has good food and a choice of forty *umeshu* plum wines. Daily 5pm–3am.

Mimi's ⓣ0261/72-4148. Fine dining comes to Hakuba at this excellent restaurant in the *Phoenix Hotel* (see opposite) serving delicious contemporary cuisine using top-grade local ingredients including oysters, fish and pork. Dec to end March daily 6–9pm.

Pizzakaya Country Road ⓣ0261/75-2889. Near Kamishiro Station, this friendly, relaxed place offers a range of tasty pizzas and pasta dishes incorporating local ingredients such as mountain vegetables, seaweed and spicy cod roe. Daily 5.30–11.30pm; closed 5th, 15th and 25th of month.

Shōya Maruhachi 庄屋丸八 ⓣ0261/75-5008. In this handsome merchant's house originally built in 1854 you can enjoy traditional Japanese dishes at reasonable prices; during the ski season free Japanese culture courses, including how to make soba, are held here. It's a short walk from Shinano Morue Station towards the Hakuba Iwatake ski area. Tues–Sun 11am–2pm & 5–9pm.

Shiga Kōgen

The complaint that Japanese ski resorts are too small certainly doesn't apply to mammoth **SHIGA KŌGEN** (志賀高原), eighteen resorts strung out along the Shiga plateau in the Jōshinetsu Kōgen National Park, 20km northeast of Nagano. The huge variety of terrain makes the one-day ¥4800 lift pass, which covers the entire lift network, terrific value. It takes several days to ski the whole area; if you're short of time head for the northern end of the mountain range to the resorts at **Okushiga-kōgen** (奥志賀高原) and **Yakebitai-yama** (焼額山), where the slalom events of the 1998 Olympics were held.

The closest **train station** to Shiga is Yudanaka (湯田中; see below) – the ski resorts are a thirty-minute bus ride away from here up a stunning mountain pass. There are also direct **buses** from the east exit of Nagano Station (1hr 15min; ¥1900) and an overnight service during ski season from Ikebukuro in Tokyo (9hr; one-way/round trip ¥4000/7500; ⓦwww.travex.co.jp).

Places to stay include the comfortable, Western-style *Okushiga Kōgen Hotel* (奥志賀高原ホテル; ⓣ0269/34-2034, ⓦwww.okushiga-kougen.com; ❺–❽). The *Shiga Kōgen Prince Hotel* (ⓣ0269/34-3111, ⓦwww.princehotelsjapan.com; ❼–❽) offers three separate wings at the foot of Yakebitai-yama: the east wing sports retro 1980s glamour while the slightly cheaper west wing, with a big outdoor bath, is geared to families and groups. The closest the area has to a ski village is Ichinose, where you could try **Villa Ichinose** (ⓣ0269/34-2704, ⓦwww.villa101.biz; ❺). For more advice on lodgings, contact the **Shiga Tourism Association** (ⓣ0269/34-2404, ⓦwww.shigakogen.gr.jp).

Yudanaka and Kambayashi Onsen

On the western fringes of the Jōshinetsu Kōgen National Park is a string of onsen villages, kicking off with **YUDANAKA** (湯田中), from where you can catch the bus to see the famous "snow monkeys" (see box, p.352) at nearby **KAMBAYASHI ONSEN** (上林温泉). Yudanaka is also the access point for the well-groomed and quiet slopes of **Gorin Kōgen** (ごりん高原) and **Kita-Shiga Kōgen Heights** (北志賀高原; ⓦwww.kitashigakogen.gr.jp), which are especially popular with snowboarders.

The Nagano–Dentetsu train line from Nagano terminates in Yudanaka (express 40min, ¥1230; local 1hr, ¥1130). From the station, it's a fifteen-minute bus journey (¥210) to Kanbayashi Onsen. There's also a direct bus from Nagano to Kanbayashi

Snow Monkeys

Yudanaka's star attraction is a troupe of some two hundred Japanese long-tailed monkeys (*Nihon-zaru*) that like to bathe in the rotemburo at the **Monkey Park**, *Jigokudani Yaen-kōen* (地獄谷野猿公苑; daily 8am–5pm; ¥500), a twenty-minute walk from **Kambayashi Onsen**. Legend goes that they started to take dips in the hot pools during the 1960s, when a local ryokan owner took pity on them and left food out in winter. A special rotemburo was eventually built for them, dubbed "snow monkeys" by *Life* magazine, even though they live beside the onsen year-round. It's curiously addictive watching these primates wallowing and fooling around by the pool; get a preview via webcam at Ⓦwww.jigokudani-yaenkoen.co.jp. The monkeys are so used to humans that they act with dignified nonchalance in the face of the paparazzi-style snapping from hordes of tourists.

Onsen (40min; ¥1300). To reach the monkey park, walk uphill from the bus stop until you find a sign for a trail leading through the woods for around 2km.

Beside the monkey park is *Kōrakukan* (後楽館; Ⓣ0269/33-4376, Ⓕ33-3244; ⑦), a rambling wooden ryokan offering homely Japanese-style accommodation; rates include two meals. Take a dip in their rotemburo for ¥500 and it's possible that the monkeys will join you. Alternatively, there's the elegant *Kanbayashi Hotel Senjukaku* (上林ホテル仙壽閣; Ⓣ0269/33-3551, Ⓦwww.senjukaku.com; ⑨), set amid the trees in Kanbayashi Onsen.

Matsumoto and around

Some 50km southwest of Nagano across the Hijiri Kōgen mountains is **MATSUMOTO** (松本), gateway to the Japan Alps. This attractive city, Nagano-ken's second largest, is famous for its splendid castle, **Matsumoto-jō**, and **Nakamachi**, an area of traditional white-walled houses, several of which have been renovated into ryokan, cafés and craft shops. Art lovers can enjoy traditional prints at the **Japan Ukiyo-e Museum** and the contemporary work of native-child Yayoi Kusama at the **Matsumoto City Museum of Art**.

Matsumoto also has a reputation as a centre for classical music. It was here that **Dr Suzuki Shin'ichi**, an internationally famous music teacher, encouraged children to learn to play instruments by using their natural gift for mimicry. His "Suzuki Method" is taught in the town's Suzuki Shin'ichi Talent Education Hall, around 1km east of Matsumoto Station. The **Saitō Kinen** (Ⓦwww.saito-kinen.com) is a major classical music festival held from mid-August to early September in memory of another local talent, Saitō Hideo, celebrated conductor and mentor to many famous musicians, including the festival's director, conductor Seiji Ozawa.

Arrival, information and city transport

Matsumoto is connected by direct **trains** with Nagano, Nagoya and Tokyo; from the latter, the fastest train is the Azusa limited express service from Shinjuku (2hr 30min). All long-distance **buses** stop in front of the train station. Matsumoto's small **airport** (Ⓣ0263/57-8818) is 8km southwest of the town centre; buses to the city centre meet all flights (25min; ¥540).

The helpful **tourist information office** (daily 9.30am–6pm; Ⓣ0263/32-2814) is inside Matsumoto Station. There's free **internet** access at M Wing (daily 9am–9pm) on Isemachi-dōri, a five-minute walk north of the station. An irreverent but good website with local info on the city is Ⓦ welcome.city.matsumoto.nagano.jp.

The main sights are within easy walking distance of the train station. Alternatively, borrow one of the **free bikes** from various locations around the city – ask the tourist office (see opposite) for details. Convenient Town Sneaker **minibuses** run along four circular routes from the JR station. One ride costs ¥190, or you can buy a ¥500 day pass on the bus; the tourist office has a map of the routes. Regular

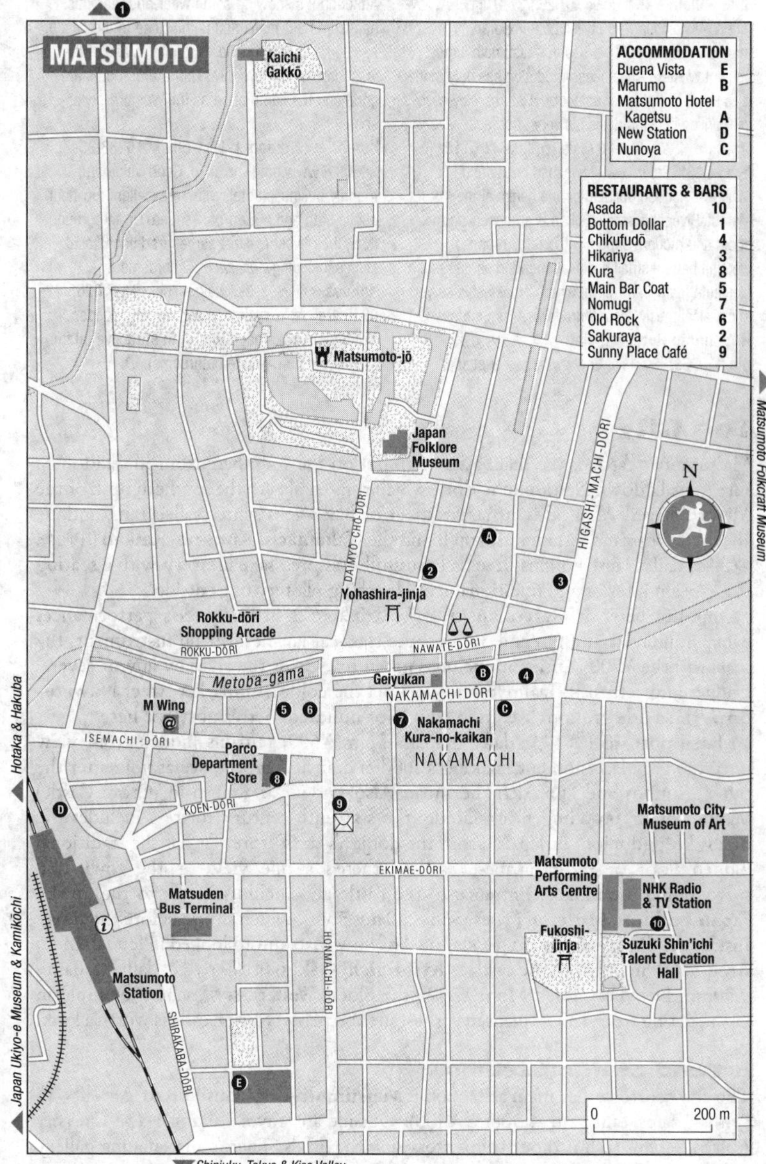

buses leave from the Matsuden Bus Terminal, under the ESPA department store opposite Matsumoto Station.

Accommodation

There are several inexpensive business hotels near the station but the nicest area to stay is Nakamichi-dōri, where there are a couple of good-value ryokan.

Buena Vista 1-2-1 Honjo ⓣ0263/37-0111, ⓦwww.buena-vista.co.jp. The stylish contemporary makeover of the public areas of Matsumoto's most opulent Western-style accommodation has only made it as far as the premier category of rooms. However, with online booking deals it's very affordable. ⑥

Marumo まるも 3-3-10 Chūō ⓣ0263/32-0115, ⓕ35-2251. Set in a whitewashed house and Meiji-era wooden building on the banks of the Metoba River, this small ryokan is an appealing mix of old and modern Japan, with tatami rooms, a wooden bath, a small enclosed bamboo garden and a nice café (daily 8am–6pm) where breakfast is served to classical music. Note there is an 11pm curfew. ⑤

Matsumoto Hotel Kagetsu 松本ホテル花月 4-8-9 Ōte ⓣ0263/32-0114, ⓦwww.hotel-kagetsu.jp. Although it's showing some wear and tear, this handsome old-fashioned hotel, close to the castle, has some stylish touches and makes use of the local dark-wood furniture. The tatami rooms are good and the same price as the Western-style ones. ⑤

Hotel New Station 1-1-11 Chūō ⓣ0263/35-3850, ⓦwww.hotel-ns.co.jp. Good-value and friendly business hotel, with an excellent top-floor public bath and a men-only sauna. On the ground floor, their lively *izakaya* serves traditional local dishes including *basashi* (raw horsemeat). ⑤

Nunoya ぬのや 3-5-7 Nakamachi ⓣ&ⓕ0263/32-0545. Delightful ryokan in a charming wooden building on Nakamachi-dōri with attractive tatami rooms (but no en-suite bathrooms). ⑤

The City

Matsumoto's castle is the main attraction, but on the way there from the station be sure to walk down **Nakamachi-dōri**, which runs parallel to the southern bank of the Metoba River. Along this attractive street of black-and-white-walled inns, antique and craft shops and restaurants, you'll find the **Nakamachi Kura-no-Kaikan** (中町蔵の会館; daily 9am–4.30pm; free), a beautifully restored sake brewery with a soaring black-beam interior and traditional cross-hatching plasterwork outside.

Opposite here, at **Geiyukan** (芸游館; ⓣ0263/32-1107), there's performances every Sunday at 1.30pm and 3pm on the classical Japanese string instrument, the *shamisen*; the ¥700 admission includes green tea. Cross the river by any of several bridges and return to Daimyō-chō-dōri via the colourful market street **Nawate-dōri**; the castle grounds are just a couple of hundred metres north of here.

Matsumoto-jō (松本城; daily 8.30am–5pm; ¥600) remains hidden from view until the very last moment, making a sudden dramatic appearance as you enter the outer grounds and approach the moat. Also known as Karasu-jō (Crow Castle) because of its brooding black facade, the sixteenth-century fortress includes the oldest keep (donjon) in Japan. From the donjon's sixth storey (it has the traditional hidden floor of most Japanese castles), there's a fine view of the town and surrounding mountains. Entrance to the castle also includes access to the quirky **Japan Folklore Museum** (Tues–Sun 8.30am–5pm), which is just before the moat. Inside, the displays include a good model of how Matsumoto looked in feudal times. Around 500m north of the castle is **Kyū Kaichi Gakkō** (旧開智学校; daily 8.30am–4.30pm, Dec–Feb closed Mon; ¥300), the oldest Western-style school building in Japan, dating from 1876; the pretty pale-blue and plasterwork facade is worth a look.

Art and craft museums

The city centre's other main attraction is **Matsumoto City Museum of Art** (松本市美術館; Tues–Sun 9am–4.30pm; ¥400). Outside are Yayoi Kusama's *The Visionary Flowers* – giant technicolour tulips crossed with triffids. There's a fascinating gallery inside devoted to this famous contemporary artist, who was born in Matsumoto, as well as ones for the calligrapher Shinzan Kamijyo and the landscape artist Tamura Kazuo. Also look out for Yayoi's polka-dotted take on a vending machine outside the gallery. The museum is about 1km directly east of the JR station along Ekimae-dōri, just past the **Matsumoto Performing Arts Centre** (Ⓣ0263/33-3800), a striking building designed by Ito Toyo that is worth a peep inside.

Some 3km west of the station, the forlorn **Japan Ukiyo-e Museum** (日本浮世絵美術館; Tues–Sun 10am–5pm; ¥1050) has woodblock prints by all the great masters including Utagawa Hiroshige and Katsushika Hokusai. Only a fraction of the museum's splendid collection of 100,000 prints is ever on display and it's likely that the amiable curator will give you a personally narrated slide show. The closest station, a fifteen-minute walk south of the museum, is Ōniwa on the Matsumoto–Dentetsu line; or catch a taxi here for around ¥1500 from the town centre.

If you've an interest in Japanese folk crafts, head to the worthwhile **Matsumoto Folkcraft Museum** (松本民芸館; Tues–Sun 9am–5pm; ¥300; Ⓣ0263/33-1569), a fifteen-minute bus ride (¥290) out of the city towards Utsukushigahara Onsen – get off the bus at Shimoganai Mingeikanguchi. Set in a traditional-style building, the museum contains some exquisite objects, including giant pottery urns, lacquerware inlaid with mother of pearl, and wooden chests. If you're here for the last weekend in May, it's worth checking out the **Crafts Fair Matsumoto** (Ⓦmatsumoto-crafts.com) in Agatanomori-kōen, a twenty-minute walk east of the JR station.

Eating and drinking

Note that several of the best **places to eat** in Matsumoto are closed on Wednesday. Soba, best eaten cold (ask for *zaru-soba*), is the local speciality. Unique to the area is *sasamushi*, eel steamed inside rice wrapped in bamboo leaves. The adventurous will also want to try horsemeat served in a variety of ways, including raw (*basashi*). For **drinking**, a popular option is the Irish bar *Old Rock* (Todoroki Bldg, 2-3-20 Chūō; Mon–Fri 11.30am–2.30pm, 6pm–midnight, Sat noon–midnight, Sun noon–11pm), which serves several draught ales; or the stylish *Main Bar Coat* (Miwa Bldg, 2-3-5 Chūō; daily 6pm–2am; ¥800 cover charge), known for its cocktails (from ¥800).

Asada あさだ 3-10-11 Fukashi. In a traditional white-walled building behind the NHK radio and TV station, this restaurant has a good reputation for soba served either *zaru* (cold) or *kinoko* (in a hot soup). Tues–Sun 11.30am–4pm.

Bottom Dollar 1-2-35 Kiri Ⓣ0263/33-3501. In the north of the city, this little wooden house decorated with fairy lights is a long-running favourite for its generous beefburgers, range of ales and live music sessions (for which there may be a cover charge). Daily 6pm–2am.

Chikufudō 竹風堂 3-4-20 Nakamachi. Local rice dishes and sweets made with chestnuts are served at this restaurant in one of the old whitewashed houses on Nakamachi-dōri. Set meals start at ¥900. Daily except Wed 9am–6pm.

Hikariya ヒカリヤ 4-7-14 Ōte Ⓣ0263/38-0186. An elegant 120-year-old *machiya* (townhouse) has been beautifully restored and converted into this very stylish complex of two restaurants: *Higashi* serving an austere but masterful *kaiseki* menu, and *Nishi* specializing in French cuisine. Lunch starts at ¥3800, dinner ¥5700. Daily except Wed 11.30am–1.30pm & 6–8.30pm.

Kura 1-10-22 Chūō. The building might be a reproduction of a white-walled storehouse (*kura*), but the food – top-notch sushi and tempura – is the real thing. Also on the English menu are local specialities including *basashi* (horsemeat sashimi) and their own brand of sake. Daily except Wed 11.45am–2pm & 5.30–10pm.

Nomugi 野麦 2-9-11 Chūō. Another celebrated soba noodle shop; you may have to queue for one of the few seats here and they close up when sold out. Mon & Thurs–Sun 11.30am–2pm.

Sakuraya 桜家 4-9-1 Ōte Ⓣ0263/33-2660, Ⓦwww.sakuraya.ne.jp. Traditional restaurant with waitresses in kimono, specializing in eel dishes, including *sasamushi*. A variety of set meals, from around ¥1800, are described on the English menu. Closed Mon.

Sunny Place Café 2-6-1 Chūō. Relaxed café-bar that snags a younger crowd – a good place to chill over a light meal or drink any time of day. Daily 10am–11pm.

Around Matsumoto

It's all about the mountains around Matsumoto. To the north is the ski centre of **Hakuba** (see p.349), while to the west is the serene lake and mountain resort of **Kamikōchi** – a place that gets so much snow that it is inaccessible all winter. A generally less crowded alternative is the nearby onsen and ski resort of **Norikura Kōgen**. The fabulous **Skyline Road** runs through this area, across to Takayama in neighbouring Gifu-ken (see p.363); drive along it and you'll see why Nagano-ken is known as the "roof of Japan". If you don't have your own wheels, look into the bus company Alpico's three-day ticket (¥6400; Ⓦ www.alpico.co.jp) for use of all its services in the area.

Kamikōchi

Tucked away in the Azusa valley at an altitude of 1500m is the beautiful mountaineering and hiking resort of **KAMIKŌCHI** (上高地). Little more than a bus station and a handful of hotels scattered along the Azusa-gawa, Kamikōchi has some stunning alpine scenery, which can only be viewed between April 27 and November 15 before heavy snow blocks off the narrow roads and the resort shuts down for winter. As a result, the place buzzes with tourists during the season and the prices at its hotels and restaurants can be as steep as the surrounding mountains.

Kamikōchi owes its fortunes to the late nineteenth-century British missionary **Walter Weston** (see box, p.358), who helped popularize the area as a base for climbing the craggy peaks known as the Northern Alps. The highest mountain here is the 3190m **Hotaka-dake** (also known as Oku-Hotaka-dake), followed by **Yari-ga-take** (3180m). Both are extremely popular climbs; one trail up Yari-ga-take has been dubbed the Ginza Jūsō ("Ginza Traverse") after Tokyo's busy shopping area, because it gets so crowded. However, the congestion on the mountain is nothing compared to that found at its base, where, at the height of the season, thousands of day-trippers tramp through the well-marked trails along the Azusa valley. The best way to appreciate Kamikōchi is to stay overnight so you can experience the valley in the evening and early morning minus the day-trippers. Alternatively, visit in June, when frequent showers deter fair-weather walkers.

Hotaka

A thirty-minute train ride north of Matsumoto lies the quiet country town of **Hotaka** (穂高), well known for its production of *wasabi*, the fiery green horseradish that, made into a paste, accompanies sushi and sashimi. The enjoyably touristy **Dai-ō Wasabi Farm** (大王わさび農場; daily 9am–5pm; free), one of the largest such in Japan, is about 2km from the station. The vast fields of *wasabi* growing in wide, waterlogged gravel trenches make an impressive sight. Within the landscaped grounds you can sample *wasabi* in all manner of foods, including ice cream, which is surprisingly tasty.

Closer to the station is the serene **Rokuzan Art Museum** (碌山美術館; Tues–Sun 9am–5pm; ¥500), comprising an ivy-covered, church-like building and a couple of modern galleries. The museum houses the sculptures of **Ogiwara Rokuzan**, known in Japan as the "Rodin of the Orient", whose career was cut short with his death at 32 in 1910.

The best way to explore this tranquil area is to pick up a map from the **tourist information office** at the station and rent a bicycle from one of the many outlets around here. Keep an eye open along the country roads for the charming *dōsojin*, small stones on which guardian deity couples have been carved.

Arrival and information

Private vehicles are banned from the valley. If you're **driving**, park your car in the village of Naka-no-yu (中の湯), 8km outside Kamikōchi. From here buses (¥1000 one-way, ¥1800 return) and taxis (¥4500 for up to four passengers) make regular runs to and from Kamikōchi, passing through narrow rock tunnels. To get here from Matsumoto, take a thirty-minute **train** journey on the Matsumoto Dentetsu line to Shin-Shimashima Station (新島々; ¥680), then transfer to a bus to Kamikōchi (75min; ¥2000). There are also a few direct buses in summer from Matsumoto bus terminal (¥2600 one-way, ¥4600 return). From Takayama there are a couple of direct buses daily (¥2200), but it's quicker to hop on the more frequent bus to Hirayu Onsen (¥1530), then transfer to the Kamikōchi bus (¥1050). There's also a daily bus between Norikura Kōgen (see p.359) and Kamikōchi. Once you've arrived, make sure you reserve your seat on a bus out of Kamikōchi – the sheer number of visitors often leaves many people at the mercy of the taxi drivers.

There's an **information centre** (8am–5pm; ⓣ0263/95-2433, ⓦwww.kamikochi.or.jp) at the bus terminal where you can pick up a good English map showing the main hiking trails. The assistants don't speak much English, so if you need more information or want to arrange accommodation, do this at the Matsumoto tourist office (see p.352) before setting out. The staff at the **national park visitor centre** (daily 8am–5pm; ⓣ0263/95-2606), just past Kappa-bashi, should be able to give some description in English of the many rare animals, plants and songbirds in the valley. There is **no ATM** or bank in Kamikōchi – bring plenty of cash.

Accommodation

The most convenient **campsite** is at Konashidaira (小梨平; ⓣ0263/95-2321, ⓦwww.nihonalpskankou.co.jp; ¥700/person/night), in a serene location just beyond Kappa-bashi and the visitor centre. Showers are available, as are self-catering cabins starting from ¥7000 per couple. Otherwise, the best budget option is in the large dorm at *Nishi-itoya Sansō* (西糸屋山荘; ⓣ0263/95-2206, ⓦwww.nishiitoya.com; ¥7700/person), which has both bunk beds and shared tatami areas. The rates here include two meals – a good deal for Kamikōchi. *Nishi-itoya Sansō* also has a pleasant ryokan, next door (❼ including meals). To escape the crowds, head for *Yamanohidaya* (山のひだや; ⓣ0263/95-2211; ❼–❽ with two meals) next to Myōjin-ike (see p.358), a delightfully rustic lodge, complete with stuffed animals as decoration and meals cooked on an ancient iron range.

Back in the main village, *Kamikochi Gosenjaku Lodge* (五千尺ロッヂ; ⓣ0263/95-2221, ⓦwww.gosenjaku.co.jp; ❼ with two meals) is the less expensive of the two very comfortable *Gosenjaku* properties. Top of the line, and worth the expense, is the *Kamikōchi Imperial Hotel* (上高地帝国ホテル; ⓣ0263/95-2001, ⓦwww.imperialhotel.co.jp; ❽), with the delightful spookiness of a grand old Western-style hotel in a wilderness setting. Putting up at the youth hostel in *Norikura Kōgen* (see p.359) and travelling into Kamikōchi for the day is also a viable option.

Hiking around Kamikōchi

With an early start, the scenic spots of the Azusa valley can all be covered in a day's hike. Pick up the English *Kamikōchi Pocket Guide* from the information office at the bus stop for a good map of all the main trails. At the entrance to the valley, the **Taishō-ike** (大正池) is a glass-like pond that reflects the snowcapped peaks: head here first. From here an hour-long amble starts along the pebbly riverbank and splits after the Tashiro bridge, one leg continuing beside the Azusa-gawa, the other following a nature-observation trail along wooden walkways, over chocolatey

Walter Weston

Born in Derbyshire, England, in 1861, the missionary **Walter Weston** was 29 years old when he first set foot in the mountains of Nagano-ken. The phrase "Japan Alps" was actually coined by another Englishman, William Gowland, whose *Japan Guide* was published in 1888, but it was Weston's *Climbing and Exploring in the Japan Alps*, which appeared eight years later, that really put the peaks on the mountaineers' maps. Previously, these mountains, considered **sacred**, were only climbed by Shinto and Buddhist priests, but in fast-modernizing Japan alpinism caught on as a **sport** and Weston became its acknowledged guru. Weston favoured Kamikōchi as a base from which to climb what he called "the grandest mountains in Japan", and he frequently visited the tiny village from his home in Kōbe. Although he is honoured in Kamikōchi with a monument and a festival in his name on the first Sunday in June (the start of the climbing season), Weston is said to have wept at the prospect of mass tourism ruining his beloved mountains. His ghost can take comfort from the fact that the area's beauty survives largely intact, despite Kamikōchi's popularity.

marshes. The Taishō-ike was formed when the Azusa-gawa was naturally dammed up after the eruption of the nearby volcano Yake-dake in 1915, and dead tree trunks still poke out of the water. Rowing boats can be rented from the *Taishō-ike Hotel* for ¥800 for thirty minutes.

Returning the way you came, cross over the Tashiro bridge to the opposite bank of the river, where the path leads past some of Kamikōchi's hotels and the rock-embedded relief statue of Walter Weston. In the centre of the village the river is spanned by the much-photographed wooden suspension bridge **Kappa-bashi** (河童橋). Cross this and continue north for a couple of minutes to the good **visitor centre** (daily 8am–5pm), where there are nature displays and some stunning photographs of the mountains.

The crowds fall away on the hike north from the visitors' centre to the picturesque pond, **Myōjin-ike** (明神池; ¥300 entry), with its tiny shrine and mallard ducks; the 7km return trip will take you around two hours at a leisurely pace. Myōjin-ike is the location of a festival on October 8 when two boats, their prows decorated with the head of a dragon and a legendary bird, float on the sacred pond. From here the really keen can follow the six-hour course up the valley to the Tokusawa campsite (徳沢) and the Shinmura suspension bridge, named after a famous climber, Shinmura Shōichi.

Climbing around Kamikōchi

Beyond Tokusawa the serious hiking begins. The steep hike up the "Matterhorn of Japan" (so called because of its craggy appearance) to the mountain huts at Ichinomata on the lower slopes of **Yari-ga-take** (槍ヶ岳) takes around five hours, and can be done in a long day from Kamikōchi. There are basic huts on the mountain for overnight stays; a futon and two meals cost around ¥8000 per person, but things can get very crowded during the season.

Reaching the summit of Yari-ga-take may well give you a taste for mountaineering. The popular route to follow is due south across the alpine ridge to **Hotaka-dake** (穂高岳), the third-highest peak in Japan, a three-day loop that will bring you back to Kamikōchi.

Even for day walks, make sure you pack warm, waterproof clothing, as the weather can change rapidly in the mountains. At the height of summer temperatures on the peaks can be freezing, especially early in the morning.

Eating and drinking

Eating options include standard soba and curry rice at inflated prices from the hotels, where fancier set meals are also served. If you're visiting for the day or are planning a hike into the mountains, bring a picnic. For lunch, *Kamonjigoya* (嘉門次小屋) beside Myōjin-ike (see opposite) is worth stopping at for the *iwana* (river trout) lunch at ¥1500. The fish are roasted on sticks beside an *irori* (charcoal fire), making this an ideal refuge if the weather turns nasty.

Norikura Kōgen Onsen

Much like Kamikōchi, **NORIKURA KŌGEN** (乗鞍高原), an alpine village some 30km southwest of Matsumoto, offers splendid mountain scenery, hiking trails and onsen. In winter, ski lifts shoot up the lower slopes of **Norikura-dake**, while in summer the hike to the peak of the same mountain can be accomplished in ninety minutes from the car park, where the Echo Line road leaves Nagano-ken and becomes the **Skyline Road** in Gifu-ken. This is the highest road in Japan, providing spectacular mountain-top views (the upper section is closed Nov–end May). The car park is an hour's drive from Norikura Kōgen.

The closest thing to a centre in this straggle of a village is the modern onsen complex, **Yukemurikan** (湯けむり館; Wed–Mon 9.30am–8pm; ¥700), which has both indoor wooden baths and rotemburo with mountain views. Nearby are the ski lifts and an hour-long trail east to **Sanbon-daki** (三本滝), where three waterfalls converge in one pool. An alternative hiking route from the ski lifts is south for twenty minutes to another beautiful waterfall, **Zengorō-no-taki** (善五郎の滝), reached along a clearly marked nature trail, with signs in English – a rainbow often forms in the spray across this impressive fall during the morning. Twenty minutes' walk further south of Zengorō, a small reflecting pond, **Ushidome-ike** (牛留池), provides a perfect view of the mountains. Continuing downhill from the pond, you can choose to walk towards another small waterhole, **Azami-ike** (あざみ池), or to the main picnic area, **Ichinose** (一の瀬), a picturesque spot at the confluence of two streams. A cycle and walking track leads directly north from Ichinose back to Yukemurikan, where the best plan of action is to soak in the rotemburo.

Practicalities

Norikura Kōgen can be reached by infrequent **buses** from both Shin-Shimashima train station on the Matsumoto Dentetsu line, and Takayama (see p.363), with a change of buses at Tatamidaira and Hirayu Onsen. From June to October there's also one daily bus between Norikura Kōgen and Kamikōchi. Check with local tourist offices for the current timetables.

There's a **tourist information office** (daily 9.30am–4.30pm; Ⓣ0263/93-2952, Ⓦwww.norikura.gr.jp) opposite the Yukemurikan onsen complex. As far as **accommodation** goes, the *Norikura Kōgen Youth Hostel* (Ⓣ0263/93-2748, Ⓕ93-2162; ¥3500 per person), ten minutes' walk north from the bus stop and next to the ski lifts, is ideally placed for quick access to the slopes. The young,

Cable car to the roof of Japan

An adventurous option for approaching Kamikōchi across the mountains from the west is to take the **cable car** (one-way ¥1500, return ¥2800; Ⓦwww.okuhi.jp) up from Shin-Hotaka Onsen (新穂高温泉) in **Gifu-ken**. This onsen resort, best reached by bus from Takayama (see p.363), is reputed to have one of the longest cable-car rides in Asia (3200m), which takes you halfway to the 2908m summit of Nishi-Hotaka-dake; from here, Kamikōchi is a three-hour hike southeast.

friendly staff can arrange ski rental and point out the most interesting hikes during the summer. Opposite the ski lifts is *Pension Chimney* (ⓣ0263/93-2902; ❻), an appealing European-style chalet with a steeply sloping roof and cosy rooms. Rates here include two meals; there's a heating charge in the winter. A similar deal is available at the large and friendly *BELL Suzurangoya* (BELL 鈴蘭小屋; ⓣ0263/93-2001, ⓕ93-2003; ❻), near the tourist information office. The *Kyūkamura Norikura Kōgen* (休暇村乗鞍高原; ⓣ0263/93-2304, ⓕ93-2392; ❻), near Ushidome pond, has fine tatami rooms and offers rates that include two meals; there is an extra heating charge in the winter.

The Kiso valley

The densely forested river valley of **Kiso**, southwest of Matsumoto, between the Central and Northern Alps, provides a glimpse of what Japan looked like before concrete and neon became the norm. Running through this valley was part of the route for the 550km Nakasendō, one of the five main highways spanning out from Edo (present-day Tokyo). Eleven post towns (*juku*) lined the Kiso-ji (Kiso road) section of the Nakasendō, and three of them – **Narai**, **Tsumago** and **Magome** – have been preserved as virtual museums of the feudal past, the latter two linked by an easy two-hour hiking trail. Another *juku*, **Kiso-Fukushima**, looks less like a samurai film set than the others, but still has attractive areas and is useful as a transport hub. For historical background see the informative website Nakasendō Way (ⓦwww.nakasendoway.com).

Narai

Attractive **NARAI** (奈良井), 30km southwest of Matsumoto, is generally less infested with tour groups than Tsumago and Magome. This was the most prosperous of the Kiso-ji *juku*, a fact that shows in the village's beautifully preserved and distinctive wooden buildings, with overhanging second floors and eaves, and *renji-gōshi* latticework. Only the cars that occasionally pass through the conservation area, which runs for about 1km south from the train station, remind you which century you're in.

Opposite the **tourist office** (daily 10am–5pm; ⓣ0264/34-3048, ⓦwww.naraijyuku.com) in the Nakamachi area of town, look out for the shop selling *kashira ningyō*, colourfully painted, traditional dolls and toys made of wood and plaster, as well as the sake brewery Sugi-no-Mori. In the Kamimachi area stands **Nakamura House** (中村邸; daily 9am–4.30pm; ¥200), dating back to the 1830s and once the home of a merchant who made his fortune in combs, still one of the area's specialities. Side streets lead off to pretty temples and shrines in the foothills and, on the other side, to the rocky banks of the Narai-gawa, crossed by the **Kiso-no-Ōhashi**, an arched wooden bridge.

Narai, a 45-minute local **train** journey from Matsumoto, can easily be visited in half a day. Dotted along the main street are several appealing cafés with soaring wooden-beamed ceilings and *irori* (central charcoal fires) serving soba noodles and other local dishes – a good one is *Kokoro-ne* (こころ音; ⓣ0264/34-3345; daily except Wed 11am–3pm). For somewhere to **stay**, try the lovely minshuku *Iseya* (伊勢屋; ⓣ0264/34-3051, ⓦwww.oyado-iseya.jp; ❻); rates include two meals.

Kiso-Fukushima

Four train stations south of Narai is **KISO-FUKUSHIMA** (木曽福島), a much more developed town than the other *juku* – hence it being a stop for the express train between Matsumoto and Nagoya. At the **tourist office** (Ⓣ0264/22-4000, Ⓦwww.kankou-kiso.com) opposite the train station, pick up a map to point you towards the hilltop **Ue-no-dan** (上の段) conservation area and the temple **Kōzen-ji** (興禅寺) with its serene raked gravel and rock garden.

If you're looking for somewhere inexpensive **to stay**, the *Kiso-Ryojōan Youth Hostel* (木曽旅情庵ユースホステル; Ⓣ0264/23-7716; ¥3000 per person), is a 25-minute bus ride from Kiso-Fukushima, in a large traditional building in the peaceful mountain village of **Ōhara**. You could use the hostel as a base from which to explore the valley's post towns. Alternatively, the *Tsutaya* (つたや; Ⓣ0264/22-2145, Ⓦwww.kisoji-tutaya.com; ⑦) is a pleasant ryokan opposite the station where the rates include two meals.

Tsumago

Given the number of tourists it now attracts, it's hard to believe that, back in the 1960s, **TSUMAGO** (妻籠), 80km south of Matsumoto, was virtually a ghost town, with most of its traditional Edo-era houses on the point of collapse. That's when locals banded together to restore the village's buildings, eventually earning Tsumago protected status and helping to spark the idea of cultural preservation across Japan. Telegraph poles and TV aerials have been banished from sight, so that the scene that greets you on the pedestrian-only street is probably very similar to that encountered by lords and their retinues passing through the village hundreds of years ago.

The walk from one end of Tsumago to the other will take you less than thirty minutes. Along the way you should drop by the **Nagiso-machi Museum** (daily 9am–4.45pm) which consists of two sections, the main one of which is the **Waki Honjin Okuya** (脇本陣奥谷; ¥600), a finely constructed two-storey mansion dating from 1877 and once one of the village's designated post inns for government officials. Attached is the **Historical Museum**, with exhibits on the history of the Nakasendō and the village, including photographs showing just how dilapidated Tsumago once was. Across the street is the **Tsumago-juku Honjin** (妻籠宿本陣; ¥300), the former home of the village headman. A combined ticket for ¥700 gains you access to both properties, but if you're staying overnight in the village check in with your accommodation first as you should qualify for a twenty percent discount.

The former site of **Tsumago castle**, destroyed sometime in the late sixteenth century, provides a bird's-eye view of the village. To get here, follow the path that

Hiking the Kiso-ji

It's traditional to hike the Kiso-ji from Magome to Tsumago in order to experience the supposedly tough initial climb up into the mountains – though it's actually not that difficult. Although the 7.7km route is frequently signposted in English, it's a good idea to pick up a map from one of the tourist information offices before you start.

There's a **baggage-forwarding** service (weekends and national holidays late March–July & Sept–Nov; daily late July to late Aug; ¥500 per piece) to and from the tourist information offices in both Tsumago and Magome. Get your bag to the offices before 11.30am and they will be delivered at the other end by 5pm.

If you choose to walk in the opposite direction, start at Nagiso Station on the Chūō line, from where Tsumago is less than an hour south through picturesque fields and small villages. Set aside a day to explore both post towns and to complete the hike. You'll enjoy the experience all the more if you stay in either Tsumago or Magome overnight.

heads north out the village on the hiking route to Nagiso (see box, p.361). A good way to relax after the Magome to Tsumago hike is to hop on the free shuttle bus from the village's northern car park to the onsen and tourist complex **Kisojikan** (木曽路館; daily 10am–8pm; ¥700); there are fine views of the valley from its rotemburo. While here, you can also participate in soba-making classes (¥1050/30min, ¥2100/hr).

The closest **train station** to Tsumago is Nagiso (南木曽), from where the village is an hour's walk south or a ten-minute bus ride. Tsumago's helpful **tourist information office** (daily 8.30am–5pm; ⓣ0264/57-3123, ⓦwww.dia.janis.or.jp/~tumago) is in the centre of the village; here you can arrange to have your bag forwarded if you're planning to hike to Magome. One of the best **places to stay** is *Fujioto* (藤乙; ⓣ0264/57-3009; ❼), a charming traditional inn with friendly English-speaking owners. Other options include the minshuku *Daikichi* (大吉; ⓣ0264/57-2595; ❺), at the northern end of the village, and the more upmarket, 140-year-old ryokan, *Matsushiro-ya* (松代屋; ⓣ0264/57-3022; ❼). All rates include two meals.

There's no shortage of lunchtime **restaurants and cafés** in Tsumago. Most places serve *sansai* soba (buckwheat noodles topped with mountain vegetables) and *gohei-mochi* (balls of pounded rice coated with a sweet nut sauce). A good place to sample these is *Yamagiri* (やまぎり) at the north end of the village near the water wheel.

Magome

With its buildings perched on a steep slope, **MAGOME** (馬籠), 5km south of Tsumago, stands 800m up in the hills above the Kiso valley. Magome means "horse basket", because this *juku* was where travellers were forced to leave their nags before tackling the mountainous stretch of road ahead. Plaster and wooden buildings line either side of the stone-flagged path – many of the wooden roofs are still held down by stone. Despite appearances, most buildings date from the twentieth century, the village having suffered a history of fires, the most recent being in 1915, when 42 houses burnt to the ground. Magome is famous for its native son, **Shimazaki Tōson** (1872–1943), whose historical novel *Yoake Mae* (*Before the Dawn*) put the town on Japan's literary map. In the middle of the village, the **Tōson Kinenkan** (藤村記念館; daily 8.30am–4.45pm; ¥500) displays fragments of the author's life; however, they're all labelled in Japanese.

To start the **hike** to Tsumago (see box, p.361), continue up the hill, past the **kōsatsu**, the old town noticeboard on which the shogunate posted rules and regulations, including the death penalty for anyone found illegally logging the forests' trees. The steepest part of the hike is over once you've reached the **Magome-tōge** (pass), where there's an old teahouse beside the road and a stone monument engraved with a lyrical verse by the haiku master Masaoka Shiki (see p.638). From here, the route enters the forest and later passes two **waterfalls**, O-dake and Me-dake.

The closest **train station** to Magome is in Nakatsugawa (中津川), a 55-minute journey northeast of Nagoya (see p.384) by limited express. **Buses** to Nakatsugawa also run from Nagoya and the spa town of Gero (下呂) on the JR Takayama Line. Buses to Magome run from platform three outside Nakatsugawa Station (30min; ¥540).

Magome's **tourist information office** (daily 8.30am–5pm; ⓣ0264/59-2336, ⓦwww.kiso-magome.com), opposite the Tōson Kinenkan, has an English map of the area; staff speak Japanese only and can help with accommodation bookings at the village's numerous minshuku. Two good **places to stay** are *Magome-chaya* (馬籠茶屋; ⓣ0264/59-2038; ❺), close to the tourist office, which also runs an attached restaurant, and *Tajimaya* (但馬屋; ⓣ0264/59-2048; ❻), a little further downhill – both places include two meals in their rates.

Takayama and around

On the Gifu-ken side of the Central Alps in an area known as Hida, the busy tourist town of **TAKAYAMA** (高山), 110km northeast of Nagoya, was once an enclave of skilled carpenters employed by emperors to build palaces and temples in Kyoto and Nara. Takayama's appeal today lies in its old merchant houses, small museums, tranquil temples and shrines clustered into a compact area. An easy day-trip is **Furukawa**, a mini version of Takayama, but generally minus the crowds. Takayama can also be used as a base from which to visit the picturesque **Shirakawa-gō** and **Gokayama valleys**, where three villages of A-frame thatched houses have been designated a UNESCO World Heritage Site.

Arrival and information

Takayama is connected by **train** to both Toyama (see p.372) in the north and Nagoya (see p.384) in the south. The long-distance bus terminal is next to JR Takayama Station, ten minutes' walk west of the San-machi Suji district, where many of the town's main sights can be found.

The Hida **tourist information office** (daily: April–Oct 8.30am–6.30pm; Nov–March 8.30am–5pm; ⓣ0577/32-5328, ⓦwww.hida.jp), immediately in front of the JR station, has clued-up, English-speaking staff; there's also a booth in the San-machi Suji area. Takayama is best explored on foot or by **bicycle**, which can

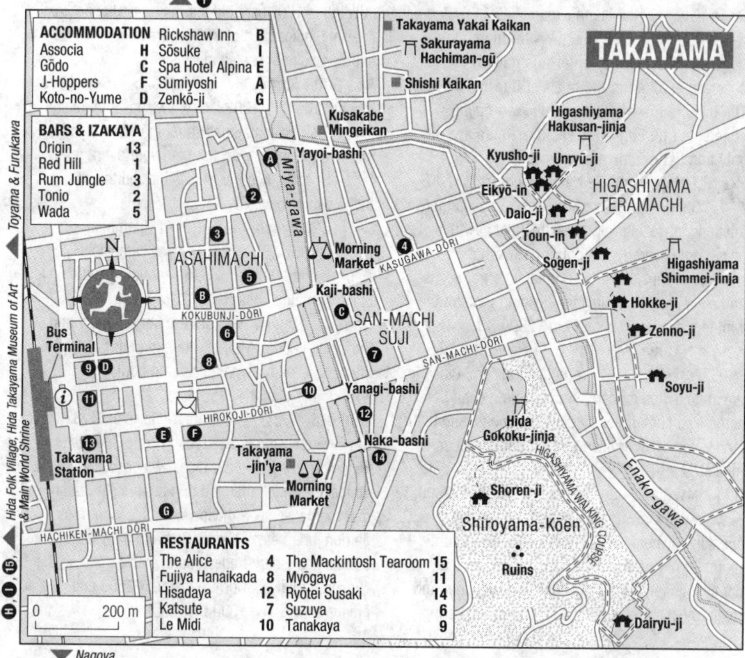

The morning markets

Every day, from 7am (6am in summer) until around noon, Takayama has two **morning markets** (*asa ichi*), which are well worth getting up early to attend. The fruit and veg market is held in front of the *jin'ya* (see opposite), while the larger, more tourist-orientated market is strung out along the east bank of the Miya-gawa, between the Kaji-bashi and Yayoi-bashi bridges. Here, apart from pickles and flowers, you can buy local handicrafts, including *sarubobo*, the little fabric baby monkeys seen all over Takayama, grab a coffee or locally brewed beer, and sample the sweet marshmallow snack *tamaten*.

be rented from the car park to the right of the station (¥200/hr, ¥1200/day). Kankakokan, 40-4 Kamininomachi (daily 10am–5pm), has a couple of **internet** terminals (¥100/30min); you can also quickly access the internet at the tourist office for free.

Accommodation

If you're planning on staying in Takayama during its festivals (see box opposite), book well ahead. Apart from the places listed below, there are several inexpensive business hotels near the train station.

Associa 1134 Echigo-chō Ⓣ0577/36-1177, Ⓦwww.associa.com/tky. Elegant luxury hotel, in the hills 5km southwest of Takayama Station but connected to town by a free shuttle bus. Offers several restaurants and bars, and a lavish spa with ten indoor and outdoor baths. ⑦–⑧

Gōdo 河渡 46 Kamisanno-machi Ⓣ&Ⓕ0577/33-0870. You pass through a low, paper-covered door to enter this quirkily decorated ryokan in the heart of San-machi Suji. The owners are friendly and used to *gaijin* guests, but no English is spoken. Rates are room only and bathrooms are shared. ⑤

J-Hoppers 5-52 Nada-machi Ⓣ0577/32-3278, Ⓦtakayama.j-hoppers.com. Is there anything that this slick, super-friendly new hostel hasn't got covered? They offer dorms and private rooms, run trips, have bike rental, internet access and even provide wellies for sloshing through the winter snow. Dorm beds from ¥2500. ④

Koto-no-Yume 古都の夢 6-11 Hanasato-chō, Ⓣ0577/32-0427, Ⓦwww.kotoyume.com. Close to the station, this modern, small-scale ryokan has some nice contemporary design touches, and both indoor and outdoor onsen baths. Rates include two meals. ⑥

Rickshaw Inn 54 Suehiro-chō Ⓣ0577/32-2890, Ⓦwww.rickshawinn.com. With friendly English-speaking owners, this relaxing place has tatami rooms furnished to a high standard. There's a comfy lounge with a daily English newspaper and magazines, and a small kitchen for self-catering. The very stylish suite room, sleeping up to four, is great value for a family. ⑤

Sōsuke 惣助 1-64 Okamoto-machi Ⓣ0577/32-0818, Ⓦwww.irori-sosuke.com. Good-value traditional minshuku, about 10min walk west of the station, opposite the *Takayama Green Hotel*. The building is 170 years old and has a traditional *irori* hearth. Singles start at ¥5040; breakfast is ¥700 extra and dinner is also available. ④

Spa Hotel Alpina スパホテルアルピナ 5-41 Nada-machi Ⓣ0577/33-0033, Ⓦwww.spa-hotel-alpina.com. The pleasant, smallish rooms offer slightly more contemporary design than your average business hotel. Another plus is the rooftop spa baths with a view. ④–⑤

Sumiyoshi 寿美吉 21-4 Honmachi Ⓣ0577/32-0228, Ⓦwww.sumiyoshi-ryokan.com. Delightful *gaijin*-friendly ryokan, in a building dating back to 1912, with a great riverside location. The staff are very friendly and the place is chock-full of interesting antiques and knick-knacks; breakfast costs an additional ¥1050, and dinner ¥3150. ④

Zenkō-ji 善光寺 4-3 Tenman-chō Ⓣ0577/32-8470, Ⓦtakayamahostelzenkoji.com. Buddha is watching you, but in the nicest way possible at this appealing hostel attached to a temple. The tatami-mat rooms, some with views of a pleasant rock garden, are a steal. Like its Nagano namesake, the temple has a dark underground corridor hiding the "key to paradise". Dorm beds are ¥2500 and private rooms just ¥500 more. ③

The Town

Takayama's main tourist draw is the **San-machi Suji**, but if you have more time there are also worthwhile attractions west of the train station, in particular the **Hida Folk Village**.

San-machi Suji and around

Around ten minutes' walk from the station, on the east bank of the Miya-gawa, is the **San-machi Suji** (三町筋) area of dark wooden merchant houses dating from the mid-nineteenth century. The quarter's main three narrow streets are most evocative at dusk, when the crowds have thinned. During the day, you'll have to negotiate your way through rickshaws and tourists pottering in and out of craft shops, cafés and sake breweries (see box, p.367).

Before you cross the Miya-gawa, drop by the town's feudal-era government complex, **Takayama-jin'ya** (高山陣屋; daily: April–Oct 8.45am–5pm; Nov–March 8.45am–4.30pm; ¥420), at the end of Hachikenmachi-dōri, five minutes' walk southeast of the station. This small-scale palace, originally built in 1615 and the only building of its kind left in Japan, was the seat of power for the Hida area's governor, appointed by the shogun. Most of the buildings seen today, including a torture chamber and a rice storehouse, date from reconstruction in 1816, and the best way to explore them is to go on one of the free guided tours in English (around 45min).

San-machi Suji has a plethora of small and generally uninteresting museums. The best is the handsome **Kusakabe Mingeikan** (日下部民芸館; daily: March–Nov 9am–4.30pm; Dec–Feb 9am–4pm; ¥500), the home of the Kusakabe family, dating from 1879, and an outstanding example of Takayama's renowned carpentry skills. In the shaded courtyard between the main home and the storehouses, now stocked with folk crafts, you'll be offered a refreshing cup of tea and a rice cracker.

Sakurayama Hachiman-gū and Higashiyama Teramachi

Five minutes' walk northeast of the Kusakabe Mingeikan is Takayama's main shrine, **Sakurayama Hachiman-gū** (桜山八幡宮), dating back to the fourth century. Here you'll find the **Takayama Yatai Kaikan** (see box below), the entrance charge to which includes the **Sakurayama-Nikkō-kan**, a hall displaying a dazzling one-tenth-scale replica of 28 buildings from Nikkō's Tōshōgū shrine, where a computer controls the lighting to reproduce sunrise and sunset.

It's also worth checking out the enjoyable demonstration of automated *karakuri* puppets in the **Shishi Kaikan** (獅子会館; daily: mid-April to mid-Nov

Takayama's festivals and Yatai

Takayama's two famous festivals are the **Sannō Matsuri** (April 14–15) and the **Hachiman Matsuri** (Oct 9–10), when eleven huge elaborate *yatai* (floats), adorned with mechanical dolls (*karakuri*), are paraded around town, a spectacle that attracts hundreds of thousands of visitors. If you're not in town for the festivals you can still view four of the *yatai* at the **Takayama Yatai Kaikan** (高山屋台会館; daily: March–Nov 8.30am–5.30pm; Dec–Feb 9am–4.30pm; ¥820), a large exhibition hall within the grounds of the shrine **Sakurayama Hachiman-gū** (櫻山八幡宮). At least once a year all eleven floats and the golden *mikoshi* (portable shrine) are displayed inside the huge glass case that you wind your way around at different levels so you can see all of the decoration closely. Many of the floats date from the seventeenth century and are usually stored in the tall storehouses (*yatai-gura*) that you'll notice around Takayama.

8.30am–5.30pm; mid-Nov to mid-April 9am–5pm; ¥600), on the south side of the shrine. A video of a *shishi* (mythical lion) dance, common to festivals in the Takayama area, is screened at regular intervals during the day, and you can also see many lion masks and musical instruments used in these dances.

Following the narrow Enako-gawa southeast, towards the hills from the Sakurayama Hachiman-gū, will bring you to the tranquil **Higashiyama Teramachi** (東山寺町) area, where thirteen temples and five shrines are dotted among the soaring pine trees and linked by a pleasant walk that goes over the river to **Shiroyama-kōen**. This wooded park stands on the remains of Lord Kanamori's castle, destroyed over three hundred years ago; you can still trace the donjon's foundations on the top of the hill. The route is signposted and you can pick up a map from the tourist information office (see p.363).

Hida Folk Village and around

West of Takayama Station are a few more worthwhile sights, the best of which is the **Hida Folk Village**, or *Hida Minzoku-mura* (飛騨民俗村; daily 8.30am–5pm; ¥700), twenty minutes' walk from the station, in a lovely hillside location overlooking the mountains. This outdoor museum of over twenty traditional buildings gathered from the Hida area is fascinating to wander around, especially if you're not planning on visiting the *gasshō-zukuri* thatched houses of the Shirakawa-gō and Gokayama districts (see p.369).

The main entrance is roughly 600m uphill, past the first car park and old houses, opposite a row of giftshops. You're free to explore inside the houses, many of which have displays of farm implements and folk crafts relating to their former owners. The four old houses next to the ticket gate offer a chance to see real artists working at traditional crafts such as lacquering and woodcarving; those at the bottom of the hill comprise the **Hida Folk Museum**, but are little different from those in the main village. If you don't fancy walking or cycling to the museum, take a bus (¥200 each way) from the terminal beside Takayama Station; they run to the village every thirty minutes during the day. The **Hida-no-Sato Setto-ken** discount ticket (¥900) includes return bus fare and entrance to the village.

On the road up to the Hida Folk Village, you'll pass the elegant and modern **Hida Takayama Museum of Art** (飛騨高山美術館; daily 9am–5pm; ¥1300), which contains a wonderful glass collection and Art Nouveau interiors. Near the entrance is a beautiful glass fountain by René Lalique, which once stood in the Paris Lido; further on, the collection includes lustrous objets d'art by Gallè, Tiffany glass lamps and the interior designs of Charles Rennie Mackintosh and the Vienna Secessionists. The museum also has a pleasant café (see opposite). Ask at the tourist office for a ¥200 discount coupon on entrance and about the free London double-decker bus that runs to the museum and back from the station.

With its golden roof, topped with what looks like a huge red snooker ball, you can't miss the enormous **Main World Shrine** (daily 9.30am–4pm, but call ☎0577/34-7008 first as it's sometimes closed for special events), roughly 1km west of Hida Folk Village. This is the headquarters of the Sūkyō Mahikari sect, which combines elements of Shintō with Buddhism and was founded in 1959 by businessman Okada Kotama, after he claimed to have received "revelations" from God. Inside, check out the shrine's stupendous architecture, built like a stage set for a cast of thousands and including a bizarre replica of Mexico City's Quetzalcoatl Fountain and two vaguely Islamic-looking towers.

Eating and drinking

The best thing to sample at Takayama's numerous **restaurants** is the area's speciality, *sansai ryōri*, dishes of local mountain vegetables, ferns and wild

Sake breweries

The Hida area has been well known for its sake for over 400 years; at one time there were some 56 breweries in Takayama. Now there are just six functioning ones in San-machi Suji – Hirata (平田), Harada (原田), Kawashiri (川尻), Niki (二木), Hirase (平瀬) and Tanabe (田邊), all easily spotted by the balls of cedar leaves hanging above their entrances. Winter is the main sake-making season, and between mid-January and the end of February each brewery takes it in turns to provide a free tour (10am–noon, 1–4pm) of their facilities – check with the tourist office for details.

plants. Also look out for *sansai soba*, buckwheat noodles topped with greens, and *hōba miso*, vegetables mixed with miso paste and roasted on a magnolia leaf above a charcoal brazier (a beef version is also served). In addition, the local *hida* beef is excellent, and a delicious snack sold around town is *mitarashi-dango* – pounded rice balls dipped in soy sauce and roasted on skewers. Note that many of the San-machi Suji tourist restaurants are only open at lunch, when they can get very busy.

Restaurants and cafés

The Alice Yashugawa-dōri. Stylish, good-value café attached to a wedding hall. Aproned waitresses serve faithfully executed *yōshoku* – Japanese takes on Western dishes such as steak and rice-filled omelettes. Daily except Wed 11.30am–2pm & 4.30–8pm.

Fujiya Hanaikada 富士屋花筏 46 Hanakawa-chō. Specializing in *wagashi* (traditional Japanese sweets), this stylish place is also a showroom for locally made wooden furniture. Its outdoor deck is a good place for a break. Daily except Thurs 10am–6pm.

Hisadaya 久田屋 11-3 Kamisanno-machi ⓣ0577/32-0216. Excellent set lunches of *sansai ryōri* (from ¥1400 per person) are served in the tatami rooms of one of the San-machi Suji's old merchants' houses. Daily except Wed 11am–3pm.

Katsute かつて 92 Kamisanno-machi, ⓦwww.wdo-kao.jp. On Takayama's most touristy street, this café serving drinks and sweets, plus a gift shop, offers a bit more style than other places and has a no-smoking section upstairs. Daily except Wed 10am–5pm.

Le Midi 2-2 Honmachi ⓣ0577/36-6386, ⓦwww.le-midi.jp. Sample top-quality *hida* beef and other local meat and fish at this sophisticated bistro that feels like a slice of Paris. Daily except Tues 11.30am–2.30pm & 6–9.30pm.

The Mackintosh Tearoom Attached to the Hida Takayama Museum of Art (see opposite). Modelled on the famous tearooms in Glasgow, which were designed by Charles Rennie Mackintosh, this place offers specially blended tea and cakes, as well as light meals. The view across the mountains is lovely, and you can eat outside. Daily except Tues 9am–5.30pm.

Myōgaya 茗荷屋 5-15 Hanasato-chō ⓣ0577-32-0426. This relaxed natural food restaurant and shop serves excellent vegetarian food. The brown rice and organic veggie set menu is good value at ¥1000, and the cook will avoid using salt and fat if you ask her. You can reserve for dinner on Sat (5–7pm). Wed–Sun 8am–3pm.

Ryōtei Susaki 料亭洲さき 4-14 Shinmei-machi ⓣ0577/32-0023, ⓦwww.ryoutei-susaki.com. This memorable *ryōtei* has been run by the same family since 1794 and serves *honzen* cuisine, which is similar to *kaiseki* in style and presentation. *Ryōtei* are famously exclusive places, but here the service is friendly, the setting serene and atmospheric, and the food worth every last yen. Lunch courses start at ¥6300, dinner ¥12,750; reservations are essential. Daily 11.30am–2pm & 5–9pm.

Suzuya 寿々や 24 Hanakawa-machi ⓣ0577/32-2484. Beamed, family-run restaurant that's a great place to sample *sansai ryōri*, and especially *hoba miso*. There's an English menu with pictures, friendly waitresses to assist you, and you can either sit at tables or on tatami. Can get really busy at night with tour groups. Daily except Tues 11am–2.30pm & 5–8pm.

Tanakaya 6-28 Hanasato-chō. Delicious sweet and savoury pastries and cakes are available at this cute shoebox of a café with a few seats inside and out. Daily except Thurs 9am–7pm.

Bars and izakaya

The Asahimachi area between the station and the Miya-gawa is packed with small **bars** – locals recommend the reggae and blues bar *Rum Jungle*, which offers a killer selection of sake.

Origin 4-108 Hanasato-chō ⓣ0577/36-4655. You can sample three local sakes for ¥525 at this rustic *izakaya*, as well as a good range of *sōchū*. The food, including sashimi and sushi, is tasty and affordable. Daily 5pm–midnight.

Red Hill 2-4 Sowa-chō ⓣ0577/33-8139. You'll get a warm welcome at this small bar, which serves a good range of bottled beer from around the world and appealing food that borrows from a global menu. Tues–Sun 7pm–midnight.

Tonio 4-65 Honmachi ⓣ0577/32-1677. This self-styled "Western bar", plastered with old film posters and other memorabilia, is a quiet place for a beer and snack. Daily 5pm–1am.

Wada 和田 Ichiban-gai ⓣ0577/33-4850. If you're wondering where the locals choose to drink and nibble on snacks in this very touristy town, search no further. Don't be put off by the menu, which features fried chicken bowels with miso, and grilled pig's trotters – there are plenty of things to try here and it's all good value. Daily 5pm–1am.

Furukawa

With its old white-walled storehouses by the canal, sake breweries and temples decorated with intricate woodcarvings, charming **FURUKAWA** (古川) is like a compact version of Takayama, without the crowds. The sleepy riverside town comes alive during its annual spring *matsuri* (see box below). You can see what the festival is like at the **Hida Furukawa Matsuri Kaikan** (飛騨古川まつり会館; daily: March–Nov 9am–5pm; Dec–Feb 9am–4.30pm; ¥800), five minutes' walk west of the station. Here you can inspect three of the nine *yatai*, as well as watch a three-dimensional film of the festival and a computer-controlled performance by one of the puppets decorating the *yatai*. Local craftsmen work here, too. The drums used in the festival are in an open hall on the square in front of the main hall. Also on the square is the **Hida Craftsmens Cultural Hall**, or *Hida-no-Takumi Bunkakan* (飛騨の匠文化館; same hours as Matsuri Kaikan, except Dec–Feb closed Tues; ¥300), which has displays highlighting local carpenters' art and skills, showing how buildings are made from jointed wooden beams without the use of nails. A ¥1000 ticket covers entry to both museums.

Immediately south of the square is the **Shirakabe-dozō** district, where a row of traditional storehouses stands beside a narrow, gently flowing canal that is packed with carp. From here, a five-minute walk east along the canal will take you to **Honkō-ji** (本光寺), an attractive temple decorated with the intricate carving and carpentry for which the town is famous. From the temple, return to the town centre along Ichino-machi-dōri, where you'll find the two-hundred-year-old

Furukawa Matsuri

One of the region's liveliest annual festivals, the **Furukawa Matsuri** (April 19 & 20) celebrates the arrival of spring with grand parades of wonderfully decorated floats (*yatai*). The highlight is the **Okoshi Daiko** procession, which starts at 9pm on April 19 and runs until about 2am: led by over a thousand people carrying lanterns, hundreds of men, clad only in baggy white underpants and belly bands, compete to place small drums, tied to long poles, atop a portable stage that bears the huge main drum, which is all the while being solemnly thumped. The men also balance atop poles and spin around on their stomachs. Extra late-night trains and buses run on festival days between Takayama and Furukawa. The *yatai* and *mikoshi* processions happen during the day. For more information see ⓦtinyurl.com/2aqnzed.

candle shop **Mishima** (三嶋); a candlemaker gives regular demonstrations. On this street, you'll also find Furukawa's two **sake breweries** – Kaba (蒲) and Watanabe (渡辺); both will happily let you sample their products whether you buy or not.

Practicalities

Furukawa is just 15km north of Takayama, and with frequent **trains** (¥230 local, ¥540 express) and **buses** (¥360) taking at most thirty minutes to reach the town it's an easy half-day trip. The JR station is called Hida-Furukawa (飛騨古川); the **Kita-Hida tourist information booth** (daily 9am–5pm; Ⓣ0577/73-3180, Ⓦwww.city.hida.gifu.jp) is located just outside – the helpful staff can assist you in finding accommodation, although with Takayama so close there's little reason to linger unless you're planning on hiking up into the surrounding mountains. The best base to do this from is the modern *Hida Furukawa Youth Hostel* (飛騨古川ユースホステル; Ⓣ0577/75-2979, Ⓦwww.d2.dion.ne.jp/~hidafyh; ¥5600/person including two meals), housed in a homely wooden cabin amid rice fields a fifteen-minute bus ride from Hida-Furukawa Station. Take a bus to Shinrin-kōen from the JR station – check times with the tourist information.

A great place for lunch is *Katsumi* (克己; Mon–Sat 11.30am–1pm & 5.30–10pm), in a grey building a minute's walk west of the station. The lunchtime *wagamama teishoku* (¥950) is a feast of delicious vegetable, tofu and fish dishes, while in the evening you can try their fish specialities (¥2000/head). If you want to sample the tender local beef, *Maeda* (まえだ; daily except Thurs 11.30am–9pm), on the right-hand corner of the junction with the road from the station, has set meals starting at ¥2100 and beef curry for under ¥1000. There's also the cute, casual *Café b* beside the canal.

Shirakawa-gō and Gokayama

Designated a World Heritage Site in 1995, the picturesque villages of the **Shirakawa-gō** (白川郷) and **Gokayama** (五箇山) areas, northwest of Takayama, were among the many fabled bolt holes of the Taira clan after their defeat at the battle of Dannoura (see p.768). Until the mid-twentieth century, these communities, with their distinctive, thatched A-frame houses, were almost entirely cut off from fast-modernizing Japan. The damming of the Shō-kawa in the 1960s, together with the drift of population away from the countryside, threatened the survival of this rare form of architecture called *gasshō-zukuri* (see box below). In

Praying-hands houses

Gasshō-zukuri means "praying hands", because the sixty-degree slope of the thatched gable roofs is said to recall two hands joined in prayer. The sharp angle is a way of coping with the heavy snowfall in this area and the size of the houses is the result of generations of the same family living together. The upper storeys of the home were used for industries such as making gunpowder and cultivating silkworms. The thatched roofs – often with a surface area of around six hundred square metres – are made of *susuki* grass, native to the northern part of the Hida region (wooden shingles were used in the south), and have to be replaced every 25 to 35 years.

Since it can cost ¥20 million to rethatch an entire roof, many of the houses fell into disrepair until the government stepped in with grants in 1976, which enabled the locals to keep up their house-building traditions. The local preservation society decides which buildings are most in need of repair each year and helps organize the *yui*, a two-hundred-strong team who work together to rethatch a roof in just one day. Despite these initiatives, however, there are now fewer than two hundred examples of *gasshō-zukuri* houses left in the Hida region.

1971, local residents began a preservation movement, which has been so successful that the trio of villages – **Ogimachi** in Gifu-ken, and **Suganuma** and **Ainokura** in neighbouring Toyama-ken – is now in danger of being swamped by visitors. It is still worth braving the crowds to see these remarkable thatched buildings, in idyllic valleys surrounded by forests and mountains, but to feel the full magic of the places, arrange to stay overnight in a minshuku in a *gasshō-zukuri* house.

Ogimachi

In the shadow of the sacred mountain Hakusan, **OGIMACHI** (荻町) is home to 114 **gasshō-zukuri** houses, the largest collection within the Shirakawa-gō area of the Shō-kawa valley. Many of the thatched houses were moved here when threatened by the damming of the Shō-kawa, and this makes for rather a contrived scene, not helped by the major road that cuts through its centre, bringing a daily overdose of tourists. Even so, this is a real village, populated by families living in most of these houses, farming rice and other crops in the surrounding fields.

Arrival, information and accommodation

Touring the region by **car** is recommended; try Toyota Rent-a-Car opposite Takayama Station (ⓣ0577/36-6110; daily 8am–8pm). Otherwise, seven direct **buses** connect Takayama to Ogimachi (50min; ¥2400 one-way, ¥4300 return), with two continuing on to Kanazawa; reserve your seat in advance. Four daily buses head north from Ogimachi to Suganuma (¥840) and Ainokura (¥1250), terminating at Takaoka (¥2350) on the JR Hokuriku line.

The main **tourist information office** (daily 9am–5pm; ⓣ05769/6-1013; ⓦwww.shirakawa-go.gr.jp) is in the car park beside the Gasshō-zukuri Folklore Park, where the buses stop. There's a second smaller office in the village centre.

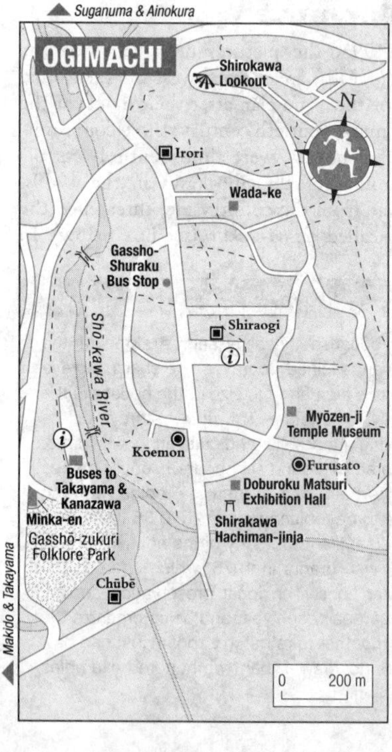

The only way of seeing Ogimachi without the crowds is to **stay** overnight. There are several nice minshuku in the thatched-roof houses to choose from; try *Furusato* (ふるさと; ⓣ05769/6-1033; ⑤), just south of Myōzen-ji, which has endearing decorative touches throughout its tatami rooms, or cosy *Koemon* (幸エ門; ⓣ05769/6-1446; ⑤), which has an English-speaking owner; bathrooms at both are shared and rates include two meals.

The Village

Start your explorations by hiking up to the Shirokawa lookout (*tenbōdai*) at the north end of the village, from where you can get a good view of Ogimachi's layout and a great photo of the thatched houses. The **Wada-ke** (和田家; daily 9am–5pm; ¥300), with a lily pond in front, is the first of several "museum" houses you'll pass on your way back to the village centre. Inside, lacquerware and other household items used by the Wada family, who lived here for over two hundred years, are displayed.

Five minutes' walk further south stands the five-storey **Myōzen-ji Temple Museum** (明善寺郷土館; daily: April–Nov 9am–5pm; Dec–March 9am–4pm; ¥300). This huge building was once the living quarters for the priests and monks of the attached temple; on its upper floors you can see where over a tonne of silk cocoons were cultivated each year. Gaps in the floorboards allowed the smoke from the *irori* fire to permeate the whole building, preserving the wood and thatch. A narrow passageway connects the main house to the thatched temple next door, and outside is a thatched bell tower.

Continuing south of the temple will bring you to the village's main shrine, **Shirakawa Hachiman-jinja** (白川八幡神社), next to which stands the **Doburoku Matsuri Exhibition Hall** (どぶろく祭りの館; April–Nov daily 9am–5pm; ¥300), devoted to the annual festival (Oct 14–19), which involves the making of *doburoku*, a rough, milky sake. The exhibition itself is small, but you can watch a good video in Japanese about life in the village and try a drop of the thick and potent alcohol on the way out.

On the west side of the Shō-kawa, reached by a footbridge, is the **Gasshō-zukuri Folklore Park** (合掌造り民家園; April–July & Sept–Nov daily except Thurs 8.40am–5pm; Aug daily 8am–5.30pm; Dec–March daily except Thurs 9am–4pm; ¥500), an open-air museum of some 25 buildings gathered together from around the region. Enjoy a rest and a free cup of tea in the Nakano Chōjirō family house near the entrance. Just outside the park is the **Minka-en** (Ⓣ05769/6-1231), the village hall where, if you make an advance booking, you can learn how to make soba noodles (April–Oct daily 10am & 1.30pm; ¥1800).

Eating

At *Irori* (いろり), opposite the petrol station on the main road at the north end of the village, you can sit around a raised hearth while enjoying the good-value set lunches (¥1000), which include fish, noodles or tofu. Overlooking the river at Ogimachi's south end is *Chūbe* (忠兵衛), offering feasts of mountain vegetable cuisine, *sansai ryōri*, from ¥1300 per person. *Shiraogi* (しらおぎ), in the village centre, has an English menu and offers a set menu of local delicacies (ask for the *shiraogi-setto*), including trout and miso bean paste, for ¥2600.

Suganuma and around

Route 156 along the Shō-kawa valley tunnels through the mountains, running for the most part alongside the frequently dammed river as it meanders north. Some 10km from Ogimachi, the road passes the quaint hamlet of **SUGANUMA** (菅沼), featuring nine *gasshō-zukuri*, beside a sharp bend in the river. Pop into the **Gokayama Minzoku-kan** (五箇山民族館; daily 9am–4pm; ¥300), made up of two houses, one displaying artefacts from daily life, the other detailing the production of gunpowder, made here because the remote location allowed the ruling Kaga clan to keep it secret.

Some 4km from Suganuma, the modern village of Kaminashi is worth a stop to inspect the **Murakami-ke** (村上家; daily except Wed 8.30am–5pm; ¥300), one of the oldest houses in the valley, dating from 1578. The owner gives guided tours around the tatami rooms, pointing out the sunken pit beside the entrance where gunpowder was once made, and finishing with spirited singing of folk tunes accompanied by a performance of the *bin-zasara*, a rattle made of wooden strips.

Ainokura

The last of the three World Heritage Site villages, and perhaps the loveliest, is **AINOKURA** (相倉; Ⓦwww.g-ainokura.com), 4km further north of Kaminashi.

The bus will drop you on the main road, a five-minute walk from the village, which nestles on a hillside and will not take you more than an hour to look around – make sure you hike up the hill behind the main car park for a great view. You could also while away a little more time in the **Ainokura Minzoku-kan** (相倉民族館; daily 8.30am–5pm; ¥200), a tiny museum of daily life, including examples of the area's handmade paper and toys.

Appealing as it is, Ainokura's charms can be all but obscured as you battle past yet another group of camera-toting day-trippers. To experience the village at its best stay overnight, making sure you reserve well in advance – they don't like people just showing up here. Seven of the *gasshō-zukuri* offer lodging, including *Nakaya* (なかや; ⓣ0763/66-2555) and *Goyomon* (五ヨ門; ⓣ0763/66-2154). If you're just visiting for the day, *Matsuya* (まつや; daily 8am–5pm), serving soba, tempura and sweets, is a friendly place for lunch and they'll look after your bags while you wander around.

If you're heading to Ainokura from the Sea of Japan coast, take a train from Takaoka to Jōhana (城端), where you can pick up the bus to the Gokayama area.

Toyama and around

Northeast of the Gokayama valley is the coastal city of Takaoka and, further west, the prefectural capital of Toyama. Neither city particularly warrants an overnight stop and you'd do well to press on south along the Sea of Japan coast to Kanazawa and the more scenic Noto Hantō peninsula (see p.381).

That said, **TOYAMA** (富山) has a handful of interesting sights and is a possible start or finish for excursions along the famous Alpine Route (see opposite) to Nagano-ken. Gathered together at the foot of the Kureha hills is the **Toyama Municipal Folkcraft Village**, or *Toyama Minzoku Mingei Mura* (富山市民族民芸村; daily 9am–4.30pm; ¥500), offering eight museums highlighting local arts, crafts and industries, as well as the atmospheric temple **Chōkei-ji** (長慶寺), with its Gohyaku Rakan terraces, containing over five hundred miniature stone statues of the Buddha's disciples. To reach the village, take a bus from stop #14 opposite Toyama Station to Minzoku Mingei Mura, and then walk for five minutes.

Alternatively, hop on the light rail tram at the north exit of the JR station and head out to the harbour suburb of **Iwase** (岩瀬), where Omachi-Niikawamachi-dōri is an attractive street lined with Edo-era buildings, including a sake brewery and a glass and ceramics workshop. Toyama castle, 1km south of the station, is a replica of the original and now houses the not overly exciting **Municipal Folk Museum** (daily 9am–4.30pm; ¥200).

Practicalities

The **tourist information booth** (daily 8.30am–8pm; ⓣ076/432-9751, ⓦvisit-toyama.com), outside to the left of the central exit at Toyama Station, has a good selection of leaflets and English-speaking staff. Between March and November you can hire a bike for free from here, as well as pick up a copy of the Toyama International Centre Foundation's newsletter *What's Happening* (ⓦwww.tic-toyama.or.jp).

The city's banks, main post office and shops are all within easy walking distance of the station. If you need **accommodation**, there are plenty of business hotels, too, including a *Tōyoko Inn* (ⓣ076/405-1045, ⓦwww.toyoko-inn.com; ❹). Toyama is known for its seafood and sushi – locals recommend the *kaitenzushi* (conveyor belt sushi restaurant) operation *Sushitama* (ⓦwww.sushitama.com; daily 11am–9.30pm), a fifteen-minute bus or taxi ride south of the station.

Tateyama-Kurobe Alpine Route

A dramatic and memorable way to travel from the Sea of Japan coast across the Alps to Nagano-ken or vice versa, using a combination of buses, trains, funicular and cable cars, is to follow the **Tateyama–Kurobe Alpine Route** (立山黒部アルペンルート; Ⓦwww.alpen-route.com). The 90km route is only open from mid-April to mid-November, depending on the snow, and is at its busiest between August and October, when on certain sections you may have to wait a while for a seat or a spot on the cable car (numbered tickets are issued for order of boarding). Delays apart, it takes about six hours to traverse the roof of Japan; the spectacular views fully justify the ¥10,560 one-way ticket. Start early so you have some time to wander around along the way.

Starting from Toyama, take the Toyama Chihō Tetsudō line to the village of **Tateyama** (立山) at the base of Mount Tateyama (45min; ¥1170), one of the most sacred mountains in Japan after Mount Fuji and Mount Hakusan. Board the Tateyama Cable Railway for the seven-minute journey (¥700) up to the small resort of **Bijo-daira** (美女平), meaning "beautiful lady plateau". One of the best parts of the journey follows, taking the Tateyama Kōgen bus (55min; ¥1660) up the twisting alpine road, which early in the season is still piled high on either side with snow, to the terminal at **Murodō** (室堂). Only five minutes north of the bus terminal is the **Mikuriga-ike**, an alpine lake in a 15m-deep volcanic crater and, twenty minutes' walk further on, **Jigokudani** (Hell Valley), an area of boiling hot springs. There are also several longer hikes that you can do around Murodō, which is the best place to end your journey along the Alpine Route, if you're short of time or money. There are several places to stay in Murodō: try *Tateyama Murodō Sansō* (立山室堂山荘; Ⓣ076/465-5763; ⑤), also a good place to head for lunch if you want to avoid the crowds at the *Hotel Tateyama* (Ⓣ076/465-3333, Ⓦwww.alpen-route.co.jp/h-tateyama; ⑧) at the head of the Tateyama tunnel.

The next section of the journey – a ten-minute bus ride to **Daikanbō** (大観峰) along a tunnel cut through Mount Tateyama – is the most expensive (¥2100). The view from Daikanbō across the mountains is spectacular, and you'll be able to admire it further as you take the Tateyama Ropeway cable car (¥1260) down to the Kurobe Cable Railway (¥840) for a five-minute journey to the edge of the Kurobe-ko lake formed by the enormous **Kurobe dam** (黒部ダム; Ⓦwww.kurobe-dam.com). Blocking one of Japan's deepest gorges, the dam is a highlight of the trip, and there are also boat trips across the lake (30min; ¥930) and some excellent hiking. An easy thirty-minute walk along the lake to the south gets you to a **campsite**, and if you have gear and the Tateyama topographical map – available in any major bookstore – you could continue for days along some of Japan's most spectacular hiking trails.

From the cable railway you'll have to walk 800m across the dam to catch the trolley bus (¥1260) for a sixteen-minute journey through tunnels under Harinoki-dake to the village of **Ōgisawa** (扇沢), across in Nagano-ken. Here you'll transfer to a bus (40min; ¥1330) down to the station at **Shinano-Ōmachi** (信濃大町), where you can catch trains to Matsumoto (see p.352) or Hakuba (see p.349). You can buy a ticket covering the whole trip at either end (¥10,560).

Kanazawa and around

Back in the mid-nineteenth century **KANAZAWA** (金沢), meaning "golden marsh", was Japan's fourth-largest city, built around a grand castle and the beautiful garden **Kenroku-en**. Today, the capital of Ishikawa-ken continues enthusiastically to cultivate the arts and contains attractive areas of well-preserved

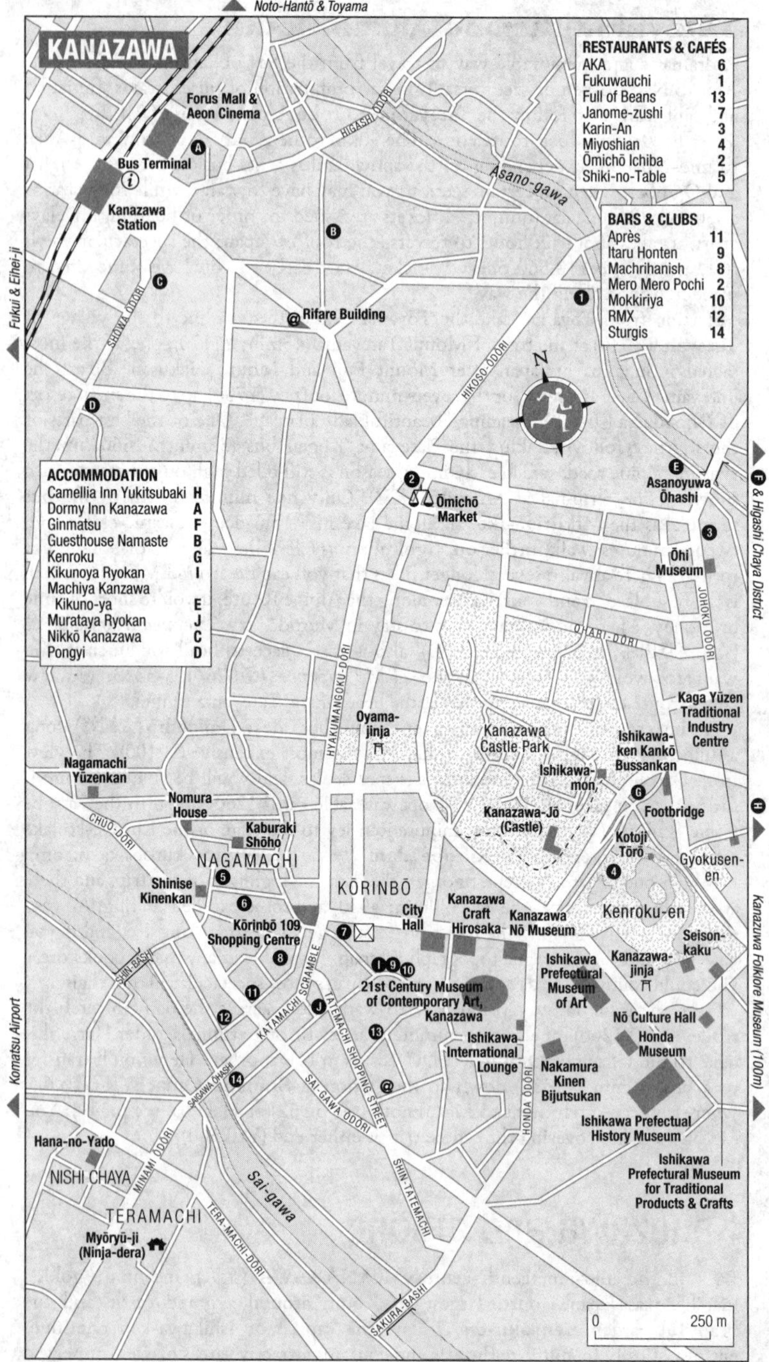
KANAZAWA
Noto-Hantō & Toyama
Fukui & Eihei-ji
Komatsu Airport
F & Higashi Chaya District
Kanazawa Folklore Museum (100m)
RESTAURANTS & CAFÉS
AKA 6
Fukuwauchi 1
Full of Beans 13
Janome-zushi 7
Karin-An 3
Miyoshian 4
Ōmichō Ichiba 2
Shiki-no-Table 5
BARS & CLUBS
Après 11
Itaru Honten 9
Machrihanish 8
Mero Mero Pochi 2
Mokkiriya 10
RMX 12
Sturgis 14
ACCOMMODATION
Camellia Inn Yukitsubaki H
Dormy Inn Kanazawa A
Ginmatsu F
Guesthouse Namaste B
Kenroku G
Kikunoya Ryokan I
Machiya Kanzawa Kikuno-ya E
Murataya Ryokan J
Nikkō Kanazawa C
Pongyi D
Forus Mall & Aeon Cinema
Bus Terminal
Kanazawa Station
Rifare Building
Asano-gawa
Higashi Ōdori
Hikoso-Ōdori
Showa Ōdori
Ōmichō Market
Asanoyuwa Ōhashi
Ōhi Museum
Johoku Ōdori
Ōhari-dōri
Hyakumangoku-dōri
Oyama-jinja
Kanazawa Castle Park
Ishikawa-ken Kankō Bussankan
Kaga Yūzen Traditional Industry Centre
Ishikawa-mon
Kanazawa-Jō (Castle)
Footbridge
Kotoji Tōrō
Gyokusen-en
Kenroku-en
Seison-kaku
Nagamachi Yūzenkan
Nomura House
Kaburaki Shōho
Chuō-dōri
NAGAMACHI
KŌRINBŌ
Shinise Kinenkan
Kōrinbō 109 Shopping Centre
City Hall
Kanazawa Craft Hirosaka
Kanazawa Nō Museum
Ishikawa Prefectural Museum of Art
Kanazawa-jinja
21st Century Museum of Contemporary Art, Kanazawa
Shin-bashi
Katamachi Scramble
Tatemachi Shopping Street
Ishikawa International Lounge
Nō Culture Hall
Honda Museum
Nakamura Kinen Bijutsukan
Honda Ōdori
Saigawa Ōhashi
Sai-gawa Ōdori
Ishikawa Prefectual History Museum
Ishikawa Prefectural Museum for Traditional Products & Crafts
Hana-no-Yado
NISHI CHAYA
Minami Ōdori
Shin-Tatemachi
Sai-gawa
TERAMACHI
Tera-machi-dōri
Myōryū-ji (Ninja-dera)
Sakura-bashi
0 250 m

samurai houses and geisha teahouses. Its modern face is ably represented by the impressive **21st Century Museum of Contemporary Art, Kanazawa** – all up, this is the one place you shouldn't miss on the Sea of Japan coast.

Kanazawa's heyday was in the late fifteenth century, when a collective of farmers and Buddhist monks overthrew the ruling Togashi family, and the area, known as **Kaga** (a name still applied to the city's exquisite crafts, such as silk-dyeing and lacquerware, and its refined cuisine), became Japan's only independent Buddhist state. Autonomy ended in 1583, when the *daimyō* Maeda Toshiie was installed as ruler by the warlord Oda Nobunaga, but Kanazawa continued to thrive as the nation's richest province, churning out five million bushels of rice a year.

Kanazawa can be used as a base to visit other places in Ishikawa-ken (Ⓦwww.hot-ishikawa.jp), including the **Noto Hantō**, the rugged peninsula north of the city and a great place to enjoy seaside vistas and a slower pace of life. To the south, in neighbouring Fukui-ken, is the working monastery **Eihei-ji**, one of Japan's most atmospheric temples.

Arrival and information

The Shinkansen is set to streak into town in 2014; until then, take the bullet **train** from Tokyo to Nagaoka and change to an express train. There's also a daily direct limited express train (6hr) from Tokyo's Ueno Station. Coming from the Kansai area, the Thunderbird express from Ōsaka, via Kyoto, does the journey in two hours and thirty minutes; there's also a direct express service from Kyoto and Nagoya.

Long-distance **buses** pull up at the bus terminal on the east side of the train station. **Komatsu airport** (Ⓣ076/121-9803, Ⓦwww.komatsuairport.jp), 30km southwest of the city, is connected to Kanazawa Station by bus (55min; ¥1100). The bus stops first in the Katamachi district, which is close to some hotels.

Providing assistance to foreign visitors is one of Kanazawa's strengths. In the JR station is an excellent **tourist information office** (daily 9am–7pm; Ⓣ076/232-3933, Ⓦwww.kanazawa-tourism.com) with English-speaking staff (daily 10am–6pm) who can arrange for a guide to show you around town for free. The **Ishikawa Foundation for International Exchange** (Mon–Fri 9am–6pm, Sat 9am–5pm; Ⓣ076/262-5931, Ⓦwww.ifie.or.jp), on the third and fourth floors of the **Rifare Building**, five minutes' walk southeast of the station, has a library with foreign newspapers and magazines and is a good place to meet Japanese who want to practise their English. The similar **Kanazawa International Exchange Foundation**, or KIEF (Mon–Fri 9am–5.45pm; Ⓣ076/220-2522, Ⓦwww.kief.jp), is also in the Rifare Building, on the second floor, while near Kenroku-en is the **Ishikawa International Lounge** (Mon–Fri 10am–5pm, Sat 10am–4pm; Ⓣ076/221-9901), offering many free cultural and Japanese-language courses, as well as courses in origami, tea ceremony, calligraphy and *ikebana*. Also look out for the free quarterly English tourist paper *Eye on Kanazawa* (Ⓦwww.eyeon.jp) and the Japanese-language mini-magazine *Kanazawa Soraaruki* (¥330; Ⓦwww.soraaruki.com).

City transport

Getting around is easy enough by foot or by **bike** (rent one near the west gate of the JR station for ¥1200 a day). Most sights are clustered within walking distance of Kōrinbō and Katamachi, the neighbouring downtown areas, ten minutes by bus from outside the east exit of Kanazawa Station. **Buses** leave frequently from stops #7, #8 and #9 at the train station for both Kōrinbō and Katamachi (¥200). The Kanazwa Loop Bus (daily 8.30am–6pm; ¥200 or ¥500 for a one-day pass) is a useful service that runs in a clockwise direction around the city from the train station and back again, covering all the main sights.

Accommodation

There's a glut of **hotels** near the train station, but it's handier to stay in the central **Kōrinbō** district, within easy walking distance of Kenroku-en and other sights. On the east side of the city, **Higashi Chaya** is also a pleasant area to overnight; for details of more ryokan than listed here see ⓦwww.yadotime.jp/english.

APA Hotel Kanazawa Chūō 1-5-24 Katamachi ⓣ076/235-2111, ⓦwww.apahotel.com. There are several branches of this classy business chain in Kanazawa including this central one. The rooms offer standard business-hotel-style comfort. Adding a little luxury is a top-floor onsen and sauna, including outdoor and hot stone baths that guests can use for free (non-guests Mon–Fri ¥500, Sat & Sun ¥1000). ⑤

Camellia Inn Yukitsubaki カメリアイン雪椿 4-17 Kosho-machi ⓣ076/223 5725, ⓦwww.camellia.jp. Laura Ashley meets traditional Japan at this charming guesthouse that offers spacious Western-style rooms and a lounge set in a *kura* (storehouse). Rates include breakfast; add ¥4000 for a dinner of French cuisine served on Kutani pottery. ⑥

Dormy Inn Kanazawa 2-25 Horai-kawa Shin-machi, ⓣ076/263-9888. Opposite the slick Forus shopping mall is this stylish business hotel, offering full and half tatami rooms, a roof-top spa, internet terminals and a pleasant lounge area where a big buffet breakfast (¥950) is served. ⑤

Ginmatsu 銀松 1-17-18 Higashi Chaya ⓣ076/252-3577, ⓔginmatsu@nifty.com. Pleasant, good-value minshuku in the lovely Higashi Chaya district, with a friendly welcome and tatami rooms at ¥3500 per person. There's a communal bathroom with shower and they also provide free tickets for the local *sentō* (public bath). ④

Guesthouse Namaste 6-14 Kasaichi-machi ⓣ076/255 1057, ⓦguesthouse-namaste.com. The cheapest backpacker accommodation in town, with dorm rooms for ¥2400 and singles for ¥3000. They also rent bicycles for ¥500 a day. ③

Kenroku ホテル兼六 2-5 Kenroku-machi ⓣ076/210-8111. A minute's walk from the northern gate of Kenroku-en, this small hotel offers good-value Western and tatami rooms, with singles from ¥6000. Their restaurant serves local-style meals and there's a chic modern café. ⑤

Kikunoya Ryokan きくのや旅館 1-1-27 Hirosaka ⓣ076/231-3547, ⓦkikunoya.ninja-web.net. A centrally located ryokan that's meticulously maintained by its friendly elderly owners. Even with rates boosted by ¥750 per person for a Saturday-night stay, it remains very good value. ④

Machiya Kanazawa Kikuno-ya 3-22 Kazue-machi ⓣ076/287-0834, ⓦwww.machiya-kanazawa.jp. In the heart of the atmospheric geisha district of Kazue-machi, this renovated teahouse sleeps up to five people. The building dates to 1898, but includes modern amenities such as internet access. Breakfast and tickets to the public bath are included in the price; cultural programmes are extra. ⑨

Murataya Ryokan 村田屋旅館 1-5-2 Katamachi ⓣ076/263-0455, ⓦwww.spacelan.ne.jp/~murataya. Although showing its age, this centrally located ryokan has some stylish touches and is run by a friendly family well used to foreign guests. Internet access, laundry and a handy map of local restaurants are available. ④

Nikkō Kanazawa 2-15-1 Honmachi ⓣ076/234-1111, ⓦwww.hnkanazawa.co.jp. Good views are guaranteed from the rooms in this thirty-storey luxury hotel opposite Kanazawa Station, sporting a sophisticated modern European design. ⑧

Pongyi 2-22 Rokumai-machi ⓣ076/225-7369, ⓦwww.pongyi.com. Five minutes from the JR station, behind the old sake shop Ichimura Magotaro, is this convivial budget guest-house beside a gurgling stream. The cosy dorms are in a converted *kura* and there's one spruce tatami room that sleeps up to four people. The very hospitable English-speaking owner donates ¥100 of each night's accommodation charge to a charity that helps poor kids in Asia. ③

The City

This is a city that rewards a more leisurely pace, so set aside at least a couple of days to see Kanazawa. Having escaped bombing during World War II, traditional inner-city areas, such as **Nagamachi** with its samurai houses and the charming geisha teahouse district of **Higashi Chaya**, remain intact and are a joy to wander around. The following sights are listed in order of importance, if you're pushed for time.

Kenroku-en

Early morning or late afternoon are the best times for experiencing Kanazawa's star attraction, **Kenroku-en** (兼六園; daily: March to mid-Oct 7am–6pm; mid-Oct to Feb 8am–4.30pm; ¥300), at its most tranquil, otherwise you're bound to have your thoughts interrupted by a megaphone-toting guide and party of tourists – such is the price of visiting one of the official top three gardens in Japan (Kairaku-en in Mito and Kōraku-en in Okayama are the other two). Kenroku-en – developed over two centuries from the 1670s – is rightly regarded as the best.

Originally the outer grounds of Kanazawa castle, and thus the private garden of the ruling Maeda clan, Kenroku-en was opened to the public in 1871. Its name, which means "combined six garden", refers to the six horticultural graces that the garden embraces: spaciousness, seclusion, artificiality, antiquity, water and panoramic views. It's a lovely place to stroll around, with an ingenious pumping system that keeps the hillside pools full of water and the fountains – including Japan's first – working. There are many carefully pruned and sculpted pine trees and sweeping views across towards Kanazawa's geisha district Higashi Chaya.

In the garden's northeast corner is the elegant **Seison-kaku** (成巽閣; daily except Wed 9am–4.30pm; ¥1000), a two-storey shingle-roofed mansion built in 1863 by the *daimyō* Maeda Nariyasu as a retirement home for his mother. Look out for paintings of fish, shellfish and turtles on the wainscots of the *shōji* sliding screens in the formal guest rooms downstairs. The view from the Tsukushi-no-rōka (Horsetail Corridor) across the mansion's own raked-gravel garden is particularly enchanting, while upstairs the decorative style is more adventurous, using a range of striking colours and materials including, unusually for a traditional Japanese house, glass windows, imported from the Netherlands. These were installed so that the occupants could look out in winter at the falling snow.

21st Century Museum of Contemporary Art

Highlighting a forward-thinking attitude that had previously been obscured by the city's love of the traditional arts is the excellent **21st Century Museum of Contemporary Art** (金沢２１世紀美術館; Tues–Sun 9am–10pm; public areas free, exhibition area charge varies; ⓣ076/220-2800), opposite Kenroku-en's southwest entrance.

The hyper-modern design by the architectural practice SANAA – a circle of glass embracing a series of galleries, a library and a free crèche – is like a giant geometry puzzle and perfectly suited to the multiple uses of the facility. Exhibitions frequently change, although there are some specially commissioned works on permanent display. James Turrell's *Blue Planet Sky* is a great place to relax and watch the clouds float by, while Leandro Elrich's *Swimming Pool* encourages fun interaction between viewers around the pool's edge and those walking beneath. The twelve tuba-shaped tubes that sprout out of the lawns surrounding the gallery are by the German artist Florian Claar; speak into one and the sound comes out of another.

Nearby is **Kanazawa Nō Museum** (Tues–Sun 10am–5.30pm; ¥300), shining light on the most refined of Japan's dramatic arts. On the ground floor is a virtual nō stage around which you can walk as if you were in a play. Upstairs are prime examples of nō's ornate costumes and inscrutable masks.

Kanazawa-jō and around

From Kenroku-en's northernmost exit a footbridge leads to the **Ishikawa-mon**, a towering eighteenth-century gateway to the castle, **Kanazawa-jō** (金沢城; daily 9am–4.30pm; ¥300 entry to the castle buildings; ⓣ076/234-3800). There's been a fortification on the Kodatsuno plateau since 1546, but the castle in its present form dates back mainly to the early seventeenth century. In 2001, part of the inner enclosure was rebuilt using traditional methods and plans from the Edo period. These included the three-storey, diamond-shaped Hishi Yagura and Hashizume-mon Tsuzuki Yagura watchtowers, the Gojukken Nagaya corridor linking them, some of the earthen walls, and the Hashizume bridge and gate leading to the enclosure. Inside the buildings you can see the intricate joinery and inspect the one-tenth-scale skeletal model carpenters used to master the complexities of the task.

Parts of the original castle are within the grounds, as well as an attractive modern garden with traditional elements – an interesting contrast to Kenroku-en. If you head for the Imori-zaka entrance at the southwest corner of the grounds, you'll emerge near the back of the **Oyama-jinja** (尾山神社), a large shrine dedicated to the first Maeda lord, Toshiie. The shrine is fronted by the **Shinmon**, an unusual square-arched gate with multicoloured stained glass in its upper tower, designed in 1875 with the help of Dutch engineers and once used as a lighthouse to guide ships towards the coast.

Alternatively, returning to Ishikawa-mon and Kenroku-en's north exit, head along the garden's eastern flank, to the small traditional garden, **Gyokusen-en** (玉泉園; April–Nov daily 9am–4pm; ¥500). Built on two levels on a steep slope, this quiet garden has many lovely features, including mossy stone paths leading past two ponds and a mini waterfall. For ¥500 extra you can enjoy green tea and a sweet in the main villa's tearoom. Next to the garden at the **Kaga Yūzen Traditional Industry Centre**, or *Kaga Yūzen Dentō Sangyō Kaikan* (加賀友禅伝統産業会館; daily except Wed 9am–5pm; ¥300; ⓣ076/224-5511), you can watch artists painting beautiful designs on silk, then try your own hand at this traditional Kanazawa craft (¥1050) or dress in a kimono made from the dyed material (¥1500).

Nagamachi

Scenic **Nagamachi** (長町), west of Kōrinbo, is a compact area of twisting cobbled streets, gurgling streams and old houses, protected by thick mustard-coloured earthen walls, topped with ceramic tiles. This is where samurai and rich merchants once lived. Many of the traditional buildings remain private homes but one that is open to the public is *Nomura House* (野村家; daily: April–Sept 8.30am–5.30pm, Oct–March 8.30am–4.30pm; ¥500), worth visiting principally for its compact but beautiful garden with flowing carp-filled stream, waterfall and stone lanterns. The rich, but unflashy materials used to decorate the house reveal the wealth of the former patrons and, in keeping with the culture of the time, there is a simple teahouse where you can enjoy *macha* and a sweet for ¥350.

Also of interest is the **Shinise Kinenkan** (老舗記念館; daily 9.30am–5pm; ¥100) a small museum in a handsome, spacious pharmacy and old merchant home. Upstairs, examples of the city's various handicrafts are displayed, including an amazing flower display made entirely of sugar, and intricate designs of the gift decorations called *mizuhiki*. At **Nagamachi Yūzenkan**, 2-6-16 Nagamachi (長町友禅館; daily 9am–5pm; ¥350; ⓣ076/264-2811), on the far western side of Nagamachi, you can learn more about the *yūzen* silk-dyeing process, paint your own design or buy pieces of the colourful fabric.

Higashi Chaya and around

Kanazawa is the only place outside of Kyoto to support the old-style training of geisha. Of the three districts in which this happens, **Higashi Chaya** (東茶屋), a fifteen-minute walk northeast from Kenroku-en across the Asana-gawa, is the largest and most scenic.

Several old teahouses are open to the public. The **Ochaya Shima** (お茶屋志摩; daily 9am–6pm; ¥400) is the most traditional, while opposite is **Kaikarō** (懐華楼;

daily except Tues 9am–6pm; ¥700), decorated in a more modern style, including an unusual Zen rock garden made entirely of broken chunks of glass and a tearoom with gilded tatami mats. At both you can take tea (without geisha, unfortunately) for a small extra fee. Tea is also part of the deal at the venerable **Shamisen-no-Fukushima** (三味線の福島; Mon–Sat 10am–4pm, closed 2nd & 4th Sat of month; ¥300), where you can learn to pluck the Japanese stringed instrument, the *shamisen*. Walk off all that tea by exploring the scores of **temples** nestling at the foot of Utatsuyama in the north area of Higashi Chaya.

On the south side of the Asanagawa bridge is the smaller, but equally scenic **Kazue-machi Chaya** geisha district; there's a teahouse you can stay in here (see p.376). Five minutes' walk south of here is the **Ōhi Museum** (大樋美術館; daily 9am–5pm; ¥700), displaying and selling exquisite examples of amber-glazed pottery refined over four centuries for the *urasenke* style of tea ceremony.

Nishi Chaya and Myōryū-ji

The third of Kanazawa's pretty geisha districts, **Nishi Chaya**, is on the south side of the Sai-gawa, ten minutes' walk from the distinctive iron bridge Sai-gawa Ohashi. It's less commercial than Higashi Chaya – to see inside the beautifully decorated teahouse **Hana-no-Yado** (華の宿; daily 9am–5pm) you need only buy a coffee (¥300) or *macha* (¥500).

Five minutes' walk east of Nishi Chaya, in the temple-packed **Teramachi** (寺町) district, you'll find **Myōryū-ji** (妙立寺; daily: March–Oct 9am–4.30pm; Jan, Feb, Nov & Dec 9am–4pm; ¥800), also known as Ninja-dera. Completed in 1643 and belonging to the Nichiren sect of Buddhism, this temple is associated with the Ninja assassins (see p.345) because of its many secret passages, trick doors and concealed chambers, including a lookout tower that once commanded a sweeping view of the surrounding mountains and coast. It's necessary to book a tour to look around the temple (Ⓣ076/241-0888), however the guides barely make an effort, so don't make this a priority.

Other museums

Should you hunger for further cultural enrichment, Kanazawa has many more museums, several of which are clustered around Kenroku-en. The best is the informative **Ishikawa Prefectural Museum for Traditional Products and Crafts**, or *Ishikawa-kenritsu Dentō-Sangyō Kōgeikan* (石川県立伝統産業工芸館; daily 9am–4.30pm; closed Thurs Dec–March & 3rd Thurs of month rest of year; ¥250; Ⓣ076/262-2020), displaying prime contemporary examples of Kanazawa's rich artistic heritage, including lacquerware, dyed silk, pottery, musical instruments and fireworks. None of the articles is for sale but all have a price tag, so if you take a fancy to one of the gold leaf and lacquer Buddhist family altars, for example, you'll know that it costs ¥4.5 million.

The **Ishikawa Prefectural History Museum**, or *Ishikawa-kenritsu Rekishi Hakubutsukan* (石川県立歴史博物館; daily 9am–4.30pm; ¥250; Ⓣ076/262-3236), housed in striking red-brick army barracks buildings dating from 1910, has displays including a detailed miniature reconstruction of a samurai parade, a grainy black-and-white film of Kanazawa from the early twentieth century, and a reconstruction of a silk-spinning factory.

On the other side of the neighbouring Honda Museum, the **Ishikawa Prefectural Museum of Art**, or *Ishikawa-kenritsu Bijutsukan* (石川県立美術館; daily 9.30am–5pm; ¥350; Ⓣ076/231-7580), has beautiful examples of calligraphy, kimono, pottery, lacquerware and other relics of the Maeda clan, displayed along with a more eclectic collection of contemporary local art. There are usually special exhibitions held here, which cost extra.

Eating

Kanazawa's refined local **cuisine**, *kaga ryōri*, includes many special seafood dishes including steamed bream, snow crab and prawns. Sushi is also great – you'll find the freshest slices of fish at the lively market, **Ōmichō Ichiba** (近江町市場). Another typical Kanazawa dish is *jibuni*, boiled duck or chicken and vegetables in a viscous broth spiced up with a dab of wasabi.

AKA RENN Bldg, 2-10-42 Kata-machi ⓣ076/231-3233. *Atelier Kitchen for Artisans* (*AKA*) offers outstandingly good modern Japanese food served in a chic yet casual setting by very friendly young staff. Their short course menu (¥3500) is brilliant value for this standard of cooking. There's some wonderful local sake to drink here, too, as well as rustic pottery for sale. Tues–Sun 6pm–midnight.

Fukuwauchi 福わ家 1-9-31 Hikoso-machi ⓣ076/264-8780. There's a warm welcome and equally warming udon, soba and *nabe* (stew) at this rustic complex of four restaurants in a 120-year-old building next to the Ko-bashi. Daily 11.30am–2.30pm.

Full of Beans 41-1 Satomi-chō. Cute café, just off the Tatemachi shopping street, specializing in *onigiri* (rice balls) in a wide variety of flavours. Their lunch sets, including several different curries, are a great deal; upstairs there's an art gallery and shop to browse. Daily except Wed 11.30am–7pm.

Janome-zushi 蛇の目寿司 1-12 Katamachi ⓣ076/231-0093. Set in an attractive building by a gurgling stream, this excellent sushi restaurant has reasonably priced set menus and also does some *kaga-ryōri* dishes. Sit at the counter to admire the chefs at work. Daily except Wed 11am–2pm & 5–10pm.

Karin-An かりん庵 2-23 Hashiba-chō, ⓣ076/224-2467, ⓦwww.kinjohro.co.jp. Part of the venerable *ryotei Kinjohro*, this less formal restaurant allows you to enjoy the same quality of cooking in comfort at a table or the counter where you can watch the chefs create their beautiful dishes. Lunch courses start at just ¥2625. Wed–Mon 11am–2.30pm, 5–9pm.

Miyoshian 三芳庵 1-11 Kenroku-machi ⓣ076/221-0127. Atmospheric 100-year-old restaurant in Kenroku-en, just past the row of shops at the north entrance. Specializes in *kaga ryōri*; try the bentō boxed lunches (from ¥1575) or come for a cup of *macha* tea and sweets (¥525), overlooking the ornamental pond. Daily except Wed 9am–4pm; dinner by reservation until 8.30pm.

Ōmichō Ichiba 近江町市場 Kanazawa's lively central market is well worth a visit. In and around it are many small sushi bars and restaurants serving rice-bowl dishes (*donburi*) – there's usually several open daily. Try the *kaitenzushi* operation *Mori Mori Sushi* (もりもり寿し; Mon–Fri 10am–4pm, Sat & Sun until 8pm) or go upstairs to find the cute French patisserie and restaurant *La Cook Mignon* (Thurs–Tues 10am–9.30pm). Daily 9am–5pm.

Shiki-no-Table 四季のテーブル 1-1-17 Nagamachi ⓣ076/265-6155, ⓦwww.aokicooking.com. Pleasant, reasonably priced restaurant where you can try the duck dish *jibuni* as well as take part in cookery classes at the school upstairs. Thurs–Tues 11am–8.30pm.

Drinking and entertainment

Nightlife revolves around buzzing Katamachi Scramble, the neon-lit drag connecting the Sai-gawa to Kōrinbō. The warren of streets around here is chock-full of **bars**. For **live music** the central café-bar *Mokkiriya* (もっきりや; daily noon–midnight) serves up top-class jazz and folk music with its coffee, drinks and snacks. *Mero Mero Pochi* (メロメロポッチ; ⓣ076/234-5556), in a basement space at Ōmichō Ichiba, stages a more hit- and- miss range of events including art exhibitions and DJ sets.

Cinemas include the art-house Cinemondo (ⓦwww.cine-monde.com) on the 4th floor of the 109 Kohrinbo Building, and the multiplex Aeon Cinema (ⓣ076/231-8650, ⓦwww.aeoncinema.co.jp) in the Forus mall.

The city's geisha put on free concerts throughout the year and perform at various festivals: check with the tourist office for details of when. Also check at the same offices for the latest on **nō plays** (enthusiastically nurtured by Kanazawa's arty citizens) and classical music performances.

Après 2-3-7 Katamachi ⓣ076/221-0002. This long-running *gaijin* bar with a pool table is now found on the 7th floor of the Space Building, while its Thai restaurant is on the 9th. From July–Sept they also run a popular beach bar out at Uchinada, on the coast a few kilometres north of the city. Tues–Sun: bar 10pm–2am; restaurant 6–11pm.

Itaru Honten いたる本店 3-8 Kakinobatake ⓣ076/221-4194. Locals tip this as Kanazawa's best *izakaya* – it's a great place to get acquainted with the area's excellent sakes and enjoy some sashimi or grilled fish. Mon–Sat 5.30–11.30pm.

Machrihanish 2F Nishino Bldg, 2-4 Kigura-machi ⓣ076/233-0072. Haba-san used to work at the Royal St Andrew's Golf Club and continues to communicate his passion for Scotch whisky and golf at this convivial bar stocking some 170 different single malts and blends. Mon–Sat 6.30pm–2am.

RMX Katamachi. There's a friendly welcome at this relatively spacious gay bar that's pronounced "remix". The cover charge is ¥1500 including one drink. Mon–Sat 8pm–2am.

Sturgis 4F Kirin Bldg, 1-7-15 Katamachi. Like stumbling into a New Year's Eve party, circa 1975, this silver-streamer-festooned bar is the domain of rocker Nitta-san who, if things are quiet, takes to the stage to play a live set or two. Daily 8pm–6am.

Shopping

Kanazawa is a fantastic place to shop for souvenirs and lovely objets d'art. The austerely rustic *Ōhi* and highly elaborate *Kutani* pottery can be bought at many shops around the city; several good options line Hirozaka, the street leading up to Kenroku-en from Kōrinbō. For unusual modern design gifts, browse the shop in the 21st Century Museum of Art, Kanazawa (see p.377). Also check out the **Tatemachi Shipping Street** (タテマチストリート) shopping street for quirky design shops and individual retailers.

Hakuza 箔座 1-26-7 Higashiyama. Kanazawa produces 98 percent of Japan's gold leaf. At this specialist shop in the heart of Higashi Chaya, you can buy all kinds of gold-leaf-decorated products, including chocolate cake. It's worth popping in just to see their gilded *kura* (storehouse). Daily except Wed 10am–5.30pm.

Ishikawa-ken Kankō Bussankan 石川県観光物産館 Kenroku-en-shita ⓣ076/222-7788. This two-storey tourist shop has a good selection of everything from food products to *washi* paper and pottery. A variety of craft classes are also held here. Daily except Tues 10am–6pm.

Kaburaki Shōho 鏑木商舗 1-3-16 Nagamachi ⓦwww.kaburaki.jp. This *kutani* pottery shop and restaurant/bar in the heart of Nagamachi occupies an elegant old house surrounded by pleasant gardens. Browse their small museum, which houses gorgeous pieces of pottery. Daily 9am–10pm.

Kanazawa Craft Hirosaka 金沢クラフト広坂 1-2-25 Hirosaka. Sells exquisite examples of Kanazawa's traditional crafts and hosts special exhibitions of work on its second floor. Tues–Sun 10.30am–5pm.

Sakuda さくだ 1-3-27 Higashiyama. Another dazzling shop specializing in gold-leaf products, from beautiful screens to gilded golf balls.

Listings

Banks and exchange Several banks can be found along the main road leading southeast from Kanazawa Station, as well as around Kōrinbō.

Car rental Toyota Rent-a-Car (ⓣ076/223-0100) and Nippon Rent-a-Car (ⓣ076/263-0919) are both close by Kanazawa Station.

Hospital Kanazawa University Hospital, 13-1 Takaramachi (ⓣ076/265-2000), is around 1km southeast of Kenroku-en.

Internet access There's free access at the library on the third floor of the Rifare building.

Police The Police Help Line (ⓣ076/225-0555) operates from 9am–5pm Mon–Fri.

Post office There are branches at Kōrinbō as well as the JR station.

Noto Hantō

Jutting out like a gnarled finger into the Sea of Japan is the **Noto Hantō** (能登半島), the name of which is said to derive from an Ainu word, *nopo*, meaning "set apart".

The peninsula's rural way of life, tied to agriculture and fishery, is certainly worlds away from fast-paced, urban Japan – there's little public transport here so the area is best explored by car or bicycle. The rugged and windswept west coast has the bulk of what constitutes the Noto Hantō's low-key attractions, while the calmer, indented east coast harbours several sleepy fishing villages, where only the lapping of waves and the phut-phut of boat engines breaks the silence.

The West Coast

Travelling up the peninsula's **west coast** from Kanazawa, drive past the wide, sandy beach Chiri-hama (千里浜), cluttered with day-trippers and their litter, and head briefly inland to the alleged UFO-hotspot of **HAKUI** (羽咋). Here, in a suitably saucerish hall near the station, you'll find **Cosmo Isle Hakui** (コスモアイル羽咋; daily except Tues 9am–4.30pm; ¥300), a fascinating museum devoted to space exploration which houses a great deal of authentic paraphernalia, most impressively the Vostok craft that launched Yuri Gagarin into space in 1961 – it looks like a giant cannonball.

Nearby, set in a wooded grove near the sea, is **Keta-taisha** (気多大社, daily 8.30am–4.30pm), Noto's most important shrine. The complex dates from the 1650s, although it is believed that the shrine was founded in the eighth century. It's attractive but the atmosphere is spoilt by the modern-day commercialization of the place, catering to young lovers who come to seek the blessing of the spirits. A few kilometres further up the coast, **Myōjō-ji** (妙成寺; daily 8am–4.30pm) is a seventeenth-century temple with an impressive five-storey pagoda (¥300). Millennia of poundings from the Sea of Japan have created fascinating rock formations and cliffs along this coastline.

Around the midpoint of the west coast is the small town of **MONZEN** (門前), famous for its temple **Sōji-ji** (総持寺; daily 9am–5pm; ¥300), a training centre for Zen monks.

Wajima

A further 16km up the coast from Monzen is **WAJIMA** (輪島), an appealing fishing port, straddling the mouth of the Kawarada-gawa. The peninsula's main tourist centre hosts the **Asa Ichi** (daily 8am–11.30pm, except for the 10th and 25th of each month), a touristy, yet colourful morning market, where around two hundred vendors set up stalls along the town's main street selling fish, vegetables and other local products.

Along the same street is also an incongruous replica of an Italian palazzo, inside which is the **Inachū Gallery** (イナチュウ美術館; daily 8am–5pm; ¥800). This bizarre museum exhibits reproductions of famous art pieces, such as the *Venus de Milo*, next to original European and Japanese antiques, including a huge pair of jet-black ornamental jars that once belonged to Tokugawa Iemitsu, the third Tokugawa shogun.

Anime and manga fans will prefer the nearby **Gō Nagai Wonderland Museum** (永井豪記念館; ⓣ0768/23-0715; ¥500; daily 9am–5pm), a new facility celebrating the locally-born creator of series such as *Mazinger Z*, *Devilman* and *Cutie Honey*. In one section you can draw your own manga character on a computer and get a print-out as a souvenir.

Wajima is also renowned for its high-quality lacquerware (know locally as *wajima nuri*), and you'll find many shops around town selling it. The best collection of pieces can be viewed at the **Ishikawa Wajima Urushi Art Museum** (石川県輪島漆芸美術館; daily 9am–5pm; ¥600), on the southwest side of town. More modern styles of lacquerware can be seen at the **Wajima Kōbō Nagaya** (輪島工房長屋; ⓣ0768/23-0011; closed Wed), a complex of traditional-style wooden buildings close to the sea in the centre of town, where you can also see the artists creating it. If you make an advance booking, it's possible to engrave lacquerware yourself. Also well worth visiting before you move on is the **Kiriko-kaikan** (キリコ会館; daily 8am–5pm; ¥600) on the east side of town. This exhibition hall houses the enormous colourful paper lanterns paraded around town in Wajima's lively summer and autumn festivals. The museum also shows videos of the festivals.

Elsewhere on the peninsula

The scenic coastline between Wajima and the cape **Rokkō-zaki** (禄剛崎) is scattered with many strange rock formations – look out for **Godzilla Rock** (ゴジラ岩) and, near the village of **Sosogi** (曽々木), the **Shiroyone no Senmaida** (白米の千枚田), where over a thousand rice paddies cling to the sea-facing slopes in diminishing terraces. Just south of the cape, a winding road leads down to the "secret onsen" inn of *Lamp-no-Yado* (see p.384).

Heading inland towards Iwakura-yama, a steep 357m mountain, are two traditional thatched-roof houses that once belonged to the wealthy Tokikuni family, supposed descendants of the vanquished Taira clan (see p.768). The family split in two in the sixteenth century, one part staying in the **Kami Tokikuni-ke** (上時國家; daily: April–Nov 8.30am–6pm; Jan–March & Dec 8.30am–5pm; ¥500), the other building the smaller **Shimo Tokikuni-ke** (下時國家; daily: Jan–March & Dec 8.30am–4pm; April–Nov 8.30am–5pm; ¥250), with its attractive attached garden.

On the Noto Hantō's gentler **east coast**, the picturesque **Tsukumo-wan** (九十九湾), meaning "99 Indentation Bay", is worth pausing at for the view. Also down this side of the coast, look out for the *Boramachi-yagura*, pyramid-shaped wooden platforms on top of which fishermen once perched, waiting for the fish to swim into their nets.

Arrival and information

Noto Airport (Ⓣ0768/26-2000), 25 minutes south of Wajima, has two flights daily to and from Tokyo's Haneda Airport. **Trains** from Kanazawa terminate at the uninteresting east-coast resort town of **Wakura Onsen** (和倉温泉), which can also be reached from Toyama, with a change of trains at Tsubata. More convenient are the **buses** (2hr, 15min; ¥2200) that cruise up the peninsula's central highway from Kanazawa to Wajima.

Local **buses** connect most other places of interest, but they're infrequent and you might want to try cycling or renting a car (the best option) instead. If you're pushed for time, there are also several daily **tour buses** (¥7200) from Kanazawa which take in all the sights, with an unrelenting Japanese commentary.

There's a **tourist information office** (daily 8am–7pm; Ⓣ0768/22-1503, Ⓦwww.wajimaonsen.com) in Wajima Bus Station, where you can also rent **bicycles** (¥800/8hr).

Accommodation and eating

Wajima has the widest choice of **accommodation** and is a good base for day-trips around the peninsula. Unless otherwise mentioned rates will include two meals. In Wajima, the seafood restaurant *Meigetsu* (名月; Ⓣ0768/22-4477; closed Thurs) is a good place to eat.

Flatt's by the Sea Ⓣ0768/62-1900, Ⓦwww.flatts.jp. In the town of Hanami at the northern tip of the Noto Hantō is this cute seaside minshuku, restaurant and bakery run by an Australian-Japanese couple. The café is closed Wed and Thurs. ⑥

Fukasan ふかさん Ⓣ0768/22-9933, Ⓦwww.wajima-minsyuku.com/fukasan. There's a friendly welcome at this newly restored minshuku with coastal views in Wajima. The four tatami-style rooms are simply furnished and share a large

Temple of Eternal Peace

A complex of over seventy buildings blending seamlessly with the forest **Eihri-ji** (永平寺; ⓣ0776/63-3640; daily: May–Oct 9am–5pm, Nov–April 9am–4.30pm; adult/child ¥500/200) is home to some two-hundred shaven-headed monks. Established by the Zen master Dōgen Zenji in 1244, this serene temple in cedar-covered mountains is one of the two headquarters of Sōtō Zen Buddhism.

Located 10km northeast of Fukui (福井), less than an hour's train ride south of Kanazawa, it's easy to make a day-trip to the temple. Eihri-ji is closed periodically for special services, so it's wise to check first with **Fukui City Sightseeing Information** (daily 9am–6pm; ⓣ0776/21-6492, ⓦwww.fuku-e.com) or with the temple before setting off. Also make an advance reservation if you'd like to enjoy a vegetarian *shōjin-ryōri* meal as part of your visit.

From JR Fukui Station, the easiest way to reach Eihri-ji is by direct bus (¥720; 35min). Alternatively, hop on the local train to Eihei-ji Guchi Station, then either walk uphill for five minutes or take a bus or taxi.

Affiliates of a Sōtō Zen Buddhist organization can arrange to stay overnight here (¥8000) and participate in the monks' daily routine, including cleaning duties and pre-dawn prayers and meditation; for serious devotees a four-day/three-night course (¥12,000) is also available. Details of how to apply can be found at ⓦtinyurl.com/2ee2dk9.

onsen bathtub. Delicious meals include plenty of local seafood. 6

Lamp-no-Yado ランプの宿 ⓣ0768/86-8000, ⓦwww.lampnoyado.co.jp. One of the peninsula's most famous ryokan, this fourteen-room place in Suzu offers rooms that each have their own *rotemburo*, and a spectacular cliffside location. 8

Noto Isaribi Youth Hostel 能登漁火ユースホステル 51-6 Ogi-yo ⓣ0768/74-0150, ⓦwww2.plala.or.jp/isaribi0150. Facing onto Tsukumo-wan in the sleepy village of Ogi (小木), this hostel has good-quality tatami dorms and is run by a friendly man who rustles up local seafood feasts. The bus from Kanazawa will drop you at Ogi-kō, an 8min walk from the hostel. Dorm beds ¥3800. 4

Nagoya

Completely rebuilt after a wartime drubbing, **NAGOYA** (名古屋) is a modern metropolis of high-rise buildings, wide boulevards, multi-lane highways and flyovers, where business takes precedence over tourism. Here you'll find the headquarters of industrial powerhouse Toyota (see box, p.389) as well as numerous other companies that exploit the local skill of *monozukuri* (making things) to the hilt.

Less overwhelming than Tokyo or Ōsaka, the capital of Aichi-ken and Japan's fourth-largest city provides an easily accessible introduction to urban Japan and all its contemporary delights, one of the highlights of which is its food scene. The grand **Tokugawa Art Museum** and attached gardens display possessions of the powerful family who once ruled Japan, and who built Nagoya's original castle back in 1610. Another highlight is the **Toyota Commemorative Museum of Industry and Technology**, an appropriate tribute to Nagoya's industrial heritage.

Excellent transport links, including an international airport, make Nagoya an ideal base from which to tour the region. Day-trip possibilities include the castle towns of **Inuyama** (p.393) and **Gifu** (p.396), both places where you can view the ancient skill of *ukai* – fishing with cormorants. The Shima Hantō (p.506) can also easily be visited from Nagoya.

Arrival and information

The lines of three **train** companies converge on Nagoya, and their stations are all close to each other on the west side of the city. The **main station** belongs to JR and is where you'll alight from Shinkansen and regular JR services. Immediately south of the JR station, beneath the Meitetsu department store, is the **Meitetsu line terminus** for trains to and from Inuyama and Gifu, while next door is the **Kintetsu line terminus** for services to Nara (p.463) and the Shima Hantō region (see p.506). Long-distance **buses** pull in at the terminal at the north end of the JR station as well as at the Oasis 21 terminal in Sakae.

All international and some domestic flights arrive at **Central Japan International Airport** (ⓣ0565/38-1195, ⓦwww.centrair.jp), commonly known as Centrair, on a man-made island in Isewan Bay some 30km south of Nagoya. The airport has become something of a tourist attraction in its own right – locals visit just to sample its restaurants and bathe in its giant bath with a view of the runways. The high-speed Meitetsu Airport line connects Centrair with the city (28min; ¥1200), while a taxi

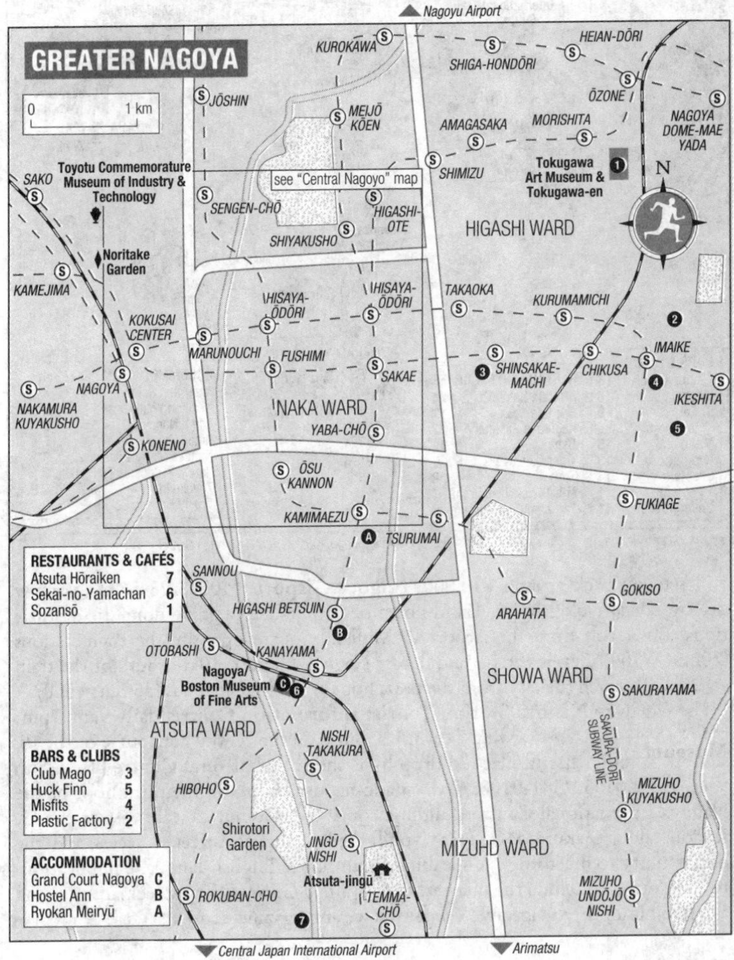

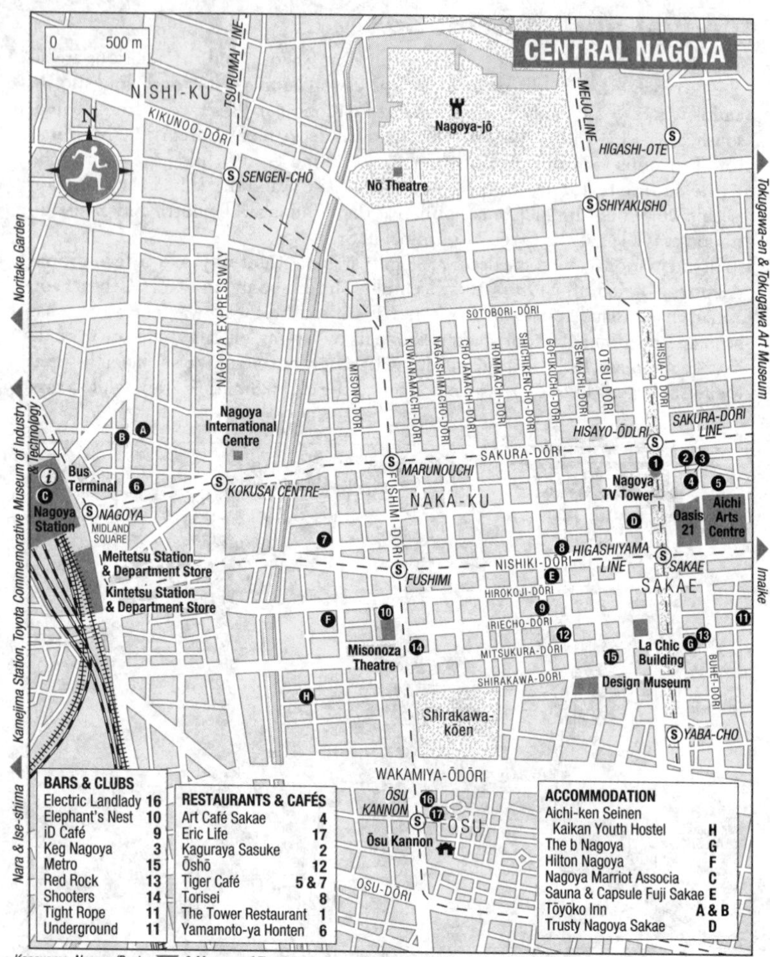

will set you back around ¥10,000. **Nagoya Airport** (ⓣ0568/28-5633, ⓦwww.nagoya-airport-bldg.co.jp), 12km north of the city, serves nine domestic destinations. Buses run from the airport to Midland Square opposite the train stations (20min; ¥700). **Ferries** arrive and depart Nagoya-kō port, 10km south of the train stations. To reach the city from the port, hop on the Meitetsu bus (35min; ¥500).

The clued-up **Nagoya Station Tourist Information Centre** (daily 9am–7pm; ⓣ052/541-4301; ⓦwww.ncvb.or.jp) is found on the central concourse of the JR station. Another useful place to drop by is the **International Centre** (Tues–Sun 9am–7pm; ⓣ052/581-0100, ⓦwww.nic-nagoya.or.jp), on the third floor of the Nagoya International Centre Building, some seven minutes' walk east of the JR station, along Sakura-dōri. Here you'll find a library, internet access and the opportunity to meet English-speaking locals. Local English-language publications to look out for include the quarterly *Nagoya Info Guide* (ⓦwww.seekjapan.jp) and the free bimonthly magazine *Ran* (ⓦwww.ranmagazine.com).

Tokai Welcome Card

The Tokai **Welcome Card** is a discount scheme for overseas tourists covering hundreds of hotels, restaurants, transportation and sightseeing facilities; it's valid in Nagoya, all of Aichi-ken and neighbouring Gifu-ken, Mie-ken and Shizuoka-ken. Cards can be ordered free from Ⓦwww.j-heartland.com. For more details on Welcome Cards, see Basics, p.70.

Orientation and city transport

In front of Nagoya JR Station, a giant sculpted air vent marks the beginning of **Sakura-dōri**, the main highway cutting directly east towards **Sakae**, the city's heart, where you'll find most hotels, department stores and restaurants. Around 1km north of Sakae lie the **castle grounds**, while a similar distance south is the temple **Ōsu Kannon**. Heading further south, you'll hit **Kanayama**, another major entertainment and business district. A kilometre or so south of here is the venerable shrine **Atsuta-jingū**. Keep heading south and you'll reach the **Nagoya-kō** port area.

The easiest way to get around is on the **subway**; the four lines you'll use the most are: Higashiyama (yellow on the subway map), Meijō (purple), Sakura-dōri (red) and Tsurumai (blue). Both the Sakura-dōri and Higashiyama lines connect with the train stations. The extensive **bus** system is also handy: **Me-guru** (メーグル; Ⓦwww.ncvb.or.jp/routebus) is a convenient service that runs from Tuesday to Sunday around Nagoya's central sights, which you can hop on and off all day for ¥500. Single journeys by subway or bus start at ¥200; if you plan to travel a lot, consider buying one of the **day tickets** (¥740 for subway only; ¥600 for buses only; ¥850 for subway and buses). There's also the Weekend Eco Pass (¥600), a one-day pass valid on buses and subways and available on weekends, national holidays and the eighth day of each month. For full details of the city's public transport systems, see Ⓦtinyurl.com/23godyf.

Accommodation

Nagoya has a good range of **accommodation**, with many places situated near the train stations. However, the city's excellent public transport system means you can stay pretty much anywhere and get around quickly; choose Sakae or Kanayama if you're after lively nightlife.

Aichi-ken Seinen Kaikan Youth Hostel 愛知県青年会館ユースホステル 1-18-8 Sakae, Naka-ku Ⓣ052/221-6001. Great location and very good value, since it's more like a hotel, with big rooms and a huge top-floor communal bath. The downside is the 11pm curfew. Dorm beds ¥2992, singles from ¥4095.

The b Nagoya 4-15-23 Sakae, Naka-ku Ⓣ052/241-1500, Ⓦwww.ishinhotels.com. A stylish makeover pushes this business hotel into boutique territory. Singles start at ¥6500, with lower rates on weekends. ❹

Grand Court Nagoya 1-1-1 Kanayama-chō, Naka-ku Ⓣ052/683-4111, Ⓦwww.grandcourt.co.jp. This fine hotel, in groovy Kanayama, is a handy base for southern Nagoya. There's a good choice of restaurants and a selection of four different pillows for your bed. ❼

Hilton Nagoya 1-3-3 Sakae, Naka-ku Ⓣ052/212-1111, Ⓦwww.hilton.com. Classy hotel with good rooms, an excellent range of facilities, and a great location. ❽

Hostel Ann 2-4-2 Kanayama-chō, Naka-ku Ⓣ052/253-7710, Ⓦhostelann.com. A 10min walk northeast of Kanayama Station is this relaxed hostel in a small old house. They have a kitchen, fussball table in the lounge, bike rental for ¥500 per day and no curfew. Dorm beds ¥2500, singles ¥3500.

Nagoya Marriot Associa Hotel 1-1-4 Meieki, Nakamura-ku Ⓣ052/584–1113, Ⓦwww.associa.com/nma. These luxurious lodgings, high above the mammoth station and twin towers complex, offer comfortable rooms with a chintzy old European look and wonderful views. There's an excellent range of restaurants and a fitness club with a 20m pool. ❽–❾

Ryokan Meiryū 旅館名龍 2-4-21 Kamimaezu, Naka-ku ⓣ052/331-8686, ⓦwww.japan-net.ne.jp/~meiryu. Friendly English-speaking owners run this ryokan. The tatami rooms have a/c and TV; bathrooms are communal and there's a little café for breakfast and dinner. Singles are ¥5250. Take exit three at Kamimaezu subway station and walk a couple of minutes east. ❹

Sauna & Capsule Fuji Sakae サウナ&カプセルフジ栄 3-22-31 Sakae ⓣ052/962-5711. Nagoya's largest capsule hotel (men only) is a snazzy affair, with its own restaurant, sauna and huge bath. If you just want to use the sauna and bath it's ¥1000 for 15min. Mon–Thurs & Sun ¥3000, Fri & Sat ¥3800 per person.

Tōyoko Inn 3-16-1 Meieki, Nakamura-ku ⓣ052/561-1046, ⓦwww.toyoko-inn.com. Two branches of this reliable business chain hotel face off against each other, about a 5min walk northeast of the station. The smaller, newer Honkan building is a bit cheaper than the larger Shinkan. ❹

Trusty Nagoya Sakae 3-15-21 Sakae, Naka-ku ⓣ052/968-5111, ⓦwww.trusty.jp. There's an old European feel to this pleasant, small, mid-range hotel in the heart of the city. Nice touches include William Morris-inspired duvets and handsome inlaid wood furniture and fixtures. ❺

The City

Nagoya's sights are quite spread out, but walking from the main hub of train stations to Sakae and around, even down to Ozu, is quite feasible. The following descriptions come in rough order of priority if your time is limited.

Tokugawa Art Museum and Nagoya-jō

Nagoya's single best sight is the **Tokugawa Art Museum** (徳川美術館; Tues–Sun 10am–5pm; ¥1200 or ¥1350 including the garden; ⓣ052/935-6262) and its lovely attached garden **Tokugawa-en** (徳川園; daily 9.30am–5.30pm; ¥300), laid out in the late seventeenth century. The museum, around 4km east of the stations, houses heirlooms from the Owari branch of the Tokugawa family, who once ruled Nagoya, and includes items inherited by the first Tokugawa shogun, Ieyasu, reconstructions of the formal chambers of the *daimyō*'s residence and a nō stage, around which beautiful traditional costumes are arranged, which enables you to really get a sense of the rich and cultured life led by the Tokugawas. The museum's most treasured piece is the twelfth-century painted scroll *The Tale of Genji* (see p.784); it's so precious and fragile that it's only displayed for a month each year from November 10 – the rest of the time you can see reproduced panels and video programmes about the scroll.

Three kilometres west of the museum, back towards the train stations, brings you to the moat surrounding **Nagoya-jō** (名古屋城; daily 9am–4.30pm; ¥500 or ¥640 including Tokugawa-en). Tokugawa Ieyasu started to build this fortress in 1610 but the original was largely destroyed during World War II – all that survived were three turrets, three gates and sequestered screen paintings. A handsome concrete replica was completed in 1959, the central donjon topped by huge gold-plated *shachi*, the mythical dolphins that are one of the symbols of Nagoya. The Hommaru Goten (本丸御殿), the palace that once stood at the foot of the donjon, is currently under reconstruction; the first stage opened in 2010 but it won't be fully finished until 2018. Eventually it will house Edo-era painted screens including the famous bamboo grove, leopard and tiger scenes.

Nagoya Station and around

The area around Nagoya's trio of train stations is like a mini-Manhattan with a clutch of tower blocks including **Midland Square**, Toyota's headquarters. Apart from the shops, restaurants and multiplex cinema here there's also the **Sky Promenade** (daily 11am–10pm), a partially open walkway that winds its

The Toyota way

No business is more closely associated with Nagoya than **Toyota** (ⓦwww.toyota.co.jp), whose 47-floor headquarters are based in the Midland Square Tower (see opposite) opposite Nagoya Station. The automobile company was started in 1937 by Kiichiro Toyoda as a spin-off from Toyoda Automatic Loom Works, founded by his father Sakichi, who invented the **wooden handloom** in 1890; the company diversified into car manufacturing in 1933. You can learn much about the company's history at the Toyota Commemorative Museum of Industry and Technology (see below). Devoted **auto enthusiasts** will also want to visit one of Toyota's factories to see its famous production processes in action. The one-hour tours are free but reservations are required – call ⓣ0565/29-3355 or see the company's website for details.

way down from the 46th to the 44th floors of the building for a panoramic view of Nagoya.

The city's industrial heritage is neatly covered in a couple of fascinating museums. Ten minutes' walk north of Nagoya Station is **Noritake Garden** (ⓣ052/561-7114). The former factory and grounds of the celebrated china manufacturer have been transformed into a very pleasant park within which you'll find a **craft centre** (daily 10am–5pm; ¥500, or ¥800 for joint entry with the Toyota Commemorative Museum of Industry and Technology, see below) where you can watch pottery being created and try your own hand at painting a plate (¥1600). In a 1904-vintage brick building, the **Morimura-Okura Museum Canvas** (daily 10am–5pm; free) reveals in ingenious ways the history and science involved in the ceramics technologies of the Morimura group (of which Noritake is a member). Elsewhere on the spacious green site there is a good café, a gallery of modern pottery and showrooms where you can buy Noritake products.

Ten minutes' walk northwest of Noritake Garden, and close to Sakō Station on the Meitetsu Nagoya line, is the **Toyota Commemorative Museum of Industry and Technology** (Tues–Sun 9.30am–5pm; ¥500; ⓣ052/551-6115). Housed in an old red-brick Toyota factory, the museum is made up of two pavilions, one housing cars, the other textile machinery (though now famous worldwide for its cars, Toyota began life as a textile producer). In the first pavilion, rows of early twentieth-century looms make an incredible racket; in contrast, a computer-controlled air-jet loom at the end of the display purrs like a kitten. In the automobile pavilion, it's the car-making robots, some of which look like giant, menacing aliens, that grab the attention.

Sakae

Sakae (栄) is Nagoya's central shopping and entertainment playground. Hisaya ōdōri-kōen, a swathe of parkland splitting the area, is punctuated more or less in the centre by the 180m **Nagoya TV Tower** (viewing deck daily 10am–10pm; ¥600). This handsome silver-painted structure, Japan's first TV signal transmission tower, built in 1954, has been designated a National Tangible Cultural Property. It's best visited for its good range of places to eat and drink (see p.392). The UFO-shaped complex immediately east of here is the bus station **Oasis 21** (ⓦsakaepark.co.jp); its oval-shaped roof, covered with a shallow pool of water, provides an attractive elevated perch from which to survey the surroundings.

Immediately behind Oasis 21 is the **Aichi Arts Centre** (ⓦwww.aac.pref.aichi.jp), a major concert and performance hall. Head to the top floor to visit the excellent **Aichi Prefectural Museum of Art** (愛知県美術館; Tues–Thurs, Sat & Sun 10am–5.30pm; Fri 10am–7.30pm; ¥500); its permanent collection provides a brisk romp through superstars of the post nineteenth-century art scene, including pieces by Picasso, Klimt, Matisse and Modigliani, as well as Japanese painters such as Kishida Ryusei and Takahashi Yuichi. The large galleries here also host good temporary exhibitions, and the museum is the focus of the Aichi Triennale international arts festival (Ⓦ aichitriennale.jp), first held in 2010.

A short walk south of the art museum is the Nadya Park Building; on the fourth floor you'll find the engrossing **Design Museum** (daily except Tues 11am–8pm; ¥300), which charts the commercial design of modern products, such as telephones and radios, and has hi-tech displays and computer simulations. Push the buttons on the display towers to shuffle through the various exhibits, including the museum's unique collection of American Art Deco items.

Ōsu and Kanayama

Five minutes' walk southwest of Nadya Park, and beside the Ōsu Kannon stop on the Tsurumai subway line, is **Ōsu Kannon** (大須観音), a vermilion-painted temple bustling with a steady stream of petitioners. A lively antiques and flea market is held in the temple's precincts on the 18th and 28th of each month; at other times it's still worth heading here to explore the bargain-hunters' district of **Ōsu**, where old-style arcades are lined with shops selling discount electronic goods, cheap clothes and used kimono – it's an area that's popular with Nagoya's youth and you'll find several funky clothing and gift shops around here, including the mega retailer *Komehyo* (Ⓦ www.komehyo.co.jp) selling everything from electronics to used clothing priced by weight.

Around 2km south of Ōsu, **Kanayama** (金山) is a major Nagoya district revolving around a busy train station (which is also on the Meitetsu Airport line). Next to the south side of the station is the excellent **Nagoya/Boston Museum of Fine Arts** (Mon–Fri 10am–7pm, Sat & Sun 10am–5pm; ¥1200, after 5pm ¥1000; Ⓣ 052/684-0101), an annex of the respected US art institution, with several different exhibitions staged at a time. The plaza in front of the museum is a favourite spot for young busking musicians and dancers to perform.

Atsuta-jingū and around

Some 5km south of central Nagoya, amid extensive wooded grounds, lies the ancient shrine of **Atsuta-jingū** (熱田神宮), home of the *kusanagi-no-tsurugi*, or "grass-cutting sword". This, along with the sacred jewels in Tokyo's Imperial Palace and the sacred mirror at Ise-jingū (see p.506), forms part of the imperial

World Cosplay Summit

Short for "costume play", **cosplay** is when fans dress up as their favourite character from anime, manga, video games or Japanese rock (J-rock) bands. It's said the word was coined by Japanese journalist Nobuyuki Takahashi in 1984 when he wrote a feature about US fans dressing up for a masquerade (a combination of a skit show and fashion parade for people in cosplay costumes) at a science fiction convention in Los Angeles. Since then, the term has caught on and it's now inconceivable for an anime convention anywhere in the world not to have a substantial cosplay element to it. At the ultimate level there's the **World Cosplay Summit** (Ⓦ www.tv-aichi.co.jp/wcs/e), held annually in early August since 2003 by the Aichi Broadcasting Company in Nagoya with participants from up to fourteen countries. The main events are a cosplay parade in the Ōsu district and the championship show itself, held in the public areas of Oasis 21 (see p.389).

regalia and remains hidden deep within the shrine, which had to be rebuilt after World War II.

Within the shrine grounds there's a small **museum** (daily 9am–4.30pm; closed last Wed & Thurs of the month; ¥300), where you can see many other swords offered to the Shinto gods at Atsuta-jingū, including a ferocious 2m-long blade in the entrance hall. Within the grounds, look out for the giant camphor tree, said to have been planted by the Buddhist saint Kōbō Daishi (see p.499) 1300 years ago. It takes around twenty minutes by subway from Nagoya Station to reach Jingū-Nishi Station on the Meijō line, the closest stop to Atsuta-jingū.

Stroll west from the subway station towards the Hori-kawa, on the other side of which is the charming **Shirotori Garden** (白鳥庭園; Tues–Sun 9am–4.30pm; closed third and fourth Wed of month; ¥300). This classical stroll-garden, arranged around ponds and streams, has an elegant traditional teahouse that is said to resemble a swan landing on the water.

Arimatsu

Dating back to 1608, **Arimatsu** (有松), once a town on the Tokaidō highway but now a suburb of southeastern Nagoya, is famous for *shibori*, an intricate and time-consuming traditional method of tie-dyeing cotton that is still practised here. One *shibori* kimono typically takes up to six months to complete, which accounts for the high price of *shibori* goods. You'll find many shops selling them along the very picturesque street lined with prime examples of old Japanese architecture that lies just south of Meitetsu Arimatsu Station. If not for the utility poles and power lines, it could be a scene from a woodblock print – the old wooden houses with intricate tiled roofs providing the perfect backdrop to spring and autumn festivals (held on the third Sunday of March and first Sunday of October) when ornate floats are paraded down the street. Find out more about the tie-dyeing industry at the **Arimatsu-Namuri Shibori Kaikan** (有松鳴海絞会館; daily except Wed 9.30am–4.30pm; ¥300; Ⓦ www.shibori-kaikan.com).

Arimatsu can be reached directly from Meitetsu Nagoya Station (20min; ¥310), but if you're already at Atsuta-jingu (see opposite) you can board the train at the closer Jingu-mae Station. The ticket collector at Meitetsu Arimatsu can give you an English map of the area, although the houses are clearly visible from the station exit. One of the first of the old wooden houses you'll pass after you turn left into the conservation area street is Kaihantei, which is also home to the delicious bakery-café *Dasenka* (Wed–Sun 10am–7pm).

Eating, drinking and nightlife

Nagoya is blessed with many food specialities, including the flat, floury noodles *kishimen*, and the succulent chicken dishes made from *Nagoya Kochin* birds. Foodies should also consult the schedule of the excellent **farmers' market** (Ⓦ www.marche-japon.org/area/2301), which is held most weekends in different parts of the city and attracts vendors from around the region.

Sakae is packed with lively **restaurants** and numerous **bars**, and is a great place to head to for the local specialities. Drinking and dining options are also plentiful around Nagoya Station, south in Kanayama or east in Imaike and Ikeshita, two districts that sport some relaxed bars and clubs.

Traditional performing arts are well supported in Nagoya, with a splendid nō **theatre** opposite the castle and the grand kabuki theatre, Misono-za, in the downtown area of Fushimi. There are also plenty of **cinemas**, including a modern multiplex in Midland Square. You could also try your hand at a game of *pachinko* – Nagoya is where the noisy pinball pastime really took off in the 1950s.

Restaurants and cafés

Art Café Sakae 森村記念館 1-10-18 Higashi Sakura, Higashi-ku ⓣ052/971-0456. Tucked away behind a grove of bamboo is this relaxed gallery and café where you can admire the traditional-themed art of Morimura-san, including a lovely ceiling painting. Wed–Sun 10am–5pm.

Eric Life 2-11-8 Ōsu, Naka-ku ⓣ052/222-1555. There's a mid-century retro look at this hipsters' café behind Ōsu Kannon where you can lounge on green velvet chairs enjoying *yoshoku* dishes such as *omu-raisu* or nursing a cappuccino. Daily except Wed noon–midnight.

Atsuta Hōraiken あつた蓬莱軒 503 Gōdo, Atsuta-ku ⓣ052/671-8686. *Hitsumabushi* is a famous Nagoya *unagi* (eel) dish and this is the best place to eat it. There's a branch next to the southern entrance of Atsuta-jingū but it's worth heading to the main one, a couple of blocks further south, in an atmospheric traditional mansion with tatami rooms. A set meal costs ¥2520: you eat the delicious eel on top of rice in three ways: first as it is; second with a sprinkling of dried seaweed, spring onion and *wasabi*; and third with the soup added. Tues–Sun 11.30am–2pm & 4.30–8.30pm.

Kaguraya Sasuke 神楽家左助 1-10-6 Higashi Sakura, Higashi-ku ⓣ052/971-6203. It feels incredible to find this charming old building overlooking lovely gardens in the heart of modern Nagoya – even better is that they serve delicious, beautifully presented traditional food. Enjoy a course lunch from ¥3000 and dinner from ¥5000. Daily 11.30am–2pm, 5–10pm.

Ōshō 王将 3-91-1 Sakae, Naka-ku. This cheap and cheerful Chinese ramen joint in the heart of Sakae is nearly always full. It has an English menu and pictures of set meals, which rarely cost over ¥1000. Mon–Sat 11am–midnight, Sun 11am–10.30pm.

Sekai-no-Yamachan 世界の山ちゃん 2-4-16 Kanayama-chō, Naka-ku. Addictively spicy chicken wings, and other cheap, tasty dishes, are served at this fun *izakaya*. Popularly known as *Yamachan*, it's a local phenomenon, with scores of branches across the city and more around Japan. Mon–Sat 5–11.30pm, Sun 5–10.30pm.

Sozansō 蘇山荘 1001 Tokugawa-chō, Higashi-ku ⓣ052/932-7887. Attached to the fancy French restaurant overlooking the beautiful Tokugawa Gardens, this chic café-bar in a reconstructed VIP guesthouse dating from 1937, with its own garden views, is the more afforable choice. During the day, sip premium teas or coffee and nibble on *temmusu*, Nagoya's own style of *onigiri* rice balls embedded with shrimp tempura. In the evening drop by to drink in sophisticated surroundings. Daily: café-bar noon–5pm & 7pm–midnight; restaurant 11am–2pm & 5–10pm.

Tiger Café 1-8-26 Nishiki, Naka-ku. This 1930s-style French café-bistro is good for a sandwich, an espresso or an after-dinner *digestif*. There's another branch at 1-9-22 Higashi Sakura, Higashi-ku. Both open Mon–Sat 11am–3am, Sun 11am–midnight.

Torisei 鳥勢 3-19-24 Sakae, Naka-ku ⓣ052/951-7337. You'll need to book ahead, especially at weekends, to enjoy the excellent *yakitori* and other chicken dishes at this restaurant, with counter seating downstairs and tatami rooms upstairs. Mon–Sat 11.30am–1.30pm & 5–10.30pm.

The Tower Restaurant 4F Nagoya TV Tower, 3-6-15 Nishiki, Naka-ku ⓣ052/951-3505. The exposed girders of the TV tower cutting through this stylish restaurant lend it a retro sci-fi feel. They serve tasty European-style food including roast beef and a pasta lunch (¥2300). The views across to Oasis 21 are great. Daily 11.30am–2.30pm & 5pm–midnight.

Yamamoto-ya Honten 山本屋本店 B1, Horiuchi Building, Meieki ⓣ052/565-0278. The chief outlet of this noodle café chain is on Sakura-dōri, a few minutes' walk from the JR station. The specialities are *miso nikomi* (thick udon noodles in a bean paste), locally reared *Nagoya kochin* (chicken) and Berkshire pork. Around ¥2000 per head. Daily 11am–7.30pm.

Bars, clubs and live music

If you're in search of *gaijin* company, the *Nagoya Info Guide* (see p.386) will help you find old standby bars and clubs such as *Shooters* (2-9-26 Naka-ku ⓦwww.shooters-nagoya.com) and *Elephant's Nest*, 1-4-3 Sakae, Naka-ku (ⓣ052/232-4360); listed below are the better places.

Nagoya also has an enthusiastically supported **live music** scene. Some venues to check out include: *Tight Rope*, downstairs from *Underground* in Sakae (ⓣ052/242-8557); *Electric Landlady* in Ōsu (ⓣ052/201-5004); and the long-running and punky *Huck Finn*, 5-19-7 in Imaike (ⓣ052/733-8347).

Club Mago 2-1-9 Shin-Sakae, Naka-ku ⓣ052/243-1818. Big-name DJs front up at this friendly and nicely decorated club, which also hosts a recovery party every Sun from 5am. The same building is home to the live house venues *Diamond Hall* and *Apollo Theatre* (ⓦwww.diamond-hall.com).

Keg Nagoya 1-10-13 Higashi Sakura, Higashi-ku ⓣ052/971-8211. Sample a great range of Japanese craft beers on tap at this appealing real-ale bar. On the food menu they do special types of curry rice. Daily 11.30am–1.30pm, Mon–Sat 5–11pm, Sun until 10pm.

iD Café 3-1-15 Sakae, Naka-ku ⓣ052/251-0382, ⓦwww.idcafe.info. Hip-hop, reggae and r'n'b can all be heard at this survivor of the Nagoya club scene. Entrance is ¥2000 including two drinks. Thurs–Sun 7pm–midnight.

Metro ⓦwww.thenagoyametroclub.com. The fabulous Madame Matty hosts this long-running *gaijin*-friendly gay and lesbian club event, a guaranteed fun time for all – it's held every second Sat of the month at *Club Wall* in Sakae; check the website for details. Entry ¥2500 including two drinks.

Misfits 4-10-16 Imaike, Chikusa-ku ⓦwww.misfitsnagoya.com. A friendly welcome, jam nights and drink-all-you-can on Wednesday nights (8–11pm; ¥1500) – no wonder this long-running bar remains a popular choice. On the third floor of a building around the corner from exit 5 of Imaike Station.

Plastic Factory 32-13 Kanda-chō, Chikusa-ku ⓣ052/723-9971, ⓦwww.plasticfactory.jp. Hosting an eclectic range of events in – guess what? – an old plastic factory, three blocks north of Imaike Station. Expect anything from progressive techno to live rock.

Red Rock 2F Aster Plaza Building, 4-14-6 Sakae, Naka-ku ⓣ052/262-7893, ⓦwww.theredrock.jp. There's an Aussie theme to this spacious, centrally located bar serving Australian ales such as Coopers, VB and Cascade, as well as traditional pub grub like shepherd's pie and fish and chips. Mon–Thurs 5.30pm–2am, Fri & Sat 5.30pm–6am, Sun 11.30am–2am.

Listings

Banks and exchange Several major bank branches can be found around the stations, along Sakura-dōri and Nishiki-dōri in Sakae. These include Citibank, whose ATMs accept some foreign-issued cards.

Bookshops English-language books are available at Maruzen, 3-2-7 Sakae (daily except Wed 9.50am–8pm), and Sanseido on 11th floor of Takashimaya department store in JR Central Towers.

Car rental Eki Rent-a-Car ⓣ052/581-0882; Nissan Rent-a-Car ⓣ052/451-2300.

Consulates Australia, 13F, Amnat Building, 1-3-3 Sakae, Naka-ku ⓣ052/211-0630; Canada, 6F, Nakatō Marunouchi Building, 3-17-6 Marunouchi ⓣ052/972-0450; USA, 6F, International Centre Building, 1-47-1 Nagono, Nakamura-ku ⓣ052/581-4501.

Emergencies The Prefectural Police Office is at 2-1-1 Sannomaru (ⓣ052/951-1611). In an absolute emergency, contact the International Centre (ⓣ052/581-0100). For other emergency numbers, see p.71.

Hospital The main hospital is the Nagoya Medical Centre, 4-1-1 Sannomaru, Naku-ku (ⓣ052/951-1111), but it's best to first call the International Centre (ⓣ052/581-0100) and they'll tell you the most appropriate place to go.

Internet access The Nagoya International Centre (see p.386) has internet terminals. Each of the four Kinko's – at Chiyogaoka, Ikeshita, Sakae and Meikei Minami – offers internet access.

Post office There's a post office (Mon–Fri 9am–7pm, Sat 9am–5pm, Sun 9am–12.30pm) at 1-1-1 Meieki, one minute's walk north of the JR station, as well as one in the station itself.

Inuyama and around

The appealing castle town of **INUYAMA** (犬山), 25km north of Nagoya, lies beside the Kiso-gawa. From May to October the river is the stage for the centuries-old practice of *ukai* (cormorant fishing; see box, p.394), to which the castle's floodlit exterior provides a dramatic backdrop. Boats sail from the dock beside the Inuyama-bashi bridge, five minutes' walk north of Inuyama Yūen Station. From

Ukai

Inuyama (see p.393) and Gifu (see p.396) are two of the main locations for **ukai**, or night-time fishing with **cormorants**, a skill developed back in the seventh century; others include Kyoto (see p.403), Iwakuni (p.560) and Ōzu in Shikoku (see p.634). The specially trained, slender-necked birds are used to catch *ayu*, a sweet freshwater fish, which is in season between May and September. Traditionally dressed fishermen handle up to twelve cormorants on long leashes, which are attached at the birds' throats with a ring to prevent them from swallowing the fish. The birds dive into the water, hunting the *ayu*, which are attracted to the light of the fire blazing in the metal braziers hanging from the bows of the narrow fishing boats.

The fast-moving show usually only lasts around thirty minutes, but an *ukai* jaunt is not just about fishing. Around two hours before the start of the fishing, the audience boards long, canopied boats, decorated with paper lanterns, which sail upriver and then moor to allow a pre-show picnic. Unless you pay extra you'll have to bring your own food and drink, but sometimes a boat will drift by selling beer, snacks and fireworks – another essential *ukai* component. Although you can watch the show for free from the riverbank, you won't experience the thrill of racing alongside the **fishing boats**, the birds splashing furiously in the reflected light of the pine wood burning in the brazier hanging from the boats' prows.

May to August the boats depart at 6pm and the fishing show begins at 7.45pm, while in September and October the start time is 5.30pm, with the *ukai* kicking off at 7.15pm. In May, June, September and October the cost is ¥2500, rising to ¥2800 during the peak months of July and August, when it's best to make a reservation (ⓣ0568/61-0057). There's no *ukai* on August 10 when Inuyama stages its riverside fireworks display.

The castle is slightly closer to Inuyama-Yūen Station, but if you approach it from the west side of Inuyama Station – which takes around ten minutes on foot – you'll pass through an area dotted with old wooden houses, some of which house craft galleries, culminating in the small **Inuyama Artefacts Museum** (犬山市文化史料館; daily 9am–5pm; ¥100). Here you can see two of the thirteen towering, ornate floats (*yatai*) that are paraded around Inuyama during the major festival on the first weekend of April. If you visit the museum on a Friday or Saturday, you can also see a craftsman demonstrating the art of making *karakuri*, the mechanical wooden puppets that perform on the *yatai*.

The museum is just in front of **Haritsuna-jinja**, the shrine at which the colourful festival takes place. One minute's walk up the hill behind will bring you to the entrance of the only privately owned castle in Japan, **Inuyama-jō** (犬山城; daily 9am–4.30pm; ¥500, joint ticket with Uraku-en ¥1200). This toy-like fortress was built in 1537, making it the oldest in Japan (although parts have been extensively renovated), and it has belonged to the Naruse family since 1618. Inside, the donjon is nothing special, but there's a pretty view of the river and surrounding country from the top, where you can appreciate the defensive role that this white castle played.

A five-minute walk east of Inuyama-jō, within the grounds of the luxury *Meitetsu Inuyama Hotel* (名鉄犬山ホテル), is the serene garden of **Uraku-en** (有楽苑; daily: March to July 14 & Sept–Nov 9am–5pm; July 15 to Aug 31 9am–6pm; Dec–Feb 9am–4pm; ¥1000 or ¥1300 for combined garden and tea ticket). The mossy lawns and stone pathways act as a verdant frame for the subdued **Jo-an**, a traditional teahouse. Originally built in Kyoto by Oda Uraku, the younger brother of the warlord Oda Nobunaga, the yellow-walled teahouse has floor space for just over three tatami mats, though it can only be viewed from the outside. Tea (¥500) is served in one of the garden's larger modern teahouses.

Meiji Mura

One of Japan's best open-air architectural museums, **Meiji Mura** (明治村; daily: March–Oct 9.30am–5pm; Nov–Feb 9.30am–4pm; ¥1600; ⓣ0568/67-0314), is 7km east of Inuyama. Dotted around a huge park are 67 structures, including churches, banks, a kabuki theatre, a lighthouse and a telephone exchange (from Sapporo). All the structures date from around the Meiji era (see p.771) when Western influences were flooding into Japan, which resulted in some unique hybrid architecture. A highlight is the front of the original **Imperial Hotel**, designed by Frank Lloyd Wright (see box below).

Allow at least half a day to see the park fully. If you don't fancy walking, there's an electric bus (¥600) that beetles from one end of the park to the other, or you could hop on an old Kyoto tram (¥300) and steam locomotive (¥500), though these only go part of the way. There are several places to snack or eat **lunch** within the park, including inside the *Imperial Hotel*.

Buses to Meiji Mura leave at regular intervals from the east side of Inuyama Station (20min; ¥410).

Practicalities

Inuyama is roughly thirty minutes from both Nagoya (¥540) and Gifu (¥440) on the Meitetsu railway. There's a **tourist information booth** (daily 9am–5pm; ⓣ0568/61-6000) beside the central exit of Inuyama Station.

With both cities so close, there's no pressing need to stay here. However, if you do decide to stay over, a good **accommodation** option is the *Inuyama International Youth Hostel* (ⓣ0568/61-1111, ⓦwww.inuyama-iyh.com; ❸), a modern hostel with a choice of Western- or Japanese-style rooms – including singles for a bargain ¥3700 – and a good restaurant; order dinner (from ¥1580) as the hostel is a couple of kilometres from town. To reach the hostel, take the monorail from Inuyama-Yūen Station to the Monkey Park (¥150) and walk north for ten minutes past the park, across the main road, and up the hill on your left.

A good place to **eat**, only five minutes' walk north of Inuyama Station, is *Narita* (なり田; ⓣ0568/65-2447; closed first Mon of month), an upmarket French restaurant set in a former kimono-weaving factory and mansion with lovely traditional gardens; the five-course set lunch is ¥2940.

Wright in Japan

Frank Lloyd Wright's fame in Japan has much to do with the fact that his grand *Imperial Hotel* in Tokyo (part of which now stands in Meiji Mura) survived the Great Kantō Earthquake, which hit Tokyo the day after the hotel opened in 1923. The US-born architect first visited Japan in 1905 and was so enamoured of the country that he pursued and eventually received the commission to build Tokyo's *Imperial Hotel*. He moved to the city to live and work on this and thirteen other projects between 1917 and 1923. Of these, only seven were built and today just five survive in total or partially: the front lobby of the *Imperial Hotel* in Meiji Mura (see above); the school Jiyu Gakuen Myonichikan (ⓦwww.jiyu.jp/index-e.html) and a portion of the Aisaku Hayashi House, both in Tokyo; JR Nikko station (see p.172); and Tazaemon Yamamura House (ⓦwww.yodoko.co.jp/geihinkan/index_e.html) in Ashiya near Kōbe. For more information see ⓦwww.wrightinjapan.org.

Gifu

On the other side of the Kiso-gawa from Inuyama is Gifu-ken, whose capital, **GIFU** (岐阜), lies 20km further west. Like Inuyama, Gifu offers *ukai* on a meandering river overlooked by a hilltop castle, but is otherwise a bigger and more modern city, rebuilt after the double whammy of an earthquake in 1891 and blanket bombings during World War II.

Ukai displays (see box, p.394) run each year from May 11 to October 15 on the Nagara-gawa (長良川), around 2km north of the town's two train stations. To book a seat on a boat, go to the boat office (ⓣ058/262-0104; ¥3000–3300) beside the Nagara-bashi, reached on buses from stands 11 and 12 (¥200) outside the JR station – take care not to get on an express (快速) bus, though.

The boat office is in the picturesque riverside area of old wooden houses known as **Kawaramachi** (川原町); you'll find some good places to eat, interesting small galleries and craft shops here.

Perched 329m up on Kinka-zan, the small white castle of **Gifu-jō** (岐阜城; daily: March 16 to May 11 9.30am–5.30pm; May 12 to Oct 16 8.30am–5.30pm; Oct 17 to March 15 9.30am–4.30pm; ¥200) is nothing special in itself but does command a panoramic view of the city. A cable car (daily: March 16 to May 11 9am–6pm; May 12 to Oct 16 8am–6pm; Oct 17 to March 15 9am–5pm; ¥600 one-way, ¥1050 return) saves you having to slog up the densely forested hill from the base of verdant **Gifu-kōen** (岐阜公園). The park is reached on the same buses that go to the Nagara-bashi. While you're out here, pop into **Shōhō-ji** (正法寺; daily 9am–5pm; ¥150), a weatherworn temple opposite the park, which houses an imposing 13.7m-tall sculpture of Buddha made of lacquered bamboo.

Gifu is also renowned for its high-quality **paper crafts**, including umbrellas, lanterns, fans and the painted rice-paper fish you'll see flying off poles like flags. The tourist information office (see below) can provide a map locating workshops selling these products where you may also be able to watch the craftsmen go about their business.

Practicalities

Gifu's two **train stations** – JR and Meitetsu – are five minutes from one another at the south end of the city's commercial district. The **tourist information office** (daily: March–Nov 9am–7pm; Dec–Feb 9am–6pm; ⓣ058/262-4415, ⓦwww.gifucvb.or.jp) is inside JR Gifu Station.

There are plenty of business hotels clustered near the train stations; try *Weekly Sho Gifu Daiichi Hotel*, 2-5 Fukuzumi-chō (ウィークリー翔岐阜第一ホテル; ⓣ058/251-2111, ⓦwww.weekly-sho.jp; ③), two blocks northwest of the station, which offers singles from ¥2900 including breakfast. At the other end of the scale, one of the nicest ryokan is *Jūhachirō* (十八楼; ⓣ058/265-1551; ⑧ including two meals), overlooking the Nagara-gawa.

Eating and drinking

There are plenty of **restaurant and bars** on the roads heading north from the JR station; check out the lively *yakitori* stands around the bar *Bier Hall*. Other good places to eat can be found in Kawaramachi.

Bunkaya 文化屋 ⓣ058/212-0132. Facing on to the Nagara-gawa, this place is particularly lovely, but bookings are essential for its course meal (¥2940). Daily 11.30am–1.30pm & 5.30–8.30pm.

Izumiya 泉屋 ⓣ058/263-6788. Specializes in *ayu*, serving the fish in a whole range of dishes. Daily except Wed 11.30am–2pm & 5–7.30pm.

Kawaramachiya 川原町屋 This pleasant café/gallery, serving udon noodles, is easily spotted by the old-fashioned red postbox outside. Daily 10am–6pm.
Natural Café & Gallery ⓣ058/269-5788. Convivial café and gallery set in an old storehouse close to the Hon-machi san-chōme bus stop. Daily 11am–midnight, closed 1st & 3rd Tues of month.
Tamaiya-honpo 玉井屋本舗 ⓣ058/262-6893. Relax over a *macha* and sweet cake at this venerable traditional confectionery shop opposite the ryokan *Jūhachirō* in Kawaramachi. Daily except Wed 8am–8pm.

Gujō Hachiman

> **It is a town of low, dark, wood-and-plaster buildings, paved lanes, and running water. The windows of the buildings are narrow and slatted. The lanes, too, are narrow, steeply walled, and end in dimly lanterned eating places or in small stone bridges that arch over splashing streams. It was like an Edo-era stage set.**
>
> Alan Booth *Looking for the Lost*, 1995

Booth's romantic description captures **GUJŌ HACHIMAN** (郡上八幡) to a tee: its bygone-days atmosphere and mountain-bound location – with two pristine rivers, the Yoshida and Nagara, running through the centre – lend it great appeal. Tucked in a valley on an old trade route that once led to the Sea of Japan, the town lies around 55km north of Gifu. It's worth visiting year-round, but the best time is during the **Gujō Odori** (see box below), one of Japan's top three dance festivals.

The tourist office (see p.398) sells a ¥1500 ticket providing access to nine places of interest around town. The best of these is the **Hakurankan** (博覧館; daily 9.30am–5pm; during Gujō Odori 9am–6pm; ¥500), on the northern side of the Yoshida River, a ten-minute stroll from the tourist office. This excellent museum has four sections detailing the town's history, arts and crafts, connection with water, and folk dance.

A good fifteen-minute climb from the Hakurankan, past several attractive temples, is **Gujō-Hachiman-jō** (郡上八幡城; daily: March–May 9am–5pm; June–Aug 8am–6pm; Nov–Feb 9am–4.30pm; ¥300). This photogenic replica of the old castle was rebuilt in 1934 on the stone foundations of the less

Gujō Odori

Bon Odori festivals are common across Japan, but nowhere is the dance so firmly rooted in the life of the community as at Gujō Hachiman, where the **Gujō Odori** has been going since the 1590s. Nearly every night from mid-July to early September, from about 8pm to 10.30pm in a different part of town (the tourist information centre can tell you exactly when and where), the locals don their *yukata* and *geta* and dance in the streets.

People dance in circles around a tall wood-and-bamboo structure from which a singer, drummers, flute player and a chorus call the tune. There are ten kinds of dances and the singer will call their name out before each one commences. Watch the hand and feet movements of those in the inner circle, as these are the people who learned these steps as children – then follow along!

During the O-bon holiday in mid-August, dancing goes on all night and thousands crowd the town to take part. Don't worry if you can't find a bed, since there's always a place for revellers to rest during the night-long festivities – again check with the tourist office.

elaborate original structure. From its ramparts you'll see that the town resembles the shape of a fish, the elegant concrete span of the motorway accenting the tail. South of the Yoshida-gawa, a ten-minute walk from the tourist office, is **Jionzen-ji** (慈恩禅寺), a sixteenth-century temple with a lovely attached garden Tetsusō-en (daily 9am–5pm; ¥300), which looks particularly spectacular in autumn.

Rafting trips are available year-round downriver at Minami with **Outdoor Support Systems** (Ⓣ058/248-4711). In summer, you might be tempted to take a swim in the sparkling river. Anglers with long poles and tall straw hats can be seen along both of the town's rivers trying their luck for the *ayu* (sweetfish) and trout for which the region is famous. Also seek out the town's natural spring, dubbed the **Fountain of Youth**, or *Sōgi-sui* (宗祇水) – it's located down the stone pathway that leads to a pretty bridge over the Kodara-gawa, about five minutes' walk northwest of the tourist office.

Practicalities

Gujō Hachiman has direct **bus** connections with Nagoya (2hr) and Gifu (1hr 10min; ¥1480). Buses also stop at the highway intersection for Gifū Hachiman, around thirty minutes west of the town centre, for services to and from Takayama (1hr 15min; ¥1600), Kyoto (2hr 30min; ¥3300) and Ōsaka (3hr 30min; ¥4150). By **train**, take the JR line to Mino-Ōta then transfer to the private Nagaragawa line (1hr 20min; one way ¥1320, day return ¥2000).

The **tourist information office** (daily 8.30am–5.15pm; Ⓣ0575/67-0002, Ⓦwww.gujohachiman.com/kanko) is set in a handsome Western-style building in the town centre, about 1km north of the train station. The best budget **accommodation** is the *Gujō-Tōsen-ji Youth Hostel* (郡上洞泉寺ユースホステル; Ⓣ0575/67-0290, Ⓕ67-0549; dorm beds ¥3300), in the grounds of Tosen-ji temple. *Nakashimaya* (中嶋屋; Ⓣ0575/65-2191; ❺) is a good traditional ryokan right on Shinmachi, the main shopping street where the all-night O-bon dancing takes place. Halfway uphill to the castle, *Hotel Sekisuien* (ホテル積翠園; Ⓣ0575/65-3101; ❼ including two meals) is more modern but offers large, bright tatami rooms, excellent meals and a big public bath.

Eating

One curiosity about Gujō Hachiman is that around eighty percent of the plastic food samples displayed in restaurant windows in Japan are made here. For somewhere to **eat** real food try the following:

Hanamura 花むら Ⓣ0575/67-0056. Around the corner from *Nakashimaya* is this rustic, friendly place where the set dinner of local dishes (*omikase*) is a great deal at ¥2500. Daily 11.30am–1.30pm & 5–10.30pm.

Uotora 魚寅 Ⓣ0575/65-3195. On the main shopping street, offering tasty fish and *unagi* (eel) dishes; a set meal here is around ¥2000. Daily except Wed 11am–2.30pm & 5–8pm.

Ristorante Suzume no Iori 雀の庵 Ⓣ0575/67-2355. The upmarket option, in an elegant house combining Western and Japanese styles, behind the tourist office; set menus of Italian dishes, big on seafood, start at ¥2800 for lunch, ¥4500 for dinner. Daily except Tues 11.30am–2pm & 5–9pm.

Soba-no-Hirajin そばの平甚 Ⓣ0575/65-2004. Expect to have to wait for a table at this popular noodle restaurant on the north side of the Yoshida River, close to the Fountain of Youth. Daily 11.30am–5pm.

Travel details

Trains

The trains between the major cities listed below are the fastest direct services. There are also frequent slower services covering the same destinations. It's usually possible, especially on long-distance routes, to get there faster by changing between services.

Kanazawa to: Echigo-Yuzawa (10 daily; 2hr 30min); Fukui (every 15min; 50min); Kyoto (every 30min; 2hr 20min); Niigata (5 daily; 3hr 40min); Ōsaka (every 30min; 2hr 45min); Tokyo (Ueno Station; daily; 6hr 5min); Toyama (every 45min; 40min).

Matsumoto to: Hakuba (11 daily; 1hr 45min); Nagano (every 30min; 45min); Nagoya (hourly; 2hr); Ōsaka (daily; 4hr); Tokyo (Shinjuku Station; hourly; 2hr 30min).

Nagano to: Matsumoto (hourly; 50min); Nagoya (hourly; 2hr 50min); Niigata (2 daily; 3hr); Obuse (9 daily; 23min); Ōsaka (daily; 4hr 50min); Tokyo (every 30min; 1hr 30min); Yudanaka (8 daily; 45min).

Nagoya to: Fukui (8 daily; 2hr 5min); Fukuoka (Hakata Station; every 30min; 3hr 25min); Gifu (every 30min; 30min); Hiroshima (every 30min; 2hr 20min); Inuyama (every 30min; 35min); Kanazawa (8 daily; 2hr 55min); Kii-Katsuura (4 daily; 3hr 20min); Kyoto (every 10min; 45min); Matsumoto (hourly; 2hr); Nagano (hourly; 2hr 50min); Okayama (every 30min; 2hr); Ōsaka (every 10min; 1hr); Takayama (9 daily; 2hr 35min); Toba (8 daily; 1hr 30min); Tokyo (every 10min; 1hr 50min); Toyama (11 daily; 3hr 40min).

Takayama to: Kyoto (daily; 4hr 20min); Nagoya (10 daily; 2hr 10min); Ōsaka (daily; 5hr); Toyama (4 daily; 1hr 20min).

Toyama to: Kanazawa (hourly; 40min); Nagoya (4 daily; 3hr 40min); Niigata (5 daily; 3hr); Ōsaka (hourly; 3hr 15min); Takayama (4 daily; 1hr 30min); Tateyama (hourly; 1hr); Tokyo (Ueno Station; daily; 5hr 40min).

Buses

The buses listed below are mainly long-distance services – often travelling overnight; local services are given where there is no alternative means of transport. For shorter journeys, however, trains are almost invariably quicker and often no more expensive.

Kanazawa to: Kyoto (5 daily; 3hr 50min); Matsumoto (2 daily; 4hr 50min); Nagoya (10 daily; 3hr); Niigata (2 daily; 4hr 40min); Ōsaka (2 daily; 3hr 40min); Sendai (daily; 8hr 30min); Takayama (2 daily; 3hr); Tokyo, Shinjuku (8 daily; 7hr 30min); Toyama (16 daily; 1hr 15min); Wajima (4 daily; 2hr).

Matsumoto to: Kanazawa (April–Nov 2 daily; 4hr 50min); Nagano (hourly; 1hr 20min); Ōsaka (2 daily; 6hr 50min); Takayama (4 daily; 2hr 30min); Tokyo (Shinjuku Station; hourly; 3hr 10min).

Nagano to: Hakuba (10 daily; 1hr); Matsumoto (hourly; 1hr 20min); Nozawa Onsen (5 daily; 1hr 15min); Togakushi (5 daily; 1hr 30min); Tokyo (hourly; 3hr 40min).

Nagoya to: Gujō Hachiman (2 daily; 2hr); Kanazawa (8 daily; 3hr); Kyoto (every 30min; 2hr 15min); Magome (daily; 2hr); Ogimachi (daily; 4hr); Ōsaka (2 daily; 3hr 20min); Takayama (9 daily; 2hr 45min); Tokyo (hourly; 6hr).

Takayama to: Gifu (4 daily; 2hr); Gujō Hachiman (11 daily; 1hr 10min); Kanazawa (2 daily; 2hr 15min); Kyoto (2 daily; 4hr); Matsumoto (4 daily; 2hr 20min); Nagoya (9 daily; 2hr 35min); Ogimachi (7 daily; 50min); Ōsaka (2 daily; 5hr); Tokyo (5 daily; 5hr 30min); Toyama (4 daily; 2hr 30min).

Toyama to: Kanazawa (16 daily; 1hr 15min); Nagoya (2–4 daily; 4hr 30min); Niigata (2 daily; 3hr 20min); Ōsaka (2 daily; 7hr 40min); Tokyo, Ikebukuro (4 daily; 6hr 30min).

Ferries

Nagoya to: Sendai (3–4 weekly; 21hr); Tomakomai (3–4 weekly; 38hr 45min).

Flights

Komatsu to: Fukuoka (2 daily; 1hr 15min); Izumo (6 weekly; 1hr 5min); Kagoshima (5 weekly; 1hr 40min); Naha (daily; 2hr 15min); Narita (daily; 1hr); Okayama (2 daily; 55min); Sapporo (daily; 1hr 35min); Sendai (daily; 1hr 5min); Tokyo (11 daily; 1hr).

Matsumoto to: Fukuoka (daily; 1hr 30min); Sapporo (daily; 1hr 30min).

Nagoya, Centrair to: Akita (daily; 1hr 10min); Aomori (2 daily; 1hr 20min); Asahikawa (daily; 1hr 40min); Fukuoka (hourly; 1hr 15min); Fukushima (daily; 1hr 5min); Hakodate (daily; 1hr 25min);

Kagoshima (8 daily; 1hr 20min); Kōchi (2 daily; 55min); Kumamoto (4 daily; 1hr 15min); Matsuyama (3 daily; 1hr 5min); Miyazaki (3 daily; 1hr 15imin); Nagasaki (2 daily; 1hr 20min); Narita (3 daily; 1hr); Niigata (3 daily; 55min); Ōita (2 daily; 1hr 10min); Okinawa (5 daily; 2hr 10min); Sapporo (12 daily; 1hr 35min); Sendai (5 daily; 1hr 5min); Takamatsu (2 daily; 1hr 5min); Tokushima (2 daily; 1hr); Toyama (2 daily; 55min); Yonago (2 daily; 1hr 10min).

Nagoya to: Akita (2 daily; 1hr 10min); Fukuoka (5 daily; 1hr 20min); Kōchi (2 daily; 1hr); Kumamoto (2 daily; 1hr 20min); Matsuyama (2 daily; 1hr); Nagasaki (2 daily; 1hr 25min); Niigata (2 daily; 50min); Tokachi-Obihiro (daily; 1hr 40min); Yamagata (daily; 1hr).

Toyama to: Fukuoka (daily; 1hr 20min); Hakodate (daily; 1hr 50min); Kansai International (daily; 1hr 15min); Nagoya (2 daily; 55min); Sapporo (daily; 1hr 20min); Tokyo (6 daily; 1hr 5min).

6

Kyoto & Nara

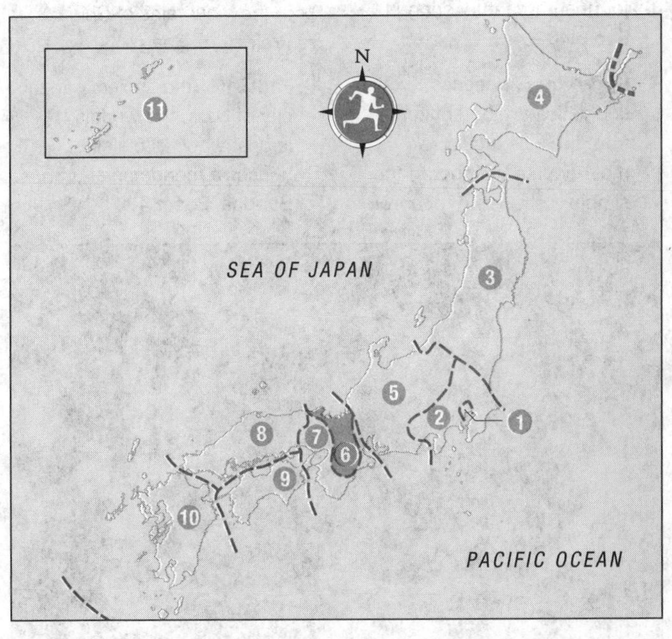

CHAPTER 6 Highlights

* **Kyoto International Manga Museum** Kyoto gets into "Cool Japan" with the first museum in the world devoted to Japanese comics. See p.419

* **Kinkaku-ji** Kyoto's most elaborate Zen temple, the Golden Pavilion, was built as a retirement home for a fourteenth-century shogun. See p.432

* **Kyō-ryōri** Experience Kyoto's sophisticated food culture from the ultimate *kaiseki* multi-course banquet to the simple pleasures of *obanzai* Kyoto home-style cooking. See p.436

* **Green tea** Visit the tea fields of Uji and later enjoy the sophisticated *macha* salons of Kyoto and a traditional tea ceremony. See p.440 & p.452

* **Miho Museum** Stunning art museum designed by I.M. Pei, in a dramatic setting deep in the mountains of Shiga Prefecture. See p.462

* **Tōdai-ji** In the ancient capital city of Nara, the world's largest wooden building houses a monumental bronze Buddha. See p.468

▲ International Manga Museum

6

Kyoto & Nara

The former imperial capitals of **KYOTO** and **NARA** are home to a sublime collection of temples, palaces, shrines and gardens. Both cities are deeply revered by the Japanese for their imperial history and renowned for their highly developed traditional arts and centuries-old festivals. Yet each has its own distinct personality. Kyoto is notoriously exclusive, whereas Nara has a more relaxed dignity; as a result, the two cities complement each other well – not least because in Nara you can see the foundations of traditional Japanese culture, which reached its zenith in Kyoto.

Until Emporer Meji decamped for the bright lights of Tokyo in 1868, **Kyoto** was Japan's imperial capital, and despite modern trappings the city still represents a more traditional version of the country than the current capital. Kyoto maintains its reputation for cultural finesse – with its cuisine and traditional arts and crafts – and continues to demonstrate its ability to fuse tradition with contemporary innovation. It's a delight to explore the exquisite **temples** and **gardens**, as well as contemporary designer shops and stylish cafés. It's also rewarding to spend at least a day in the surrounding districts; meander through rice fields in **Ohara**, tea fields in **Uji** or view the city from atop **Hiei-zan**, where the temples of Enryaku-ji are nestled in a cedar forest.

Before Kyoto even existed, the monks of **Nara** were busily erecting their great Buddhist monuments under the patronage of an earlier group of princes and nobles. In 2010, this relaxed, appealing town celebrated the thirteen-hundredth anniversary of **Heijō-kyō**, the site close to the centre of modern-day Nara city, where Japan's first permanent capital was founded in the early eighth century. A surprising number of buildings survive – notably the great **Tōdai-ji** with its colossal bronze Buddha – but Nara's real glory lies in its wealth of statues. Nowhere is this more evident than at the nearby temple complex of **Hōryū-ji**, a treasure-trove of early Japanese art.

Kyoto

The capital of Japan for more than a thousand years, **KYOTO** (京都) is endowed with an almost overwhelming legacy of ancient Buddhist temples, majestic palaces and gardens of every size and description, not to mention some of the country's most important works of art, its richest culture and most refined cuisine. For many people the very name Kyoto conjures up the classic image of Japan: streets of traditional wooden houses, the click-clack of *geta* (traditional wooden sandals) on the paving stones, geisha passing in a flourish of brightly coloured silks and temple pagodas surrounded by cherry blossom trees.

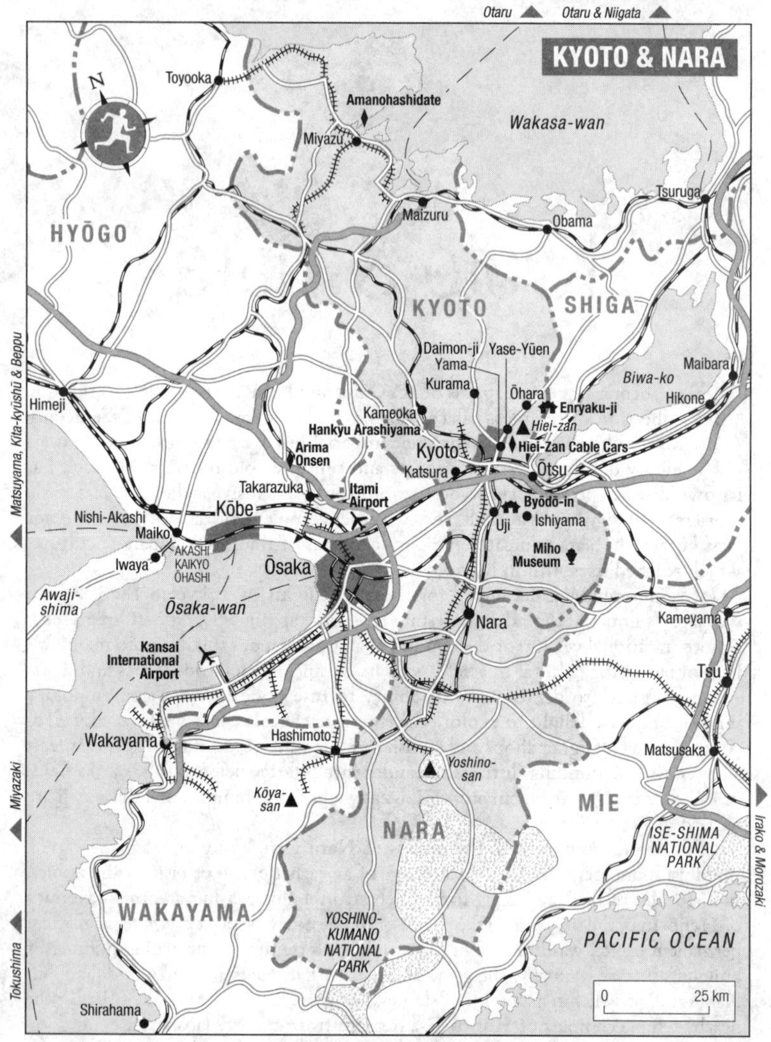

While you can still find all these things, and much more, first impressions of Kyoto can be disappointing. Decades of haphazard urban development and a conspicuous industrial sector have affected the city, eroding the distinctive characteristics of the townscape. However, current regulations limiting the height of new buildings and banning rooftop advertising indicate that more serious thought is being given to preserving Kyoto's visual environment. Yet, regardless of all the trappings of the modern world and the economic realities of the lingering recession, Kyoto remains notoriously exclusive, a place where outsiders struggle to peek through the centuries-thick layer of cultural sophistication into the city's traditional soul.

The vast amount of culture and history to explore in Kyoto is mind-boggling, yet it's perfectly possible to get a good feel for the city within a couple of days. Top

Applications to visit restricted sights

To visit some of Kyoto's most famous palaces and gardens it's necessary to apply in advance. Usually this is a simple procedure and well worth the effort. Tours of the **Imperial Palace**, **Sentō Gosho**, **Katsura Rikyū** and **Shūgaku-in Rikyū** are all handled by the **Imperial Household Agency** (IHA; Mon–Fri 8.45am–noon & 1–4pm; ⓣ075/211-1215, ⓦwww.kunaicho.go.jp). Their office is on the west side of the Imperial Park, near Imadegawa subway station. It's best to book your tour two days in advance, though it is possible to visit the Imperial Palace itself on the same day that you make a booking, provided that you get to the IHA at least half an hour in advance. You can apply online up to three months in advance. All tours are free and conducted in Japanese, with the exception of the Imperial Palace, where there are tours in English. Note that anyone under 20 years old (still a minor in Japanese law) has to be accompanied by an adult when visiting the Sentō Gosho, Katsura Rikyū or Shūgaku-in Rikyū. Don't forget to take your passport with you to the office and also for the tour itself.

Other sights in Kyoto that require reservations in advance are **Nijō-jin'ya** (see p.418) and **Saihō-ji** (see p.435).

priority should go to the eastern, Higashiyama, district, where the walk north from famous **Kiyomizu-dera** to **Ginkaku-ji** takes in a whole raft of fascinating temples, gardens and museums. It's also worth heading for the northwestern hills to contemplate the superb Zen gardens of **Daitoku-ji** and **Ryōan-ji**, before taking in the wildly extravagant Golden Pavilion, **Kinkaku-ji**. The highlight of the central sights is **Nijō-jō**, a lavishly decorated seventeenth-century palace, while nearby **Nijō-jin'ya** is an intriguing place riddled with secret passages and hidey-holes. Also worth seeing are the imperial villas of **Shūgaku-in Rikyū** and **Katsura Rikyū**, and the sensuous moss gardens of **Saihō-ji**, in the outer districts. Take time to walk around the city's old merchant quarters; one of the best is found in the **central district**, behind the department stores and modern shopping arcades north of **Shijō-dōri**, and across the river in **Gion** you'll find the traditional **crafts shops**, selling everything from handmade bamboo blinds to geisha hair accessories, and beautiful old **ryokan** for which the city is justifiably famous.

Spring and autumn are undoubtedly the **best times to visit** Kyoto, though also the busiest; after a chilly winter, the cherry trees put on their finery in early April, while the hot, oppressive summer months (June–Aug) are followed in October by a delightful period of clear, dry weather when the maple trees erupt into fiery reds.

Some history

Kyoto became the **imperial capital** in the late eighth century when Emperor Kammu relocated the court from Nara (see p.463). His first choice was Nagaoka, southwest of today's Kyoto, but a few inauspicious events led the emperor to move again in 794 AD. This time he settled on what was to be known as **Heian-kyō**, "Capital of Peace and Tranquillity". Like Nara, the city was modelled on the Chinese Tang-dynasty capital Chang'an (today's Xi'an), with a symmetrical north–south axis. By the late ninth century **Heian-kyō** was overflowing onto the eastern hills and soon had an estimated population of 500,000. In 894, imperial missions to China ceased and earlier borrowings from Chinese culture began to develop into distinct Japanese forms.

The city's history from this point is something of a rollercoaster ride. In the late twelfth century a fire practically destroyed the whole place, but two centuries later the **Ashikaga shoguns** built some of the city's finest monuments, among them the Golden and Silver Pavilions (Kinkaku-ji and Ginkaku-ji). Many of the great

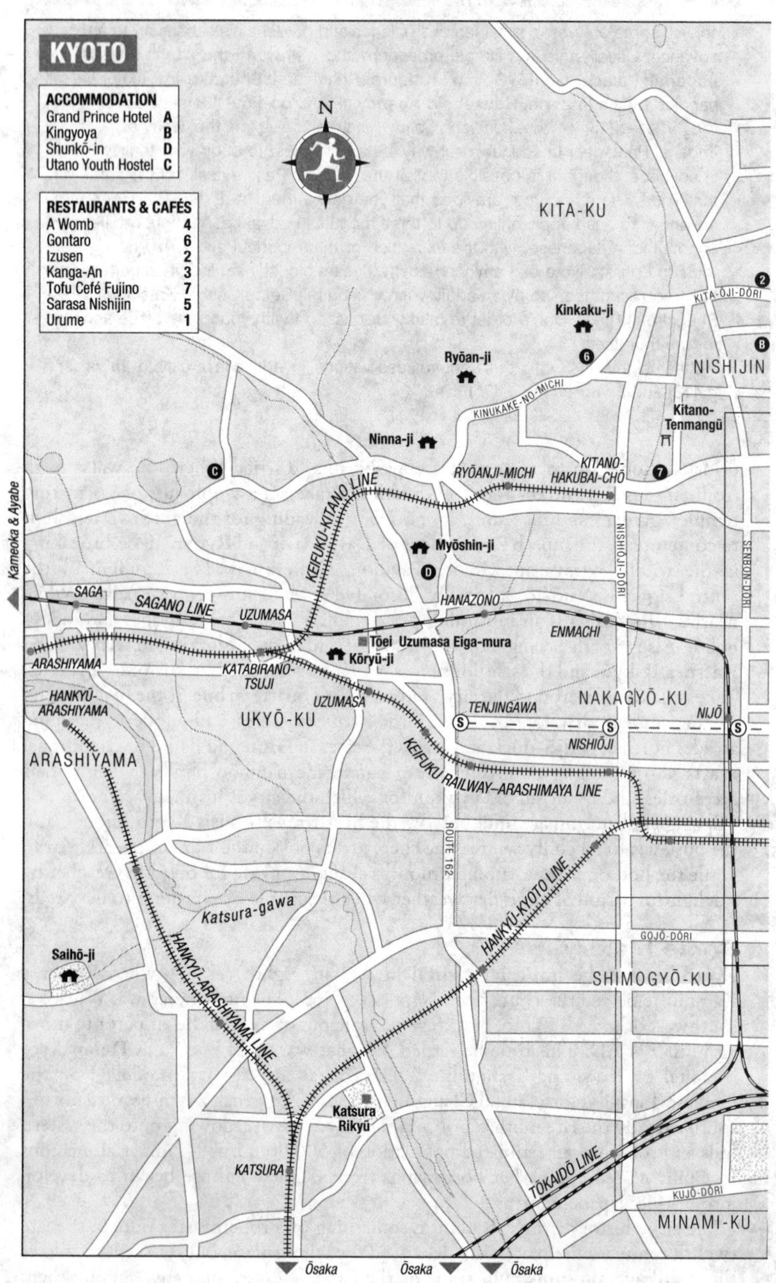
KYOTO
ACCOMMODATION
Grand Prince Hotel A
Kingyoya B
Shunkō-in D
Utano Youth Hostel C
RESTAURANTS & CAFÉS
A Womb 4
Gontaro 6
Izusen 2
Kanga-An 3
Tofu Cefé Fujino 7
Sarasa Nishijin 5
Urume 1
N
KITA-KU
KITA-ŌJI-DŌRI
Kinkaku-ji
Ryōan-ji
NISHIJIN
KINUKAKE-NO-MICHI
Kitano-Tenmangū
Ninna-ji
KITANO-HAKUBAI-CHŌ
RYŌANJI-MICHI
KEIFUKU-KITANO LINE
Kameoka & Ayabe
Myōshin-ji
NISHIŌJI-DŌRI
SENBON-DŌRI
SAGA
SAGANO LINE
UZUMASA
HANAZONO
ENMACHI
Tōei Uzumasa Eiga-mura
Kōryū-ji
ARASHIYAMA
KATABIRANO-TSUJI
HANKYŪ-ARASHIYAMA
UZUMASA
UKYŌ-KU
NAKAGYŌ-KU
TENJINGAWA
NIJŌ
NISHIŌJI
ARASHIYAMA
KEIFUKU RAILWAY–ARASHIMAYA LINE
ROUTE 162
HANKYŪ-KYOTO LINE
Katsura-gawa
GOJŌ-DŌRI
Saihō-ji
HANKYŪ-ARASHIYAMA LINE
SHIMOGYŌ-KU
Katsura Rikyū
KATSURA
TŌKAIDŌ LINE
KUJŌ-DŌRI
MINAMI-KU
Ōsaka
Ōsaka
Ōsaka

6 KYOTO & NARA

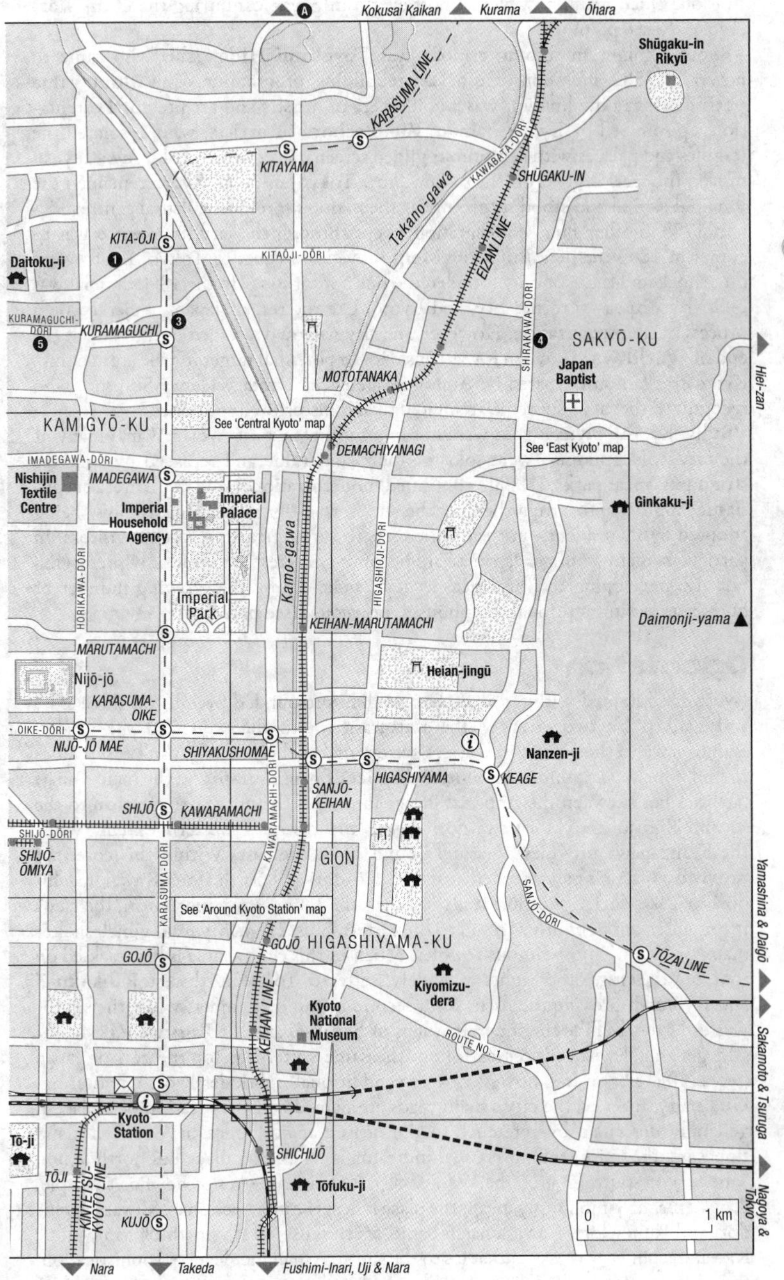

Kokusai Kaikan
Kurama
Ōhara
Shūgaku-in Rikyū
KARASUMA LINE
KITAYAMA
KAWABATA-DŌRI
SHŪGAKU-IN
Takano-gawa
EIZAN LINE
KITA-ŌJI
Daitoku-ji
KITAŌJI-DŌRI
KURAMAGUCHI-DŌRI
KURAMAGUCHI
SHIRAKAWA-DŌRI
SAKYŌ-KU
Hiei-zan
Japan Baptist
MOTOTANAKA
KAMIGYŌ-KU
See 'Central Kyoto' map
DEMACHIYANAGI
See 'East Kyoto' map
IMADEGAWA-DŌRI
Nishijin Textile Centre
IMADEGAWA
Imperial Palace
Imperial Household Agency
Ginkaku-ji
HIGASHIOJI-DŌRI
Kamo-gawa
HORIKAWA-DŌRI
Imperial Park
Daimonji-yama
KEIHAN-MARUTAMACHI
MARUTAMACHI
Nijō-jō
Heian-jingū
KARASUMA-OIKE
OIKE-DŌRI
NIJŌ-JŌ MAE
SHIYAKUSHOMAE
Nanzen-ji
HIGASHIYAMA
KEAGE
SANJŌ-KEIHAN
SHIJŌ
KAWARAMACHI
SHIJŌ-DŌRI
SHIJŌ-ŌMIYA
KAWARAMACHI-DŌRI
GION
KARASUMA-DŌRI
SANJŌ-DŌRI
Yamashina & Daigo
See 'Around Kyoto Station' map
GOJŌ
HIGASHIYAMA-KU
TŌZAI LINE
Kiyomizu-dera
KEIHAN LINE
Kyoto National Museum
ROUTE NO. 1
Sakamoto & Tsuruga
Kyoto Station
Tō-ji
SHICHIJŌ
TŌJI
KINTETSU-KYOTO LINE
Tōfuku-ji
Nagoya & Tokyo
KUJŌ
0
1 km
Nara
Takeda
Fushimi-Inari, Uji & Nara

Zen temples were established at this time and the arts reached new levels of sophistication. Once again, however, almost everything was lost during the **Ōnin Wars** (1467–78; see p.769).

Kyoto's knight in shining armour was **Toyotomi Hideyoshi**, who came to power in 1582 and sponsored a vast rebuilding programme. The **Momoyama period**, as it's now known, was a golden era of artistic and architectural ostentation, epitomized by Kyoto's famous **Kanō school of artists**, who decorated the temples and palaces with sumptuous gilded screens. Even when **Tokugawa Ieyasu** moved the seat of government to Edo (now Tokyo) in 1603, Kyoto remained the imperial capital and stood its ground as the nation's foremost cultural centre.

In 1788 another huge conflagration swept through the city, but worse was to come; in 1869 the new **Emperor Meiji** moved the court to Tokyo. Kyoto went into shock and the economy foundered – but not for long. In the 1890s a canal was built from Biwa-ko to the city, and Kyoto, like the rest of Japan, embarked on a process of industrialization. However, the city narrowly escaped devastation at the end of **World War II**, when it was considered a potential target for the atom bomb. Kyoto was famously spared by American Defence Secretary Henry Stimson, who recognized the city's supreme architectural and historical importance.

Sadly, Kyoto's own citizens were not so mindful and post-World War II many of the city's old buildings were sold for their land value and replaced by concrete structures or car parks. Despite continued modernization, however, a more enthusiastic approach to strengthening the city's traditional heritage is now being adopted by its residents, not least in efforts towards attracting foreign visitors. In particular, many younger Japanese are becoming interested in not only preserving but also developing this historical legacy, evidenced by the growing number of businesses set in traditional townhouses, or *machiya* (see p.428).

Orientation

Kyoto is contained within a wide basin valley surrounded by hills on three sides and flanked by two rivers – the Katsura-gawa to the west and the smaller Kamo-gawa to the east. A grid street system makes this one of Japan's easier cities to find your way around. The **central district** of banks, shops and the main tourist facilities lies between the Imperial Palace in the north and **Kyoto Station** to the south. Nijō-jō and Horikawa-dōri define the district's western extent, while the Kamo-gawa provides a natural boundary to the east. Within this core, the **downtown** area is concentrated around Shijō-dōri and north along Kawaramachi-dōri to Oike-dōri. Shijō-dōri leads east over the Kamo-gawa into **Gion**, the city's major entertainment district, and to the eastern hills, **Higashiyama**, which shelter many of Kyoto's most famous temples. Much of this central area is best tackled on foot, but the city's other sights are widely scattered. To the northwest, **Kinkaku-ji** and **Ryōan-ji** provide the focus for a second group of temples, while the southwestern suburbs hide the superb gardens of **Saihō-ji** and the **Katsura Rikyū**.

In general, Kyoto **addresses** follow the same pattern as for the rest of Japan (see p.40). There are, however, a few additional subtleties worth mastering. Unusually, most of the city's main roads are named and the location of a place is generally described by reference to the nearest major junction. Since the land slopes gently south, the most usual indicator is whether a place lies north (*agaru*, "above") or south (*sagaru*, "below") of a particular east–west road. For example, Kawaramachi Sanjō simply means the place is near the intersection of Kawaramachi-dōri and Sanjō-dōri; Kawaramachi Sanjō-agaru tells you it's north of Sanjō-dōri; Kawaramachi Sanjō-sagaru, that it's to the south. At a higher level of sophistication, the address might also indicate whether a place lies east (*higashi*) or west (*nishi*) of the north–south road.

Arrival

Most visitors arrive at the impressive **Kyoto Station**. The city is linked by Shinkansen to Tokyo and Nagoya to the east and Ōsaka, Hiroshima and Fukuoka to the west. If you're coming direct from **Kansai International airport** (see p.483), the quickest and easiest option is a JR Haruka Limited Express train, which whisks you direct to Kyoto in just over an hour (¥3490 reserved, ¥2980 unreserved); JR rail passes are valid on this service for unreserved seats. For those not travelling with a JR rail pass, a cheaper option is to take an express from the airport as far as Ōsaka Station, changing there to an express train on the JR Kyoto line. This method takes a little under two hours and costs about ¥1600. Alternatively, comfortable **airport limousine** buses do the journey in under two hours, traffic permitting, terminating on the south (Hachijō-guchi) side of Kyoto Station (1–2 hourly 6am–8pm; ¥2300). Limousine buses also run direct from Ōsaka's **Itami airport** to Kyoto Station (every 30min 6am–7.30pm; 55min; ¥1280), from where local buses and a two-line subway system fan out to all destinations around the city.

Information

The station area is home to Kyoto's main information service, the **Kyoto Tourist Information Centre** (daily 8.30am–7pm; ⓣ075/343-6655), on the second floor of the station building next to the main entrance of Isetan department store. Closer to the city centre, near Nanzen-ji, **Kyoto International Community House** (9am–9pm; closed Mon; ⓣ075/752-3010, ⓦwww.kcif.or.jp) is aimed primarily at foreign students and longer-term residents, but will happily assist tourists where possible. Detailed bilingual maps of Kyoto are available free from Seven-Eleven stores and *Starbucks* city-wide.

The free monthly tourist magazine, *Kyoto Visitor's Guide* (ⓦwww.kyotoguide.com), is the best source of information regarding **what's on** in Kyoto and also has useful maps for sightseeing. It includes details of festivals and cultural events; you can usually pick it up in tourist information offices, major hotels and other tourist haunts. The free monthly *Kansai Scene* magazine also has a good listings section, with the latest on Kyoto clubs.

There are excellent **online resources** for Kyoto too. For general travel, cultural, accommodation, eating and shopping information, try Kyoto Travel Guide

Moving on from Kyoto

If you're heading from Kyoto direct **to Kansai International airport**, it's a good idea to reserve your transport in advance. Limousine buses depart (hourly 6am–8pm; 1hr 45min; ¥2300; ⓣ075/682-4400) from outside the *New Miyako Hotel* and the Avanti department store, both on the south side of Kyoto Station; tickets are available from the ground floor of the nearby *Keihan Hotel*. You can buy tickets at ordinary JR ticket offices for JR's Haruka Limited Express trains. Anther option for getting to the airport is to take a "door-to-door" taxi shuttle bus (¥3500): the MK Skygate shuttle (ⓣ075/702-5849, ⓦwww.mk-group.co.jp) or the Yasaka Kansai Airport Shuttle (ⓣ075/803-4800, ⓦwww.yasaka.jp/taxi/shuttle-e/). The ride time varies, depending on the traffic, but will be calculated to get you there on time for check-in.

Long-distance **buses** depart from terminals either side of Kyoto Station. JR Highway buses and other services to Tokyo, Nagoya and Kanazawa depart from a stand on the north side of the station, while Keihan Bus uses a terminal on the south side, outside the *Keihan Hotel*. Keihan services cover Nagasaki, Kumamoto, Fukuoka, Tokyo and Kanazawa.

(Ⓦ www.kyoto.travel), Kyoto Kyoto (Ⓦ www.kyotokyoto.jp) or Eat Drink Kyoto (Ⓦ www.eatdrink-kyoto.com). Art See Kyoto (Ⓦ www.artsee-kyoto.com) is the only English guide to the city's art museums, commercial galleries and shops, while Deep Kyoto (Ⓦ www.deepkyoto.com) is an expat blog covering the author's favourite people and places.

City transport

Kyoto's two **subway** lines are the quickest way to scoot around the city, but often walking is the best way to explore if you don't want to utilize the bus network, which can get very congested during spring and autumn's peak visitor seasons. **Taxis** are useful for hopping short distances; the minimum fare is ¥580 for 2km. Renting a **bike** is a viable option for exploring central Kyoto, though not much use along the eastern hills, where you're better off walking; see p.448 for rental information.

Subway

Kyoto's subway (5.30am–11.30pm; ¥210–340) consists of two lines. The **Karasuma line** runs from southerly Takeda, via Kyoto Station and Kita-ōji, to Kokusai Kaikan in the north, while the **Tōzai line** starts at Tenjingawa in the west and cuts east through Sanjō-Keihan and Higashiyama to Daigō in the southeast suburbs; the two lines intersect at Karasuma-Oike Station. As well as single tickets, you can also buy stored-fare cards (*Torafika Kyō Kādo*) for ¥1000 or ¥3000, which you can use to buy subway tickets and on City Bus services. This card is available from the Kyoto Bus Information Center in front of Kyoto Station, as well as from train and subway stations and from bus drivers. Another option is the Surutto Kansai Miyako Card, which can be used on city buses, the subway, and the Keihan and Hankyū train lines; it's available in ¥1000, ¥2000, ¥3000 and ¥5000 denominations from large hotels and tourist and bus information centres. If you are planning day-trips from Kyoto to other parts of Kansai, the Kansai Thru Pass (¥3800/two days, ¥5000/three days) is a good option as it allows you to use almost any bus, subway or private railway in the whole of the region.

Trains

Several private railways also operate within the city. Trains on **Hankyū railway**'s Kyoto line for Ōsaka (Umeda) run beneath the city centre from Kawaramachi

Jinrikisha

Jinrikisha (人力車), which means "man-powered vehicle", were a common form of transportation in Kyoto from the 1880s until the early twentieth century, when it became more fashionable to use bicycles, automobiles and street trams. A local company is now producing two-seater Meiji-period-style *jinrikisha*, and has revived this more environmentally friendly form of transportation for tourists. Strapping, sun-tanned lads, and occasionally a few young women, pull *jinrikisha* around Kyoto's main tourist areas. It's a fun way to see the sites and to discover a few hidden spots in any season – they all have hoods to protect passengers from sun and rain. There are *jinrikisha* stations in front of Heian-jingu, near Nanzen-ji and at Arashiyama on the northwest side of Togetsu-kyo bridge, covering three routes: Kiyomizu-dera to Yasaka-jinja, Heian-jingū to Ginkaku-ji and around Arashiyama. Tours last from ten minutes (¥2000 for one, ¥3000 for two) to an hour (¥9000 for one, ¥15,000 for two), depending on the route and whether you want to stop and take photos. Some of the *jinrikisha* pullers speak English and will be able to give you a commentary on the sights. *Jinrikisha* are available every day from 10am until sunset (Kyoto ⓣ075/533-0444, Arashiyama ⓣ075/868-4444).

Station west along Shijō-dōri; a branch line heads northwest from Katsura Station in west Kyoto to Arashiyama (see p.449). Arashiyama is also served by the **Keifuku Railway** from Shijō-Ōmiya Station, with another branch line (the Kitano Line) looping north. In northeast Kyoto, Demachiyanagi is the terminus for the **Eizan line**, which covers Shūgaku-in Rikyū and Yase-yūen, one of the routes up Hiei-zan (see p.454). **Keihan mainline services** start from a separate station in Demachiyanagi and then head south via Sanjō-Keihan to Ōsaka (Yodoyabashi). Finally, trains on the **Kintetsu-Kyoto line** depart from the south side of Kyoto Station, from where they link into the main Kintetsu network, with services to Nara, Kōya-san and Ise.

Buses

Kyoto's excellent **bus system** is relatively easy to use. The buses are colour-coded, the majority show their route numbers on the front and the most important stops are announced in English, either on the electronic display or over the internal speakers. Within the city there's a flat fare of ¥220, which you pay on exit. You enter via the back door, where you may need to take a numbered ticket if the bus is going into the suburbs, though the flat fare still applies within the central zone. Most services stop running around 11pm, or earlier on less popular routes.

Before leaping on board, get hold of the English-language route map from the information office (see p.409) or the bus terminals. This shows the central zone boundary and routes operated by both **Kyoto City Bus** (light green with a darker stripe) and the far less comprehensive **Kyoto Bus** (cream with a red stripe). You'll need to use Kyoto Bus services for Ōhara and Arashiyama, but otherwise you can stick to City Bus for the central districts. The **main bus terminal** is outside Kyoto Station's Karasuma exit. Most routes loop around the city; the most useful is #206, with stops near the National Museum, Gion, Heian-jingū, Daitoku-ji and Nijō-jō. Buses running clockwise leave from stand B-4, anticlockwise from A-2. The other major terminals are at **Sanjō-Keihan**, in east Kyoto, and **Kita-ōji** in the north.

The **Raku bus routes** are ideal if you want to cover a lot of the sights in a short amount of time. These are tourist buses that stop at major sightseeing spots and have English-language commentary. All Raku routes start from Kyoto Station; Raku #100 travels up the east side of Kyoto from Kiyomizu-dera to Ginkakuji, Raku #101 towards Nijo and then Kinkakuji, and Raku #102 goes towards Ginkakuji and then across to Kinkakuji. The buses only operate from 9am to 5pm, and while the #100 buses run every ten minutes, the #101 and #102 only run once an hour. You can use any of the prepaid card systems on the Raku buses or it's ¥220 per ride.There is also a central area ¥100 bus service at the weekend and on national holidays. This one-direction-only, circular bus route runs in a loop from Kyoto City Hall to Karasuma Oike, Shijō Karasuma and Shijō Kawaramachi before heading back to Kyoto City Hall (every 10min 11am–5.50pm). Buses are easy to spot as they have "¥100" written on the side in big letters.

Discount bus tickets and subway-bus passes

The bus companies offer a range of **discount tickets**. The simplest, *kaisūken*, are booklets of five ¥220 tickets available at a small reduction at the bus terminals for ¥1000, valid on all buses. Next up are the one-day passes (*shi-basu ichi-nichi jyōshaken*; ¥500), which allow unlimited travel on City Bus services within the central zone; available at information centres, hotels, bus terminals and from the bus driver. To validate the pass, put it through the machine beside the driver when you get off the first bus – after that, just show it as you exit. Finally, there are combined subway and bus passes, either one-day (*shi-basu chikatetsu ichi-nichi*

City tours

Kyoto is best appreciated at a leisurely pace, and there is a variety of tours that can show you different aspects of the city. **Johnnie Hillwalker** (otherwise known as Hirōka Hajime), a veteran English-speaking tour guide, takes small groups on a slow amble through southern Kyoto from Higashi-Hongan-ji to Kiyomizu-dera, starting at 10am and finishing mid-afternoon (March–Nov Mon, Wed & Fri, except national holidays; ¥2000/person; ⓣ075/622-6803, ⓦweb.kyoto-inet.or.jp/people/h-s-love).

Long-term resident **Peter Macintosh** offers Geisha Walking Lectures, a ninety-minute stroll through the Gion and Miyagawa-chō districts that provides a chance to see where geisha live, study and entertain, alongside Macintosh's entertaining personal anecdotes. Geisha parties, where you have the chance to meet a *maiko* or geisha in person, can be arranged by Macintosh after the tour; check the website for details (¥3000/person; call from noon–3pm to reserve; ⓣ090/5169-1654, ⓦwww.kyotosightsandnights.com). Another long-term resident, **Mark Hovane**, specializes in small, group visits to Kyoto's more secluded and difficult to access traditional gardens (Fri–Sun; half day ¥25,000, full day ¥40,000; ⓦkyotogardentours.com).

If you'd rather travel around on two wheels, the **Kyoto Cycling Tour Project** (ⓣ075/354-3636, ⓦwww.kctp.net) offers daily guided English tours of Kyoto's backstreets and hidden alleyways (¥3800/person for groups of four), as well as a home-cooking tour, where you shop for ingredients in Nishiki food market and learn to cook in a *machiya* (¥8400/person for groups of four). The cost includes bicycle rental and any admission fees. Reservations must be made three days in advance.

jyōshaken; ¥1200) or two-day (*shi-basu chikatetsu futsuka jyōshaken*; ¥2000), covering unlimited travel on the subways, City Bus and Kyoto Bus within a wider area marked on the bus maps in white. They're sold at hotels, tourist information offices, bus terminals, subway information windows or travel agents.

Accommodation

Kyoto's **accommodation** options range from basic guesthouses, youth hostels and temple lodgings (*shukubō*) to luxurious international hotels and top-class **ryokan**. One night in a full-blown Kyoto **ryokan**, enjoying the world's most meticulous service, is an experience not to be missed. The ongoing recession has made many establishments that were previously difficult to access more affordable and welcoming to international guests. Recently, a number of old Kyoto houses (*machiya*) have been developed into guesthouses, offering visitors the chance to experience traditional Kyoto life. It's essential to make **reservations** at these places as far in advance as possible, but all accommodation in Kyoto gets pretty busy during spring and autumn, at holiday weekends and around the major festivals (see p.442); room rates may rise considerably during these times.

Central Kyoto

Central Kyoto is obviously a popular choice, with its easy access to the main shopping and nightlife districts as well as good transport links to sights around the city. The following listings are marked on the map on p.416.

First Cabin ファーストキャビン 4F 331 Kamiyanagi-chō ⓣ075/361-1113, ⓦwww.first-cabin.jp. Newly opened capsule hotel, for both men and women, close to Karasuma-Shijō, with a first-class air travel theme. Cabins are bigger than the business capsules and all have their own TV and internet connections. Excellent bath and café/bar facilities. ❷

Hotel Gimmond Takakura Oike, Nakagyō-ku ⓣ075/221-4111, ⓦwww.gimmond.co.jp/kyoto.

Elegant mid-range hotel with pleasant, though slightly pokey, rooms and smart in-house Japanese and Italian restaurants. ❺

Hiiragiya 柊家旅館 Fuyachō Anekoji-agaru ⓣ075/221-1136, ⓦwww.hiiragiya.co.jp. One of the city's most famous ryokan, since the mid-nineteenth century it has hosted the rich and famous, including Elizabeth Taylor, Charlie Chaplin and Mishima Yukio. You need to book well in advance, but it's worth it for a quintessential Kyoto experience. ❾, or ❻ for slightly less grand accommodation in the annexe (without meals).

Kyoto Brighton Hotel 京都ブライトンホテル Shinmachi Nakadachiuri-dōri ⓣ075/441-4411, ⓦwww.kyotobrighton.com. Top-end hotel a stone's throw from the Imperial Palace. The lobby and rooms are decorated in a style reminiscent of the 1980s, but even standard rooms have a lounge area that gives the impression of being in a suite. ❼

Kyoto Hotel Okura ホテルオークラ Kawaramachi-Oike ⓣ075/211-5111, ⓦokura.kyotohotel.co.jp. Offers an elegant mix of European and Japanese style. Rooms are of a good size and offer great views of the city. Facilities include a fitness centre and swimming pool. ❽

Kyoto Townhouse Stays 庵京町家スティ ⓣ075/352-0211, ⓦwww.kyoto-machiya.com; check website for various locations. Conceptualized by *Lost Japan* author Alex Kerr (see p.811), this collection of restored *machiya* (see p.428) offers visitors the chance to stay in ten unique properties each decorated with antiques from Kerr's personal collection. They vary in character and size, making them a good option for groups as large as fourteen; some even have tearooms and small gardens. Prices start from ¥6000–41,000 per night per person depending on group size.

Mitsui Garden Hotel Kyoto Sanjō 三井ガーデンホテル京都三条 80 Mikura-chō, Sanjō Karasuma Nishi-iru, Nakagyō-ku ⓣ075/256-3331, ⓦwww.gardenhotels.co.jp. Conveniently located very close to Karasuma-Oike shopping area, this superior mid-range hotel is surprisingly good value (especially off-peak when prices drop sharply). There's free internet access in the hotel lobby. ❹

Hotel Monterey ホテルモントレ京都 Karasuma Sanjō-sagaru ⓣ075/251-7111, ⓦwww.hotelmonterey.co.jp/kyoto. This conveniently located hotel has a stylish, classic European interior, Japanese and French restaurants and a "British Library" themed café. ❼

9h Nine Hours ナインアワーズ Teramachi-dōri Shijō-sagaru ⓣ075/353-9005, ⓦ9hours.jp. The design of this newly opened capsule hotel is minimalist bordering on sci-fi, and the capsules are actually quite spacious sleeping pods. After check-in, female and male guests take separate elevators to pods and shower rooms. Impeccably clean and comfortable. ❷

Palace-Side Hotel ザ・パレスサイドホテル Shimodachiuri Karasuma, Kamigyō-ku ⓣ075/415-8887, ⓦwww.palacesidehotel.co.jp. Large hotel overlooking the Imperial Palace, with good views from the higher, more expensive rooms. Excellent value for the location and substantial discounts if you stay six days or more. Three minutes north of Marutamachi subway station. ❹

Yoshikawa Ryokan 吉川旅館 Tominokoji Oike-sagaru, Nakagyō-ku ⓣ075/221-5544, ⓦwww.kyoto-yoshikawa.co.jp. Intimate, traditional inn that's renowned for its tempura *kaiseki* cuisine. Cypress-wood bath, immaculate garden and all the understated luxury you could want, including two meals. ❽

Around the station

The **station area** is less picturesque than other parts of Kyoto but undoubtedly convenient, with an abundance of inexpensive accommodation options. The following listings are marked on the map on p.420.

Capsule Ryokan カプセル旅館京都 204 Tsuchihashi-chō ⓣ075/344-1510, ⓦwww.capsule-ryokan-kyoto.com. Newly opened modern-style ryokan with the world's first tatami capsules with futon (¥3500), and en-suite rooms for two. Free internet, security lockers and kitchen. Run by the same friendly team who run Tour Club (see below). ❹

Hotel Granvia Kyoto ホテルグランヴィア京都 657 Higashi-Shiokoji-chō ⓣ075/344-8888, ⓦwww.granvia-kyoto.co.jp/e/index.html. Sleek hotel incorporated into the Kyoto Station building, with rooms on the upper floors. Facilities include a good range of restaurants and bars, indoor swimming pool, boutiques and business suites. Excellent value in this price range. ❻

Hana Hostel 花宿 51-2 Nakagoryō-chō ⓣ075/371-2282, ⓦkyoto.hanahostel.com. Newly opened "hybrid" hostel that aims for a budget ryokan style. Bunk bed dorm rooms (¥2500/person) and single (❷) and double tatami rooms which are slightly more expensive with en suite. ❸

J-Hoppers ジェイホッパーズ 51-2 Nakagoryō-chō ⓣ075/681-2282, ⓦkyoto.j-hoppers.com. Clean and well-organized backpackers' hostel with dorm beds (¥2500/person) and private rooms (❸), plus bike rental, internet access, laundry facilities and satellite TV.

New Hankyū Hotel 新阪急ホテル JR Kyoto-eki-mae ⓣ075/343-5300, ⓦwww.newhankyu.co.jp/kyoto-e. Large, recently refurbished hotel conveniently located opposite Kyoto station offering comfortable rooms and efficient service. Non-smoking rooms and a women-only floor are available. There are five in-house restaurants including one specializing in Kōbe beef. 7

Tour Club ツアークラブ 362 Momiji-chō ⓣ075/353-6968, ⓦwww.kyotojp.com. Popular backpacker hostel with a solid reputation. Conveniently located and a great source for sightseeing information. Dorms (¥2450/person) and en-suite double, twin and triple rooms are available. Facilities include a Japanese-style communal living room, internet access, coin laundry, showers, money-changing facilities, the chance to try on a kimono and very reasonable bicycle rentals. Rates get cheaper the longer you stay. 3

East Kyoto

Many places in **eastern Kyoto** are within walking distance of Gion and the city centre, while also being in quieter, more attractive surroundings. The following listings are marked on the map on p.423.

B&B Juno Imadegawa Kita-shirakawa nishi-iru ⓦwww.gotokandk.com/casa. Close to the Philosopher's Path area, this friendly guesthouse is in a stately old home and has traditional-style rooms with futon and shared facilities. Full breakfast included. Free wi-fi with your own PC. Reservations by internet only. 3

Gion Hatanaka 祇園畑中 Yasaka-jinja Minamimon-mae ⓣ075/551-0553, ⓦwww.thehatanaka.co.jp. Elegant ryokan in a fabulous location with spacious rooms. Effortlessly blends traditional service with modern style. Don't miss their Kyoto cuisine and *maiko* evening (See p.443). 8

Hyatt Regency Kyoto ハイアットリージェンシー京都 ⓣ075/541-1234, ⓦkyoto.regency.hyatt.com. Right next to Sanjūsangen-dō, this is Kyoto's top modern luxury hotel with an emphasis on contemporary Japanese style. Guest-room interiors are sleekly decorated with traditional Kyoto fabrics. There are three in-house restaurants to choose from and the spa specializes in traditional Japanese therapies. 8

Kiyomizu Sansō 清水山荘 3-341 Kiyomizu ⓣ075/551-3152, ⓦwww.kyo-yado.com/kiyomizu-sansou/english.html. There are only four rooms in this friendly and comfortable hundred-year-old family inn, hidden down an alley off the Sannen-zaka pedestrian street. Meals are optional, but excellent value. Reservations essential. 5

Waraku-An 和楽庵 19-2 Sannō-cho ⓣ075/771-5575, ⓦgh-project.com. Nicely restored *machiya* (see p.428) guesthouse, conveniently located to the northwest of Heian-jingū. All rooms are traditional style and have shared bath and no a/c. The deluxe room next to the garden is recommended for its pleasant outlook and can sleep up to four. Dorm beds ¥2500/person. 3

Westin Miyako Hotel ウェスティン都ホテル Sanjō Keage ⓣ075/771-7111, ⓦwww.westinmiyako-kyoto.com. Huge, efficient, top-class hotel complete with landscaped gardens, bird sanctuary and a range of restaurants. There's a choice of elegant Japanese-style rooms, some in the garden annexe, or Western-style accommodation, where higher rates get you balconies with views over the city. Free shuttle buses operate between the hotel, Sanjō-dōri and Kyoto Station. 7

Yoshida Sansō 吉田山荘 59-1 Shimo Ōji-chō ⓣ075/771-6125, ⓦwww.yoshidasanso.com. Located on Mt Yoshida, this high-class ryokan is the former second residence of the current emperor's uncle. With such imperial associations, don't be surprised if your room has an historical connection, if not a lovely garden view. *Kaiseki* cuisine is served and there's also an in-house tea salon. 8

North and northwest Kyoto

It's also worth considering one or two nights in **northern** Kyoto to explore the region around Kinkaku-ji and west to Arashiyama. The following listings are marked on the map on pp.406–407.

Grand Prince Hotel Kyoto グランドプリンスホテル Takaragaike ⓣ075/712-1111, ⓦwww.princehotels.com/en/kyoto. This is one of the city's oldest top-class Western-style hotels – and certainly the only one shaped like a doughnut. Rooms are large, the service is efficient and surroundings are pleasantly green and relaxing, but the location is not so convenient for exploring the city. ⑧

Kingyoya 金魚家 243 Kanki-chō ⓣ075/411-1128, ⓦkingyoya-kyoto.com. Small and friendly guesthouse in a tastefully restored *machiya* located in the heart of Nishijin, the weaving district. Dorm rooms (¥2500/person) and private rooms have traditional interiors. Dinner and breakfast are also served. ③

Shunkō-in 春光院 42 Myōshinji-chō ⓣ075/462-5488, ⓦwww.shunkoin.com. Welcoming and peaceful temple lodging in the atmospheric Myōshinji complex, run by a young American-educated Zen scholar. Some rooms have private bath and rates include a temple tour and a Zen meditation session. ④

Utano Youth Hostel 宇多野ユースホステル 29 Nakayama-chō, Uzumasa, Ukyō-ku ⓣ075/462-2288, ⓦyh-kyoto.or.jp/utano. Recently renovated and award-winning hostel with a good atmosphere and helpful, English-speaking staff. Set in its own grounds on Kyoto's western outskirts, it has an excellent range of facilities. Dorm rooms (¥3300/person) are comfortable and there are also Japanese and Western-style private rooms. ④

The City

The spirit of old Kyoto reveals itself in surprising places. The key to enjoying this ancient city is to leave the tourist haunts behind and delve into the **quiet backstreets**, to explore **age-old craft shops** and distinctive *machiya* houses (see p.428) or seek out the peaceful garden of some forgotten temple. However, the city is not all temples and tradition; the recently opened **Kyoto International Museum of Manga**, alongside the increasing number of innovative **designer shops** and **stylish cafés**, are examples of Kyoto's modern spirit, showing how the city manages to combine its heritage with contemporary culture.

The account below starts in central Kyoto and then heads south to the station before crossing east over the Kamo-gawa to work anticlockwise around the outer districts. Much of the city centre and the eastern hills can be covered on foot, but you'll need to hop on a few trains and buses to explore the more scattered sights to the north and west.

Central Kyoto

Before the emperor moved to Tokyo in 1868, Kyoto's **Imperial Palace** symbolized the nation's physical and spiritual centre. Today's palace is by no means a high priority among Kyoto's wealth of sights, but it's a good idea to come here early in your stay to make arrangements for visiting the city's more rewarding imperial villas and gardens (see p.405). The **Sentō Gosho** garden, also in the Imperial Park, is worth seeing, and it's not far from here to **Nijō-jō**'s magnificent screen paintings and the intriguing **Nijō-jin'ya**.

The Imperial Park and Palace

Dun-coloured earth walls enclose the **Imperial Park**, inside which wide expanses of gravel and clipped lawns have replaced most of the former palaces and subsidiary buildings. In the park's northwest corner, the **Imperial Household Agency** handles applications to visit the former royal palaces (see p.405); the nearest subway station is Imadegawa, or you can take a bus to Karasuma Imadegawa. As long as you arrive thirty minutes in advance, it's usually possible to sign up for the next tour of the nearby **Imperial Palace**, or *Kyōto Gosho* (京都御所; English tours Mon–Fri 10am & 2pm; free). The tour lasts around one hour and is quite detailed, though it's still worth investing in the English-language guidebook (¥200) for the photos of some of the interior sections that you won't be able to access. The palace originally stood about 2km further west, at Nijō-jō, but was relocated to its present site in the late twelfth century. However, nearly all of the buildings date from the mid-nineteenth century and the overwhelming impression is rather monotonous – wide spaces of pure white gravel, set against austere Meiji-period

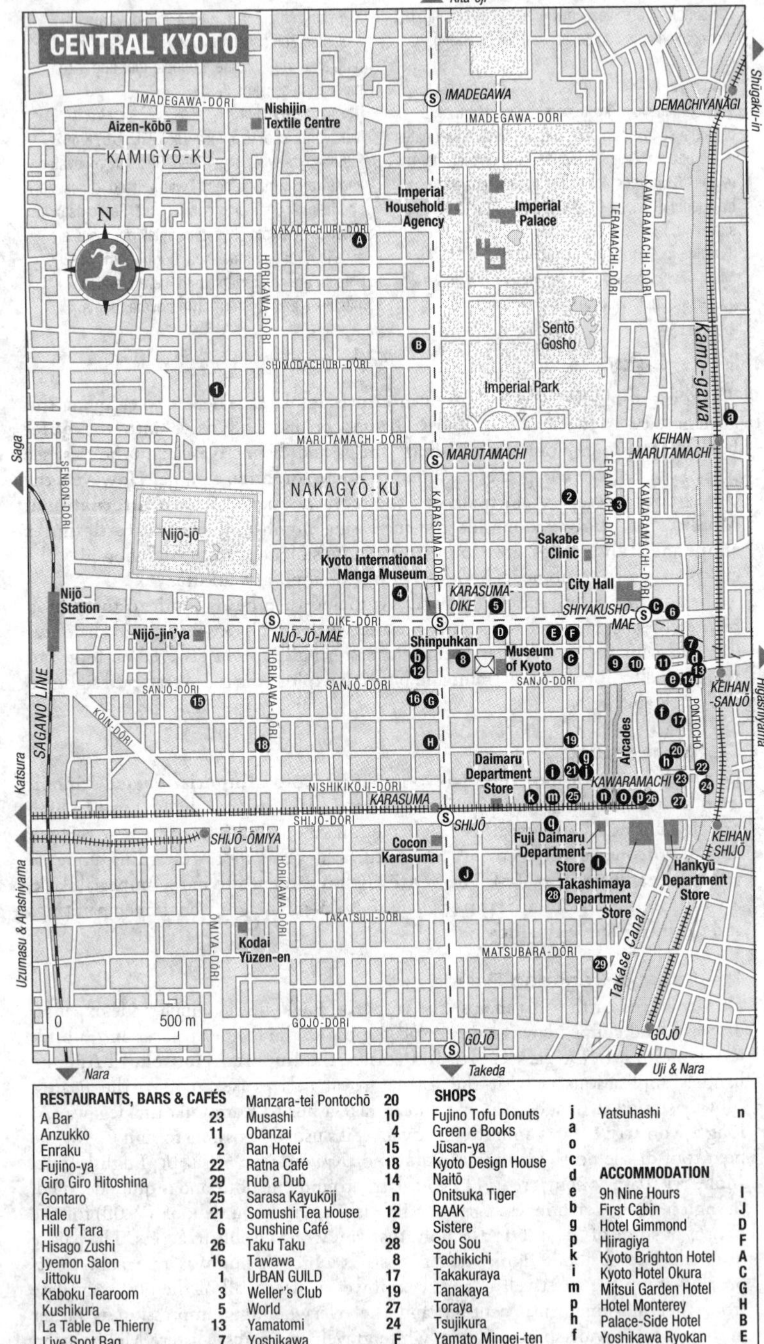

RESTAURANTS, BARS & CAFÉS

A Bar	23
Anzukko	11
Enraku	2
Fujino-ya	22
Giro Giro Hitoshina	29
Gontaro	25
Hale	21
Hill of Tara	6
Hisago Zushi	26
Iyemon Salon	16
Jittoku	1
Kaboku Tearoom	3
Kushikura	5
La Table De Thierry	13
Live Spot Rag	7
Manzara-tei Pontochō	20
Musashi	10
Obanzai	4
Ran Hotei	15
Ratna Café	18
Rub a Dub	14
Sarasa Kayukōji	n
Somushi Tea House	12
Sunshine Café	9
Taku Taku	28
Tawawa	8
UrBAN GUILD	17
Weller's Club	19
World	27
Yamatomi	24
Yoshikawa	F

SHOPS

Fujino Tofu Donuts	j
Green e Books	a
Jūsan-ya	o
Kyoto Design House	c
Naitō	d
Onitsuka Tiger	e
RAAK	b
Sistere	g
Sou Sou	p
Tachikichi	k
Takakuraya	i
Tanakaya	m
Toraya	p
Tsujikura	h
Yamato Mingei-ten	f
Yatsuhashi	n

ACCOMMODATION

9h Nine Hours	I
First Cabin	J
Hotel Gimmond	D
Hiiragiya	F
Kyoto Brighton Hotel	A
Kyoto Hotel Okura	C
Mitsui Garden Hotel	G
Hotel Monterey	H
Palace-Side Hotel	B
Yoshikawa Ryokan	E

The Kamo-gawa

Used for hundreds of years for rinsing out kimono fabric that had been dyed using the *kyō-yūzen* hand-dyeing technique, it's no surprise that by the early 1990s the **Kamo-gawa** (鴨川), which runs through central Kyoto, was polluted. However, at the end of the decade the city government undertook a rejuvenation programme and now all 35 kilometres of the river and its surroundings have become home to an abundance of bird and plant life.

At weekends, Kyoto's inhabitants flock to the banks of the Kamo-gawa for sport and relaxation, such as t'ai chi and barbecues. It's a great place to stretch out and do some people-watching, or sit on a *yuka* (wooden platforms that extend out from the restaurants of Pontochō) and enjoy *kyō-ryōri* cuisine. The **4.5km route** below will take you along part of the river from Shijō bridge, in the south, and up to Takano bridge, in the north, in around two hours, including refreshment stops.

A good place to start your walk is at **Shijō bridge**, where from late spring the western bank of the Kamo-gawa, up until just north of **Ōike bridge**, is covered with *yuka*, a perfect spot for catching cooling river breezes during the humid summers. Three hundred metres north of here, the **Sanjō bridge** area is very popular at weekends with young people, and you can often see buskers performing to large crowds.

Proceeding north, at **Marutamachi bridge**, *Rue Ergo Café* (daily 10.30am–7.30pm) has a pleasant outdoor seating area and good coffee. As you continue up the western bank, listen out for the cacophony of Kyoto University music students practising everything from trombones to electric guitars on the river banks. A little further on, large turtle-shaped stepping stones stretch across the river at **Kōjin bridge** – this is a good place to cross or even sit for a while. Between here and Imadegawa, there are tennis courts, and other sports areas.

The river splits into two at **Imadegawa bridge**, where there is a large picnic and barbecue area, a good place to bring a bentō and enjoy the view of the eastern hills. Near here, on the west bank, is *Al Sole Café* (daily noon–10pm), which has a semi-open terrace and good-value pasta lunch sets (¥800). The left fork of the river continues up to Kyoto's **Botanical Gardens** and more picnicking and sports areas, but it's nicer to cross over to the less developed right fork which skirts the edge of **Shimogamo-jinja**, one of Kyoto's oldest Shinto shrines. This side is quieter and has more birdlife. It's also mostly a residential area so as you meander north you can peek into some of the local gardens that spill out onto the riverbank. Finally, at **Takano bridge** you'll find *Café & Bar Air* (daily noon–11pm), which has a very pleasant glass conservatory at the front and serves sandwich and pasta sets (¥1300). This is a nice sunny spot to sit and while away a few hours in autumn or winter. From here you can either turn northeast and head up to **Shūgaku-in Rikyū** or loop back through Shimogamo-jinja into central Kyoto.

replicas of Heian-style (794–1185) architecture. The most important building is the ceremonial **Shishin-den**, flanked by two cherry and citrus trees, where the Meiji, Taishō and Shōwa emperors were all enthroned. Further on, you can peer inside the Seiryō-den, which was once the emperor's private residence, while beyond there's a tantalizing glimpse of a pond-filled stroll-garden designed by the landscape gardener Kobori Enshū (1579–1647).

You can enjoy Enshū's work to the full in the **Sentō Gosho**, which occupies the southeast quadrant of the Imperial Park. Again, you have to join a guided tour (same hours as palace tour), but this time it's all in Japanese. Originally built as a retirement home for former emperors, the palace burnt down in 1854 and now only the peaceful garden remains. Apart from several graceful pavilions, its main features are a zigzag bridge – stunning when its wisteria trellis is in full bloom – and a cobbled "seashore", which lends the garden an extra grandeur.

Nijō-jō and Nijō-jin'ya

One kilometre southwest of the Imperial Park, the swaggering opulence of **Nijō-jō** (二条城; daily 8.45am–4pm, closed Tues in Jan, July, Aug & Dec; ¥600) provides a complete contrast to imperial understatement. Built as the Kyoto residence of Shogun Tokugawa Ieyasu (1603–16), the castle's double moats, massive walls and watchtowers demonstrate the supreme confidence of his new, Tokyo-based military government. Inside, the finest artists of the day filled the palace with sumptuous gilded screens and carvings, the epitome of Momoyama style (see p.785), leaving the increasingly impoverished emperor in no doubt as to where power really lay. The castle took 23 years to complete, paid for by local *daimyō*, but Nijō-jō was never used in defence and was rarely visited by a shogun after the mid-1600s.

The main entrance to Nijō-jō is the East Gate on Horikawa-dōri, near the Nijō-jō-mae subway station and bus stop. After entering here head to the **Ninomaru Palace**, whose five buildings face onto a lake-garden and run in a staggered line connected by covered corridors. Each room is lavishly decorated with **screen paintings** by the brilliant Kanō school of artists, notably Kanō Tanyū and Naonobu.

Ieyasu built Nijō-jō in the grounds of the original Heian-era Imperial Palace, of which only a tiny fragment today remains – a pond-garden, **Shinsen-en** – trapped between two roads immediately south of the castle walls. Walk through the garden, continuing south down Ōmiya-dōri, to find the mysterious **Nijō-jin'ya** (二条陣屋) behind a fence on the right-hand side. It was built in the early seventeenth century as an inn for feudal lords who came to pay homage to the emperor. As these were days of intrigue and high skulduggery, it is riddled with trap doors, false walls and ceilings, "nightingale" floors (floors that squeak when trodden on), escape hatches, disguised staircases and confusing dead ends to trap intruders. Since this is a private house, **tours** (daily except Wed; 10am, 11am, 2pm & 3pm; 1hr; ¥1000; ⓣ075/841-0972, ⓦnijyojinya.net) are strictly by appointment only and must be booked by phone, in Japanese, a day before; they also ask that non-Japanese-speakers bring an interpreter. Nijō-jin'ya has been **closed for renovations** since mid-2009 and is not due to reopen till sometime in 2012.

Downtown Kyoto

Kyoto's **downtown** district is contained within the grid of streets bounded by Oike-dōri and Shijō-dōri to the north and south, Karasuma-dōri to the west and the Kamo-gawa in the east. While there are few specific sights, the backstreets still hide a number of traditional wooden buildings, including some of Kyoto's best ryokan (see p.412). You'll also come across fine old craft shops (see p.445) among the boutiques and department stores, while the colourful arcades of **Teramachi-dōri** and neighbouring **Shinkyōgoku** are worth a browse. The alleys east of Shinkyōgoku are home to a scattering of forgotten temples that were banished to this area in the late sixteenth century. Beyond here, towards the Kamo-gawa, lies the geisha district of **Pontochō** – best at night, when lantern-light fills the district's narrow lanes. In July and August Pontochō restaurants open terraces over the cooling Kamo-gawa – their mellow lamplight a memorable feature of Kyoto's sweltering summer nights.

A little further west, **Nishiki-kōji street market**, also known as "Kyoto's kitchen", greets you with tantalizing smells and sights. Since the early seventeenth century this narrow covered alley has been one of Kyoto's main fish and vegetable markets; nowadays these wares are supplemented by the city's famous *tsukemono* – great vats of brightly coloured pickled vegetables. Where the stalls end, turn north on Takakura-dōri to find the **Museum of Kyoto** (10am–7.30pm, 10am–6pm for

Manga in Kyoto

The excellent **Kyoto International Manga Museum** (10am–6pm; closed Wed; ¥500; Ⓦwww.kyotomm.jp) is the world's first museum entirely devoted to **Japanese comics**. A joint project between Kyoto City and Seika University, it's housed in an old elementary school, which has been remodelled to accommodate the huge, all-encompassing collection of manga (see *Manga & anime* colour section), as well as provide plenty of space for art workshops (held at weekends) to teach the techniques of manga, as well as international conferences to discuss research. The great thing about the museum is that most of the manga can be taken outside and read on the lawn, and there is also a small international section with some English-language manga.

At Kyoto station don't miss **Tezuka Osamu World** (daily 10am–7pm; ¥200; Ⓦwww.kyoto-station-building.co.jp/kyototezuka), near the *Granvia Hotel*, which continuously shows **anime** by comic-book genius Tezuka (see *Manga & anime* colour section), plus that of other artists, in their smallish but comfortable theatre. If you don't have time to visit the museum devoted to Tezuka at Takarazuka, near Ōsaka, this is a good place to see some of his work. The shop next door is filled with a surprisingly tasteful array of AstroBoy and other Tezuka-associated character goods.

special exhibitions; closed Mon; ¥500; Ⓦwww.bunpaku.or.jp), in a trendy area of galleries and cafés. The museum incorporates a Meiji-era bank building and a replica Edo-period shopping street with craft shops and some reasonable restaurants. Upstairs, the main display halls deal with local history, culture and modern crafts. Despite the charming historical dioramas, the exhibitions are rather disappointing as there is very little detailed explanation about the exhibits in Japanese or English – ask for one of the museum's volunteer guides if you want an English-language explanation. However, the small section on Kyoto's film industry is enlivened by screenings of classic movies (in Japanese) at 1.30pm and 5pm on weekdays.

Around the station

Historically, the principal entrance to Kyoto lay through its great southern gate, so it's only fitting that this district, south of the city centre, should be home to the monumental **Kyoto Station** (京都駅). Rebuilt and enlarged in the 1990s by Tokyo architect Hara Hiroshi, it was initially the source of much local controversy, but over time many people have come to appreciate its shiny black bulk. Uncompromisingly modern, with its marble exterior and giant central archway, the station building also houses the Isetan department store, restaurants and underground shopping malls, plus a hotel and theatre.

The 131m-high **Kyoto Tower**, built in the 1960s, is also considered by many to be rather unsightly, though it does prove a useful landmark when walking around the city. Rather than heading for the tower's observatory (daily 9am–9pm; ¥770), visit the station's twelfth-floor Sky Garden instead: the views may be less dramatic, but it's free and the building's extraordinary central atrium, with its grand stairways and suspended walkway, is well worth exploring.

This area also contains a few of the city's more venerable temples. In their day, when their massive wooden halls were filled with shimmering gold, **Nishi-Hongan-ji** and **Higashi-Hongan-ji** were probably just as awe-inspiring as the modern train station. Across the tracks, **Tō-ji** boasts Japan's tallest original wooden pagoda and some of the city's oldest surviving buildings.

Nishi-Hongan-ji and Higashi-Hongan-ji

One of Japan's most popular and wealthy Buddhist sects is the Jōdo Shinshū (True Pure Land), founded by the Kyoto-born priest Shonin Shinran (1173–1262). His

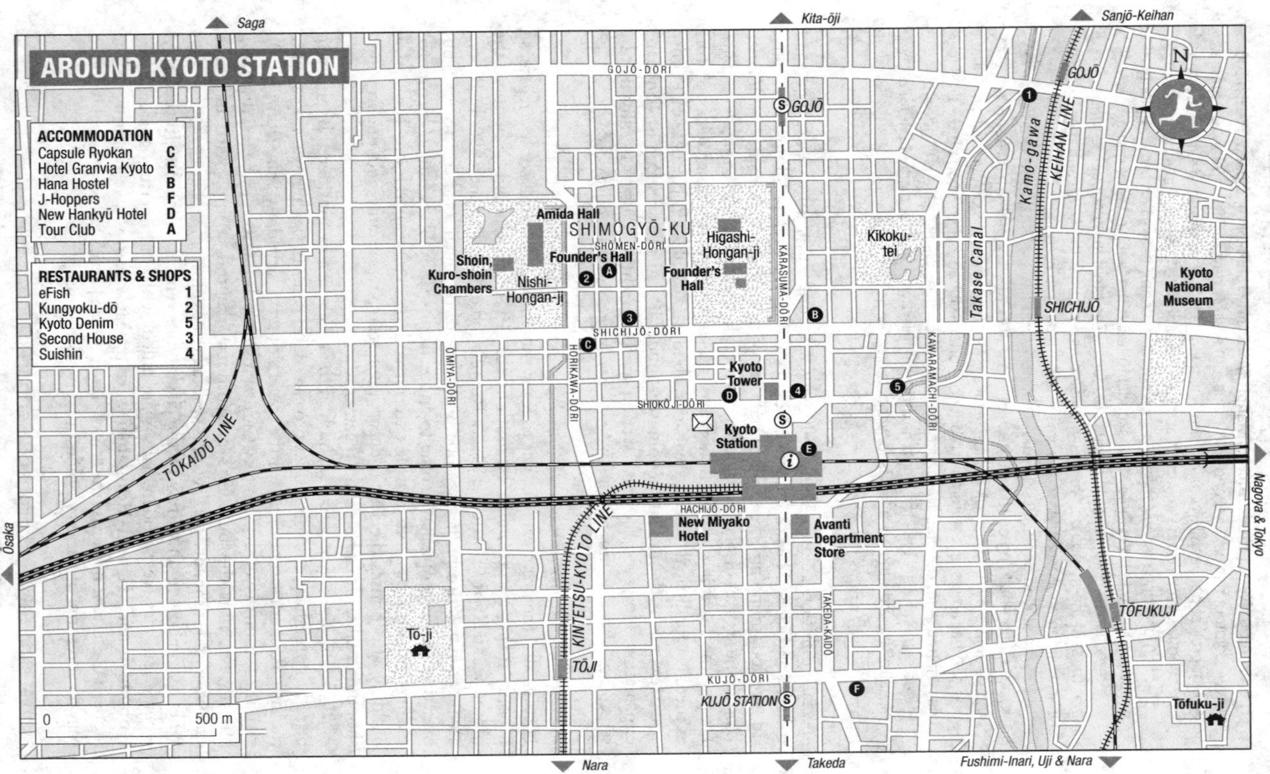
AROUND KYOTO STATION
ACCOMMODATION
Capsule Ryokan C
Hotel Granvia Kyoto E
Hana Hostel B
J-Hoppers F
New Hankyū Hotel D
Tour Club A
RESTAURANTS & SHOPS
eFish 1
Kungyoku-dō 2
Kyoto Denim 5
Second House 3
Suishin 4
Saga
Kita-ōji
Sanjō-Keihan
Ōsaka
Nagoya & Tokyo
Nara
Takeda
Fushimi-Inari, Uji & Nara
GOJŌ-DŌRI
GOJŌ
SHICHIJŌ
TŌFUKUJI
KEIHAN LINE
Kamo-gawa
Takase Canal
Kikoku-tei
Kyoto National Museum
Tōfuku-ji
Amida Hall
SHIMOGYŌ-KU
SHŌMEN-DŌRI
Founder's Hall
Shoin, Kuro-shoin Chambers
Nishi-Hongan-ji
Higashi-Hongan-ji
Founder's Hall
KARASUMA-DŌRI
SHICHIJŌ-DŌRI
ŌMIYA-DŌRI
HORIKAWA-DŌRI
KAWARAMACHI-DŌRI
Kyoto Tower
SHIOKŌJI-DŌRI
Kyoto Station
TŌKAIDŌ LINE
KINTETSU-KYOTO LINE
HACHIJŌ-DŌRI
New Miyako Hotel
Avanti Department Store
TAKEDA-KAIDŌ
Tō-ji
TŌJI
KUJŌ-DŌRI
KUJŌ STATION
0
500 m
N

simple creed, which at the time was regarded as heresy, asserts that merely chanting the *nembutsu*, "Praise to Amida Buddha", can lead to salvation. Not surprisingly, the sect grew rapidly, despite opposition from the established hierarchy, until eventually Toyotomi Hideyoshi granted them a plot of land in southern Kyoto in 1591. Yet by 1602, Shogun Tokugawa Ieyasu was sufficiently alarmed at the sect's power to sponsor a splinter group, Higashi-Hongan-ji, which is just a few hundred metres to the east. Even today, the two groups continue to differ over doctrinal affairs.

The more interesting of the two temples is the original **Nishi-Hongan-ji** (西本願寺; daily: March–Oct 5.30am–5.30pm; Nov–Feb 6am–5pm; free; Ⓦ www.hongwanji.or.jp/english), which faces onto Horikawa-dōri, about ten minutes' walk north of Kyoto Station. The gravel courtyard contains two huge halls, the oldest of which is the Founder's Hall, **Goeidō** (1636), on the left, dedicated to Shinran and recently restored, while the **Amida Hall** dates from 1760. Both are decked with gold, including screens by Kanō artists in the Amida Hall. The temple's real highlights, the even more ornate **Shoin** and **Kuro-shoin Chambers**, are only open to guided tours (daily 10.45am & 2.45pm; free; Ⓣ 075/371-5181) – ask in the green-roofed building, to the left of the Founder's Hall.

Shōmen-dōri leads east from Nishi-Hongan-ji, past shops selling Buddhist accessories, to the back wall of **Higashi-Hongan-ji** (東本願寺; daily: March–Oct 5.50am–5.30pm; Nov–Feb 6.20am–4.30pm; free). Though similar in style to its rival, Higashi-Hongan-ji had to be completely rebuilt after a fire in 1864, and only the two main halls are open to the public. The more northerly **Goeidō**, also recently restored, is among Japan's largest wooden buildings – when the new halls were built, ordinary ropes proved too weak to lift the massive roof beams, so female devotees from around the country sent in enough hair to plait 53 ropes; an example of these black coils is preserved in the open corridor connecting the halls. Two blocks further east, the temple's shady **Kikoku-tei** garden (daily 9am–4pm; free) provides a welcome respite from the surrounding city blocks.

Tō-ji

Ten minutes' walk southwest of Kyoto Station is **Tō-ji** (東寺; daily: mid-March to mid-Sept 8.30am–5.30pm; mid-Sept to mid-March 8.30am–4.30pm). This historic temple, founded by Emperor Kammu in 794, contains some of Japan's finest esoteric Buddhist sculpture. The best time to visit is during the **monthly flea market** (the 21st of each month), when Tō-ji is thronged with pilgrims, hustlers and bargain hunters.

The main entrance to eighth-century Heian-kyō lay through the great south gate, Rashō-mon, which stood at the junction of Kujō-dōri and Senbon-dōri After the problems in Nara (see p.463), Emperor Kammu permitted only two Buddhist temples within the city walls: Tō-ji and Sai-ji, the East and West temples. Standing either side of Rashō-mon, they were charged with the young capital's spiritual wellbeing. While Sai-ji eventually faded in the thirteenth century, Tō-ji prospered under **Kōbō Daishi**, the founder of Shingon Buddhism (see p.499), who was granted the stewardship of the temple in 823. Over the centuries, the temple gathered a treasure-trove of calligraphy, paintings and Buddhist statuary, the oldest of which were supposedly brought from China by the Daishi himself.

Tō-ji's most distinctive feature is a **five-storey pagoda** – Japan's tallest – which was erected in 826 and last rebuilt in the mid-seventeenth century. It now stands in an enclosure alongside Tō-ji's greatest treasures, the Kō-dō and more southerly Kon-dō (¥500, or ¥800 including the Hōmotsu-kan). These solid, confident buildings both date from the early seventeenth century, but it's the images inside, such as Heian-period Buddhist statues, that are the focus.

Kōbō Daishi is said to have lived in the **Miei-dō**, the Founder's Hall, located in the temple's northwest corner. The present building, erected in 1380, houses a thirteenth-century statue of him, which can be seen on the 21st of each month. On this day, which marks the entry of the Daishi into Nirvana, hundreds of pilgrims queue up to pay their respects. Beyond the Miei-dō, the modern **Hōmotsu-kan** contains Tō-ji's remaining treasures, including priceless mandala, portraits of Kōbō Daishi and a 6m-tall Senju Kannon (thousand-armed Buddhist Goddess of Mercy), carved in 877. The museum opens for two seasons (March 20–May 25 & Sept 20–Nov 25 daily 9am–4.30pm; ¥500), with a different exhibition each time.

East Kyoto

If you only have one day in Kyoto, it's best to concentrate on the wealth of temples and museums lining the eastern hills. Not only does this district include many of Kyoto's more rewarding sights, but it's also fairly compact and contains areas of attractive lanes and traditional houses set against the wooded slopes behind. Beginning in the south, the massed statues of **Sanjūsangen-dō** are a tremendous sight, as are the autumn leaves of Tōfuku-ji and Fushimi-Inari's thousands of vermilion-red *torii*. However, if you're pushed for time head straight for **Kiyomizu-dera**, with its distinctive wooden terrace, and then follow cobbled **Sannen-zaka** north. **Gion**, the famous entertainment district traditionally associated with geisha and teahouses, has retained a surprising number of wooden facades and photogenic corners, though its seductive charms are best savoured after dark. Further north, **Heian-jingū** rings the changes as both a major shrine and a relatively recent addition to the cityscape, while the nearby **Fureaikan** provides a comprehensive introduction to Kyoto's myriad traditional crafts. It's worth seeking out the quiet gardens of **Murin-an** and **Konchi-in**, before taking the philosopher's path north to **Ginkaku-ji** – the Silver Pavilion may be unexpectedly low-key, but it makes a startling combination with the garden's mass of sculpted white sand. Garden lovers should also arrange to visit **Shūgaku-in Rikyū** on the northeast edge of Kyoto, for its inspired use of borrowed scenery on a grand scale – you'll need to allow a half-day for this.

Fushimi-Inari

The spectacularly photogenic **Fushimi-Inari Taisha** (伏見稲荷大社; free), about 2.5km southeast of Kyoto Station, is the head shrine of the Inari cult, dedicated to the god of rice and sake. In 711, the local Hata clan established a shrine on top of Inari-san, the mountain, although this was eventually moved in the ninth century to the site of the current sanctuary at the foot of the mountain. Don't linger here too long though – the real highlight is the **4km maze of paths** that wind their way up through the deep forest to the summit of the mountain. More than 10,000 vermilion *torii* gates frame the paths, forming a mysterious tunnel that in some places cuts out most light, even on the brightest days. These painted wooden gates are replaced every ten years, each one an offering by local and national companies asking for success in business – the black lettering on each gate indicates the company that has donated it. At times you will emerge out of the gloom into bright sub-shrines, with hundreds of thousands of miniature wooden gates hanging from every available space, flanked by stone foxes, which are believed to be the messengers of the rice gods. It's quite a steep climb up to the top, but you'll be rewarded with great views of Kyoto, and along the way you can stop for tea and grab some *inari-zushi* – rice balls in pockets of fried tofu.

Fushimi-Inari is best **reached by train**: from Kyoto station take either the JR Nara line to Inari Station, or the Keihan line to Fushimi-Inari Station. If you have

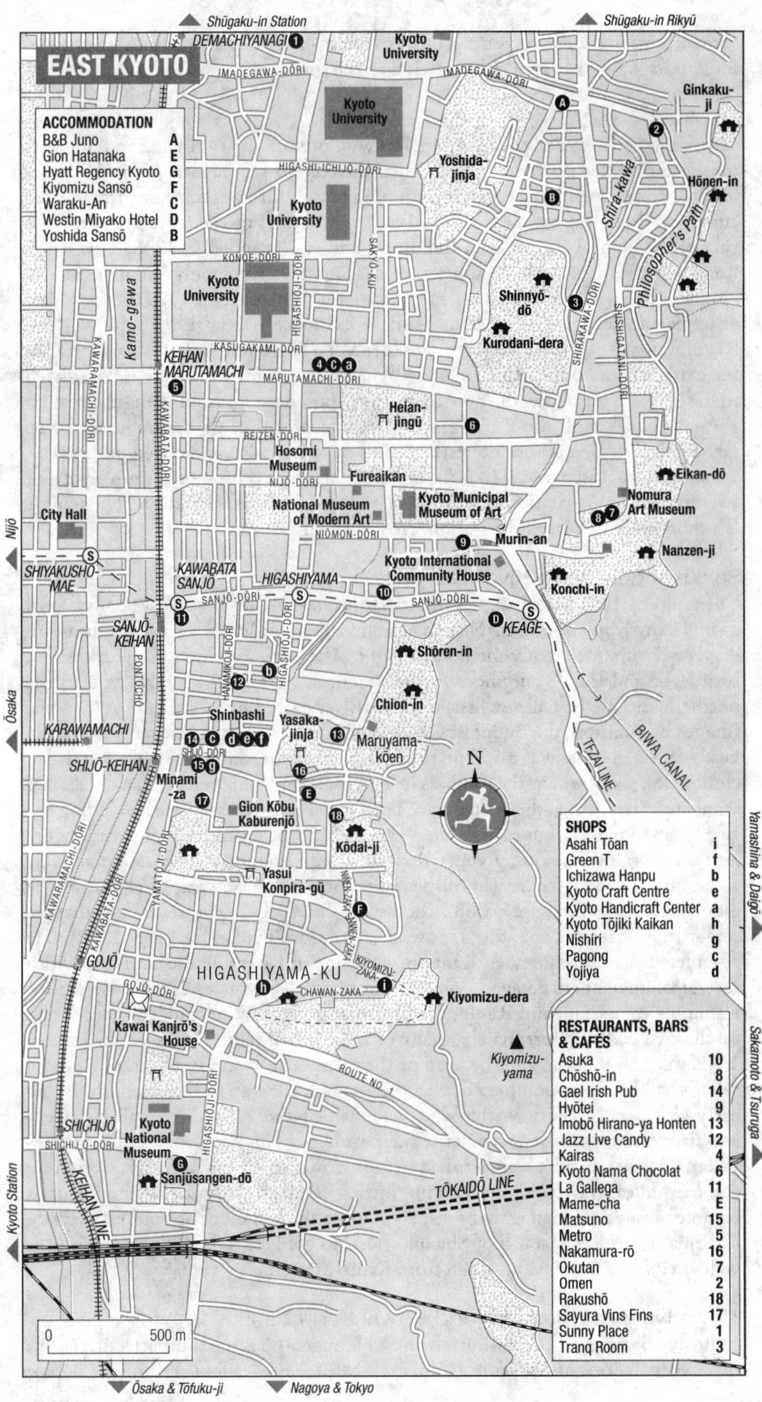
EAST KYOTO
ACCOMMODATION
B&B Juno A
Gion Hatanaka E
Hyatt Regency Kyoto G
Kiyomizu Sansō F
Waraku-An C
Westin Miyako Hotel D
Yoshida Sansō B
SHOPS
Asahi Tōan i
Green T f
Ichizawa Hanpu b
Kyoto Craft Centre e
Kyoto Handicraft Center a
Kyoto Tōjiki Kaikan h
Nishiri g
Pagong c
Yojiya d
RESTAURANTS, BARS & CAFÉS
Asuka 10
Chōshō-in 8
Gael Irish Pub 14
Hyōtei 9
Imobō Hirano-ya Honten 13
Jazz Live Candy 12
Kairas 4
Kyoto Nama Chocolat 6
La Gallega 11
Mame-cha E
Matsuno 15
Metro 5
Nakamura-rō 16
Okutan 7
Omen 2
Rakushō 18
Sayura Vins Fins 17
Sunny Place 1
Tranq Room 3
Shūgaku-in Station
Shūgaku-in Rikyū
DEMACHIYANAGI
Kyoto University
IMADEGAWA-DŌRI
Ginkaku-ji
Yoshida-jinja
HIGASHI-ICHIJŌ-DŌRI
Hōnen-in
Shira-kawa
Philosopher's Path
SAKYŌ-KU
KONOE-DŌRI
HIGASHIOJI-DŌRI
Kamo-gawa
Shinnyō-dō
Kurodani-dera
SHIRAKAWA-DŌRI
SHISHIGATANI-DŌRI
KASUGAKAMI-DŌRI
KEIHAN MARUTAMACHI
MARUTAMACHI-DŌRI
KAWARAMACHI-DŌRI
KAWABATA-DŌRI
Heian-jingū
REIZEN-DŌRI
Hosomi Museum
Fureaikan
NIJŌ-DŌRI
Eikan-dō
Kyoto Municipal Museum of Art
Nomura Art Museum
National Museum of Modern Art
City Hall
NIŌMON-DŌRI
Murin-an
Nijō
Kyoto International Community House
Nanzen-ji
SHIYAKUSHO-MAE
KAWABATA SANJŌ
HIGASHIYAMA
SANJŌ-DŌRI
Konchi-in
KEAGE
SANJŌ-KEIHAN
Shōren-in
HANAMIKOJI-DŌRI
PONTOCHŌ
Chion-in
Ōsaka
Shinbashi
Yasaka-jinja
KARAWAMACHI
Maruyama-kōen
BIWA CANAL
TOZAI LINE
SHIJŌ-DŌRI
SHIJŌ-KEIHAN
Minami-za
N
Gion Kōbu Kaburenjō
Kōdai-ji
YAMATOJI-DŌRI
Yasui Konpira-gū
NINEN-ZAKA
SANNEN-ZAKA
Yamashina & Daigo
GOJŌ
HIGASHIYAMA-KU
KIYOMIZU-ZAKA
GOJŌ-DŌRI
CHAWAN-ZAKA
Kiyomizu-dera
Kawai Kanjrō's House
Kiyomizu-yama
ROUTE NO. 1
Sakamoto & Tsuruga
SHICHIJŌ
SHICHIJŌ-DŌRI
Kyoto National Museum
HIGASHIOJI-DŌRI
Sanjūsangen-dō
KEIHAN LINE
TŌKAIDŌ LINE
Kyoto Station
0 500 m
Ōsaka & Tōfuku-ji
Nagoya & Tokyo

come from eastern Kyoto you can bus to Tōfuku-ji Station and get on a train there. It's a short walk east from either station to the shrine.

Tōfuku-ji

Tōfuku-ji (東福寺; daily 9am–4pm; ⓦwww.tofukuji.jp; ¥400), a Zen temple, is most often visited during autumn, when the colours of the *momiji* (maple) leaves in the man-made mini valley in the temple grounds turn a spectacular array of red and gold, though it is well worth a visit at other times of the year. The temple is part of the Rinzai sect of Zen Buddhism and was founded in 1236. This large, sprawling complex with 23 sub-temples is significant not only for its medieval temple architecture – the two-storey San-mon gate, built in 1425, is the oldest example of Zen gate architecture still in existence – but also for its gardens. Revolutionary twentieth-century gardener Mirei Shigemori designed and installed the gardens around the **Hōjō** (main hall) in 1939, and his work here is considered to be a great example of **contemporary Japanese garden** design, creating abstract shapes with moss and gravel. His interpretation of the traditional Zen raked gravel garden is also interesting – lots of extra swirls and coned peaks.

To **get here**, catch a #202, #207 or #208 bus from central or eastern Kyoto or a train from Kyoto Station on the JR Nara line to Tōfuku-ji Station. The temple is a short walk east from the station, crossing a busy road.

Sanjūsangen-dō to Kiyomizu-dera

The ranks of 1001 gilded statues inside **Sanjūsangen-dō** (三十三間堂; daily: April to mid-Nov 8am–5pm; mid-Nov to March 9am–4pm; ¥600), on the southeastern edge of Kyoto, are a truly memorable sight. After you are through the turnstiles, turn right and leave your shoes in the porch; a short corridor takes you to the northern end of the hall. At first, the impassive, haloed figures appear as identical **images of Kannon**, the Buddhist Goddess of Mercy, usually portrayed with eleven heads and a thousand arms. But they all have subtle differences in their faces, clothes, jewellery and in the symbols held in their tiny, outstretched hands. Rather than a thousand arms, the statues have been given only forty apiece (excluding the two hands in prayer), but each of these can save 25 worlds. In addition, every figure represents 33 incarnations, giving a total of 33,033 Kannon to help save mankind.

Commissioned by the devout former emperor Go-Shirakawa in 1164, during the bloody Genpei Wars (see p.768), they were carved by some seventy craftsmen under the direction of the renowned sculptor **Tankei** (c.1173–1256). He completed the central, seated Kannon at the age of 82 and is also attributed with several of the superb images along the front row. Of these, 28 are disciples of Kannon, while Fūjin and Raijin, the muscular gods of Wind and Thunder, bring up the two ends. Unfortunately, many of the original statues were lost in a fire in 1249, but 156 Kannon and the head of the main image were saved, and by 1266 a replica hall had been completed with the Kannon back up to full strength. In the early seventeenth century, the west verandah of the 118m-long hall became a popular place for samurai to practise their **archery**. This developed into a competition, **Tōshiya**, in which archers had to fire arrows from a squatting position along the length of the building without hitting a pillar. Nowadays, the event is commemorated with an archery display outside the hall on or around January 15.

Sanjūsangen-dō lies south of Shichijō-dōri; to get here, take Raku bus #100, as well as city buses #206 and #208 from Kyoto Station.

Kyoto National Museum and Kawai Kanjirō's House

Immediately across Shichijō-dōri from Sanjūsangen-dō is the southern entrance to the **Kyoto National Museum** (京都国立博物館; 9am–4.30pm, Fri until 7.30pm;

closed Mon; ¥500, plus extra for special exhibitions; ⓦ www.kyohaku.go.jp). The permanent collection, covering Kyoto culture from prehistory up to 1868, is held in the modern wing, while the original hall, built in 1895, is reserved for special exhibitions. Many of the items on display are national treasures and the museum is a manageable size, though the displays and lighting are rather old-fashioned.

Heading north along Higashiōji-dōri, anyone interested in Japanese folk crafts should make a brief detour to **Kawai Kanjirō's House** (河井寛次郎記念館; 10am–5pm; closed Mon, and Aug 11–20 & Dec 24 to Jan 7; ¥900), the tastefully rustic home of the innovative potter Kawai Kanjirō (1890–1966), who helped revive *mingei* (folk crafts) in the 1930s. The house is as he left it, beautifully furnished with ceramics and sculptures from his long career, including the kilns where many of these pieces were made. To find the house, turn west off the main road shortly before the Gojō-dōri flyover.

Kiyomizu-dera

Just north of the flyover a right fork brings you to **Chawan-zaka** (茶わん坂), a road lined with shops selling local pottery. This is also a quieter, back entrance to **Kiyomizu-dera** (清水寺; daily 6am–6pm; ¥300). If you'd rather use the traditional approach, continue on to Kiyomizu-zaka, where you'll find a colourful, crowded parade of souvenir shops and craft galleries. The closest bus stops are Kiyomizu-michi or Gojō-zaka on Higashiōji-dōri served by buses #100 (Raku bus), #202, #207 and #206.

With its trademark wooden platform overhanging the valley, Kiyomizu-dera is one of Kyoto's defining sights. There's been a temple here since 778, when a visionary priest came across its fount of clear water (*kiyo-mizu*); however, nearly all the buildings you see today date from 1633. Pass the three-storey pagoda and step for a moment into the monumental **Hon-dō** (Main Hall) to enjoy the surprisingly peaceful interior. There's actually little to see in here – its principal image, an eleven-headed Kannon, only goes on show every 33 years (next time will be 2033), so head for the terrace in front, originally a stage for sacred dances, to soak up the famous view over the wooded gorge and Kyoto beyond.

On the hill behind the Hon-dō a jumble of shrine buildings competes for the attention of people looking for luck in love. **Jishu-jinja** (地主神社; 9am–5pm) is dedicated to several Shinto gods, of whom the most popular is Okuninushi-no-mikoto, an ancient deity in charge of love and good marriages; his messenger is a rabbit. To test your current love life, try walking in a straight line between the two "blind stones", set 18m apart, with your eyes closed and intoning your partner's name. If you arrive at the other stone without erring, all is well. If not, well, it's time for a new relationship. Finally, head down beside the wooden terrace to the **Otowa waterfall**, a sip of which is reputed to cure any illness, or make you beautiful, and then follow the short path up the opposite hillside from where you get the best views of Kiyomizu-dera.

Sannen-zaka and Ninen-zaka

Leaving Kiyomizu-dera via Kiyomizu-zaka, head north down a set of stone steps and along a couple of inviting, cobbled lanes. Known as **Sannen-zaka** (三年坂; "Three-Year Slope") and **Ninen-zaka** (二年坂; "Two-Year Slope"), these lanes preserve some of the last vestiges of the old Kyoto townscape (see p.428). There has been a path here since the ninth century, while the two-storey wooden townhouses date from the late 1800s. Many still cater to passing pilgrims and souvenir hunters in time-honoured fashion, peddling Kiyomizu pottery, bamboo-ware, pickles and refreshments. Just at the bottom of the steps, look out for Hyōtan-ya, which has been selling gourd flasks (*hyōtan*) for two hundred years. Be careful walking along these two lanes, though: according to popular belief, a fall here brings two or three years of bad luck.

Kōdai-ji

At the north end of Ninen-zaka, walk straight ahead up the steps and through the car park to find the entrance to the peaceful gardens of **Kōdai-ji** (高台時; daily 9am–5pm; ¥600; Ⓦwww.kodaiji.com). This temple was granted to Kita-no-Mandokoro, the wife of Toyotomi Hideyoshi, when she became a nun after his death in 1598. Kōdai-ji owes its finery, however, to the generosity of Hideyoshi's successor, Tokugawa Ieyasu, who donated buildings from his own castles and financed paintings by Kanō artists, before he wiped out the Toyotomi dynasty at Ōsaka in 1615. Nowadays, the temple buildings blend beautifully into their attractive hillside garden, its two ponds graced by a moon-viewing pavilion and the aptly named "Reclining Dragon Corridor". Between the two, the ceilings of the pretty **Kaisan-dō** hall are made from recycled panels from Ieyasu's ship and from the carriage of Kita-no-Mandokoro. But the temple's most important building lies at the top of the **Reclining Dragon Corridor** – you have to walk round by path – where statues of Hideyoshi and his widow are enshrined. The exquisite gold-inlay lacquer work is among the finest of its kind in Japan.

Maruyama-kōen and around

About 200m to the north of Kōdai-ji, a phoenix-tipped tower is a 1920s replica of a float from the Gion Matsuri (see p.442). A right turn in front of it brings you to an attractive public park called **Maruyama-kōen** (円山公園), beyond which lies a

Living dolls

Arthur Golden's *Memoirs of a Geisha* and similar books have sparked a curiosity in the Western world about the centuries-old institution of the geisha. Often mistakenly considered to be high-class prostitutes, **geisha** (which means "practitioner of the arts") are in fact refined women who entertain affluent men with their various accomplishments, such as singing, dancing, conversation and playing a traditional instrument such as a *shamisen* (three-string banjo). English conversation skills are also becoming important, as a result of the international attention generated by the Hollywood film of *Memoirs of a Geisha* (see p.810), which has brought overseas visitors into the teahouses of the *hanamachi* ("flower towns"), where geisha live and work.

It takes five years for an apprentice geisha – known as **maiko** – to master her art, training with the same focus and dedication of an Olympic athlete in the various arts and living according to a strict code of dress and deportment, almost like living dolls. The world of the geisha is shrinking, however: from a pre-World War II peak of eighty thousand there are now reckoned to be no more than a few thousand geisha left, the majority concentrated in Kyoto, the centre of the tradition. Though few fifteen-year-olds are tempted to sign up as apprentices, the internet is beginning to change this – some geisha houses have established websites to recruit apprentices, with successful results. Geisha have also started blogging; one Kyoto *maiko* has even translated her musings on life in a *hanamachi* into English (Ⓦwww.ichi-kyoto.jp).

It's also becoming more common to be able to meet and talk with geisha and *maiko* in person. Many hotels and ryokan now offer exclusive dinner shows (see p.443), where it is possible to experience a little of the elegant yet fun entertainment that has until recently been the exclusive playground of wealthy male customers. Don't be fooled by daylight groups of "geisha" in Kyoto tourist spots: they are likely to be visitors who have paid for the chance to don the distinctive white make-up, lacquered hairdos and fabulously expensive kimono that constitute the epitome of geisha beauty.

pair of markedly different temples. The first, **Chion-in** (知恩院), is a big, busy complex where everything is built on a monumental scale. Founded in 1175 by the priest Hōnen, it is the headquarters of his popular Jōdo (Pure Land) sect of Buddhism. On entering via the huge San-mon gate, look up to the right, and you'll see the colossal Daishō-rō bell, the biggest in Japan, hanging in its belfry; at New Year it takes seventeen priests to ring this 67-tonne monster. Behind the cavernous main hall – all dark wood and sumptuous gold – red arrows lead to the entrance of the **Ōhōjō** and **Kohōjō** halls and a garden representing Amida's paradise (daily: March–Nov 9am–3.30pm; Dec–Feb 9am–4pm; ¥400; Ⓦwww.chion-in.or.jp). The main feature of both halls is the Momoyama-period screens that fill them; since you can only peer in, they've placed replicas of the screens in a room behind the ticket desk – the most famous features a cat with uncannily lifelike eyes.

Next door, **Shōren-in** (青蓮院; daily 9am–5pm; ¥500) is a quiet little place surrounded by gardens and ancient camphor trees. The temple started life in the ninth century as lodgings for Tendai-sect priests from Enryaku-ji (see p.455) and later served as a residence for members of the imperial family. After seeing the collection of painted screens, there's not a lot to do here apart from enjoy the paths that wind through the hillside garden.

Gion and around

Back in Maruyama-kōen, take any path downhill to come to the back of **Yasaka-jinja** (八坂神社). The main entrance to this bustling shrine faces west onto Higashiōji-dōri where, instead of the usual *torii*, there's a brightly coloured Buddhist-style gate – a legacy of the days before 1868 when Buddhism and Shinto often cohabited. Yasaka-jinja lies on the eastern edge of **Gion** and each July hosts one of Kyoto's biggest spectacles, the **Gion Matsuri** (祇園祭). This festival dates back to the ninth century, since when the ritual purification to ward off plague in the humid summer months has developed into a grand procession of richly decorated floats.

From Yasaka-jinja, Shijō-dōri runs west through the heart of Gion and across the Kamo-gawa into Kyoto's main downtown district. One of the most distinctive buildings along here, on the corner overlooking the river, is the **Minami-za** (南座). This famous kabuki theatre was established in the early seventeenth century, though last rebuilt in 1929; each December it is the venue for a major kabuki festival featuring Japan's most celebrated actors. Kabuki has been an integral part of Gion life since the late sixteenth century when a female troupe started performing religious dances on the river banks. Eventually this evolved into an equally popular, all-male theatre, and, patronized by an increasingly wealthy merchant class, kabuki joined geisha and the teahouses in Kyoto's vibrant **pleasure quarters**. Of these, **Gion** was perhaps the most famous, and you can still get a flavour of this "floating world", as these districts were referred to during the eighteenth century, if you walk south along Hanamikōji-dōri, where many of the lovely wooden buildings still function as exclusive teahouses where geisha hold court. It's best after dark when red lanterns hang outside each secretive doorway, allowing the occasional glimpse down a stone-flagged entranceway; early evening is also a good time to spot geisha and trainee *maiko* arriving at the teahouses for an appointment.

During April's Miyako Odori (都をどり), local geisha give performances of traditional dance at the **Gion Kōbu Kaburenjō** (祇園甲部歌舞練場), a theatre near the south end of Hanamikoji-dōri. This is also the venue for a touristy display of traditional arts known as **Gion Corner** (ギオンコーナー; March–Nov daily 7pm & 8pm; ¥3150; Ⓦwww.kyoto-gion-corner.info). Though it's far better to spend a

Machiya

Kyoto's traditional townhouses, *machiya*, were built in a unique architectural style and remain an enduring symbol of the city's **cultural heritage**. These long, wooden houses are made up of a succession of rooms, connected by a single corridor, sometimes stretching as far back as 100m from the front. Their design is a result of the taxes that were levied on buildings during the Edo period according to the size of their street frontage. *Machiya* were generally built by merchants, encompassing a front shop space, living quarters in the middle and a warehouse at the rear. A courtyard garden was also included to aid the flow of light and air through the centre. Their long, thin shape lead to their colloquial name, *unagi no nedoko*, or "bedroom of eels".

Machiya were built almost entirely out of wood, which means that because of fire and earthquakes few that remain today are more than a century old. Some of the best examples are protected by law, but this has not stopped others being demolished at an alarming rate (some figures estimate by more than ten percent a year) since the end of World War II as land values increased and modern development was encouraged. However, you can still walk along **Sannen-zaka** (see p.425), **Shinbashi** (see below) or through the **Nishijin** weaving district in Western Kyoto and find some almost complete rows of these beautiful old houses, each dark facade showing subtle variations on the same overall design. Note the distinctive gutter-guards made of curved bamboo, and the narrow-slatted ground-floor windows, which keep out both the summer heat and prying eyes.

Encouragingly, though they are still being demolished, many *machiya* now seem to be experiencing a period of revitalization, having been remodelled as restaurants, guesthouses, boutiques and galleries, particularly in the central area north of Shijō and west of Kawaramachi. You can find a selection of the best of these in the accommodation and restaurant listings (see pp.412–415 & pp.436–439).

little extra to see the real thing, this is an opportunity to see brief extracts of court dance, *bunraku* puppet theatre and the slapstick *kyōgen*. See p.441 for further details of events in Kyoto.

Gion north of Shijō-dōri consists mainly of high-rise blocks packed with clubs, bars and restaurants. But walk up Kiritoshi, one block west of Hanamikoji-dōri, and you eventually emerge into another area of teahouses, known as **Shinbashi** (新橋). Although it only comprises two short streets, the row of slatted facades reflected in the willow-lined Shirakawa Canal makes a delightful scene, day or night.

Heian-jingū

In the late nineteenth century, after Emperor Meiji moved his imperial court to Tokyo, Kyoto authorities felt the need to reaffirm their city's illustrious past. The result was **Heian-jingū** (平安神宮; daily: March–Nov 8.30am–5.30pm; Dec–Feb 8.30am–4.30pm; free; Ⓦwww.heianjingu.or.jp), an impressive though rather garish shrine that was modelled on a scaled-down version of the original eighth-century emperor's Hall of State. Completed in 1895 to commemorate the 1100th anniversary of the founding of the city, it was dedicated to emperors Kammu and Komei (1846–67), Kyoto's first and last imperial residents. The present buildings are reconstructions from 1979, but this is still one of Kyoto's most famous landmarks. The shrine lies about ten minutes' walk north of Higashiyama subway station, or you can take one of the many bus routes along Higashiōji-dōri.

The shrine's bright orange and white halls have an unmistakably Chinese air. Two wings embrace a huge, gravelled courtyard, at the north end of which sits the main worship hall flanked by a couple of pretty two-storey towers representing the protective "Blue Dragon" and "White Tiger". More interesting are the **gardens** behind (same hours; ¥600), which were also designed in Heian style. They're divided into four sections, starting in the southwest corner and ending beside a large pond in the east. The south garden features a collection of plants mentioned in Heian literature, while the middle (third) garden is famous for a row of stepping stones made from the columns of two sixteenth-century bridges. The more spacious east garden boasts the shrine's most attractive buildings – the graceful Taihei-kaku pavilion and its covered bridge.

Museums around Heian-jingū

Heian-jingū faces south towards a large vermilion *torii* across a park dotted with museums and other municipal buildings. The most rewarding of these is the **Fureaikan** (ふれあい館; 10am–6pm; closed Mon; free), a museum of traditional crafts in the basement of the modern Miyako Messe building. Well designed and informative, the museum provides an excellent introduction to the whole range of Kyoto crafts, from roof tiles and metalwork to textiles, confectionery and ornamental hairpins. Allow plenty of time to take it all in.

Close to Fureaikan, the **National Museum of Modern Art** (京都国立近代美術館; 9.30am–5pm and April–Oct until 8pm on Fri; closed Mon; ¥420, extra for special exhibitions; Ⓦwww.momak.go.jp) and the brick-built **Kyoto Municipal Museum of Art** (京都市美術館; 9am–5pm; closed Mon; varying prices; Ⓦwww.city.kyoto.jp/bunshi/kmma) stand on opposite sides of the big *torii*. The modern art museum focuses on local twentieth-century artists, while the Municipal Museum hosts temporary exhibitions from its vast collection of post-1868 fine arts.

Also in this area, west of the Fureaikan, is the cube-shaped **Hosomi Museum** (細見美術館; 10am–6pm; closed Mon; Ⓦwww.emuseum.or.jp; ¥700–1000), a private establishment with an inspiring collection of Japanese painting, sculpture and decorative art from all major periods. There are seasonal exhibitions, curated from the museum's collection, and seminars and workshops are also held here in the tearoom on the top floor – check the website for details on English-language events. The downstairs Artcube shop has an excellent selection of contemporary crafts and art books. The museum's *Café Cube* serves Italian dishes till 5pm.

Murin-an and Nanzen-ji

At the same time that Heian-jingū was being built, Marshal Yamagata Aritomo, a leading member of the Meiji government, was creating a delightful haven for himself beside the Biwa Canal. From the large *torii* between the two art museums, walk east along the canal to find his villa, **Murin-an** (無鄰庵; daily 9am–4.30pm; ¥350; Ⓣ075/771-3909), where the road bends to the right. Even today, as you look east from the garden to the Higashiyama hills beyond, it's hard to believe that you're in the middle of a busy city. Designed by Yamagata himself, the unusually naturalistic garden incorporates a meandering stream, pond and lawns in a surprisingly small space. There are also three buildings: take a look upstairs in the two-storey brick house, where parquet floors and wood panelling blend beautifully with Kanō-school painted screens.

Continuing east, cross over the canal again in front of **Kyoto International Community House** (see p.409), and head uphill towards **Nanzen-ji** (南禅寺). This large, active temple belongs to the Rinzai sect of Zen Buddhism and is one of the most important in Kyoto. Before entering the main compound, however, it's worth exploring its quiet sub-temple, **Konchi-in** (金地院; 8.30am–5pm; ¥400), on the right in front of the first gate. An arched gate leads straight into one of Kyoto's most beautiful dry gardens – one of the rare works by famed landscape gardener Kobori Enshū, with documents to prove it. Its centrepiece is a large rectangle of raked gravel with two groups of rocks set against a bank of clipped shrubs. The right-hand, vertical rock group represents a crane, in balance with the horizontal "tortoise"-shaped rock topped by a twisted pine, on the left; both these animals symbolize longevity.

Erected in 1628 to commemorate the soldiers killed during the siege of Ōsaka Castle (see p.488), the looming bulk of **San-mon** (三門; ¥500; 9am–5pm), the main gate to Nanzen-ji, seems excessively monumental after Konchi-in. Nanzen-ji's prize possessions can be found in the **Hōjō** (March–Nov 8.40am–5pm; Dec–Feb 8.40am–4.30pm; ¥500), up to the right behind the San-mon. These include the "Leaping Tiger" garden, also attributed to Enshū, though working in a much more confined space, and a series of screens painted by Kanō Tanyū that depict tigers in a bamboo grove. Nanzen-ji is also famous for its **shōjin-ryōri**, Buddhist vegetarian cuisine, which can be sampled in a number of its sub-temples (see p.438).

The Philosopher's Path to Ginkaku-ji

The final sight along this stretch of Kyoto's eastern hills is the famous Ginkaku-ji. Though you can get there by bus (see p.411), by far the best approach is to walk alongside the canal on the **Philosopher's Path**, which starts just north of Nanzen-ji (see p.429). The name of the 2km-long path refers to a respected philosopher, Nishida Kitarō (1870–1945), who took his daily constitutional along the path through the wooded hillside.

To reach the path from Nanzen-ji, follow the road curving northeast past the small, extremely esoteric **Nomura Art Museum** (野村美術館; mid-March to mid-June 10am–4.30pm & Sept–Dec 10am–4pm; closed Mon; ¥700), which holds rotating exhibitions of tea-ceremony utensils and related paraphernalia.

A little further on, you might want to pop in to **Eikan-dō** (永観堂; Dec–Oct daily 9am–5pm; ¥600; Nov daily 8.30am–5pm & 5.30–9.30pm; Ⓦwww.eikando.or.jp), also known as Zenrin-ji for its unusual Amida statue. Eikan-dō was founded in the ninth century by a disciple of Kōbō Daishi (see p.499), but later became the headquarters of a sub-sect of Jōdoshū (Pure Land Buddhism). In 1082 the then head priest, Eikan, was circling the altar and chanting the *nembutsu*, "Praise to Amida Buddha", when the Amida statue stepped down and started walking in front of him. When Eikan stopped in his tracks, Amida turned to encourage him. Soon after, the priest commissioned the statue you see today of Amida looking over his left shoulder. Eikan-dō is also a popular location for **maple leaf viewing** during November. Viewing the floodlit leaves in the evening is quite magical, if you don't mind sharing the experience with big crowds; weekends during this period are best avoided.

On exiting Eikan-dō, the first right turn leads to the Philosopher's Path. Every so often stone bridges link it to the tempting residential lanes on either side, while the occasional souvenir shop or bijou teahouse provides an additional distraction. **Hōnen-in** (法然院; daily 7am–4pm; free) makes for a pleasant stop before the crowds of Ginkaku-ji. Restored in 1680 by the then head priest of Chion-in, it is a tranquil place with a pleasing carp pond and small garden, which attracts few visitors. Occasional events and exhibitions are held here. Without too many stops, however, you should emerge beside the Ginkaku-ji bridge about thirty minutes later. Alternatively, bus routes #5, #203 and #204, and Raku buses #100, #102, stop nearby at Ginkaku-ji-michi.

Ginkaku-ji

The Temple of the Silver Pavilion, **Ginkaku-ji** (銀閣寺; daily: mid-March to Nov 8.30am–5pm; Jan to mid-March & Dec 9am–4.30pm; ¥500; Ⓦwww.shokoku-ji.or.jp/english), is one of Kyoto's most celebrated sights. Though modelled on its ostentatious forebear, the golden Kinkaku-ji (see p.432), this simple building sits quietly in the wings while the garden takes centre stage, dominated by a truncated cone of white sand whose severity offsets the soft greens of the surrounding stroll-garden. Ginkaku-ji originally formed part of a much larger villa built in the fifteenth century for Shogun **Ashikaga Yoshimasa** (1436–90), the grandson of Kinkaku's Ashikaga Yoshimitsu. Interrupted by the Ōnin Wars (1467–77) and plagued by lack of funds, the work continued for thirty years, until Yoshimasa's death in 1490. During that time, however, it became the focal point of Japanese cultural life. Yoshimasa may have been a weak and incompetent ruler, but under his patronage the arts reached new heights of aesthetic refinement; in this mountainside retreat, significantly turned away from the city, he indulged his love of the tea ceremony, poetry and moon-viewing parties while Kyoto succumbed to war. After 1490, the villa became a Rinzai Zen temple, **Jishō-ji**, and eventually fires razed all except two buildings, one of which was the famous pavilion.

The approach to Ginkaku-ji creates a wonderful sense of anticipation as you're funnelled between tall, thick hedges down an apparently dead-end lane. Turning the corner, a high wall now blocks the view except for one small, low window that offers a teasing glimpse. Inside, you're directed first to the **dry garden**, comprising a raised, rippled "Sea of Silver Sand" – designed to reflect moonlight – and a large "moon-facing" cone of sand. The jury's out on whether these enhance the garden or intrude, but it's almost certain that they weren't in the original design, and were probably added in the early seventeenth century. Behind the cone to the west, the small, dark two-storey building with the phoenix topknot is **Ginkaku-ji**, or "Silver Pavilion", despite its lack of silver plating.

Shūgaku-in Rikyū

In the far northeast of Kyoto, the foothills of Hiei-zan (see p.454) provide a superb setting for one of Japan's finest examples of garden design using "borrowed scenery"; a technique which incorporates the existing landscape to give the impression of a much larger space. Entry to **Shūgaku-in Rikyū** (修学院離宮), an imperial villa, is by appointment only (see p.405), on a guided tour (five daily, Mon–Fri at 9am, 10am, 11am, 1.30pm & 3pm; free). To get here, hop on City Bus #5 to the Shūgaku-in Rikyū-michi stop on Shirakawa-dōri, from where the villa is a signed ten-minute walk to the east. Alternatively, take a train on the private Eizan line from Demachiyanagi Station (in northeast Kyoto) to Shūgaku-in Station (10min), located a couple of minutes west of Shirakawa-dōri.

Emperor Go-mizuno'o, who reigned between 1611 and 1629, built Shūgaku-in Rikyū in the late 1650s as a pleasure garden rather than a residence. Just 15 years old when he ascended the throne, the artistic and highly cultured Go-mizuno'o fiercely resented the new shogunate's constant meddling in imperial affairs – not least being forced to marry the shogun's daughter. After Go-mizuno'o abdicated in 1630, however, the shogun encouraged him to establish an imperial villa. He eventually settled on the site of a ruined temple, Shūgaku-in, and set about designing a series of gardens, which survived more than a century of neglect before the government rescued them in the 1820s. Though some of the original pavilions have been lost, Go-mizuno'o's overall design remains – a delightfully naturalistic garden that blends seamlessly into the wooded hills.

In fact, Shūgaku-in Rikyū is made up of three separate gardens, each in their own enclosure among the terraced rice-fields. Of these, the top lake-garden is the star attraction. Climbing up the path towards the upper villa, you pass between tall, clipped hedges before suddenly emerging at the compound's highest point. An airy pavilion, **Rin-un-Tei**, occupies the little promontory, with views over the lake, the forested, rolling hills in the middle distance and the mountains beyond.

Walking back down through the garden, the grand vistas continue with every twist and turn of the path, passing the intricate Chitose bridge, intimate tea-ceremony pavilions and rustic boathouses.

West Kyoto

Compared to east Kyoto, sights in the city's **western districts** are more dispersed and therefore require a little more effort to get to. Nevertheless, it's well worth devoting one day to this area, particularly the northwest fringes, where the city meets the encircling hills. Here you'll find the outrageously extravagant **Kinkaku-ji**, the Golden Pavilion, rubbing shoulders with **Ryōan-ji**'s supreme example of an austere, enigmatic Zen garden. If puzzling over Zen riddles is your thing, then don't miss the dry gardens of **Daitoku-ji**, where **Daisen-in** attracts all the attention, though several other sub-temples allow quieter contemplation.

Kōryū-ji, to the south, houses one of Japan's most perfect images, a serene statue of the Future Buddha, carved fourteen centuries ago. Nearby **Tōei Uzumasa Eiga-mura**, on the other hand, celebrates the celluloid world, with a theme park of working film sets and studios. The city's southwestern suburbs contain two outstanding gardens: **Katsura Rikyū**, one of Japan's first stroll-gardens, belongs to the languid world of moon-viewing parties and tea ceremonies, while the dappled mosses of **Saihō-ji** herald from an older tradition of Buddhist paradise gardens.

Daitoku-ji

Lying halfway between the Kamo-gawa and the Kitayama hills, **Daitoku-ji** (大徳寺) is one of Kyoto's largest Zen temple complexes, with over twenty sub-temples in its large, walled compound. Of these only four are open to the public, but within them you'll find a representative sampler of the dry gardens (*kare-sansui*) for which Japanese Zen Buddhism is renowned. The temple lies roughly 1500m west of Kita-ōji subway station (on the Karasuma line), or can be reached by City Bus #101, #205 and #206 – get off at Daitoku-ji-mae.

Entering from the east, head through the huge San-mon gate to **Daisen-in** (大仙院; daily: March–Nov 9am–5pm; Dec–Feb 9am–4.30pm; ¥400) in the north of the compound. This sub-temple contains two gardens, the most famous of which is on the right as you enter the main hall. It replicates a Chinese landscape painting, and the garden uses carefully selected rocks, pebbles and a few scaled-down plants to conjure up jagged mountains.

It pays to visit Daisen-in early in the day before the crowds arrive. However, Daitoku-ji's other sub-temples remain surprisingly quiet; probably the most interesting of these is **Ryōgen-in** (龍源院; daily 9am–4.30pm; ¥350), lying just south of the San-mon gate. The temple was also founded in the early sixteenth century and is home to **Japan's smallest Zen rock garden**. The minuscule Tōtekiko garden, on your right-hand side as you continue along the corridor from the entrance, consists of waves of sand round a rock, symbolizing a Zen saying that the harder a stone is thrown, the bigger the ripples.

Kinkaku-ji and around

West of Daitoku-ji, the wooded hills of Kitayama are home to **Kinkaku-ji** (金閣寺; daily 9am–5pm; ¥400; Ⓦwww.shokoku-ji.or.jp/english), the famous Temple of the Golden Pavilion. The pavilion originally formed part of a larger retirement villa built by the former Shogun Ashikaga Yoshimitsu (1358–1408) on the site of an earlier aristocratic residence; it was converted into a Zen temple on his death. A noted scholar of Chinese culture, Yoshimitsu incorporated various Chinese motifs into the pavilion and its surrounding garden, the focus of which is a lake studded with rocks and pine-covered islets.

Even the crowds can't diminish the impact of seeing the temple for the first time – a hint of gold glimpsed though the trees, and then the whole, gleaming apparition floating above the aptly named **Kyōko-chi** (Mirror Pond). If you're lucky enough to see it against the autumn leaves, or on a sunny winter's day after a dusting of snow, the effect is doubly striking. Note the different architectural styles of the pavilion's three floors and the phoenix standing on the shingle roof. It's an appropriate symbol: having survived all these years, Kinkaku-ji was torched in 1950 by an unhappy monk. The replica was finished in just five years, and in 1987 the building was gilded again, at vast expense. Kinkaku-ji lies on several bus routes, of which the most convenient are #12 and #59.

The **Kyoto Museum for World Peace** (9.30am–4.30pm; closed Mon; ¥400; Ⓦ www.ritsumei.ac.jp/mng/er/wp-museum/e/eng.html), located halfway between Kinkaku-ji and Ryōan-ji on the campus of Ritsumeikan University, makes for an interesting diversion. The museum unflinchingly examines the roots of Japan's militarization and its devastating effects on other Asian countries, as well as considering what could have happened if the US plan to drop an atomic bomb on Kyoto had not been abandoned in favour of Nagasaki. The displays in the main exhibition room have English-language descriptions and include a replica of a wartime-era house, showing blacked-out windows and other precautions. The two large reliefs on the wall depicting the mythical phoenix were painted by noted manga artist Tezuka Osamu (see *Manga & anime* colour section) and symbolize the living energy of all creatures on earth.

Ryōan-ji

While Kinkaku-ji is all about displays of wealth and power, the dry garden of **Ryōan-ji** (龍安寺; daily: March–Nov 8am–5pm; Dec–Feb 8.30am–4.30pm; ¥500; Ⓦ www.ryoanji.jp) hides infinite truths within its riddle of rocks and sand. Thought to date back to the late fifteenth century, and said by some to be the work of Sōami, the most famous artist, landscape gardener and tea ceremony master of the time, it was largely unknown until the 1930s. Now it's probably Japan's most famous garden, which means you're unlikely to be able to appreciate the Zen experience thanks to intrusive loud-speaker announcements and almost constant crowds, though very early morning tends to be better. To get to Ryōan-ji, either hop back on a #59 bus or walk southwest along Kitsuji-dōri for about twenty minutes.

The garden consists of a long, walled rectangle of off-white gravel, in which fifteen stones of various sizes are arranged in five groups, some rising up from the raked sand and others almost completely lost. In fact, the stones are placed so that wherever you stand one of them is always hidden from view. The only colour is provided by electric-green patches of moss around some stones, making this the simplest and most abstract of all Japan's Zen gardens. It's thought that the layout is a *kōan*, or riddle, set by Zen masters to test their students, and there's endless debate about its "meaning". Popular theories range from tigers crossing a river to islands floating in a sea of infinity. Fortunately, it's possible to enjoy the garden's perfect harmony and in-built tension without worrying too much about the meaning. Walk round the veranda of the main hall and you'll find a stone water basin inscribed with a helpful thought from the Zen tradition: "I learn only to be contented".

Leaving the main hall, it's definitely worth strolling round Ryōan-ji's refreshingly quiet lake-garden. This dates back to the twelfth century, when a noble of the Fujiwara clan built his villa here, before the estate was donated to the Rinzai Buddhist sect in the fifteenth century.

Kōryū-ji and around

The **Uzumasa** district, due south of Ryōan-ji, is home to the art treasures of Kōryū-ji and the Tōei film studios (see box below). The easiest way to get here is to take a train on the private Keifuku Arashiyama line from Shijō-Ōmiya Station in central Kyoto to Uzumasa Station. If you're coming straight from Ryōan-ji, it's probably quickest to backtrack into Kyoto and pick up the train or a bus; City Bus #11 and Kyoto Bus #71, #72 and #73 all stop outside Kōryū-ji.

Kōryū-ji (広隆寺; daily 9am–5pm; ¥700) is said to have been founded in the early seventh century by Nara's Prince Shōtoku (see p.767), but some scholars believe that the real founder was actually a friend of the prince's by the name of Hata no Kawakatsu, who had a lineage that stretched back to Korea, and possibly all the way to Turkestan.

The Kōdō (Lecture Hall) – straight ahead once you've entered the compound from the Heian-period gate – dates from 1165 and is one of the oldest buildings in Kyoto. The three Buddhas inside are imposing enough, but Kōryū-ji's main attractions are the statues kept in the modern **Reihōden** (Treasure House) at the back of the compound. The "newest" of these images is a thirteenth-century statue of Prince Shōtoku aged 16, his sweet face framed by bun-shaped pigtails. The oldest is the exquisite **Miroku Bosatsu**, the Future Buddha rendered as a Bodhisattva pondering how to save mankind. Originally, it was probably gilded and it is thought to have been a gift to Shōtoku from the Korean court in the early seventh century; its soft, delicate features are certainly unlike any other Japanese images from the time. The small, slim figure sits, elbow on knee, leaning forward slightly and head tilted in a pose of utter concentration.

Katsura Rikyū

In the southwest corner of Kyoto are two magnificent gardens, though in both cases admission is by appointment only. The more accessible garden belongs to **Katsura Rikyū** (桂離宮; Mon–Fri and occasionally Sat; six tours daily at 9am, 10am, 11am, 1.30pm, 2.30pm, 3.30pm; free), a former imperial palace; applications to visit should be made through the Imperial Household Agency (see p.405). Located on the west bank of the Katsura-gawa, it's fifteen minutes' walk from Katsura Station, on the private Hankyū line from central Kyoto. Alternatively, City Bus #33 will drop you at Katsura Rikyū-mae, the first stop after crossing the river, from where it's a five-minute walk north to the gate; this bus stop lies just outside the bus-pass zones, so if you want to save a few yen, get off before the river and walk over.

Tōei Film Studio Park

At **Tōei Uzumasa Eiga-mura** (東映太秦映画村; daily: March–Nov 9am–5pm; Dec–Feb 9.30am–4pm, closed Dec 21–Jan 1; ¥2200, plus extra charges for some attractions; ⓦwww.toei-eigamura.com), one of Japan's major film companies opens its sets to the public. At the entrance is **Padios**, an amusement arcade aimed at children, with 3D roller-coaster rides, games and souvenir shops. The **studios** behind, where directors such as **Kurosawa Akira** filmed their classics, hold more general appeal and are worth a visit. One of the indoor studios is usually in action, nowadays mostly making historical TV dramas but also the occasional film (most recently, the 2009 historical drama *Hiten no Shiro* – "*The Castle of Heavenly Flames*") while the outdoor sets – an Edo-period street, thatched farms, Meiji-era Western-style buildings and so on – are enlivened by roaming geisha, battling samurai and a superbly cheesy "special effects" zone. On the way out, don't miss the Movie Museum, where Japanese film buffs can take a nostalgic romp through the archives.

Katsura palace, unfortunately not open to the public, was built in the early seventeenth century as a residence for the imperial Prince Toshihito, and then expanded by his son, Toshitada, in the 1650s. Toshihito was a highly cultured man, who filled his villa and garden with references to *The Tale of Genji* and other literary classics, while also creating what is considered to be Japan's first **stroll-garden**. As the name suggests, these gardens were to be enjoyed on foot – rather than from a boat or from a fixed viewpoint – and designed to look "natural". In fact they were planned in minute detail so that scenes unfold in a particular order as the viewer progresses. Focused on a large, indented lake, the Katsura garden is famed for its variety of footpaths and stone pavings, and for its stone lanterns, all of which helped create the desired mood of relaxation. Several tea pavilions occupy prime spots around the lake, the most attractive of which is **Shokin-tei**, but perhaps the most interesting aspect of the garden is the sheer ingenuity of the designer – Toshihito managed to wrestle a splendidly harmonious, seemingly spacious garden out of an unexciting bit of floodplain.

Saihō-ji

Three kilometres northwest of Katsura Rikyū, in a narrow, tree-filled valley, you'll find the voluptuous and tranquil moss gardens of **Saihō-ji** (西芳寺; daily; ¥3000; ⓣ075/391-3631), also known as Koke-dera (苔寺; the "Moss Temple"). If you've got time to spare after the major sights, this temple is well worth visiting, though you have to make an **application** (see p.405). Japanese speakers can try phoning a few days before to see if there's space – or ask someone to phone on your behalf. The more assured method is to write to Saihō-ji, 56 Kamigatani, Matsuo, Nishikyō-ku, Kyoto-shi, 615-8286, giving your name, address, age, occupation and proposed date of visit. It's best to allow one or two weeks' notice – longer if sending from abroad – and remember to enclose a stamped-addressed postcard or international reply coupon. Within Japan you can buy special reply-paid "double postcards", or *ōfuku hagaki* (往復はがき), for this type of application (from post offices).

Saihō-ji lies at the terminus of the #73 Kyoto Bus route, which takes a circuitous course from Kyoto Station via Arashiyama (see p.449). Unless you're visiting Arashiyama at the same time, it's quicker to take a City Bus (#28 and #29) to Matsuo Taisha-mae (松尾大社前), just west of the river, and then change to the #73. At the end of the line, walk up the road for a minute or so – the temple gate is on your right. All visitors are required to attend a short Zen service during which you'll chant a sutra, trace the sutra's characters in *sumi-e* ink and finally write your name, address and "wish" before placing the paper in front of the altar. After that you're free to explore the garden at your leisure.

Like Kōryū-ji (see opposite), the temple apparently started life in the seventh century as another of Prince Shōtoku's villas. Soon after, Jōdo Buddhists adopted the site for one of their "paradise gardens", after which the gifted Zen monk, **Musō Kokushi**, was invited to take over the temple in 1338. The present layout dates mostly from his time, though the lakeside pavilion – the inspiration for Kinkaku-ji (see p.432) – and nearly all Saihō-ji's other buildings burnt down during the Ōnin Wars (1467–77). In fact, given the temple's history of fire, flooding and periods of neglect, it seems unlikely that today's garden bears much resemblance to Musō's. Saihō-ji was in complete ruins by the eighteenth century and some sources even attribute the famous mosses to accident, arguing that they spread naturally as the garden reverted to damp, shady woodland.

Whatever their origin, the swathes of soft, dappled moss – some 120 varieties in all – are a magical sight, especially after the rains of May and June, when the greens take on an extra intensity.

...ng

...th treating yourself to a meal in a traditional *Kyo-ryōri* (Kyoto cuisine) ...nt, such as **kaiseki** (a multi-course banquet of seasonal delicacies), **shōjin-ryōri** (Buddhist vegetarian cuisine) or **yūdōfu** (simmered tofu). **Nishin soba**, a big bowl of soba noodles with a part-dried piece of herring on top, and **saba-zushi**, made with mackerel, are two of the more everyday Kyoto dishes. **Reservations** are nearly always essential at top-end *kaiseki* restaurants in the evening; elsewhere it's not a bad idea to book ahead at weekends and during peak holiday times.

Central Kyoto

The central shopping district around **Shijō-dōri and Kawaramachi-dōri**, and the backstreets north of Shijō are the best places to look for somewhere to eat while in central Kyoto. Among the ubiquitous fast-food chains there are a number of decent restaurants specializing in international cuisine and also several old Kyoto establishments hiding down narrow alleys. The following listings are marked on the map on p.416.

Anzukko 杏っ子 2F Le Shisemme Building Ebisu-chō ⓣ075/211-3801.This is the place to go for gourmet-style *gyōza* in Kyoto. Mouthwatering variations on fried, grilled and steamed dumplings. The pan-grilled 12 *gyōza* set (¥980) and the boiled shrimp dumplings dribbled with spicy oil (¥840) are recommended. Open 6pm–1am; closed Mon.

Enraku 燕楽 Ebisugawa Fuyachō Higashi-iru ⓣ075/254-8488. This is a great place to sample very reasonably priced Kyoto-style *oden* (from ¥160) in a traditional building; the *nabe* and tempura are also recommended. There are cosy rooms downstairs and massive banquet spaces on the upper floor. Don't be put off by the formal-looking exterior – there's an English menu inside. Daily 5.30–11pm.

Fujino-ya 藤の家 Pontochō Shijō-agaru ⓣ075/221-2446. One of Pontochō's more affordable restaurants, with the added attraction of a river view. The simple menu (in English) offers either tempura or *kushi-katsu* (deep-fried pork skewers), with standard sets from around ¥2800. In the summer you can eat on the *yuka* riverside terrace, but the price of dinner increases to ¥3800 for the minimum set. Open 5–10pm; closed Wed.

Giro Giro Hitoshina 枝魯 枝魯ひとしな Nishi Kiyamachi Matsubara-sagaru ⓣ075/343-7070. This is the hippest place in Kyoto for an innovative ten-course meal at the unbelievable price of ¥3680. Dishes are a superb fusion of traditional Japanese and European cuisine, making this is a fun and unforgettable dining experience. Reservations are essential well in advance. Daily 5.30–11pm.

Gontaro 権太呂 Fuyachō Shijō-agaru ⓣ075/221-5810. Despite the elegant entrance, prices are reasonable at this specialist noodle restaurant just north of busy Shijō-dōri, starting at under ¥1000 for standard dishes and rising to around ¥4000 for the house speciality, *Gontaro nabe* (hotpot). Open 11am–9.30pm; closed Wed.

Hale 晴 Nishiki-koji Fuyachō Nishi-iru ⓣ075/231-2516. Organic and vegan restaurant in a quaint *machiya* with a garden, just off Nishiki food market, good for a healthy and relaxing meal. Lunch sets are very reasonable at ¥1000, and six-course dinner sets (¥2200), with deliciously fresh tofu and steamed vegetables, can be shared between two. Open 11.30am–2pm & 6–9pm; closed Mon.

Hisago Zushi ひさご寿し Kawaramachi Shijō-agaru ⓣ075/221-5409. Top-quality Kyoto-style sushi conveniently located in the central shopping area. Superbly presented lunch (¥2400) and dinner sets (¥4200), as well as takeaway bentō (¥1680). Counter seating downstairs and table seating upstairs. Daily 9.30am–8.30pm.

Kushikura Takakura-dōri Ōike-agaru ⓣ075/213-2211. Premium *yakitori* and other skewer foods in a nicely restored old Kyoto house. Sit at the counter and watch the chefs grill your food over charcoal, or enjoy the privacy of the small dining rooms. Sets start at ¥1600, or you can order by skewers separately from ¥160. Daily 11am–2.30pm & 5–10pm.

La Table De Thierry 9F Takase Building Sanjō Ohashi ⓣ075/212-0069. Enjoy fabulous views of the eastern hills, the Kamo-gawa and Pontochō, while savouring the seasonal flavours of chef Thierry Houngues' Kyoto-influenced French cuisine. The "quick plate lunch" (¥1500) includes a drink, while exquisitely presented dinner courses start at ¥5000, and a sommelier can help with your wine selection. Open 11.30am–2pm & 6–9pm; closed Mon.

Manzara-tei Pontochō まんざら亭先斗町 Pontochō Shijō-agaru ⓣ075/212-0028. Elegant *izakaya* with a welcoming atmosphere and English menu. Serves seasonal dishes as well as local specialities such as tofu, *yuba* (tofu skin) and *nama-fu* (wheat gluten). Also stocks local beers, sake and *shōchū*. Table seating downstairs and tatami rooms upstairs. Reservations advised. Daily 5pm–midnight.

Musashi むさしKawaramachi Sanjō-agaru ⓣ075/222-0634. The original branch of the reliable, region-wide *kaitenzushi* (conveyor-belt sushi) chain. Located right on the junction, it also does a brisk trade in takeaway bentō. Unless you're ravenous, lunch – or dinner – shouldn't set you back more than ¥1000, and the cheapest dishes are just ¥120.

Obanzai おばんざい Koromonotana-dōri Ōike-agaru ⓣ075/223-6623. It's well worth searching out this nicely designed and very popular buffet-style restaurant east of Nijō-jō for their excellent-value vegetarian buffets (¥840–1050 for lunch, ¥2100 in the evening). Daily 11am–2pm & 5–8.30pm; closed Wed eve.

Ratna Cafe ラトナカフェ Takoyakushi-sagaru, Iwagami-dōri ⓣ075/812-5862. Delicious south Indian cuisine in an award-winning *machiya* restoration, which hasn't lost any of its traditional Kyoto character. Curry lunch sets from ¥800; various chai and lassi from ¥450. The café is north of Shijō, one street west of Horikawa. Open 11.30am–8.00pm; closed Tues & Wed.

Sarasa Kayukoji さらさ花遊小路 Shinkyōgoku Shijō-sagaru ⓣ075/212-2310. Tranquil café in an old building tucked away off hectic Shijō serving an eclectic range of curries, fried rice dishes and soups. The daily lunch set (¥890) is good value and includes two dishes, rice, soup and a drink. Daily noon–11.30pm.

Sunshine Café 5F Izumi Biru, Sanjō-dōri, Teramachi Nishi-iru ⓣ075/251-1678. High above the Sanjō shopping street, this light and breezy organic café serves generous portions of tasty, innovative variations on Western-style cooking using Japanese vegetables such as burdock root and mountain yam. There's a daily lunch set (¥790), a longer evening menu (around ¥800 for a main dish), plus curry, bagels, sandwiches, salads, herbal teas and organic beer. Daily 11am–11pm.

Tawawa 3F Shinpuhkan, Karasuma-dōri Anekōji-sagaru ⓣ075/257-8058. All-you-can-eat buffet of dishes based on Kyoto vegetables. Pasta, salads, bread and fresh fruit desserts also served. The lunch buffet (11am–1pm; ¥1000) is a great deal. Dinner can be the "100 minute" buffet (¥3000) or *a la carte*. They serve coffee and cake in the afternoon. Daily 11am–11pm.

Yamatomi 山とみ Pontochō Shijō-agaru ⓣ075/221-3268. Another tourist-friendly Pontochō restaurant a few doors down from *Fujino-ya*. There's plenty of good, wholesome food on offer (English menu available), such as tofu, *nama-fu* (wheat gluten) and *kushi-age* (skewer food). Count on about ¥4000 for dinner, including drinks. In summer you can eat on their riverside terrace. Open noon–11.30pm; closed Mon.

Yoshikawa 吉川 Tominokōji Ōike-sagaru ⓣ075/221-5544. The best tempura restaurant in Kyoto is located inside this eponymous ryokan. Definitely worth sitting at the counter to watch the chefs expertly deep-fry your meal. Lunch sets (¥3000) include hearty portions of seafood and vegetables. In the evenings, the tempura supper (¥6000) or tempura *kaiseki* course (¥12,000) are both recommended. Open 11am–2pm & 5–8.30pm; closed Sun.

Around the station

The area immediately around **Kyoto Station** isn't particularly well endowed with restaurants, but the enormous station complex has well over a hundred eating options. Apart from the places recommended below, your best bet is the eleventh-floor *Eat Paradise* food court in the station's Isetan department store, The Cube shopping mall's eleventh-floor restaurant mall (adjoining *Eat Paradise*) or the Porta underground shopping mall, where there are a number of coffee-shop and fast-food chains. The following listings are marked on the map on p.420.

efish Nishi-hashizumi-cho ⓣ075/361-3069, ⓦwww.shinproducts.com/efish/cafe.php. Riverside café east of the station near Gojo bridge, serving chunky bread sandwich sets (¥800), cheesecake, juice and coffee in a very stylish interior, designed by the owner. A good place to gaze out at the river and eastern hills from a comfortable chair. Daily 11am–10pm.

Second House Shichijo-dōri Nishinotoin Nishi-iru ⓣ075/342-2555. Casual and friendly café specializing in Japanese-style spaghetti dishes and elaborate cakes in a majestic old building that was once a bank. Lunch (¥890) and dinner (¥1260) sets are very reasonable and include a drink. Daily 10am–11pm.

Suishin すいしん 1F SK Building, Kyoto-eki-mae ⓣ075/365-8888. The ground floor of this large restaurant houses a clean, modern sushi bar (it's better value at lunchtime). In the evening head for the huge, popular *izakaya* in the basement. Daily 11.30am–11.30pm.

East Kyoto

If you want to treat yourself to traditional Kyoto cuisine, head for the city's **eastern districts**. One or two of the more affordable restaurants are recommended below, and these still offer a glimpse into the world of kimono-clad waitresses, elegant tatami rooms, carp ponds and tinkling bamboo water spouts. The following listings are marked on the map on p.423, unless otherwise noted.

A Womb 35-2 Ichijōji Hinokuchi-chō ⓣ075/721-1357, ⓦwww.awomb.com. See Kyoto map, pp.406–407. Ultra-modern cavernous restaurant and bar a street back from Shirakawa-dōri serving contemporary interpretations of *kaiseki*, sushi and *donburi* rice bowls. Dinner courses from ¥5000. Open noon–3pm & 6–9pm; closed Wed.

Asuka 明日香 Sanjō-dori Jingumichi-nishi-iru ⓣ075/ 751-9809. If you are in the Higashiyama area, this friendly establishment, run by six Kyoto *obasans* (aunties), is an excellent lunch stop. Sit at the counter or at low tables and enjoy the tempura lunch set (¥1000) or the slightly more expensive *yūdōfu* (simmered tofu) set (¥1800) – both are highly recommended.

Chōshō-in 聴松院 Fukuchi-chō, Nanzen-ji ⓣ075/761-2186. A sub-temple of Nanzen-ji which offers Zen *yūdōfu* cuisine in its attractive gardens, with the option of sitting on the outside terrace in fine weather. If you don't want the full "Matsu" meal (around ¥3200), there are individual dishes such as *fu-no-dengaku*, three wheat-gluten cakes with different toppings. English menu available. Open 11am–4pm; closed Tues.

Hyōtei 瓢亭 Nanzen-ji ⓣ075/771-4116. Next to Murin-an garden, this sublime thatch-roofed garden-restaurant started serving *kaiseki* cuisine in 1837. Their specials are *asagayu*, a summer breakfast, and *uzuragayu* (rice gruel with quail eggs) in winter. Prices are lower in the new annexe, but even here expect to pay ¥4000 for the cheapest meal. Reservations essential and English spoken. Daily 8–10am (summer breakfast) & 11am–7.30pm; closed second & fourth Tues of the month.

Imobō Hirano-ya Honten いもぼう平野屋本店 Maruyama-kōen-uchi ⓣ075/561-1603. Delightful, three-hundred-year-old restaurant located inside the north entrance to Maruyama park. Their speciality is *imobō* (dried cod stew) incorporating an unusual type of potato (*ebi-imo*), and finding ingenious ways to make preserved fish taste superb. Try an *imobō* set for ¥2520, but expect to pay upwards of ¥7000 for a wonderful *kaiseki* experience. Daily 10.30am–8pm.

Kairas カイラス Sannō-cho Shōgoin ⓣ075/752-3127. Vegetarian café in a quant old *machiya* next to *Waraku-An* guesthouse (see p.414). Healthy daily lunch sets are ¥850 and the only other food served till closing are cakes (¥400). Open 11.30am–8pm; closed Wed.

Mame-cha 豆ちゃ Yasaka-jinja Nanmon-sagaru Ishibeikōji ⓣ075/532-2788. Elegant *obanzai* (Kyoto-style home cooking) restaurant in a modern-designed *machiya* up a narrow alleyway just south of Yasaka-jinja. The ¥3675 eleven-course dinner has a wonderful combination of flavours and is beautifully presented. Counter seating or tatami rooms upstairs, plus English-speaking staff and menu. Reservations are essential. Daily 5–11pm.

Matsuno 松乃 Shijō-dōri ⓣ075/561-2786, ⓦwww.matsuno-co.com. This century-old *unagi* (eel) shop is family-run and very friendly. Eels are traditionally eaten in the hot summer months to revive one's stamina, and the menu here has some surprising variations on eel cuisine. Sets start at around ¥2000. English menu. Open 11.30am–9pm; closed Thurs.

Nakamura-rō 中村楼 Gion-machi minami-gawa ⓣ075/561-0016. This wonderful four-hundred-year-old restaurant at the south gate of Yasaka-jinja serves exquisite Kyoto cuisine. It's surprisingly relaxed and informal, with tatami rooms overlooking a lush garden and a modern room with counter seating. However, even just a lunchtime bentō will set you back ¥5250. Full *kaiseki* dinners start at ¥13,000. Try to get there before 7pm for dinner; reservations essential. Open 11.30am–10pm; closed Thurs.

Okutan 奥丹 Fukuchi-chō, Nanzen-ji ⓣ075/771-8709. If *Chōshō-in* (see above) is full, try this smaller *yūdōfu* restaurant half hidden in a bamboo grove on the east side of the same garden. The *yūdōfu* sets start at ¥3000. Open 11am–5pm; closed Thurs.

Omen Jōdo-ji Shibashi-chō ⓣ075/771-8994. Excellent udon restaurant near Ginkaku-ji, serving bowls of thick white noodles topped with the nutritious combination of fresh ginger, sesame seeds and pickled *daikon* radish. Side dishes of tempura vegetables, tofu and grilled *hamo* (conger eel) are also delicious. Open 11am–9pm; closed Thurs.

Sunny Place Tanaka Oi-chō ⓣ075/711-7617, ⓦsunnyplace.okoshi-yasu.net. One of Kyoto's longest-running and most popular vegan restaurants. There's a daily set menu for ¥850 with a variety of Japanese-style dishes served with brown rice, but the Teriyaki *tempeh* (Indonesian soy cake) burger (¥900) is very tasty. Open noon–2pm & 6–10pm; closed Tues.

Tranq Room Shirakawa-dōri Shinyo-chō ⓦhome.att.ne.jp/sun/tranqroom. Neo-Asian café between Nanzen-ji and Ginkaku-ji, with white vinyl sofas signed by famous visitors such as American star Vincent Gallo. Set menus, including Indian curry, from ¥700. The *nama-yūba* (soy bean skim) rice bowl (¥700) is recommended. There's a gallery on the second floor, and live events are held regularly. Open late; closed Tues.

Northwest Kyoto

The **northwestern district** covers a huge area and there's no particular centre to aim for food-wise; the restaurants below are chosen for their proximity to Daitoku-ji, Kinkaku-ji and Kitano Tenmangū shrine. The following listings are marked on the map on pp.406–407.

Gontaro 権太呂 Kinukake-no-michi ⓣ075/463-1039. Suburban branch of the Shijō soba shop in an old house just a few minutes' walk west of Kinkaku-ji. Fresh, well-priced noodle dishes and welcoming atmosphere. Open 11am–9pm; closed Wed.

Izusen 泉仙 Daitoku-ji ⓣ075/491-6665. Located in the garden of Daiji-in, a sub-temple of Daitoku-ji, this is one of the nicest places to sample vegetarian *shōjin-ryōri* at an affordable price, though it's still around ¥3500 for the simplest lunch. Reservations are recommended in spring and autumn. They also have a cheaper branch near Kyoto Station (see p.419). Open 11am–5pm; closed Thurs.

Kanga-An 閑臥庵 Kuramaguchi-dōri ⓣ075/256-2480. *Fucha-ryōri* (Chinese-influenced *shōjin-ryōri*) restaurant and bar in a stately old temple with private dining rooms. Dinner courses are over ¥12, 000, but well worth the experience. This is the only temple in Kyoto serving food at night; reservations essential. Daily noon–3pm & 5–9pm.

Sarasa Nishijin さらさ西陣 Kuramaguchi-dōri ⓣ075/432-5075. Spacious restaurant and bar in a converted *sento* (public bathhouse) in the Nishijin weaving district, with its original tiled interior still intact. The menu is mostly *yōshoku* – Western-style Japanese dishes, such as *omuraisu* (ketchup-flavoured fried rice wrapped in an omelette, ¥980), as well as salads (from ¥700). Monthly live music performances. Open noon–11pm; closed Wed.

Tofu Café Fujino Imadegawa-dōri ⓦwww.kyotofu.co.jp/shop/cafe_kitano. West of Kitano Tenmangu shrine, this modern café serves innovative soy bean cuisine. The Fujino lunch plate (¥1050) is very filling. Extremely busy on the 25th of the month, when the shrine market is held. Daily 11am–8pm.

Urume うるめ 51 Ōno-chō Kitaōji-dōri ⓣ075/495-9831. This friendly soba restaurant in a converted *machiya* (see p.428) is run by a young couple and makes a good stop for a generous lunch while sightseeing, with dishes such as *Zaru-soba* from ¥740 and tempura with soba from ¥1680. The private room at the back has a nice garden view. Northside of Kitaōji-dōri between Shinmachi and Horikawa. Open 11am–5pm; closed Tues.

Drinking and nightlife

Kyoto isn't all about high culture. After you've finished tramping the streets, there are plenty of **tea houses**, **coffee shops** and cosy **bars** where you can kick back and quench your thirst. And, if your aching feet can stand it, Kyoto's late-night scene offers a fair range of **clubs, discos** and **live music** venues. It may not compete with the likes of Ōsaka and Tokyo, but you should be able to find somewhere to party until the wee hours. The prime entertainment districts are **Kiyamachi** and **Gion**, both of which are stuffed with bars and clubs. But be warned: even fairly innocuous-looking establishments can be astronomically expensive (many have a "seating" fee of over ¥1000), so check first to make sure you know exactly what you're letting yourself in for. Some of the more upmarket establishments used to require an introduction by a regular customer, before you could even set foot inside, but the ongoing recession has loosened the formalities to some extent.

The teahouses of Kyoto

The world of tea tends to have a reputation for rigidity and rules, but fortunately there are now some innovative and modern ways in which to experience this quintessential Japanese drink. Whether you want just a relaxing cuppa or a full-blown tea ceremony, both are easily accessible.

You can start by going straight to the heart of Kyoto tea commerce, at the historic Ippodo on Teramachi, which has been in business since 1717. The shop sells all grades of Japanese green teas, locally grown in Uji. However, just past the counter is the **Kaboku Tearoom** (daily 11am–5pm; ⓣ075/211-3421, ⓦwww.ippodo-tea.co.jp), a wonderful place to sample different types and grades of green tea. The tearoom has a hushed atmosphere but the staff are friendly and happy to guide you through the extensive menu. If you are keen to experience a tea ceremony, head to **Ran Hotei** on the Sanjō-Horikawa shopping arcade (daily 10am–8pm; ⓣ075/801-0790), a tea salon decorated in the Taisho-Art Deco style. If you book in advance it's possible to have a 90-minute tea ceremony lesson (¥2500) in the tatami tearoom with the owner, a Canadian-born tea master.

Roaring into the internet age is the **Iyemon Salon** (daily 8am–11pm; ⓣ075/221-1500), on Sanjō-dōri, just west of Karasuma, possibly Kyoto's trendiest teahouse and a complete contrast to the meditative atmosphere of a tea ceremony. It's large and bustling, with a free internet café, bookshop, tea counter and a kitchen serving tea-inspired cuisine. Just across the road is **Somushi** (10am–8pm; closed Wed; ⓣ075/253-1456), an artfully rustic Korean tea house that's an incredibly calm space to try a variety of medicinal teas, such as ginseng and jujube (red dates), as well as healthy vegetarian Korean dishes. In eastern Kyoto, don't miss **Rakushō** (daily 9am–5pm; ⓣ075/561-6892), a charming old teashop between Kiyomizu-dera and Yasaka-jinja. Enjoy a bowl of *macha* and *warabi mochi* (jelly-like cakes rolled in sweet soybean flour) while gazing out over the pond of enormous carp. East of the Heian-jingu is the **Kyoto Nama Chocolat Organic Tea House** (Wed–Sun noon–5pm; ⓣ075-751-267, ⓦwww17.plala.or.jp/kyotochocolat), in an elegant old house with a rambling garden. They serve a variety of teas and coffee, as well as their own brand of delectable fresh soft chocolate, which they make on the premises.

Bars, clubs and live music

From boisterous *izakaya* to trendy wine **bars**, Kyoto is well endowed with places to while away the evening. The epicentre of this activity is found either side of the Kamo-gawa in downtown Kyoto, in the two traditional pleasure quarters of Gion and Pontochō. In the evening you might be lucky enough to see a *maiko* or a geisha as she hurries between teahouse assignations. The Kiyamachi area between Sanjō and Shijō is where most of the clubs are, and is brimming with buskers, fortune-tellers and bar touts at weekends. In summer, look out for rooftop **beer gardens** on top of the big hotels and department stores.

The contemporary music scene is also alive and well in Kyoto. The city has enough **clubs**, discos and **live music** venues to satisfy most tastes. To find out who or what's on, check online (see p.409) or pick up a free copy of the *Kyoto Visitors' Guide* or *Kansai Scene*. Kyoto has very few gay and lesbian venues, compared with Ōsaka; however, Diamond Night, held monthly at *Metro* (see opposite), is a mainstay of the local LGBT scene.

Central Kyoto and Pontochō

The following listings are marked on the map on p.416.

A Bar 2F Reiho Biru Nishi Kiyamachi ⓣ075/213-2129. Serving a large selection of inexpensive *izakaya* food, draught beer and cocktails, this establishment is a popular choice with the younger crowd. The log-cabin interior, shared tables and funky T-shirts worn by the waiters make for a fun, relaxed evening. Open till midnight weekdays and 1am on weekends.

Hill of Tara Ōike-dori Kawaramachi higashi-iru ⓣ075/213-3330, ⓦwww.thehilloftara.com. Right next to the *Kyotō Hotel Okura*, this very popular Irish pub has Kilkenny and Guinness on tap, voluminous portions of hearty Irish food, and an enjoyable atmosphere, especially on the regular live music nights. Happy hour 5–8pm.

Jittoku 拾得 Ōmiya Marutamachi-agaru ⓣ075/841-1691. A little bit out of the way, north of Nijō-jō, this wonderful old *kura* (storehouse) with good acoustics hosts mostly rock and blues bands. Cover charge ¥800–3000. Closed Tues.

Live Spot Rag 5F Empire Biru ⓦwww.ragnet.co.jp. Well-established musicians' hangout (they have rehearsal rooms and recording studios here as well) which hosts local and international bands, mainly playing jazz. Live music daily from 7pm. Entry from ¥1600.

Rub a Dub B1 Tsujita Biru, Kiyamachi Sanjō-sagaru ⓣ075/256-3122. Sip a piña colada in this compact reggae beach bar decked out with fairy lights, palm trees and plastic fruit. DJ nights occur occasionally. It's at the north end of canalside Kiyamachi-dōri – look for a small signboard on the pavement. Open late.

Taku Taku 磔磔 Tominokoji Bukkōji-sagaru ⓣ075/351-1321. In the blocks southwest of Takashimaya department store, this *kura* makes a great live venue. The music's pretty varied but tends towards rock and blues, including the occasional international artist. Cover charge from ¥1600 (depending on performer), including one drink. Doors 6pm, performances 7–9pm.

UrBAN GUILD 3F New Kyoto Biru, Kiyamachi Sanjō-sagaru ⓣ075/212-1125. Avant-garde club, with a good local reputation for hosting interesting underground local and international acts playing psych-rock, acid folk and lo-fi electronica. Entry ¥1500–3000.

The Weller's Club 5F Rapport Building, Takoyakushi-dōri Fuyachō Nishi-iru ⓣ075/253-0753, ⓦwww.wellersclub.com. A shrine to all things mod, celebrating Paul Weller in his various incarnations, with strict observance of his birthday. Occasional Northern Soul nights. Daily 8pm–3am.

World B1-B2 Imagium Building ⓦwww.world-kyoto.com. Cavernous basement club attracting big-name house, hip-hop and techno DJs from Japan and abroad. Weekday nights are quieter, but the place heaves at the weekend. Average entry is ¥2000–2500 (including one drink). Open most nights from 9pm.

Gion and east Kyoto

The following are marked on the map on p.423.

The Gael Irish Pub 2F Ōto Bldg, Keihan Shijō Station ⓣ075/525-0680, ⓦwww.irishpubkyoto.com. Popular expat hangout with a warm and friendly atmosphere. There's good-quality food and a decent range of beers. Weekly live music and other events.

Jazz Live Candy B1 Hanamikōji Shinmonzen-agaru. Well-established jazz bar with top, mostly local, live acts every night. Seating charge of ¥735, plus cover charge (¥1000–2500). Open 7pm–1am.

La Gallega Kyouen Complex, Keihan Shijō Station ⓣ075/533-7206. Spacious Spanish tapas and standing bar which looks out onto a Zen-style rock garden. Monthly flamenco shows. Excellent value at happy hour (6–8pm).

Metro Keihan Marutamachi Station ⓦwww.metro.ne.jp. In the heart of the train station (take exit 2), this progressive club offers an eclectic selection of music, from local guitar bands and big-name foreign techno DJs to drag shows and hardcore dub reggae parties. It's small, loud and very popular. Entrance ¥500–2000 (more for foreign DJs or bands), including one drink. Daily from around 9pm.

Sayura Vins Fins 570 Gion-machi ⓣ075/551-1599. Elegant wine bar in a *machiya* right opposite Gion Kōbu Kaburenjō. The interior is ultra-modern – sleek wood and dim lighting with the spotlight on an internal garden. They offer a sophisticated wine list that won't blow your budget. There's no sign, so look out for the giant wine glass at the gate. Closed Mon.

Dance, theatre and cinema

Kyoto is famous for its traditional **geisha dance** shows. Performances of kabuki and nō plays are more sporadic but worth attending if you happen to be in town when they are on.

Geisha Odori

Geisha (or *geiko*, as they are known locally) and *maiko* (trainee geisha) from each of the city's former pleasure quarters (see p.426) have been putting on *Odori* (dance performances) during spring and autumn since the late nineteenth century, though the music and choreography are much older. By turns demure and coquettish, they glide round the stage in the most gorgeous kimono, straight out of an Edo-period woodblock print of Japan's seductive "floating world". If you're in Kyoto during these seasonal dances, it's well worth going along. Performances take place several times a day, so it's usually possible to get hold of tickets; you can buy them from the theatre box offices and major hotels. At all of the *Odori*, you can also buy tickets that combine the show with a tea ceremony conducted by geisha and *maiko*, which is well worth the extra cost (¥3800–6000, depending on the district). Make sure you get there early enough to enjoy your bowl of *macha* (powdered green tea).

The annual dance performances in the geisha districts kick off with the **Miyako Odori** (April 1–30) performed by the geisha and *maiko* of Gion. This is the most prestigious and well known of the *Odori*, mainly because it is the oldest, having started in 1872. The dances are based on a seasonal theme and have lavish sets and costumes. Live musicians playing *shamisen*, flutes and drums, as well as singers, perform in alcoves at each side of the stage. Miyako Odori is held at Gion Kōbu Kaburenjō (see p.427; ⓣ075/541-3391, ⓦwww.miyako-odori.jp; tickets from ¥2000).

Also at this time is **Kyo Odori**, held in the Miyagawa-chō district, south of Gion. This is a smaller, more intimate production than Miyako Odori, though equally as

Major Kyoto festivals and annual events

Thanks to its central role in Japanese history, Kyoto is home to a number of important **festivals**; the major celebrations are listed below. The **cherry-blossom** season hits Kyoto in early April – famous viewing spots include the Imperial Park, Yasaka-jinja and Arashiyama – while early November brings dramatic **autumn colours**. Many **temples** hold special **openings** in October and November to air their inner rooms during the fine, dry weather. This is a marvellous opportunity to see paintings, statues and other treasures not normally on public display; details are available in the free *Kyoto Visitors' Guide*. Kyoto gets pretty busy during major festivals and national holidays, especially Golden Week (April 29–May 5).

Febuary 2–4 Setsubun. Annual bean-throwing festival celebrated at shrines throughout the city. At Yasaka-jinja, "ogres" scatter beans and pray for good harvests, while Heian-jingū hosts performances of traditional *kyōgen* theatre (see p.788) on Feb 3.

April 1–30 Miyako Odori. Performances of traditional geisha dances in Gion (see p.427).

April 7–22 Kyo Odori. Performances by the geisha and *maiko* of the Miyagawachō district (see above).

May 15 Aoi Matsuri. The "Hollyhock Festival" dates back to the days when this plant was believed to ward off earthquakes and thunder. Now it's an occasion for a gorgeous, yet slow, procession of people dressed in Heian-period costume (794–1185). They accompany the imperial messenger and an ox cart decked in hollyhock leaves from the Imperial Palace to the Shimo-gamo and Kami-gamo shrines, in north Kyoto.

May 1–24 Kamo-gawa Odori. Performances of traditional dances by geisha in Pontochō (see p.417).

June 1–2 Takigi Nō. Nō plays performed by torchlight at Heian-jingū.

July 17 Gion Matsuri. One of Kyoto's great festivals dates back to Heian times, when ceremonies were held to drive away epidemics of the plague. The festivities opulent (April 7–22; tickets from ¥3,800 with tea; ⓣ075/561-1151). The ladies of Pontochō stage their **Kamo-gawa Odori** once a year (May 1–24) in Pontochō Kaburenjō, at the north end of Pontochō-dōri (ⓣ075/221-2025; tickets from ¥2000) – Jean Cocteau and Charlie Chaplin were both fans.

Autumn brings a whole flurry of activity, though the dances are more like recitals, and not as extravagant as the spring dances. The **Onshukai** dances are held during the first week in October at the Gion Kaikan theatre, near Yasaka-jinja (ⓣ075/561-0224; from ¥4000), closely followed by **Kotobukikai** (around Oct 8–12) in northwest Kyoto's Kitano Kami-shichiken Kaburenjō (ⓣ075/461-0148; ¥6000), and **Mizuekai** (mid-Oct) at the Miyagawa-chō Kaburenjō (ⓣ075/561-1151; from ¥3000). Finally, the **Gion Odori**, performed by the *maiko* and geisha of the smaller Gion Higashi district, wraps things up in early November (Nov 1–10; from ¥3300), at the Gion Kaikan (ⓣ075/561-0160) theatre near Yasaka-jinja.

If your visit doesn't coincide with any of these, you can see *maiko* dancing, as well as a sampler of other traditional performance arts, from March to November at **Gion Corner**, held at Gion Kōbu Kaburenjō (see p.427). As well as dances by *maiko*, there are short extracts from court dances, a puppet play (*bunraku*), *kyōgen* theatre, and demonstrations of the tea ceremony and flower arranging (*ikebana*). English-language guided commentary is available to rent at the entrance. Alternatively, the **Gion Hatanaka Ryokan** (see p.414) holds Kyoto Cuisine and Maiko Evening events (6pm Mon, Wed, Fri & Sat; ⓣ075/541-5315; ⓦwww.kyoto-maiko.jp; ¥18,000; reservations essential) which non-guests are welcome to attend. This is a great chance to see *maiko* performing at close range and take photos.

focus on Yasaka-jinja and culminate on July 17 (though there are related events throughout the whole of the month), with a grand parade through central Kyoto of tall, pointy *yama-boko* floats, richly decorated with local Nishijin silk. Night festivals are held three days prior to the parade, when the floats are lit with lanterns. Some can be viewed inside for a few hundred yen.

August 16 Daimonji Gozan Okuribi. Five huge bonfires etch *kanji* characters on five hills around Kyoto; the most famous is the character for *dai* (big) on Daimonji-yama, northeast of the city. The practice originated from lighting fires after Obon (see p.59).

October 22 Jidai Matsuri. This "Festival of the Ages" was introduced in 1895 to mark Kyoto's 1100th anniversary. More than two thousand people, wearing costumes representing all the intervening historical periods, parade from the Imperial Palace to Heian-jingū.

October 22 Kurama-no-Himatsuri. After the Jidai parade, hop on a train north to see Kurama's more boisterous Fire Festival. Villagers light bonfires outside their houses and local lads carry giant, flaming torches (the biggest weighing up to 100kg) to the shrine. Events climax around 8pm with a mad dash up the steps with a *mikoshi*, after which there's heavy-duty drinking, drumming and chanting till dawn. To get there, take the Eizan line from Kyoto's Demachiyanagi Station (30min); it's best to arrive early and leave around 10pm unless you want to see it through.

December 1–25 Kabuki Kaomise. Grand kabuki festival.

December 31 Okera Mairi. The best place to see in the New Year is at Gion's Yasaka-jinja. Apart from the normal festivities (see *Festival fun* colour section), locals come here to light a flame from the sacred fire, with which to rekindle their hearths back home. As well as general good luck, this supposedly prevents illness in the coming year.

Kabuki and nō

Colourful and dramatic, **kabuki** theatre is said to have originated in Kyoto. Unfortunately, performances these days are fairly sporadic, but in December there's a major kabuki-fest at Gion's eye-catching Minami-za theatre (see p.427; ⓣ075/561-1155). During this *kaomise*, or "face-showing" (Dec 1–25), big-name actors give snippets from their most successful roles.

Nō theatre is a far more stately affair; though it is often incomprehensible, even to the Japanese, it can also be incredibly powerful. Kyoto's main venue for nō is the Kanze Kaikan (ⓣ075/771-6114), south of Heian-jingū, with performances of nō or *kyōgen* most weekends (tickets from ¥2500, occasional free performances). Both the Kongo Nō-gakudō (ⓣ075/221-3049; around ¥6000), near west Kyoto's Karasuma Shijō junction, and Kawamura Nō Kaikan (ⓣ075/451-4513; from ¥4000), put on plays every month or so. The latter is a lovely old theatre run by the Kawamura family – a long line of famous nō actors – located on Karasuma-dōri near Doshisha University.

An important part of the local arts scene is the **Kyoto Art Center** (ⓣ075/213-1000, ⓦen.kac.or.jp), a large space that hosts a range of exhibitions and art performances as well as lectures, field trips and a well-regarded series of "Traditional Theatre Training" workshops (held every July) for those who want to find out more about nō and other Japanese performing arts.

Cinema

As nearly all of Kyoto's stately old **cinemas** have been demolished in recent years, the mulitplexes are the place to see mainstream films and include Movix Kyoto (ⓣ075/254-3215), south of Sanjō, and Toho Cinemas at Nijō Station (ⓣ075/813-2410, ⓦwww.tohotheater.jp/theater/nijo/index.html). For art-house films, try Minami Kaikan (ⓣ075/661-3993), near the junction of Ōmiya and Kujō, southeast of Kyoto Station, or Kyoto Cinema (ⓣ075/353-4723, ⓦwww.kyotocinema.jp), in the Cocon Karasuma shopping complex.

Shopping

Kyoto's main shopping district is focused around the junction of **Shijō-dōri** and **Kawaramachi-dōri**, and spreads north of Shijō along the Teramachi and Shinkyōgoku covered arcades. You'll find the big-name **department stores**, notably Takashimaya, Hankyū and Daimaru, all on Shijō. Souvenir shops, smart boutiques and even a few traditional craft shops are mostly situated on **Sanjō-dōri**, just west of the river. In recent years, two trendy shopping complexes have opened on Karasuma-dōri. Shinpuhkan, just south of Ōike, consists of four levels of boutiques, restaurants and variety goods shops, built around an inner courtyard. Cocon Karasuma, south of **Shijō**, has designer furniture and contemporary Japanese craft shops, as well as restaurants and cafés. The station area is home to the huge Isetan department store and a revamped underground shopping mall, Porta, under the northern bus terminal.

East Kyoto is best known for its wealth of shops around Kiyomizu-dera, which sell the local pottery, while nearby Sannen-zaka hosts a lovely parade of traditional craft shops. Further north, Gion's Shinmonzen-dōri specializes in antiques – prices are predictably high, but it's a good area to browse.

Textiles and fashion

Kyoto has long been famous for its high-quality **weaving**. The centre of the city's textile industry is the **Nishijin** district, located northwest of the Imperial Palace. Even today you'll still hear the clatter of looms in dozens of family-run workshops as you walk through the area. Due to the lingering recession, the number of kimono- and *obi*- related businesses in Nishijin is believed to be now just over six hundred, compared with more than twelve hundred in 1980.

In Nishijin weaving, silk threads are dyed before being woven into their intricate patterns. Originally, only the aristocracy could afford these fabrics, and when merchants began to patronize the same tailors in the late seventeenth century the shogun promptly forbade such extravagance. However, an enterprising Kyoto craftsman, Yūzensai Miyazaki, soon came up with a method for hand-dyeing fabrics to create the same elaborate effect. **Yūzen dyeing** is still an incredibly complex process, involving successive applications of glutinous-rice paste and dye to produce detailed, multicoloured designs. Afterwards, the pattern is often augmented with powdered gold or silver leaf, or embroidered with gold threads. You can see samples of these gorgeous fabrics and demonstrations of traditional Nishijin weaving at the **Nishijin Textile Centre** (daily 9am–5pm; free; Ⓦwww.nishijin.or.jp/eng/eng.htm), just south of the Horikawa Imadegawa junction. The centre also puts on daily kimono shows (hourly; 10am–4pm) showcasing the season's fashions.

Some of these wonderful techniques have been revitalized by young Kyoto fashion designers. The shops listed below offer top-quality locally designed and made clothes and accessories.

Green T 281-1 Gion-machi Ⓦwww.green-t.jp; see East Kyoto map, p.423. Funky original T-shirt designs inspired by traditional Kyoto motifs in a range of colours and sizes.

Kyoto Denim 373 Koinari-chō; see Around Kyoto Station map, p.420. Fashionable denim jeans and clothing incorporating local fabrics, including cotton, silk and brocade.

Onitsuka Tiger 373 Kiyomoto-chō Gion Ⓦwww.asics.co.jp/onitsukatiger; see Central Kyoto map, p.416. Unique and much sought-after sports shoes made with Nishijin brocade and kimono fabric.

Pagong 373 Kiyomoto-chō Gion; see East Kyoto map, p.423. Traditional Yūzen dyer now producing aloha shirts, camisoles, dresses, scarves and T-shirts with traditional patterns and designs.

Sistere 2F 381-1 Funaya-chō Ⓦwww.sistere.jp; see Central Kyoto map, p.416. Ultra-cool modern Kyoto designer, focusing less on the kimono tradition of pattern and colour and more on sleek lines and top-quality craftsmanship.

Sou Sou 565-72 Nakano-chō Ⓦwww.sousou.co.jp; see Central Kyoto map, p.416. A winning combination of traditional footwear and modern style, the shop designs and sells *jikatabi*, split-toe workmen's shoes, in funky fabrics and styles. Also sells sportswear and kimono.

Traditional arts and crafts shops

You can still find **shops** in Kyoto producing crafts in the traditional way, using skills passed down the generations; these offer superb, if often pricey, souvenirs of the city. There's also no shortage of innovative shops and galleries which expertly fuse time-honoured traditional techniques with modern design.

Asahi-do 朝日堂1-287-1 Kiyomizu; see East Kyoto, map, p.423. The best and most famous of several pottery shops on the road up to Kiyomizu-dera, established in the Edo period and selling a wide variety of locally produced *Kiyomizu-yaki*.

Ichizawa Hanpu 一澤帆布 Higashi-ōji Shijō-agaru Furumon-mae; see East Kyoto map, p.423. Long-established canvas bag manufacturer, famous for a family feud over the brand name when the partriarch died. Now three of the brothers have stores on opposite sides of Higashi-ōji – essentially producing the same product. The hand-stitched bags have functional designs and come in a variety of colours. Prices start at ¥3000. Arrive early to beat the crowds. Daily except Sun 9am–5.30pm.

Jūsan-ya 十三や Shijō Teramachi higashi-iru; see Central Kyoto map, p.416. This little shop on Shijō-dōri is crammed with beautiful combs and hair ornaments in plain boxwood or covered in lacquer. All the items are handcrafted using traditional techniques.

Kungyoku-dō 薫玉堂 Horikawa-dōri, Nishi-Hongan-ji-mae; see Around Kyoto Station map, p.420. Though you wouldn't guess it from its modern, grey-stone frontage, this shop has been selling incense since 1594 – their original customers were Buddhist temples and court nobles indulging in incense parties (players had to guess the ingredients from the perfume). The shop lies opposite the west gate of Nishi-Hongan-ji. Closed 1st and 3rd Sun of the month.

Kyoto Craft Centre Shijō-dōri; see East Kyoto map, p.423. This large, modern shop showcases the best of Kyoto's contemporary designers working with traditional crafts and is great for unusual, stylish souvenirs. It's located in Gion, towards the east end of Shijō-dōri. Open daily except Wed 11am–7pm.

Kyoto Design House Tominokōji-dōri Sanjō-agaru; see Central Kyoto map, p.416. Premium selection of contemporary local designs – from sleek tableware to functional purses and wallets. Daily 11am–8pm.

Kyoto Handicraft Center Marutamachi-dōri ⓦwww.kyotohandicraftcenter.com; see East Kyoto map, p.423. Five floors packed with souvenirs from all over Japan, with a range of prices. The smaller Amita Plaza, next door, is also worth a look for its selection of foodstuffs. Both shops offer tax-free prices for goods over ¥10,000 (see p.667 for more about this). Find them near the northwest corner of Heian-jingu.

Kyoto Tōjiki Kaikan Gojō-zaka; see East Kyoto map, p.423. West of Kiyomizu-dera, this place stocks a good selection of *Kiyomizu-yaki* and other local ceramics. It's also worth popping into the next-door gallery to see what's on display.

Naitō 内藤 Sanjō-ōhashi; see Central Kyoto map, p.416. You might not be in the market for a broom, but this old shop just west of the Sanjō bridge is a treasure-trove of beautifully made hemp brushes of every size and description (from ¥700). The traditional shop selling rice crackers and confectionery next door is also a delight.

RAAK Muromachi Sanjō-agaru ⓦwww.raak.jp; see Central Kyoto map, p.416. The main store of this traditional *tenugui* (cotton hand cloth) manufacturer, which now reproduces stylish Taisho designs from the 1920s, can be found on Muromachi, but there are smaller branches on Shijō, on both sides of the bridge. Modern styles are also produced; the *tenugui* can be worn as a scarf or framed and hung on the wall. Daily 11am–8pm.

Tachikichi たち吉 Shijō Tominokoji ⓦwww.tachikichi.co.jp; see Central Kyoto map, p.416. An elegant shop on Shijō-dōri, selling fine ceramics and china on three floors and modern crafts in the basement. Looks expensive but seasonal sales are surprisingly good for bargains. Closed occasionally on Wed.

Tanakaya Shijō Yanaginobanba; see Central Kyoto map, p.416. Dolls of all shapes and sizes fill this shop on Shijō-dōri. There's also a gallery upstairs with changing exhibitions of antique dolls. Closed Wed.

Tsujikura Kawaramachi Shijō-agaru; see Central Kyoto map, p.416. Traditional paper and modern

Experiencing Kyoto culture

It's possible to learn about various traditional crafts and Kyoto culture at venues around the city. For *yūzen* dyeing head to the **Kodai Yūzen-en** gallery (daily 9am–5pm; ¥500; ⓦwww.kodaiyuzen.co.jp), located on Takatsuji-dōri, southwest of the Horikawa Shijō junction. Ask to see their introductory video in English, first and then, if you're inspired, you can try **yūzen hand-dyeing** for yourself, on a handkerchief or table centrepiece (from ¥1600). Two blocks west of the Nishijin Textile Centre, on Nakasuji-dōri, you can learn about another hand-dyeing technique at the lovely old **Aizen-kōbō** workshop run by the Utsuki family (Mon–Fri 10am–5.30pm, Sat & Sun 9am–4pm; free; reservation essential at weekends; ⓣ075/441-0355, ⓦweb.Kyoto-inet.or.jp/people/aizen). Aizen-kōbō's owner, Kenichi Utsuki, gives explanations in English of the intricate and time-consuming techniques involved in **indigo hand-dyeing**. The cloth is dyed with natural indigo and then sun-dried to give it a glorious, rich shade of blue or green. The **Kyoto Handicraft Centre** (see opposite) offers **demonstration classes** for beginners in *cloisonné* (enamel-work) and woodblock printing (¥1890 for 1hr; book at the ground-floor information desk 1–4pm). The **Uzuki Cooking School** in northeastern Kyoto holds classes in seasonal **Kyoto cuisine**, mostly on weekday afternoons. The enthusiastic English-speaking instructor, Emi Hirayama, brings you into her own kitchen and takes you through the steps of creating a delicious four-course meal (¥4000/person; ⓦwww.kyotouzuki.com). Finally, **WAK Japan** (¥3500–5500/person; ⓦwww.wakjapan.com) offers 55-minute courses with English-speaking female teachers in **tea ceremony, kimono, calligraphy, flower arrangement** and **musical instruments** at their *machiya* school near the Imperial Palace. More expensive "home visit" lessons are also available (from ¥10,500).

plastic umbrellas spill out of this shop (established in 1690) onto the pavement of Kawaramachi-dōri. They also stock jaunty paper lanterns in a variety of styles. Closed Wed.

Yamato Mingei-ten やまと民芸店 Kawaramachi Takoyakushi-agaru; see Central Kyoto map, p.416. The best place in Kyoto to buy folk crafts. The main shop has two floors stuffed full of tempting items from all over Japan, while the annexe round the corner displays furniture and more modern designs. Find them on Kawaramachi-dōri, near Jankara Karaoke. Closed Tues.

Yojiya よーじや Shijō-dōri, Gion Ⓦwww.yojiya.co.jp; see East Kyoto map, p.423. Traditional Kyoto cosmetic manufacturer with branches now all over the city. Powders, lipsticks and brushes, just like those used by geisha, as well as cute make-up pouches and hand-mirrors. There is another branch on Sanjō, which has an excellent in-house Italian café. Daily 10am–8pm.

Books

A small but useful range of foreign-language **books and magazines** can be found on the seventh floor of the Junkudo store (Ⓣ075/253-6460), in the BAL building on Kawaramachi-dōri, north of the Shijō junction. The Kyoto Handicraft Center (Ⓣ075/761-8001, Ⓦwww.kyotohandicraftcenter.com) also stocks an excellent selection of books on Japan on the fifth floor. Green e Books (Ⓣ075/751-5033, Ⓦwww.greenebooks.net,) on the northeastern corner of the Marutamachi and Kawabata intersection, is Kyoto's only secondhand English-language bookshop, with an eclectic range of fiction, non-fiction, magazines and children's books.

Food

Kyoto is as famous for its beautiful **foodstuffs** as it is for crafts, all made with the same attention to detail and love of refinement. You can see this in even the most modest restaurant, but also in the **confectionery** shops, where the window displays look more like art galleries. A popular local delicacy is **pickled vegetables** (*tsukemono*), which accompany most meals. If you take a walk down **Nishiki-kōji** market street (see p.418), you'll notice that pickles predominate among all the vegetables, tofu and dried fish. The shops listed below sell souvenir packaging of their famous products.

Fujino Tofu Donuts Nishiki-kōji; see Central Kyoto map, p.416. Delicious small doughnut rings made with tofu and very lightly deep-fried.

Nishiri 西利 Shijō-dōri, Gion; see East Kyoto map, p.423. Renowned Kyoto pickle company popular for their crispy *nasu* (aubergine) pickles.

Takakuraya 高倉屋 Nishiki-kōji; see Central Kyoto map, p.416. Famous for their thinly sliced white radish pickles, among other local vegetables which they expertly prepare.

Toraya とらや Gokomachi nishi-iru Shijō-dōri Ⓦwww.toraya-group.co.jp; see Central Kyoto map, p.416. Superbly artistic creations of seasonal sweets made from *mochi* (pounded rice) and sweet white beans.

Yatsuhashi 八つ橋 Shinkyōgoku Shijō-agaru; see Central Kyoto map, p.416. Sweet cinnamon-flavoured crackers. The smell of them baking in this shop is divine.

Temple and shrine flea markets

If you're in Kyoto towards the end of the month, don't miss the two big **flea markets**. On the 21st, Kōbō-san (in honour of the founder) is held at **Tō-ji** temple (see p.421), and on the 25th, Tenjin-san (in honour of the enshrined deity) is held at **Kitano Tenmangū**, a large shrine in northwest Kyoto (entrance on Imadegawa-dōri). Both kick off before 7am and it's worth getting there early if you're looking for special treasures. There's a fantastic carnival atmosphere at these markets, where stalls sell everything from used kimono to dried fruit and manga. Tō-ji has an antiques market on the first Sunday of every month.

A monthly market is also held at **Chion-ji** on the 15th of every month (16th if raining), which focuses more on crafts and other handmade goods. Chion-ji sits on the corner of Imadegawa-dōri and Higashiōji-dōri, close to Kyoto University.

Listings

Airports Itami (Ōsaka International) ⓣ06/6856-6781; Kansai International ⓣ072/455-2500, ⓦwww.kansai-airport.or.jp.

Banks and exchange The main banking district is around the Karasuma Shijō junction, where Sumitomo Mitsui Banking Corporation, Citibank and Bank of Tokyo Mitsubishi UFJ (MUFG) banks all have foreign-exchange facilities. At the station, the Central Post Office (see below) also handles foreign exchange (Mon–Fri 9.30am–6pm).

Bike rental Kyo no Raku Chari (ⓣ0120/318-319; daily 9am–5pm), on the riverbank just north of Sanjō-Keihan Station, charges ¥2000/day. Kyoto Cycling Tour Project (ⓣ075/354-3636; 9am–7pm) rents various kinds of bikes from ¥1000/day and also arranges tours (see p.412).

Car rental Nippon Rent-a-Car (ⓣ075/671-0919), Nissan Rent-a-Car (ⓣ075/351-4123) and Eki Rent-a-Car (ⓣ075/371-3020) all have offices near Kyoto Station.

Emergencies The main police station is at 85-3 Yabunouchi-cho, Shimodachiuri-dori, Kamanza Higashi-iru, Kamigyo-ku (ⓣ075/451-9111). In an absolute emergency, contact the Foreign Advisory Service on ⓣ075/752-3010. For other emergency numbers, see p.71.

Hospitals and clinics The main Kyoto hospital with English-speaking doctors is the Japan Baptist Hospital, 47 Yamanomoto-chō, Kitashirakawa, Sakyō-ku (ⓣ075/781-5191). Sakabe Clinic, 435 Yamamoto-chō, Gokomachi Nijō-sagaru (closed Thurs & Sat afternoons and all day Sun; ⓣ075/231-1624), is run by English-speaking staff. For more information about medical facilities with English-speaking staff in Kyoto or throughout the region, call the AMDA International Medical Information Centre (ⓣ06/6636-2333).

Immigration To renew your tourist or student visa, apply to the Immigration Bureau, 4F, 34-12 Higashi Marutamachi, Kawabata Higashi-iru, near Keihan Marutamachi Station (ⓣ075/752-5997).

Internet The Kyoto Tourist Information Center on the second floor of Kyoto Station next to the Isetan department store charges ¥100/10min. Kyoto International Community House has free usage. Downtown, you can use PCs or Macs (¥250/10min) at Kinkos on Karasuma-dōri (ⓣ075/213-6802) or at C. Coquet Communication Service (ⓣ075/212-0882) on Marutamachi-dōri, south of the Imperial Palace (ⓣ075/212-0882). The *Gael Irish Pub* in Gion (p.441) has free access to two computers and wi-fi.

Language courses Kyoto Japanese Language School, Ichijō-dōri Muromachi-nishi, Kamigyō-ku ⓣ075/414-0449, ⓦwww.kjls.or.jp; Kyoto Institute of Language and Culture, 21 Kamihate-chō, Kitashirakawa, Sakyō-ku ⓣ075/722-5066, ⓦwww.kicl.ac.jp; Kyoto YMCA Japanese Language School, Sanjō Yanaginobanba ⓣ075/255-3287, ⓦwww.kyotoymca.or.jp; and Kyoto International Academy, Kitano Tenman-gu ⓣ075/466-4881, ⓦwww.kia-ac.jp. The Kyoto International Community House, 2-1 Torii-chō Awataguchi, Sakyō-ku ⓣ075/752-3010, ⓦwww.kcif.or.jp; Trademark, 15 Naginomiya-chō, Nakagyō-ku ⓣ075/201-6139, ⓦj-space.sakura.ne.jp.

Post office The Central Post Office, 843-12 Higashi Shiokoji-chō, Shimogyō-ku, Kyoto-shi, is located in front of Kyoto Station. Downtown, the Nakagyō Ward Post Office, 30 Hishiya-chō, Nakagyō-ku, is near the Museum of Kyoto. Both have a 24hr window for stamps and express mail.

Around Kyoto

There's so much to see in Kyoto itself that most people don't explore the surrounding area. First priority should probably go to **Arashiyama**, to the west side of Kyoto, which is famous for its gardens and temples, as well as the Hozu-gawa gorge boat ride and the monkey park. **Uji**, to the south of Kyoto, is another quiet pocket of history and home to the magnificent **Byōdō-in**, whose graceful Phoenix Hall is a masterpiece of Japanese architecture, as well as the tea fields which support Kyoto's cultural traditions. In the northeast of Kyoto is **Hiei-zan**, atop a mountain overlooking the city, where age-old cedars shelter the venerable temples of **Enryaku-ji**. Below Hiei-zan, **Ōhara** contains a scattering of beguiling temples in an attractive valley.

Slightly further afield, but definitely worth the effort, are **Amanohashidate**, the "Bridge to Heaven", on the northern coast of Kyoto prefecture and one of the trio of top scenic views in Japan; the attractive castle town of **Hikone** on Biwa-ko, Japan's largest lake; and the architecturally stunning **Miho Museum**, nestled in the Shigaraki mountains.

Arashiyama

Western Kyoto ends in the pleasant, leafy suburb of **ARASHIYAMA** (嵐山). Set beside the Hozu-gawa, Arashiyama was originally a place for imperial relaxation, away from the main court in central Kyoto, where aristocrats indulged in pursuits such as poetry-writing and hunting, but the palaces were later converted into Buddhist temples and monasteries. The most famous of these is **Tenryū-ji**, noted for its garden, while the smaller, quieter temples have a more intimate appeal. In contrast with Tenryū-ji's somewhat introspective garden, that of **Ōkōchi Sansō** – the home of a 1920s movie actor – is by turns secretive and dramatic, with winding paths and sudden views over Kyoto. For a break from temples and gardens, take the Torokko train up the scenic Hozu valley to **Kameoka**, from where boats ferry you back down the fairly gentle **Hozu rapids**.

A good way to explore the area is to rent a bike and spend a day pottering around the lanes and through magnificent bamboo forests; alternatively, it is possible to see some of the main sights by *jinrikisha* (see p.410). If you're pushed for time, you could consider combining Arashiyama with the sights of western Kyoto (see p.432).

Arrival and information

Three train lines and several bus routes connect Arashiyama with central Kyoto. Unless you've got a bus or JR rail pass, the quickest and most pleasant way to get here is to take a **train** on the private Keifuku Electric Railway from Kyoto's Shijō-Ōmiya Station (every 10min; 20min; ¥200). This brings you into the main Arashiyama Station in the centre of town – pick up a free bilingual map of the town at the station. Keifuku offers a one-day pass (¥650) covering unlimited travel on this Arashiyama line and also the Keifuku Kitano line, which connects with Kitano-Hakubai-chō Station in northwest Kyoto. Alternatively, the JR Sagano line runs from Kyoto Station to Saga-Arashiyama Station (every 20min; 15min; ¥230), which is handy for the Torokko trains, but it's roughly fifteen minutes' walk to central Arashiyama from here; make sure you get on a local JR train from Kyoto and not the express, which shoots straight through. Finally, there's the less convenient Hankyū Electric Railway; from central Kyoto you have to change at Katsura Station, and you end up in the Hankyū Arashiyama Station on the south side of the river.

Buses are slightly more expensive and take longer, especially when the traffic's bad. However, Arashiyama is on the main Kyoto bus network and falls within the limits for the combined bus and subway pass (see p.411). City Bus routes #11, #28 and #93, and Kyoto Bus routes #61, #71, #72, #73 and #83, all pass through central Arashiyama. If you plan to do more than just the central sights, it's worth considering **bike rental**. There are rental outlets at each of the train stations (¥500–1000 per day).

Most people visit Arashiyama from their Kyoto lodgings but there is some **accommodation** available in the area, though it is very expensive and difficult to make reservations during peak tourist seasons. Check with the tourist office at Kyoto Station (see p.409) if you are keen to stay overnight.

The Town

Arashiyama is centred on the long **Togetsu-kyō** (渡月橋) bridge, which spans the Hozu-gawa (known as the Katsura-gawa east of the bridge). This is a famous spot for viewing spring cherry blossoms or maples in autumn. The town's most interesting sights, as well as the majority of its shops, restaurants and transport facilities, lie north of the Hozu-gawa. Note that central Arashiyama can get unbearably crowded, particularly on spring and autumn weekends; however, if you head north along the hillside you'll soon begin to leave the crowds behind.

Tenryū-ji

The first major sight is the Zen temple of **Tenryū-ji** (天龍寺; daily 8.30am–5pm; ¥600, or ¥500 for the garden only; ⓣ075/881-1235, ⓦtenryuji.org), which started life as the country retreat of Emperor Kameyama (1260–74), grandfather of the more famous **Emperor Go-Daigo** (1318–39). Go-Daigo overthrew the Kamakura shogunate (see p.768) and wrested power back to Kyoto in 1333 with the help of a defector from the enemy camp, **Ashikaga Takauji**. The ambitious Takauji soon grew exasperated by Go-Daigo's incompetence and staged a counter-coup. He placed a puppet emperor on the throne and declared himself shogun, thus also gaining the Arashiyama palace, while Go-Daigo fled south to set up a rival court in Yoshino, south of Nara. After Go-Daigo died in 1339, however, a series of bad omens convinced Takauji to convert the palace into a temple to appease Go-Daigo's restless soul.

The temple buildings are nearly all twentieth-century reproductions, but the **garden** behind dates back to the thirteenth century. It's best viewed from inside the temple, from where you get the full impact of the pond and its artfully placed rock groupings against the tree-covered hillside. The present layout of the garden is the work of **Musō Kokushi**, the fourteenth-century Zen monk also responsible for Saihō-ji (see p.435), who incorporated Zen and Chinese motifs into the existing garden. There's still an argument, however, over who created the garden's most admired feature, the dry, Dragon Gate waterfall on the far side of the pond. Apparently inspired by Chinese Sung-dynasty landscape paintings, the waterfall's height and bold vertical composition are extremely unusual in Japanese garden design. The temple is also home to **Shishiku-no-niwa** ("The Garden of the Lion's Roar"), a noted Zen garden of the dry, landscape type, with some particularly striking fence-work. Dating back to the Muromachi period (1338–1573), the garden opened to the public for the first time in 130 years in 2003, albeit for limited periods in spring and autumn (mid-March to mid-May & mid-Sept to mid-Dec). It's especially attractive in the autumn, when the maple trees are turning red.

Ōkōchi Sansō

Leaving Tenryū-ji, follow the paths through the garden to its back (north) entrance, where you'll emerge into some of the bamboo groves for which Arashiyama is renowned. Heading northwest along the hillside, look out on the left for the entrance to **Ōkōchi Sansō** (大河内山荘; daily 9am–5pm; ¥1000, including green tea; ⓣ075/872-2233), just before you reach the train tracks. Once the home of Ōkōchi Denjirō, a silent-film idol of the 1920s, this traditional Japanese villa has a spectacular location. The path through the villa's expansive grounds takes you winding all over the hillside, past tea-ceremony pavilions, a moss garden, a dry garden and stone benches, up to a ridge with views over Kyoto on one side and the Hozu gorge on the other. Finally, you drop down to a small museum devoted to the actor.

Seiryō-ji and Daikaku-ji

Further off to the west are two temples of significance. **Seiryō-ji** (清凉寺; daily 9am–4pm; ¥400) is worth the trek to see the statue of Shaka Nyorai (the Historical Buddha). The statue is currently on public display in April, May, October and November; at other times, a donation of ¥1000 will enable you to view it. The image was carved in China in 985 AD and is a copy of a much older Indian statue, which in turn was said to have been modelled on the Buddha while he was alive.

The rest of the time you'll only be able to see the statue's "internal organs" – when it was opened in 1953 several little silk bags in the shape of a heart, kidneys and liver were found, and these are now on display in the temple museum.

One kilometre northeast from here, the more impressive **Daikaku-ji** (大覚寺; daily 9am–4.30pm; ¥500) was founded in 876, when Emperor Saga ordered that his country villa be converted to a Shingon-sect temple. The main Shin-den hall was moved here from Kyoto's Imperial Palace in the late sixteenth century and still contains some fine screens painted by renowned artists of the Kanō school. Behind this building is the Shoshin-den, also noted for its panels of a hawk and an endearing group of rabbits. Afterwards you can wander along the banks of Ōsawa-ike, Emperor Saga's boating lake.

Along the Hozu-gawa

Northwest of Arashiyama the **Hozu-gawa** (保津川) flows through a fairly narrow, twisting gorge just over 15km long. It's a popular, though fairly expensive, half-day excursion to take the old-fashioned Torokko train upriver to **Kameoka** and come back down by boat. You can board the train at Torokko Arashiyama Station, just north of Ōkōchi Sansō (see opposite), or at the Torokko Saga terminus one stop further east. Wherever you get on it's the same price (¥600 one-way) for the 25-minute journey, which takes you through tunnels and crisscrosses the river. It's a good idea to reserve seats in advance during the main holiday periods, especially when the cherry blossoms and autumn colours are at their peak, though at other times you should be able to buy tickets on the day. Reservations can be made through JTB and other major travel agents, at JR's Green Windows or at Saga Torokko Station (Ⓣ075/861-7444, Ⓦwww.sagano-kanko.co.jp/eng). Trains leave hourly between 9.50am and 4.50pm (daily except Wed March–Dec).

At the Torokko Kameoka terminus buses wait to take you to the landing stage (15min; ¥280), from where chunky wooden **punts** set off down the Hozu-gawa (March 10–Nov 30 9am–3.30pm; Dec 1–March 9 10am–2.30pm; ¥3900; Ⓣ0771/22-5846, Ⓦwww.hozugawakudari.jp). The **rapids** aren't the most fearsome in the world, but it's a fun trip and the gorge is that much more impressive from water level. Back in Arashiyama, the boats land on the river's north bank just short of the Togetsu-kyo bridge. Regular **sightseeing boats** depart from this same landing stage for a very overpriced thirty-minute jaunt to the mouth of the gorge (¥1100/person), or you can rent your own three-person rowing boat for ¥1400 per hour.

Just over the Togetsu-kyo bridge, near the south bank landing stage, is the entrance to the **Arashiyama Monkey Park Iwatayama** (嵐山モンキーパークいわたやま; daily: March 15–Nov 20 9am–5.30pm; Nov 21–March 14 9am–4.30pm; Ⓣ075/872-0950, Ⓦwww.kmpi.co.jp; ¥500). A steep path winds up Mount Arashiyama to the observation deck, where the monkeys are fed; over 150 live in the park, which is also a research centre. From the deck there are good views of Arashiyama, Kyoto and the river, and the park is well worth a visit for a break away from the crowds.

Eating

Arashiyama is famous for its Buddhist vegetarian cuisine, *shōjin-ryōri*, and particularly for *yūdōfu* (simmered tofu), which is closely associated with the Zen tradition. Some of the top-end places are very pricey but Arashiyama also has plenty of cheaper places to eat, mostly clustered around the main station.

Arashiyama Yoshimura 嵐山よしむら; Ⓣ075/863-5700, Ⓦwww.arashiyama-yoshimura.com. This soba restaurant, near the Togetsu-kyō bridge, has fantastic views of the river and Mt Arashiyama from the second-floor dining area. Lunch sets start from ¥1575. Daily 10.30am–5pm.

Nishiki 錦 Ⓣ075/871-8888. One of the best-known restaurants in Kyoto, Nishiki is on the eastern end of Nakanoshima, the low island in the middle of the Hozu-gawa. Specializing in Kyoto cuisine, it serves exquisite seven- to thirteen-course meals, starting at ¥4400. Reservations essential at weekends. Open 11am–7.30pm; closed Tues.

Sagano 嵯峨野 ⓣ075/871-6946. In a graceful bamboo grove south of Tenryū-ji, Sagano is a tranquil place for lunch or an early dinner. The walls are lined with Imari chinaware, and their *yūdōfu* set meal is superb, accompanied by lots of sauces and vegetarian side dishes (¥3800). Daily 11am–7pm.

Shigetsu 天龍寺篩月 ⓣ075/882-9725. Located within Tenryū-ji, this is a truly authentic *shōjin-ryōri* experience. There's a choice of three courses (from ¥3000) and reservations are recommended; note that if you're eating in the restaurant the temple's ¥600 entry fee will be waived. Daily 11am–2pm.

Uji

The town of **UJI** (宇治), thirty minutes' train ride south of Kyoto, has a long and illustrious past and boasts one of Japan's most fabulous buildings, the **Byōdō-in** – for a preview, look at the reverse side of a ¥10 coin. Somehow this eleventh-century hall, with its glorious statue of Amida Buddha, survived war, fire and years of neglect, and today preserves a stunning display of Heian-period art at its most majestic. Uji is also famous for being the setting of the final chapters of *The Tale of Genji*, and there is now a museum entirely devoted to this aspect of the town's past. While you're here, see the tea fields and sample some of Uji's famous **green tea**; since the fourteenth century, this area's tea leaves have been rated among the best in the country. Uji can easily be visited on a half-day excursion from Kyoto, and it's only a little bit further from Nara (see p.463).

Arrival and information

Uji lies on the JR Nara line between Kyoto and Nara, with **trains** running roughly every fifteen minutes from Kyoto (15–30min) and every twenty minutes from Nara (30–50min). The Keihan line, which runs between Kyoto and Ōsaka, stops at Chushojima where you can change for the Keihan Uji line.

The **tourist information office** (daily 9am–5pm; ⓣ0774/23-3334) is further along the riverbank from Byōdō-in, next door to a traditional **teahouse**, *Taihou-an* (対鳳庵), where you can try Uji's famous green tea with a seasonal sweet (daily 10am–4pm; closed Dec 20–Jan 10; ¥500). On summer evenings the river here is used for demonstrations of **cormorant fishing** (see p.394); it's best experienced from one of the fishing boats (mid-June to early Sept daily 7–8.30pm; ⓣ0774/21-2328; ¥1500).

Byōdō-in

Arriving at JR Uji Station, cross over the main road and turn left along the next, parallel, road for a quieter route down to the Uji-gawa. Just before the bridge – a

The tea fields of Uji

Uji is the second-biggest **tea-growing** region in Japan (the largest is Shizuoka in the east of the country) and the area's tea leaves have supplied Kyoto's tea culture since the fourteenth century, when seeds brought over from China were first planted. It has become possible only quite recently to visit Uji's tea fields and tea-processing factories, and the best time to do so is in May, when the first leaves of the season, later drunk as *shin-cha* ("new tea"), are being picked. **Obubu Tea Plantations** (ⓦwww.obubutea.com) and **Shohokuen** (ⓦwww.ujicha.com) are two growers which have recently started offering field and factory tours to tourists during the picking season; check their websites for details.

The Tale of Genji Museum

The small but engaging **The Tale of Genji Museum** (源氏物語ミュージアム; 9am–5pm; closed Mon; ¥500; ⓣ0774/39-9300, ⓦwww.uji-genji.jp) is a delightful place to connect with Japan's literary history. *The Tale of Genji* (see p.784) was written in the early eleventh century by Murasaki Shikibu, the daughter of an official of the Imperial Court in Kyoto, and is regarded as the world's first novel. It is an epic saga of love affairs, court intrigues and political machinations, centring on Genji, the Shining Prince, the beautiful son of an emperor and his concubine. The book's finale is set in Uji, which Murasaki Shikibu would have known intimately – she was a distant relative of Fujiwara Michinaga and she served as lady-in-waiting to his daughter, Empress Akiko. At the museum, you can learn about the fictional world of Genji in 3-D format, which includes a reproduction of a Heian-period home and an animated film based on the heroine of the Uji chapters, Ukifune. Pick up one of the English-language pamphlets which explain the basics of the museum at the entrance. To get to the museum, cross over Uji bridge, north of Byōdō-in, towards Keihan Uji Station, and take a right turn up the hill.

modern successor to the seventh-century original – turn right on to a narrow shopping street and follow the river southeast through a fragrant haze of roasting tea. Then, where the lane forks left up onto the embankment, continue straight ahead and you'll find the entrance to the **Byōdō-in** (平等院; daily 8.30am–5.30pm; ¥600; ⓣ0774/21-2861, ⓦwww.byodoin.or.jp), roughly ten minutes' walk from the station.

After the imperial capital moved to Kyoto in 794 AD, Uji became a popular location for aristocratic country retreats. One such villa was taken over in the late tenth century by the emperor's chief adviser, **Fujiwara Michinaga**, when the Fujiwara clan was at its peak (see p.767). His son, Yorimichi, continued developing the gardens and pavilions until they were the envy of the court. Those pavilions have long gone, but you can still catch a flavour of this golden age through the great literary masterpiece, *The Tale of Genji* (see box above), written in the early eleventh century. In 1052, some years after *The Tale of Genji* was completed, Yorimichi decided to convert the villa into a temple dedicated to Amida, the Buddha of the Western Paradise. By the following year the great Amida Hall, popularly known as the **Phoenix Hall** (*Hōō-dō*), was completed. Miraculously, it's the only building from the original temple to have survived.

The best place to view the Phoenix Hall (daily 9.30am–4.10pm; ¥300) is from the far side of the pond, where it sits on a small island. The hall itself is surprisingly small, but the architect added two completely ornamental wings that extend in a broad U, like a pair of open arms. Inside, the gilded statue of **Amida** dominates. It was created by a sculptor-priest called Jōchō, using a new method of slotting together carved blocks of wood, and is in remarkably fine condition. At one time the hall must have been a riot of colour, but now only a few traces of the **wall paintings** remain, most of which are reproductions. If you look very carefully, you can just make out faded images of Amida and a host of heavenly beings descending on billowing clouds to receive the faithful. Meanwhile the white, upper walls are decorated with a unique collection of 52 carved Bodhisattvas, which were also originally painted. The original wall paintings, as well as the temple bell and two phoenixes, are now preserved in the excellent modern **treasure hall**, *Hōmotsu-kan,* partially submerged into a hill behind the Phoenix Hall. It's worth seeing them up close, especially as these are now the oldest examples of the *Yamato-e* style of painting (see p.784) still in existence.

Eating

You'll find plenty of snack shops and **restaurants** as you walk down towards Byōdō-in from JR Uji Station. *Magozaemon* (孫左エ門; daily 11am–3pm: closed Thurs; ☎0774/22-4068), opposite the entrance to Byōdō-in, has especially good and inexpensive handmade noodle dishes – try their green-tea udon, either hot or cold. In fine weather it's nice to buy a bentō from one of the local shops and eat it in the park on the little island in the middle of Uji-gawa.

Hiei-zan

Protecting Kyoto's northeastern flank (traditionally considered the source of evil spirits threatening the capital), the sacred mountain of **Hiei-zan** (比叡山) is the home of Tendai Buddhism, the headquarters of which are housed in an atmospheric collection of buildings, **Enryaku-ji**. Also on top of the mountain is the kitsch Garden Museum Hiei, an outdoor museum devoted to re-creating garden scenes from famous paintings by Monet and Renoir. Away from the commercialization, Enryaku-ji is still a pleasant place to meander along ancient paths through cedar forests. Though there are several ways of getting to Enryaku-ji (see opposite), the easiest route is by bus from Kyoto, wriggling up the mountainside and then following a ridge road north. On a clear day you'll be rewarded with huge views west over **Biwa-ko**, Japan's largest lake and the second-oldest freshwater lake in the world after Lake Baikal in Siberia.

Arrival

The quickest and simplest way of getting to Enryaku-ji is to take a **direct bus** (1hr; ¥750) from either Kyoto Station or Sanjō-Keihan Station in east Kyoto. The timetable varies according to the season, so check in Kyoto for the latest schedule and note that in winter the road is sometimes closed by snow. Enryaku-ji lies about 800m above sea level and can get pretty chilly in winter; even in summer you'll find it noticeably cooler than Kyoto.

The alternative is to take one of two **cable cars** up the mountain. The most convenient of these is the eastern **Sakamoto Cable** (坂本ケーブル; every 30min; 11min; ¥840, or ¥1570 return), which has the added benefit of views over Biwa-ko. To reach the cable car, take a JR Kosei line train from Kyoto Station to Hiei-zan Sakamoto Station (比叡山坂本駅; every 15min; 20min; ¥320), then a bus (¥220). From the top station it's a 700m-walk north to the central Tō-tō area along a quiet road. The main disadvantage of the western **Eizan Cable** (叡山ケーブル; every 30min; 20min; ¥840 one-way, or ¥1640 return) is that it dumps you about 1.5km from the Tō-tō, at the Sanchō Station (山頂駅), from where you can catch a shuttle bus (see below), or walk along a footpath from behind the Garden Museum Hiei. Eizan Cable leaves from near Yase-Hiei-zan-guchi Station (八瀬比叡山口駅) on the private Eizan line; to get there, either take a Kyoto Bus headed for Ōhara, or a train from Kyoto's Demachiyanagi Station (every 12min; 14min; ¥260). If you travel on the Keihan line to Demachiyanagi Station before connecting to the Eizan line, there are significant savings on the Hieizan one-day ticket, available at all local stations (except Demachiyanagi). A day return pass with unlimited shuttle-bus usage is ¥1720–2000, depending on which Keihan station you embark from.

Getting around on the mountain

Once you've arrived on the mountain, the best way to get around is on foot. If you're in a hurry take a **shuttle bus** (March 23–Nov 30; every 30min), which runs during most of the year from Sanchō via the central Tō-tō car park to Sai-tō and Yokawa. The whole journey only takes about twenty minutes and costs ¥740. A one-day pass (*hiei-zan-nai ichi-nichi jyōshaken*; ¥800) is available from the bus driver or at the Tō-tō bus terminal; this allows unlimited travel and also entitles you to a ¥100 discount on entrance to Enryaku-ji.

Enryaku-ji

The top of Hiei-zan consists of a narrow ridge, at the south end of which stand the central halls of **Enryaku-ji** (延暦寺; daily 9am–4pm; ¥550 covering the main compounds; ⓣ077/578-0001, ⓦwww.hieizan.or.jp). From this core area, known as the **Tō-tō** (Eastern Pagoda), the ridge slopes gently northwest down to the **Sai-tō** (Western Pagoda). A third compound, **Yokawa**, lies further north again, but this was a later addition and contains little of immediate interest. Buses from Kyoto loop around the rather uninteresting **Garden Museum Hiei** and then stop at the Enryaku-ji Bus Centre, where the main entrance is. To find the ticket office, walk behind the car park and souvenir shop.

Enryaku-ji was founded in 788 AD by a young Buddhist monk called Saichō (767–822), who was later sanctified as **Dengyō Daishi.** Saichō built himself a small hut on the mountain and a temple to house an image of Yakushi Nyorai (the Buddha of Healing), which he carved from a fallen tree. He then went to China for a year to study Buddhism; on his return to Hiei-zan in 805 AD he founded the Japanese **Tendai sect**. Based on the Lotus Sutra, Tendai doctrine holds that anyone can achieve enlightenment through studying the sacred texts and following extremely rigorous practices. Its followers went on to establish a whole host of splinter groups: Hōnen (who founded the Jōdo sect), Shinran (Jōdo Shinshū), Eisai (Rinzai Zen) and Nichiren all started out as Tendai priests.

In the early days, Enryaku-ji received generous imperial funding and court officials were sent up the mountain for a twelve-year education programme. As the sect expanded it became enormously rich and politically powerful, until there were three thousand buildings on the mountain. It owned vast areas of land and even maintained an army of several hundred well-trained **warrior monks** – many of whom were not really monks at all. They spent a good deal of time fighting other Buddhist sects, notably their great rivals at Nara's Kōfuku-ji (see p.467). In 1571, the warlord **Oda Nobunaga** (see p.769) put a stop to all this, leading 30,000 troops up Hiei-zan to lay waste to the complex, including the monks and their families. Nobunaga died eleven years later and his successor, Toyotomi Hideyoshi, was more kindly disposed to the Tendai sect, encouraging the monks to rebuild.

Tō-tō

Enryaku-ji's most important buildings are concentrated in the southerly **Tō-tō** (東塔) compound. Immediately inside the entrance you'll find a modern treasure hall, the **Kokuhō-den** (国宝殿; ¥450). Its most interesting exhibits are a fine array of statues, including a delicate, thirteenth-century Amida Buddha and a lovely Senjū Kannon (Thousand-Armed Kannon) of the ninth century. You can also see a scroll apparently recording Saichō's trip to China in 804 AD. Up the hill from the museum, the first building on your left is the **Daikō-dō**, the Great Lecture Hall, where monks attend lectures on the sutras and discuss doctrinal subtleties. Keeping an eye on them are life-size statues of Nichiren, Eisai, Hōnen, Shinran and other great names from the past – a sort of Tendai Hall of Fame.

Continuing uphill, you can take your turn at the huge bell, whose thundering peal reverberates around the mountain, and then go down the steps to the temple's most sacred hall, the **Konpon Chū-dō** (根本中堂). This powerful, faded building marks the spot where Saichō built his first hut; his statue of Yakushi Nyorai is kept inside, though hidden from view. Despite the crowds, the atmosphere in the dark, cavernous hall is absolutely compelling. Unusually, the altars are in a sunken area below the worship floor, where they seem to float in a swirling haze of incense smoke lit by low-burning lamps. It's said that the three big lanterns in front of the main altar have been burning ever since Saichō himself lit them 1200 years ago. Some sources hold that the lanterns did go out after Nobunaga's attack, and that a monk was sent up to Yamadera, in northern Honshū, to bring back a light from their sacred flame, which had itself originally come from Enryaku-ji. Monks tending the flames nowadays wear a mask in case they sneeze and accidentally blow the flame out.

From Konpon Chū-dō, walk ahead to the paved road and then follow it generally west, passing the bell again on your right. The next little hillock sports the pretty **Kaidan-in**, the Ordination Hall, and beyond it stands the recently reconstructed **Amida-dō** and its two-storey pagoda. Behind this bright-red hall, a path leads off through the woods to the Sai-tō compound.

Sai-tō

It takes around thirty minutes to walk from the Amida-dō to the centre of the **Sai-tō** (西塔) compound, with a few stops en route. The first of these is the **Jōdo-in** (浄土院), which you'll come to after about ten minutes on the path through the woods at the bottom of a lantern-lined staircase. Inside the temple's courtyard, behind the main hall, **Saichō's mausoleum**, a red-lacquered building, stands in a carefully tended gravel enclosure.

Continuing northwest, the path eventually leads to two identical square halls standing on a raised area. These are commonly known as **Ninai-dō** (にない堂), which roughly translates as "shoulder-carrying hall"; this refers to the legendary strength of a certain Benkei, who's said to have hoisted the two buildings onto his shoulders like a yoke. Their official names are Jōgyō-dō, the Hall of Perpetual Practice, and the Hokke-dō, or Lotus Hall. They're used for different types of meditation practice: in the former, monks walk round the altar for days reciting the Buddha's name, in the latter they alternate between walking and sitting meditation while studying the Lotus Sutra.

Walk between the pair of buildings and down more steps to reach the **Shaka-dō** (釈迦堂), another imposing hall, which marks the centre of the Sai-tō area. Though smaller and not so atmospheric as Konpon Chū-dō, this building is much older. It was originally erected in the thirteenth century on the shores of Biwa-ko, but was moved here in 1595 to replace the earlier hall destroyed by Nobunaga's

Marathon monks

Followers of the Buddhist **Tendai sect** believe that the route to enlightenment lies through chanting, esoteric ritual and extreme physical endurance. The most rigorous of these practices is the "thousand-day ascetic mountain pilgrimage", in which **marathon monks**, as they're popularly known, are required to walk 40,000km through the mountains and streets of Kyoto in a thousand days – the equivalent of nearly a thousand marathons. The thousand days are split into hundred-day periods over seven years; during each period the monk has to go out every day in all weathers, regardless of his physical condition. He must adhere to a strict vegetarian diet and, at one point during the seven years, go on a week-long fast with no food, water or sleep, just for good measure.

Not surprisingly, many monks don't make it – in the old days they were expected to commit ritual suicide if they had to give up. Those that do finish (nowadays, about one person every five years) are rewarded with enlightenment and become "living Buddhas". Apparently, the advice of modern marathon monks is much sought after by national baseball coaches and others involved in endurance training.

armies. It enshrines an image of Shaka Nyorai (Sakyamuni, the Historical Buddha), which is also attributed to Saichō, but again you can't see it. Otherwise, the Shaka-dō is similar to the Tō-tō, with its sunken centre and three lanterns. It's a lovely, quiet place to rest before you start heading back.

Ōhara

Though only a short bus ride north from Kyoto, the collection of temples that make up **ŌHARA** (大原) is almost in a different world. All are sub-temples of Enryaku-ji (see p.455), but the atmosphere here is quite different: instead of stately cedar forests, these little temples are surrounded by maples and flower-filled gardens, fed by tumbling streams. The sights are divided into two sections: the easterly **Sanzen-in** and the melancholy **Jakkō-in** across the rice fields.

Arrival and information

To reach Ōhara from central Kyoto, take a cream-and-red **Kyoto Bus** either from Kyoto Station (#17 and #18), Sanjō-Keihan Station (#16 and #17) or Kita-ōji Station (#15). The journey takes between thirty and fifty minutes and costs a maximum of ¥580, or you can use the Kyoto-wide subway and bus pass (see p.410). The route takes you past Yase-yūen, the starting point of the Eizan cable car up Hiei-zan (see p.454), making it possible to visit both places in one rather hectic day.

Sanzen-in and around

From the Ōhara bus terminal, cross over the main road and follow the lane leading east, uphill beside a small river and between stalls selling "beefsteak-leaf" tea (*shiso-cha*), mountain vegetables and other local produce. At the top of the steps, roughly ten minutes from the bus terminal, a fortress-like wall on the left contains Ōhara's most important temple, **Sanzen-in** (三千院; daily 8.30am–4.30/5pm; ¥700). The temple is said to have been founded by Saichō, the founder of Tendai Buddhism, but its main point of interest is the twelfth-century **Hon-dō**, a small but splendid building standing on its own in a mossy garden. Inside is an astonishingly well-preserved tenth-century Amida Buddha flanked by smaller statues of Kannon (on the right as you face them) and Seishi, which were added later.

The hillside behind Sanzen-in is covered with hydrangeas, which are at their best in June, but at other times of the year walk out the entrance and north along the lane for a short distance to **Shōrin-in** (勝林院; daily 9am–5pm; ¥300) where, if you're lucky, you might hear monks chanting. The main hall, reconstructed in the 1770s and containing another image of Amida, is used for studying *shōmyō*, the Buddhist incantations practised by followers of Tendai. *Shōmyō* were first introduced from China in the eighth century and have had a profound influence on music in Japan such as *gagaku* (court music); press the button in the booth on the left side of the altar and you can hear a short recitation.

The last temple in this section, **Hōsen-in** (宝泉院; daily 9am–5pm; ¥800, including green tea), lies at the end of the lane, on the left. Like Jakkō-in, the highlight here is the garden, although this one is much more enclosed and nearly swamped by a magnificent pine that is almost seven hundred years old. The temple's ceiling is made from planks that were originally in Fushimi Castle, where more than three hundred samurai committed *seppaku* (ritual suicide) after losing a battle in 1600. If you look carefully, traces of blood are still visible.

Jakkō-in

To reach Ōhara's other major temple, **Jakkō-in** (寂光院; daily 9am–5pm; ¥600; ⓣ075/744-334), make your way back to the bus station and follow the path along the river, past small souvenir shops, and then up the hill through the rice paddies for about fifteen minutes. Situated in a quiet garden, which was landscaped in the late Edo period and is fringed by a row of tufted pines, the main hall of the temple was destroyed in an arson attack in May 2000. This unfortunately damaged its Jizo *bodhisattva* and also its one-thousand-year old pine tree, mentioned in the *Tale of Heike*, which withered and died in 2004. The hall has now been completely rebuilt, and the temple and the area that surrounds it have been reinvigorated; photos of the devastating fire are on display in the Homotsuden. On your way back down the hill, look out for the **Ohara Sanso Ashiyu Café** (大原山荘足湯カフェ), where you can either cool your heels in summer or warm them up in winter (in the footbath) while sipping tea or coffee (from ¥700).

Practicalities

There are numerous small **restaurants** in Ōhara; one of the nicest places to eat is *Seryō* (芹生; daily 11am–5pm), on the left at the bottom of the steps up to Sanzen-in. They serve a beautifully presented bentō of seasonal vegetables (¥2756) as well as more expensive meals; in good weather you can eat outside on a riverside terrace. A cheaper option is *Seryō Chaya* (daily 9am–5pm), at the top of the steps, just before the entrance to Sanzen-in. Their tasty soba lunch set is ¥1000.

Seryō Chaya also has a fine **ryokan** with a choice of tatami or Western-style rooms and both open-air and indoor baths (Ⓣ075/744-2301, Ⓦwww.seryo.co.jp/english.html; ¥21,000/person, including two meals), worth considering if you want to enjoy Ōhara once the crowds have gone.

Amanohashidate

At the northern tip of Kyoto-fu (Kyoto prefecture), the stubby peninsula of Tango-hantō (丹後半島) leans protectively over Wakasa Bay, shielding the sand spit of **Amanohashidate** (天橋立), the "Bridge to Heaven". As one of the trio of top scenic views in Japan (the other two are Matsushima and Miyajima), Amanohashidate has a lot to live up to. The "bridge" is actually a 3.6km ribbon of white sand and pine trees slinking its way between the touristy villages of **Monju** and **Fuchū** across the bay.

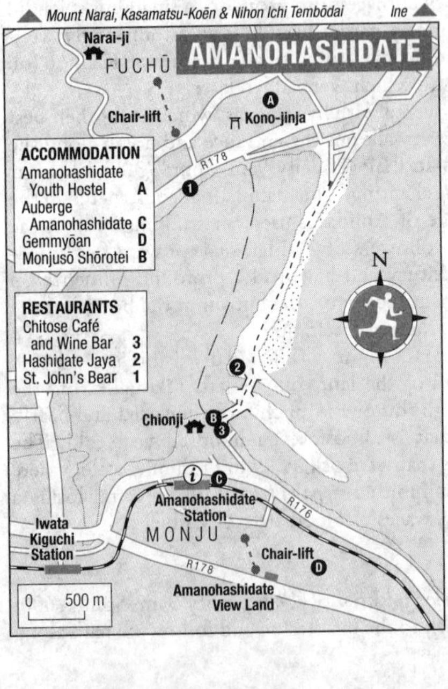

On Mount Nariai above Fuchū, the splendidly atmospheric **Nariai-ji** is one of the 33 temples on the Saigoku Kannon pilgrimage route, while closer to the summit there is a fantastic view of the bay and coast as far away as the Noto-hantō, some 500km northeast. East along the Tango-hantō lies the picturesque fishing hamlet of **Ine**, while across the bay in Monju is another attractive wooden temple, **Chion-ji**, standing on the brink of the sandbar – a lovely area for a quiet stroll or cycle ride, or simply lazing on the beach.

Arrival, information and local transport

Trains to Amanohashidate Station (天橋立駅) in Monju run along the scenic Kita-kinki Tango Tetsudō line (北近畿丹後鉄道). When taking the express service from Ōsaka (2hr; ¥5440; hourly) and Kyoto (2hr; ¥4580; hourly) in the Kansai region, you may be required to switch in Fukuchiyama. There are a few direct JR trains from Amagasaki, Kyoto and Ōsaka, which take around two hours and thirty minutes, but you'll have to pay for the Kita-kinki Tango Tetsudō portion of the journey if you're using a JR pass (¥1380 for the express service). **Buses** from both Kyoto (¥2700; twice daily) and Ōsaka (¥2460; three daily) take around two hours and forty minutes.

The assistants at the **tourist information desk** (daily 10am–6pm; ⓣ0772/22-8030) inside Amanohashidate Station are fairly helpful but don't speak much English, although they can provide a couple of English-language pamphlets on the area and help with accommodation bookings.

Buses across the bay to Fuchū (府中; 20min; ¥510) and around the Tango-hantō leave from outside the station until 7pm. Alternatively, you can take the more regular and faster **ferries** (5–6min; ¥500; last ferry 4.45pm) from the jetty beside Chion-ji, five minutes' walk from the station, to the Fuchū-side jetty at Ichinomiya. If you fancy some exercise, **bicycles** can be rented from various shops close to the station and jetty (¥400–500 for 2hr), or you could stroll the 4km across the sandbar.

Accommodation

Monju (文殊) is the main tourist hub of Amanohashidate and has the widest range of **accommodation**, including several inexpensive minshuku near the station and a couple of top-class ryokan. The youth hostel is across the bay in Fuchū.

Amanohashidate Youth Hostel 天橋立ユースホステル Fuchū ⓣ0772 /27-0121, ⓦwww.hashidate-yh.jp. This hostel is a 15min hike uphill to the right from the ferry and bus stop at Ichinomiya, but it's worth it for the wonderful views. It has bunk-bed dorms, a comfy lounge, helpful English-speaking staff and cheap bike rental (¥500/day). Dorm beds ¥2950/person.

Auberge Amanohashidate オーベルジュ天橋立 Eki-dōri ⓣ0772/22-0650. Very basic Western-style hotel, with a surprisingly decent in-house French restaurant. Opting for the cheaper rooms (without bathrooms) means you'll have to use the public bath in the hotel next door. Scheduled for renovation. ❹

Genmyōan 玄妙庵 ⓣ0772/22-2171, ⓦwww.genmyoan.com. On the hillside above Monju, with superb views of the sandbar, this pricey ryokan has the feel of an English cottage, with dark wooden beams and white plaster walls. The rooms are traditional tatami and there's an outdoor pool in the summer. ❾

Monjusō Shōrotei 文殊荘松露亭 ⓣ0772/22-2151. Exquisite ryokan behind Chion-ji temple, surrounded by private gardens at the tip of a mini-peninsula overlooking the sandbar. Rates can climb as high as ¥60,000/person, depending on the room and your choice of meals. The service is excellent. ❾

The Town

Five minutes' walk north of Amanohashidate Station, at the end of a shopping street leading towards the sand spit, is the attractive temple **Chion-ji** (智恩寺), dedicated to the Buddhist saint Chie-no-Monju. Between the main gate and the hall (Monjudo), which houses a revered image of the saint, stands the Tahoto, a squat wooden pagoda dating from 1500. In the temple precincts, near the ferry jetty, you'll also see the Chie-no-wa Torō, a granite ring monument symbolizing wisdom, which has been adopted as an emblem of the town.

To reach the pine-forested sand bar, **Amanohashidate**, cross the red bridge, Kaisenkyō, which swings around to allow boats through the narrow channel to the open sea. The sandy, crescent-shaped beaches on the east side of the spit are at their busiest from July to August. The best place from which to view the sand spit in its entirety is Kasamatsu-kōen above Fuchū (see below), but if you're pushed for time there's also a lookout point in the hills behind **Monju**. A five-minute walk over the rail tracks and up the hill behind Amanohashidate Station brings you to the **chair lift** (daily 8.30am–5pm; ¥850 return), which takes six minutes to reach the touristy **Amanohashidate View Land**, a mini-amusement park where loudspeakers pump out a 1950s musical soundtrack.

Fuchū and around

The walking trail (or ferry ride) across Amanohashidate brings you into the Fuchū area (府中). The highlight is **Kono-jinja** (籠神社), the oldest shrine in the area, guarded by a pair of stone dogs dating from the Kamakura era (1185–1333). Note that the roofs of the shrine buildings are reminiscent of the architecture of Ise-jingu (see p.506). A short walk up the hill to the left, past a row of souvenir stalls, is the station for both the funicular railway and chair lift (daily 8am–5.30pm; ¥1740 return, including bus to and from Nariai-ji) up the lower slopes of Mount Nariai to **Kasamatsu-kōen**, the principal lookout point over Amanohashidate, where tourists gather for official group photos in rather amusing poses. Signs demonstrate how best to stand: bent over with your head between your legs, so that the view of the sand spit seems to float in midair like a bridge.

From the park you can either catch a bus or walk for twenty minutes further up the mountain to the gate to **Nariai-ji** (成相寺; daily 8am–5pm; ¥500), a charming rustic temple surrounded by lofty pines, founded in 704 AD and dedicated to Kannon, the Buddhist goddess of mercy. This is one of the 33 temples on the Saigoku Kannon pilgrim route, and so attracts a steady stream of visitors, many of whom clutch elaborate hanging scrolls which are specially inscribed at each temple. Legend has it that if you pray at the temple and make a vow to Kannon, your prayer will be granted.

As you climb the stone steps leading up to the main temple building you'll pass a 33m-tall pagoda, recently rebuilt for the first time since it burnt down five hundred years ago, and a small wooden bell tower. An interesting legend is attached to the bell, which has only been rung once since it was first cast in 1609. A mother who claimed to be too poor to contribute money to the temple accidentally dropped her baby into the vat of molten copper being cast as the bell. When the bell was first struck, it is said that the people could hear the baby calling out for its mother, so it was decided never to ring the bell again.

It really is worth making the effort to continue on to the **Nihon Ichi Tembōdai** (日本一展望台), a panoramic lookout spot around 1km further up the mountain from Nariai-ji. The sublime view across Amanohashidate and Wakasa Bay, as far away as the Noto-hanō and the sacred mountain Hakusan on the Hokuriku coast, is straight out of a woodblock print.

If you have time, back down in **Fuchū** (府中) you can catch a bus 16km up the coast (¥1350 return) to the charming fishing hamlet of **INE** (伊根), sheltering in a hook-like inlet towards the eastern end of the Tango-hantō. The best way to see the traditional wooden houses built over the water, with space beneath for boats to be stored, is to take a yellow sightseeing boat from Ine harbour (daily 9am–4.30pm; closed Feb; ¥660) on a thirty-minute tour of the inlet.

Eating and drinking

You'll find more **restaurants** and **cafés** in Monju than Fuchū, although there are few stand-out options. One of the nicest places is *Chitose Café and Wine Bar* (daily 11am–8pm), just near the bridge going over to the sand spit. It serves set lunches, cakes, good coffee and the award-winning local wine. Nestling amid the pines at the Monju end of the sand spit is the *Hashidate Jaya* (はしだて茶屋; 9am–5pm; closed Thurs), which serves good-value meals and snacks, including *asari-don* (small shellfish and spring onions on a bowl of rice). Over in Fuchū, try *St John's Bear* (daily 8.30am–8pm) at the water's edge down from the chair-lift station, a friendly Western-style café-bar that also serves pizza.

Hikone

On the northeastern shore of Biwa-ko, Japan's largest lake, lies the stately castle town of **HIKONE** (彦根). Often overlooked by international visitors, Hikone (not to be confused with Hakone, the resort town near Mount Fuji, see p.189) is an easy day-trip from Kyoto or Ōsaka. This attractive town not unreasonably claims that it has retained the look and feel of the Edo period more than any other place in the country. The town's castle is one of the few in Japan to have remained intact since the early 17th century. With Himeji-jō's donjon under renovation till sometime in 2016 (see p.521), it's well worth a visit. Hikone is also known for its *butsudan* (Buddhist altar) industry and the town has an abundance of shops with elaborate altars on display. Hikone's main attractions can all be seen on foot and, except during the cherry blossom season when the castle is engulfed by hordes of tourists, the town can be enjoyed at a leisurely and crowd-free pace.

Arrival and information

While Hikone is an easy day-trip by train from Kyoto or Ōsaka, it's a nice place to stay overnight if you are also planning to visit either the Miho Museum (see p.462) or Amanohashidate (see p.458). Express JR trains take 90 minutes from Ōsaka (¥1890) and 50 minutes from Kyoto (¥1100). On the Shinkansen Tokaido line, get off at Maibara Station (25 min from Kyoto; ¥3300) and change for the JR Biwako line to Hikone Station (5 min; ¥180). From here, it's about a ten-minute walk to the castle area. There's a helpful **tourist office** (daily 9am–6pm; ⓣ0749/22-2954) at JR Hikone Station, on your left-hand side as you exit.

Hikone-Jō

Very little has changed in the 400 years and more that **Hikone-jō** (彦根城; daily 8.30am–5pm; ¥500) has stood on the hill looking out onto the town and the lake. One of the most authentic castles remaining in Japan, it is also one of only four designated as a National Treasure. There are spectacular views of Biwa-ko from the donjon on a clear day, and with very few modern buildings and little pollution to obscure the panorama it is possible to imagine something of what people in the Edo period may have seen.

Hikone-jō was built between 1602 and 1622 by the Ii family from the ruins of other castles in the area, including one on the original site. If you look at the stone walls as you climb up the hill, you can see that the style is inconsistent. The lower levels were constructed by untrained labourers while the upper levels have been assembled using the patchwork-like *gobo-zumi* masonry technique. Although the walls look rather precarious, they have successfully protected the castle from earthquake damage since their construction. The fortress is double-moated and also features many *yagura* or turrets. In particular, the *tenbin-yagura*, in the unique shape of a *tenbin* (Japanese scales), and the *taikomon-yagura*, so called because a *taiko* or Japanese drum was kept there to send warnings, are both architecturally significant.

Hikone-jō Museum (彦根城博物館; daily 9am–5pm; ¥500) is located just inside the main gate of the castle. It was reconstructed in 1987 and is an exact copy of the Edo-period official quarter of the castle. Inside you can see how the Ii family lived. Their nō stage, tea room and living area have been re-created, and there are a large number of artefacts on display including nō costumes, weaponry, calligraphy manuscripts and other artworks.

On the northeast side of the castle is the **Genkyū-en** garden (玄宮園; 8.30am–5pm; same ticket). Built in 1677, it is modelled on the ancient Chinese palace of Tang dynasty emperor Genso and features a large pond full of carp. Genkyu-en has many imitation scenes of the region and the pond is Biwa-ko in miniature. The *Hoshō-dai* tea house, where the Ii Lords entertained, is a good place to stop for a bowl of *macha* and a sweet (¥500) while enjoying pleasant views of the garden and castle.

Around the castle

The **Yume-Kyōbashi Castle Road** (夢京橋), just south of Hikone-jō, is a charming imitation of a bustling Edo-period merchant area. The 350m stretch has modern reconstructions of traditional Japanese shops on both sides, housing a variety of cafés, restaurants, bars and souvenir shops. At the end of the road farthest from the castle, turn left into **Yonban-chō**, another reconstructed shopping and dining area. Here, dozens of small shops and restaurants have been built in a style reminiscent of the Taishō era of the 1920s.

The Zen temple **Ryōtanji** (龍潭寺;9am–5pm; ¥400), located on the eastern edge of the town, was founded in 733 and was the family temple of the Ii lords. Its gardens were designed by monks in training and it was once an important centre for Zen gardening. The Fudaraku stone garden, dating from 1670, is considered to be a fine example of the genre. Another Zen temple is **Tennei-ji** (天寧寺; 9am–5pm; ¥400), southeast of JR Hikone Station, where 500 Buddhist disciples who reached Nirvana are enshrined as *Gohyaku Rakan* wooden statues. It is said that you should be able to find a face that resembles someone you know among the statues.

Practicalities

The best place to stay is the *Hikone Castle Hotel* (彦根キャッスルホテル; Ⓣ0749/21-2001, Ⓦwww.hch.jp; ❼), overlooking the moat. The rooms are spacious and most have clear views of the castle. Near the station, the friendly and efficient *Hotel Estacion Hikone* (ホテルエスタシオンひこね; Ⓣ0749/22-1500, Ⓦwww.estacion-hikone.com; ❺) is a recently renovated business hotel with free internet and bike rental.

For dinner, *Hokkoriya* (ほっこりや; Ⓣ0749/21-3567), on the Yume Kyōbashi Castle Road, is a popular *izakaya* in an atmospheric traditional-style house serving *yakitori* and *donburi* dishes. In Yonban-chō square, the stylish *Germoglio di Bambu* (Ⓣ0749/27-7373) is a great place for Italian cuisine, as well as *izakaya*-style meals. Hikone's liveliest bar is *Paraiso*, near the Hikone Castle Hotel. It has a large cocktail menu and serves Okinawan cuisine, as well as occasionally hosting DJ events.

Miho Museum

The I.M. Pei-designed **Miho Museum** (ミホミュージアム; Tues–Fri & Sun 10am–5pm; ¥1000; Ⓣ0748/82-3411, Ⓦwww.miho.jp/english) is one of the architectural highlights of the Kansai region, although it's only open for a few months every year – exact dates vary; check the website for details. Located in a rural, mountainous part of Shiga Prefecture, which is best known for its Shigaraki pottery, the museum provides an unlikely setting for an incredible collection of artworks belonging to Koyama Mihoko and her daughter Hiroko. Koyama is the head of one of Japan's so-called "new religions", Shinki Shumeikai, founded in 1970, which has an estimated 300,000 followers worldwide, hundreds of whom live and work here at the museum. The central tenet of Shinki Shumeikai's philosophy is that spiritual fulfilment lies in art and nature, hence the setting.

From the entrance and restaurant (serving excellent, if pricey, organic vegetarian cuisine), access to the museum proper is on an electric shuttle bus through a tunnel that opens onto a beautiful valley spanned by a 120m-high bridge; alternatively, you can walk – it takes about fifteen minutes on foot. Opposite is a series of tetrahedrons, which is all that can be seen of the museum, as most of it is actually built inside the mountainside due to planning restrictions. Inside, a continually shifting pattern of light and shadow is created by the innovative use of skylights, pyramid-shaped wall lights and ever-so-slightly uneven corridors which look out – through windows fitted with aluminium screens – onto bamboo gardens and tranquil green landscapes.

The museum has two wings. The **north wing** houses Japanese art, including priceless porcelain, scrolls, screens and Buddhist relics; the **south wing** has antiquities from the rest of the world, including jewellery, frescoes, textiles and statues produced by a range of civilizations, from ancient Egyptian to classical Chinese. Among the numerous treasures are a three-thousand-year-old silver-and-gold cult figure of a falcon-headed deity from Egypt's 19th dynasty, a limestone Assyrian relief unearthed in Nimrud and the splendid Sanguszko Carpet from Iran. Each artwork is labelled in English and Japanese and there are explanatory leaflets in some of the galleries, but the overall effect is one of art that is meant to be experienced for its intrinsic beauty rather than its historical or cultural import.

There are tours available to the museum but it is better (and very much cheaper) to get there by yourself. From JR Kyoto Station, take a local train on the JR Biwako line (for Nagahama or Maibara) two stops to JR **Ishiyama Station** (every 10–15min; 13min; ¥230). Buses (50min; ¥800), run by the Teisan Bus Company, leave for the museum from outside Ishiyama Station's south exit. On weekdays, buses leave at ten minutes past the hour between 9.10am and 1.10pm. If you miss the last bus, you'll have to take a taxi, which is quite expensive (¥6000). On Saturdays, Sundays and national holidays, the weekday timetable is supplemented by buses at 9.50am and 2.55pm.

Nara

Before Kyoto became the capital of Japan in 794 AD, this honour was held by **NARA** (奈良), a town some 35km further south in an area that is regarded as the birthplace of Japanese civilization. During this period, particularly the seventh and eighth centuries, Buddhism became firmly established within Japan under the patronage of court nobles, who sponsored magnificent temples and works of art, many of which have survived to this day. Fortunately, history subsequently left Nara largely to its own devices and it remains today a relaxed, attractive place set against a backdrop of wooded hills. Its greatest draw is undoubtedly the monumental bronze Buddha of **Tōdai-ji**, while **Kōfuku-ji** and several of the smaller temples boast outstanding collections of Buddhist statuary. However, even these are outclassed by the images housed in **Hōryū-ji**, a temple to the southwest of Nara, which also claims the world's oldest wooden building. The nearby temples of **Yakushi-ji** and **Tōshōdai-ji** contain yet more early masterpieces of Japanese art and architecture.

Nara has the added attraction of packing all these sights into a fairly compact space. The central area is easily explored on foot, and can just about be covered in a long day, with the more distant temples fitting into a second day's outing. Many people visit Nara on a day-trip from Kyoto, but it more than deserves an overnight stop, not least to enjoy it once the crowds have gone. If at all possible, try to avoid Nara on Sundays and holidays.

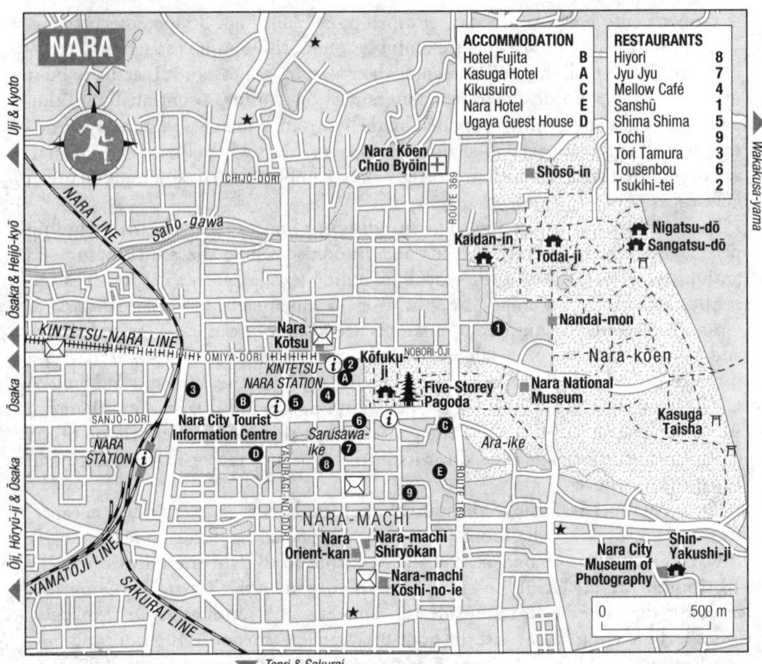

Some history

During the fifth and sixth centuries a sophisticated culture evolved in the plains east of Ōsaka, an area known as **Yamato**. Close contact between Japan, Korea and China saw the introduction of Chinese script, technology and the Buddhist religion, as well as Chinese ideas on law and administration. Under these influences, the regent **Prince Shōtoku** (574–622) established a strictly hierarchical system of government. However, he's probably best remembered as a devout Buddhist who founded numerous temples, among them the great **Hōryū-ji**. Though Shōtoku's successors continued the process of centralization, they were hampered by the practice of relocating the court after each emperor died, in line with purification rites. In 710 AD, therefore, it was decided to establish a permanent capital modelled on China's imperial city, Chang'an (today's Xi'an). The name chosen for this new city was **Heijō-kyō**, "Citadel of Peace", today known as **Nara**. In fact, Heijō-kyō lasted little more than seventy years, but it was a glorious period in which Japanese culture began to take shape. A frenzy of building and artistic creativity during this period culminated in the unveiling of the great bronze Buddha in **Tōdai-ji** temple by **Emperor Shōmu** in 752 AD. But beneath the surface things were starting to unravel. As the temples became increasingly powerful, so the monks began to dabble in politics, until one, Dōkyō, seduced a former empress and tried to seize the throne in 769. In an attempt to escape such shenanigans Emperor Kammu decided to move the court out of Nara in 784, and eventually founded Kyoto.

Arrival and information

Nara has two competing **train stations**: the JR Nara Station, on the west side of the town centre, and the private Kintetsu-Nara Station which is close to the main sights. Arriving **from Kyoto**, the quickest option is a Limited Express train on the private Kintetsu–Kyoto line (every 30min; 40min; ¥1110); the ordinary express takes a little longer and you have to change at Yamato-Saidaiji (1–2 hourly; 50min; ¥610). JR also has a choice of express trains (8 daily; 45min; ¥740) and regular trains (every 30min; 1hr 20min; ¥690) from Kyoto. Travelling **from Ōsaka**, trains on the private Kintetsu–Nara line (from Ōsaka's Kintetsu-Namba Station) arrive at the Kintetsu-Nara Station (every 15min; 30–40min; ¥540–1040). Alternatively, take a JR line train from Ōsaka Station (every 20min; 40min; ¥780) or from JR Namba Station (every 20min; 30–40min; ¥740) to JR Nara Station. If you're coming here **from Kansai International airport** you can go into central Ōsaka to pick up a train or hop on a limousine bus (hourly; 1hr 35min; ¥1800), which stops at both of Nara's train stations.

Nara is well provided with **information offices**. The most useful of these is the Nara City Tourist Information Centre (daily 9am–9pm; ⓣ0742/22-5595, ⓦnarashikanko.jp), located on Sanjō-dōri. There's also an office in the JR Station (daily 9am–5pm; ⓣ0742/22-9821) and another in Kintetsu Station (daily 9am–5pm;

Festivals and annual events

Several of Nara's **festivals** have been celebrated for well over a thousand years. Many of these are dignified court dances, though the fire rituals are more lively affairs. In spring and autumn the New Public Hall (ⓣ0742/27-2630, ⓦwww.pref.nara.jp/koukaido-e) in Nara-kōen stages a series of **nō dramas**, while the biggest cultural event of the year is undoubtedly the autumn exhibition of **Shōsō-in treasures** at the National Museum (see p.467).

January 15 Yama-yaki (Grass-burning festival). On a winter evening at 6pm, priests from Kōfuku-ji set fire to the grass on Wakakusa-yama – supervised by a few hundred firemen. The festival commemorates the settlement of a boundary dispute between Nara's warrior monks.

February 3 Mantoro Lantern Festival To mark *setsubun*, the beginning of spring, three thousand stone and bronze lanterns are lit at Kasuga Taisha (from 6pm).

March 1–14 O-Taimatsu and O-Mizutori (Torch lighting and water drawing). A 1200-year-old ceremony that commemorates a priest's dream about Kannon drawing water from a holy well. The climax is on the night of March 13 when, at around 6.30pm, priests on the second-floor veranda light huge torches and scatter sparks over the assembled crowds to protect them from evil spirits. At 2am the priests collect water from the well, after which they whirl more lit flares round in a frenzied dance.

May 11–12 Takigi Nō Outdoor performances of nō dramas by firelight at Kōfuku-ji.

August 14–15 Chugen Mantoro To celebrate Obon, the festival of souls, Kasuga Taisha's lanterns are spectacularly lit.

September Uneme Matsuri On the night of the harvest moon, this festival takes place at the Sarusawa-ike Pond as a dedication to Uneme, a court lady who drowned herself here after losing the favour of the emperor. At around 7pm two dragon-bowed boats bearing costumed participants and *gagaku* musicians commemorate the lady's death in multicoloured splendour. The festival lasts until 9.30pm.

Early to mid-October Shika-no-Tsunokiri (Antler cutting). This is the season when the deer in Nara-kōen are wrestled to the ground and have their antlers sawn off by Shinto priests. It all takes place in the Roku-en deer pen, near Kasuga Taisha. Check locally for exact dates.

December 15–18 On-matsuri At around midday a grand costume parade sets off from the prefectural offices to Kasuga Wakamiya-jinja, stopping on the way for various ceremonies. It ends with outdoor performances of nō and courtly dances.

ⓣ0742/24-4858). *Nara Explorer* (ⓦwww.naraexplorer.jp), a free quarterly English-language magazine available at tourist offices, hotels and shops, carries the latest information about **what's on**, as does the free monthly *Kansai Scene*.

City transport

The centre of Nara is small enough to be covered on foot, though you'll need to use local **buses** for some of the more far-flung sights – the main termini for these are outside the JR and Kintetsu-Nara train stations. The standard fare is ¥200 within the city centre, which you usually pay as you get on, though buses going out of central Nara employ a ticket system – take a numbered ticket as you board and pay the appropriate fare on exit. If you're heading for the sights around Nara, there is a range of **bus passes**, of which the most helpful is the *Nara Nishinokyō Ikaruga Furii-ken* (¥1600). This covers unlimited travel for one day in central Nara and the western districts, including Hōryū-ji, Yakushi-ji and Tōshōdai-ji. A cheaper version, which excludes Hōryū-ji, is available for ¥810.

There are a number of bus tours which take in Nara's seven World Heritage sites, but the best way is to walk and take public transport when needed. The Nara SCG Club (ⓦnarashikanko.jp/sgg) and the Nara YMCA EGG (ⓦwww4.kcn.ne.jp/~eggymca/egghomepage.html) both offer free guided walking tours in English, with interesting historical anecdotes. Reservations are required at least a day in advance. Another option for central Nara is **bike rental**. You'll find Eki Rent-a-Cycle (daily 9am–5pm; ¥1000/day) outside the JR Station, and Sunflower Rent-a-Cycle (daily 9am–5pm; ¥1000–1200/day, or ¥2000 for two days) southeast of the Kintetsu Station.

Accommodation

Nara has a range of **accommodation** options, from budget guesthouses in traditional homes to the grand old *Nara Hotel*, whose guests have included Albert Einstein and the Dalai Lama. There's plenty of choice in the city centre, but you'll need to book ahead at weekends and during the spring and autumn peaks.

Hotel Fujita ホテルフジタ 47-1 Sanjō-chō ⓣ0742/23-8111, ⓦwww.fujita-nara.com/e. Reasonably smart and affordable business hotel right on Sanjō-dōri. The rooms are plain, but comfortable, and there's free bike rental. 5

Kasuga Hotel 春日ホテル 40 Noborioji-chō ⓣ0742/22-4031, ⓦwww.kasuga-hotel.co.jp. This luxurious ryokan-like hotel is only a short walk from Kintetsu-Nara Station. There are Japanese- and Western-style rooms, and some have their own private outdoor baths. Locally sourced *kaiseki* cuisine is served for the evening meal. 8

Kikusuiro 菊水楼 11-30 Takahata-chō ⓣ0742/23-2001. Rambling old ryokan conveniently located near Nara-kōen serving highly-rated French and Japanese cuisine. Rooms are quaintly decorated and spacious. Only a little English spoken but the service is friendly. 7

Nara Hotel 奈良ホテル 1096 Takabatake-chō ⓣ0742/26-3300, ⓦwww.narahotel.co.jp. Nara's most historic hotel occupies a classic building, set in its own gardens within Nara-kōen. Rooms in the old wing, with high ceilings, fireplaces, period furniture and original baths, are recommended for their Meiji-era ambience. 8

Ugaya Guest House 奈良ウガヤゲストハウス 4-1 Okukomori-chō ⓣ0742/95-7739, ⓦwww.ugaya.net. This small and friendly guesthouse, located between the JR and Kintetsu stations, was once a pharmacy. There are dorm rooms with bunk beds (¥2500) as well as private rooms – all with shared shower facilities. There's also an in-house library and organic coffee shop. 3

Yougendo 涌玄堂 13-25 Kudo 2 chome Oji-chō ⓣ0745/32-0514, ⓦwww.yougendo.com. Relaxed guesthouse in a stately old walled compound with gardens. Rooms and communal areas have been tastefully renovated, preserving many of the mansion's traditional features, such as hand-painted *fusuma* (sliding doors). *The Dining Bar*, in a converted *kura* (storehouse), serves Mediterranean-style food with Guinness on tap, plus there's free bike rental and internet access. Its approximately 15min west of town on JR from Nara station. 3

The City

More a large town than a city, Nara is an enjoyable place to explore. The grid street system is well signposted in English, and the main sights are all gathered on the city's eastern edge in the green expanse of **Nara-kōen**. The route outlined below starts with the most important temples, **Kōfuku-ji** and **Tōdai-ji**, before ambling south along the eastern hills to Nara's holiest shrine, **Kasuga Taisha**, and splendid displays of Buddhist statuary in two historic temples, **Sangatsu-dō** and **Shin-Yakushi-ji**. With an extra hour or two to spare, it's worth wandering the streets of southerly **Nara-machi**, a traditional merchants' quarter where some attractive old shophouses have been converted into museums and craft shops.

Nara-kōen

The most pleasant route into **Nara-kōen** (奈良公園) is along Sanjō-dōri, which cuts across the central district and brings you out near Sarusawa-ike (猿沢池) with the **Five-Storey Pagoda** rising from the trees to your left. The pagoda belongs to **Kōfuku-ji** (興福寺), which in the eighth century was one of Nara's great temples. Founded in 669 AD by a member of the Fujiwara clan, it was moved to its present location when Nara became the new capital in 710.

The prime draw here is the fine collection of **Buddhist statues** contained in the Tōkon-dō (東金堂; daily 9am–5pm; ¥300) and the Kokuhōkan (国宝館; same hours; ¥500). The **Tōkon-dō**, a fifteenth-century hall to the north of the Five-Storey Pagoda, is dominated by a large image of Yakushi Nyorai, the Buddha of Healing. He's flanked by three Bodhisattvas, the Four Heavenly Kings and the Twelve Heavenly Generals, all beady-eyed guardians of the faith, some of which date from the eighth century. Perhaps the most interesting statue, though, is the seated figure of Yuima Koji to the left of Yakushi Nyorai; depicting an ordinary mortal rather than a celestial being, it's a touchingly realistic portrait.

The modern **Kokuhōkan** is a veritable treasure-trove of early Buddhist statues. The most famous image is the standing figure of **Ashura**, one of Buddha's eight protectors, instantly recognizable from his three red-tinted heads and six spindly arms. Look out, too, for his companion Karura (Garuda) with his beaked head. Though they're not all on display at the same time, these eight protectors are considered to be the finest dry-lacquer images of the Nara period. The large **bronze Buddha head**, with its fine, crisp features, comes from an even earlier period. Apart from a crumpled left ear, the head is in remarkably good condition considering that the original statue was stolen from another temple by Kōfuku-ji's warrior priests sometime during the Heian period (794–1185). Then, after a fire destroyed its body, the head was buried beneath the replacement Buddha, only to be rediscovered in 1937 during renovation work.

Nara National Museum

Heading east from Kōfuku-ji you'll soon see a Western-style building, which houses the main exhibits of the **Nara National Museum** (奈良国立博物館; 9am–5pm;

> **Nara-kōen's deer**
>
> The large, grassy areas of the park are kept trim by more than a thousand semi-wild **deer**. They were originally regarded as divine messengers of one of Kasuga-jinja's Shinto gods, and anyone who killed a deer was liable to be dispatched shortly after.
>
> During World War II their numbers dwindled to just seventy, but now they're back with a vengeance – which can make picnicking difficult and presents something of a hazard to young children; try to avoid areas where vendors sell special *sembei* (crackers) for feeding the deer.

closed Mon; ¥500, ¥1000 for special exhibitions; ⓦwww.narahaku.go.jp). As you'd imagine, the museum's strong point is its superb collection of statues, of which only a small part is on display at any one time. They're arranged chronologically, so you can trace the development of the various styles, and there's plenty of English-language information available. Each autumn (late Oct to early Nov) the museum is closed for two weeks while an exhibition of the **Shōsō-in treasures** takes place in this annexe. This priceless collection was donated to Tōdai-ji in 756 by Empress Kōmyō, on the death of her husband Emperor Shōmu, and then added to with more treasures in 950. It contains unique examples of Buddhist art and ritual objects, musical instruments, household utensils, glassware and games, not only from eighth-century Japan but also from China, Korea, India and Persia. The exhibition takes a different theme each year, so what you see is very much the luck of the draw. In the lower-level passageway between the original building and the annexe you'll find an informative display that explains the forms, techniques and other characteristics of Buddhist art.

Tōdai-ji

For many people Nara is synonymous with **Tōdai-ji** (東大寺). This great temple was founded in 745 by **Emperor Shōmu**, ostensibly to ward off the terrible epidemics that regularly swept the nation, but also as a means of cementing imperial power. In doing so he nearly bankrupted his young nation, but the political message came across loud and clear; soon an extensive network of sub-temples spread throughout the provinces, where they played an important role in local administration. It took more than fifteen years to complete Tōdai-ji, which isn't surprising when you learn that the main hall is still the world's largest wooden building. Even so, the present structure (last rebuilt in 1709) is only two-thirds the size of the original. Avoid visiting Tōdai-ji at weekends, especially during the spring and autumn, the two peak times for visiting Nara, when the temple is overrun with thousands of tourists and school groups.

The Daibutsu-den

The main entrance to Tōdai-ji lies through the suitably impressive **Nandai-mon** (南大門), or Great Southern Gate. Rebuilt in the thirteenth century, it shelters two wonderfully expressive guardian gods (*Niō*), each over 7m tall. Beyond, you begin to see the horned, sweeping roof of the **Daibutsu-den**, the Great Buddha Hall (大仏殿; daily: March 20–Sept 19 8.30am–5pm; Sept 20–March 19 8.30am–4pm; ¥500), which houses Japan's largest bronze statue. A 15m-tall blackened figure on a lotus throne, the great Buddha (*Daibutsu*) seems to strain at the very walls of the building. It depicts Rushana (later known as Dainichi Nyorai), the Cosmic Buddha who presides over all levels of the Buddhist universe, and was a phenomenal achievement for the time. Not surprisingly, several attempts at casting the Buddha failed, but finally in 752 the gilded statue was officially dedicated by symbolically "opening" its eyes. To achieve this, an Indian priest stood on a special platform and "painted" the eyes with a huge brush, from which coloured strings trailed down to the assembled dignitaries, enabling them to participate in the ceremony. Not only were there hundreds of local monks present, but also ambassadors from China, India and further afield, bearing an amazing array of gifts, many of which have been preserved in the Shōsō-in treasury – as has the original paintbrush.

The Buddha has had a rough time of it since then. As early as the ninth century an earthquake toppled his head, then it and his right hand melted in a fire in 1180 and again in 1567. As a result, only tiny fragments of the original statue remain intact, the rest being made up of patchwork parts put together over the centuries. Nonetheless, the remodelled giant is definitely large, and it's hard not to be impressed by the technological triumph involved in re-creating it. As you walk round the hall, don't be surprised to see people trying to squeeze through a hole in one of the rear supporting pillars – success apparently reserves you a corner of paradise.

The Kaidan-in

Walk west from the Daibutsu-den compound and you'll find the more modest **Kaidan-in** (戒壇院; daily 8am–4.30pm; ¥500), which was established in 754 as Japan's first, and foremost, ordination hall. It was founded by a Chinese high priest, Ganjin, who Emperor Shōmu hoped would instil some discipline into the rapidly expanding Buddhist priesthood. He had to be patient, however; poor Ganjin's ship took six attempts to arrive here, by which time the priest was 67 years old and completely blind. His ordination hall was rebuilt in the Edo period, but the statues inside include eighth-century representations of the Four Heavenly Kings (*Shi-Tennō*), crafted in clay.

Along the eastern hills

Two of Tōdai-ji's sub-temples were built on the slopes of Wakakusa-yama, which forms Nara's eastern boundary. Northerly **Nigatsu-dō** (二月堂; daily 8am–5pm; free) offers good views over the city from its wooden terrace. Next door, **Sangatsu-dō** (三月堂; daily 8am–5pm; ¥500), completed in 729, is Nara's oldest building and contains another rare collection of eighth-century dry-lacquer statues. The main image is a dimly lit, gilded figure of Kannon, bearing a silver Amida in its crown, while all around stand gods, guardians, Bodhisattvas and other protectors of the faith.

From Sangatsu-dō it's a pleasant stroll south along the Wakakusa hillside, past a few snack stands and up the lantern-lined approach to **Kasuga Taisha** (春日大社; Kasuga Grand Shrine). This was founded in 768 as the tutelary shrine of the Fujiwara family and, for a while, held an important place in Shinto worship; indeed, the emperor still today sends a messenger here to participate in shrine rituals. The four sanctuaries are just visible in the inner compound, while the thousand beautifully crafted bronze **lanterns** hanging round the outer eaves are easier to admire. Donated over the years by supplicants, they bear intricate designs of deer, wisteria blooms, leaves or geometric patterns. The best time to see them is when they are lit up twice a year for the Mantoro ("Ten-thousand lantern") festivals – on February 3 marking *setsubun*, the beginning of spring, and during Obon, the festival of souls, in mid-August (Aug 14–15) for the Chugen Mantoro festival. The bronze lanterns and the nearly two thousand stone lanterns, which line the path leading up to the shrine, are lit at dusk. Just before the entrance to the inner shrine is the **Kasuga Taisha Shin-en garden** (春日大社神苑 萬葉植物園; 9am–4pm; ¥525), especially charming in early May when the dozens of varieties of wisteria are in bloom. The garden is also a living museum of over nine hundred flowers, herbs and other plants mentioned in the verses of the *Manyōshū* ("Collection of Ten Thousand Leaves") poetry anthology, compiled in the Nara and early Heian periods.

Continuing south through the woods from Kasuga Taisha, cross over the main road into a quiet residential area. Five minutes further on you'll come to the venerable **Shin-Yakushi-ji** (新薬師寺; daily 9am–5pm; ¥600). This quiet temple stands in a courtyard full of bush clover, much as it has done for the last 1250 years. It was founded by Empress Kōmyō to pray for Emperor Shōmu's recovery from an eye infection; she apparently had some success since he lived for another decade. Inside the modest-looking hall you'll find some intriguing Buddhist statues. The central image is a plump-faced, slightly cross-eyed Yakushi Nyorai (the Buddha of Healing), carved from one block of cypress wood. He's surrounded by clay statues of the Twelve Heavenly Generals; it's worth the walk just to see their wonderful expressions.

The **Nara City Museum of Photography** (奈良市写真美術館; 9.30am–5pm; closed Mon; ¥500) is just to the west of Shin-Yakushi-ji, in a sleek, modern and almost completely underground building. Its core collection consists of some eighty thousand photos by the late Irie Taikichi, who spent most of his life capturing Nara and its temples on film.

Nara-machi

The southern district of central Nara is known as **Nara-machi** (ならまち). It's a quaint area of narrow streets, worth exploring for traditional shops and lattice-front houses. The best approach is to start by the southwest corner of willow-fringed Sarusawa-ike, a good spot for views of the Five-Storey Pagoda, and then head south. At the end of the road is an enticing little shop, **Kikuoka Kampō Yakkyoku** (菊岡漢方薬局; 9am–7pm; closed Mon), selling all sorts of traditional Chinese medicines and, next door, **Nara-machi Monogatari-kan** (奈良町物語館; daily 10am–5pm; free), which shows changing exhibitions of local crafts. Turn right (west) in front of these two and you'll find **Nara-machi Shiryōkan** (奈良町資料館; 10am–4pm; closed Mon; free) on the next corner. Marked by strings of red-cloth monkeys (good-luck charms) hanging outside, this small museum occupies the former warehouse of a mosquito-net manufacturer and houses a wonderful jumble of household utensils, shop signboards, Buddhist statues, pots and so forth from the local area.

Turn left (south) beside Nara-machi Shiryōkan for the **Nara Orient-kan** (奈良オリエント館; 10am–5pm; closed Mon), an interesting old merchant's house consisting of two traditional storehouses (*kura*) linked by a long corridor. Follow this road round to the left and turn south again, past a sub-post office. Just before the next corner is **Nara-machi Kōshi-no-ie** (ならまち格子の家; 9am–5pm; closed Mon; free), which stands out as one of the area's best-preserved traditional houses. This Edo-period merchant's dwelling has a long and narrow interior, including an inner courtyard garden; the front door and kitchen skylights have a clever operating mechanism, which the staff will happily demonstrate.

You're now near the southern limits of Nara-machi. To return to central Nara, take the next road parallel to the west, which will eventually lead to the shopping arcades and Sanjō-dōri. On the way, look out for **Ashibi-no-sato** (あしびの郷; daily 10am–5pm), an old-style shop selling pickles and tea, where you can also have light meals, and **Esaki** (エサキ; daily except Wed 10am–6pm) on the corner – unmissable thanks to its colourful lanterns and traditional umbrellas.

Eating

The central Higashimuki arcade is particularly convenient for eating, as is Sanjō-dōri, where you'll find a range of cafés and a clutch of decent **restaurants** serving classy local cuisine. Like Kyoto, Nara has its own brand of *kaiseki*, the elaborate meals that originally accompanied the tea ceremony, but **local specialities** also include some rather bland dishes. *Cha-ga-yu* may have evolved from the breakfast of poor people into a fairly expensive delicacy, but there's no escaping the fact that it's basically a thin rice gruel, boiled up with soya beans, sweet potatoes and green tea leaves. It's best as part of a set meal, when the accompaniments such as pickles add a bit of flavour. *Tororo* is pretty similar: thickened grated yam mixed with soy sauce, seaweed and barley, then poured over a bowl of rice – full of protein and rather sticky. Less of an acquired taste is *kakinoha-zushi*, sushi wrapped in persimmon leaves, and *Nara-zuke*, vegetables pickled in sake.

Hirasō 平宗 30-1 Imanikadō-chō ⓣ0742/22-0866. *Hirasō* specializes in *kakinoha-zushi* (persimmon-wrapped sushi), though you'll also find all sorts of other tasty delicacies on the menu. Sushi sets start at ¥820, with more varied meals from around ¥3000, including *cha-ga-yu*. Closed Mon.

Hiyori ひより 26 Nakanoshinya-chō ⓣ0742/24-1470. Specializes in *yamato-yasai,* the vegetable cuisine of Nara. Lunch sets start at ¥1575 and multi-course dinners are from ¥3675. Open 11.30am–2.30pm & 5–10pm; closed Tues.

Jyu Jyu 樹樹 27-1 Mochidono-chō ⓣ0742/27-6121, ⓦwww.jyujyunara.com. Up a narrow alleyway off the arcade south of Sanjo-dori, this friendly *izakaya* is in an old geisha house and serves Japanese home-style cooking. Try the fermented soy bean and onion omelette (¥730) or avocado sashimi (¥680). Closed Mon and every first and third Tues of the month.

Mellow Café Axe Unit, 1–8 Konishi-chō ⓣ0742/27-9099, ⓦwww.mellowcafe.jp. Fifty metres south of the Vivre department store, located in a faux-Spanish-style shopping arcade, is this large, spacious Italian café-restaurant, specializing in oven-fired pizza. Lunch specials start at ¥1100. Daily 11am–11pm.

Sanshū 三秀 Isui-en ⓣ0742/25-0781. *Tororo* isn't everyone's cup of tea, but this is an attractive place to seek out all the same, located in an old wooden house overlooking the secluded, Meiji-era Isui-en garden. There are just two meals on the menu: plain *mugi tororo* (¥1800) or *unagi* (eel) *tororo* (¥2800). Open 11.30am–1.30pm; closed Tues.

Shima Shima しましま Hayashikōji-chō ⓣ0742/26-8805. Just opposite the city tourist office, this is a great place for lunch – daily sets of Japanese-style home cooking are ¥800 – or home-made cakes for afternoon tea (¥450). Mon–Fri 10am–4.30pm.

Tochi 栃 15-3 Kasagi-cho ⓣ0742/27-2600. Elegant Chinese restaurant in a beautiful old house in Nara-machi. Set menu only – lunch from ¥6000 and dinner from ¥8000. Reservations are essential.

Tori Tamura 鶏 田村 1 Shonami-chō ⓣ0742/26-7739. This bustling restaurant, not far from the JR station, offers 30 different kinds of *yakitori*, served with locally brewed sake. Open 11.30am–2pm & 5–11pm; closed Mon.

Tousenbou 豆仙坊 2F Na Ra Ra Konishi-chō ⓣ0742/26-0633. Delicious tofu restaurant with an eclectic menu – everything from soups and noodles to desserts are made with soybeans. Tasty lunch sets (from ¥1200) are served with rice, miso soup and local *Nara-zuke* pickles. Daily 11am–8pm.

Tsukihi-tei 月日亭 2F Nara-ken Keizai Kurabu Biru, Higashimuki-dōri ⓣ0742/23-5470. This is one of the best places to sample Nara *kaiseki* at an affordable price. A full *kaiseki* course starts at ¥6000, with mini-*kaiseki* from ¥3990. At lunchtime they do cheaper sets from ¥1050. There's another branch (ⓣ0742/26-2021) deep in the forest behind Kasuga Taisha, which is worth making a trip to for its tranquil location; however, it is more expensive, with prices starting at ¥10,000.

Listings

Banks and exchange Kinki Ōsaka Bank, Mizuho Bank and Nara Bank, all on Sanjō-dōri, have foreign exchange desks. The *Hotel Fujita* is also able to change most major currencies and travellers' cheques.

Buses Long-distance buses for Tokyo (Shinjuku) and Yokohama stop outside both the Kintetsu and JR Nara train stations.

Car rental Eki Rent-a-Car (ⓣ0742/26-3929) is next door to JR Nara Station. Toyota (ⓣ0742/22-0100) and Nippon Rent-a-Car (ⓣ0742/24-5701) have branches near the Kintetsu Station.

Hospital Nara's main hospital is the Nara Koen Chuo Byōin, 2 Imakoji-chō (ⓣ0742/26-0277), with a 24hr emergency department. It's located on the main road, Tegai-dōri, northwest of Tōdai-ji.

Internet Nara City Tourist Information Centre has a full list of places offering internet access. The Shalala comic and internet café chain has branches in front of JR Nara and Kintetsu Nara.

Post offices Nara's Central Post Office is on Ōmiya-dōri, a fair walk west of centre. It has 24hr mail services, but for other purposes the sub-post offices in the centre of town (see map on p.464) are more convenient.

Shopping Among a range of local crafts, Nara is particularly renowned for its high-quality *sumi-e* ink, calligraphy brushes (*fude*), tea whisks (*chasen*) and bleached hemp cloth (*sarashi*). You'll find all these on sale along the main shopping streets, or try the Nara Prefectural Commerce, Industry and Tourist Hall, on Ōmiya-dōri to the east of Kintetsu-Nara Station, which stocks the full range of Nara crafts. The Nara Kogeikan Craft Museum, southwest of JR Nara, also has good displays and local work on sale.

Around Nara

Even before Nara was founded, the surrounding plains were sprinkled with burial mounds, palaces and temples. A few of these still survive, of which the most remarkable is **Hōryū-ji**, an historic temple about 10km southwest of Nara in Ikaruga district, which also includes the **Chūgū-ji** nunnery. Closer to Nara, the two temples of Nishinokyō district, **Yakushi-ji** and **Tōshōdai-ji**, continue the story of the transition from Chinese to Japanese art and architecture. The route described below starts at Hōryū-ji and then works back towards Nara. All of these temples are served by the same **buses** (routes #52 and #97) from Nara's JR and Kintetsu stations.

Hōryū-ji and around

As you walk round the UNESCO World Heritage Site of **Hōryū-ji** (法隆寺; daily: Feb 22–Nov 3 8am–5pm; Nov 4–Feb 21 8am–4.30pm; ¥1000; Ⓦwww.horyuji.or.jp), completed in 607 AD, it's worth bearing in mind that Buddhism had only really got going in Japan some fifty years earlier. The confident scale of Hōryū-ji and its superb array of Buddhist statues amply illustrate how quickly this imported faith took hold. One of its strongest proponents was Prince Shōtoku (574–622), the then-regent, who founded Hōryū-ji in accordance with the dying wish of his father, Emperor Yōmei. Though the complex burnt down in 670, it was soon rebuilt, making this Japan's oldest-surviving Buddhist temple.

The main approach to Hōryū-ji is from the south, which takes you past the helpful **information centre** (daily 8.30am–6pm; Ⓣ0745/74-6800). Walk north

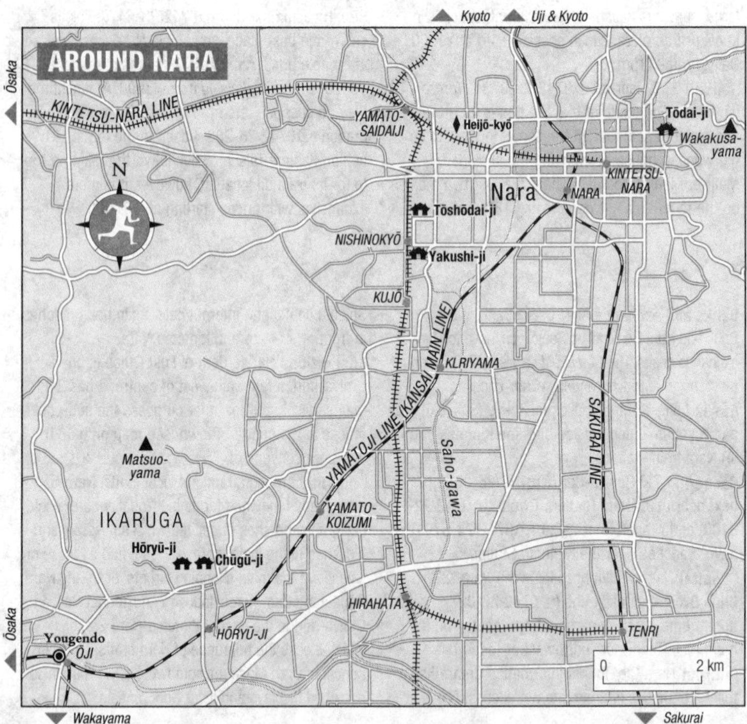

Getting to Hōryū-ji

The simplest way of getting to Hōryū-ji from Nara is by bus (every 30min; 50min; ¥760); get off at the Hōryū-ji-mae stop. Alternatively, Ōsaka-bound trains from JR Nara stop at Hōryū-ji Station (every 10min; 15min; ¥210), from where it's a good twenty-minute walk to the temple on a fairly busy road, or you can catch a #72 bus (weekdays 2–3 hourly, weekends every 10min; 10min; ¥170).

from here along a wide, tree-lined avenue to **Nandai-mon** (Great South Gate), which marks the outer enclosure. Inside lies a second, walled compound known as the **Sai-in Garan**, or Western Precinct. Within the Sai-in Garan's cloister-gallery, the **Five-Storey Pagoda** will inevitably catch your eye first. This is Japan's oldest five-tier pagoda, and inside you can see the early eighth-century clay images of Buddha entering nirvana. However, it's actually the right-hand building, the **Kon-dō** (Golden Hall), which is Hōryū-ji's star attraction. This is the world's oldest wooden structure, dating from the late seventh century, and although it's not very large, the building's multi-layered roofs and sweeping eaves are extremely striking.

Entering the Kon-dō's east door, you're greeted by a bronze image of Shaka Nyorai (Historical Buddha) flanked by two Bodhisattvas still bearing a few touches of original gold leaf that they were once covered in; this **Shaka triad** was cast in 623 AD in memory of Prince Shōtoku, who died the previous year. To its right stands **Yakushi Nyorai**, the Buddha of Healing, to which Hōryū-ji was dedicated, and to the left a twelfth-century **Amida Buddha** commemorating the Prince's mother.

Exiting the Sai-in compound, walk east past two long, narrow halls, to the **Daihōzō-den** (Gallery of Temple Treasures), which houses Hōryū-ji's priceless temple treasures in two halls. Look out for the bronze **Yume-chigae Kannon**. This "Dream-Changing" Kannon is credited with turning bad dreams into good, and has a soft, secretive smile. Connecting the two museum halls is the **Kudara Kannon Dōi**, which houses the wooden **Kudara Kannon** statue, thought to date from the seventh century. Nothing is known about this unusually tall, willowy figure, but it has long been recognized as one of the finest Buddhist works of art in Japan.

Chūgū-ji

A gate in the northeast corner of the Tō-in Garan leads directly into **Chūgū-ji** (中宮寺; daily 9am–4pm; ¥500; ⓣ0745/75-2106). This intimate, tranquil nunnery was originally the residence of Prince Shōtoku's mother, which he converted into a temple on her death in 621. The main reason for coming here, however, sits inside a modern hall facing south over a pond. If you've already visited Kyoto's Kōryū-ji (see p.434), you'll recognize the central image of a pensive, boy-like **Miroku Bosatsu** (Future Buddha) absorbed in his task of trying to save mankind from suffering. In this case the statue is of camphor wood, burnished black with age, and is believed to have been carved by an immigrant Korean craftsman in the early seventh century.

Chūgū-ji marks the eastern extent of the Hōryū-ji complex. If you exit from here it's about an eight-minute walk south down to the main road and the Chūgū-ji-mae bus stop, one stop east of the Hōryū-ji-mae stop; alternatively, trek back and exit from the Nandai-mon, which will take you down to the Hōryū-ji bus depot. Buses heading south will take you back to JR Hōryū-ji

The Hidden Buddha of Hōryū-ji

Tō-in Garan is the eastern precinct of Hōryū-ji, which was added in 739. At its centrepiece is the octagonal **Yume-dono** (Hall of Dreams), with its magnificent statue, the **Kuze Kannon**. Until the late nineteenth century, this gilded wooden figure, said to be the same height as Prince Shōtoku (perhaps even modelled on him in the early seventh century), was a *hibutsu*, a hidden image, which no one had seen for centuries. Somewhat surprisingly, it was an American art historian, Ernest Fenellosa, who in the 1880s was given permission by the Meiji government, against the wishes of the temple, to unwrap the Kannon from the bundle of white cloth in which it had been kept. He revealed a dazzling statue in an almost perfect state of repair, carrying a sacred jewel and wearing an elaborate crown, with the famous enigmatic smile of the Kon-dō's Shaka Nyorai on its youthful lips. Unfortunately, the Kannon is still kept hidden for most of the year, except for brief spells in spring and autumn (April 11–May 15 & Oct 22–Nov 22).

Station, while those going north pass Yakushi-ji en route to Nara; in either case, you'll want a #60 or #97 bus.

Yakushi-ji

Six kilometres northwest of Hōryū-ji, the Nishinokyō area is home to two great temples that are again famed for their age and wealth of statuary – Yakushi-ji and Tōshōdai-ji.

The older of the pair is southerly **Yakushi-ji** (薬師寺; daily 8.30am–5pm; ¥800). Emperor Tenmu first ordered its construction sometime around 680 AD when his wife was seriously ill. Although she recovered, Tenmu himself died eight years later, leaving the empress to dedicate Yakushi-ji herself in 697. Over the centuries, fires have destroyed all but one of the original buildings, though the statues themselves have fared better.

Arriving by **bus** from Hōryū-ji (35min; ¥560) or Nara (20min; ¥240) – buses #52 and #97 – get off at the Yakushi-ji Chusha-jo stop, from where it's a short walk to the temple's south gate. Alternatively, Kintetsu-line **trains** run from Nara to Nishinokyō Station (¥250) with a change at Saidai-ji; the north gate is a three-minute walk east of the station.

The only building of historical note in Yakushi-ji's inner compound is the three-storey **East Pagoda**, which was famously described as "frozen music" by Ernest Fenellosa (see box above). He was referring to the rhythmical progression of the smaller double roofs that punctuate the pagoda's upward flow. It's the sole surviving remnant of the original temple and contrasts strongly with the spanking red lacquer of the new West Pagoda, the Daikō-do (Great Lecture Hall) and the Kon-dō (Golden Hall), all of which have been rebuilt during the last thirty years. However, inside the Kon-dō the temple's original seventh-century bronze **Yakushi triad** sits unperturbed. Past fires have removed most of the gold and given the statues a rich black sheen, but otherwise they are in remarkably fine condition.

Continuing through the outer compound you come to a long, low wooden hall on your left, the **Tōin-dō**. Rebuilt around 1285, the hall houses a bronze image of **Shō-Kannon**, an incarnation of the goddess of mercy, which dates from the early Nara period. This graceful, erect statue, framed against a golden aureole, shows distinctly Indian influences in its diaphanous robes, double necklace and strands of hair falling over its shoulders.

The last building, in the compound's northeast corner, is the Daihōzō-den, a modern **treasure hall**. It's only open for three short periods each year (Jan 1–15, late March–early April & Oct 8–Nov 10; ¥500), and during two of those periods (Jan & Oct–Nov) a rare, Nara-period painting of Kissho-ten, the Buddhist goddess of peace, happiness and beauty, is the prime attraction. She is portrayed as a voluptuous figure with cherry-red, butterfly lips, and dressed in an intricately patterned fabric whose colours are still remarkably clear.

Tōshōdai-ji

After exiting from Yakushi-ji's north gate, head straight ahead for five minutes and you'll find the front entrance to **Tōshōdai-ji** (唐招提寺; daily 8.30am–4.30pm; ¥600). The weathered, wooden halls in their shady compound are superb examples of late eighth-century architecture. The temple was founded in 759 by the eminent Chinese monk Ganjin – he of Nara's Kaidan-in (see p.469) – when he was granted permission to move from the city to somewhere more peaceful.

The first thing you'll see on entering the south gate is the stately Chinese-style Kon-dō (main Hall), which has recently been restored. Craftsmen who accompanied Ganjin from the mainland are responsible for the three superb dry-lacquer statues displayed here. The **Kō-dō** (Lecture Hall) behind the Kon-dō also dates from the late eighth century, and is more Japanese in styling. During the Nara period, this hall was a major centre of learning and religious training. On the compound's east side is the concrete **Shin-Hōzō** (daily 8.30am–4pm; ¥100), where, each spring and autumn, Tōshōdai-ji's treasures go on display (March–May & Sept–Nov). Again, these are mostly statues, of which the most celebrated is a headless Buddha known as the "Venus of the Orient". Just once a year – on June 6, the anniversary of Ganjin's death – the doors of the **Miei-dō** (Founder's Hall), in the northern section of the compound, are opened to reveal a lacquered image which was carved just before he died in 763 at the grand age of 76. He's buried next door, in the far northeast corner of the compound, in a simple grave within a clay-walled enclosure.

Afterwards, walk back to the main gate and then east for about five minutes to the main road where you can pick up a bus back to Nara – the #60 or #97 (20min; ¥240). Alternatively, head back to Yakushi-ji and catch a Kintetsu-line train, changing at Saidaiji.

Travel details

Trains

Kyoto to: Amanohashidate (7 daily; 2hr 30min); Fukuoka (Hakata Station; 1–2 hourly; 2hr 50min); Hikone (every hour; 50min); Himeji (1–3 hourly; 50min); Hiroshima (1–2 hourly; 1hr 40min); Ise (hourly; 2hr); Kanazawa (1–2 hourly; 2hr); Kansai International (every 30min; 1hr 15min); Kashikojima (hourly; 2hr 45min); Kōbe (& Shin-Kōbe) (1–3 hourly; 30min); Nagoya (every 15min; 40min); Nara (every 15–20min; 40min); Ōsaka (& Shin-Ōsaka) (every 15min; 17min); Toba (hourly; 2hr 20min); Tokyo (every 15min; 2hr 10min); Toyama (hourly; 2hr 40min); Uji (every 10–15min; 20min).

Nara to: Ise (every 15–20min; 2–3hr); Kōya-san (every 15–20min; 3hr); Kyoto (every 15–20min; 40min); Ōsaka (Kintetsu-Namba & Shin Ōsaka) (every 15min; 30min).

Buses

The buses listed below are mainly long-distance services – often travelling overnight – between the major cities, and local services where there is no alternative means of transport. For shorter journeys, however, trains are almost invariably quicker and often no more expensive.

Kyoto to: Amanohashidate (2 daily; 2hr 40min); Fukuoka (1 daily; 9hr 35min); Kanazawa (5 daily; 4hr); Kansai International (hourly; 1hr 45min); Kumamoto (1 daily; 11hr); Nagasaki (1 daily; 11hr); Nagoya (16 daily; 2hr 30min); Ōsaka (Itami; every 30min; 55min); Tokyo (3 daily; 8hr); Tottori (3 daily; 4hr); Yokohama (1 daily; 7hr 30min).

Nara to: Fukuoka (1 daily; 10hr); Tokyo (1 daily; 8hr); Yokohama (1 daily; 9hr).

Kansai

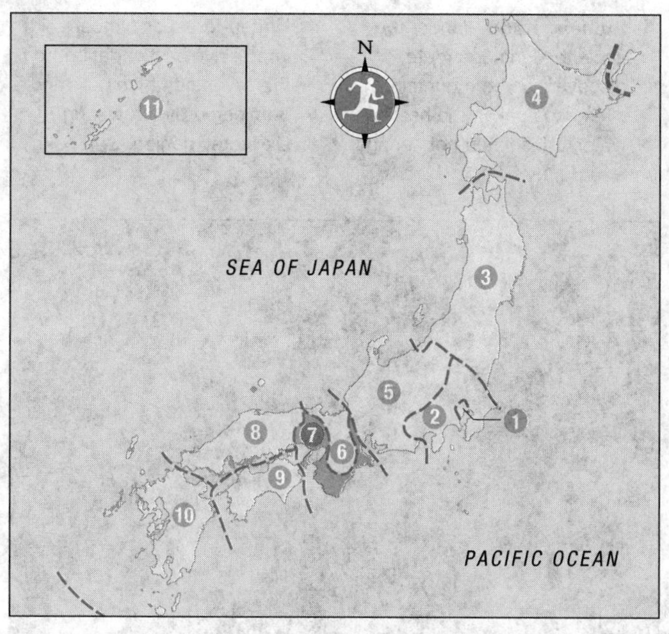

CHAPTER 7 Highlights

* **Ōsaka Aquarium** The country's best aquarium, housed in an unusual, butterfly-shaped building. See p.491
* **Takarazuka** See the popular all-female revue troupe gender-bend their way through classic musicals. See p.497
* **Kumano Kodō** Wander the ancient pilgrimage route, discover sacred mountain sites and soak in the healing waters of isolated hot springs. See p.503
* **Shima Hantō** Visit the Grand Shrine at Ise, Japan's spiritual heartland, and later eat fresh seafood with the *ama* women divers of Toba. See p.506
* **Kōbe** Enjoy a meal of tender Kōbe beef in one of this harbourside city's sophisticated restaurants. See p.513
* **Himeji-jō** Japan's most impressive castle, dating from the seventeenth century and dominated by a towering six-storey donjon. See p.521

▲ The ancient Kumano Kodō pilgrimage trail

Kansai

In a country so devoid of flat land, the great rice-growing plains of **KANSAI** (関西), the district around Ōsaka and Kyoto, are imbued with an almost mystical significance. This was where the nation first began to take root, in the region known as Yamato, and where a distinct Japanese civilization evolved from the strong cultural influences of China and Korea. Kansai people are tremendously proud of their pivotal role in Japanese history and tend to look down on Tokyo, which they regard as an uncivilized upstart. Today, its diverse legacy of temples, shrines and castles, combined with an increasing array of exciting modern architecture, makes Kansai one of Japan's top tourist destinations. The former imperial capitals of Kyoto and Nara, with their enduring historical and cultural importance, are naturally a major part of the region's appeal, and are covered in the previous chapter.

Although **Ōsaka** has been much maligned as an "ugly" and "chaotic" city, it is not short of attractions and easily makes up for its aesthetic shortcomings with an excess of commercial spirit – the source of its long-established wealth – and an enthusiastic love of eating, drinking and its own style of comedy.

South of Ōsaka, the temples of **Kōya-san** provide a tranquil glimpse into contemporary religious practice in Japan. This mountain-top retreat – the headquarters of the Shingon school of Buddhism – has been an active centre of pilgrimage since the ninth century. People of all faiths are welcome to stay in the quiet old temples and join in the morning prayer service. Afterwards, you can walk through the atmospheric **Okunoin** cemetery to visit the grave of Shingon's founder, Kōbō Daishi, wreathed in incense smoke under towering cryptomeria trees.

Shinto, Japan's native religion, also has deep spiritual roots in Kansai. Not far from **Kōya-san** is the **Kumano Kodō**, an ancient pilgrimage route through the "Land of the Gods", where for centuries both emperors and peasants sought purification and healing at sacred sites and hot springs. Over on the far eastern side of the region is **Ise-jingū**, one of the country's most important Shinto shrines, dedicated to Amaterasu, the Sun Goddess, from whom all Japan's emperors are descended. **Ise** itself is the gateway to an attractive peninsula called **Shima Hantō**. Here, *ama* women divers still use traditional fishing methods to collect shellfish. The unspoiled scenery of **Agō-wan**, the bay at the southern tip of the peninsula, is a rewarding destination for scenic boat rides which give a bird's-eye view of the cultured pearl industry.

The port of **Kōbe**, now fully recovered from 1995's devastating earthquake, is less than thirty minutes west of Ōsaka in a dramatic location on the edge of Ōsaka Bay. Kōbe's sights are less of a draw than its relaxed cosmopolitan atmosphere, best experienced with a stroll around its shops and harbourside developments. Close by

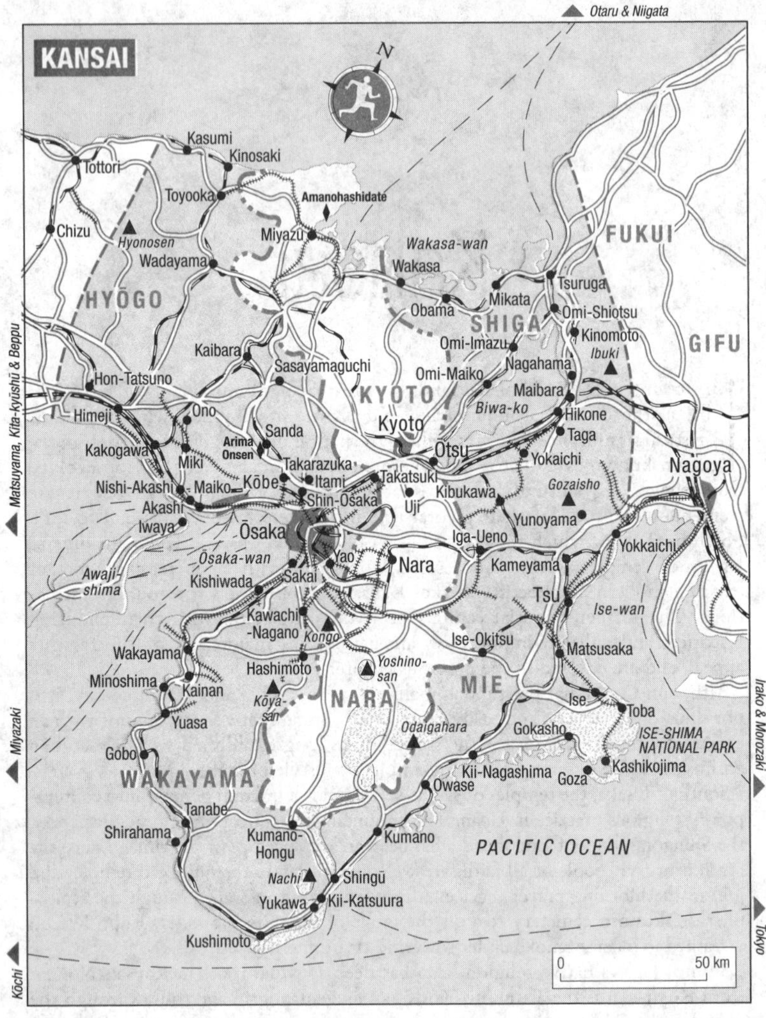

is the ancient hot-spring resort **Arima Onsen**, which has managed to retain some old-world hospitality in its elegant ryokan.

Wherever you choose to stay in Kansai, don't miss the opportunity to visit **Himeji**, on the area's western edge, to explore **Himeji-jō**, Japan's most impressive castle. Himeji also has a couple of intriguing museums in buildings designed by top contemporary architects, and the lovely **Himeji Kōko-en**, nine connected gardens laid out according to traditional principles.

The most convenient way of **getting around** the Kansai district is by train. The area is crisscrossed by competing JR and private rail lines, while the Tōkaidō Shinkansen provides a high-speed service between Ōsaka, Kyoto, Kōbe and Himeji. If you plan to travel intensively around the region, you might want to buy JR-West's **Kansai Area Pass**. Valid for between one and four consecutive days (¥2000–6000), the pass allows unlimited travel on all local services operated by JR

West, apart from the Shinkansen. It also offers discounts on admission to various cultural and tourist sights, including art museums and amusement parks along JR lines. For those travelling on to Fukuoka, the **San'yō Area Pass** covers JR services from Kansai Airport via Ōsaka, Kōbe and Himeji, including the Shinkansen (four consecutive days ¥20,000, eight consecutive days ¥30,000). Another option is to take advantage of the loose alignment which the region's private railway lines, subway networks and bus companies have made with the *Kansai Thru Pass* (two-day ticket, ¥3800; three-day ticket, ¥5000) and the stored-value card, which enable travellers to ride on almost any bus, subway or private railway in the whole of the region. Even if you have a JR Rail Pass these cards are handy, as they save the hassle of buying tickets each time you jump on a bus or ride the subway.

Ōsaka and around

Having received a bad rap as a tourist destination for many years, **ŌSAKA** (大阪), Japan's third-largest city after Tokyo and Yokohama, has used public money to try and "re-brand" itself. The city is hoping to successfully improve its image, mainly through urban revitalization and ambitious architectural projects, to become a more attractive destination. It may still lack the pockets of beauty and refinement found in nearby Kyoto, but Ōsaka is a vibrant metropolis, inhabited by famously easy-going citizens with a taste for the good things in life.

Ōsakans speak one of Japan's more earthy dialects, **Ōsaka-ben**, and are as friendly as Kyoto folk can be frosty. They may greet each other saying "Mō kari-makka?" ("Are you making any money?"), but Ōsakans also know how to enjoy themselves once work has stopped. There are large entertainment districts in the north and south of the city, and the Ōsaka live music scene showcases eclectic local talent as well as international acts. In a city that cultivated high **arts**, such as *bunraku* puppetry, the locals also have a gift for bawdy comedy; Takeshi "Beat" Kitano, the internationally famous film director, started his career as a comedian here. The city continues to produce successful comedy duos who dominate national TV variety shows, and Ōsakans are very proud that their dialect has now become popular as the language of comedians. Ōsaka is also one of Japan's great **food** cities, but Ōsakans are not snobby about their cuisine; a typical local dish is *takoyaki*, grilled octopus dumplings, usually sold as a street snack.

The city also feels a welcoming place for foreigners. It has Japan's largest community of Koreans and a growing *gaijin* population. There's also a willingness to face up to uncomfortable social issues, exemplified by the city's admirable civil rights museum, **Liberty Ōsaka**, which among other things focuses on Japan's untouchables, the Burakumin. Similarly, Ōsaka's homelessness problem has not been ignored, at least by citizens, and the *Big Issue Japan* started here in 2003.

If you want to escape Ōsaka's urban landscape for a day, take a trip out to **Takarazuka**, home of the eponymous musical drama troupe. As well as taking in one of the all-female troupe's glitzy shows, you can check out the imaginative artwork at the **Tezuka Osamu Manga Museum**, a showcase for local artist Tezuka, widely regarded as the god of manga.

Some history

Ōsaka's history stretches back to the fifth century AD, when it was known as **Naniwa** and its port served as a gateway to the more advanced cultures of Korea and China. For a short period, from the middle of the seventh century, the thriving city served as Japan's capital, but in the turbulent centuries that followed it lost its status, changed its name to Ōsaka and developed as a temple town. It was on the site of the temple Ishiyama Hongan-ji that the warlord **Toyotomi Hideyoshi** decided to build his castle in 1583 (see box, p.489) and it became a key bastion in his campaign to unite the country.

With Toyotomi's death in 1598, another period of political instability loomed in Ōsaka for his supporters, as rival **Tokugawa Ieyasu** shifted the capital to Edo. The shogun's troops besieged the castle in 1614 and destroyed it a year later. With Japan firmly under their control, the Tokugawa shoguns were happy to allow the castle to be rebuilt and for Ōsaka to continue developing as an economic and commercial centre. The wealth of what became known as the "kitchen of Japan" led to

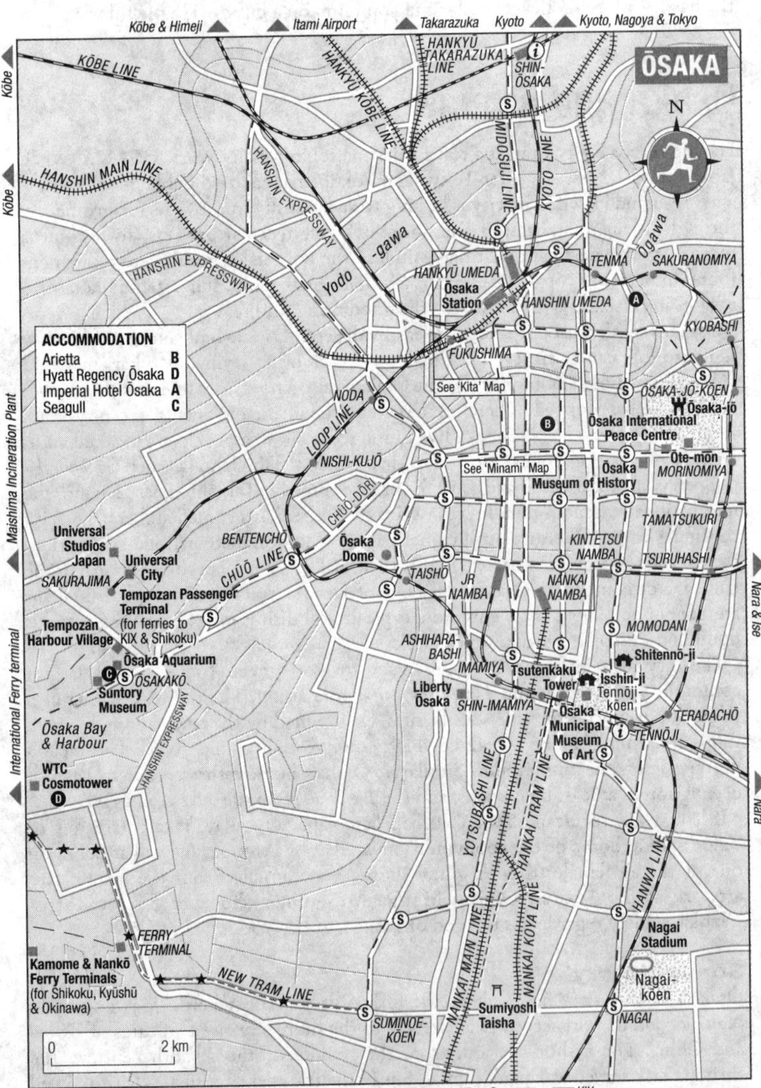

patronage of the arts, such as kabuki and *bunraku*, and a deep appreciation of gourmet pursuits (the origin of the expression "kuidaore", to eat oneself bankrupt) still exists today.

Despite having a gross domestic product comparable to that of Canada, and despite the city's commercial activity, the local government has been in the red for over a decade. Governor Toru Hashimoto is a controversial figure; a former lawyer and TV celebrity who was elected in 2008, he has initiated severe cost-cutting measures affecting education and community programmes.

Arrival

Served by two airports, numerous ferries and buses, not to mention a slew of railway companies, you can arrive in Ōsaka from almost any point in Japan and, via Kansai International Airport, from many places overseas, too. There's also a weekly ferry service between Ōsaka and Shanghai in China.

By plane

International and many domestic flights arrive at **Kansai International Airport** (KIX; 関西国際空港; Ⓦ www.kansai-airport.or.jp), on a man-made island in Ōsaka Bay, some 35km south of the city centre. International arrivals are processed on the first floor of the sleek modern building, where you'll also find the small **Kansai Tourist Information Centre** (daily 9am–9pm; Ⓣ 0724/56-6025), a separate desk where you can make hotel reservations, and several **bureaux de change**.

The fastest way into the city is by train. Services depart from the station connected to the second floor of the passenger terminal building. The regular **Nankai Express**, or *kaisoku* (快速; ¥890), takes 45 minutes to reach Nankai Namba Station (南海難波駅), although it's hard to resist the chic **Rapi:t**, designed like a train from a sci-fi comic, which costs ¥1390 and does the journey in just over thirty minutes. From Nankai Namba Station you can take a subway or taxi to other parts of the city.

JR also runs trains directly to several stations in and around Ōsaka from KIX, and if you have a rail pass voucher you can exchange it at Kansai Airport Station. For pass holders, the services to JR Namba Station (JR難波駅; 1hr; ¥1010) are a good alternative to the Nankai Express. The **Haruka** limited express is a convenient but pricey option, stopping at Tennōji Station (天王寺駅; 30min; ¥2270), Shin-Ōsaka Station (新大阪駅; 45min; ¥2980), where you can catch the Shinkansen, and then on to Kyoto (1hr 15min; ¥3490). If you're in no hurry, the regular JR express trains to Tennōji Station (45min; ¥1030) and Ōsaka Station (70min; ¥1160), in the Umeda area of the city, are worth considering.

To avoid the hassle of dragging your luggage on and off trains, there are also **limousine buses** and taxis for various locations around Ōsaka, including several hotels, departing from international arrivals. All central city locations take forty minutes to one hour to reach, depending on the traffic, and cost ¥1500. There's also a direct bus to Itami airport (see below; 1hr 20min; ¥1900), and services to Kyoto, Kōbe and Nara. **Taxis** to central Ōsaka are expensive (from ¥10,000), and no faster than the buses.

Itami Airport (伊丹空港), or Ōsaka Airport (大阪空港), as it is also confusingly known, is 10km north of the city centre and only handles **domestic flights**. From the airport there are regular buses into the city (25–50min depending on destination; ¥340–680) and also to Shin-Ōsaka Station (25min; ¥480), where you can connect to the Shinkansen. There are also direct limousine buses to KIX (1hr 20min; ¥2000) and on to Kyoto and Kōbe. A taxi to Umeda in central Ōsaka costs around ¥5000. There's also a **monorail** (tickets from ¥190), which links the airport with parts of north Ōsaka, connecting at various points to the city subway system and both the Hankyu and Keihan private railways.

By train

Shinkansen pull into **Shin-Ōsaka Station**, north of the city centre. You can transfer here to other JR services around the area or to the city's subway lines.

JR services, along the Tōkaidō line connecting Nagoya, Kyoto and Kōbe with Ōsaka, arrive at the central **Ōsaka Station** (大阪駅) in Umeda (梅田), where you'll also find the termini for the Hankyū (阪急) and Hanshin (阪神) lines, both of which provide cheaper connections with Kyoto and Kōbe than JR if you're not using a rail pass. Services from Nara (see p.463) on the Kintetsu line arrive at **Kintetsu Namba Station** (近鉄難波駅), in the heart of the Minami district. Those from Ise (see p.506) arrive at Uehonmachi, also on the Kintetsu network.

By bus

Ōsaka has various long-distance **bus stations.** These are located beside the JR Ōsaka Station in Umeda; at the Namba Kaisoku Bus Terminal and Ōsaka City Air Terminal in Namba; at Kintetsu Uehonmachi, south of the castle; and at Abenobashi near Tennōji, 1km further south of the castle. All are beside or near subway and train stations for connections around the city.

By boat

Ōsaka is still a major port of call for many of the **ferries** plying routes around Japan, and sailing into Ōsaka Bay is a memorable way of approaching the city. The port is west of the city centre and has good transport links via the subway and train network. Most ferries use the Ōsaka Nankō Terminal (大阪南港フェリーターミナル), close to Ferry Terminal Station on the New Tram monorail, which connects to the city's subway network. The nearest station to the less busy Tempozan East Wharf (天保山東岸壁) is Ōsaka-kō (大阪港) on the Chūō subway line, a ten-minute walk away.

Orientation

Like all big Japanese cities, Ōsaka is divided into wards (*ku*), but you'll often hear locals talking of Kita (north) and Minami (south), the split being along Chūō-dōri. **Kita** covers the areas of **Umeda,** where all the main railway companies have stations, and **Shin-Ōsaka**, north of the Yodo-gawa River and location of the Shinkansen station. On the east side of this area is **Ōsaka-jō**, the castle. The

Moving on from Ōsaka

The international departure lounge at **Kansai International Airport** is on the fourth floor. The ¥2650 departure tax is generally included in the price of tickets, except for some cheap discount tickets, in which case you'll have to pay it when you check in. Domestic departures are on the second floor.

If you plan to depart from Ōsaka by **bus**, check first with one of the tourist information centres (see opposite) for timetables and which station to go to.

There are **ferry** services from Ōsaka to Beppu, Miyazaki and Shin-Moji on Kyūshū (see p.649), and to Kōchi, Matsuyama and several other destinations on Shikoku (see p.591). In addition, there's a slow boat to Shanghai, China, which leaves once a week from Ōsaka Nankō International Ferry Terminal, close to Cosmosquare Station, where the Techno Port line meets the New Tram line. Check current timetables and fares with the tourist information office.

shopping and entertainment districts of Shinsaibashi, Dōtombori and Namba are all part of **Minami**.

Slightly further south is **Tennōji**, where you'll find Tennōji-kōen and the temple Shitennō-ji and, further south again, the ancient shrine Sumiyoshi Taisha. West of these districts lies the patchwork of landfill islands edging Ōsaka Bay; the Ōsaka Aquarium is at **Tempozan Harbour Village**, while the Kansai area's tallest building, the WTC Cosmotower, is further south at **Nankō**.

Information

The Ōsaka Tourist Association beats those of Tokyo and Kyoto hands down. There are **tourist information** offices all over the city, as well as at KIX. All are open daily from 9am to 8pm, have English-speaking staff and can help you book accommodation.

There's an office in Shin-Ōsaka Station (ⓣ06/6305-3311), handy if you've arrived by Shinkansen, while the main office is in Umeda's JR Ōsaka Station (ⓣ06/6345-2189), in a cabin beside the Midōsuji South Gate opposite the Hankyū department store. You'll also find tourist information counters in Nankai Namba Station (ⓣ06/6631-9100) and in JR Tennōji Station (ⓣ06/6774-3077). If you're going to be in Ōsaka for a while, it's well worth visiting the **Ōsaka International House** (大阪国際交流センター), at 8-2-6 Uehonmachi (ⓣ06/6772-5931, ⓦwww.ih-osaka.or.jp), which has a well-stocked library and cultural exchange facilities.

At all the information counters and in most top hotels you'll find the free quarterly booklet *Meet Ōsaka*, and the bimonthly *Ōsaka Guide*, both of which carry basic **listings** of traditional events and performances. Information on contemporary cultural events is listed in the free monthly *Kansai Scene* (ⓦwww.kansaiscene.com), an English-language magazine that also has interesting features, while the nationwide *Japanzine*, another free monthly, includes information on the Ōsaka club scene. Both are available from tourist offices, as well as main bookstores and pubs.

City transport

Ōsaka's extensive **subway and train system** operates exactly like Tokyo's, and the city also has a JR Loop line. The latter is handy if you're using a rail pass, but most of the time you'll find the subway more convenient and quicker for getting around the city. You can transfer between the nine subways and the New Tram line on the same ticket, but if you switch to any of the railway lines at a connecting station you'll need to either buy another ticket or a special transfer ticket when you start your journey. Most journeys across central Ōsaka cost ¥230. See the back of the book for a **map** of the Ōsaka subway.

Because Ōsaka's attractions are widely scattered, investing in a **one-day pass** (¥850) is worth considering if you're up for a hectic round of the sights. The pass is valid on all the subway lines and buses, and will be date-stamped when you first pass through the gate machines. You could also buy a one- or two-day **Ōsaka Unlimited Pass** (¥2000–2700), valid for both trains and buses, and including free admission to 26 popular tourist sites. These can be bought at subway-ticket vending machines as well as station kiosks. There are plenty of **buses**, but you'll find the subways and trains with their English signs and maps much easier to use.

Accommodation

As a commercial city, Ōsaka's **accommodation** is predominantly Western-style hotels. The **Umeda** area hosts the bulk of the city's luxury hotels, while the shopping and nightlife districts of **Shinsaibashi** and **Namba** have a greater range of accommodation options, catering to all budgets. There are a decent number of youth hostels in the city, though they aren't convenient if you're keen to experience the city's nightlife, due to their strict curfews. Local transport is so efficient, however, that it's no great problem to be based even outside the central area.

Kita

The following are marked on the map on p.486.

Dōjima 堂島ホテル 2-1-31 Dōjimahama ⓣ06/6341-3000, ⓦwww.dojima-hotel.com. Ōsaka's first boutique hotel, with starkly elegant decor, a cigar bar and an all-day diner. All rooms have wide-screen TVs and large designer bathtubs. ❼

Hearton Hotel Nishi-Umeda ハートンホテル西梅田 3-3-55 Umeda ⓣ06/6342-1111, ⓦwww.hearton.co.jp. Popular business hotel just behind the main post office next to JR Ōsaka Station. Rooms are smart, clean and functional, and come with cable TV and internet access. ❹

Imperial Hotel Ōsaka 帝国ホテル大阪 1-8-50 Tenmabashi ⓣ06/6881-1111, ⓦwww.imperialhotel.co.jp. This opulent hotel, overlooking the Ōkawa River, is just as luxurious as its famous Tokyo parent. Purified air, a golf driving range and a range of elegant restaurants are all part of the experience. ❽

J-Hoppers Ōsaka ジェイホッパーズ大阪 7-4-22 Fukushima ⓣ06/6453-6669, ⓦosaka.j-hoppers.com. This is Kita's best budget option, in a handy location for exploring Ōsaka. Rooms are clean, the staff are happy to help with travel information, and the breezy rooftop garden is very popular. Dorm beds are ¥2500, and there are double and twin rooms as well. ❸

Ritz Carlton Ōsaka リッツカールトン大阪 2-5-25 Umeda ⓣ06/6343-7000, ⓦwww.ritzcarlton.com. Luxury hotel with the intimate feel of a European country house, liberally sprinkled with antiques and Japanese objets d'art. Rooms have fantastic views across the city, there's a great range of restaurants and the pool and gym are free to guests. ❼

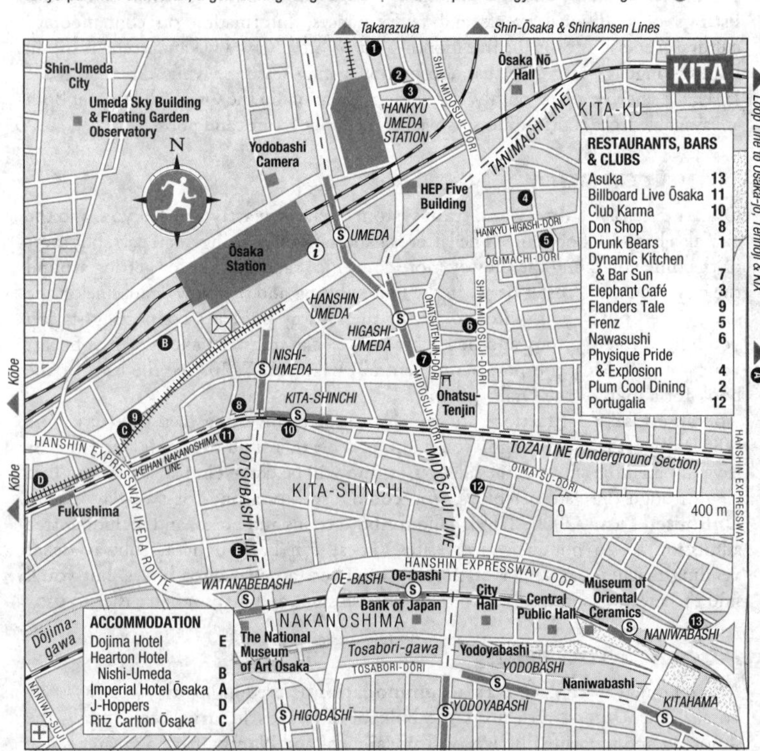

Minami

The following are marked on the map on p.487.

Arietta アリエッタホテル 3-2-6 Azuchimachi ⓣ06/6267-2789, ⓦwww.thehotel.co.jp/en/arietta_osaka. Clean and smart business hotel with a light and breezy Mediterranean-style lobby. Conveniently located close to three subway lines. Free breakfast and internet access. ❹

Cross Hotel Ōsaka クロスホテル大阪 2-5-15 Shinsaibashi ⓣ06/6213-8281, ⓦwww.crosshotel.com/osaka. A stylish hotel with efficient service, just minutes away from the Minami shopping and nightlife scene. The decently sized rooms are tastefully decorated and include internet access. ❺

First Cabin ファーストキャビン 4-2-1 Namba ⓣ06/6631-8090, ⓦwww.first-cabin.jp. Smart capsule hotel for both men and women in the heart of Namba, with a first-class air travel theme. Cabins are bigger than the business capsules but all have their own TV and internet connection. Excellent bath, café/bar and communal lounge facilities. ❷

Nikkō Ōsaka ホテル日航大阪 1-3-3 Nishi-Shinsaibashi ⓣ06/6244-1281, ⓦwww.hno.co.jp. Top-class hotel close to nightlife and shopping arcades, with spacious and comfortable rooms, attentive service and a good range of restaurants, including a coffee shop that has an excellent buffet breakfast. ❽

Swissôtel Nankai Ōsaka スイスホテル南海大阪 5-1-60 Namba ⓣ06/6646-1111, ⓦwww.swissotel.com. Currently Ōsaka's top international hotel, located directly above Nankai Station, which makes it ultra-convenient for direct airport access. Rooms are fresh and modern and the service is impeccable. ❽

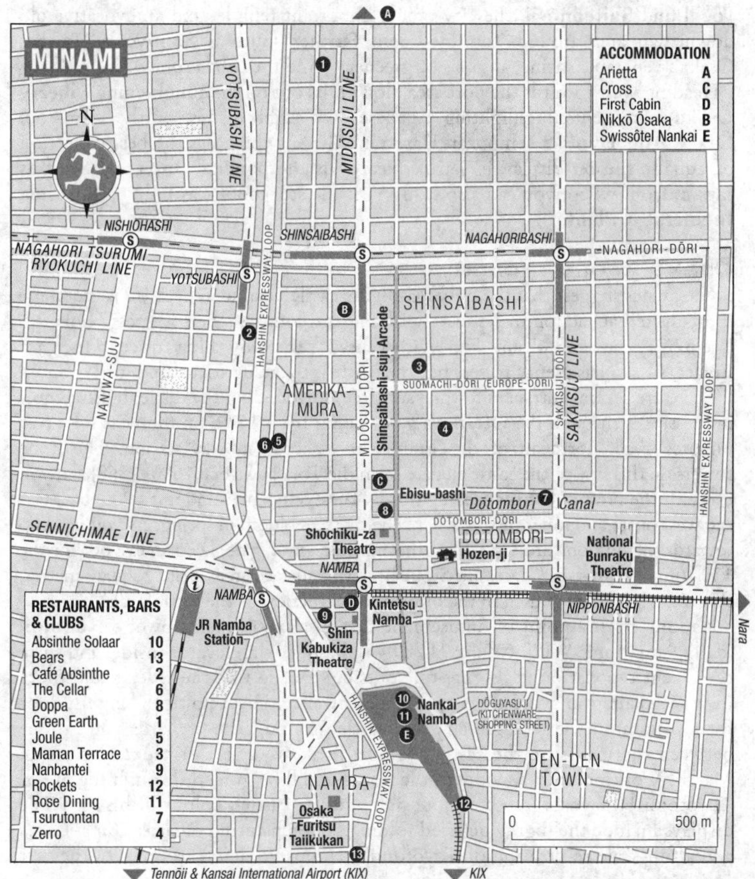

Other areas

The following are marked on the map on p.482.

Hyatt Regency Ōsaka ハイアットリージェンシー大阪 1-13-11 Nankō-Kita ⓣ06/6612-1234, ⓦwww.hyattregencyosaka.com. Good luxury choice near the port area, offering well-equipped rooms with a minimalist design, elegant public areas and restaurants, and indoor and outdoor pools. ❼

Seagull ホテルシーガル 1-5-15 Kaigan-dōri ⓣ06/6575-5000. Stylish contemporary hotel that is convenient for visiting the Ōsaka Aquarium and Universal Studios. Rooms are individually decorated and there's a cheerful lobby restaurant with pleasant views. ❼

The City

Ōsaka's best sights are scattered far and wide, but there are some areas worth exploring on foot. A fine place to start is the castle **Ōsaka-jō** and its immediate environs. **Umeda** (梅田), north of the centre, also has a few attractions, such as the rarefied **Museum of Oriental Ceramics** and the soaring skyscrapers near the clutch of train stations. The areas south of the Ogawa, including Shinsaibashi, Dōtombori, Amerika-mura and Namba, are almost exclusively shopping, eating and entertainment districts, which come to life at night (see p.493).

Another good area for strolling around is **Tennōji**, south of the centre, where you'll find **Shitennō-ji**, the city's most important temple, and an evocative old downtown area around **Tennōji-kōen**. Further south is **Sumiyoshi Taisha**, Ōsaka's venerable shrine, an oasis of greenery amid the urban sprawl.

Heading west towards the port area, don't miss out on the enlightening **Liberty Ōsaka**, a museum highlighting Japanese civil rights issues, or the ultra-cool **Ōsaka Aquarium** at Tempozan Harbour Village, which has the best collection of aquatic life on display in Japan. Nearby is the popular **Universal Studios Japan**, from where you can also easily visit the storybook-castle-like **Maishima Incinerator Plant**.

Ōsaka-jō and around

Some cynics suggest that the only reason the castle **Ōsaka-jō** (大阪城) is the single most-visited attraction in Japan – outdoing the country's best fortress Himeji-jō (see p.521) and even Mount Fuji – is because it's the only thing to see in the city. In fact, Ōsaka has plenty to see, but the castle is the main focus, and justly so.

There are several entrances to the park (free) surrounding the castle, but the most impressive is through the **Ōte-mon** gate, dating from 1629, on the west side, two minutes' walk northeast of the Tanimachi 4-chōme subway station. The stone towers on this side of the castle all date from the Tokugawa era (1600–1868) and you can visit the pretty **Nishinomaru garden** (Tues–Sun 9am–4.30pm; ¥200) between the west outer and inner moats, where cherry trees bloom in spring. As you head up towards the donjon through the southern Sakura-mon gate, keep an eye out for the 130-tonne **Tako-ishi** ("Octopus Stone"): with a surface area of sixty square metres, this is the largest rock used in the original construction of the castle walls.

It's long been a point of amusement that Ōsaka-jō's main tower, or **donjon** (daily 9am–5pm; ¥600; ⓣ06/6941-3044), has its own elevator inside, and since the recent renovation it also has one outside, too, so that the elderly and those in wheelchairs can avoid the steps to the entrance. Head up to the eighth floor for a panoramic view of the city and castle grounds; the orchards you can see between the moats on the castle's eastern flank are a riot of plum blossom in March. Working your way down the floors you'll be guided through the life of Toyotomi Hideyoshi (see box opposite) and the castle's colourful history. The displays include the highly detailed folding screen painting *Summer War of Ōsaka* and a full-scale re-creation of Toyotomi's famous golden tearoom. On the first

The indomitable fortress

Despite being largely a concrete reconstruction, Ōsaka-jō can be counted a great survivor, a tangible link with the city's illustrious past as Japan's one-time seat of power. The castle's roots go back to the early sixteenth century, when an influential Buddhist sect built its fortified temple headquarters **Ishiyama Hongan-ji** beside the confluence of the Ōgawa and Neya-gawa rivers. For a decade the monks held out against warlord Oda Nobunaga (see p.769), before handing their fortress over in 1580. Nobunaga's successor, **Toyotomi Hideyoshi**, decided to build the grandest castle in Japan on the temple site. For three years from 1583, tens of thousands of men laboured on the enormous castle, and craftsmen were drafted in from around Japan to give the eight-storey central donjon the finest gold-leaf decoration.

Toyotomi died in 1598, and his son and heir Hideyori was immediately under threat from rival **Tokugawa Ieyasu**. In 1614, the would-be shogun laid siege to the castle, even though his favourite granddaughter Senhime, wife of Hideyori, was inside. A year later he breached the castle and reduced it to ruins. Hideyori and his mother committed suicide rather than surrender, but Senhime survived and went on to become mistress of Himeji-jō (see p.522). When Ieyasu allowed the castle to be rebuilt in the 1620s, he made sure it was not on the same scale as his own residence in Edo. In 1665, the donjon was again burnt to the ground after being struck by lightning. It was not rebuilt until the 1840s and then only lasted another thirty years before the Tokugawa troops set fire to the castle during the civil war that briefly raged before the Meiji Restoration of 1868. Ōsaka's citizens, however, had grown fond of their castle, so the donjon was rebuilt once more in 1931 – this time from concrete – and it has remained standing despite the heavy bombing of the city during World War II.

floor, it's worth dropping by the mini-theatre to see the free history videos screened with English subtitles.

From the donjon, there's a choice of directions through the park. Returning through the Sakura-mon and turning left past the dry moat through the Tamatsukuri-mon will bring you to the sobering **Ōsaka International Peace Centre** (大阪国際平和センター; Tues–Sun 9.30am–5pm; ¥250; Ⓣ06/6947-7208) in the southern corner of the park. As at similar museums in Hiroshima and Nagasaki, the worthy but heavy-going displays attempt to square the destruction of Ōsaka with Japan's provocative actions before and during World War II. Another possibility is to take the route north from the main tower, across the Gokuraku-bashi bridge and past the circular concert hall towards the exit for Ōsaka-jō-kōen Station (大阪城公園駅). On Sunday, between noon and 6pm, **amateur rock bands** crank out their music in front of the station to hordes of fans. It's a great place for people-watching.

To the southwest of the castle is the stunning **Ōsaka Museum of History** (大阪歴史博物館; Mon & Wed–Sun 9.30am–5pm, Fri until 8pm; ¥600; Ⓣ06/6946-5728), a twelve-storey concrete and glass structure in the shape of a giant ship's funnel – the "edge" pointing towards the castle is made of glass and offers excellent views. One of the city's premier attractions, the museum is built on the site of the Asuka-period Naniwa-no-Miya Palace, remains of which have been preserved in the museum's basement. Above that are four storeys of excellent displays featuring antique manuscripts and intricate scale models of street scenes and long-vanished buildings which once played important roles in the city's cultural and social life.

Umeda and Nakanoshima

Around 1km west of the castle, sandwiched between the Dojima and Tosabori rivers, is **Nakanoshima** – a thin island that is surrounded by Ōsaka's business district and home to many of the city's most impressive art museums. At the eastern end, you'll find the **Museum of Oriental Ceramics** (東洋陶磁美術館; Tues–Sun 9.30am–4.30pm; ¥500; ⓣ06/6223-0055), housing an exemplary collection of ancient Chinese and Korean pottery in a hushed, reverential atmosphere, a world away from the bustling city outside. At the western end of Nakanoshima is **The National Museum of Art Ōsaka** (国立国際美術館; Tues–Sun 10am–5pm; ¥420; ⓣ06/4860-8600), which holds engaging exhibitions of contemporary Japanese art in its subterranean galleries.

Heading northeast from here, and connecting with the broad Midōsuji-dōri, brings you to the heart of the **Umeda** area, the meeting point of the JR, Hankyū and Hanshin railway lines. Tucked into a side street just before the stations is the **Ohatsu-Tenjin** (お初天神), an atmospheric shrine where local shopkeepers pray for good business and which has a flea market on the first and third Friday of each month.

Even if you don't plan to take a train, the Baroque entrance hall of the **Hankyū Umeda Station** (阪急梅田駅) is worth a look, as is the nearby **HEP Five** eleven-storey shopping and dining extravaganza, complete with a Ferris wheel (daily 11am–11pm; ¥700) on its roof, which offers excellent vistas of the city. Immediately west of the station, a tunnel leads under the railway sidings to the twin towers of the **Umeda Sky Building** (梅田スカイビル), one of the city's more striking skyscrapers, where you can take a glass elevator up to the **Floating Garden Observatory** (daily 10am–10.30pm; ¥700; ⓣ06/6440-3855), 170m above the ground, and enjoy 360-degree views of north Ōsaka, including the castle.

Around Tennōji

Some 2km southeast of Namba lies **Shitennō-ji** (四天王寺), one of the first Buddhist temples in Japan. The temple has retained its classical layout but contains none of the buildings originally erected in 593 AD; the oldest feature of this windswept, concrete complex, with turtle ponds and a five-storey pagoda at its centre, is the late thirteenth-century *torii* at the main entrance gate. The **treasure house** (Tues–Sun 8.30am–4pm; ¥200; ⓣ06/6771-0066), in the modern white building behind the central courtyard, contains gorgeous orange costumes and enormous mandalas, carved with fantastic birds and dragons, which are used for the ceremonial *bugaku* dances held at the temple on April 22, August 8 and October 22. The main entrance to the temple is five minutes' walk south of Shitennō-ji-mae subway station and fifteen minutes north of the Tennōji overground station.

Festival days apart, spacious Shitennō-ji swallows up visitors with ease, but the more compact precincts of nearby **Isshin-ji** (一心寺), five minutes' walk west, are always bustling with crowds of petitioners. This atmospheric temple is adorned with striking modern sculptures of the gods of thunder and wind (Raijin and Fūjin) and bare-breasted dancing girls on the steel gate doors.

Leave the temple through its adjacent graveyard and walk south to reach the **Ōsaka Municipal Museum of Art** (大阪市立美術館; Tues–Sun 9.30am–4.30pm; ¥300; ⓣ06/6771-4874), which contains fine examples of ancient and modern Oriental art in its permanent collection and usually has special exhibitions. Behind the gallery is **Keitakuen**, a pretty traditional Japanese garden arranged around a central pond. The garden, donated to the city by Baron Sumitomo, whose family owned the trading company of the same name, is now part of **Tennōji-kōen** (天王寺公園; Tues–Sun 9.30am–5pm; ¥150; ⓣ06/6771-8401), which also includes the modern Great Conservatory, a giant glasshouse brimming with plants and flowers from around the world.

On the western side of Tennōji-koen, near the zoo, soak up the low-rent atmosphere of **Shin-Sekai** ("New World"; 新世界), a raffish district of narrow shopping arcades, cheap bars, restaurants and *pachinko* parlours. At its centre stands the retro **Tsūtenkaku Tower** (通天閣; daily 9am–8.30pm; ¥600; ⓣ06/6641-9555). This city landmark was rebuilt in the 1950s after it was destroyed in World War II, though at just 103m it's long been surpassed by Umeda's skyscrapers to the north and the 256m WTC Cosmotower by Ōsaka Bay. A few minutes' walk to the south of the tower is the intriguing **Spa World** (daily 10am–9am of the next day; ¥2400/3hr, ¥2700 all day; ⓣ06/6631-0001, ⓦwww.spaworld.co.jp), which offers a bizarre array of baths and saunas, from faux-Roman to mysterious Atlantis. Special offers are sometimes available, reducing tickets to ¥1000; check the website for details.

Sumiyoshi Taisha and Liberty Ōsaka

From Ebisuchō Station (恵美須町駅), immediately north of Shin-Sekai, it's a fifteen-minute subway or tram ride south to **Sumiyoshi Taisha** (住吉大社), Ōsaka's grandest shrine, home of the Shinto gods of the sea. Built in 211 AD, after the grateful Empress Jingō (so the legend goes) returned from a voyage to Korea, its buildings, with logs jutting out at angles from the thatched roofs, exemplify *sumiyoshi zukuri*, one of Japan's oldest styles of shrine architecture. Unlike similar complexes at Ise (see p.506) and Izumo Taisha (see p.585), Sumiyoshi Taisha is painted bright red, in sharp contrast with its wooded surrounding. The approach to the complex takes you over the elegant humpbacked Sori-hashi bridge, donated to the shrine by Yodogimi, the warlord Toyotomi Hideyoshi's lover.

Some 2km west of Tennōji is the city's most stimulating museum, **Liberty Ōsaka** (リバティ大阪; Tues–Sun 10am–4.30pm; ¥250; ⓣ06/6561-5891). Its longer name is the Ōsaka Human Rights Museum and it contains remarkable exhibits that tackle Japan's most taboo subjects. There's an excellent English-language leaflet and a portable audio guide that explains the displays, which include the untouchable caste (the Burakumin), Japan's ethnic minorities, the disabled, the sexist treatment of women, and the effects of pollution, most tragically seen in the exhibition about Minamata disease (see p.799). The museum is an eight-minute walk south of Ashiharabashi Station on the JR Loop line.

Ōsaka Bay

To reach the **Ōsaka Bay** area, take the JR Loop line to Bentenchō Station (弁天町); on the way you'll pass the UFO-like **Ōsaka Dome**, home of the Kintetsu Buffaloes baseball team. From Bentenchō Station, take the Chūō line subway to Ōsaka-kō Station (大阪港駅) – the subway will bring you all the way from other parts of the city – and walk north towards the huge Ferris wheel beside Tempozan Harbour Village (天保山ハーバービレッジ). Inside an exotic butterfly-shaped building, decorated with a giant fish-tank mosaic, is the fabulous **Ōsaka Aquarium** (大阪海遊館; daily 10am–7pm; ¥2000; ⓣ06/6576-5501). The aquarium is constructed so that you wind down between fourteen elongated tanks, each representing a different aquatic environment, from Antarctica to the Aleutian Islands. The beauty of the design means you can, for example, watch seals basking on the rocks at the top of the tank and see them swimming, torpedo-like, through the lower depths later. The huge central tank represents the Pacific Ocean and is home to a couple of whale sharks and several manta rays, among many other fish. The giant spider crabs, looking like alien invaders from *War of the Worlds*, provide a fitting climax to what is undoubtedly Japan's best aquarium.

While at Tempozan, check out what's showing at the **Suntory Museum** (サントリーミュージアム; Tues–Sun 10.30am–7pm; ¥1000; ⓣ06/6577-000), housed in a striking inverted glass-and-concrete cone, designed by star local architect Andō Tadao. The museum specializes in twentieth-century graphic art and has a collection

Technology, ecology and art

A more unusual sightseeing destination in the bay area is the **Maishima Incineration Plant** (舞洲工場), which was commissioned after Ōsaka's bid for the 2008 Olympics failed. With bulbous ceramic columns, gold-plated turret roofs and tiered gardens, this extraordinary building was designed by the Austrian conservation architect and artist Friedensreich Hundertwasser, and completed in 2001. It looks more like a storybook castle than a hi-tech garbage combustor, and is often mistaken for an extension of the nearby Universal Studios Japan. Inside, 450 tonnes of waste are processed daily. Free tours of the plant are given on weekdays at 10am, 1pm or 3pm, and while there are some interesting displays detailing Hundertwasser's "technology, ecology and art" concept, the tour mainly focuses on the incineration process. However, it is worth gaining access to the building for a closer inspection of the architectural detail of the upper levels. The tour is in Japanese but there are plenty of English explanations on the displays, as well as an informative pamphlet. Bookings must be made at least a week in advance with the Ōsaka Environmental Management Bureau (90min; free; ⓣ06/6630-3353, ⓔja0003@city.osaka.lg.jp). To get there, take a train to JR Sakurajima Station (桜島駅), one stop after Universal City, and catch the #56 bus to Konohana-Ohashi Nishizume (此花大橋西詰), or the Hokko Bus to Kankyo-kyoku Mae (環境局前); both stop in front of the incinerator.

of over ten thousand posters. There's also an IMAX movie theatre (Tues–Sun 11am–7pm; ¥1000) showing films on a 20m-high screen.

Covering some 140 acres on Ōsaka's western waterfront, **Universal Studios Japan** (ユニバーサル・スタジオ・ジャパン; daily 10am–7pm; ¥6100; ⓣ06/6465-3000) is one of the nation's leading theme parks. It is served by the Universal City Station on the JR Yumesaki line, which connects to the JR Loop line at Nishikujō Station. Direct express trains run to Universal City Station from JR Ōsaka Station (every 10min; 14min).

Eating

Ōsaka has a reputation as a foodies' paradise, but it can be a daunting task finding the best places to eat in a city crammed with so many restaurants. The trick is to stick to particular areas and to hunt around until something takes your fancy. Both **Umeda** and **Dōtombori** offer rich pickings, while **Tsuruhashi**, on the JR Loop line to the east, is the main place to head for Korean food.

There are many excellent local specialities. You shouldn't leave town without going to an **okonomiyaki** restaurant, preferably one where you can fry the thick pancakes yourself, or grabbing some piping hot **takoyaki** (octopus dumplings) from a street stall. Ōsaka's own style of **sushi** is *oshizushi*, layers of vinegared rice, seaweed and fish cut into bite-size chunks, and the city also has a favourite way of cooking chunky udon noodles, simmering them in a veggie, seafood or meat broth.

Restaurants and cafés

The best choice of **restaurants and cafés** is around the Kita areas of Umeda and Chayama, and the Minami areas of Shinsaibashi, Dōtombori and Namba. Strolling around the narrow streets dotted with stand-up noodle and *takoyaki* bars, and restaurants with flickering neon signs and crazy displays – especially along Dōtombori-dōri (道頓堀), with its redeveloped promenade – is an appetizing experience in itself. The major **hotels** and **department stores** are also worth checking out, especially at lunchtime, when many restaurants offer special deals.

Kita

The following are marked on the map on p.486.

Asuka 4-3 Sugahara-chō ⓣ06/6361-6150. Simple and cosy Japanese vegetarian home-style cooking. Only one daily lunch (¥950) and dinner (¥3500) set on the menu – the chef's selection. Tues–Sat 11.45am–2pm & 6–9pm.

Dynamic Kitchen & Bar Sun 27F 4-5-10 Nishi-Tenma-3 ⓣ06/6367-5512. With stunning night views over the Kita area, this is a great place to enjoy modern Japanese cuisine. You can choose to sit at either *ozashiki* floor tables, or at the counter. Excellent-value dinner courses of fresh seafood and Kyoto vegetables from ¥3500 and Ōsaka beef from ¥6500. Mon–Fri 11.30am–2pm & 5–11pm, Sat & Sun 11.30am–2pm & 5–10.30pm.

Elephant Café エレファントカフェ 2-28 Chayamachi ⓣ06/6359-0136. Asian-fusion restaurant in the Chayama area with an exotically decorated interior of hanging lamps and fabrics, serving curries, noodles, dumplings and salads. The delicious set lunch (¥1080) is good value. Daily 11.30am–11.30pm.

Nawasushi 縄寿司 2-14-1 Sonezaki ⓣ06/6312-9891. Generous servings of super-fresh sushi (around ¥400/plate) in a traditional atmosphere. Don't be shy to yell out your order. Mon–Sat 5–10pm.

Plum Cool Dining 3F 4-6 Chayamachi ⓣ06/6377-0701, ⓦwww.plum.co.jp. Everything on the menu here includes one of the staples of Japanese cuisine – *umeboshi* (pickled plums) – and the dishes are cooked in a variety of ways. Try the delicious shrimp dumplings with spicy plum sauce (¥450) or the sour plum fried rice (¥850); there's also an extensive *umeshu* (sweet plum wine) menu, from ¥280 a glass. Daily 5.30–11.30pm.

Portugalia 14-12-11 Nishi-tenma ⓣ06/6362-6668, ⓦwww.portugalia.jp. Authentic Portuguese cuisine near the American Consulate. Their ¥1250 lunch sets (fish, chicken or pork) are excellent value, but the evening menu can be a little pricey. Good selection of wine and sherry. Mon–Sat 11.30am–10.30pm.

Minami

The following are marked on the map on p.487.

Absinthe Solaar Namba Dining Maison 8F, 5-1-18 Namba ⓣ06/6633-1445. Newly opened rooftop restaurant with outdoor lounge area, great for enjoying the evening breeze during the hot summer months. The Mediterranean menu includes Greek salads (¥1100), moussaka (¥1250) and Moroccan-style lamb chops (¥2300). Daily 11am–11.30pm.

Doppa 2F 1-6-9 Dōtombori ⓣ06/6212-0530. A fun restaurant that is a good mix of Italian and Ōsakan sensibilities – hearty portions served without fuss. There are thirty kinds of pasta dishes (from ¥800), as well as pizza (¥600) and risotto (¥980). Daily 11.30am–10.30pm.

Green Earth 4-2-2 Kitakyuhoji-machi ⓣ06/6251-1245. This narrow café is one of the city's most popular vegetarian establishments. The jumbo sandwiches (¥500) either come on their own or as part of a set meal (¥700), which also includes soup, salad and a drink. Good pasta and pizza dishes too. Mon–Sat 11.30am–5pm.

Maman Terrace 1-5-4 Shinsaibashi-suji ⓣ06/6282-2774. Stylish macrobiotic restaurant serving fish and vegetable dishes. The plate lunch (¥1100) uses local seasonal ingredients such as *nanohana* (mustard flowers) in spring, and *yamaimo* (mountain yams) in autumn. Excellent cakes, tarts and tofu ice cream (¥500). Tues–Sun 11am–9pm.

Nanbantei 南蛮亭 4-5-7 Nanba ⓣ06/6631-6178. In the alleyway behind the Shin Kabukiza Theatre, this popular *yakitori-ya* has a huge range of skewer food (from ¥250), an English menu and a friendly atmosphere. Because of its popularity, dining time is limited to two hours. Daily 5pm–midnight.

Rose Dining Namba Dining Maison 9F, 5-1-18 Namba ⓣ06/6633-1034. Elegant restaurant in the dining complex on top of the Takashimaya department store, serving an eclectic range of Japanese, Chinese and Western dishes, including dim sum, sushi and pasta. The lunch menu starts at ¥1680 and there are good-value set dinner courses from ¥2500. Daily 11am–10pm.

Tsurutontan つるとんたん 3-17 Soemon-chō ⓣ06/6211-0021, ⓦwww.tsurutontan.co.jp. Fabulous udon restaurant that serves an amazing range of traditional and modern fusion dishes in extremely large bowls. The *umeboshi* (pickled plum) udon is unbeatable for its classic home-style cooking taste (¥850), whilst the carbonara udon (¥1300) really pushes the fusion boundaries by serving the thick white noodles with creamy seafood. Daily 11am–7.30pm.

Nightlife and entertainment

The epicentre of Ōsaka's frenetic nightlife is **Ebisu-bashi**, a dazzling area to wander around, if only to check out the wild youth fashions on view, and pose for a photo with locals in front of the landmark Glico Man sign (see box, p.494).

The Glico Man sign

At night, Dōtombori–dori is ablaze with the neon lights of large billboards and TV screens, all flashing modern commercial messages. However, the one sign that has lasted the longest, for over 70 years, is the 33m Glico Man sign at the Ebusubashi bridge. It's a simple graphic showing an athlete in a victory pose, but it looks somewhat out of place amongst the slick contemporary advertising that surrounds it. Glico Man still has enduring popularity amongst the locals, who congregate here to celebrate sporting victories. The company behind the ad, Ezaki Glico, are a confectionery manufacturer based in the city, best known for their caramel candy and Pocky pretzel snacks. Coincidentally, they were the original sponsor of the anime series Tetsujin 28, a giant robot which is a new landmark in Kōbe (see box, p.517).

Don't miss out on strolling through **Amerika-mura**, immediately west of Shinsaibashi, a street crowded with extremely cool shops and bars. In contrast, the **Hozen-ji Yokochō** area, around the paper-lantern-festooned temple Hozen-ji, is old-time Ōsaka, a narrow alley of tiny watering holes.

The city's **gay scene** is much smaller than that in Tokyo, and historically it's tended to be in the Doyama-cho area of Kita rather than Minami. Check the free magazine *Kansai Scene* for the latest info on clubs, bars and one-off dance events.

Bars and clubs

Bears B1 Shin-Nihon Namba Building, 3-14-5 Namba-naka ⓣ06/6649-5564. The heart of the city's underground music scene, with a diverse range of experimental and avant-garde acts playing every night. Gigs start and end early (6.30–10pm) so as not to irritate the *yakuza* upstairs. Entrance from ¥1500.

Billboard Live Ōsaka B2 Herbis Plaza Ent Building, 2-2-2 Umeda ⓣ06/6342-7722, ⓦwww.billboard-live.com/club/o_index.html. Top-flight jazz, soul, R&B and folk performers regularly play at this small-scale supper club. It's pricey though, with tickets often in excess of ¥7000. Still, the sound system is excellent and the food's reasonable. Daily 6.30–9.30pm.

Café Absinthe 1-2-27 Kita-Horie ⓣ06/6534-6635. Mediterranean-style bar with live music, DJs and photography exhibitions. Tabbouleh and hummus (¥900) are on the menu, and they serve absinthe cocktails (¥1400). Daily 1pm–1am.

The Cellar B1 Dai-3 Hirata Building, 2-17-13 Nishi-Shinsaibashi ⓣ06/6212-6437. Comfortable neighbourhood bar with reasonably priced drinks and a daily happy hour (6–8pm), plus live music on Wednesday, Friday and Saturday, and a popular jam session on Sunday afternoons. Mon–Thurs 6pm–2am, Fri & Sat 6pm–4am, Sun 6pm–midnight.

Club Karma Kasai Building, 1-5-18 Sonezaki-Shinchi ⓣ06/6344-6181. Stark yet roomy bar and club that hosts a range of up-to-the-minute music and dance nights, with the added bonus of a good menu and a happy hour until 9pm. The all-night techno and house events are usually held on Friday and Saturday, when there's a cover charge of ¥2500 (more if big-name foreign DJs are in town). *Karma* is the most gay-friendly of the mainstream clubs and stages occasional gay or lesbian events. Daily 6pm–late.

Don Shop B1 Shimazu Building, 2-4-11 Umeda ⓣ06/6341-2605. If *Billboard Live Ōsaka* over the road is too expensive, catch live jazz (nearly always free; very occasionally a ¥1500 cover charge) any night of the week at this legendary all-night jazz club with its bohemian, 1960s atmosphere. Big-name performers from *Billboard Live* sometimes hop over the road for impromptu late-night jam sessions. Good food and reasonable drinks.

Drunk Bears BF 10-12 Chayamachi ⓣ06/6372-7275. Friendly tapas bar in the NU Chayamachi shopping centre. Three times a month (usually the 8th, 16th & 24th) it's "*megane* day" – customers wearing glasses get a ¥200 discount. Belgian beers on tap. Daily 11am–late.

Explosion Sanyo Kaikan B1F 8-23 Doyama-cho ⓦwww.ex-osaka.com. In the same building as *Physique Pride Ōsaka* (see opposite), this club hosts men only, women only and mixed nights, with drag shows and film showings. ¥2000 cover charge, with two drinks for Japanese and three drinks for non-Japanese customers. Daily 8pm–4am.

Flanders Tale 2-5-25 Umeda ⓣ06/6344-5258. Spacious Belgian beer house with a good selection of premium draught and bottled beers. Excellent food selection too, including steamed mussels (¥1350) and "blooms" – onions fried in flower shapes (¥750). Unusually for this area, last order is at 10.30pm.

Frenz 2F 8-14 Kamiyacho. This is the first gay bar in Japan to be run by a non-Japanese, and *Frenz* has firmly established itself at the centre of the Kansai gay community. It's a relaxed and friendly place to drop by on your own or with friends, especially if you enjoy retro disco music. Sister bar *Frenzy* is in the same building but only open at weekends. Daily 8pm–2am.

Joule 2,3,4F Minami-sumiymachi Building, Nishi-Shinsaibashi. This very popular Shinsaibashi club has a fairly mainstream music policy but a more laidback atmosphere. There's a third-floor lounge for relaxing in when the dancefloor gets too full. Entrance ¥2500–3000. Daily 8pm–late.

Physique Pride Ōsaka Sanyo Kaikan, 8-23 Doyama-chō ⓣ06/6361-2430. Well-established Ōsaka gay bar that's foreigner-friendly and has English-speaking staff. No cover charge. Daily 9pm–late.

Rockets 2-8-13 Nambanaka ⓣ06/6649-3919. Alternative club nestling under the railway tracks running south from Namba Station. DJs spin everything from drum 'n' bass to reggae and punk, depending on the night of the week. It's best to phone in advance as it's not open every night. Entrance ¥2500 including one drink. Daily 7pm–late.

Zerro 2-3-2 Shinsaibashi ⓣ06/6211-0439. Popular bar with foreign and Japanese staff, and hosting DJ events on Saturday nights. Drinks are rather pricey but there's no extra charge for enjoying Zerro's music and dance on weekends. Daily 8pm–late.

Traditional performing arts

Ōsaka is where **bunraku** puppetry flourished during the seventeenth century and performances are still held in Namba at the **National Bunraku Theatre** (国立文楽劇場; ⓣ06/6212-2531, ⓦwww.ntj.jac.go.jp/english/index.html; performances in Jan, April, June–Aug and Nov at 11am and 4pm). Tickets (price depends on performance) sell out quickly, but you can try at the theatre box office, a three-minute walk from exit seven of Nipponbashi Station.

The place to catch **kabuki** plays is the handsomely restored **Ōsaka Shōchiku-za Theatre** (大阪松竹座; ⓣ06/6214-2211; tickets from ¥400), five minutes' walk north of Namba Station, beside the Dōtombori canal. If you're interested in sampling the more difficult **nō** plays, the **Ōsaka Nō Hall** (大阪能楽会館; ⓣ06/6373-1726), near Nakazakichō Station on the Tanimachi line, or a short walk east of Hankyū Umeda Station, often shows free performances on weekends and national holidays, usually beginning around 9.30am. Full details of all traditional arts performances appear in the free quarterly booklet *Meet Ōsaka*, available at all the tourist offices, and also in *Kansai Scene*, which you can pick up from pubs and large bookstores.

Shopping

While Umeda, Shinsaibashi and Nanba attract hordes of shoppers to their covered malls, there are other places in Ōsaka where window-shopping is just as interesting as picking up a bargain. Yodobashi Camera (ヨドバシカメラ; daily 9.30am–9pm) is directly across the street from the north exit of Ōsaka Station. It has five floors of the latest camera and other electronic equipment – there's an overwhelming range of choice and you can bargain here for a good deal. In the Minami area, Den Den Town (でんでんタウン), south of Nipponbashi Station, has long been the focus for electronic gear enthusiasts. Increasingly, this is a handy place to pick up "character goods" for all your favourite manga and anime heroes. If you are keen on Japanese cuisine, Dōguyasuji (道具屋筋), just west of Nankai Namba Station, is the place to pick up an interesting souvenir – it's an entire street of kitchen and tableware shops, all stocked full with every kind of pot, pan, dish and chopstick required for Japanese cooking.

Listings

Airport information Kansai International ⓣ072/455-2500, ⓦwww.kansai-airport.or.jp; Itami (Ōsaka) Airport ⓣ06/6856-6781.

Banks and exchange There are plenty of banks around Umeda, Shinsaibashi and Namba. Major department stores also have foreign exchange desks, as does the Central Post Office, beside JR Ōsaka Station.

Bookshops Kinokuniya, behind the main entrance to Hankyu Umeda Station, is open daily 10am–9pm, except the third Wed of the month. Athens, in the Shinsaibashi shopping arcade, has a particularly good selection of art books.

Car rental Several major car rental firms can be found at both Shin-Ōsaka and Ōsaka stations (both daily 8am–8pm) including Eki Rent-a-Car (Shin-Ōsaka ⓣ06/6303-0181, Ōsaka ⓣ06/6341-3388). Alternatively, try Nippon Rent-a-Car (Ōsaka Reservation Center ⓣ06/6344-0919) and PanaLife (ⓣ06/6949-1822).

Consulates Australia, 29F, Twin 21 MID Tower, 2-1-61 Shiromi, Chuō-ku (ⓣ06/6941-9271); Canada, 12F Daisan Shoho Building, 2-2-3 Nishi-Shinsaibashi, Chuō-ku (ⓣ06/6212-4910); China, 3-9-2 Utsubohommachi, Nishi-ku (ⓣ06/6445-9481); Russia, 1-2-2 Nishimidorigaoka, Toyonaka-shi (ⓣ06/6848-3451); South Korea, 2-3-4 Nishi-Shinsaibashi, Chuō-ku (ⓣ06/6213-1401); UK, 19F Epson Ōsaka Building, 3-5-1 Bakuromachi, Chuō-ku (ⓣ06/6120-5600); USA, 2-11-5 Nishitemma, Kita-ku (ⓣ06/6315-5900).

Emergencies The main police station is at 3-1-16 Otemae, Chuō-ku (Mon–Fri 9.15am–5.30pm; ⓣ06/6943-1234). In an absolute emergency, contact the Foreign Advisory Service on ⓣ06/773-6533. For other emergency numbers, see p.71.

Home visits Ōsaka runs a programme which allows you to meet local people in their homes for a few hours so you can learn a bit more about Japanese life. If you want to participate you need to take your passport to either of the tourist information desks at Ōsaka or Shin-Ōsaka stations (see p.485) and allow a couple of days for visiting arrangements to be made.

Hospitals and medical advice Yodogawa Christian Hospital, 2-9-26 Awaji, Higashi-Yodogawa-ku (ⓣ06/6322-2250), or the more central Sumitomo Hospital, 5-2-2 Nakanoshima, Kita-ku (ⓣ06/6443-1261). Otherwise contact one of the tourist information counters (see p.485).

Immigration Ōsaka's immigration bureau is a 3min walk from exit 3 of Tenmabashi Station on the Keihan line at 2-1-17 Tanimachi, Chuō-ku (ⓣ06/6941-0771).

Internet There are four branches of Kinko's around the city offering internet access (¥200/10min). The Umeda branch is 5min from the Sakurabashi exit of JR Ōsaka, opposite the Herbis Plaza. Other branches can be found in Minami-Morimachi, Shinsaibashi, Shin-Ōsaka and on Sakaisuji-Honmachi. Also try *Bean's B:t Café*, 6-2-29 Uehonmachi, Tennōji-ku (daily 8.30am–9pm), which offers special rates for foreigners. The closest subway station is Tanimachi 9-chōme, and it's also close to Uehonmachi on the Kintetsu line.

Lost property The lost and found department for Ōsaka's buses and subways is at 1-17 Motomachi (ⓣ06/6633-9151).

Post office The Central Post Office is immediately west of JR Ōsaka Station and open 24 hours.

Sports Ōsaka's fifteen-day sumo tournament is held mid-March at Ōsaka Furitsu Taiikukan, a ten-minute walk from exit 5 of Namba Station. Seats for the bouts, which begin at 10am and run through to 6pm, sell out quickly, and you'll need to arrive early to snag one of the standing-room tickets (¥1500), which go on sale each day at 9am. The Kintetsu Buffaloes play at the huge Ōsaka Dome during the professional baseball season, but the highlight of the city's sporting summer is the All-Japan High School Baseball Championship, held at Kōshien Stadium, a 5min walk from Kōshien Station on the Hanshin line. For ticket availability, check first with tourist information (ⓣ06/6345-2189).

Takarazuka

When the Hankyū railway tycoon Kobayashi Ichizū laid a line out to the tiny spa town of **TAKARAZUKA** (宝塚), 20km northwest of Ōsaka, in 1911, he had an entertainment vision that extended way beyond soothing onsen dips. By 1924 he'd built the **Takurazuka Grand Theatre** (宝塚大劇場), which has been home ever since to the all-female musical drama troupe the **Takarazuka Revue** (see box opposite). Some 2.5 million people – mainly women – flock to the town each year to see the revues and musicals at the theatre, ten minutes' walk southeast of the train stations, through the Hana-no-michi, or Flower Road, an elevated platform

The wonderful world of Takarazuka

There's a long tradition of men performing female roles in Japanese theatre, acting out a male fantasy of how women are supposed to behave. It's not so strange, then, that actresses playing idealized men have struck such a chord with contemporary female audiences. This has been the successful formula of the seven-hundred-strong, all-female **Takarazuka Revue Company** (宝塚歌劇団), who have been thrilling audiences with their Broadway-style shows since 1914.

The company's founder, Kobayashi Ichizō, was mightily impressed by performances of Western operas he'd seen in Tokyo. He sensed that Japanese audiences were ripe for lively Western musical dramas, but he also wanted to preserve something of Japan's traditional theatre. So, as well as performing dance reviews and musicals, Takarazuka also act out classical Japanese plays and have developed shows from Western novels, including *Gone with the Wind* and *War and Peace*. Even manga have been adapted, with *The Rose of Versailles* still one of Takarazuka's most successful and enduring productions.

Thousands of young girls apply annually to join the troupe at the age of 16, and devote themselves to a punishing routine of classes that will enable them to embody the "modesty, fairness and grace" (the company's motto) expected of a Takarasienne, as Takarazuka members are called. They must also forsake boyfriends, but in return are guaranteed the slavish adoration of an almost exclusively female audience. The male impersonators or *otoko-yaku* attract the most attention from the fans, who buy so many cut flowers for their idols that the town's shops and restaurants receive free daily deliveries of unwanted bouquets.

along an avenue of cherry trees, which is supposed to be like a passage leading onto the stage. Depending on the day, shows start at 11am and 3pm, or 1pm only, with no performances on Wednesday. Tickets cost ¥3500–10,000; reservations should be made via the ticket office up to a month before performances (daily 10am–5pm except for four-day closures between performances; ⓣ0570/00-5100; no English spoken, but tourist offices can often check availability on your behalf). Alternatively, tickets can be purchased from Ticket Pia outlets (ⓦkageki.hankyu.co.jp/english/index.html). Shows are also staged regularly in Tokyo (see p.159), but most fans prefer to see the troupe on their home ground, and perhaps glimpse one of the stars on her way to and from the theatre.

As the Takarazuka Revue has both inspired and been inspired by manga, a visit to the **Tezuka Osamu Manga Museum** (手塚治虫記念館; daily except Wed 9.30am–5pm; ¥500; ⓦtezukaosamu.net), just beyond the Grand Theatre, is worthwhile. The museum celebrates the comic-book genius **Tezuka Osamu** (1928–89), creator of *Astro Boy* and *Kimba the White Lion* among many other famous manga and anime series. Tezuka was raised in Takarazuka, and this colourful museum charts his career, displays art from his books, comics and animated films, screens cartoons and gives you the chance to become an animator in the basement workshop (40min session; 10am–4pm). If you want to see more of Tezuka's animated works, check out Kyoto's Tezuka Osamu World (see p.419).

Practicalities

The fastest **train** on the Hankyū Takarazuka line from Ōsaka's Umeda Station takes less than thirty minutes to reach Takarazuka Station (¥270). There are also direct trains on the JR Fukuchiyama line, taking a few minutes more from JR Ōsaka Station to JR Takarazuka Station, next to the Hankyū terminus and department store. The town's **tourist information office** (daily 9am–5pm; ⓣ0797/81-5344) is in front of the second-floor Hankyū Station entrance; you can pick up a map of development and there are no convenience or fast-food stores. By early evening, the shops are shuttered and the streets almost deserted. Be aware that while the mountain can be pleasantly cool in summer, winter temperatures often fall below freezing.

The biggest **festival** in Kōya-san takes place on the 21st day of the third lunar month (usually mid-April), when all the monks gather for a service at the Mie-dō, which is fully opened to the public, and worshippers make flower and candle offerings. Everyone's out in force again for the street parade on Kōbō Daishi's birthday (June 15), while during Obon several thousand lanterns light the route through Okunoin cemetery as part of Japan's festival for the dead (Aug 13). During these festivals it is extremely difficult to find accommodation. If you plan to visit Kōya-san at any of these times it would be wise to book well in advance.

Some history

The first monastery on Kōya-san was founded in the early ninth century AD by the monk Kūkai (774–835), known after his death as **Kōbō Daishi**. As a young monk, Kūkai travelled to China to study esoteric Buddhism for two years. On his return in 806 he established a temple in Hakata (now Fukuoka) before moving to Takao-san near Kyoto, where his ardent prayers for the peace and prosperity of the nation won him powerful supporters. Kūkai was soon granted permission to found the **Shingon** school which, in a break from contemporary belief, held that enlightenment could be achieved in one lifetime (see below for more on Shingon Buddhism). But city life was too disruptive for serious meditation, so Kūkai set off round Japan to find a suitable mountain retreat.

According to legend, when Kūkai left China he prayed for guidance on where to establish his monastery. At the same time he flung his three-pronged *vajra* (the ritual implement of Shingon monks) clear across the ocean. Later, as he drew near **Kōya-san**, he met a giant, red-faced hunter, who gave him a two-headed dog. The dog led Kūkai to the top of the mountain where, of course, he found his *vajra* hanging in a pine tree. In any event, the historical records show that Kūkai first came to Kōya-san in 816 and returned in 819 to consecrate the first temple. For a while after 823 he presided over Kyoto's Tō-ji temple (see p.421), but eventually

Kōbō Daishi

Kōbō Daishi (known during his lifetime as Kūkai) was born in 774 AD in the town of Zentsūji, 30km from Takamatsu on the island of Shikoku. This pious man walked all over Shikoku as an itinerant priest and spent two years in Tang dynasty China studying esoteric Buddhism, before apparently gaining enlightenment at Muroto Misaki in Kōchi-ken and founding the **Shingon** ("True Word") school of Buddhism. Shingon was influenced by the Tibetan and Central Asian tantric Buddhist traditions and this is reflected in the Shikoku temples, with their exotic decor and atmosphere.

In addition to his significant efforts in the development of Japanese Buddhism, Kōbō Daishi is often referred to as the father of Japanese culture; in many ways, he was the Japanese Leonardo da Vinci. He is credited with a phenomenal number of cultural and technological achievements: devising the kana syllabary, opening the first public school, inventing pond irrigation, discovering mercury, and compiling the first dictionary. In addition, he was also renowned as a master calligrapher, poet, sculptor and healer.

Kōbō Daishi died on April 22, 835, the exact day he predicted he would. For his achievements, he was posthumously awarded the title Daishi ("Great Saint") by the imperial court. Soon after his death, his disciples began a tour around the temples of Shikoku associated with the Daishi, thus establishing the pilgrimage as it is known today (see p.593).

returned to Kōya-san, where he died in 835. Even without his religious work it seems that Kūkai was a remarkable man (see box, p.499). After his death, Kūkai's disciple **Shinzen** continued developing the monasteries, then collectively known as **Kongōbu-ji**, until there were more than 1500 monasteries and several thousand monks on the mountain-top. The sect then had its ups and downs, of which the most serious was during the anti-Buddhist movement following the 1868 Meiji Restoration. Today there are 117 temples atop Kōya-san and it is once again a major centre of pilgrimage.

Arrival and information

Access to Kōya-san's mountain-top hideaway is via a cable car which departs every thirty minutes from **Gokurakubashi Station** (極楽橋駅), arriving at Kōya-san Station five minutes later. Direct express and super-express trains on the private Nankai line run from Ōsaka's **Namba Station** (every 20–30min; 1hr 15min–1hr 40min; ¥1230–1990), connecting with the cable car (price included in the ticket); note that reservations are required on the limited express. From Nara and Kyoto you can either travel via Ōsaka or use the JR network as far as Hashimoto (橋本) and then change onto the Nankai line.

At the top cable-car station you'll find **buses** waiting for the ten-minute ride into town (every 20–30min; ¥280). All buses stop at the central Senjuin-bashi crossroads (千手院橋), where the routes then divide, with the majority of services running east to Okunoin and fewer heading past Kongōbu-ji to the western, Dai-mon, gate. **Taxis** also wait outside the station, or call Kōya-san Taxi on ⓣ0736/56-2628. Once you're in the centre it's more pleasant to explore on foot, but if you plan on doing a lot of bus journeys, you can buy a one-day pass, or *ichi-nichi furii kippu* (¥800), at the station terminus.

The **Kōya-san Tourist Association** office (daily 8.30am–5pm; ⓣ0736/56-2616, ⓦwww.shukubo.jp) is beside the Senjuin-bashi junction. You can book accommodation here, or in advance through their English website. They also offer **bikes** for rent (¥1200 per day) and the Kōya-san Audio Guide (8.30am–4.30pm; ¥500), which has a commentary in English of Kōya-san's places of interest, corresponding to a numbered guide post system throughout the town. A better way to learn the stories and the secrets of this sacred site is with the **Kōya-san Interpreter Guide Club** (ⓣ0736/56-2270, ⓔmail@koyasan-ccn.com). Their walking tours encompass Okunoin, as well as Kongōbuji and the Garan. Reservations must be made at least a day in advance (¥1000 plus transportation). The recently opened **Kōya-san Visitor Information Center** (April–Oct Mon, Tues & Fri 10am–4pm; ⓣ0736/56-2270, ⓦkoyasan-ccn.com) near Kongōbu-ji also has helpful staff and free internet access.

Accommodation and eating

More than fifty monasteries on Kōya-san offer **accommodation** in *shukubō* – temple lodgings run by the monks, and occasionally also by the nuns. The rooms are all Japanese-style and usually look out over beautiful gardens or are decorated with painted screens or antique hanging scrolls; most have communal washing facilities. In recent years, some of the temples have upgraded rooms to include private bathing facilities, Western-style toilets, mini-refrigerators, TVs and internet connections. These are primarily places of worship, so don't expect hotel-style service, and you'll be asked to keep to fairly strict meal and bath times. Guests are usually welcome to attend the early-morning prayers (around 6am). At some temples this also includes a fire ceremony – the burning of 108 pieces of wood which are said to represent the number of "defilements" that need to be overcome in order to gain enlightenment. All the *shukubō* offer excellent **vegetarian meals** (*shōjin-ryōri*), which consist of seasonal vegetable and tofu-based dishes cooked without meat, fish, onion or garlic seasoning. Due to the number of foreign tourists making the journey to Kōya-san, there is usually someone at the temples who can speak English.

It's a good idea to make accommodation reservations in advance, either through the Kōya-san Tourist Association (see opposite) or by approaching the temples recommended below directly. Prices generally start at around ¥9500 per person per night, including two meals.

For lunch try *Bon On Sha* (梵恩舎; ⓣ0736/56-5535), a welcoming café and art gallery run by a young Japanese and French couple, serving organic vegetarian lunch sets (¥1200). It's east of the Senjuin-bashi intersection. In the evening, *Miyasan* (みやさん; ⓣ0735/56-2827), south of Senjuin-bashi, is a cheap and friendly *izakaya* serving fried chicken, omelettes, salads and locally distilled plum wine.

Accommodation

Ekō-in 恵光院 ⓣ0736/56-2514, ⓔekoin@mbox.co.jp. Simple but comfortable rooms overlooking a garden. Has a meditation hall for after-dinner sessions, which anyone can attend. Internet available. ⑥

Fukuchi-in 福智院 ⓣ0736/56-2021, ⓦwww.fukuchiin.com. This temple is famous for its modern dry landscape garden by Mirei Shigemori, who controversially used concrete and avant-garde shapes in the design. Even if you're not staying here, it's worth a visit to see the garden. ⑦

Ichijō-in 一乗院 ⓣ0736/56-2214. Elegant and recently refurbished lodgings; all rooms have internet connection and some have en-suite facilities. The meals are especially good. ⑦

Kōya-san Youth Hostel 高野山ユースホステル ⓣ0736/56-3889, ⓦwww2.ocn.ne.jp/~koyasan. The best budget accommodation in Kōya-san. Comfortable dorm rooms in a former temple. Meals are extra. ②

Muryōkō-in 無量光院 ⓣ0736/56-2104, ⓦmuryokoin.org. Highly recommended for its spacious rooms and international atmosphere. The morning service here, including a fire ceremony (see opposite), is well worth rising at dawn for. ⑥

Sekishō-in 赤松院 ⓣ0736/56-2734. One of the larger temples, with rambling corridors, an elevator and some unusual historical and modern artwork. ⑥

The Town

The road into Kōya-san from the cable-car station winds through cool, dark cryptomeria forests for about 2km before passing a small temple called **Nyonin-dō** (女人堂). This "Women's Hall" marks one of the original seven entrances to the sacred precincts, beyond which women weren't allowed to proceed; the practice continued until 1906 despite an imperial edict against it issued in 1872. In the meantime, female pilgrims worshipped in special temples built beside each gate, of which Nyonin-dō is the last remaining. Beyond the hall, you begin to see the first monasteries and, 1km further on, you reach the main **Senjuin-bashi crossroads**. This junction lies at the secular centre of Kōya-san. Nearby you'll find the information office, post office, police station and restaurants, alongside shops peddling souvenirs and pilgrims' accessories. By early evening, most businesses are shuttered and the streets almost deserted. The main sights are located either side of this crossroads: head west for Kōya-san's principal temple, **Kongōbu-ji**, and its religious centre, the **Garan**, or east for the mossy graves of **Okunoin cemetery**. Be aware that while the mountain can be pleasantly cool in summer, winter temperatures often fall below freezing.

Kongōbu-ji and the Garan

Though it originally applied to the whole mountain community, the name **Kongōbu-ji** (金剛峯寺), meaning "Temple of the Diamond Mountain" (daily:

May–Oct 8.30am–5pm; Nov–April 8.30am–4.30pm; ¥500, or combination ticket for all six major sites, valid for two days ¥1500; ⓣ0736/56-2011), now refers specifically to the Shingon school's chief monastic and administrative offices, located three minutes' walk west of the central crossroads. In fact, this temple was a late addition to the complex, founded in 1592 by the ruler Toyotomi Hideyoshi in honour of his mother. It only later became Shingon's headquarters.

Rebuilt in 1861 in the original style, the graceful building is famous largely for its late sixteenth-century **screen paintings** by Kyoto's Kanō school of artists. The best of these are the cranes and pine trees by Kanō Tanyū decorating the Great Hall, and Kanō Tansai's *Willows in Four Seasons* two rooms further along. Beside the temple's front entrance, the **Rokuji-no-kane** (六時の鐘) or "Six O'Clock Bell", cast in 1535, sits on a castle-like foundation; a monk comes out to ring it every even hour (6am–10pm). Opposite the bell a gravelled path leads into the **Garan** (伽藍), Kōya-san's sacred precinct. This large sandy compound, filled with cryptomeria trees, lanterns and wooden halls wreathed in incense, is where Kōbō Daishi founded his original monastery.

The Garan's most important building is the monumental **Konpon Daitō** (根本大塔; ¥200), the Fundamental Great Stupa, covered in strident, orange lacquer; it was last rebuilt in the 1930s. South of the stupa, the more restrained **Kon-dō** (金堂; ¥200), also rebuilt in the 1930s, marks the spot where Kūkai gave his first lectures. He reputedly lived where the **Miei-dō** (御影堂) now stands, just to the west, which is regarded as one of the mountain's most holy places. Note the two sacred pines in front which are said to be offspring of the tree in which Kūkai's *vajra* (ritual implements) landed.

The main road in front of the Garan eventually leads to the **Dai-mon** (大門), or Great Gate, which was Kōya-san's main entrance until the cable car was built in the 1930s. The huge, rust-red gate sits on the mountain's western edge, where on a clear day you can see right out to sea. Follow the main road back towards town to see the temple's greatest treasures in the **Reihōkan** (霊宝館; daily 8.30am–4.30pm; ¥600). Though the old buildings don't really do the exhibits justice, this collection includes a number of priceless works of esoteric Buddhist art. The displays are changed five times a year, but look out for a triptych of Amida welcoming souls to the Western Paradise, painted in 965, and a Heian-era silk painting of Buddha entering nirvana.

Okunoin

About 1km east of Kōya-san's central crossroads, the buildings give way once more to stately cedar trees. Turn left here over a white bridge, **Ichi-no-hashi**, to follow the path into a mysterious, mossy forest. This is **Okunoin** (奥の院), Kōya-san's vast **cemetery**. Stretching away to either side, the forest floor is scattered with more than 200,000 stone stupas of all shapes and sizes. Here and there you'll also find Jizō statues and the occasional war memorial. A large number of historical characters are also buried here, among them the great general Oda Nobunaga.

It's best to walk through Okunoin in the early morning or around dusk, when lamps light up the path; at these times the only other people you're likely to meet are the occasional white-garbed pilgrims with their tinkling bells. Wandering slowly along the mystical 2km path, it takes about 45 minutes to reach the cemetery's spiritual centre, beyond the little **Tama-gawa** River.

Across the bridge you begin the approach to the **mausoleum of Kōbō Daishi**. First comes the **Hall of Lanterns**, where ten thousand oil lamps donated by the faithful are kept constantly alight. Two of them are said to have been burning since the eleventh century, one donated by the former Emperor Shirakawa and another by an anonymous poor woman. After this blaze of light and colour, the **tomb** itself is surprisingly restrained. Indeed, it's only just visible within a gated enclosure behind the hall, sheltered by lofty cryptomeria trees and clouds of incense.

According to Shingon tradition, the Great Master, Daishi, did not die in 835 but rather entered "eternal meditation". He's now waiting to return as Miroku, the Future Buddha, when he will help lead the faithful to salvation – which is one reason why so many Japanese wish to have their ashes buried on Kōya-san. Next to the Daishi's tomb you'll see the octagonal ossuary where ashes are collected. Many of these are destined for the **modern cemetery**, which lies south of the Tama-gawa bridge on a short cut back to the main road. Large companies maintain plots on Kōya-san for past employees – the space rocket and UCC's coffee cup are probably the most famous memorials. And note also the "letter boxes" on some monuments for company employees to leave their *meishi* (business cards).

You emerge at Naka-no-hashi (中の橋), on the main road beside a clutch of restaurants and a bus park. If you don't want to walk back, take any bus heading west from the Okunoin-mae stop across the road towards **Senjuin-bashi**.

Kumano Kodō

Set amongst the isolated mountain ranges of the **Kii Hantō** (紀伊半島) peninsula, in southern Wakayama prefecture, southeast of Ōsaka, is a network of ancient pilgrimage routes known as the **Kumano Kodō** (熊野古道). In 2004, Kumano Kodō, literally the "Kumano ancient road", became a UNESCO World Heritage Site. An area of stunning natural beauty – old-growth forests, charming mountain tea fields, magnificent waterfalls and healing hot springs – it is also the spiritual heartland of Japanese mythology and religion, and unique for its synthesis of Shintoism and Buddhism, in which indigenous Japanese deities were accepted as manifestations of Buddhist deities. This is where the mountain-worshipping Buddhist-Shinto practice of Shugendō evolved and is still active today.

Four pilgrimage routes

The Kumano Kodō is actually a rubric for the network of four pilgrimage routes; the Imperial Nakahechi route, the mountainous Kohechi route, the coastal Ohechi route and the eastern Iseji route. The Kohechi and Iseji routes link up Kumano with Kōya-san and Ise-jingū, respectively.

The Nakahechi is the most popular route to the Grand Shrines. Beginning in Tanabe, it traverses the mountains eastwards towards Hongū, where it splits into a river route to Shingu and a mountain route to Nachi. The Nakahechi passes through some remote villages but has excellent accommodation facilities for multi-day walks. This route has many *oji*, small roadside shrines for worshipping various deities, hence many of the villages are named accordingly. Most pilgrims take a bus from Kii-Tanabe station to Takijiri-oji, a major trailhead, and walk to Chikatsuyu (6hr) on the first day, stopping at Takahara Kumano-jinja to see the wonderful vista of clouds and mountains. The second full-day walk leads to Hongū and its onsen. Many pilgrims continue on the trail for another few days, also taking in Kumano Nachi Taisha and its amazing waterfall, before arriving at the final destination in Shingū. It is also possible to use a combination of buses and selected trail walks to experience the Nakahechi route – either way, it takes in some of the most tranquil natural scenes in Western Japan, and is a great way to visit the Kumano Sanzan Grand Shrines. Remember, however, that this is a mountainous area and the weather can change quickly, so it's important to be prepared for different temperatures. Detailed information on all the routes, as well as suggested itineraries, are available in English; see p.504.

Though mentioned in the eighth-century *Kojiki* historical record as the "Land of the Dead", where the spirits of the gods reside, Kumano Kodō became popular from the tenth century mainly through Imperial pilgrimages by retired emperors and aristocrats, who made the trek from Kyoto to worship at the **Kumano Sanzan** (熊野三山), a set of three important Grand Shrines of **Kumano Hongū Taisha**, **Kumano Hayatama Taisha** and **Kumano Nachi Taisha**, and to perform rites of purification in the surrounding rivers and waterfalls. The working classes were also attracted to worshipping here, and consequently, by the fourteenth century pilgrims from all over the country had forged routs here from other parts of the county. Unlike nearby Kōya-san, some seventy kilometres away, female pilgrims have always been welcomed in Kumano from its earliest history.

Another reason for the historical popularity and significance of the Kumano Kodō is the number of excellent **hot springs**, many in remote villages, which since ancient times have been known for their healing and restorative powers. The Kumano Kodō is a special place to visit both for its serene natural beauty and its ancient spiritual atmosphere. Despite its remoteness from modern, hi-tech Japan, it is an incredibly friendly place, with a good transport and accommodation infrastructure that caters well to international visitors.

Arrival and information

The main access point for the Kumano Kodō is the city of Tanabe (田辺); its JR station is Kii-Tanabe (紀伊田辺); express train services run from Kyoto and Ōsaka. If coming from eastern Japan, trains from Nagoya go to Shingū (新宮). There are also JR Nishi-Nihon and Meiko buses from Ōsaka to Tanabe (10 daily; ¥2600). From April 1 to November 30, there are buses between Kōya-san and Tanabe (2 daily; ¥4430). During the summer months, buses also run from Kōya-san to Hongū (2 daily; ¥3800), but it is advisable to check times well in advance on the tourism bureau website (see below). Otherwise, you can get the train from Kōya-san, changing at Hashimoto for services towards Wakayama city and Tanabe.

There is a small **tourist information office** just outside Kii-Tanabe Station where you can pick up an excellent array of English-language pamphlets on the ancient routes. The best source for the latest information on Kumano Kodō, translated into English, including transport timetables and an accommodation reservation system, is the comprehensive **website** of the Tanabe City Kumano Tourism Bureau (Ⓦtb-kumano.jp/en). There are also **visitor information centres** at Takiri-oji, the spiritual entrance to the sacred Kumano mountains, and also at the Kumano Hongū Heritage Center, near Kumano Hongū Taisha, the crossroads of the four ancient routes.

Pilgrims are usually intent on walking the Kumano Kodō, but there is also a good network of fairly regular **bus services**, depending on the season, which connect the main sights of the pilgrim routes and the surrounding areas; see the Tourism Bureau website for timetables. **Bike rental** is available at Kii-Tanabe Station (9am–6pm; ¥1000/2 days) and also from the Kumano Hongū Heritage Center (8.30am–5pm; ¥1500/day).

Accommodation

Along the Kumano Kodō there is a range of good-quality accommodation options for all budgets. Many ryokan or minshuku have their own onsen, or are close to one, and most places can provide dinner and breakfast, as well as a boxed lunch to take on the trail the next day. The increasing number of international visitors to the area also means that some very reasonably priced guesthouses have opened, especially along the Nakahechi route.

Altier アルティエホテル Tanabe ⓣ0739/81-1111, ⓦwww.altierhotel.com. If you are starting your journey in Tanabe, this comfortable business hotel near the station, with free breakfast and internet, is an excellent choice. ❺

Blue Sky Guesthouse 蒼空げすとはうす Hongū ⓣ0735/42-0800, ⓦwww.kumano-guesthouse.com. In a spacious new building with tatami rooms and excellent facilities. Friendly and international atmosphere. ❹

Kamigoten Ryokan 上御殿 Ryujin Onsen ⓣ0739/79-0005, ⓦwww.aikis.or.jp/~kamigoten. High-class ryokan at Ryujin Onsen in an exquisite Edo-period building and serving multi-course dinners of hearty mountain cuisine. Onsen facilities are modern with superb river valley views. ❼

Kiri no Sato Takahara 霧の郷たかはら Takahara ⓣ0739/64-1900. Newly built mountain lodge in Takahara village on the Nakahechi route. The comfortable rooms have fantastic views looking directly out over the valley. ❹

Minshuku Chikatsuyu 民宿ちかつゆ Chikatsuyu ⓣ0739/65-0617. This minshuku on the Nakahechi route has comfortable private and shared tatami rooms, as well as its own onsen with water as smooth as silk. ❸

Minshuku Omuraya 民宿大村屋 Kawayu Onsen ⓣ0735/42-1066. At Kawayu Onsen, near Hongū, this family-run inn is steps away from the Sennin-buro river bath, and offers a delicious evening meal, as well as a gourmet boxed lunch the next day. The clean and spacious tatami rooms all have their own WC. ❸

Yoshinoya よしのや Yunomine ⓣ0735/42-0101, ⓦwww.yunomine.com. A clean and friendly inn right on the narrow stream near the ancient Tsuboyu, with its own pleasant outdoor bath. ❺

Hongū

In Hongū, the four pilgrimage routes converge at the **Kumano Hongū Taisha** (熊野本宮大社; daily 8am–5pm; free), a stately shrine similar in style to the architecture of **Ise-jingū**. This is the spiritual and geographical centre of Kumano and is a major destination for pilgrims. It was moved to its current, and slightly more elevated, location after a massive flood in 1889 almost completely destroyed it at nearby Oyunohara, a sandbank on the Kumano-gawa. Today, an enormous *torii* gate stands on the site, visible from many kilometres around. You can see photos and models of the shrine before the flood, and learn more about its history, at the **Kumano Hongū Heritage Center** (世界遺産熊野本宮館; daily 9am–5pm; free; ⓦwww.city.tanabe.lg.jp/hongukan/en), just across the road from the shrine entrance. This is a great place to get a deeper understanding of the culture and religion of the Kumano Kodō, with informative and multilingual displays. There are buses from Tanabe to Hongū that stop at the shrine and Heritage Center (2hr; ¥2000), as well as from Shingū, which depart from the station (80min; ¥1500).

Hongū boasts three unique onsen. At the 1800-year-old **Yunomine Onsen** (湯の峰温泉), the main attraction is *Tsuboyu* (つぼ湯) – the only hot spring in Japan to be registered as a UNESCO World Heritage Site. It is a small spring, built out of the narrow stream that runs through the town, and is covered by a wooden cabin that you can use privately for thirty minutes (daily; 6am–9.30pm; ¥750). The river at **Kawayu Onsen** (川湯温泉) is transformed during winter into a piping-hot giant outdoor bath called the *Sennin-buro* (仙人風呂; 6.30am–10pm; free), while not far away is **Wataze Onsen** (渡瀬温泉; 6am–9.30pm; ¥700), whose claim to fame is having the largest rotenburo (outdoor bath) in western Japan. It's not as historic as the other two, but its garden setting is just as picturesque. **Ryujin Onsen** (龍神温泉) is slightly outside of Hongū, in a more remote mountain area, but is worth considering for a visit if you are travelling from Kōya-san towards Hongū and Shingū. Its waters are well known for their beautifying effects on the skin, and the views from the outdoor baths in spring and autumn are sublime.

Shingū and Nachi-Katsuura

The other two Grand Shrines of the Kumano Sanzen are located to the southeast of Hongū. **Kumano Hayatama Taisha** (熊野速玉大社; daily 8am–5pm; free) is close to the centre of coastal Shingū city, and not far from the mouth of the Kumano-gawa. The shrine buildings are much less austere than Kumano Hongū Taisha, and the shrine itself is in a very pleasant setting, among ancient trees – look out for the 800-year-old Nagi-no-ki tree. It is easily accessible from the train station on foot. Walking inland in a northerly direction, it should take about fifteen minutes.

Just outside the town of Nachi-Katsura is the Grand Shrine of **Kumano Nachi Taisha** (熊野那智大社; daily; 8.30am–4.30pm; free) and the Buddhist temple of **Seiganto-ji** (青岸渡寺; daily; 8.30am–4pm; free). Perched on the side of Nachi Mountain, they are fine examples of the interconnectivity of Shinto and Buddhist faiths in the Kumano region, exemplified by the fact that they have been situated next to each other for centuries and attract large numbers of pilgrims, especially from the western pilgrimage routes. The shrine is dedicated to the god of the nearby **Nachi-no-Otaki** (daily; 9am–5pm; free), which at 133m is said to be the tallest waterfall in Japan and is also an important place of worship for Shugendō followers. If you don't have time to trek down to the waterfall, you can still enjoy the superb view from Seiganto-ji. The best way to get to Kumano Nachi Taisha is to take a bus from JR Kii-Katsuura Station (30min; ¥600).

Shima Hantō

East of the Kii Hantō mountain ranges, on the far side of the Kii Peninsula, a small knuckle of land sticks out into the ocean. Known as **Shima Hantō** (志摩半島), this peninsula has been designated a national park, partly for its natural beauty but also because it contains Japan's spiritual heartland, **Ise-jingū**. Since the fourth century the Grand Shrine of Ise, on the edge of **Ise** town, has been venerated as the terrestrial home of the Sun Goddess Amaterasu, from whom it was once believed all Japanese emperors are descended. Beyond Ise it's **pearl** country. The world-famous Mikimoto company started up in **Toba** when an enterprising restaurant owner discovered the art of cultivating pearls. Now there's a whole island dedicated to his memory, including a surprisingly interesting museum. Most of today's pearls are raised further east in **Ago-wan**, where hundreds of rafts are tethered in a beautiful, island-speckled bay.

Ise

The town of **ISE** (伊勢) wears its sanctity lightly, and many visitors find the town a disappointingly ordinary place. However, at **Ise-jingū** (伊勢神宮), Japan's most sacred Shinto shrine, even non-Japanese visitors can appreciate a deeply spiritual atmosphere. Apart from their historical importance, there is an unquestionable sense of awe and mystery about these simple buildings, with their unusual architecture, deep in the cedar forest. Ise-jingū is naturally a top choice for the first shrine visit of the New Year (*hatsu-mōde*) on January 1. This is followed by more than 1500 annual **ceremonies** in honour of Ise's gods. The most important of these revolve around the agricultural cycle, culminating in offerings of sacred rice (Oct 15–17). In spring (April 5–6) and during the autumn equinox (Sept 22 or 23), ancient Shinto dances and a moon-viewing party take place at the inner shrine.

Arrival and information

There are regular **trains** to Ise from Nagoya, Kyoto and Ōsaka. In all cases the private Kintetsu network offers the quickest and most convenient service, particularly if you're travelling from Kyoto or Ōsaka. Note that there are two stations in central Ise. The more easterly, **Uji-Yamada Station**, is Kintetsu's main station.

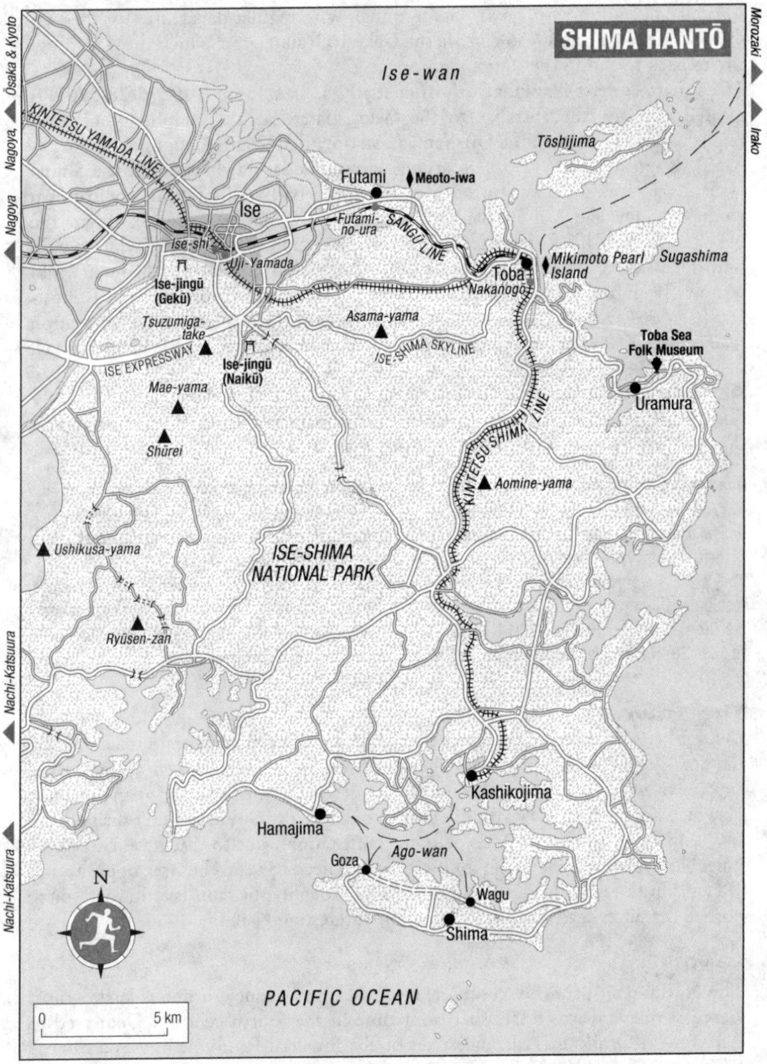

However, some Kintetsu trains also stop at **Ise-shi Station**, which is shared with JR. **From Nagoya** the fastest option is an express on the Kintetsu-Ise line to Uji-Yamada Station (hourly; 1hr 25min; ¥2690). If you've got a JR Rail Pass, you can use JR's limited express trains direct from Nagoya to Ise-shi (hourly; 1hr 30min), but note that you have to pay a small supplement (¥440) for travelling on a section of Kintetsu track. Kintetsu also runs direct trains **from Ōsaka**'s Tsuruhashi Station (every 15min; 1hr 45min; ¥3030) and **from Kyoto** (hourly; 2hr; ¥3520). For those planning on spending a few days in the area, a ¥3800 three-day Kintetsu-line rail pass spanning the whole of the extensive Kintetsu network is available, but this doesn't include the surcharge for using the fastest, special express trains.

Each train station has its own **bus** terminal, with regular departures for the two shrines; buses #51 and #55 run via the Gekū to Naikū, after which the #51 route circles back round to the stations.

Ise's main **tourist information office** (daily 8.30am–5pm; ⓣ0596/28-3705) is located opposite the entrance to the Gekū. There's also a helpful office with English-speaking staff in the Uji-Yamada Station (daily 9am–5.30pm; ⓣ0596/23-9655), where staff can also help arrange accommodation throughout the Shima Hantō area. Ise's main **shopping area** lies south of Ise-shi Station. For **foreign exchange**, try the Daisan Bank opposite the JR Station, or walk down the pleasant, lantern-lined street leading from the station to the Gekū, where you'll find the Bank of Tokyo-Mitsubishi UFJ. **Car rental** is available through Kinki Nippon Rent-a-Car (ⓣ0596/28-0295), at Uji-Yamada Station, and Eki Rent-a-Car (ⓣ0596/25-5019), at Ise-shi Station. **Bike rental** is available at Ise-shi Station (9am–5pm; ¥1030 per day) and from the *Hoshidekan* (see below) for ¥300 per day.

Accommodation

Surprisingly, Ise doesn't have a great choice of **accommodation**; if you plan to visit during New Year or other important holiday times, it's advisable to book ahead.

Hoshidekan 星出館 2-15-2 Kawasaki ⓣ0596/28-2377, ⓦwww.hoshidekan.jp. This eccentric old ryokan offers tatami rooms centred around a garden, all with shared bath and toilet facilities. They serve delicious macrobiotic food in their restaurant. ⑤

Ise City 伊勢シティホテル 1-11-31 Fukiage ⓣ0596/28-2111. Fairly bland business hotel with English-speaking staff, rather small rooms and an in-house steak restaurant. They have a slightly more expensive annexe just along the road towards the Kawasaki district (⑥). ⑤

Town Hotel Ise タウンホテル伊勢 1-8-18 Fukiage ⓣ0596/23-4621. Small and economical business hotel right next to the train tracks; rooms are functional and double-glazed. ④

The Town

Central Ise is bounded to the north by the JR and Kintetsu-line train tracks and by the Seta-gawa River to the east. The southwestern quarter is taken up by a large expanse of woodland (which accounts for a full third of the town's area), in the midst of which lies the first of **Ise-jingū**'s two sanctuaries, the **Gekū**, or outer shrine. This is within easy walking distance of both train stations, but to reach the **Naikū**, or inner shrine, some 6km to the southeast, you'll need to take a bus (see opposite and "Practicalities", p.511). The two shrines follow roughly the same layout, so if you're pushed for time, head straight for the more interesting Naikū.

Naikū

The **Naikū** (内宮; sunrise to sunset; free), Ise-jingū's inner shrine, is Japan's most sacred shrine and was established sometime in the fourth century. Dedicated to **Amaterasu Ōmikami**, the ancestress of the imperial family, it houses a **mirror** that Amaterasu gave her grandson Ninigi-no-Mikoto when she sent him to rule Japan. At first it was stored in the Imperial Palace, along with the sacred sword and beads (these are now held in Nagoya's Atsuta-jingū and Tokyo's Imperial Palace), but the goddess gave instructions to move her mirror to somewhere more remote. Eventually they settled on a wooded spot beside Ise's Isuzu-gawa, which has been the mirror's home ever since.

After crossing the Uji-bashi bridge, turn right and walk through a small, formal garden to reach the purification fountain just in front of the first sacred *torii*. A little further on, the path goes down to the river where, traditionally, pilgrims would purify themselves. The path loops round to approach the **inner sanctum** from the south. The main building is contained within four increasingly sacred enclosures, with the inner sanctum the furthest from view, making it difficult to see the details. Nevertheless, the architecture's pure, strong lines hold the same mystical power. Only members of the imperial family and head priests can enter the inner sanctuary where Amaterasu's **sacred mirror** is enshrined. It's wrapped in layers of cloth and, according to the records, no one has laid eyes on it for more than a thousand years.

According to custom, both the **Naikū** and **Gekū** (outer shrine) are rebuilt every twenty years in order to re-purify the ground. Each is an exact replica of its predecessor, following a unique style of architecture that has been passed down the centuries and is free of any of the Chinese or Korean influences usually found in Buddhist architecture. Only plain *hinoki* (Japanese cypress) and grass thatch are used, plus a few gold embellishments. When the buildings are dismantled, the old timbers are passed on to other shrines around the country to be recycled. The next rebuilding is scheduled for 2013.

If you've got time to spare after exploring the Naikū, turn right immediately over the Uji-bashi and take a stroll down the shopping street known as **Oharai-machi** (おはらい町). This pedestrian-only area replicates the late Edo and early Meiji-era merchants' quarter which was on this exact site; it's all rather touristy, but the buildings look authentic and there are some decent places to eat (see below). Across the road is the Okage-Yokochō (おかげ横町) area, with more replica Edo and Meiji-era buildings, including the quaint **Okageza history museum** (おかげ座; daily 9am–4.30pm; ¥300). The museum re-creates the encounters between pilgrims and the people of Ise during the Edo period, using scale models and recordings of Edo-period stories and street sounds (in Japanese). There's a short introduction by the staff in Japanese but after that you are free to wander through the museum. The English-language pamphlet adequately explains the main features of the museum.

To return to central Ise and the **Gekū** from the Naikū area, take a bus (#51 or #55) from stop 1 (every 30min; 15–20min; ¥410).

Gekū

The **Gekū**, or outer shrine (外宮; sunrise to sunset; free), is located close to the southern edge of the modern business district of Ise city, and has a much smaller scale, and fewer crowds, than Naikū. Its entrance lies over a small humped bridge and along a gravel path leading into the woods. It was constructed in the fifth century to honour the goddess **Toyouke-no-Ōmikami**, who was sent by Amaterasu to look after the all-important rice harvests. Another of her duties is to provide Amaterasu with sacred food, so twice a day priests make offerings to Toyouke in a small hall at the back of the compound. Having paid their respects to Toyouke by bowing deeply twice, clapping and bowing deeply a third time, most people hurry off to visit the Naikū, if they haven't already. Buses heading east leave from a stand on the main road opposite the Gekū's main entrance; hop on either a #55 or #51 for the Naikū stop (every 10–15min; ¥410).

Eating

Ise's **speciality foods** include lobster (*Ise-ebi*) and the rather salty *Ise udon*, which consists of thick, handmade noodles served in a thin soy sauce. Matsuzaka beef, marbled and fatty like its Kōbe cousin, is another local favourite. Oharai-machi makes the Naikū area a better, and more interesting, choice for lunch than the Gekū area.

Akafuku 赤福本店 26 Ujinakanokiri-chō ⓣ0596/22-7000. A 300-year-old sweet shop near the Shinbashi bridge that serves the local speciality – *akafuku mochi*, deliciously fresh pounded rice cakes covered with red bean paste (¥340 for three pieces including tea). Daily 9am–5pm.

Daiki 大喜 143-3 Kusube-chō ⓣ0596/28-0281, ⓦwww.ise.ne.jp/daiki. Touted as "Japan's most famous restaurant", *Daiki* has made its name catering to the Imperial Family. In a dreary location near Uji-Yamada Station, it serves rather average *kaiseki* and *Ise-ebi* sets, both from ¥5000. Daily 9am–10pm.

Okadaya 岡田屋 31 Ujimazaike-chō ☎0596/22-4554. Popular *Ise udon* restaurant in the main part of Oharai-machi. Their lunch sets (¥1250) are good value. Daily 10.30am–5pm.

Toramaru 虎丸 2-13-6 Kawasaki ☎0596/22-9298. Friendly, non-smoking *izakaya* in a restored *kura* (warehouse) in the Kawasaki merchant area, serving sashimi, lotus root tempura and aubergine dumplings. Daily except Thurs 5–10pm.

Yamaguchi-ya 山口屋 1-1-18 Miyago ☎0596/28-3856. Very friendly *Ise udon* restaurant down a shopping street near the JR station, serving excellent, tasty noodles. They also offer soba and tempura sets. Daily except Thurs 10am–7pm.

Toba and Ago-wan

East of Ise, the ragged Shima Peninsula juts out into the Pacific Ocean. Most of this mountainous area belongs to the Ise-Shima National Park, whose largest settlement is the port of **Toba**, home to the famous **Mikimoto Pearl Island**. After learning everything you ever wanted to know about cultured pearls, you can head on south to **Kashikojima** on the shores of **Ago-wan**, a huge, sheltered bay scattered with wooded islands between which float banks of oyster rafts – magical at sunset.

Travelling from Ise, there's a choice of routes into the area. If the weather's clear then the best option is via the **Ise-Shima Skyline bus** (伊勢志摩スカイライン), which runs between Ise and Toba over the summit of Asama-yama. From the top you get excellent views over Ise-wan and, on an exceptional day, you can see Mount Fuji. **Buses** depart twice a day (12.05pm & 2.20pm; 40min; ¥1220) from outside Ise's Naikū shrine (see p.508). Alternatively, the "Canbus" bus service (Mon–Fri hourly, Sat & Sun every 30min) departs from Uji-Yamada Station and stops at all the major sights and train stations between Ise and Toba, including the inner and outer shrines, wedded rocks at Futami, and Mikimoto Pearl Island. One-day (¥1000) and two-day (¥1600) passes are available; both passes come with a book of coupons offering further discounts to attractions. Passes are available at major train stations and on the bus.

Alternatively, both Kintetsu (¥290) and JR (¥230) **trains** continue east of Ise. Of these, the JR services are less frequent and don't go beyond Toba. However, their lines run closer to the coast, where they pass through **FUTAMI** (二見), which is famous for its "wedded rocks", **Meoto-iwa** (夫婦岩). Joined by a hefty, sacred rope, this pair of "male" and "female" rocks lies just offshore, about twenty minutes' walk northeast of Futami-no-ura Station (二見浦駅). They're revered as representations of Izanagi and Izanami, the two gods who created Japan, and it's the done thing to see the sun rise between them – the best season to do this is from May to August. On a clear day, you can also see Mount Fuji in the distance from above the rocks.

Toba

Although it's on an attractive bay, the main reason to stop in the town of **TOBA** (鳥羽) is to pay homage to the birthplace of cultured pearls. The seafront is mostly a strip of car parks, ferry terminals and shopping arcades, behind which run the main road and train tracks. However, there are a number of interesting museums that have opened in recent years, and the abundance of good seafood restaurants is also worth considering should you wish to stop over.

In 1893, **Mikimoto Kokichi** (1858–1954), the son of a Toba noodle-maker, produced the world's first cultivated pearl using tools developed by a dentist friend. Just six years later he opened his first shop in Tokyo's fashionable Ginza shopping district, from where the Mikimoto empire spread worldwide. His life's work is commemorated – and minutely detailed – on **Mikimoto Pearl Island** (ミキモト真珠島; daily: April–Oct 8.30am–5.30pm; Nov–March 9am–4.30pm;

The ama women divers

The female diving culture of Ise-shima dates back to the earliest annals of Japanese history. Known as *ama,* the women free-dive for shellfish, such as oysters and abalone, as well as harvesting seaweed. On average they'll spend three to four hours a day in the water, going down to a depth of 10–15m without any breathing apparatus, and some are still diving past the age of 70. *Ama* usually dive year-round either in small groups, or from boats skippered by their husbands. The reason for women-only divers is that they can hold their breath longer than men and are blessed with an extra layer of insulating fat, which protects them from the freezing waters.

Traditionally, *ama* harvested seafood in Ise Bay and transported it to Ise-jingū, where they presented their catch as an offering. They played a major role in the development of the cultured pearl industry in the nineteenth century, helping to gather the *akoya* pearl oysters. Today, there are approximately 1300 *ama* in the Toba area; they still wear the customary white outfits, which apparently scare off sharks, and which are also marked with special protective star-shaped charms to ward off bad luck.

Sunrise Tours (Ⓣ03/5796-5454, Ⓦwww.jtb-sunrisetours.jp) offers a unique opportunity on their "Women Pearl Divers and Ise Shinto Shrine" one-day tour to meet the *ama* in person. The tour starts at **Naikū**, Ise-jingū's inner shrine, and also takes in the Mikimoto Pearl Museum, where you can see the *ama* pearl divers demonstration (see below). Down the coast at Osatsu, the tour ends at a specially arranged visit to the *ama* huts in the fishing port, where you can hear their stories of the sea while they barbecue the seafood they caught a few hours earlier. As the *ama* don't speak English, your tour guide will interpret your questions and the fascinating answers of the *ama.*

¥1500; Ⓣ0599/25-2028), lying just offshore, five minutes' walk south of Toba's train and bus stations. Even if you're not a pearl fan, the museum is extremely well put together, with masses of information in English describing the whole process from seeding the oyster to grading and stringing the pearls. There's also a section devoted to Mikimoto's extraordinary pearl artworks. The unsung heroines of all this are the **ama women divers** (see box above) who stoically come out every hour in all weathers to demonstrate their skills.

Further along the seafront is the **Toba Aquarium** (鳥羽水族館; daily: April–Oct 9am–5pm; Nov–March 9am–4.30pm; ¥2400). The steep entry fee is off-putting but it is one of only two places in the world where you can see a captive dugong. The **Toba Sea Folk Museum** (海の博物館; daily: April–Nov 9am–5pm; Dec–March 9am–4.30pm; ¥800; Ⓣ0599/32-6006), further down the coast road in Uramura, is housed in an award-winning wooden building overlooking the ocean. The museum, both inside and out, has been constructed to resemble the upturned hull of a wooden fishing boat. It has some informative 3D exhibits on the historical relationship between the people of Toba and the sea, and if you are interested in the *ama* women divers, there are some good displays here providing more historical background. The museum is 10km south of Toba on the Pearl Road driveway. Take the Sanco bus for Ijika (石鏡) from the bus terminal in front of Toba Station, getting off at the Umi-hakubutsukan-mae (海博物館前) bus stop. From here, it's a seven-minute walk down the hill.

Practicalities

Toba's JR and Kintetsu **stations** and the bus terminal are all located next door to each other in the centre of town. There's a very helpful **information booth** (daily 9am–5pm; Ⓣ0599/25-2844) beside the taxi stand at the bottom of the Kintetsu Station steps. The staff don't speak much English, but can help with accommodation.

Toba doesn't have many convenient or inexpensive **accommodation** options, but it is worth staying over to enjoy an excellent seafood dinner. One of the most reasonable places to stay is *Road Inn Toba* (ロードイン鳥羽; ⓣ0599/26-5678; ❹), behind the station. It's a standard business hotel with free internet, a sauna and swimming pool. Otherwise, the choice is a pricey resort hotel, such as the *Toba International Hotel* (鳥羽国際ホテル; ⓣ0599/25-3121, ⓦwww.tobahotel.co.jp; ❼), in a fine position on the headland overlooking Toba Bay. It takes about ten minutes on foot from the station.

Eating in Toba is less of a problem. Seafood restaurants abound, with fresh oysters and abalone on offer. Though it looks a bit grim, the Pearl Building, opposite Toba Station, makes a pretty good lunch choice with its third-floor *Ichibangai* restaurant floor, mostly serving local seafood (daily except Thurs; 10am–4pm). *Tenbinya* (天びん屋) is the best recommendation here, with their well-priced and supremely fresh seafood *teishoku set lunch* (¥1550). You'll also find noodle shops here, such as *Kippei* (吉平), which does a hearty bowl of *asari* (shellfish) *soba* for ¥850. *Tenbinya*'s main restaurant (天びん屋 てんびん屋本店; Tues–Sun 11.30am–2pm & 5–10.45pm; ⓣ0599/25-2223), in the streets just inland from Mikimoto Pearl Island, makes a great choice for a very reasonably priced seafood dinner for as little as ¥1350. Nearby, *Nagatokan* (長門館; Tues–Sun 11.30am–2pm & 5–10.45pm; ⓣ0599/25-2006) is another popular seafood restaurant with slightly more expensive, but hearty, lunch and dinner set menus (lunch ¥1900; dinner ¥3500).

Ago-wan

The Shima Hantō ends in a bay of islands known as **Ago-wan** (あご湾). This large, sheltered bay has myriad coves and deep inlets. For centuries, divers have been collecting natural pearls from its warm, shallow waters, but things really took off when Mikimoto (see p.510) started producing his cultured pearls in Ago-wan early in the twentieth century. Nowadays, hundreds of rafts moored between the islands trace strangely attractive patterns on the water, while, in the nets beneath, thousands of oysters busily work their magic.

The main reason to visit Ago-wan is to take a **boat trip** round the bay. Boats depart from the tiny port of **KASHIKOJIMA** (賢島) at the end of the Kintetsu train line (40min; ¥460). The station lies just one minute north of the harbour, where you'll find a choice of sightseeing boats and ferries. For ¥1500 you can cruise in a very tacky mock-Spanish galleon (50min; every 30min; 9am–4pm, according to demand), which stops off at a pearl farm. There are also small boats called *yūransen* (遊覧船), which take you further in among the islands (50–60min; from ¥1400). The cheapest option is one of the infrequent passenger **ferries** called *teikisen* (定期船). There are two ferry routes: across to **Goza** (御座), on the long arm forming the bay's southern edge, and back via **Hamajima** (浜島) to the west of Kashikojima (1hr 15min; ¥1800 for the round-trip); or via Masaki island (間崎) in the middle of the bay to **Wagu** (和具), a village east of Goza (25min; ¥600 one-way). You can get tickets and information about the ferries and Spanish cruise boats from an office beside the harbour – on the right as you walk down from the station – or buy *yūransen* tickets from one of the small booths opposite.

For local maps and general **information**, head to the Kashikojima Ryokan Annaijo (賢島旅館案内所; Tues, Wed & Fri–Sun 9am–4.30pm; ⓣ0599/43-3061), on the right-hand side as you come down the escalator leading from the station to the pier. They can help with all types of **accommodation**. The recently refurbished *Shima Kankō Hotel* (志摩観光ホテル; ⓣ0599/43-1211, ⓦwww.miyakohotels.ne.jp/shima; ❼) is a luxury hotel in a magnificent position overlooking the bay; the spacious rooms have wonderful views. At the other end of the scale, the secluded *Ryokan Ishiyama-sō* (旅館石山荘; ⓣ0599/52-1527, ⓔlosman-gili@ab.aeonnet.ne.jp; ❹) is a great place to spend the night on the small island of Yokoyama-jima (横山島). It's two minutes by boat from Kashikojima pier, where the English-speaking owner will collect you. After dining on a scrumptious feast of fresh seafood in their restaurant (from ¥3000), you can watch the sun go down over Ago-wan.

Kōbe and around

A historic port and distinct city in its own right, **KŌBE** (神戸), the capital of Hyōgo-ken, now seems more like a fashionable western suburb of sprawling Ōsaka. Kōbe's cosmopolitan atmosphere, eclectic food scene and dramatic location on a sliver of land between the sea and Rokkō-san are the main reasons to visit this friendly harbourside city.

Although it is more than fifteen years since the 1995 **earthquake**, Kōbe has far from forgotten this horrific event – the oddly named **Disaster Reduction and Human Renovation Institution** documents the quake and its aftermath, while the new **Tetsujin** robot monument is a reminder of the continuing spirit and effort of Kōbe citizens in rebuilding their city. The **Kōbe City Museum**, covering the port's earlier illustrious history, is also worth a look, as is the space-age **Fashion Museum** on the man-made Rokkō Island, east of the city harbour.

Heading into the hills, you can relax at **Arima Onsen**, one of Japan's oldest spa resorts. West of the city is the **Akashi Kaikyō Ōhashi**, the longest single-span suspension bridge in the world (see p.520), linking Kansai directly with Shikoku via Awaji-shima. Travelling some 55km further west of here, along the coast, you'll arrive at **Himeji**, home of Japan's best original castle, Himeji-jō, a UNESCO World Heritage Site since 1993.

Some history

Kōbe's history is dominated by two important events; the opening of Japan's ports to foreign trade in 1868 and the Great Hanshin Earthquake of 1995. Although it had been a port as long ago as the eighth century AD, Kōbe's fortunes really took off when **foreign traders** set up shop in the city in the latter part of the nineteenth century, bringing their new ways and styles of living with them. Japan got its first taste of beef and football in 1871 in Kōbe, the first cinema film was shown here in 1896, and the first golf course was laid down close to the city in 1903, designed by Arthur Gloom, a Brit.

This trendsetting nature and booming trade made Kōbe a very popular place and, despite suffering heavy bombing during World War II, by the 1960s the city was bursting out of its narrow stretch of land between the mountains and the sea. A solution was found by levelling the hills and dumping the rubble in the sea to create Port Island and Rokkō Island in the bay. All this came to a sudden halt, though, at 5.46am, January 17, 1995, when a devastating **earthquake** struck the city and surrounding area. As dawn broke, Kōbe resembled a war zone, with buildings and highways toppled, whole neighbourhoods in flames, some 5500 people dead and tens of thousands homeless. While the authorities were criticized for not responding promptly to the disaster, Kōbe has recovered well and today the city bears little physical sign of the tragedy.

Nonetheless, a lingering recession still affects the city, and economic growth is somewhat stalled. The primary source of angst for many of the city's residents is Kōbe Airport, which opened in 2006 on a man-made island off the coast. The airport only handles domestic flights, and with two perfectly good airports already in service within an hour of the city centre, it has failed to spark increased prosperity.

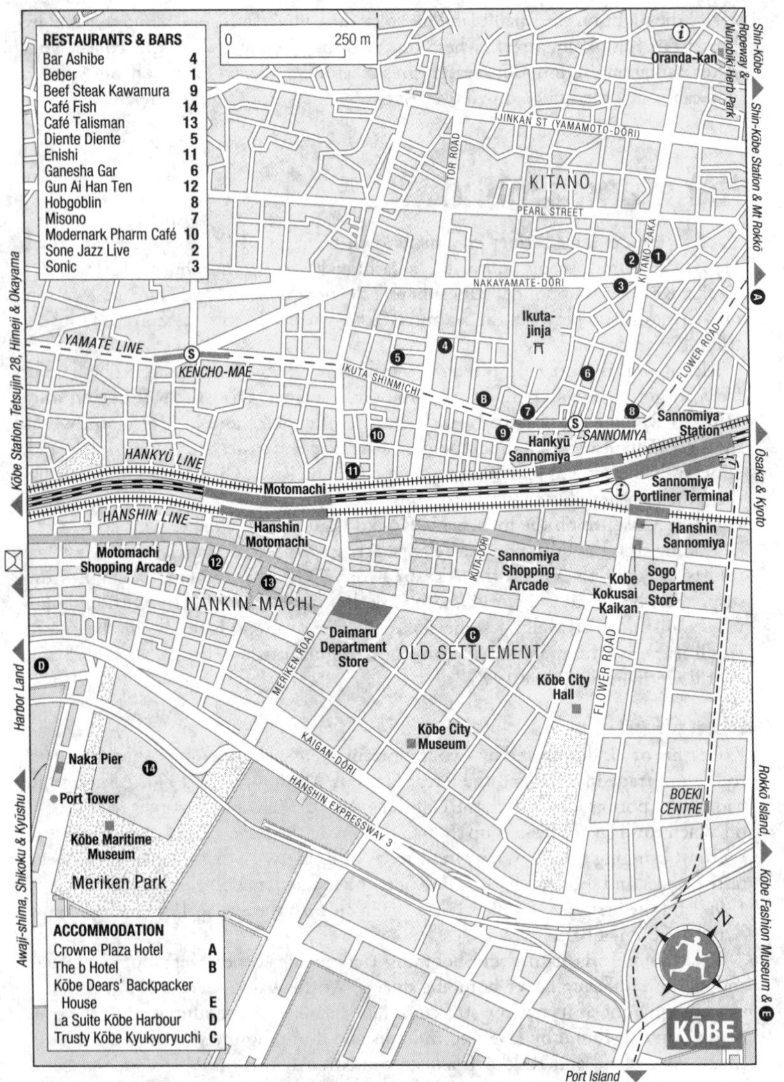

Arrival, information and city transport

Shinkansen **trains** stop at Shin-Kōbe Station at the foot of Rokkō-san, around 1km north of Sannomiya Station in downtown Kōbe. As well as JR trains, those on the Hankyū and Hanshin lines also stop at Sannomiya Station, and are the cheaper way of connecting with Ōsaka and Kyoto to the east if you're not using a JR pass. The fastest way of getting directly to Kōbe from Kansai International Airport is by **limousine bus** (1hr; ¥1900), which drops passengers at Sannomiya Station and the *Kōbe Bay Sheraton Hotel*. **Ferries** from Shikoku, Kyūshū and Awaji-shima arrive at Naka Pier next to the Port Tower, ten minutes' walk south of Motomachi Station, and at Rokkō Island Ferry Terminal, east of the city. From here you can take the Rokkō Liner monorail to JR Sumiyoshi or Hanshin Uozaki stations, from where it's ten minutes to either JR Sannomiya or Hanshin Sannomiya stations. To get to Kōbe Airport, which is attached to Port Island, take the Port Liner monorail from Sannomiya (18min; ¥320). The main **tourist information** office (daily 9am–7pm; ⓣ078/322-0220), is at the south exit of JR Sannomiya Station, but there's a much more helpful **information counter** inside Shin-Kōbe Station (daily 9am–6pm; ⓣ078/241-9550). As it's less than 3km wide, Kōbe is a great city for **walking** around. If you feel like taking things easy, hop on the **city loop** tourist bus (¥250 per ride, or ¥650 for a day pass, offering substantial discounts to many of the city's major sights), which runs a regular circuit around Kōbe's main sights.

Accommodation

There's plenty of top-end and mid-range **accommodation** in Kōbe, but very few budget options.

ANA Crowne Plaza Hotel Kōbe ANAクラウンプラザホテル神戸 1-7-14 Kitano-chō ⓣ078/291-1121, ⓦwww.anacrowneplaza-kobe.jp. This upmarket hotel occupies a soaring skyscraper next to Shin-Kōbe Station, with fantastic views from all rooms, great service and a good range of restaurants both in the hotel and the connected shopping plaza. ❼

The b Hotel ザ・ビー神戸21-5 Shimoyamate-dōri ⓣ078/333-4480, ⓦwww.ishinhotels.com/theb-kobe/en. An excellent mid-range choice right in the middle of Sannomiya. Their stylish rooms are comfortable though on the small side. Internet access is free, and there's a coffee lounge for guests in the lobby. ❺

Kōbe Dears' Backpacker House 4-2-1 Minami Uozaki ⓣ070/6453-1583, ⓦwww.kobe-dears.com. Located in the Nada sake-brewing district, this is Kōbe's best budget option. Only 10min away by train from the Sannomiya area, it has a friendly atmosphere, as well as internet access, laundry, a kitchen, and no curfew. Dorm beds are ¥2500, but there are also singles (¥3900), doubles/twins (¥3200) and triples (¥3000). ❸

La Suite Kōbe Harborland ホテルラ・スイート神戸ハーバーランド 7-2 Hatoba-chō ⓣ078/371-1111, ⓦwww.l-s.jp/eng. Kōbe's newest luxury hotel has great harbour views from its sweeping terraces and balconies. The rooms are lavishly decorated in a classic modern style with comfortable lounges. The in-house French and *tepanyaki* restaurants emphasize local produce but are very pricey. ❽

Trusty Kōbe Kyukyoryuchi ホテルトラスティ神戸旧居留地 63 Naniwamachi ⓣ078/330-9111, ⓦwww.trusty.jp/kobe. Located in the Motomachi district, not far from Chinatown, this is another stylish hotel that's a good mid-range option. The rooms are clean but rather pokey. On the second floor there's an outdoor terrace café with a good breakfast buffet. ❻

The City

Kōbe's sights are split into three main areas. South of the band of rail lines passing through Sannomiya Station is the city's commercial centre covering the old settlement area and, to the west, **Nankin-machi**, Kōbe's Chinatown. Immediately south of here are the **harbour** developments of Meriken Park, Kōbe Harbor Land, Port Island and Rokkō Island. North of Sannomiya Station lies Shin-Kōbe Station and **Kitano** where the *ijinkan* (foreigners' houses), dating from the turn of the twentieth century (though most were reconstructed after the 1995 earthquake), are clustered on the slopes of Maya-san. For the best view of the whole city and the Inland Sea, take the **Shin-Kōbe Ropeway** up Rokkō-san to the Nunobiki Herb Garden, where you might also be lucky enough to see one of the many wild boars that roam the city's mountainous northern districts.

Sannomiya Station and Kitano

Around a century ago, the area south of Sannomiya Station (三宮駅) was Kōbe's principal foreign settlement, although there's little evidence of it today. To get a better idea of what it once looked like, head for the **Kōbe City Museum** (神戸市博物館; Tues–Sun 10am–4.30pm; ¥200; ⓣ078-391-0035), ten minutes' walk south of either Sannomiya or Motomachi stations, which contains a finely detailed scale model of early twentieth-century Kōbe and many woodblock prints from the same era. The highlight of the museum, however, is its collection of *Namban* (southern barbarian) art. These paintings, prints and screens – some of extraordinary detail and beauty – by Japanese artists of the late sixteenth and seventeenth centuries, show how they were influenced by the art of the first Europeans, or "southern barbarians", to come to Japan.

Immediately west of the museum is **Nankin-machi** (南京町), Kōbe's Chinatown, the entrance to which is marked by the ornate Choan-mon gate opposite the Daimaru department store. The area is packed with Chinese restaurants and colourful street stalls. It's better to visit in the day as most of the restaurants are closed by mid-evening.

Of primary interest to the hordes of Japanese visitors to Kōbe are the *ijinkan*, or Western-style brick and clapboard houses of **Kitano** (北野), 1km north of Sannomiya Station. The area's steep, narrow streets, lined with fashionable cafés, restaurants and shops, are pleasant to explore and occasionally throw up odd surprises, such as a mosque and a Jain temple. However, virtually all the *ijinkan* had to be reconstructed after the 1995 earthquake and most are now fairly tacky reconstructions heavily focused on souvenir sales. Entry fees are ¥500–700, but it is possible to buy a passport for three of the houses from a booth outside the Orandakan (the former home of the Dutch consul-general) for ¥1300.

From the top of Kitano, it's a short walk across to the **Shin-Kōbe Ropeway** (新神戸ロープウェー; daily: March 20 to July 19 & Sept–Nov Mon–Fri 9.30am–5.30pm, Sat & Sun 9.30am–9pm; July 20 to Aug 9.30am–9pm; Dec to March 19 9.30am–5.30pm; ¥550 one-way, ¥1000 return). The cable car provides sweeping views of the bay on the way up to the restful **Nunobiki Herb Park** (opens 30min later and closes 30min earlier than the cable car; ¥200), a flower garden with a field of lavender and glasshouses stocked with more exotic blooms. Hiking up the hill along the course, starting behind Shin-Kōbe Station, takes around thirty minutes.

Kōbe Harbour

Kōbe's **harbour** lies directly south of Nankin-machi. Here you'll find the city's most striking architectural feature – the filigree roof of **Kōbe Maritime Museum** (神戸海洋博物館; Tues–Sun 10am–4.30pm; ¥500, or ¥800 including entrance to the Port Tower; ⓣ078/327-8983), a swooping white framework symbolizing waves and sails. It's quite a contrast with the tapered red casing of the adjacent Port Tower, which makes a dramatic sight when viewed at dusk from the wharf of the Harbor Land development. The museum itself contains detailed models of a wide range of ships and intriguing audiovisual displays, and has good English explanations, although it lacks the impact of its exterior. If you just want a bird's-eye view of the city, go up to the observation lounge on the 24th floor of **Kōbe City Hall** (神戸市役所; Mon–Fri 8.15am–9pm, Sat & Sun 10am–9pm; free), back on Flower Road, rather than pay ¥600 to enter the Port Tower.

The surrounding **Meriken Park** (メリケンパーク) is a pleasant place to chill out and take in the harbour views, as is the newer **Harbor Land** development, directly across the bay, where spruced-up brick wharf buildings are joined by modern shopping malls, a cinema complex and a huge Ferris wheel.

The rest of the city

East of the city centre, **Rokkō Island** (六甲アイランド) is something of a *gaijin* ghetto of multinational offices and expat apartments. The main tourist attraction

Kobe Tetsujin Project

Perhaps only in Japan would $1.4 million be spent on building a giant-sized statue of a fictional robot as a symbol of a city's revival following a major catastrophe. That's exactly what has happened in Kōbe, where the latest must-see attraction is an impressive 18m-tall, fifty-tonne replica of the famous manga and anime robot **Testujin 28**. Located in Wakamatsu Park, an area of the city that was hardest hit by the 1995 earthquake, the full-scale robot dwarfs the neighbouring Daimaru department store as it strides across a plaza, his metal fists striking a punch.

Mitsuteru Yokoyama (1934–2004), the manga artist who created Tetsujin 28, was a native of Kōbe. His Tetsujin, literally "iron man", was the first giant robot to appear in manga, in 1956. Later, the manga was adapted into an animated television series, which was first broadcast in 1963. Set in the then distant year 2000, its heroes were the plucky boy detective Shōtarō Kaneda and his radio-controlled robot, Tetsujin 28, which he used to battle the usual cast of deranged villains. The inspiration for Yokoyama's work apparently came from his childhood experience of World War II, when Kōbe was severely bombed. To get to Wakamatsu Park, take the JR line from Nishinomiya to Shin Nagata Station (10min).

here is the **Kōbe Fashion Museum** (神戸ファッション美術館; daily except Wed 10am–5.30pm; ¥500; ⓣ078-858-0050). Housed inside what looks like a docked *Starship Enterprise*, this museum is a must for fashionistas, with regular special exhibitions that mainly focus on historical developments and classic couture collections, as well as an extensive multilingual library of fashion magazines. To reach the Fashion Museum, take the Rokkō Line monorail from JR Sumiyoshi or Hanshin Uozaki stations to Island Centre Station (¥240), from where it's a couple of minutes' walk from the southeast exit.

On the way back from Rokkō Island, hop off the Rokkō Liner train at Minami Uozaki Station and walk five minutes east to the Uozaki-Gō area (魚崎郷), part of the Nada sake-brewing district. Here you can visit two **breweries** and see the production of sake, as well as sample a few free thimblefuls. Hamafukutsuru (浜副鶴; Tues–Sun 10am–5pm; ⓣ078/411-0942) has good explanations in English of the brewing process, which you can observe from decks overlooking the production area. Sakuramasamune (櫻正宗; daily 10am–10pm; ⓣ078/436-3030) has some historical exhibits on display, as well as an in-house restaurant, *Sakuraen*, where you can enjoy lunch and dinner with the house brews.

Located about ten minutes' walk from Hanshin Iwaya or JR Nada stations' south exits (both stations are east of Sannomiya on their respective lines) is the **Disaster Reduction and Human Renovation Institution** (人と防災未来センター; Tues–Sun 9.30am–4.30pm, Fri & Sat 9.30am–7pm; ¥800 for both museums, ¥500 for one; ⓣ078/262-5050), two conjoined museums dedicated to the **Great Hanshin-Awaji Earthquake**. The Disaster Reduction Museum is the more interesting of the two, and its hi-tech multimedia facilities, interactive exhibits and film screenings devoted to the 1995 disaster make this one of Kōbe's highlights. Queue in the lobby for guidance to the fourth floor, where you'll see two short films before proceeding to the incredibly detailed exhibits. Audio guides are available but there are often English-speaking volunteers on hand, some of them quake survivors, who are happy to answer questions.

If you're able to spare the time, a visit to the nearby Andō Tadao-designed **Hyogo Prefectural Museum of Art** (兵庫県立美術館; Tues–Sun 10am–5.30pm; ¥500, ¥1200 for special exhibitions; ⓣ078/262-0901) is highly recommended. Exhibitions tend to focus on artists from the prefecture, but as this includes the postwar Gutai – a controversial group of loosely aligned 1950s artists who went very much against the local grain with their stunts and visceral visual art – the quality is extremely high.

Eating, drinking and nightlife

Kōbe's long history of international exchange has given it a reputation for having the best Western-style and ethnic cuisine **restaurants**, all aimed at Japanese palates. Despite the density of restaurants catering to Chinese and Indian cuisine, it can be difficult to find a good curry or authentic dim sum. The most cosmopolitan dining area is between Sannomiya Station and Kitano-zaka, where you can also find the local delicacy, Kōbe beef – expensive slices of meat heavily marbled with fat. While Kōbe doesn't have as strong a club scene as neighbouring Ōsaka, it does have a good range of **bars**, most clustered around Sannomiya and Motomachi, and all within easy walking distance of each other. There are also several **cinemas** around Sannomiya.

Restaurants and cafés

Beef Steak Kawamura 6F 1-10-6 Kitanagasa-dōri ⓣ078/335-0708. Kawamura serves award-wining local beef in an opulent setting complete with Greco-Roman statues and chandeliers. The deluxe Kōbe beef lunch sets start at ¥9000, while set dinner courses are from ¥18,000. It's also possible to order a la carte. Daily 11.30am–3pm & 5–9.30pm.

Café Fish 2-8 Hatoba-chō ⓣ078/334-1820. Easily recognizable by the giant metal fish outside, this funky warehouse-style café in the Harbor Land development serves tasty fish and seafood burgers (¥1050) and is a relaxing place to while away a few hours gazing out on the harbour. Daily 11.30am–8pm.

Diente Diente 3-12-2 Kitanagasa-dōri ⓣ078/332-3131. Trendy Spanish café and restaurant with an excellent wine list and a good tapas menu (dishes from ¥650). A fun place for an evening with friends. Daily 5pm–5am.

Enishi 8F 3-2-3 Kitanagasa-dōri ⓣ078/326-8655. Classy Japanese lounge restaurant with great night views over JR Motomachi Station and the surrounding area, serving fresh seafood dishes (from ¥1500) and a wonderful range of local sake and *shōchū*. No English menu but foreigners are welcome. Daily 5pm–1.30am.

Ganesha Ghar 4F 1-6-21 Nakayamate-dōri ⓣ078/391-9060. Popular Indian restaurant serving fresh naan bread and delicious lunch (¥1000) and dinner sets (¥2800). Call ahead to reserve. There's also a branch in Kitano. Tues–Sun 11am–9.30pm.

Gun Ai Han Ten 群愛飯店 2-4-3 Motomachi-dōri ⓣ078/332-3635. In the heart of Nankin-machi, this no-frills Chinese restaurant has great lunch deals which include dim sum and tasty beef and chicken dishes ((¥900). Mon, Wed–Fri 11.30am–3pm & 5–8.30pm, Sat & Sun 11.30am–8.30pm.

Misono 8F 1-1-2 Shimoyamate-dōri ⓣ078/331-2890. This restaurant proudly boasts that it is the originator of the *tepanyaki* grilling technique, but it also has a reputation for serving top-quality local beef. Locals flock here for the 100g fillet (¥8400), grilled expertly on the counter hotplates. Daily noon–9.30pm.

Modernark Pharm Cafe 3-11-15 Kitanagasa-dōri ⓣ078/391-3060, ⓦwww.chronicle.co.jp/shop/shop_MODcafe.html. This vegetarian restaurant is spacious and light with lots of indoor plants. The daily "plate lunch" (¥1050) and quiche set (¥850) are great choices. Also recommended are the organic fresh juices and scrumptious desserts. Daily 11am–10pm.

Bars and clubs

Bar Ashibe 2-12-21 Shimoyamate-dōri ⓣ078/391-2039. Dark and moody bar with lots of intimate seating space plus an extensive cocktail menu. Popular with both locals and the expat crowd. Daily 6pm–3am.

Beber B1 & 6F 1-22-10 Nakayamate-dōri ⓣ078/231-6262, ⓦwww.beber-kobe.com. Weekend-only club specializing in r'n'b, hip-hop and reggae. Events are held simultaneously on both floors (¥3000 cover charge each floor), and attract large crowds of fashionable Kōbe youth. Fri & Sat 9pm–5am.

Café Talisman 1-3-12 Motomachi-dōri ⓣ078/391-3353. Funky tapas bar serving mixed olives (¥380) and garlic prawns (¥800), as well as a decent selection of Spanish wine, near the central Chinatown square. Live flamenco and jazz at weekends. Austrian hemp beer (¥600) and Portuguese sherries (¥800) are also on the menu.

Hobgoblin 4-3-2 Kano-chō ⓣ078/325-0830. Bustling British pub with live music and sports broadcasts. There's a range of local and imported draught beers as well as a large bar-food menu that includes fish & chips (¥1500) and tortilla wraps (¥1200). Daily from 5pm until late.

Sone Jazz Live & Restaurant Kitano-zaka Kitano-zaka ⓣ078-221-2055. The birthplace of Japanese jazz, attracting many top international artists as well as local talent. The first live set starts around 7pm; ¥1000 cover charge. Daily from 5pm.

Sonic B1 1-13-7 Nakayamate-dōri ⓣ078/391-6641, ⓦwww.sonic-kobe.com. During the week it's a sports bar but at weekends *Sonic* hosts popular DJ and dance music events, mixing house, world music and hip-hop (¥2500 cover charge). Daily 8pm–5am.

Listings

Banks and exchange MUFJ Bank and Sumitomo-Mitsubishi Bank are 5min walk south of Sannomiya Station, just off Flower Road. There's also a City Bank branch northwest of Kōbe City Hall.

Bookshops Kinokuniya (daily 11am–8pm) is on the fifth floor of the Loft department store, next to the Kōbe Kokusai Kaikan. Junkudo (daily 10am–9pm) also stocks English books and magazines in its Sannomiya shopping arcade branch.

Car rental Nippon Rent-a-Car (ⓣ078/231-0067), Kōbe Rent-a-Car (ⓣ078/241-5151) and Eki Rent-a-Car (ⓣ078/241-2995) all have branches near Sannomiya Station.

Emergencies The main police station is at 5-4-1 Shinoyamate-dōri (ⓣ078/341-7441). There's also a police box right opposite the tourist information centre at the Sannomiya Station south exit. In an absolute emergency, contact the Foreign Advisory Service on ⓣ078/291-8441. For other emergency numbers, see p.71.

Hospital and medical advice Kōbe Adventist Hospital, at 8-4-1 Arinodai, Kita-ku (ⓣ078/981-0161), has many English-speaking staff, but is a 30min drive north of the city. Kōbe Kaisei Hospital, at 3-11-15 Shinohara Kitamachi, Nada-ku (ⓣ078/871-5201), has an international division with many English-speaking staff, but, like the Adventist Hospital, is a little awkward to reach, being a 15min walk uphill from Hankyū Rokko Station. Kōbe University Hospital, at 7-5-2 Kusunoki-chō (ⓣ078/382-5111), is 10min walk north of Kōbe Station.

Internet Netsquare, under the tracks of JR Sannomiya Station, close to Flower Road, has both Mac and Windows terminals (7am–9pm; ¥100 for 10min).

Post office Kōbe Central Post Office is a 2min walk northeast of Kōbe Station. There's also a convenient branch in the Kōbe Kokusai Kaikan Building, directly south of Sannomiya Station, as well as a small postage-only branch under JR Sannomiya Station.

Shopping Kōbe has several large department stores, including Daimaru, south of Motomachi Station, and Kōbe Hankyū, part of the Harbor Land development beside Kōbe Station. The shopping arcades shadowing the train tracks between Motomachi and Sannomiya stations are a favourite cruising ground of Kōbe's youth, while the arcades around Nankin-machi have several cut-price electrical outlets.

Arima Onsen

On the northern slopes of Rokkō-san, northeast of Kōbe, is one of Japan's oldest hot-spring resorts, **ARIMA ONSEN** (有馬温泉). Since the seventh century AD, Arima has been famous for attracting emperors, shoguns and, in more modern times, the literati, all of whom have come to bathe in its gold and silver waters. It's even mentioned in the ancient chronicle the *Nihonshoki*. Hideyoshi Toyotomi brought the tea master Sen no Rikyu here in the sixteenth century to perform a tea ceremony, an event commemorated annually in November with the Arima Great Tea Ceremony. Arima has two kinds of mineral-rich hot springs, both recognized for their health benefits – the sludgy brown *ginsen* (gold spring) and the clear *kinsen* (silver spring) waters are believed to be effective for curing everything from rheumatism to high blood pressure, as well as improving appetite.

There are some top-class ryokan in Arima, where you can soak yourself in luxury on an overnight trip. However, if you can only visit Arima by day, you should take a dip in the **public baths**. The **Kin no Yu** public bath (金の湯; daily

8am–9.30pm; closed second and fourth Tues of the month; ¥650) is five minutes' walk uphill from the train station, close to the bus station and **tourist information office** (daily 9am–7pm; Ⓣ078/904-0708, Ⓦarima-onsen.com). Here you can relax in the kinsen waters, at the source, in a modern bathhouse. Outside there is a free footbath area, as well as a fountain of drinkable spa water. Heading up the Negai-zaka slope, lined with lots of small wooden ryokan and shops selling local crafts, you'll find the **Gin no Yu** public bath (銀の湯; daily 9am–8.30pm; closed first and third Tues of the month; ¥550) at the top, just past Nenbutsu-ji temple. Gin no Yu is much quieter than Kin no Yu and has a high ceiling with skylights; the light streaming in through the mist is mesmerizing. For more than double the price, it is also possible to visit the spas of some of Arima's ryokan and hotels, but opening days and times depend on the season. Check at the tourist information office to find out which private spas you can enter.

Practicalities

To reach the resort by **train** from Kōbe, take the subway from Sannomiya to Tanigami, then transfer to the Kōbe Dentetsu line to Arima Guchi (有馬口), where you may have to change again (same platform) to reach the terminus at Arima Onsen. The journey takes around 45 minutes and costs ¥900. There are also direct **buses** from Sannomiya and Shin-Kōbe stations to Arima; they take around forty minutes and cost ¥680. If you're coming from Ōsaka, take a local JR train to Sanda (JR Fukuchiyama line), where you can change to the Kōbe Dentetsu line. The journey costs ¥1290 and takes about 80 minutes. Alternatively, comfortable air-conditioned coaches from Ōsaka's Hankyū Bus Station underneath Hankyū Umeda Station cost ¥1330 and take just over an hour.

The tourist office has a detailed English map of the town and can help arrange **accommodation** should you wish to stay, although it is best to book in advance. *Tosen Goshobo* (陶泉御所坊; Ⓣ078/904-0551; ⑧) is the top place to stay in Arima – there have been lodgings in this exact location since the twelfth century, and its current incarnation – a fusion of Japanese and Western styles – is the height of onsen sophistication. Fortunately, they serve lunch to non-guests (daily 11am–2pm; from ¥2950), which is a great opportunity to experience the tasteful surroundings. *Nakanobo Zui-en* (中の坊瑞苑; Ⓣ078/904-0787, Ⓦwww.zuien.jp; ⑦) is another top Arima resort, which once hosted Princess Grace of Monaco; both the rooms and bathing areas look out onto gardens. One of the more traditional small ryokan is *Kami-ō-bō* (上大坊; Ⓣ078/904-0531; ⑤ including two meals), just up the main street from Kin no Yu.

The longest suspension bridge in the world

The **Akashi Straits Suspension Bridge** (明石海峡大橋), at 3.91km, is the longest suspension bridge in the world, linking mainland Hyogo-ken to Awaji-shima, the largest island in the Inland Sea after Shikoku. The bridge was still under construction when the 1995 earthquake hit (Awaji-shima was the epicentre), which caused the bridge to lengthen by an extra metre. Since opening in 1998, this commanding concrete-and-steel engineering feat, with a central span of 1.99km, has become a tourist draw in its own right, with fishermen and artists gathering on the promenades around its imposing base. You can enter one of the bridge's pylons and wander out 150m along the undercarriage of the structure. If you're a serious bridge-spotter, though, you might want to bus across the bridge to Iwaya on Awaji-shima and take a ferry back in order to fully comprehend the structure in its entirety. If you want more facts and figures on this marvel of civil engineering, visit the **Bridge Exhibition Centre** near Maiko Station, twenty minutes west of Kōbe by train.

Himeji

Of Japan's twelve surviving feudal-era fortresses, by far the most impressive is the one in **HIMEJI** (姫路), 55km west of Kōbe. The fortress, **Himeji-jō**, made the memorable backdrop to the Bond adventure *You Only Live Twice*, as well as countless feudal-era dramas and the Tom Cruise film, *The Last Samurai*, part of which was also filmed here and around the city. The splendid gabled donjons of Himeji-jō – also known as Shirasagi-jō, or "white egret castle", since the complex is supposed to resemble the shape of the bird in flight – miraculously survived the World War II bombings that laid waste to much of the city, and in 1993 it was added to UNESCO's World Heritage list.

Major **renovation work** is currently taking place at Himeji-jō on the central donjon, and isn't due for completion until sometime in 2016. During this period, visitors will still be able to enter the castle, and also inspect the repair process from inside protective scaffolding that will cover the donjon. While here, it's worth visiting the beautiful **Himeji Kōko-en**, nine linked traditional-style gardens, and there's also a couple of intriguing **museums** around the fortress walls.

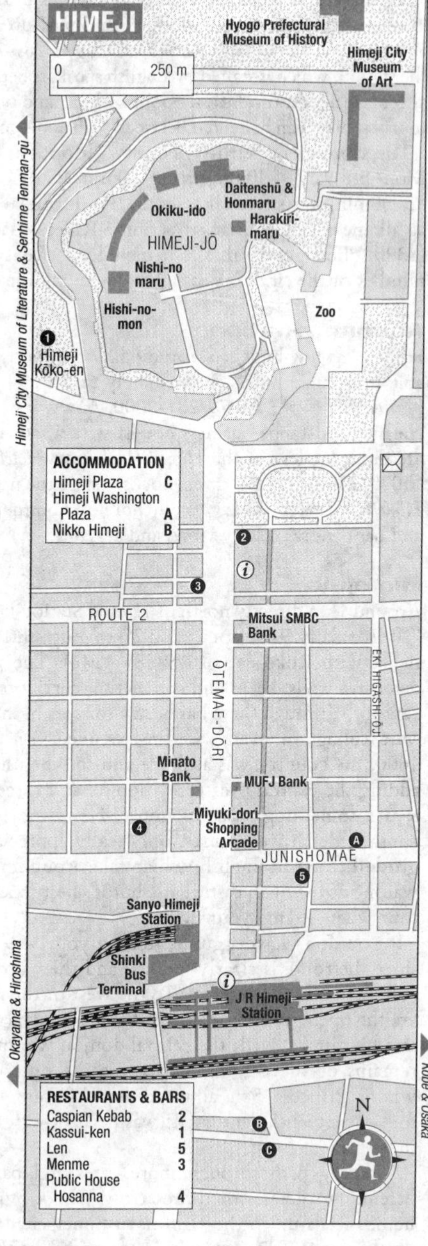

Arrival, information and city transport

Himeji is a stop on the **Shinkansen** line between Ōsaka and Okayama, and is also served by slower but cheaper *shinkaisoku* **trains**, which take forty minutes from Kōbe or an hour from Ōsaka. Long-distance **buses**, from Tokyo, Ōsaka and Kōbe, also stop beside the train station, which is around 1km south of the castle at the end of Ōtemae-dōri (大手前通り), the main boulevard.

Himeji's major sights are within easy walking distance of the station. Stash your bags in one of the station's coin lockers, and pick up a map from the excellent **Himeji Kanko Navi Port** (daily 9am–5pm; Ⓣ079/287-3658, Ⓦwww.himeji-kanko.jp) in the station, which is staffed by English speakers between 10am and 3.30pm. They can also make **accommodation** bookings here, and offer a free **bicycle rental** service to tourists; bikes can be rented between 9am and 4pm and must be returned by 6pm.

The convenient retro-styled city **"loop bus"** (ループバス; daily: March–Nov Mon–Fri 9am–4.30pm, every 30min; Jan–Dec Sat & Sun 9am–5pm, every 15–30min) starts from the Shinki Bus Terminal outside Himeji Station and stops at all the major tourist attractions. Rides cost ¥100, though the one-day pass (¥300) offers good value as it includes a twenty percent discount on entry to a number of the city's major sights, including the castle and some of the museums.

Accommodation

Himeji has few budget accommodation options but there are some quite reasonable mid-range hotels. Immediately south of Himeji Station is the *Himeji Plaza* (ホテル姫路プラザ; Ⓣ079/281-9000, Ⓦwww.himeji-plaza.co.jp; ④), one of the cheaper mid-range business hotels, with a sauna and communal bath. The rooms are more modern at the *Himeji Washington Hotel Plaza* (姫路ワシントンホテルプラザ; Ⓣ079/225-0111; ⑤), three blocks east of the north side of the station. The *Nikko Himeji* (ホテル日航姫路; Ⓦwww.hotelnikkohimeji.co.jp; ⑦) is a bit more upmarket and has panoramic city views and a gym.

Himeji-jō

Around 1km directly north of Himeji Station lies the main gateway to **Himeji-jō** (姫路城; daily 9am–4pm, Apr 27 to Aug until 5pm; ¥600, or ¥720 combined ticket with Kōko-en; Ⓣ079/285-1146). The present complex of moats, thick defensive walls, keeps and connecting corridors dates from the early seventeenth century, although there has been a fortress in the town since around 1346. By the time Tokugawa Ieyasu's son-in-law, Ikeda Terumasa, took control of the area in 1600, the country was at peace and so when he set about rebuilding Himeji-jō, adding the central five-storey donjon and three smaller donjons, the aim was to create something visually impressive. Even so, the castle incorporates many cunning defensive features, only really appreciated if you go on one of the **free guided tours** in English, which take around ninety minutes; guides are usually waiting at the main castle gate, but it's best to ask about the start time of the next tour when buying your ticket.

If you don't have a guide, finding your way around the castle is no problem, since the route is clearly marked and there are English explanations on plaques at many points of interest. To the west of the main gateway, the Hishi-no-mon, are the open grounds of the **Nishi-no-maru** (western citadel), where the *daimyō* and his family lived; the central donjon was only used in times of war. All that remains of the original palace are the outer corridor and "cosmetic tower", where Princess Sen adjusted her kimono and powdered her nose in the mid-seventeenth century. It was Sen's dowry that enabled the castle to be built in its present form.

A zigzag path through more gates and past turrets and walls from which defending soldiers could fire arrows, shoot muskets and drop stones and boiling liquids leads up to the **Honmaru** (inner citadel), dominated by the magnificent central donjon, **Daitenshū**. There are six levels within the dark and chilly keep, supported by a framework of huge wooden pillars, one of which is made from a 780-year-old cypress tree; touch it and it's said you'll have long life. On the top level, where the lord and his family would have committed suicide if the castle was captured (which it never was), you can usually look out across the city and see as far as the Inland Sea on clear days.

The rest of the town

Himeji's other sights are conveniently located around Himeji-jō's moats. On the west side of the castle is the splendid **Himeji-jō Kōko-en** (姫路城好古園; daily: Jan–May & Sept–Dec 9am–4.30pm; June–Aug 9am–5.30pm; ¥300, or ¥720 combined ticket with the castle), nine connected Edo-era style gardens built in 1992 on the former site of the Nishi Oyashiki, the *daimyō*'s west residence for his samurai. The gardens are separated by mud walls topped with roof-tiles, like those which would have stood around each samurai villa, and include mini-forests, carp-filled pools, rockeries and an elegant teahouse where you can experience the tea ceremony (¥500).

Ignore the depressing zoo on the east side of Himeji-jō and follow the moat grounds north past the red-brick building that once housed an armoury and is now the **Himeji City Museum of Art** (姫路市立美術館) to the informative **Hyōgo Prefectural Museum of History** (兵庫県立歴史博物館; Tues–Sun 10am–4.30pm; ¥200), in a striking building designed by the founding father of modern Japanese architecture, Tange Kenzō. The museum includes detailed scale models of the twelve castle donjons across Japan that survive in their original form. There's also a display of children's culture, beginning in the Edo period, an interesting multimedia exhibition on Himeji's festivals, and three opportunities a day to try on a Heian-style twelve-layered court kimono and samurai armour (free; 10.30am, 1.30pm & 3.30pm).

Tange's contemporary rival, Andō Tadao, has made his mark on Himeji at the city's **Museum of Literature** (姫路文学館; Tues–Sun 10am–4.30pm; ¥300; ⓣ079/293-8228), some 600m directly west of the Museum of History across the moat and just beyond the entrance to Princess Sen's shrine, **Senhime Tenman-gū** (千姫天満宮). The exhibits inside the museum are all in Japanese (the English-language leaflet only outlines the concept of the museum) and their authors are mostly unknown in the West, but the displays are imaginative. If nothing else, come here to admire Andō's ultra-modern design – a disjointed arrangement of squares, circles and walkways made from rough concrete – which also respects traditional principles, such as the *shakkei* (borrowed scenery) of the castle behind the museum and the use of water.

Eating and drinking

The Miyuki-dōri covered shopping arcade (みゆき通り), one street east of Ōtemae-dōri, is a good place to stop for a snack, pick up a bentō to enjoy within the castle grounds, or have an evening meal. There are also several good lunch options closer to the castle.

Caspian Kebab 68-170 Honmachi ⓣ079/285-1776, ⓦwww5f.biglobe.ne.jp/~caspian. Persian and Turkish restaurant close to the castle serving a variety of kebabs (¥980–2100), falafel (¥980) and curries (¥1575). Tues–Sun 11am–10pm.

Kassui-ken 活水軒 ⓣ079/2289-4131. Classic teahouse within Himeji Kōko-en; the *anago* bentō (grilled conger eel) is a delicious local speciality (¥1575). Daily 9.30am–4.30pm.

Len 324 Ekimae-chō ⓣ079/225-0118. This friendly restaurant has bamboo-lined floors and walls, and serves a variety of Thai, Vietnamese and Okinawan cuisine. Lunch sets from ¥900. Daily 11.30am–11.30pm.

Menme めんめ 68 Honmachi ⓣ079/225-0118. A specialist udon shop with noodles made on the premises throughout the day and a variety of healthy toppings such as tofu and vegetables to choose from. Menu items start at ¥400. Daily except Wed 11.30am–7pm.

Public House Hosanna 9 Tachi-machi ⓣ079/288-3299. British-style pub-restaurant with a cosy and authentic interior that's heated with a wood-fired stove. There are eight kinds of local and imported draught beer on tap, while the food is a mishmash of typical *izakaya* fare, British fish and chips (¥1500), and Italian pizza (¥850). Daily 5pm–midnight.

Travel details

Trains

The trains between the major cities listed below are the fastest direct services. There are also frequent slower services.

Himeji to: Fukuoka (Hakata Station; hourly; 2hr 15min); Hiroshima (every 30min; 1hr); Kōbe (every 30min; 20min); Kyoto (every 30min; 1hr); Nagoya (30 daily; 1hr 50min); Okayama (every 30min; 20min); Ōsaka (every 30min; 30min); Tokyo (hourly; 3hr 40min).

Ise to: Futaminoura (1–3 hourly; 6min); Kashikojima (1–3 hourly; 50min–1hr); Kyoto (hourly; 2hr); Nagoya (every 20–30min; 1hr 20min–1hr 35min); Nara (every 15–20min; 2–3hr); Ōsaka (every 15min; 1hr 45min); Toba (every 20–30min; 15–20min).

Kashikojima to: Ise (1–3 hourly; 50min–1hr); Kyoto (hourly; 2hr 45min); Nagoya (hourly; 2hr 15min); Ōsaka (hourly; 2hr 20min).

Kōbe (Shin-Kōbe) to: Fukuoka (Hakata Station; every 15min; 2hr 10min); Himeji (every 30min; 20min); Hiroshima (every 30min; 1hr 10min); Kyoto (every 10min; 30min); Nagoya (every 10min; 1hr 10min); Okayama (every 30min; 35min); Shin Ōsaka (every 10min; 15min); Tokyo (every 10min; 2hr 50min).

Kōya-san (Gokurakabashi) to: Hashimoto (every 20–30min; 45min); Nara (every 15–20min; 3hr); Ōsaka (every 20–30min; 1hr 15min–1hr 40min).

Ōsaka (Hankyu Umeda) to: Takarazuka (every 30min; 30min).

Ōsaka (Kintetsu-Namba) to: Nara (every 15min; 30min).

Ōsaka (Namba) to: Kansai International Airport (every 30min; 35min); Kōya-san (every 20–30min; 1hr 15min).

Ōsaka (Ōsaka Station) to: Akita (daily; 12hr); Aomori (daily; 15hr); Kanazawa (24 daily; 2hr 30min); Kii-Tanabe (hourly; 2hr); Matsumoto (daily; 4hr); Nagano (daily; 4hr 50min); Takarazuka (every 30min; 30min); Toyama (14 daily; 3hr 5min).

Ōsaka (Shin-Ōsaka) to: Fukuoka (Hakata Station; every 30min; 2hr 20min); Himeji (every 20min; 35min); Hiroshima (every 15min; 1hr 15min); Kansai International (every 30min; 45min); Kōbe (every 15min; 15min); Kyoto (every 15min; 20min); Nagoya (every 15min; 1hr 10min); Okayama (every 15min; 1hr 5min); Tokyo (every 15min; 2hr 30min).

Ōsaka (Uehonmachi) to: Ise (every 15min; 1hr 45min); Kashikojima (1–2 hourly; 2hr 20min); Toba (every 20–30min; 2hr).

Toba to: Kashikojima (every 30min; 30–40min); Kyoto (hourly; 2hr 20min); Nagoya (every 20–30min; 1hr 45min); Ōsaka (every 20–30min; 2hr).

Buses

The buses listed below are mainly long-distance services – often travelling overnight – between the major cities, and local services where there is no alternative means of transport.

Himeji to: Tokyo (Shibuya; daily; 9hr).

Ise to: Toba (7 daily; 1hr).

Kōbe to: Fukuoka (daily; 10hr); Kagoshima (daily; 12hr); Kumamoto (daily; 9hr); Tokyo (30 daily; 8hr); Tottori (7 daily; 3hr 10min); Uwajima (2 daily; 7hr 30min); Yokohama (8 daily; 9hr); Yonago (6 daily; 4hr).

Ōsaka to: Beppu (daily; 9hr); Fukuoka (daily; 9hr 30min); Hagi (daily; 12hr); Kagoshima (daily; 12hr); Kansai International (every 15min; 40min); Kumamoto (daily; 11hr); Miyazaki (daily; 12hr); Nagano (daily; 8hr); Nagasaki (1 daily; 10hr); Niigata (daily; 9hr); Ōsaka (Itami; every 20–30min; 50min); Tokyo (30 daily; 8hr 50min); Tottori (20 daily; 4hr); Yonago (18 daily; 5hr).

Ferries

Kōbe to: Imabari (daily; 6hr 40min); Matsuyama (2 daily; 8hr); Ōita (daily; 12hr); Shinmoji (daily; 12hr); Takamatsu (5 daily; 3hr 30min).

Ōsaka to: Ashizuri (daily; 9hr 20min); Beppu (daily; 11hr 30min); Kannoura (daily; 5hr); Kōchi (daily; 9hr 10min); Matsuyama (daily; 9hr 20min); Miyazaki (daily; 12hr 50min); Shibushi (daily; 14hr 40min); Shinmoji (2 daily; 12hr).

Toba to: Irago (8 daily; 50min).

Flights

Ōsaka (Itami) to: Akita (2 daily; 1hr 20min); Aomori (2 daily; 1hr 30min); Fukuoka (11 daily; 1hr); Kagoshima (8 daily; 1hr 10min); Kumamoto (7 daily; 1hr 5min); Miyazaki (5 daily; 1hr 5min); Nagasaki (5 daily; 1hr 10min); Niigata (5 daily; 1hr); Ōita (3 daily; 1hr); Okinawa (Naha; 5 daily; 2hr 20min); Sapporo (Chitose; 3 daily; 2hr); Sendai (12 daily; 1hr 10min); Tokyo (Haneda; 29 daily; 1hr); Tokyo (Narita; 3 daily; 1hr 15min); Yamagata (4 daily; 1hr 20min).

Ōsaka (Kansai International) to: Akita (daily; 1hr 30min); Fukuoka (2 daily; 1hr); Ishigaki (2 daily; 2hr 50min); Kagoshima (2 daily; 1hr 10min); Kōchi (2 daily; 40min); Kumamoto (daily; 1hr 5min); Matsuyama (2 daily; 50min); Miyako (daily; 2hr); Miyazaki (2 daily; 1hr); Nagasaki (daily; 1hr 10min); Niigata (daily; 1hr 10min); Ōita (daily; 1hr); Okinawa (Naha; 6 daily; 2hr); Sapporo (6 daily; 2hr); Tokyo (Haneda; 14 daily; 1hr).

Western Honshū

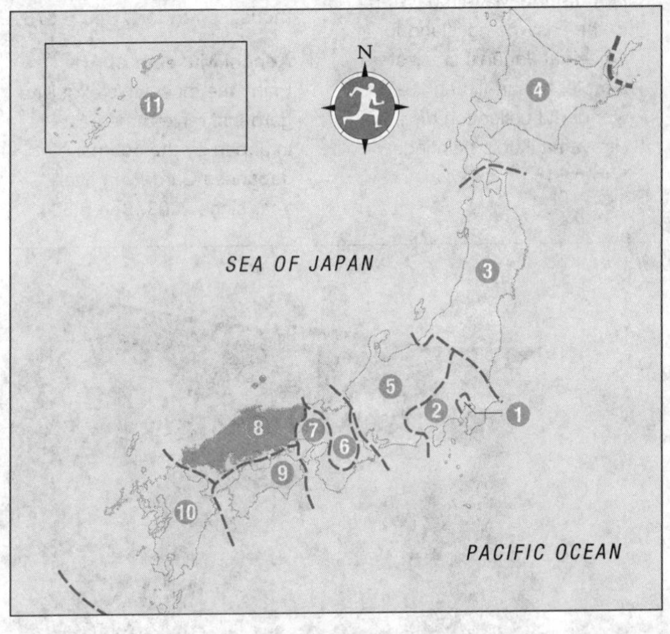

CHAPTER 8 Highlights

* **Washū-zan** Climb Washū-zan and watch the sun set over the Seto Ōhashi bridge and the islands of the Inland Sea. **See p.540**

* **Tomonoura** Wander the narrow, twisting streets of this picturesque port with a famous view of the Inland Sea. **See p.541**

* **Ikuchi-jima** Make a day-trip to the easy-going island for a peek at Japan's craziest temple, Kōsan-ji, and the wonderful collection of Hirayama Ikuo's paintings. **See p.546**

* **Miyajima** Watch the summer fireworks explode over Itsukushima-jinja's magnificent *torii*, or view the island's spectacular autumn foliage. **See p.557**

* **Tsuwano** Explore this picturesque old castle town by bicycle, then climb up to the Taikodani Inari-jinja through a tunnel of over a thousand red *torii*. **See p.575**

* **Adachi Museum of Art** Enjoy the museum's exquisite gardens, ranked the best in Japan by the Journal of Japanese Gardening every year since 2003. **See p.584**

▲ Itsukushima-jinja, Miyajima

Western Honshū

Also known as *Chūgoku*, meaning "middle country", **western Honshū** used to be at the centre of the Japanese nation, lying between the country's earliest settlements in Kyūshū and the imperial city of Kyoto. The region is split geographically into two distinct areas. The southern **San'yō coast** is blighted by heavy industry but borders the enchanting **Inland Sea**, while the rugged and sparsely populated northern **San'in** coast boasts some delightful small towns and a generally pristine landscape. The southern coast is easy to travel around, with Shinkansen lines, good local railway services and highways, while the northern coast takes more planning to tour by public transport, but easily repays the effort.

Though western Honshū is rich in history, with burial mounds on both coasts dating from the first century, it's a more contemporary event that brings most visitors to the region. Lying midway along the San'yō coast, **Hiroshima**, site of the first atom bomb attack and the region's largest city, is the one place you'll want to stop off en route to or from Kyūshū. At the eastern end of the San'yō coast, **Okayama** has one of Japan's most famous gardens, **Kōrakuen**, and makes a good base for visiting the beautifully preserved Edo-era town of **Kurashiki** or the island art project on **Inujima**. As you head west along the coast, one of the treasures of Hiroshima-ken is the timeless fishing village of **Tomonoura** with its gorgeous views across the Inland Sea. The port of **Onomichi**, just to the north, is also the jumping-off point for the Shimanami Kaidō, or Sea Road, which connects Honshū via a series of breathtaking bridges and islands to Imabari on Shikoku, taking in the laidback island of **Ikuchi-jima** en route.

The one island of the Inland Sea you won't want to miss is **Miyajima**, just west of Hiroshima and site of the ancient shrine **Itsukushima-jinja**. On the southern coast of neighbouring Yamaguchi-ken, pause to admire the elegant Kintai-kyō bridge at **Iwakuni** and the spectacular view across the narrow Kanmon Straits to Kyūshū from Hino-yama in the port of **Shimonoseki**, at the tip of Honshū. Inland, the highlights of the prefecture's small capital, **Yamaguchi**, are an impressive pagoda and classic Zen rock and moss garden.

East along the frequently deserted San'in coast, the old castle town of **Hagi** boasts a lovely cluster of samurai houses and atmospheric temples. Perhaps even more beautiful is **Tsuwano**, another small castle town nestling in a tranquil valley inland, further east in Shimane-ken. This prefecture is the heartland of Japan's eight million Shinto deities, who are believed to gather each year in November at the ancient shrine Izumo Taisha, near the appealing capital of **Matsue**. Matsue has the region's only original castle tower, as well as some old samurai houses and interesting museums. In neighbouring Tottori-ken you'll find **Mount Daisen**, the highest peak in the Chūgoku region, with great hiking in the summer and skiing in winter.

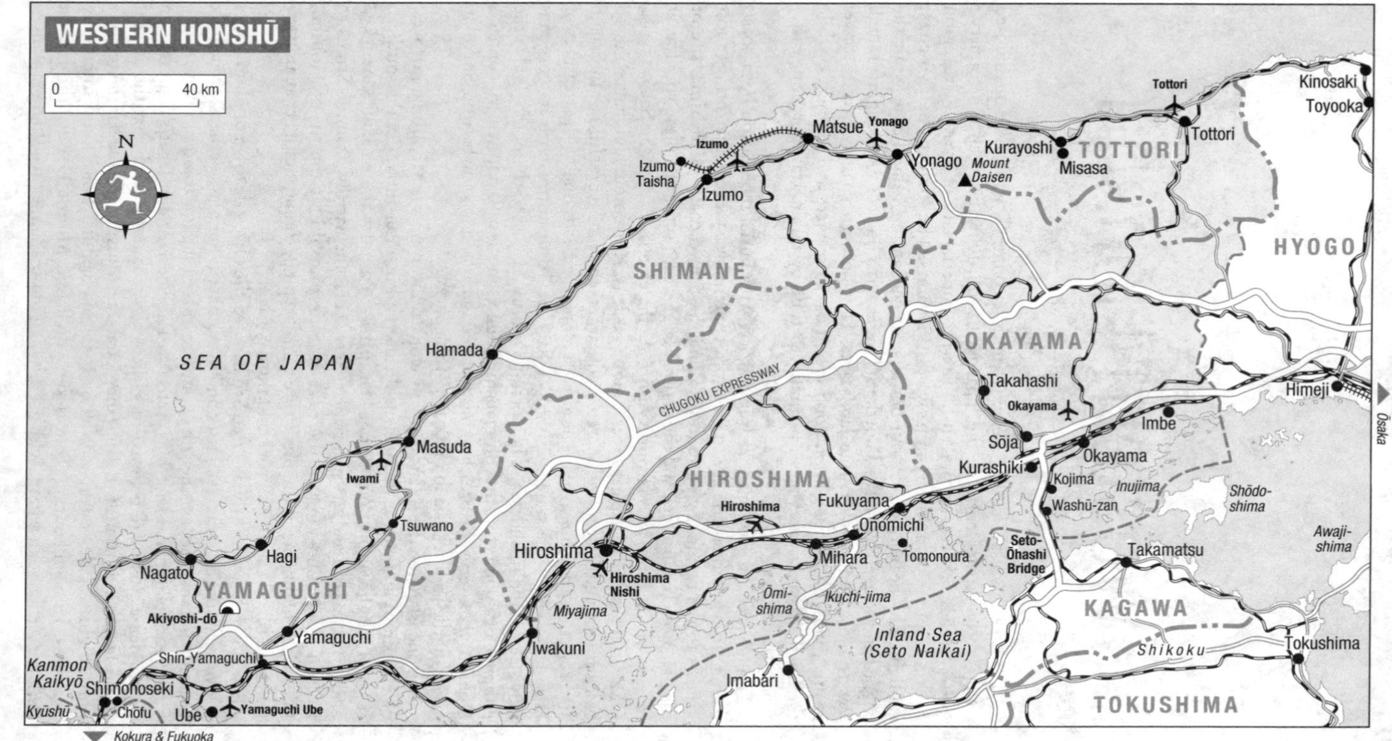
WESTERN HONSHŪ
0
40 km
N
SEA OF JAPAN
SHIMANE
TOTTORI
HYOGO
OKAYAMA
HIROSHIMA
YAMAGUCHI
KAGAWA
TOKUSHIMA
Kinosaki
Toyooka
Tottori
Tottori
Kurayoshi
Misasa
Mount Daisen
Yonago
Yonago
Matsue
Izumo
Izumo
Izumo Taisha
Hamada
Masuda
Iwami
Tsuwano
Hagi
Nagato
Akiyoshi-dō
Yamaguchi
Shin-Yamaguchi
Kanmon Kaikyō
Shimonoseki
Chōfu
Kyūshū
Ube
Yamaguchi Ube
Kokura & Fukuoka
CHUGOKU EXPRESSWAY
Takahashi
Okayama
Sōja
Kurashiki
Okayama
Imbe
Himeji
Ōsaka
Kojima
Washū-zan
Inujima
Shōdo-shima
Awaji-shima
Seto-Ōhashi Bridge
Takamatsu
Tokushima
Shikoku
Fukuyama
Onomichi
Tomonoura
Mihara
Hiroshima
Hiroshima
Hiroshima Nishi
Miyajima
Ōmi-shima
Ikuchi-jima
Inland Sea (Seto Naikai)
Imabari
Iwakuni

The Inland Sea

"They rise gracefully from this protected, stormless sea, as if they had just emerged, their beaches, piers, harbors all intact...Wherever one turns there is a wide and restful view, one island behind the other, each soft shape melting into the next until the last dim outline is lost in the distance."

Donald Richie, *The Inland Sea*, 1971.

It's difficult to improve on Richie's sublime description of the **Inland Sea** (Seto Naikai) and, despite his fears that it would all be ruined in Japan's rush to the twenty-first century, this priceless panorama has changed remarkably little. Boxed in by the islands of Honshū, Kyūshū and Shikoku, and dotted with more than three thousand other islands, the sea is one of Japan's scenic gems, often likened to the Aegean in its beauty.

Several islands are now connected by bridges and fast ferries to the mainland, reducing their isolation and much of their charm, but on many others you'll be struck by the more leisurely pace of life and the relative lack of modern-day blight. The best islands to head for are **Naoshima** (p.605), **Inujima** (p.534), **Ikuchi-jima** (p.546), **Ōmi-shima** (p.548), **Miyajima** (p.557) and **Shōdo-shima** (p.603), all popular for their relaxed atmosphere and beautiful scenery.

If you don't have time to linger, consider a boat trip across the sea or heading to a vantage point such as Washū-zan (p.540) or Yashima (p.602) to look out over the islands. There are also several sightseeing cruises, though these are expensive for what they offer; you're better off putting together your own itinerary using individual ferry services.

If you only have a few days, aim to take in Kurashiki and Matsue, as well as Hiroshima and Miyajima. In a couple of weeks, you could make a circuit of both coasts taking in most of the region's highlights.

Getting around western Honshū

A regular JR Rail Pass is the most convenient way of getting around the region, but if you plan to stick only to the San'yō coast consider the cheaper **JR West San'yō Area Pass** (see p.481). For quicker access to the region there are several **airports**, including two near Hiroshima, plus others at Okayama, Ube (close to Shimonoseki), Yonago (near Matsue) and Tottori. If time isn't an issue, then schedule a leisurely **ferry** ride across the Inland Sea (see above). **Renting a car** is a good idea, especially if you're planning to tour the quieter San'in coast, as you can make good use of the fast **Chūgoku Expressway**, which threads its way through the region's central mountainous spine, from where you can branch off to sights on either coast.

Okayama and around

The main reason for stopping off in the capital of Okayama-ken, **OKAYAMA** (岡山), 730km west of Tokyo, is to stretch your legs in its famous garden, **Kōrakuen**, considered one of Japan's top three. It's overlooked by the castle, **Okayama-jō**, around which the city developed in the Edo period, but aside from the intriguing **Okayama Orient Museum** there's little else of note in this modern town.

Okayama is also the transport hub for trips out to surrounding attractions. **Kurashiki** has a well-preserved enclave of picturesque old merchant houses and canals. From there you can head inland to **Takahashi** to discover Japan's highest

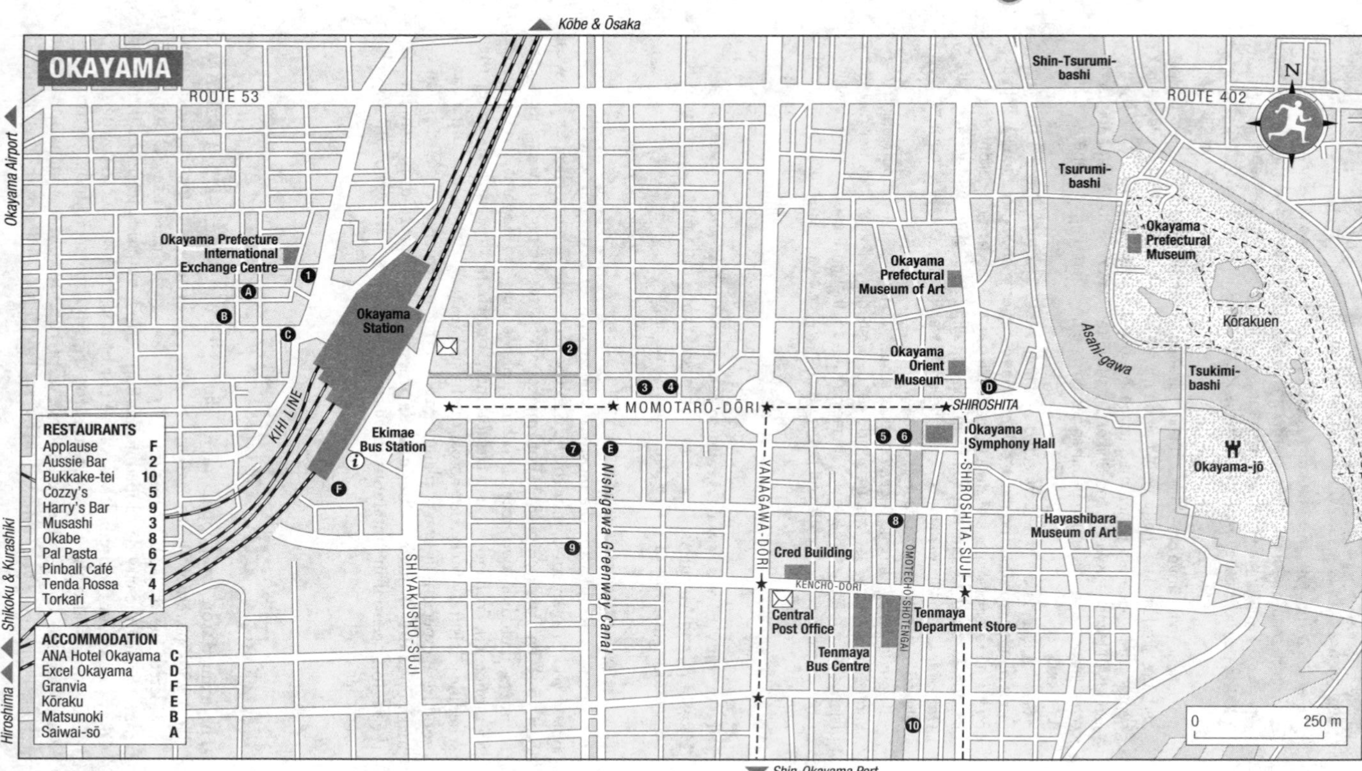
OKAYAMA
Kōbe & Ōsaka
Okayama Airport
Shikoku & Kurashiki
Hiroshima
Shin-Okayama Port
ROUTE 53
ROUTE 402
N
Shin-Tsurumi-bashi
Tsurumi-bashi
Tsukimi-bashi
Asahi-gawa
Okayama Prefectural Museum
Kōrakuen
Okayama-jō
Okayama Prefecture International Exchange Centre
Okayama Station
KIHI LINE
Ekimae Bus Station
Okayama Prefectural Museum of Art
Okayama Orient Museum
Okayama Symphony Hall
Hayashibara Museum of Art
Cred Building
Central Post Office
Tenmaya Bus Centre
Tenmaya Department Store
MOMOTARŌ-DŌRI
SHIROSHITA
SHIROSHITA-SUJI
YANAGAWA-DŌRI
KENCHO-DŌRI
ŌMOTECHŌ-SHŌTENGAI
SHIYAKUSHO-SUJI
Nishigawa Greenway Canal
0
250 m
RESTAURANTS
Applause F
Aussie Bar 2
Bukkake-tei 10
Cozzy's 5
Harry's Bar 9
Musashi 3
Okabe 8
Pal Pasta 6
Pinball Café 7
Tenda Rossa 4
Torkari 1
ACCOMMODATION
ANA Hotel Okayama C
Excel Okayama D
Granvia F
Kōraku E
Matsunoki B
Saiwai-sō A

castle, Bitchū Matsuyama, looking down from its mountain-top over a town of old temples. For a spectacular view of both the Inland Sea and the Seto Ōhashi bridge, aim for the mountain of **Washū-zan** on the southern tip of the prefecture, while fragments of the area's ancient history can be seen along the Kibi Plain bicycle route, which runs past fifth-century burial mounds and rustic temples and shrines.

Arrival and information

Shinkansen and regular **trains** stop at Okayama Station, just over 1km west of Kōrakuen. If you're heading across to Shikoku, change here from the Shinkansen to the JR Seto Ōhashi line. Long-distance **buses** arrive either at the Ekimae bus station on the east side of Okayama Station or the Tenmaya Bus Centre, in the heart of the city's shopping district. Okayama **airport** is 20km northwest of the train station; regular buses run from the airport into the city (¥740; 30min). Ferries arrive at Shin-Okayama Port, 10km south of the city; from the port, buses go to Tenmaya Bus Centre every hour or so (30min).

You'll find **tourist information** at the Momotarō Kankō Sentā (daily 9am–8pm; ⓣ086/222-2912) in the shopping mall beneath the station, near the *Hotel Granvia* exit. The **Okayama Prefecture International Exchange Centre**, 2-2-1 Hokan-chō (information centre 9am–5pm, closed Mon; library 10am–7pm, closed Sun; ⓣ086/256-2914, ⓦwww.opief.or.jp), two minutes' walk from the west exit of the station, has English-speaking staff, a good library and information centre, plus free internet access.

Kōrakuen and the city's other main sights are clustered around the Asahi-gawa, twenty minutes' walk down Momotarō-dōri, the main road heading east from Okayama Station, which **trams** run along. If you don't fancy walking, you can **rent bicycles** from several outlets by the station, behind *Hotel Granvia*, from ¥300 a day.

Accommodation

There are plenty of inexpensive business **hotels** around Okayama Station. If you want to stay in a ryokan or minshuku, head for nearby Kurashiki (see p.534).

ANA Hotel Okayama 全日空ホテル 15-1 Ekimoto-chō ⓣ086/898-1111, ⓦwww.anahotel-okayama.com. This plush hotel attached to the Okayama Convention Centre offers spacious, elegant rooms, two restaurants and great views of the city from the twentieth-floor bar. ⑦

Excel Okayama エクセル岡山 5-1 Ishiseki-chō ⓣ086/224-0505, ⓕ224-2625. Good-value mid-range hotel, smartly decorated and conveniently located near Kōrakuen and Okayama's shopping arcades. ⑤

Hotel Granvia ホテルグランヴィア 1-5 Ekimoto-chō ⓣ086/234-7000, ⓦwww.granvia-oka.co.jp. A close second to *ANA Hotel Okayama* in terms of luxury, with large, tastefully furnished rooms and several restaurants, bars and shops. ⑥

Kōraku Hotel 後楽ホテル 5-1 Heiwa-machi ⓣ086/221-7111, ⓦwww.hotel.kooraku.co.jp. Large, simple and stylish rooms. There's a Japanese restaurant on the second floor, computers in the lobby and business centre, and internet in all rooms. ⑤

Matsunoki まつのき旅館 19-1 Ekimoto-chō ⓣ086/253-4111, ⓦww3.tiki.ne.jp/~matunoki. This hotel has both Western-style and tatami rooms, the cheaper ones with shared bath. A Japanese-style breakfast (¥600) is served in the communal dining hall. ④

Saiwai-sō 幸荘 24-8 Ekimoto-chō ⓣ086/254-0020, ⓕ9438. Small, good-value business hotel with tatami and Western rooms – the cheaper ones share a bathroom. ④

The City

Although you can hop on a tram and travel the length of **Momotarō-dōri** to Shiroshita (¥140), the closest stop to Kōrakuen, the walk from the station is easy enough and takes you across the tree-lined **Nishigawa Greenway Canal**, a pleasant spot for a stroll. At the main crossroad, Shiroshita-suji, turn north and you'll soon arrive at the atmospheric **Okayama Orient Museum** (岡山市立オリエント美術館; 9am–5pm; closed Mon; ¥300), an unusual and well-presented collection of Near Eastern antiquities, ranging from Mesopotamian pottery and Syrian mosaics to Roman sculptures. A block further north, you'll see an angular modern building which is home to the **Okayama Prefectural Museum of Art** (岡山県立美術館; 9am–5pm; closed Mon; ¥300), a collection of more recent and local art. As well as dreamy ink paintings by the fifteenth-century artist and priest Sesshū Tōyō, there are examples of the local pottery style, *Bizen-yaki*, and regularly changing special exhibitions, for which you'll have to pay an additional fee.

Just north of the museum, turn east and head across the Tsurumi-bashi to the northern end of the comma-shaped island on which you'll find Okayama's star attraction, **Kōrakuen** (後楽園; daily: April–Sept 7.30am–6pm; Oct–March 8am–5pm; ¥350; ¥440 combined ticket with Okayama Prefectural Museum; Ⓦwww.okayama-korakuen.jp). Founded in 1686 by Lord Ikeda Tsunamasa, this landscaped garden is notable for its wide, lush lawns, which are highly unusual in Japanese garden design. Otherwise, all the traditional elements, including teahouses, artificial lakes, islands and hills, are present, and the black keep of Okayama-jō has been nicely incorporated into the scenery. The strange bleating sound you'll hear on entering the garden comes from a flock of caged red-crested cranes. Fortunately, Kōrakuen is large enough to soak up the kinds of crowds that deluge other famous gardens, such as Kenroku-en in Kanazawa and Ritsurin-kōen in Takamatsu.

Kibi Plain bicycle road

The 15min-long **Kibi Plain bicycle road** (吉備路サイクリングロード), accessed from either Okayama or Kurashiki (see p.534), is an enjoyable way to see an area of countryside studded with ancient burial grounds, shrines and temples. Running from Bizen-Ichinomiya Station in the east to Sōja Station in the west, the route takes about four hours to cycle, or a full day to walk. Bikes can be rented at either station (¥200/hr, or ¥1000/day) and dropped off at the other end.

In the fourth century this area, known as Kibi-no-kuni, was the centre of early Japanese civilization. Lords were buried in giant keyhole-shaped mounds known as *kofun*, one of which can be visited along the cycle route. Starting from **Bizen-Ichinomiya Station** (備前一宮駅), three stops from Okayama on the JR Kibi line, cross the tracks and follow the cycle path to Kibitsuhiko-jinja, an ordinary shrine beside a pond notable only for its huge stone lantern, one of the largest in Japan. Around 300m further southwest is the much more impressive **Kibitsu-jinja** (吉備津神社), dating from 1425 and dedicated to Kibitsu-no-mikoto, the valiant prince who served as the inspiration for the legend of **Momotarō**, the boy who popped out of the centre of a giant peach rescued from a river by a childless farmer's wife. This shrine nestles at the foot of Mount Naka and has a magnificently roofed outer sanctum, with twin gables.

Several kilometres further west is the **Tsukuriyama-kofun** (造山古墳), a burial mound constructed in the fifth century in the characteristic keyhole-shape (only really appreciated from the air). Measuring 350m in length and 30m at its highest point, this wooded mound in the midst of rice fields is the fourth-largest *kofun* in Japan. Around 1km east of here is a cluster of sights, including the foundation stones of Bitchū Kokubun-niji, an eighth-century convent, another burial mound and the five-storey pagoda of **Bitchū Kokubun-ji** (備中国分寺), a temple dating from the seventeenth century.

It's another couple of kilometres to the train station at **Sōja** (総社), from where you can return to either Okayama or to Kurashiki. Before leaving, check out **Iyama Hōfuku-ji** (井山宝福寺), a pretty Zen Buddhist temple, 1km north of Sōja Station along a footpath that follows the railway line. The celebrated artist and landscape gardener Sesshū Tōyō (1420–1506) trained here as a priest.

Outside the main gate to Kōrakuen is the lacklustre **Okayama Prefectural Museum** (岡山県立博物館; Tues–Sun: April–Sept 9am–6pm; Oct–March 9.30am–5pm; ¥200; ¥440 combined ticket with Kōrakuen), where the historical exhibits are presented with little ceremony and no English captions. Better to head for the smartly renovated castle, **Okayama-jō** (岡山城; daily 9am–5pm; ¥300), reached by walking round the island and crossing the Tsukimi-bashi ("Moon-viewing Bridge"). Its nickname, U-jō ("Crow Castle"), refers to the black wood cladding of the donjon, from the top of which you get an excellent view of the surrounding area. Founded in 1573 by Lord Ukita Hideie, the adopted son of the great warlord Toyotomi Hideyoshi, the castle fell foul of both the Meiji restoration and World War II bombings, with the only original bit of the building now being the Tsukimi Yagura ("Moon-Viewing Turret"), at the western corner of the compound. You can pick up a good English-language leaflet from the ticket desk at the entrance to the donjon, and inside there's the chance to dress up in kimono as a samurai lord or lady for no extra charge.

A final stop on the way back to the station is the small **Hayashibara Museum of Art** (林原美術館; 9am–5pm; closed Mon; ¥300), 2-7-15 Marunouchi, which displays selections from the Oriental art collection of local businessman Hayashibara Ichiro. There are some beautiful items in the collection, including delicate ink scroll paintings and exquisite nō theatre robes from the sixteenth century, but they're not always on display, so take a moment to leaf through the catalogue while sipping a free cup of green tea in the lounge.

Eating, drinking and nightlife

Okayama has the widest range of **eating** and **drinking** options between Kōbe and Hiroshima. The main districts to head for are immediately east of Okayama Station, where you'll find all the usual fast-food outlets and many other restaurants, and along Omotechō-shōtengai, the covered shopping street closer to the river. Local dishes include *somen*, handmade noodles dried in the sun and often served cold in summer, and *Okayama barazushi* (festival sushi), a mound of vinegared rice covered with seafood and regional vegetables.

There's not a huge variety of **nightlife**, but several jolly *izakaya* cater to a mainly younger crowd. The mauve cylindrical building at the start of the Omotechō-shōtengai is the **Okayama Symphony Hall**; check with tourist information as to what concerts are on. Towards the southern end of the arcade several cinemas show mainstream films.

Restaurants

Applause *Hotel Granvia* (see p.531), 1-5 Ekimoto-chō. The main lounge bar on the nineteenth floor of this upmarket hotel does good-value buffet lunches between 11.30am and 2.30pm. The cityscape view, especially at night, is unbeatable.

Bukkake-tei ぶっかけ亭 2-6-59 Omotechō-shōtengai. Located inside the main shopping arcade, this restaurant specializes in udon noodles, served in cheap set menus (around ¥800) with tempura on rice. Open 11am–7.30pm; closed Tues.

Cozzy's 1-1-40 Omotechō. A rival to the myriad coffee chains in the Omotechō area, this chic little café has espresso drinks, sandwiches and a wide range of gourmet hamburgers including ones with avocado or *teriyaki* sauce. Lunchtime sets around ¥900.

Musashi 武蔵 Momotarō-dōri ⓣ086/222-3893. This traditional restaurant is the best place to try Okayama cuisine. The set lunches at ¥750–1200 are the best value, while dinner starts at ¥3000. Closed Sun.

Okabe おかべ 1-10-1 Omotechō. All forms of tofu are celebrated in this little restaurant on a side street off the shopping arcade. Recommended dishes are daily *teishoku* (¥700) and the *yuba* (tofu skin) *donburi* (¥750). Open 11.30am–2pm; closed Thurs.

Pal Pasta パルパスタ Omotechō-shōtengai. Stock up on carbs at this cheerful corner café serving good-value pasta sets and coffee. Daily 11am–7pm.

Tenda Rossa Momotarō-dōri. Plaid tablecloths and rustic decor complement the pseudo-traditional

Italian menu at this large pink restaurant. The menu (Japanese only) includes pastas, pizzas and grilled meats and fish from ¥1200. Open 11.30am–2pm & 5.30–9.30pm; closed Mon.

Torkari 30-10 Ekimoto-chō. Great little Indian restaurant with good-value lunch and dinner specials ranging from *dal tarka* to chicken *masala* with rice and *naan* (¥600–1350). Daily 11.30am–10pm.

Bars and izakaya

Aussie Bar ⓣ086/223-5930. By the Nishigawa Greenway Canal, north of Momotarō-dōri. Popular with foreigners, and busiest on weekends. Look for the ubiquitous Australian yellow road sign hanging outside. Daily 7pm–3am.

Harry's Bar 2F Felice Building, Nishiki-machi ⓣ086/231-0727. Soft lighting and exposed brick feature at this upmarket bar, which overlooks the canal below. Open 2pm–12.30am; closed Sun.

Pinball Café 2F Honmachi ⓣ086/222-6966. Pinball's not on the menu in this casual café which turns bar in the evenings, though Guinness is, and often attracts a foreign crowd. Daily 11.30am–3pm & 5pm–2am.

Listings

Banks and exchange There are several banks along Momotarō-dōri, and you can also change money at the Central Post Office (see below).

Bookshop In the Omotechō-shōtengai entrance of Symphony Hall, Maruzen (daily 10am–8pm; closed second Tues of month) has a good selection of English books and magazines.

Car rental Nippon Rent-a-Car ⓣ086/235-0919 or Toyota Rent-a-Car ⓣ086/254-0100.

Hospital Okayama University Medical Research Hospital, 2-5-1 Shikata-chō ⓣ086/223-7151.

Internet You can get 30min free at the Okayama Prefecture International Exchange Centre, 2-2-1 Hokan-chō (9am–5pm; closed Mon; ⓣ086/256-2914).

Police Okayama Prefectural Police HQ, 2-4-6 Uchisange ⓣ086/234-0110.

Post office Central Post Office, 2-1-1 Nakasange (Mon–Fri 9am–7pm, Sat 9am–5pm, Sun 9am–12.30pm).

Shopping The Okayama Tourist Product Centre (daily 10am–8pm) on Omotechō-shōtengai opposite Symphony Hall is a good place for local foods and crafts, including *Bizen-yaki* pottery, masks and weaving.

Kurashiki

At first sight, **KURASHIKI** (倉敷), 26km west of Okayama, looks like just another bland identikit Japanese town. But ten minutes' walk south of the station, the modern

Inujima

Just off the coast of Okayama-ken lies the tiny island of **INUJIMA** (犬島), home to the Inujima Art Project "Refinery" (犬島アートプロジェクト精錬所; March–Nov 10am–4.30pm; closed Mon; during Dec, Jan & Feb Fri–Sun only; ¥1000; ⓦwww.inujima-ap.jp), the latest in a series of projects by the Bennesse Art Corporation to encourage regional revitalization through architecture and contemporary art (see p.607). Using local granite and waste products from the smelting process, architect Sambuichi Hiroshi has transformed the long-abandoned buildings and smokestacks of an old copper refinery into a strikingly beautiful eco-building and art space, where solar power and geothermal cooling create a naturally air-conditioned environment. Working closely with the architect, the artist Yanagi Yukinori has used the dismantled childhood home of the novelist Mishima Yukio as the basis for a site-specific artwork. Doors, windows and sliding screens are taken out of context and suspended from the ceiling in a dimly lit industrial space, while porcelain bathroom fittings are juxtaposed against a raked gravel surround, creating an installation that symbolizes the contradictions inherent in the modernization of Japan.

To **get here**, take a bus from Okayama Station to Saidaiji (Platform 9; ¥390; 35min), then change onto a bus for Nishi-Honden (¥500, 40min), where you can catch the ferry over to Inujima (¥300, 5min). Detailed timetable and visitor information is available at the island's website. There's also a shuttle ferry service from Naoshima (¥2000; 45min).

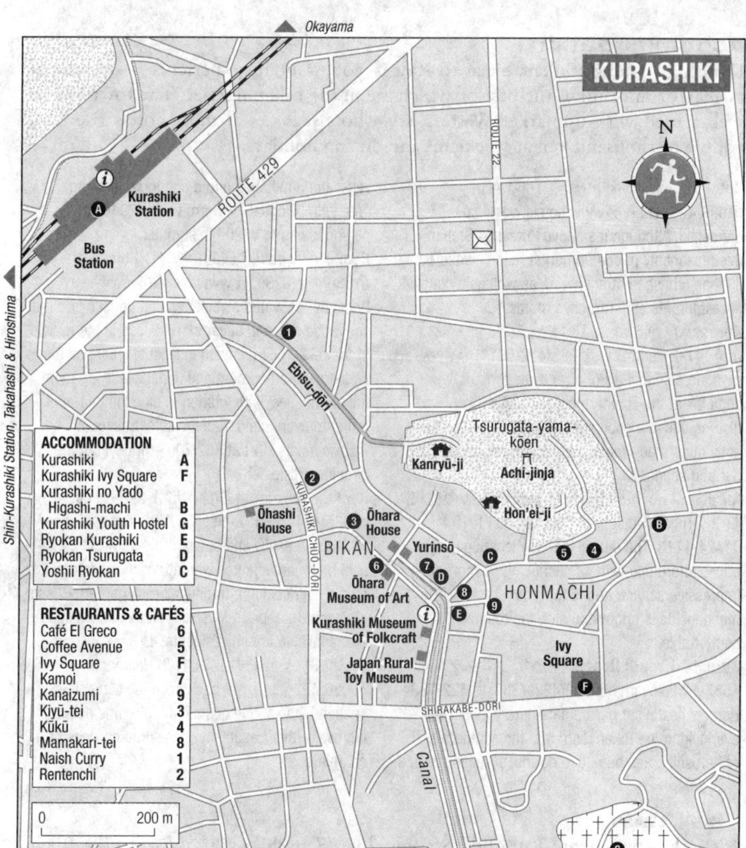

buildings and shops are replaced by a delightful enclave of black-and-white walled merchants' homes (*machiya*) and storehouses (*kura*) dating from the town's Edo-era heyday, when it was an important centre for trade in rice and rush reeds. The compact **Bikan** historical area (美観地区), cut through by a narrow, willow-fringed canal, in which swans drift and carp swim, is full of museums and galleries, the best of which is the excellent **Ōhara Museum of Art**, containing four separate halls for Western art, contemporary Japanese art and local crafts. Kurashiki is hugely popular with tourists and can get very busy during the day; to really appreciate the town's charm it's best to stay overnight and take an early-morning or evening stroll through the Bikan district.

Arrival and information

Local trains arrive at Kurashiki Station, fifteen minutes west of Okayama on the San'yō line (¥320). Kodama Shinkansen stop at Shin-Kurashiki, from where you can change to a local train (¥190). Regular buses from Okayama and Kojima (see p.540) stop in front of Kurashiki Station. The **tourist office** (daily 9am–7pm; ⓣ086/426-8681) is on the second floor of the brown building attached to the southwest corner of Kurashiki Station. There's another helpful tourist information office in the Bikan district (daily 9am–6pm; ⓣ086/422-0542), beside the canal.

Accommodation

Kurashiki is an excellent place to stay if you want to experience a traditional ryokan or minshuku, the best of which are in the Bikan district. The town is also well served with upmarket Western-style hotels. Rates at most hotels rise by a couple of thousand yen at weekends and during holidays.

Hotel Kurashiki ホテル倉敷 1-1-1 Achi ⓣ086/426-6111, ⓦwww.hotels.westjr.co.jp/kurashiki. Although it's above Kurashiki Station, this reasonably priced upmarket hotel, owned by JR, has a hushed atmosphere, as well as a couple of restaurants and attractive rooms. ⑤

Kurashiki Ivy Square Hotel 倉敷アイビースクエアホテル 7-2 Honmachi ⓣ086/422-0011, ⓦwww.ivysquare.co.jp. Part of a renovated factory complex at the southern corner of the Bikan district, this is a good mid-range hotel with pleasantly decorated rooms, a couple of restaurants, a bar and shops. ⑥

Kurashiki no Yado Higashi-machi 倉敷の宿東町 2-7 Higashi-machi ⓣ086/424-1111, ⓕ424-1118. The out-of-the-way location keeps prices affordable without sacrificing comfort or impressive service at this top-notch ryokan. The mood inside is bright and airy, the rooms clean and comfortable. ⑧

Kurashiki Youth Hostel 倉敷ユースホステル 1537-1 Mukoyama ⓣ086/422-7355, ⓕ422-7364. Homely hostel set beside a cemetery atop a hill overlooking the Bikan district at the southern end of Kurashiki. Has bunk bed dorms, excellent food, a self-catering kitchen and a comfortable lounge area with bilingual TV. Dorm beds ¥2940 per person, rising to ¥4200 in summer.

Ryokan Kurashiki 旅館倉敷 4-1 Honmachi ⓣ086/422-0730, ⓦwww.ryokan-kurashiki.jp. Recently renovated swanky ryokan housed in three converted rice and sugar storehouses in the middle of the Bikan district. Each individual suite has a Western-style bedroom and Japanese living room full of antiques, with women in blue kimono ministering to every need. Rates with extravagant *kaiseki* meals start at ¥32,200 – pricey, but the genuine article. ⑨

Ryokan Tsurugata 旅館鶴形 1-3-15 Chūō ⓣ086/424-1635, ⓦbit.ly/b37VRS. Cheaper than *Ryokan Kurashiki* and set in a 250-year-old canal-side merchant's house with atmospheric tatami rooms overlooking a traditional rock garden. Guests are served top-class *kaiseki ryōri* meals, which are also available to non-residents. ⑦

Yoshii Ryokan 吉井旅館 1-29 Honmachi ⓣ086/422-0118. Set back from the canal, this peaceful little abode has eight big rooms peering out over either beautifully manicured gardens or a courtyard. ⑨

The Town

It's a 1km walk from Kurashiki Station along Kurashiki Chūō-dōri to the Bikan district of seventeenth-century granaries and merchant houses, but first peel off west after the fourth set of traffic lights to check out **Ōhashi House** (大橋家住宅; 9am–5pm; closed Mon; ¥500). A rich merchant family, the Ōhashi prospered through salt production and land holdings. When they built their home in 1796 it was designed like those of the high-ranking samurai class, indicating how wealth was beginning to break down previously rigid social barriers. After passing through a gatehouse and small courtyard, and listening to a recorded history of the house (in Japanese), you're free to wander through the spacious, unfurnished tatami rooms.

Returning to the main road, the start of the **Bikan** district is marked by the inevitable cluster of shops and dawdling tourists. Either side of the willow-lined canal are beautifully preserved houses and warehouses, including the **Ōhara House**, with its typical wooden lattice windows, and the adjacent **Yūrinsō**, the Ōhara family guesthouse with its distinctive green roof tiles. Opposite, across a stone bridge decorated with carved dragons, is the **Ōhara Museum of Art** (see opposite), the best of Kurashiki's many galleries and museums. The next most engaging is the **Kurashiki Museum of Folkcraft** (倉敷民芸館; Tues–Sun: March–Nov 9am–5pm; Dec–Feb 9am–4.15pm; ¥700), in a handsomely restored granary around the canal bend, next to a stylish Meiji-era wooden building that houses the tourist information centre. The museum displays a wide range of crafts, including

Festival fun

Stately processions, fire rituals and phallus worship: Japanese festivals (*matsuri*) take many forms and are a central part of the local culture. Many have a religious origin, and with every shrine and temple observing its own celebrations chances are you'll stumble across a festival at some stage during your visit. Don't stand back – anyone prepared to enter into the spirit of things will be welcome. There's a list of major festivals and events on pp.57–59, while the following pages highlight some of the most important, unusual and fun *matsuri* that you won't want to miss.

Women dressed in *furisode* for Adult's Day, Kyoto ▲

Cherry blossom-viewing season, Tokyo ▼

Oshōgatsu

The year kicks off with Oshōgatsu (Jan 1), **New Year's Day**. In preparation, people clean their homes to sweep away the previous year's bad luck and decorate them with bamboo and pine sprigs. They also visit temple fairs to buy lucky charms such as *daruma*, chubby little red dolls with blank white eyes; the idea is to make a wish while drawing in one eye – the other eye is completed when the wish comes true.

On New Year's Eve, after watching the annual song show *Kōhaku Uta Gassen* on television and slurping a bowl of *toshi-koshi* soba – extra long noodles that symbolize longevity – people hurry to the nearest shrine or temple. At midnight, temple bells ring out 108 times to cast out the 108 human frailties recognized by Buddhism. The last chime heralds the New Year and a clean slate when everyone wishes each other *akemashite omedetō gozaimasu* ("please have a good year").

A year of festivals

The second Monday in January is **Adult's Day**, when 20-year-olds mark their entry into adulthood with a visit to the local shrine, with women dressed in gorgeous, long-sleeved kimono called *furisode* (swinging sleeves). Come early March, nature takes over as the trees burst with the first cherry blossoms; people gather for **blossom-viewing parties** (*hanami*), picnicking under the trees with copious amounts of sake.

In late July and early August, the skies blaze with **fireworks**, poetically known as *hanabi*, or fire-flowers. Traditionally, such displays were part of "river-opening" ceremonies, marking the start of pleasure boating, cormorant fishing (*ukai*, see p.394) and other summer activities. In mid-August the ancestral spirits are welcomed back to earth with special dances during **Obon**, the Buddhist Festival of the Souls; in particular, Tokushima's **Awa Odori** (see p.614) and Gujō Hachiman's **Gujō Odori** (see p.397) are the big dance events well worth attending.

Shichi-go-san (Nov 15) is a special festival for boys aged 3 and 5 and girls aged 3 and 7 – the ages when it's believed they are particularly prone to bad luck. Dressed in kimono, they go to the shrine to pray for a healthy and happy life.

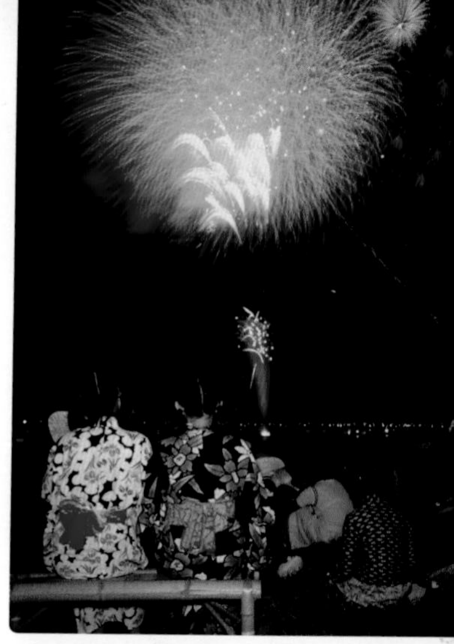

▲ Summer fireworks, Chiba

Local festivities

Towns and villages hold at least one local *matsuri* each year. Chiefly Shinto in origin, these celebrations focus on the village shrine and typically involve purification rituals, offerings and other religious rites. This will usually include parading the *mikoshi* (portable shrines) around the streets, various competitive games and much feasting and drinking.

Tokyo's **Sanja Matsuri** (p.158) is among the biggest local bashes, taking place on the third weekend in May when over one hundred *mikoshi* are jostled through the streets of Asakusa in a wildly exuberant parade. Kyoto's festivals are rather more sedate affairs, including the **Gion Matsuri** (July 17), one of the city's oldest festivals, which culminates in a stately procession of richly decorated floats; this originated in mid-summer purification rituals held to ward off the plague. The origins of August's **Nebuta Matsuri**, in Aomori (p.252), have been lost in the mists of time, but that doesn't stop everyone having a jolly good knees-up. As dusk falls, huge illuminated floats are escorted through the streets by thousands of dancers, accompanied by flutes and drums.

▼ Sanja Matsuri, Tokyo

Kanamara Matsuri, Kawasaki ▲

Mud wrestling at the Hadaka Matsuri, Yotsukaido ▼

Fertility festivals

Kawasaki's **Kanamara Matsuri**, a fertility festival held on the first Sunday in April, features a tumescent pink phallus and all sorts of phallic fun, from riding giant wooden penises to sucking on suitably sculpted lollipops. Similar genitalia-worshipping festivals happen at the **Ōagata-jinja** and **Tagata-jinja** near Inuyama (see p.383) every March.

There's also a fertility aspect to the **Warabi Hadaka Matsuri** (March), held in Yotsukaido, Chiba-ken, under an hour from central Tokyo. Men clad only in *fundoshi* (loincloths) splash around in a giant mud pool, daubing the crowd with mud for good luck. It's one of Japan's so-called "naked festivals", the most famous of which is the **Saidai-ji Eyo Hadaka Matsuri** held at Saidai-naka, Okayama-ken, on the third Saturday in February, in which some nine thousand men wrestle for two sacred sticks.

Fire festivals

Fire is celebrated in numerous festivals known as *hi-matsuri*. The sake-fuelled **Dōso-jin Matsuri** (Jan 15), in Nozawa Onsen (see p.348), combines purification rites with prayers for the coming year. Villagers wielding flaming torches attempt to set light to a wooden *mikoshi* built around a sacred tree, while men aged 25 and 42 (auspicious ages) fight them off. The sparks also fly at **Kurama**, near Kyoto, on October 22, as villagers carry giant brands of burning pine through the darkened streets in commemoration of the imperial torchbearers sent to make offerings at the local shrine. Five huge bonfires in the shape of *kanji* are set alight on the mountains surrounding Kyoto for the **Daimonji Gozan Okuribi** (Aug 16) – the aim is to guide ancestral spirits back "home" after Obon.

Bizen-yaki pottery, baskets and traditional clothes, and has a small shop selling souvenirs a cut above those found in most of Kurashiki's other giftshops.

A few doors down from the folkcraft museum, another excellent giftshop attached to the **Japan Rural Toy Museum** (日本郷土玩具館; daily 9am–5pm; ¥500) sells colourful new versions of the traditional playthings on display in the museum. Among a vast collection of dolls, spinning tops, animals and suchlike – most faded and tatty with age and use – the best displays in the museum are of huge kites and masks in the hall across the garden, at the back of the shop.

Kurashiki's other museums are lacklustre, so instead retrace your steps north over the canal and amble past the seventeenth-century merchant houses in the district of **Honmachi**, where you'll find some artsy craft shops, or stroll up the hillside to **Tsurugata-yama Park** (鶴形山公園), which includes the grounds of the simple **Achi-jinja** shrine and **Hon'ei-ji** and **Kanryū-ji** temples. You could also potter around **Ivy Square**, east of the canal, where the ivy-covered late nineteenth-century Kurashiki Cotton Mill has been redeveloped into a shopping, museum and hotel complex. There's another good craft shop here, as well as an atelier where you can try your hand at pottery (¥2100).

Ōhara Museum of Art

The impressive **Ōhara Museum of Art** (大原美術館; 9am–5pm; closed Mon; ¥1000) is easily spotted by its creamy Neoclassical facade. This is the entrance to the original gallery, established in 1930 by local textile tycoon Ōhara Magosaburō to house his collection of Western art, including works by Cézanne, El Greco, Matisse, Monet, Picasso and Rodin, hand-picked by his friend, the painter Kojima Torajirō, in Europe in the 1920s. The first gallery to exhibit Western art in Japan, it was a roaring success and has been continually expanded ever since, with Magosaburō's heirs adding contemporary Western and Japanese art to the collection, as well as ancient Chinese artworks and an excellent range of top-class Japanese folkcrafts.

The entrance to the **main gallery** is flanked by bronze sculptures of St John the Baptist and the Burghers of Calais by Rodin – both were nearly melted down to make armaments during World War II. Starting with Ōhara's nineteenth-century purchases, the paintings are displayed in roughly chronological order, with works by Kandinsky, Pollock, Rothko and Warhol included in the twentieth-century and contemporary art sections. Despite the impressive range of artists displayed, however, there are few truly memorable works in this collection.

In contrast, the **Craft Art Gallery**, housed in an attractive quadrangle of converted wooden-beamed storehouses, leaves a much stronger impression. The ceramics rooms display beautiful and unusual works by four potters who were prime movers in the resurgence of interest in Japanese folk arts (*mingei*) earlier last century: Hamada Shōji, Kawai Kanjirō, Tomimoto Kenkichi and Bernard Leach, the British potter who worked with Hamada both in Japan, at Mashiko (see p.179), and in England at St Ives. A room filled with the strikingly colourful and sometimes abstract woodblock prints of Munakata Shikō follows, with the last section devoted to Serizawa Keisuke, a textile dyer and painter whose exquisite work features on kimono, curtains and fans, and who designed both the craft galleries and the adjoining **Asian Art Gallery**. This smaller collection, on two levels, provides another change of pace with its displays of ancient East Asian art, including seventh-century Tang Dynasty ceramics and sculptures, and serene Buddhas.

The ground floor of the **Annex**, in a separate building behind the main gallery, displays unmemorable pastiches of modern Western-style art by Japanese artists, while downstairs you'll find bizarre contemporary works, made from Day-Glo perspex and the like.

Eating, drinking and nightlife

There's a bewildering choice of **restaurants** in Kurashiki, with the Bikan district being the place to head to for excellent-value set-lunch deals. In the evenings many places are closed, so you might have to head towards the station area. The town's signature dish is *mamakari-zushi*, a vinegared sardine-like fish on top of sushi rice.

Bars and evening entertainment aren't Kurashiki's strong point. *Coffee Avenue* is a coffee shop in the middle of a street of old merchant houses that transforms into *Robert Brown Jazz Avenue* bar with live jazz from 8pm (closed Mon; cover charge ¥500). And in July and August you can chill out at the beer garden in the inner courtyard of the red-brick, ivy-clad complex of **Ivy Square** (daily 6–9.30pm).

Café El Greco カフェエルグレコ Next to the Ōhara Museum of Art, this classic Bikan café in an ivy-clad building facing the canal is a popular pit stop for tea and cake. Seating is at shared tables and a coffee will set you back ¥400. Open 10am–5pm; closed Mon.

Kamoi カモ井 1-3-17 Chūō. Good-value sushi shop in an old granary facing the canal. Choose from the plastic food display in the restaurant window. Open 10am–6pm; closed Mon.

Kanaizumi かな泉 Honmachi. Koto music tinkles in the background at this traditional restaurant, specializing in freshly made noodles and serving excellent-value set meals throughout the day, all illustrated in a photo menu. A good place to sample *mamakari-zushi* at only ¥840 for a set meal. Open 11.30am–8pm; closed Mon.

Kiyū-tei 亀遊亭 Chūō. Rustic steak restaurant at the head of the canal that runs through the Bikan district. Lunches start at ¥1000 for curry rice or there's a three-course lunch or dinner menu for ¥2850. Daily 11am–3pm & 5–8.30pm.

Kūkū 空空 Honmachi. This quaint restaurant, located away from the bustle of the tourist track, serves up great Indian and Thai curries (from ¥650) with chai and lassis at ¥400. Open 11.30am–7.30pm; closed Wed.

Mamakari-tei ままかり亭 3-12 Honmachi ⓣ086/427-7112. A good place to try the local speciality *mamakari-zushi* – a set lunch including the sushi, alongside baked fish, tofu and soup, is ¥2500. Open 11am–2pm & 5–10pm; closed Mon.

Naish Curry ナッシュカリー Nishinaka-shinda 78-2. Just off the Ebisu-dōri arcade, this great little curry restaurant and bar gets pretty lively at night. Delicious sets from ¥800 – they'll ask you how spicy you want your curry and how much rice. Mon–Fri 6pm–3am, Sat & Sun 11.30am–3am.

Rentenchi 煉天地 Kurashiki Chūō-dōri. Intimate, dimly lit Italian restaurant with pasta and pizza meals for around ¥1500. It's sandwiched between two other restaurants, so look for the green awning marked "Enoteca Osteria Rentenchi". Open 12.30–4pm & 6–10pm; closed Tues.

Terrace de Ryokan Kurashiki 4-1 Honmachi. Elegant café inside the *Ryokan Kurashiki* (see p.536), opening out onto a beautiful traditional garden complete with moss-covered rocks, gnarled pines and stone lanterns. Indulge in tea and biscuits for ¥800. Daily 2–5pm.

Pottery in Imbe

Only dedicated lovers of ceramics will want to linger in drab **IMBE** (伊部), 30km east of Okayama and home of *Bizen-yaki*, Japan's oldest method of making pottery, developed here over a thousand years ago. The ceramics' distinctive earthy colour and texture are achieved without the use of glazes by firing in wood-fuelled kilns, whose brick chimneys you'll see dotted around Imbe Station. Beside the station is a **tourist information** counter (9am–6pm; closed Tues; ⓣ0869/64-1100), where you can pick up an English leaflet about *Bizen-yaki* and get directions to the local pottery museums, the best being the **Bizen Pottery Traditional and Contemporary Art Museum** (9.30am–4.30pm; closed Mon; ¥500), in the grey concrete block immediately north of the station; it displays both old and new examples of the ceramics, providing an overview of the pottery's style and development. There are plenty of kilns with attached shops in which you can mooch around, and at some there are studios where you can sculpt your own blob of clay, for around ¥3000. This is then fired and shipped to your home (for overseas deliveries you'll need to pay extra). The most convenient place to try your hand at making pottery is the **Bizen-yaki Traditional Pottery Centre** (ⓣ0869/64-1001), on the third floor of Imbe Station, where workshops are held each weekend and on holidays.

Takahashi

Some 40km northwest of Okayama, in the foothills of the mountain range that divides western Honshū, **TAKAHASHI** (高梁) is a small and charming time-warped castle town. Few visitors venture here despite the fine old buildings and temples in the **Ishibiya-chō Furusato Mura** ("Hometown Village") area, a name evoking images of a long-lost Japan. Except for the steep hike up to the castle – Japan's highest – all of Takahashi's sights are within easy walking distance of Bitchū Takahashi Station and can be covered in half a day. Finding your way around is simple, since there are plenty of direction signs in English.

Arrival and information

Takahashi's train station, Bitchū-Takahashi (備中高梁駅), is on the JR Hakubi line, just under an hour from Okayama (¥820) or 25 minutes on an express train from Kurashiki (¥520). You can pick up a Japanese map of the town from the tiny information office (9am–3pm; ⓣ0866/21-0461) at the bus terminal, next to the station.

The Town

The temples, ranged attractively at staggered levels along the hillside on the eastern side of the train tracks, extend north towards Furusato Mura. The single most impressive is **Raikyū-ji** (頼久寺; daily 9am–5pm; ¥300), ten minutes' walk from the train station, with its serenely beautiful raked-gravel garden. The exact date of the temple's construction is uncertain, though it is known that in 1604 Kobori Enshū, governor of the province and expert gardener, lived in the temple. The Zen garden he designed is maintained today exactly as he left it, with its islands of stones, plants and trimmed azalea hedges carefully placed to resemble a crane and a tortoise in the "well-wishing garden" style, and featuring the distant borrowed scenery of Mount Atago.

Rest by Raikyū-ji's garden before tackling the strenuous hour-long hike up to the castle, **Bitchū Matsuyama-jō** (備中松山城), following a shaded track through the hillside forest; even if you take a taxi from the station (¥1250), it's still a steep fifteen-minute walk from the car park. Takahashi's fortunes prospered from the mid-thirteenth century, when warlord Akiba Saburoshigenobu built the original fortress on top of nearby Mount Gagyū. Don't bother paying to go into the **donjon** (daily 9am–4.30pm; ¥300), restored this century, since there are few relics inside and not much of a view from its narrow windows. The vistas on the walk back downhill make the effort of hiking up worthwhile.

On returning to the town, if you have time, explore the **Ishibiya-chō Furusato Mura** area of old houses and buildings, sandwiched between the rail tracks and the Takahashi-gawa, and cut through by a stream crossed by stone bridges topped with miniature shrines. Of the several buildings here which have been turned into museums, the most interesting are the two **Buké-yashiki-kan samurai houses** (武家屋敷館; daily 9am–5pm; ¥400 for both) and the clapboard Meiji-era Takahashi Elementary School, now the **Local History Museum** (郷土資料館; daily 9am–5pm; ¥300), housing a jumble of items running from *mikoshi* (portable shrines) to a morse code machine. At the back of the ground floor are some evocative black-and-white photos of the town, while on the second floor you should look out for the dancing doll models made from old cigarette packets – a nod to Japan Tobacco, which has a factory in Takahashi.

Accommodation and eating

If you want to stay, try the *Takahashi Kokusai Hotel* (高梁国際ホテル; ⓣ0866/21-0080, ⓕ0075; ⑤), two minutes' walk north of the station.

Eating options in Takahashi are centred around the station, where there are several restaurants with plastic food displays. *Jūjū-tei* (closed Thurs), near the *Takahashi Kokusai Hotel*, is an inexpensive *okonomiyaki* restaurant, while across the road is *Kōzō Sushi* (daily until 7pm), a take-out sushi shop, ideal for a picnic lunch at the castle.

Kojima and Seto Ōhashi

About 25km south of Okayama, **KOJIMA** (児島), with its sprawling shopping centres and newly laid roads, has boomed since the opening in 1988 of the nearby 12.3km-long **Seto Ōhashi** (瀬戸大橋), a series of six bridges and four viaducts hopping from island to island across the Inland Sea to Shikoku. One of the most memorable ways to view this engineering wonder is to take a 45-minute-long boat tour (daily March–Nov 9am–3pm; Dec–Feb Sat & Sun 9am–3pm; ¥1550) from the sightseeing pier immediately to the east of Kojima station.

If you'd prefer to view the Seto Ōhashi and islands from dry land, head 4km south of Kojima to **Washū-zan** (鷲羽山), a 134m-high hill jutting out into the Inland Sea. Regular buses run to the lookout point from Kojima station. Stay on the bus past the fishing hamlet of **Shimotsui** and Washū-zan Highland, a tacky amusement park, and get off at the car park by the official lookout spot. From here you can climb to Washū-zan's summit and take in what has to be one of Japan's most glorious panoramas. If you have time, stop off in Shimotsui and check out the interesting **Mukashi Shimotsui Kaisendonya** (むかし下津井回船問屋; 9am–5pm; closed Tues; free), a museum of fisherfolk life, and wander around the old streets, taking in the castle ruins, the covered wells from which passing boats stocked up on fresh water and the Gion-jinja shrine.

Back in Kojima the **Bridge Museum** (瀬戸大橋記念館; 9am–10pm; closed Mon; free), a fifteen-minute walk west of the train station, is an unusual attraction, displaying scale models of bridges from around the world. You can actually walk over the arched museum building, inspired by a *taiko-bashi* (drum bridge), and enjoy the small park over the road containing eleven amusingly miniature bridges, a chessboard-like square decorated with bizarre silver statues (supposedly symbolizing the seasons) and a model of Stephenson's famous steam engine, the *Rocket*. Inside the museum, the eye is drawn immediately to the ceiling, painted with a lively mural of Edo-era travelling performers, craftsmen, merchants and priests.

Practicalities

Kojima is on the Seto Ōhashi line, twenty minutes by express train from Okayama (¥480). The **tourist office** (daily 9am–5.30pm; ⓣ086/472-1289) in Kojima Station can provide you with an English map and booklet on the area.

The best **place to stay** hereabouts is at the *Washū-zan Youth Hostel* (鷲羽山ユースホステル; ⓣ086/479-9280, ⓦwww.washuzan-yh.com), which has bunk-bed dorms (¥2100/person) and good food (breakfast ¥525, dinner ¥945), as well as impressive views of the Seto Ōhashi and the Inland Sea from its location at the tip of a promontory. It takes twenty minutes to reach the hostel on one of the hourly buses (last bus 5.30pm) leaving for Washū-zan from platform #4 outside Kojima Station.

Fukuyama and around

Some 65km west from Okayama along the industrialized San'yō coast is the old castle town of **Fukuyama** (福山), now the key industrial city of Hiroshima-ken's Bingo district and a jumping-off point for the lovely seaside town of **Tomonoura**.

Arrival and information

Fukuyama Station is on both the Shinkansen and JR San'yō **train** lines. The bus terminus, from where services run to Tomonoura (see below), is beside the station's south exit.

Inside the station, beside the north exit, is the **tourist information desk** (daily 9am–5.30pm; ⓣ084/922-2869), which has English maps and leaflets on Fukuyama and Tomonoura.

The Town

One of Japan's less interesting castles, **Fukuyama-jō** (9am–5pm; closed Mon; ¥200), immediately north of the train station, can be safely ignored in favour of the more memorable **Hiroshima Prefectural Museum of History** (広島県立歴史博物館; 9.30am–5pm; closed Mon; ¥290), just west of the station. Designed around the excavation of the ruins of **Kusado Sengen**, a medieval town buried in the nearby riverbed of the Ashida-gawa, the museum has some imaginatively displayed artefacts and haunting background music, as well as a reconstructed village street from Kusado Sengen, lit to re-create twilight in May. Next door is the **Fukuyama Museum of Art** (ふくやま美術館; 9.30am–5pm; closed Mon; ¥300), with a permanent collection of mainly Japanese art, focusing on contemporary works by local artists. The most striking pieces of sculpture are in the surrounding gardens.

Accommodation and eating

If you need to **stay** overnight, there are plenty of hotels near the station. The *Marunouchi Hotel* (丸の内ホテル; ⓣ084/923-2277, ⓕ923-6557; ④) has the cheapest rates, while the *Fukuyama Oriental Hotel* (福山オリエンタルホテル; ⓣ084/927-0888, ⓕ927-0991; ⑤) offers smart, spacious en-suite rooms.

There are plenty of **restaurants** along the south side of the JR station, while Tenmaya Department store, two minutes' walk south of Fukuyama Station, has restaurants on the seventh floor.

Tomonoura

There are few more pleasant ways to spend half a day or more in Japan than exploring the enchanting fishing port of **TOMONOURA** (鞆の浦), at the tip of the Numakuma Peninsula, 14km south of Fukuyama, and the inspiration for Hayao Miyazaki's 2008 film *Ponyo*. The town has one of the most beautiful locations on the Inland Sea, and its narrow, twisting streets and surrounding hills are easily explored on foot or by bicycle. Boats unload their catch daily beside the horseshoe-shaped **harbour**, which has hardly changed since the town's Edo-era heyday, when trading vessels waited here for the tides to change direction or rested en route to mainland Asia. Today, you're just as likely to see locals dreaming the day away on the sea walls, rod in hand, waiting for the fish to bite, or selling catches of prawns, squirming crabs and other seafood on the streets.

Arrival and information

Buses leave platform 11 at Fukuyama bus terminus roughly every fifteen minutes, and take around thirty minutes to reach Tomonoura (¥510). They stop just down the road from the tiny ferry landing building, inside which is an **information desk** (daily 9am–5.45pm), where you can pick up an English map of the town. **Bikes** can be rented from the adjoining car park (¥300/2hr, plus ¥500 deposit).

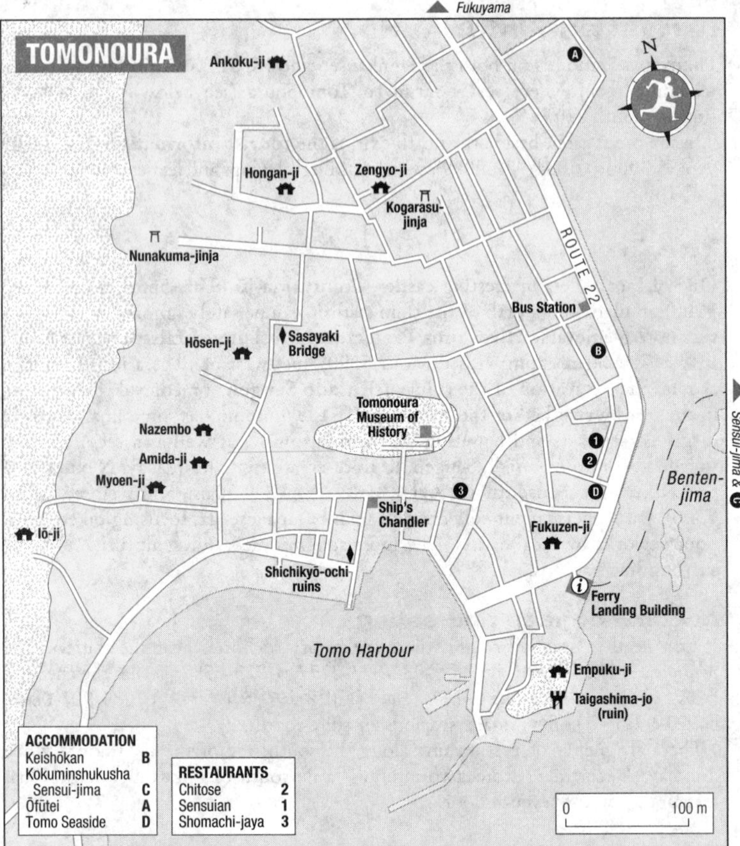

Accommodation

Accommodation in Tomonoura is limited to expensive ryokan-type hotels in charmless modern buildings.

Keishōkan 景勝館 ⓣ084/982-2121, ⓕ982-2510. Luxurious accommodation and a selection of indoor and outdoor baths make this seafront hotel an attractive option. ⑧

Kokuminshukusha Sensui-jima 国民宿舎仙酔島 ⓣ084/970-5050, ⓕ5035. Probably the best option for a night's accommodation isn't even in Tomonoura proper, but in Sensui-jima, the island that's a five-minute ferry ride (¥240 return) to the east. It has superior-quality tatami rooms and a relaxing set of public baths, including an outdoor rooftop pool. Unusually for a Japanese hotel, there are no TVs in the rooms; instead, you'll find pens and paper and a note encouraging guests to write a letter or even a poem. At a small visitors' centre beside the hotel, you can pick up a map showing four trails around the island, including one across its hilly centre and another passing secluded beaches. Breakfast and dinner are around ¥3000/person extra. ⑥

Hotel Ōfūtei ホテル鴎風亭 ⓣ084/982-1123. The most upmarket choice in town, whose highlight is its collection of huge roofop baths; thankfully at least the strikingly ugly hotel building is safely out of view at the north end of the town. ⑨

Tomo Seaside Hotel 鞆シーサイドホテル ⓣ084/983-5111, ⓕ982-3121. Traditional tatami rooms with sea views at a reasonable price, though the hotel is looking a bit frayed around the edges. ⑤

The Town

Get your bearings by climbing up to the ruins of the castle **Taigashima-jō** on the headland immediately above the ferry landing, where you'll find a small monument to the celebrated haiku poet Bashō and great views from Empuku-ji temple. To the west, you can see the gentle sweep of the harbour and the temple-studded slopes of Taishiden hill, while to the east is tiny **Benten-jima**, an outsized rock crowned with a temple to the Buddhist deity, and the larger island **Sensui-jima** (仙酔島), the best place to stay the night (see opposite).

Heading west into the town from the bus station, you'll soon hit the steps leading up to the **Tomonoura Museum of History** (鞆の浦歴史民俗資料館; 9am–5pm; closed Mon; ¥150), which has a few mildly diverting exhibits, including a miniature model of the sea bream-netting show held every day in May, when the local fishermen use age-old methods to herd the fish into their nets. The view from its hilltop location in the middle of the town, across a patchwork of grey and blue tiled roofs dropping away to the harbour, is one of Tomonoura's most pleasant.

Returning to the foot of the hill, follow the narrow road west past the Ship's Chandler shop and then turn left into the street lined with wood and plaster warehouses dating from the eighteenth and nineteenth centuries, some of which have been converted into gift and coffee shops. At the end of the street are the **Shichikyō-ochi Ruins** (10am–5pm; closed Tues; ¥400), a perfectly intact old sake brewery that briefly sheltered a band of anti-shogun rebels in the turbulent times prior to the Meiji Restoration. The water-washed steps of the harbour, topped off by a handsome stone lantern, are directly ahead.

Returning towards the town, keep an eye open for the sign pointing up a narrow pedestrian alley up Taishiden hill to the pretty temple **Iō-ji** (医王寺). If you're cycling it's best to leave your bike on the main road before hiking up to the temple, one of many founded by the revered Buddhist priest Kōbō Daishi (see p.499). You can hike down the hill eastwards past several more temples, including **Hōsen-ji** (法宣寺), where only a truncated stump remains of the previously 14.3m-wide Tengai pine tree. As the street turns the corner, just beyond Hōsen-ji, glance down to see the mini stone bridge **Sasayaki** where, as legend has it, a couple of ill-fated lovers fed up with the town's incessant gossip and intolerance, drowned themselves.

Continuing north for a couple of minutes, you'll arrive at the hillside approach to **Nunakuma-jinja** (沼名前神社), a large shrine which, although ancient, was recently rebuilt in concrete. More impressive is the traditional wooden nō stage within the shrine grounds that used to be taken around battlefields so the warlord Toyotomi Hideyoshi could be entertained. A couple of minutes' walk further north is **Ankoku-ji** (安国寺; daily 8am–5pm; ¥150), founded around 1270, and containing two wooden statues of Buddha, designated as national treasures, though neither they nor the temple's tatty sand and rock garden are worth going out of your way for.

Either wind your way back to the ferry landing along the narrow streets or follow the seafront to the south, then hike up the hill immediately to the north to take in one more view from the Taichōrō reception hall of **Fukuzen-ji** temple (福禅寺; daily 9.30am–5pm). It costs ¥200 to enter the airy tatami space with paper screens that open to reveal a striking panorama of the Inland Sea, a view which has changed little since 1711, when a visiting Korean envoy hailed it "the most beautiful scenery in Japan".

Eating

Being a fishing port, Tomonoura has a decent range of seafood **restaurants**, the best being *Chitose* (千とせ 11.30am–3.30pm & 5.30–9pm; closed Tues), a friendly place just behind the car park on the town's eastern waterfront. A delicious set meal of many dishes, including the trademark catch of *tai* (sea bream), costs ¥2320. In the same row of shops, pop into the charming *Sensuian* (仙酔庵), a café serving *macha* tea and *dango* rice balls in winter and shaved ice desserts in the summer. Also worth checking out is *Shomachi-jaya* (11.30am–2pm & 5–9pm; closed Mon), which serves tempura set meals (¥1400) in an atmospheric wooden building near the Chandler Shop on the east side of the harbour. On the dock south of the Shichikyō-ochi ruins, a café serves coffee and tea, and has some outdoor seating overlooking the harbour.

Onomichi

Twenty kilometres west of Fukuyama lies the enchanting port of **ONOMICHI** (尾道), overlooked by the houses and temples that tumble down the steep face of the wooded hill, Senkōji-san. Many Japanese come here to linger along the town's vertiginous byways, imagining scenes from their favourite films by local director Ōbayashi Nobuhiko. Onomichi is also a gateway to some of the islands of the Inland Sea, including **Ikuchi-jima** and **Ōmi-shima** (see p.546), and to Shikoku via ferry or by road along the Shimanami Kaidō Expressway.

Arrival and information

Trains on the JR San'yō line take twenty minutes from Fukuyama to Onomichi Station (¥400), a minute's walk from the waterfront. Shinkansen take nine minutes to Shin-Onomichi (¥400), 3km north of the town; from here a regular bus (¥180) takes fifteen minutes to reach Onomichi Station. **Buses** leave from outside Onomichi Station for Ikuchi-jima (see p.546, 1hr; ¥1250) and Hiroshima airport (1hr 40 min; ¥800; see p.551), thirty minutes west. Ferries to Setoda on Ikuchi-jima leave from the jetty immediately in front of Onomichi Station (40min; ¥800 one-way).

Tourist **information** is available inside the station (daily 9am–6pm; ⓣ0848/20-0005, ⓕ20-1361), where you can pick up an English map showing the walking route around the town's temples.

Accommodation

The cheapest **accommodation** options are business hotels, of which there are several immediately west of the station, including the *Alpha-1* (アルファ・ワン; ⓣ0848/25-5600; ❺) and the *Dai-Ichi Hotel* (第一ホテル; ⓣ0848/23-4567, ⓕ2112; ❺), just round the corner; rooms at the latter have sea views. *View Hotel Seizan* (ビュウホテルセイザン; ⓣ0848/23-3313, ⓕ22-3780; ❺) is a friendly place up by the castle with great views out over the Inland Sea and discounted off-peak rates.

The Town

There's a pleasant **temple walk** from Onomichi Station past most of the town's 25 temples; to complete the full course takes the better part of a day, by which time you'll be sick of temples, so skip those at the start by hopping on the regular bus from stand 1 outside Onomichi Station and heading east for five minutes to the Nagaeguchi stop (¥140). From here, you can catch the **ropeway** (daily 9am–5.15pm; ¥280 one-way, ¥440 return) up to **Senkōji-kōen** park (千光寺公園), which blooms with cherry blossom and azaleas each spring. The views from its hilltop observatory across the town and narrow sea channel to the nearest island Mukai-shima are impressive.

The most colourful temple on the hill is the scarlet-painted **Senkō-ji** (千光寺), packed with *jizō* statues and doing a lively trade in devotional trinkets, particularly heart-shaped placards on which visitors scribble a wish and leave dangling in the temple for good luck. Heading back downhill from here, you can follow the section of the temple walk known as the "literary path", so called because famous writers' words are inscribed on stone monuments along the way. The most

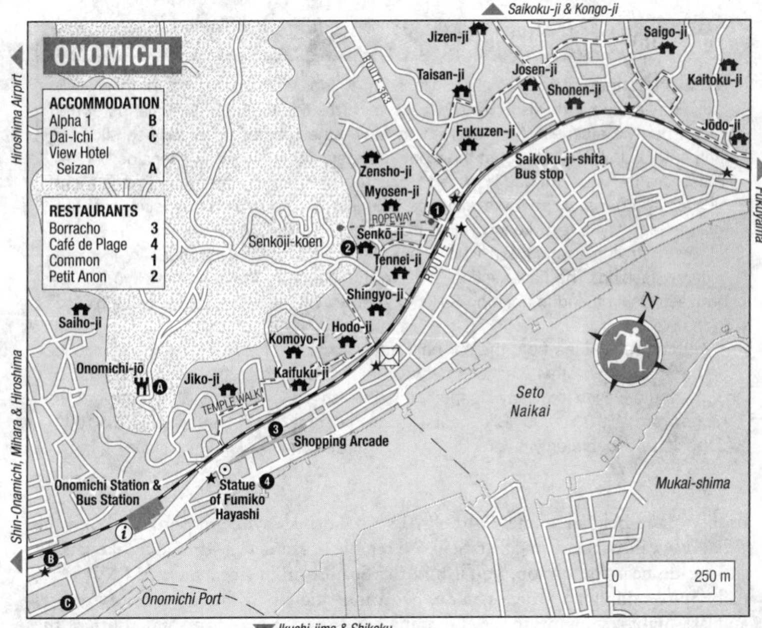

celebrated of the local writers is **Hayashi Fumiko**, a female poet who lived in Onomichi from 1917 and whose bronze statue can be found crouching pensively beside a wicker suitcase and umbrella at the entrance to the shopping arcade a minute east of the station.

The "literary path" continues past the pagoda at the temple **Tennei-ji**, just behind the ropeway base station, from where you can head east back up the hill towards **Fukuzen-ji** (福善寺). Dating from 1573, it has a vast spreading pine tree in its grounds, said to be shaped like an eagle, and its main gate is decorated with beautiful woodcarvings of cranes and dragons. Once inside the temple, look out for **Tile-ko-michi** (Little Tile Street), a narrow alley back down the hill which has been plastered over the last 25 years with ceramic slabs inscribed by visitors.

Continuing east along the flagstoned streets, head north up the hill when you hit the next main crossroads and you'll arrive at **Saikoku-ji** (西国寺), one of the largest temple complexes in western Japan and easily spotted by the giant straw sandals which hang either side of its imposing entrance gate; pray here and it's said that you'll find the strength to continue your journey.

The last temple worth visiting is **Jōdo-ji** (浄土寺), at the eastern end of the route. Pigeons flock around its squat two-storey pagoda, and there's an elegant Zen garden, with a tea-ceremony room transported from Kyoto's Fushimi castle, hidden behind the main hall of worship. To see the garden you'll have to pay the attendant ¥500.

Eating

Onomichi fancies itself as something of a gourmet destination and the tourist office produces a map in Japanese detailing an impressive range of **eating** options. Being a port, fresh seafood is the thing to go for, especially at the sushi restaurants clustered along the harbour front east of the station. Further along you can get a cheap lunch of salad and a drink at the trendy *Café de Plage*, which also opens in the evenings at weekends. At the base of the ropeway, *Common* (daily 10am–5pm) specializes in

The Shimanami cycling road

Onomichi is the gateway to the Shimanami Kaidō, which connects Honshū with Shikoku via the 65km Nishi-Seto Expressway. This ties together nine islands of the Inland Sea via a series of ten bridges, including the Tatara Ōhashi between Ikuchi-jima and Ōmi-shima, at 1480m the world's longest cable-stayed suspension bridge. These are the only bridges between Honshū and Shikoku over which cyclists are allowed to ride, and the route makes a stunning way to explore the islands of the Inland Sea. If you're a keen cyclist, it's possible to do the whole thing in a day, although staying overnight in Ikuchi-jima allows you to enjoy the scenery in more leisurely fashion. The final section takes in the 4km-long Kurushima-Kaikyō bridge between Ōshima and Imabari on Shikoku, the longest three-span suspension bridge in the world.

You can **rent bikes** from the car park attached to the ferry terminal in Onomichi, and from a dozen other locations between here and Imabari; they all provide maps of the route, which is clearly signposted in English along the way. Bridge cycle tolls range from ¥50 to ¥200. Bike rental along the route is ¥500/day, plus a ¥1000 deposit, refundable only if you return your bike to the place where you hired it.

freshly made Belgian waffles (¥400–670 with a drink), while in **Senkōji-kōen** the *Petit Anon* café at the turn-off to Senkō-ji temple has ramen, *donburi* and cake sets. In the arcade near the station, you'll find the Spanish-influenced *Borracho* (ボラーチョ; daily 5pm–midnight), where you can get drinks and tapas. There are plenty of bars and late-night restaurants in the entertainment district, Saikoku-ji-shita, south of the bus stop, in the narrow streets between the railway line and the waterfront.

Ikuchi-jima and Ōmi-shima

Among the Geiyo archipelago of islands clogging the Inland Sea between Onomichi and the northwest coast of Shikoku, **IKUCHI-JIMA** (生口島) and **ŌMI-SHIMA** (大三島) are both worth a visit. Of the two, Ikuchi-jima is the place to stay and has the best attractions, including **Kōsan-ji**, a dazzling, kaleidoscopic temple complex, and the exquisite **Hirayama Ikuo Museum of Art**.

While part of the fun of visiting these islands is the **ferry** ride there, you can also get to Ikuchi-jima by bus or bicycle from Onomichi along the Shimanami Kaidō (see above). Both islands are best explored by bicycle.

Ikuchi-jima

Sun-kissed **IKUCHI-JIMA** (生口島), covered with citrus groves, attracts plenty of tourists each summer to its palm-fringed beaches, in particular the sweeping man-made Sunset Beach on the west coast. The island can comfortably be toured by bicycle in a day, as can the islet Kōne-shima, which is linked by bridge to Ikuchi-jima's main settlement, the quaint **Setoda** (瀬戸田) on the island's northwest coast. Around the island, look out for the fourteen bizarre contemporary outdoor sculptures, including a giant saxophone and a stack of yellow buckets, which form part of Ikuchi-jima's "Biennale" modern art project.

Arrival and information

There are **ferries** to Ikuchi-jima from Onomichi (40min; ¥800 one-way) and Mihara, further west along the coast, which is on both the San'yō rail line and Shinkansen (25 min; ¥800 one-way). The **bus** from Onomichi (1hr; ¥1250) leaves from platform 7 in front of Onomichi Station and terminates at the southern end of Setoda; you have to change buses at the terminus on Inno-shima along the way.

The **tourist information** booth (daily 9am–5pm; ⓣ0845/27-0051, ⓕ26-4001), across from the Hirayama Ikuo Museum of Art, has maps of Ikuchi-jima and a well-illustrated brochure on the island's attractions, partly in English. **Bikes** can be rented from here (¥500/day, plus ¥1000 deposit).

Accommodation

The slightly run-down *Ikuchi-jima Shimanami Youth Hostel* (生口島しまなみユースホステル; ⓣ0845/27-3137; ❶), beside Sunset Beach a couple of kilometres south of Setoda, has the cheapest accommodation, rents bikes, offers meals and will pick you up from the ferry port. Setoda also has several ryokan: *Sazanami* (さざなみ; ⓣ&ⓕ0845/27-3373; ❺), just off the main approach to the Kōsan-ji a couple of blocks from the waterfront, is one of the cheapest, while the nicest is *Ryokan Tsutsui* (旅館つつ井; ⓣ0845/27-2221, ⓕ27-2137; ❼), a traditional establishment next to the ferry terminal, with recently refurbished spacious tatami rooms and a deliciously invigorating lemon bath. Rates at both include two meals.

Kōsan-ji

A giftshop-lined street leads directly from the waterfront just west of Setoda's ferry landing to the unmistakeably gaudy entrance of Ikuchi-jima's most famous attraction – the technicolour temple complex of **Kōsan-ji** (耕三寺; daily 9am–5pm; ¥1200), the creation of steel-tube manufacturer Kanemoto Kozo, who made much of his fortune from the arms trade. When his mother died, the bereft Kanemoto decided to build a temple in her honour, so bought a priesthood from Nishi-Hongan-ji temple in Kyoto and took over the name of a minor-league temple, Kōsan-ji, in Niigata. He resigned from his company, grew his hair, changed his name to Kōsanji Kozo, and began drawing up plans for the new Kōsan-ji – a collection of copies of the most splendid examples of Japanese temple buildings – which includes about ten halls, three towers, four gates, an underground cave and an enormous statue of Kannon, the Goddess of Mercy. Although many of the re-creations are smaller than the originals, Kanemoto cut no corners when it came to detail, even adding his own embellishments – most famously to the already over-the-top replica of the Yōmei-mon from Nikkō's Tōshō-gū, earning Kōsan-ji its nickname Nishi-Nikkō, the "Nikkō of the west".

The entrance gate is modelled on one from the imperial palace in Kyoto. To the right of the main temple building is the entrance to the **Senbutsudō** ("Cave of a Thousand Buddhas") and the Valley of Hell. An underground passage leads past miniature tableaux showing the horrors of damnation, followed by the raptures of a heavenly host of Buddhas. You then wind your way up to emerge beneath the beatific gaze of a 15m-tall statue of Kannon. From here you can walk up to the **Hill of Hope**, a collection of unusual modern marble sculptures with names like "Flame of the Future" and "Stage of the Noble Turtle".

Kōsan-ji's five-storey pagoda, modelled on the one at Murō-ji in Nara, is the last resting place of Kanemoto's beloved mother, whose holiday home, **Chōseikaku** (潮聲閣), is right by the exit (included in admission to the temple). The home is a fascinating combination of Western and traditional styles, with two of the rooms having beautiful painted panels on their ceilings and a Buddha-like model of Mrs Kanemoto resting in one of the alcoves. Opposite the mother's retreat is Kōsan-ji's **art gallery**, a plain building housing sober displays of mainly religious paintings and statues.

Hirayama Ikuo Museum of Art and around

Topping Kōsan-ji's treasures takes some doing, but the **Hirayama Ikuo Museum of Art** (平山郁夫美術館; daily 9am–5pm; ¥800; ⓦwww.city.onomichi.hiroshima.jp),

Moving on from Ōmi-shima

There are **ferries** from Miyaura (宮浦) to Imabari (今治) on Shikoku. You can reach Miyaura by local bus from the ferry port of Inokuchi – the bus station is located just below the Tatara Ōhashi (the bridge linking Ōmi-shima with Ikuchi-jima). There's also a **bus** back to Onomichi from Inokuchi (¥1500 one-way, with a change at Inno-shima), or you can catch a bus on to Imabari (¥1180 one-way).

next door to the temple's art gallery, eclipses it with a superior calibre of art. Hirayama Ikuo (1930–2009) was born in Setoda and was a junior-high-school student in Hiroshima when the bomb dropped – his famous painting *Holocaust at Hiroshima* can be seen in the Hiroshima Prefectural Museum of Art (see p.554). Despite travelling the world and becoming famous for his series of paintings on the Silk Road, he continually returned to the Inland Sea for inspiration. Hirayama used a traditional Japanese painting technique for his giant canvases, working very quickly with fast-drying paint – the resultant swift brush strokes give the finished paintings a distinctively dreamy quality. Because the special paint (*iwaenogu*) needed for this method is much less flexible and dries faster than oil paint, each picture has its own series of preparatory sketches. These full-sized blueprints for the final painting are known as *oshitazu*, and this museum contains many such sketches of Hirayama's most celebrated works, as well as original paintings and watercolours.

After the Hirayama museum, you can take in the view that inspired one of the artist's most beautiful paintings by hiking up to the summit of the hill behind Setoda. A small park here overlooks the attractive three-storey pagoda of **Kōjō-ji**, breaking out of the pine trees below, with the coloured tiled roofs of the village and the islands of the Inland Sea beyond.

Eating

Most of Setoda's **eating** options are along the Shiomachi-shōtengai shopping street leading up to the temple, but almost everything in this area is closed on Wednesdays. Opposite Kōsan-ji, *Mansaku* (万作) and *Chidori* (ちどり) are two smart fish restaurants serving pricey set lunches (¥1000–2500) of local cuisine. For something cheaper, head back towards the ferry terminal for sushi at the down-to-earth *Keima* (桂馬). If you're cycling around the island, pack a picnic from Setoda's shops.

Ōmi-shima

While Ikuchi-jima's top attraction is a temple, the big draw of neighbouring **Ōmi-shima** (大三島) is one of the oldest shrines in the country, **Ōyamazumi-jinja** (大山祇神社), dating back to the end of the Kamakura era (1192–1333). Dedicated to Ōyamazumi, the elder brother of the Shinto deity Amaterasu, the shrine is around a fifteen-minute walk from the small, undistinguished port of **Miyaura**, on the west side of the island. Between the twelfth and sixteenth centuries it used to be a place of worship for pirates, who used the island as a base before being brought to heel by the warlord Toyotomi Hideyoshi.

To the right of the main shrine grounds you'll find three modern buildings comprising Ōyamazumi-jinja's **museum** (大山祇神社宝物館; daily 8.30am–5pm; ¥1000, including entrance to the Kaiji Museum). The Shiyōden hall and connected Kokuhō-kan are reputed to contain the largest collection of armour in Japan, but unless you're a samurai freak you'll find the dry displays dull. More intriguing is the **Kaiji Museum** next door, which houses the Hayama-maru, the boat built for Emperor Hirohito so he could undertake marine biology research.

Beside the boat are some meticulously catalogued displays of fish, birds and rocks, some of the sea life looking like pickled aliens.

After visiting the shrine, you can explore the coast by bike (the best way of getting around the island) – which will take half a day – or linger on some of Ōmi-shima's rather average beaches. The interior is hilly, but there is a decent 5km, mainly downhill, cycle track from **Inokuchi**, the ferry port closest to Ikuchi-jima, across the island from Miyaura.

Hiroshima and around

Western Honshū's largest city needs little introduction. Since August 6, 1945, **HIROSHIMA** (広島) has become a byword for the devastating effects of the atomic bomb, and for this reason alone millions visit the city every year to pay their respects at the Peace Park and museum. But more than either of these formal monuments, the reconstructed city – bigger, brighter and more vibrant than ever – is an eloquent testimony to the power of life over destruction. Where once there was nothing but ashes as far as the eye could see, there now stands a modern city that still retains an old-world feel with its trundling trams and sunny disposition.

Poised on the coast at the western end of the Inland Sea, Hiroshima is also the jumping-off point for several islands, including **Miyajima**, home of the beautiful shrine **Itsukushima-jinja**. The view out to the red *torii* gate standing in the shallows in front of the shrine is rightly one of Japan's most celebrated, and although the island is often swamped by day-trippers it's a delightful place to spend the night.

Some history

During the twelfth century, the delta of the Ōta-gawa on which Hiroshima now stands was known as **Gokamura** ("Five Villages"). The delta was ruled by Taira no Kiyomori, a scion of the Taira clan who was for a while the power behind the emperor's throne in Kyoto and who commissioned the Ikutsushima-jinja shrine on Miyajima. All this ended when the Taira were vanquished by the Minamoto clan (or Genji) at the Battle of Dannoura in 1185. However, Gokamura continued to grow and became crucial during warlord **Mōri Motonari**'s campaign to take control of Chūgoku during the latter half of the fifteenth century. When Motonari's grandson Terumoto built his castle, the city was renamed **Hiroshima** ("Wide Island"), and by the Meiji era the city had become an important base for the imperial army, a role that placed it firmly on the path to its terrible destiny.

As a garrison town, Hiroshima was an obvious target during World War II, but until August 6, 1945, it had been spared Allied bombing. It's speculated that this was an intentional strategy by the US military so that the effects of the atom bomb when exploded could be fully understood. Even so, when the B29 bomber *Enola Gay* set off on its mission, Hiroshima was one of three possible targets (the others being Nagasaki and Kokura) whose fate was sealed by reconnaissance planes above the city reporting clear skies.

When "Little Boy", as the bomb was nicknamed, exploded 580m above the city at 8.15am it unleashed the equivalent of the destructive power of 15,000 tonnes of TNT. Beneath, some 350,000 people looked up and saw what must have looked like the sun falling to the earth. In less than a second a kilometre-wide radioactive fireball consumed the city. The heat was so intense that all that remained of some victims were their shadows seared onto the rubble. Immediately some 70,000 buildings and 80,000 people were destroyed. By the end of the year, 60,000 more had died from burns, wounds and radiation sickness. The final death toll is still

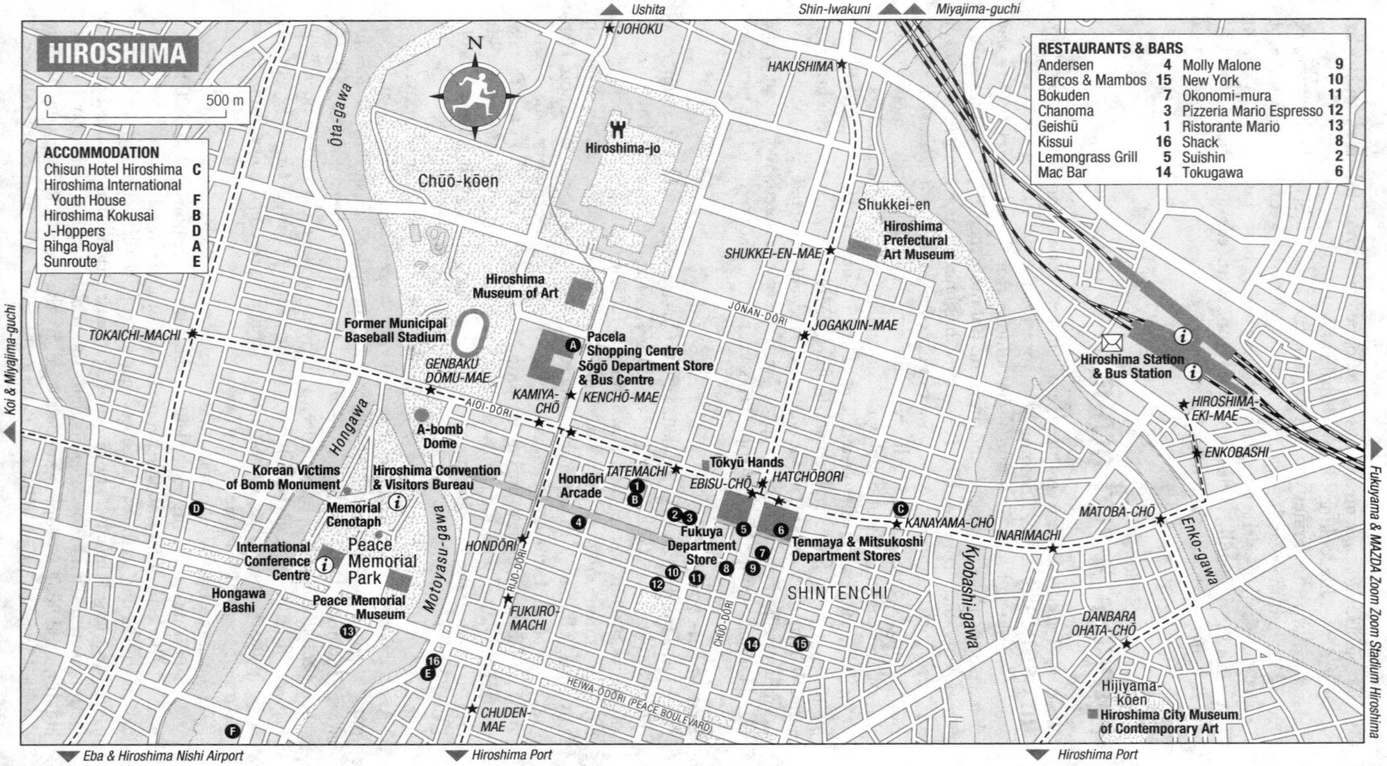

HIROSHIMA

0 500 m

ACCOMMODATION

Chisun Hotel Hiroshima	C
Hiroshima International Youth House	F
Hiroshima Kokusai	B
J-Hoppers	D
Rihga Royal	A
Sunroute	E

RESTAURANTS & BARS

Andersen	4	Molly Malone	9
Barcos & Mambos	15	New York	10
Bokuden	7	Okonomi-mura	11
Chanoma	3	Pizzeria Mario Espresso	12
Geishū	1	Ristorante Mario	13
Kissui	16	Shack	8
Lemongrass Grill	5	Suishin	2
Mac Bar	14	Tokugawa	6

N
Ushita
Shin-Iwakuni
Miyajima-guchi
Koi & Miyajima-guchi
Fukuyama & MAZDA Zoom Zoom Stadium Hiroshima
Eba & Hiroshima Nishi Airport
Hiroshima Port
Hiroshima Port
JOHOKU
HAKUSHIMA
Ōta-gawa
Chūō-kōen
Hiroshima-jo
Shukkei-en
Hiroshima Prefectural Art Museum
SHUKKEI-EN-MAE
Hiroshima Museum of Art
JŌNAN-DŌRI
JOGAKUIN-MAE
Former Municipal Baseball Stadium
Pacela Shopping Centre
Sōgō Department Store & Bus Centre
Hiroshima Station & Bus Station
TOKAICHI-MACHI
GENBAKU DŌMU-MAE
KAMIYA-CHŌ
KENCHŌ-MAE
AIOI-DŌRI
HIROSHIMA-EKI-MAE
ENKOBASHI
Hongawa
A-bomb Dome
Korean Victims of Bomb Monument
Hiroshima Convention & Visitors Bureau
TATEMACHI
Hondōri Arcade
Tōkyū Hands
EBISU-CHŌ
HATCHŌBORI
Memorial Cenotaph
Fukuya Department Store
Tenmaya & Mitsukoshi Department Stores
KANAYAMA-CHŌ
MATOBA-CHŌ
INARIMACHI
Enko-gawa
International Conference Centre
Peace Memorial Park
Motoyasu-gawa
HONDŌRI
RIJO-DŌRI
Hongawa Bashi
Peace Memorial Museum
FUKURO-MACHI
CHŪŌ-DŌRI
SHINTENCHI
Kyobashi-gawa
DANBARA OHATA-CHŌ
HEIWA-ŌDORI (PEACE BOULEVARD)
CHUDEN-MAE
Hijiyama-kōen
Hiroshima City Museum of Contemporary Art

unknown, the figure offered by the Hiroshima Peace Memorial Museum being "140,000 (plus or minus 10,000)". (For all Hiroshima's symbolic importance, it's important to put the number of those killed into context – in Tokyo, close to 20,000 died in a single night of bombing in 1945.)

Many survivors despaired of anything growing again for decades in the city's poisoned earth, but their hopes were raised on seeing fresh buds and blossom on the trees less than a year after the blast. The reborn Hiroshima, with its population of more than a million, is now a self-proclaimed "city of international peace and culture", and one of the most memorable and moving days to visit the city is August 6, when a **memorial service** is held in the Peace Park and 10,000 lanterns for the souls of the dead are set adrift on the Ōta-gawa delta.

Arrival and information

Hiroshima Station, on the east side of the city, is where local **trains** and Shinkansen arrive. Long-distance **buses** also arrive beside Hiroshima Station, although some also terminate at Hiroshima Bus Centre on the third floor of Sogō department store in the city centre. **Ferries** from Imabari and Matsuyama in Shikoku, and various other locations around the Inland Sea, arrive at Hiroshima Port, 4km south of Hiroshima Station and connected to the city by regular trams (¥150).

Two airports serve the city, the closest being **Hiroshima Nishi airport**, on the bay around 4km southwest of the city centre, which handles services to smaller regional airports, such as Niigata and Miyazaki; buses from the airport to the city centre leave roughly every forty minutes (30min; ¥240); a taxi will set you back around ¥3000. Flights from Tokyo Haneda airport and several other cities arrive at **Hiroshima airport**, some 40km east of the city; regular buses run from here to Hiroshima Station and the central bus centre (50min; ¥1300), or you can take a bus to nearby Shiraichi Station and transfer to a local train to the city.

There are two small **tourist information** booths in Hiroshima Station; one in the concourse at the south (*minami*) entrance and one on the second floor of the north (*kita*) Shinkansen entrance (both daily 9am–5.30pm). Hiroshima's main tourist office, the **Hiroshima Convention & Visitors Bureau** (daily: April–Sept 9.30am–6pm; Oct–March 8.30am–5pm; Ⓣ082/247-6738, Ⓦwww.hiroshima-navi.or.jp), is in the *Hiroshima Rest House* beside the Motoyasu bridge in the Peace Park. It has the best range of tourist literature, including information on other areas of Hiroshima-ken, and a small souvenir shop.

If you want to arrange a **home visit**, you should apply in person at the International Exchange Lounge of the International Conference Centre (daily: April–Sept 9am–7pm; Oct–March 9am–6pm; Ⓣ082/248-8879, Ⓔinternat@pcf.city.hiroshima.jp), at the southwest end of the Peace Park, at least a day in advance. The centre also has information on local events and an excellent library and reading area with magazines and newspapers, plus thirty minutes' free internet access.

City transport

The city is well served by public transport, with nine **tramlines**, an extensive network of **city buses** and the zippy Astram **monorail** line which transforms into a subway in the city centre, terminating beneath the Hondōri arcade. In practice, however, traffic can make catching a bus or a tram a frustratingly slow business; to get around the central sights quickly, you're often better off **walking**.

Within the city centre the minimum tram and city bus fares are ¥150. From the station, trams #1 and #5 head south to Hiroshima Port past Hijiyama-kōen, while #2 and #6 head west to the Peace Park and beyond. Tram #9 shuttles back and forth from Hatchōbori past the Shukkei-en garden. If you need to transfer from one tram to another to get to your destination, ask for a *norikae-kippu* from the driver; drop this in the fare box when you leave the second tram. If you need to transfer again, a second *norikae-kippu* costs ¥50.

With fares so cheap, neither of the one-day tram tickets is worth buying. A better option is the **pre-paid travel card**, which can be used on the buses, trams and monorail/subway – the ¥1000 card gets you ¥1100-worth of travel. These cards can only be bought at the tram terminus at Hiroshima Station, the Bus Centre and the main JTB office on Rijo-dōri (Kamiya-chō Biru, 2-2-2 Kamiya-chō ⓣ082/542-5005).

Accommodation

Hiroshima has plenty of inexpensive **accommodation,** and the only time of year you might have a problem finding somewhere to stay is August 6, when the annual peace ceremony is held. Although there are many business hotels in the charmless area around Hiroshima Station, it's better to stay closer to the Peace Park, west of which are more business hotels, minshuku and, if all else fails, love hotels.

Chisun Hotel Hiroshima チサンホテル広島 14-7 Nobori-chō, Naka-ku ⓣ082/511-1333, ⓦwww.solarehotels.com. Spotless accommodation right by the Kanayama-chō streetcar stop on Aioi-dōri, refreshingly devoid of typical business hotel drabness. There's internet access in the rooms and lobby. ③

Hiroshima International Youth House アステールプラザ国際ユースハウス 4-17 Kakomachi, Naka-ku ⓣ082/247-8700, ⓦhiyh.pr.arena.ne.jp. Accommodation at this municipal culture centre south of the Peace Park is meant for students (there's a midnight curfew), but is also available to foreign tourists. The large, comfortable Western and tatami rooms have en-suite bathrooms and good views. ④

Hiroshima Kokusai Hotel 広島国際ホテル 3-13 Tatemachi, Naka-ku ⓣ082/248-2323, ⓦwww.kokusai.gr.jp/front/english/E-stay/newstay2.html. Good-value mid-range hotel, in a great location just off the Hondōri shopping arcade. It's showing a bit of wear, but has economy singles, plus a fourteenth-floor revolving restaurant and a good Japanese restaurant (see p.555 for both). ⑤

J-Hoppers Hostel 5-16 Dobashi-chō, Naka-ku ⓣ082/233-1360, ⓦhiroshima.j-hoppers.com. Great little hostel west of the Peace Park with dorms and tatami rooms, internet access, self-catering kitchen and laundry facilities. If full, try the *Hana Hostel* near Hiroshima Station, run by the same management. ③

Rihga Royal Hotel リーガロイヤルホテル 6-78 Motomachi, Naka-ku ⓣ082/502-1121, ⓦwww.rihga.com/hiroshima. Hiroshima's grandest hotel soars 33 floors and was designed in the image of its neighbour, the reconstructed castle. It has spacious rooms, six restaurants, a pool, a gym and a stunning painting of Itsukushima-jinja by Hirayama Ikuo (see p.547) in the plush lobby. ⑦

Hotel Sunroute ホテルサンルート 3-3-1 Ōtemachi, Naka-ku ⓣ082/249-3600, ⓦwww.sunroute.jp. One of the more upmarket branches of this nationwide chain of business hotels, with two good restaurants (the Italian *Viale* and the Japanese *Kissui*) and rooms specially equipped for disabled guests. ⑥

World Friendship Centre (WFC) ワールドフレンドシップセンター 8-10 Higashi-Kannonmachi, Nishi-ku ⓣ082/503-3191, ⓦhomepage2.nifty.com/wfchiroshima. This small and homey non-smoking B&B has tatami rooms and is run by a friendly American couple who can also arrange meetings with A-bomb survivors and guided tours around the Peace Memorial Park for non-guests. Breakfast is included. ③

The City

Many of Hiroshima's top attractions – the **Peace Memorial Park and Museum**, the **A-bomb Dome** and the **Hiroshima Museum of Art** – are all within walking distance of the Genbaku Dōmu-mae tram stop. **Hiroshima-jō**, **Hiroshima Prefectural Museum of Art** and **Shukkei-en** lie north of the Hondōri Arcade and Shintenchi district, where there is a high concentration of hotels, restaurants and bars. The **Hiroshima City Museum of Contemporary Art**, the most far-flung point of interest, is best explored on foot from the station or by public transportation.

The Peace Memorial Park

The most appropriate place to start exploring Hiroshima is beside the twisted shell of the Industrial Promotion Hall, built in 1914 and now better known as the **A-bomb Dome**, or *Genbaku Dōmu* (原爆ドーム). Almost at the hypocentre of the blast, the hall was one of the few structures in the surrounding 3km that remained standing. It's been maintained ever since in its distressed state as a historical witness to Hiroshima's suffering and packs a powerful punch as you emerge from the modern-day hustle and bustle of the Hondōri arcade.

On the opposite bank of the Motoyasu-gawa is the verdant **Peace Memorial Park**, or *Heiwa Kinen-kōen* (平和記念公園), dotted with dozens of statues and monuments to the A-bomb victims. One of the most touching is the **Children's Peace Monument**, a statue of a young girl standing atop an elongated dome and holding aloft a giant origami crane – the symbol of health and longevity. The monument's base is eternally festooned in multicoloured garlands of origami cranes, folded by schoolchildren from all over Japan and many other countries, a tradition that started with radiation victim Sasaki Sadako who fell ill with leukaemia in 1955. The 12-year-old started to fold cranes on her sick bed in the hope that if she reached 1000 she'd be cured; she died before reaching her goal, but her classmates continued after her death and went on to build this monument.

The main monument – a smooth concrete and granite arch aligned with the A-bomb Dome and the Peace Memorial Museum – is the **Memorial Cenotaph**, designed by architect Kenzō Tange in the style of protective objects found in ancient Japanese burial mounds. Underneath the arch lies a stone coffin holding the names of all the direct and indirect A-bomb victims, and beside it burns the **Flame of Peace**, which will be put out once the last nuclear weapon on earth has been destroyed. It is before this monument that a memorial service is held every August 6, when white doves are released.

One final monument to take note of before proceeding to the museum is the **Monument in Memory of the Korean Victims of the Bomb**, on the eastern bank of the Hongawa, inside the Peace Park, just north of the Hongawa-bashi. Some two thousand forced labourers from Korea, a Japanese colony at the time of the war, died anonymously in the A-bomb blast, but it took decades before this monolith, mounted on the back of a turtle, was erected in their memory.

The Peace Memorial Museum

The **Peace Memorial Museum**, or *Heiwa kinen-shiryōkan* (平和記念資料館; daily: March–July & Sept–Nov 8.30am–6pm; Aug 8.30am–7pm; Dec–Feb 9am–5pm; ¥50), deserves to be seen by every visitor to Hiroshima; it presents a balanced picture of why the atrocity took place, as well as of its harrowing effects. The newer displays in the **east building** revolve around two models of the city before and after the explosion, and explain the lead-up to the bombing, including Japan's militarism. A watch in one case is forever frozen at 8.15am. There's a video theatre showing two short documentary films in English; in one a doctor's voice breaks as he recalls his realization that vast numbers of childhood leukaemia cases were caused by radiation.

On the third floor, after displays on the nuclear age post-Hiroshima, a connecting corridor leads to the old museum in the **west building**. You can rent a taped commentary (¥300) in one of sixteen different languages – worth doing, although the appalling injuries shown in photographs and re-created by models need no translation, shirking none of the horror of the bomb's aftermath. At the end, you'll walk along a corridor overlooking the Peace Park and the resurrected city, providing a chance for contemplation on the bomb that once wiped it all out.

The Hibakusha

I saw, or rather felt, an enormous bluish white flash of light, as when a photographer lights a dish of magnesium. Off to my right, the sky split open over the city of Hiroshima.

Ogura Toyofumi, *Letters from the End of the World*

As of March 2009 there were 235,000 **hibakusha** (A-bomb survivors) in Japan who, like Ogura, lived through the A-bomb, including some 73,000 still living in Hiroshima. Ogura's poignant account – a series of letters penned to his dead wife in the immediate aftermath of the war – stands alongside many others, including the videotaped testimonies of survivors, which can be viewed at the Peace Museum.

Through the museum it's also possible to meet a *hibakusha*. To do this you need to make a request in writing to the Heiwa Bunka Centre (Ⓣ082/241-4004, Ⓦwww.pcf.city.hiroshima.jp/hpcf), stating the dates you'd prefer and whether you'll need an interpreter. You'll be asked to cover their taxi costs of ¥8–10,000. The World Friendship Centre (see p.552) also arranges meetings and occasionally hosts discussions with experts and visiting scholars.

North of the Peace Park

Ten minutes' walk northeast of the Genbaku Dōmu lies the **Hiroshima Museum of Art** (ひろしま美術館; daily 9am–5pm; ¥1000; Ⓦwww.hiroshima-museum.jp), which specializes in late nineteenth- and twentieth-century French art, including minor works by Monet, Renoir and Matisse. If you have limited time, skip this and head for some of Hiroshima's better art museums such as the Hiroshima Prefectural Museum of Art or the Hiroshima City Museum of Contemporary Art.

If you've seen other castles in Japan, there's little reason to proceed to **Hiroshima-jō** (広島城; daily: March–Nov 9am–6pm; Dec–Feb Mon–Fri 9am–5pm, Sat & Sun 9am-6pm) ¥360 whose main entrance is directly behind the museum, next to three reconstructed turrets containing temporary exhibitions and fronting the Ninomaru compound beside the castle moat. The original castle was built in 1589 by Mōri Terumoto, one of Toyotomi's Hideyoshi council of "five great elders", but just eleven years later he was forced to retreat to Hagi (see p.570) following defeat in the battle of Sekigahara. Eventually the shogun passed control of Hiroshima to the Asano clan who held sway until the Meiji Restoration. Inside the smartly rebuilt five-floor donjon are various historical displays, the most entertaining of which is the combined model and video show with a guard giving a comical English commentary.

Shukkei-en and the Hiroshima Prefectural Art Museum

Ten minutes' walk east of Hiroshima-jō (or catch tram #9 from the Hatchōbori stop, getting off at Shukkei-en-mae) is a much better post-bomb reconstruction, **Shukkei-en** (縮景園; daily: April–Sept 9am–6pm; Oct–March 9am–5pm; ¥250), a beautiful stroll-garden with a central pond and several teahouses. Built originally by Asano Nagaakira after he had been made *daimyō* of Hiroshima in 1619, the garden aims to present in miniature the Xihu lake from Hangzhou, China, and its name literally means "shrunk scenery garden".

Adjacent to the garden is **Hiroshima Prefectural Art Museum** (広島県立美術館; Tues–Fri & Sun 9am–5pm, Sat 9am–7pm; ¥500; Ⓦwww1.hpam-unet.ocn.ne.jp), an impressive modern facility worth visiting to see two paintings alone: the fiery, awe-inspiring *Holocaust at Hiroshima* by Hirayama Ikuo (see p.547), who was in the city when the bomb dropped, and the floppy watches of Salvador Dalí's surreal piece *Dreams of Venus*. Check out what's showing in the temporary exhibition area, too, for which you'll pay an extra fee. A combined ticket for the museum and garden costs ¥600.

Hiroshima City Museum of Contemporary Art

Around 1km south of Hiroshima Station, on the crest of Hiji-yama, is the thought-provoking **Hiroshima City Museum of Contemporary Art** (広島市現代美術館; 10am–5pm; closed Mon; ¥360; Ⓦwww.hcmca.cf.city.hiroshima.jp), with its ultra-modern collection of art inspired in part by the atomic bombing. The surrounding leafy park, **Hijiyama-kōen**, is dotted with more modern sculptures, including some by Henry Moore, and provides splendid views across the city.

To reach the museum, take trams #1, #3 or #5 to Hijiyama-shita and hike up the hill. On Saturday, Sunday and holidays, there's a free shuttle bus from the Bus Centre to the museum.

Eating

Hiroshima's excellent selection of **restaurants** is the best you'll find in this part of Japan. The Pacela (パセーラ) shopping complex connecting the *Rihga Royal Hotel* and Sogō department store also has four floors of restaurants and a food court in the basement, mostly fast-food places and cafés.

Hiroshima's specialities are fresh seafood from the Inland Sea, in particular **oysters**, which are cultivated on thousands of rafts in Hiroshima Bay, and **okonomiyaki**. The local tradition is to make these delicious batter pancakes with the diner's choice of separate layers of cabbage, bean sprouts, meat, fish and noodles, unlike in Ōsaka, where all the ingredients are mixed up – don't leave Hiroshima without sampling one. Where the reviews below list a telephone number, it's a good idea to book.

Andersen 7-1 Hondōri. With its ground-floor deli full of quality imports, top-notch bakery and café, and second-floor restaurants (European, Chinese and pizzeria), this is a true gourmet foodie's paradise. Worth the visit for their Danish pastries alone.

Bokuden ボクデン Takata Arei Biiru, 4-20 Horikawa-chō, on the covered arcade just behind Tenmaya department store ⓣ082/240-1000. The glossy, post-modern decor of this trendy Korean restaurant is an interesting contrast to the sizzling barbecue meat dishes (from ¥1100) and fiery *chijimi*, a kind of omelette with leeks, meat and chilli (¥790). Daily 5pm–1am.

Geishū 芸州 2F *Hiroshima Kokusai Hotel* (see p.552) 3-13 Tatemachi. Pricey but beautifully presented local seafood dishes. *Le Train Blue*, the revolving restaurant on the top floor of the same hotel, is worth dropping by for a romantic evening cocktail.

Kissui 吉水 15F *Hotel Sunroute* (see p.552) 3-3-1 Ōte-machi ⓣ082/249-3600. Elegant *shabu shabu* (beef) restaurant overlooking the Peace Park, where the waitresses wear pale-green kimono. Dinner (last orders at 8.30pm) is pricey, but the ¥1800 lunch is much more affordable.

Lemongrass Grill 4F Mozart House Building, Chūō-dōri. Authentic Thai restaurant above the posh *Mozart* cake shop and café. The chef's most popular requests are *Tom Yam Kung* soup (¥1365) and green curry (¥1150). Daily 11am–2pm & 5–11pm.

Okonomi-mura お好み村 5-13 Shin-tenchi. Behind the Parco department store in the heart of the lively entertainment district, this building has 28 small *okonomiyaki* stalls crammed into three floors. *Hasshō* on the second floor and *Itsukushima*, the first stall you see on emerging from the elevator on the fourth floor, are two of the best in town. Daily 11am–9pm.

Pizzeria Mario Espresso 7-9 Fukuro-machi. Lively pizzeria with outside tables overlooking a small park. A nice spot to chill out over a coffee and dessert if you don't fancy a full meal.

Ristorante Mario 4-11 Nakaji-machi ⓣ082/248-4956. Authentic and deservedly popular Italian restaurant in the ivy-clad mock-Tuscan villa beside the Peace Bridge. The set lunches for ¥1200 and

¥1800 offer the best deal, but it's not too expensive for dinner.

Suishin 酔心 6-7 Tatemachi ⓣ082/247-2331. Long-established fish restaurant that serves dishes in the local style, in particular *kamameshi* (rice casseroles, from ¥735). Closed Wed.

Tokugawa 徳川 2F Tohgeki Building, Ebisu-chō. Cook your own *okonomiyaki* for around ¥800 at this restaurant, halfway down the covered arcade running behind Tenmaya department store. Has an English menu and a bright, family-oriented atmosphere. Daily 11am–3am.

Drinking

Come sundown, the thousands of **bars** crammed into the Nagarekawa and Shintenchi areas of the city, at the east end of the Hondōri arcade, fling open their doors. In summer, several beer gardens sprout on city rooftops, including one at the *ANA Hotel*.

Barcos & Mambos 2F, 3F, Sanwa Building 2, Yagenbori 7-9. This is the place to come if you want to mingle with an international crowd; head to Mambos (closed Sun) on the third floor for some Latin vibes and salsa dancing. ¥1000 cover gets you one drink, and Barcos has a food menu too.

Chanoma チャノマ 2F, 2-19 Honden, above the Cine Twin Cinema. Relax on soft mattresses and enjoy the wide range of cocktails and Asian-fusion food menu served in this unusual café-bar. Daily noon–2am.

Mac Bar 2F Hiroshima Rakutenchi Building, Chūō-dōri. Laidback second-floor bar with a vast CD collection and beers from ¥500.

Molly Malone 4F Teigeki Building, Chūō-dōri. This popular Irish bar is a good place to meet local expats, and the Irish chef rustles up generous-sized portions of tasty Irish food – try the Jameson chicken.

New York 7-2 Fukuro-machi. Industrial-style but with hints of traditional Japan; this all-day *izakaya* has dim lighting and comfortable seats. You can find just about anything on the expansive cocktail menu, and the food includes pastas, pizzas and snacks.

Shack 6F Takarazuka Building, Chūō-dōri. Popular place for beers, burgers and Tex-Mex food, with a pool table and a couple of dartboards for when you're pining for a bit of pub-style entertainment.

Listings

Banks and exchange There are several banks clustered around the Hondōri arcade as it crosses Rijo-dōri, including Hiroshima Bank, Sumitomo Bank and Tokyo Mitsubishi Bank. You can make cash withdrawals with cards including Visa and Mastercard at the Tokyo Mitsubishi Bank (Mon–Fri 9am–3pm). Foreign exchange is also available at the central post office (see below) and Higashi post office next to Hiroshima Station.

Bookshops There's a small selection of English-language books and magazines at Kinokuniya, on the 6th floor of Sogō department store. The Book Nook Global Lounge, 2F Nakano Building, 1-5-17 Kamiya-chō, Naka-ku, near the *Hiroshima Kokusai Hotel*, has an excellent selection of secondhand books in English and internet available at ¥200/15min.

Car rental Eki Rent-a-Car is at Hiroshima Station (ⓣ082/263-5933). Otherwise, try local branches of Avis (ⓣ0120-390784) and Budget (ⓣ082/262-4455).

Cinema Salon Cinema (ⓣ082/241-1781), near the city hall, shows European and American art-house films and revivals.

Emergencies The main police station is at 9-48 Moto-machi (ⓣ082/224-0110). In an absolute emergency, contact the Foreign Advisory Service on ⓣ082/247-8007. For other emergency numbers, see p.71.

Hospital Hiroshima Municipal Hospital, 7-33 Moto-machi ⓣ082/221-2291.

Internet You can get thirty minutes free at the International Exchange Lounge in the Peace Park (daily 10am–6pm). There's 24hr access at the *Chai Garden* on the 5th floor of the same building as the Tokugawa restaurant (¥200 for the first 30min, ¥63 for every 10min after that; drinks are free) and at Futaba@café on the 6th floor of the GIGA/Futaba building on your left as you walk out of the south exit of Hiroshima Station.

Post office The main central post office is on Rijo-dōri near the Shiyakusho-mae tram stop (Mon–Fri 9am–7pm, Sat 9am–5pm & Sun 9am–12.30pm). Other convenient branches are the Higashi post office beside the south exit of Hiroshima Station (also open Sat until noon) and the Miru Paruku post office next to Sogō department store.

Sports The Big Wave sports centre, with a swimming pool in summer and two ice rinks during the winter, sits beside the Ushita stop on the Astram line. There's also a pool and other fitness facilities at the Hiroshima Prefectural Sports Centre behind the former Municipal Baseball Stadium. Just east of the station is the MAZDA Zoom Zoom Stadium Hiroshima, home of the Toyo Carp, Hiroshima's professional baseball team. Tickets start from ¥1600 and can be bought at the gate and from convenience stores.

Miyajima

The most famous attraction on **MIYAJIMA** (宮島), officially known as Itsukushima, is the venerable shrine of **Itsukushima-jinja**, where the vermilion gate rising grandly out of the sea is considered to be one of Japan's most beautiful views. In the right light, when the tide is high and the many day-trippers have left, you may be tempted to agree.

The shrine and temples clustered around Miyajima's only village at the northern tip of this long, mountainous island can comfortably be seen in a half-day trip from Hiroshima. If you have more time, there are plenty of other attractions, including beaches to laze on and hikes over **Mount Misen**, whose summit provides panoramic views across the Inland Sea. Consider splashing out on a night's accommodation at one of the island's classy ryokan so that you can enjoy the after-hours atmosphere with only tame deer and a few other guests for company. Autumn is a particularly beautiful time to visit, when the myriad maple trees turn a glorious red and gold, perfectly complementing Itsukushima-jinja.

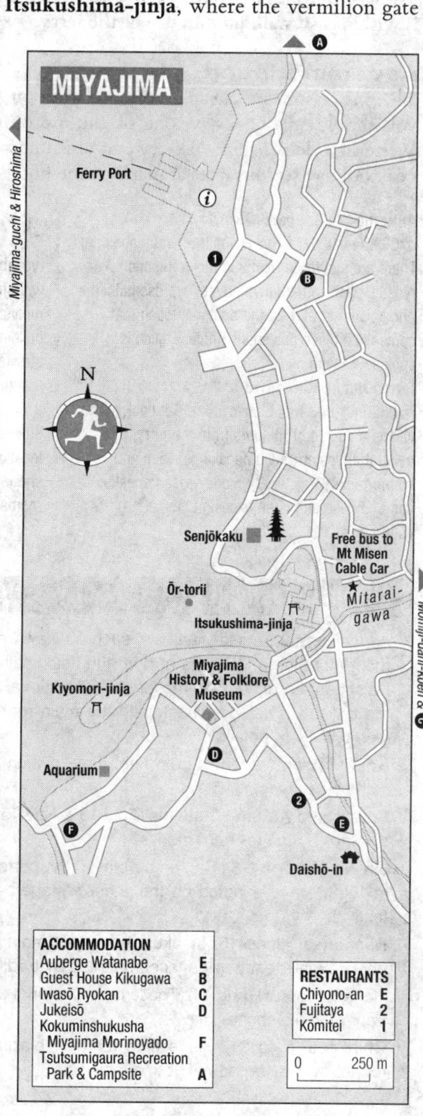

Arrival and information

From Hiroshima you can get to Miyajima either directly by ferry or by a combination of tram and ferry or train and ferry. High-speed **ferries** (¥1460) from Hiroshima's port – connected by tram #5 to Hiroshima Station and tram #3 to the city centre – take twenty minutes. Alternatively, tram #2 will take you to the ferry terminal at Miyajima-guchi, a 55-minute journey. A one-way trip costs ¥270, and the ten-minute ferry fare is ¥170. If you plan to return to Hiroshima the same day and travel a bit around the city, you'll save money buying a ¥840 one-day ticket. The **train** plus ferry route is only worth considering if you have a rail pass or special excursion ticket that will cover the cost of both the thirty-minute journey from Hiroshima to Miyajima-guchi Station and the crossing on the JR-run ferry.

There's a **tourist information** booth (daily 9am–7pm; ⓣ0829/44-2011) inside the island's ferry terminal, where you can pick up a basic map and book accommodation. You can also **rent bikes** from the JR ticket counter in the terminal (from ¥320 for 2hr), if you want to pedal to the northern beaches – everything else is within easy walking distance of the ferry.

Accommodation

There is reasonably cheap accommodation on Miyajima, but if you can afford it you should splash out on one of the more upmarket **ryokan** or the excellent Western-style pension. Also try and visit midweek, since at weekends and during peak holiday seasons rates at many of the hotels rise.

Auberge Watanabe 四季の宿わたなべ ⓣ0829/44-0234, ⓦwww.auberge-watanabe.com. There are just three rooms in this traditional ryokan, each with its own private cypress bath. It's pricey, but worth it for the personal touch that comes in a place this small. Some English is spoken. ⑧ with meals.

Guest House Kikugawa ゲストハウス菊川 ⓣ0829/44-0039, ⓦbit.ly/cyd6vz. Set back in the village a couple of minutes from the ferry, this delightful Western-style pension is clean and comfortable. The owner Kikugawa-san speaks some English and is an excellent chef. ⑤, or ⑦ with meals.

Iwasō Ryokan 岩惣旅館 ⓣ0829/44-2233, ⓦwww.iwaso.com. The most famous ryokan on the island, and by far the most luxurious, with immaculate tatami rooms and sumptuous meals. Rooms overlooking the gorge behind the building are booked solid throughout autumn when the view transforms into a sea of red, yellow and orange. with meals ⑨.

Jukeisō 聚景荘 ⓣ0829/44-0300, ⓦwww.jukeiso.com. This ryokan has an excellent hillside location south of Itsukushima-jinja, overlooking the shrine. There's a choice of Western and tatami rooms. ⑥, or ⑦ with meals.

Miyajima festivals

As well as the regular festivals, such as New Year, there are special **festivals** held most months on Miyajima at both the Itsukushima-jinja shrine and the main temple Daishō-in. From time to time, *bugaku* (traditional court dancing) is also performed on the shrine's nō stage; check with the main tourist information offices in Hiroshima (see p.551) for details.

Kaki Matsuri (second Sat in Feb): Free oysters, an island speciality, are served to sightseers.

Spring and Autumn festivals (April 15 & Nov 15): at Daishō-in, including firewalking displays by the resident monks.

Jin-Nō (April 16–18): Sacred nō plays, first performed for the *daimyō* Mōri Motonari in 1568, are re-enacted on the shrine's stage as part of the spring peach-blossom festival.

Kangensai (June 16): Itsukushima-jinja's main annual festival includes an atmospheric night-boat parade, accompanied by traditional music.

Hanabi Matsuri (Aug 14): The largest fireworks display in western Japan explodes in front of Itsukushima-jinja.

Chinkasai (Dec 31): Huge pine torches, blazing in front of Itsukushima-jinja, are fought over by groups of young men.

Kokuminshukusha Miyajima Morinoyado 国民宿舎みやじま杜の宿 ⓣ0829/44-0430, ⓦwww.morinoyado.jp. This minshuku, on the island's quiet southern end, is the best deal on Miyajima, but you'll have to book well in advance. There are both Western and Japanese rooms, and a good public bath which non-residents can use for ¥500. ❼ with meals.

Tsutsumigaura Recreation Park and Campsite ⓣ0829/44-2903. The only real budget accommodation option on the island is at its northern end. It has fairly plush cabins (from ¥15,210 for a four-person cabin) with air conditioning, kitchen and bathroom, as well as tent space (¥300/person/night; tent rental available).

The Town

The heart of Miyajima is **Itsukushima-jinja**, just to the south of the port. The iconic **Ō-torii**, seemingly floating atop the water, is visible from the shore, while the peaceful **Daishō-in** keeps a watchful eye from its perch on the hill above. The trek up **Misen-san** makes a pleasant afternoon hike, or is just a quick ropeway ride from the grassy **Momiji-dani-kōen**.

Itsukushima-jinja and around

Ancient records tell that a sea deity has been worshipped on Miyajima since the sixth century, but it wasn't until 1168 that **Itsukushima-jinja** (厳島神社; daily: March to mid-Oct 6.30am–6pm; mid-Oct to Feb 6.30am–5pm; ¥300) took on its present splendid form, courtesy of the warlord Taira-no-Kiyomori. When the sea is lapping beneath its low-slung halls and red-colonnaded, lantern-fringed corridors, you can see why it's called the "floating shrine". More than likely, though, the tide will be out and the muddy sea bed revealed. Still, the classical beauty of the architectural ensemble, modelled after the *shinden*-style villas of the Heian period, endures, although the shrine is at its most enchanting come dusk, when the lights of the surrounding stone lanterns flicker on.

From the ferry landing the shrine is a ten-minute walk south either along the seafront, where the island's many tame deer amble, or through the parallel shopping arcade crammed with giftshops and cafés. There's only one way to walk through the shrine, from its most northern entrance to its southern exit beside the Nishi-matsubara sand spit. Most of the attached halls are closed, but in the centre, 200m ahead of the projecting stage for nō plays, you'll see the famed 16m-tall **Ō-torii**, dating from 1875. This is the seventeenth incarnation since the original gate was erected by Taira-no-Kiyomori; its position in the sea indicates that the entire island is a Shinto holy place.

Just before the shrine, head up the hill towards the red-painted five-storey pagoda that you'll see poking through the trees. Beside this is the "hall of a thousand tatami", **Senjōkaku** (千畳閣; daily 8.30am–4.30pm; ¥100), part of Hokoku-jinja, a shrine started by Toyotomi Hideyoshi but left unfinished when the warlord died. Votive plaques decorate the inside of the large, airy hall, which was originally a library for Buddhist sutras. Better still is the island's main temple **Daishō-in** (大聖院), on the hillside around ten minutes' walk south of Itsukushima-jinja. This attractive temple complex, with ornate wooden pavilions, arched bridges across lily-pad-dotted ponds and stone lanterns, belongs to the Shingon sect of Buddhism associated with the revered Kōbō Daishi, who blessed the island with a visit in the ninth century. Look out for the "universally illuminating cave" towards the back of the complex, hung with hundreds of lanterns and packed with mini-Buddhas laden down with lucky talismans.

Misen-san and around

If you're feeling energetic, the 530m **Misen-san** (弥山), Miyajima's sacred mountain, can be climbed in a couple of hours. Otherwise a two-stage **ropeway** (daily: March–Oct 9am–5pm; Nov–Feb 9am–4.30pm; ¥1000 one-way, ¥1800 return) provides a thrilling and somewhat scary 1.7km cable-car ride up to within easy walking distance of the summit. The ropeway base station is beside **Momiji-dani-kōen** (紅葉谷公園), a leafy hillside park around a twenty-minute hike from the ferry terminal; a free minibus runs here from opposite the *Iwasō Ryokan*.

Around the Shishiwa station on top of the mountain, you'll see a colony of wild **monkeys** as well as more deer. Cute as they may look, it's important to keep your distance from the monkeys, which can occasionally become aggressive. There's an excellent lookout spot across the Inland Sea near the station, but the actual summit is a good twenty minutes further on. The path initially drops down but then starts to climb past various small temples built in honour of Kōbō Daishi. Opposite the Misen Hondō, the main hall of worship on the mountain, is the **Kiezu-no-Reikadō**, in which a sacred fire said to be originally lit by the Daishi has burnt for over 1200 years. Legend has it that if you drink tea made from the boiling water in the suitably blackened iron pot which hangs over the fire, all your ills will be cured.

Five more minutes' climb will take you past mysterious giant boulders to the rest-house at the summit; if you haven't packed refreshments you can buy them here, but at accordingly high prices. The main route down passes more small temples and provides stunning views over Itsukushima-jinja, especially as you near Daishō-in.

If you have enough time, the beachside walks along a pine-tree-lined sand spit south of the shrine are pleasant; the aquarium here was being refurbished at time of writing, but is scheduled to reopen in August 2011. Opposite the aquarium, the marginally diverting **Miyajima History and Folklore Museum** (宮島歴史民族資料館; 8.30am–5pm; closed Mon; ¥300) has a mishmash of exhibits, including traditional boats, farm equipment and furniture.

Several kilometres north of the ferry landing is the **Tsutsumigaura Recreation Park**, with a long stretch of sandy beach and shallow waters ideal for paddling in. Further north still, you'll find beautiful empty beaches with crystal-clear water and fantastic views.

Eating and drinking

Because most people dine at their hotels, non-lunch **eating** options on the island are limited. Besides oysters, another local speciality is **anago**, a long eel-like fish, cooked and served sliced on top of rice (*anagoburi*). The most famous place to sample this is the refined *Fujitaya* (ふじたや), a small, busy restaurant a couple of minutes' walk northwest of Daishō-in. A large serving of *anagoburi*, accompanied by soup and pickles, costs ¥2300. Less expensive is the *Chiyono-an* (千代乃庵) restaurant (on the first floor of the *Auberge Watanabe*), beside the main gate to Daishō-in, which has *anago* set lunches for ¥1600, as well as rice bowls and noodle soups for about half the price.

The arcade of tourist shops leading to the shrine has several restaurants, all with plastic food displays. *Kōmitei* (好み亭), on the seafront close to the ferry terminal, serves *okonomiyaki*, has an English menu and a pretty ornamental garden at the back. You can have your *okonomiyaki* Hiroshima-style (layered and cooked for you) or Kansai-style (cook it yourself).

Iwakuni

Heading south along the coast from Miyajima, you'll soon cross the border into western Honshū's last prefecture, Yamaguchi-ken. The first place to pause briefly is the pleasant old castle town of **IWAKUNI** (岩国), 40km southwest of Hiroshima and home to an American military base, as well as one of Japan's top three bridges, a scattering of samurai houses and a mildly interesting museum; it's also one of the best places in the country to watch the ancient practice of cormorant fishing.

Arrival and information

Shinkansen stop at Shin-Iwakuni Station, ten minutes by bus west of the bridge, while trains on the JR San'yō line stop at Iwakuni Station, a fifteen-minute bus journey east of the centre. Buses operate from both stations; the fare to Iwakuni is ¥240, to Shin-Iwakuni, ¥280.

There's a **tourist office** by the bridge with some English-language leaflets (8.30am–5pm; ⓣ0827/41-2037). All Iwakuni's sights can be comfortably seen in a couple of hours.

The Town

Two kilometres west of the present town centre and roughly between the Shinkansen and local train stations, is one of the country's top three bridges, **Kintai-kyō** (錦帯橋), an elegant five-arched structure, spanning the rocky Nishiki-gawa like a tossed pebble skipping across the water. It was *daimyō* Kikkawa Hiroyoshi who ordered the bridge's construction in 1673 to solve the problem of crossing the Nishiki-gawa every time it flooded. The first bridge was quickly washed away during the rainy season of 1674, but the second attempt – a 210m-long structure built without a single nail and bound together with clamps and wires – survived until Typhoon Kijiya swept it away in 1950. What you see today – and can walk across for ¥300 – is the 1953 reconstruction, no less impressive for that. For once, the hordes of tourists add something to the bridge's attraction, as they parade across the steep arches like figures in an *ukiyo-e* print.

Out of regular office hours, you either drop the bridge toll in the box beside the ticket office, or avoid it altogether by crossing the river on the nearby modern concrete span, the Kinjō-kyō, a good vantage point for a photo. It's also worth checking out the bridge at night, when it's glamorously floodlit. The ticket office sells a **combination ticket** (¥930) for the bridge, the return cable-car ride up Shiro-yama and entry to the castle, which, if you do all three, gives you a small saving.

Adjoining the bridge on the west bank of the Nishiki-gawa is a landscaped park, **Kikkō-kōen** (吉香公園), once the estate of the ruling Kikkawa clan. With its grass lawns and cooling fountains, the park preserves some of the layout and buildings of the former estate. Immediately ahead from the bridge, on the right, is the **Nagaya-mon**, the wooden gate to the home of the Kagawa family, samurai to the Kikkawa *daimyō*; there are also several other samurai houses you can wander around in the same area. There's a mildly interesting collection of old maps and plans from feudal times, photos and prints featuring the bridge through the centuries, as well as craftwork from Iwakuni's past, on display at the **Chōko-kan** (徴古館; 9am–5pm; closed Mon; free), at the north end of the park. Just round the corner from there is the **Kikkawa Historical Museum** (吉川史料館; 9am–5pm; closed Wed; ¥500), which has various artefacts from the Kikkawa family collection, including swords, jewellery and hanging scrolls, although the explanations are all in Japanese.

The **cable car** (¥320 one-way, ¥540 return; marked "tram" on town maps) saves a forty-minute hike up Shiro-yama – the route begins beside the youth hostel. An impressive view of the meandering river, town and Inland Sea from the summit makes the effort worthwhile. Unless you're interested in displays of armour, swords and a miniature wooden model of the Kintai-kyō, however, the **castle** (daily 9am–4.45pm; ¥260) isn't worth entering.

If you are in Iwakuni overnight between June 1 and August 31, don't miss the **cormorant fishing** (*ukai*), which takes place on the Nishiki-gawa beside the bridge between 6.30pm and 9pm. This colourful and exciting method of fishing with birds (see p.394) can be watched from boats for ¥3500, or for free from the pebbly riverbank.

Practicalities

If you decide to **stay** the night, the cheapest option is *Iwakuni Youth Hostel* (岩国ユースホステル; ⓣ0827/43-1092, ⓕ0123; dorm beds ¥2835/person), in the peaceful southwest corner of the park, ten minutes' walk from the bus stop by the bridge; it has shared Japanese-style rooms with TVs. The best ryokan is the pretty *Shiratame Ryokan* (白為旅館; ⓣ0827/41-0074, ⓦbit.ly/avY0Zx; ❽), with rooms overlooking the bridge; even if you can't afford to stay, try to go for lunch. The *Iwakuni Kokusai Kankō Hotel* (岩国国際観光ホテル; ⓣ0827/43-1111, ⓦbit.ly/9TmYTh; ❼) has branches on both sides of the river.

There are several **eating** options on the east side of the bridge; try the local fish dishes, such as *Iwakuni-zushi*, a block of vinegared rice topped with bits of cooked fish and vegetables, at *Yoshida*, which lies just beyond some interesting antique shops leading up to the Kintai-kyō. *Kikkō*, across from the cable-car station, has picture menus of *Iwakuni-zushi* sets and deep-fried *renkon* (lotus root), another regional speciality. In the summer be sure to try the *ayu*, a sweet fish caught by cormorants, available at many of the restaurants near the bridge. Otherwise, pack a picnic and enjoy it in the park.

Yamaguchi and around

The coastal route west of Iwakuni is blighted by heavy industry, but head inland to the hills and you'll find an old-world atmosphere hanging over the sleepy prefectural capital, **YAMAGUCHI** (山口), It's a modern city, but one can see why it's also known as the "Kyoto of western Japan". Highlights are the beguiling temple garden of **Jōei-ji**, designed by the fifteenth-century artist and priest Sesshū, the handsome five-storey pagoda at **Rurikō-ji** and the recently reconstructed **St Francis Xavier Memorial Cathedral**, an ultra-contemporary church commemorating the first Christian missionary to Japan.

The closest of the surrounding attractions is the hot-spring resort **Yuda Onsen**, just one train stop to the west of Yamaguchi, and practically a suburb of the city. Some 20km northwest are the intriguing caverns and rocky plateau of **Akiyoshi-dai** Quasi-National Park.

Some history

Many of the temples spread around Yamaguchi, not to mention its artistic sensibilities, date from the late fifteenth century, when war raged around Kyoto, and the city became an alternative capital for fleeing noblemen and their retinues. The

SL Yamaguchi-gō

A highly popular steam-train service, the SL Yamaguchi-gō runs on weekends and holidays between mid-March and November, passing through Yamaguchi on its way to the delightful castle town of Tsuwano (see p.575). A gleaming 1937 locomotive, pulling restored antique carriages, takes two hours to run from Shin-Yamaguchi to Tsuwano, where it waits for just under three hours before making the return journey. The fare from Shin-Yamaguchi to Tsuwano is ¥1620, and reservations are essential. For the current schedule, check with JR and tourist information offices.

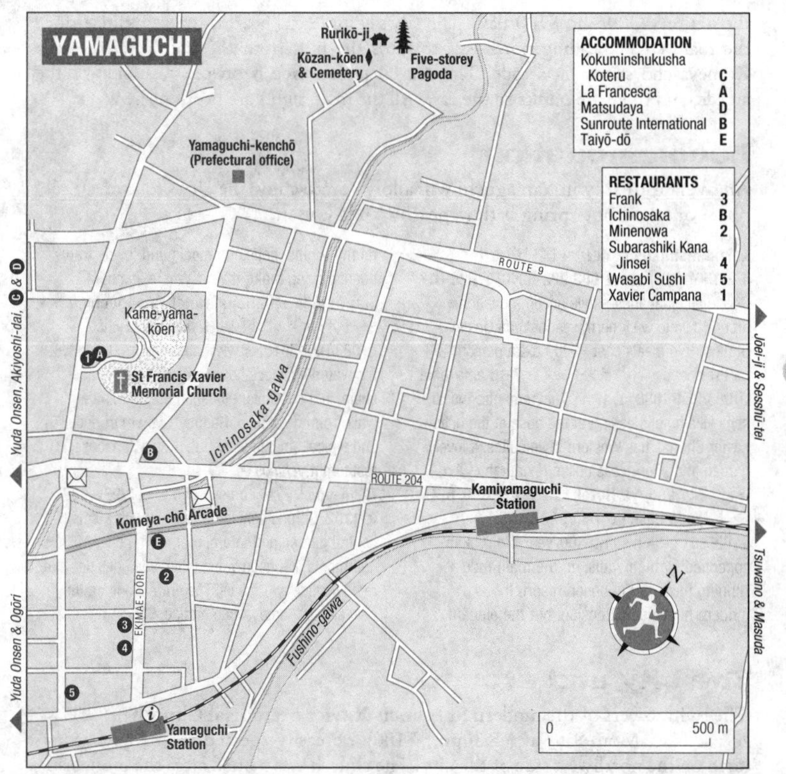

tolerant ruling family of **Ōuchi Hiroyo**, who settled in the area in 1360, allowed the missionary Francis Xavier to stay in Yamaguchi in 1549. By the Edo period, the **Mōri** clan had gained power over the whole of western Japan, and several of the Mōri lords are buried in Kōzan-kōen, including Mōri Takachika, who was a key figure in the overthrow of the Tokugawa government in 1867.

Arrival and information

Yamaguchi is twenty minutes by **train** from Shin-Yamaguchi (¥230) on the branch JR Yamaguchi line, which runs between **Shin-Yamaguchi** (新山口) on the southern coast (a Shinkansen stop) and the north-coast town of Masuda in Shimane-ken. Regular **bus** services run to the city from Hagi (p.570), and there are also connecting buses for flights into **Yamaguchi Ube Airport**, some 40km south near the coastal city of Ube. All buses stop in front of Yamaguchi Station.

The **tourist office** (daily 9am–6pm; ⓣ083/933-0090) is on the second floor of Yamaguchi Station. English maps and leaflets are available and you can use the internet here. There's also an information counter at Shin-Yamaguchi Station beside the exit from the Shinkansen tracks, where you can get English leaflets on most attractions in Yamaguchi-ken.

Yamaguchi might be the smallest of Japan's prefectural capitals, but its main sights are too widely spread out to walk between them. There are plenty of local buses, but the easiest way to get around is to rent a **bicycle** from the shop across the street from the station (¥300/2hr, ¥700/day). The city's commercial heart is where Ekimae-dōri, the main street heading northwest towards the hills from the station, crosses the Komeya-chō shopping arcade. The central **post office** is on the west side of the arcade, and there are **banks** to the east. All the main sights are north of here.

Accommodation

An **overnight stay** in Yamaguchi will allow you to enjoy the city's relaxed atmosphere or take a hot-spring bath in nearby Yuda Onsen.

Kokuminshukusha Koteru 国民宿舎小てる 4-3-15 Yuda Onsen ⓣ083/922-3240, ⓕ928-6177. Good-value Japanese-style accommodation, around 10min walk northwest of Yuda Onsen Station. Two meals cost ¥2000 extra/person. ⑤

La Francesca ラ・フランチェスカ 7-1 Kameyama ⓣ083/934-1888, ⓕ1777. This romantic Tuscan-style villa hotel, nestling at the base of the hilltop Xavier Church, has Western-style suites, a lovely garden and a top-class Italian restaurant. ⑧

Matsudaya Hotel 松田屋ホテル 3-6-7 Yuda Onsen ⓣ083/922-0125, ⓕ925-6111. A historic 300-year-old ryokan, cocooned by high walls, on the main road running through the onsen resort. It has a modern high-rise extension, but the elegant tatami rooms, delicious meals and lovely traditional garden make it worth the expense. ⑨

Sunroute International Hotel Yamaguchi サンルート国際ホテル山口 1-1 Nakagawara-chō ⓣ083/923-3610, ⓦwww.sunroute.jp. Recently renovated business hotel, part of a nationwide chain, in a convenient location fifteen minutes' walk from the station. Rooms have smart decor and typical amenities, and there's a Japanese restaurant, *Ichinosaka*. ⑤

Taiyō-dō 太陽堂 Komeya-chō ⓣ083/922-0897, ⓕ1152. Surprisingly large ryokan, with a small central garden and tatami rooms with shared bathrooms. It's good value when you consider that rates include two meals. The entrance is on the east side of Komeya-chō arcade. ⑥

The city and around

The twin towers of the modern **St Francis Xavier Memorial Church** (山口サビエル記念聖堂; Mon–Sat 9am–5.30pm; ¥100) are easily spotted atop Kame-yama-kōen on the northwest side of the city. The church was named after the pioneering Spanish missionary Francis Xavier who, having already had success in Goa and Malacca, landed in Japan on August 15, 1549, and in the following year was granted leave to preach in Yamaguchi. When he left, the city had a community of more than five hundred Christians, many of whom later died for their beliefs under the less tolerant Tokugawa government. In 1991, the original church (built in 1952 to commemorate the four-hundredth anniversary of Xavier's visit) burnt down, but was replaced in 1998 by a striking contemporary structure incorporating a pyramid-like main building, and twin square towers topped by metallic sculptures, one hung with nine bells.

A more traditionally Japanese place of worship is the charming temple and park of **Rurikō-ji** (瑠璃光寺) and **Kōzan-kōen**, in the foothills around 1km north of Kame-yama-kōen. Its highlight is a beautifully preserved **five-storey pagoda** (designated one of the top three in the country), made from Japanese cypress and picturesquely sited beside an ornamental pond. Beside the temple is a small exhibition hall (daily 9am–5pm; ¥300) containing a diverting collection of model pagodas, photographs of the other 53 pagodas scattered around Japan, and strange masks.

Next to Rurikō-ji, the park of **Kōzan-kōen** (香山公園), with its peaceful and atmospheric graveyard, is the last resting place of the *daimyō* Mōri Takachika and his offspring. Takachika was one of the prime movers in planning the overthrow of the Tokugawa government at the end of the Edo era, and there are a couple of old wooden houses preserved in the park where he secretly met fellow plotters. The closest bus stop to Rurikō-ji is Kimachi.

Some 2km east of the park, along the major road Route 9, is the enchanting **Sesshū-tei** garden (雪舟庭) at the **Jōei-ji** temple (常榮寺; daily 8am–5pm; ¥300). The priest and master-painter Sesshū, born in Okayama-ken in 1420, settled in Yamaguchi at the end of the fifteenth century. After travelling to China to study the arts, he was asked by the *daimyō* Ōuchi Masahiro to create a traditional garden for the grounds of his mother's summer house. Sesshū's Zen-inspired rock and moss design remains intact behind the temple and, if you're fortunate enough to avoid the arrival of a tour group, you'll be able to sit in quiet contemplation of the garden's simple beauty, looking for the volcano-shaped rock that symbolizes Mount Fuji. The surrounding forest and the lily-pad pond add brilliant splashes of colour, particularly in autumn, when the maple trees flame red and gold. Orimoto, the closest bus stop to Jōei-ji, is around ten minutes' walk south of the temple.

On the way back to the city centre, follow the meandering path of the **Ichino-saka-gawa**, a pretty stream crossed by pedestrian bridges. The cherry trees along the riverbanks turn candyfloss pink each spring, while in early summer fireflies buzz around the azaleas and reeds.

Yuda Onsen

One train stop west of Yamaguchi or a short bus ride south of the city centre is **Yuda Onsen** (湯田温泉), easily spotted by the cluster of large (and not particularly attractive) hotels. A cute legend about a white fox curing its injured leg in the natural springwater explains both how the onsen and the town's mascot, immortalized by an 8m-high cartoon-like fox statue beside the station, developed. **Onsen no Mori** (温泉の森; daily 10am–midnight; ¥1000), a modern spa complex, has several different jacuzzi baths, a sauna and a rotemburo; you're given a small towel to use when you enter. Take a left at the intersection in front of Yuda Onsen Station, then your first right and follow the road for about ten minutes to get here. The *Kamefuku Hotel* (かめ福ホテル; daily 11.30am–10pm;

Akiyoshi-dai

Midway between Yamaguchi and the northern coast city of Hagi are the vast caverns and rock-strewn tablelands of **AKIYOSHI-DAI** (秋吉台). The main attraction of this bleak landscape is **Akiyoshi-dō** (daily 8.30am–4.30pm; ¥1200; ⓦenglish.karusuto.com), the largest limestone cave in Japan, stretching around 10km underground, although only about a tenth of it is open to the public. The main entrance is a five-minute walk from Akiyoshi-dō bus station along a pedestrianized street of gift shops.

A raised walkway through a copse of lofty, moss-covered pine trees provides an atmospheric introduction to the gaping cavern mouth. Inside, however, the booming loudspeakers of competing tour-group leaders, combined with unimaginative lighting, detract from the huge cave's potential impact. It took more than 300,000 years of steady erosion and dripping to create some of the rock walls and formations, which have since been given names like "Big Mushroom" and "Straw-Wrapped Persimmon".

From the bowels of the earth an elevator whisks you up to the alternative cave entrance **Yano-ana**, a short walk from Akiyoshi-dai, Japan's largest karst plateau. A lookout point commands an impressive view of rolling hills, and there is a range of hikes you can follow across the 130 square kilometres of the plateau. If you return to the cave in the elevator, you'll be charged ¥100, but you can just as easily walk down the hill or catch a bus back to Akiyoshi-dō Station.

Buses run to Akiyoshi-dō from Higashi-Hagi (¥1760), Shin-Yamaguchi (¥1140), Shimonoseki (¥1730) and Yamaguchi (¥1130). The fastest connection is from Shin-Yamaguchi Station, a Shinkansen stop (43min). If you have a JR Rail Pass, it's best to take the JR bus service from Yamaguchi. **Tourist information** is available from the counter inside the bus centre (daily 8.30am–5pm; ⓣ0837/62-1620).

¥800) along Route 204 also has good facilities, with individual turtle-shaped baths outside.

Eating

There's a limited range of **restaurants** in Yamaguchi, with most options clustered along Ekimae-dōri and the Komeya-chō arcade, and a few cafés along the riverside beyond the arcade. Many shops also sell the local speciality, *uirō*, a glutinous sweet made from pounded rice, a supposed favourite of the ruling Ōuchi clan six hundred years ago.

Frank フランク 2F, Ekimae-dōri. Reasonably priced and serving staple Japanese café food including curry rice and pilaf. The entrance is off the side-street. Closed Tues.

Ichinosaka いちの坂 1-1 Nakagawara-chō. Handy restaurant in the *Sunroute International Hotel* (see p.564) serving good-value set meals. Last orders at 9pm.

La Francesca 7-1 Kameyama ⓣ083/934-1888. Top-class Italian restaurant attached to the hotel of the same name (see p.564) which does excellent-value pasta lunches (from ¥1260) and more expensive dinners. Sometimes closed for weddings.

Minenowa 峰乃輪 Komeya-chō. This inexpensive and authentic noodle operation is identifiable by its traditional wooden exterior. Bowls of tempura, udon and soba cost as little as ¥470. Daily 11.30am–5.30pm.

Subarashiki Kana Jinsei 素晴らしきかな人生 Ekimae-dōri. Lively little spot, serving all the usual *izakaya* staples.

Wasabi Sushi Cheap and cheerful conveyor-belt sushi stop near the station. Daily until 8.30pm.

Xavier Campana 5-2 Kameyama ⓣ083/923-6222. Mouthwatering bakery and restaurant serving a wide range of breads, cakes, salads and a mixture of European meals, including German-style dishes, fondue and pasta.

Shimonoseki and around

Most travellers pass through the port of **SHIMONOSEKI** (下関) at the southern tip of Honshū, 65km west of Yamaguchi, as quickly as possible en route to Kyūshū, or to Pusan in South Korea on the daily ferry. However, this unpretentious city is not without its attractions. The narrow **Kanmon Channel**, which separates Honshū from Kyūshū, is best viewed from Hino-yama, the mountain park that rises above the port. The channel was the scene of the battle of Dannoura, the decisive clash between the Taira and Minamoto clans in 1185, and the colourful shrine **Akama-jingū** is dedicated to the defeated Taira. If you have enough time, make the short trip to the neighbouring town of **Chōfu**, with its authentic enclave of samurai houses and streets, sleepy temples and lovely garden.

Arrival, information and city transport

If you're travelling by **Shinkansen**, you'll need to change **trains** at Shin-Shimonoseki Station, and go two stops on the San'yō line to Shimonoseki Station. Long-distance **buses** arrive at the bus station in front of Shimonoseki Station.

The fastest way of connecting with Kyūshū is by train or road across Kanmon suspension bridge; traditionalists can still make the short ferry hop (¥390) from Karato Pier, around 1.5km east of Shimonoseki Station, to Moji on Kyūshū's northwest tip. If you arrive by ferry from South Korea, you'll come in at the Shimonoseki Port International Terminal.

Maps and local sightseeing literature in English are available from the **tourist information** booth (daily 9am–7pm; ⓣ&ⓕ0832/56-3422) in Shin-Shimonoseki

The Kampu Ferry to South Korea

The Kampu Ferry service to Busan in South Korea (Ⓦwww.kampuferry.co.jp) leaves daily at 7pm from the **Shimonoseki Port International Terminal**, five minutes' walk from Shimonoseki Station. The ticket booking office is on the second floor of the terminal building (daily 9am–5pm; Ⓣ0832/24-3000); the cheapest one-way ticket is ¥9000 (¥7200 student fare) for the tatami resting areas, ¥12,000 for beds. Although there's a ten percent discount on a return ticket, it's still cheaper to buy another one-way ticket in Pusan.

The ferry is one of the cheapest routes in and out of Japan, and is often used by people working illegally who need to renew their tourist visas. For this reason, the immigration officials at Shimonoseki have a reputation for being tough on new arrivals. Note also that if you need a visa for South Korea, you must arrange it before arriving in Shimonoseki; the nearest consulate is in Hiroshima.

There is also a twice-weekly ferry service to Qingdao (Orient Ferry Ⓣ0832/32-6615) and a weekly ferry service to Shanghai (Shanghai-Shimonoseki Ferry Ⓣ0832/32-6615).

Station by the Shinkansen exit. There's another tourist office (daily 9am–7pm; Ⓣ&Ⓕ0832/32-8383) on the concourse of Shimonoseki Station. The **Yamaguchi International Exchange Association** (9am–5.30pm; closed Mon), on the second floor of the Kaikyō-yume Tower complex, also has information in English.

Shimonoseki's main sights don't take long to see, but are several kilometres east along the waterfront from the station so it's best to use the local **buses** to get around; if you're staying at the youth hostel you can hire a bike (¥300/day, ¥350/day for a mountain bike). The buses departing from platforms 1 and 2 outside Shimonoseki Station are the most convenient, passing Akama-jingū and Hino-yama on their way to Chōfu (¥340).

Accommodation

There's the usual cluster of business **hotels** around Shimonoseki Station and the international ferry terminal. More spectacular views can be had from the youth hostel and the *kokuminshukusha* on the slopes of Hino-yama, around 2km east of the station, near the Kanmon Bridge.

Kaikyō View Shimonoseki 海峡ビューしものせき 3-58 Mimosusogawa-chō Ⓣ0832/29-0117, Ⓕ0114. This low-rise concrete block has a fantastic view across the Kanmon Channel and a choice of spacious tatami rooms or Western-style suites. With meals, 7

Shimonoseki Grand Hotel 下関グランドホテル 31-2 Nabe-chō Ⓣ0832/31-5000, Ⓕ35-0039 Ⓦbit.ly/9fgjh0. Comfortable upmarket hotel beside Karato Pier with Western-style rooms and a couple of restaurants, one French and one Japanese. 6

Shimonoseki Hinoyama Youth Hostel 下関火の山ユースホステル 3-47 Mimosusogawa-chō Ⓣ0832/22-3753, Ⓦwww.e-yh.net/shimonoseki. Fine hostel with bunk-bed dorms (¥3200), views across to the Kanmon Bridge and free wi-fi. The friendly English-speaking manager is a reasonable cook. From Shimonoseki Station, take the bus from platform 1 to the Hino-yama ropeway, from where the hostel is a 2min walk downhill. More buses stop at the base of Hino-yama at Mimosuso-gawa; it's a 10min hike up to the hostel from here. There's a 9.30pm curfew.

Shunpanrō 春帆楼 4-2 Amida-dera Ⓣ0832/23-7181, Ⓕ32-7980. Top-notch hotel near the Akama-jingū, with large suites of Western-style bedrooms and tatami sitting rooms overlooking the Kanmon Channel. The meals include lavish *fugu* dishes. 9

Via Inn Shimonoseki ヴィアイン下関 4-2-33 Takezaki-chō Ⓣ0832/22-6111, Ⓕ24-3261. One of the newest of the many business hotels close to the station, with wide and comfortable beds. If it's full, try the nearby *Shimonoseki Station Hotel* or *Hotel 38 Shimonoseki*, both of which offer much the same deal. 4

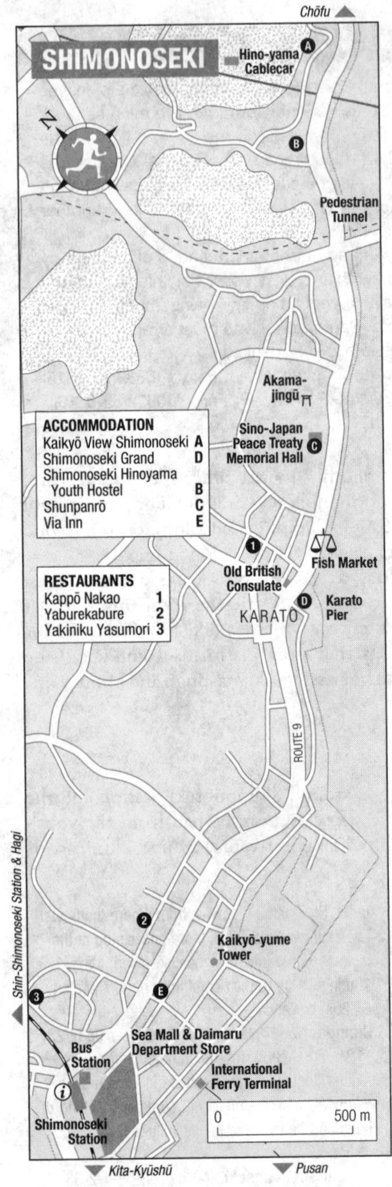

The City

The one thing you should do while in Shimonoseki is head up Hino-yama to take in the panoramic view over the Kanmon Channel (see below). If you're pushed for time, a similar view can be had ten minutes' walk east of Shimonoseki Station from the top of **Kaikyō-yume Tower** (海峡ゆめタワー; daily 9.30am–9.30pm; ¥600), a 153m-high observation tower made of glass which looks like a giant golf tee with a ball resting on top. The tower is at its most striking at night, when the interior glows green and points of light dot the spherical observation deck, which also has a restaurant.

On the way to Hino-yama you'll pass through **Karato** (唐戸), the early twentieth-century port area, which still has a handful of handsome brick and stone buildings, including the former British Consulate. On the waterfront is the **Karato Fish Market**, a lively place early in the morning.

Ten minutes' stroll further east is **Akama-jingū** (赤間神宮), the shrine dedicated to Antoku, an 8-year-old emperor who drowned along with the Taira clan when they were routed in the naval battle of Dannoura. The clash took place in the straits overlooked by the striking vermilion, gold and pale-green shrine, originally built as a Buddhist temple to appease the souls of the dead Taira warriors, and known at the time as Amida-ji. When Shinto and Buddhism were separated in the Meiji period, the temple became a shrine and was renamed Akama-jingū.

Beyond the Chinese-style arched gate is a courtyard, the scene of the colourful **Sentei Matsuri**. Held on April 23–25, this festival is based around the legend that the surviving Taira women, who after their clan's defeat were forced to turn to prostitution, came to the shrine each year to purify themselves. In a small graveyard to the left of the courtyard are fourteen ancient graves for notable Taira warriors and a small statue of the blind and deaf priest, Hōichi Miminashi – the "earless Hōichi" in one of the Irish writer Lafcadio Hearn's most famous ghost stories (see p.582). There's also a small museum of armour and scrolls, with an honesty box for the ¥100 donation requested for entry.

If you've got time, nip up the hillside road before the shrine to check out the **Sino-Japan Peace Treaty Memorial Hall** (daily 9am–5pm; free), in an ornate, gabled building next to the *Shunpanrō* hotel. Built in 1936, the hall includes a re-creation of the room in the hotel where a peace treaty was signed between China and Japan on April 17, 1895, after nearly a month of negotiations. Around 1km further east, just beside the Kanmon Bridge, is a kilometre-long pedestrian tunnel (6am–10pm) through which you can walk under the straits to Moji, on Kyūshū.

Uphill from the bridge is **Hino-yama** (火の山), with a number of trails leading up to the 268m summit. There is a cable car (¥200) to the top, which is only open in July and August, with buses running the rest of the year (hourly 9.15am–6.15pm). The view from the top of the mountain takes in the whole of the Kanmon Straits and the islands to the west of Shimonoseki – particularly memorable towards sunset. Over a thousand ships a day sail through this narrow waterway, making it one of Asia's busiest maritime crossroads.

Chōfu

Heading east along Route 9 from Hino-yama for around 3km, ignore the lacklustre aquarium and amusement park in favour of the elegant garden **Chōfu-teien** (長府庭園; daily 9am–5pm; ¥200), which makes a civilized introduction to **CHŌFU** (長府), an old castle town of the Mōri family. The garden dates from the Taishō era and has several teahouses dotted around an ornamental pond and babbling river.

After the garden, branch off from the main road at the next turning and head inland towards a compact enclave of old **samurai houses**, shielded by wooden gates and crumbling earthen walls, topped with glazed tiles, with the roads bordered by narrow water channels. Further up the hill in a leafy glade approached by a broad flight of stone steps is **Kōzan-ji** (功山寺), the Mōri family temple dating from the fourteenth century. Next to the temple, you'll see the small **Chōfu Museum** (9.30am–5pm; closed Mon; ¥200), which displays beautiful scrolls decorated with calligraphy and intriguing old maps.

One of the joys of Chōfu is its relative lack of tourist development, making it easy to feel you have slipped back several centuries while wandering round the samurai district. The one shop you should search out is **Chayashō**, a marvellous antique emporium selling kimono, pottery and other colourful knick-knacks, with a special display area in the *kura* (storehouse) at the back; it also serves

Fugu

Shimonoseki revels in its role as Japan's centre for **fugu**, the potentially deadly blowfish or globefish, which provides inspiration for many local sculptures and souvenirs of spiky, balloon-shaped fish. It is known in Shimonoseki as *fuku*, homonymous with the character for fortune and wealth, in order to attract good luck and happiness. About half the entire national catch (3000 tonnes a year) passes through Haedomari, the main market for *fugu*, at the tip of the island of Hiko-shima, some 3km west of Shimonoseki Station.

Chomping on the translucent slivers of the fish, which are practically tasteless, you may wonder what all the fuss is about. However, it is the presence of tetrodotoxin – a poison more lethal than potassium cyanide – found in the *fugu*'s ovaries, liver and a few other internal organs, that make this culinary adventure both dangerous and appealing. *Fugu* chefs spend up to seven years in training before they can obtain a government licence to prepare the fish. Even so, a small number of people do die, the most famous fatality being kabuki actor Bandō Mitsugorō – a national treasure – who dropped dead after a globefish banquet in Kyoto in January 1975.

coffee and tea in an atmospheric lounge (see below). Look for the large red-paper umbrella by the entrance to the century-old house, downhill from Kōzan-ji.

Buses to Chōfu (25min; ¥340) run from platforms 1 and 2 at Shimonoseki Station, every fifteen minutes or so. For Chōfu-teien get off at Shiritsu Bijutsukan-mae bus stop; for the samurai district, get off at **Jōkamachi** bus stop and head uphill.

Eating

Shimonoseki is packed with **restaurants** specializing in *fugu* (see box opposite), but the daily ferry connection with Pusan means Korean cuisine is almost as popular. Several restaurants around the Green Mall near the station specialize in Korean barbecue dishes, called *yakiniku*, while for *fugu* head for the parade running parallel to Route 9, northwest of the Kaikyō-yume Tower. Another good area for fish restaurants is Karato.

The area around the station has plenty of **fast-food** options, while the seventh floor of Daimaru department store has a variety of inexpensive restaurants.

Chayashō 茶屋祥 Chōfu. Delightful café in a kimono shop in Chōfu (see p.569), where the gracious hosts serve tea and coffee with cakes for ¥500. The delicious chocolate cake comes on indigo china plates and is decorated with a gold maple leaf. Look for the large red-paper umbrella by the entrance to the century-old house, downhill from Kozan-ji.

Furue Shōji 古江小路 Chōfu ⓣ0832/45-5233. Elegant *kaiseki ryōri* restaurant in an old samurai house on a street of the same name. The light but visually splendid lunch for ¥2625 is worth trying (11.30am–2.30pm). Dinner is at least twice the price. Closed Wed.

Kappō Nakao 割烹なかお 4-6 Akama-chō, Karato ⓣ0832/31-4129. Excellent fish restaurant set back from the road where a team of motherly waitresses serves hearty set lunches for around ¥1200. The *fugu* course is ¥5000 at dinner. Closed Sun except during *fugu* season (Nov–Mar).

Yaburekabure やぶれかぶれ 2-2-5 Buzenda-chō ⓣ0832/34-3711. Look out for the large plastic *fugu* and red signs hanging outside this restaurant on the shopping parade east of the station. The speciality is a meal including seven different *fugu* dishes for ¥6300.

Yakiniku Yasumori 焼肉やすもり 2-1-13 Takezaki-chō. One of Shimonoseki's best *yakiniku* restaurants: order plates of raw meat and vegetables to sizzle on a tabletop cooker. Also try *pivinpa*, a traditional mix of rice and vegetables in a stone bowl. Around ¥2000/person. Closed Thurs.

Hagi and around

Heading east from Shimonoseki along the **San'in** coast, the landscape becomes much more rugged and sparsely populated. Here the savage Sea of Japan has eroded the rocks into jagged shapes, and if you take the train you'll see some marvellously bleak shorelines. The next town of any consequence is **HAGI** (萩), some 70km northeast of Shimonoseki, which dates back to 1604 when warlord Mōri Terumoto built his castle at the tip of an island between the Hashimoto and Matsumoto rivers. Hagi's castle is long ruined, but the atmospheric graveyards of the Mōri *daimyō*, the layouts of the samurai and merchants' quarters – **Horiuchi** and **Jōkamachi** – and the temple district of Teramachi remain, with several significant buildings intact. These attractive plaster-walled streets are the town's main attraction, together with its renowned pottery, **Hagi-yaki**, considered Japan's next-best style of ceramics after Kyoto's *Raku-yaki* – you can hardly move around Hagi without coming across a shop selling the pastel-glazed wares. The town is also famous for the role that some of its citizens played in the Meiji Restoration, such as Yoshida Shōin (see p.573), who was executed by the Tokugawa Shogunate for his radical beliefs and is now enshrined at **Shōin-jinja**.

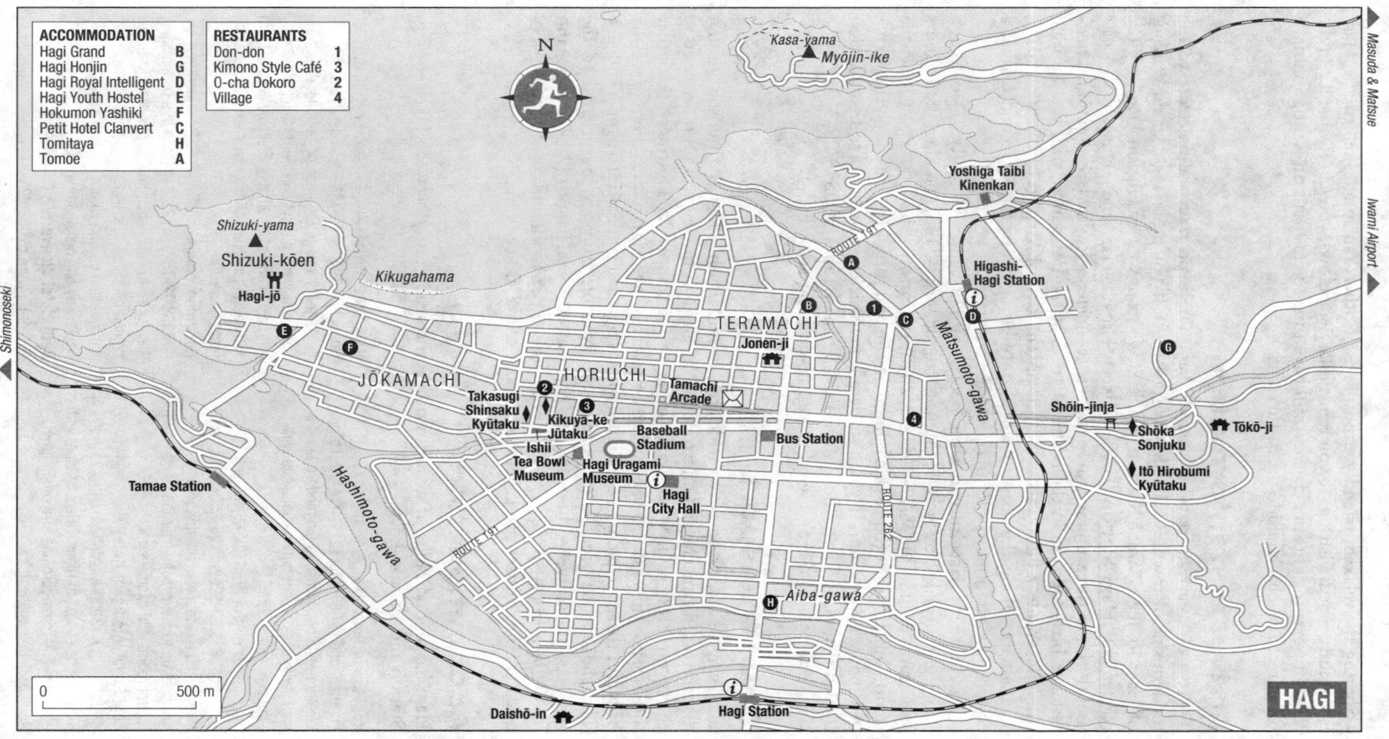
HAGI
ACCOMMODATION
Hagi Grand B
Hagi Honjin G
Hagi Royal Intelligent D
Hagi Youth Hostel E
Hokumon Yashiki F
Petit Hotel Clanvert C
Tomitaya H
Tomoe A
RESTAURANTS
Don-don 1
Kimono Style Café 3
O-cha Dokoro 2
Village 4
N
Kasa-yama
Myōjin-ike
Masuda & Matsue
Iwami Airport
Shimonoseki
Yoshiga Taibi Kinenkan
Higashi-Hagi Station
Shizuki-yama
Shizuki-kōen
Hagi-jō
Kikugahama
TERAMACHI
Jonen-ji
HORIUCHI
JŌKAMACHI
Matsumoto-gawa
Takasugi Shinsaku Kyūtaku
Kikuya-ke Jūtaku
Tamachi Arcade
Ishii Tea Bowl Museum
Baseball Stadium
Bus Station
Hagi Uragami Museum
Hagi City Hall
Shōin-jinja
Shōka Sonjuku
Tōkō-ji
Itō Hirobumi Kyūtaku
Tamae Station
Hashimoto-gawa
ROUTE 191
ROUTE 262
Aiba-gawa
0
500 m
Daishō-in
Hagi Station

Sharing the relaxed, friendly atmosphere of other Yamaguchi-ken towns, Hagi is certainly worth visiting. If you rent a bike (see below), you can easily take in the most important sights in a day and still have time to crash out on **Kikugahama**, a fine stretch of beach beside the castle ruins.

Arrival and information

There are three train stations around Hagi. The main train station, close to the modern side of town, is **Higashi-Hagi** (東萩駅). If you're staying near the remains of Hagi-jō, then **Tamae Station** (玉江駅), two stops west of Higashi-Hagi, is more convenient. **Hagi Station** (萩駅), between Higashi-Hagi and Tamae, is the least useful of the three unless you're staying at *Tomitaya Ryokan* (see oppoite). Long-distance **buses** all stop in the centre of town at the bus station, near the Tamachi shopping arcade, a short walk east of Jōkamachi. **Iwami Airport** (Ⓣ0856/24-0010), an hour east along the coast, is served only by flights from Tokyo and Ōsaka; a connecting bus (80min; ¥1560) runs to the bus station.

There are **tourist information** booths at Higashi-Hagi (daily: Dec–March 9am–5pm; April–Nov 9am–5.45pm; Ⓣ&Ⓕ0838/25-3145) and Hagi (same hours as Higashi-Haji; Ⓣ0838/25-1750, Ⓕ2073) stations, to the left as you leave the station buildings. Both provide bilingual maps and pamphlets, although they don't get updated very often. If you have detailed enquiries, contact the tourism section (desk 14) at Hagi City Office (Mon–Fri 8.30am–5.15pm; Ⓣ0838/25-3131) in the City Hall, where there's a helpful English-speaking assistant.

Town transport

Hagi's sights are spread over a wide area. From Higashi-Hagi Station, the samurai district of Jōkamachi and the remains of Hagi-jō in Shizuki-kōen are a good thirty minutes' walk west, while other major temples and shrines are similar distances to the east and south. The best way of getting around, therefore, is by **bicycle**; there are plenty of rental shops at Higashi-Hagi Station (from ¥150/hr). The cheapest day rentals (¥800/day) are available from the outfit next to the station. Alternatively, there are two **bus** routes – *nishi mawari* (西回り; west) and *higashi mawari* (東回り; east) – that cover the entire town and its attractions in a circular route. Buses run twice hourly and cost ¥100 per ride.

Accommodation

Hagi has a good range of **accommodation** spread evenly between Higashi-Hagi Station and Shizuki-kōen.

Hagi Grand Hotel 萩グランドホテル 25 Furuhagi-chō Ⓣ0838/25-1211, Ⓕ4422. Large Western-style hotel close to the modern heart of town, with dated decor but spacious and well-furnished rooms. ❻

Hagi Honjin 萩本陣 385-8 Chintō Ⓣ0838/22-5252, Ⓕ25-3594. This super-swish hotel has fabulous rotemburo baths, a monorail up to a viewpoint over the city, beautiful tatami rooms and exquisite meals. ❼

Hagi Royal Intelligent Hotel 萩ロイヤルインテリジェントホテル 3000-5 Chintō Ⓣ0838/21-4589. Business hotel next to Higashi-Hagi Station, with an onsen and rotemburo and in-room internet. Rates include breakfast. ❹

Hagi Youth Hostel 萩ユースホステル 109-22 Horiuchi Ⓣ0838/22-0733. This hostel has bunk-bed dorms (¥2940/person) around a central open courtyard. It's not a modern place, but staff are helpful and bike rental is available (¥500). From Tamae Station, walk 15min north across the Hashimoto-gawa. ❶

Hokumon Yashiki 北門屋敷 210 Horiuchi Ⓣ0838/22-7521, Ⓕ25-8144. Set in a picturesque area close to the castle ruins, Hagi's most luxurious ryokan combines traditional Japanese rooms, gardens and cuisine with a Western-style lobby backed by an English garden. ❾

Petit Hotel Clanvert プチホテルクランベール 370-9 Hijiwara Ⓣ0838/25-8711. Good-value modern hotel with comfy Western-style rooms, all with twin beds. There's also a kids' play area and a smart café. Breakfast and dinner cost ¥3600 extra. ⑤

Tomitaya 冨田屋 Hashimoto-chō 61 ⓣ0838/22-0025, ⓕ25-8232. Friendly ryokan with spotless rooms, each with an alcove featuring a suitably seasonal hanging scroll as well as a sitting room. Breakfast, served in front of the big-screen television in the communal dining room, is beautifully presented; you can opt out of dinner for a cheaper rate. ⑦

Tomoe 常茂恵 Hijiwara ⓣ0838/22-0150, ⓦwww.tomoehagi.jp. Along with Hokumon Yashiki (see above), this is the best option for enjoying traditional Japanese hospitality and cuisine, albeit at a hefty price. The warm orange walls of this swanky modern ryokan offset the Zen minimalism of the rest of the decor. Rooms overlook the surrounding raked-gravel gardens. ⑨

The Town

Much of Hagi's charm is as a place for meandering strolls and bike rides. The tourist map suggests several cycling routes, and if you set off early the main sights can be seen in a day. There's no shortage of English direction signs, and at each of the sights you'll usually find an English explanation.

If time is limited, head first to the scenic **Jōkamachi** district. If you're starting from Higashi-Hagi Station, you'd be wise first to check out the temples and shrines in the hills to the south or the coastal routes, leaving Jōkamachi as the final stop, to be enjoyed once most of the day-trippers have gone home.

Jōkamachi and around

From Higashi-Hagi Station, the most direct route to the **Jōkamachi** district (城下町) is along the main road heading west across the river, which will take you through Hagi's central shopping area and the **Teramachi** district (so-called because it contains some twenty temples, or *tera*). Bordering Jōkamachi is the surprisingly clean and picturesque **Kikugahama** beach (菊ヶ浜), officially open for swimming only from mid-July to mid-August, after which you'll have to watch out for jellyfish.

At the end of the beach, across a narrow channel, rises Shizuki-yama, a 143m-high hill surrounded by **Shizuki-kōen** (指月公園; daily: March 8.30am–6pm; April–Oct 8am–6.30pm; Nov–Feb 8.30am–4.30pm; ¥210). The park is home to the rustic *Hananoe* teahouse (tea costs ¥500), an atmospheric shrine and the moat and sloping stone walls of **Hagi-jō**, all that remains of the castle destroyed in 1874 when Mōri Takachika shifted court to Yamaguchi (see p.562).

Yoshida Shōin

Born into a Hagi **samurai** family in 1830, the charismatic **Yoshida Shōin** believed that the only way self-isolated, military-ruled Japan could face up to the industrialized world – knocking at the country's door in the insistent form of Commodore Perry (see p.771) – was to ditch the Tokugawa government, reinstate the emperor and rapidly emulate the ways of the West. To this end, he tried to leave Japan in 1854 on one of Perry's ships, together with a fellow samurai, but was handed over to the authorities who imprisoned him in Edo (Tokyo) before banishing him back to Hagi.

Once at home, Yoshida didn't let up in his revolutionary campaign to "revere the emperor, expel the barbarians". From 1857 he was kept under house arrest in the Shōka Sonjuku (now within the shrine grounds of Shōin-jinja), where he taught many young disciples, including the future Meiji-era prime minister Itō Hirobumi. Eventually Yoshida became too big a thorn in the shogunate's side and he was executed in 1860, aged 29, for plotting to assassinate an official.

Five years later, samurai and peasants joined forces in Hagi to bring down the local Tokugawa government. This, and similar revolts in western Japan (see p.771), led to Yoshida's aim being achieved in 1867 – the restoration of the emperor to power.

It takes twenty minutes to hike to the top of Shizuki-yama, or you can relax beside the quiet cove with modern sculptures on the west side of the park.

Immediately south of the park are several large pottery factories with showrooms and a long wood and plaster tenement building where soldiers of the Mōri clan once lived. Entry to the soldiers' residence is covered by the same ticket as for Shizuki-kōen, and as you walk the path outside the building you can look into the various rooms and imagine life here two centuries ago. Return east through the picturesque **Horiuchi** quarter, with narrow lanes lined by whitewashed buildings decorated with distinctive black-and-white lattice plasterwork. High- and low-ranking samurai, along with rich merchants, once lived in this area – you'll notice the *natsu mikan* (summer orange) trees heavily laden with fruit behind the high stone and mud walls; these were planted in 1876 as a way for the redundant samurai to earn some money. Several of the old houses are open to the public, the most interesting being the **Kikuya-ke Jūtaku** (菊屋家住宅; daily 9am–5pm; ¥500), built in 1604 for a wealthy merchant family. It has a particularly lovely garden, which you can see from the main tatami guest room, as well as displays of many household items. Just south of the Kikuya residence is the **Takasugi Shinsaku Kyūtaku** (高杉晋作旧宅; daily: Nov–March 9am–4pm; April–Oct 8am–5pm; ¥100), home of Takasugi Shinsaku, a leading figure in the fight to restore the emperor to power. Like his mentor, Yoshida Shōin (see box, p.573), Takasugi died tragically young at 29, a year before the Meiji Restoration in 1868.

The tiny **Ishii Tea Bowl Museum** (石井茶碗美術館; 9am–noon & 1–4.45pm; closed Tues; ¥500), at the southern end of Jōkamachi, contains a few prime examples of *Hagi-yaki* tea bowls, as well as a jumble of knick-knacks including toys, lamps and old cameras. A little further south is the **Hagi Uragami Museum** (萩浦上記念館; 9am–5pm; closed Mon; ¥300), which houses a collection of *ukiyo-e* prints and oriental ceramics, as well as a display of the tools and processes employed in *ukiyo-e* print making.

South of Higashi-Hagi Station

One kilometre southeast of Higashi-Hagi Station, on the mountain side of the Mastumoto-gawa, is **Shōin-jinja** (松陰神社), Hagi's largest shrine, dedicated to the nineteenth-century scholar and revolutionary figure Yoshida Shōin (see box, p.573). Within the shrine grounds is **Shōka Sonjuku** (松下村塾), the small academy where Yoshida lived and taught during the final years of his life, the **Yoshida Shōin History Museum** (吉田松陰歴史館; daily 9am–5pm; ¥500), illustrating various scenes from Yoshida's life and also the **residence** (daily 9am–5pm; free) where he was held under house arrest following his attempt to leave Japan in 1854.

Following the riverside cycle path uphill from the shrine leads you to one of the family temples of the Mōri clan, **Tōkō-ji** (東光寺; daily 8.30am–5pm; ¥300), where there's an atmospheric graveyard packed with neat rows of more than five hundred moss-covered stone lanterns. The temple, founded in 1691, has a Chinese flavour to its many handsome buildings and gates. Look out for the giant wooden carp gong hanging in the courtyard as you walk behind the main hall towards the graveyard. Here you'll find the tombs of five Mōri lords, all odd-numbered genertions, save the first lord buried with the even-numbered generations in nearby Daishō-in (see opposite), guarded by an army of lanterns. During the Obon (Aug 15), the lanterns are lit to send off the souls of the dead. Cycling up the hill behind the temple will bring you to **Tanjōchi**, the birthplace of Yoshida Shōin, marked by a bronze statue of the samurai revolutionary and one of his followers. Take in the view of the town before heading back downhill, past the small thatched home of **Itō Hirobumi** (伊藤博文旧宅), another Yoshida disciple who later became prime minister and drafted the Meiji constitution. Cross over to the west bank of the Matsumoto-gawa and follow the river south to the start of the **Aiba-gawa**, a narrow canal teeming with carp.

The final sight to check out on a tour of this side of Hagi is the **Daishō-in** temple (大照院; daily 8am–5pm; ¥200), around ten minutes' bike ride from the Aiba-gawa, west of Hagi Station on the south bank of the Hashimoto-gawa. The temple was built after the death of Mōri Hidenari, the first lord of the Hagi branch of the Mōri clan. A rickety gate leads to another lantern-filled graveyard, where you'll find the tombs of all the even-numbered Mōri lords, as well as Hidenari's and those of eight samurai who committed *seppuku* (ritual suicide) on his death.

North to Kasa-yama

Along the coastal route Highway 191, directly north of Higashi-Hagi Station, is **Yoshiga Taibi Kinenkan** (吉賀大眉記念館; daily 9am–5pm; ¥500), one of Hagi's most respected pottery kilns, with an attached museum displaying an outstanding collection of *Hagi-yaki*. If you call in advance (Ⓣ0838/26-5180) you can make your own pottery for ¥2000, which will be fired and sent to you for an extra fee after a couple of months. Unlike some other kilns, this one will post pottery abroad.

A fifteen-minute bike ride further north along the indented coast will take you past several fishing villages, where drying squid hang on lines like wet underwear, out along a narrow peninsula to the **Myōjin-ike**, a saltwater pond teeming with fish, at the foot of a small, extinct volcano, **Kasa-yama** (笠山). Set back from the pond, beside a small shrine, is an interesting natural phenomenon: the **Kazeana**, a shaded glade cooled by cold air rushing from cracks in the lava. Naturally, you'll find a café in this amenable spot, which is a good place to cool down after hiking the 112m up Kasa-yama. At the summit there are panoramic views along the coast and you can inspect the 30m crater, one of the smallest in the world.

Eating and drinking

You'll find many of Hagi's **restaurants** around the central Tamachi shopping arcade and the main cross street, Route 262. There's not a huge choice, but you won't go wrong if you opt for a cheap noodle bar or fish restaurant. The local speciality is whitebait, and in spring you'll see fishermen on the Matsumoto-gawa sifting the water with giant nets hung from their narrow boats.

Don-don どんどん 177 Hijiwara 3-ku. Bustling, inexpensive noodle joint near the Hagi-bashi across the Matsumoto-gawa. A bowl of udon noodles plus *taki-kome gohan* (vegetable rice) and pickles costs ¥700. Order at the counter, and point at the plastic dishes in the window if you can't read the menu.

Kimono Style Café 2-39 Gofuku-machi, Jōkamachi. Café, shop and kimono experience all in one: delicious cake and coffee sets for ¥700, soup and toast from ¥580 and kimono rental experience from ¥2480. 9am–6pm; closed Thurs.

O-cha Dokoro お茶処 Gofuku-machi, Jōkamachi. A pleasant place to rest and sample various types of Japanese tea (from ¥500). Sit either on the tatami or at a low table, admire the mini-garden and enjoy tea and sweets served by waitresses in kimono.

Village 291-1 Hijiwara. Laidback café-bar on the second floor of a white building on the way to the Matsumoto-bashi. Serves cheap meals of spaghetti and pilaf as well as yummy yoghurt drinks, and alcohol. There are often live jazz performances here at the weekend. Closed Tues.

Tsuwano

Some 80km east of Hagi, in the neighbouring prefecture of Shimane-ken, is the older and even more picturesque castle town of **TSUWANO** (津和野). Nestling in the shadow of the 908m-high extinct volcano, **Aono-yama**, around which mists swirl moodily each autumn, this is yet another small town that touts itself as a "Little

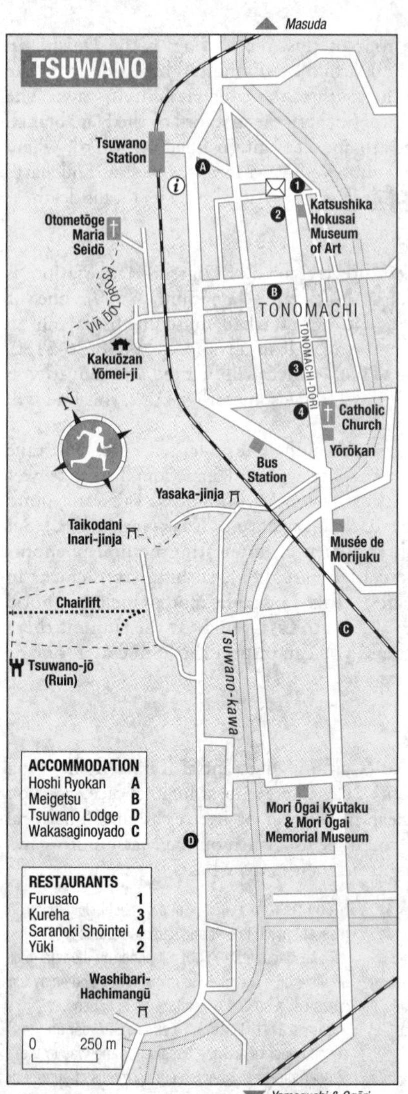

Kyoto". Thankfully (for once), there really is an air of courtly affluence along the tourist-jammed streets of **Tonomachi**, the well-preserved central area of samurai houses, with their distinctive cross-hatched black-and-white plaster walls.

Arrival and information

By **train**, Tsuwano is reached on the cross-country JR Yamaguchi line. From Shin-Yamaguchi, where the Shinkansen stops, the fastest journey takes just over an hour, while from Masuda (near Iwami Airport; see p.572), on the San'in coast, express trains take thirty minutes, just ten minutes faster than the local service. Tsuwano Station is also the terminus for the **SL Yamaguchi-gō** steam-train service (see p.562). There are also direct **bus** services to Tsuwano from Hagi (5 daily; ¥2080, 1hr 45min). The bus station is a few minutes' walk from Tonomachi, the heart of the old samurai district.

To the right of the train station is the **tourist office** (daily 9am–5pm; ⓣ0856/72-1771, ⓔtsuwanok@iwami.or.jp). It's worth picking up the excellent English guidebook to the town (¥200), which is updated every April.

Tsuwano's sights are somewhat spread out, so if you intend to explore beyond Tonomachi, rent a **bicycle** from one of the many operations around the station (¥500/2hr, ¥800/day). Alternatively, infrequent **buses** run to the southern end of town, from where you can walk back towards the station, seeing most of the sights in a couple of hours.

Accommodation

There's little more than a day's leisurely sightseeing and walks around Tsuwano, but an **overnight stay** is recommended if you want to sample a traditional ryokan or minshuku, of which the town has several. Rates mostly start at a reasonable ¥7000 per person including two meals, and the tourist office by Tsuwano Station can help you find a place if the ones below are full.

Hoshi Ryokan 星旅館 Ekimae ⓣ0856/72-0136, ⓕ0241. Slightly run-down but friendly ryokan near the station. The reasonable rates include two delicious meals. ⑤

Meigetsu 明月 Uochō ⓣ0856/72-0685, ⓕ0637. Tsuwano's most charming ryokan, with an attractive flower display at the front door, polished wood fittings, spacious tatami rooms and a small traditional garden. Rates include two meals, which feature seasonal mountain vegetables and carp. ⑦

Tsuwano Lodge 津和野ロッジ Washibara ⓣ0856/72-1683, ⓕ2880. Friendly hotel set on the west bank of the Tsuwano-kawa. Meals included, and there's a small rotemburo. ⑥

Wakasaginoyado 若さぎの宿 Mori ⓣ&ⓕ0856/72-1146. Homely minshuku with an English-speaking owner and good tatami rooms with TV and a/c. Inexpensive rates include breakfast and dinner but you can also pay ¥4500 per person without meals. ⑤

The Town

Head first to the old streets of **Tonomachi** (殿町), southeast of the station. At the north end of the main pedestrian thoroughfare, Tonomachi-dōri, pause at the small **Katsushika Hokusai Museum of Art** (葛飾北斎美術館; daily 9.30am–5pm; ¥500) to view its refined collection of woodblock prints, illustrations and paintings by the famous nineteenth-century artist Hokusai Katsushika.

Tonomachi's streets are bordered by narrow, carp-filled canals; the fish (which outnumber the town's nine thousand residents by more than ten to one) were originally bred as emergency food supplies in the event of famine. The town's prosperity, born of peace and enlightened rule by local *daimyō*, is evident from the handsome buildings. Look out for sake breweries and shops selling traditional sweets, including *genji-maki*, a soft sponge filled with sweet red-bean paste.

Easily spotted behind the white, tile-capped walls is the grey spire of the **Catholic Church**, built in 1931, which combines stained-glass windows and an organ with tatami flooring. Further along, near the banks of the Tsuwano-kawa, is the **Yōrōkan** (養老館), the former school for young samurai, now containing an uninspiring folk art museum (8.30am–5pm, closed Wed; ¥250).

Make a short detour across the Tsuwano-gawa to the **Musée de Morijuku** (杜塾美術館; daily 9am–5pm; ¥500), a restored farmhouse fronted by raked-gravel gardens that has been converted into a smart modern gallery showing works by local contemporary artists, plus a small collection of etchings by Goya. Upstairs, the attendant will show you the pinhole camera in the *shōji* screen, capturing an image of the garden outside.

Back across the river, just west of the train tracks, is the **Yasaka-jinja** shrine, where each July 20–27 the ancient *Sagi-Mai* ("Heron Dance") is performed by men dressed as the white birds, complete with flapping wings and long-necked hats. Nearby, a path covered by a tunnel of over a thousand red *torii* leads uphill towards the **Taikodani Inari-jinja** (太鼓谷稲成神社), one of the five largest Inari shrines in Japan. The bright-red and gold shrine bustles with tourists who say prayers to the local Shinto deities outside the splendid main hall.

The views of Tsuwano from the shrine's hillside location are good, but not as dramatic as those from the top of the hill where the ruins of the town's castle, **Tsuwano-jō**, stand. The castle was built in 1295 by Lord Yoshimi Yoriyuki as protection against potential Mongol invaders. The castle was dismantled at the start of the Meiji era, but you can still walk around the remnants of the walls. If you fancy an energetic hike, follow the pathway leading up to the old castle grounds (around a 30min walk), or take the **chairlift** (daily 10am–5pm; ¥450 return).

Going downhill from the bottom of the chairlift, you'll find yourself at the southern end of Tsuwano. If you cross over the river and head south along the main road, you'll soon reach **Mori Ōgai Kyūtaku**, the preserved wood and mustard-plaster home of a famed Meiji-era novelist. Personal effects of the writer, and his death mask, are displayed next door in the modern **Mori Ōgai Memorial**

Museum (森鴎外記念館; daily 9am–5pm; ¥600). Crossing back over the river again and following it southwest, you'll reach the **Washibari Hachimangū** shrine. It's well worth braving the crowds to see its annual Yabusame Horseback Archery Competition, held on the second Sunday in April.

Otometōge Maria Seidō to Kakuōzan Yōmei-ji

If you have some time to spare, there's a pleasant woodland hike in the hills behind Tsuwano Station. Head southwest and cross the train tracks at the first opportunity, then double back and continue to the car park, from where a footpath leads up to the cosy chapel of **Otometōge Maria Seidō** (乙女峠マリア聖堂), nestling in a leafy glade. In 1865, the Tokugawa shogunate transported some 150 Christians from Nagasaki to Tsuwano; 36 were eventually put to death for their beliefs before the new Meiji government bowed to international pressure, lifting the ban on the religion in 1874. This chapel was built in 1951 to commemorate the martyrs, and the quaint wooden building is the scene of the **Otometōge festival** on May 3.

From the chapel a series of wooden signs counts down the Stations of the Cross along the **Via Dolorosa footpath**, winding up the hillside. The path emerges from the forest onto a wider dirt track leading downhill to the charming temple of **Kakuōzan Yōmei-ji** (覚皇山永明寺; daily 8.30am–5pm; ¥300). Stone steps lead up to the elegant collection of thatched wooden buildings, used by generations of Tsuwano lords since 1420. Inside, look out for the lovely screen paintings decorating some of the tatami rooms and take a moment to sit and admire the verdant traditional garden. From the temple it's a five-minute walk back to Tsuwano Station.

Eating

Tsuwano isn't short of **restaurants**, with several *shokudō* and noodle shops close to the station and around the scenic Tonomachi area. Finding an evening meal can be tricky, since most visitors who stop over eat in their ryokan or minshuku. *Uzume-meshi*, the traditional local dish of rice in a broth with shredded green mountain vegetables, pieces of tofu and mushrooms, is worth trying, as is the carp.

Furusato ふる里 Gion-chō. This small restaurant, in a traditional plaster house, specializes in *uzume-meshi*, served as part of a set meal (¥1500) with slices of white root-vegetable jelly coated in lemon sauce and pickles. Daily 11am–3pm.

Kureha 紅葉 Yamane-chō. Cakes and omelettes are the speciality at this cute little coffee house, which has English-speaking staff. Avoid the lunch rush at noon. Tues–Fri 10am–6pm, Sat & Sun 9am–6pm.

Saranoki Shōintei 沙羅の木松韻亭 Yamane-chō. From the large tatami room you can gaze out on a lovely traditional garden while eating a set meal (¥2625 or ¥5250) of *kaiseki ryōri* haute cuisine. There's an attached *omiyage* shop and café that overlooks the main street. Daily until 4pm.

Yūki 遊亀 Honmachi. This famous restaurant has a carp-filled stream running through the dining room. Some of the fish end up on the plate as sashimi or in the miso soup. Try the ¥2000 *Tsuwano teishoku*, a set meal of local dishes. Daily until 7pm; closed Fri.

Matsue and beyond

Straddling the strip of land between the lagoons of Nakaumi and Shinji-ko is **MATSUE** (松江), the appealing prefectural capital of Shimane-ken, 180km east of Tsuwano, and one of the highlights of the San'in coast. Although the city's main sights – one of Japan's few original castles, **Matsue-jō**, an area of samurai residences and the museum and one-time home of nineteenth-century expat writer **Lafcadio Hearn** (see p.582) – are so closely grouped together that they can all easily be seen in half a day, it's worth lingering here. The lakes, rivers and castle moat lend this modern city a soothing, faintly Venetian atmosphere, and it's still possible to catch glimpses of the old Japan that so enchanted Hearn a century ago, such as fishermen casting their nets in **Shinji-ko**, or prodding the lake bed with poles, searching out shellfish.

There's also plenty to see in the area around Matsue, including the stunning landscapes at the **Adachi Museum of Art**, the shrines and burial mounds at **Fudoki-no-Oka**, and **Izumo Taisha**, one of Japan's most important shrines, holiday home of the Shinto pantheon of deities, and the reason that Matsue was dubbed "chief city of the province of the gods" by Hearn. Some 130km east of Matsue, **Mount Daisen**, the cluster of hot-spring resorts around **Kurayoshi** and the coastal sand dunes around the Tottori prefecture's eponymous capital all offer stunning scenery.

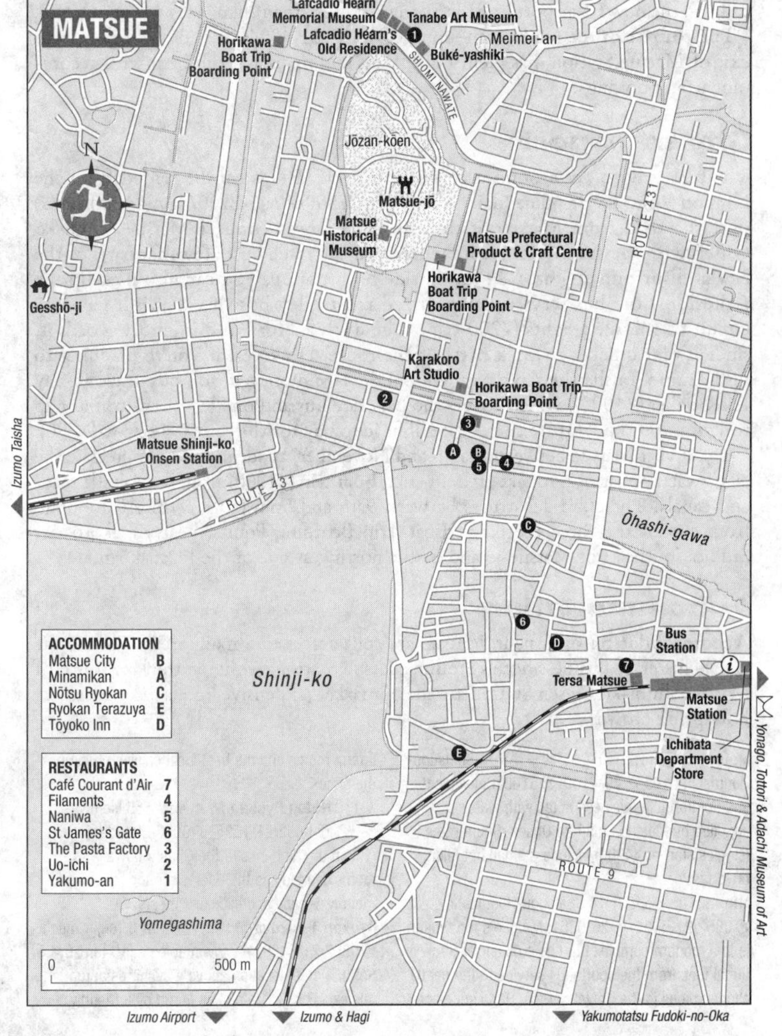

Arrival and information

JR **trains** arrive at **Matsue Station**, south of the Ōhashi-gawa, while **Matsue Shinji-ko Onsen Station** (complete with public hot-spring footbath outside), just north of where the river flows into Lake Shinji, is the terminus for Ichibata trains from Izumo Taisha (see p.585). The most convenient Shinkansen stop is Okayama, from where local trains run to Matsue (the fastest takes 2hr 20min). There are also sleeper train services from Tokyo via **Yonago**, the main San'in coast railway junction, some 25km east of Matsue. Most long-distance **buses** arrive beside Matsue Station; the rest go to Matsue Shinji-ko Onsen Station. There are overnight services from Tokyo (¥11,550) and Fukuoka (¥8800) and daily services from Ōsaka (¥5100) and Hiroshima (¥4000). For **flights**, the closest airport is **Izumo Airport**, 35km west, although **Yonago Airport** to the east is also an option. Direct buses run from Izumo to Matsue Station (¥1000), while from Yonago you can catch a train on the new JR airport link for Yonago Station, then change for Matsue (¥740).

The **tourist office** (daily 9am–6pm; ⓣ0852/21-4034), just outside the north exit of Matsue Station, has plenty of leaflets and maps and can help with accommodation bookings.

City transport

The best way to get around is to walk or cycle. **Bikes** can be rented from the Nippon Rent-a-Car office (daily 8am–8pm; ¥500/2hr, ¥1100/day, ¥1600/24hr) over the road from Matsue Station. Regular **buses** connect Matsue Shinji-ko Onsen with Matsue Station, from where you can catch buses to other parts of the city and surrounding area. From outside both stations you can also pick up the **Lakeside Line** bus service, a motorized red trolley bus that makes a leisurely circuit of Matsue's sights (¥200/trip). The day-pass for ¥500 is hardly worth it, since it's far quicker to walk parts of the route. However, if you're planning to visit Izumo Taisha the same day, you might save money if you buy the one-day L&R ticket (¥1000), which covers the Lakeside bus and one leg of the round trip to Izumo on the Ichibata train – you'll have to pay for the return journey (¥790).

If you visit Matsue between March and November, an ideal way to appreciate the city's watery charms is to take an hour-long **boat** trip (¥1200) around the castle moat and canals. There are departures between 9am and 5pm (July & Aug 9am–6pm) from any of the three Horikawa Boat Trip Boarding Points: near Karakoro Art Studio, southeast of Matsue-jō and on the northwest side of the Jōzan-kōen.

Accommodation

Accommodation options in Matsue are split across two main areas. There's the usual cluster of business hotels around Matsue Station, while on the lake south of Matsue Shinji-ko Onsen Station are the upmarket, expensive hotels catering to the hot-spring crowd.

Matsue City Hotel 松江シティーホテル Suetsugu-Honmachi ⓣ0852/25-4100, ⓕ5100. Convenient and comfortable business hotel, with water supplied by Matsue Shinji-ko Onsen. Room rates (singles start at ¥4900) include a small but filling breakfast bentō. 5

Minamikan 皆実館 14 Suetsugu-Honmachi ⓣ0852/21-5131, ⓕ26-0351. Matsue's top ryokan is in a modern complex but has a distinctly traditional feel, from the courteous service to the neatly clipped pines in the gravel garden. Huge suites of tatami rooms and the best local cuisine push up the prices. 8

Nōtsu Ryokan 野津旅館 555 Isemiya-chō ⓣ0852/21-1525, ⓕ9096. Smart new ryokan on the banks of the Ōhashi-gawa with rooms overlooking the river, a rooftop rotemburo, friendly service and excellent meals. 9

Ryokan Terazuya 旅館寺津屋 60-3 Tenjin-machi ⓣ0852/21-3480, ⓦwww.mable.ne.jp/~terazuya. Set in a quiet location above a sushi restaurant, this excellent-value ryokan is run by a friendly

English-speaking couple and has well-kept Japanese-style rooms with a/c and TV. Room only, ¥4000; with meals ⑤

Tōyoko Inn 東横イン 498-10 Asahi-machi ⓣ0852/60-1045, ⓦwww.toyoko-inn.com. This budget accommodation is clean, reliable and offers in-room internet access and complimentary Japanese breakfast. ④

The Town

Clustered together around **Jōzan-kōen** and **Shiomi Nawate**, the latter a parade of samurai residences, are Matsue's finest attractions: **Matsue-jō**, the **Matsue Historical Museum**, a handsome samurai district and the museum and former residence of **Lafcadio Hearn** (see box, p.582). If you plan to visit all the main sights, it's best to buy the **Universal Pass** (¥920) at the first of the sights you visit; it's valid for three days, will save you money on the separate entrance fees and get you discounts at other attractions around the city. The best place to head at the end of the day, especially if the weather is good, is the eastern shore of **Shinji-ko**, where a mass of photographers often gathers to capture the golden sunset behind Yomegashima, a tiny pine-studded island in the lake.

Matsue-jō and around

The brooding, five-storey donjon of **Matsue-jō** (松江城; daily: April–Sept 8.30am–6.30pm; Oct–March 8.30am–5pm; ¥550, half-price for foreign visitors), standing on top of the hill, Oshiro-yama, is still the focal point of the city, as it was when the *daimyō* Horio Yoshiharu first built his castle in 1611. Compared to Himeji-jō's donjon (see p.521), this one looks as if it's been squashed, but it is, in fact, the largest of the twelve remaining original castle towers scattered around Japan – its sinister aspect is enhanced by the black-painted wood decorating the walls. The castle was extensively renovated in the 1950s, and the surrounding grounds, defined by the inner moat, have been turned into a pleasant park, **Jōzan-kōen**. English-speaking guides are available at weekends, and on weekdays if you book at the tourist information office (see opposite).

If you're taking a bus from Matsue Station to the castle, get off at Kenchō-mae and you'll see the castle grounds dead ahead. Leave your shoes at the entrance to the donjon, and climb the slippy wooden stairs to the fifth-floor *Tengu* ("Long-Nosed Goblin") room in your socks. This is where the lords would have commanded their armies from if there had been any battles (which there weren't). On the second floor there are displays of armour, weapons and other artefacts, including the original *shachi* (mythical dolphins) that topped the roof. The views across the city towards the lake and sea are still splendid.

Within Jōzan-kōen you'll also find the **Matsue Historical Museum** (松江郷土館; daily 8.30am–5pm; free), in an elegant whitewashed wooden building, whose combination of pillars, verandas and ornate gabled roof is typical of the hybrid style of the Meiji era. The two-storey mansion was built in 1903 to accommodate the emperor on the off chance that he might visit the city, which he never did. It now contains an interesting collection of colourful local arts and crafts, including plenty of tea-ceremony utensils.

Shiomi Nawate and around

Leave the park by the bridge in the northwest corner, follow the moat as it turns east and you'll come to **Shiomi Nawate**, where a number of samurai residences have been converted into museums and remain protected by high walls capped with grey tiles. On the corner is the **Lafcadio Hearn Memorial Museum** (小泉八雲記念館; daily: April–Sept 8.30am–6.30pm; Oct–March 8.30am–5pm; ¥300, half-price for foreign visitors), which provides an excellent introduction to

Lafcadio Hearn

"There is some charm unutterable in the morning air, cool with the coolness of Japanese spring and wind-waves from the snowy cone of Fuji..."

Lafcadio Hearn, *My First Day in the Orient*

The journalist **Lafcadio Hearn** was enchanted by Japan, and of all expat writers is by far the most respected by the Japanese. Celebrated by Matsue as an adopted son, his books, including *Glimpses of Unfamiliar Japan* and *Kwaidan*, are considered classics.

The offspring of a passionate but doomed liaison between an Anglo-Irish army surgeon and a Greek girl, and named after the Greek island of Lefkada on which he was born on June 27, 1850, Hearn grew up in Dublin, a contemporary of Bram Stoker and Oscar Wilde. A schoolyard accident in 1866 left him permanently blind in his left eye, and in 1869 the young and penniless Hearn decided to chance his fortune in the United States. Over the course of the next fourteen years Hearn worked as a reporter and writer in Cincinatti, New Orleans and the West Indian island of Martinique (where he penned his first novel, *Chita),* with a brief marriage to an African-American girl along the way.

Commissioned by *Harper's Monthly* to write about Japan, Hearn arrived in Yokohama on April 4, 1890. By the end of the day he had decided to stay, get a teaching job and write a book. The teaching post brought Hearn to Matsue, where he met and married Koizumi Setsu, the daughter of an impoverished samurai family.

Hearn would happily have stayed in Matsue, but the freezing winter weather made him ill and in 1891 they moved south to Kumamoto, in Kyūshū, closer to Setsu's relatives. The couple had four children and in 1896 he adopted the name Koizumi Yakumo (Eight Clouds) and secured Japanese nationality. By the turn of the century, Hearn's novels and articles had become a great success; he had started teaching at Tokyo's prestigious Waseda University, and was invited to give a series of lectures at London University and in the United States. But, on September 30, 1904, at the age of 54, Hearn suffered a series of heart attacks and died. His gravestone in Zoshigaya cemetery near Ikebukuro in Tokyo proclaims him a "man of faith, similar to the undefiled flower blooming like eight rising clouds who dwells in the mansion of right enlightenment".

Hearn's books stand as paeans to the beauty and mystery of old Japan, something he believed worth recording because it seemed to be fast disappearing in the nonstop modernization of the early Meiji years.

the life and works of the revered writer (see above) and is curated by Hearn's great-grandson, Bon Koizumi. There are lots of English captions and you can also see Hearn's favourite writing desk and chair, specially designed so that he could better use his one good eye. Next door is **Lafcadio Hearn's Old Residence** (小泉八雲旧居; daily 9am–5pm; ¥350), the small, old samurai house where the writer lived from May to November 1891 and in which he began work on two of his most famous books, *Glimpses of Unfamiliar Japan* and the ghost story collection *Kwaidan*. Sit in the calm of the tatami rooms, read the English leaflet containing extracts from Hearn's essay, "In a Japanese Garden", which is about the house, and see how little has changed.

The next high wall shields the contemporary building of the **Tanabe Art Museum** (田部美術館; 9am–5pm; closed Mon; ¥600), established by the late prefectural governor Tanabe Chōemon XXIII, who was also a respected artist with a particular interest in the aesthetics of the tea ceremony. The museum contains the Tanabe family's refined collection, centred around pottery tea bowls and tea utensils. There's a pleasant, airy café where you can have tea (¥350) overlooking the museum's garden.

Further along Shiomi Nawate is the largest samurai house remaining in Matsue, the **Buké-yashiki** (武家屋敷; daily: April–Sept 8.30am–6.30pm; Oct–March 8.30am–5pm; ¥300, half-price for foreign visitors), built in 1730 as the home of the Shiomi family, high-ranking retainers to the ruling Matsudaira clan. The attractive complex of buildings has been well preserved and you can wander round the exterior, looking into tatami and wood rooms, which give some sense of what eighteenth-century samurai life was like.

The dusty grounds of the Buké-yashiki are a contrast to the precise Zen beauty of the raked gravel and artfully positioned stones around the **Meimei-an teahouse** (明々庵; grounds daily 9am–5pm; ¥300), a short walk up the hill directly behind Shiomi Nawate. Originally designed by the *daimyō* Matsudaira Fumai to exact tea-ceremony principles, the tiny cottage has creamy beige plaster walls which hardly look capable of holding up the heavily thatched roof. In 1966, to celebrate its 150th anniversary, Meimei-an was restored and moved to this spot beside an existing samurai mansion with a good prospect of the castle. You can't enter the teahouse itself, but it's still worth taking time to admire it from the veranda of the adjoining mansion.

Karakoro Art Studio

Near the Kyobashi Bridge is the **Karakoro Art Studio** (daily 9.30am–6.30pm; free), housed in a stately former bank. The complex contains a small gallery exhibiting locally produced glass art, kimono and fabric, and a number of craft shops (some close at 5pm) selling jewellery, clothing and stained glass. There's also a classy restaurant with affordable lunchtime specials, and a café serving cappuccino and mouthwatering Italian ice cream that can be enjoyed in the breezy courtyard.

Eating and drinking

Matsue's range of restaurants isn't wide, but they are of high quality and reasonably priced; a good place to head for is the Suetsugu Honmachi area beside the canal just south of the castle. If you're on a budget, pack a picnic to enjoy in the castle grounds or at Meimei-an.

You'll find various **drinking** options in the Isemiya district near Matsue Station and the side streets of Tohonchō between the canal and the Ōhashi-gawa. *Filaments* is generally recommended as a *gaijin*-friendly bar, but can be a little expensive, and *St James's Gate* is a *gaijin*-run Irish pub.

Café Courant d'Air 494-13 Asahi-machi. Sophisticated café, with subdued lighting, classical music and classy decor, offering thick slices of creamy sponge cake and fancy coffees. Daily until 9pm.

Naniwa. なにわ 21 Suetsugu-Honmachi ⓣ0852/21-2835. Popular, classy restaurant perched on the edge of Shinji-ko that serves beautiful *kaiseki* meals and more modest "ladies"

Kyōdo ryōri in Matsue

Epicureans flock to Matsue for its **Kyōdo ryōri**, seven types of dishes using fish and seafood from Shinji-ko. The dishes, best sampled in winter when all the fish are available and tasting their freshest, are: *amasagi*, smelt either cooked as tempura or marinated in teriyaki sauce; *koi*, carp baked in a rich, sweet sauce; *moroge-ebi*, steamed prawns; *shijimi*, small shellfish usually served in miso soup; *shirauo*, whitebait eaten raw as sashimi or cooked as tempura; *suzuki*, bass wrapped in paper and steam-baked over hot coals; and *unagi*, grilled freshwater eel. To sample the full seven courses, make an advance reservation with one of the top ryokan, such as *Minamikan* (ⓣ0852/21-5131), and be ready to part with at least ¥10,000.

set dinners. It's also one of the best places to try *Kyōdo ryōri*, with prices ranging between ¥4200 and ¥7350, depending on the size.
The Pasta Factory 82 Suetsugu-Honmachi. Build your own pasta (¥830), salad or hot sandwich at this fun, casual restaurant by filling out (English) order forms with a pencil.
Uo-ichi 魚一 78 Katahara-chō. This is a good place to try some of the *Kyōdo ryōri* fish dishes. The set menu costs ¥4200, but there are cheaper meals, starting at around ¥1050, which include sashimi and tempura. Friendly service either at the counter or at tables on tatami. Closed Tues.
Yakumo-an 八雲庵308 Kitabori-chō, Shiomi Nawate. Popular, picturesque restaurant in a former samurai residence, with a central garden, teahouse and carp-filled pond, specializing in good-value soba and udon noodles, including *warigo soba*. Daily until 4.30pm.

Yakumotatsu Fudoki-no-Oka

The area around Matsue, once known as Izumo, is one of the longest settled in Japan, with a written history dating back to the seventh-century *Izumo-no-Kuni Fudoki* (*The Topography of Izumo*). Keyhole-shaped burial mounds (*kofun*) from this period can be seen in the rice-field-dotted countryside at **Yakumotatsu Fudoki-no-Oka** (八雲立つ風土記の丘), a museum and park thirty minutes by bus south of Matsue Station (platform 4; 30min). The **museum** (9am–5pm; closed Tues; ¥200) is mainly of interest to archeology and history buffs, with a small display of finds from nearby excavations, including impressive pottery horses and some first- and second-century bronze daggers and bells. The park has several pleasant forest and nature walks, plus the **Izumo Kanbe-no-sato** (出雲かんべの里), a couple of buildings promoting local culture where you can watch woodworkers, basket-makers, weavers, potters and a specialist in *temari*, the art of making colourful thread-decorated balls. With an advance reservation (Ⓣ0852/28-0040) you can even take craft lessons here.

Before leaving, check out the nearby fourteenth-century shrine, **Kamosu-jinja** (神魂神社), dedicated to the Shinto mother deity Izanami. The impressive raised wooden structure, in a glade of soaring pines reached via stone steps lined by cherry trees, is one of the few remaining examples of *Taisha-zukuri* or "Grand shrine style" left in Japan.

Adachi Museum of Art

While in Matsue, don't miss taking a trip to the stunning **Adachi Museum of Art** (足立美術館; April–Sept 9am–5.30pm; Oct–March 9am–5pm; ¥2200, half-price for foreign visitors), some 20km east of the city near the village of Yasugi, en route to Yonago. The large collection of Japanese artworks, dating from 1870 to the present day, includes masterpieces by Yokoyama Taikan and Uemura Shoen. The surrounding gardens are also exquisite, covering 43,000 square metres.

The museum's founder, Adachi Zenkō, was an enthusiastic gardener, and his passion for the artform shows through in the beautiful landscapes that envelop the galleries and steal your attention at every turn. The museum is designed so that as you move around, the views of the Dry Landscape Garden, the White Gravel and Pine Garden, the Moss Garden and the Pond Garden appear like living picture scrolls when viewed through carefully placed windows. A couple of the gardens have traditional teahouses where you can take *macha* and sweets (from ¥1500). *Juryū-an* is a copy of a teahouse in the former Imperial Palace, Katsura Rikyū, in Kyoto, and looks over a peaceful moss-covered garden; in the smaller *Juraku-an* visitors are served a bowl of green tea made with water boiled in a kettle of pure gold, said to aid longevity. The two coffee shops in the museum are less atmospheric but cheaper, and the views just as fine.

Give yourself plenty of time here because, once you've dragged yourself away from the gardens, the art itself isn't bad either. The museum has the largest collection of paintings by **Yokoyama Taikan**, whose delicate ink drawings and deep colour screens set the standard for modern Japanese art. There is also a section on kitsch art from children's books, and a ceramics hall which includes works by Kawai Kanjirō – a brilliant local potter who participated actively in the *mingei* (folk art) movement begun by Yanagi Sōetsu – and Kitaōji Rosanjin, a potter and cook, whose pieces were designed to complement and enhance the food served on them.

Direct buses from Matsue's and Yonago's JR stations take around fifty minutes to reach the museum (get off at Saginoyu Onsen), or you can take a train to Yasugi (¥400 from Matsue, ¥190 from Yonago), twenty minutes from the museum by free shuttle bus (8 daily); the tourist information offices in Matsue and Yasugi Station can provide timetables.

Izumo Taisha and around

The grand, graceful shrine of Izumo Oyashiro, second only in importance to that at Ise, is better known as **IZUMO TAISHA** (出雲大社), after the town it's situated in, 33km west of Matsue. Although most of the current buildings date from the nineteenth century, the original shrine was built – if you believe the legend – by Amaterasu, the Sun Goddess, and is still visited each November by all eight million Shinto deities for their annual get-together. In this region the tenth month of the lunar calendar is traditionally known as the "month with gods", while in all other parts of Japan it's known as the "month without gods". Since the shrine is dedicated to Okuninushi-no-mikoto, the God of Happy Marriage, many couples visit in the hope that they will live happily ever after; visitors to the shrine clap their hands four times to summon the deity rather than the usual two.

Arrival and information

From Matsue, the easiest way to reach Izumo Taisha is by **train** on the Ichibata line from Matsue Shinji-ko Onsen Station (松江しんじ湖温泉駅). You'll have to change at Kawato for the final leg to Izumo Taisha. The journey takes an hour and costs ¥790. If you're travelling round both Matsue and Izumo Taisha in the same day you can save some money by buying the ¥1000 L&R Free Kippu (see p.580). JR trains stop at Izumo-shi Station, from where you'll have to transfer to the Ichibata line, changing again at Kawato. The Izumo Taisha-mae terminus is five minutes' walk south of the shrine. There's also a direct Ichibata bus from Izumo-shi Station (¥510; 25min). The Izumo Taisha bus station, from where you can catch buses to Hinomisaki (see p.586), is a minute's walk west of the shrine. A regular bus leaves Izumo Airport for Izumo Taisha daily (35min; ¥850).

The **tourist office** (daily 9am–5.30pm; ⓣ0853/53-2298) is in the train station and has English leaflets. It's only worth renting a bicycle at the station (¥500/3hr, ¥800/day) if you plan to cycle out to Hinomisaki, which takes around thirty minutes.

The shrine and around

A giant concrete *torii* stands at the southern end of Shinmon-dōri, the main approach to the shrine. More in keeping with the shrine's natural grace is the

Izumo Taisha festivals

Apart from the usual Shinto festival days (see pp.57–59), the important festivals at Izumo Taisha are:

Imperial Grand Festival (May 14–16): The welcome mat is rolled out for an envoy from the imperial family.

Kamiari-sai (End of Nov): Celebration for the annual gathering of the Shinto gods.

wooden *torii* that marks the entrance to the forested grounds at the foot of Yakumo-yama. Closer to the central compound, to the right of the Seki-no-Baba, an avenue of gnarled pine trees leaning at odd angles, is a large, modern statue of the deity Okuninushi.

Straight ahead, beyond the bronze *torii*, is the shrine's central compound, the **Oracle Hall**, in front of which hangs a giant *shimenawa*, the traditional twist of straw rope. Inside the hall, Shinto ceremonies take place all day, with accompanying drumming and flute-playing. To the right is a modern building containing the **treasure hall** (daily 8am–4.30pm; ¥150), on the second floor of which you'll find a small collection of swords, statues, armour, painted screens and a map of the shrine, dating from 1248, painted on silk and in remarkably good condition. There's also an illustration of the shrine as it was supposed to have been in the Middle Ages, when it was 48m tall and the highest wooden structure in Japan, topping Nara's Tōdai-ji, home of the great statue of Buddha. It's still the country's tallest, at 24m in height, with projecting rafters that shoot out from the roof.

The inner shrine, or **Honden**, was undergoing one of its periodic reconstructions at the time of writing but is due to be completed in May 2013, when the shrine spirit now temporarily housed in the Oracle Hall will be relocated to its usual home. Unless you've paid to take part in a Shinto ceremony, you'll have to stand outside the **Eight-Legged East Gate** entrance, decorated with beautiful unpainted wooden carvings, and peer through to the inner courtyard. Even pilgrims are not allowed anywhere near the central Holy of Holies hall, buried deep within the Honden – only the head priest can enter.

The branches of the trees surrounding the shrine, on which visitors tie *omikuji* (fortune-telling) papers for good luck, are so heavily laden they look as if they have been coated with snow. In the woods behind the Honden is the **Shōkōkan** (closed until May 2013), the former treasure house, which displays many jolly statues of Daikoku (one of the guises of Okuninushi), and his *bon viveur* son Ebisu, who usually has a fish tucked under his arm.

Leaving the shrine by the west exit (the closest to the bus station and main car park), you'll see a large modern hall, where more daily ceremonies take place and which is also used for the sacred kagura dances performed on festival days. In front of the hall hangs another *shimenawa* into which people fling coins, hoping they will stick and bring them luck.

Apart from the shrine, there are only a couple of other sights worth seeing in Izumo Taisha. Near the cement *Ōtorii* is the **Kichō-kan** (daily 9am–5pm; free), a modern hall with colourful exhibits on the town's festival, including costumes, banners and video films. Also look out for **Iwaidakoten**, where traditional Izumo kites have been made for over seventy years (the large ones cost ¥40,000); it's on the same street as the soba shop *Arakiya* (see opposite), close to Shinmon-dōri.

If you have time, head 10km northwest to the scenic cape of **Hinomisaki** (日御碕), where you'll find a quieter shrine complex, **Hinomisaki-jinja**, built in 1644 under the shogun Tokugawa Ieyasu, and boasting a 44m-tall white stone lighthouse dating from 1903. Climb the steep spiral staircase to the top of the lighthouse (daily 9am–4.30pm; ¥150) for a splendid view out to the nearby islands (you can't go up in bad weather). Around the cape are several bathing beaches. Hinomisaki is a twenty-minute bus ride (¥530) from Izumo Taisha bus station.

Practicalities

With Matsue so close, there's no pressing reason to **stay overnight** in Izumo Taisha. If you do, the *Hinode-kan* (日の出館; Ⓣ0853/53-3311, Ⓕ2014; ❼) and the slightly more expensive but better-kept Takenoya (竹野屋; ⓣ0853/53-3131, ⓕ3134; ❼) are both attractive, friendly places on the main Shinmon-dōri approach to the shrine.

There are lots of bland tourist **restaurants** around the bus station near the shrine. For something more interesting, try the local speciality, **warigo soba**, cold buckwheat noodles seasoned with seaweed flakes, served in three-layer dishes, over which you pour *dashi* stock. The best place to try it is at *Arakiya* (荒木屋), a hospitable outfit about five minutes' walk south of the main throng of tourist canteens. You'll pay ¥780 for *warigo soba*, or you can try one layer of noodles for just ¥250. Both are served with a cup of hot soba-water soup, which you can flavour with *dashi*.

Kurayoshi and around

An hour further east along the coast by train brings you to **KURAYOSHI** (倉吉), a small town in central Tottori-ken and the jumping-off point for the hot-spring resort of **Misasa** and the temple hike up to **Nageire-dō** on Mount Mitoku.

The **tourist information** booth (daily 8.30am–5pm; ⓣ0858/26-9095), to the left outside the station at the end of the bus stands, has maps and Japanese information on the surrounding area and free bikes with which to explore the town.

If you have an hour or two to spare, head for the picturesque **Akagawara** area (赤瓦), a twenty-minute cycle ride from the station (follow signs for **Shirokabe-dozō-gun**; 白壁土蔵群), where a number of recently refurbished Edo- and Meiji-era black-and-white storehouses stand next to the shallow Tama-gawa. These are now home to various souvenir and craft shops selling local goods including beautiful *Kurayoshi-gasuri* items made from the locally woven, indigo-dyed cloth.

Café Mela (closed Thurs), on the second floor of the Sadar Chowk (サダルチョーク) crafts shop opposite the storehouses, serves up authentic Indian curry, lassi and chai, while a little way along the river either side of the storehouses you'll find a couple of peaceful little temples.

Misasa

The hot-spring resort **MISASA** (三朝) is situated in the mountains twenty minutes by bus (platform 3; ¥460) south of Kurayoshi. Take advantage of the free **rotemburo** in the river if you're passing through and feeling brave – there are

Mount Daisen

The main rail and road routes along the coast east of Matsue cross into the neighbouring prefecture of Tottori-ken and through the uninteresting industrial city of **Yonago** (米子); trains from Okayama on the JR Hakubi line terminate here. Yonago is the gateway to **Mount Daisen** (大山), at 1711m the highest mountain in the Chugoku region, and home to beautiful beech forests and ancient temples. Buses (9 daily) depart from bus stop 4 outside Yonago Station for the village of **DAISEN-JI** (大山寺; 8–9 daily; 50min; ¥800), the main hub for accommodation on Mount Daisen, with access to the ski slopes in winter and hiking paths in summer.

Daisen has the largest **ski slopes** in western Japan and sees heavy snowfall from November to April; it's also known for the **Daisen Ice and Snow Festival**, which takes place over three days at the end of January, with fireworks lighting up the night sky and an amazing display of ice sculptures. A couple of minutes' walk east from the bus stop, the **tourist information** booth (Mon–Fri 8.30am–5pm, Sat & Sun 8.30am–6.30pm; ⓣ0859/52-2502) has plenty of maps of the area and staff can help book accommodation.

bamboo screens by the pools, but as onlookers from the nearby bridge have a bird's-eye view of proceedings, this is one communal bathing experience that's not for the shrinking violet.

West of the river is the **Misasa Museum of Art** (みささ美術館; Fri–Mon: April–Nov 9.30am–6pm, Dec–March 9am–5pm; free), home to a collection of wonderful contemporary woodblock prints by local artist Hasegawa on the second floor, and rotating exhibits downstairs.

Misasa is a picturesque place to spend the night, and you'll come across *yukata*-clad visitors wandering through the streets from inn to rotemburo or bar and back again. *Kiya Ryokan* (木屋旅館; ⓣ0858/43-0521, ⓕ0523; ❼ including meals) is a friendly place with fine food and a choice of baths, located on the narrow street dotted with craft shops and tea rooms east of the river. You'll recognize its mint-green roofs from the bus stop.

Mount Mitoku and Nageire-dō

While in the area it's worth taking the bus from Misasa (15min; ¥370) 8km up the road to **Mount Mitoku** (三徳山) to visit the famous **Nageire-dō** (投入堂) temple, part of the Sanbutsu-ji temple (山佛寺); the main Sanbutsu-ji temple complex is just over the road from the bus stop. From here it's an hour's climb up a rugged path (there are chains in places to help you scramble over the massive boulders) past a belfry and a number of smaller temple buildings including Monju-dō (文殊堂) and Jizō-dō, both spectacularly perched on a precipice and with marvellous views. At the very top is Nageire-dō, a wooden structure nestling under an overhanging rock and balanced precariously on stilts which grip the cliff face below. It's an incredible feat of engineering, and no one knows quite how it was built. Legend has it that it was thrown into place by an ascetic priest named Ennogyoja; certainly Sanbutsu-ji has been a centre for Buddhism since the eighth century, and Nageire-dō is thought to date back to the eleventh or twelfth century.

On your way down, try the local speciality of *sansai-ryōri*, mountain vegetables and tofu, at one of the restaurants at the foot of the main temple complex, near the bus stop. Make sure you check bus times for the return trip, however, or you could end up with a long wait for the next bus back to Misasa.

Tottori and around

At the easternmost end of the prefecture, an hour's train ride from Kurayoshi, lies the provincial capital of **TOTTORI** (鳥取), famous in Japan for the 16km-long **sand dunes** (砂丘), part of the San'in Coast National Park, at nearby Hamasaka. Designated a national monument, the dunes themselves are quite atmospheric and come complete with imported camels for would-be Lawrence of Arabias to pose on.

Arrival and information

Tottori Station, on the San'in line, is the terminal of the JR Tsuyama line from Okayama. The **bus station** next to the station is where long-distance buses from Tokyo, Himeji, Hiroshima, Kyoto, Kōbe and Ōsaka stop. Tottori **airport** (ⓣ0857/28-1150), 10km northwest of the city, has daily flights to Tokyo. A bus to the city from the airport takes twenty minutes and costs ¥450.

The **tourist information** booth (daily 9.30am–6.30pm; ⓣ0857/22-3318) by the north exit of Tottori Station has English leaflets and maps of the city and prefecture.

Seeing the dunes and the San'in Coast National Park

Buses to the dunes (¥360; 20min) leave from platform 4 at the bus station next to the Tottori train station and pass through the city centre on the way to either Sakyū Kaikan, beside the dunes, or the Sakyū Centre, overlooking them from a hill. The centre is nothing more than a souvenir and food stop for the tour buses that pile in daily. There's a **chairlift** (daily 8am–5pm; ¥200), which runs between the centre and the edge of the dunes, but you can just as easily walk between the two.

More scenic is the **Uradome coastline** (浦富海岸), covering the 15km between the edge of the sand dunes and the eastern edge of the prefecture, and which, together with the dunes, forms part of the **San'in Coast National Park**. The shore is fringed with strangely shaped rocks and islands jutting out of the water, some topped with pine trees, and many sculpted with wave-carved tunnels, caves and openings. Taking a sightseeing boat is a popular way to enjoy the scenery (daily March–Nov 9.10am–4.10pm; ¥1200; ⓣ0857/73-1212). To do so, take a bus (40min; ¥590) bound for Iwai-onsen from platform 4 outside Tottori Station and get off at **Yuronsen-noriba-mae**; boats depart every half hour or so on forty-minute tours of the coastline, but don't sail in bad weather.

The views from the cliff-top paths along much of the pine-covered coastline looking out over the blue-green Sea of Japan are also stunning, and if you follow one of the steep paths down through the trees to the shore you'll find numerous sandy bays and bathing beaches. If you have a car you can drive along the coast from the sand dunes on Route 178, stopping at any of the many parking places along the way to enjoy the beautiful views from the cliff top, or follow one of the many paths down to the secluded beaches below. If using public transport, continue on the bus bound for Iwai-onsen for another ten minutes and get off at **Uradome-kaigan-guchi**, from where you can explore the cliff-top paths and beaches at your leisure, before catching a bus back to the city.

Practicalities

There are several **accommodation** choices close to the station's north side. *Tottori Green Hotel Morris* (鳥取グリーンホテルモーリス; ⓣ0857/22-2331, ⓕ26-5574; ❺) is a good-value business hotel behind the Daimaru department store across from the station; it has neat rooms and serves Western-style breakfast for ¥550. Nearby is the ever-reliable *Washington Hotel* (ワシントンホテル; ⓣ0857/27-8111, ⓕ8125; ❺), while the upmarket *Hotel New Ōtani Tottori* (ホテルニューオータニ鳥取; ⓣ0857/23-1111, ⓦwww.newotani.co.jp; ❻) sits next to Daimaru. Of the places by the dunes, the old-fashioned *Sakyū Centre Hotel* (砂丘センターホテル; ⓣ0857/22-2111, ⓕ24-8811; ❺) has good-value Japanese-style rooms overlooking the coast, with two meals included in the rates and, in summer, an outdoor pool.

Although there is a handful of **restaurants** at the dunes, you'll be better served by the choice near Tottori Station. Several restaurants can be found in the shopping arcades that run under the train tracks, all with plastic food displays. On the fifth floor of the Daimaru department store you'll find *Marguerite* (11am–6.30pm), a Japanese restaurant with a good range of set meals and special daily dishes.

Travel details

Trains

The trains between the major cities listed below are the fastest direct services.

Hagi to: Masuda (7 daily; 1hr 20min).

Hiroshima to: Fukuoka (Hakata Station) (every 15min; 1hr 10min); Kyoto (every 15min; 1hr 50min); Matsue, via Okayama (1 hourly; 4hr); Okayama (every 15min; 40min); Shin-Ōsaka (every 15min; 1hr 30min); Tokyo (at least 25 daily; 4hr 50min).

Matsue to: Izumo Taisha (10 daily; 1hr); Shin-Yamaguchi (3 daily; 3hr 45min); Okayama (14 daily; 2hr 20min); Tottori (5 daily; 1hr 30min); Tokyo (daily; 13hr); Tsuwano (3 daily; 2hr 30min).

Okayama to: Kurashiki (every 15min; 15 min); Hiroshima (every 15min; 40min); Matsue (hourly; 2hr 20min); Shin-Ōsaka (every 30min; 55min); Takamatsu (3 hourly; 1hr); Tokyo (every 20min; 3hr 53min); Yonago (hourly; 2hr 10min).

Tottori to: Okayama (5 daily; 1hr 25min); Ōsaka (15 daily; 2hr 20min); Yonago (7 daily; 1hr 40min).

Yamaguchi to: Tsuwano (17 daily; 50min–1hr 20min); Shin-Yamaguchi (every 20min; 20min).

Buses

The buses listed below are mainly long-distance services, often travelling overnight – between the major cities – and local services where there is no alternative means of transport. For shorter journeys, however, trains are almost invariably quicker and often no more expensive.

Hagi to: Ōsaka (daily; 12hr); Tokyo (daily; 14hr 30min); Akiyoshi-dai (2 daily; 1hr 10min).

Hiroshima to: Hagi (4 daily; 4hr); Izumo (8 daily; 3hr 30min); Kyoto (daily; 8hr); Matsue (14 daily; 3hr 30min); Ōsaka (daily; 7hr 30min); Tokyo (daily; 12hr).

Kurashiki to: Ōsaka (2 daily; 5hr); Tokyo (daily; 11hr).

Okayama to: Chiba (1 daily; 10hr 55min); Fukuoka (1 daily; 9hr); Kōbe (2 daily; 2hr 50min); Kōchi (8 daily; 2hr 30min); Matsue (7 daily; 3hr 50min); Matsuyama (6 daily; 2hr 40min); Ōsaka (2 daily; 4hr); Tokyo (2 daily; 10hr 20min); Yonago (6 daily; 2hr 10min).

Onomichi to: Imabari (Shikoku) (10 daily; 1hr 30min); Matsuyama (Shikoku) (2 daily; 2hr 50min); Ōmi-shima (10 daily; 55min).

Shin-Yamaguchi to: Akiyoshi-dai (12 daily; 40min); Hagi (6 daily; 1hr 26min).

Tottori to: Hiroshima (5 daily; 4hr 50min); Kyoto (3 daily; 4hr); Ōsaka (13 daily; 3hr 30min); Tokyo (daily; 10hr 30min).

Yamaguchi to: Akiyoshi-dai (19 daily; 55min); Hagi (11 daily; 1hr 15min).

Ferries

Hiroshima to: Beppu (daily; 3hr 10min); Matsuyama (25 daily; ferry 2hr 40min, hydrofoil 1hr 10min); Miyajima (every 20min; 10min).

Okayama to: Shōdo-shima (hourly; 1hr 10min).

Onomichi to: Ikuchi-jima (9 daily; 30min).

Shimonoseki to: Pusan (daily; 13hr 30min); Shanghai (China) (weekly; 39hr); Qingdao (China) (2 weekly; 16hr).

Flights

Hiroshima to: Beijing (China) (4 weekly; 3hr 15min); Dalian (China) (4 weekly; 1hr); Okinawa (2 daily; 1hr 50min); Sapporo (2 daily; 2hr); Sendai (daily; 1hr 20min); Seoul (daily; 1hr 35min); Tokyo Haneda (15 daily; 1hr 15min); Tokyo Narita (daily; 1hr 20min).

Hiroshima Nishi to: Kagoshima (3 daily; 1hr); Miyazaki (daily; 1hr).

Iwami (Hagi) to: Ōsaka (daily; 1hr); Tokyo (daily; 1hr 30min).

Izumo to: Fukuoka (2 daily; 1hr 15min); Ōsaka (7 daily; 1hr); Tokyo (5 daily; 1hr 20min).

Okayama to: Beijing (China) (3 weekly; 4hr 30min); Kagoshima (2 daily; 1hr 15min); Okinawa (2 daily; 2hr); Sapporo (daily; 2hr); Seoul (daily; 1hr 30min); Shanghai (China) (daily; 2hr 10min); Tokyo (9 daily; 1hr 20min).

Tottori to: Tokyo Haneda (4 daily; 1hr 10min).

Yamaguchi Ube to: Tokyo Haneda (7 daily; 1hr 30min).

Yonago to: Nagoya (daily; 1hr 10min); Tokyo Haneda (5 daily; 1hr 15min); Seoul (3 weekly; 1hr 30min).

Shikoku

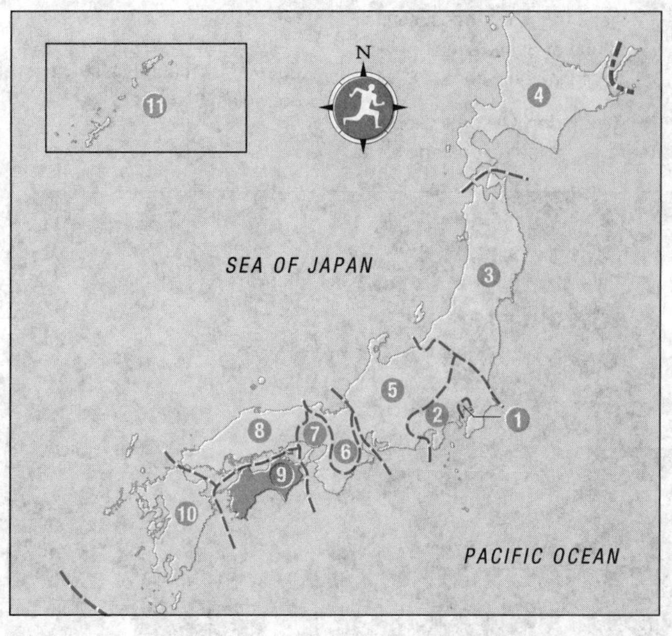

CHAPTER 9 Highlights

* **Ritsurin-kōen** A century in the making, Japan's largest garden is Takamatsu's verdant highlight. See p.598

* **Naoshima** Contemporary art and architecture combine with serene fishing villages on this idyllic Inland Sea island. See p.605

* **Kompira-san** Climb 1346 steps to the innermost shrine of one of Shinto's major places of pilgrimage. See p.608

* **Awa Odori** Over a million revellers let their hair down at Tokushima's annual summer dance festival. See p.614

* **Ōboke Gorge** Go whitewater rafting on the crystal-clear Yoshino River through this spectacular gorge hidden in the island's central mountains. See p.618

* **Matsuyama** This castle city boasts good nightlife, a strong literary history, a famous hot-spring resort and one of the country's strangest temples. See p.636

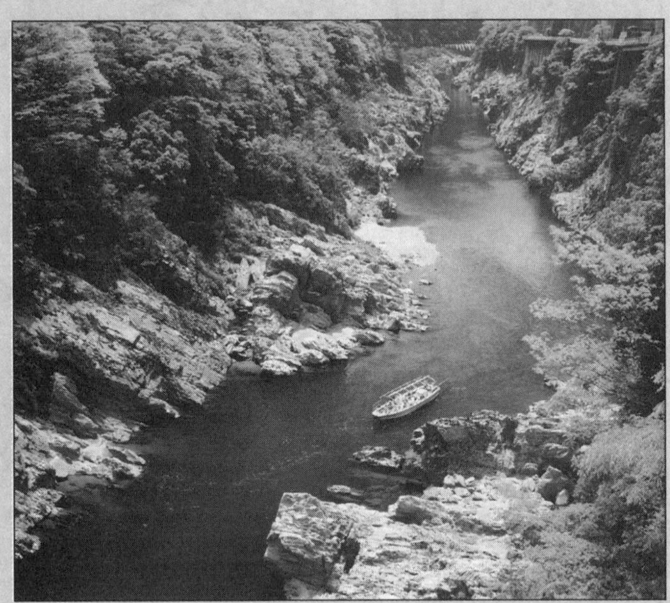

▲ Yoshino River, Ōboke Gorge

9

Shikoku

It has beautiful scenery, a laidback atmosphere, friendly people and several notable sights, yet **SHIKOKU** (四国), Japan's fourth main island, is usually at the bottom of most visitors' itineraries – if it appears at all. This is a shame, since this tranquil island, nestling in the crook between Honshū and Kyūshū, offers elements of traditional Japan that are often hard to find elsewhere. An ancient Buddhist pilgrimage, original castles and distinctive arts and crafts are some of Shikoku's attractions – but equally appealing are the island's rural pace of life and little-visited villages and smaller surrounding islands. Set aside a week or so to get around all Shikoku's four prefectures. If you only have a day or two, though, head straight for **Matsuyama**'s splendid castle and the hot springs at nearby **Dōgo**; or pay a visit to the landscape gardens of **Ritsurin-kōen** in Takamatsu, before hopping on a ferry over to the idyllic, contemporary art-filled island of **Naoshima**.

The Shikoku pilgrimage

Wherever you are in Shikoku, you'll seldom be far from Japan's longest and most famous pilgrimage, established by disciples of the Buddhist saint **Kōbō Daishi**, founder of Shingon Buddhism (see box on p.499 for more on Daishi). It usually takes over two months to walk the 1400km between the 88 temples on the prescribed route, and plenty of pilgrims, known as *henro-san*, still complete the journey this way, though far more follow the route by car, train or on bus tours. The number of temples represents the 88 evils that, according to Shingon Buddhism, bedevil human life.

Henro-san are easy to spot, since they usually dress in traditional short white cotton coats, coloured shoulder bands and broad-rimmed straw hats, and generally clutch rosaries, brass bells and long wooden staffs – for support on the steep ascents to many of the temples. The characters on their robes and staffs translate as "Daishi and I go together". Most pilgrims are past retirement age, as few younger Japanese have the inclination or the vacation time needed for such a pilgrimage.

The present-day headquarters of the Shingon sect is **Kōya-san**, in Wakayama-ken (see p.498), and this is the traditional start of the pilgrimage. The first temple visited on Shikoku is **Ryōzen-ji**, near Naruto in Tokushima-ken. Pilgrims then follow a circular route that winds its way clockwise around the island, stopping at all the temples en route to the 88th, **Ōkubo-ji**, in Kagawa-ken. Many temples allow pilgrims to stay for around ¥4000 per person including meals. It's a lucrative business: you'll see many pilgrims dropping coins by the thousands of Buddhas along the way, and they fork out again at the temples, where an official stamp costs around ¥300.

Several books in English describe the 88-temple hike, including Oliver Statler's classic *Japanese Pilgrimage*. For more up-to-date details, check out Ⓦwww.shikokuhenrotrail.com, created by the American *henro* David Turkington.

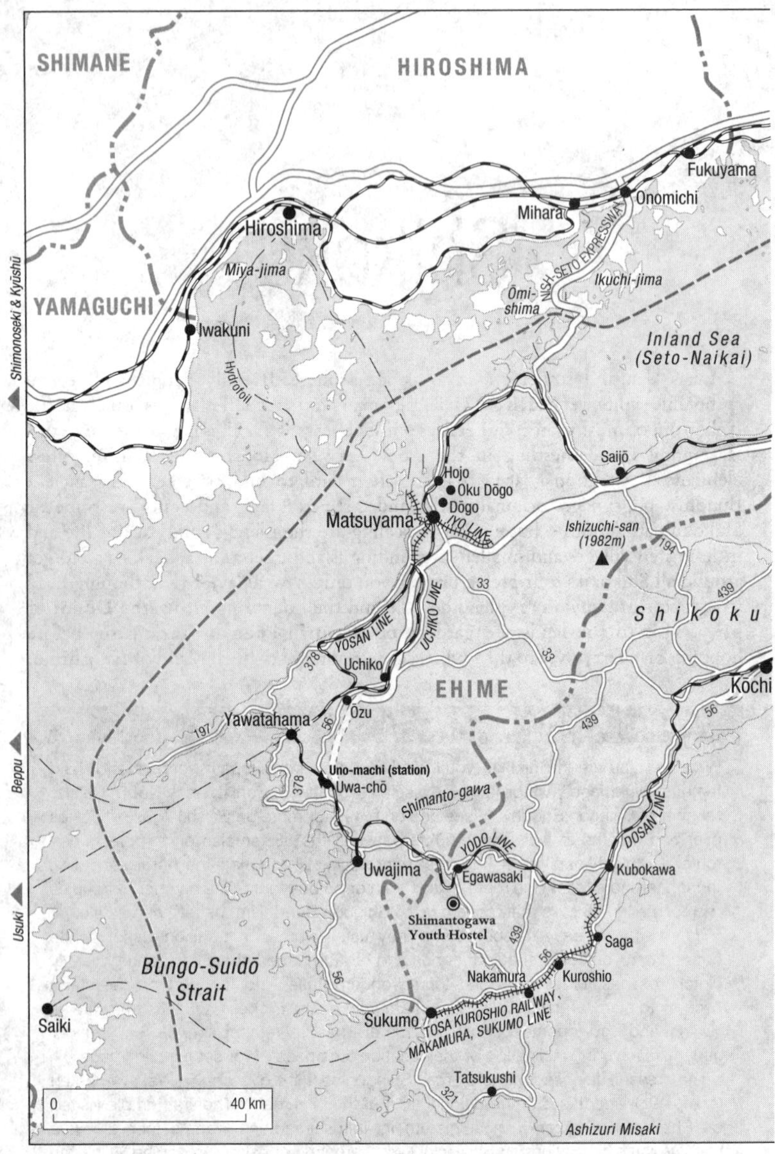

According to legend, Shikoku was the second island (after Awaji-shima) born to Izanagi and Izanami, the gods who are considered to be Japan's parents. Its ancient name was Iyo-no-futana and it was divided into four main prefectures: Awa (now Tokushima-ken), Iyo (Ehime-ken), Sanuki (Kagawa-ken) and Tosa (Kōchi-ken). These epithets are still used today when referring to the different prefectures' cuisines and traditional arts. Apart from being the scene of a decisive battle

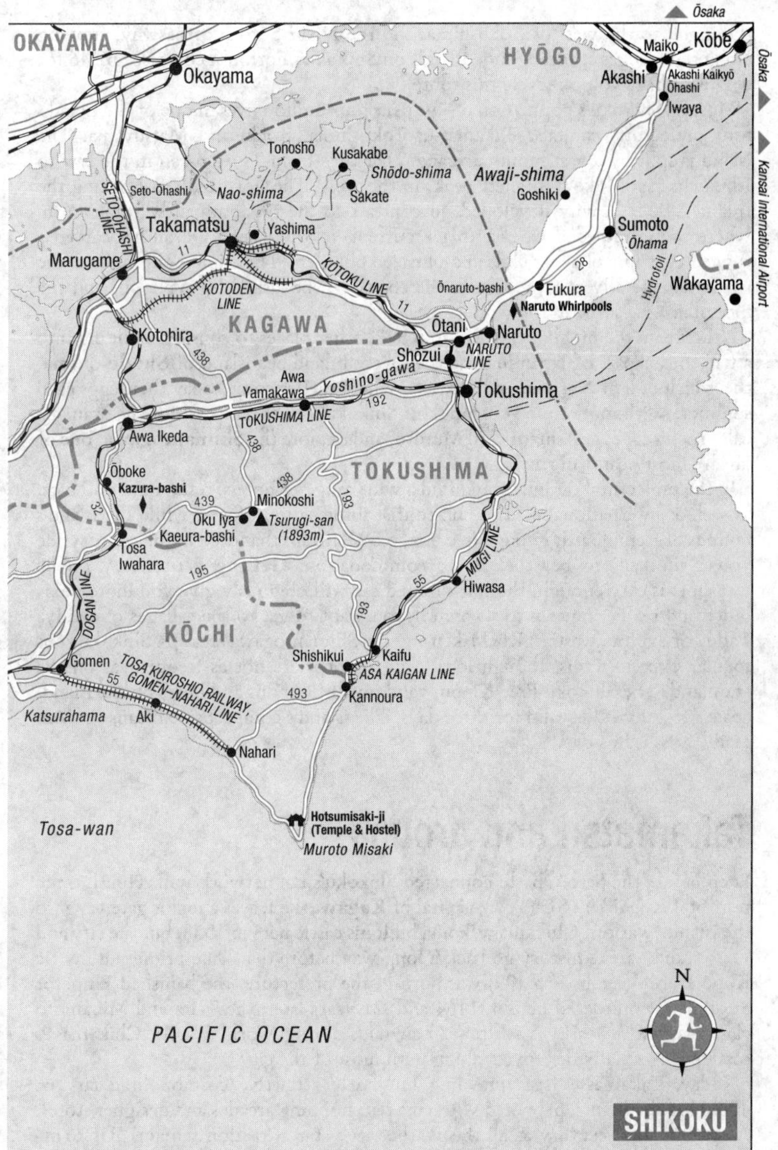

between the Taira and Minamoto clans in the twelfth century (see p.768), Shikoku has had a relatively peaceful history, due in part to its isolation from the rest of Japan. The physical separation ended with the opening of the **Seto Ōhashi** in 1989, a series of six bridges that leapfrog the islands of the Inland Sea, carrying both trains and cars. It has since been joined by the **Akashi Kaikyō Ōhashi suspension bridge** (see p.520), connecting Shikoku to Honshū via Awaji-shima, the island to the west of Tokushima, and the **Nishi Seto Expressway**, running along ten bridges spanning nine islands on Shikoku's northern coast (see p.546 for details of how you can cycle this route).

Most of Shikoku's population of just over four million lives in one of the island's four prefectural capitals: Takamatsu, Tokushima, Kōchi and Matsuyama. The island is split by a vast mountain range that runs from Tsurugi-san in the east to Ishizuchi-san, Shikoku's tallest peak, in the west. The northern coast, facing the Inland Sea, is heavily developed, in contrast to the predominantly rural south, where the unimpeded *kuroshio* (black current) of the Pacific Ocean has carved a rugged coastline of sheer cliffs and outsized boulders. The climate throughout the island is generally mild, although the coasts can be lashed by typhoons and the mountains see snow in the winter.

Apart from the highlights listed on p.592, other places to consider building into a trip to this part of Japan include the lovely Inland Sea island of **Shōdo-shima**, the whirlpools at **Naruto**, and **Hiwasa**, where turtles come to lay their eggs each summer. With more time you could hit Shikoku's southern coast for the dramatically rocky capes at Ashizuri and Muroto, and explore the **Shimantogawa**, one of Japan's most beautiful rivers.

In the prefectural capitals you'll find a wide range of hotels, restaurants and bars, as well as international centres and tourist information offices, while the island's famous 88-temple **pilgrimage** (see box, p.593) means that even in the countryside you're unlikely to be stuck for accommodation. **Getting around** by public transport is easy enough, though a rented car will obviously give you more flexibility and really comes into its own if you want to get to the villages of the Iya Valley or explore western Kōchi-ken and the Shimantogawa area. JR Shikoku runs regular express trains, though local train services are not as frequent as on the mainland. The Shikoku Free Kippu, valid on all JR trains and buses on the island, costs ¥15,700 and is valid for three days. The island's compact size means you can easily cross it in a day.

Takamatsu and around

Even before the Seto Ōhashi connected Shikoku's rail network with Honshū, the port of **TAKAMATSU** (高松), capital of **Kagawa-ken**, was a major gateway into the island. Warlord Chikamasa Ikoma built his castle here in 1588, but the city and surrounding area's history go back a long way before that. The priest and mystic Kōbō Daishi (see box, p.499) was born in the prefecture, the banished Emperor Sutoku was murdered here in 1164 and, 21 years later, the Taira and Minamoto clans clashed at nearby **Yashima**. In air raids during World War II, Chikamasa's castle was virtually destroyed, along with most of the city.

Today, Takamatsu is a sprawling but fairly attractive cosmopolitan city of 420,000 inhabitants, peppered with covered shopping arcades and designer stores. As twenty-first-century as all this is, the city's star attraction remains **Ritsurin-kōen**, one of Japan's most classical, spacious and beautifully designed gardens. The gardens are easily accessible on a day-trip from Honshū, but it's well worth staying overnight so you can also take in **Shikoku Mura**, the open-air museum of traditional houses at Yashima, or **Kotohira-gū** (see p.610), the ancient shrine an hour's train ride west of the city. Takamatsu is also a gateway to two of the most appealing islands in the Inland Sea: **Shōdo-shima**, a mini-Shikoku with its own temple circuit and scenic attractions; and delightful **Naoshima**, a must for contemporary art and architecture fans with several outstanding galleries designed by Andō Tadao (see p.605).

Arrival, information and city transport

The JR **train** station is at the northern, seaside end of the central thoroughfare, Chūō-dōri, and ten minutes' walk from the heart of the city. Long-distance and most local **buses** pull in nearby, at the north end of Chūō-dōri. **Ferries** from Kōbe (¥1800 one way, ¥2990 return; Ⓦwww.ferry.co.jp) dock a ten-minute bus ride from the city centre at Takamatsu-East; a free shuttle bus transports passengers to JR Takamatsu Station. Ferry connections with Shōdo-shima and Naoshima are at the Sunport ferry terminal, a five-minute walk east of the train station. Takamatsu **airport** (Ⓣ087/835-8110, Ⓦwww.takamatsu-airport.com) lies 16km south of the city, 35 minutes away by bus (¥740) or taxi (¥4700).

There's a helpful **tourist information office** (daily 9am–6pm; Ⓣ087/851-2009), on the west side of the plaza outside the train station. You can also pick up a free **Kagawa Welcome Card** (Ⓦwww.21kagawa.com/visitor/kanko) here, and at other tourist offices in the prefecture, which provides non-Japanese with discounts of up to twenty percent on a good range of hotels, restaurants and tourist attractions. Also useful is the Kagawa International Exchange Centre, better known as **I-PAL** (Tues–Sun 9am–6pm; Ⓣ087/837-5908, Ⓦwww.i-pal.or.jp). This excellent facility has a library of foreign-language books, magazines and newspapers and free internet access (30min). It's also a good place to meet Japanese who speak English and foreigners who live in town, and you can pick up the free information sheets *Kagawa Journal* and *Takamatsu Information Board* (TIA), which carry details of what's on in town. I-PAL is at the northwest corner of Chūō-kōen, 750m south of Takamatsu Station.

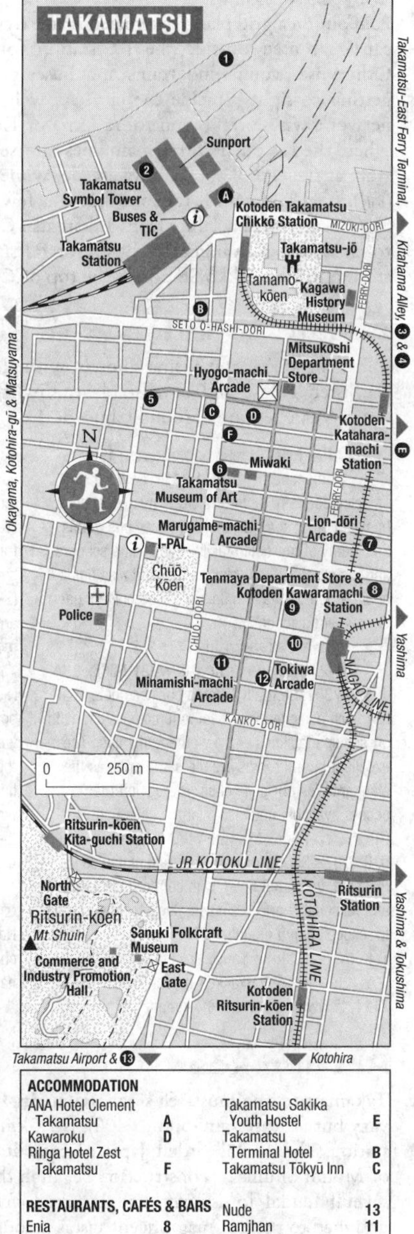

ACCOMMODATION

ANA Hotel Clement Takamatsu	A	Takamatsu Sakika Youth Hostel	E
Kawaroku	D	Takamatsu Terminal Hotel	B
Rihga Hotel Zest Takamatsu	F	Takamatsu Tōkyū Inn	C

RESTAURANTS, CAFÉS & BARS

Enia	8	Nude	13
Fumiya	9	Ramjhan	11
Gowariyasu	7	Ruff House	11
Izara Moon	3	Szechwan Restaurant Chin	2
Kanaizumi	6	Tenkatsu	5
King's Yawd	10	Tokiwa Saryō	12
Mikayla	1	Umie	4

City transport

Laid out on a grid plan, Takamatsu is an easy city to walk or cycle around. Bicycles can be rented outside the JR station for just ¥100 (see "Listings", p.601). Otherwise, you'll find trains and buses perfectly user-friendly, and good for getting to sights outside the city. As well as JR, Takamatsu has the **Kotoden** network whose trains run to Yashima or Kotohira. Kawaramachi Station (瓦町), where the Kotoden's three main lines intersect, is beside the Tenmaya department store at the end of the Tokiwa arcade, while Kotoden Takamatsu Chikkō Station (高松築港) is next to Tamamo-kōen, a few minutes' walk from JR Takamatsu Station. If you're heading from Takamatsu Chikkō Station to Yashima, you'll need to change at Kawaramachi. Buses for Ritsurin-kōen and Yashima run from the stops outside Chikkō Station at the top of Chūō-dōri.

Accommodation

Takamatsu has many business hotels, with plenty near the station – the better ones are listed below and have single rooms from around ¥6000. More upmarket options can be found around Chūō-dōri.

ANA Hotel Clement Takamatsu 1-1 Hamanchō ⓣ087/811-1111, ⓦwww.anaclement.com. By far the city's swankiest hotel, boasting great sea views, stylish, spacious rooms and plenty of top-notch facilities including six bars and restaurants. From May to August it also has a beer garden on the fifth floor. JR Pass holders get a ten percent discount. ❻

Kawaroku ホテル川六エルステージ; 1-2 Hyakken-machi ⓣ087/821-5666, ⓕ821-7301. Centrally located business hotel that has been designed to appeal to female visitors with on-site spa facilities and a women-only floor. The excellent tatami rooms are the same price as the standard Western-style ones. There's internet access available and also a large public bath. ❺

Rihga Hotel Zest Takamatsu 9-1 Furujin-machi ⓣ087/822-3555, ⓦwww.rihga-takamatsu.co.jp. Pleasant, upmarket hotel, with comfortable rooms and reasonably priced singles. Conveniently located for shopping and nightlife. ❻

Takamatsu Sakika Youth Hostel 高松さきかユースゲストハウス 6-9 Hyakken-machi ⓣ087/822-2111, ⓦwww.netwave.or.jp/~nmimatsu. Occupying an ageing but still serviceable hotel, this youth hostel offers plenty of privacy and large rooms – some of which combine Japanese- and Western-style spaces – at bargain rates. Also has free bicycle rental. Guests can use the large public bath in the sister hotel *New Grand Mimatsu* (2-3 Hyakken-machi; ⓣ087/823-4111; ❹), around the corner, which also has good tatami rooms and a lively *izakaya*. ❹

Takamatsu Terminal Hotel 10-17 Nishinomaru-chō ⓣ087/822-3731. There are both Western- and Japanese-style rooms at this welcoming business hotel. The rooms are clean, though unspectacular, and some double rooms have a sofa that can be turned into a bed if you want to share a room between three and bring the cost down. Also has free internet access in the lobby. ❺

Takamatsu Tōkyū Inn 9-9 Hyogo-machi ⓣ087/821-0109, ⓦwww.tokyuhotelsjapan.com. Nothing fancy, but the rooms at this well-placed chain hotel are modern, reasonably priced and have a good range of facilities. ❻

Ritsurin-kōen

Takamatsu's one must-see sight, **Ritsurin-kōen** (栗林公園; daily; opening hours vary but at least 7am–5pm; ¥400), is 2.5km south down Chūō-dōri from the JR station. The formal garden, Japan's largest at 750,000 square metres, lies at the foot of Mount Shuin. Its construction began in the early seventeenth century and took several feudal lords over one hundred years to complete. The gardens were designed to present magnificent vistas throughout the seasons, from an arched red bridge amid a snowy landscape in winter, to ponds full of purple and white irises in early summer.

The East Gate is the garden's main entrance but JR trains stop at least once an hour at Ritsurin-kōen Kita-guchi, close by the North Gate. At either entrance you can pick up a free English map of the gardens and buy tickets that combine entrance with tea in the *Kikugetsu-tei* Pavilion. From the East Gate you can either follow a route through the Nantei (South Garden) to the left or Hokutei (North Garden) to the right. The more stylized **Nantei** garden has paths around three lakes, dotted with islands with carefully pruned pine trees. The highlight here is the delightful *Kikugetsu-tei*, or "Scooping the Moon", teahouse overlooking the South Lake (entry to the teahouse is free, but the experience is all the better if you stop there for a cup of *sencha* or *macha*; ¥250/¥350). Dating from around 1640 and named after a Tang-dynasty Chinese poem, the teahouse exudes tranquillity, with its screens pulled back to reveal perfect garden views. Viewed from across the lake it's just as impressive, swaddled in trees that cast a shimmering reflection over the water. The Nantei also has the less elaborate but more secluded *Higurashi-tei* teahouse, set in a shady grove.

Hokutei has a more natural appearance, and is based around two ponds – Fuyosho-ike, dotted with lotus flowers, and Gunochi-ike, where feudal lords once hunted ducks and which now blooms with irises in June. Keep an eye out for the Tsuru Kame no Matsu, just to the left of the main park building, a black pine tree shaped like a crane spreading its wings and considered to be the most beautiful of the 29,190 trees in the gardens. Behind this is a line of pines called the "Byōbu-matsu", after the folding-screen painting (*byōbu*) they are supposed to resemble.

After you've viewed the gardens, head back towards the East Gate, where you'll find the **Sanuki Folkcraft Museum** (daily 8.45am–4.30pm, Wed until 4pm; free), displaying good examples of local basketwork, ceramics, furniture and huge, brightly painted banners and kites. The neighbouring **Commerce and Industry Promotion Hall**, housed in an impressive two-storey traditional building, is little more than a glorified giftshop, but sometimes food stalls are set up outside, making for a pleasant place to stop for a snack.

Tamamo-kōen and around

A couple of minutes' walk east of the JR station is **Tamamo-kōen** (玉藻公園; times vary through the year but always 7am–5pm; ¥200), a pleasant park which contains the ruins of the city's castle, **Takamatsu-jō**. Four hundred years ago this was one of the three major Japanese fortresses protected by sea, with three rings of moats surrounding the central keep. Like many of Japan's castles, Takamatsu-jō was decommissioned in 1869 following the Meiji Restoration (see p.771); all that remains today are a couple of turrets, parts of the moat, and grounds that are only a ninth of their original size. At the time of research much of this was a construction site due to ongoing restoration work. Still, it has a fantastic display of blossom on the cherry trees in spring and, if you climb the raised mound on which once stood the keep, you'll get a great view out across the Inland Sea. At the park's east end you can also look around the very traditional **Hiunkaku**, a sprawling wooden mansion surrounded by stunted pines. Rebuilt in 1917, it's now used as public rooms.

Immediately east of the park is the **Kagawa History Museum** at Kagawa-ken Rekishi Hakubutsukan (香川県歴史博物館; Tues–Sun 9am–4.30pm; ¥400), built on part of the old castle grounds. Head to the fourth floor to see the main exhibition, which has lots of hi-tech displays and some impressive relics and life-size replicas of local landmarks, such as the 7m-tall copper lantern from Marogame. On the third floor is a special section relating to Kōbō Daishi (see box, p.499), with some amazing giant mandala paintings and ancient statues. On the ground floor you can try on a multi-layered kimono or a samurai warrior's armour and have your photo taken.

Next to Takamatsu JR station, you can't miss the thirty-storey **Takamatsu Symbol Tower**. The city's tallest building anchors the **Sunport** complex of offices, shops, convention halls and ferry piers. Northwest of here, the red-glass brick lighthouse at the end of the Tamamo breakwater is a good place to aim for if you're out for a seaside stroll or want to join local runners for a jog, but the mall has been a dead duck ever since a larger, newer mall opened to the west of the city. If shopping's your thing you'd do best to head east to **Kitahama Alley** (北浜アリー), a small area of brick warehouses and old buildings that have been converted into appealing cafés (see below) and boutiques.

Just off Chūō-dōri on Bijutsukan-dōri is the modern **Takamatsu Museum of Art** (Tues–Sun 9.30am–5pm; ¥200). The small permanent collection includes Sanuki lacquerware and Western and Japanese contemporary art. There's also a library of art books and videos – some in English – and the spacious entrance hall is used for dance and music performances. Around here are Takamatsu's main commercial and entertainment districts, threaded through with covered shopping arcades (*shotengai*) – one stretches for 2.7km and is said to be the longest in Japan.

Eating, drinking and nightlife

Takamatsu has a wide range of **restaurants** and **cafés**, many conveniently concentrated around the central arcade district, just off Chūō-dōri. Like Shikoku's other seaside cities, this is a great place to sample **fish** and **seafood** – in some restaurants it is served live and still wriggling on your plate. The other local speciality is **sanuki udon**, thick white noodles usually served with a separate flask of stock and condiments.

Among the city's many **bars** is *Ruff House* at B1F Minami-Biru, 2-3 Tamachi (☎087/835-9550; daily 7pm–3am), a relaxed place popular with the city's expat population, and *King's Yawd* at 1-2-2 Tokiwa-chō, which serves a spicy Caribbean-style curry to a nonstop soundtrack of reggae. A couple of kilometres south of the city centre, *Nude* (☎087/851-1515) is Takamatsu's premier **club** hosting big-name DJs and dance events.

Fumiya ふみや 2-2-35 Kawaramachi ☎087/831-5090. Main branch of a popular chain that serves excellent *okonomiyaki* at bargain prices (from ¥550); you'll struggle to spend more than ¥1500 on food. Daily except Tues 11.30am–2.30pm & 4–7.30pm.

Gowariyasu 吾割安 6-3 Fukudamachi ☎087/851-5030. This atmospheric *izakaya*, decorated with old film posters, record covers and other memorabilia, offers a wide range of tasty inexpensive dishes such as *yakitori*. Daily 6pm–3am, Sun till midnight.

Izara Moon Kitahama Alley, 3-2 Kitahama-chō ☎087/811-4530. This stylish café-bar makes good use of its former warehouse space. It specializes in small plates of Chinese food including dim sum, and offers good set lunches and Chinese tea during the day. A meal will cost around ¥2000. Daily except Tues 11am–midnight.

Kanaizumi かな泉 9-3 Konyamachi ☎087/822-0123. This busy branch of a noted *sanuki udon* chain is a great place to fill up if you're on a budget. It's self service, but the chefs are happy to help you choose from the wide choice of noodle toppings (¥500 for a large bowl of udon with a topping). Daily 9.30am–5pm.

Mikayla 8-40 Sunport ☎087/811-5357. This Italian restaurant/café/bar has a prime position in a stand-alone site at the start of the breakwater jutting off the side of the Sunport development. On a fine day it's a very pleasant place to sample pasta, pizza or an espresso. Evening set menus start at ¥4500 (a la carte also available), lunch from ¥980. Daily 11am–9.30pm.

Ramjham Minami Building, 2-3 Tamachi ☎087/834-8505. Friendly, Indian-run place serving good Indian curries, tandoori-cooked meats and naan. Dinner shouldn't cost more than ¥2000. Daily 11am–2.30pm & 5–10pm.

Szechwan Restaurant Chin 29th floor Maritime Plaza, 2-1 Sunport ☎087/811-0477. The most appealing and certainly the most welcoming of Sunport's top-of-the-tower trio of restaurants. The Chinese cuisine is authentically spicy, the decor chic and the views spectacular. Expect to pay around ¥3000 for dinner. Daily 11am–2pm & 5–9pm.

Tenkatsu 天勝 Nishizumi Hiroba, 7-8 Hyogo-machi ⓣ087/821-5380. The interior of this reputable fish restaurant is dominated by a central sunken tank around which you can sit either at the jet-black counter bar or in tatami booths. Kimono-clad waitresses will bring you your pick of the fish served raw, as part of a sushi platter, or cooked in a *nabe* (stew). Set meals start from as little as ¥1000. Mon–Fri 11am–2pm & 5–9.40pm. Sat & Sun 11am–9pm.

Tokiwa Saryō ときわ茶寮 1-8-2 Tokiwa-chō ⓣ087/861-5577. Much of the lovely interior decoration of this old ryokan has remained intact in its transformation into a restaurant. Set courses of local delicacies start at as little as ¥1050 for lunch, from ¥3500 for dinner. It can be difficult to find, so look out for the giant white lantern hanging outside. Daily 11am–2.30pm & 5–9.30pm.

Umie Kitahama Alley, 3-2 Kitahama-chō ⓣ087/811-7455. Relax over great coffee or tasty meals (mains from ¥600) such as hearty beef stew and pizza at this cool joint decorated with mismatched furniture and stacks of old books and magazines. They sometimes host live music events, and within the same complex are a gift and stationery shop, gallery and secondhand furniture store. Mon–Fri 9am–11.30pm, Sat & Sun 10am–11.30pm.

Listings

Banks and exchange The main branch of Hyaku-jyushi Bank is at 5-1 Kameichō; Kagawa Bank is at 6-1 Kameichō; and Sumitomo Mistui Bank is at 10 Hyōgo-machi. The main post office (see below) and most smaller branches have ATMs that accept foreign cards; the main branch of the post office is accessible Mon–Fri 7am–11pm, Sat & Sun 9am–7pm.

Bike rental From the cavernous rent-a-cycle offices and parking lot beneath JR Takamatsu Station. At ¥100 for 24 hours this is an absolute steal and the best way to see the city. You need to register first, but it's a very quick and simple process; the paperwork can be done in English.

Bookshop Miawaki, 4-8 Marugame-chō (daily 9am–10pm), has English-language books and a smattering of magazines on the sixth floor.

Car rental Eki Rent-a-Car (ⓣ087/821-1341) and Toyota Rent-a-Car (ⓣ087/851-0100) both have offices at Takamatsu JR Station.

Hospital Kagawa Kenritsu Chūō Byōin (Prefectural Central Hospital) is at 5-4-16 Banchō (ⓣ087/835-2222).

Internet There are free terminals at I-PAL (see p.597). Right next door to the *Tokyu Inn* (see p.598) there is also Planet Media Café, where access starts at ¥90/15min.

Laundry Flower Coin Laundry, 1-11-15 Hananomiya-chō (daily 8am–10pm).

Police The main police station is at 4-1-10 Banchō (ⓣ087/833-0110). Emergency numbers are listed on p.71.

Post office The main post office (Mon–Fri 9am–7pm, Sat 9am–5pm, Sun 9am–12.30pm) is at the north end of the Marugame arcade, opposite the Mitsukoshi department store.

Shopping Sanuki lacquerware and papier-mâché dolls are the main local crafts. Apart from the giftshops in Ritsurin-kōen and the Kagawa History Museum, shops in the arcades and the Mitsukoshi and Tenmaya department stores are good places for souvenirs. Mingei Fukuda at Hyakean-machi, opposite the *Kawaroku Hotel* (Tues–Sun 10am–5.30pm; ⓦmingei-fukuda.com), is a fine emporium packed with folk crafts, pottery and paper goods.

Isamu Noguchi

Born in Los Angeles in 1904 to an Irish-American mother and a Japanese father, **Isamu Noguchi** spent part of his childhood in Japan before returning to the States, aged 13. In his late 20s he settled in New York, where his main studio (also a museum) can be found. It was here that he began to establish his reputation through his iconic designs for paper lanterns and furniture, as well as high-profile commissions for sculptures and landscape works around the world. Noguchi returned to Japan after World War II, creating numerous site-specific pieces such as the two bridges in the Hiroshima Peace Park (1952) and the lobby of the Sogestu Kaikan in Tokyo (1977). In the year that he died he completed his design for Moerenuma Park in Sapporo (see p.295). Apart from the work at his studio in Mure, another of Noguchi's sculptures, *Time and Space*, stands at Takamatsu Airport.

Yashima and around

Literally meaning "rooftop island" (which thousands of years ago it was), the plateau **YASHIMA** (屋島) lies 6km east of Takamatsu's city centre. A trip here and to nearby **MURE** (牟礼) to see the Isamu Noguchi Garden Museum Japan is a great way to spend a day. It was at Yashima that, in 1185, the Taira and Minamoto clans famously battled to determine who ruled Japan (see p.768). A small detachment of Minamoto forces surprised the Taira by attacking from the land side of the peninsula – the Taira had expected the attack to come from the sea. Within a month the Taira were defeated at the Battle of Dannoura and forced to flee to the mountainous hinterland of Shikoku.

Buses run to the top of the 293m-high volcanic lava plateau, or you can spend an hour hiking up a steep, winding path starting to the west of the decommissioned cable car. Once at the top, apart from expansive views (weather permitting) of the Inland Sea, you might be a little disappointed, as on the southern ridge of the plateau are some rather dingy tourist hotels, souvenir shops and the tacky **New Yashima Aquarium** (daily 9am–4.30pm; ¥1200), where dolphins and sea lions are kept in appallingly small pools. More appealing is **Yashima-ji** temple (屋島寺), supposedly constructed in 754 AD and number 84 on the Shikoku pilgrimage. Look out for the saucy granite carvings of raccoons next to the temple. Yashima-ji's **Treasure House** (daily 9am–5pm; ¥500) is worth popping into for its collection of screens, pottery and a mixed bag of relics from the battle between the Taira and Minamoto. There's also a traditional garden behind the Treasure House, with the distinctly unbloody "Pond of Blood", believed to be the spot where the Minamoto soldiers cleansed their swords.

A much better reason for visiting Yashima is **Shikoku Mura** (四国村; daily: April–Oct 8.30am–5pm; Nov–March 8.30am–4.30pm; ¥800 or ¥1000 including Shikoku Mura Gallery), which lies at the base of the plateau, five minutes' walk north of the Kotoden Yashima Station. Some twenty-odd traditional houses and buildings from across the island and Inland Sea were relocated here in an imaginatively landscaped park rising up the hill. The route around the park, which takes about an hour, starts with a small and slightly dilapidated replica of the Iya Valley's Kazura-bashi (see p.619), a bridge made of vines and bamboo which crosses a pond to an impressive thatched-roof kabuki theatre from Shōdo-shima. Plays are occasionally performed here – check with the tourist information office in Takamatsu (see p.597). Look out also for the circular Sato Shime Goya (Sugarcane Press Hut) with a conical roof – a unique feature in Japanese architecture. Each of the houses has an excellent English explanation of its history.

Snug against the hillside near the top of the park is the Ando Tadao-designed **Shikoku Mura Gallery** (same hours as Shikoku Mura; ¥500). Inside the polished concrete building is a single long gallery featuring original paintings by the likes of Marc Chagall and Pablo Picasso, as well as regularly changing themed exhibitions. Tumbling down the hill outside is a water garden, designed so that the sound of the water changes in intensity as you walk up and down the steps, from a gentle trickle to a raging torrent.

Practicalities

From Takamatsu JR trains run at least every hour to Yashima Station (15min; ¥210), from where it's a fifteen-minute walk north to the base of the plateau. More convenient is the Kotoden line (every 20min; 20min; ¥310 from Kotoden Takamatsu Chikkō Station), as Kotoden Yashima Station is only a five-minute walk from Shikoku Mura. Between 9am and 5pm there's a bus every hour from outside both the JR and Kotoden stations running to the top of the plateau (¥100).

There are a few good **restaurants** in Yashima. *Ikkaku* (一鶴; Mon–Fri 11am–2pm & 4–10pm, Sat & Sun 11am–10pm), a minute's walk east of Kotoden Yashima

Station, is a contemporary beer hall specializing in spicy chicken served with raw cabbage leaves, for around ¥1000 a head. *Waraya* (わらや) is a famous *udon* restaurant beside the entrance to Shikoku Mura, in a building with a thatched roof and water wheel. You can sit and slurp a variety of udon dishes at shared tables (from ¥410); they also serve tempura.

Mure

A few kilometres east of Yashima in **Mure**, the streets resound to the clack of hammer on stone and are lined with fantastic stone sculptures and designs – everything from traditional lanterns to pot-bellied Buddhas and long-necked giraffes.

It was in this long-established stonemasons' town that the celebrated American-Japanese sculptor Isamu Noguchi (see box, p.601) created a traditional-style home and sculpture studio during the latter part of his life. Although you must make an appointment (preferably two weeks in advance by email) and the entrance fee is more expensive than most museums, a visit to the **Isamu Noguchi Garden Museum Japan** (イサムノグチ庭園美術館; Tues, Thurs & Sat 10am, 1pm & 3pm; ¥2100; ⓣ087/870-1500, ⓔmuseum@isamunoguchi.or.jp) is highly recommended. The house, gardens and studio have been left exactly as they were when Noguchi died. Scattered around is a collection of 150 of Noguchi's sculptures (some only partly finished), including the signature pieces *Energy Void*, a 3.6m-tall work that looks more like a giant rubber tube than solid black granite, and the two-coloured stone ring *Sun at Midnight*. Exactly an hour is granted to wander the studio and grounds soaking up the singular atmosphere. To get here, hop on the Kotoden train either in Takamatsu or at Kotoden Yashima Station, alighting at **Yakuri Station** (八栗駅) from where the museum is a twenty-minute walk northeast.

Shōdo-shima

It may not have quite the same idyllic appeal as its smaller Inland Sea neighbour Naoshima (see p.605), but thanks to its splendid natural scenery and a collection of worthwhile sights **Shōdo-shima** (小豆島) should still be high on any list of places to visit in Shikoku. The mountainous, forested island styles itself as a Mediterranean retreat, and has a whitewashed windmill and mock-Grecian ruins strategically placed in its terraced olive groves. But native culture also gets a look-in, since Shōdo-shima – which translates as "island of small beans" – promotes its own version of Shikoku's 88-temple pilgrimage and its connection with the classic Japanese book and film *Nijūshi-no-Hitomi* (*24 Eyes*). This tear-jerking tale of a teacher and her twelve young charges, set on Shōdo-shima between the 1920s and 1950s, was written by local author Tsuboi Sakae. A trip to the island also offers a rare opportunity to visit a centuries-old soy sauce factory (see p.605), where traditional methods are still employed.

Arrival, information and getting around

Shōdo-shima is best reached by **ferries** from Takamatsu (1hr; ¥670) and **high-speed boats** (35min; ¥1140) that depart daily for several ports on the island. If you're coming from Honshū, there are also ferries from Himeji (1hr 40min; ¥1480), Hinase (1hr; ¥1000), Okayama (1hr; ¥1000) and Uno (1hr 30min; ¥1200), and Ōsaka (3hr 25min; ¥3900) to Sakate. The island's main port of Tonoshō, on the west coast, is served by the most services. If you intend to stay at the youth hostel (see p.604), take a ferry from Takamatsu to Kusakabe and, if you're heading for the *Shōdo-shima Cycling Terminal* (see p.604), take the boat to Sakate. There's a helpful **tourist information desk** (daily 9am–5pm; ⓣ0879/62-0649) inside Tonoshō's ferry terminal, but if you're coming from Takamatsu, you can pick up information on the island from the tourist information centre there (see p.597).

Buses for main points around the island depart from the terminal next to the Tonoshō Port building. Here you can buy a one-day ticket for ¥1980 or a two-day ticket for ¥2550 – only worthwhile if you intend to do a lot of sightseeing by bus. Note that the frequency of the bus services changes seasonally, and some routes around the island don't operate in January, February or June; check with the tourist information desk before setting off. Renting a car, bicycle or scooter in Tonoshō is easily arranged, and there are rental **bicycles** available at both the youth hostel and the *Shōdo-shima Cycling Terminal*.

Accommodation

Tonoshō has plenty of business and tourist **hotels** charging around ¥8000 per person, including two meals. A good option is *Maruse* (マルセ; Ⓣ0879/62-2385; ❸, ❹ with two meals), a small, clean minshuku next to the Tonoshō post office (which has a cash machine). If they're full, ask for a room at the marginally more expensive *New Port* nearby (ニューポート; Ⓣ0879/62-6310; room only ❸, with two meals ❹), a business hotel run by the same people, which has both Japanese- and Western-style rooms. The upmarket choice is *Shōdoshima International Hotel* (小豆島国際ホテル; Ⓣ0879/62-2111; ❼), a big resort-style hotel with some chic rooms and a beautiful location on the south side of Tonoshō next to "Angel Road", a slinky sand bar linking three tiny islands.

The real flavour of Shōdo-shima, however, is perhaps best appreciated at the smaller seaside villages along the southern coast. The *Shōdo-shima Olive Youth Hostel* (小豆島オーリブユースホステル; Ⓣ0879/82-6161, Ⓦhttp://www.jyh.gr.jp/shoudo; sometimes closed for maintenance in Jan, Feb & June – check in advance; ❹), a ten-minute walk west of Kusakabe port, has clean dorms (¥2730 per person) and private tatami rooms. The very friendly, English-speaking manager whips up good *teishoku* (set menu including a main dish, rice, miso soup and pickles) dinners and goes out of his way to help you get the best out of your time on the island. A fine alternative are the simple but clean tatami mat rooms at the *Shōdo-shima Cycling Terminal* (小豆島サイクリングターミナル; Ⓣ&Ⓕ0879/82-1099; ❷), beside Sakate port. This welcoming place is run by Yokoyama Iwao, president of Shōdo-shima's International Friendship Club (Ⓣ&Ⓕ0879/82-0469) and author of an informative, though slightly dated, free English booklet on the island. Shōdo-shima doesn't have many good places to eat, so it's best to plan on eating dinner and breakfast at your hotel.

The Island

Midweek, Shōdo-shima makes a peaceful escape, and you may well be tempted to linger. During the summer, however, and at weekends for much of the rest of the year, the island absolutely teems with tourists. Though the main sights can be covered in a day, it's a bit of a rush if you don't have your own transport, in which case it's better to spend at least one night on the island. If you're short of time, from the main port of **Tonoshō** (土庄) head up into the mountains on the bus bound for the 612m-high spot of **Kanka-kei** (寒霞渓). Along the way, the bus stops for thirty minutes at the monkey park **Choshi-kei** (銚子渓; daily 10am–4.30pm; ¥370), where apes from Africa, Southeast Asia and South America are kept in cages while the local wild monkeys roam free. It's rather unsettling to be surrounded by so many monkeys, especially as the apes often fight viciously among themselves over the food. The bus makes a five-minute stop at a lookout point before arriving at the park at Kanka-kei, which has breathtaking vistas across the Inland Sea.

Another way of getting up to Kanka-kei is by **cable car** (times change through the year but at least daily 8.30am–4.30pm; ¥700 one way, ¥1250 return) from Kōuntei (紅雲亭), a fifteen-minute bus ride from the port of Kusakabe (草壁) on the south of the island. From the cable car you can look down into the three-million-year-old granite gorge, where the rocks sprout trees that explode in a palette of brown, gold and red every October. It's a fairly easy forty-minute hike up the gorge from Kōuntei, while to continue up to the summit of Hoshigajō (星ヶ城), the island's highest point at 817m, will take another hour. The youth hostel (see opposite) can provide a basic hiking map in Japanese, though it's not necessary if you're just going from Kōuntei to Kanka-kei. Note that if you decide to hike or take the cable car up to Kanka-kei with the intention of catching the bus to Tonoshō, the last bus doesn't make the thirty-minute stop at the monkey park.

Along the main Highway 436 heading east from Tonoshō and around the south of the island lies **Olive-kōen** (オリーブ公園; daily 8.30am–5pm; free), a pleasant but touristy park of olive groves and fake Grecian ruins where, among other things, you can buy green-olive chocolate or take an onsen bath (¥700) followed by a moisturising session with olive-oil creams. Just as touristy, but far more interesting, is **Nijūshi-no-Hitomi Eigamura** (二十四の瞳映画村; daily 9am–5pm; ¥700). This fake village, a film set used in the 1980s remake of *24 Eyes*, is now a mini-theme park dedicated to the film, which is played in one of the evocative buildings. The location, at the tip of a crooked isthmus sticking out into Uchinomi Bay on the south of the island, is idyllic. Also in the village you'll find a museum dedicated to the prolific author Tsuboi Sakae, best known for the novel the film was based on, and the very stylish *Café Shinema Kurabu*, a good place for lunch and part of a display devoted to classic Japanese films of the 1950s and 1960s. Just before Eigamura is the rustic fishing village of **Tanoura** (田の浦), where the original schoolhouse that served as an inspiration for the book is also open to visitors (daily 9am–5pm; ¥200).

Scattered around the southeastern part of the island, between Eigamura and the youth hostel, you'll find several **soy sauce** factories, the most worthwhile of which is **Yamaroku** (ヤマロク醤油; ⓣ0879/82-0666; daily 9am–5pm; free). Here each batch of the local sauce is fermented for two years in hundred-year-old, 2m-high wooden barrels, and carefully watched over by a fifth-generation soy master. The staff don't speak much English, but are happy to show visitors around and let you climb up and peer into the pungent, bacteria-coated barrels; note when you climb the ladder how the aroma becomes sweeter the higher you get. They also have a small souvenir shop where you can sample their different sauces.

Naoshima

The living canvas for a dynamic ongoing art project (see box, p.607), idyllic **NAOSHIMA** (直島), 13km north of Takamatsu, is home to three stunning Andō Tadao-designed galleries as well as several large-scale installations and outdoor sculptures from major international and Japanese talent. In the island's main town and ferry port, **Miyanoura** (宮浦), is an amazing bathhouse, while around the southern Gotanji area there are sheltered beaches with glorious Inland Sea views – all making Naoshima a blissful escape.

Arrival, information and getting around

Regular **ferries** sail to Miyanoura from Takamatsu (1hr; ¥510) and Uno (20min; ¥280), one hour by train from Okayama (see p.529). **Cycle rental** is available at the ferry terminal (¥500/day) and elsewhere, and there's a regular **minibus** (¥100) that runs between Miyanoura and the Chichū Art Museum via Honmura and

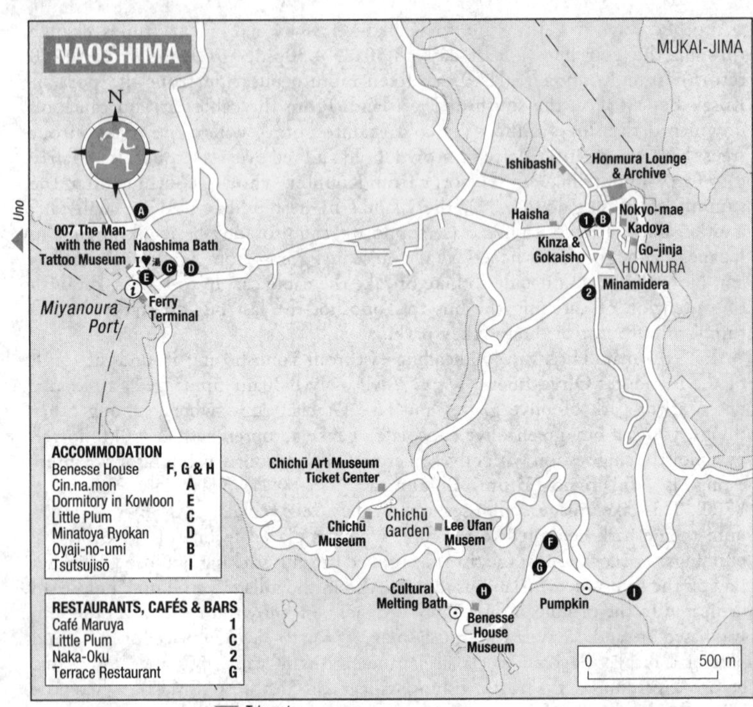

Benesse House. The bus timetable plus an English map and guide to the island is available from the **tourist information** desk in the ferry terminal (daily 8.30am–6pm; ⓣ087/892-2299).

Accommodation and eating

New places to **stay** keep popping up, several also serving as places to **eat**, but most only have a few rooms so reserve well in advance, especially if you plan to visit on a weekend. In Honmura, *Café Maruya* (カフェまるや; Tues–Sun 11am–5pm) in the village centre, and *Naka-Oku* (Wed–Mon 11.30am–9pm) on the hillside west of Minamidera, are both lovely places to eat or just enjoy a quiet drink. Offering wonderful Inland Sea views, the *Terrace Restaurant* at Benesse House's newer hotel complex serves appealing Mediterranean cuisine, while the museum itself has a café and a restaurant serving *kaiseki-ryōri* from ¥3500 for lunch and ¥6000 for dinner.

Accommodation

Benesse House Gotanji ⓣ087/892-2030, ⓦwww.naoshima-is.co.jp. Fine hotel offering comfortable, spacious rooms in four separate blocks in and around the museum (see opposite), all with sea views. The hotel's newer complex is closer to the water and has a Scandinavian feel to the decor, as well as a spa, library and guest lounge. At both properties guests get to see artworks not available to the general public. 6–9

Cin.na.mon Miyanoura ⓣ087/840-8133, ⓦwww.cin-na-mon.jp. Stylishly renovated wooden house that has three smart, though slightly damp, tatami bedrooms, all sharing a bathroom, and a trendy café-bar (Tues–Sun 11am–11pm) decorated with a collection of colourful plastic models of characters from *Star Wars*, *Dragon Ball* and the like. They offer a selection of curry dishes (¥900) and have a 90min all-you-can-drink deal for ¥2000. Rates include breakfast. 4

Seto Inland Sea Project

Since 1989, the **Seto Inland Sea Project**, partly sponsored by the cultural foundation of publishing company Benesse, has been a major force for revitalizing island communities that were dying out due to depopulation. Naoshima continues to be the foundation's main focus, but for 2010's Setouchi International Art Festival (ⓦsetouchi-artfest.jp) contemporary art projects were launched on a couple of other islands, including **Inujima** (see p.534). At the time of research, a gallery designed by Nishizawa Ryue of SANAA and located amid the terraced rice paddies of **Teshima**, east of Naoshima, was yet to open but will feature works by Christian Boltanski, Mori Mariko and Olafur Eliasson among others. It's likely that there will be ferry services connecting up the islands.

Dormitory in Kowloon Miyanoura ⓣ087/892-2424. Simple hostel, steps from the ferry terminal, with self-catering facilities and free internet access. Dorm bed ¥2800.

Little Plum Miyanoura ⓣ087/892-3751. Behind the bathhouse is this cute hostel and café-bar (Tues–Sun 3–10pm) made out of shipping crates. There are four comfortable bunk beds in each of the crates, and a shared bathroom/shower. In the evening it's about as buzzing as sleepy Miyanoura gets. Dorm bed ¥2700.

Minatoya Ryokan みなとや旅館 Miyanoura ⓣ087/892-3044. Run by friendly people, rates at this traditional inn include breakfast and dinner. ❺

Oyaji-no-umi おやじの海 Honmura ⓣ090-892-2269, ⓦoyajinoumi.web.fc2.com. A delightful garden fronts this comfortable minshuku with tatami rooms in the heart of the village. Rates include breakfast. ❸

Tsutsujisō つつじ荘 Gotanji ⓣ087/892-2838, ⓕ892-3871. Choose between chalets with tatami floors, or pau, spacious Mongolian circular tents with four beds, table and chairs at this great seaside-facing camp. It gets busy with school groups in July and August, but at other times you might end up having the place pretty much to yourself. ❹

Benesse House

Overlooking the Inland Sea, the spacious contemporary art gallery and hotel **Benesse House** (ベネッセハウス; daily 8am–9pm, last entry 8pm; ¥1000; see opposite for hotel details), 5km southeast of Miyanoura, is home to some stunning art including works by Bruce Nauman, Jasper Johns, Jean Michel Basquiat, David Hockney and Frank Stella. Scattered around the museum are seventeen outdoor sculptural works ranging from Kusama Yayoi's *Pumpkin*, an icon for the island, to Cai Gui Quang's witty and practical *Cultural Melting Bath*, an open-air jacuzzi in a glade surrounded by 36 jagged limestone rocks imported from China. Guests of Benesse House can book to use the jacuzzi (Wed, Fri & Sun 4–5pm; ¥1000).

Chichū Art Museum and Lee Ufan Museum

The serene **Chichū Art Museum** (地中美術館; Tues–Sun March–Sept 10am–5pm; Oct–Feb 10am–4pm; ¥2000) is a twenty-minute walk northwest around the coast from Benesse House. A naturally lit gallery housing four paintings from Monet's *Water Lily* series is the climax of a winding tour through towering corridors of polished concrete connecting spaces dedicated to a dazzling installation by Walter de Maria and three signature "playing with light" pieces by James Turrell. The museum's lovely café offers a spectacular panorama of the Inland Sea. On the approach to the museum, the pretty, and free, **Chichū Garden** has been planted with flowers and plants similar to those cultivated by Monet at his famous garden in Giverny.

Sited between Benesse House and the Chichū Art Museum is the new **Lee Ufan Museum**. Nearing completion at the time of research, this three-room gallery and courtyard garden, also designed by Andō Tadao, will showcase the work of major Korean artist Lee Ufan.

Honmura: Art House Project

The charming fishing village of **Honmura** (本村), located midway down Naoshima's east coast, is the base for **Art House Project**, in which several old wooden houses, a temple and a shrine have been turned into art installations. To buy an entry ticket (¥400 per site, or ¥1000 for a combined ticket), head first to the **Honmura Lounge and Archive** (Tues–Sun 10am–4pm; ⓣ087/840-8273), around the corner from the Nokyo-mae bus stop. There's a library of information on the different artists represented around the island here and it is the starting point at weekends for guided tours of the installations (¥500).

Kadoya (角屋) is the forum for a trio of works by Miyajima Tatsuo, including the beguiling light-and-water installation *Sea of Time '98*. On the small hill to the east stands the Edo-era shrine **Go-ō-jinja** (護王神社), renovated to include a stone chamber and a glass staircase. **Minamidera** (南寺) is a collaboration between Andō Tadao and American artist James Turrell. Andō designed the stark building that stands on the site of a long-since-demolished temple and incorporates the charred wooden walls that are typical of the village. Inside, it takes about ten minutes for your eyes slowly to adjust to the darkness and see Turrell's artwork – an enigmatic blue void. A former dental clinic now houses the scrapbook-style **Haisha** (はいしゃ) by Ōtake Shinro, which includes a partial life-size copy of the Statue of Liberty; **Ishibashi** (石橋) is decorated with beautiful waterfall paintings by Senju Hiroshi; and **Gokaisho** (碁会所) displays amazingly realistic wooden sculptures of camellias by Suda Yoshihiro in tatami rooms. Prior booking and an extra fee (¥500) is required for **Kinza** (きんざ); as one's eyes become accustomed to the lack of light in the darkened space, the collections of small wood, glass and stone objects slowly reveal themselves.

Naoshima Bath I ♥ 湯 and around

Ōtake Shrinro collaborated with design studio Graf on the incredible *sentō* **Naoshima Bath I ♥ 湯** (Tues–Fri 2–9pm, Sat & Sun 10am–9pm; ¥500), a minute's walk from Miyanoura's sleek SANAA-designed ferry terminal. As with his Haisha (see above), there's a wealth of detail both inside and out this public bath (I ♥ 湯 is a pun on the Japanese word *yu*, meaning hot water), including recycled ceramic tile mosaics, pop art paintings and photo collages, video, erotica and a small elephant perched on the divide between the male and female baths.

James Bond fans will want to drop by Miyanoura's tiny **007 The Man with the Red Tattoo Museum** (daily 9am–5pm; free). Plastered with posters, photos and other memorabilia, it feels like a shrine created by an obsessive teenage fan and is part of the island's campaign to feature as a location in a future Bond film – not too big a stretch since Raymond Benson set his 007 novel *The Man With The Red Tattoo* on Naoshima.

Kotohira

Approximately 30km southwest of Takamatsu, **KOTOHIRA** (琴平) is home to the ancient shrine Kotohira-gū, popularly known as **Kompira-san**. Along with the Grand Shrines of Ise and Izumo Taisha, Kotohira is one of the major Shinto pilgrimage sites, attracting some four million visitors a year. Despite the crowds, it is still one of Shikoku's highlights. The town itself is pleasantly located, straddling the Kanakura-gawa at the foot of the mountain Zozu-san, so called because it is said to resemble an elephant's head (*zozu*). Kotohira can easily be visited on a day-trip from Takamatsu, one hour away by train, or en route to Kōchi or the mountainous interior.

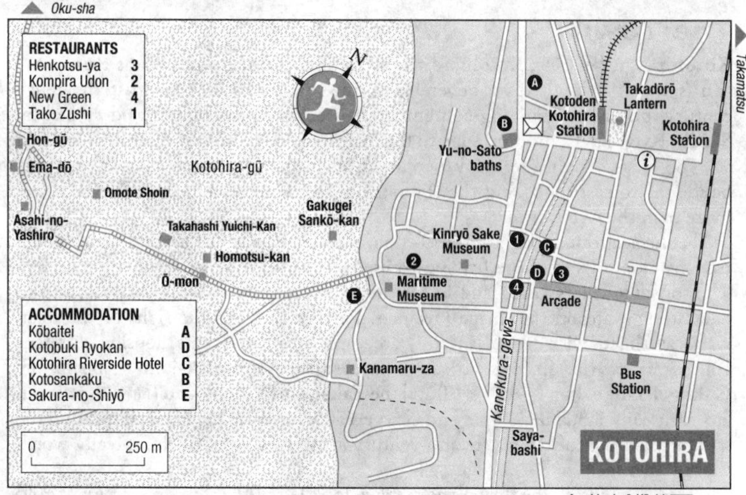

Arrival and information

JR Kotohira Station is a ten-minute walk northeast of the town centre. Left of the exit is a cloakroom for left luggage (daily 6.30am–9pm; ¥200/bag). If you've travelled by Kotoden train from Takamatsu, you'll arrive at the smaller station closer to the town centre on the banks of the Kanekura-gawa. The **tourist information** office (daily 10am–7pm) is on the main street between the two stations; very little English is spoken here, but you can get a map and some English-language information. They also rent bicycles (¥100/hr, ¥500/day).

Accommodation

Accommodation in Kotohira is in high demand, and prices can rise substantially on weekends and public holidays. The town is famed for its top-notch ryokan; unless mentioned, rates include breakfast and dinner, usually of high quality. The nearest youth hostel is in Awa Ikeda (see p.621), 20km south.

Kōbaitei 紅梅亭 ⓣ0877/75-1111, ⓦwww.hananoyu.co.jp. Charming ryokan with lovely public areas including a tea lounge, traditional garden, small swimming pool and public onsen bath. There's a choice of tatami and Western-style rooms. ⑦

Kotobuki Ryokan ことぶき旅館 ⓣ&ⓕ0877/73-3872, ⓔwelcome-kotobuki@be.wakwak.com. The best deal in Kotohira, this small and attractive ryokan is run by a friendly couple and oozes tradition. It's conveniently located by the river and shopping arcade. ⑤

Kotohira Riverside Hotel 琴平リバーサイドホテル; ⓣ0877/75-1880. This small Western-style hotel with fairly spacious modern rooms, on the west bank of the Kanekura-gawa, is a good mid-range option. ⑤

Kotosankaku 琴参閣 685-11 Kotohira-chō ⓣ0877/75-1000, ⓦwww.kotosankaku.jp. Enormous complex, located 5min walk west of the JR station, with top-notch facilities including a rooftop swimming pool, luxurious spa baths and restaurants. ⑧

Sakura-no-Shō 桜の抄 ⓣ0877/75-3218, ⓦwww.hananoyu.co.jp. At the foot of the steps leading up to Kompira-san, with comfortable Japanese- and Western-style rooms and some nice public baths. If you fancy a splurge, it's also worth visiting for the beautifully presented mix of traditional and contemporary Japanese dishes at its main restaurant, *Ikuri* (いくり), a large, sleek affair with an open kitchen in its centre and romantic views out over the illuminated Ō-mon at night. ⑦

The Town

Kotohira-gū (琴平宮), Kotohira's star attraction, is usually known as **Kompira-san** (see box below). It's a venerable shrine, dating back to at least the tenth century, but award-winning contemporary steel and glass buildings designed by Suzuki Ryoji lend a modern edge to the mainly wooden hillside complex, reached via 785 steps. You'll see many people huffing and puffing on the lower slopes beside the tourist shops, but the climb is not so strenuous and shouldn't take you more than thirty minutes.

The shrine grounds begin at the Ō-mon, a stone gateway just beyond which you'll pass the Gonin Byakushō – five red-painted stalls shaded by large white umbrellas. The souvenir sellers here stand in for the five farmers who were once allowed to hawk their wares in the shrine precincts. Further along to the right of the main walkway, lined with stone lanterns, are three small museums housing different collections of the shrine's artistic treasures: the **Hōmotsu-kan** (宝物館), the **Gakugei Sankō-kan** (学芸参考館) and the **Takahashi Yuichi-kan** (高橋由一館). All are open daily 8.30am–4.30pm and charge ¥500, but only the latter, displaying the striking paintings of the nineteenth-century artist Takahashi Yuichi, is really worth the entrance fee.

Before climbing to the shrine's next stage, look left of the steps to see a giant gold ship's propeller, a gift from a local shipbuilder. To the right is the entrance to the serene reception hall **Omote Shoin** (表書院; daily 8.30am–4.30pm; ¥500), built in 1659. Delicate screen paintings and decorated door panels by the celebrated artist Okyo Maruyama (1733–95) are classified as Important Cultural Assets; they're so precious you have to peer through glass into the dim interiors to see them. At the rear of the complex is a series of wall-panel paintings of crimson camellias by local artist Takubo Kyoji.

Returning to the main ascent, the next major building reached is the grand **Asahi-no-Yashiro** (Sunshine Shrine) dedicated to the sun goddess Amaterasu, decorated with intricate woodcarvings of flora and fauna and topped with a green copper roof. Two flights of steep steps lead from here to the thatched-roof **Hon-gū**, the main shrine, built in 1879 and the centre of Kompira-san's daily activities. Priests and their acolytes in traditional robes rustle by along a raised wooden corridor linking the shrine buildings. Many visitors stop here, but the hardy, and truly faithful, trudge on up a further 583 steps to the **Oku-sha**

Kompira's Buddhist connection

Kompira-san, the unofficial but more commonly used name for Kotohira-gū, comes from the nickname for Omono-nushi-no-Mikoto, the spiritual guardian of seafarers. Kompira was originally Kumbhira, the Hindu crocodile god of the River Ganges, and was imported as a deity from India well before the ninth century, when Kōbō Daishi chose the shrine as the spot for one of his Buddhist temples. For one thousand years Kompira-san served as both a Buddhist and Shinto holy place and was so popular that those who could not afford to make the pilgrimage themselves either dispatched their pet dogs, with pouches of coins as a gift to the gods, or tossed barrels of rice and money into the sea, in the hope that they would be picked up by sailors who would take the offering to Kompira-san on their behalf.

When the Meiji Restoration began, Shinto took precedence, and the Buddhas were removed from the shrine, along with Kompira, who was seen as too closely associated with the rival religion. While there are no representations of Kompira at the shrine today, an open-air gallery decorated with pictures and models of ships serves as a reminder of the shrine's original purpose, and the Chinese flavour of some of the buildings hints at the former Buddhist connection.

following a path to the left of the main shrine. When you reach this inner shrine, located almost at the top of Zozu-san, look up at the rocks on the left to see two rather cartoonish stone carvings of the demon Tengu.

From the main shrine area, head to the wooden platforms for magnificent views of the surrounding countryside – on a clear day you can see as far as the Inland Sea. To the left of the main shrine is the open-air **Ema-dō gallery**, which displays votive plaques, paintings and models of ships. These are from sailors who hope to be granted good favour on the seas. The commendations extend to one from Japan's first cosmonaut, a TV journalist who was a paying passenger on a Russian Soyuz launch in 1990.

Kompira-san is one of only two places in Japan (the other is Kyoto) where you can see the ancient sport of *kemari* performed. Deemed an Intangible Cultural Property, this ninth-century forerunner of soccer is played by the shrine's monks on May 5, July 7 and in late December.

The Takadōrō Lantern to Saya-bashi

Compared with Kompira-san, Kotohira's other sights are rather minor. The **Takadōrō Lantern**, a 27.6m-tall wooden tower next to the Kotoden station, was built in 1865 and served as a warning beacon in times of trouble. The **Kinryō Sake Museum** (金陵の郷; daily except Wed 9am–at least 4pm; ¥310), at the start of the shrine approach, is also well worth a look. There has been a sake brewery on this spot since 1616, and the buildings arranged around a large courtyard have changed little over the centuries. Inside, the well-presented exhibition runs step by step through the sake-making process, using life-size displays and a fascinating Japanese-language audio guide that includes traditional brewers' songs. You can also sample three types of sake for ¥100 per shot.

Closer to the shrine steps, a road to the left leads past the lacklustre **Maritime Museum** (daily 9am–5pm; ¥400) up the hill to the **Kanamaru-za** (金丸座; daily 9am–5pm; ¥500). This performance hall, built in 1835, is said to be the oldest-surviving kabuki theatre in Japan and was fully restored when it was moved to this location from the centre of Kotohira in 1975. Plays are only performed here in April, but the theatre itself merits a visit, especially for its wooden-beamed and lantern-lit auditorium.

Just before the turning up the hill to the Kanamaru-za, a twisting path leads down to the river, and if you head south along the banks you'll soon come to the **Saya-bashi** (鞘橋), an attractive arched wooden bridge with a copper-covered roof. The bridge is only used during the grand Otaisai festival held every October, in which sacred *mikoshi* are paraded through the town.

After climbing up to Kompira-san and exploring the rest of Kotohira, you might want to rest your aching bones at the luxurious **Yu-no-sato baths**, part of the *Kotosankaku* hotel complex and open to the public daily from 10.30am to 3.30pm (¥1200; closed 2nd and 4th Thurs of each month).

Eating

Note that many places to **eat** in Kotohira shut up shop by 5pm. On the main approach to the shrine you'll find several tourist-oriented places dishing up Kagawa-ken's famous udon noodles; try *Kompira Udon* (金比羅うどん; daily 8am–5pm) where a bowl topped with *tempura* or *tonkatsu* costs around ¥650. If you fancy sushi, there's *Tako Zushi* (たこ寿司), easily spotted on the main shopping street by the large red octopus (*tako*) above the door. If you're looking for somewhere to eat after 5pm, a good choice is *New Green* (ニューグリーン; Tues–Sun 8am–8pm). This friendly café, at the foot of the main approach to the shrine, serves Japanese and Western food including good-value set menus for around ¥1000. A pleasant place for a refreshing cup of *macha* and some *manju* (set ¥650) after climbing Kompira-san is *Henkotsu-ya* (へんこつ屋; daily 8.30am–6.30pm). You'll find it on the same street as the *Kotobuki Ryokan* (see p. 609).

Tokushima and around

Built on the delta of the Yoshino-gawa – Shikoku's longest river – and bisected by the Shinmachi-gawa, **TOKUSHIMA** (徳島), the capital of Tokushima-ken, is known across Japan for its fantastic summer dance festival, the **Awa Odori**, which is attended every year by over one million people (see box, p.614). If you're not among them then don't worry, as Tokushima does its best to provide a flavour of the Awa Odori experience year-round at the Awa Odori Kaikan, at the foot of **Mount Bizan**, a parkland area providing sweeping views of the city.

Home to the first temple of the Shikoku pilgrimage, Tokushima has a long history of welcoming visitors and you'll find it a noticeably friendly and relaxed place, as well as a good base to explore the rest of the prefecture. North of the city are the whirlpools of **Naruto**, while heading south there's the pretty coastal village of **Hiwasa**, where turtles lay their eggs on the beach each summer, popular surf beaches, and, across the border in Kōchi-ken, the jagged cape at **Muroto**. Inland, the best place to head is the spectacular **Iya Valley**, including the river gorge at **Ōboke**.

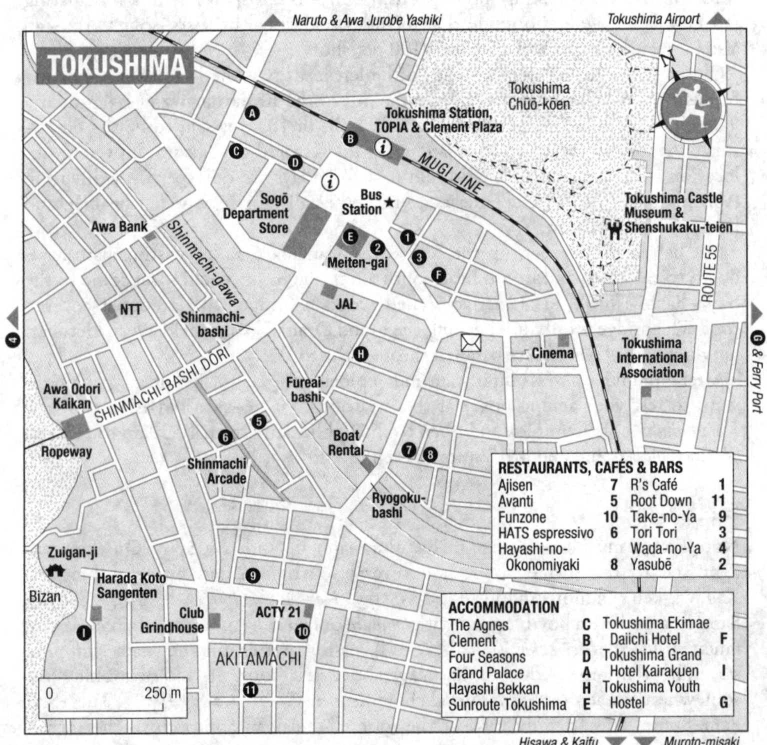

9

SHIKOKU | Tokushima and around

Arrival and information

Trains pull in at Tokushima Station, next to the Clement Plaza shopping centre, at the head of Shinmachibashi-dōri, the main thoroughfare. Tokushima's **airport** (Ⓣ088/699-2831, Ⓦwww.tokushima-airport.co.jp) lies 8km north of the city centre; there are buses from here to Clement Plaza (30min; ¥430). **Ferries** arrive at Okinosu port, 3km east of the centre, while long-distance **buses** come and go from the bus station in front of the train station. The city's sights are all within easy walking distance of Clement Plaza.

Although there is a **tourist information** booth outside Clement Plaza, it's better to go to Tokushima Prefecture International Exchange Association (TOPIA), on the plaza's sixth floor (daily 10am–6pm; Ⓣ088/656-3303, Ⓦwww.topia.ne.jp), where the English-speaking staff are very helpful. There's also a small library of English books and magazines, as well as internet access (¥50/10min). The Tokushima International Association (Mon–Fri 9am–6pm; Ⓣ088/622-6066), one block beyond the city hall to the east of the JR station, offers similar services and, for longer-term visitors, both facilities offer Japanese classes.

Accommodation

Tokushima has a decent range of **accommodation**, most of it of a high standard and conveniently located around the JR station. Book well in advance if you plan to visit during the Awa Odori in August. If you're having problems finding somewhere to stay, pop into TOPIA (see above), which can make enquiries for you.

The Agnes 1-28 Terashima Honchō Nishi Ⓣ088/626-2222, Ⓕ626-3788. From the same family of hotels as the *Grand Palace* and *Four Seasons* (see below) comes this cool, monochrome number with decent-sized, well-equipped rooms and a trendy patisserie on the ground floor. ⑤

Clement 1-61 Terashima Honchō Nishi Ⓣ088/656-3111. Upmarket hotel next to the station with spacious, tastefully furnished rooms. There's an eighteenth-floor bar and restaurant with a grandstand view of Mount Bizan. JR Pass holders get ten percent discount on the rates. ⑥

Grand Palace 1-60-1 Terashima Honchō Nishi Ⓣ088/626-1111, Ⓔmail@gphotel.jp. Going for the sleek black look in a big way, this boutiquish hotel offers larger than average rooms. The same company also operates the small and stylish *Four Seasons* business hotel, nearby (Ⓣ088/622-2203; ⑤). ⑥

Hayashi Bekkan はやし別館 2-22 Naka Torimachi Ⓣ088/622-9191, Ⓕ626-3346. Tucked away in the side streets between the station and the Shinmachi-gawa, this colourful place has spacious tatami rooms and friendly management. All rooms have en-suite bathrooms, but there's also a large communal bath. Rates include free tickets to the evening show at Awa Odori Kaikan (see p.614). ⑤, with two meals ⑦

Sunroute Tokushima 1-5-1 Moto-machi Ⓣ088/653-8111, Ⓦwww.sunroute.jp. Reception for this slick modern hotel is on the third floor of the Meiten-gai block opposite Tokushima Station. Pleasant rooms are decorated in monochrome hues and each one has its own personal computer. There's also free access to the rooftop onsen bath, jacuzzi and sauna (¥700 for non-guests). ⑤

Tokushima Ekimae Daiichi Hotel 徳島駅前第一ホテル 2-21 Ichibanchō Ⓣ088/655-5005, Ⓕ655-5003. You'll find tiny, but clean, rooms at this convenient and modern business hotel. Rates are substantially lower on Fri, Sat and Sun. Breakfast is extra, but there are non-smoking rooms and free internet access. ④

Tokushima Grand Hotel Kairakuen 徳島グランドホテル偕楽園 1 Igachō Ⓣ088/623-3333. This traditional Japanese-style hotel, in a secluded spot at the base of Bizan, offers large tatami rooms with lovely garden views. Rates include two meals. ⑦

Tokushima Youth Hostel 徳島ユースホステル 7-1 Hama, Ohama-machi Ⓣ088/663-1505, Ⓦwww.jyh.gr.jp. Next to a crescent-shaped stretch of beach fringed by pine trees, this large hostel has a peaceful location and friendly English-speaking management. Meals and bike rental are available. The only drawback is getting there; take the bus bound for Omiko (the last one leaves from outside Tokushima Station around 6pm), then catch the bus to Omiko-guchi and walk the remaining 3km to the beach. Dorm beds are ¥2940.

The City

Five minutes' walk to the east of the JR station is the attractive **Tokushima Chūō-kōen** (徳島中央公園), a park on the site of the fortress of *daimyō* Hachisuka Iemasa. From 1586 his clan lived in the castle for 280 years, creating the town that is now Tokushima. All that remains of the castle, which was destroyed in 1896, are a few stone walls, part of the moat and the **Shenshuku-teien**, a beautiful formal garden (daily 9am–5pm; ¥50). Beside the garden is the small **Tokushima Castle Museum** (Tues–Sun 9.30am–5pm; ¥300; ⓣ088/656-2525), with informative, modern displays explaining the history of the Hachisuka clan and a large model that gives a good idea of what the fortress and its surrounding compound once looked like.

Walking directly south out of the JR station along the main road brings you to the **Shinmachi-gawa** (新町川). There are several bridges spanning the river, including the Shinmachi-bashi, on which you'll see street mosaics of Awa Odori dancers reflected in the metallic bollards. Several hundred metres south, beside the Ryogoku-bashi, you can rent boats (¥500/30min) and there are also free sightseeing boat trips several times a day.

Five minutes' walk southeast of the river, at the base of the 280m-high **Mount Bizan** (眉山), is the **Awa Odori Kaikan** (阿波踊り会館; daily 9am–6pm). The complex houses a good gift shop on the ground floor, a **ropeway** (April–Oct daily 9am–9pm, Nov–March daily 9am–5.30pm; one way ¥600, return ¥1000) on the fifth floor that goes to the top of Mount Bizan, a museum on the third floor (daily 9am–5pm; ¥300), and the **Awa Odori Hall** (¥500), where there are at least four live performances daily of the city's famous dance, including one slightly more expensive evening performance from 8pm (¥700); audience participation is encouraged at all performances, so don't be surprised if you end up on stage. If you plan to do the lot, buy the ¥1500 ticket which covers all the attractions (though not the evening dance).

On a clear day, it's worth ascending Bizan for the panoramic view, and it's not too difficult a hike if you want to save on the ropeway fee or fancy the exercise; a route starts from the temple to the left of the *kaikan* at the end of Shinmachibashi-dōri. At the summit there's a park with a stupa, called **Tokushima Pagoda**, in memory of the Japanese soldiers who served in Burma

The dancing fools

Every year in mid-August many Japanese return to their family homes for **Obon** (Festival of the Dead), which is as much a celebration as a remembrance of the deceased. Towns all over the country hold *bon* dances, but none can compare to Tokushima's **Awa Odori** – the "Great Dance of Awa" – a four-day festival that runs every year from August 12 to 15. Over a million spectators come to watch the eighty thousand participants, dressed in colourful *yukata* (summer kimono) and half-moon-shaped straw hats, who parade through the city, waving their hands and shuffling their feet to an insistent two-beat rhythm, played on *taiko* drums, flutes and *shamisen* (traditional stringed instruments). With plenty of street parties and sideshows, this is as close as Japan gets to Rio's Mardi Gras, and there's plenty of fun to be had mingling with the dancers, who famously chant, "The dancing fool and the watching fool are equally foolish. So why not dance?"

If you plan to attend the festival, book accommodation well in advance or arrange to stay in one of the nearby towns and travel in for the dances, which start at 6pm and finish at 10.30pm (street parties continue well into the night). To take part as a dancer, contact the Tokushima International Association (see p.613), which organizes a dance group on one of the festival nights.

during World War II, and the marginally interesting **Moraesu-kan** (daily 9.30am–5pm; ¥200; ⓣ088/623-5342), a tiny museum dedicated to Wenceslão de Morães, a Portuguese naval officer and former consul-general in Kōbe. Morães lived in Tokushima for sixteen years until his death in 1929 and wrote many books on Japan.

Walk east around the base of Bizan and you'll come to the delightful Buddhist temple, **Zuigan-ji** (瑞巌寺). Built in the Momoyama-style, Zuigan-ji dates from 1614 and has an elegant traditional garden with carp-filled pools, a waterfall and rock paths across mossy lawns leading up to a picturesque red pagoda. While here, drop by the small shop Harada Koto Sangenten (原田琴三絃店; ⓣ088/652-5625; Mon–Sat 8.30am–6.30pm), opposite *Tokushima Grand Hotel Kairakuen*, which specializes in *shamisen* and *koto*. If you are lucky, the friendly staff might give you a demonstration.

If you're interested in *bunraku* puppetry, known locally as *ningyō jōruri*, head for the historic premises of the Jūrobei family, **Awa Jūrōbē Yashiki** (阿波十郎兵衛屋敷; ⓣ088/665-2202; daily 9.30am–at least 5pm; ¥400), 4km to the north of Tokushima Station. This former samurai residence, with an enclosed garden and display room of beautifully made antique puppets, was once the home of the tragic figure Jūrōbē, immortalized in *Keisei Awa no Naruto*, the epic eighteenth-century play by Chikamatsu. You can see part of the play performed here, usually the classic scene where Jūrōbē's wife, Oyumi, turns away their daughter Otsuru as a stranger. Live performances are held daily at 11am in the wooden outdoor theatre, with an additional performance at 2pm on Saturdays and Sundays. A video of the play is also shown inside a large tatami hall. To reach the building, take a twenty-minute bus journey from stop number 7 at the bus terminal.

Eating, drinking and nightlife

Tokushima has a good choice of **restaurants** and no shortage of **bars**, with the densest concentration in **Akitamachi**, Tokushima's lively entertainment area. Rooftop beer gardens open during the summer at several hotels, including the *Clement*. For **dancing** try *Funzone* (ⓣ088/656-0085) in the basement of the ACTY Ijinkan building, just down from the ACTY21 building, which hosts drum 'n' bass and other club events at the weekends. For **live music**, fans of rock and indie should head to the small club *Club Grindhouse* (ⓣ088/655-5175), where all manner of local bands play most nights of the week; admission depends on the act (¥1000–4000).

Ajisen 味扇1-29 Minami Uchimachi ⓣ088/624-0005. Appealing traditional restaurant that's not too formal and serves good-value set meals (around ¥2000) with lots of little dishes that change by the season. Seating is in private booths. Mon–Fri 11am–2pm & 5–9.30pm, Sat 5–9.30pm.

Avanti 1-18 Higashi Semba ⓣ088/655-6038. Stylish contemporary Italian bistro serving pasta, risotto, pizza and – for something a bit different – couscous. Dishes are around ¥1000. Mon & Wed–Sat 11.30am–9pm, Sun 11.30am–5.30pm.

HATS espressivo 1-16-4 Higashi-shinmachi ⓣ088/635-4698. Trendy café-bar on two levels in the city's central covered arcade that's a popular hangout and a good lunch spot. Their take on the Tokushima burger (¥600), a local burger that ditches ketchup in favour of a sweetish sauce containing thin strips of beef, comes highly recommended. Daily 11am–midnight.

Hayashi-no Okonomiyaki はやしのお好み焼き 1-30 Minami Uchimachi. Relaxed *okonomiyaki* joint, where you can cook your own meal from ¥700. Mon–Sat 11am–8pm.

R's Café Second floor, 3-30 Ichiban-chō ⓣ088/623-4787. R speaks English and whips up simple, inexpensive dishes such as pasta, pizza and sandwiches, as well as his own version of the local Tokushima Burger. Also has a good range of drinks, including cocktails. Tues–Sun 11am–2.30am.

Root Down 1-26-1 Takasho-machi. There's always a warm welcome at this café-bar that's popular with Tokushima's expat community

Naruto

The 88-temple pilgrimage (see p.593) first reaches Shikoku at **NARUTO** (鳴門), around 13km north of Tokushima. However, the town is more famous for the **whirlpools** that form as the tides change and water is forced through the narrow straits between Shikoku and Awaji-shima. This is one of Tokushima's most heavily hyped attractions, but it's not a consistently reliable phenomenon. The whirlpools are at their most dramatic on days of the full and new moon; to avoid a wasted journey, check first on the tidal schedule with tourist information in Tokushima (see p.613). To see the whirlpools up close you can either hop on one of the tourist **cruise boats** (¥2200 for around 30min), or traverse the **Uzu-no-Michi** (渦の道; daily April–Sept 9.30am–5.30pm; Jan–March & Oct–Dec 9.30am–4.30pm; ¥500), a walkway under Naruto-Ōhashi bridge, which puts you 45m directly above the maelstrom. The cheaper alternative is a bird's-eye view from Naruto-kōen, the park on Oge Island, just to the north of Naruto town. Although there are several trains daily from Tokushima to Naruto, the bridge is a fair way from the station. It's more convenient to hop on the regular direct bus from Clement Plaza, which takes around an hour and costs ¥690.

and which is found in one of the city's raunchier areas. The American owner turns out a mean burger and all food and drinks are ¥500. Mon–Sat 7pm–3am.

Take-no-ya 竹の家 Konya-chō ☎088/623-5262. This lively *izakaya* specializing in *yakitori* near ACTY21 runs late into the night and has bargain prices. Dishes start from ¥320 and they do a good *yakitori* set for ¥980. Daily 5.30pm–2.30am.

Tori Tori とりとり 2-16 Ichiban-chō. Serried ranks of sake bottle-keeps and fading Awa Odori posters set the tone at this convivial *izakaya*, across the street from *R's Cafe*. *Yakitori* is the speciality – if you're feeling adventurous, go for the pizza-flavoured chicken, pig's stomach or *wani* (alligator).

There's an English menu and dishes start from ¥600. Mon–Sat 5pm–1am.

Wada-no-Ya 和田の屋 Teramachi. Delightful teahouse at the foot of Bizan with a view onto a rock garden. *Macha* and Tokushima's signature *yaki-mochi* (small, lightly toasted patties of pounded rice and red beans) costs ¥650. Daily except Thurs 10am–5pm.

Yasubē 安兵衛 ☎088/622-5387. Well-priced *izakaya* with larger than average servings. The emphasis is on chicken and seafood dishes, such as *yakitori* (from ¥220) and *sashimi* (set ¥1200). If you fancy something with a hint of danger attached, try their *fugu* course (¥10,500; serves three people). Daily 10.30am–9.30pm.

Listings

Banks and exchange The main branch of Awa Bank, beside the Kasuga-bashi, offers the full range of foreign exchange services. There's an ATM accepting foreign cash cards at the post office (see below).

Bookshop Kinokuniya has an outlet stocking English books and magazines on the eighth floor of Sogō department store (daily 10am–7.30pm) opposite Clement Plaza.

Car rental Eki Rent-a-Car (☎088/622-1014) is situated in front of Tokushima Station, while Nippon Rent-a-Car (☎088/699-6170) is at the airport.

Hospital Tokushima Prefectural Central Hospital (Kenritsu Chūō Byōin), 1-10-3 Kuramoto-chō ☎088/631-7151.

Internet Available at TOPIA (see p.613; ¥50/10min).

Laundry A 10min walk from the station is the Aozara coin laundry, at 3-3 Nakajo-sanjima, open daily 8am–10pm.

Police The main police station is close to Kachidoki-bashi ☎088/622-3101. Emergency numbers are listed on p.71.

Post office The central post office is just south of the JR station at 1-2 Yaoya-chō (Mon–Fri 9am–7pm, Sat 9am–5pm & Sun 9am–12.30pm).

Hiwasa and around

Picturesque **HIWASA** (日和佐), 55km south of Tokushima, is worth pausing at for its intriguing temple, quaint harbour and pretty beach. **Yakuō-ji** (薬王寺), the 23rd temple on the Shikoku pilgrimage, is on the hillside as you pull into the train station; the temple's base is surrounded by hotels and gift shops catering to the hordes of pilgrims who regularly pass through. Climbing the steps to the main temple, you can't fail to notice lots of ¥1 coins on the ground: some pilgrims place a coin on each step for luck as they head up. At the top of the steps is the main temple area, whose buildings date from 815 AD and where there's a striking statue of a goddess carrying a basket of fish and flanked by lotus blooms. Off to the right is a more recently built single-storey pagoda. There's a good view of Hiwasa's harbour from the platform, but the highlight here is to descend into the pagoda's darkened basement, where for ¥100 you can fumble your way around a pitch-black circular corridor to a central gallery containing Brueghel-like painted depictions of all the tortures of hell. In a second gallery is a long scroll showing the steady decay of a beautiful, but dead, young woman.

About 1km south of the harbour, the reconstructed castle **Hiwasa-jō** (日和佐城; Tues–Sun 9am–5pm; ¥200) is only worth visiting for its impressive view of the town. The better option is to head directly to Ōhama beach, north of the harbour, where **turtles** lay their eggs between May and August. During this time, the beach is roped off and spectators must watch the action from a distance. For a closer look at the turtles, make your way to the **Sea Turtle Museum** at Umigame Hakubutsukan Karetta (うみがめ博物館カレッタ; daily 9am–5pm; ¥600; Ⓣ0884/77-1110), beside the beach. The displays are mainly in Japanese, but are very visual, with step-by-step photos of turtles laying eggs; you can also see some turtles swimming in indoor and outdoor pools.

The popular surfing spot of **KAIFU** (海部), 26km south of Hiwasa, is where the JR train line ends and is replaced with the private Asa Kaigan railway. You'll nearly always have to change trains here to continue toward the southern cape (simply cross over to the opposite platform). Even if you don't, you'll have to pay ¥270 extra to travel the remaining two stops – the first is **SHISHIKUI** (宍喰), Tokushima's top surf beach, where there's a good range of accommodation including the reasonable *Kokuminshukusha Mitoko-sō* (国民宿舎みとこ荘; Ⓣ0884/76-3150, Ⓕ76-3609; ❺ including two meals). The end of the line is **KANNOURA** (甲浦), a sleepy village with a pleasant stretch of gravelly sand framed with rocky outcrops.

Practicalities

Limited express and local **trains** link Hiwasa to Tokushima. You can leave your bags (¥200 a bag) at the small **tourist information office** at the station, where you can also pick up a map of the town and rent a bicycle for the day for ¥500 – a good idea, as the sights are a bit spread out. For somewhere to **stay**, close to the museum is a national lodge, *Umigamesō* (うみがめ荘; Ⓣ0884/77-1166, Ⓕ77-1167; room only ❹, including two meals ❻). Otherwise, there's also the basic *Hiwasa Youth Hostel* (Ⓣ&Ⓕ0884/77-0755; dorm bed ¥2885), or the comfortable *White Lighthouse* (ホテル白い燈台; Ⓣ0884/77-1170, Ⓕ77-1174; room only ❺, with two meals ❼–❽).

For lunch, there are a couple of big udon **restaurants** on the main road near Yakuō-ji, as well as *Hisayama Shokudō* (ひさやま食堂), a clean, friendly establishment serving staple fare like curry rice. It's on the left as you walk out of the station.

Muroto Misako and on to Kōchi

From Kannoura, buses continue south to the black-sand beaches and rugged cape of **MUROTO MISAKI** (室戸岬), an important stop on the pilgrimage route. On the way look out for **Meotoiwa** – two huge rock outcrops between which a ceremonial rope has been strung, creating a natural shrine. Virtually at the cape, a towering white **statue of Kōbō Daishi** commemorates the spot where the priest gained enlightenment when he had a vision of the Buddhist deity Kokūzō in a nearby cavern. Pilgrims pay their respects here before tackling the stiff climb up to

Deep sea therapy

In recent years Muroto Misaki (see p.617) has attracted pilgrims of a different ilk to those hiking the *henro* trail. Unusual currents off the cape push pure and mineral-rich sea water from as deep as 1000m closer to the surface. Near the Kōbō Daishi statue this deep-sea water is pumped into **Searest Muroto** (シレストむろと; daily except Wed 10am–9pm; ¥1400; ⓣ0887/22-6610), a state-of-the-art bathing complex where you can be pummelled by high-pressure water jets, relax in a spa bath or follow a workout video on a pool-side touch-controlled screen. Searest is part of Deep Sea World, which also includes the stylish **Utoco Deep Sea Therapy Centre & Hotel** (ⓣ0887/22-1811, ⓦwww.utocods.co.jp; ❽–❾ including breakfast). Here high-end beauty treatments and sophisticated baths using the same waters have been designed by the renowned Japanese cosmetics artist Shu Uemura; treatment packages cost from ¥9000. The attached contemporary hotel has seventeen chic rooms, all with unimpeded views of the Pacific. Meals using local seafood and deep-sea water products can be enjoyed at the hotel's classy *Bonne Peche* restaurant, where a set lunch starts at ¥1500. The restaurant *Kaido* in Searest is also good, offering set meals for around ¥1000.

a glade of lush vegetation swaddling **Hotsumisaki-ji** (最御崎寺). This appealingly shabby Buddhist temple, known locally as Higashi-dera (East Temple), is the 24th on the pilgrimage circuit. There's a hostel (ⓣ0887/23-0024, ⓕ22-0055; dorm beds ¥3885 per person, ¥5985 with two meals) just behind the temple, offering spacious tatami rooms with separate bathrooms and toilet; unsurprisingly, its main custom is from coach-loads of OAPs on pilgrimage. Order your meals when you book, or bring your own food, because there's nothing else up here.

Apart from taking a dip at **Searest Muroto** (see box above) there's not much else to do at Muroto Misaki other than follow a series of pathways along the shore and up the mountainside to the temple. The **information centre** (daily except Tues 8.30am–5pm; ⓣ0887/22-0574), beneath the wooden lookout platform close to the bus stop, may be able to assist if you're stuck for somewhere to stay.

Heading towards Kōchi, regular buses run to Nahari (奈半利), where you can continue by train on the Gomen-Nahari line of the **Tosa Kuroshio Railway**. Before doing that, though, consider making a short diversion to the **Jardin de Monet Marmottan du Village de Kitagawa** (北川村モネの庭マルモッタン; daily except Tues 10am–5pm; ¥700), a pretty impressive re-creation of parts of Claude Monet's gardens at Giverny. The complex, a blaze of technicolour blooms atop a hill with sweeping views of the surrounding countryside, also includes a winery selling vile-tasting fruit wines and a bakery and café that sell more palatable fare. A shuttle bus (¥230) makes short work of the 3km to the gardens from Nahari Station.

Most trains run from Nahari all the way to Kōchi, though the Gomen to Kōchi stretch is on JR lines. From Nahari it costs ¥1040 to get to Gomen and takes about an hour. With an early start from Tokushima, it's possible to visit the cape and make it all the way to Kōchi in a day (and vice versa), but you should allow two days if you plan to linger en route.

Inland to the Ōboke Gorge

Highway 192 shadows the JR Tokushima line for around 70km inland from Tokushima to the railway junction at **AWA IKEDA** (阿波池田), also easily reached from Kotohira (see p.608). If you want to explore the mountainous heart of Shikoku, this is where you'll need to change trains.

From Awa Ikeda the road and railway enter the spectacular **Ōboke Gorge** (大歩危), cut through by the sparkling Yoshino-gawa. The vertiginous mountains here and in the adjacent **Iya Valley** can be coated in snow during the winter, while less than one hour south, the palms of Kōchi sway in the sunshine. This remoteness from the rest of the island made the gorge an ideal bolt-hole for the Taira clan after their defeat at Yashima in 1185. Here the warriors traded their swords for farm implements and built distinctive thatched-roof cottages on the mountainsides. Few of these remain in their original form, their thatched roofs now covered in rusty tin and their wooden walls in plastic sheeting, but one that does is **Chiiori** (ちいおり; daily except Wed 11am–5pm; ⓣ0883/88-5290, ⓔenfo@chiiori.org; ¥500; call or email in advance), a 300-year-old house in the village of Tsurui (釣井). Tsurui is some 20km east from JR Ōboke, the nearest train station. This delightfully rustic building is the base for **The Chiiori Project** (ⓦwww.chiiori.org), which fosters community-based tourism in the Iya Valley and has established a small organic farm. Regular volunteer weekends and workshops on traditional crafts are hosted here, and it's also possible to stay overnight (Fri–Mon), a communal experience where guests and staff cook, eat and wash up together, and everyone shares a dorm. The suggested rates are ¥7000 for the first night and ¥4000 per subsequent night; rates may be reduced if you're involved in one of their volunteer projects. Full details can be found on the website.

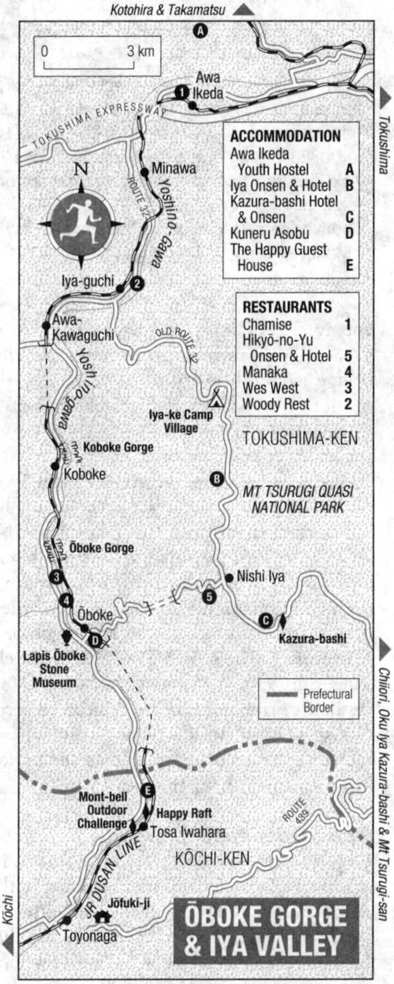

ŌBOKE GORGE & IYA VALLEY

ACCOMMODATION
Awa Ikeda Youth Hostel A
Iya Onsen & Hotel B
Kazura-bashi Hotel & Onsen C
Kuneru Asobu D
The Happy Guest House E

RESTAURANTS
Chamise 1
Hikyō-no-Yu Onsen & Hotel 5
Manaka 4
Wes West 3
Woody Rest 2

To get to Chiiori and many of the area's other attractions, you'll need your own transport – either a car or bicycle (though pedalling up and down these valleys is tough work). With your own transport you'll have the choice of taking the quieter old Route 32 through the Iya Valley – this is the road that starts across the blue bridge at Iya-guchi, and continues past the *Iya Kei Camp Village* and **Iya Onsen** (祖谷温泉), where you can take a short funicular train ride down to the hot spring right beside the river (7.30am–5pm; ¥1500 if you're not staying at the attached *Iya Onsen* hotel). The road eventually ends up at **Nishi Iya** (西祖谷) where you'll find the **Kazura-bashi** (かずら橋), one of several bridges in the area whose style dates from Taira times, when they were made out of *shirakuchi* (mountain vines) and bamboo so that they could easily be cut down to block an

Riding Ōboke's rapids

With thrilling rapids and spectacular rocky scenery, a **boat trip** (daily 9am–5pm unless there is heavy rain or strong wind; 30min; ¥1050) down the Yoshino-gawa is the best way to view the Ōboke Gorge. Boats leave from the *Manaka* restaurant (Ⓣ0883/84-1211), a five-minute walk past the Lapis Ōboke Stone Museum. More exciting **rafting and canyoning trips** are offered between March and November by the Australian-run *Happy Raft* (Ⓣ0887/75-0500, Ⓦwww.happyraft.com) further upriver near Tosa Iwahara Station; half-day trips start at ¥5500, full day at ¥10,000. MontBell Outdoor Challenge (Ⓣ0887/70-2334) also offers whitewater rafting trips.

enemy. The Taira would have a tougher time chopping down the Kazura-bashi today, since it's strengthened with carefully concealed steel cables. The 45m-long bridge is rebuilt every three years and, though it is not that high, the swaying motion as you cross induces enough of a thrill to justify the ¥500 entry fee. Otherwise, you can get a perfectly good view for free from the secure footing of the adjacent concrete bridge.

Even more picturesque are the **Oku Iya Kazura-bashi** (奥祖谷かずら橋), a pair of vine bridges also known as the "Fufu-bashi" (husband and wife bridges), some 30km further into the Iya Valley from Nishi Iya and en route to **Tsurugi-san** (剣山) – at 1955m, Shikoku's second-highest mountain. A four-hour round-trip climb starts at **Minokoshi** (見ノ越), from where there's a ropeway part of the way up the mountain, if you want to save time and effort.

To learn more about the area's geology, pop into the **Lapis Ōboke Stone Museum** (ラピス大歩危石の博物館; March–Nov daily 9am–4.30pm, Dec–Feb Tues–Sun 9am–4.30pm; ¥500; Ⓣ0883/84-1489), in a modern building with a distinctive rippling roof that's situated across the river and about 1km north from Ōboke Station. Inside there's a model of the gorge and all manner of stones, including a meteorite from Mars and various glittering gems, as well as a café and information desk for the area.

Practicalities

Regular **express trains** from Okayama and Kōchi stop at Awa Ikeda (most also stop at Ōboke). Several daily **local trains** ply the route through the Iya Valley between Awa Ikeda and Ōboke, but they are infrequent, as are buses – the information office beside Awa Ikeda Station has details, and they're also posted at Ōboke Station and at Lapis Oboke, which doubles as a tourist information centre for the area. It's possible to rent a car for as little as ¥3000 for three hours from the *Manaka* restaurant (see box, above). The Shikoku Transit Information Bureau (Ⓣ0883/72-1231) runs "Bonnet Bus" tours from March to the end of November, starting and finishing in Awa Ikeda and taking in most of the area's sights for ¥5200 or ¥6300, depending on the route.

Several tourist **restaurants** around the Kazura-bashi serve *yakisakana* – fish roasted on sticks over hot coals; set meals start at around ¥1000. The management at *Woody Rest* (daily except Wed 11am–8pm), near Iya-guchi Station, speak English; it's a rustic place serving good, inexpensive food. In Ōboke, *West West* (daily 10am–5pm) is an attractive modern complex including a café with a great view and a MontBell outdoor gear shop beside the Yoshino-gawa. Next door is an atmospheric soba noodle restaurant, with a water wheel outside and a thatched roof. Further upriver, *Manaka* serves set Japanese meals starting at ¥1200, and also individual dishes such as soba from ¥400. A handy restaurant at Awa Ikeda Station is *Chamise*; it serves the local speciality, *Iya soba*, as well as staple dishes like udon and curry rice for about ¥500.

Accommodation

With its rustic onsen and river-rafting possibilities, the Iya Valley is a popular tourist spot that offers a good range of **accommodation**. Apart from the listings below it's also possible to stay at Chiiori (see p.619) and at several campsites in the area.

Awa Ikeda Youth Hostel 阿波池田ユースホステル Ikeda-chō ⓣ0883/72-5277, ⓦwww.jyh.or.jp. Part of a temple, in a spectacular location on the side of the mountain overlooking the town. The manager will pick you up at the station if you call. Accommodation is in high-standard tatami rooms; there's a cosy lounge with TV, and the meals (breakfast ¥500, dinner ¥1000) are excellent. ❸

The Happy Guest House Otoyo-chō ⓣ0887/75-0500, ⓦwww.happyraft.com. You don't need to be on one of their rafting or canyoning trips to enjoy the guesthouse run by Teru from *Happy Raft* (see opposite). It's a lovely old house on the mountainside overlooking the valley on the Kōchi-ken side of Ōboke, and you'll need to bring your own food. Dorm beds in tatami rooms are ¥3500 per person (¥3000 if you join one of *Happy Raft*'s tours).

Hikyō-no-Yu 秘境の湯 Nishi Iya-yama ⓣ0883/87-2300. Not far from the Kazura-bashi, this onsen complex with a large public bath and rotemburo (daily except Tues 10am–9pm; open to non-guests for ¥1000) offers both Japanese- and Western-style rooms. Their restaurant has tables with *irori* (charcoal fires) in the centre. ❽

Iya Onsen ホテル祖谷温泉 Ikeda-chō ⓣ0883/75-2311, ⓦwww.iyaonsen.co.jp. One of the most stylish ryokan in Shikoku, *Iya Onsen* has a spectacular location that it makes the most of. It's highly recommended for its luxurious rooms with beautiful riverside views, and fine food. ❽

Kazura-bashi ホテルかずら橋 Nishi Iya-yama ⓣ0883/87-2171. This fine ryokan on the main road about 20min walk before the bridge has open-air baths on the hillside above the hotel, which are open to non-guests for ¥1000 (daily 10am–4pm). ❽

Kūneru Asobu 空音遊 Nishi Iya-yama ⓣ090-9778-7135, ⓦwww.k-n-a.com. Three kilometres' walk south of JR Ōboke Station (call and someone will come and pick you up), this casual guesthouse, also known as *K & A*, offers large tatami dorms in a 90-year-old house by the river. There's no shower, but the friendly owners will take you to the local onsen for ¥500 extra. Dorm bed ¥2600.

Kōchi and around

Sun-kissed **KŌCHI** (高知) lies dead in the centre of the arch-shaped southern prefecture of Shikoku. With its palm-lined avenues, network of rivers and shopping arcades, and gently trundling trams, it's a pleasant town to explore. The area's old name of Tosa is still used by people today, particularly when referring to the local cuisine. It wasn't until 1603, when ruling *daimyō* Yamauchi Katsutoyo named his castle Kōchiyama (now Kōchi-jō), that the city adopted its present name.

The **castle** remains Kōchi's highlight. To see other places of interest requires a short journey out of the city centre. The most immediately rewarding trip is to **Godai-san-kōen**, a mountain-top park overlooking the city, and the nearby **Chikurin-ji**, the 31st temple on the pilgrimage circuit. South of the city lies **Katsurahama**, with its over-hyped beach, and the **Sakamoto Ryōma Memorial Museum**, dedicated to a local hero of the Meiji Restoration (see box, p.625). In the right season Kōchi can be a base from which to take a whale-watching tour (see box, p.628). The weekly **Sunday market** (7am–5pm) on Kōchi's Otesuji-dōri, when farmers from all over the prefecture bring their produce to town, is worth attending, as is the colourful **Yosakoi Matsuri** (around Aug 9 to 12), when fourteen thousand dancers parade along the city's streets.

Arrival, information and city transport

All **trains** and most **buses** arrive at Kōchi Station, at the head of Harimaya-bashi-dōri, around 500m north of the city centre. **Kōchi Ryoma Airport** (ⓣ088/863-2906,

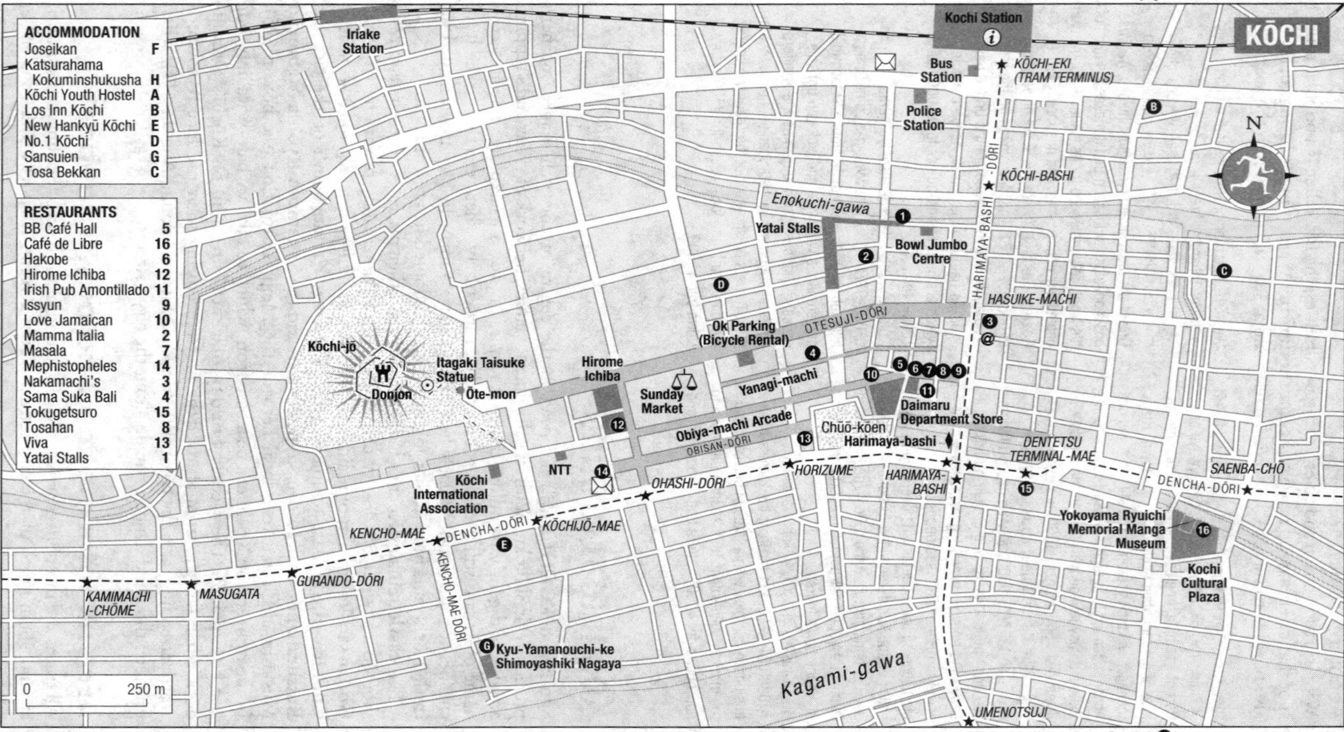
KŌCHI
ACCOMMODATION
Joseikan F
Katsurahama Kokuminshukusha H
Kōchi Youth Hostel A
Los Inn Kōchi B
New Hankyū Kōchi E
No.1 Kōchi D
Sansuien G
Tosa Bekkan C
RESTAURANTS
BB Café Hall 5
Café de Libre 16
Hakobe 6
Hirome Ichiba 12
Irish Pub Amontillado 11
Issyun 9
Love Jamaican 10
Mamma Italia 2
Masala 7
Mephistopheles 14
Nakamachi's 3
Sama Suka Bali 4
Tokugetsuro 15
Tosahan 8
Viva 13
Yatai Stalls 1
Ryūga-dō, Awa Ikeda & Takamatsu
Nakamura, Uwajima & A
Kōchi Prefectural Museum of Art & Godai-san-kōen
Ferries, Katsurahama Beach & H
F
Kochi Station
Iriake Station
Bus Station
Police Station
KŌCHI-EKI (TRAM TERMINUS)
KŌCHI-BASHI
HARIMAYA-BASHI-DŌRI
Enokuchi-gawa
Yatai Stalls
Bowl Jumbo Centre
HASUIKE-MACHI
OTESUJI-DŌRI
Ok Parking (Bicycle Rental)
Kōchi-jō
Donjon
Itagaki Taisuke Statue
Ōte-mon
Hirome Ichiba
Sunday Market
Yanagi-machi
Obiya-machi Arcade
OBISAN-DŌRI
Chūō-kōen
Daimaru Department Store
Harimaya-bashi
DENTETSU TERMINAL-MAE
HARIMAYA-BASHI
HORIZUME
OHASHI-DŌRI
NTT
Kōchi International Association
KŌCHIJŌ-MAE
KENCHO-MAE
DENCHA-DŌRI
KENCHO-MAE DŌRI
GURANDO-DŌRI
MASUGATA
KAMIMACHI I-CHŌME
SAENBA-CHŌ
Yokoyama Ryuichi Memorial Manga Museum
Kochi Cultural Plaza
Kyu-Yamanouchi-ke Shimoyashiki Nagaya
Kagami-gawa
UMENOTSUJI
N
0 250 m

Ⓦ www.kochiap.co.jp) is a forty-minute drive east of the city; a bus (¥700) runs at least hourly from the airport to opposite Kōchi Station, while a taxi into the city will cost around ¥4000.

Just outside the south exit of the station, in a swanky wooden building it shares will several souvenir shops, you'll find Kōchi's excellent **tourist information centre** (daily 9am–5pm, hotel information by phone until 8pm; Ⓣ 088/879-5489). Also helpful is the **Kōchi International Association (KIA)**, close to the castle on the second floor of the Marunouchi Biru, 4-1-37 Honmachi (Mon–Sat 8.30am–5.15pm; Ⓣ 088/875-0022, Ⓦ www.kochi-f.co.jp/kia), which also has a small library of English books and magazines as well as free internet access.

While central Kōchi is easily negotiated on foot, the distances between the major sights make catching a **tram** or **bus** a sensible option. The tram terminus is immediately outside the south exit of Kōchi Station. The system consists of two lines, one running north to south from the station to the port, crossing the east–west tracks at Harimaya-bashi. To travel within the city area costs a flat ¥190, paid to the driver on leaving the tram; you'll need to ask for a transfer ticket (*norikae-ken*) when you switch lines at Harimaya-bashi. A one-day ticket covering the central city area costs ¥500; a ¥800 ticket gives you access to everywhere on both lines.

Accommodation

There's the usual cluster of identikit business **hotels** close to the train station. More convenient for the shopping and entertainment districts are the hotels between Dencha-dōri and the city's principal river, Kagami-gawa. If you want to stay by the beach, head for the good *kokuminshukusha* (national lodging house) at Katsurahama.

Jōseikan 城西館 2-5-34 Kamimachi Ⓣ 088/875-0111, Ⓦ www.jyoseikan.co.jp. This elegant ryokan may be housed in a large modern building but it has a long history and offers top-grade, spacious tatami rooms with service fit for an emperor – which is why he stays here when he visits town. Its public bath is open to non-guests (4–11pm; ¥1000). ❽ including two meals.

Katsurahama Kokuminshukusha 桂浜国民宿舎 Katsurhama Ⓣ 088/841-2201, Ⓕ 841-2249. Located 13km south of central Kōchi, this modern hotel has spectacular views across the beach from its cliff-top location and good-value, high-standard tatami rooms. Non-guests can use its public bath (10am–3pm; ¥570). ❻ including two meals.

Kōchi Youth Hostel 高知ユースホステル 4-5 Fukui Higashi-machi, Ⓣ 088/823-0858, Ⓦ www.kyh-sakenokuni.com. One of Shikoku's best youth hostels, in a modern but rustic-styled building with lots of character. The friendly English-speaking manager used to work in a sake brewery and offers sake tasting courses after dinner each evening (¥500). There are both single rooms and dorms. The nearest train station is Engyouji, two stops west of Kōchi Station, then a 5min walk. Dorm ¥2835.

Los Inn Kōchi ロスイン高知 2-4-8 Kitahonmachi Ⓣ 088/884-1110, Ⓔ hotel@losinn.co.jp. Close to the station, this friendly place has kitsch decor (a mixture of reproduction antiques, heavy leather sofas and 1970s-style chandeliers), an English-speaking manager and comfortable Western- and Japanese-style rooms. Singles are a bargain ¥4400. ❹

New Hankyū Kōchi 高知新阪急ホテル 4-2-50 Honmachi Ⓣ 088/873-1111, Ⓦ hotel.kochi-newhankyu.co.jp. Handily located luxury Western-style hotel, with well-appointed rooms, a good selection of restaurants, a fitness centre and swimming pool. Book online for good discounts. ❻

No.1 Kōchi ホテルNo.1高知 16-8 Nijōdai- chō Ⓣ 088/873-3333. Both this business hotel and its annexe opposite have open-air rooftop baths offering a view of the castle – very atmospheric when it's lit up at night. The annexe offers preferential service to women, including a female-only floor. ❹

Sansuien 三翠園 1-3-35 Takajō-machi Ⓣ 088/822-0131, Ⓦ www.sansuien.co.jp. Don't judge it by the modern exterior; this ryokan has a refined interior, while the attached traditional gardens and buildings beside the Kagami-gawa add some atmosphere. They also have some slightly cheaper Western-style rooms. The onsen bath complex is open to non-residents (10am–4pm; ¥900). ❻ room only, ❽ including two meals.

Tosa Bekkan とさ別館 1-11-34 Sakurai-chō Ⓣ 088/883-5685. Friendly and relaxed Japanese-style hotel. The clean tatami rooms have TV, a/c and toilet, though bathrooms are communal. Meals are available, and there's a coin-operated laundry outside. ❹

The Town

A fable associated with Kōchi concerns a romantic monk who courted a lady beside the **Harimaya-bashi** (はりまや橋), a bridge that is ten minutes' walk south from the station. The original bridge is long gone, but the same-named crossroads is the city's apex and a small re-creation of the old red-railed bridge can be found nearby. Follow the covered Obiya-machi shopping arcade west of Harimaya-bashi to reach the hilltop castle of **Kōchi-jō** (高知城; daily 9am–4.30pm; ¥400 to enter the donjon; ⓣ088/824-5701). Construction was begun in 1601 by the feudal lord Yamauchi Katsutoyo but what you see today dates mainly from 1748, when reconstruction of the donjon turrets and gates was completed, following a major fire 21 years earlier.

The main approach is through the Ōte-mon, an impressive gateway flanked by high stone walls at the end of Otesuji-dōri. On the walk up to the donjon you'll pass a statue of Itagaki Taisuke, the founder of the People's Rights Movement, which promoted democracy in Japan during the early years of the Meiji era. For his efforts, Itagaki suffered an assassination attempt, during which he reputedly cried out "Itagaki may die, but liberty never!" The politician survived the knife attack, living to the ripe old age of 82, and his defiant phrase was adopted across Japan as the patriotic *cri de coeur* for democracy.

In the anti-feudal fervour that heralded the start of the Meiji era, almost all the castle's buildings were demolished, leaving the steeply sloping walls surrounding empty courtyards. The exception was the three-storey donjon, within the inner citadel (*honmaru*). To the left of the entrance there's an exhibition of old samurai armour and a scroll from 1852 showing the English alphabet, written by John Mung (see p.629). In the main building, look out for a beautifully painted palanquin before you ascend to take in the superb view from the uppermost storey.

From the castle, it's only a five-minute walk south along Kenchomae-dōri to Kōchi's other main building of historic note: the **Kyū-Yamanouchi-ke Shimo-yashiki Nagaya** (旧山内家下屋敷長屋; daily 7am–5pm; free), located on the banks of the Kagami-gawa, and next to the *Sansuien Ryokan*. Once the barracks of foot soldiers during the late Tokugawa period, the narrow two-storey wooden building is now a National Treasure. It houses a small museum with models of boats and displays showing the original use of the rooms.

Kōchi Prefectural Museum of Art and Yokoyama Ryuichi Memorial Manga Museum

A fifteen-minute tram journey east of Harimaya-bashi (ask to get off at Kenritsu Bijutsukan-dōri) is the **Kōchi Prefectural Museum of Art** (高知県立美術館; Tues–Sun 9am–4.30pm; ¥350; ⓣ088/866-8000), a stylish modern building set in landscaped grounds. Here you'll find an impressive collection of modern Japanese and Western art, including a gallery of lithographs and paintings by Marc Chagall, and a theatre with a specially designed stage for nō plays. Films and other performances are occasionally held here too. Closer to the town centre, a five-minute walk east of the Harimaya-bashi tram stop, Kōchi Cultural Plaza is home to the **Yokoyama Ryuichi Memorial Manga Museum** (横山隆一記念まんが館; Tues–Sun 9am–6pm; ¥400; ⓣ088/883-5029). Though Tezuka Osamu (see *Manga & anime* colour section) is credited with revolutionizing the world of manga after World War II, it was Yokoyama (1909–2001) who paved the way for Tezuka's success by founding the *Shinmanga ha Shudan* manga group in Tokyo in 1932. It was the members of this group who brought a freshness and vitality to the previously staid world of Japanese cartoons. The museum is full of examples of Yokoyama's work, including his signature creation, "Eternal Boy" Fuku-chan, a comic strip that clocked up a record 5534 serializations before bowing out in 1971. There's also an exact replica of one of his ateliers, as well as a mock-up of the bar he used to have in his house.

Sakamoto Ryōma

You'd have to be blind to miss the scowling features of Kōchi's favourite son, **Sakamoto Ryōma,** on posters and other memorabilia around the city. Born in 1835 to a half-samurai, half-farmer family, Sakamoto directly challenged the rigid class structure of the Shogunate years by leaving Kōchi to start a trading company in Nagasaki (samurai never normally dirtied their hands in business). In his travels around Japan, he gathered support for his pro-Imperial views, eventually forcing the shogun, Tokugawa Yoshinobu, to agree to give supreme power back to the emperor. But one month later, on November 15, 1867, Sakamoto was assassinated in Kyoto. Although he was just 33 at the time, his writings included an enlightened plan for a new political system for Japan, aspects of which were later embraced by the Meiji government.

Godai-san-kōen and Chikurin-ji

Perched on the wooded mountaintop overlooking Kōchi's harbour, 2km south of the city centre, is the attractive park of **Godai-san-kōen** (五台山公園). Buses run from Harimaya-bashi to Aoyogi-bashi Higashi-zume (around 20min), from where it's a thirty-minute walk up the hill. On weekends and public holidays a bus runs directly to the park from Kōchi Station and continues on to Katsurahama (one day pass ¥700).

Alongside Godai-san-kōen lie the equally pleasant grounds of the **Chikurin-ji** (竹林寺) temple. This was founded in 724 AD, making it one of the oldest temples in the prefecture, and its atmospheric main building, decorated with intricate carvings of animals, dates from the Muromachi period. The pagoda, built in the 1970s, is said to contain a bone of the Buddha from Bodh Gaya in India, but there's no way of verifying this since the tower is closed to the public. The **Treasure House** (daily 8.30am–4.30pm; ¥400), to the right of the temple's main entrance gate, is worth a visit for its tranquil traditional gardens, overlooked by an Edo-era villa, and small collection of Tantric statues and Buddhas.

Opposite the temple lies the large **Makino Botanical Garden** (牧野植物園; daily 9am–5pm; ¥700; ⓣ088/882-2601), which has lovely views out to the coast and is dedicated to celebrated local botanist Dr Makino Tomitaro, who died in 1957 aged 95. Apart from the large greenhouse and a fossil gallery, easily spotted since it has a giant model of a tyrannosaurus rex outside, there's the rather more tasteful **Makino Museum of Plants and People**, designed to harmonize with the environment. While you're out here, the garden's café and restaurant, *Arbre* (アルブル), is worth trying.

Katsurahama

About 13km south of Kōchi, **Katsurahama** (桂浜) is famous for two things: its beach and the Tosa fighting dogs that compete in mock sumo tournaments. Neither attraction is what it's cracked up to be. The crescent-shaped beach, though capped off at one end with a picturesque cliff-top shrine, is rather pebbly and swimming isn't allowed. Equally, animal lovers will want to give the vicious canine bouts a wide berth.

Far more interesting is the **Sakamoto Ryōma Memorial Museum** (高知県立坂本龍馬記念館; daily 9am–5pm; ¥500; ⓣ088/841-0001), the architecturally stunning building on the headland above the beach. Dedicated to local hero Sakamoto (see box above), the building uses bold colours and a radical freestanding design for the main exhibition halls. Inside there are state-of-the-art displays using computers, as well as the blood-spotted screen from the room in which Sakamoto was assassinated in Kyoto. If the weather is good, you can walk out onto the top of the building for spectacular views of the Pacific.

Next to the beach is a large statue of Sakamoto and the small **Katsurahama Aquarium** (daily 9am–5.30pm; ¥1100), which has dolphin and sea-lion shows. Frequent **buses** head to Katsurahama from Kōchi's Harimaya-bashi (¥610; 40min). Buses also leave from beside Kōchi Station, but they're very infrequent.

Eating, drinking and entertainment

The best area for **eating and drinking** in Kōchi is around the Obiya-machi arcade, although on Wednesdays you'll find several places closed. The warm weather and a convivial atmosphere mean locals tend to favour the many cheap *yatai* (street stalls) around town, serving *oden*, ramen, *gyōza* and beer – a good location on a balmy night is beside the Enokuchi-gawa near the Bowl Jumbo centre. If you want to push the boat out, *sawachi-ryōri* is Kōchi's most refined style of cuisine, featuring lots of fresh seafood dishes.

Check with the tourist office (see p.623) to see whether there are any **cultural performances**, including classical music and traditional Japanese performing arts, happening at the Museum of Art. You could also try your hand at tenpin bowling at Bowl Jumbo. There's sometimes **live music** at *Mephistopheles* and *BB Café Hall*.

Restaurants and cafés

Café de Libre 3F Kōchi Cultural Plaza, 2-1 Kutanda ⓣ088/882-7750. In the same building as the Yokoyama Memorial Manga Museum, this stylish and spacious café serves a good range of light meals and some very tasty desserts and cakes. Dishes are around ¥1000. For a similar price, *Tendre Table* (タンドルターブル) on the first floor does good Italian and French lunches. Tues–Sun 9am–7pm.

Hakobe はこべ 1-2-5 Harimaya-chō. In the Obiya-machi arcade, this casual place offers *okonomiyaki* and *yakisoba*. You cook up the dishes yourself at the hotplate on your table; it's difficult to spend over ¥1500.

Hirome Ichiba ひろめ市場 At the end of the Obiya-machi arcade. Indoor market with over sixty stalls selling a range of Japanese food, as well as Indian, Chinese and even toasted sandwiches; you'll eat well for under ¥1500. The cheap beer and lively atmosphere mean you're almost always guaranteed to find members of the local expat community here. Daily 8am–11pm.

Issyun 2-1-3 Harimaya-chō ⓣ088/824-2030. Appealing contemporary *izakaya* with a long counter bar and discreet nooks. It specializes in sake from around Shikoku as well as local beers and nicely presented seasonal food. Lunchtime set meals are good value (from ¥680). Mon–Fri 11.30am–11pm, Sat & Sun 11.30am–midnight.

Mamma Italia Nijudai-chō ⓣ088/873-3131. Stylish Italian restaurant run by an English-speaking chef who learned his craft in Rome. The speciality is pizza baked in a wood-fired oven. Around ¥2500 a head. Tues–Sat 11.30am–2pm & 5.30–9pm.

Masala Obiya-machi arcade ⓣ088/885-0065. This Indian restaurant, an expat favourite, is found in the basement of the Obiya-machi arcade opposite Daimaru. Lunches cost from ¥750. Daily 11am–10pm.

Mephistopheles 2-5-23 Obiya-machi. Dark, comfy and convivial, this café serves a wide range of coffees and set-meal menus from ¥750. Also has occasional live music. Daily 7am–9.30pm.

Sama Suka Bali 1-9-18 Obiya-machi, ⓣ088/871-3370. This laidback Indonesian restaurant has good lunch sets (from ¥980) as well as a decent selection of reasonably priced a la carte dishes. Dinner shouldn't cost more than ¥2000. Daily 11.30am–2pm & 6–11.30pm.

Tokugetsuro 得月楼 1-17-3 Minami Harimaya-chō ⓣ088/882-0101. This highly traditional restaurant with kimono-clad waitresses and tatami rooms is the place to sample a *sawachi-ryōri* meal (lunch from ¥6300, dinner ¥8400). The lunch bentō (from ¥2635) are a more affordable option. Bookings essential. Daily 11am–2pm & 5–10pm.

Tosahan 土佐藩 1-2-2 Obiya-machi. The place to go to savour *Tosa ryōri*, local speciality fish dishes, including *katsuo no tataki* (seared skipjack tuna). The decor is all dark-wood beams and red lanterns, and the set lunches are good value at around ¥1000. Daily 11.30am–10pm.

Bars and clubs

As the largest city on Shikoku's southern coast, Kōchi attracts many people looking for a night on the town, so it's not short of a **bar** or ten and has a lively atmosphere, especially at weekends. The city's famous drinking street is **Yanagi-machi**, which runs parallel to the Obiya-machi arcade. During summer Kōchi's many *yatai* and rooftop beer gardens are the ideal places to relax with a cold brew on a sultry night. For **dancing**, try *Love Jamaican*, just off Obiya-machi arcade (entry around ¥1000).

BB Café Hall 1-2-1 Obiya-machi ⓣ088/823-2277. A basement club just off the Obiya-machi arcade, which attracts a trendy young crowd and triples up as a café, bar and live music venue. The cover charge for the live music ranges from ¥500 to ¥2500, depending on who is playing.

Irish Pub Amontillado 1-1-17 Obiya-machi ⓣ088/875-0599. Owner Shimai-san's fascinating tale of how this Irish bar ended up with a Spanish name trundles on for at least a couple of pints of Guinness or Kilkenny (¥900 a pint). There's decent fish 'n' chips and Irish stew, and occasional live music. Daily 5pm–1am.

Nakamachi's Funky hangout on the second floor of a building just off Harimaya-bashi-dōri, on the east side of Otesuji-dōri – look for the wooden sliding door. Spacious interior with cushions scattered around low tables on one side and a long bar on the other. Also serves food. Daily 8pm–3am.

Viva 1-1-11 Honmachi ⓣ088/823-6362. Cosy basement restaurant-cum-bar with quirky decor that turns into a club after midnight on Saturdays. Mon–Fri 6pm–1am, Sat 6pm–5am.

Listings

Banks and exchange Shikoku Bank is on the corner at Harimaya-bashi; there's a branch of Kōchi Bank further west, along Dencha-dōri. Foreign cards can be used in the ATM at the post office next to the JR station.

Bike rental Bikes are available for ¥500/day from OK Parking (OKパーキング; ⓣ088/871-4689) 100m east of the Sunday market site along Otesuji-dōri.

Car rental Try Eki Rent-a-Car ⓣ088/882-3022; Toyota Rent-a-Car ⓣ088/823-0100; or Nissan ⓣ088/883-6444.

Hospital The Red Cross Hospital (ⓣ088/822-1202) is behind Kōchi Station.

Internet There's free access at the Kōchi International Association (see p.623). Otherwise, try the 24-hr internet café Hot Station (ほっとステーション) on the fifth floor of the Bei-epokku Biru at 1-3-1 Otesuji-dōri (¥105/15min).

Laundry There are coin-operated machines outside the *Tosa Bekkan* (see p.623).

Police The main police station is opposite Kōchi Station. Emergency numbers are listed on p.71.

Post office The main post office is just to the west of Kōchi Station (Mon–Fri 9am–7pm, Sat 9am–5pm, Sun 9am–12.30pm).

Shopping The main department store is Daimaru on the Obiya-machi arcade. On Harimaya-bashi Shotengai, Hana Usagi (花うさぎ) sells beautiful secondhand and antique kimono and *obi*. For Kōchi's handmade *washi* paper, try Papie at 2-8-11 Harimaya-chō.

Western Kōchi-ken

Some of Shikoku's best scenery is in western Kōchi-ken. Inland you can raft or kayak down the beautiful **Shimanto-gawa**, while along the indented coast, carved by the savage Pacific Ocean, there are several fishing communities, including **Kuroshio** (黒潮), from where you can take **whale-watching tours** (see box, p.628). The rocky cape at **Ashizuri Misaki**, 180km southwest of Kōchi, with its twisting scenic roads, temple and lush foliage, is well worth the journey. Continue around the coast to reach **Tatsukushi**, where outlandish rock formations stretch out towards coral reefs. To get the most out of this area it helps to have your own transport since bus and train services are relatively scarce.

Shimanto-gawa

Often claimed to be the last free-flowing river in Japan, the **Shimanto-gawa** (四万十川) actually has one small dam along its 196km length, though this

Whale-watching tours

It's said that the whaling industry in Kōchi dates from 1591, when the local *daimyō* Chokosabe Motochika gifted the warlord Toyotomi Hideyoshi in Ōsaka a whale and in return received eight hundred bags of rice. Japan and whales have, in recent times, become a controversial combination, but along Kōchi-ken's coast few are complaining, as whale-watching tours are replacing the old way of making a living. Tours typically last three hours and cost around ¥5000 per person in small boats holding eight to ten people. The best time to see whales is May and August, though the season runs from spring through to autumn. Nothing's guaranteed, but with a good skipper expect to see the large Bryde's whales and medium-sized false killer whales, as well as schools of white-sided and Risso's dolphins. For details, contact the Ōgata Town Leisure Fishing Boats Owners' Association (ⓣ0880/43-1058, ⓦwww.sunabi.com/kujira) or Saga Town Fishermen's Association (ⓣ0880/55-3131).

doesn't detract from the wide river's beauty, winding through green countryside, past pine-clad slopes and terraced rice fields. This is the place to head for tranquil boating, canoeing and fishing. As a base, try the charming *Shimantogawa Youth Hostel* (四万十川ユースホステル; ⓣ0880/54-1352; ❷), run by a friendly couple and about as far off the beaten track as you could wish for. It sleeps eleven people, has good food and a regular programme of canoeing trips down the river (from ¥5775, full tuition and equipment included). The nearest train station is Ekawasaki (江川崎) on JR's plodding Yodo line, which runs from Kubokawa (窪川) on the bay side of Kōchi-ken, to Uwajima along a very scenic route. In August and most weekends from March to November, you can ride part of the line in open-air carriages (*torroko ressha*). From Ekawasaki you'll need to catch a bus (Mon–Sat, 3 daily) to Kuchiyanai (口屋内), from where the hostel is 4.5km across the river; if you call the hostel manager he will arrange to meet you. There are also a few buses (Mon–Sat) to Kuchiyanai from Nakamura (see opposite) on the Tosa Kuroshio train line.

Ashizuri Misaki

The tourist trail has beaten a steady path to **ASHIZURI MISAKI** (足摺岬), a friendly village spread thinly around Shikoku's most southerly point. Pilgrims have long been coming here to pay their respects at picturesque **Kongōfuku-ji** (金剛福寺), the 38th temple on the sacred circuit. Dedicated to the Buddhist deity Kannon, who symbolizes infinite compassion, the temple has a two-storey pagoda and is situated amid a palm grove at the eastern end of the village. Ashizuri's white-painted lighthouse stands atop 80m-high cliffs, while at shore level there's a natural rock arch, crowned by a small shrine. All these sights are within easy walking distance of each other, along cliff-top pathways that burst forth with crimson camellia blossoms each February.

Opposite Kongōfuku-ji is a statue of Nakahama Manjirō, also known as **John Mung** (see box opposite). At **John Mung House** (ジョン万次郎資料館; daily except Wed 8.30am–4pm; ¥200; ⓣ0880/82-3155), opposite the *Ashizuri Youth Hostel*, you can learn more about the local lad who travelled the world and pioneered relations between Japan and the USA in the early years of the Meiji Restoration. The small museum includes some of Mung's personal possessions and miniature tableaux describing his life and the whaling industry he was once part of. Overlooking the village from the headland is **Ashizuri Thermae** (足摺テルメ; daily 11am–10pm, except Thurs 4–10pm; ¥500; ⓣ0880/88-0301), an onsen, swimming pool and spa complex that's a great place to relax.

John Mung

In the normal course of life, Nakahama Manjirō, born in 1827 into a poor family living in Tosa Shimizu, near Ashizuri Misaki, would have lived and died a fisherman. His fortunes changed when he was marooned on an uninhabited volcanic island some 580km south of Tokyo, along with five shipmates. After nearly five months, they were saved by a landing party from a passing US whaling ship, who had come to the island in search of fresh water.

Mung ended up serving with the American crew for four years, before returning with the captain, John Whitfield, to his home in Bedford, Massachusetts. The bright lad mastered English, mathematics, surveying and navigation, and undertook journeys to Africa, Australia and around southeast Asia. After making some money in the California Gold Rush of 1849, Mung returned to Japan in 1851, where he soon found himself serving as an advisor to the feudal lord of Tosa. Two years later Mung was summoned to Tokyo to assist with the drawing up of international trade treaties, and in 1860 he returned to the US as part of a national delegation.

Before his death in 1898 he taught at the Kaisei School for Western Learning in Tokyo (later to become part of the prestigious Tokyo University), sharing the knowledge he had accumulated during a period when Japan was still living in self-imposed isolation from the rest of the world.

Practicalities

To reach the cape by public transport, take a **train** to Nakamura (中村), then transfer to a bus (7 daily; ¥1930; 1hr 45min) directly outside the station. If you have to wait for a connection, there's a good tourist office (daily 8.30am–5.30pm; ⓣ0880/35-4171) five minutes' walk southeast from the station, along Route 439, or head to the good *unagi* (eel) restaurant **Hiratomi** (ひら富). The bus journey becomes progressively more spectacular the closer to the cape you get, the driver whipping the bus around the narrow, cliff-hugging road. In your own car, you can opt for the less hair-raising but equally scenic Skyline Road down the middle of the peninsula to the cape. The buses all go to Kongōfuku-ji, but a couple of stops before there's Ashizuri's tiny bus station, where you can also get some tourist information on the area. The post office opposite has an ATM.

All those pilgrims means there's no shortage of accommodation at the cape. *Ashizuri Youth Hostel* (あしずりユースホステル; ⓣ0880/88-0324) is a basic but friendly and relaxed place next to a small shrine. Accommodation is in small tatami dorms (from ¥3360 per person) and meals are available. Most other places include two meals in their rates; recommended options include *Minshuku Kan* (民宿冠; ⓣ0880/88-0559; ❺) and the more deluxe *Ashizuri Kokusai Hotel* (足摺国際ホテル; ⓣ0880/0201; ❼), which has ocean views and plenty of facilities. The *Ashizuri Thermae* (❼; see opposite) offers both good-standard Western- and Japanese-style rooms, and has a restaurant (closed Thurs). Higher up the hill, in the heart of the Ashizuri-Uwaji National Park, is the *Ashizuri Resort* (ⓣ0880-88-1185; apartments/cottages for two ❹/❺) offering self-catering accommodation either in apartments or lovely cottages, all with stunning views. The manager here is English.

Tatsukushi and Sukumo

Heading northwest for 24km around the coast from Ashizuri Misaki brings you to the small town of **TATSUKUSHI** (竜串), which gets its name (meaning "dragon's skewers") from the remarkable rock pillars that protrude, like fossilized dinosaur bones, from the sea. The honeycombed rocks, split by swirling indentations where the sea water has sluiced in, are fascinating.

The Minokoshi coastline (見残し海岸) around Tatsukushi was designated a national underwater park in 1970, the first of its kind in Japan. It's possible to take glass-bottomed boats (¥1260; 30min) from the jetty near the bus station to view the coral reefs and explore the weird rock formations along the coast, created over tens of thousands of years. Don't expect much from the reefs – they're hardly up to tropical standards, but the oddly shaped cliffs on what is dubbed the "hidden coast" make it worth the trip.

Between Tatsukushi bus station and the ocean, in a strikingly angular concrete and wood building surrounded by trees, the **Seashell Gallery** (海のギャラリー; daily except Thurs: Sept–June 9am–4pm, July & Aug 9am–5pm; ¥500) houses a collection of eighty thousand seashells from around the world. It's the building, however, that steals the show. Built in 1967, the Hayashi Masako-designed structure is included on the Architectural Institute of Japan's list of one hundred "modern movement sites in Japan", while the dark aqua interiors, designed to create a sense of being under water, make for a very peaceful atmosphere. Five minutes' walk around the coast, past a sandy beach and an unremarkable aquarium, is the **Ashizuri Submarine Lookout** (Jan–March & Sept–Dec 9am–5pm; April–Aug 8.30am–5pm; ¥900), a red and white cross-shaped pod, marooned in the ocean, and reached along a gantry from the rocks. Inside the pod you descend a spiral staircase to the sea floor to watch the fish swirling around the observation room's windows.

Tatsukushi is a twenty-minute bus ride (¥560) from Tosa Shimizu (土佐清水), a small town on the bus route between Nakamura and Ashizuri. Buses from Tatsukushi continue up the coast for 50km to **SUKUMO** (宿毛), from where ferries sail to Saiki (佐伯) in Kyūshū. Bypassing the cape, the Tosa Kuroshio train line links Sukumo with Kubokawa on the JR line with through-trains from Kōchi. Buses also run to Uwajima several times a day (¥1750; 1hr 50min), departing from outside Sukumo Station.

Uwajima and around

From Sukumo, Route 56 continues through countryside before emerging on the coast. The cliff-side road, passing though small fishing communities, provides spectacular views of the deep-blue sea, carpeted with nets held up by a crisscross network of buoys. Pearls are cultivated here, and at the port of **UWAJIMA** (宇和島), 67km north of Sukumo, there are plenty of shops selling them. The town's main sights – which include a castle and a fertility shrine – can be seen easily in half a day, though it's worth staying a night and using Uwajima as a base from which to explore the small country town of Uwa-chō (see p.633) to the north.

Renting a bike to get around is a good idea (see below). The castle is a fifteen-minute walk south of the JR station, while the Taga-jinja sex shrine, across the Suka-gawa River, is a ten-minute walk to the north. The municipal bullfighting ring is a twenty-minute walk up the hill to the east.

Arrival and information

Uwajima Station is the terminus for both the JR Yodo line running from Kubokawa and the JR Yosan line from Matsuyama. Buses to and from Sukumo stop in front of the station as well as at the main bus centre at the foot of the castle hill on Route 56.

Inside the JR station is a **tourist information booth** (daily 9am–6pm), which can help arrange bicycle rental (¥100/hr). You can change money at Iyo Bank just

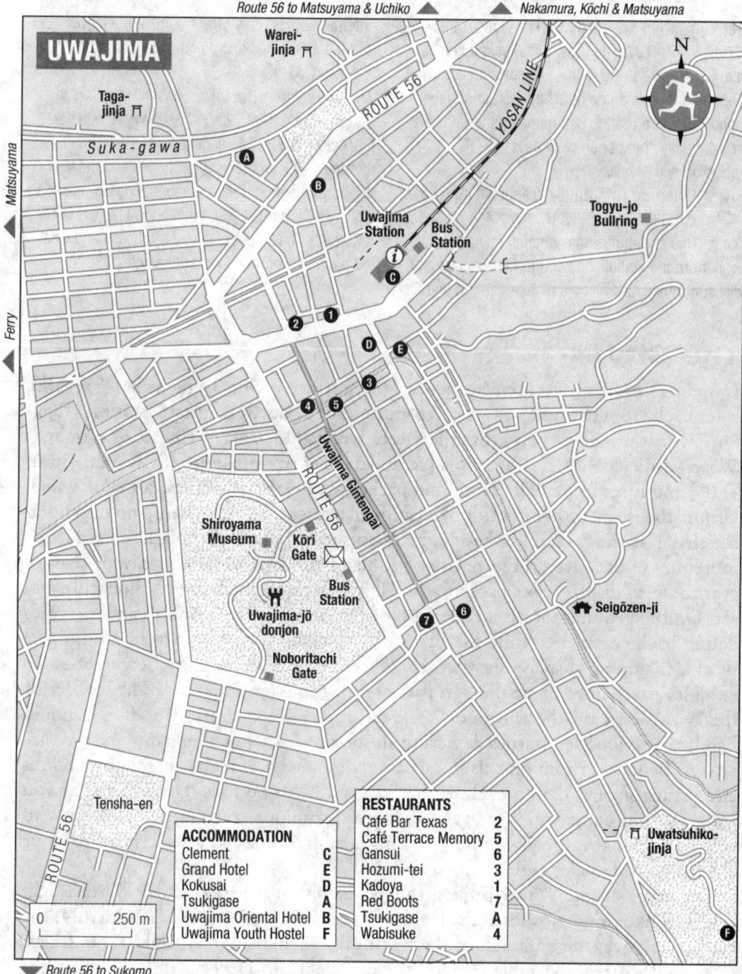

off the Gintengai, and there's an ATM at the main post office near the Kōri Gate to the castle.

Accommodation

There are several **hotels** near the station and even more towards the port area. The youth hostel is at the top of a steep hill, twenty minutes' walk south of the JR station. If you're carrying heavy luggage, it's best to take a taxi there (around ¥900).

Clement 10-1 Nishiki-machi ⓣ0895/23-6111, ⓕ23-6666. Smart mid-range hotel, directly above the JR station, with mainly Western-style rooms but also a few Japanese-style ones. There's a rooftop beer garden in summer (May–Sept) and a ten percent discount on rates for Japan Rail Pass holders. ⑤

Kokusai 国際ホテル 4-1 Nishiki-machi ⓣ0895/25-0111, ⓕ25-0715. Close to the station, this friendly and traditional hotel offers large, well-appointed Japanese rooms, as well as some Western-style rooms with outlandish 1970s decor. They also run the business-style *Grand Hotel* (ⓣ0895/24-3911; ⑤) across the road. ⑤

Tsukigase 月ヶ瀬 1-5-6 Miyukimachi ⓣ0895/22-4788, ⓕ22-4787. The town's top ryokan is a little old-fashioned but the rooms are spacious and well kept, and there's a fine attached restaurant (see opposite) and a rooftop communal bath. Rates are substantially cheaper on weekdays. ❼–❽ including two meals.

Uwajima Oriental 6-10 Tsurushima-chō ⓣ0895/23-2828, ⓔuwajima@oriental-web.co.jp. This stylish business hotel, a few minutes' walk from the station, has comfortable rooms and discount rates. As well as a nice restaurant and internet access, they offer free use of a bicycle for three hours. Rates are slightly cheaper at the weekend. ❹–❺

Uwajima Youth Hostel 宇和島ユースホステル Atago-kōen ⓣ0895/22-7177, ⓦwww2.odn.ne.jp/~cfm91130. The building's a tad institutional, but the views on the way up the hill and the friendly reception from the young, English-speaking couple who run the place make the hike worth the effort. Also has a pool table, a treehouse and free bike rental. Dorm beds ¥2100; singles ¥3500.

The City

Uwajima's most provocative attraction, the fertility shrine **Taga-jinja** (多賀神社), is set back from the Suka-gawa, a ten-minute walk north of the JR station. Taga-jinja is to the left as you cross the river, while the larger shrine to the right is **Warei-jinja** (和霊神社). Taga-jinja has an attached **sex museum** (daily 8am–5pm; ¥800) and is set in a small compound packed with various statues, some of which assume the shape of penises if looked at from a certain angle – there's no mistaking the shape of the carved log beside the main shrine building, though. The shrine's museum, spread over three floors of a bland modern building, is wall-to-wall erotica, with display cases packed with all manner of sexual objects, literature and art. On the ground floor is a collection of Japanese fertility symbols and figurines dating back centuries, while the first floor holds similar objects from around the world, including displays devoted to Tibet, India, Europe and elsewhere; some exhibits are claimed to be the best part of two thousand years old. The smaller of the two rooms on the top floor hosts an impressive collection of five hundred hand-carved wooden statues depicting all sorts of sexual shenanigans – no two are alike. The larger room on this floor has a large selection of Japanese erotic books and prints (*shunga*) dating back to the Edo and Meiji periods. Downstairs, as you leave the museum, you'll see two of the most unique souvenirs Shikoku has to offer – rock-hard, life-size candies, unmistakably fashioned after certain parts of the male and female body.

The other shrine, **Warei-jinja**, is the focal point of the spectacular Warei Taisai, one of Shikoku's major festivals. Held from the evening of July 22 to July 24, the festival involves huge models of devil bulls (*ushi-oni*) being paraded in the streets, along with ornate portable shrines, the aim being to dispel evil. The bulls, like giant pantomime horses, eventually do battle in the river, while at the shrine there's much banging of *taiko*, bonfire burning and a fireworks finale.

Walking back into the town, keep an eye out for the rather forlorn-looking **Uwajima-jō** (宇和島城; daily 9am–4pm; ¥200), at the top of the hillside park that rises west of Route 56. The compact, three-storey donjon may be original and certainly gives a fine view of the surrounding city and port, but there's little other reason to pay the entrance charge. There are two routes up to the donjon, either from the north through the gate of the Kōri samurai family (transferred to the castle ground in 1952), tucked back from the main road behind the post office, or from the Noboritachi-mon gate on the south side of the castle hill.

A short walk south of the castle park is the small formal garden of **Tensha-en** (天赦園; daily: April–July 8.30am–5pm; Aug–March 8.30am–4.30pm; ¥300). Dating from 1866, the pretty garden is laid out in circular style with a feature made of a wisteria trellis. Nearby, you can also explore the narrow residential streets immediately southeast of the centre. Here shrines, temples and graveyards are

Japanese-style bullfighting

Although it's said that the novelty wears thin fast, the best time to visit Uwajima is for one of its **bullfights**, or *tōgyū*, the bovine equivalent of sumo wrestling. Some accounts date the sport back four hundred years, while others pinpoint the origins in the nineteenth century, when a Dutch captain made a gift of bulls to the town, after local fishermen came to his ship's aid during a typhoon. The bulls, weighing in at up to a tonne and treated like pampered pets by their owners, lock horns and struggle either to push each other to the floor or out of the tournament ring. The fights are held five afternoons a year (Jan 2, the first Sun in April, July 24, Aug 14 and the fourth Sun in Oct; details at Ⓦwww.tougyu.com) at the **Tōgyū-jō**, a white-walled arena in the hills above the city. Get there an hour early to soak up the atmosphere and watch the bulls being paraded around the ring. The bouts are very good-natured and the enthusiastic crowd is welcoming and friendly. Tickets cost ¥3000 and can be bought on the day at the arena.

huddled on the slopes leading up to the *Uwajima Youth Hostel*. Even if you're not staying at the hostel, the hill is worth climbing for sweeping views of the town.

Eating and drinking

Not surprisingly for a port, Uwajima offers ample opportunity to eat **fresh fish** – two popular dishes are *taimeshi* (sashimi of sea bream on top of hot rice) and *satsuma-jiru* (strips of fish mixed with a white miso sauce and eaten with rice). For a **drink**, apart from some of the places listed, you could try *Red Boots* (closed Mon), which has a Wild West vibe and very lively management, or *Café Bar Texas*, where you can also play darts. For cheap lunch options and cafés, explore Uwajima Gintengai.

Café Terrace Memory Shin-machi ⓣ0895/22-8004. Bright place on the second floor of a building just outside the arcade, serving mainly Japanese takes on Western dishes, such as spaghetti and pilaf, with lunch costing around ¥800. Daily except Wed 8am–7pm.

Gansui 丸水 2-3-10 Honmachi Ote ⓣ0895/22-3636. Upmarket *izakaya* east of the Gintengai, with a picture menu and daily set dishes from as little as ¥1300. It's known for its *taimeshi*. Daily except Tues 11am–2pm & 5–8.30pm.

Hozumi-tei ほづみ亭 2-3-8 Shin-machi ⓣ0895-22-0041. Appealingly rustic fish restaurant with tables and tatami seating areas overlooking a stream. A meal will cost around ¥2000. Mon–Sat 11am–1.30pm & 5–9.40pm.

Kadoya かどや Tsurushi-machi ⓣ0895/22-1543. With reasonable prices and friendly service, this is one of the best places in town to sample seafood dishes, including *taimeshi*, with various set menus for around ¥1000. There's a useful picture menu. Mon–Sat 11am–2.30pm & 5–9pm, Sun 11am–9pm.

Tsukigase 月ヶ瀬 1-5-6 Miyuki-machi. Bamboo grows in the centre of this restaurant specializing in *fugu* (in winter) and tempura. Set lunch starts from as low as ¥790. Their *satsuma-jiru* meal is ¥1500. Daily 11am–10.30pm.

Wabisuke 和日輔 1-2-6 Ebisu-chō ⓣ0895-24-0028. This large restaurant near the castle combines traditional decor with a friendly welcome and a range of set meals, including sashimi sets, soba, udon and *kamameshi* (a kind of pilaf). Lunch from ¥840. Mon–Sat 11am–2pm & 5–9.30pm, Sun 11am–9.30pm.

Uwa-chō

Less than 20km north of Uwajima, the small country town of **UWA-CHŌ** (宇和町) makes a very pleasant half-day trip from Uwajima. The highlight is the excellent **Museum of Ehime History and Culture** (愛媛県歴史文化博物館; Tues–Sun 9am–5.30pm; ¥500). Inside this ultra-modern building sticking out from the hillside is ample space for the spectacular displays inside, which include full-sized replicas of buildings, including a Yayoi-era (330 BC to 300 AD) hut, a street of Meiji-era shops and a small wooden temple. In the centre of the museum is a folklore exhibit, which includes examples of the fabulous portable shrines, costumes and other decorations used in local festivals, such as Uwajima's Warei Taisai. TV screens also show videos of the festivals.

The **train** station for Uwa-chō is Uno-machi, less than twenty minutes from Uwajima by the hourly limited express. The museum can be reached by an infrequent bus (¥150) from the stop about five minutes' walk south of the JR station, along Route 56. To walk up the hill to the museum takes around twenty minutes. On the way, you'll pass the other reason for visiting this town, a street of well-preserved, white-walled houses known as **Naka-chō**, which is also the name given to this part of town. Along here is **Kaimei School** (開明学校; Tues–Sun 9am–5pm; ¥200), a lovely and well-preserved example of a Meiji-period school and one of the oldest extant in western Japan; there's also a temple and a church house you can look into. Opposite the old schoolhouse is the **Uwa Folkcraft Museum** (宇和町民具館; Uwa-chō Mingu-kan; Tues–Sun 9am–5pm; free), an immaculate museum that contains a wide range of interesting items that were once in daily use in the town, from bamboo swords and deer costumes used in local festivals to record players and dioramas depicting life during the Edo period.

You can pick up a simple map-cum-guide to the town's sites in English here, as well as a special ¥400 ticket offering entry to the school, the nearby **Memorial Museum of Great Predecessors** at Uwa-chō Sentetsu Kinenkan (宇和町先哲記念館; Tues–Sun 9am–5pm; ¥200), and the **Rice Museum** at Uwa-chō Kome Hakubutsukan (宇和町米博物館; Tues–Sun 9am–5pm; ¥200) on the other side of town. If you're in a hurry, the latter two can be safely skipped, as there's little in the way of English explanations, though the rice museum is housed in a lovely 109m-long wooden school building. To reach this street, walk straight ahead from the station through the arch and turn right at the pedestrianized shopping street. Take the first left and then follow the road as it forks right.

For **lunch** there's a takeaway sushi joint and a coffee shop offering light meals in the small branch of the Takashimaya department store on the main road, a minute's walk from the station, but your best bet is the *Ristorante Station*, which serves pizza and Yebisu beer and is bang opposite the station.

Ōzu

Further north along the Yosan line the train hits the coast at **Yawatahama** (八幡浜), where there are ferries to Beppu and Usuki in Kyūshū. It then turns inland to reach **ŌZU** (大洲) on the banks of the Hiji-kawa. The town's billing as a mini-Kyoto is overselling the place; still Ōzu has its charms, particularly so from June 1 to September 20 when the river is the location for *ukai* – fishing with cormorants (see box, p.394). To view the display from a boat costs ¥3000; for bookings call **Ōzu tourist office** (see opposite).

At other times of the year, the town is worth visiting to see the picturesque **Ōzu Castle** (大洲城; daily 9am–4.30pm; ¥500 or ¥800 with entry to Garyū Sansō). Destroyed in 1888, the four-storey donjon of this fortress commanding a bend in the river was rebuilt in 2004 to its original sixteenth-century specifications. The grounds are a riot of pink in cherry blossom season.

From the castle, follow the river for around fifteen minutes as it bends southeast to reach steps leading up to **Garyū Sansō** (臥龍山荘; daily 9am–4.30pm; ¥500), a prime example of a traditional villa built in the *sukiya kenchiku* architectural style with a triangular thatched roof. Beautifully detailed woodcarvings and fixtures inside are matched by a lovely moss-and-stone garden outside leading to a teahouse and a separate moon-viewing platform overlooking the river. Head directly west back into Ōzu from the river to locate **Ohanahan-tōri** (おはなはん通り), a short street lined with traditional houses including one that has been converted into a good restaurant (see below). Also worth a look before leaving town is the gallery, gift shop and café **Ōzu Akarengakan** (おおず赤煉瓦館; daily 9am–5pm), housed in a handsome red-brick complex dating from 1901 and once used as a bank.

Ōzu is forty minutes by express train from either Uwajima or Mastuyama. The town's train station, **Iyo Ōzu** (伊予大洲), is around 2km northwest of the Hiji-kawa and the castle. The **tourist information** desk (daily at least 8.30am–5pm; ⓣ0893/24-2664) is on the south side of Ōzu. The assistants here can advise where to find bicycle rental and suggest places to stay should you get the unlikely urge to linger overnight. For **eating**, *Shun* (旬; ⓣ0893/23-4031; daily except Thurs 11.30am–2pm & 6–10pm), on Ohanahan-tōri, is a **restaurant** in an attractive traditional house facing a neatly tended garden. Its speciality is beef *satsuma-jiru* (¥1260). On the north side of the Hiki-kawa-bashi is *Tarui* (たる井; ⓣ0893/24-3000; Tues–Sun 11.30am–2.30pm & 5–8.30pm), a restaurant in a large wooden-beamed building specializing in *unagi* (eel) dishes. Also worth trying here is the rich, savoury rice porridge, called *zousui* (ぞうすい; ¥630).

Uchiko

A trip to Ōzu can easily be combined with one to the appealing small town of **UCHIKO** (内子), ten minutes by express train north along the Yosan line. Uchiko was once an important centre for the production of Japanese **wax** (*moku-rō*), made from the crushed berries of the sumac tree. The wax is still used in candles, polishes, crayons, cosmetics, food and even computer disks. The wealth generated by the industry has left Uchiko with many fine houses preserved in the picturesque **Yōkaichi** (八日市) district of the town, where craftsmen can still be seen making candles by hand.

The best place to start your tour of Uchiko – which is easily explored on foot – is at the handsomely restored kabuki theatre **Uchiko-za** (内子座; Tues–Sun 9am–4.30pm; ¥300; ⓣ0893/44-2840), which lies around 500m northeast of the train station. Performances are held once or twice a week at the theatre, which was built in 1916 to celebrate the accession of the Emperor Taisho; during the day you can wander around the auditorium and stage.

Closer to Yōkaichi, at Akinai-to-Kurashi Hakubutsukan, is the **Museum of Commercial and Domestic Life** (商いと暮らし博物館; daily 9am–4.30pm; ¥200), set in a charmingly converted merchant's house, and with mechanical talking dummies that help show the daily life of a shopkeeper during the Taishō era (1912–26). The mannequins, which are electronically activated to start speaking, include a moaning pharmacist in the upstairs storeroom.

Just before heading northwest uphill into the **Yōkaichi** district, take a detour towards the Oda-gawa to admire the venerable **Takahashi Residence** (高橋邸; daily except Tues 9am–4.30pm; free), the birthplace of Takahashi Ryutaro, a politician and founder of the Asahi Beer company. The elegant two-storey building with castle-like stone walls has a lovely garden, which you can admire from the café inside.

Return to Yōkaichi, walking uphill past touristy shops selling souvenirs and tea, to reach the **Machiya Shiryōkan** (町家資料館; daily 9am–4.30pm; free), dating from 1793 and restored as a typical merchant's townhouse. Further along, on the left after the kink in the road, are two of Uchiko's most photographed buildings: the **Ōmura Residence** (大村家), the Edo-era home of a dyehouse merchant, and neighbouring **Hon-Haga Residence** (本芳我邸; daily except Thurs 9am–4.30pm;

free), home of the main family behind Uchiko's wax industry. This is more elaborate than the other houses, with ornate gables, a facade decorated with intricate plaster sculptures, and a small, attractive garden. Next on the right is another grand house once belonging to the Hon-Haga family, the **Kami Haga Residence** (上芳我邸; daily 9am–4.30pm; ¥400). Its size and elegant interior decoration give a good indication of how wealthy they must have been. Unlike most of the other buildings along the street, the plaster walls are a golden sand colour, and there's a spacious courtyard surrounded by exhibition halls. If you plan to enter all the buildings and museums around town, a small saving can be made by purchasing the ¥700 combination ticket from Uchiko-za, the Kami Haga Residence or the Museum of Commercial and Domestic Life.

Practicalities

By the fastest **trains** Uchiko is one hour from Uwajima and 25min from Matsuyama. JR offers a handy ¥2700 day-pass ticket covering Matsuyama, Uchiko and Ōzu. Several **buses** a day run from Matsuyama, Ōzu and Uwajima, stopping a couple of hundred metres to the east of Yōkaichi. Bicycle rental is available at the train station (daily 9.30am–5pm; ¥300/hr). There's also an old-fashioned bus that shuttles back and forth from the station to Yōkaichi (Fri–Sun; ¥800 for round-trip ticket).

Although there's no need to **stay overnight** in Uchiko, there are some colourful ryokan and minshuku in and around town. *Matsunoya* (松乃屋; ⓣ0893/44-5000; ❺, ❼ with two meals,) is a pleasant, traditional ryokan on the main road leading up to Yōkaichi. Some 2km north of Yōkaichi, *Farm Inn Raum Kokuriko* (ファームインRAUM古久里来; ⓣ0983/44-2079; ❻ with two meals) is a rather cultured farmhouse-minshuku where you can help the owners cultivate rice and harvest from various fruit orchards. For alternatives, contact **Uchiko Tourist Association** (ⓣ0893/44-3790) or the **International Association** (ⓣ0893/44-6137) on the third floor of Uchiko Town Hall (内子市役所; Mon–Fri 8.30am–5pm).

For food, be aware that many of the **restaurants** along Yōkaichi are overpriced tourist traps; one exception is *Komachi* (こまち; daily except Wed 9am–5pm & 6pm–midnight), a charming teahouse serving green tea and snacks such as sweet bean cake. It's also a gift shop and turns into a bar at night. Down on the island in the river there is also *Karari* (からり), a modern restaurant, fresh-produce market and ice-cream parlour. Uchiko's twin-town links with Germany are celebrated here with a menu heavy on sausages, and at lunchtime they also run a small udon restaurant and a hamburger bar on the island.

Matsuyama and around

Historic **MATSUYAMA** (松山), with a population of over 450,000, is Shikoku's largest city and single best destination. Despite its size, Matsuyama is a convivial, friendly place that's easy to get around, thanks to a tram network that bestows an old-fashioned grace to a city that also proudly promotes its literary connections (see box, p.638). Most points of interest are centred on the impressive castle, **Matsuyama-jō**, and the popular hot-spring suburb of **Dōgo**, 2km east of the centre, home to one of Japan's most magnificent bathhouses.

Local warlords from the Kono clan built a fortress in Dōgo in the fourteenth century, while Matsuyama was created in 1602 by *daimyō* Katō Yoshiakira when he built his castle on Katsuyama Hill. In 1635, the Matsudaira clan took charge of the castle and ruled the area until the Meiji Restoration in 1868. Rebuilt following

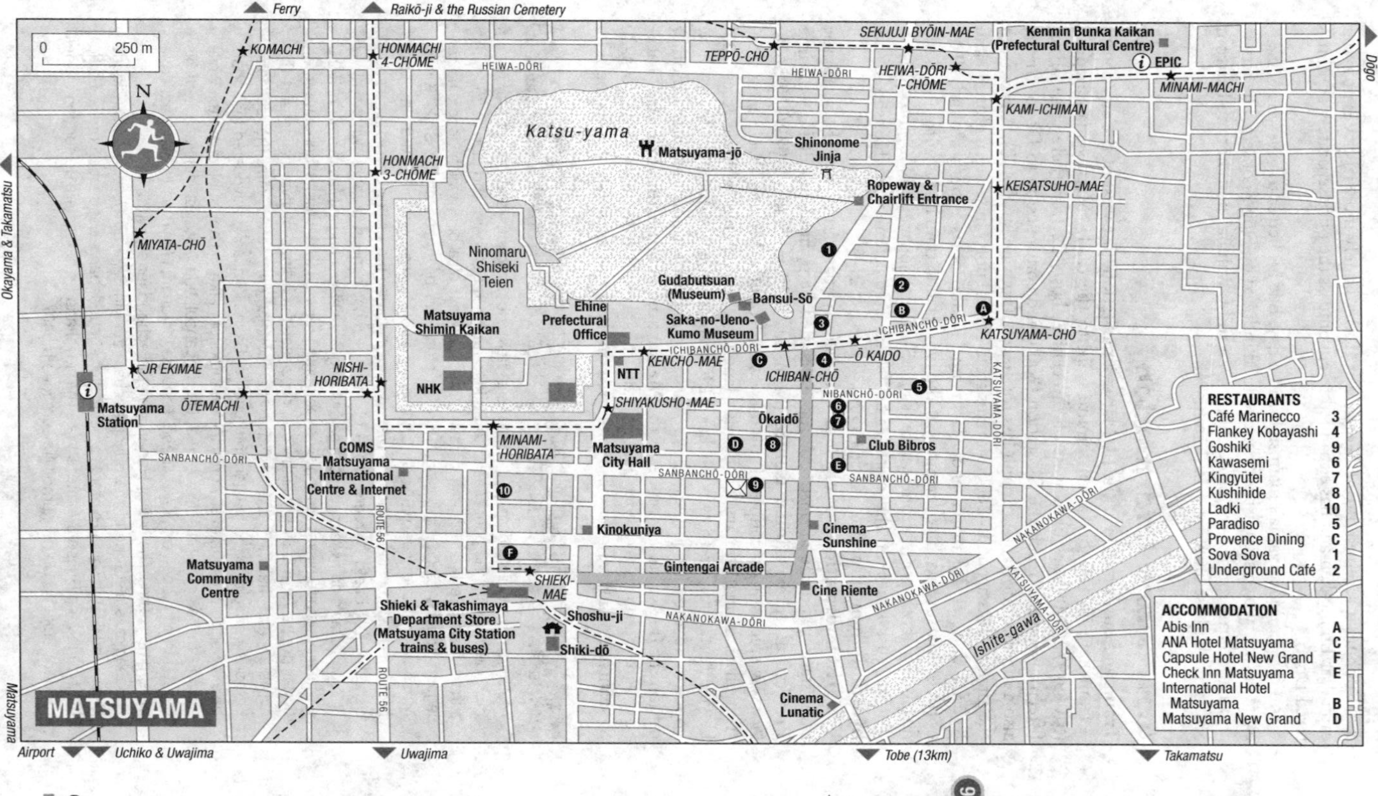
MATSUYAMA
0 250 m
N
Ferry
Raikō-ji & the Russian Cemetery
Dōgo
Okayama & Takamatsu
Matsuyama
Airport
Uchiko & Uwajima
Uwajima
Tobe (13km)
Takamatsu
KOMACHI
HONMACHI 4-CHŌME
HONMACHI 3-CHŌME
MIYATA-CHŌ
JR EKIMAE
ŌTEMACHI
NISHI-HORIBATA
MINAMI-HORIBATA
SHIYAKUSHO-MAE
KENCHŌ-MAE
ICHIBAN-CHŌ
Ō KAIDO
KATSUYAMA-CHŌ
KEISATSUHO-MAE
KAMI-ICHIMAN
MINAMI-MACHI
HEIWA-DŌRI I-CHŌME
SEKIJUJI BYŌIN-MAE
TEPPŌ-CHŌ
SHIEKI-MAE
HEIWA-DŌRI
ICHIBANCHŌ-DŌRI
NIBANCHŌ-DŌRI
SANBANCHŌ-DŌRI
KATSUYAMA-DŌRI
NAKANOKAWA-DŌRI
ROUTE 56
Ishite-gawa
Katsu-yama
Matsuyama-jō
Shinonome Jinja
Ropeway & Chairlift Entrance
Ninomaru Shiseki Teien
Gudabutsuan (Museum)
Bansui-Sō
Saka-no-Ueno-Kumo Museum
Ehine Prefectural Office
Matsuyama Shimin Kaikan
NHK
NTT
Matsuyama City Hall
Ōkaidō
Club Bibros
COMS Matsuyama International Centre & Internet
Kinokuniya
Cinema Sunshine
Gintengai Arcade
Cine Riente
Cinema Lunatic
Matsuyama Community Centre
Matsuyama Station
Shieki & Takashimaya Department Store (Matsuyama City Station trains & buses)
Shoshu-ji
Shiki-dō
Kenmin Bunka Kaikan (Prefectural Cultural Centre)
EPIC
RESTAURANTS
Café Marinecco 3
Flankey Kobayashi 4
Goshiki 9
Kawasemi 6
Kingyūtei 7
Kushihide 8
Ladki 10
Paradiso 5
Provence Dining C
Sova Sova 1
Underground Café 2
ACCOMMODATION
Abis Inn A
ANA Hotel Matsuyama C
Capsule Hotel New Grand F
Check Inn Matsuyama E
International Hotel Matsuyama B
Matsuyama New Grand D

the drubbing it received during World War II, this largely modern city is now the capital of Ehime-ken and has expanded to encompass the once separately administered Dōgo.

You can see Matsuyama's main sights in a day, but it's better to give yourself an extra day or two to savour the relaxed mood induced by Dōgo's onsen. The city is also a good base for day-trips to Uchiko, Ōzu and Uwajima and is not too far from Shikoku's highest mountain, **Ishizuchi-san**.

Arrival and information

Trains and **buses** pull in at the JR Matsuyama Station, just west of the city centre – from here it's roughly a ten-minute walk to the castle. Matsuyama's **airport** (Ⓣ089/972-5600) lies 6km west of the centre; bus #52 from here takes about fifteen minutes to reach the JR station (¥300) and continues on to Dōgo; there's also a more comfortable, though less frequent, limousine bus (¥400). A taxi from the airport costs around ¥2000. **Ferries** from several ports in western Honshū and Kyūshū dock at Takahama and Matsuyama Kankō ports – both around 10km north of Matsuyama. The terminus of the Iyo Tetsudō train line is within walking distance of both ports, from where it's a 25-minute journey (¥400) into Shi-eki Station, just south of the castle. The fastest connection with Honshū is the **hydrofoil** from Hiroshima (1hr; ¥6900).

Tourist information is available all over Matsuyama, starting with booths at the train station and the airport. For more detailed help, head for **EPIC – Ehime Prefectural International Centre** (Mon–Sat 8.30am–5pm; Ⓣ089/917-5678, Ⓦwww.epic.or.jp), a couple of minutes' walk from the Minami-machi tram stop. As well as a small library of English-language books, free internet access and bicycle rental (for up to two weeks), EPIC can arrange goodwill guides to show you around the city and also hosts classes on Japanese traditional arts. Another option for free volunteer guides is the **Matsuyama International Centre** (Tues–Sun 9am–5.30pm; Ⓣ089/943-2025), on the ground floor of COMS, 6-4-20 Sanbanchō. They also publish the free monthly *What's Going On?* booklet

Masaoka Shiki

Matsuyama heavily promotes its Japanese literary connections and one of the most prominent is with the poet **Masaoka Shiki**, a rather tragic figure who died at 35 from tuberculosis. He took his pen name, Shiki, from that of a bird, which according to legend coughs blood as it sings. His life story can be traced at the **Shiki Kinen Museum** in Dōgo (see p.643) and there are two houses connected with the poet preserved as tourist attractions in Matsuyama, including the villa he shared for a short period with **Sōseki Natsume**, one of Japan's most famous authors, whose novel *Botchan* draws on his experiences as a young teacher working in Matsuyama in 1895.

Masaoka made his reputation by encouraging reforms to the then hidebound traditional poetic form haiku, which comprises just three lines of five, seven and five syllables and has a subject matter traditionally connected with the seasons. Famously criticizing the master of the genre, Bashō, Masaoka advocated that poets be allowed to use whatever words they wanted for haiku, on any subject matter, while striving to be more reflective of real life. Encapsulating his approach is one of his most famous poems: *"Kaki kueba kane-ga narunari Hōryū-ji"* ("I was eating a persimmon. Then, the bell of Hōryū-ji temple echoed far and wide").

Masaoka is also one of the principal characters in *Saka no Ue no Kumo* (Clouds Over the Hill) by Shiba Ryotaro, a bestseller about Japan's destruction of the Baltic fleet during the Russo-Japanese War. The novel and its heroes are celebrated at the modern Saka no Ue no Kumo Museum (see p.640).

(Ⓦ home.e-catv.ne.jp/wgo), available here and at EPIC. Finally, the **Dōgo tourist information office** (daily April–Sept 8am–9pm, Oct–March 8am–8pm; Ⓣ 089/921-3708, Ⓦ www.dogo.or.jp), across the road from the **Dōgo tram terminus**, has English maps and leaflets, as well as bicycle rental (¥300/day).

City transport

Matsuyama's city centre is easily covered on foot, but to travel between here and Dōgo you'll most likely use the **tram** network. There are four tram routes: one loop line and three other routes all running through the city centre at Ichiban-chō, past the castle and ending at the delightfully old-fashioned Dōgo terminal. **Fares** are a flat ¥150 and must be paid to the driver on leaving the tram. A **one-day ticket**, offering unlimited travel on the trams and the Loop Bus, is a bargain at ¥400, and can be bought on the trams. A couple of special tram services are pulled by the **Botchan Ressha**, designed like the steam trains that ran through the city during the Meiji era; a single trip on these costs ¥300, a day pass ¥500. Retro-fans might also want to experience the **Madonna Bus** (single trip ¥200, day pass ¥400), an old-fashioned bus named after the heroine of Botchan that runs a circuit of Matsuyama's main sights on weekends and national holidays. Regular **buses** are most useful for reaching further-flung areas of the city, such as the airport and Oku Dōgo. Apart from the castle hill, Matsuyama is reasonably flat, making this a good city to **cycle** around (for rental see above).

Accommodation

With its baths and great range of accommodation, the most pleasant **place to stay** in Matsuyama is Dōgo. If you want to be based more centrally, you'll find plenty of cheap business hotels around the JR station as well as in the city centre – expect to pay around ¥5000 for a single room or ¥8000 for a double or twin.

Matsuyama

Abis Inn 2-3-3 Katsuyamachō Ⓣ 089/998-6000. The small singles are smart and well maintaned, and rates include a light breakfast. Internet access is also available. ❸

ANA Hotel Matsuyama 3-2-1 Ichiban-chō Ⓣ 089/933-5511, Ⓦ www.anahotelmatsuyama.com. The best hotel in the city centre offers a range of stylish rooms, several restaurants and a shopping arcade. Rates for the less flash rooms in the annexe are substantially cheaper, especially the singles. ❻–❼

Capsule Hotel New Grand Minato-machi Ⓣ 089/945-7089. Opposite Takashimaya department store, this hotel is clean and spacious, if a little shabby, and capsules cost just ¥2800.

Check Inn Matsuyama チェックイン松山 2-7-3 Sanbanchō Ⓣ 089/998-7000, Ⓦ www.checkin.co.jp. Emerald-green leather sofas, a Rococo-style grandfather clock and chandeliers in the lobby, plus even more chandeliers in the rooms, give this comfortable, well-priced business hotel in the centre of the city more than a touch of elegance. Rooftop onsen baths are also a plus. ❻

International Hotel Matsuyama 1-13 Ichiban-chō Ⓣ 089/932-5111, Ⓕ 945-2055. Good-value mid-range hotel near the castle, with comfortably furnished rooms and some striking interior design in its public areas and restaurants. The retro-to-the-max top-floor Chinese restaurant has to be seen to be believed. ❺

Matsuyama New Grand 3-4-10 Niban-chō Ⓣ 0120-404-810. Not so new, nor that grand, but it does have single rooms and cheaper doubles in its older section (ask for the *honkan*) if you're on a budget. The newer doubles are a bit more comfortable and there's one cheap, but spacious, tatami room. Guests can also use the large communal baths and sauna. ❸–❹

Dōgo

Dōgo Yamanote Hotel 道後山の手ホテル 1-13 Dōgo Ⓣ 089/998-2111, Ⓕ 998-2112. The rooms at this faux English-style hotel offer Laura Ashley-esque decor with floral print wallpaper and parquet floors. Some have great views towards the city and castle. Basic rates include breakfast. ❻

Matsuyama Youth Hostel 松山ユースホステル 22-3 Dōgo Himezuka Ⓣ 089/933-6366,

Ⓦ www.matsuyama-yh.com. A fantastic hostel, where the management goes out of its way to make your stay enjoyable: there's a good-value restaurant, a sauna, free 24hr internet access and free tea and snacks are served every evening in the comfy lounge. Also has private tatami rooms big enough for several people with TVs and washbasins. Dorm beds ¥2625 per person. ❸

Patio Dōgo Dōgo Honkan-mae Ⓣ 089/941-4128, Ⓦ www.patio-dogo.co.jp. You couldn't get more convenient than this modern mid-range hotel, opposite the Honkan, with friendly staff. The attached sushi restaurant is good value, and there's free internet access. A ten-percent discount voucher is available on the website. ❺

Yamatoya Honten Hotel 大和屋本店 20-8 Dōgo Yunomachi Ⓣ 089/935-8880. Hotels with their own nō stage are few and far between, but not only does the Yamatoya Honten have one, it also stages two short nightly performances (30min and 10min). The tatami rooms are well up to deluxe standard, but there are also more modest, slightly dated Western-style single rooms and a rotemburo in the basement. If this place isn't ritzy enough for your tastes, try their even more traditional *Yamatoya Besso* (大和屋別荘; 2-27 Sagidani-chō Ⓣ 089/931-7771; with two meals ❾), a smaller ryokan nearby. Room only ❻, including two meals ❽–❾.

The City

The 132m-high Katsu-yama dominates the centre of Matsuyama and on its summit stands the city's prime attraction, **Matsuyama-jō** (松山城; daily 9am–5pm; ¥500; Ⓣ 089/921-2540). Warlord Katō Yoshiakira began building his fortress in 1602, but by the time it was finished, 26 years later, he had moved to Aizu in Tōhoku. Like many Japanese castles hailed as "original", this one has gone through several incarnations during its lifetime. The main five-storey donjon was destroyed by lightning on New Year's Day in 1784 and rebuilt two storeys shorter in 1820 – the three lesser donjons are all modern-day reconstructions. Despite this, the castle is one of Japan's more impressive fortresses and its location certainly provides commanding views of the city and Inland Sea.

You can get up to the castle using the ropeway or rickety chairlift (both ¥260 each way; ¥500 return) on the eastern flank of the hill. There are also several steep walking routes, the main one starting just beside the ropeway, at the steps up to **Shinonome-jinja** (東雲神社), also on Katsu-yama's east side. This picturesque shrine is famous for its Takigi festival, held every April, when nō plays are performed by the light of fire torches. Other routes run up the west side of the hill, and can be combined with a visit to the Ninomaru Shiseki Teien (see below). Whichever route you take, you'll end up at the Tonashi-mon gateway to the castle, past which you emerge onto a long plateau surrounded by walls and turrets and planted with blossom trees. Inside the main donjon, climb up to the top floor for the view and, on the way down, pass through the museum with displays of calligraphy, old maps, samurai armour and some gorgeously painted screens.

Heading down the western side of the hill leads to the tranquil gardens of the **Ninomaru Shiseki Teien** (二之丸史跡庭園; Feb–July & Sept–Nov 9am–5pm; Aug 9am–5.30pm, Dec–Jan 9am–4.30pm; ¥100). Looking a bit like a giant geometry puzzle, the gardens are built on the site of the Ninomaru, the outer citadel of the castle. The pools and pathways at the front of the gardens represent the floor plan of the former structure, which succumbed to fire in 1872. To the rear, as the grounds climb Katsuyama, the design becomes more fluid, with rockeries, a waterfall and two tea-ceremony houses, one of which serves tea and *wagashi* (a sweet cake) for ¥300.

At the base of the south side of the hill is the modern **Saka no Ue no Kumo Museum** (坂の上の雲ミュージアム; Tues–Sun 9am–6pm; ¥400), devoted to the famous novel by Shiba Ryotaro (see box, p.638). To non-Japanese speakers the most interesting thing about this museum will be the highly contemporary polished concrete-and-glass building it's housed in, designed by Andō Tadao. It contrasts nicely with the striking French-style villa, **Bansui-sō** (萬翠荘), further up the hill. Built in 1922 for Count Sadakoto Hisamatsu, the fifteenth lord of Matsuyama-jō, the villa now houses the **Annexe of the Prefectural Art Museum** (Tues–Sun 9am–6pm; ¥100; ⓣ089/921-3711). The twentieth-century Japanese art displayed inside is changed every three months, but it's the exterior of the building which is most impressive, particularly the juxtaposition of trees pruned like poodles and the wild palms on the forecourt. Sadly, visitors can no longer see (or take tea in) the charming **Gudabutsuan** (愚陀佛庵), the relocated and restored lodging house briefly shared by Masaoka Shiki and Sōseki Natsume; formerly nestled in the woods behind the villa, it was destroyed in a mudslide in July 2010. At the time of writing, plans to rebuild it were uncertain.

From the exit to Bansui-sō you are well placed to start exploring the main shopping arcade of Ōkaidō, at the entrance of which is a branch of the Mitsukoshi department store. At the end of the arcade, cross the main road and turn right into the Gintengai arcade, which eventually leads to the Shi-eki Station and Takashimaya department store. A couple of minutes' walk south of here, across the Iyo Tetsudō rail line, is the **Shiki-dō** (子規堂; daily 8.30am–5pm; ¥50; ⓣ089/945-0400), an evocative re-creation of the poet Masaoka Shiki's home sandwiched between his family's local temple, Shoshu-ji, and the cemetery. Inside the tiny one-storey house are some of the poet's personal effects, his writing desk and examples of his calligraphy.

In the Yamagoe district lie a number of temples whose purpose it was to defend the area immediately to the north of the castle. The most worthy of a visit is **Raikō-ji** (来迎寺), originally located in Dōgo but reconstructed in its present location in the eighteenth century. Beside the temple, up a steep incline, is the so-called **Russian Cemetery** (ロシア人の墓地). Some six thousand Russian prisoners were interned at the POW camp here during the Russo-Japanese War of 1904–5. The prisoners – being something of a novelty and having little chance of escaping back to Russia – were allowed a fair amount of freedom. Ninety-eight prisoners died from natural causes during their imprisonment, and their graves are still kept immaculate, with fresh flowers placed in front of each of the crosses. An impressive commemorative bust of a fierce-looking, bearded Russian officer stands watch at the entrance to the cemetery. Raikō-ji is a fifteen-minute walk northeast of the Takasago-chō tram stop.

Dōgo

Like many other onsen resorts, **DŌGO** (道後) has its strip shows and a deluge of hostess clubs and snack bars, as well as mundane tourist gift shops lining its arcade. However, Dōgo's bathtime delights more than make up for this. Once you've sampled the **onsen**, there are also a couple of interesting museums to explore, along with the appealing **Isaniwa-jinja** shrine and over-the-top **Ishite-ji** temple.

The onsen

"If you went first class, for only 8 sen they lent you a bathrobe, an attendant washed you, and a girl served you tea in one of those elegant, shallow cups that they use in the tea ceremony. I always went first class."

Botchan, by Sōseki Natsume, 1906

It may no longer be so cheap, nor do the attendants scrub your back, but a bath at the grand **Dōgo Onsen Honkan** (道後温泉本館) is still a treat. This is the oldest

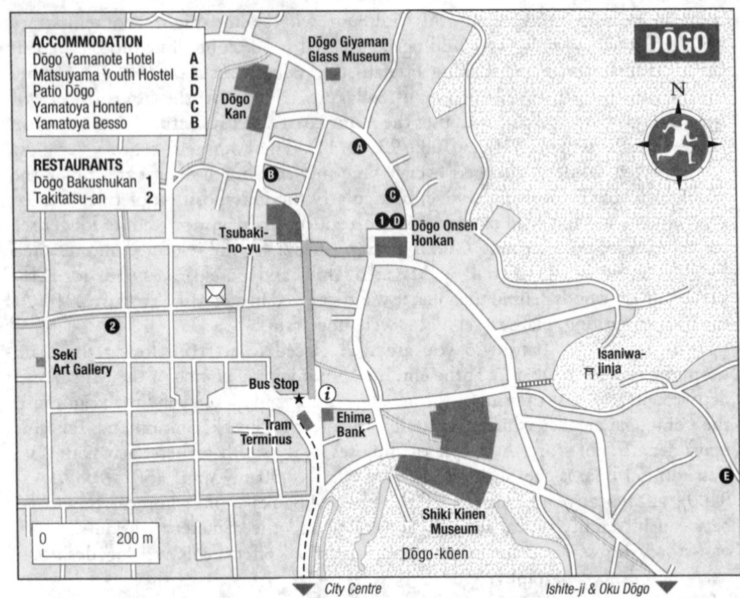

hot springs in Japan, mentioned in the 1300-year-old history book *Nihon-shoki*. According to legend, a white heron dipped its injured leg into the hot water gushing out of the rocks and found that it had healing properties. By the sixth century the onsen's fame reached the ears of Prince Shōtoku, and his royal patronage cemented its reputation. By the seventeenth century the local *daimyō* Matsudaira Sadayuki had segregated the baths into those for monks and samurai and those for the lower-class merchants and craftsmen. He also introduced women-only baths and created facilities for animals to soak away their ills (the animal baths were only closed in 1966).

The present architectural extravaganza was built in 1894 and the heron, which has become the symbol of the baths, is commemorated in a statue astride the three-storey building's ornate roof. Inside there are two types of bath, plus the Yushinden, a special bath built in 1899 for the imperial family, but now drained of water. The cheapest way to soak at the Honkan is to use the rather raucous **Kami-no-yu** (神の湯; daily 6am–10.30pm; ¥400), or "Hot Water of the Gods", a section with two identical baths, decorated with mosaics of the heron, on each side of the changing rooms. For ¥800, you still bathe in the Kami-no-yu, but get to relax afterwards in the second-floor public room, where you'll be served green tea and rice crackers, and you also get to borrow a cotton *yukata* robe. The next level up is the **Tama-no-yu** or "Hot Water of the Spirits" (霊の湯; daily 6am–9pm; ¥1200), a more exclusive bath at the back of the complex. There's a view of a small garden from the changing room and you relax afterwards in a separate section on the second floor. The first-class experience recommended by the title character of *Botchan* entitles you to a **private room** (daily 6am–8.40pm; ¥1500) on the third floor, where you'll be offered green tea and three-coloured *dango* (sweet rice-dough balls on a stick) after your dip.

Even if you opt for the no-frills bath, the staff will allow you to explore the rest of the building. On the second floor, look out for a display of tea-ceremony items and old calligraphy scrolls to the side of the large tatami resting-room with carved wooden verandas. On the third floor, the corner room has a small exhibition (all in Japanese) of items related to *Botchan* and his creator **Sōseki**. You'll need to return to the second floor to gain entrance to the **Yushinden** (又新殿; daily 6am–9pm; ¥250); the extra fee is waived if you've opted for the Tama-no-yu bath. Yushinden has been empty since 1950 (it was only ever used ten times), but the imperial apartments, with their silver- and gilt-coated screens and ornamental gardens, have been preserved. You'll be guided around by one of the no-nonsense female attendants who'll explain, in Japanese, how the rooms were specially constructed to foil any would-be assassins.

A minute's walk along the arcade from the Honkan is the separate modern bathhouse **Tsubaki-no-yu** (椿の湯; daily 6am–10.30pm; ¥360), meaning "Hot Water of Camellia". The granite bath here is much larger than those at the Honkan and uses water from the same hot-spring source. You won't find so many tourists here; rather, elderly locals who take their bathing seriously.

Most of the top-class ryokan in Dōgo also have their own baths, some open to non-residents, including **Dōgo Kan** (道後館; ⓣ089/941-7777), which has a sumptuous series of classically designed indoor and outdoor onsen (daily 11am–11pm; ¥1500). The most exotic baths are at **Oku Dōgo** (奥道後), 4km towards the hills northeast of Dōgo, where the **Jungle Onsen** (ジャングル温泉; daily 7am–10pm; ¥550) lives up to its name, offering no fewer than eleven different bathing pools in a botanical garden setting; there's even a sake bath, smelling a little too pungently of the rice liquor. Several pretty walks lead through the gardens beside the baths, where lengthy trellises bloom with lilac wisteria in May. Buses #52 and #53 (¥300) run out to Oku Dōgo roughly every hour from beside the Dōgo tram terminal.

Other sights

Just before Dōgo's old-fashioned tram terminus you'll pass **Dōgo-kōen** (道後公園), a pleasantly landscaped park, built on the former site of Yuchiku-jō, the fourteenth-century castle of the Kono clan. The summit of the mound in the centre of the park gives a good view of the surrounding area. In the park's eastern corner is the **Shiki Kinen Museum** (子規記念博物館; Tues–Sun 9am–4.30pm; ¥400; ⓣ089/931-5566), which houses rather dry displays telling the life story – with English translations – of Masaoka Shiki (see box, p.638), and setting his literature in its cultural context.

Walking directly up the hill from the tram terminus, you'll see a flight of 140 old stone steps with lanterns, leading up to the beautiful **Isaniwa-jinja** (伊佐爾波神社). It hardly feels appropriate that this enchanting shrine, built by Matsudaira Sadanaga in 1667 and decorated with delicately painted carvings of animals, birds, plants and the sea, was once called Yuzuki Hachiman-gū and is still dedicated to Hachiman, the god of war. Returning to the Dōgo shopping arcade, take the first turning on the left along the arcade, and walk down past the Nikitatsu beer and sake brewery to the **Seki Art Gallery** (セキ美術館; Wed–Sun 10am–5pm; ¥500; ⓣ089/946-5678), a small but worthwhile museum containing the collection of a local printing tycoon. Inside is a room of sketches and two statues by Rodin, as well as some good examples of twentieth-century Japanese art. From here, backtrack to the Dōgo Onsen Honkan and head uphill to the north to find the **Dōgo Giyaman Glass Museum** (道後ぎやまんの庭; daily

9am–9.30pm; ¥800; ⓣ089/933-3637), which displays exquisite pieces of glass from the Edo and Taisho periods in a three-floor gallery. The attached building houses a dazzling display of chandeliers as well as a shop, stylish café (9am–11.30pm) and garden studded with glass works.

Ishite-ji

Eight of the 88 temples on Shikoku's sacred circuit are in Matsuyama, but the most famous – and without a doubt the most unusual – is the 51st, **Ishite-ji** (石手寺). Unlike the pilgrimage's other 87 temples, Ishite-ji has used its accumulated wealth to branch out into surreal forms of religious expression. Tucked away behind the main temple buildings are dimly lit tunnels lined with hundreds of Buddhas and other icons. Condensation drips heavily from the tunnel ceiling if it's been raining, adding to the slightly foreboding atmosphere. Further on, in the tunnel which heads upwards, flashing fairy and strobe lights, activated as you approach, and the piped sound of a priest wailing mantras, create the impression that you've stumbled into an esoteric rave.

The main tunnel emerges from behind a rock on the hill above the temple, close to the crumbling entrance to a park containing more bizarre statues, at the centre of which is a squat, golden-domed 3-D mandala. Enter this dimly lit circular hall and you'll be confronted by a two-hundred-strong congregation of wooden *jizō*, between 1m and 3m high, carved with Buddhist sexual symbols, and arranged in tiered circles. Oddly, while the main temple is usually heaving with pilgrims, very few bother to head up to the park, making it a nice place to relax for a few minutes and take in your unusual surroundings. Climbing up the slope from the mandala will lead to a large graveyard and, on the summit of the adjoining hill, the looming statue of Buddhist saint Kōbō Daishi, founder of Shikoku's pilgrim trail (see p.593).

Next to all this, the temple's classical Kamakura-era architecture, which includes a three-storey pagoda, seems almost mundane. Behind the main gate, Niō-mon, built in 1318, are two giant straw sandals, along with many normal-sized ones, left by pilgrims who hope to have their feet and leg ailments cured. There's also a drab **museum** (¥300) on the east side of the complex, where the temple's treasures are rather poorly presented.

To get to Ishite-ji, you can either walk for fifteen minutes east of the Dōgo tram terminus along the main road or hop on the #8 or #52 bus (¥150) to Oku Dōgo from the tram terminus, which will drop you outside the temple gate.

Eating, drinking and entertainment

As befits a big city, Matsuyama has a wide range of restaurants, cafés and bars. Local specialities include the sponge roly-poly cake called *taruto* (タルト), inspired by a Portuguese confection introduced to Japan 350 years ago through the port of Nagasaki; the three-coloured rice dumplings on sticks called *Botchan dango*, after the character's favourite sweet; and *goshiki somen*, thin noodles made in five colours.

The tight grid of streets between Niban-chō and Sanban-chō in the centre heaves with **bars** and, in the summer, beer gardens appear on the roofs of several hotels including the *ANA Hotel Matsuyama*. In Dōgo, though, note that many of the bars are pricey hostess joints and best avoided. Various **dance** events are held at *Club Bibros* (usually with a ¥1500 cover charge), east of Ōkaidō on the seventh floor of a building between Nibanchō and Sanbanchō. The **cinemas** in and around Ōkaidō arcade show mainstream Hollywood and Japanese films, while you can usually catch independent foreign films at Cinema Lunatic (ⓣ089/933-9240), south of the city centre, close to the Tachibana-bashi across the River Ishite-gawa. Theatre, dance and orchestral performances are held at the Matsuyama Shimin Kaikan (松山市民会館; ⓣ089/931-8181) and the Prefectural Cultural Centre at Kenmin Bunka Kaikan (県民文化会館; ⓣ089/923-5111). Check *What's Going On?* (see p.638) for details.

Matsuyama

CAFE Marinecco 3-1-3 Ōkaidō ⓣ089/935-5896. Convivial café-cum-wine bar with stylish wooden interiors and menus handwritten on chalk boards. Has a good selection of lunch dishes such as pasta (from ¥680), while the outdoor tables are the perfect place for watching the world go by with a pint of Guinness or Kilkenny (¥800). Daily 11.30am–3pm & 5pm–2am.

Flankey Kobayashi フランキー小林 2-3 Ichiban-chō. Lively standing bar that acts like a drop-in centre for Matsuyama's expat community. Drinks are a bargain, with beers and sake starting at ¥250. Also has dirt-cheap but fairly decent food, such as pasta and curry (from ¥300). Daily 11am–3am.

Goshiki 五色 3-5-4 Sanban-chō ⓣ089/933-3838. The most famous place in town to sample *somen*, the five-coloured noodles. In front of the restaurant is a shop where you can buy the noodles, packed as souvenir sets, for around ¥300. Lunchtime set menus start at ¥880; noodles on their own are cheaper. Daily 11am–11pm.

Kawasemi 川瀬見 2-5-18 Niban-chō ⓣ089/933-9697. Zen-like *kaiseki* (Japanese haute cuisine) restaurant. The portions are small, but your taste buds will be subtly challenged. Look for the world "club" in English on the mauve sign and go up to the second floor. *Kaiseki*-style lunch/dinner from ¥1500/4300. Daily noon–2pm & 5–10pm.

Kingyūtei 金牛亭 2-5-18 Niban-chō ⓣ089/921-0007. This Japanese take on Korean barbecue (*yaki-niku*) in the heart of Niban-chō is worth seeking out if you fancy gorging on grilled beef and spicy Korean side dishes such as *kimchi*. You cook the beef yourself on grills at your table. Expect to pay around ¥4000. Mon–Sat 5–11pm.

Kushihide くし秀 3-2-8 Niban-chō ⓣ089/921-1587. This rustic restaurant is a top place to try *yakitori*, while a few doors down is its equally good sister operation *Iyo-ryori Kushihide* (伊予料理くし秀; ⓣ089/941-9410; Mon–Sat 5–11pm), serving fish dishes with the seafood picked out of a central tank. Around ¥3500 for a meal. Tues–Sun 5–11pm.

Ladki ラルキー 5-9 Hanazono-machi ⓣ089/948-0885. Indian restaurant serving great curries and huge, freshly baked naan breads. You can fill up for around ¥1000. They also have a second, larger, shop at 1-11-7 Ichiban-chō; several hundred metres east along Ichibanchō-Dōri from the north end of Ōkaidō. Daily 11am–2.30pm & 5–10pm.

Paradiso 1-10-1 Niban-chō ⓣ089/941-5077. Occupying two corner spots facing each other, this highly rated pizzeria has some outdoor tables and keeps late hours. A meal is around ¥2000. Daily 5.30pm–3am.

Provence Dining *ANA Hotel Matsuyama*, 3-2-1 Ichiban-chō ⓣ089/933-5511. The best thing about the *ANA*'s top-floor restaurant is its grand-stand view of Katsuyama Hill and the Bansui-sō villa, especially romantic when the buildings are spotlit at night. The lunch buffet (¥1600) offers a selection of Mediterranean dishes. For top-quality Japanese cuisine served by kimono-clad waitresses, *Unkai* (daily 11.45am–2.30pm & 5–9.30pm) on the sixth floor is a good option with lunches from ¥1200 and dinner courses from ¥4000. Daily 6.30am–9pm.

Sova Sova 3-2-35 Ōkaidō ⓣ089/945-5252. Stylish, laidback café-bar serving a range of simple dishes such as cold soba and rice bowls for under ¥1000. In the evening it's a pleasantly quiet place for a drink. Daily except Wed 11am–9pm.

Underground Café 3-3-6 Ōkaidō ⓣ089/998-7710 . Retro-chic café-bar in a side street on the way to the castle chairlift, with a very laidback vibe. Look out for the large Union Jack flag hanging outside. The food is reasonable and there are occasional club events. Daily noon–4am, closed second and fourth Wed of each month.

Dōgo

Dōgo Bakushukan 道後麦酒館 Opposite Dōgo Onsen Honkan ⓣ089/945-6866. An *izakaya* owned by the same independent brewery that runs *Nikitatsu-an* (see below). Try their *yakitori* set (¥1500) along with one of the brewery's sakes or three ales: the light Botchan lager, a stout and the slightly sweet Madonna ale (¥470 for a small glass), all very refreshing after an onsen dip. Daily 11am–10pm.

Takitatsu-an たきたつ庵 3-18 Dōgo Kitamachi ⓣ089/924-6617. Seating is on tatami or at the modern, dark wooden counter, and the imaginative modern Japanese cooking complements their own-brewed beers and sake. Set lunch/dinner starts at ¥1300/2800 and includes a range of tasty morsels, beautifully presented on an oversized wood plate that almost looks like one of Honkan's wash basins and accompanied by special rice and soup. There's also an outdoor deck for quaffing beer on balmy nights. Daily 11am–2pm & 5–8.30pm. Closed Mon.

Listings

Banks and exchange Ehime Ginkō has several branches in downtown Matsuyama. There's also a branch by the Dōgo tram terminus.
Bookshop Kinokuniya, 5-7-1 Chifune-machi, has English books and magazines (daily 10am–7.30pm).
Car rental Budget Rent-a-Car has a branch at the airport (℡089/974-3733).
Hospital The central prefectural hospital, Ehime Kenritsu Chūō Byōin (℡089/947-1111), is in Kasuga-machi, south of the Shi-eki Station.
Internet Free at EPIC and Matsuyama International Centre (see p.638).
Laundry Okaya Coin Laundry, 43 Minami-Mochida (daily 6am–10.30pm).
Police The main police station is at 2 Minami Horibata (℡089/941-0111). Emergency numbers are listed on p.71.
Post office Matsuyama's main post office is at 3 Sanban-chō (Mon–Fri 9am–7pm, Sat 9am–5pm & Sun 9am–12.30pm). There's also a branch in Dōgo (Mon–Fri 9am–5pm), to the west of the shopping arcade. Both have ATMs that accept credit cards.
Shopping Local products that make good souvenirs include *iyo-gasuri*, an indigo-dyed cloth; *hime temari*, colourful thread-covered balls that bring good luck; and *Tobe-yaki*, distinctive blue-patterned pottery. Check out Ōkaidō and Gintengai arcades for souvenir shops, and Mitsukoshi and Takashimaya department stores.
Tobe-yaki pottery is distinguished by its robust feel and simple blue-and-white glaze. The centre of the local pottery industry is Tobe-chō, 13km from Matsuyama. Take a #18 or #19 bus here from Shi-eki Station (45min; ¥600) to visit the Tobe-yaki Kankō Centre (℡089/962-6145; daily 9am–5pm; closed Thurs), where you can watch pottery being made and make or decorate some pieces yourself.

Ishizuchi-san

Some 50km east of Matsuyama is **ISHIZUCHI-SAN** (石鎚山), Shikoku's tallest peak. Legend has it that the 1982m mountain was climbed in 797 by Kōbō Daishi. Women were once strictly forbidden from setting foot on the sacred mountain and this tradition is still upheld for the annual official opening ceremony on July 1, when *yamabushi* (Buddhist ascetics) hike to the shrine at the summit. It's possible to climb Ishizuchi-zan from April, once the winter snow has melted, but the official climbing season runs from July until the end of August; there are more frequent bus connections to the trails during this time, enabling you to get up and down the mountain in a day, as long as you set off early.

The **Ishizuchi Quasi National Park**, in which the mountain stands, was established in 1955 and has several hiking trails, plus limited skiing in the winter. The relatively warm climate means there are trees on the slopes of the mountain, almost to the summit. There's a **cable car** (times vary throughout the year: at least 9am–5pm; ¥1000 one way, ¥1900 return) at **Nishi-no-Kawa** (西之川), which cuts out some of the foot-slogging, taking you to within three hours' hike of the top. A short walk from the cable car is a **chairlift** (late April to mid-Nov; 9am–4.30pm; ¥300 one way, ¥500 return), which saves a little bit more effort on the way up to **Jōju** (成就), where you'll find the **Ishizuchi-jinja** shrine, plus several places to eat and buy souvenirs. There are good views from here, if you don't wish to go any further.

The 3.5km route from Jōju to the summit is clearly marked. Along the way are several spots where *kusari*, thick metal chains, have been hammered into the rock to help you climb. If this doesn't appeal then there's a marginally easier walking path, which doesn't require climbing chains. Most people stop at the mountain-top shrine, but the official summit is the even higher peak of Tengu-dake, approached along a razor-edge ridge, about ten minutes away. If you don't want to retrace your steps, follow the alternative signposted route down the mountain to **Tsuchigoya** (土小屋), from where infrequent buses (you might have to change buses at Kuma) run back to Matsuyama.

Plenty of trains from Matsuyama go to Iyo-Saijō, on the Yosan line, from where it's a 55-minute bus ride (¥970) to Nishi-no-Kawa via the scenic Omogo-kei Gorge (the first bus is 7.43am; the next isn't until 10.23am). Alternatively, you can take a bus from Matsuyama to Tsuchigoya (3hr; ¥3160); to do the climb in a day you'll need to be on the first bus at 8am. The last bus back to Matsuyama from Tsuchigoya is at 4.30pm, but double-check this before setting out.

On the mountain, Jōju's *Shiraishi Ryokan* (白石旅館; ⓣ0897/59-0032; ④) serves decent food and is also a reasonable place to bunk down, with large tatami rooms.

Travel details

Trains

The trains between the major cities listed below are the fastest, direct services.

Kōchi to: Awa Ikeda (14 daily; 1hr 5min); Kotohira (16 daily; 1hr 30min); Nakamura (9 daily; 1hr 50min); Okayama (hourly; 2hr 25min); Takamatsu (5 daily; 2hr 15min).

Matsuyama to: Okayama (hourly; 2hr 45min); Takamatsu (hourly; 2hr 30min); Uwajima (14 daily; 1hr 20min).

Takamatsu to: Matsuyama (hourly; 2hr 30min); Kōchi (6 daily; 2hr 5min); Kotohira (7 daily; 55min); Okayama (every 30min; 1hr); Tokushima (16 daily; 1hr 5min); Uwajima (daily; 4hr).

Tokushima to: Awa Ikeda (6 daily; 1hr 20min); Kaifu (3 daily; 1hr 40min); Naruto (14 daily; 40min); Takamatsu (17 daily; 1hr).

Uwajima to: Kubokawa (6 daily; 2hr 20min); Matsuyama (14 daily; 1hr 25min).

Buses

Kōchi to: Okayama (9 daily; 2hr 30min); Ōsaka (21 daily; 5hr 35min); Takamatsu (14 daily: 2hr 10min); Tokyo (daily; 11hr 40min).

Kotohira to: Tokyo (daily; 11hr 40min).

Matsuyama to: Kōbe (9 daily; 2hr 50min); Kōchi (11 daily; 2hr 30min); Kyoto (2 daily; 5hr 30min); Nagoya (daily; 10hr 40min); Okayama (6 daily; 2hr 50min); Onomichi (2 daily; 2hr 10min); Ōsaka (15 daily; 5hr 20min); Takamatsu (15 daily; 2hr 40min); Tokyo (daily; 11hr); Tokushima (7 daily; 3hr 10min).

Takamatsu to: Kōchi (14 daily; 2hr 10min); Matsuyama (15 daily; 2hr 40min); Ōsaka (16 daily; 3hr 25min); Kōbe (6 daily; 2hr 35min); Tokyo (daily; 11hr); Yokohama (daily; 10hr 30min).

Tokushima to: Awaji-shima IC (4 daily; 45min); Matsuyama (7 daily; 3hr 10min); Ōsaka (every 30min; 2hr 40min); Takamatsu (12 daily; 1hr 35min); Tokyo (3 daily; 10hr 40min).

Uwajima to: Matsuyama (15 daily; 2hr 20min); Sukumo (11 daily; 2hr).

Ferries

Matsuyama to: Beppu (daily; 3hr 30min); Hiroshima (hydrofoil: 14 daily; 1hr 10min; ferry: 10 daily; 2hr 40min); Kita-kyushu/Kokura (daily; 7hr); Oita (daily; 3hr 45min); Ōsaka (daily; 9hr); Yanai (4 daily; 2hr 20min).

Sukumo to: Saiki (3 daily; 3hr).

Takamatsu to: Kōbe (4 daily; 3hr 40min); Naoshima (6 daily; 1hr); Shōdo-shima (hydrofoil: 21 daily; 35min; ferry: 28 daily; 1hr); Uno (48 daily; 1hr).

Tokushima to: Kita-Kyūshū/Kokura (daily; 17hr); Tokyo (daily; 17hr 30min); Wakayama (8 daily; hydrofoil 1hr, ferry 2hr).

Yawatahama to: Beppu (6 daily; 2hr 50min); Usuki (7 daily; 2hr 25min).

Flights

Kōchi to: Fukuoka (3 daily; 50min); Nagoya (2 daily; 1hr); Ōsaka Itami (8 daily; 40min); Tokyo (8 daily; 1hr 25min).
Matsuyama to: Fukuoka (4 daily; 45min); Kagoshima (daily; 1hr); Nagoya (4 daily; 1hr 10min); Naha (daily; 1hr 55min); Ōsaka (13 daily; 50min); Seoul (3 weekly; 1hr 40min); Shanghai (2 weekly; 50min); Tokyo (11 daily; 1hr 15min).
Takamatsu to: Kagoshima (daily; 1hr 25min); Naha (daily; 1hr 55min); Seoul (3 weekly; 1hr 50min); Tokyo (10 daily; 1hr 15min).
Tokushima to: Fukuoka (2 daily; 1hr 40min); Nagoya (daily; 55min); Tokyo (6 daily; 1hr 15min).

10

Kyūshū

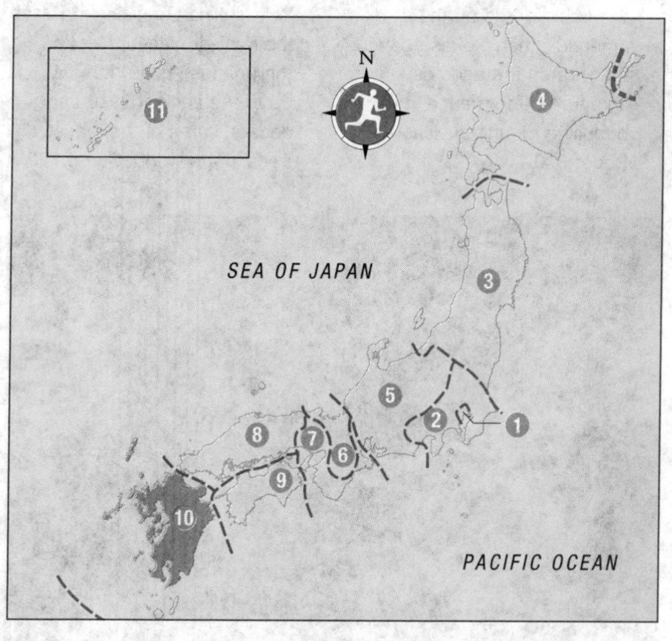

CHAPTER 10 Highlights

* **Fukuoka** Slurp a bowl of ramen noodles at one of the open-air *yatai* stalls along the Tenjin River. **See p.654**

* **Aso-san** The peaks of this active volcano offer great hiking and superb views across the largest caldera in the world. **See p.688**

* **Takachiho** Go boating through a gorge on the emerald-green Gokase-gawa, then watch the gods cavort at a kagura performance in this beguiling mountain village. **See p.690**

* **Usuki** Contemplate Japan's finest stone-carved Buddhas, sitting serenely in their wooded valley for more than seven hundred years. **See p.699**

* **Beppu's hidden onsen** Escape the Beppu crowds by hiking up to a secluded array of onsen in the western hills. **See p.696**

* **Yakushima** Go hiking in the rainiest place in Japan, through lush green forests up to the ancient yaku-sugi cedars, some of the oldest trees in the world. **See p.720**

▲ Nakasu Island food stalls, Fukuoka

10

Kyūshū

The spectacular array of natural attractions on **KYŪSHŪ** makes this, Japan's third-largest island, a feasible holiday destination on its own, providing a thrilling alternative to the regular Kanto and Kansai circuits. Here visitors can find themselves hiking the rim of the world's largest caldera, taking a lonesome onsen dip in the forest, surfing Japan's gnarliest waves, tracking down moss-coated cedar trees that predate Christianity or being showered with ash from a live volcano. It's perfectly possible to just scoot round the main cities in a week, but you'll need more like two to do the region justice, allowing time for the splendid mountainous interior and a few of the more far-flung islands.

Closer to Korea than Tokyo, Kyūshū has long had close links with the Asian mainland, and its chief city, **Fukuoka**, is an important regional hub. An energetic city on the island's heavily developed north coast, Fukuoka is worth a stop for its museums, modern architecture and vibrant nightlife. If you've only got a couple of days on Kyūshū, however, **Nagasaki** represents the best all-round destination. Though its prime draw is the A-Bomb museum and related sights, the city also has a picturesque harbour setting, a laidback, cosmopolitan air and a spattering of temples and historical museums. From here it's a short hop east to **Kumamoto**, famous for its castle and landscaped garden, and the spluttering, smouldering cone of **Aso-san.** This is great hiking country, while hot-spring enthusiasts will also be in their element – from **Kurokawa Onsen's** delightful rotemburo to the bawdy pleasures of **Beppu** on the east coast. The mountain village of **Takachiho** requires a fair detour, but it's worth it to see traditional dance performances depicting the antics of Japan's ancient gods. The island's southern districts contain more on the same theme – volcanoes, onsen and magnificent scenery. Highlights include **Sakurajima**, one of the world's most active volcanoes, which looms over the city of **Kagoshima**, while the lush island of **Yakushima**, roughly 100km south of Kyūshū, sports towering, thousand-year-old cedar trees.

Getting around Kyūshū

Kyūshū is connected to Honshū by road and rail. Fukuoka's Hakata Station receives Shinkansen from the mainland, and fires its own out on a new line heading south to Kagoshima. From Hakata, JR Kyūshū (Ⓦ www.jrkyushu.co.jp) trains fan out to all the major cities, and the company offers its own three- and five-day **rail passes** (¥13,000 and ¥16,000) for travelling round the island; see p.34 for more on JR passes and discount tickets.

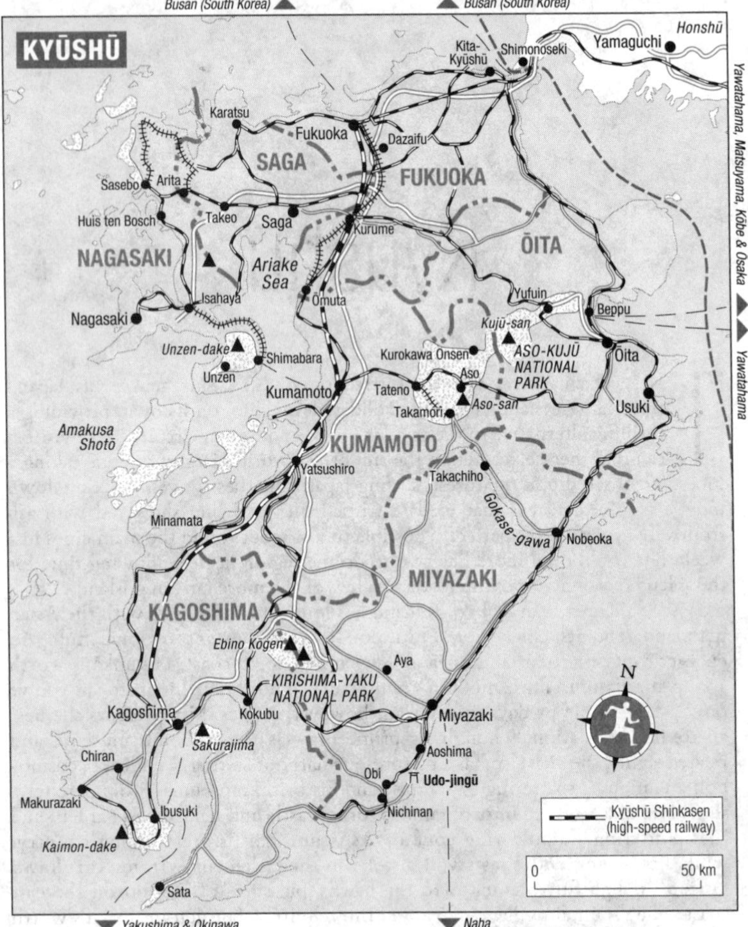

In the central uplands and southern Kyūshū, you'll be more reliant on a limited number of private train lines and on **local buses**. If you're on a whistle-stop tour, you might want to consider one of the three-day SunQ **bus passes** (Ⓦwww.rakubus.jp), which offer unlimited travel on most highway buses and local services throughout Kyūshū (¥10,000) or just the five northern prefectures (¥8000). Not all bus companies are covered, nor are some of the fastest express services between cities. The passes can be purchased at the main bus terminals in Fukuoka, Kumamoto, Nagasaki, Kagoshima, Ōita and Miyazaki.

For exploring the more remote areas, **car rental** is an excellent option; there are car rental outlets in almost every town and in all the main tourist areas.

Some history

The ancient chronicles state that **Emperor Jimmu**, Japan's legendary first emperor, set out from southern Kyūshū to found the Japanese nation in 660 BC.

To Korea by sea

Fukuoka is connected by ferry and hydrofoil to Busan, Korea's second-largest city, which is less than three hours from Seoul by high-speed train. Most travel on one of Beetle's **hydrofoils** (Ⓣ092/281-2315, Ⓦwww.jrbeetle.co.jp), which take just three hours. There are at least four daily services, costing ¥13,000 one-way; round-trips can be as low as ¥20,000, though booking the return leg in Korea will also save money. Some find the journey uncomfortable – it's a little like sitting on a washing machine for a few hours – but a more leisurely trip can be enjoyed on the daily Camellia Line **ferry** (Ⓣ092/262-2323, Ⓦwww.camellia-line.co.jp), which costs from ¥9000 one-way. The ferry heads to Busan by day in under six hours, then back to Fukuoka overnight. With both ferry and hydrofoil, travellers must pay a ¥700 **departure tax** from a machine in the terminal, and around the same is added to the ticket price as a **fuel surcharge**. Korean tourist visas – ranging from one to six months in length, depending on nationality – are available on arrival.

Though the records are open to dispute, there's evidence of human habitation on Kyūshū from before the tenth century BC, and by the beginning of the Yayoi period (300 BC–300 AD) the small kingdom of **Na** (as it was then known) was trading with China and Korea. Local merchants brought rice-farming and bronze-making techniques back to Japan, while in the twelfth century monks introduced Zen Buddhism to northern Kyūshū. Less welcome visitors arrived in 1274 and 1281 during the **Mongol invasions** under Kublai Khan. The first ended in a narrow escape when the Mongols withdrew, and the shogun ordered a protective wall to be built around Hakata Bay. By 1281 the Japanese were far better prepared, but their real saviour was a typhoon, subsequently dubbed *kami kaze*, or "wind of the gods", which whipped up out of nowhere and scattered the Mongol fleet on the eve of their massed assault.

Three hundred years later, in 1543, the first **Europeans** to reach Japan pitched up on the island of Tanegashima, off southern Kyūshū. Finding an eager market for their guns among the local *daimyō*, the Portuguese sailors returned a few years later, bringing with them **missionaries**, among them the Jesuit priest Francis Xavier. Within fifty years the Catholic Church, now also represented by Spanish Franciscans and Dominicans, was claiming some 600,000 Christian converts. The centre of activity was **Nagasaki**, where Chinese, Dutch and British merchants swelled the throng. In the early 1600s, however, the government grew increasingly wary of the Europeans in general and Christians in particular. By fits and starts successive shoguns stamped down on the religion and restricted the movement of all foreigners, until eventually only two small communities of Dutch and Chinese merchants were left in Nagasaki.

This period of isolation lasted until the mid-1850s, when Nagasaki and Kagoshima in particular found themselves at the forefront of the modernizing revolution that swept Japan after the **Meiji Restoration**. Indeed, it was the armies of the Satsuma and Chōshū clans, both from Kyūshū, which helped restore the emperor to the throne, and many members of the new government hailed from the island. In 1877, however, Kagoshima's **Saigō Takamori** led a revolt against the Meiji government in what became known as the **Satsuma Rebellion**. Saigō's army was routed, but he's still something of a local hero in Kyūshū.

North Kyūshū

Kyūshū's five northern prefectures (Fukuoka, Saga, Nagasaki, Kumamoto and Ōita) contain the bulk of the island's population, industry and economic power. They are also home to some of the island's foremost sights – Fukuoka and Nagasaki are justly two of Japan's most popular cities, and one can head from the latter via **Unzen-dake**, one of Kyūshū's several active volcanoes, to the castle-town of **Kumamoto**. This is the main jumping-off point for exploring **Aso-san**'s vast caldera, which dominates the island's wild, relatively empty central highlands. Most people then continue on to **Beppu**, on Kyūshū's east coast, where bathing is taken to such an extreme that it's earned the accolade of Japan's hot-spring capital. Further south, on the edge of the central highlands, the isolated village of **Takachiho** is a bit of a trek, but the effort is amply rewarded with a dramatic journey and the opportunity to see lively folk dances recalling the ancient gods and goddesses.

Fukuoka

The recent renaissance of **FUKUOKA** (福岡), Kyūshū's largest city, has been rather remarkable. Not too long ago this was an industrial nonentity, notable only for its transport connections to Korea and the rest of the island. Fast forward a few years, however, and we see a squeaky-clean metropolis whose energetic yet carefree atmosphere has propelled it into many a best-place-to-live list – witness the locals slurping happily away on their **ramen** at a rustic streetside *yatai*. Casual visitors may find actual sights thin on the ground, but Fukuoka boasts an undeniable charm that makes for a great introduction to Kyūshū, or indeed Japan as a whole, and it deserves a day or two of any traveller's time.

Highlights here include one or two excellent museums and ranks of eye-catching modern architecture – most notable in the latter category are **Canal City**, a self-contained cinema, hotel and shopping complex built around a semicircular strip of water, and **Hawks Town**, which forms part of a major seafront redevelopment incorporating venues for shopping, eating and entertainment. The city is also renowned for its festivals and folk crafts, which are presented at **Hakata Machiya Folk Museum**. As with any self-respecting Japanese city of this size, Fukuoka maintains a lively entertainment district, in this case crammed onto the tiny island of **Nakasu**, though it's safer on the wallet to head for the less glitzy bars and restaurants of **Tenjin**, the city's main downtown area.

There are a couple of excellent sights just to the south of Fukuoka. First up is the ancient temple town of **Dazaifu**, once the seat of government for all of southern Japan, but now a pleasant backwater best known for its collection of temples and shrines, set against a backdrop of wooded slopes. For centuries, Dazaifu's monks, priests and officials sought solace in the healing waters of nearby **Futsukaichi Onsen**. Both towns are easily accessible by train and can either be combined as a day-trip from Fukuoka or as a stopover en route to Nagasaki.

Arrival

Central Fukuoka is split in two by the Naka-gawa. To the east of this river, **Hakata** district centres on Fukuoka's main **train station**, confusingly known as

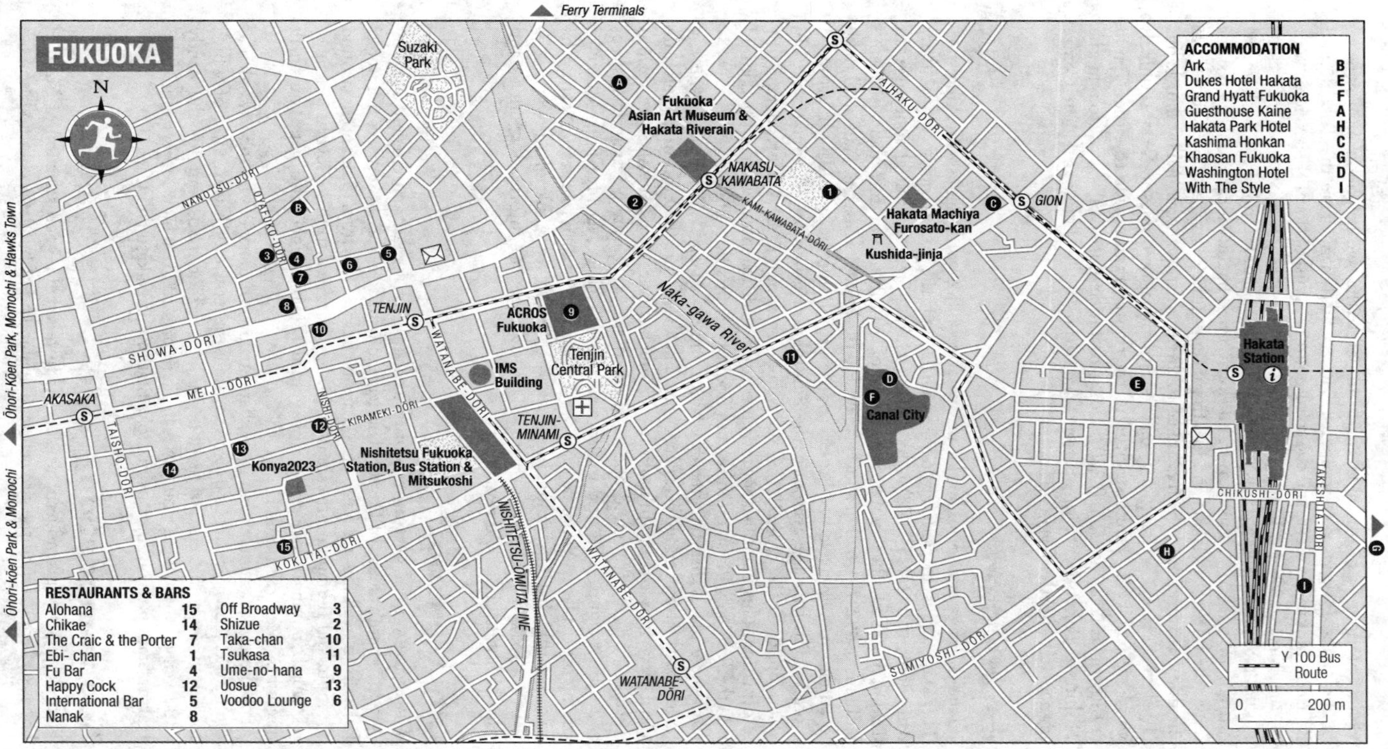

FUKUOKA

N

Ferry Terminals

Suzaki Park

Fukuoka Asian Art Museum & Hakata Riverain

NAKASU KAWABATA

TAIHAKU-DŌRI

GION

Hakata Machiya Furosato-kan

Kushida-jinja

KAMI-KAWABATA-DŌRI

NANOTSU-DŌRI

OYAFUKO-DŌRI

TENJIN

ACROS Fukuoka

Naka-gawa River

SHOWA-DŌRI

Tenjin Central Park

IMS Building

WATANABE-DŌRI

MEIJI-DŌRI

AKASAKA

NISHI-DŌRI

KIRAMEKI-DŌRI

TENJIN-MINAMI

TAISHO-DŌRI

Nishitetsu Fukuoka Station, Bus Station & Mitsukoshi

Konya2023

Canal City

Hakata Station

CHIKUSHI-DŌRI

TAKESHITA-DŌRI

NISHITETSU-ŌMUTA LINE

KOKUTAI-DŌRI

WATANABE-DŌRI

SUMIYOSHI-DŌRI

Ōhori-Kōen Park, Momochi & Hawks Town

Ōhori-kōen Park & Momochi

G

ACCOMMODATION

Ark	B
Dukes Hotel Hakata	E
Grand Hyatt Fukuoka	F
Guesthouse Kaine	A
Hakata Park Hotel	H
Kashima Honkan	C
Khaosan Fukuoka	G
Washington Hotel	D
With The Style	I

RESTAURANTS & BARS

Alohana	15
Chikae	14
The Craic & the Porter	7
Ebi- chan	1
Fu Bar	4
Happy Cock	12
International Bar	5
Nanak	8
Off Broadway	3
Shizue	2
Taka-chan	10
Tsukasa	11
Ume-no-hana	9
Uosue	13
Voodoo Lounge	6

Y 100 Bus Route

0 200 m

Hakata Station – a historical legacy from before the two neighbouring towns of Fukuoka and Hakata were combined. Hakata Station is where the Tōkaidō and Kyūshū Shinkansen meet, and the focal point of Kyūshū's local JR services. West of the Naka-gawa, in **Tenjin**, the city's commercial heart, stands Nishitetsu-Fukuoka Station, where trains from Dazaifu (see p.662) terminate. These central districts are linked by subway to **Fukuoka airport**, handily located only two stops down the line from Hakata and five from Tenjin; the subway station is located in the domestic terminal, which is linked to the international terminal by shuttle bus (10–15min; free). Arriving at Hakata international or domestic **ferry** terminals you have to take a Nishitetsu city bus for the ten-minute ride to either Tenjin (¥180) or Hakata Station (¥220). **Long-distance buses** call at a stop in the Nishitetsu-Fukuoka Station, before terminating at the Fukuoka Kōtsu Centre immediately north of Hakata Station.

Information

Fukuoka has a good sprinkling of **information** offices with English-speaking staff. There are desks in both airport terminals, but the main tourist office (daily 8am–8pm; Ⓣ092/431-3003) is located on Hakata Station's central concourse. In Tenjin, there's an office on the ground floor of the Mitsukoshi store (daily 10.30am–6.30pm; Ⓣ092/751-6904), above the Nishitetsu-Fukuoka Station. Staff at all these locations can help make hotel reservations but only for the same day. If you need more English-language assistance, the **Fukuoka International Association** (daily 10am–8pm: Ⓣ092/733-2220, Ⓦwww.rainbowfia.or.jp) offers a broad range of information, plus English-language newspapers and free internet access; you'll find it in the Rainbow Plaza, on the eighth floor of Tenjin's IMS Building.

All these places dish out free city **maps** and the *Fukuoka City Visitor's Guide*, a handy booklet outlining the main sights. They also issue the **Fukuoka Welcome Card** (Ⓦwww.welcome-fukuoka.or.jp), which entitles overseas visitors to various discounts or gifts at around one hundred participating hotels, restaurants, shops and tourist sights. The card is also available at Hakata Machiya Folk Museum, among other places. You'll need to show a passport or alien registration card. The free monthly **listings magazine** *Fukuoka Now* (Ⓦwww.fukuoka-now.com) is worth a look for local events; you'll find it at tourist information offices and various hotels, shops and restaurants.

City transport

The easiest way of **getting around** Fukuoka is on its fast and efficient **subway** system. There's plenty of English-language information and most places of interest fall within walking distance of a station. Trains run from 5.30am to around 11.45pm and the minimum fare is ¥200. If you expect to make several journeys, it's worth buying a one-day **subway** card (¥600), which also gets you small discounts at several museums.

For those places not within immediate striking distance of the subway, such as the Hawks Town area, you'll need to use Nishitetsu **city buses**, most of which funnel through the Hakata Station–Tenjin corridor. Look out for the handy "100-yen bus" – where you pay a flat fare of ¥100 – which loops round from Hakata Station to Nishitetsu-Fukuoka Station via Nakasu and Canal City.

Accommodation

Fukuoka has several modern, world-class **hotels** and a good selection of business hotels scattered around the city centre. The standard of budget accommodation has also improved recently, mostly located around Hakata Station. You can make hotel **reservations** at the Hakata Station and Tenjin information offices and at the airport, though only for the same day. Weekend rates tend to be slightly more expensive.

Ark Hotel 3-7-22 Tenjin ⓣ092/781-2552. Fairly-priced business hotel located in the thick of the Tenjin restaurant and bar district. Singles occasionally dip below ¥5000, including breakfast. ❹

Canal City Fukuoka Washington Hotel 1-2-20 Sumiyoshi ⓣ092/282-8800, ⓦwww.fukuoka-wh.com. This slightly upmarket member of the Washington chain is centrally located and has relatively spacious rooms with TV, free internet access and spacious bathrooms. ❻

Dukes Hotel Hakata 2-3-9 Hakata-eki-mae ⓣ092/472-1800. A lobby heavy with the scent of flowers sets a suitable tone for this elegant business hotel, whose lovingly decorated rooms are excellent value for the price and location. ❹

Grand Hyatt Fukuoka 1-2-82 Sumiyoshi ⓣ092/282-1234, ⓦfukuoka.grand.hyatt.com. Can't-miss-it hotel occupying a large chunk of Canal City. The oval-shaped lobby and plunging atrium are worth a visit even if you're not staying, though the rooms don't disappoint – large and beautifully designed with Japanese touches, such as *shōji* screens and contemporary artwork. Find hefty discounts online. ❼

Hakata Park Hotel 4-1-18 Hakataekimae ⓣ092/451-1151. Everything you want from a business hotel, but throw in sleek design, hearty buffet breakfasts and a quiet location near Hakata Station. ❸

Kashima Honkan 鹿島本館 3-11 Reisen-machi ⓣ092/291-0746, ⓔkashima-co@mx7.tiki.ne.jp. This homely, ninety-year-old ryokan is located on a pleasant backstreet, just round the corner from Gion subway station. The 27 tatami rooms are elegant, with antique screens and wall-hangings, though none is en suite. Rooms are available with or without meals. There's free internet access and English is spoken. ❺

Khaosan Fukuoka 11-3 Hie-machi ⓣ092/404-6035, ⓦwww.khaosan-fukuoka.com. A short walk east of Hakata Station, this laidback hostel is the ideal place to meet some travel buddies. Rooms are more than adequate, while way up near the roof is a relaxed common area with internet access and a beanbag-filled TV room. Dorms ¥2400, bunk-bed twins ❶

With The Style 4-1-18 Hakataeki-minami ⓣ092/433-3900, ⓦwww.withthestyle.com. So hip it hurts, this snazzy boutique hotel is a favourite with young, moneyed Japanese. You're unlikely to get change from ¥40,000, but those zoning out in the rooftop spa or sipping cocktails in the private penthouse bar tend to find it worth the splurge. ❾

The City

Even today the old cultural and economic divide between the original castle town, Fukuoka, and the former merchants' quarter of Hakata can be traced, albeit faintly, in the city's streets. Much of **Hakata** (博多) consists of dull office blocks, but the district is also home to the city's oldest **shrine** and its most rumbustious festival. You'll also still find the occasional wooden building, narrow lane or aged wall, while some of the unique Hakata culture is showcased in its well-presented **folk museum**. Not surprisingly, many **craft industries** originated in this area, most famously Hakata dolls and *ori* silks, while geisha still work the traditional **entertainment district** of Nakasu. Hakata is also home to one of Fukuoka's most famous landmarks, the futuristic **Canal City** complex, a startling contrast to the rest of the district.

West of the Naka-gawa, **Tenjin** (天神) has upmarket boutiques, department stores and "fashion buildings", but there's little in the way of sights until you go further west to the ruins of Fukuoka castle in **Ōhori-kōen**. As well as an attractive lake, this park also contains an **art museum** with an important collection of twentieth-century works.

Hakata

At the south end of **Kami-Kawabata-dōri**, a covered shopping arcade, a left turn under a *torii* brings you to the back entrance of Hakata's principal shrine, **Kushida-jinja** (櫛田神社), founded in 757 AD. This is the home of Hakata's annual **Gion**

Yamakasa festival (July 1–15), which climaxes in a 5km dawn race finishing at Kushida-jinja, in which seven teams manhandle one-tonne floats through the streets while spectators douse them with water. Like Kyoto's Gion festival, this harks back to the Kamakura period (1185–1333 AD) when Buddhist priests sprinkled sacred water to drive away summer epidemics. There's a small **museum** (daily 10am–5pm; ¥300) of shrine treasures in the grounds, not of great interest, but it does stock English-language leaflets about Kushida-jinja and the festival.

Turn east out of Kushida-jinja and you can't miss the traditional whitewashed walls and grey roofs of **Hakata Machiya Furusato-kan** (博多町家ふるさと館; daily 10am–6pm; Ⓦwww.hakatamachiya.com), a folk museum which evokes the Hakata of the late nineteenth century. One block houses a museum (¥200) featuring a twenty-minute video of the Gion Yamakasa festival.

Turning west out of Kushida-jinja will take you to **Nakasu** (中洲), an entertainment district built on a sandbank in the middle of the Naka-gawa. Most atmospheric at night, the district can still make for an interesting wander during daylight. Its size is a mere 1500m long by 250m wide but is deceptive – somehow around two thousand restaurants and bars manage to squeeze themselves onto it. The weird and wonderful multicoloured blocks of **Canal City** (Ⓦwww.canalcity.co.jp), a showpiece urban renewal project inaugurated in 1996, lie near Nakasu's southernmost point. Apart from two large hotels, a major theatre and a thirteen-screen cinema with seating for nearly 2600, the complex also houses shopping arcades and a host of bars and restaurants. The liveliest part, however, is the interior court, where the pink, purple and blue buildings wrap round the "canal", which erupts on the hour with five-storey-high jets of water.

Tenjin

From Nakasu, a pedestrian bridge leads west across the Naka-gawa to Tenjin. Immediately over the river is the unusual **ACROS Fukuoka building**; meaning "Asian Crossroads Over the Sea", this was completed in 1995 as a cultural centre. Its terraced south side forms a "step garden" (daily 10am–dusk; free), giving it the vague air of an Inca ruin, while inside there is a symphony hall, an information centre (see p.656) with an interesting prefectural crafts exhibition space, shops and restaurants.

In the next block north, the **Akarenga Cultural Centre** (赤煉瓦文化館; 9am–9pm, closed Wed; free) was erected in 1909 for a life insurance company. It was designed by Tatsuno Kingo, one of Japan's first modern architects, who went in for busy, white stone detailing, domes and turrets. The interior offices, now given over to exhibition space, are more sedate and have some attractive touches, particularly the wooden ceilings and iron grillwork.

Crossing back over the Naka-gawa from here, the **Fukuoka Asian Art Museum** (福岡アジア美術館; 10am–8pm; closed Wed; ¥200; Ⓦfaam.city.fukuoka.lg.jp) is located on the seventh floor of the ritzy Hakata Riverain shopping complex. It boasts a modest but interesting collection of contemporary art from Asia, as well as temporary exhibitions. You can occasionally see artists at work in the studio upstairs. On a similarly arty bent, the **Konya2023** project – set off one of Tenjin's main pedestrian drags – is well worth popping into, its various galleries and workshops filled with youthful local fare.

Ōhori-kōen and beyond

In 1601, the Kuroda lords built their castle on a low hill sitting among coastal marshes to the west of the Naka-gawa. Today, just a few old stone walls and ruined watchtowers remain, but the castle grounds have been landscaped to form **Ōhori-kōen** (大濠公園), a large public park. It's most easily accessible from the subway; exit 3 of

Ōhori-kōen Station brings you up beside a large lake spanned by a pleasing necklace of islets and bridges. The park's foremost attraction is the **Fukuoka Art Museum** (福岡市美術館; July & Aug Tues–Sat 9.30am–7.30pm, Sun 9.30am–5.30pm; Sept–June 9.30am–5.30pm; closed Mon; ¥200; Ⓦwww.fukuoka-art-museum.jp), situated in its southeast corner. Its three ground-floor rooms contain a hotchpotch of early Japanese and Asian art, including the Kuroda family treasures and several eye-catching statues of Buddhism's twelve guardian generals (Jūni Jinsho), each crowned with his associated zodiacal beast. Upstairs you leap a few centuries to the likes of Dalí, Miró and Chagall in a great retrospective of twentieth-century Western art, displayed alongside contemporary Japanese works.

The district west of here, known as **Momochi** (モモチ), has only recently been reclaimed from the sea and handed over to ambitious city planners. By far their most striking building is the 234m, pencil-thin **Fukuoka Tower** (福岡タワー; Ⓦwww.fukuokatower.co.jp), which has become one of the city's most famous icons. The closest subway station is Nishijin, about fifteen minutes' walk to the south, or you can catch city bus #305 from Hakata and Tenjin, which stops right outside. Primarily a communications tower, its first section is an empty shell coated with 8000 sheets of mirror glass, while the top third bristles with radio transmitters. In between, at 123m, the architects slipped in an observation deck (daily 9.30am–9pm; ¥800) to capitalize on the spectacular views of Fukuoka and Hakata Bay.

Five minutes' walk south of the tower, the excellent **Fukuoka City Museum** (福岡市博物館; July & Aug Tues–Sat 9.30am–7.30pm, Sun 9.30am–5.30pm; Sept–June 9.30am–5.30pm; closed Mon; ¥200) occupies an imposing, late-1980s structure of mirrored glass and grey stone. The museum's most famous exhibit is the two-centimetre-square **Kin-in gold seal**, ornamented with a dumpy, coiled snake. According to its inscription, the seal was presented by China's Han emperor to the King of Na (see p.653) in 57 AD – it was only rediscovered in 1784 in a grave on an island in Hakata Bay.

Eating

Not surprisingly for such a cosmopolitan city, Fukuoka boasts a range of international cuisines. However, Fukuoka's most notorious **speciality food** is *fugu*, the poisonous blowfish eaten only in winter (Nov–March); though you'll find *fugu* throughout Japan, the best is said to come from the waters off northern Kyūshū. Cheaper food is on offer at the city's characteristic **yatai kitchens** (see box, p.660).

Tenjin is a good bet for traditional restaurants, particularly the **Daimyō** district, immediately west of Tenjin Nishi-dōri, which is packed with little bars and funky designer boutiques.

Alohana 2F, 1-11-4 Daimyō ⓣ092/724-0111. There's scarcely a floral shirt in sight in this contemporary, Hawaiian-owned restaurant in the thick of Daimyō. The Japanese–Hawaiian menu includes Huli-Huli barbecue chicken and *loco moco* (Hawaiian hamburger with egg, gravy and rice), washed down with Kona beer or a coconut cocktail. Lunch plates at ¥700, or count on ¥2000 upwards in the evening. Reservations recommended at weekends. Mon–Thurs noon–2pm & 6pm–3am, Fri & Sat noon–4pm & 6pm–5am, Sun 6pm–3am.

Chikae 稚加榮 2-2-17 Daimyō ⓣ092/721-4624. Famous fish restaurant where you sit at a counter overlooking the fish tanks, or at tables to the side. Kimono-clad staff bustle about bearing platters laden with ultra-fresh sashimi and sushi, adding to the spectacle. It's a good place to try the local speciality *Karashi mentaiko* (spicy fish eggs), as well as *fugu*. Sashimi platters start at around ¥2000, sushi at ¥2700. Daily 11am–10pm.

Nanak 2F, 1-1-4 Maizuru. On the corner of Showa-dōri and Oyafukō-dōri, this branch of the reliable, long-established Indian chain offers excellent-value lunchtime sets and reasonable evening menus. Outside of these special deals, count on around ¥2000/head. Mon–Fri 11am–5.30pm, Sat & Sun 11am–10.30pm.

Yatai

Forget the sights – *this* is Fukuoka. Come evening, steam billows out from more than one hundred **mobile street-kitchens**, each cocooning a fascinating little world of their own. Customers push their way through a thin drape of plastic sheets to find a garrulous clutch of locals, crammed onto narrow benches and filling up on scrumptious food – pork-based **tonkotsu ramen** is the meal of choice (¥600 or so), usually accompanied by flasks of sake and a few new friends. Mobile in nature, none of these **yatai** has a fixed location, but this being Japan they rarely venture too far from their original mark, and you'll usually find them open from 7pm–3am. The greatest concentrations of *yatai* are around the intersection of Tenjin Nishi-dōri and Shōwa-dōri, and along the southwest bank of Nakasu Island. These are some of the most enjoyable places to eat in all Japan, and the focus on merry-making means that any noisy *yatai* is worth a go, but a few certainly stand out from the crowd.

Ebi-chan えびちゃん. All *yatai* have beer and sake, but this goes further, its menu containing no fewer than fifty cocktails, as well as Italian-themed food. There's a ¥400 sit-down charge.

Shizue しずえ. The tricolour on the outside isn't just a decoration: amazingly, this *yatai* serves no ramen; even more amazingly, its menu is based upon French cuisine. Beef in red wine sauce at a *yatai*? Somehow, it works.

Taka-chan たかちゃん. *Kokin-chan* is a local institution, having dished out ramen for over four decades. But here's the secret – the place next door is just as good, and you won't have to queue for an hour to get in.

Tsukasa 司 ⓦyatai-tsukasa.com. The best of a clutch on the riverside (it even has a website), this shack specializes in *mentaiko* tempura – spicy cod roe fried in batter. Mmm...oishii.

Ume-no-hana 梅の花 B2, ACROS Building, 1-1-1 Tenjin ⓣ092/725-9022. Popular chain restaurant specializing in melt-in-the mouth tofu creations. Try their *yudōfu* set lunch (¥1600), where you boil the tofu at the table, then eat it with grated ginger and a sprinkling of ground sesame, accompanied by all sorts of other delicacies. They also have an attractive branch in Dazaifu (see p.662). Daily 11am–2.30pm & 5–9pm.

Uosue 魚末 2-1-30 Daimyō ⓣ092/713-7931. Small, traditional sashimi restaurant famous for having the freshest fish in town. Menus change daily and you should expect to pay at least ¥3000 for a satisfying meal – stick to items with a price tag (indicating the day's market price) to avoid any nasty shocks. Even on weekdays it pays to make a reservation, or get here at 6pm. Tues–Sun 6pm to late.

Drinking

Fukuoka's famous **Nakasu** nightlife district is crammed full of clubs, restaurants and bars, as well as a whole clutch of seedier establishments aimed at Japanese businessmen. It's a great area to wander round, but most places are extortionately expensive and only take customers by recommendation, if they accept foreigners at all. A happier hunting ground lies around Tenjin's main crossroads, particularly **Oyafukō-dōri** and the streets immediately to the east, which are packed with bars and clubs. Roughly translated, Oyafukō-dōri means "street of disobedient children", originally referring to a local school but nowadays more applicable to groups of drunken college kids who gather here at weekends under the blind eye of the *kōban* on the corner.

The Craic and the Porter 2F, 3-5-16 Tenjin. Still going strong thanks to a superb, ever-changing roster of draught beers and ales (¥900/pint), this tiny Irish pub makes a nice change from the norm, and is a good place for a chat. Mon–Wed 2pm–2am, Thurs–Sun 7pm–4am.

Fu Bar 4F, 3-6-12 Tenjin. This DJ bar is popular with foreigners and locals alike, largely thanks to a winning cocktail of good music and cheap booze – drink all night for ¥3000 if you're a chap, ¥2000 if you're a lady. 9pm–late; closed Mon.

Happy Cock 9F, 2-1-51 Daimyō ⓣ092/734-2686. It's elbow room only at weekends in this large, laidback bar just off Tenjin Nishi-dōri. DJs, party nights and all-you-can-eat-and-drink deals pull a younger crowd. Cover charge Fri & Sat ¥1200 including two drinks. Wed–Thurs 7pm–1am, weekends to 5am.

International Bar 4F, 3-1-13 Tenjin. This ordinary little bar is a good place to meet local *gaijin*. No cover charge and inexpensive bar food. Look out for the English sign on the main street opposite the Matsuya Ladies store, north of the main Tenjin crossroads. Daily from 6.30pm.

Off Broadway 2F, 1-8-40 Maizuru ⓣ092/724-5383. Imagine a processed chunk of New York – fries, burgers and buffalo wings fill up a sophisticated, multinational clientele, who find themselves serenaded by jazz and Latin music (live most weekends). 7.30pm–late; closed Mon.

Voodoo Lounge 3F, 3-2-13 Tenjin. Boogie the night away or chill out among the jungle palms in this capacious bar tucked off Oyafukō-dōri. Stages an eclectic programme of DJs, live bands and other events. Entry charges and opening times vary.

Entertainment

Fukuoka is large enough to be on the circuit for pop stars, musicals and major theatre productions. The main venues are Canal City's Fukuoka City Theatre (ⓣ092/271-1199, ⓦwww.shiki.gr.jp), ACROS Symphony Hall (ⓣ092-725-9113), Hakata-za in the Hakata Riverain complex (which occasionally stages kabuki; ⓣ092/263-5858, ⓦwww.hakataza.co.jp), and, for the real biggies, the Fukuoka Dome and Zepp (ⓣ092/832-6639, ⓦwww.zepp.co.jp) in Hawks Town. To find out what's on, consult the *Rainbow* newsletter and *Fukuoka Now* (see p.656) or ask at any of the tourist offices; tickets are available through PIA (ⓣ092/708-9999), which has an outlet next to the tourist office on the second floor of the ACROS Building.

Film fans should check the current week's showings at United Cinema's thirteen-screen multiplex on Canal City's fourth floor (¥1800 all day Sat and before 9am Sun–Fri, ¥1000 after 9pm Sun–Fri. They also operate a ten-screen cinema in Hawks Town.

Listings

Airport information Domestic flights ⓣ092/621-6059, international flights ⓣ092/483-7007; ⓦwww.fuk-ab.co.jp. Fukuoka airport has separate terminals for domestic and international flights, linked by a free shuttle-bus service (10–15min). The subway station is located in the domestic terminal.

Banks and exchange There are ATMs in both airport terminals. You can change money at Fukuoka Bank in the international terminal. Fukuoka Bank also offers foreign exchange facilities at its branches outside the front west entrance of Hakata Station and next to the IMS Building in Tenjin. You can also change money at the two main post offices (see p.662).

Bookshops For foreigh-language books, try: Maruzen, in Tenjin on the corner of Watanabe-dōri

Fukuoka festivals and events

Hakata celebrates a whole host of **festivals**, of which the biggest are the **Gion Yamakasa** (July 1–15) and the **Hakata Dontaku**, now held during Golden Week (May 3 & 4). In feudal times, Hakata townspeople were permitted across the river once a year to convey New Year greetings to their lord. Today's festival centres on a parade along Meiji-dōri to the old castle (see p.658). On a similarly traditional theme, the sumo circus comes to town each November for Japan's last *basho* of the season, at Fukuoka's Kokusai Centre (ⓦwww.sumo.or.jp). A much more recent invention is the **Isla de Salsa** (ⓦwww.tiempo.jp), a Latin music festival held mid-August on Nokonoshima island, a ten-minute ferry ride from Fukuoka.

and Meiji-dōri; Junkudō, in the next block east in the MMT Building; or Kinokuniya, near Hakata Station.

Buses Long-distance buses depart from the bus centre next to Hakata Station, with a stop at Tenjin. There are connections to major cities on Kyūshū, as well as express buses to Ōsaka.

Car rental Budget (Ⓣ092/473-0543), Eki Rent-a-Car (Ⓣ092/431-8775) and Toyota Rent-a-Car (Ⓣ092/441-0100) all have offices in or near Hakata Station.

Consulates Australia, 7F, 1-6-8 Tenjin Ⓣ092/734-5055, Ⓦwww.consular.australia.or.jp/fukuoka; China, 1-3-3 Jigyohama Ⓣ092/713-1121, Ⓔchinaconsul_fuk_jp@mfa.gov.cn; South Korea, 1-1-3 Jigyohama Ⓣ092/771-0461, Ⓔfukuoka@mofat.go.kr; US, 2-5-26 Ōhori Ⓣ092/751-9331, Ⓦjapan.usembassy.gov.

Emergencies The main police station is at 7-7 Higashikoen, Hakata-ku (Ⓣ092/641-4141). In an absolute emergency contact the Foreign Advisory Service on Ⓣ092/733-2220. For other emergency numbers, see p.71.

Hospitals The largest general hospital with English-speaking staff is National Kyūshū Medical Centre, 1-8-1 Jigyohama (Ⓣ092/852-0700), near Hawks Town. More centrally, there's Saiseikai Fukuoka General Hospital, 1-3-46 Tenjin (Ⓣ092/771-8151), south of the ACROS building.

Immigration For visa renewals, contact Fukuoka Regional Immigration Bureau, 1–22 Okihama-chō, Hakata-ku (Ⓣ092/281-7431).

Internet The Fukuoka International Association (8F, IMS Building, 1-7-11 Tenjin; daily 10am–8pm, closed third Tues of the month; take your passport or other ID) has free internet, as does the basement of Hakata Riverain shopping mall (daily 10am–7pm). *Café Estación* (daily 7am–10.20pm), just inside the east entrance of Hakata Station, has almost-free access – the cost is the price of a drink.

Police Ⓣ092/641-4141.

Post offices Fukuoka Central Post Office (4-3-1 Tenjin), just north of Tenjin subway station, offers foreign exchange and a 24hr mail service. There's another big branch beside the west exit of Hakata Station.

Shopping Fukuoka's big department stores are grouped around the main crossroads in Tenjin and south along Watanabe-dōri, and around Hakata Station. They all sell a selection of local crafts, the most famous of which are Hakata *ningyō*, hand-painted, unglazed clay dolls fashioned as samurai, kabuki actors, or demure, kimono-clad women. *Champon* are long-stemmed, glass toys with a bowl at the end which make a clicking sound when you blow into them, while Hakata *ori* is far more transportable – slightly rough silk fabric traditionally used for *obi* (sashes worn with kimono), but now made into ties, wallets and bags. Apart from the big stores, try Hakata Machiya Furusato-kan (p.658), the Kawabata-dōri arcade (p.657) or Hakata Station's underground arcades for local souvenirs.

Travel agents For domestic travel, JTB (Ⓣ092/733-1300) has English-speaking staff; there are branches in the two train stations and another in the basement of Iwataya department store to the west of Nishitetsu Fukuoka Station. International travel can be arranged through H.I.S, 2F, 2-7-9 Tenjin (Ⓣ092/736-8661, Ⓦwww.his-j.com), by the junction of Tenjin Nishi-dōri and Meiji-dōri, and No 1 Travel, 3F, ACROS Building, 1-1-1 Tenjin (Ⓣ092/761-9203, Ⓦwww.no1-travel.com/fuk).

Dazaifu and Futsukaichi Onsen

A mere 15km southeast of Fukuoka, **DAZAIFU** (太宰府) only just breaks free of the urban sprawl, but manages to retain a definite country air. The town is very much on Kyūshū's tourist map, thanks to the important **Kyūshū National Museum**. The crowd of art lovers and historians gets a boost in late February and March, when plum blossoms signal both the start of spring and the onset of the exam season, and anxious students descend on **Tenman-gū**, Japan's foremost shrine dedicated to the god of learning. Thankfully, the nearby **temples** and other historical relics remain surprisingly peaceful. Everything is within easy walking distance of the station, making it possible to cover the main sights in a day. A popular stop en route to or from Dazaifu is **Futsukaichi Onsen**, around 3km further south, where you can take a dip in its healing waters.

Dazaifu rose to prominence in the late seventh century, when the emperor established a regional seat of government and military headquarters (known as the Dazaifu) here, responsible for defence, trade and diplomatic ties, particularly with

China and Korea. For more than five hundred years successive governor generals ruled Kyūshū from Dazaifu, protected by a series of ditches, embankments and hilltop fortresses, until political circumstances changed in the twelfth century and the town gradually fell into decline.

Arrival and information

The easiest way of **getting to Dazaifu** from Fukuoka is on a private Nishitetsu train from Tenjin's Nishitetsu-Fukuoka Station (30min; ¥390), while those heading to the onsen should take a train from JR Hakata Station to JR Futsukaichi Station (15–20min; ¥270). Ten minutes' walk north of this there's a station on the Nishitetsu line (Nishitetsu-Futsukaichi), making it possible to combine Dazaifu and the onsen with a five-minute train ride and a gentle stroll.

Right outside Dazaifu station is a **tourist office** (daily 9am–5.30pm; ⓣ092/925-1880) with local maps and brochures in English. Ask at the station ticket window if you'd like to rent a **bike** (from ¥300/3hr; 9am–6pm) for visiting the western sights. Futsukaichi's **tourist office** (daily 9am–6pm; ⓣ092/922-2421) is inside the JR station.

Accommodation

Most travellers visit the area on a day-trip from Fukuoka, but there are accommodation options in Dazaifu and Futsukaichi Onsen for those wanting a break from city life.

Daimaru Bessō 大丸別荘 Futsukaichi Onsen ⓣ092/924-3939. An atmospheric old ryokan on the south side of town, set round a traditional garden of pine trees and carp ponds. The beautifully appointed tatami rooms include two meals, and the use of their huge hot-spring bath. ❾

Guest House Dazaifu ゲストハウス太宰府 ⓣ092/922-8740. A convenient, relaxed and welcoming B&B in a grand position up on a hill 10min walk north of Dazaifu Station. ❹

Ivy Hotel Futsukaichi Onsen ⓣ092/920-2130. This ivy-clad business hotel next to the Baden House public bath (see p.666) offers somewhat more ordinary accommodation than *Guest House Dazaifu*, but its functional Western- and Japanese-style rooms – two with their own private onsen bath – are a good option for those on a tighter budget. ❹

Masuya Dong Dazaifu ⓣ092/929-1225. A B&B on the far west side of town, about 10min walk north of Tofurō-mae Station on the Nishitetsu line. The private rooms (not en suite) and dorms are spick-and-span and grouped around an attractive patio. You can rent bikes here (¥500/day) for visiting the sights. ❸

The Town

It's a short walk east from the tourist office up Tenjin-sama-dōri to Dazaifu's main historical sight, **Tenman-gū** (天満宮; daily 7am–7pm; free; Ⓦwww.dazaifutenmangu.or.jp), a tenth-century shrine dedicated to Tenjin, the guardian deity of scholars, also known as Sugawara-no-Michizane (see box, p.664).

The approach to Tenman-gū lies over an allegorical stone bridge, **Taiko-bashi**; its first, steep arch represents the past, the present is flat, while the final, gentler hump indicates difficulties yet to come. While negotiating the bridge, take a close look at the second of the two little shrines on the right, which was constructed in 1458 – its intricate, Chinese-style roof shelters some particularly fine carving. Beyond, a two-storey gate leads into a courtyard dominated by the main **worship hall**, built in 1591 but resplendent in bright red and gold lacquer under its manicured thatch. A twisted plum tree stands immediately to the right (east) of the hall. Known as the "flying plum tree", it's said to be over a thousand years old and, according to legend, originally grew in Michizane's Kyoto garden. On the eve of his departure he wrote a farewell poem to the tree, but that night it upped roots and "flew" ahead of him to Dazaifu. To the left and behind the worship hall, a

The story of Tenjin

Tenjin is the divine name of **Sugawara-no-Michizane**, a brilliant scholar of the Heian period, who died in Dazaifu in 903 AD. By all accounts, Michizane was a precocious youngster – composing *waka* poems at five years old and Chinese poetry by the age of eleven – and went on to become a popular governor of Shikoku before rising to the second-highest position at court as "Minister of the Right". Not surprisingly, he found no favour with his powerful superior, Fujiwara Tokihira, who persuaded the emperor to banish Michizane. So, in 901 Michizane, accompanied by his son, daughter and a retainer, travelled south to take up a "post" as deputy governor of Dazaifu. He was kept under armed guard until he died in despair – though still loyal to the emperor – two years later. Soon after, a succession of national disasters was attributed to Michizane's restless spirit, so in 919 Tenman-gū was founded to pray for his repose. This was the first of an estimated 12,000 shrines dedicated to Tenjin in Japan.

modern building houses a small **museum** (9am–4.30pm; closed Tues; ¥200) detailing the life of Michizane through a series of tableaux. And you can see a few older portraits, alongside a poem supposedly written by Michizane and other historical items, in the **treasure house** (9am–4.20pm; closed Mon; ¥300), set back to your left as you leave the main compound.

Kyūshū National Museum and Kōmyōzen-ji

A path beside the treasure house leads to an escalator that tunnels through the rock to emerge beside a magnificent, wave-shaped building that houses the **Kyūshū National Museum** (九州国立博物館; 9.30am–5pm; closed Mon; ¥420; Ⓦwww.kyuhaku.com). Japan's fourth national museum after Tokyo, Kyoto and Nara, it focuses on the history of Japan's cultural trade with other Asian countries and illustrates the profound impact these interactions had on local art and culture. It's fascinating to see Chinese, Korean, Japanese and Egyptian ceramics side by side, and to compare Japanese Buddhist statues, musical instruments and lacquer ware with those from neighbouring countries. The permanent exhibition hall, on the fourth floor, is beautifully laid out, comprising five themed spaces and auxiliary galleries covering prehistoric times to the Edo period; before going in, make sure you pick up a free audio guide at the desk. The museum also hosts major temporary exhibitions.

Returning to Tenman-gū, walk south from the shrine entrance for about 100m to find the small, serene temple of **Kōmyōzen-ji** (光明禅寺; daily 8am–5pm; ¥200 donation), founded in the mid-thirteenth century. It's an appealing collection of simple, wooden buildings whose tatami rooms contain Buddha figures or works of art. There's usually no one around, but you're welcome to explore – take your shoes off and follow the polished wooden corridors round to the rear, where there's a contemplative garden made up of a gravel sea swirling round moss-covered headlands and jutting rocks, caught against a wooded hillside. The stones in the garden at the front of the temple are arranged in the character for "light", referring to the halo of the Buddha.

Kanzeon-ji and Kaidan-in

Dazaifu's two other major sights lie about twenty minutes' walk – or a short bicycle ride – west of the station; to avoid the main road, turn right in front of the post office to pick up a riverside path and then follow signs pointing you along a quiet lane. Take a left down a footpath just before a set of old foundation stones lying in the grass and the route brings you to the back of **Kanzeon-ji** (観世音寺). Founded in 746 AD by Emperor Tenji in honour of his mother, Empress Saimei, at one time Kanzeon-ji was the largest temple in all Kyūshū and even rated a mention in the great eleventh-century novel *The Tale of Genji* (see p.784). Only some Buddhist statues and the bronze **bell**, the oldest in Japan, remain from the original temple, while the present buildings – unadorned and nicely faded – date from the seventeenth century.

Kanzeon-ji's main hall holds a graceful standing Buddha, but you'll find its most magnificent statues in the modern **treasure house** (daily 9am–5pm; ¥500), to the right as you face the hall. The immediate impression is of the sheer power of the huge wooden figures, of which even the newest is at least 750 years old. The oldest is Tobatsu-Bishamonten, standing second in line, which was sculpted from a single block of camphor wood in the eighth century. An informative English brochure provides further details, starting with the **jizō** figure facing you as you come up the stairs and working clockwise from there.

From the treasure house, walk west in front of Kanzeon-ji towards the two-tiered roof of **Kaidan-in** (戒壇院), built in the late eighth century for the

Takeo and Huis ten Bosch

Those heading between Fukuoka and Nagasaki by train may care to stop off at two beguiling sights on the way. Squeezed into a narrow valley is the pleasant resort of **TAKEO** (武雄), whose onsen buildings are ten minutes' walk northwest of the station behind a squat, Chinese-style gate. First on the left through the gate is Moto-yu (元湯; daily 6.30am–midnight; ¥300), the most traditional of the **public baths**. If you prefer outdoor bathing, the nearby *Ryokan Kagetsu* (旅館花月; ⓣ0954/22-3108, ⓦwww.kagetsu-r.jp; ❺) has a beautiful rotemburo (daily 3–9pm; ¥700). Takeo often tempts its visitors to stay the night, and there are several ryokan gathered round } the onsen.

Opened in 1992 at a cost of ¥250 billion, the resort town of **HUIS TEN BOSCH** (ハウステンボス; ⓦenglish.huistenbosch.co.jp) is a meticulously engineered replica of an old Dutch port. Part theme park, part serious experiment in urban living, it owes its existence to the drive and vision of **Kamichika Yoshikuni**, a local entrepreneur who was so impressed with Dutch land reclamation and environmental management that he persuaded his financiers it could work in Japan as a commercial venture. While the result may seem quaintly old world, it's equipped with the latest technology to manage its sophisticated heating systems, wave control, desalination, water recycling and security. All the pipes, cables and wires are hidden underground and it's designed to be as environmentally benign as possible.

The town (daily 9am–8.30pm) is divided into an exclusive residential district, Wassenaar, and public areas where you'll find a raft of museums and attractions, plus dozens of souvenir shops and numerous restaurants. The basic **ticket** (¥3200) covers entry only, although once inside you can buy a pass card covering most attractions (¥2400), or pay for them individually. Three of these stand out – the **Great Voyage Theatre** screens a short film about the first Dutch ships to reach Japan, during which the whole seating area pitches and rolls; in **Mysterious Escher** you enter a topsy-turvy world to watch a sickly sweet but well-executed 3D film based on Escher's famous graphics; and **Horizon Adventure** stages a real-life flood with 800 tonnes of water cascading into the theatre.

The easiest way of getting to the resort is on JR's special **Huis ten Bosch Express** direct from Fukuoka (1hr 45min; ¥2070) or the *Seaside Liner* from Nagasaki (90min; ¥1430). For those in a hurry, high-speed boats zip across Ōmura Bay direct to Huis ten Bosch from Nagasaki airport (3 daily; 50min; ¥1600). Huis ten Bosch can easily be explored in a day, but should you decide to stay there are hotels on-site, as well as a huge choice of restaurants and cafés.

ordination of Buddhist priests. This is one of only three such ordination halls in Japan – the other two being in Tochigi and Nara – and again the statuary is of interest, in this case an eleven-headed Kannon from the Heian period, dressed in fading gold.

Futsukaichi Onsen

People have been coming to **FUTSUKAICHI ONSEN** (二日市温泉) since at least the eighth century to soothe muscle pain, skin complaints and digestive troubles in its healing waters. Despite being the closest hot spring to Fukuoka, the resort is still surprisingly undeveloped. There are three **public baths** (daily 9am–9pm), all grouped together in the centre of Futsukaichi, about ten minutes' walk south of JR Futsukaichi Station. The first, and easiest to spot by its English sign, is Baden House (¥460) – it's also the biggest, with a small rotemburo and sauna as well as a variety of other pools, though it is beginning to show its age. In the attractive, old-style building next door, Hakata-yu (博多湯; ¥300) is a small but spruce bathhouse favoured by Futsukaichi's senior citizenry, while over the road Gozen-yu (御前湯; ¥200) is another good option with three large pools.

Eating

By far the best restaurant in Dazaifu is *Ume-no-hana* (梅の花; daily 11am–3.30pm & 4.30–9pm; ⓣ0120-28-7787, ⓦwww.umenohana.co.jp), in the lanes east of Kōmyōzen-ji, which is worth tracking down for its melt-in-the-mouth tofu creations served in tatami rooms overlooking a pretty garden. Set meals start at ¥2500, or ¥3000 on Sundays; try to arrive before noon if you haven't got a reservation. Otherwise, there are a number of places along Tenjin-sama-dōri, where *Yasutake* (やす武; daily 10am–6pm) is popular for its inexpensive handmade soba dishes; find it on the right just beyond the first *torii*. Afterwards, try the local delicacy, *Umegae-mochi*, a steamed rice cake stuffed with sweet, red-bean paste on sale all along Tenjin-sama-dōri. In Futsukaichi Onsen, the *Daimaru Bessō* (see p.663) is a grand place in which to enjoy a gourmet meal.

Nagasaki

Not particularly ancient, nor possessing any absolutely compelling sights, **NAGASAKI** (長崎) is nevertheless one of Japan's more picturesque cities, gathered in the tucks and crevices of steep hills rising from a long, narrow harbour. Nagasaki's appeal lies in its easy-going attitude and an unusually cosmopolitan culture, resulting from over two centuries of contact with foreigners when the rest of Japan was closed to the world, and cemented by its distance from Tokyo.

Nagasaki would probably have remained little more than a pleasant, attractive city with a bustling harbour if a chance break in the clouds on August 9, 1945, hadn't seared it into the world's consciousness as the target of the second **atomic bomb** dropped on Japan. It's the A-Bomb hypocentre and nearby museum, as harrowing as that in Hiroshima, that brings most people to Nagasaki, yet the city has much else to offer. Successive communities of Chinese, Dutch, Portuguese and British have left their mark here, building colourful **Chinese temples**, Catholic **churches** and an array of European-style houses gathered in Glover Garden, as well as imported cuisines and festivals. Despite efforts to stamp out another European import, the Catholic faith, Nagasaki remains Japan's centre of **Christianity**, claiming one-sixth of the country's believers. It's possible to cover the two main areas – the hypocentre and around Glover Garden – in a day, but Nagasaki deserves at least one extra night's stopover to explore its backstreets, soak up some atmosphere and sample a few of the city's culinary treats.

Some history

Portuguese traders first sailed into Nagasaki in 1570, establishing a trading post and **Jesuit mission** in what was then a small fishing village of just 1500 inhabitants. For a brief period, Christianity was a major influence here, but in the late sixteenth century Toyotomi Hideyoshi, fearing the missionaries would be followed by military intervention, started to move against the Church. Though the persecutions came in fits and starts, one of the more dramatic events occurred in Nagasaki in 1597 when Hideyoshi ordered the crucifixion of 26 Franciscans.

After 1616 the new shogun, Tokugawa Hidetada, gradually took control of all dealings with foreigners, and by the late 1630s only Chinese and Portuguese merchants continued to trade out of Nagasaki. The latter were initially confined to a tiny island enclave called **Dejima**, but in 1639 they too were expelled following a Christian-led rebellion in nearby Shimabara (see p.679). Two years later, their place on Dejima was filled by Dutch merchants who had endeared themselves to the

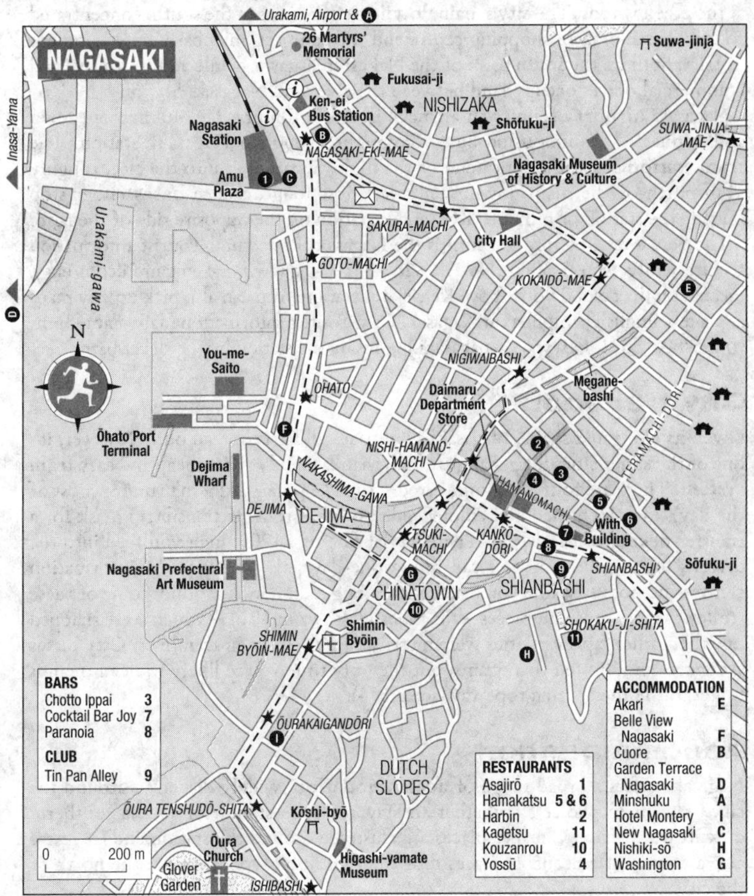

shogun by sending a warship against the rebels. For the next two hundred years this tiny Dutch group, together with a slightly larger Chinese community, provided Japan's only link with the outside world. Dutch imports such as coffee, chocolate, billiards and badminton were introduced to Japan via Dejima.

Eventually, the restrictions began to ease, especially after the early seventeenth century, when technical books were allowed into Nagasaki, making the city once again Japan's main conduit for **Western learning**. Nevertheless, it wasn't until 1858 that five ports, including Nagasaki, opened for general trade. America, Britain and other nations established diplomatic missions as Nagasaki's foreign community mushroomed and its economy boomed. New inventions flooded in: the printing press, brick-making and modern shipbuilding techniques all made their Japanese debut in Nagasaki. Then came high-scale industrial development and, of course, the events of 1945 (see p.671).

Arrival and information

Nagasaki is a long, thin city that fills the flatland beside the harbour, spreads its tentacles along tributary valleys and is slowly creeping up the hillsides, eating away at the green woods. The city's main **downtown** area lies in the south, concentrated round Hamanomachi shopping centre and the compact Shianbashi entertainment district, both on the south bank of the Nakashima-gawa, while administrative and commercial offices occupy land between the river and Nagasaki Station.

Nagasaki **airport** occupies an artificial island in Ōmura Bay, 40km from town and connected by limousine bus (40min–1hr; ¥800) to Nagasaki Station. The **train station** sits at the south end of the highway running into the city, roughly 1km north of the main downtown area. Most long-distance **buses** either stop outside the station or pull into Ken-ei bus station on the opposite side of the road.

The best source of **information** is the Nagasaki Prefectural Tourist Information Centre (daily 9am–5.30pm; ⓣ095/828-7875, ⓦwww.ngs-kenkanren.com/eng), located on the second floor above Ken-ei bus station. You can also pick up city maps and a few English pamphlets at Nagasaki City Tourist Information (daily 8am–8pm; ⓣ095/823-3631, ⓦwww.at-nagasaki.jp), inside the station by the ticket barrier.

City transport

Given its elongated shape, Nagasaki's sights are all fairly spread out. However, it's one of the easier cities for getting around, thanks mainly to its cheap and easy **tram system**. There are four lines, numbered #1 to #5 (line #2 doesn't run for most of the day), each identified and colour coded on the front. If transferring, ask for a transfer ticket (*norikae-kippu*). There's a flat fare of ¥120 which you feed into the driver's box on exit, or you can buy a one-day pass (¥500) at the information centres and hotels. While you're clanking along, take a look around: some of these trolley cars are museum pieces – the oldest dates from 1911 – which were snapped up when other Japanese cities were merrily ripping up their tramlines. **City buses** are more complicated than trams, but the only time you're likely to need them is to get to the Inasa-yama ropeway (see p.674).

Accommodation

Nagasaki offers a broad range of **accommodation**, widely dispersed around the city. The main choice is whether to stay near the station or in the southern, downtown district. Cheaper places are clustered around the station and there are also a couple of reasonable places near the A-Bomb Hypocentre, in the north of the city.

Akari 2-2 Kojiya-machi ⓣ095/801-7900, ⓦwww.nagasaki-hostel.com. A real backpacker favourite, with clued-up, super-friendly staff, comfy dorms, a cool common room and a pleasant canalside location. Dorms from ¥2500, doubles ❸

Hotel Belle View Nagasaki 1-20 Edo-machi ⓣ095/826-5030. Reasonably priced business hotel with friendly and efficient service plus a restaurant, bar and free internet access in all rooms. Rates include a buffet breakfast. ❸

Hotel Cuore 7-3 Daikoku-machi ⓣ095/818-9000. Spruce business hotel opposite the station. Everything you could possibly need, including trouser press and tea-making equipment, is squeezed into the smallest space imaginable in the single rooms; doubles and twins are slightly more spacious. Rates include a good buffet breakfast. ❹

Garden Terrace Nagasaki 1-20 Akizuki-machi ⓣ095/864-7777. Imagine a giant Rubik's Cube made of pine, and you're halfway to visualising award-winning architect Kengo Kuma's classy boutique hotel. Sitting halfway up a mountain on the "other" side of the bay, its various suites are decked out with angular furniture, and each provides a wonderful city view – in some cases, even from the bathtub. ❾

Minshuku Tanpopo 民宿たんぽぽ 21-7 Hoei-chō ⓣ095/861-6230, ⓦwww.tanpopo-group.biz/tanpopo. Tidy minshuku near Peace Park, with good-value tatami rooms and well-priced meals. If you phone in advance, a pick-up service from JR Urakami Station is sometimes available. ❻

Hotel Monterey 1-22 Ōura-machi ⓣ095/827-7111, ⓦwww.hotelmonterey.co.jp. Good location, smartly designed rooms, attentive service and free internet connections – not bad, in other words. Big discounts often await those who book online. ❻

Hotel New Nagasaki 14-5 Daikoku-machi ⓣ095/826-8000, ⓦwww.newnaga.com. Central Nagasaki's top hotel, conveniently placed just outside the station, has all the trimmings: grand marble lobby, shopping arcade, restaurants, bar and fitness centre with swimming pool. The rooms are mostly Western-style, some boasting harbour views. ❼

Nishiki-sō にしき荘 1-2-7 Nishikoshima ⓣ095/826-6371, ⓕ828-0782. If you're after a bit of Japanese flavour, try this welcoming budget guesthouse on the far east side of town, up a short flight of steps. There's a choice of well-kept tatami rooms with or without views or en-suite facilities. ❸

Washington Hotel 9-1 Shinchi-machi ⓣ095/828-1211, ⓦwww.nagasaki-wh.com. Located in Chinatown, this is a standard member of the *Washington* chain, but with a good selection of rooms. Facilities include a restaurant and coffee lounge. ❺

The City

Nagasaki's principal sights are widely spread, starting in the north with the Peace Park and the gruelling but informative **Atomic Bomb Museum**. From there it's a tram ride down to Nagasaki Station and a gentle stroll along the slopes of **Nishizaka** from the **26 Martyrs' Memorial**, via Nagasaki's informative new history museum, to its most imposing shrine, Suwa-jinja. The focus of interest in the central district is a row of quiet **temples**, and the former Dutch enclave of **Dejima**.

Down in the far south, several European houses have been preserved on the former hilltop concession, now known as **Glover Garden**, overlooking Nagasaki's magnificent harbour and a colourful Confucian shrine. To round it all off, take a twilight ropeway ride up to the top of **Inasa-yama** before hitting the bars and clubs of **Shianbashi**.

The Atomic Bomb Museum and around

As you walk around the district of **Urakami** (浦上) it's hard to link the quiet, reasonably prosperous residential suburban streets with the scenes of utter devastation left by the atomic explosion on August 9, 1945. If you've already visited Hiroshima (see p.549), which was destroyed by a similar bomb three days earlier, Nagasaki's memorials might seem a little less striking. However, the museum is notable for its balanced approach.

One enters the **Atomic Bomb Museum** (長崎原爆資料館; 8.30am–5.30pm; ¥200; ⓦwww1.city.nagasaki.nagasaki.jp/peace) via a symbolic, spiralling descent. Views of prewar Nagasaki then lead abruptly into a darkened room full of twisted iron girders, blackened masonry and videos constantly scrolling through horrific

photos of the dead and dying. It's strong stuff, occasionally too much for some, but the most moving exhibits are always those single fragments of an individual life – a charred lunchbox, twisted pair of glasses or the chilling shadow of a man etched on wooden planks.

The purpose of the museum isn't only to shock, and the displays are packed with information, much of it in English, tracing the history of atomic weapons, the effects of the bomb and the heroic efforts of ill-equipped emergency teams who had little idea what they were facing. There's a fascinating video library of interviews with survivors, including some of the foreigners present in Nagasaki at the time; figures vary, but probably more than 12,000 of these were killed in the blast, mostly Korean forced-labour working in the Mitsubishi shipyards, as well as Dutch, Australian and British prisoners of war. The museum then broadens out to examine the whole issue of nuclear weapons and ends with a depressing video about the arms race and test ban treaties.

Just outside the museum is **Hypocentre Park**, where an austere black pillar marks the exact spot where the bomb exploded 500m above the ground. The neighbouring **Peace Memorial Hall** (daily: May–Aug 8.30am–6.30pm; Sept–April 8.30am–5.30pm; free), also buried underground, is another place for quiet reflection, its centrepiece a remembrance hall where the names of victims are recorded in 141 volumes.

The Peace Park

A short way further north, a long flight of steps leads up into the **Peace Park**, or *Heiwa-kōen* (平和公園) – as popular among anti-nuclear lobbyists trawling for signatures as it is for young kids skateboarding among the donated plaques and memorials – watched over by sculptor Kitamura Seibō's muscular **Peace Statue**. The figure, right hand pointing skyward at the threat of nuclear destruction, left extended to hold back the forces of evil, was unveiled in 1955. As Kazuo Ishiguro remarked in *A Pale View of the Hills* (see p.817), from a distance the figure resembles a "policeman conducting traffic", but when some elderly figure pauses on the way past, head bowed, it's not easy to remain cynical.

From the Peace Park you can see the twin red-brick towers of **Urakami Cathedral** (浦上大聖堂), dominating a small rise 400m to the east. The present building is a postwar replica of the original, which was completed in 1925 and destroyed when the atomic bomb exploded only 500m away. The blast left scorch marks on the statues now preserved at the top of the steps, and tore off huge chunks of masonry, including a section of the bell tower which still rests on the bank under the north wall. Inside the south door, a chapel is dedicated to the "Bombed Mary", from whose charred face stare sightless eyes.

Along Nishizaka

East of Nagasaki Station, a quiet lane hugs **Nishizaka** hillside, starting in the north at a bizarre, mosaic-clad church dedicated to Japan's first Christian martyrs. In 1597, six foreign missionaries and twenty Japanese converts were the unlucky victims of the shogunate's growing unease at the power of the Church. They were marched from Kyoto and Ōsaka to Nagasaki, where they were crucified on February 2 as a warning to others. The group was canonized in 1862, and a century later the **26 Martyrs' Memorial** (日本二十六人殉教地), was erected on the site, together with a small **museum** (daily 9am–5pm; ¥250) telling the history – mostly in Japanese – of the martyrs and of Christianity in Japan. A surprising amount survives, including tissue-thin prayer books hidden in bamboo and statues of the Virgin Mary disguised as the goddess Kannon. One document records the bounties offered to informers: 500 silver pieces per priest, down to 100 for a lowly catechist.

Heading southeast along Nishizaka, a giant statue of Kannon marks **Fukusai-ji** (福済寺; daily 7am–4pm; ¥200). The original Zen temple, founded in 1628, was destroyed in 1945 by the bomb and replaced with a tasteless, turtle-shaped building topped by the 18m-tall, aluminium-alloy goddess and a circle of supplicating infants. Inside, a 25m-long Foucault's pendulum represents a perpetual prayer for peace, oscillating over the remains of 16,500 Japanese war-dead buried underneath. Of much greater interest is nearby **Shōfuku-ji** (聖福寺), another early seventeenth-century Zen temple, although it was rebuilt in 1715 and survived the bomb. Inside the imposing gateway you'll find an attractive collection of aged wooden buildings surrounded by rustling bamboo stands and shady trees. Its main attributes are some detailed carving on the gates and unusual decorative features such as the red balustrade around the worship hall.

Next stop is the engaging **Nagasaki Museum of History and Culture** (長崎歴史文化博物館; daily 8.30am–7pm; closed 3rd Tues of month; ¥600; Ⓦwww.nmhc.jp), which focuses on the city's role as a conduit for cultural exchange; make sure you pick up a free audio guide at the ticket desk. Alongside scale models and videos, there are plenty of original materials, including an exquisite seventeenth-century folding screen depicting British and Dutch ships in Nagasaki harbour, and the first Japanese–English dictionary compiled by Dutch interpreters in 1814. There's a room devoted to local crafts, some showing distinctly foreign influences, and you exit through a reconstruction of the Nagasaki Magistrate's office.

From the museum it's a short walk northeast along the hillside to find Nagasaki's major shrine **Suwa-jinja** (諏訪神社) at the top of steep steps. Ask at the office (beside the bronze horse by Kitamura Seibō) for their comprehensive English brochure. Suwa-jinja was founded in 1625 when the shogunate was promoting

August 9, 1945

In the early twentieth century Nagasaki became an important naval base with huge munitions factories, which made it an obvious target for America's second **atomic bomb** in 1945. Even so, it was only poor visibility at Kokura, near Fukuoka, that forced the bomber, critically short of fuel, south to Nagasaki. The weather was bad there too, but as the *Bock's Car* B-29 bomber flew down the Urakami-gawa at 11am on August 9, a crack in the cloud revealed a sports stadium just north of the factories and shipyards. A few moments later "Fat Boy" exploded. It's estimated that over 70,000 people died in the first seconds, rising to 140,000 from radiation exposure by 1950, while 75,000 were injured and nearly forty percent of the city's houses destroyed in the blast and its raging fires. Horrific though these figures are, they would have been higher if the valley walls hadn't contained the blast and a spur of hills shielded southern Nagasaki from the worst. An American naval officer visiting the city a few weeks later described his awe at the "deadness, the absolute essence of death in the sense of finality without resurrection. It's everywhere and nothing has escaped its touch." But the city, at least, did rise again to take its place with Hiroshima as a centre for anti-nuclear protest and hosts many ardent campaigns for world peace.

Shintoism in opposition to the Christian Church. Its main hall, rebuilt in 1869, is fresh and simple, but for most foreigners its greatest attraction is the English-language fortune papers on sale beside the collecting box (¥200). The grounds are scattered with unusual subsidiary shrines, notably two *koma-inu* (guardian lions) known as the **stop lions**, where people vowing to give up unwanted habits fasten paper strings around the front legs, like plaster casts; you'll find them in a small garden to the left as you face the main hall.

Each autumn, Suwa-jinja hosts the famous **Kunchi Matsuri** (Oct 7–9). This festival is believed to have originated in 1633 when two courtesans performing a nō dance attracted huge crowds during celebrations to mark the ninth day of the ninth lunar month. Gradually, European and Chinese elements were incorporated – this was one of the few occasions when Dutch merchants were allowed to leave Dejima – and the jollities now consist of dragon dances and heavy floats, some fashioned as Chinese and Dutch ships, being spun round outside the shrine.

Down the Nakashima-gawa

Below Suwa-jinja, the **Nakashima-gawa** flows west through central Nagasaki under a succession of stone bridges linked by a pleasant riverside walk. The most noteworthy of these is the double-arched **Megane-bashi** (眼鏡橋), aptly named "Spectacles Bridge", which is Japan's oldest stone bridge, dating from 1634. Across **Megane-bashi**, Teramachi-dōri (Temple-town Street) parallels the river along the valley's eastern slopes.

Turn right along this street, lined with temples on one side and neighbourhood shops on the other, to pick up signs pointing left to **Sōfuku-ji** (崇福寺; daily 8am–5pm; ¥300). This is Nagasaki's most important Chinese Zen temple, founded in 1629 by Fujian immigrants and containing rare examples of Ming-period Chinese architecture.

In the seventeenth century, Nagasaki's Chinese community comprised over fifteen percent of the population. Like the Europeans, they were restricted to a designated area that lay just inland from Dejima, near today's **Chinatown**. Four elaborate gates signpost this colourful grid of six blocks packed with shops and restaurants, while a bare earth park over on the south side houses an older wooden gate and a Chinese pavilion where old men sit and gossip over chess pieces.

There's more to see immediately to the northwest, where traces of **Dejima** (出島; daily 9am–6pm; ¥500), the Portuguese and (later) Dutch enclave, can still be found along a curve of the old sea wall. Created in 1636, this tiny artificial island provided Japan's only access to the Western world for over two hundred years (see p.770). The island was swallowed up in later land reclamations, but has recently been re-created in its original style. It's best to start at the far, west gate, where the **Chief Factor's residence** is one of the grandest buildings, its dining room laid out for a lavish and – to Japanese eyes – exotic Christmas dinner.

A couple of minutes' walk southwest of Dejima is the new **Nagasaki Prefectural Art Museum** (daily 10am–8pm; closed 2nd & 4th Mon of month; ¥400; Ⓦwww.nagasaki-museum.jp), occupying a splendidly airy building on the waterfront. It's particularly strong on Spanish art, including works by Picasso, Dalí and Miró, and Meiji-era art from Nagasaki, though only part of the collection is on show at any one time.

Glover Garden

From the Ōura Tenshudō-shita tram stop (Line 5), a parade of souvenir shops leads up to Japan's oldest church, **Ōura Catholic Church** (daily 8am–6pm; ¥300). A pretty little white structure, with nothing much to see inside, it was built by French missionaries in 1864 to serve Nagasaki's growing foreign community.

Thomas Glover

Scotsman **Thomas Glover** arrived in Nagasaki from Shanghai in 1859, aged just 22, and became involved in various enterprises, including arms dealing. In the mid-1860s, rebels seeking to overthrow the shogun approached Glover for his assistance. Not only did he supply them with weapons, he also furthered their revolutionary cause by smuggling some of them abroad to study, including Ito Hirobumi, who eventually served as prime minister in the new Meiji government. For this, and his subsequent work in modernizing Japanese industry, Glover was awarded the Second Class Order of the Rising Sun – a rare honour – shortly before his death in Tokyo, aged 73.

Glover built the bungalow now known as **Glover House** in 1863, where he lived with his wife Tsuru, a former geisha, and his son from an earlier liaison, Tomisaburo. After his father's death, Tomisaburo was a valued member of both the Japanese and foreign business communities, but as Japan slid towards war in the mid-1930s his companies were closed and he came under suspicion as a potential spy. Forced to move out of Glover House, with its bird's-eye view of the harbour, and kept under virtual house arrest, he committed suicide two weeks after the atomic bomb flashed above Nagasaki.

A few months later Father Petitjean was astonished to find outside his door a few brave members of Nagasaki's "hidden Christians" who had secretly kept the faith for more than two centuries.

The path continues on up to **Glover Garden** (グラバー園; daily: April 27 to May 7 & July 15–Oct 9 8am–9.30pm; May 8 to July 14 & Oct 10–April 26 8am–6pm; ¥600; Ⓦwww.glover-garden.jp). Despite the crowds and piped music, the garden is worth a visit for its seven late nineteenth-century, European-style buildings, each typically colonial with wide verandas, louvred shutters and high-ceilinged, spacious rooms. The houses also contain odds and ends of furniture and evocative photos of the pioneering inhabitants they once housed.

The best approach is to start at the top – there are moving walkways up the hill – and work down. The first building you'll come across is Walker House, a modest bungalow built in the 1870s for the British-born captain of a Japanese passenger ship after he helped provide transport for government troops in the Satsuma Rebellion (see p.712). On retiring from the sea in 1898 he joined Thomas Glover, the bluff's most colourful and illustrious resident (see box opposite), in setting up Japan's first soft drinks company, which produced a popular line in "Banzai Lemonade" and "Banzai Cider" and eventually became Kirin Brewery. Glover's old house is worth a look around, as are those formerly belonging to Frederick Ringer, founder of the Nagasaki Press, and tea merchant William Alt.

The exit from Glover Garden takes you through the **Museum of Traditional Performing Arts** (same ticket), which displays the beautifully fashioned floats and other paraphernalia used during the Kunchi festivities (see p.672).

The Dutch Slopes

Back at Ōura Church, take the footpath heading east through a little graveyard and along the valley side until you pick up signs to the **Dutch Slopes** (オランダ坂) and Higashi-yamate (東山手). Though it's only five minutes' walk, few visitors bother to venture into this area where several more Western-style period houses have been preserved on the terraced hillsides, which are reached by roads still paved with their original flagstones. The first group of wooden houses you see on the left consists of two neat rows: the lower row houses a **photography museum** (9am–5pm; closed Mon; ¥100) displaying fascinating early photos of Nagasaki, while the **Higashi-yamate Museum** (same hours; free), the second building in the

Madame Butterfly

Puccini's opera, written in the early twentieth century, tells the story of an American lieutenant stationed in Nagasaki who marries a Japanese woman known as **Madame Butterfly**. Whereas she has given up her religion and earned the wrath of her family to enter the marriage, Lt. Pinkerton treats the marriage far less seriously, and is soon posted back to the US. Unknown to Pinkerton, Butterfly has given birth to their son and is waiting faithfully for his return when he arrives back in Nagasaki three years later. Butterfly pretties up her house and prepares to present her child to the proud father. Pinkerton, meanwhile, has remarried in America and brings his new wife to meet the unsuspecting Butterfly. When he offers to adopt the child, poor Butterfly agrees and tells him to come back later. She then embraces her son and falls on her father's sword.

The opera was adapted from a play by David Belasco, though some attribute it to a book by Frenchman Pierre Loti who wrote *Madame Chrysanthème* after spending a month in Nagasaki in 1885 with a young Japanese woman called Kane. Whatever its origin, the opera was not well received at its debut and Puccini was forced to rewrite Pinkerton and his American wife in a more sympathetic light. Efforts to trace the real Pinkerton have led to a William B. Franklin, but there are many contenders; it was common practice in the late nineteenth century for Western males stationed in Japan to "marry" a geisha in order to secure their companion's faithfulness and reduce the spread of venereal disease. In return, they provided accommodation plus some remuneration. As soon as the posting ended, however, the agreement was considered null and void on both sides.

upper row, exhibits Japanese-language materials about the district and efforts to rescue the old buildings.

Walking along the Dutch slopes you can't miss the bright yellow roofs of **Kōshi-byō** (孔子廟; daily 8.30am–5pm; ¥525), nestling at the foot of the hill within its stout, red-brick wall. Interestingly, the land beneath this **Confucian shrine**, completed in 1893, belongs to China and is administered by the embassy in Tokyo. Its present pristine state is due to an extensive 1980s rebuild using materials imported from China, right from the glazed roof tiles to the glittering white marble flagstones and statues of Confucius's 72 disciples filling the courtyard.

Inasa-yama

Nagasaki is not short of good viewpoints, but none can compare with the spectacular night-time panorama from **Inasa-yama** (稲佐山), a 333m-high hill to the west of the city. A **ropeway** (daily: March–Nov 9am–10pm; Dec–Feb 9am–9pm; closed early Dec; ¥700 one-way, ¥1200 return) whisks you up there in just five minutes; cars run every twenty minutes. To reach the ropeway, take Nagasaki Bus #3 or #4 from outside the train station and get off across the river at Ropeway-mae bus stop, from where the entrance is up the steps in the grounds of a shrine.

Eating

Nagasaki's international heritage extends to its most famous culinary **speciality**, *shippoku*, in which various European, Chinese and Japanese dishes are served almost like tapas at a lacquered round table. It's not a cheap meal, starting at around ¥4000 per head, and for the best *shippoku* you need to reserve the day before, although most of the big hotels also offer a less formal version. Nagasaki's other home-grown dishes include the cheap and cheerful *champon*, in which morsels of seafood, meat and vegetables are served with a dollop of thick noodles in piping-hot soup. *Sara udon* blends similar ingredients into a thicker sauce on a pile of crispy noodle strands.

The most popular local souvenir is Castella (*kasutera*) sponge cake – the best-known Castella bakeries are Fukusaya and Bunmei-dō, both of which have outlets all over the city. If you want to buy it at source, try Fukusaya's original shop (daily 8.30am–8pm) in a picturesque building on the edge of Shianbashi – look for its distinctive bat logo.

Asajirō 朝次郎 4F, Amu Plaza 1-1 Onoue-machi. Good, modern *izakaya* with picture windows overlooking the harbour and an extensive menu, plus a selection of daily dishes. Daily 11am–11pm.

Hamakatsu 浜勝 1-14 Kajiya-chō. Popular restaurant on Teramachi-dōri specializing in juicy *tonkatsu* (pork cutlets). Though it looks smart, with its gold signboard and iron lantern, prices are reasonable and you can eat all you want of the extras – soup, rice and salad. Daily 11am–midnight.

Hamakatsu 浜勝 6-50 Kajiya-chō ⓣ095/826-8321. This smarter *Hamakatsu* offers good-value *shippoku* meals. You can try a mini-*shippoku* for ¥3800 or the real thing from ¥4800 up to over ¥10,000/person; it's best to reserve, and for a full *shippoku* they require a minimum of two people.

Harbin 2F, 4-13 Yorozuya-machi ⓣ095/824-6650. Above the *Doutor* café on Kankō-dōri pedestrian arcade, this Nagasaki institution has been serving French and Russian cuisine since 1959. Portions aren't huge, but the food's tasty and there's plenty of choice, from borscht to Russian-style *pot au feu*, and over 30 different vodkas. Lunchtime sets from ¥1000; count on at least ¥3000 in the evening. 11.30am–2.30pm & 5–11pm; closed Wed.

Kagetsu 花月 2-1 Maruyama-machi ⓣ095/822-0191, ⓦwww.ryoutei-kagetsu.co.jp. Set in an exquisite traditional garden, this lovely, 360-year-old restaurant is the best spot in town for *shippoku*. Lunchtime prices start at ¥5220 for a *shippoku* bentō or ¥10,000 for the full meal; in the evening you'll pay upwards of ¥13,900. Booking is essential and you need at least two people to order the full *shippoku*. Noon–3pm & 6–10pm; closed one day a week.

Kouzanrou 江山楼 12-2 Shinchi-machi ⓣ095/824-5000. Chinatown is packed with tempting restaurants, but this Fukien establishment is recommended for its reasonably priced *champon* and *sara udon*, as well as more mainstream Chinese dishes. Daily 11am–9pm.

Yossō 吉宗 8-9 Hamano-machi ⓣ095/821-0075. Famous old restaurant specializing in *chawan-mushi*, a steamed egg custard laced with shrimp, shiitake mushroom, bamboo shoots, shrimp and other goodies. You'll pay around ¥750 for a basic bowl, or ¥1260 with rice and pickles, while a *teishoku* will set you back ¥1800. Tinkling *shamisen* music sets the tone. Daily 11am–9pm.

Battleship Island

Jutting out of the sea about 15km off Nagasaki lies the city's newest attraction, and perhaps its most fascinating. Properly known as Hashima, it's more commonly referred to as **Gunkan-jima**, or "Battleship Island"; this may sound like a board game or pirate film, but the reality is far more interesting.

Gunkan-jima was once one of Japan's most important sources of coal, and from 1890 to 1974 was inhabited by hundreds of miners and their families. This dense concentration of people gave Japan a sneak preview of what it has become today – Gunkan-jima boasted the country's first ever high-rise concrete buildings, which together with the island's high sea walls make it appear from a distance like some huge and rather monstrous ship, hence the name. For a time it functioned quite well, with just enough schools, shops and housing to keep its tiny population satisfied. However, mainland Japan soon raced ahead development-wise, giving this brave attempt at urban utopia a relatively improverished appearance. Its fate was sealed when the domestic coal industry collapsed in the mid-1970s; the island was abandoned and left to decay.

Gunkan-jima was only opened up to tourism in 2009, and it is now possible to visit on half-day trips, organized through the tourist office (p.668). It's wise to book at least a couple of days ahead, and trips can be cancelled in bad weather. There are two tours available – a three-hour one which includes a brief stop on the island (¥4300), or a two-hour version which merely scoots around it (¥3300).

Drinking and entertainment

Nagasaki's entertainment district, **Shianbashi** (思案橋), is sandwiched between Hamanomachi shopping district and Chinatown, in the south of the city. Ironically, *shi-an* translates as something like "peaceful contemplation", which is the last thing you'll find in this tangle of lanes, packed with bars, clubs, *pachinko* parlours, *izakaya* and "soaplands" (seedy massage parlours), where nothing really gets going until 10pm and ends at dawn. The choice is bewildering and prices can be astronomical, but a safe place to start is the With Building, on the east edge of the district on Kankō-dōri. It's a one-stop night out, starting in the basement and working upwards through a host of restaurants, bars and nightclubs.

Chotto Ippai 2-13 Motoshikkui-machi. Meaning "a little drunk" but also known as "Ken's Bar" on account of its affable American owner. It's a real rarity among foreign-owned bars, since it's just as likely to be filled with elderly locals as English teachers. A huge shōchū selection – mainly from Amami-Ōshima – keeps everyone entertained. Come after 10pm.

Cocktail Bar Joy 7F 10-21 Hamano-machi. A sophisticated air, with jazz pouring from the speakers, and over 400 kinds of vodka (they say) pouring into customers' glasses – cocktails are also superbly made. If the booze gets you in the mood for a dance, pop one floor down to throw some shapes at *Bar G Soul*. Open 8pm–late.

Paranoia 3F, 5-36 Yorozuya-machi ⓣ095/821-0987. Music bar with occasional live music and a great record collection, run by a young and friendly *mama-san*. Depending on the band, there may be a music charge of ¥2500 including one drink. Mon–Thurs 7.30pm–3am, Fri & Sat 7.30pm–5am.

Tin Pan Alley 4F, 5-10 Motoshikkui-machi ⓣ095/818-8277, ⓦwww.tin-pan-alley.jp. The house band struts its stuff nightly with a playlist ranging from mellow groove to rock and pop classics. Entry charge ¥1500 for men, ¥1000 for women. Tues–Sun 7pm–3am.

Listings

Airport information ⓣ095/752-5555.

Banks and exchange The 18th Bank, next to the *New Nagasaki Hotel*, is the closest foreign exchange service to the train station; its main branch is at 1-11 Dōza, on the banks of the Nakashima–gawa just north of Chinatown. You can also change money at the central post office.

Bookshops Kinokuniya, on the fourth floor of the You-me-saito shopping centre, and Metro Books, on the third floor of Amu Plaza; don't expect a great English-language choice at either.

Car rental Eki Rent-a-Car ⓣ095/826-0480; Nippon Rent-a-Car ⓣ095/821-0919; Nissan Rent-a-Car ⓣ095/825-1988; Toyota Rent-a-Car ⓣ095/825-0100.

Festivals Chinese New Year is celebrated in Chinatown with a Lantern Festival, dragon dances and acrobatic displays (late Jan to mid-Feb). Dragon-boat races, here called *Peiron*, were introduced by the Chinese in 1655 and are still held in Nagasaki harbour every summer (June–July). The last evening of Obon (Aug 15) is celebrated with a "spirit-boat" procession, when recently bereaved families lead lantern-lit floats down to the harbour. The biggest bash of the year occurs at the Kunchi Matsuri held in early Oct at Suwa-jinja (see p.672).

Hospital Shimin Byōin, 6-39 Shinchi-machi (ⓣ095/822-3251) is an emergency hospital on the western edge of Chinatown.

Internet There are a number of places along the main road near Daimaru, or try Cybac, southeast of the Hamanomachi arcade (¥300 membership plus ¥300 for 30min; open 24hr; passport required). *Chikyu-kan* café, next to the Higashiyamate Museum, offers 30min use with your order (10am–5pm; closed Wed).

Police 6-13 Okeya-machi (ⓣ095/822-0110). Emergency numbers are listed on p.71.

Post office Nagasaki Central Post Office is 300m east of the station at 1-1 Ebisu-machi.

Shopping The main department stores, Daimaru and Hamaya, are in the Hamanomachi shopping arcades, while Amu Plaza and You-me-saito are the two biggest shopping malls.

Travel agencies For domestic travel, the main JTB office is on the ground floor of the *New Nagasaki Hotel* (ⓣ095/824-5194). International tickets can be bought at H.I.S., 2F, 4-22 Tsuki-machi (ⓣ095/820-6839, ⓦwww.his-j.com), across the river from the north end of the Hamanomachi arcade.

Shimabara Hantō

East of Nagasaki, the **Shimabara Hantō** bulges out into the Ariake Sea, tethered to mainland Kyūshū by a neck of land just 5km wide. The peninsula owes its existence to the past volcanic fury of **Unzen-dake**, which still grumbles away, pumping out sulphurous steam, and occasionally spewing lava down its eastern flanks. Buddhist monks first came to the mountain in the eighth century, followed more than a millennium later by Europeans from nearby Nagasaki, attracted by the cool, upland summers and mild winters. Even today, **Unzen**, a small onsen resort surrounded by pine trees and billowing clouds of steam, draws holidaymakers to its hot springs, malodorous "hells" and scenic hiking trails. One of the most popular outings is to the lava dome of **Fugen-dake**, which roared back into life in 1990 after two centuries of inactivity, and now smoulders menacingly above the old castle town of **Shimabara** – this was protected from the worst of the eruption by an older lava block, but still suffered considerable damage to its southern suburbs. Previously, Shimabara was famous largely for its association with a Christian-led rebellion in the seventeenth century when 37,000 peasants and their families were massacred. Both towns can be covered on a long day's journey between Nagasaki and Kumamoto, but if time allows, Unzen makes a relaxing overnight stop.

Unzen

Little more than a village, the lofty town of **UNZEN** (雲仙) sits contentedly on a plateau of the same name. Its name means "fairyland among the clouds", perhaps inspired by the pure mountain air and colourful flourishes of vegetation – azaleas in spring and autumn leaves – against which the **onsen** and their alter egos, the spitting, scalding **jigoku** ("hells"), compete for attention. Unzen town – little more than a village – consists largely of resort hotels and souvenir shops strung out along the main road, but fortunately there's plenty of space around and a variety of **walking trails** leads off into the surrounding national park. The best hikes explore the peaks of Unzen-dake; from the top of **Fugen-dake** you're rewarded with splendid views of the Ariake Sea and, if you're lucky, Aso-san's steaming cauldron.

Arrival and information

Without your own transport, the best way of **getting to Unzen** is by bus. Six direct services depart from Nagasaki's Ken-ei bus station (¥1900) every day, or JR pass holders can take the train to Isahaya Station (諫早) and pick up a Nagasaki Ken-ei bus from the other side of the road (¥1300). Unzen has two **bus stations**: Ken-ei buses from Nagasaki and Isahaya pull in at the far north end of town, while Shimatetsu buses for the onward journey to Shimabara depart from a square a little further back down the main road.

For general **information** about accommodation and transport, try Unzen Information Centre (daily 9am–5pm; ⓣ0957/73-3434, ⓦwww.unzen.org), located at the south end of town, next to Unzen Spa House. The **post office** opposite has an **ATM** that accepts international cards (Mon–Fri 9am–5.30pm, Sat 9am–12.30pm).

Accommodation and eating

Most **accommodation** in Unzen consists of upmarket resort hotels, but there are a few reasonable mid-range choices, as well as a **campsite** (ⓣ0957/73-3636; closed Dec–March) downhill from the post office. **Dining** options are more limited, so you're best off taking meals in your hotel, but the restaurant at *Fukuda-ya* serves sizzling plates of *yōgan* (lava) soba noodles big enough for two and delicious sweet potato ice cream, among other inexpensive dishes (daily 11am–10pm).

Fukuda-ya 福田屋 ⓣ0957/73-2151, ⓦwww.fukudaya.co.jp. A modern hotel with well-sized rooms decked out in warm ochre colours and a choice of rotemburo (non-guests noon–9pm; ¥700). ❻

Kaseya かせや ⓣ0957/73-3321, ⓕ0957/73-3322. The pleasingly worn-around-the-edges tatami rooms of this ryokan have been housing guests for decades. Reservations are recommended, as are the delicious meals. Internet access available. ❺

Unzen Kankō Hotel 雲仙観光ホテル ⓣ0957/73-3263, ⓦwww.unzenkankohotel.com. With a wonderful garden setting, this is one of the original European-style hotels, built in 1935, with lots of dark, highly polished wood and spacious public areas. The cheaper rooms are all Western-style; small but comfortable, and equipped with large, old-fashioned bathtubs. ❻

The Town

Unzen is pretty much a one-street town. The main road enters from the southwest, doglegs east and then north, and exits east towards Shimabara. Unzen's commercial centre lies in the north, concentrated between the two bus stations, while its geographical centre consists of a steaming, barren area known as **jigoku** (地獄); the *jigoku* and an assortment of **onsen baths**, renowned for their silky smooth water, constitute Unzen's foremost attractions.

A Shingon Buddhist priest is credited with "founding" Unzen when he built a temple here in 701 AD; the area developed into a popular retreat where monks could contemplate the 84,000 tortures awaiting wrongdoers in the afterlife as they gazed at Unzen's bubbling mudpools. The first commercial onsen bath was opened in 1653, while two hundred years later Europeans arriving from Nagasaki, Hong Kong, Shanghai and east Russia prompted the development of a full-blown resort, complete with mock-Tudor hotels and one of Japan's first golf courses, laid out in 1913. The volcanic vents are less active nowadays but still emit evil, sulphurous streams and waft steam over a landscape of bilious-coloured clay. Only the hardiest of acid-tolerant plants can survive, and local hoteliers have added to the satanic scene by laying a mess of rusting, hissing pipes to feed water to their onsen baths.

The nicest of Unzen's **public baths** is the old-style **Kojigoku Onsen** (小地獄温泉; daily 9am–9pm; ¥400), which occupies two octagonal wooden buildings roughly ten minutes' walk south of town; take the left turn just past the *Fukuda-ya* hotel. More in the centre of things, **Shin-yu** (新湯; daily 10am–11pm; ¥100) is a small but traditional bathhouse overlooking a car park at the southern entrance to the *jigoku*. Lastly, there's the more glitzy **Unzen Spa House** (daily 10am–6pm; ¥800), offering a sauna and a variety of baths, including a rotemburo, in a half-timbered building on the main road into town. In addition, most hotels also open their baths to non-residents during the day, for a fee.

The *jigoku* provide an interesting hour's diversion, particularly the more active eastern area. The paths are well signposted, with lots of maps and information along the way, and there's also a descriptive English-language brochure, *Around in Unzen Jigoku*, available free at the information centre (see p.677). The highest and most active *jigoku*, **Daikyōkan Jigoku**, takes its name ("great shout") from the shrill noise produced as it emits hydrogen sulphide steam at 120°C. The noise is likened to the cries of souls descending to hell, but could well be the howls of the 33 Christian martyrs commemorated on a nearby monument, who were scalded to death here around 1630 by the Shimabara lords (see p.680). Another unhappy end is remembered at **Oito Jigoku**, which, according to legend, broke out the day a local adulteress, Oito, was executed for murdering her husband. The tiny, bursting bubbles of **Suzume Jigoku**, on the other hand, supposedly resemble the twittering of sparrows. Over in the western section, the main point of interest is **Mammyō-ji** temple, beside the Shimatetsu bus station. Founded nearly 1300 years ago, the temple is now home to a large gilded Shaka Buddha sporting a natty blue hairdo.

Fugen-dake

While Unzen-dake is the name of the whole volcanic mass, **Fugen-dake** (普賢岳; 1488m) refers to a newer cone on its east side that now forms the highest of the Unzen peaks. Fugen-dake erupted suddenly in November 1990 and reached a crescendo in June 1991 when the dome collapsed, sending an avalanche of mud and rocks through Shimabara town. Forty-three people were killed and nearly 2000 homes destroyed. There have been some minor rumbles since, but the eruption officially ended in 1996 and for now Fugen-dake just steams away gently.

A **ropeway** (daily 8.50am–5.20pm; ¥1220 return) takes visitors up from Nita Pass to an observation platform to the west of Fugen-dake. Cars run every twenty minutes, though not in bad weather or if the volcano is misbehaving; the last ride down is just after 5pm. From the top station, you can walk up Fugen-dake (1347m) in about an hour for views of the 1990 lava dome, though check beforehand that the path is open. Buses to the ropeway (at Nita Pass) depart from Unzen's Ken-ei bus terminal (25min; ¥740 return; 6 daily). The last bus down to Unzen leaves at 5.20pm (Nov–Dec 4.30pm), after which you'll have to walk, which takes an hour.

Shimabara

The port town of **SHIMABARA** (島原) has had a chequered history. Following the ructions of the **Shimabara Rebellion** (see p.680) it was decimated when Unzen-dake erupted in 1792, sending rock and hot ash tumbling into Shimabara Bay. An estimated 15,000 people died in the disaster, mostly from huge tidal waves that swept the Ariake Sea. The volcano then lay dormant until Fugen-dake burst into life again in 1990 (see p.677) and cut a swathe through the town's southern reaches. While the brooding mountain makes a dramatic backdrop, the main reason to stop here is to visit its castle, **Shimabara-jō**, which hosts an interesting museum about Japan's early Christians and the local rebellion.

Arrival and information

Shimabara straggles along the coast for more than 2km from its southerly **Shimabara-kō ferry terminal** to the main centre, **Ōte**, just below the castle. **Buses** from Unzen call at the Shimabara-kō Station before proceeding into town, where they either terminate at the Shimatetsu bus station or stop a little further on in Ōte. **Trains** running south from Isahaya on the private Shimabara line stop at the main Shimabara Station, a couple of minutes' walk east of Ōte, and then continue three more stops to Shimabara-Gaikō Station near the ferry port.

Shimabara's **tourist office** (daily 8am–5.30pm; Ⓣ0957/62-3986, Ⓦwww.shimabaraonsen.com) is inside the Shimabara-kō station building. They provide good English-language maps and brochures, and also offer **bike** rental (¥150/hr, ¥750/5hr), handy for scooting into town or out to the southern sights. For **onward transport**, there's a choice of a high-speed ferry (6–7 daily; 30min; ¥800) or a regular service (10 daily; 1hr; ¥680) to Kumamoto-kō, from where buses take you into the city.

Accommodation

Shimabara isn't exactly awash with accommodation options, and considering its proximity to Nagasaki and Kumamoto, many opt for a day-trip. However, there are a few decent places to stay.

Business Hotel Toraya ⓣ0957/63-3332, ⓕ64-0097. Cheap and cheerful business hotel next to the ferry terminal, offering either Western- or tatami-style rooms, and views out towards Kumamoto if you crane your head to the left. There's a decent restaurant on-site. ❸

Hanamizuki 花みずき ⓣ0957/62-1000. Bright business hotel, 5min walk southwest from Shimabara Station. The on-site spa is delightful, as are the breakfasts – rise early to savour them both. ❹

New Queen Hotel ⓣ0957/64-5511, ⓕ63-0051. Smart option perched up above the main road just north of the ferry terminal, its airy, understated rooms possessing a pleasantly old-fashioned seaside atmosphere. ❹

Shimabara Youth Hostel ⓣ0957/62-4451. There's something delightful about a youth hostel with an onsen – just what's on offer at this chalet-like building behind Shimabara-Gaikō Station. Dorm beds ¥2850/person.

The Town

Completed in 1625, **Shimabara-jō** (島原城) took seven years to build – it was partly the taxes and hard labour demanded for its construction that provoked the Shimabara Rebellion. Entry to the grounds is free, while the reconstructed turrets contain a **museum** (April–Oct daily 9am–5.30pm; ¥520), spread among three buildings – most interesting are the main keep's local history exhibits, including relics of clandestine Christian worship. The modern building in the northwest corner shows a short film about Fugen-dake, while fans of Nagasaki's Peace Statue (see p.670) will be interested in the Kitamura Seibō Memorial Museum located in the southeast turret. Kitamura, a local sculptor who died in 1987, specialized in powerful bronzes, the best of them gripped by a restless, pent-up energy.

A few remnants of the old castle-town still exist. A couple of minutes' walk northwest of the castle, **Bukéyashiki** (武家屋敷) is a pretty little street of samurai houses. You can wander round the gardens and peek inside three of the grander, thatched houses at the street's northern end (daily 9am–5pm; free). Those willing to pay the price of a drink or snack can poke their noses into another old house, **Mizuyashiki** (see opposite).

To the outsider, there's little visible evidence now of the devastation wreaked by the mud flows that ripped through southern Shimabara in 1990, beyond some heavy-duty retaining walls aimed at channelling any future flows directly down to the sea. Just before the Mizunashi River, 5km south of central Shimabara along Highway 251, the **Mount Unzen Disaster Memorial Hall** (雲仙岳災害記念館; daily 9am–6pm; ¥1000; ⓦwww.udmh.or.jp), contains a moderately interesting museum commemorating the eruption. English-speaking staff are on hand to guide you through the exhibits, of which the most accessible are videos of the disaster and a technologically impressive but ultimately rather tacky Great Eruption Theatre

The Shimabara Rebellion

In 1637, exorbitant taxes and the oppressive cruelty of two local *daimyō* sparked off a large-scale **peasant revolt** in the Shimabara area, though the underlying motive was anger at the **Christian persecutions** taking place at the time. Many of the rebels were Christian, including their leader, a 16-year-old boy known as Amakusa Shirō, who was supposedly able to perform miracles. His motley army of 37,000, which included women and children, eventually sought refuge in abandoned Hara castle, roughly 30km south of Shimabara town. For three months they held off far-superior government forces, but even Shirō couldn't save them when Hara was stormed in April 1638 and, so it's said, all 37,000 were massacred. Rightly or wrongly, Portuguese missionaries were implicated in the rebellion and soon after all foreigners were banished from Japan as the country closed its doors.

Manga & anime

Manga (comic books) and anime (animation) are as much a part of Japan as chopsticks and rice. From doe-eyed, punk-haired teenage girls with mystical powers to morphing, metallic-limbed robots, cartoons are loved by young and old throughout the country. Top manga titles sell millions, anime movies consistently break box-office records and practically every institution has a cartoon mascot. The dynamic duo have even been co-opted by the government as part of their "soft power" offensive to tune the rest of the world into contemporary Japanese pop culture.

Hokusai's *Sazai Hall of the Five-Hundred-Rakan Temple* ▲

Comic illustration on a locker, Tokyo ▲

Scene from *Howl's Moving Castle* ▼

Visual culture

The word **manga** (meaning "whimsical pictures") is attributed to the great nineteenth-century artist Hokusai. Today, it covers comics, graphic novels, cartoon strips and even creations such as Hello Kitty. Japan's love of images is ingrained in the culture – **ukiyo-e** (woodblock prints), many of which depict lively scenes of common life and imaginative renditions of fables and fantasy, were as popular two centuries ago as manga is today. Indeed, Hokusai's erotic print *The Dream of the Fisherman's Wife* (1824), which depicts a naked woman being pleasured by a couple of rather randy octopuses, could be straight out of contemporary pornographic manga (*hentai*).

International opinion of the medium can be clouded by the graphic porn and violence seen in some cartoons, and it is often presumed that subject matter is exclusively limited to sci-fi and fantasy. In reality, manga (and anime) covers an enormous range of stories, and is even used to explain complicated current-affair topics. Cartoon images appear everywhere, from billboards to the packaging of countless consumer products, and throughout the country you can pop into a 24-hour **manga café** (see p.150), stacked with magazines, books and DVDs (and players on which to watch them), and dip into a universe of graphic adventures.

International success

Anime encompasses movies, television series and straight-to-video releases. Around sixty per cent are based on previously published manga, while others, like *Pokemon*, are inspired by video games. Anime has been a staple of Japanese TV since the 1960s, with some series such as *Astro Boy* (see box) and *Space Battleship*

Yamato (known in the US as *Star Blazers*) becoming popular overseas. However, it was the critical international success of Ōtomo Katsuhiro's feature-length film *Akira* and the rise of **Studio Ghibli**, purveyors of some of the most successful anime of all time, including *Howl's Moving Castle* and the Oscar-winning *Spirited Away*, that has ignited the current global interest in all things anime; see p.805 for more on cinema anime.

At anime **conventions** across the world, fans turn up in tens of thousands to celebrate the medium. The **Adult Swim** programme, on the US cable channel Cartoon Network, showcases adult-oriented anime and has been a huge success, undoubtedly playing a role in generating US interest. Many choose to watch anime downloaded from the internet from sites such as **Anime News Network** (Ⓦwww.animenewsnetwork.com) and **Crunchyroll** (Ⓦww.crunchyroll.com).

The Tezuka effect

Many of anime and manga's stylistic traits – exaggerated facial features, episodic storytelling and the cinematic quality of presentation – are credited to the seminal manga artist **Tezuka Osamu** (1928-1989) creator of *Astro Boy*, or *Tetsuwan Atomu* as he's known in Japan. Astro is a boy robot with rockets for feet and a memory bank of human experiences who forever ponders his relationship to humans; such philosophical character traits and dark, complex themes are a prominent feature throughout the genre. Tezuka is credited with jump-starting anime in the 1960s, when he turned his comic *Astro Boy* into a TV series. The flat 2-D look of anime, which is still common today, was a result of the need to keep production budgets low, using fewer images per second.

▲ Stained glass in the Ghibli Museum

▼ *Akira* film poster

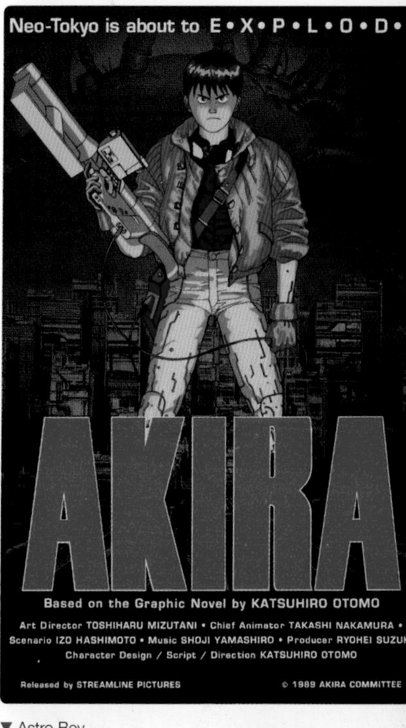

▼ Astro Boy

Tezuka Osamu character mural, Tokyo ▲

The head of the 15m-high Tetsujin statue, Kōbe ▲

Manga Museum, Kyoto ▼

Japan's anime and manga circuit

Manga and anime fans visiting Japan should make a beeline for Tokyo's **Akihabara** (see p.107), a shopping district that, given its mass of shops selling manga, anime and video games, as well as *figua* (scaled down plastic models of game and anime characters), is *otaku* (hardcore fan) central. In western Tokyo, the Suginami Animation Museum (see p.127) provides a great overview of the genre and a chance to view some anime for free, while the Ghibli Museum in Mitaka (see p.127) brings Studio Ghibli's creations to life in a theme park to rival Disneyland.

Kyoto's **Manga Museum** (see p.419), which has one of the largest manga collections in the country, and the Tezuka Osamu Manga Museum in Takarazuka (see p.497), devoted to this key manga artist and displaying wonderful original examples of his work, are also worth seeing. While down in the Kansai area, swing by Kōbe to view the giant statue of anime robot **Tetsujin 28** (see p.517). In Wajima (p.382), on Japan's northern coast, there's the Gō Nagai Wonderland Museum celebrating the locally born creator of series such as Mazinger Z and Cutie Honey, while in Ishinomaki there's the entertaining **Mangattan Museum** (p.239).

It's also worth planning your trip around two annual Tokyo-based **events**. In March, the Tokyo International Animation Fair (ⓦwww.tokyoanime.jp) is the world's biggest such event and, although held mainly for the trade, is open to the public for two days of its run. The comic convention Comiket (ⓦwww.comiket.co.jp), held over three days in August and again in December, is a public event that's attended by a staggering quarter of a million people.

which places you in the middle of the pyroclastic flows. A more solemn memorial to the dead is the small area of **half-buried houses**, signed as "Suffer House Preservation Park" (土石流被災家屋保存公園; daily 9am–5pm; free), preserved under two plastic domes about ten minutes' walk across the river from the hall. The best way to get here is to rent a bike (see p.679). Otherwise, take a Shimatetsu bus heading south from Ōte via Shimabara-kō ferry terminal and get off outside the Memorial Hall at the Arena-iriguchi stop (hourly; 15min; ¥240).

Eating

A little hard to find these days, though well worth hunting down, Shimabara's signature dish is **guzōni**, a delicious clam broth packed with rice cakes, fish, pork, lotus root, tofu and egg.

Aoi Rihatsu-kan 青い理髪館 Eighty-year-old venue immediately east of the castle (look out for the blue building) that's part barber shop, part coffee shop. They serve a limited range of set lunches and delightful home-baked cakes and cookies. 10.30am–7pm; closed Wed.

Himematsu-ya 姫松屋 Popular restaurant opposite the entrance to Shimabara-jō. They serve Shimabara's speciality food, *guzōni* (see above), as well as a choice of well-priced sets and mainstream Japanese dishes. Daily 10am–7pm.

Hōjū ほうじゅう An attractive and welcoming little place beside a carp stream a couple of blocks east of the shopping arcade; try the Shimabara *teishoku* (¥1350) for a sampler of local delicacies. Daily 11am–11pm.

Shimabara Mizuyashiki しまばら水屋敷 Meiji-era house serving drinks and snacks above a delightful garden, incongruously located on the shopping arcade southeast of the castle. Daily 11am–5pm.

Kumamoto

A fair proportion of travellers to Kyūshū find themselves in **KUMAMOTO** (熊本) at some point. Not only is the city handily located between Fukuoka in the north and Kagoshima down south, but it also lies within striking distance of Aso to the east and Unzen to the west. As well as making a good base or stopover, the city itself is reasonably attractive and boasts a couple of worthwhile sights. Chief among these is the fearsome, fairy-tale **castle** dominating the town centre, and **Suizenji-jojuen**, one of Japan's most highly rated gardens, in the western suburbs. Wars and development have meant that little else of particular note survives, though you've got to admire a city which invented the endearingly offbeat "Kobori-style" swimming which "involves the art of swimming in a standing posture attired in armour and helmet".

Some history

Kumamoto owes its existence to the Katō clan, who were given the fiefdom in the late sixteenth century in return for supporting Tokugawa Ieyasu during his rise to power. **Katō Kiyomasa**, first of the feudal lords, not only built a magnificent fortress but is also remembered for his public works, such as flood control and land reclamation. However, political intrigue resulted in the Katō being ousted in 1632 in favour of the **Hosokawa** clan, who had previously held Kokura. Thirteen generations of Hosokawa lords ruled Kumamoto for more than two centuries, during which time the city thrived as Kyūshū's major government stronghold, until feudal holdings were abolished in 1871. Six years later, the final drama of the Meiji Restoration was played out here when Saigō Takamori's rebel army was defeated by government troops, but not before destroying much of Kumamoto's previously impregnable castle.

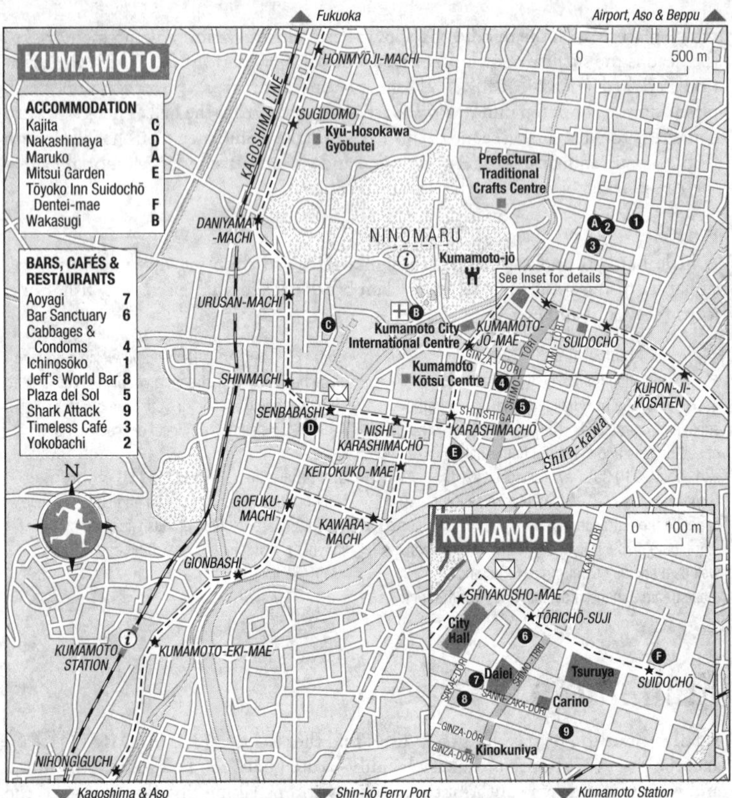

Arrival and information

Central Kumamoto occupies the north bank of the **Shira-kawa**, between the river and the castle. This is where you'll find the main shopping arcades, Shimo-tōri and Kami-tōri, as well as major hotels, banks and Kumamoto Kōtsū Centre (熊本交通センター), the city's central bus station. The main station, however, lies 2km to the south, creating a secondary hub, with its own hotels and bus services.

From Kumamoto **airport**, roughly 15km northwest, limousine buses shuttle into town in roughly an hour (¥670), stopping at Shimo-tōri and the Kumamoto Kōtsū Centre before ending up at the train station. Most long-distance buses terminate at the Kōtsū Centre, though a few continue to Kumamoto Station; in addition, most buses from the ferry **port**, Kumamoto-kō (熊本港), stop at the station first.

Kumamoto's helpful **tourist information** service (daily 8.30am–7pm; ⓣ096/352-3743, ⓦwww.kumamoto-icb.or.jp) occupies a desk inside the train station's central exit. There are also branches in the airport (daily 6.50am–9pm) and beside the main entrance to the castle (April–Oct 8.30am–6pm; Nov–March 8.30am–5pm; ⓣ096/322-5060).

City transport

Getting around central Kumamoto is made fairly easy thanks to a **tram** system, which covers most sights. There are just two lines (#2 and #3), both of which run from the eastern suburbs through the city centre before splitting near the Kōtsū Centre. Line #2 then heads off south to Kumamoto Station, while Line #3 loops north round the castle. You can change from one line to another at Karashimachō, where the lines split; if you haven't got a day pass (see below), ask for a transfer ticket (*norikae-kippu*) to avoid paying twice. Trams run every five to ten minutes between approximately 6.30am and 11pm, with a flat fare of ¥150. Alternatively, if you're moving about a lot, you can buy a one-day pass (*ichi-nichi jōshaken*; ¥500), which also entitles you to discounted tickets to various sights.

Accommodation

Kumamoto has accommodation options to suit all budgets. The train station area has plenty of cheap places to sleep, but the Shinkansen upgrade meant that it resembled a building site at the time of writing – it may be best to stay elsewhere until gentrification is complete.

Kajita 梶田 1-2-7 Shin-machi ⓣ&ⓕ096/353-1546. Tucked away on the castle's west side, this homely minshuku is one of the few budget places within walking distance of central Kumamoto, with good prices and helpful owners. The tatami rooms are a little aged and none is en suite, but all have a TV, phone and heater. ❸

Maruko Hotel 11-10 Kamitōri-chō ⓣ096/353-1241, ⓦwww.maruko-hotel.jp. Modern hotel in an interesting area to the north of the centre. Rooms are mostly Japanese-style and all en suite, and there's a Japanese bath with views on the sixth floor. ❻

Mitsui Garden Hotel 1-20 Koyaima-machi ⓣ096/352-1131, ⓦwww.gardenhotels.co.jp. Despite the grand marble lobby, prices at this mid-range business hotel on the south edge of the centre aren't too bad, and the comfortable rooms come with bathroom, TV and internet access. ❺

Nakashimaya 中島屋 2-11-6 Shin-machi ⓣ096/202-2020, ⓦnakashimaya.ikidane.com. A wonderful hostel: cheap, friendly, decorated with traditional flourishes, free internet... and you can have a dab at dyeing your own shoes or T-shirts. Tatami berths ¥2500, or ¥2000 if you have a sleeping bag.

Tōyoko Inn Suidochō Dentei-mae 1-1 Suido-chō ⓣ096/325-1045, ⓦwww.toyoko-inn.com. Typically good-value option from the business hotel chain, handily located on Kumamoto's main shopping street, right beside the Suidochō tram stop. There's another branch next to the train station. ❸

Wakasugi 若杉 1-14 Hanabatachō ⓣ096/352-2668. Rooms here won't win prizes for design, though they're cheap and do the job, and some have views of the castle walls. Breakfast included at the ground-floor café. ❸

The City

Completed in 1607 after only seven years' work, **Kumamoto-jō** (熊本城; daily: April–Oct 8.30am–5.30pm; Nov–March 8.30am–4.30pm; ¥500) is Japan's third-largest castle (after Ōsaka and Nagoya) and one of its most formidable. It was designed by lord **Katō Kiyomasa**, a brilliant military architect who combined superb fortifications with exquisitely graceful flourishes – as Alan Booth observed in *The Roads to Sata* (see p.815), the main keep seems like "a fragile bird poised for flight". At its peak, Kumamoto-jō had an outer perimeter of 13km and over 5km of inner wall built in what's called *musha-gaeshi* style, meaning that no invading warrior could scale their smooth, gently concave surfaces. In case of prolonged attack, 120 wells were sunk, while camphor and ginkgo trees provided firewood and edible nuts. These defences were severely tested during the 1877 **Satsuma Rebellion** (see p.712), when Saigō Takamori's army besieged Kumamoto-jō for fifty days. Government reinforcements eventually relieved the garrison, soon after trouncing the rebels. Though the castle held, most of its surrounding buildings were burnt to the ground and left in ruins until 1960, when the main keep was magnificently restored around a concrete shell; turrets and various other buildings are now also in good shape.

The best approach to the castle is from its south side, which brings you up into the grassy expanse of **Ninomaru** and the main, west, gate into the **inner citadel**. Inside to the left, **Uto Yagura** was the only turret to survive the 1877 battle, while straight on, a high-sided defile leads to the imposing central keep, which hosts an excellent historical **museum** about the castle and the Hosokawa lords. Immediately south of the keep, the low-lying **Go-ten Ōhiroma** – the main reception hall – is resplendent after its recent restoration.

Opposite the northeastern Akazu-no-mon gate, the **Prefectural Traditional Crafts Centre** (熊本県伝統工芸館; 9am–5pm; closed Mon) hosts free exhibitions promoting local artists and an excellent display of Kumamoto crafts on the second floor (¥200). The most famous traditional craft is *Higo zogan*, a painstaking method of inlaying gold and silver in a metal base. Developed in the seventeenth century for ornamenting sword hilts, it's now used for jewellery, decorative boxes and the like. Look out among the toys for a little red-faced fellow with a black hat, the ghost Obake-no-kinta – try pulling the string.

The last of the city-centre sights is over in the northwest corner of the castle grounds, roughly fifteen minutes' walk from the Crafts Centre and near the Sugidomo tram stop. The effort is rewarded with **Kyū-Hosokawa Gyōbutei** (旧細川刑部邸; daily: April–Oct 8.30am–5.30pm; Nov–March 8.30am–4.30pm; ¥300, or ¥640 including entry to the castle), an immaculately restored and unusually large high-ranking samurai residence set in traditional gardens. It's one of the few buildings of its kind remaining in Japan.

Suizenji-jojuen

It pays to visit **Suizenji-jojuen** (水前寺成趣園; daily: March–Nov 7.30am–6pm; Dec–Feb 8am–5.30pm; ¥400; Ⓦwww.suizenji.or.jp) early, before crowds arrive. In any case, the garden is at its best with an early-morning mist over the crystal-clear, spring-fed lake, its surface broken by jumping minnows or the darting beak of a heron. Plump, multicoloured carp laze under willow-pattern bridges, while staff sweep the gravel paths or snip back an errant pine tuft. Considered to be one of Japan's most beautiful stroll-gardens, Suizenji-jojuen was created over eighty years, starting in 1632, by three successive Hosokawa lords. The temple from which the garden took its name is long gone, but the immaculate, undulating landscape, dotted with artfully placed shrubs and trees, has survived. The design supposedly mimics scenes on the road between Tokyo and Kyoto, known as the "53 stations of the Tōkaidō" – the ones you're most likely to recognize are Fuji and Lake Biwa.

Considering Suizenji's prestige, it's surprising to find the garden cluttered with souvenir stalls, and it's also quite small, taking only thirty minutes to walk round. On the way, you'll pass the Izumi shrine, dedicated to the Hosokawa lords, and a four-hundred-year-old **teahouse** (March–Nov 9am–5.30pm; Dec–Feb 9am–5pm) overlooking the lake. If it's not too early, you can drink a cup of green tea on the benches outside (¥500) or in the tea ceremony room (¥600), while admiring one of the best views of the garden; the price includes an *izayoi*, a white, moon-shaped cake made using egg white.

Eating, drinking and nightlife

Local **speciality foods** include horsemeat sashimi (*basashi*) eaten with lots of garlic, and *karashi renkon*, which consists of lotus-root slices stuffed with a mustard and bean paste, dipped in batter and deep-fried. In addition to the restaurants listed below, you'll find a good variety on the 7th floor of Tsuruya department store's main building.

Cafés and restaurants

Aoyagi 青柳 1-2-10 Shimotōri-chō ⓦwww.aoyaginet.com. Large, elegant restaurant behind the Daiei store, with a choice of counter, tatami room or tables. Despite appearances, prices aren't astronomical; lunch sets start at ¥1000, though you could spend a lot more. Beautifully presented house specialities include *basashi* (from ¥2100). Daily 11.30am–10pm.

Cabbages & Condoms 1-9-13 Shimotōri-chō. Delicious, fairly-priced Thai cuisine – it's around ¥1100 for a tom yum or pad thai. Ah yes, the name – apparently a share of the profits go to Thailand in the form of prophylactics. Daily noon–3pm & 6pm–midnight.

Ichinosōko 壱之倉庫 2-8 Kachikōji. A tiny door leads into this spacious, wood-beamed beer restaurant, which started life as a silk-weaving workshop. The food is a typical mix of Western and Japanese, with both snacks and full meals available, and you should be able to eat well for around ¥2000. Daily 11.30am–11.30pm.

Plaza del Sol B1, 1-10-27 Shimotōri-chō. Locals swear by the burritos (veggie version available on request) at this Mexican restaurant. Other classics include quesadillas, ceviche and enchiladas, and they stock a mean range of tequilas. Set meals at ¥1300 or count on around ¥2500 from the menu. 6–11pm; closed Wed.

Timeless 11-3 Kamitōri-chō. Artistic café with a soothing, semi-European atmosphere, serving a global range of coffees. As a little bonus, you get to choose your own cup from a delightful selection. 11am–10pm, Sun to 7pm.

Yokobachi 11-40 Kamitorōri-chō. Chow down on *karashi renkon* or *basashi* at this bustling *izakaya* around the corner from the *Maruko Hotel*, where tatami-mat rooms overlook a pretty Japanese garden. Daily 5pm–midnight.

Bars and clubs

Bar Sanctuary 4-16 Tetori-honmachi. Kumamoto's one-stop party venue, from a dance club on the ground floor (entry charge ¥1500 Fri & Sat) and bar to darts room, karaoke and pool. Daily 8pm–6am.

Jeff's World Bar 2F, 1-4-3 Shimodōri. Foreigners' favourite, good for a pint or cocktail and some friendly conversation. You can drink as much as you please for ¥3000. Daily 8pm–late.

Shark Attack 8F, Anty Rashin Building, 6-3 Anzei-machi. Another cosy little bar, this time with a surfing theme, even down to sand on the floor. Daily 9pm–5/6am.

Listings

Airport information ⓣ096/232-2810.

Banks and foreign exchange The best bet for foreign-exchange services is Higo Bank and Kumamoto Family Bank, both of which have branches on the main road near Tsuruya department store.

Bookshops Kinokuniya, on Shimo-tōri, near the corner with Ginza-dōri, and Tsutaya & Books, in the Carino Building on Sannenzaka-dōri, east of the Daiei store, both have small selections of English-language books.

Car rental Nippon Rent-a-Car (ⓣ096/359-0919), Toyota Rent-a-Car (ⓣ096/311-0100) and Eki Rent-a-Car (ⓣ096/352-4313) all have branches near Kumamoto Station.

Ferries Kumamoto Ferry (ⓣ096/311-4100, ⓦwww.kumamotoferry.co.jp) operates high-speed ferries from Kumamoto-kō to Shimabara (6–7 daily; 30min; ¥800), while Kyūshū Shōsen (ⓣ096/329-6111, ⓦwww.kyusho.co.jp) runs a regular service (10 daily; 1hr; ¥680). To get to the port, take a bus from Kumamoto Station (1–3 hourly; 30min; ¥420).

Festivals Kumamoto's main events are the Hinokuni Festival (Aug 11–13), celebrated with folk dances, a city-centre parade and fireworks, and the Fujisaki Hachiman-gū autumn festival (Sept 11–15). On the final day, there are two processions, morning and afternoon, when some twenty thousand people parade through the streets in historical garb.

Hospital Kumamoto National Hospital (ⓣ096/353-6501) is immediately south of Ninomaru Park.

Internet Kumamoto City International Centre, 4–8 Hanabatacho (ⓦwww.kumamoto-if.or.jp), offers 30min free – but slow – access on the second floor (Mon–Fri 9am–8pm, Sat & Sun 9am–7pm), plus English-language newspapers and TV. Media Café Popeye, on Kami-tōri, offers 30min for ¥240 (open 24hr).

Police Kumamoto Prefectural Police Headquarters, 6-18-1 Suizenji ⓣ096/381-0110.

Travel agents JTB (ⓣ096/322-4111) is a good bet for domestic travel, while HIS (ⓣ096/351-0561) handles international tickets.

Aso and the central highlands

Central Kyūshū is dominated by sparsely populated, grassy highlands, in places rising to substantial peaks, which offer some of the island's most magnificent scenery and best walking country. These mountains are relics of ancient volcanic upheavals and explosions of such incredible force that they collapsed one gigantic volcano to create the **Aso caldera**, the world's largest crater. Today the floor of the caldera is a patchwork of fields like many tatami mats, and the surrounding uplands form a popular summer playground, but the peaks of Aso-san at its centre provide a potent reminder that the volcano is still very much alive. Most people come here to peer inside its steaming crater, eruptions permitting, and then scale some of the neighbouring peaks or walk over the lush green meadows at its base.

All this subterranean activity naturally means a wealth of hot springs to wallow in, mostly within the caldera itself, although there are a few gems hidden deep in the highlands. One is the picturesque village of **Kurokawa Onsen**, squeezed in a narrow gorge on the Senomoto plateau, which makes a great overnight stop on the road to Beppu. The village lies a few kilometres off the **Yamanami Highway**, the main route between Aso and Beppu, providing a spectacular mountain ride through the **Aso-Kujū National Park**. Heading in the opposite direction, another dramatic road climbs over the crater wall and heads southeast to **Takachiho**. Perched above an attractive gorge of angular basalt columns, this is where the mythical Sun Goddess Amaterasu hid, according to legends about the birth of the Japanese nation. A riverside cave and its neighbouring shrine make an easy excursion, but a more compelling reason to stop here is to catch a night-time performance of the story told through traditional folk dances.

Regional transport

The Aso region is one place where having your own **transport** is a definite advantage; it's perfectly feasible to get around by public transport, but everything takes a lot longer. From Kumamoto it's recommended to take the JR Hōhi line across the caldera floor and to spend a night or two in Aso Town. This is a great journey in its own right, but for an added bit of fun, you can travel on the *Odan Express*, a cute red diesel train which makes four daily round trips between Kumamoto and Aso. Make sure to reserve a seat in advance (¥300, or ¥500 in high season). It's possible to visit Aso-san on a day-trip from Kumamoto, or to break the journey here en route to Beppu. If you're heading that way, the Yamanami Highway offers the most scenic option, though the train continues via Bungo-Taketa and Ōita to Beppu and is a good alternative for JR pass holders, providing another magnificent journey through lush green forest deep in the mountains before dropping down to the coast. You'll have to overnight in Aso, however, if you're combining the crater with Takachiho.

The Aso Caldera

The train from Kumamoto changes direction twice as it zigzags up the formidable wall of the **Aso Caldera**. This ancient crater, measuring 18km from east to west, 24km north to south and over 120km in circumference, was formed about 100,000 years ago when a vast volcano collapsed. As the rock cooled, a lake formed, but the eruptions continued, pushing up five smaller cones, today known collectively as **Aso-san** (阿蘇山). Eventually the lake drained and the area became inhabited; local people attribute their fortune to the god Takeiwatatsu-no-mikoto, grandson of Emperor Jimmu, who kicked a gap in the western wall – the same gap the train uses – to give them rice-land. Now some 70,000 people live within the

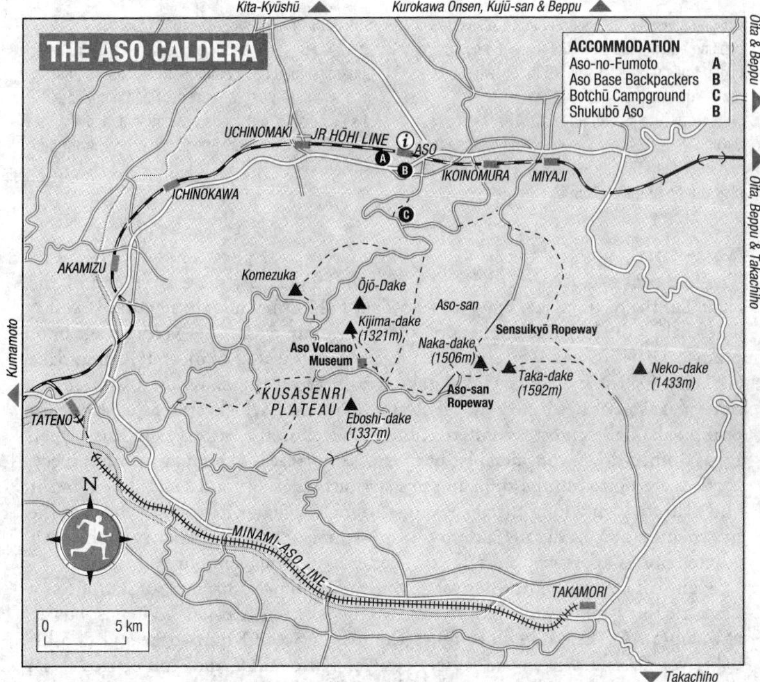

crater, working the rich volcanic soils, while cattle and horses graze the higher meadows in summer.

Arrival and information

Aso Town (阿蘇市) is a grandiose name for a scattered group of villages located in the northern caldera, including a tourist area around Aso Station, which represents the centre of local life. The **bus** station is to the right as you exit the train station, while to the left there's a well-organized **tourist office** (daily 9am–6pm; ⓣ0967/35-5077, ⓦwww.aso-denku.jp), with helpful, English-speaking staff and a wealth of information on local transport, walks and accommodation. In the same building you'll also find **internet** terminals (daily 9am–6pm; free) and a **car rental** desk (ⓣ0967/34-1001; same hours).

Accommodation and eating

Despite Aso's excellent accommodation options, there are a just a couple of **restaurants**. *Coffee Plaza East* (daily 9am–10pm) has a good range of well-priced Japanese and Western meals, including substantial breakfast sets; they're on the main highway, two minutes' walk straight ahead from Aso Station, and opposite a 24-hour convenience store. There are a few interesting options within a fifteen-minute walk – *Aso Base Backpackers* (below) give out excellent maps.

Aso Base Backpackers ⓣ0967/34-0408, ⓦwww.aso-backpackers.com. A short walk south of the train station, this squeaky-clean, pine-lined venue is one of the best hostels in Japan. Friendly staff, comfy beds and internet access are augmented by a pleasing lodge-style atmosphere. Dorm beds ¥2800, doubles ❷

Botchū Campground 坊中キャンプ場 ⓣ0967/34-0351, ⓦwww.aso.ne.jp/~jp6hck. About 1km south of the station – just within comfortable walking distance. You can rent tents, blankets and cooking equipment here, and there are some great hiking trails up to Aso-san. ¥930 for two. Open April–Nov.

Minshuku Aso-no-Fumoto 民宿阿蘇のふもと ⓣ0967/34-0624. Welcoming option offering bed and breakfast. The owners speak English and will pick you up at the station. ❸

Shukubō Aso 宿坊あそ ⓣ0967/34-0194, ⓕ1342. By far the fanciest place to stay in Aso, this minshuku has beautiful, traditional rooms in a wonderful old farmhouse. Good meals are also available, but these are optional, and the English-speaking owner will collect you from the station. ❺

Aso-san

The five peaks of **Aso-san** line up across the caldera. At the eastern end of the chain lies the distinctively craggy Neko-dake (1433m), while the next peak west is Taka-dake (1592m), the highest of the five summits, and its volcanic offshoot Naka-dake (1506m). West of here lie Eboshi-dake (1337m) and Kijima-dake (1321m). Of the five, only **Naka-dake** is still active; it's really just a gash on the side of Taka-dake, formed by a volcanic explosion which created a secondary peak. Naka-dake's most recent eruptions occurred in the early 1990s, since when it has calmed down considerably, but it's wise to treat the mountain with respect. Notices are posted in the train and bus stations when Naka-dake is closed, but if you plan to do any long-distance walks around the crater it's wise to check at the information office. Anyone suffering from asthma or other respiratory problems is advised not to approach the crater rim because of strong sulphur emissions.

Seven daily **buses** shuttle visitors from the terminal outside Aso Station on a dramatic forty-minute journey up towards the peaks of Aso-san (¥540; last bus up at 3.20pm). As the road climbs up to the pass between Kijima-dake and Eboshi-dake, you look down on the perfect cone of **Komezuka**, the "hill of rice" – its dimpled top is said to have been created when Takeiwatatsu-no-mikoto scooped up a handful of rice to feed his starving people. Turning the other way, you get your first glimpse of Naka-dake's gaping mouth across the grassy bowl of **Kusasenri plateau**, speckled with shallow crater lakes.

On the plateau, the bus stops outside the missable **Aso Volcano Museum** (阿蘇火山博物館; daily 9am–5pm; ¥840), though you might want to get off here to climb **Kijima-dake** (杵島岳; 1321m), which rises behind the museum. The paved path from the far northeast corner of the car park takes you on an easy thirty-minute climb, rewarded with more views over the caldera, and then down into Kijima-dake's extinct crater. From here, you can descend via a ski slope to join a path alongside the road to Naka-dake; the whole walk should take under ninety minutes.

Buses terminate at the foot of **Naka-dake** (中岳) in a scruffy area of souvenir shops and restaurants, while a toll road continues to the top for cars. You can walk up in twenty minutes, or there's a **ropeway** (daily 9am–5pm; ¥410) running every fifteen minutes or so from the bus terminus up to the crater; though the ropeway looks rather aged, the cables were replaced recently. However you arrive, the multi-coloured rocks and glimpses of a seething grey lake through turbulent, sulphurous clouds of steam are a forbidding sight. Most activity takes place in a 100m-deep crater at the northern end, and this area is strictly off limits. Near the ropeway, however, you can approach the crater lip and then walk south beside barren, dormant craters and across the lava fields – mercifully out of earshot of the loudspeakers.

Rather than backtracking, you could take a great **hiking trail** round the crater's southern rim to the summit of Naka-dake, followed by a possible side trip to **Taka-dake** (高岳) and then down to the northeastern Sansuikyō Ropeway (every 25min; ¥750). It's not too difficult as long as you've got good boots, plenty of water and you keep well away from the edge. To pick up the path, follow the boardwalks heading south round the crater across the Sunasenri plateau. Allow two to three hours, depending on whether you include Taka-dake, to the Sansuikyō Ropeway. With any luck, you'll coincide with a cable car down, but from the bottom you'll have to hitch a ride or set off on the ninety-minute downhill trot to Miyaji Station (宮地駅), two stops east of Aso.

North on the Yamanami Highway

From Aso the **Yamanami Highway** heads north over the Kujū mountains to Beppu. The road breaches the caldera wall at Ichinomiya, from where the classic profile of Aso-san's five peaks supposedly conjures up a sleeping Buddha with head to the east and Naka-dake's steaming vent at his navel, although it's a little more convincing from Daikambō lookout further west. North of here, **Kurokawa Onsen** (see below) offers a choice of rotemburo along a picturesque valley. The highway then climbs again through the Kujū range, which for some reason receives far less attention than Aso-san or Ebino-Kōgen (see p.706), although it offers good hiking and the Kyūshū mainland's highest peaks. The tallest, Kujū-san (1787m), is no longer active, but even here wisps of steam mark vents high on the north slopes. More spa towns lie strung along the route from here, and then start again at **Yufuin** (see p.698) before the road makes its final descent into Beppu.

While the Yamanami Highway is best avoided during peak holiday periods, for the most part it's fairly traffic free. Every day, four buses ply the route between Kumamoto and Beppu, stopping at Aso, Kurokawa Onsen, Senomoto, Yufuin and a few other places en route.

Kurokawa Onsen

One of the most popular hot-spring resorts in Japan, **KUROKAWA ONSEN** (黒川温泉) is made up of twenty-odd ryokan, which lie higgledy-piggledy at the bottom of a steep-sided, tree-filled valley scoured into the **Senomoto Kōgen** plateau (瀬の本高原), some 6km west of the Yamanami Highway. The village is completely devoted to hot-spring bathing and most of its buildings are at least traditional in design, if not genuinely old, while *yukata*-clad figures wandering the lanes add to its slightly quaint atmosphere. The village is particularly famous for its rotemburo: there are 24 different locations in total, offering rocky pools of all shapes and sizes. Out of the main tourist season, when the crowds have gone, it's well worth making the effort to get here, and Kurokawa makes an excellent overnight stop, if you don't mind paying a little extra for accommodation.

Arrival and information

Though it helps if you have your own **transport**, it's possible to reach Kurokawa Onsen on one of the six daily buses from Aso Town (1hr; local bus ¥940, Yamanami Highway bus ¥960). The first bus to Kurokawa from Aso departs at 10.10am and

Kurokawa's baths

All the baths in town are attached to ryokan and you can either buy tickets at reception (from ¥500) or get a day pass (¥1200) from the tourist office or the ryokan allowing entry to any three. If you only have time for one, try the central *Okyaku-ya Ryokan* (see p.690) for all-round atmosphere, or *Yamabiko Ryokan* (see p.690) for its unusually large rotemburo. *Yumotosō* (湯本荘) has a gorgeous little rotemburo and women can bathe in old-fashioned iron tubs. If you have your own transport, it's worth travelling a few kilometres out of central Kurokawa to try the riverside baths at *Yamamizuki* (山みず木) or *Hozantei* (帆山亭), set in wooded hills away from the crowds.

the last bus back leaves Kurokawa at 5.55pm, so there is time to explore a few of the ryokan baths in a day, though it's wise to check current bus times locally before setting off. If you're heading on to Beppu, on the other hand, you can take the last, mid-afternoon bus at around 4.45pm from Kurokawa along the Yamanami Highway. Make sure you're at the stop at least ten minutes early since these buses occasionally run ahead of schedule.

The **tourist office** (daily 9am–6pm; Ⓣ0967/44-0076, Ⓦwww.kurokawaonsen.or.jp) is beside a car park and taxi rank on the north side of the river, just uphill from the bus stop. They can provide a good English map showing the location of all the **public rotemburo** (daily 8.30am–9pm) with a key indicating whether they're mixed or segregated; the Japanese version has photos.

Accommodation and eating

There are some excellent ryokan in town – rates listed below include two meals. If you're looking for a lunch spot, try *Ajidokoro-naka* (味処なか; 11am–11pm; closed Wed), a sweet little **restaurant** down by the river that serves simple but good-value dishes along the lines of ramen and *donburi*. To find it, walk down the path behind the tourist office until you reach the river, turn right and it's almost immediately on your right.

Aso Kujū-kōgen Youth Hostel 阿蘇くじゅう高原ユースホステル Ⓣ0967/44-0157. The closest acceptable budget accommodation lies 5km away, near the Senomoto Kōgen junction; buses bound for Kurokawa stop at the end of the drive. Meals are available and staff can provide good hiking information. Dorm beds ¥2800.

Okyaku-ya Ryokan 御客屋旅館 Ⓣ0967/44-0454. Founded in 1603, this ryokan occupies a lovely wooden building right in the centre of things, and (trinket shop aside) maintains a pleasant Edo-era atmosphere. The on-site baths are nothing short of spectacular, particularly as evening encroaches. ⑦

Oyado Kurokawa お宿玄河 Ⓣ0967/44-0651. Contemporary styles take precedence over traditional trimmings in this well-designed facility, a short walk west along the river. The on-site baths are also superb. ⑦

Yamabiko Ryokan やまびこ旅館 Ⓣ0967/44-0311, Ⓦwww.yamabiko-ryokan.com. Grand riverside ryokan set in spacious grounds – the place for a splurge. The meals are simply delectable, and the outdoor rotemburo make heavenly places for a relaxing bathe. ⑧

Takachiho

The small town of **TAKACHIHO** (高千穂) lies on the border between Kumamoto and Miyazaki prefectures, where the Gokase-gawa has sliced a narrow channel through layers of ancient lava. In winter, when night temperatures fall below freezing, local villagers perform time-honoured **Yokagura dances** in the old farmhouses, bringing back to life the gods and goddesses who once inhabited these mountains (see p.692). The main reason for visiting Takachiho is to see a few excerpts from this dance-cycle, but combine that with **Takachiho gorge**, a pretty spot whose strange rock formations are woven into local myths, plus a dramatic journey from whichever direction you arrive, and Takachiho becomes somewhere to include on any Kyūshū tour.

To **get here** from Aso Town and points west, you need to take a private Minami-Aso line train from Tateno (立野), three stops west of Aso on the JR line, round the caldera's south side as far as Takamori (高森; ¥470), from where three buses a day continue to Takachiho (1hr; ¥1280). Check the connection times locally before setting off. The east coast is the main access route; Miyazaki Kōtsu buses track the Gokase valley from Nobeoka (延岡), on the JR line between Beppu and Miyazaki, up to Takachiho (hourly; 1hr 10min–1hr 30min; ¥1710). Sadly, the spectacular JR Takachiho line between Nobeoka and Takachiho was closed after a typhoon washed away parts of the track in 2005. There are tentative plans to reopen the line; check with the local ryokan (see below) for up-to-date information.

Arrival and information

Takachiho **bus station** lies about 100m south of the central Honmachi crossroads. Staff at the ticket window can provide sketch maps of the town, which is just as well since the **tourist office** (daily 9.30am–5pm; ⓣ0982/73-1213, ⓦwww.takachiho-kanko.jp) is inconveniently located on the bypass a good kilometre northwest of town. And, since none of the staff speaks English, you're best off in any case talking to the owners at one of the two ryokan mentioned below for information in English. There's an international ATM at the **post office**, buried in the backstreets to the northeast of the Honmachi crossing. Local **shops** are full of dried mushrooms, sweet potatoes, *shōchū* and other local produce alongside *kagura* dolls and locally crafted camphor-wood masks, which make unusual souvenirs.

Accommodation

Youth hostel aside, the accommodation prices below include meals, though discounts can be had if you choose to forgo them.

Kamino-ya かみの家 ⓣ0982/72-2111, ⓦinter-net.co.jp/miyazaki/kaminoya/index.htm. Homely ryokan with a nice, rustic atmosphere, and rooms decorated with original ink paintings. None is en suite, but you can use the lovely traditional baths. The meals are also good value, though you can opt for room only. ❻

Hotel Takachiho ⓣ0982/72-3255. On a promontory overlooking the gorge, just beyond Takachiho-jinja, this grand hotel is a good option if you want to sleep in a bed. It has spick-and-span Western-style en-suite rooms; if you phone ahead they'll collect you from the bus station. ❼

Takachiho Youth Hostel 高千穂ユースホステル ⓣ0982/72-3021. About 3km out of town to the east, and run by a wonderfully friendly woman who will happily pick you up and take you back out for the Yokagura dances. Dorm beds ¥2800/person.

Yamato-ya 大和屋 ⓣ0982/72-2243. Welcoming ryokan with en-suite tatami rooms, 100m southwest of the Honmachi crossroads. While you don't have to eat in, it's well worth opting for the evening meal. ❻

The Town

Takachiho sits on the north bank of the **Gokase-gawa**, grouped around the central Honmachi crossroads. Both the gorge and Takachiho-jinja, where nightly Yokagura dances are held, are on the southwest edge of town, within easy walking distance, while its other main sight, a mildly interesting riverside cave, lies a short bus ride to the east. It's possible to cover both areas in a day, see a Yokagura performance in the evening and travel on the next morning.

The road southwest to the gorge first passes **Takachiho-jinja** (高千穂神社), at the top of mossy steps roughly 800m from the Honmachi crossing. It's a simple wooden building, engulfed in ancient cryptomeria trees and mainly of interest for a high-relief carving of the guardian deity dispatching a demon; to find the carving, facing the shrine, walk round to the right of the building. The new, wooden **Kagura-den** next door is where the nightly sampler (8pm; ¥500) of **Yokagura** dances is held (see box p.692).

Takachiho gorge and Amano Iwato-jinja

Continuing along the road heading southwest, take the first lane left, corkscrewing down in a series of hairpin bends to emerge at the south end of the **Takachiho gorge** (高千穂峡). At its narrowest point the gorge is just 3m wide and plunges 100m between cliffs of basalt columns, which in one place fan out like a giant cockleshell. If you want to see what it looks like from below you can hire rowing boats at the southern end (daily 8.30am–4.20pm; ¥1500 for 30min; three people/boat); though it's a little pricey, the gorge is impressive when viewed from the

Myths and dance in Takachiho

Takachiho's famous **traditional dances** have their roots in local legend. The story goes that the Storm God, Susano-ō, once destroyed the rice fields of his sister, the Sun Goddess **Amaterasu**, and desecrated her sacred palace. Understandably offended by these actions, Amaterasu hid in a cave and plunged the world into darkness. The other gods tried to entice her out with prayers and chants, but nothing worked until, finally, a goddess named Ama-no-uzume broke into a provocative dance. The general merriment was too much for Amaterasu, who peeped out to see the fun, at which point the crowd grabbed her and hauled her back into the world. Takachiho locals also claim that nearby mountain Takachiho-no-mine – not the mountain of Ebino Kōgen (see p.706) – is where Amaterasu's grandson, Ninigi-no-mikoto, descended to earth with his mirror, sword and jewel to become Japan's first emperor.

A visit to Takachiho is not complete without viewing a sample of this dance at the Kagura-den (see p.691). In one hour you see three or four extracts from the full cycle, typically including the story of Amaterasu and her cave, and ending with an explicit rendition of the birth of the Japanese nation in which the two "gods" leave the stage to cavort with members of the audience – to the great delight of all concerned. The performers are drawn from a pool of around 550 local residents, aged from 5 to 80 years, who also dance in the annual **Yokagura festival** (mid-Nov to mid-Feb). In a combination of harvest thanksgiving and spring festival, 24 troupes perform all 33 dances in sequence in private homes and village halls, lasting through the night and into the next day.

emerald-green river. Otherwise, follow the path along the east bank, which takes you along the gorge's most scenic stretch, crossing and recrossing the river. Six hundred metres later you come out at an old stone bridge and the main road back into Takachiho, which soars high above. Before tackling the climb, you might want to stop off at *Araragi-no-chaya* (あららぎ乃茶屋; daily 8.30am–5pm), the restaurant-cum-souvenir shop beside the stone bridge, for a taste of the local speciality, *kappo saké* – sake heated in a pipe of fresh green bamboo.

Suitably revived, head back to the central bus station to board a bus for the attractive ride east along the Iwato-gawa to **Amano Iwato-jinja** (天岩戸神社), some 8km from Takachiho (hourly; 15min; ¥300). The shrine buildings are closed to the public, but it's an attractive setting among venerable cedars, and from behind the shrine it's just possible to make out Amaterasu's cave on the river's far bank. Unfortunately, you can't reach it, but, when her fellow gods were deciding their strategy, they convened in the more accessible **Amano Yasugawara**, which is on the same side as the shrine. It's about a fifteen-minute walk east, down some steps and beside the river, to find the cave with its diminutive shrine beneath a sacred rope.

Eating

Hatsu-e 初栄. Up towards the post office, this restaurant provides a warm welcome on cold evenings with its table-top braziers for cooking *yakiniku*; sets start at ¥1200. Tues–Sun 11am–2pm & 5–9pm.

Kenchan けんちゃん. Cosy *yakitori* bar opposite *Kamino-ya* (see p.691). A good meal, excluding drinks, will set you back about ¥2000/person. 5pm–midnight; closed Sun.

Ten-an 天庵. Rustic noodle joint serving excellent home-made soba – for just ¥850, the *Ten-an* soba set is a real feast. To find it, walk southwest from the Honmachi junction, straight over the next set of lights (the Shiroyama crossing) and take the first right. 11am–8pm; closed Sun.

Tentsukuten てんつくてん. This popular *izakaya* is hidden behind a shack-like door just south round the corner from the bus station. You can sample some of Takachiho's well-rated *shōchū*, and eat well. 5pm–midnight; closed Sun.

Beppu and around

Walking around the relaxed, coastal city of **BEPPU** (別府), it is at times tempting to think that the place was built atop the den of some giant dragon – spirals of steam billow skywards from a thousand holes, lending certain streets a magical, otherworldly air. However, this is no myth or fairytale, simply one of the world's most geothermically active regions. Over one hundred million litres of near-boiling water gush out of more than three thousand springs each day, harnessed for use by local homes and swimming pools, for heating and medicinal purposes, or to fill the dozens of public and private baths that make this one of Japan's most popular **onsen** resorts. The place is unashamedly commercial in nature, yet despite receiving over ten million visitors per year, it manages to feel like a town in decline – largely built during the domestic tourism boom of the 1970s, it seems half-forgotten by modern Japan. Still, the humble, throwback air that this creates enhances the city's pleasure, and it's easy to escape from the crowds.

There's not a lot more to do in Beppu than soak in a tub or be buried in hot sand. The most popular attractions are the nine **jigoku**, which spew out steaming, sulphurous mud and form simmering lakes in lurid hues. Despite the hype, only two or three are of any real interest; you'd do better to head for a clutch of **secret onsen** hiding away in the western hills (see p.696). However, recent years have seen a burst in artistic creativity thanks to the **Beppu Project** (Ⓦ www.beppuproject.com), a venture which has roped in all sorts of locals – from painters to former prostitutes – in a noble effort to vent some of the city's character. Projects have varied from art exhibitions to the remodelling of traditional buildings, but these come and go, so pick up a pamphlet at the tourist office, or go straight to their tiny base in the alley behind Takeya (see p.697).

Arrival and information

Beppu is served by **Ōita airport**, 40km away on the north side of the bay; frequent airport buses run south to Ōita city, stopping at Kitahama on the way (40min; ¥1450), and a few of these buses terminate at Beppu Station. **Ferries** from Honshū and Shikoku dock a couple of kilometres north of the centre at the

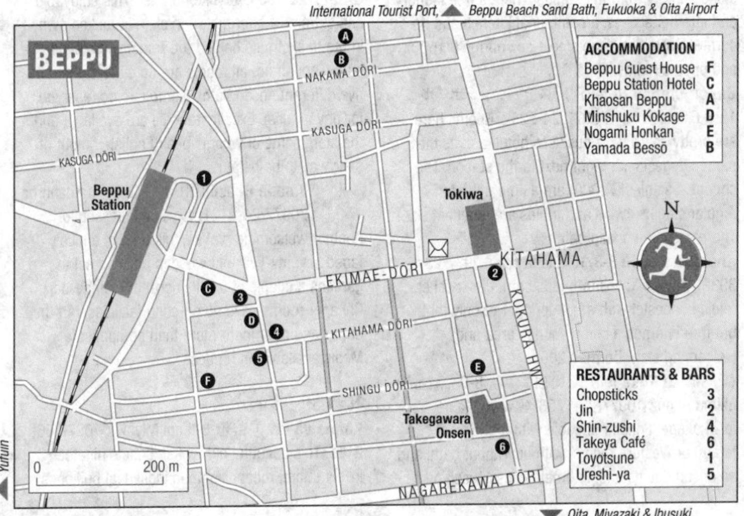

International Tourist Port; see p.726 for details. **Long-distance buses** mostly stop at Kitahama, although some services from Aso terminate at Beppu Station.

The town's main **tourist office** (daily 9am–5pm; ⓣ0977/21-1119, ⓦwww17.ocn.ne.jp/~ftio) lies just inside the central east exit of Beppu Station and has maps, brochures and information on local bus routes. The English-speaking staff can also assist with hotel reservations and there's a computer you can use to access the **internet** (free for ten minutes).

City transport

Local buses are the best way of getting around Beppu. Fortunately, they're not too complicated and there's a fair amount of information in English for the major routes. In general, Kamenoi buses, in blue and white livery with route numbers indicated on the front, cover most places within the city limits. They all start at Beppu Station, but could leave from either the west or east sides – ask to make sure you're waiting in the right place. It may be worth investing in a one-day "Mini Free Pass" (¥900), available at the station information desk or the Kamenoi bus station in Kitahama. The pass includes all buses within the city centre, which covers the *jigoku*, Suginoi Palace, sand baths and even the ropeway. It also entitles you to a ten percent discount on entry to the main sights, including the *jigoku* day pass (see opposite).

Accommodation

The most convenient place to look for **accommodation** is around Beppu Station, where you'll find a clutch of business hotels, a couple of appealing ryokan and some good-value budget options. Though less central, the **Kannawa** area offers a few atmospheric alternatives buried among its old streets. Prices tend to go up at weekends, when it can be hard to find a room anywhere in Beppu – make sure you book ahead.

Around the station

Beppu Guest House 1-12 Ekimae-chō ⓣ0977/76-7811. Perfectly acceptable hostel just a stone's throw from the station. There's free laundry and internet access, a communal kitchen and no curfew. Basic but clean single-sex dorms (¥1500) and private rooms. ❶

Beppu Station Hotel 別府ステーションホテル 12-8 Ekimae-chō ⓣ0977/24-5252. Rooms here are pretty sharp for a business hotel, and as the name suggests, it's right next to the station. The cheapest singles (¥3900) are a little tight, but regular singles, twins and triples are a decent size. There's also an onsen bath. ❹

Khaosan Beppu 3-3-10 Kitahama ⓣ0977/23-3939, ⓦwww.khaosan-beppu.com. Backpackers rejoice: a hostel with a hot spring. Not only that, but free internet, a comfy lounge area and welcoming staff. Dorms ¥2000.

Minshuku Kokage 国際民宿こかげ 8-9 Ekimae-chō ⓣ0977/23-1753, ⓦww6.tiki.ne.jp/~kokage. Popular cheapie with a choice of tatami or Western rooms, with or without bath, and an onsen downstairs. Internet access, washing machines and bike rental are thrown in for free. There is a midnight curfew. ❷

Nogami Honkan 野上本館 1-12-1 Kitahama ⓣ0977/22-1334, ⓦyukemuri.net. This enjoyable – and extremely affordable – ryokan is tucked away in the backstreets behind the Takegawara sand bath. Though not all rooms are en suite, there are five different onsen baths (some can be reserved for private use). Excellent meals are available and the staff, some of whom speak English, go out of their way to be helpful.

Yamada Bessō 山田別荘 3-2-18 Kitahama ⓣ0977/24-2121, ⓦyamadabessou.jp. Another welcoming ryokan, this time in a nicely faded seventy-year-old wooden building set in gardens a couple of blocks north of Ekimae-dōri. Cheaper rooms have no en-suite facilities, but the onsen and rotemburo more than compensate. Meals available on request.

Kannawa

Kannawa-en 神和苑 6-kumi Miyuki ⓣ0977/66-2111. This beautiful old ryokan boasts nineteen lovely tatami rooms, some in individual buildings, set in a classic, hillside garden with beautiful rotemburo. Rates include breakfast and an evening meal. ⑨

Sakae-ya サカエ家 2-kumi Ida ⓣ0977/66-6234. The century-old *Sakae-ya* is another elegant ryokan hidden in the eastern, less touristy part of Kannawa. They offer twelve rooms at either minshuku rates (④), with optional meals, or in the more upmarket ryokan including two meals. There are ovens for steaming *jigoku mushi* (see p.697) at the back – order in advance if you'd like to try it. ⑦

Shinki-ya しんき屋 2-kumi Furimoto ⓣ0977/66-0962, ⓦwww.shinkiya.jp. Three minutes downhill from the bus terminal, on the right, tucked up a lane behind a coin laundry, near the *Sakae-ya*. This little ryokan has been beautifully renovated with gleaming tatami rooms (none is en suite), *hinoki* onsen baths and a rotemburo. Meals are offered, including home-steamed *jigoku mushi* on request. ③

The Town

There are eight distinct hot-spring "towns" dotted about Beppu, each characterized by the varying proportions of iron, sulphur and other minerals in the water. Most activity, however, is concentrated in **Kannawa** (鉄輪). Not only is this northern district home to seven of the ten *jigoku*, but it's also a spa in its own right with a beautiful garden rotemburo, as well as an outrageously tacky museum of erotica. Dedicated bathers might want to try one of Beppu's **sand baths** or take a dip in one of the many on offer at the **Suginoi Palace**. Alternatively, you can ride the ropeway to the top of **Tsurumi-dake** for superb views over Beppu bay and inland to the Kujū mountains.

Kannawa and the jigoku

Noxious pools of bubbling mud, super-heated lakes, geysers and other geothermal outpourings are generally known in Japan as **jigoku**, after the word for the Buddhist notion of hell. Beppu's *jigoku* (daily 8am–5pm) are located in three clusters: seven in central Kannawa, one on Kannawa's western edge and two in Shibaseki Onsen, 3km further north. Though each *jigoku* has its own "personality" and you could cover them all in two to three hours, only those recommended below are really worth it – any more and you'll tire of the tacky commercialism, loudspeakers and tour groups. You can buy individual tickets (¥400) as you go round, or get a day pass (¥2000) covering all except Hon-Bōzu Jigoku and Kinryu Jigoku. Frequent buses ply between Beppu Station and Kannawa (20min; ¥360). If you plan to visit any of the district's **public baths**, it's a good idea to bring a towel, though you can always buy one on the spot for a couple of hundred yen.

To get here, take one of the many buses from Beppu Station to the *Umijigoku-mae* stop, which drops you at the top of Kannawa's main *jigoku* area. Here, **Umi Jigoku** (海地獄) is the most attractive, set in a bowl of hills among well-tended gardens. Its main feature is a sea-blue pool – 120m deep and, at 90°C, hot enough to cook eggs – set off by a bright-red humped bridge and *torii* swathed in clouds of roaring steam. The next-door **Oniishi-Bōzu Jigoku** (鬼石坊主地獄) takes its name from the resemblance between mud bubbles and the bald pate of a Buddhist monk, a *bōzu*. The speciality here is mud – boiling, smelly, steaming, hiccuping pools of it.

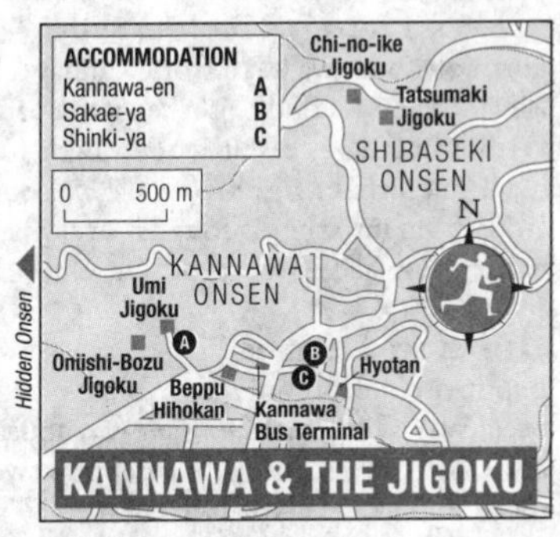

The remaining Kannawa *jigoku* are generally best avoided, being full of gaudy statues of unfortunate elephants,

Beppu's hidden onsen

It wasn't always this way. Taking a dip in an onsen should be the most natural thing in the world – add human bodies to hot water – but Beppu has seen most of its hot springs appropriated for commercial gain, whether it be heating a home on the cheap, boiling eggs for sale, or pointing guests towards their *omiyage* (souvenir gifts) at a five-star hotel. However, a few "hidden" baths lurking in the western hills allow some unsullied enjoyment of Beppu's raison d'être – not exactly holes in the ground, but close enough.

The first step is to get to Myoban (明礬), an onsen area accessible from Beppu Station on buses #5, #9, #24, #41 and #43 (25min; ¥360). From here directions are a little tough; it's best to arm yourself with a suitably rough map from the tourist office, or one of the two hostels (p.694). A twenty-minute walk on a road heading up and left from Myoban bus stop will bring you to a fork. Take a right, then scramble up the rock path at the second gate to get to **Nabeyama-no-yu** (鍋山の湯), a pair of onsen sitting in a forest-like setting. The first is a black-water pool, the second filled with clay that you can use for a free mud bath. Beppu is visible below, yet all one can hear are the sounds of nature – there isn't even a place to put your clothes. Turning left instead at the aforementioned fork will eventually bring you to **Hebin-yu** (へびん湯), a valley-based cascade of pools attended by a ramshackle hut. To hit the third spring, **Tsuru-no-yu** (鶴の湯), you'll have to get off the bus just before it passes under the highway, and head up the dirt track alongside a graveyard. Not easy – but it's Beppu at its purest.

crocodiles and monkeys in their own personal hell. If you fancy an onsen, it's definitely worth heading for the *Kannawa-en* ryokan (see p.694), whose picturesque, milky-white rotemburo are open to the public (daily 10am–2.30pm; ¥800). Built on a hillside to the east of Umi Jigoku, the ryokan has a beautiful, classic garden enclosing a small lake and hidden rocky pools reached by winding paths.

Continuing downhill, you might like to join the giggling young couples at **Beppu Hihōkan** (別府秘宝館; daily 9.30am–5pm; ¥1000), a sex museum. Buxom statuary grace the entrance, while inside there's a collection of erotic *ukiyo-e*, sacred phalluses from Shinto shrines, and then it descends rapidly into pornographic videos and tableaux, notably a gleeful Snow White and her seven dwarfs, which grind into action at the push of a button. Finally, if you fancy trying another of Kannawa's baths, **Hyōtan Onsen** (ひょうたん温泉; daily 9am–1am; ¥700, or ¥550 after 6pm; ⓣ0977/66-0572, ⓦwww.hyotan-onsen.com), a modern complex at the bottom of the hill, offers a rotemburo, sauna, a range of indoor pools and a sand bath (*yukata* rental ¥200). Should you be feeling peckish, you can even buy *jigoku mushi* to snack on.

Beppu's last two *jigoku* are in **Shibaseki Onsen** (柴石温泉), five minutes' bus ride north of Kannawa (#16 from Kannawa bus terminal). **Chi-no-ike Jigoku** (血の池地獄), "Blood Pond", is the better of the two, a huge bubbling pool whose vermilion fringes result from a high iron-oxide content. Fifty metres down the road, **Tatsumaki Jigoku** (龍巻地獄) consists of an unimpressive geyser that spouts around 5m into the air roughly every half-hour; it used to reach 50m until a stone block was placed over it for safety.

The sand baths

Beppu is one of only two places in Japan where it's possible to take a real, oceanside **sand bath**, or *suna-yu*. Ibusuki (see p.717) may be more famous and have the better scenery, but Beppu's two sand baths are less touristy and far more relaxed. **Takegawara Onsen** (竹瓦温泉) is a grand old Meiji-era edifice in the backstreets south of Ekimae-dōri. Its ordinary bath (daily 6.30am–10.30pm; ¥100) is nicely traditional, but try the **sand bath** first (8am–9.30pm; ¥1000). After rinsing in hot water, you lie face up – take a towel to cover your front – on a bed of coarse, black sand while an attendant gently piles sand onto you – a heavy, warm cocoon (around 42°C) that comes up to your neck. Then just relax as the heat soaks in for the recommended ten minutes, before another rinse and then a soak in the hot tub.

On a fine day, the seaside location of **Beppu Beach Sand Bath** (別府海浜砂湯; daily 8.30am–5pm; ¥1000) at first sounds preferable, but it's slightly marred by the busy main road behind and a concrete breakwater that dominates the view – the end result after a bath here, however, is still an overall sense of wellbeing. You'll need a swimsuit, but they provide *yukata* to wear in the "bath". It's on Shoningahama beach, near Beppu Daigaku Station, on Kamenoi bus route #20 or #26 from central Beppu (20min; ¥230); ask for the *Rokushoen* stop.

Kankaiji and Tsurumi-dake

Kankaiji onsen (観海寺温泉) spews out its hot water high up on a hill overlooking western Beppu, where it feeds the multifarious baths of *Suginoi Hotel*'s **Tana-yu** (daily 9am–10.30pm; ¥2000; free to hotel guests). This is Beppu's foremost bathing extravaganza, with an enormous terraced outdoor bath boasting fantastic views over the city and Beppu Bay, plus a separate spa complex and the Aquabeat resort, a huge indoor pool with a spiral water slide.

On the way up to Kankaiji, you pass the pencil-thin **Global Tower** (daily: March–Nov 9am–9pm; Dec–Feb 9am–7pm; ¥300), which serves as both viewing platform and a landmark for **B-Con Plaza**, Beppu's lavish convention centre and concert hall. The 100m-high, open observation deck provides giddying views, but if you've got time you'll get a better all-round panorama from the western hills. Here, a **ropeway** (daily 9am–4.30pm; ¥1400; ⓦ www.beppu-ropeway.co.jp) carries you to the top of **Tsurumi-dake** (鶴見岳; 1375m) in ten minutes, from where you can see Shikoku on a clear day. Kamenoi buses #33 to #37 depart Beppu Station every half-hour for the forty-minute ride to the ropeway (¥420), passing near the *Suginoi Hotel* en route.

Eating and drinking

Beppu's **speciality foods** include *fugu* (blowfish) and *karei* (flounder), both winter dishes, and the piping-hot *dango-jiru*. This cheap, filling soup comes with thick white noodles, assorted vegetables and chunks of either chicken or pork. You might also like to try *jigoku mushi*, a name given to a whole assortment of comestibles (vegetables and eggs are most prominent) slow-cooked in steam from Beppu's hells. You'll find it on sale at stalls and supermarkets in the Kannawa area, though the best is served in Kannawa's ryokan (see p.694). When it comes to finding a **restaurant**, you're best off in the downtown area.

Chopsticks 2F, 13-16 Ekimae-chō. Watch the world go by from the picture windows of this bar-restaurant, which is popular with a young, arty crowd. The extensive cocktail list ranges from regular rum- or beer-based concoctions to milk and *macha* (powdered green tea). Daily 11.30am–3pm & 6pm–1am.

Jin 仁 1-15-7 Kitahama. Lively "*robata* and beer pub" at the east end of Ekimae-dōri with an English menu listing a good range of fish, vegetable and tofu dishes, as well as *yakitori* skewers and local specialities. You should be able to eat for around ¥2000. Daily 5pm–midnight.

Shin-zushi 新鮨し 8-15 Ekimae-chō. Sushi fans should head to this pristine *sushi-ya* round the corner from *Minshuku Kokage*. It has a good choice of sushi, sashimi and tempura sets from ¥1500, while individual sushi start at ¥200. 2pm–midnight; closed Sun.

Takeya 15-7 Gen-chō. Sweet café with a bamboo theme (hence the name) and tasty coffee. A good place to meet prominent characters from the Beppu Project (see p.693).

Toyotsune とよ常 3-7 Ekimae-chō. Unpretentious restaurant opposite Beppu Station specializing in *fugu*, either as sashimi (¥2625/person) or a full, two-hour-long meal (from ¥5250). Less exotic dishes include well-priced tempura or sashimi sets (¥1100), and a good range of local *shōchū*. 11am–2pm & 5–10pm; closed Thurs.

Ureshi-ya うれしや 7-12 Ekimae-chō. Tables fill up early at this small, friendly restaurant where you can choose from a tempting display of ready-prepared dishes, such as vegetable tempura, sashimi, salads and fried fish. They also serve up standard rice and noodle dishes, all at very reasonable prices. 5.30pm–2am; closed Mon.

Listings

Airport information ⓣ0978/67-1174.
Banks and exchange Ōita Bank, on Ekimae-dōri, accepts the widest range of currencies, in cash and travellers' cheques.
Car rental Eki Rent-a-Car (ⓣ0977/24-4428), Nippon Rent-a-Car (ⓣ0977/22-6181) and Toyota Rent-a-Car (ⓣ0977/22-7171) all have offices near Beppu Station.
Ferries Uwajima Unyu Ferry (ⓣ0977/21-2364) runs six services a day from Beppu's International Tourist Port to Yawatahama on Shikoku (2hr 50min; ¥3020). Kansai Kisen (ⓣ0977/22-2181, ⓦwww.ferry-sunflower.co.jp) operates a daily ferry from the same port to Ōsaka (13hr; from ¥9100), via Matsuyama (4hr; from ¥3300). To reach Beppu port, take Kamenoi bus #20 or #26 and get off at *Kansai Kisen-mae*.
Hospital Beppu National Hospital (ⓣ0977/67-1111) is in north Beppu's Kamegawa district, inland from Kamegawa Station.
Police The main police station (ⓣ0977/21-2131) is opposite the post office on Route 10.
Post office The most convenient post office is on Ekimae-dōri.
Shopping The Beppu region is famed for its bamboo handicrafts, which you'll find in the station malls and department stores on Ekimae-dōri. Another popular souvenir is *yu-no-hana*, natural bath salts to create that instant hot-spring feel back home. These are on sale all over town.

Yufuin

The small resort town of **YUFUIN** (湯布院) sits in a mountain-surrounded hollow just 25km inland from Beppu. The fact that this is perfect day-trip distance is evidenced by the hordes of tourists who converge here each day, reaching their peak on weekends and holidays – this is one of those places that begs for an overnight stay, its charming thatched roof-lined alleyways better augmented by silence and streetlights than the *omiyage*-frenzy of the daytime. That said, Yufuin has made great efforts to protect its original character, and it makes a pleasing complement, or even alternative, to Beppu.

Like its noisier neighbour to the east, Yufuin's appeal centres around tripping from one **onsen** to the next – the most popular is **Shitan-yu** (下ん湯), a lakeside onsen with rustic thatched roofing. Hot springs aside, there are few sights as such, though Yufuin boasts a number of picturesque temples, as well as the opportunity to climb **Yufu-dake**, the double-headed volcano that rears up above town.

Practicalities

The best approach to Yufuin is on the Yananami Highway from Aso (see p.688), but most visitors arrive by **train**. There are local services from Beppu, as well as the Yufuin-no-mori, a gleaming green machine which runs a limited express service from Hakata (2hr 10min; ¥4600). There's a **tourist information** booth in the station (daily 9am–7pm; ⓣ0974/84-2446), and a post office with **ATM** close by.

Most **accommodation** options in Yufuin are ryokan catering to upscale travellers. One of the most atmospheric options is *Makiba-no-ie* (牧場の家; ⓣ0974/84-2138), whose thatched-roof huts sit around a charming rotemburo. Those travelling on a budget should head straight to *Country Road Youth Hostel* (ⓣ0974/84-3734), a superb place with its own onsen and a rarified location on a hillside above town – try to arrange pick-up from the station in advance.

Usuki

After all the self-indulgence of Beppu, the small and attractive castle town of **USUKI** (臼杵), some 40km to the south, offers a reminder of the spiritual side of life, and makes a pleasant stop on the coastal route to or from Miyazaki. Between the twelfth and fourteenth centuries, in a little valley around 5km southwest of town, skilled craftsmen sculpted some sixty Buddha statues in the soft lava tuff. The weather has taken its toll since then, but restoration work has saved several of these serene statues, which continue their vigil unperturbed.

The **stone Buddhas**, or *Seki butsu* (石仏; daily 6.30am–6pm; ¥530), are grouped around the sides of a narrow north–south valley and divided into four clusters, of which the first and last are the most interesting. Following the path anticlockwise, the first you reach is the Hoki Second Cluster, dominated by a 3m-tall figure of **Amitabha Buddha** and his two attendants, each individually expressed. The path then takes you round via the Hoki First Cluster – comprising over twenty statues – and the rather worn Sannōsan trinity of Buddhas, to the Furuzono Cluster. Here, the central **Dainichi Nyorai** is considered one of Japan's finest stone-carved Buddhas. While the lower body has partly rotted away, the Buddha's face, picked out with faded pigment, is still sublime.

After you've walked round the Buddhas, which won't take much over thirty minutes, it's worth taking a quick stroll through the **old centre** of Usuki on the way back to the station; if you're travelling by bus (see below), ask to get off at the *Hirasōzu* stop on the west side of town. From here, a stone-paved street leads northeast between high mossy walls and past temples and samurai houses. You'll eventually come out on a traditional shopping street, where the local speciality, *fugu*, is much in evidence, either for sale dried in shops or on restaurant menus. Where you come to the big red *torii* on the far east side of town, turn right and you'll be back at the station.

Practicalities

Usuki is a stop on the JR Nippō Line, forty minutes south of Beppu by express train, with services roughly every hour; make sure you get a train which stops at Usuki. From the station you can pick up a **bus** to the *Seki-butsu* (7 daily; 20min; ¥300) or, if you're feeling energetic, you can rent a **bicycle** – just ask at the JR ticket window. It takes about thirty minutes to cycle out to the Buddhas, though much of the route is along a busy main road. A taxi from the station will cost in the region of ¥1400. Staff at the station hand out basic sketch maps, but for anything more complicated, you'll need to walk into the centre of town (around ten minutes) to the **tourist office** (daily 9am–7pm; ⓣ0972/64-7271) on the main shopping street.

South Kyūshū

Southern Kyūshū consists of two huge prefectures, which offer plenty of stunning scenery – mostly of the volcanic variety – and further stops on the onsen trail. Heading down the east coast from Beppu the first place of note is Miyazaki; an agreeable place, it has little to detain the traveller, but serves as a useful base for exploring the surrounding countryside, notably south along the coast to **Aoshima**'s subtropical gardens and the celebrated cave-shrine of **Udo-jingū**. On the way west to Kagoshima, it's worth stopping at Kirishima National Park, which has a famous shrine, as well as excellent hiking terrain on **Ebino Kōgen**, a high, open plateau ringed by volcanic peaks. Kagoshima city itself sits in the shadow of a grumbling, ash-spewing volcano, **Sakurajima**. Some people come simply to view this troublesome beast, but the city also has one or two worthwhile museums celebrating its role in the Meiji Restoration, and it is also a gateway to the Satsuma Peninsula. Here, the small town of **Ibusuki** is devoted to hot-spring bathing, including a seaside sand bath, while nearby **Chiran** houses another of Japan's disturbing war museums. In this case it commemorates the kamikaze suicide bombers who rallied to the imperial cause at the end of World War II. From either Kagoshima or Ibusuki, ferries ply south to **Yakushima**; a paradise for botanists and hikers, this mountainous island is covered in ancient, misty forests that are home to five-thousand-year-old cedar trees.

Miyazaki and around

There's a relaxed, summery feel to **MIYAZAKI** (宮崎). This breezy city boasts palm trees, flower-lined streets and the longest sunshine hours in Japan, factors which make its surrounding coast all the more appealing to the **surfers** who head here in droves in warmer months (see p.15). While the city itself has few draws bar the odd shrine, park and museum, it makes a good base for exploring the **Nichinan coast**. A short train ride south, the island of **Aoshima** is a subtropical garden ringed by platforms of heavily scored rocks, while further along the coast, **Udo-jingū**'s main shrine nestles in a sacred cave. From here you can continue down the peninsula to **Cape Toi**, or turn inland to circle round via **Obi**, an attractive castle town with a passable collection of museums and old houses.

Arrival and information

Arriving in Miyazaki by **train**, you end up at Miyazaki Station, to the east of the city centre. **Long-distance buses** tend to stop at the Miyazaki Eki-mae Bus Centre just across the road, though some arrive at Miyakō City terminal, south of the river near JR Minami-Miyazaki Station. The **airport** is 5km south of the city centre and connected by both train (1–3 hourly; 10min; ¥340) and bus (every 30min; 30min; ¥400) to Miyazaki Station. Finally, **ferries** from Ōsaka dock at Miyazaki Port Ferry Terminal, east of the city centre. You'll find buses waiting outside the terminal buildings to bring you to Miyazaki Station (15–20min; ¥240).

Miyazaki is well provided with English-language information at both the main **tourist office** inside Miyazaki Station (daily 9am–6pm; ⓣ0985/22-6469) and the airport desk (daily 7am–9pm; ⓣ0985/51-5114). The International Plaza on the eighth floor of the Carino shopping mall (Tues–Sat 10am–7pm; ⓣ0985/32-8457, ⓦwww.mif.or.jp) is another useful resource, aimed primarily at long-term residents.

City transport

To **get around**, local buses depart from either the Miyazaki Eki-mae Bus Centre or from the Miyakō City terminal, south of the river. However, since almost all buses call at stops around the city's central crossroads, the best thing is to head for this junction (*Depāto-mae*) and ask which stop you need; the minimum fare is ¥150. The city provides free **bikes** to reduce the number of cars on the roads. You can pick up a bike at the Wheels outlet (daily 9am–6pm) to the west of the station on Hiroshima-dōri, and at Yotten Plaza (よってんプラザ; daily 11am–6.30pm) on

Tachibana-dōri beside the *Kensington Hotel*. There's a ¥500 deposit and the first three hours are free – the cost for the rest of the day is ¥200.

Accommodation

The best accommodation is around Tachibana-dōri, south of the central crossroads, where you'll find a sprinkling of mid-range business hotels. Cheaper places cluster round Miyazaki Station.

Green Rich Hotel 1-5-8 Kawaramachi ⓣ0985/26-7411. Excellent value on offer at this business hotel, indeed green in hue, near the river. Rooms are spick-and-span and internet-ready. ❷

Miyazaki Kankō Hotel 1-1-1 Matsuyama ⓣ085/27-1212. Central Miyazaki's poshest hotel boasts a riverside location, shopping mall, choice of restaurants and onsen spa complete with a rotemburo. Rooms are smarter – and considerably more expensive – in the newer east wing, but all are very comfortable. Ask for a river view. ❻

Hotel Kensington 3-4-4 Tachibana-dōri Higashi ⓣ0985/20-5500. South of Miyazaki's central crossroads, this smartish business hotel promises "nostalgic days of England" and has a few twin and double rooms. Cheaper rooms lack windows, but they're all equipped with phone, TV and en-suite bath. ❺

Miyazaki-ken Fujin-kaikan 1-3-10 Asahi ⓣ0985/24-5785. Miyazaki's youth hostel consists of shared tatami rooms in the Prefectural Women's Centre, though men are welcome. You can use the kitchen (¥100), but there's a 10pm curfew. Dorm beds ¥2750/person.

Phoenix Seagaia Resort Hamayama, Yamasaki-cho ⓣ0985/21-1111, ⓦwww.seagaia.co.jp. Miyazaki's most luxurious accommodation by far – there are four separate facilities to choose from at this lengthy beachside resort, most pertinent of which is the *Sheraton Grande*, housed in a distinctive 154m-tall skyscraper. The complex also features a golf range, onsen and a Banyan Tree spa. ❼

Hotel Plaza 1-1 Kawaramachi ⓣ0985/27-1111. Good mid-range choice, with river-facing rooms, delectable food and a lush onsen that's probably the best in the city. ❺

Tōyoko Inn Miyazaki Eki-mae 2-2-31 Oimatsu ⓣ0985/32-1045, ⓦwww.toyoko-inn.com. This business hotel boasts the low prices and excellent location typical of the chain – it's right outside Miyazaki Station's west entrance. ❷

The City

Though they won't appear on anyone's must-see list, the city's sights are sufficiently interesting to fill a leisurely day. In the northern suburbs, **Heiwadai-kōen** is a hilltop park with a delightful collection of clay *haniwa* figurines – replicas of statues found in ancient burial mounds. The grounds of nearby **Miyazaki-jingū**, the city's foremost shrine, contain a good municipal museum, while the city's sleek **art museum** lies nearby. In the city centre, near Miyazaki Station, is the entertaining Science Centre. Further south, much is made of the riverside **Tachibana Park**; by day it's just a narrow strip of green with a few tables and chairs, but at dusk it comes into its own, when the palm trees glitter with fairy lights.

In the city centre there's little to see bar the excellent **Science Centre** (科学技術館; 9am–4.30pm; closed Mon; ¥520, or ¥730 including planetarium), which covers everything from microorganisms, wind power and pulleys to robots and satellite imagery, making use where possible of examples from the island. The museum boasts one of the world's largest **planetariums** – 27m in diameter – which is well worth the extra expense. The shows (Tues–Sat 3 daily, Sun 4 daily) give you a superb fifty-minute ride through the heavens.

The northern districts

Low hills rise to the north of Miyazaki, where the rather Stalinist "Tower of Peace" dominates a large public park, **Heiwadai-kōen** (平和台公園). To reach the park take a Heiwadai-bound bus from *Depāto-mae* stop #1 outside Bon Belta department store (10–20min; ¥270). Behind the tower you'll find the **Haniwa Garden**, where dozens of clay statues of houses, animals and people populate a mossy wood. Look out for the charming warriors with elaborate uniforms and the pop-eyed, open-mouthed dancers. These are copies of the *haniwa* figures discovered in fourth-century burial mounds at nearby Saitobaru; it's believed the statues were used to "protect" aristocratic tombs.

Around 1km southeast of Heiwadai-kōen, and close to Miyazaki-jingū JR Station, the **Miyazaki Prefectural Museum of Nature and History** (宮崎県総合博物館; 9am–5pm; closed Tues; free) is worth visiting for its displays of local folklore. The same complex includes an archeological centre, where you can watch people patiently glueing together pottery shards, and the **Minka-en** (daily 10am–4.30pm; free), a collection of four thatched farmhouses from around the area. Don't miss the two traditional stone baths; the water was heated by lighting a fire underneath, like giant cauldrons. These museums stand in the extensive woodlands surrounding **Miyazaki-jingū** (宮崎神宮), a shrine dedicated to Japan's first emperor, Jimmu Tennō. An unusually large shrine at the end of an imposing avenue, the sanctuary itself is typically understated, though if you're lucky you'll catch a festive ceremony, or at least spot some of the colourful, semi-wild chickens scurrying round the raked-gravel compound.

Art lovers should walk five minutes west to a complex of public buildings, including a concert hall (home to Japan's largest pipe organ), theatre and library, in the aptly named Culture Park. Here, the monumental **Prefectural Art Museum** (宮崎県立美術館; 10am–6pm; closed Mon; free) hosts temporary exhibitions of twentieth-century Japanese and Western painting. To get back into central Miyazaki, catch a bus from the main road east of the Culture Park, or from the southern entrance to Miyazaki-jingū (¥160).

Eating, drinking and entertainment

Beef, wild boar, *ayu* (sweet fish), shiitake mushrooms from the mountains, clams, flying fish and citrus fruits – Miyazaki has a good spread of edible delicacies.

There's also the local sushi – *retasu-maki* – containing shrimp, lettuce and mayonnaise; chicken *Namban* – deep-fried, succulent chicken morsels with tartar sauce; and, in summer, *hiyajiru*, an aromatic soup of fish, tofu, cucumber and sesame, served ice-cold and then poured over hot rice. Another popular **speciality food** is cheese *manju*, consisting of a small, sweet almond butter-cake bun filled with melt-in-the-mouth cream cheese; you can buy them at the Hidaka cake shop on Tachibana-dōri (daily 9am–10pm). While you're at it, try their *Nanjya-kora Daifuku* – a chilled package of soft white rice-flour, filled with red-bean paste, a strawberry, a chestnut and cream cheese; it's absolutely divine.

The best choice of **restaurants** is in the streets either side of Tachibana-dōri and particularly those behind the Bon Belta department store, which is also where you'll find Miyazaki's energetic **nightlife** district. Most foreigners make a beeline for *The Bar*, a place that, though hit-and-miss, is a good base from which to organise operations. *Weather King* is a good place for live music at weekends, while from April to September you can also quaff a beer on the rooftop beer-garden of the Carino Building.

Gunkei ぐんけい 8-12 Chūō-dōri ⓣ0985/28-4365, ⓦwww.gunkei.jp. Tender *jidori* chicken seared over coals and brought sizzling to the table is the order of the day in this great restaurant, decorated in traditional rustic style. There's no English menu, but ask for the *jidori* set (¥2600) and you won't be disappointed. Reservations strongly recommended. Daily 5–11.30pm.

Kokoro 心 6-24 Chūō-dōri. Stylish vegetarian *izakaya* where the friendly English-speaking owner will guide you through the extensive menu. Portions aren't huge but the food is lovingly prepared and presented. The ¥2000 course menu represents good value. It's behind a low, wooden door and a bit tricky to spot. 5pm–2am; closed Mon.

Ogura おぐら 3-4-24 Tachibana-dōri Higashi. A diner-style restaurant offering good, cheap food, which has hardly changed since they invented chicken *Namban* (¥950) here in 1968. They also serve burgers, fried pork cutlets, curry rice and other comfort food in generous portions. 11am–3pm & 5–8.30pm; closed Tues.

Sangam 1-2-25 Tachibana-dōri Nishi. Decent curries on offer at this local favourite, and they'll add extra spices if you like it fiery. Lunch sets from ¥1000, dinner around ¥2000. Daily noon–2pm & 6.30–11pm.

Suginoko 杉の子 2-1-4 Tachibana-dōri Nishi ⓣ0985/22-5798. One of the city's most famous restaurants, at the southern end of Tachibana-dōri, serving tasty country cooking in elegant surroundings. Try their lunchtime *Kuroshio teishoku* or *Shokado bentō* sampler (both ¥1600). Evening course menus start at ¥4200. Daily 11.30am–2pm & 4–10.30pm; closed for lunch once a week, usually Mon; phone to check.

Listings

Airport information ⓣ0985/51-5114.

Banks and exchange Mizuho Bank and Fukuoka City Bank, both on Tachibana-dōri, just north of the central crossroads, have foreign exchange desks.

Car rental Eki Rent-a-Car (ⓣ0985/24-7206) and Nippon Rent-a-Car (ⓣ0985/25-0919) have outlets near the station. The latter has an airport outlet (ⓣ0985/56-5007).

Ferries Miyazaki Car Ferry (ⓣ0985/29-5566, ⓦwww.miyazakicarferry.com) operates a daily overnight service to Ōsaka (12hr; from ¥11,600), departing from Miyazaki-kō Ferry Terminal, a short bus ride east of central Miyazaki (15–20min; ¥240). You can buy tickets at local travel agents (see below).

Hospitals and medical care The Prefectural Hospita (ⓣ0985/24-4181) 1, 5-30 Kita-takamatsu-chō, is on Takachiho-dōri, west of the central crossroads. Staff at the International Plaza should be able to help find English-speaking doctors.

Internet e-planet (24hr; membership ¥100, ¥250 for 30min, then ¥100/15min) is on Tachibana-dōri south of the central crossroads; there's a smaller branch west of Miyazaki Station on Hiroshima-dōri.

Police Miyazaki-Kita Police Station, 2-10-1 Higashi, Tachibana-dōri Miyazaki (ⓣ0985/27-0110).

Post office Miyazaki Central Post Office, 1-1-34 Takachiho-dōri, is on the main road east of the Tachibana junction. They operate a 24hr service for express mail.

Travel agents For domestic travel arrangements, try JTB (ⓣ0985/29-2111) in Miyazaki Station. For international tickets, contact H.I.S. (ⓣ0985/31-6686) on Tachibana-dōri south of the main crossroads.

Around Miyazaki

South of Miyazaki, the hills close in as road and railway follow the coast down to **Aoshima**, a small island surrounded by peculiar rock formations. As you head down the Nichinan coast to Cape Toi, famed for its wild horses, there are more sandy coves and picturesque islands, as well as the castle remains and old samurai houses of **Obi**, a small, attractive town lying 6km inland.

Both Aoshima and Obi are stops on the JR Nichinan Line, but unless you're just heading to Aoshima, you'll save money by buying a one-day **bus pass** (¥1000), which covers all Miyazaki Kōtsū buses throughout the prefecture. You can buy the "Free Pass" at the train station, or the Miyazaki Eki-mae Bus Centre across the road.

Aoshima

Fourteen kilometres south of Miyazaki, the tiny island of **AOSHIMA** (青島), just 1500m in circumference, is little more than a heap of sand capped by a dense forest of betel palms and other subtropical plants. It's best at low tide when you can explore the rock pools trapped on the surrounding "devil's washboard" shelf of rocks, scored into deep grooves as if by a giant's comb. After that, the only other thing to do is walk round the island – it takes all of fifteen minutes – and drop in at its small shrine, **Aoshima-jinja**. Swathed in vegetation, this is dedicated to Yamasachi Hiko, a god of mountain products. Each year he's honoured with a couple of lively festivals: on the last weekend in July portable shrines are paraded round the island on boats and then manhandled back to Aoshima, while mid-January sees men rushing semi-naked into the sea. Come warmer weather, countless souls do likewise, though armed with surfboards – Aoshima is a prime base for the surfing fraternity (see below).

The island is a five-minute walk across a causeway from the neighbouring town, also known as Aoshima. Though it has no other sights worth stopping for, you could wander through the **botanical garden** (daily 8.30am–5pm; free), beside the causeway, while you're waiting for onward transport.

Practicalities

Aoshima is accessible by **bus** and **train** from Miyazaki. Buses depart from Miyazaki Eki-mae Bus Centre (hourly; 50min; ¥670), with a stop at *Depāto-mae*,

Surfin' Miyazaki

To scores of adventurous young Japanese, Miyazaki prefecture is inextricably linked to **surfing**. These are Japan's best and warmest waters, and though few foreigners get in on the action, this makes a trip here all the more appealing. The peak season runs from August to October, when most weekends will have a surfing event of some description.

There's decent surfing in the waters immediately west of Aoshima (see above) – protected by the island, these smaller swells are perfect for beginners. **Nagisa Store** (☎0985/65-1070), between Kodomonokuni Station and *Grand Hotel Qingdao*, rents boards (¥3000) and wetsuits (¥2000), while a few minutes' walk north of the same station similar prices are on offer at **Wellybird** (☎0985/65-1468). A little further towards Miyazaki is Kisaki-hama (木崎浜), a decent beach popular with surfers, and a ten-minute walk from Undōkōen Station. Equipment here can be rented at **Blast Surf World** (☎0985/58-2038), frustratingly located behind the Mos Burger just about visible from the station exit.

Experienced surfers with their own equipment should head instead to the reefs and reef breaks south of Aoshima, though these can be hard to get to without a local friend. Far to the north of Miyazaki, there are similarly ferocious waters surrounding **Hyūga** (日向), just south of Nobeoka.

and drop you beside the west entrance to the botanical garden. Alternatively, you can take the JR Nichinan Line train from Miyazaki Station (hourly; 30min; ¥360). The island lies 800m east from Aoshima Station; the map outside the station will point the way. There are plenty of cheap **minshuku** around Aoshima Station, which can be hunted down using the same map.

Udo-jingū

Eighteen kilometres south of Aoshima, a cleft in the rock hides one of this area's most famous sights, **Udo-jingū** (鵜戸神宮; free). The main **shrine** fills the mouth of a large, low cave halfway down the cliff face, its striking, vermilion *torii* and arched bridges vivid against the dark rock. According to legend, Udo-jingū was founded in the first century BC and marks the spot where Emperor Jimmu's father was born. The rounded boulders in front of the cave are said to represent his mother's breasts – expectant women come here to pray for an easy birth and newlyweds for a happy marriage. It's also supposed to be lucky if you land a small clay pebble (*undama*; five for ¥100) in the hollow in the top of the nearest "breast"; women throw with their right hand, men with their left.

The shrine is accessible by **bus** from Miyazaki (hourly; 1hr 30min; ¥1440) or Aoshima (hourly; 40min; ¥990), and it's best to arm yourself with a day-pass (see opposite). Buses on towards Obi (6 daily; 40min; ¥880) are less frequent – check the schedules in Miyazaki.

Obi

An old **castle town** 45km south of Miyazaki, **OBI** (飫肥) is a pristine little place with a number of samurai houses and a fine collection of traditional whitewashed warehouses, many of them immaculately restored, clustered under the castle walls. Obi's heyday was under the Itō family, who were granted the fiefdom in 1588 and then spent much of their time feuding with the neighbouring Shimazu clan of Kagoshima. Only the walls of their once formidable castle remain, though the main gate and lord's residence have been rebuilt in the original style.

Arrival and information

The quickest way to reach Obi is by **train** on the JR Nichinan line from Miyazaki (hourly; 1hr 15min; ¥910) via Aoshima. Obi Station lies on the east side of town, about fifteen minutes' walk across the river from the castle – staff at the ticket office can provide a sketch map. Alternatively, **buses** from Aoshima and Udo-jingū stop on the main road five minutes' walk south of the castle; ask for *Obi-jō*.

The Town

Central Obi lies in a loop of the Sakatani-gawa, with its historic core concentrated north of the main east–west highway. Here you'll find a few streets of **samurai houses** and carp streams, as well as the castle, **Obi-jō** (飫肥城; free), on the low hill behind. Walking north up Ōte-mon-dōri, enter the castle via its great southern gate and follow the path round to the right to find a white-walled **history museum** (daily 9.30am–4.30pm; ¥600 including Yoshōkan and Komura Memorial Hall), which has a small but impressive collection of Itō family heirlooms. On the hill behind stands the **Matsu-no-maru** (same ticket and hours), an exact replica of the rambling Edo-period buildings where the lords once lived, including the reception rooms, women's quarters, tea-ceremony room and a lovely "cooling-off" tower, where the lord could catch the summer breezes after his steam bath.

The rest of the castle grounds are now just grass and trees, but on the way out take a quick look at Obi's largest samurai house, the **Yoshōkan** (豫章館; same ticket and hours), immediately west of Ōte-mon gate. When the Meiji reforms abolished feudal holdings in the late nineteenth century, the Itō family moved to this more modest villa, which had previously belonged to their chief retainer. Though you can't go in, the house is a lovely, airy building surrounded by a spacious garden that's looking a bit worse for wear.

On the opposite side of Ōte-mon-dōri from the Yoshōkan, the **Komura Memorial Hall** (小村記念館; same ticket and hours) commemorates a famous Meiji-era diplomat who was born in Obi in 1855. He's best remembered for his part in concluding the 1905 peace treaty following the Russo-Japanese War; the museum's most interesting material, much of it in English, revolves around this period.

Eating

Obi has its own **speciality food**, *Obi-ten*, which consists of minced flying fish mixed with tofu, miso and sugar, rolled into a leaf shape and deep-fried. *Obi-ten chaya* (おび天茶屋; daily 9am–5pm), a nicely rustic **restaurant** in a garden immediately south of the Komura Memorial Hall, has a good-value *teishoku*, including rice, soup and pickles for ¥950.

Kirishima National Park

On the border between Kagoshima and Miyazaki prefectures, **Kirishima National Park** is Japan's oldest and comprises no fewer than 23 volcanic mountains, ten crater lakes and numerous hot springs. The park's main centre is the plateau village of **Ebino Kōgen**, a cluster of shops, hotels and a campsite, from where it's a short scramble up the park's highest peak, Karakuni-dake (1700m). The park's easternmost peak, Takachiho-no-mine, however, holds greater significance, since according to legend this is where Ninigi-no-mikoto, grandson of the Sun Goddess Amaterasu (see p.767) and legendary founder of the Japanese imperial line, descended to earth. The traditional approach to Takachiho is from the park's southern gateway, **Kirishima Jingū**, stopping first at a shrine shrouded in cryptomeria trees. The peaks are linked by a skein of **hiking** trails – it's worth scaling at least one of them for superb views over jagged craters filled with perfectly round, cobalt-blue lakes and Sakurajima puffing angrily on the southern horizon.

Arrival and information

The best way to reach Kirishima Jingū is by train to Kirishima-jingū Station, in the valley 7km to the south of the town. Buses from the station (7–11 daily; 15min; ¥240) drop you in the main square at the top of the town, just below the red-lacquer bridge. There's a small **tourist office** (daily: April–Sept 9am–6pm; Oct–March 9am–5pm; ⓣ0995/57-1588, ⓔinfo@kirishimacho.com) beside the big *torii* at the south end of this square. Here you'll also find convenience stores, a **post office** and a smattering of **restaurants**, though most stop serving around 5pm or 7pm.

The Kirishima range itself is best tackled by car, since public transport is patchy. A daily **sightseeing bus** leaves Kirishima Jingū Station at 9.55am (3hr; ¥2220), calling at Maruo and Hayashida Onsen on the way up to Ebino Kōgen. A better option if you want to see much on the plateau is to visit on a Saturday or Sunday, when a "Trekking Bus" departs at 8am and 10.20am from Kirishima-jingū Station for Takachiho-gawara and Ebino Kōgen (1hr; ¥740). Coming down, buses leave the plateau at 1pm and 3.30pm, but make sure you double-check bus times locally before setting off.

Kirishima Jingū and around

The small town of **KIRISHIMA** (霧島), built on the southern slopes of Takachiho-no-mine, makes a possible alternative base to Ebino Kōgen. The town is named after **Kirishima-jingū**, a beautiful shrine at its top end, an appealingly village-like area partly enveloped in cedar forests and focused around a cheerful, red-lacquer bridge. Kirishima also boasts a number of reasonable accommodation options and a couple of mildly interesting sights.

Accommodation

If you want to stay overnight, head to the top end of Kirishima Jingū, where you will find a cluster of minshuku. There are some excellent options in the surrounding area, though these can be hard to get to on public transport.

Sakura Sakura Onsen さくらさくら温泉 ⓣ0995/57-1227. This quality hotel has several rotemburo, but its speciality is volcanic mud – especially popular with young women for its skin-softening effects. The stunning baths are open to non-residents (daily 10am–8pm; ¥700). The hotel is roughly 3km west of Kirishima Jingū; a taxi will cost around ¥720. ❼

Tenku-no Mori 天空の森 ⓣ0995/76-0777, ⓦtenkunomori.net. Perfection at a price. With superb mountain views, all-pervasive scents and sounds of the outdoors and pampering at every turn, it would be hard to come away from this swish, remote resort feeling anything but a state of Zen-like bliss. Until, at least, you get your credit card bill – rack rates are a jaw-dropping ¥200,000. ❾

Tozan-guchi Onsen 登山口温泉 ⓣ0995/57-0127. Spruce little minshuku tucked just off the square – take the road heading east from the roundabout. It has a rooftop rotemburo and also doubles as a youth hostel (¥3500/person, or ¥5000 including meals), with accommodation in shared tatami rooms. ❺

The Town

The first sight of any interest in Kirishima Jingū is **Kirishima Tengu-kan** (霧島天狗館; daily 9am–5pm; ¥350) at the top of the central square – look for the building sprouting long-nosed goblin-like creatures. These are *tengu*, supernatural mountain spirits that often appear in folktales, nō plays and, more recently, manga and video games. Inside, some 1600 masks are on display, including a monster over 2m in length carved from local camphor wood. Across the square, the small **craft village** *Kirishima Mingei-mura* (霧島民芸村; daily 9am–5.30pm; free) is a little touristy, though some of the items on display are worth a quick look.

Heading over the lacquered bridge, walk under the bright vermilion *torii* and up a steep flight of steps to the shrine, **Kirishima-jingū (霧島神宮)**, after which the town is named. A surprisingly imposing complex, it's dedicated to Ninigi-no-mikoto and his fellow gods who first set foot in Kirishima at the dawn of Japan's creation.

Although there are fine views of Kagoshima Bay from the shrine, they're better from the summit of **Takachiho-no-mine** (高千穂峰; 1574m) itself, roughly three hours' walk to the northeast. With your own transport you can halve the walking time by driving 7km up the road to **Takachiho-gawara** (高千穂河原). It's then a steady climb on a well-marked path, ending in a short scramble on scree to the crater rim where a replica of Ninigi's sacred sword points skywards. Takachiho last erupted in 1913, and now only faint wisps of steam indicate that it's still active. Before setting off, you might want to take a brief look at the displays in the **visitors' centre** (daily 9am–5pm; ⓣ0995/57-2505), where you can also get local maps and other tourist information.

Ebino Kōgen

Whichever route you take to **EBINO KŌGEN** (えびの高原) the views are stunning. At 1200m above sea level, temperatures on the plateau rarely exceed 20°C in summer and dip well below freezing when winter gives the peaks a dusting of snow and hoarfrost and the tennis courts morph into an ice-skating rink. This is the best time to appreciate the local **onsen** – Kirishima is Japan's highest hot-spring resort – while spring and autumn provide perfect hiking weather.

Arrival and information

The centre of Ebino Kōgen consists of a large car park, around which everything happens: buses stop outside a souvenir shop to the south; there's a restaurant upstairs in the **Rest Centre** to the west; and you can get **information** at the visitors' centre (9am–5pm; closed Mon; ⓣ0984/33-3002) to the northeast. The centre also provides local sketch maps and sometimes has more detailed trekking maps, though it's safer to bring one with you if you're doing the longer hikes, just in case they've run out. While you're here, take a look at the 3D model of the area – it's handy for getting the lie of the land.

Exploring the plateau

If it's a clear day, try tackling **Karakuni-dake** (韓国岳) at the very least. The trails are signposted from the car park, heading northeast, with the quickest trail running beside a steaming, sulphurous scar known as Sai-no-kawara and then climbing steeply along a heavily eroded ridge. It's not a difficult climb, taking under two hours, though you'll want good footwear on the loose stones. From here you can circle south to Ōnami-no-ike (大波の池), Japan's largest crater lake, and then back to Ebino Kōgen, which will take about another three and a half hours. The classic walk, however, is east along Kirishima's magnificent volcanic peaks from Karakuni-dake to Takachiho-gawara; allow about five hours for the hike and remember to carry plenty of water. The path leads over Shishiko-dake (獅子戸岳; 1428m), the still-active Shinmoe-dake (新燃岳; 1421m) and Naka-dake (中岳; 1345m) with its two grassy hollows, and then descends to Takachiho-gawara. From here it's a 7km trot down to the comforts of Kirishima Jingū (see p.707), though if you time it right, at weekends you may be able to catch the bus (see p.707).

There are also more gentle ambles across the Ebino plateau. The most rewarding is a 4km walk starting from behind the Rest House, through forests of white fir and maple, and past three beautiful **crater lakes** before emerging beside Sai-no-kawara. If you are here in May or June, head southeast to where wild azaleas give the hillsides a dusty-pink tinge. As a reward for all this exercise, you can't do better than wallow in an **onsen**. The best is the smart **rotemburo** (daily 11.30am–8pm; ¥500 to non-guests) at *Ebino-kōgen-sō* (see opposite). If you don't fancy a full onsen, you can always ease aching feet in the free hot-spring footbath next to the Rest Centre.

Accommodation and eating

In Ebino Kōgen itself there are just two **hotels**. If you're not staying, it's a good idea to bring food with you to the plateau, since the few shops sell little more than souvenirs, snacks and drinks. The Rest Centre (daily 8am–5pm, last orders 4.30pm) offers either ramen or bentō downstairs and an array of set lunches in the restaurant upstairs.

Ebino-kōgen Campground えびの高原キャンプ村 ⓣ0984/33-0800. Open from April–Oct, this campground has tents and cheap wooden cabins among the pine forests. ❶

Ebino-kōgen-sō えびの高原荘 ⓣ0984/33-0161. A couple of minutes' walk west of the central car park, this is by far the swisher of the two hotels, with comfortable Western and Japanese rooms and a decent restaurant. ❼

Karakuni-sō からくに荘 ⓣ0984/33-0650. A 5min walk north of the visitor centre, comprising mostly Japanese rooms, including one in the annexe with a private onsen and mountain views. ❻

Kagoshima and around

Imagine having an onsen in waters heated by a live volcano. It sounds almost too good to be true, but this is more than possible in **KAGOSHIMA** (鹿児島), one of Japan's sunniest and most likeable cities. Kagoshima curls round the west shore of Kagoshima Bay, while on the other side of the water, and just fifteen minutes away by ferry, is the smouldering cone of **Sakurajima** – one of the world's most active volcanoes, and home to the aforementioned hot springs. Frequently to be seen billowing an enormous cloud of ash into the southern Kyūshū sky, this is the city's most obvious and compelling attraction, but Kagoshima contains a few sights of its own which justify a day's exploration. Foremost of these are its classical garden, **Sengan-en**, which uses Sakurajima in the ultimate example of borrowed scenery, and several excellent **museums** of local history and culture.

South of Kagoshima, the great claw of the Satsuma Peninsula extends into the East China Sea. Here lies the town of **Ibusuki**, whose trademark is a piping-hot, open-air sand bath on Surigahama beach; and **Kaimon-dake**, whose volcanic cone makes a good hike. Farther north is the town of **Chiran**, which contains a strip of beautifully preserved samurai houses, each with a diminutive traditional garden. Those staying in Kagoshima can tour both Chiran and Ibusuki in a single day, though if using public transport, bus schedules decree that Chiran must come first.

Some history

Originally known as **Satsuma**, the Kagoshima region was ruled by the powerful **Shimazu** clan for nearly seven centuries until the Meiji reforms put an end to such fiefdoms in 1871. The area has a long tradition of overseas contact and it was here that Japan's first Christian missionary, the Spanish-born Jesuit **Francis Xavier**, arrived in 1549. Welcomed by the Shimazu lords – who were primarily interested in trade and acquiring new technologies – he spent ten months working in Kagoshima, where he found the poorer classes particularly receptive to Christian teachings. After just a few months Xavier declared "it seems to me that we shall never find among heathens another race to equal the Japanese".

Soon after, Japan was closed to foreigners and remained so for the next two hundred years. As central control crumbled in the mid-nineteenth century, however, the far-sighted **Shimazu Nariakira** began introducing Western technology, such as spinning machines, the printing press and weapons manufacture, and it was Kagoshima that saw Japan's first gas light, steamships, electric lights, photographs and Morse code transmission. However, not all relations were cordial.

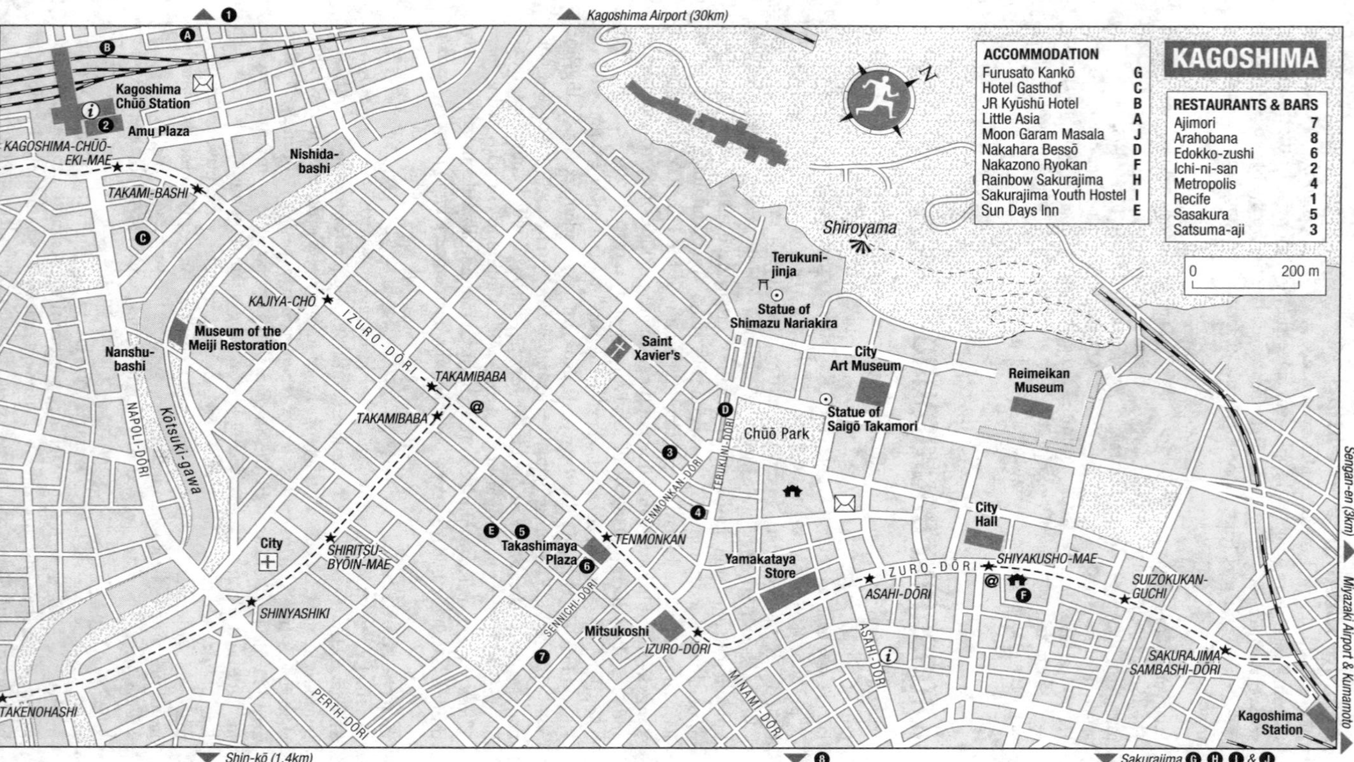
KAGOSHIMA
ACCOMMODATION
Furusato Kankō G
Hotel Gasthof C
JR Kyūshū Hotel B
Little Asia A
Moon Garam Masala J
Nakahara Bessō D
Nakazono Ryokan F
Rainbow Sakurajima H
Sakurajima Youth Hostel I
Sun Days Inn E
RESTAURANTS & BARS
Ajimori 7
Arahobana 8
Edokko-zushi 6
Ichi-ni-san 2
Metropolis 4
Recife 1
Sasakura 5
Satsuma-aji 3
0 200 m
Kagoshima Airport (30km)
Chiran & Ibusuki
Sengan-en (3km)
Miyazaki Airport & Kumamoto
Shin-kō (1.4km)
Sakurajima, G, H, I & J
Kagoshima Chūō Station
Amu Plaza
KAGOSHIMA-CHŪŌ-EKI-MAE
TAKAMI-BASHI
Nishida-bashi
Shiroyama
Terukuni-jinja
Statue of Shimazu Nariakira
KAJIYA-CHŌ
IZURO-DŌRI
Museum of the Meiji Restoration
Saint Xavier's
City Art Museum
Reimeikan Museum
Nanshu-bashi
TAKAMIBABA
TAKAMIBABA
Statue of Saigō Takamori
Chūō Park
NAPOLI-DŌRI
Kōtsuki-gawa
TERUKUNI-DŌRI
TEMMONKAN-DŌRI
City Hall
City
SHIRITSU-BYŌIN-MAE
Takashimaya Plaza
TENMONKAN
Yamakataya Store
SHIYAKUSHO-MAE
ASAHI-DŌRI
SUIZOKUKAN-GUCHI
SHINYASHIKI
SENNICHI-DŌRI
Mitsukoshi
IZURO-DŌRI
ASAHI-DŌRI
SAKURAJIMA SAMBASHI-DŌRI
TAKENOHASHI
PERTH-DŌRI
MINAMI-DŌRI
Kagoshima Station

In 1862 an Englishman was decapitated in Yokohama by a Shimazu retainer for crossing the road in front of the *daimyō*'s procession. When the Shimazu refused to punish the loyal samurai or pay compensation, seven **British warships** bombarded Kagoshima Bay in 1863. Fortunately there was little loss of life and the Shimazu were so impressed by this show of force that three years later they dispatched nineteen "young pioneers" to study in London – many of these young men went on to assist the new Meiji government in its mission to modernize Japan. Easily Kagoshima's most famous son, however, is **Saigō Takamori** (see p.712).

Arrival and information

Kagoshima **airport**, served by flights to Seoul and Shanghai as well as domestic routes, is located some 30km north of the city, and actually far closer to Kirishima National Park if you're headed that way. **Buses** depart every ten or twenty minutes for town (¥1200); express services (40min) head straight to the gleaming Kagoshima Chūō Station, while regular services (1hr) stop at central Kagoshima's Tenmonkan crossroads en route. The new Tsubame **Shinkansen** heads from Kagoshima Chūō Station to Kumamoto and Hakata; local trains use the same station (and sometimes Kumamoto Station, east of the city centre), while intercity buses usually arrive at a terminal opposite the east exit.

Kagoshima's main **tourist office** (daily 8.30am–7pm; ⓣ099/253-2500, ⓦwww.city.kagoshima.lg.jp), located inside Kagoshima Chūō Station, provides the useful *Kagoshima Course Guide*, which comprises a city map and recommended itineraries; they can also assist with accommodation and provide information about Kirishima (see p.706) and Yakushima (p.720).

City transport

Moving around central Kagoshima is simplified by a highly efficient two-line **tram system** that has been in operation since 1912 – some of the original cars are still used. There's a flat fare of ¥160, which you pay on exit; trams run roughly every eight minutes from 6.30am–10.30pm.

The local **bus system** is a lot more complicated, with services run by five different companies. However, easily recognizable, retro-style **City View** tourist buses depart every half-hour (9am–5pm) on a circuit of the main sights from Kagoshima Chūō Station (stand #9) via the Museum of the Meiji Restoration, Reimeikan and Shiroyama observatory to Sengan-en, before returning via Dolphin Port and Tenmonkan. You can buy individual tickets (¥180) or a one-day pass (¥600), which also covers the trams; it's available at the tourist information centre, or on board the buses and trams, and entitles you to discount tickets to various sights.

Local **ferries** to Sakurajima depart from a pier to the east of the city centre. The nearby Minami-Futō (South Pier) is used by services to Yakushima and Ibusuki, while those to Okinawa currently operate out of the quite separate and even more southerly Shin-kō, though it's possible they may move to Kita-Futō (North Pier), which lies between Minami-Futō and the Sakurajima pier.

Accommodation

Kagoshima is well provided with mid- and lower-range business hotels, offering comfortable if unexciting **accommodation**. It also has a smattering of Japanese-style places and there are a few decent options over on Sakurajima (see p.715).

Hotel Gasthof 7-1 Chūō-chō ⓣ099/252-1401. Remodelled in an eclectic mix of foreign styles, this hotel is excellent value. The attention to detail is admirable – think bathrooms lined with pearlescent tiling, chunky beds and tartan frills – while there are some superb restaurants in the same building. ❺

JR Kyūshū Hotel Kagoshima Chūō Eki ⓣ099/213-8029. Rooms in the new north wing of this station hotel have been designed along the lines of the award-winning JR Kyūshū trains – sleek contours, soft lighting and dark wood. Perfect for the style-conscious, or those with an early train to catch. ❺

Little Asia 2-20-8 Nishida ⓣ099/251-8166, ⓦwww.cheaphotelasia.com. A backpacker's delight – clean, cheap as chips, free internet and within spitting distance of the train station. The only drawback is the somewhat surly nature of the staff. Dorms ¥1500.

Nakahara Bessō 15-19 Higashi-Sengoku-chō ⓣ099/225-2800, ⓦwww.nakahara-bessou.co.jp. Nicely decorated onsen hotel in the city centre overlooking Chūō Park. The Japanese-style rooms are better value, and though they do offer room-only rates, the meals are highly recommended. ❼

Nakazono Ryokan 1-18 Yasui-chō ⓣ099/226-5125, ⓔshindon@satsuma.ne.jp. There's always service with a smile at this homely ryokan, tucked behind a temple opposite Kagoshima City Hall. The tatami rooms are clean and large enough, though facilities are shared. ❸

Sun Days Inn 9-8 Yamanokuchi-chō ⓣ099/227-5151. Stylish rooms, friendly staff and low prices make this nicely contemporary business hotel a real treat. You can often get hefty discounts by booking online – staff have been known to let guests use the lobby computer for this purpose – but try to get a room with views of Sakurajima. ❹

The City

Kagoshima's handful of central sights are gathered round the informative **Reimeikan** museum at the foot of Shiroyama. From here, you can either walk or take a tram south to the banks of the Kōtsuki-gawa, where there's a gimmicky but entertaining **Museum of the Meiji Restoration**. A few kilometres north of town, the **Sengan-en** area is of interest not only for its traditional garden, but also for a museum celebrating the modernizing zeal of the enterprising Shimazu lords. All these sights are served by the City View bus (see p.711), while you'll need to catch a ferry to visit **Sakurajima** (p.715).

Chūō Park and around

There are a few interesting sights in the area around Chūō Park, though the best place from which to kick off a walking tour is the delightful **Terukuni-jinja** (照国神社). The greenery and mossy tree trunks surrounding this shrine enable it to blend seamlessly into Shiroyama, the mountain rearing up behind the complex (see p.713). The main hall of the shrine is somewhat disappointing – its surrounding buildings and statues are of more interest. The first statue you'll come to is of Shimazu Nariakira (see p.709), to whom the shrine is dedicated,

Saigō Takamori

Born in 1827, **Saigō Takamori** made his name as one of the leading figures in the **Meiji Restoration**. Though aware of the need for Japan to modernize, he grew increasingly alarmed at the loss of traditional values and eventually left the government to set up a military academy in Kagoshima. He soon became a focus for opposition forces – mainly disaffected samurai but also peasants protesting at punitive taxes. Things came to a head in January 1877 when Saigō led an army of 40,000 against the government stronghold in Kumamoto, in what came to be known as the **Satsuma Rebellion**. After besieging the castle for nearly two months, the rebels were forced to withdraw before the 60,000-strong Imperial Army. They retreated to Kagoshima where they were gradually pinned down on Shiroyama. On September 24, the imperial forces closed in and Saigō, severely wounded, asked one of his comrades to kill him. His courage, idealism and heroic death earned Saigō enormous popular support – so much so that he was officially pardoned by imperial decree in 1891.

while just to the north is a statue of his half-brother Hisamitsu, his successor in power, if not title.

Zigzagging northeast will bring you to the **City Art Museum** (鹿児島市立美術館; 9.30am–6pm; closed Mon; ¥200). This spacious modern building houses a good collection of Impressionist and twentieth-century Western art, besides highly rated local artists such as Kuroda Seiki and Fujishima Takeji. Outside the museum, and facing south across Chūō Park, is a bronze statue of the close-cropped, portly Saigō Takamori (see box opposite). Unlike the more relaxed portrait in Tokyo's Ueno-kōen (see p.117), this shows Saigō as an uncompromising military leader. Behind him, carp-filled moats and some bullet-pocked walls are all that remain of **Tsurumaru-jō** following the 1877 Satsuma Rebellion.

Walking north from here, you will reach an arched stone bridge that leads up to the **Reimeikan** museum (黎明館; 9am–5pm; closed Mon; ¥300), which provides a good introduction to local history and culture. Apart from a delightful mock-up of Tenmonkan arcade as it would have looked in the 1930s, the most interesting displays cover local festivals and the southern islands' distinct traditions, showing the influence of Melanesian culture from the islands of the West Pacific. Behind the museum is a path leading up through impressive stands of mature, subtropical trees to the top of **Shiroyama** (城山). The twenty-minute climb is worth it for superb views over Kagoshima and the smouldering cone of Sakurajima.

From the Reimeikan, it's a ten-minute seaward walk to the **City Aquarium** (かごしま水族館; daily 9.30am–6pm; ¥1500), on a man-made island in the harbour. Thanks to the warm Kuroshio current sweeping across from the East China Sea, the waters around Kagoshima's southern islands are rich in temperate and subtropical aquatic life, a broad range of which is on show in this well-designed installation, from Sakurajima's unique tube worm to colourful sea anemones.

Around the Kōtsuki-gawa

The engaging **Museum of the Meiji Restoration** (維新ふるさと館; daily 9am–5pm; ¥300) sits beside the tranquil Kōtsuki-gawa. No expense has been spared to re-create the "golden age" of Kagoshima, when Saigō and other local luminaries were instrumental in returning power to the emperor and then spearheading the Meiji reforms. The highlight is a 25-minute sound and light show in which robots – including a wild-eyed Saigō – re-enact scenes from the restoration. The show takes place roughly once an hour (9.15am–4.30pm) in the basement theatre and headsets are available for an English-language translation. Upstairs, don't miss listening to the original version of the Japanese national anthem, recorded by the Satsuma Military Band in 1870, composed a couple of years earlier by an Irish bandmaster, John William Fenton.

Sengan-en

When their base at Tsurumaru-jō was destroyed during the Satsuma Rebellion, the Shimazu lords set up residence in their lovely garden-villa Iso Tei-en, now known as **Sengan-en** (仙巌園; daily 8.30am–5.30pm; ¥1000, or ¥1500 including entry to the residence; Ⓦwww.senganen.jp), 3km east of the city centre. Though the villa itself is beautiful, the main points of interest are the garden, with its views of Sakurajima, unfortunately now interrupted by the main road and train tracks, and the neighbouring history museum.

The easiest way to reach Sengan-en is to take the City View tourist bus or a regular bus from Kagoshima Chūō Station or Tenmonkan (every 30min; 15–20min; ¥180); check the destination when you get on, as a few buses skip Sengan-en.

Eating

Kagoshima's most popular **speciality foods** are *Satsuma-age*, a deep-fried, slightly sweet patty of minced fish and sake, eaten with ginger and soy sauce, and steaks of succulent *kurobuta* pork. The prettiest local dish is *kibinago sashimi*, in which slices of a silvery, sardine-like fish are arranged in an eye-catching flower head. *Keihan* mixes shredded chicken with carrot, egg, mushroom and spring onions over a bowl of rice in a hot, tasty broth, while *sake-zushi* consists of sushi with a drop of sake. For snacks, there's *Satsuma-imo* ice cream (made with sweet potato) and *jambo mochi* – rice cakes smothered in sweet sauce and impaled on a pair of bamboo skewers.

Ajimori あぢもり 13-21 Sennichi-chō. This nicely informal restaurant, specializing in *tonkatsu* and *shabu-shabu*, has a good choice of set meals (from around ¥700, or ¥3200 for *shabu shabu*). Noon–2.30pm & 5.30–9.30pm; closed Wed.

Arahobana 新穂花 Dolphin Port, 5-4 Honkōshin-machi ⓦwww.fenyworld.com/arahobana. There's a breezy, tropical atmosphere to this restaurant specializing in the food of the Amami islands, off Kagoshima's south coast. Choose from an extensive range of well-priced set meals, including *keihan* and all sorts of black-pork dishes, from around ¥1000, washed down with some local *shōchū*.

Edokko-zushi 江戸ッ子寿司 2-16 Sennichi-chō ⓦwww.edokoo-susi.jp. Long-established and justifiably popular sushi bar on a street corner to the west of Izuro-dōri. Prices are reasonable, with sushi sets starting at around ¥1100. It also does sashimi and tempura; an English menu is available. Daily 11.30am–midnight.

Ichi-ni-san 5F, Amu Plaza, 1-1 Chūō-chō. An attractive place on Amu Plaza's restaurant floor, with decoration skating the line between traditional and contemporary. Kagoshima specialities such as *kurobuta* with ginger can be ordered from an English menu (of sorts), and there's an excellent range of local *shōchū* . Daily 11am–11pm.

Satsuma-aji さつま路 6-29 Higashi-Sengoku-chō ⓦwww.satumaji.co.jp. If you're after a more relaxed dining experience, try this elegantly rustic restaurant serving fairly pricey but top-quality local food. Lunch deals start at ¥1575 and there's a picture-menu. Daily 11.30am–2.30pm & 5.30–10pm.

Drinking

Kagoshima prefecture is also Japan's biggest producer, and consumer, of *shōchū* (see box opposite). Its **nightlife district fills** the lanes either side of the Sennichi arcade, to the east of Izuro-dōri.

Metropolis 3F, 16-18 Higashi-Sengoku-chō. Visually appealing venue with colourful chandeliers, bright red walls, comfy floor-cushions and bizarre egg-like lights. Various (all-you-can-drink) courses make it possible to select your desired level of inebriation. Daily 6pm–3am.

Recife 2-1-5 Takashi. An expat favourite, this English-owned bar has a mix of tasty Western and Mexican dishes, and a highly impressive drinks list. Has fun theme nights during the week. 6pm–late.

Sasakura 酒々蔵 9-17 Yamanokuchi-chō. There are over 150 different types of Kagoshima *shōchū* available in this traditionally styled *izakaya*. Prices start at a very reasonable ¥300/glass, and there's good, inexpensive food to soak it up with. Daily 6.30pm–3am.

Listings

Airport information ⓣ099/558-2740.

Banks and exchange Banks offering foreign exchange are along Izuro-dōri. The Central Post Office has international ATMs, and there's another in the Amu Plaza.

Bookshops Kinokuniya, on Amu Plaza's fourth floor, has the largest selection of English-language books and magazines.

Car rental Eki Rent-a-Car (ⓣ099/258-1412), Budget (ⓣ099/250-0543) and Japaren (ⓣ099/257-3900) all have offices near Kagoshima Central Station.

Ferries A Line (ⓣ099/226-4141) and Marix Line (ⓣ099/225-1551, ⓦwww.marix-line.co.jp) ferries sail to Okinawa from Kagoshima Shin-kō, the city's southern port (25hr; ¥14,200). Services to Yakushima and Ibusuki use the adjacent Minami-Futō (South Pier): Toppy (ⓣ099/256-7771, ⓦwww.toppy.jp) operates hydrofoils to both Yakushima (2hr–2hr 40min; ¥6500) and Ibusuki

Kagoshima shōchū

With the possible exception of Miyazaki residents, Japanese are in near-unanimous agreement that Kagoshima's **shōchū** is the best in the land, and there are more than 800 local varieties available. These are usually made from **sweet potato** rather than rice, which makes for a heavier flavour, and a higher alcohol content – 25 percent, rather than the national norm of 20 percent. As is the case elsewhere, one can have the hooch served straight, with soda, heated, mixed with hot water, or on the rocks. Like wine, each variety has its own specific taste, but lengthy *izakaya* lists will mean nothing to the average foreign visitor – so here are a few top picks to get you started.

Kaidō 海童 Served in a distinctive red bottle, this is perhaps the best low- to mid-range choice, and has a clean, crisp taste that works best on the rocks.

Kojika 小鹿 Cheap but high-quality option, whose slightly dry taste is magnified when served heated.

Kuro 黒 Popular with young and old alike, this tasty cheapie is available in pretty much every *izakaya* and convenience store across the prefecture. Best served heated.

Maō 魔王 Running Mori Izō a close second for quality, this slightly sweet variety is a favourite with Kagoshima connoisseurs.

Mori Izō 森伊蔵 The king of local *shōchū*, this high-roller favourite can cost over ¥70,000 per bottle in a Tokyo *izakaya*, but is usually available here for a fraction of the price. Have it neat, or with hot water.

Nofū 野風 A rarity in Kagoshima *shōchū* terms, in that it's made from corn rather than sweet potato. Though, being 35 percent alcohol by volume, you may not notice.

Shiranami 白波 The most famed variety in Kagoshima city itself, this is available in over a dozen different grades, including the somewhat hazardous 37 percent-alcohol Genshū variety.

(40min; ¥2100); Cosmo Line (Ⓣ099/223-1011, Ⓦwww.cosmoline.jp) runs the cheaper Rocket hydrofoil service to Yakushima only (2hr; ¥6500); and there are also regular ferries to Yakushima (4hr; ¥3800) with Orita Kisen (Ⓣ099/226-0731), and Yakushima Maru (4hr; ¥3200).

Hospital The most central hospital with English-speaking staff is the Kagoshima City Hospital, 20-17 Kajiya-chō (Ⓣ099/224-2101), near the Shiritsu Byōin-mae tram stop (line #1).

Internet The International Exchange Plaza (Tues–Sun 9am–5pm; take your passport or other ID) offers free access. Otherwise, try *Aprecio* (24hr; from ¥480 for 1hr including free soft drinks and curry rice), on Izuro-dōri – look for the mock castle exterior.

Police Kagoshima-Chūō Police Station, 13-1 Yamashita-chō Ⓣ099/222-0110.

Post office Kagoshima Central Post Office is right next to Kagoshima Chūō Station. There's also a handy sub-office on Asahi-dōri near Chūō-kōen. Both have ATMs which take international bank cards.

Sakurajima

Kagoshima's most stirring sight, the volcanic cone of **Sakurajima** (桜島) grumbles away just 4km from the city centre, pouring a column of dense black ash into the air. This is one of the world's most active volcanoes, and hiking its peak has been prohibited since 1955 – adventurous sorts should know that security cameras have been installed around the mountain. However, Sakurajima remains a great place to head for an onsen: unlike most such facilities around the country, the island's smouldering cone provides tangible proof of just how its water has been heated.

Ferries from Kagoshima (15min; ¥150) dock at a small pier on Sakurajima's west coast. The service operates 24 hours a day, with sailings every ten to fifteen minutes from 7am–8pm; you pay at the Sakurajima end. There's an **information** desk (daily 8.30am–5pm; Ⓣ099/293-4333) upstairs in the terminal building,

Explosive island

Major **eruptions** of Sakurajima have been recorded from the early eighth century until as recently as 1947, though the most violent in living memory was that of 1914, during which enough lava spilled down the southeast slopes to fill the 400m-wide channel that previously separated Sakurajima from the mainland. Volcanic activity varies from year to year: there were just 18 eruptions in 2005, but this increased to an all-time record of more than two thousand eruptions in 2010 – around half-a-dozen every single day. During periods of high activity, the likely direction of the resultant **ash** forms part of the weather forecasts on TV – it usually heads northeast during colder months, and west (ie towards Kagoshima city centre) in the summer, when you may find yourself crunching granules of dust that were, just a few hours beforehand, several hundred metres below the surface of the earth, and considerably hotter. Sakurajima's prime **viewing point** is its eastern coast at night-time – if you're in luck, you may well see the faraway glow of molten lava.

though more useful is a visitor centre (daily 9am–5pm) a ten-minute walk away, just beyond the *Rainbow Sakurajima* hotel.

The island

A single road (40km) circles Sakurajima at sea level, past lava fields, onsen baths and a couple of observation points. The island is much too large to walk, but Sakurajima Rent-a-Car (ⓣ099/293-2162) rents **cars** (¥8500 for a half day) and **bikes** (¥300/hour) just outside the ferry terminal. Most, however, get around using **sightseeing buses**, which depart twice daily (9.40am & 2.20pm; ¥1700) from Sakurajima ferry terminal and Kagoshima Chūō Station (9am & 1.40pm; ¥2200 including return ferry tickets) on an anticlockwise circuit of the volcano. They kick off their **tour** of the island with a tortuous route up the volcano's west flank to the **Yunohira Observatory** (373m). This is the closest you can get to the deeply creviced summit, which in fact comprises three cones, from the highest, northerly Kita-dake (1117m), to Minami-dake (1040m), the most active, in the south. Weather permitting, you'll also be treated to sweeping views of Kagoshima Bay. You then drop down to **Furusato Onsen** (古里温泉), where resort hotels capitalize on the abundant supplies of hot water. The best of these, *Furusato Kankō Hotel* (see below), features a large, cliff-side **rotemburo** (8am–8pm, till 3pm on Thurs; ¥1050) shaded by a sacred camphor tree; the hotel runs a free shuttle service from the ferry port to the hotel between 8.45am and 5pm.

Continuing along the south coast, Sakurajima's brooding presence becomes more apparent as you start to see the lava fields around the **Arimura Observatory**, barren since the devastating explosion of 1914 (see box, above). A little further on, past the narrow neck of land, look out on the left for the buried *torii* of Kurokami-jinja. Originally 3m tall, now just the top crossbars protrude from a bed of ash and pumice. Turning up the north coast, the slopes get gentler and you'll see plenty of crops growing in the fertile volcanic soils, which produce not only the world's largest radishes – up to 40kg in weight and over 1m in diameter – but also its smallest mandarins, measuring a mere 3cm across.

Accommodation

Furusato Kankō Hotel 1076-1 Furusato-chō ⓣ099/221-3111. Most head to this ryokan simply to use the wonderful waterside rotemburo – not a bad idea, since its rooms are crying out for renovation. It's on the south coast of the island, fifteen minutes from the ferry pier by shuttle bus (8.45am–5pm; free). ❼

Moon Garam Masala 1722 Yokoyama-chō ⓣ090/9952-3513. Just around the corner from the ferry terminal and doubling as a café, this curious venue is something like a Thai beach hut transported to a Japanese car park. Run by a renowned Okinawan musician, who pops by from time to time, it's presided over by a delightful former hippy whose travels took her across most of the world. Just two dorm beds here, each ¥1300/night.

Rainbow Sakurajima レインボー桜島 1722-16 Yokoyama-chō ⓣ099/293-2323. This modern hotel on the seafront, less than 10min walk south round the harbour from the Sakurajima ferry terminal, makes a good base for exploring the island. It offers a mix of Japanese and Western rooms and a big onsen bath (¥300 for non-guests; 10am–10pm). ❻

Sakurajima Youth Hostel 桜島ユースホステル 189 Yokoyama-chō ⓣ&ⓕ099/293-2150. This big, relaxed hostel with dorm beds (¥2650/person) and an onsen bath is a 10min walk uphill from the ferry terminal – just follow the signs. Meals available. ❶

Ibusuki

Claiming to be Japan's third-largest hot-spring resort by volume of water, the small town of **IBUSUKI** (指宿) is a much more low-key affair than its northerly rival, Beppu (see p.693). Its main attributes are an attractive setting on a sweeping bay and a **sand bath** where you get buried up to the neck in hot sand – a more enjoyable experience than it sounds. Once you've rinsed off the grains and strolled the promenade, however, there's nothing much to do except head off to Chiran and other places in the neighbourhood (see pp.718–719).

Arrival and information

The easiest and quickest way to reach Ibusuki is by JR train (1–2 hourly; 50min–1hr 20min; ¥970) or Toppy hydrofoil (daily; 40min; ¥2100) from Kagoshima – both offer good views across Kagoshima Bay to Sakurajima and the Sata Peninsula, though note that reservations are a good idea if going by sea.

Ibusuki's **train station** lies on the west side of town, and there's a small **tourist information** desk inside. **Buses** stop on the road outside the station, while the Kagoshima Kōtsū bus office is across the road. If you're planning to move on to Yakushima, you can walk to Ibusuki port in fifteen minutes from the train station or take a taxi (around ¥800); for more detailed information on getting to Yakushima by boat, see p.722.

As Ibusuki is so spread out, it's worth **renting bikes** to get around the central district. Eki Rent-a-Car (daily 8am–5pm; ¥300/2hr, up to ¥900/day; ⓣ0993/23-3879), next to the station, rents electric bikes and also offers **car rental**.

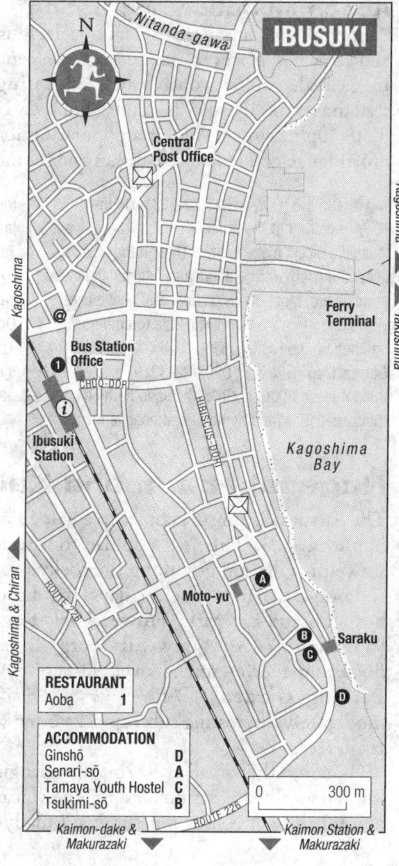

The town

Ibusuki's main north–south avenue, palm-tree-lined Hibiscus-dori, is shadowed a few hundred metres inland by a road passing in front of the JR station. Chūō-dōri, which counts as Ibusuki's prime shopping street, leads from the station to meet the sea at the bay's midpoint. Ten minutes' walk south of here, there's a second clutch of shops and restaurants gathered around the famous sand bath.

This southern stretch of beach is known as **Surigahama** (摺ヶ浜). Like much of Japan's coast, it is protected by concrete breakwaters, but a few stretches of black, volcanic sand remain, from which wisps of scalding steam mark the presence of hot springs. It's the done thing in Ibusuki to take a **sand bath** (*suna-mushi*), which is best at low tide when everyone is buried on the beach itself, leaving a row of heads under snazzy sunshades; at high tide a raised bed beside the sea wall is used. You can buy tickets and change into a *yukata* in the modern **Saraku** (砂楽) bathhouse immediately behind the beach (daily 8.30am–8.30pm; ¥900, including sand bath and *yukata* rental). You then troop down to the beach and lie down – take a small towel to wrap round your head. At over 50°C, the sand temperature is much hotter than Beppu's rival bath (see p.696) and most people find it difficult to last the recommended ten minutes. All sorts of claims are made as to the sand bath's medical benefits, but if nothing else it leaves you feeling wonderfully invigorated.

Accommodation and eating

Among the big, upmarket resort **hotels**, Ibusuki does have a number of reasonable and attractive places to stay in the town centre; prices given below include meals. In general, you're probably best off **eating** in your hotel, since the choice of restaurants in Ibusuki is pretty limited. However, *Aoba* (青葉; 11am–3pm & 5.30–10pm; closed Wed) is a popular option, just north of the station, serving a broad range of inexpensive dishes and set meals.

Ginshō 吟松 ⓣ093/22-3231. On the seafront at the far south end of town, this is Ibusuki's nicest place to stay. Though the building itself is modern, inside it has a traditional Japanese atmosphere. Most of the tatami rooms have ocean views and there's a wonderful little rotemburo perched on the rooftop. ❽

Sennari-sō 千成荘 ⓣ0993/22-3379, ⓕ3753. Budget place 200m north of the sand bath on Hibiscus-dori, with a home-like atmosphere, friendly staff and small but sparkling en-suite tatami rooms. ❺

Tamaya Youth Hostel 圭屋ユースホステル ⓣ0993/22-3553. Acceptable venue opposite the sand bath, about 15min walk from the station. Dorm beds ¥2725/person.

Tsukimi-sō 月見荘 ⓣ0993/22-4221. Spick-and-span new ryokan across the road from the sand bath, and fair value for the price. ❼

Nagasaki-bana and Kaimon-dake

The Satsuma Peninsula comes to a halt 13km southwest of Ibusuki at **Nagasaki-bana** (長崎鼻). This is a popular tourist spot and it's worth walking past the souvenir stalls and out along the rocky promontory to enjoy the classic view of Kaimon-dake and, on clear days, the distant peaks of Yakushima. Next to the bus stop and car park, **Flower Park Kagoshima** (フラワーパークかごしま; daily 9am–5pm; ¥600; ⓦwww.fp-k.org) lives up to its name with nearly 2500 flowering species spread over 90 acres. Also here is the rather oddly named **Parking Garden** (長崎鼻パーキングガーデン; daily 8.20am–5pm; ¥1200), a moderately interesting subtropical garden where parrots, monkeys and flamingos roam free.

Though rather small at 922m, the triangular peak of **Kaimon-dake** (開聞岳) is known locally as "Satsuma Fuji". The volcano last erupted some 15,000 years ago and much of it is now a nature park (daily: Feb–Oct 7.30am–5.30pm; Nov–Jan

7.30am–5pm; ¥350) inhabited by wild Tokara ponies. The classic route up Kaimon-dake is from Kaimon Station, the start of a 5km-long path which spirals round the cone. It takes about two hours and the effort is rewarded with views south to the Satsunan Islands of Yakushima and Tanegashima, and north beyond Sakurajima to Kirishima. Kaimon Station is on the JR line between Ibusuki and Makurazaki (6 daily; 35min).

Chiran

A small town lying in a broad valley, **CHIRAN** (知覧) owes its fortune to the Shimazu lords of Kagoshima (see p.709). In the eighteenth century, the Shimazu's chief retainers, the Sata family, were permitted to build a semi-fortified village, and a number of their handsome **samurai houses** survive today. Two hundred years later, an airfield on the outskirts of Chiran became the base for kamikaze suicide bombers during World War II. The site has now been turned into a **museum**, documenting the history of the kamikaze and commemorating the hundreds of young pilots who died. The road to it is lined with stone lanterns, one for each pilot.

Arrival and information

Coming from Ibusuki, you arrive first on the southwest side of Chiran at an expanse of car parks and souvenir shops that marks the entrance to the town's two museums. Here you'll also find the town's **information** office (daily 9am–4pm; Ⓣ0993/83-2511, Ⓦwww.town.chiran.kagoshima.jp), on the far side of the car parks, where you can pick up handy maps and bus timetables and arrange a taxi if needed. If you are travelling by bus, note that these services are fairly infrequent, so keep a careful eye on the times of onward buses if you don't want to get stranded.

The museums

The **Special Attack Peace Hall** (特攻平和会館; daily 9am–5pm; ¥500, or ¥600 including Museum Chiran; audio guide ¥100), marks the site of a military airfield that was established in 1942. Two years later Chiran was chosen as the base for the "Special Attack Forces", better known in the west as the **kamikaze**.

The hall, which was established in 1975, is essentially a memorial to the pilots' undoubted courage and makes little mention of the wider context or moral argument. That aside, the photos, farewell letters and the pilots' often childish mascots are tragic mementoes of the young lives wasted. Several pilots' letters

Divine wind

In 1944, Chiran etched itself into Japanese history, the town becoming a main base for a somewhat novel breed of fighter pilot whose mission was to crash their bomb-laden planes into American ships – they're better known in the West as the **kamikaze**, in reference to a "divine wind" which saved Japan from Mongol invasions in the late thirteenth century (see p.769). Hundreds of young men, most of them mere teenagers, rallied to the call, eager to die for the emperor in true samurai style. Their opportunity came during the battle of Okinawa (see p.732), when 1036 pilots died; their photos line one wall of the museum. Before leaving, they were given a last cigarette, a drink of sake and a blessing, after which they donned their "rising sun" headband and set off on the lonely, one-way mission with enough fuel to last for two hours. It seems that many never reached their target: the toll was 56 American ships sunk, 107 crippled and 300 seriously damaged.

reveal that, though they knew the war was lost, they were still willing to make the ultimate sacrifice – you'll see many older Japanese people walking round in tears and it's hard not to be moved, despite the chilling overtones. Since very little is translated into English, make sure you pick up an audio guide (¥100) at the ticket desk.

If you have time you might like to visit the more cheerful **Museum Chiran** (ミュージアム知覧; Wed 9am–5pm; closed Wed; ¥300) beside the Peace Hall. Concentrating on local history and culture, the exhibits are beautifully displayed, with the most interesting showing the strong influence of Okinawan culture on Kagoshima's festivals and crafts.

Hotaru-kan and the samurai houses

Chiran town centre is a five-minute ride by bus (get off at *Nakagōri* bus stop) or around ¥700 by taxi away from the Peace Hall. The main road runs roughly east–west through the middle of town. Just before it crosses the river for the second time you'll find **Hotaru-kan** (ホタル館; daily 9am–5pm; ¥350), opposite the *Nakagōri* bus stop. During the war this old wooden house was a restaurant, run by a motherly figure called Torihama Tome, who saw hundreds of young pilots pass through on their way to certain death. Many left personal possessions and messages for their families with Tome-san, some of which are now on display, alongside deeply moving pictures, letters and personal effects. Unfortunately, there are no English-language translations.

Continuing east across the river, the **samurai houses**, or *buké-yashiki* (武家屋敷; daily 9am–5pm; ¥500), are scattered along an attractive lane that runs parallel to and south of the main road, behind ancient stone walls topped by neatly clipped hedges. Since many of the houses are still occupied, you can't see inside, but the main interest lies in their small but intricate **gardens**, some said to be the work of designers brought from Kyoto. Seven gardens, indicated by signs in English, are open to the public. Though each is different in its composition, they mostly use rock groupings and shrubs to represent a classic scene of mountains, valleys and waterfalls taken from Chinese landscape painting. In the best of them, such as the gardens of Hirayama Katsumi and Hirayama Ryoichi, the design also incorporates the hills behind as "borrowed scenery". Look out, too, for defensive features such as solid, screened entry gates and latrines beside the front gate – apparently, this was so that the occupant could eavesdrop on passers-by.

Eating

One of the nicest places to **eat** in Chiran is *Nagōmi* (和; daily 10am–3pm), set in gardens on a lane behind the Hotaru-kan. It offers a range of well-priced set lunches from ¥780. Alternatively, you could take a pit stop at *Taki-an* (高城庵; daily 10.30am–4.30pm), in a thatched building set in another garden at the east end of the samurai street; their speciality is soba and udon, or try the sweet *jambo-mochi* (pounded rice on bamboo skewers).

Yakushima

Craggy mountain peaks; wave after wave of dripping, subtropcial rainforest; towering cedar trees which predate the Roman Empire; the all-pervasive scent of moss and flowers. If this sounds a little like the setting for an anime, rather than real-life Japan, you'd be half-right – Miyazaki Hayao was said to have taken his inspiration from Yakushima's lush forests when creating Princess Mononoke

(see p.809). Mystical deer are sadly off the agenda (though there's no harm in looking), but the aforementioned natural charms of Yakushima (屋久島) are usually enough to knock the socks off the few foreign travellers who make it to this island, which climbs steeply from the sea some 60km off Kyūshū.

Pray, however, that the weather cooperates – locals joke that it rains "35 days a month". Yakushima greedily gobbles up almost every passing cloud, resulting in an average annual rainfall of at least 4m on the coast and a staggering 8–10m in its mountainous interior. This feeds tumbling streams and a lush, primeval forest famous for its magnificent **Yaku-sugi** cedar trees, the oldest of which are well over 2000 years and honoured with individual names (trees under 1000 years are known as *ko-sugi*, or "small cedars"). **Jōmon-sugi** is known to be at least 2300 years old and thought to be the oldest; it grows high in the mountains. Logging companies worked Yakushima's forests until the early 1970s, but much of the island is now protected within the Kirishima-Yaku National Park, now a UNESCO World Heritage Site.

Yakushima's population of around 13,600 is concentrated in the two main towns of **Miyanoura** and **Anbō** or scattered in small settlements around the coast. An increasingly popular tourist destination, Yakushima now boasts a number of swish resort hotels in addition to simpler accommodation. Most people, however, come to hike and camp among the peaks, where the older cedars are found. For the less adventurous, **Yaku-sugi Land** contains a few more accessible trees and can be reached by public bus. Otherwise, there are a couple of good **local museums**, a

Getting to the island

Kagoshima serves as the main **access** point for Yakushima. There are five JAL (Ⓦwww.jal.co.jp) **flights** daily from Kagoshima airport (35min; ¥13,900 one-way), and two daily flights from Ōsaka's Itami airport. Yakushima airport (Ⓣ0997/42-1200) lies on the island's northeast coast roughly midway between the two main towns, Miyanoura and Anbō, and is served by local buses and taxis.

By the time you've included transport to and from the airports, however, the two **hydrofoil** services from Kagoshima's Minami-Futō terminal are almost as speedy. Toppy (Ⓣ099/256-7771, Ⓦwww.toppy.jp) operates five sailings daily (2hr–2hr 40min; ¥6500). Some of these hydrofoils also stop at Tanegashima en route and, while most dock at Miyanoura, one or two use Anbō port, so check beforehand. In addition, Cosmo Line (Ⓣ099/223-1011, Ⓦwww.cosmoline.jp) runs the Rocket hydrofoil (¥6500, or ¥10,600 return) to Miyanoura via Tanegashima, with one direct sailing daily (1hr 50min) and two via Tanegashima (2hr 50min). Reservations are required in both cases and can be made through a travel agent or with the ferry company, or you can buy advance tickets at the terminal in Kagoshima. For information and reservations on Yakushima call the Toppy office in Miyanoura (Ⓣ0997/42-0034) or Anbō (Ⓣ0997/46-3399) and Cosmo Line on Ⓣ0997/42-2003. Bear in mind that hydrofoils stop running in bad weather.

Finally, daily **ferries**, operated by Orita Kisen (Ⓣ099/226-0731; Ⓣ0997/42-1660 in Yakushima), also depart from Kagoshima's Minami-Futō (4hr; from ¥5200 one-way, ¥8200 return), as do the cheaper Yakushima Maru services (4hr; from ¥3200 one-way, ¥6400 return). If you're not in a hurry, these ships are a great way to travel and reservations are not required unless you want a private cabin. You might want to bring your own food, however, since there's not a great choice; there's also very little seating, just tatami mats or carpets.

seaside **onsen** and several **beaches**, two of which – Isso and Nakama – offer decent snorkelling. There are no dry months here, but the best time to visit is May or during the autumn months of October and November. June sees by far the highest rainfall, though this is when the rhododendrons are at their best, followed by a steamy July and August. Winter brings snow to the peaks, although sea-level temperatures hover around 15°C.

Information

Both of Yakushima's main towns have **tourist offices**. The most useful is in Miyanoura (daily 8.30am–5pm; Ⓣ0997/42-1019), in the circular white building at the end of the ferry pier, which has English-speaking staff. You can pick up bus timetables, hotel lists, maps and brochures here and they can book accommodation for you if you need it. Anbō's tiny tourist office (daily 8.30am–5pm; Ⓣ0997/46-2333) is located on the main crossroads in the centre of town just north of the river. There's also a small desk at the airport (daily 8.30am–5pm; Ⓣ0997/49-4010), while Yakumonkey (Ⓦwww.yakumonkey.com) has good, up-to-date information.

There are a number of **dive shops** on the island that rent gear; enquire at the Miyanoura tourist office for details. The Yakushima Nature Activity Centre (Ⓣ0997/42-0944, Ⓦwww.ynac.com) on the main drag in Miyanoura offers various guided **adventure tours**, with a choice of walking, hiking, paddling, canyoning, kayaking and scuba diving.

Miyanoura is the largest centre for supermarkets and other facilities. The main **post office** is located in the town centre, just west of the river. Although it now has an international **ATM** (Mon–Fri 8.45am–6pm, Sat 9am–5pm, Sun 9am–3pm), it's best not to rely on it – stock up with cash in Kagoshima. Both Anbō and

Onoaida have sub-post offices and small supermarkets. **Internet** access is available upstairs in the Yakushima Kankō Centre (屋久島観光センター), on the main road opposite Miyanoura ferry pier. A **left-luggage** service is also available here at the shop downstairs (¥300/bag/day).

Island transport

Yakushima's road system consists of one quiet highway circumnavigating the island, plus a few spurs running up into the mountains. **Buses** depart from outside the Toppy terminal on Miyanoura ferry pier for Nagata (永田) in the west (7 daily; 30min; ¥890), or on the more useful route east via the airport and Anbō (hourly; 40min; ¥810) to terminate at the *Iwasaki Hotel* in Onoaida (hourly; 1hr; ¥1250), in Kurio (栗生; 8 daily; 1hr 30min; ¥1700), or a little further on at Ōko-no-taki (大川の滝; 2 daily; 1hr 35min; ¥1820). The last service from Miyanoura to Kurio leaves around 6pm, and 5pm from Kurio back to Miyanoura. The last bus is sometimes cancelled in the off-season and these buses regularly run ahead of schedule, so it pays to get to the stop at least ten minutes early. For most of the year (March–Nov) buses also operate twice daily from Anbō to Yaku-sugi Land (1hr; ¥720, or ¥910 to the terminal at Kigen-sugi). The timetable varies according to the season so check locally.

It's worth renting your own transport. A day's **car rental** costs ¥5000–10,000 for the smallest car, depending on the season. Local companies are generally cheaper, such as Suzuki Rent-a-Car in Miyanoura (Ⓣ0997/42-1772) and Shinyama Rent-a-Car in Anbō (Ⓣ0997/49-7277), while national companies such as Nippon Rent-a-Car (Ⓣ0997/49-4189) have offices at the airport. Make sure you keep the tank topped up since there are no petrol stations on west Yakushima between Hirauchi and Nagata; those on the rest of the island close at 5pm or 6pm and many close on Sundays.

Motorbikes are available for rent at Suzuki Rent-a-Car (see above) and at You Shop (April–Oct; Ⓣ0997/46-2705) on the main road in Anbō; count on around ¥4000 per day (up to 9hr) for a 125cc bike. You can rent **mountain bikes** (¥800/day) at the Yakushima Kankō Center (屋久島観光センター; daily: March–Oct 8am–7pm; Nov–Feb 8am–6pm), on the main road opposite the Miyanoura ferry terminal, and at *Backpackers' Support* (see Accommodation, below).

The three main **taxi** companies on the island are Yakushima Kōtsū Taxi (Ⓣ0997/46-2321), Anbō Taxi (Ⓣ0997/46-2311) and Matsubanda Kōtsū Taxi (Ⓣ0997/42-0027).

Accommodation

Yakushima has a fair range of **accommodation**, but you still need to plan well ahead during holiday periods. Other than the hostels, prices listed include meals. Note that those hiking the interior can make use of mountain huts (p.725).

Miyanoura

Miyanoura Portside Youth Hostel 宮之浦ポートサイドYH Ⓣ0997/49-1316, Ⓕ41317, Ⓦwww.yakushima-yh.net. Conveniently located just 5min walk round the harbour from the ferry pier. Dorm beds ¥3800, ¥3200 for members.

Seaside Hotel Yakushima シーサイドホテル屋久島 Ⓣ0997/42-0175, Ⓔyoyaku@ssh-yakushima.cp.jp. Hugely convenient, having been built on the promontory overlooking the ferry port. It's a comfortable place with spacious Western and tatami rooms, plus a pool and restaurant. ❼

Anbō

Backpackers' Support Ⓣ0997/49-7101, Ⓕ7102. Otherwise known as Midori-no-hidomari (森の陽どまり), this offers dorm accommodation (¥1800/person) for hikers. Though the manager speaks limited English, he rents walking boots, rainwear, snorkelling gear and camping equipment, though not tents. It's on the corner opposite Anbō information office. ❶

Minshuku Shiho 民宿志保 Ⓣ0997/46-3288. The best option in the area – a white bungalow shaded by palm trees, it's the first building you come to on the road up from the pier, and provides spick-and-span, no-frills tatami rooms with breakfast only. ④

Sankara ⓣ0997/47-3488. Yakushima's first boutique hotel opened in 2010, and is likely to be the island's most appealing accommodation for some time; rooms have been designed in keeping with Yakushima's natural vibe, and all have balconies with sea view. The attached spa is rather heavenly, while the on-site restaurant serves local ingredients in a distinctively French style. ⑨

Onoaida

Chinryu-an 枕流庵 ⓣ0997/47-3900, ⓦwww.chinryu.com. Excellent place offering dormitory bunks or private tatami rooms in a cedar-wood chalet buried among trees. The cheerful, English-speaking owner is a fount of local information and also provides hearty meals, though you can use the kitchen for a small fee. To get here, Kurio-bound buses will drop you at the entrance, beside the Yaishi stop, or you can take the more frequent service that terminates at the *Iwasaki Hotel* and walk west for a few minutes, keeping your eyes peeled for a sign on the right. Dorms ¥4900/person, room ⑤

Sōyō-tei 送陽邸 ⓣ&ⓕ0997/45-2819. Located on Inaka Beach (いなか浜) in the northwest of the island, this tasteful, antique-decorated ryokan was painstakingly constructed using new materials and hundred-year-old beams. The best rooms boast verandas and stunning views of the finest beach in Yakushima, and there's also a rotemburo for a perfect sunset soak. The ryokan is located at the western tip of Inaka Beach next to the road leading to Nagata. ⑧

Yakushima Youth Hostel 屋久島ユースホステル ⓣ0997/47-3751, ⓦwww.yakushima-yh.net. Despite being run along military lines, with a strict policy of lights out at 10pm, the hostel is popular, so make sure you book ahead. It's 5km west of Onoaida in Hirauchi, 5min walk east from the Hirauchi-irigichu stop, sign-posted down a quiet lane. Dorm beds ¥2940/person.

The coast

The first impressions of the scruffy little port of **MIYANOURA** (宮之浦), Yakushima's main town, aren't very favourable. It is, however, home to the informative **Yakushima Environmental and Cultural Village Centre** (屋久島環境文化村センター; 9am–5pm; closed Mon; ¥500), in a modern building two minutes' walk up from the ferry pier. The exhibits are arranged in a spiral, proceeding from the ocean up through village life and the cedar forests to the mountain tops. Allow time to see the film (hourly; 25min), projected onto a huge screen, which takes you on a fabulous helicopter ride over the island – not recommended for anyone prone to motion sickness.

From Miyanoura, the main road leads east past the airport to **ANBŌ** (安房), a much more attractive place to stay, and the best place from which to tackle the island's interior (see below). On the southern coast there's **ONOAIDA** (尾之間), which also has some good accommodation options. Around here you'll see orchards of tropical fruits, such as mango, papaya and lychee, alongside the more traditional orange groves, while bright sprays of bougainvillea and bird-of-paradise flowers decorate the villages. A few kilometres west of Onoaida, **Hirauchi Kaichū onsen** (平内海中温泉; free) makes the perfect place to kick back with the locals in a hot rockpool overlooking the sea. You just have to get the timing right – the pool is only uncovered for an hour or so either side of low tide. At other times, head 500m west along the coast to **Yudomari Onsen** (湯泊温泉; ¥100).

The interior

From Anbō you can turn inland for a wonderful forty-minute ride up into the mountains. The single-track road, in places almost washed away or blocked by fallen trees, corkscrews up into a lost world wreathed in drifting cloud banks. Every so often there are glimpses of plunging, tree-filled valleys, the lush greens accentuated by cascading, ice-white torrents. If you've got your own transport, you might want to stop on the way up to visit the **Yaku-sugi Museum**, or *Yaku-sugi Shizen-kan* (屋久杉自然館; daily 9am–5pm; ¥600), 2km from the main road. Buses do stop here –

Shizenkan-mae – but, with only two a day, it's not possible to cover the museum and Yaku-sugi Land in one outing. The well-designed museum is full of fascinating displays about the cedars, including a stump and cross section of a 1660-year-old tree.

Ten kilometres higher up, and 1000m above sea level, a wooden resthouse marks the entrance to **Yaku-sugi Land** (屋久杉ランド; daily 9am–5pm; ¥300). This forest reserve contains four **walking trails** varying in length from 800m (around 30min) to 3km (around 2hr 30min). The three shortest and most popular walks wind along an attractive river valley that is home to several thousand-year-old cedar trees, their gnarled roots clinging to the rock. If you've got the time and energy, the longest course is by far the most interesting, taking you deeper into the forest and past another three ancient Yaku-sugi, of which the oldest is the 2600-year-old **Hahako-sugi**. Alternatively, continue up the paved road from the resthouse for about 6km to the **Kigen-sugi**, a grand old lady of 3000 years. Travelling by bus, you can save yourself the walk by staying on the bus to the terminus, near Kigen-sugi, and then walk back down. All these trees are mere saplings compared with the great **Jōmon-sugi** (縄文杉), whose mossy, tattered trunk, 16.4m in circumference, looks more like rock face than living tissue. The tree is at least 2300 years old, but since the centre has rotted away it's impossible to tell exactly. Growing 1300m up and five-hours' hike from the nearest road, the tree was only discovered in 1968, an event which sparked moves to protect the forests and also created the tourist industry that now accounts for over half the island's economy. The Jōmon-sugi stands on the north face of **Miyanoura-dake** (宮之浦岳; 1935m), the highest of Yakushima's seven peaks and the highest mountain in Kyūshū. There are two main routes up to the tree: the Kusugawa Hiking Path from east of Miyanoura, and the eastern Arakawa trail starting at the Arakawa Dam. In both cases you can get a fair way up by road if you've got your own transport.

Eating and drinking

In general you're best off **eating** in your accommodation, especially in the evenings, but there are a few interesting options dotted around the island.

Rengaya れんが屋 Anbō. Pleasantly rustic venue on the road down to the harbour. It offers a varied menu, including *yakiniku* (meat barbecued at your table) and *tonkatsu* (pork cutlets), with set meals from around ¥1500. Try the sashimi set, which comes complete with deep-fried flying-fish "wings" set at a jaunty angle. Daily 10am–2pm & 6–10pm.

Shimamusubi 島むすび Miyanoura. Run by an affable Argentinian of Japanese extraction, this offers bentō box lunches to take on your walking trips; cross the river and keep going along the main road towards Anbō for about five minutes until you see the log cabin exterior on your left. Daily 5am–5pm.

Travel details

Trains

Aso to: Beppu (4 daily; 2hr); Kumamoto (1 hourly; 1hr 10min).

Beppu to: Aso (4 daily; 2hr); Fukuoka (1–3 hourly; 2hr–3hr 20min); Kumamoto (4 daily; 3hr–3hr 20min); Miyazaki (1 hourly; 3hr 30min); Ōita (2–4 hourly; 10min); Usuki (1–3 hourly; 30min–1hr 15min).

Fukuoka to: Beppu (1–3 hourly; 2hr–3hr 20min); Dazaifu (from Nishitetsu-Dazaifu station every 30min; 30min); Futsukaichi (every 10min; 10–20min); Hiroshima (every 15min; 1hr 10min–1hr 50min); Huis ten Bosch (8 daily; 1hr 40min); Kagoshima (every 30min; 1hr 20min–2hr 30min); Kumamoto (every 30 min; 40min–1hr 20min); Kyoto (every 30min; 2hr–2hr 45min); Miyazaki (2 daily; 5hr 35min–8hr); Nagasaki (every 30min–1hr; 2hr); Ōsaka (every 15–20min; 2hr 40min); Takeo (7 daily; 1hr); Tokyo (every 30min; 5hr–5hr 20min).

Isahaya to: Shimabara (1–2 hourly; 1hr 10min).

Kagoshima to: Fukuoka (every 30min; 1hr 20min–2hr 30min); Ibusuki (1–2 hourly; 50min–1hr 20min); Kirishima Jingū (10 daily; 40–50min); Kumamoto (every 30 min; 40min–1hr 15min);

Miyazaki (7 daily; 2hr–2hr 15min); Shin-Yatsushiro (2 hourly; 30–40min).

Kumamoto to: Aso (1 hourly; 1hr 30min); Beppu (4 daily; 3hr); Fukuoka (every 30min; 40min–1hr 20min); Kagoshima (every 30min; 40min–1hr 15min).

Miyazaki to: Aoshima (1 hourly; 30min); Beppu (1 hourly; 3hr 10min–3hr 30min); Fukuoka (2 daily; 5hr 35min–6hr 30min); Kagoshima (7 daily; 2hr–2hr 10min); Nobeoka (1 hourly; 1hr); Obi (1 hourly; 1hr 15min).

Nagasaki to: Hakata, Fukuoka (every 30min–1hr; 2hr); Huis ten Bosch (1 hourly; 1hr 30min); Isahaya (1–2 hourly; 20min).

Tateno to: Takamori (1–2 hourly; 30min).

Usuki to: Beppu (1–3 hourly; 30min–1hr 15min); Nobeoka (1 hourly; 1hr 30min).

Buses

Aso to: Beppu (5 daily; 3hr); Kumamoto (1 hourly; 1hr 30min); Kurokawa Onsen (6 daily; 40min–1hr); Senomoto Kōgen (5 daily; 45min–1hr).

Beppu to: Aso (5 daily; 3hr); Fukuoka (every 30min–1hr; 2hr 30min); Hiroshima (2 daily; 5hr 15min); Kumamoto (4 daily; 4hr 40min); Nagasaki (7 daily; 3hr 40min); Nagoya (1 daily; 11hr); Ōita (frequent; 20min).

Fukuoka to: Beppu (every 30min–1hr; 2hr 30min); Kagoshima (every 30min–1hr; 3hr 40min); Kumamoto (every 10–20min; 2hr 20min); Kyoto (1 daily; 9hr 30min); Miyazaki (every 30min–1hr; 3hr 40min); Nagasaki (every 15–30min; 2hr); Ōsaka (2 daily; 9hr 40min).

Isahaya to: Unzen (9 daily; 1hr 20min).

Kagoshima to: Chiran (7–8 daily; 1hr 20min); Fukuoka (every 30min–1hr; 3hr 40min); Ibusuki (6–7 daily; 1hr 30min); Kumamoto (10 daily; 3hr 10min); Miyazaki (9 daily; 3hr); Ōsaka (1 daily; 12hr).

Kirishima-jingū Station to: Ebino Kōgen (Sat & Sun 2 daily; 1hr 10min); Hayashida Onsen (7–9 daily; 35min); Kirishima Jingū (9–11 daily; 15min).

Kirishima Jingū to: Ebino Kōgen (Sat & Sun 2 daily; 50min); Hayashida Onsen (7–9 daily; 20min); Kirishima-jingū Station (9–11 daily; 15min).

Kumamoto to: Aso (1 hourly; 1hr 30min); Beppu (4 daily; 4hr 40min); Fukuoka (every 10–20min; 2hr 20min); Kagoshima (10 daily; 3hr 10min); Kumamoto-kō (1–3 hourly; 30min); Miyazaki (1 hourly; 3hr); Nagasaki (8 daily; 3hr); Takachiho (3 daily; 2hr 50min).

Miyazaki to: Aoshima (1 hourly; 50min); Aya (every 30min; 50min); Fukuoka (1–2 hourly; 4hr–4hr 15min); Kagoshima (9 daily; 2hr 40min); Kumamoto (1 hourly; 3hr); Udo-jingū (hourly; 1hr 30min).

Nagasaki to: Beppu (7 daily; 3hr 10min–4hr 40min); Huis ten Bosch (1–2 hourly; 1hr 15min); Kumamoto (8 daily; 3hr); Unzen (7 daily; 1hr 40min).

Takachiho to: Kumamoto (3 daily; 2hr 40min); Nobeoka (1–2 hourly; 1hr–1hr 30min); Takamori (3 daily; 1hr).

Unzen to: Isahaya (9 daily; 1hr 20min); Nagasaki (7 daily; 1hr 45min–2hr); Shimabara (6 daily; 45min).

Ferries

Beppu to: Matsuyama (1 daily; 3hr 45min); Ōsaka (1 daily; 13hr); Yawatahama (6 daily; 2hr 40min).

Fukuoka to: Busan (South Korea) by hydrofoil (6–8 daily; 3hr), by ferry (Mon–Sat 1 daily; 5hr 30min).

Ibusuki to: Kagoshima (1 daily; 40min); Yakushima (1 daily; 1hr 15min).

Kagoshima to: Ibusuki (1 daily; 40min); Naha (4–6 weekly; 24hr); Yakushima by hydrofoil (9 daily; 1hr 50min–2hr 50min), by ferry (1 daily; 4hr).

Kumamoto to: Shimabara (1–2 hourly; 30min–1hr).

Miyazaki to: Ōsaka (1 daily; 12hr).

Shimabara to: Kumamoto (1–2 hourly; 30min–1hr).

Yakushima to: Ibusuki (1 daily; 2hr); Kagoshima by hydrofoil (9 daily; 1hr 40min–3hr 15min), by ferry (1 daily; 4hr).

Flights

Fukuoka to: Aomori (4 weekly; 2hr); Bangkok (1–2 daily; 4hr 50min); Beijing (1–2 daily; 2hr 30min); Ho Chi Minh (6 weekly; 4hr 30min); Kagoshima (5 daily; 45min); Kansai International (4 daily; 1hr); Manila (4 weekly; 3hr 40min); Miyazaki (7 daily; 40min); Nagoya (1–2 hourly; 1hr 10min); Naha (1 hourly; 1hr 40min); Niigata (1 daily; 1hr 30min); Ōsaka (Itami; hourly; 1hr 10min); Sapporo (4 daily; 2hr 10min); Sendai (5 daily; 1hr 40min); Seoul (5 daily; 1hr 15min); Shanghai (3 daily; 1hr 40min); Singapore (1 daily; 6hr 15min); Taipei (3 daily; 2hr); Tokyo (2–4 hourly; 1hr 30min).

Kagoshima to: Fukuoka (5 daily; 50min); Nagoya (7 daily; 1hr 15min); Naha (3 daily; 1hr 25min); Ōsaka (Itami; hourly; 1hr 10min); Seoul (3 weekly; 1hr 40min); Shanghai (2 weekly; 1hr 20min); Tokyo (1–2 hourly; 1hr 35min); Yakushima (5 daily; 35min).

Kumamoto to: Nagoya (5 daily; 1hr 15min); Naha (1 daily; 1hr 30min); Ōsaka (Itami; 8 daily; 1hr 5min); Seoul (3 weekly; 1hr 40min); Tokyo (1–2 hourly; 1hr 35min).

Miyazaki to: Fukuoka (7 daily; 45min); Nagoya (3 daily; 1hr 10min); Naha (1 daily; 1hr 25min); Ōsaka (Itami; 6 daily; 1hr); Seoul (3 weekly; 1hr 40min); Tokyo (1–2 hourly; 1hr 30min).

Nagasaki to: Nagoya (3 daily; 1hr 15min); Naha (1 daily; 1hr 35min); Ōsaka (Itami; 6 daily; 1hr 5min); Seoul (2–3 weekly; 1hr 25min); Shanghai (2 weekly; 1hr 35min); Tokyo (1–2 hourly; 1hr 30min).

Ōita to: Nagoya (2 daily; 1hr 5min); Naha (1 daily; 1hr 45min); Ōsaka (Itami; 5 daily; 55min); Tokyo (10 daily; 1hr 30min).

Yakushima to: Kagoshima (5 daily; 30–35min).

11

Okinawa

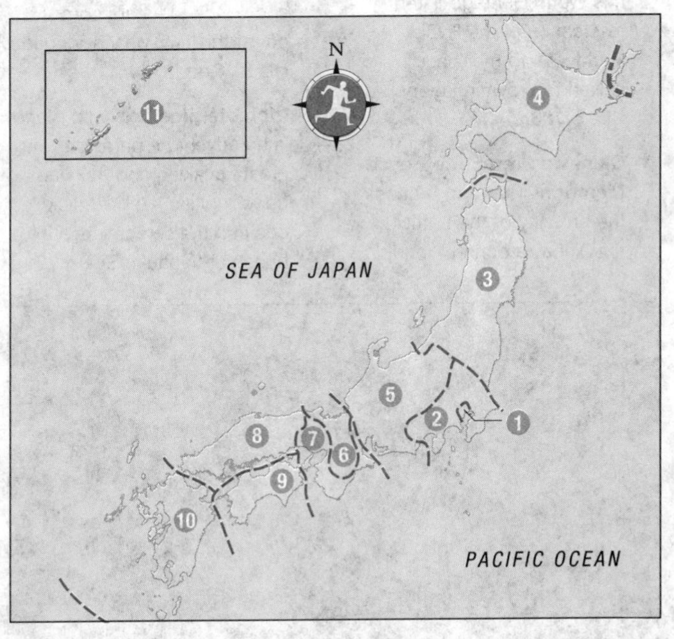

CHAPTER 11 **Highlights**

* **Diving** From the soft corals and tropical fish around the Kerama islands to the enigmatic rocks near Yonaguni-jima, Okinawa offers a wealth of outstanding diving experiences. See p.730

* **Shuri-jō** Perhaps the most distinctive of Japan's wonderful array of castles, this World Heritage-listed re-creation of the Ryūkyū kingdom's former base is Naha's crowning glory. See p.736

* **Okinawa Prefecture Peace Memorial Museum** Witness the brutality of the battle for Okinawa during World War II at this well-presented museum. See p.743

* **Okinawa Churaumi Aquarium** Get to grips with Okinawa's diverse sea life without the need to don diving gear at this fabulous aquarium. See p.746

* **Taketomi-jima** Wave goodbye to the day-trippers and watch the stars come out at this tiny, beach-fringed island. See p.759

* **Iriomote-jima** This wild island is an adventure paradise, with great kayaking and trekking opportunities – or just kick back on the serenely beautiful beach at Funauki. See p.761

▲ Okinawa Churaumi Aquarium

11

Okinawa

Mention **OKINAWA** (沖縄) to a mainland Japanese and you'll likely receive a wistful sigh in return. Perpetually warm weather, clear seas bursting with fish, fantastic food, gentle people, unspoilt beaches and jungle…the list could go on. More than one hundred subtropical islands, collectively known as the Ryūkyū Shotō, stretch over 700km of ocean from Kyūshū southwest to Yonaguni-jima, almost within sight of Taiwan, and provide one of Japan's favourite getaways. Getting here may be a little costly, but Okinawa's lush vegetation, vision-of-paradise beaches and superb coral reefs can charm the most jaded traveller – if you've had your fill of shrines and temples and want to check out some of Japan's best beaches and dive sites (see box, p.730), or simply fancy a spot of winter sun, then Okinawa is well worth a visit.

The largest island in the group, **Okinawa-Hontō**, usually referred to simply as Okinawa, is the region's transport hub and home to its prefectural capital, **Naha**. It's also the most heavily populated and developed of the Ryūkyū chain, thanks largely to the controversial presence of **American military bases** (see box, p.742). Okinawa-Hontō boasts a number of historical sights, many of them associated with the **Battle of Okinawa** at the end of the Pacific War (see p.773). But the island has more to offer than battle sites, particularly in its northern region, where the old way of life still survives among the isolated villages.

To see the best of the region, you'll have to hop on a plane or ferry and explore the dozens of **outer islands** away from Okinawa-Hontō, many of them uninhabited. Even quite close to Naha, you'll find gorgeous beaches and fantastic dive spots

Getting to and around Okinawa

By far the majority of visitors arrive by plane. Most come from the Japanese mainland, though there are **international flights** (see p.769). **Domestic airlines** operate between Naha and Tokyo, Ōsaka and a number of other Japanese cities (see p.764), while a few fly direct to Ishigaki and Miyako. Though flying can be expensive, discounts are becoming increasingly common – Skynet Asia (ⓦwww.skynetasia.co.jp) has been known to offer limited ¥10,000 flat fares to Okinawa for foreigners, while overseas visitors can also take advantage of the airpasses offered by JAL and ANA (see p.36). The other option is a **ferry** to Naha from Tokyo, Ōsaka, Kōbe or one of several cities on Kyūshū.

These days, **getting around** between the island groups is almost entirely done by plane, since the ferry network has sadly been scaled down in recent years. Using Naha as the main hub, **inter-island flights** are operated by Japan Transocean Air (JTA), Ryūkyū Air Commuter (RAC) and Air Nippon (ANK), with connections to all the major islands.

around the **Kerama islands**, just 30km off Okinawa-Hontō. Divers and beach connoisseurs will want to visit **Miyako-jima** and **Ishigaki-jima**, way down the Ryūkyū chain. If you're looking for an idyllic retreat, **Taketomi-jima** can't be beaten, while the adventurous will want to explore **Iriomote-jima**, coated in thick groves of mangrove and steamy rainforest, and home to the elusive Iriomote lynx.

It's on these outer islands that you'll also find the strongest evidence of the much-vaunted **Ryūkyū culture**, born of contact with Taiwan and China, as well as the rest of Japan. The most obvious expressions of this culture are found in the islands' cuisine and in a vibrant use of colour and bold tropical patterns, while the Chinese influence is clearly visible in the region's architecture, traditional dress and the martial art of karate – the Ryūkyū warriors' preferred mode of protection. Ancient religious beliefs are kept alive by shamen (called *yuta*) and, in central Okinawa-Hontō, there are sumo bouts between bulls. There's also a Ryūkyū dialect, with dozens of variations between the different islands, unique musical instruments, and a distinctive musical style that has reached an international audience through bands such as Nēnēs, Diamantes and Champloose (see pp.791–793). If you're lucky, you'll stumble on a local festival, such as giant rope tug-of-war contests or dragon-boat races, while the biggest annual event is the Eisā

Diving in Okinawa

With scores of dive sites around Okinawa-Hontō – and many more around the outer islands – one of the best reasons for visiting Okinawa is to go **diving**. There are plenty of dive shops, but only at a few will you find instructors who speak English. A useful website is Ⓦwww.divejapan.com, which includes links to operators, articles, dive-site maps and photo galleries. PADI courses are available on Okinawa-Hontō from *Maeda Misaki Divers House* (see p.745) and the American-run *Reef Encounters* (Ⓦwww.reefencounters.org). Once you have your certificate the islands are yours for the taking. Prices vary, but equipment hire is generally ¥3000–5000, first dives ¥8000–11,000, and second dives usually available for a couple of thousand more. To rent equipment, you should know the metric readings of your height, weight and shoe size.

There are great diving opportunities every way you turn on the islands, but the following sites are particularly notable.

Zamami-jima Fantastic hard corals, more reef fish than you could count in a week and lots of big fan corals. Head to Zamami-jima (see p.749), a particularly laidback spot from which to organize a dive with the instructors at *Joy Joy* (Ⓦkeramajoyjoy.com/eg).

Miyako-jima There are over fifty different dive spots to choose from around Miyako-jima (see p.750), with cave dives being particularly popular: start off by hooking up with *Good Fellas Club* (Ⓣ0980/73-5483, Ⓔfellas@goodfellas.co.jp).

Ishigaki-jima Dotted around the Yaeyamas are 360 species of corals and sea anemones, including the rare blue coral reefs off Shiraho-no-umi on Ishigaki-jima (see p.759). Among the thousand-odd species of fish you can expect to swim with are barracuda, butterfly fish, redfin fusiliers, spadefish and manta rays in the waters between Iriomote-jima and Kohama-jima. Try *Sea Friends* (Ⓣ0980/82-0863) in Ishigaki City, or *Umicoza* (Ⓣ0980/88-2434, Ⓦwww.umicoza.com/english) in Kabira.

Iriomote-jima There's easily accessible coral in the waters surrounding this enchanting island (see p.762). Both youth hostels can put you in touch with local diving operations.

Yonaguni-jima For the ultimate dive experience consider lugging your gear out here (see p.763) to see sea turtles and hammerhead sharks, and to explore the enigmatic rocks that some claim are the remains of a sunken civilization. *Reef Encounters* (see above), on Okinawa-Hontō, organizes trips to this distant island, or contact *Marine Club Sa-Wes* on the island itself (Ⓣ0980/87-2311, Ⓔsawes@yonaguni.jp).

festival (fifteenth day of the seventh lunar month), when everyone downs tools and dances to the incessant rhythms of drums, flutes and the three-stringed sanshin.

Besides Hokkaidō, Okinawa contains Japan's largest areas of unspoilt natural environment and its greatest biodiversity. Much of this wealth of **wildlife** is underwater, spawned by the warm Kuroshio Current that sweeps up the east coast and allows coral reefs to flourish. But there are a number of endemic species on land, too, including turtles, a crested eagle and the *noguchigera* (Pryer's woodpecker), in addition to Iriomote's wild cat, the *yamaneko*. A less welcome local resident is the highly venomous **habu snake**. It measures around 2m in length, is dark green with a yellow head, and usually lurks in dense vegetation or on roadsides, though rarely ventures into urban areas. As long as you're careful – especially during spring and autumn – you should have no problems; if you are bitten, make for the nearest hospital, where they should have antiveni.

With its subtropical **climate**, Okinawa stays warm throughout the year. Average annual temperatures are around 23°C, with a winter average of 17°C and a minimum of 10°C. Winter lasts from December to February, while the hot, humid summer starts in April and continues into September. Temperatures at this time hover around 34°C and the sun can be pretty intense, though the sea breezes help. The **best time to visit** is in spring or autumn (roughly March to early May and late Sept to Dec). The rainy season lasts from early May to early June, while typhoons can be a problem in July and August, and occasionally into October.

Some history

In the fifteenth century, the islands that now make up Okinawa were united for the first time into the **Ryūkyū kingdom**, governed from Shuri Castle in present-day Naha. This period is seen as the golden era of Ryūkyū culture. Trade with China, the rest of Japan and other Southeast Asian countries flourished, while the traditionally non-militarized kingdom maintained its independence by paying **tribute to China**. But then, in 1609, the **Shimazu** clan of Kagoshima (southern Kyūshū) invaded. The Ryūkyū kings became **vassals** to the Shimazu, who imposed punitive taxes and ruled with an iron hand for the next two hundred years, using the islands as a gateway for trade with China when such contact was theoretically outlawed by the Togukawa Shogunate. When the Japanese feudal system was abolished in the 1870s, the islands were simply annexed to the mainland as **Okinawa Prefecture**. Against much local opposition, the Meiji government established a military base and tried to eradicate local culture by forcing people to speak Japanese and swear allegiance to the emperor, forbidding schools to teach Ryūkyū history.

By the early twentieth century, Okinawa had been fairly successfully absorbed into Japan and became a key pawn in Japan's last line of defence during the **Pacific War**. Following the battle of Iwō-jima in March 1945, the American fleet advanced on Okinawa and, after an extensive preliminary bombardment, referred to locally as a "typhoon of steel", the Americans invaded on **April 1, 1945**. It took nearly three months of bitter fighting before General Ushijima, the Japanese commander, committed suicide and the island surrendered. The **Battle of Okinawa** left 12,500 American troops dead (plus 37,000 injured) and an estimated 250,000 on the Japanese side, nearly half of whom were local civilians.

It's estimated that one third of the population of Okinawa died in the war, many in **mass suicides** that preceded the surrender, and others from disease and starvation. But the islanders' subsequent anger has been directed at the Japanese government rather than America. Most people feel that Okinawa was sacrificed to save the mainland – this was the only major battle fought on Japanese soil – and that they were misled by Japanese assurances that they were luring the American fleet into a trap. Compounding this was the behaviour of Japanese troops, who are accused of denying locals shelter and medical treatment, and ultimately of abandoning them to the Americans.

By comparison, the American invaders were a welcome relief, despite the islanders' worst fears. They brought in much-needed food supplies – Spam was an instant hit in this pork-loving country, and a precursor of the processed luncheon meat found in pork *champurū* – and gradually helped restore the local economy. This wasn't wholly altruistic, of course, since Okinawa was ideally placed for monitoring events in Southeast Asia. As the 1950s Korean War merged into the Vietnam War, so the **American bases** became a permanent feature of the Okinawa landscape (see box, p.742).

In fact, Okinawa remained under **American jurisdiction** until 1972, when local protests led to the restoration of **Japanese sovereignty**. Since then, the two governments have colluded to maintain an American military presence on the island despite growing opposition, which reached a peak when three American servicemen were found guilty of raping a 12-year-old schoolgirl in 1995.

Okinawa has since borne witness to some curious political shifts. In 2007, local elections brought **Aiko Shimajiri** to power; interestingly, his focus was on the local economy rather than military issues. These were, however, to come to the fore in national elections two years down the line, with Yukio Hatayama elected Prime Minister on a pledge to remove, rather than relocate, the Futenma air base – his failure to do so saw him step down in disgrace less than a year later (see p.742 for more).

Okinawa-Hontō

Once the centre of the Ryūkyū kingdom, **Okinawa-Hontō** (沖縄本島), or Okinawa Main Island, is a strangely ambivalent place. Locals are fiercely proud of their Ryūkyū heritage, and yet the competing cultures of Japan and America are far more prevalent. To some extent, the island still feels like occupied territory, especially central Okinawa-Hontō, where the **American bases** and the nearby "American" towns, with their drive-ins and shopping malls, have become a bizarre tourist attraction for mainland Japanese, who come to soak up a bit of American culture.

Fascinating though all this is, it doesn't make Okinawa-Hontō the most obvious holiday destination. However, if you're drawn by the more appealing outer islands (see p.748), the chances are you'll spend some time on the main island waiting for plane or ferry connections. Okinawa-Hontō's chief city and the former Ryūkyū capital is **Naha**, whose prime attraction is its reconstructed castle, **Shuri-jō**, the ruins of which were awarded World Heritage status in 2001. There are also some interesting market streets and a pottery village to explore, and you'll want to take advantage of its banks – not to mention excellent bars and restaurants – before heading off to remoter regions.

Southern Okinawa-Hontō saw the worst fighting in 1945, and the scrubby hills are littered with **war memorials**, particularly around Mabuni Hill, where the final battles took place. North of Naha, the island's central district has little to recommend it, but beyond Kadena the buildings start to thin out. Here you'll find one of the better "Ryūkyū culture villages", **Ryūkyū-mura**, and the island's best beaches. The largest settlement in northern Okinawa-Hontō, **Nago** is an appealing town that provides a base for visiting the stunning Okinawa Churaumi Aquarium and exploring the scenic coastline and mountainous tip of the island, culminating in the dramatic cape of **Hedo Misaki**.

Long and thin, Okinawa-Hontō measures just 135km from tip to toe, so you can drive the whole length in a matter of hours. The best way to get around is to rent your own car or motorbike, particularly if you want to explore the northern hills. But be warned – the speed limit on many of the narrow roads that wind around the island is 40 or 50kph, and the roads around the southern and central strip are gridlocked during rush hour, so allow plenty of time for your journey and take the expressway if you're in a hurry. Otherwise most places are accessible by local bus – eventually.

Naha

The Okinawan capital of **NAHA** (那覇) should, in fairness, be a place to get things done and be on one's way. This is the only large city in a region of Japan that leans heavily on nature – despite being capital of the Ryūkyū kingdom for over four hundred years, wartime destruction and rampant commercialization have colluded to ensure that there's precious little to see bar bland residential blocks and souvenir shops catering to a near-constant stream of Japanese holiday-makers. Yet, somehow, it's a great place to kick back – a fair proportion of the locals you meet will be mainland Japanese, here to trade in a hefty chunk of their previous salary, at least temporarily, for a relaxed lifestyle. Foreign travellers often end up staying far longer than they planned – the weather's great, the food's terrific, beaches and bars are never far away, and busting a gut to get somewhere else just wouldn't be in the Okinawan spirit of things.

There are, of course, a few things to see while you're here. The beautifully reconstructed **Shuri-jō**, the old Ryūkyū kings' small, solid castle, constitutes the city's major sight and is well worth visiting, the Tsuboya pottery district is fun for a wander, and the Shuri area contains a moderately informative prefectural museum, as well as some original royal graves and stone-paved lanes. Then there's Naminoue beach, a short curl of sand that would boast grand sea views were it not for the roads firing across the waves a few dozen metres offshore.

Arrival and information

Naha Airport (那覇空港) occupies a promontory some 3km southwest of the city centre. One terminal handles flights from mainland Japan and to Okinawa's outer islands, while the adjacent building is for overseas flights. From the airport you can either take a taxi (around ¥1500) or the monorail (¥230) for the short journey into central Naha, or one of several frequent local buses departing from outside the terminal buildings (¥200).

The **ferry port**, Naha Shin-kō (那覇新港), lies north of the city. Most ferries from mainland Japan dock here, while slow boats from Kagoshima pull in further south at the old Naha Port Terminal (那覇埠頭). Naha Shin-kō is on the #101 bus route (1–3 hourly; 25min; ¥200), while Naha Port is more conveniently located about fifteen minutes' walk from the main Naha Bus Terminal.

Naha's **tourist information** service has desks in both the domestic (daily 9am–9pm; ⓣ098/857-6884) and international (daily 10.30am–7.30pm; ⓣ098/859-0742) terminals at the airport. Both have English-speaking staff, plentiful maps and brochures, and can help with hotel reservations. There are **car rental** desks at both terminals. In downtown Naha, the only other information office is located on Okiei-dōri (daily 8.30am–8pm; ⓣ098/862-1442), where you'll be lucky to find an English-speaker.

City transport

The smart **monorail** (daily 6am–11.30pm; ¥200 minimum fare) is a useful way to get around, linking the airport with Shuri 13km away. Otherwise, there are plenty of **local buses**, though services can be confusing and traffic often gridlocks at peak times. There's a flat fare of ¥200 within the city, but on other buses take a numbered ticket on entry and pay at your destination. If you plan to use the buses a lot, pick up the island-wide Naha City Bus Route Map (in English) from the tourist information offices. Taxi fares start from around ¥500.

NAHA

RESTAURANTS

Cinnamon Café	5
Dai-ichi Kōsetsu Makishi Ichiba	12
Dao	6
Harbor Diner	15
Inaka	11
Orion	2
Spicy Kitchen	13
Suimui	3
Yūnangii	14

BARS & CLUBS

Chakra	9
Helios	7
Hinotama Hall	1
Live House Shimauta	8
Oni-san	10
Rehab	4

ACCOMMODATION

Base Okinawa	B
Comfort	G
Guesthouse Kerama	A
Lohas Villa	C
NaHaNa Hotel & Spa	D
Rocore	F
Tōyoko Inn	E

N
Tokashiki-jima & Zamami-jima
Kadena, Nago & Naha Shin-kō (2km)
Okinawa City
3 & Shuri-jō (2.9km)
Naha Immigration Office
15, Itoman & Naha Airport
Kagoshima
Tomari Port
Tomarin
San-A Naha Main Place
OMOROMACHI
NAMINOUE SEASIDE ROAD
Naminoue Beach
Urashima Kaikan
WAKASA O-DORI
WAKASA NAKA-DORI
ROUTE 58
MATAYOSHI-DORI
MIEBASHI
OKIEI DORI
Mitsukoshi Department Store
MAKISHI
ASATO
MATSUYAMA-DORI
KUME O-DORI
Yotsu-dake
KUMOJI
KOKUSAI-DORI
ICHIBA-DORI
HEIWA-DORI
Naha Municipal Arts & Crafts Museum
KENCHŌ-MAE
Palette Kumoji
Tsuboya Pottery Museum
Kiln
Takaesu Pottery
Kiln
HIMEYURI-DORI
TSUBOYA
Tsuboya Pottery Association
SUNSHINE-DORI
ASAHIBASHI
Prefectural Assembly Hall
Higashi-machi Kaikan
Naha Bus Terminal
TSUBOKAWA-DORI
Naha Port Terminal
0 500 m

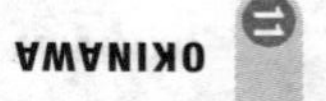

Accommodation

Naha has a good range of accommodation, especially for backpackers – there are more than a dozen hostels charging just ¥1000 for a dorm bed. Rooms are hard to come by in the peak holiday seasons – Golden Week, August and New Year – when rates may rise by up to forty percent. Don't assume, however, that Naha is the only place on Okinawa-Hontō with accommodation, as there are some great alternatives around the island.

Base Okinawa ベースオキナワ 1-17-5 Wakasa ⓣ098/868-2968, ⓔbaseokinawa@gmail.com. Make no bones about it – this is one of those backpacker flophouses your mother may have warned you about. However, it's a clean and very appealing flophouse, with free internet, free bike rental and chain-smoking young owners, while Naminoue beach (yes, the one with the road) is so close you don't even need to don your flip-flops. Dorm beds ¥1000.

Comfort コンフォートホテル 1-3-11 Kumoji ⓣ098/941-7311, ⓦwww.choice-hotels.jp. Popular business hotel within spitting distance of the monorail. Rooms have been decorated with gentle pastel colours, and you can usually score hefty discounts from the rack rates. ❺

Guesthouse Kerama ゲストハウスけらま 3-12-21 Maejima ⓣ098/863-5898, ⓦwww.guesthouse-okinawa.com. The diametric opposite of *Base*, with super-energetic staff and super-comfy beds, the latter laid out in capsule style. Beach parties and nights out are plotted from a large common room that, alas, has nowhere comfortable to sit. Dorm beds ¥1000.

Lohas Villa ロハスヴィラ 2-1-6 Makishi ⓣ098/867-7757. Tremendous value to be had at this immaculate and superbly located guesthouse, which has two dormitory rooms on its lower level (¥1500), then a few floors of superb tatami rooms, some of which are duplex. Singles ¥2500. ❷

NaHaNa Hotel & Spa ナハナホテル 2-1-5 Kume ⓣ098/866-0787, ⓦwww.ishinhotels.com. An appealingly retro exterior – replete with a ledge that may have been envisioned as a hovercar parking space – conceals surprisingly swish rooms, each mixing modern design with Okinawan motifs. Guests get special rates at the attached spa. ❼

Rocore ホテルロコアナハ 1-1-2 Matsuo ⓣ098/868-6578. Sleek, well-located hotel designed along a pine-black-white tricolour. The tastefully decorated rooms, while not over-large, are extremely comfortable, right down to the complimentary pyjamas. Some of the third-floor rooms have enclosed balconies. ❼

Tōyoko Inn 東横イン那覇旭橋駅前 2-1-20 Kume ⓣ098/951-1045, ⓦwww.toyoko-inn.com. Obligatory branch of the ubiquitous budget hotel chain – most of the rooms are good-value singles (from ¥6500). They have laundry facilities and free internet. ❹

The City

Central Naha is bordered to the south by the Kokuba-gawa, which flows into Naha Port, and to the west by Highway 58. About 500m north of the river, **Kokusai-dōri** (国際通り), the city's main thoroughfare, cuts northeast from the highway, past the Palette Kumoji department store and Prefectural Assembly Hall. Nearly 2km long, Kokusai-dōri is lined with a strange mix of classy boutiques, souvenir stalls and army-surplus outlets selling American military leftovers. Follow the road northeast and it eventually leads uphill to **Shuri-jō**, where the castle lies hidden behind stout walls. Alternatively, head east from Kokusai-dōri through the backstreets to the **Tsuboya** district, a pleasing area of little workshops and dusty galleries that is famous for its pottery kilns.

Shuri-jō

Perched on a hill 3km northeast of central Naha, **Shuri-jō** (首里城; daily 9am–6.30/8.30pm; ¥800) served as the royal residence of the Ryūkyū kings from the early fifteenth century until 1879. Elaborate ceremonies took place in the castle's opulent throne room, on occasion attended by envoys from China and, later, from Kyūshū. Very little of the original remains, but the present buildings, painstakingly restored in the early 1990s, are certainly worth seeing for their distinctive blend of Chinese and Japanese architecture. To reach the castle, take bus #1 from Kokusai-dōri or #17 from Naha Bus Terminal (every 15–20min; 30min) and get off near the modern **Suimuikan** information and shopping centre. Alternatively, you can take the monorail to Shuri Station, where it terminates, and walk fifteen minutes to the castle. You can get a fairly sketchy English-language map of the area from the Suimuikan. It's also worth popping into the small exhibition room for the interesting bilingual display and the short video about Shuri-jō and Ryūkyū culture (every 20min; free).

The castle's main entrance lies across the road from the Suimuikan, through the decorative **Shurei-mon**. This outer gate is a popular spot for group photos, but the inner **Kankai-mon** is a far more impressive structure, its no-nonsense guard tower flanked by sun-baked limestone walls. Inside there's yet another defensive wall and no fewer than three more gates – the last now housing the ticket office – before you reach the central courtyard. Pride of place goes to the **Seiden**, a double-roofed palace with an immense, colourful porch and two throne halls. From the more elaborate upper throne room, the king, surrounded by gilded dragons writhing against lustrous red and black lacquer, would review his troops or watch ceremonies in the courtyard below. Other buildings house remnants of the dynasty and details of the restoration work, though with only a smattering of English explanations to bring them alive.

Exiting Shuri-jō, a quiet park featuring a stone-walled pond and old trees lies across the road. The pond's pretty, island pavilion once belonged to **Enkaku-ji**, which was built in 1492 as the local headquarters of the Rinzai sect; it was said to have been the most impressive structure in the kingdom. Nowadays only a few shell-pocked walls remain of the original temple, east of the pond. Heading northwest, along the banks of an elongated lake, you soon reach the **Okinawa Prefectural Museum**, or Okinawa-kenritsu Hakubutsukan (沖縄県立博物館; Tues–Sun 9am–5pm; ¥210), which provides a good overview of local history and culture. Buses back into central Naha (#1 and #17) stop outside the museum.

Naha Municipal Arts and Crafts Museum and Ichiba-dōri

If you're interested in local crafts, drop by the **Naha Municipal Arts and Crafts Museum** (那覇市伝統工芸館; daily 9am–6pm; ¥300) on the second floor of the Tembusu building on Kokusai-dōri near Mitsukoshi. The entrance fee will get you into a small gallery with prime examples of fabrics, ceramics, glass and lacquerware, but more interestingly (and without paying the entrance fee) you can watch artisans fashion these objects in the adjoining workshops and studios. You can try your hand at weaving, bingata dyeing, glass-blowing, pottery and lacquerware for ¥1500–3000 depending on the craft, and there's also a well-stocked gift shop.

Just west of the Tembusu building, look out for the **Ichiba-dōri** and **Heiwa-dōri** shopping arcades. Among the souvenir stalls and discount outlets, these streets host a number of lively **markets**, of which the best is Ichiba's food market, **Dai-ichi Kōsetsu Makishi Ichiba** (第一公設牧志市場; daily 9am–8pm; closed every fourth Sun of the month). The ground-floor stalls are piled high with sweet-smelling tropical fruits, every conceivable part of pig and ice-packed arrays of multicoloured fish and mysterious, spiny crabs. You'll see fishmongers deftly slicing sashimi, some of it destined for the **food stalls** upstairs (see p.738).

Tsuboya

From the market, walk north onto Heiwa-dōri and follow it east. After a few minutes you'll emerge in the pottery district of **Tsuboya** (壺屋). This compact area has been the centre of local ceramics production since 1682, when the government gathered a number of workshops together, of which around ten are still in operation. Traditionally, the potters here produced large jars for storing the local liquor (*awamori*) and miso paste, but nowadays they concentrate on smaller items for the tourist market, typically half-moon-shaped sake flasks and snarling *shiisā* lions.

To get an overview of the area's history, drop into the **Tsuboya Pottery Museum** (壺屋焼物博物館; Tues–Sun 10am–6pm; ¥315), less than 100m from the end of the covered arcade. Next to the museum, on the embankment above the main road on your left, is a traditional climbing kiln dating from the 1880s, one of the oldest still intact.

Eating

Naha undoubtedly has Okinawa-Hontō's widest choice of **restaurants**, spanning the range from international cuisine to delectable **local dishes**. The latter includes *sōki soba*, a noodle soup with hunks of tender pork rib; *gōya champuru*, a fried mix of bitter melon, egg and pork; and *tundā-bun*, banquets once enjoyed by **Ryūkyū** kings. The latter is generally served with an accompanying show; see opposite.

Cinnamon Café 1-4-59 Makishi. Great spot to while away a quiet afternoon over a good coffee and the best chocolate cake in Naha. They do a mean curry, too, and prices are reasonable (coffee is ¥350 and curry rice ¥720).

Dai-ichi Kōsetsu Makishi Ichiba 第一公設牧志市場 Low prices and super-fresh fish – this array of small, atmospheric restaurants is a must for sushi fans. Choose from the menu or hunt around in the market downstairs for the fish of your choice, which is then prepared and sent upstairs for you to eat. Daily 10am–8pm.

Dao ダーオ 2F, Matsuo 2-8-28. A short way down Ichiba-dōri you'll spot a flag pointing up to this popular second-floor Vietnamese restaurant, where you'll find a good selection of authentic Vietnamese dishes. Tasty garlic chicken with rice is a steal at ¥720. Daily 11am–11pm.

Harbor Diner ハーバーダイナー Banyan Town, Ōnoyama. Those facing the right way on the monorail from the airport will find this restaurant hard to miss – it's located inside a towering fake banyan tree. Italian cuisine is on the menu, and while prices are a little high, there are some good-value lunch specials on offer.

Inaka 田舎, Matsuo 2-10-20. This hard-to-find market den dates from just after Okinawa's handover to Japan and, amazingly, prices haven't changed since 1976: it's still just ¥350 for a bowl of *sōki soba*. If you're still in the retro mood, spider your way up any neighbouring staircase to drink in some throwback architecture. Daily 9am–9pm.

Orion オリオン 2-18-1 Makishi. There's usually old Japanese rock playing on the radio at this 24-hour den, which serves huge, cheap portions of Okinawan staples such as *sōki soba*, *taco rice* (rice with Tex-Mex taco ingredients slapped on top; particularly recommended) and *gōya champuru*, all for around ¥600.

Spicy Kitchen Sakurazaka-dōri, Makishi 3-chōme. Look out for the chilli-pepper mural on this cheery Indian restaurant up a hilly lane near the east end of Heiwa-dōri. The simple menu includes chicken, lamb and seafood curries from ¥500, plus a range of vegetarian dishes and a good lunch deal for ¥800. The lassis are particularly tasty.

Suimui レストラン首里杜 Suimuikan, Shuri-jō. Surprisingly good restaurant in the Shuri-jō information centre (see p.737), serving Okinawa dishes as well as mainstream Japanese and Western meals, with set lunches between ¥900 and ¥1000. Not to be confused with the castle's noisy snack bar. Daily 9am–4.30pm.

Yūnangii ゆうなんぎい 3-3-3 Kumoji. Country-style restaurant, offering a warm welcome and serving Okinawa cuisine, including Okinawa soba, *champuru* and various pork dishes. Set meals go from around ¥1300, with free rice refills. Mon–Sat 9am–6pm.

Drinking and nightlife

As you'd expect, with plenty of off-duty GIs and footloose young Japanese tourists and locals, Naha's entertainment scene is far from dull.

If you want to hear **live music**, especially funky Okinawan pop and traditional sounds, head to *Chakra* on Kokusai-dōri (チャクラ; daily 7pm–1am; ¥2100–3100; ⓣ098/869-0283), owned by local music legend Kina Shoukichi. *Live House Shimauta* (ライブハウス島唄; daily 6–11pm; ¥2000; ⓣ098/863-6040) is located a few doors up from *Chakra*, above the Okinawa-ya gift shop; it's run by another local music luminary, China Sadao, who brought the all-female group Nēnēs to world attention, and the concerts here get rave reviews.

Helios 1-2-25 Makishi, Kokusai-dōri ⓣ098/863-7227. Stylish "craft beer pub" belonging to a local microbrewery and offering several types of home brew including pale ale, Weissen, Pilsner and porter. A small taste of three costs ¥900. Also serves bar snacks.

Hinotama Hall 4-9-10 Omoro-machi. Late-night dance venue offering an eclectic mix of music through the week – anything from acid jazz to hip-hop, with a smattering of live sets. Closed Wed & Thurs.

Oni-san 鬼さん B1, 3-12-4 Kumoji. Noisy, upbeat *izakaya* with a grotto-style entrance leading down to a basement complete with devil masks and fake burning torches hanging off the walls. The food's good, prices are reasonable and there's always a free sweet on the way out.

Rehab 3F, 2-4-14 Makishi, Kokusai-dōri. Follow the sign up the stairs to find this friendly little *gaijin* bar, whose staff have long been helping out foreign residents and visitors – it's a good place to ask about anything from scuba diving to teaching English in Naha. Tues–Sun 7pm–2/3am.

Entertainment

Naha is a good place to catch performances of traditional **Ryūkyū court dance**, particularly the weekly show in the Prefectural Dance Theatre (かりゆし芸能公演) in the Higashi-machi Kaikan, just north of the Kokuba-gawa. Performances are on Fridays (7pm; ¥2500), but check with the tourist office for the current schedule, and note that there's a ¥500 discount if you buy tickets from the box office in advance. The alternative is a more expensive dinner show where you'll pay from ¥3000 for a meal, sometimes including *tundā-bun* – beautifully presented royal hors d'oeuvres. Although somewhat touristy, *Yotsu-dake* on Kokusai-dōri (四つ竹; ⓣ098/863-4444; two shows nightly at 6.30pm & 8.30pm; 40min) provides an enjoyable night out and the food isn't bad. The staff are friendly and they have a printed English explanation of the food and dances. Other dinner-dance venues include another *Yotsu-dake*, at 2-22-1 Kume (ⓣ098/866-3333), and *Urashima Kaikan* (うらしま会館), at 14-8 Wakasa (ⓣ098/861-1769), both in the backstreets west of Highway 58.

Listings

Banks and exchange Ryūkyū Bank in the airport (Mon–Fri 9am–4pm) exchanges major currencies; when they're closed the central information counter can change up to US$50 cash. The post office cash machine (Mon–Fri 9am–9pm, Sat & Sun 9am–5pm) in the airport also accepts foreign cash and credit cards, as does the one at the central post office. In Naha itself, banks along Kokusai-dōri have foreign exchange desks.

Naha festivals

Shuri-jō is the venue for traditional **Ryūkyū New Year** celebrations (Jan 1–3) and the **Shuri-jō Festival** (Nov 1–3), featuring a parade of Ryūkyū-dynasty clothing, dance displays and other performing arts. The **Naha Dragon Boat Race** takes place on May 5, while **The Naha Festival** (Oct 10) includes the world's largest tug-of-war – using a rope 180m long and 1.5m in diameter – as well as a ten-thousand-strong Eisa folk dance parade down Kokusai-dōri.

Okinawan souvenirs

Those in search of local **crafts** will find beautiful *bingata* textiles the most appealing. Originally reserved for court ladies, *bingata* fabrics are hand-dyed with natural pigments from hibiscus flowers and various vegetables, in simple but striking patterns. Also worth searching out are the fine *jōfu* cloths of Miyako-jima and the Yaeyama Islands, once gifted in tribute to the local monarchs. Ceramics are thought to have been introduced to the region from Spain and Portugal in the fifteenth century, but Ryūkyū potters concentrated on roof tiles and fairly rustic utensils. Nowadays, they churn out thousands of sake flasks and *shiisā* – the ferocious lion figures that glare down at you from every rooftop. The exquisite local lacquerware has a long history in the islands, too, having been introduced over five hundred years ago from China, but the glassware you'll find is much more recent: it's said production took off in the postwar years when Okinawans set about recycling the drinks bottles of the occupying US forces.

Bookshops *Libro* on the seventh floor of Palette Kumoji has a limited selection of English-language books and magazines. You can also try Kokusai-dōri's *Tower Records* in the OPA building, where you'll find a few English-language magazines.

Car and bike rental Nippon Rent-a-Car (☎098/868-4554), Japaren (☎0120-413900) and Toyota (☎098/857-0100) all have representatives in both Naha Airport and the city centre. You can rent motorbikes and scooters at Helmet Shop SEA, 3-15-50 Makishi (☎098/864-5116), west of Kokusai-dōri, from ¥1700 for 3hr.

Consulates United States, 2564 Nishihara, Urasoe City (☎098/876-4211).

Ferries Marix Line (☎098/868-9098) specializes in slow boats through the Satsunan islands to Kagoshima, while Maru A Ferry (☎098/861-1886) does the same, and has additional sailings to Kōbe, Ōsaka and Tokyo. For details of ferries to other Okinawa islands, see the individual accounts later in this chapter.

Hospitals and medical care Izumizaki Hospital, 1-11-2 Kumoji ☎098/867-2116. If you need an English-speaking doctor your best bet is the Adventist Medical Centre, 4-11-1 Kohagura, on Route 29 northeast of Naha ☎098/946-2833.

Immigration office To renew your visa apply to the Naha Immigration Office, 1-15-15 Hikawa (☎098/832-4185), on Route 221 southeast of Kokusai-dōri.

Internet There are a number of internet cafés on Kokusai-dōri, some open round the clock, and terminals at the airport (¥100/10min).

Police 1-2-9 Izumizaki (☎098/836-0110). Emergency numbers are listed on p.71.

Post offices Naha Central Post Office is located on the south side of town around 500m down Naha Higashi Bypass from the Meiji Bridge. For ordinary services, you'll find a sub-post office in Palette Kumoji and another at the north end of Kokusai-dōri beside the *Nansei Kankō Hotel*.

Taxis Okitō Kōtsū (☎098/946-5654) has English-speaking drivers, and you can arrange sightseeing taxi tours with English-speaking drivers through Okinawa-ken Kojin Taxi ☎098/868-1145.

Travel agents Okinawa Tourist (☎098/862-1111) can help with domestic or international tickets.

Southern Okinawa-Hontō

During the long, drawn-out Battle of Okinawa (see p.732), it was the area south of Naha that saw the worst fighting and received the heaviest bombardment. Not only were the **Japanese Naval Headquarters** dug deep into the hills here, but the region's many limestone caves also provided shelter for hundreds of Japanese troops and local civilians, many of whom committed suicide rather than be taken prisoner. One of these caves has been preserved as a memorial to the young Himeyuri nurses who died there, and the area is dotted with peace parks and prayer halls. It's not completely devoted to war sights, however. **Okinawa World**, over on the southeast coast, combines 890m of extraordinary stalactite-filled caves

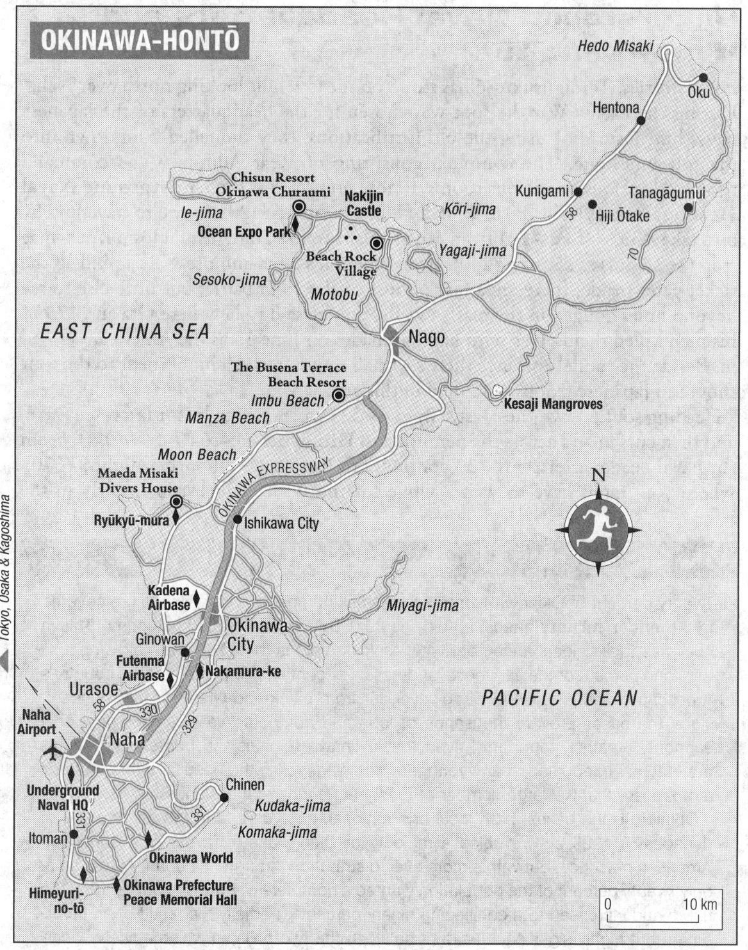

with a tourist village dedicated to Ryūkyū culture, and there's also the lovely **Komaka Island**, a great spot for snorkelling.

Getting around the island

By far the best way of **getting around** Okinawa-Hontō is by **car**, allowing you the freedom to explore some of the coves and beaches on the east coast; see p.734 for operators in Naha. Exploring by **bus** involves a lot of waiting for connections (see individual accounts for details), but an easy alternative is to join one of the organized **bus tours** out of Naha, which pack a lot into a short time at a reasonable price, and come with a practically nonstop Japanese commentary. Naha Bus (Ⓣ098/868-3750) runs three separate full-day tours from Naha's bus terminal, costing from ¥4700 to ¥5800. You can buy tickets at the bus terminal, or from their counter in the airport's domestic terminal.

Underground Naval Headquarters and Himeyuri-no-tō

For centuries, Tomigusuku-jō has stood on the low hills looking north over Naha. During the Pacific War the spot was chosen for the headquarters of the Japanese navy, but, instead of using the old fortifications, they tunnelled 20m down into the soft limestone. The complex, consisting of Rear Admiral Ōta's command room and various operations rooms, is now preserved as the **Underground Naval Headquarters** (旧海軍司令部壕; daily 8.30am–5pm; ¥420). If you're travelling by bus, take #33, #46 or #101 from central Naha to the Tomigusuku Jōshi Kōen-mae stop (1–2 hourly; 25min; ¥240), from where it's a ten-minute walk uphill to the ticket gate. Inside, there are a few photos of the 1945 battle, but little else to see beyond holes gouged in the plaster walls; they're said to be where Ōta and 175 of his men killed themselves with hand grenades on June 13 as the Americans closed in. Beside the tunnel entrance there's a small museum and a monument to the four thousand Japanese troops who died in this area.

Heading south down the coast, Highway 331 passes through **Itoman** town (糸満) and then cuts inland across the peninsula to **Himeyuri-no-tō** (ひめゆりの塔). From the naval headquarters, bus #33 continues to Itoman (1–2 hourly; 40min; ¥370), where you might have to wait a while for the #108, which runs mostly in the

The American question

Twenty percent of Okinawa-Hontō and a small number of outer islands are covered by **American military bases**, employing 27,000 American military personnel. This in itself has fuelled local anger, but what rankles most is that Okinawa makes up less than one percent of the Japanese landmass, yet contains 75 percent of the country's American bases. The issue is, however, far from black-and-white for the islanders, since the bases provide thousands of jobs and contribute vast sums to the local economy – rather important, given that Okinawa remains the poorest of Japan's prefectures. In addition, many younger Okinawans relish the peculiar hybrid cultural atmosphere that the large number of foreigners brings to the islands.

Opinion to the bases, both local and national, has yo-yoed in the past couple of decades. A 1995 poll revealed a majority of Okinawans in favour of a continued American presence, but with a more even distribution throughout Japan. At that time, only twenty percent of the population wanted a complete withdrawal, but by 1996 the figure had increased to a convincing ninety percent – partially the result of an unfortunate but highly significant incident between the two polls, in which a twelve-year-old schoolgirl was **raped** by three American servicemen (see p.733). Mass protests against American military presence were the inevitable result.

Manoeuvrings since then have been largely political in nature, and focused on **Futenma**, a large US Marine Corps air base just northeast of Naha. In 1996, the American and Japanese governments announced a joint plan to relocate the base to Henoko, a bay to the north of Okinawa-Hontō. This led to protests from the environmental lobby, aghast that the move would demolish precious **coral reef** in Henoko, as well as having an injurious effect on the bay's sea life. eighty-three percent of Okinawans voted against the plan in a referendum. In 2005, the two governments agreed to move the relocation site to Camp Schwab, an existing Marine Corps base, though this will have similar environmental ramifications. In 2009, **Yukio Hatoyama** was elected Prime Minister on a campaign promise to move the base outside Japan entirely as the first step in a systematic removal of the American military presence. However, torn between Okinawa and Washington, Hatoyama reneged on his promise, and resigned just eight months after taking office. Regardless of what happens with Futenma, the American issue is likely to rumble on for some time.

morning and late afternoon (20min; ¥200). Himeyuri-no-tō is a deeply moving war memorial dedicated to more than two hundred schoolgirls and their teachers who committed suicide here in a shallow cave. The nearby **museum** (daily 9am–5pm; ¥300) describes in Japanese (though there are detailed English leaflets) how the high-school students, like many others on Okinawa, were conscripted as trainee nurses by the Japanese army in the spring of 1945. As the fighting became more desperate the girls were sent to a field hospital, gradually retreating south from cave to cave, and were then abandoned altogether as the Japanese army disintegrated. Terrified that they would be raped and tortured by the Americans, the women and girls killed themselves rather than be captured.

Mabuni Hill, Okinawa World and Komaka-jima

The final battle for Okinawa took place on **Mabuni Hill** (摩文仁の丘), on the island's southeast coast. The site is now occupied by a cemetery and grassy park containing monuments (known as the "Cornerstone of Peace") to the more than 200,000 troops – both Japanese and American – and civilians who died on the islands during the war. A distinctive white tower crowns the **Peace Memorial Hall** (平和記念堂; daily 9am–5/5.30pm; ¥500; ⓣ098/997-3011), which contains a 12m-high lacquered Buddha and small museum. You'll learn more (though not the full story) if you visit the **Okinawa Prefecture Peace Memorial Museum** (沖縄県立平和記念資料館; Tues–Sun 9am–4.30/5pm; ¥300), which has full English translations throughout. This interesting museum, planned under the anti-establishment regime of Governor Ōta, but completed by the more conservative Governor Inamine, doesn't shirk the uncomfortable fact that Japanese soldiers ruthlessly killed Okinawan civilians. Generally, however, the whole build-up to the war is treated in the usual euphemistic way, and the exhibition ends on an upbeat note with displays on the postwar history of Okinawa to the present day. The entrance to the park lies on bus route #82 from Itoman (9 daily; 30min; ¥220).

Bus #82 will also take you on to **Okinawa World** (おきなわワールド; daily 9am–6pm; ¥600 for the village, ¥1200 for the village and cave, ¥1600 including Habu Park snake exhibit). This quirky "village" showcases local crafts and culture, including *bingata* dyeing, *awamori* brewing and performances of Eisā dances (11am & 12.30, 3 & 4pm). It's built over an 890m-long cave with an impressive array of rock formations along an underground river, but the most popular attraction is the **Habu Park** (¥600), where you can learn about the Okinawan venomous snake and pose for the cameras with a python wrapped around your shoulders. You can also try your hand at the various local crafts for ¥100–200. Afterwards, bus #83 and #54 will take you back to central Naha in around one hour (8 daily; ¥490). If you just want to chill out, you may prefer to take a high-speed boat from the Chinen Kaiyo Leisure Centre (知念海洋レジャーセンター) in Chinen village (知念村) to tiny **Komaka-jima** (コマカ島), an uninhabited island surrounded by golden sands and a coral reef, 3km off the Chinen Peninsula; it's an ideal snorkelling spot. To get to Chinen, take bus #38 from Naha terminal.

Central Okinawa-Hontō

North of Naha, traffic on Highway 58 crawls up the coast of **central Okinawa-Hontō** between a strip of *McDonald's*, *Shakey's Pizza* and used car lots on one side, and neat rows of artillery on the other. This is army country, with huge tracts of land occupied by the **American military** (see box opposite). Camps and bases extend along the coast as far north as the Maeda peninsula, where beach resorts take over. You can avoid the coastal strip by taking the expressway or Highway 330 up the island's less crowded centre past Okinawa City – this is the best way to reach the north of the island quickly. A bizarre mix of American and Japanese life, Okinawa City is the region's main urban centre, but there's little reason to stop. Heading north, though difficult to get to, **Nakamura-ke** is one of the few genuinely old buildings still standing on Okinawa-Hontō, and the nearby ruins of **Nakagusuku Castle** offer commanding views. On the district's northern fringes lies **Ryūkyū-mura**, a quieter, more interesting culture village than Okinawa World (see p.743).

Kita-Nakagusuku

About 10km north of Naha, Highway 330 skirts east of Futenma Airbase before hitting a major junction. A little further north, a road cuts east through the hills to **KITA-NAKAGUSUKU** (北中城) village where, in the early fifteenth century, Nakamura Gashi served as a teacher to a local lord, Gosamaru. In the early eighteenth century, after a rocky patch, one of Gashi's descendants was appointed village leader and started building his family's large, beautifully solid residence, **Nakamura-ke** (中村家; daily 9.30am–5.30pm; ¥300 including tea; ⓣ098/935-3500). Protected by limestone walls, a thick belt of trees and a growling *shiisā* perched on the red-tile roof, the house is typical of a wealthy landowner's residence, with its barns, a lovely grain store and the inevitable rows of pigsties. Inside, there are a few family heirlooms, and the enterprising owners have set up a small shop and restaurant next door.

To reach Nakamura-ke by public transport, take one of the many buses from Naha north to Okinawa City (#23, #25, #31 and #90 are all fairly frequent) for the hour's ride to the Futenma junction. Then hop on the next #59 bus heading north (hourly; 15min; ¥140) and ask the driver to let you off at the Nakamura-ke turning, from where it's a 1500m walk uphill. Alternatively, a taxi from Futenma costs about ¥1500 one-way.

While you're up here, it's worth walking five minutes west to where the limestone cliffs merge into the crumbling walls of **Nakagusuku-jō** (中城城跡; daily 8.30am–5pm; ¥300), designated a World Heritage Site in 2000. These impressive fortifications, consisting of six citadels on a spectacular promontory, were originally built in the early fifteenth century by Lord Gosamaru. But they weren't enough to withstand his rival, Lord Amawari, who ransacked the castle in 1458 and then abandoned the site. Nowadays you can walk through the grassy, tree-filled park and scramble among the ruins to admire the views clear across the island. Taxis usually hang around the castle entrance to whisk visitors back down to Futenma.

Ryūkyū-mura

The final sight in Okinawa-Hontō's central region lies on the west coast, where **Ryūkyū-mura** (琉球村; daily 8.30am–5.30pm; ¥840) preserves several old Okinawa farmhouses brought from all over the islands and reassembled here to showcase the remnants of Ryūkyū culture. Though some will find it too touristy, the village provides a hint of what Okinawa was like before the war. In addition to performances of Eisā dances and traditional music, you can see people weaving, dyeing textiles and milling sugar cane for molasses – try the freshly fried local doughnuts. Ryūkyū-mura occupies a wooded hillside west of Highway 58, some 30km north of Naha. Bus #120 (or the much rarer #20) takes you right to the door (every 15–20min; 1hr 20min; ¥970); coming from Okinawa City, take bus #62 to Kadena (every 15–30min; 30min; ¥400), then change to the #120 northbound.

Fifteen minutes' walk northwest of Ryūkyū-mura, in Onna village, *Maeda Misaki Divers House* (真栄田岬ダイバーズハウス; ⓣ098/964-2497) is a great place to stay, particularly if you've come to Okinawa to dive. The building – an old youth hostel – is a bit run-down, but it's in a quiet location, with walks along the cliffs and down to the white, sweeping curve of Moon Beach. Accommodation is in bunk-bed dorms (¥2000/person) and they do good meals. You can rent bikes (¥1000/day) and they run diving trips, starting from ¥9500 for an introductory dive, including all equipment. Five-day PADI courses are ¥51,000, accommodation included. The nearest bus stop is Kuraha, on bus route #120, from where the hostel is ten minutes' walk northwest.

Northern Okinawa-Hontō

North of Okinawa-Hontō's pinched waist, the scenery begins to improve as classy resort hotels line the western beaches. Bleached-white, coral-fringed Moon Beach merges into Tiger Beach and then there's the rocky, wild Onna promontory before you rejoin the sands at Manza and up through Imbu Beach. Beyond this strip, **northern Okinawa-Hontō**'s only major settlement, **Nago**, sits at the base of the knobbly **Motobu peninsula**. A generally quiet, workaday place, there's not a lot to see in Nago, but the small city makes a good base for exploring the island region's mountainous north and visiting the impressive **Okinawa Churaumi Aquarium** at the far western tip of the peninsula. The district boasts the island's most attractive scenery, particularly around **Hedo Misaki**, the northern cape, and on through sleepy **Oku** village down the rugged northeast coast. It's possible to travel up the west coast by slow local bus, but after Oku you're on your own.

Nago and the Motobu peninsula

Apart from weekends, when off-duty soldiers come up from the bases, **NAGO** (名護) sees few foreigners. If the proposed heliport goes ahead (see box, p.742) all this will change, but for the moment Nago is a slow-moving, fairly pleasant city – more a large town – best known for its huge banyan tree and a spectacular display of spring cherry blossoms. Its other sights consist of a marginally interesting local museum and views from the former castle hill.

Arrival and information

Arriving by bus, most services stop near Nago's central crossing before terminating at the **bus terminal** on the main highway to the west of town. However, some stop on the seafront, notably the Express Bus from Naha Airport, via Naha Bus Terminal (hourly; 2hr; ¥2000), which ends up outside Nago's Lego-block City Hall, roughly 500m west of the central crossroads. You'll find the **tourist information office** (Mon–Fri 8.30am–5.30pm, Sat & Sun 10am–5pm; ⓣ0980/53-7755) in Nago City Hall, which has English-language maps and pamphlets on the area. The Ryūkyū Bank, just north of the central junction, can **exchange** dollar and sterling cash and travellers' cheques, and there's a small post office with an ATM a couple of blocks to the west.

Accommodation

Nago

Tōwa ホテル東和 ⓣ0980/52-3793. In the backstreets northeast of Nago crossroads – walk east along the main street and take the second left. Suprisingly large rooms for the price and amiable service. ❸

Yamada-sō 山田荘 ⓣ0980/52-2272. Clean and friendly, and a good alternative if the nearby Tōwa is full. ❹

The Motobu peninsula

Beach Rock Village ⓣ0980/56-1126, ⓦwww.shimapro.com. A little artsy gem. Accommodation here is in tents, with rates varying from ¥690 to ¥6000 per person depending upon your required level of luxury, while you can also drop by for coffee or tea, served on balconies with commanding views. Superb.

Busena Terrace Resort ザ・ブセナテラスリゾート ⓣ0980/51-1333, ⓦwww.terrace.co.jp. Still proudly displaying evidence of its hosting of the G8 Summit in 2000, this resort has simple but tastefully designed rooms, charming staff and impressive facilities, including six restaurants, an enormous landscaped pool and a nice beach. If you want to see what's going on under the waves you can visit the Busena Resort Underwater Observatory (see below). ❾

Chisun Resort Churaumi チサンリーゾト沖縄美ら海 ⓣ0980/48-3631, ⓦsolarehotels.com. This swanky hotel is ideally located for the aquarium, which is right next door. In addition, all rooms have a sea view, and there's a fantastic on-site pool to splash around in. ❻

Nago

Nago curves round a south-facing bay. Highway 58 runs along the seafront and then turns north again on the west side of town, while behind the harbour a road strikes inland to the central **Nago crossroads**, where it cuts across the city's main shopping street. Near here is the **Orion Brewery** (Mon–Fri 9–11am & 1–3.30pm; ⓣ0980/52-2137) – phone to arrange a free factory tour and tasting of Okinawa's very drinkable home brew. To reach **Nago Castle Hill**, follow the road northeast from the brewery, along the river and up a long flight of stairs. Nothing remains of the castle, but turn left at the top for an attractively landscaped children's park and views over Nago bay.

The Motobu peninsula

Some 10km southeast at the tip of the promontory occupied by the *Busena Terrace Beach Resort* (see above), there's an **Underwater Observatory** (daily 9am–6pm; ¥1000). This is a good way to see some of the area's marine life, if you're not going diving, but not as good as a visit out to **Ocean Expo Park** (海洋博公園), on the northwestern tip of the hilly, mushroom-shaped **Motobu peninsula**. The highlight here is the **Okinawa Churaumi Aquarium** (沖縄美ら海水族館; daily: Jan–Feb & Oct–Dec 8.30am–6.30pm; March–Sept 8.30am–8pm; last admission one hour before closing; ¥1800), a spectacular facility showcasing the marine life of the Kuroshio Current. The main tank holds 7500 tonnes of water and is home to several whale sharks – the largest sharks in the world – as well as shoals of manta ray and many other fish; the cinema-scope view will hold you entranced. Most explanations are in English and there's an informative section on sharks that dispels many myths about these extraordinary creatures. There are other things to do around the sprawling park, several of them free, including dolphin shows, an ocean nursery and a tank for manatee, and a good beach at the north end. In the middle of the park you'll find the **Oceanic Culture Museum** (¥170) containing a vast collection of boats and artefacts from southeast Asia and the South Pacific, and the **Tropical Dream Centre** (¥670), containing two thousand types of orchids and flowers. All these places are connected by an electric bus (¥200 for a day-long ticket).

To escape the crowds, continue clockwise around the coast and up into the hills to the newly restored **Nakijin-jō ruins** (今帰仁城跡; daily 9am–5pm; ¥400), a lovely, peaceful spot with good views north to Hentona and Iheya. There's also a small **museum** if you want to find out more about the history of the hamlet and castle. Buses #65 and #66 circle Motobu clockwise and anticlockwise respectively in roughly two hours, with departures every hour or so from central Nago. These buses stop at the Ocean Expo Park and on the main highway, from where the castle is a gentle 1km climb up a quiet country road.

Eating

Akachōchin 赤提灯 Head down towards the harbour from *Hotel Tōwa* and you can't miss the cheerful red lanterns of this lively *izakaya*, offering cheap, filling food on the far side of the shopping street. Daily 5pm–1am.

Shinzan Shokudo 新山食堂. An unlikely-looking shack next to Yamada-sō, which draws many plaudits for its noodles. Buy a ticket from the machine – their ¥750 set lunch is a great deal. Daily 9am–6pm.

Yamabuki 山吹 ⓣ0980/52-2143. Upmarket restaurant in a grey, modern building one block east of *Hotel Tōwa*, where they serve an Okinawa set meal, *champurū* (*Regional cuisines* colour section) and other local dishes. Prices are reasonable and there's a picture menu, but you'll need to arrive before 7.30pm or make a reservation. Mon–Sat 11am–10pm.

Hiji Ōtake, Hedo Misaki and the east coast

North of Nago, Highway 58 hugs the mountainside as the cliffs rise higher, and the only settlements are a few weather-beaten villages in sheltered coves. At the village of **Kunigami** (国頭), head inland along the road that follows the river to reach the start of the walk to **Hiji Ōtaki** (比地大滝), a picturesque 26m waterfall. The undulating 1.5km trail here (entry ¥200, last entrance 3.30pm) starts from the campsite (ⓣ0980/41-3636; ¥2000), which has good washing and cooking facilities plus a small restaurant-cum-shop. About halfway along the trail you'll cross a 17m suspension bridge, with lovely views across the river; further up and at the falls themselves there are excellent swimming spots.

From Kunigami it's another 20km to Okinawa-Hontō's northern cape, **Hedo Misaki** (辺戸岬). Ignoring the unsightly restaurant block and cigarette butts, this is a good spot to stretch your legs and wander over the headland's dimpled limestone rocks while the waves pound the cliffs below. On clear days you can see northerly Yoron-tō, the first island in Kagoshima Prefecture, and lumpy Iheya-jima to the west, over a churning sea where the currents sweeping round Okinawa collide. If you're travelling by **bus**, take #67 from a stop near central Nago's Ryūkyū Bank to Hentona (辺土名; 1–2 hourly; 1hr; ¥880), then change to #69 for the last leg to Hedo Misaki Iriguchi (8 daily; 45min; ¥670); it's a twenty-minute walk out to the point from where the bus drops you.

Eight kilometres east of Hedo Misaki, the bus terminates in a large fishing village, **OKU** (奥; 15min; ¥330), with an attractive array of traditional Okinawa houses with low, tiled roofs. A quiet, seemingly deserted place, there's nothing to do but wander the lanes and peer at the neat, walled gardens protected to the seaward side by thick stands of trees. In January and February the surrounding hills are clothed in bright cherry blossoms – and in early April you can feast on the ripened fruit. Most of Oku's inhabitants are elderly, but one young couple run the delightful *Minshuku Miyagi* (民宿みやぎ; ⓣ&ⓕ0980/41-8383; ❺ including two meals) beside the river mouth; there are only three rooms, two tatami and one Western, so make sure you book early. From the bus terminus, outside the wonderful village shop, the minshuku's red roof is clearly visible beside the bridge, a few minutes' walk down a sandy track.

Route 70 snakes its way along the east coast, through forests and pineapple groves with the occasional sea view, all of which makes for a pleasant drive. There are few sights here, but one place to aim for is **Tanagāgumui** (タナガーグムイ), a gorgeous swimming hole and small waterfall in a glade reached by a perilous scramble down a 200m clay slope. There are ropes strung down the slope to help, but you still need to be sure-footed. Further south just beyond Tairawan Bay is the **Kesaji mangrove forest** (慶佐次マングローブ), where a boardwalk runs alongside the river. This is a good spot to arrange a kayak trip – ask at the tourist offices in Naha (see p.734).

The outer islands

The beaches on Okinawa-Hontō can't compare with the gems lying offshore among the dozens of **outer islands** that make up the rest of the prefecture. Here, you'll find superb white sands, limpid water and some of the best **diving** in Asia (see box, p.730). Most of these islands also escaped damage during the battles of 1945, and there are no American bases here, so you'll see much more evidence of Ryūkyū culture and traditions. Not that they're completely unspoilt; even here the paradise image is punctured by eyesore developments and a good deal of rubbish along the shore, while July and August bring plane-loads of holidaymakers.

Fortunately, there's plenty of choice and, outside the main holiday season, few tourists. One of the most accessible places to head for is **Zamami-jima**, part of the **Kerama Islands** and just a short ferry ride west of Naha, which offers great beaches and diving and has recently become a centre for whale-watching. For a real sense of escape, however, you need to head further south, to **Miyako-jima** and the **Yaeyama Islands**, including the emptier, more mountainous **Ishigaki-jima** and nearby **Iriomote-jima**, often described as Japan's last wilderness. In all these islands, it's the scenery and watersports that provide the main attractions, but Iriomote has the added distinction of its unique wildlife population and lush, almost tropical rainforest.

The Kerama Islands

The **KERAMA ISLANDS** (慶良間諸島) are the closest group to Naha, lying some 30km offshore. A knot of three large, inhabited islands and numerous pinpricks of sand and coral, the Keramas offer some of the most beautiful and unspoilt beaches in Okinawa and superb diving among the offshore reefs. **Zamami-jima** (座間味島) is a sleepy place home to mere hundreds of people, yet has recently become hugely popular with international tourists thanks to the recent boom in winter whale-watching, as well as the demise of ferries heading from Naha to Miyako and the Yaeyamas – many travellers are now choosing the Keramas over costly flights south.

Dogs and dolphins

Zamami-jima has sourced much of its fame from the animal kingdom. The millions of fish enjoyed by divers (and diners at local restaurants) are an obvious draw, but dogs and whales have also made their mark. Historically, **whaling** was an important part of the local economy, but in the 1960s the whales disappeared and the industry died. Then, towards the end of the last century, the humpbacks started coming back to their winter breeding grounds – which the locals have been quick to exploit, though this time for tourism rather than hunting (see box, p.750). In addition, most young Japanese associate the Keramas with the cutesy 1988 film *I Want to See Marilyn*. Based on a true story, it tells of a **romance between two dogs** on neighbouring islands: Shiro on Aka-jima, and Marilyn some 3km away on Zamami. They met when Shiro travelled to Zamami in his owner's boat, but the passion was such that he started swimming over every day to rendezvous with Marilyn on Zamami's Ama beach – or so the story goes. So enduring is this story that the pup's supposed route is often featured on local maps.

Zamami-jima

A whale statue greets ferries pulling in to **Zamami-jima**'s new harbour, behind which lies tiny **ZAMAMI village** (座間味村), the only settlement of any size on the island, with seven hundred inhabitants out of a total population of one thousand. They speak their own dialect and maintain a fierce rivalry with the people of the much larger island of Tokashiki-jima, a couple of kilometres away to the east. A fine place to get away from it all, Zamami-jima has spectacular **beaches**, both on the island itself or a short boat ride away. You can **dive** year-round, but the best time to visit is in autumn, when most tourists have gone and the water is still warm enough for swimming and snorkelling.

Arrival and information

The islands are served by **ferry** from Naha's Tomari Port. The high-speed Queen Zamami departs twice daily for Zamami, calling at Aka-jima either on the outward or return journey (55min–1hr 15min; ¥2750/¥5230 return; ⓣ098/868-4567); alternatively, there's the slower Ferry Zamami (daily; 2hr 15min; ¥1860/¥3540 return; same phone number). Note that there are more frequent services in high season. Coming off the ferry, the new buildings on the left contain the ferry booking office, **tourist information office** (daily 9am–5pm; ⓣ098/987-2277), where you can pick up a good English map of the island, and the Whale-Watching Association office.

There's one **car rental** outlet, Zamami Rent-a-Car (daily 9am–6/7pm; ⓣ&ⓕ098/987-3250), in the sandy lanes on the village's eastern edge, but they only have a few vehicles so it's a good to reserve in advance. You can rent **scooters** (¥3000/day) and **pedal bikes** (¥500/hr) at one of several shops.

Accommodation

Accommodation on Zamami comprises a reasonable choice of family-run minshuku with a few simple Japanese- and Western-style rooms. It's wise to book ahead at any time of year.

Joy Joy ジョイジョイ ⓣ098/987-2445, ⓦwww.keramajoyjoy.com. Very friendly place on the northwest edge of the village with a handful of decent rooms and a small garden. They're also the people to go to if you're looking for a diving trip. ⑤

Shirahama Islands Resort シラハマアイランズリゾート ⓣ098/987-2915, ⓕ0987-2655. On the road out to Furuzamami, this is Zamami's biggest, smartest hotel. Even if you're not staying here, note that its upstairs bar is one of Zamami's cheaper and more appealing places to drink. ⑤

Whale-watching

From late January through to April, Zamami is Okinawa's main centre for **whale-watching**. The Whale-Watching Association (Ⓣ098/896-4141, Ⓦwww.vill.zamami.okinawa.jp) arranges **boat trips** from Zamami port every day at 10.30am and 12.30pm depending on the weather (2hr 30min; ¥5000). Reservations are essential, and you should bring rain gear as you'll be out in the open sea. With a good pair of binoculars you can even spot humpbacks spouting and cavorting off Zamami's north coast. There's a special **whale observatory** about 3.5km northwest of Zamami village, one of several lookout points scattered round the cliffs and on the island's highest peak, **Takatsuki-yama**.

Summer House Yu Yu 民宿サマーハウス遊遊 Ⓣ098/987-2016. A few steps from Joy Joy, this minshuku offers good-value rooms, but those on a budget can lop almost half of the price away by declining meals. ⑤

Zamami Campsite Ⓣ098/987-3259. Twenty minutes' walk east along the coast road, featuring pleasing six-berth cabins. Otherwise, a pitch costs ¥300 per person, and you can rent tents (¥500) and other equipment.

The island and around

Even allowing for stops, it only takes a couple of hours to explore every road on Zamami, after which there's nothing to do but head to the beach. Roughly 1km southeast of the village, **Furuzamami beach** (古座間味ビーチ) is the best on the island, with excellent coral and shoals of multicoloured fish. In season, you can rent snorkels at the small shop, and there's also a restaurant and showers. However, the beaches get even better on the tiny **offshore islands**, such as **Gahi-jima** (嘉比島) and **Agenashiku-jima** (安慶名敷島), just south of Zamami. In summer (June to mid-Sept) small boats take day-trippers out to these islands (around ¥1000 return), but out of season you'll have to charter your own boat. As for diving, there are dozens of places offering trips and courses, but *Joy Joy* (see p.749) are recommended for their friendly, reliable service.

Eating

It's best to arrange **meals** at your accommodation, though Zamami does have one decent restaurant, the *Marumiya* (まるみや; closed Wed), next door to *Joy Joy*, which does a ¥650 lunch special and reasonable evening meals. The alternatives are a cheap cafeteria upstairs in the old information office building facing the harbour, serving basic noodle and rice dishes, and, in the summer months, the snack bar at Furuzamami beach. At night, you can repair to the friendly *Urizun* bar (うりずん), opposite *Shirayama Islands Resort*.

The Miyako Islands

One has to feel sorry for the **MIYAKO ISLANDS**. Centred around **Miyako-jima** (宮古島), this small cluster boasts some of the best beaches in all Japan, but these are graced by precious few international visitors. Long overshadowed by Zamami-jima and the Yaeyama group, its appeal took another knock with the closure of ferry services to Naha and Ishigaki, making Miyako an expensive add-on to an Okinawan tour. However, it remains a time-out favourite with mainland Japanese, some of whom stay for weeks or months on end, chalking off beach after beach and dive after dive.

The flat, triangular-shaped island of **Miyako-jima** is roughly 35km from tip to tip – its most immediately notable aspect is field after field of sugar cane. **HIRARA** (平良), the main town, lies on the island's northwest coast, from where roads fan out through the fields.

Arrival, information and island transport

Most flights to Miyako come from Naha, though there are also a few direct services from the mainland. From the airport, there are only three buses per day into the main town of Hirara, meaning that you'll most likely have to get a taxi (¥1500), as it's too far to walk. However, if you arrange **motorbike** or **scooter hire** at the airport, the agents will ferry you to your hotel in Hirara for free first, before you pick up your chosen mode of transport. The airport has **car-hire** stalls aplenty, and a helpful **information** desk (9am–5.30pm; ⓣ0980/72-0899), while a **cash machine** accepting foreign cards can be found at Hirara's post office (Mon–Sat 8.45am–7pm, Sun 9am–5pm).

In Hirara, irregular **buses** for the north of the island depart from Yachiyo bus station, a few blocks north of the central post office, while buses south to Maehama and Higashi Henna-zaki leave from Miyako Kyoei bus station on McCrum-dōri, around 1km east of the post office. Most hotels will be able to hook you up with a **dive operator**.

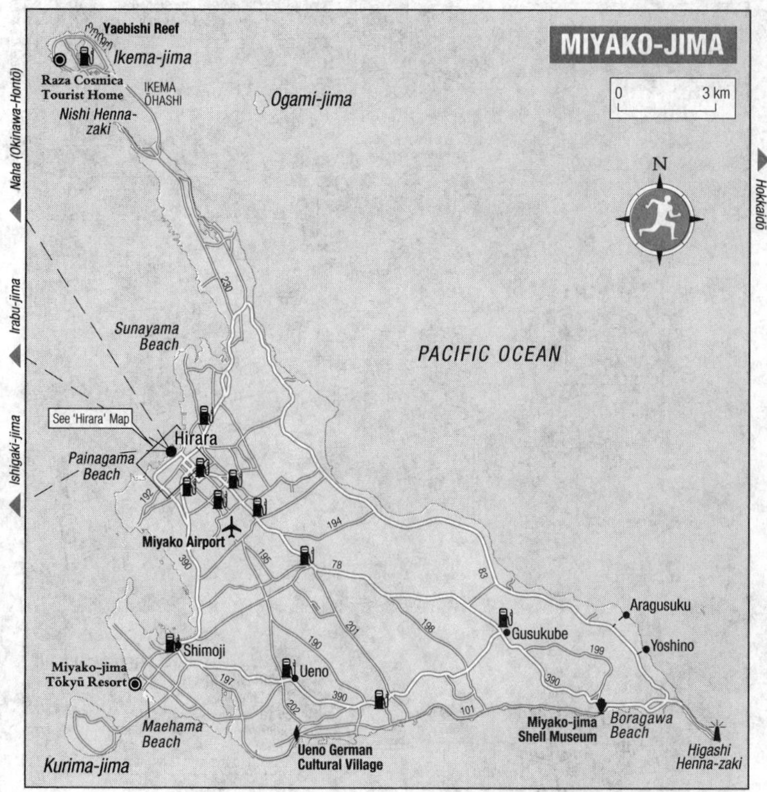

Accommodation

Hirara boasts a good range of **accommodation**, including plenty of cheap minshuku, with prices typically around ¥4000 without meals. If you fancy staying out of town, try the *Miyako-jima Tokyū Resort* at Maehama (see opposite) or the *Raza Cosmica Tourist Home* on Ikema-jima (see opposite).

Hirara

Atoll Emerald ホテルアトールエメラルド ⓣ0980/73-9800. Right beside the ferry terminal, this upmarket option is the classiest place in downtown Hirara, with spacious rooms, a pool, and a smart Japanese restaurant with waitresses in kimono. ❼

Fu-ya 風家 ⓣ0980/75-4343. Run by an impossibly cute family who have converted the ground floor of their house into a mini-hostel. They don't seem too concerned about turning a profit – they'll pick up from the airport for ¥500, let you in on their family dinner for the same price, and get this…dorm beds are just ¥980. Superb.

Hiraraya ひららや ⓣ0980/75-3221. Backpacker decadence – the bunk-beds at this hostel are simply huge. Service is friendly and staff can help to organize trips, but the common areas may be too smoky for some. Dorm beds ¥2000.

Kyōwa ホテルキョウワ ⓣ0980/73-2288, ⓕ73-2285. Tucked into a quiet area behind the Harumizu Utaki shrine, this hotel has a range of decent-value Western-style rooms. ❹

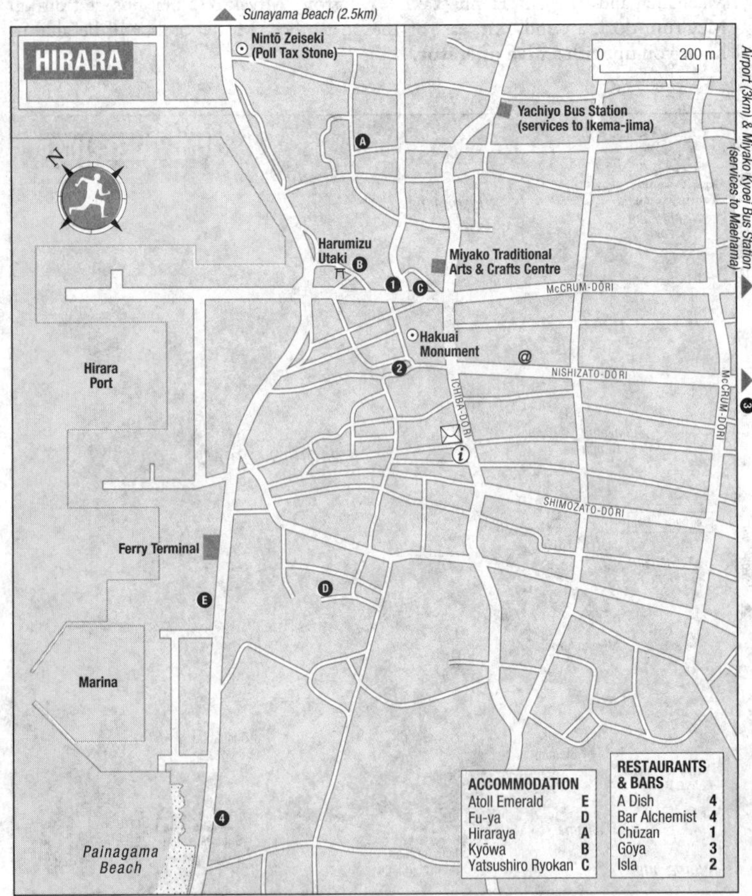

Yatsushiro Ryokan 八城旅館 ⓣ0980/72-1950, ⓕ73-1735. Nothing special, but solo travellers will find particularly good value (single rooms ¥4000) in large tatami rooms featuring bathrooms, TV and a/c. ❸

Around the island

Miyako-jima Tōkyū Resort 宮古島東急リゾート ⓣ0980/76-2109, ⓦwww.tokyuhotels.co.jp. Top-class resort sitting pretty on delectable Maehama beach (see below), to which there's a free shuttle bus from the airport. Watersports enthusiasts won't be disappointed by the range of activities on offer. ❽–❾

Raza Cosmica Tourist Home ラサコスミカツーリストホーム ⓣ0980/75-2020. There's a vague hippy feel to this delightful South Asian-themed adobe pension, perched above a secluded beach on Ikema-jima (see below). The five guest rooms are Western-style, rates include two organic vegetarian meals, and snorkelling equipment and bikes are available for free. It's popular, so booking well in advance is essential. ❼

The island

It won't take long to tick off Hirara's paltry collection of sights before scooting off to the beaches, and few bother. Most appealing is the newly tarted-up **Miyako Traditional Arts and Crafts Centre** (宮古伝統工芸品研究センター; Mon–Sat 9am–6pm), where you can watch women weaving the delicate Miyako-jōfu fabric, designated an Important Intangible Cultural Asset.

Maehama and around

Hirara has its own beach, **Painagama** (パイナガマビーチ), immediately south of the harbour, but there are much better ones around the island. Top of the list is **Maehama** (前浜ビーチ), around 10km south of Hirara, a long and remarkably pristine strip of soft white sand that is hailed as Japan's best beach. Naturally, a prime chunk of it has been requisitioned by the swanky *Miyako-jima Tōkyū Resort* (see above).

Continuing in an anticlockwise direction around the coast, the next sight you'll hit is the Disneyland-like **Ueno German Cultural Village** (うえのドイツ文化村). It was here that eight German sailors were saved from the wreck of the *Robertson*, but otherwise this kitsch mini theme park is of little interest bar a shop selling premium bottled beers from Germany.

Boragawa

The next place of note is **Boragawa beach** (保良川ビーチ), reached by a steep, twisting road from Route 390. It's a good spot for snorkelling and kayaking, and equipment for both is available from the attractive beachside complex that includes a refreshment hut and a freshwater swimming pool. If you fancy a more substantial lunch, the restaurant next to the missable shell museum on the cliffs above does hearty set menus for under ¥1000. Just east of here lies beautiful **Higashi Henna-zaki** (東平安名崎), a 2km-long peninsula renowned for its wild flowers and panoramic views. Head out to the lighthouse at the very tip, where you can climb to the top and check out the views (9am–4.30pm; ¥150).

Heading north up the east side of the island, duck off the coastal road to find the quiet beaches at **Yoshino** (吉野) and **Aragusuku** (新城), both excellent snorkelling spots with corals and a plethora of tropical fish.

Ikema-jima

At the far north of the island, a bridge connects Miyako with tiny **Ikema-jima** (池間島). Ikema has a lazy fishing port and more deserted beaches and good coral reefs, including the extensive Yaebishi reef, which is exposed annually during the low spring tides. You can take a fifty-minute glass boat tour out there for ¥2000. The best reason for detouring here, however, is the *Raza Cosmica Tourist Home* (see above).

On the way back to Hirara is another lovely beach, **Sunayama** (砂山ビーチ), which some find the best of the lot. It's 2.5km north of the town, and accessed on a steep path that worms its way through trees and over a large sand dune; the beach, when you first catch sight of it, looks nothing short of heavenly. Western-facing, it's a good spot to come for sunset, which at certain times of year can be viewed through a naturally eroded stone arch.

Eating and drinking

The best place to look for **restaurants** is in the streets immediately inland from the harbour, particularly Nishizato-dōri, which runs parallel to the main road, Highway 390, but two blocks west.

A Dish ⓣ0980/72-7114. The menu changes daily at this stylish and relaxed restaurant 500m south of the ferry terminal. There's good pasta and fine thin-crust pizza for ¥800–1000, as well as local dishes with a contemporary spin. Tues–Sat 6pm–midnight, Sun 5–11pm.

Bar Alchemist After finishing your meal at *A Dish*, nip upstairs to this convivial bar, decorated with a telescope, piano and world globe. The owner organizes live events twice a month, including folk and classical music. Daily 6pm–2am.

Chūzan 中山 McCrum-dōri ⓣ0980/73-1959. Authentic *izakaya*, specializing in fish and sushi as well as what they call "ethnic" food. A meal shouldn't cost more than ¥1000. Daily 4pm–midnight.

Gōya 郷家 Friendly *izakaya* and *minyō* house further east along Nishizato-dōri. Be warned – you may well end up dancing your way around the venue with the rest of the clientele. Daily except Thurs 5.30pm–midnight.

Isla カリブの酒場 Hirara's obligatory reggae bar, a short stroll away from the west end of Nishizato-dōri, is a cut above the average, conjuring an appropriately tropical vibe. Great cocktails, weekly salsa nights and regular gigs make this well worth a visit. Daily 8pm–5am.

The Yaeyama Islands

Star-sand beaches to pad along, waterfalls tumbling down emerald mountains, and not a soldier in sight…it's no wonder that even Okinawans go misty-eyed when talking about the **YAEYAMA ISLANDS** (八重山諸島). Japan finally fizzles out at this far-flung spray of semi-tropical islets, 430km south of Okinawa-Hontō and almost 3000km from northern Hokkaidō, and those lucky enough to make it this far are in for quite a finale. The bad news is that the Yaeyamas are no longer accessible by ferry, meaning that you'll have to take a flight from Naha or the mainland – but it's worth it, especially if you're into diving, hiking, kayaking or meeting "alternative" Japanese.

Most flights arrive at **Ishigaki-jima**, the most populous Yaeyama island by far. Travellers tend to base themselves here for convenience, but while Ishigaki has its charms, you'd be mad to come this far and not go that little bit further – a fifteen-minute ferry-ride away is tiny **Taketomi-jima**, essentially a freeze-frame of traditional Ryūkyū life, while a little further away is **Iriomote-jima**, almost entirely cloaked with jungle and about as wild as Japan gets. Even more remote are **Hateruma-jima**, to the south, and **Yonaguni-jima**, stuck out on its own between Ishigaki and Taiwan.

Ishigaki-jima

Yaeyama life revolves around **Ishigaki-jima** (石垣島), the islands' main transport hub and population centre. Most travellers base themselves here, making use of the excellent accommodation and dining options to be found in **ISHIGAKI** (石垣), the only Yaeyama settlement large enough to warrant description as a town. The rest of the island is a predominantly rural and mountainous landscape, fringed with rocky peninsulas, stunning beaches and easily accessible reefs, while its interior is scored with the gorgeous walls of hand-stacked stone which gave Ishigaki its name.

Arrival and information

Currently, the only way into Yaeyama is by plane. Ishigaki's homely airport handles daily **flights** from Tokyo and a handful of other mainland cities, though far more arrive from Naha. **Buses** make the short journey to Ishigaki town every twenty minutes or so (¥200), and a taxi will cost around ¥800. Note that a new airport is scheduled to open in 2013, at a location further towards the east of the island.

The **ferry terminal** serving Taketomi-jima and Iriomote-jima is just across the road from the bus terminal, while a smaller wharf serving Yonaguni-jima and Hateruma-jima is a ten-minute walk around the dock.

There's a small **information** booth at the airport, though more useful are the staff at Hirata Tourism (daily 7.30am–6pm; Ⓣ0980/82-6711, Ⓦwww.hirata-group.co.jp/english), located in the new ferry terminal. Internet cafés around town come and go – an outlet of the popular Gera Gera chain lies on the street behind the bus station. The post office has cash machines (daily 9am–7pm), which accept foreign cards.

Getting around

If you're planning on getting around the island by bus, it's worth investing in one of the two **Free Passes** (¥1000 & ¥2000), both valid for five days; the cheaper one allows as many round trips as you like between the airport, Kabira Bay and the resorts at Sukuji Beach; the more expensive covers all of the island's buses. Otherwise, guided **bus tours** (4hr 30min; ¥4350; Japanese only) visit all the island's main sights, departing from the bus terminal daily at 9am, but you'll find it easier to use either the buses (see above) or, better still, hire your own transport. **Car rental** is easy to organize at the airport, or prior to arrival. Good-value **bike and scooter rental** is available at *Ai Ai* (9am–7pm, closed when weather is poor; Ⓣ0980/83-9530), diagonally opposite the post office. Note that on Sunday most of the island's petrol stations are closed except for those in Ishigaki; make sure you fill up before setting off around the island.

Accommodation

Most **accommodation** is located in Ishigaki town, where you'll find several other cheap options, as well as decent mid-range hotels. The upper-end accommodation is at the resorts, the best of which is *Club Med Kabira*. Rates can rise significantly during the main holiday periods.

Ishigaki town

Chisun Resort Ishigaki チサンリゾート石垣 1 Tonoshiro Ⓣ0980/82-6161, Ⓦwww.solarehotels.com. Smart hotel in a convenient location with simple but elegantly furnished rooms. Also has a large communal bath and sauna. ❼

Minshuku Parkside Tomo 民宿パークサイドトモ 6-4 Shinei-chō Ⓣ0980/88-8388. Clean tatami rooms at a reasonable price – dorms cost just ¥1500, while singles (¥2500) have their own TV and a/c. They also rent out bikes and scooters for reasonable rates. ❸

Rakutenya 楽天屋 291 Ōkawa Ⓣ&Ⓕ0980/83-8713. English-speaking hosts Ren and Miyako have created a cosy guesthouse with both tatami and Western-style rooms. Booking is essential since it's small and popular. ❸

Super Hotel Ishigaki-jima スーパーホテル石垣島 36 Ishigaki Ⓣ0980/83-9000, Ⓕ83-9003. Smart business hotel with single rooms only. All have TV, a/c and small bathrooms, and there's a free light breakfast served in the lobby; great value at ¥4500.

Yashima Ryokan Youth Hostel 八洲旅館ユースホステル 117 Tonoshiro Ⓣ0980/82-3157, Ⓕ82-4546. Located in a traditional house, this secluded hostel gets guests into the Okinawan spirit, whether it be

11 OKINAWA | The Yaeyama Islands

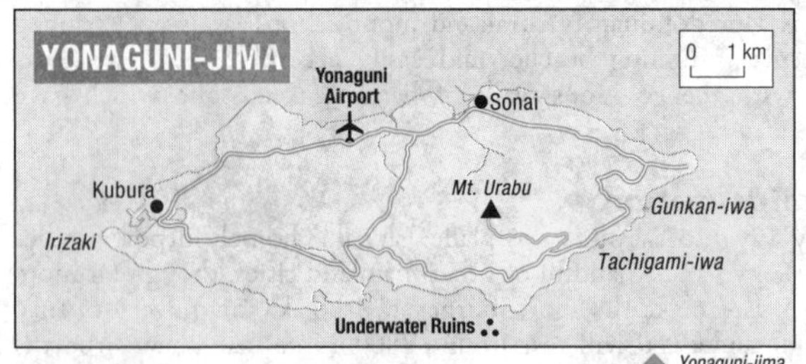

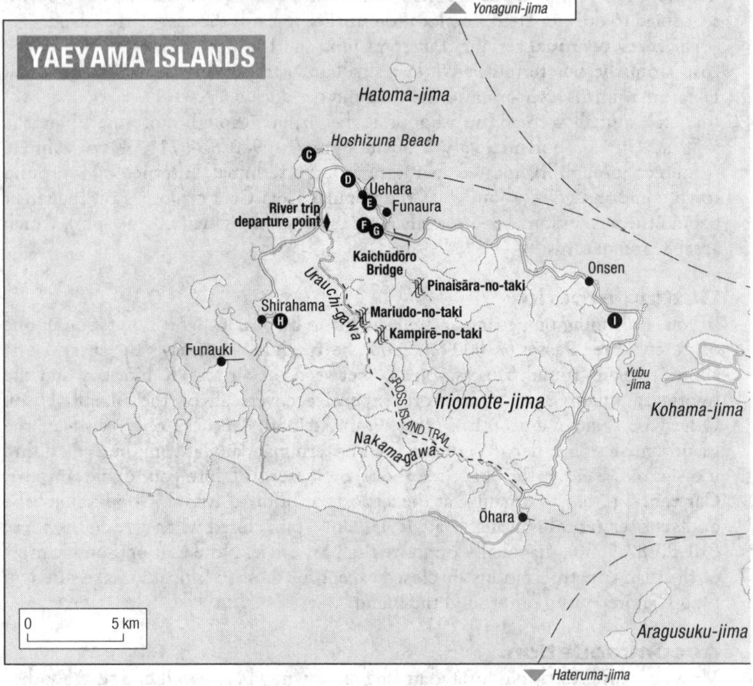

through dance, song or an alcohol-fuelled "*awamori* time" in the evening. Dorm beds ¥2500.

Kabira Bay

B&B Kabira B&B カビラ 934-4 Kabira Bay ⓣ0980/88-2229. Classy boutique hotel with modern Western-style rooms and a pleasant restaurant-bar, all with fabulous views of Kabira Bay. There are some cheap doubles, but the larger twin rooms are going on for resort prices. ⑤

Club Med Kabira クラブメッドカビラ Kabira Bay ⓣ0980/84-4600, ⓦwww.clubmed.com. A good resort option, with all the creature comforts one might expect – all staff speak English or French and there are excellent facilities, including a trapeze artist on hand to teach you the ropes. They've also got one of the best beaches on the island. ⑧

Minshuku Maetakaya 民宿前高屋 934 Kabira Bay ⓣ0980/88-2251, ⓕ88-2473. This delightful minshuku offers good tatami rooms with shared facilities, tasty Asian meals and a beautiful view of the famed bay from its spacious wooden deck. ⑤ including two meals.

Ishigaki town

Apart from hosting the Yaeyamas' best range of tourist facilities, Ishigaki town has a number of minor sights that shouldn't delay you more than an hour before you

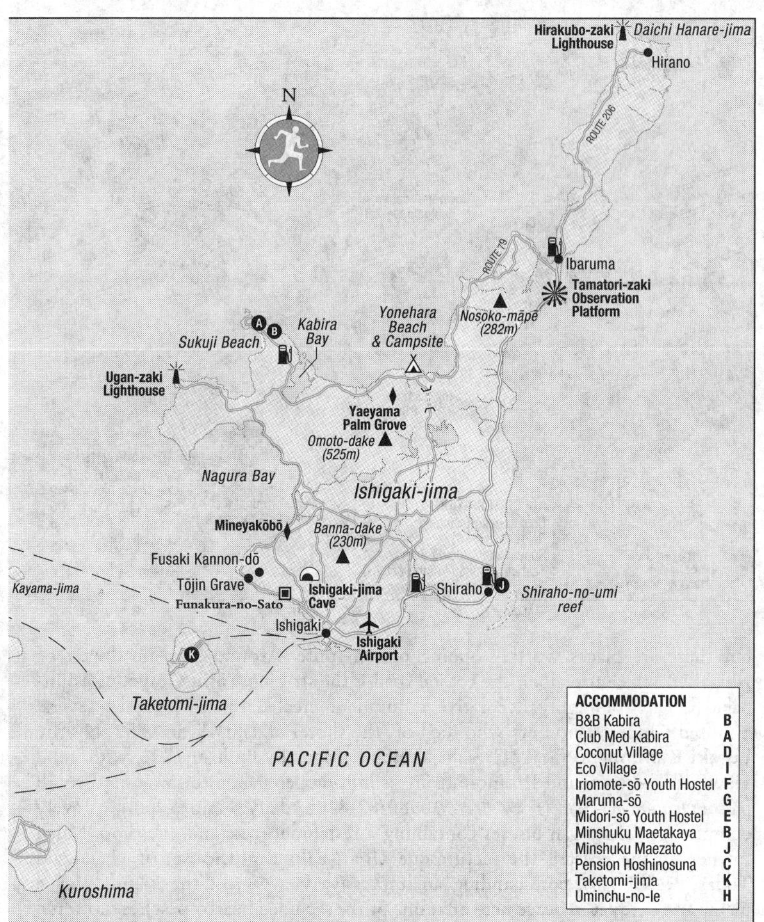

hit the beaches. The first of these, the small **Yaeyama Museum** (八重山博物館; Tues–Sun 9am–5pm; ¥200), lies five minutes' walk inland from the harbour, and contains a moderately interesting collection of local artefacts, including a pile of traditional canoes, shaggy *shiisā* masks used in local festivals, and a rather gruesome scroll depicting the tortures of hell. Ten minutes' walk northwest, **Miyara Dunchi** (宮良殿内; daily except Tues 9am–5pm; ¥200) was built in 1819 and modelled on a traditional samurai residence; it's surrounded by a coral rock garden, designated a National Scenic Beauty. As the family still lives there you can't enter the house itself but only look into the rooms that open onto the traditional garden. On the town's northwest outskirts is **Tōrin-ji** (桃林寺), an attractive Zen temple founded in 1614 where meditation is still practised. Its two Deva king statues (called *Niōzo*) are now worshipped as the island's protectors.

Along the coast to Kabira Bay

Locals and tourist literature will urge you to head straight to **KABIRA BAY**, or Kabira-wan (川平湾), home of cultured black pearls and gorgeous emerald waters,

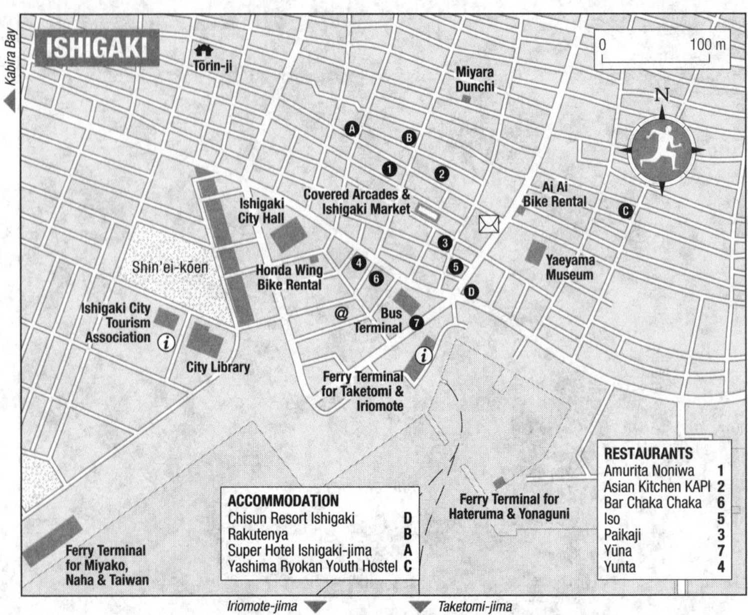

but there are places worth stopping off en route. Around 2km northwest of Ishigaki town centre along the coastal road is the striking **Tōjin Grave**, or Tōjin-baka (唐人墓), a highly decorative monument erected in 1971 to the several hundred Chinese labourers who died off the shores of Ishigaki in 1852. Nearby **Fusaki Kannon-dō** (冨崎観音堂) is a temple originally built in 1701, with good views of Taketomi and Iriomote from its hillside perch. On the way here you'll pass *Funakura-no-Sato* (舟蔵の里; ⓣ0980/82-8108, daily 11am–10pm), a lovely complex of Okinawan houses containing a restaurant, café and gift shop. Much further up the coast is the picturesque **Ugan-zaki Lighthouse**, or Ugan-zaki Tōdai (御神崎灯台), commanding an impressive view across the island. Pack a picnic and enjoy it in peace here or at one of the secluded nearby beaches, scattered with giant shells; the sunsets are often spectacular.

Kabira Bay itself is overcommercial in feel, though it's still worth battling through the *omiyage* stands for superb views of the pearl farms and surrounding confetti of islands. You can also head out on a glass-bottom boat tour; ¥1000 will buy you a fish-filled view. North of the bay is **Sukuji Beach** (底地ビーチ), one of the nicest on Ishigaki, and home to some great accommodation options (see p.756).

Yonehara beach

Ishigaki's most rewarding beach experience by far lies some 5km east of Kabira at **YONEHARA** (米原). Here you can wade out across a broad expanse of dead coral (make sure you're wearing some foot protection), teeming with sea life, to the very edge of the reef, which drops off to the sea floor and is full of tropical fish. You'll need to be wary of jellyfish here, which can pack a fatal sting. Snorkelling gear can be rented from shops on the main road for ¥1000, and there's a **campsite**, with basic toilet facilities, in the trees beside the beach. You also won't fail to notice the colourfully painted giant *shiisā* statues outside *Yoneko Yaki Kōbō* (daily 9am–6pm), a cottage industry factory and shop churning out the traditional Okinawan guardians in a range of cartoon-like styles.

Behind Yonehara, Ishigaki's mountainous interior holds several **trekking** possibilities, including the hike up **Omoto-dake**; not far north of Yonehara is the turn-off to a grove of Yaeyama palms from where a trail runs up the slopes of the mountain to an observation platform.

Ibaruma and around

At Ibaruma Bay, Route 79 swings east to the opposite side of the island. At the fork you have a choice. Head north through a pastoral landscape and you'll eventually hit the pretty viewpoint of **Hirakubo-zaki** (平久保岬), the end of the line on Ishigaki-jima, punctuated by a dazzling white lighthouse overlooking the tiny island, Daichi Hanare-jima. Otherwise turn south on Route 390 and take the turn-off for the **Tamatori-zaki Observation Platform**, or Tamatori-zaki Tembōdai (玉取崎展望台). The views from here are splendid and the landscaped grounds burst with crimson hibiscus blooms. Naturally, it's a favourite stop for tour buses. If you're heading up here by public transport, the infrequent bus #9 from Ishigaki will drop you at the foot of the hill at the Tamatori stop.

Shiraho-no-umi

One of Ishigaki's main attractions lies offshore – **Shiraho-no-umi**, a patch of reef containing the rare Ao (blue) and Hama corals. The village of **SHIRAHO** (白保) has several minshuku where you can stay and arrange boat trips (around ¥2000) at high tide to snorkel over the reef; one recommendation is *Minshuku Maezato* (民宿まえざと; ⓣ0980/86-8065; ❹ including two meals), next to the post office. If you're coming here by bus, get off at the Shōgaku-mae stop.

Eating and drinking

Ishigaki is well served with **restaurants**, some of them surprisingly smart for such an out-of-the-way place. For self-catering and local colour, check out the market in the covered arcade just north of the central Shiyakusho-dōri. There are also a few decent **bars**, including the hip Bar *Chaka Chaka* (daily from 9pm), and *Paikaji* (南風), a bustling *izakaya*.

Amurita Noniwa あむりたの庭 Ōkawa 282. This smart yet laidback venue serves local dishes with a contemporary twist – perhaps the most delectable example is Yaeyama-soba in green curry soup. Also good for coffee or an evening drink – they'll prove that the galaxy of Okinawan beer extends far beyond Orion. The friendly young hosts take holidays when they feel like it, otherwise open 11am–midnight.

Asian Kitchen Kapi Yui Road. It's worth heading to this rustic restaurant for lunch, since around ¥1000 will buy you one of their tasty southeast Asian platters. Dinners, however, are overpriced. Daily except Tues 11.30am–3pm, 5.30–11pm.

Iso 磯 9 Ōkawa. Appealingly gloomy, this is one of the best places for traditional Yaeyama cuisine. Has a photo-menu, and dishes start at ¥700. Daily 11am–10.30pm.

Yūna ゆうな 3 Misaki-chō. Some of the best *Yaeyama-soba* (similar to *sōki soba*) on the island, this spacious yet surprisingly intimate venue is highly convenient if you're waiting for a ferry or a bus. A bowl of noodles will come to ¥630, and a set with pickles and rice is ¥800. Daily 11am–11pm.

Yunta ゆんた 9-2 Misaki-chō ⓣ0980/82-7118. Popular fish restaurant on Ishigaki's main street. The sets for ¥700 are a good deal, or treat yourself to a sushi platter. Daily 5pm–midnight.

Taketomi-jima

Just before six o'clock each evening, the tiny island of **Taketomi-jima** (竹富島) undergoes a profound, magical transformation. This is the time of the last ferry back to Ishigaki-jima – after that, you're marooned, but there are few better places to be stuck. Just over 1km wide and home to fewer than three hundred people, the island's population swells during the day with folk eager to see its traditional houses, ride on buffalo-drawn carts and search lovely sandy beaches for the famous minuscule star-shaped shells. When the day-trippers are safely back in Ishigaki, those who have chosen to stay on will have Taketomi almost to themselves – it's possible to walk its dirt paths at night for hours on end without seeing a single soul.

There's only one village on Taketomi – also called **TAKETOMI** (竹富) – and it's a beauty. Practically all its houses are built in traditional bungalow style with low-slung terracotta-tiled roofs, crowned with bug-eyed *shiisā*. Surrounding them are rocky walls, draped with hibiscus and bougainvillea: these are the *ishigaki* that gave a certain neighbouring island its name, yet these days they're far more prevalent on Taketomi.

Arrival, information and island transport

Ferries from Ishigaki (¥1100 return) run regularly from 7.30am–5.30pm. There's a small **information** booth inside the terminal, but more interesting is the adjacent visitor centre (ゆがふ館; daily 8am–5pm; free), which has displays and short films about the island's unique lifestyle.

If you've booked accommodation and given advance warning of your arrival time, you'll be met at the terminal and taken to your room. Otherwise, it's a ten-minute walk to Taketomi village, or you can hitch a ride with one of the touts renting **bicycles** (¥300/hr). Another way to get around is on **buffalo-driven carts** known as *suigyūsha* (¥1400/person for 30min), while being serenaded by a *sanshin*-plucking local or, more commonly, young mainlanders on a gap year.

Accommodation

Taketomi has some great accommodation options, almost all of which are in the village. Rates at all, except the youth hostel, include breakfast and dinner.

Je t'aime ⓣ0980/85-2555. A little bit of Thailand transported to the Yaeyamas, this rickety but pleasing little hostel has decent bunk beds (¥2000/person), a smoky common room and geckos patrolling the walls.

Nohara-sō のはら荘 ⓣ0980/85-2252. A fantastic place to stay, with a very laid-back atmosphere, excellent food and free snorkelling gear. Come sundown, a bottle of *awamori* (an Okinawan hooch) is likely to appear, the three-stringed *sanshin* comes out and an Okinawan singsong begins. ❺

Takana Ryokan 高那旅館 ⓣ0980/85-2151, ⓕ85-2129. Well-run place with a mix of tatami dormitory and ryokan rooms – the ryokan side of the building is slightly fancier and you get served a better standard of meal. Dorms ¥2900 per person, rooms ❻

Villa Taketomi ⓣ0980/84-5600, ⓕ85-5601. There's a real sense of remoteness at this cluster of en-suite pine chalets, sitting in solitude to the west of the island, and perfect for those who want to unwind. They also run an excellent nearby restaurant. ❼

The island

Apart from soaking up the atmosphere, the main thing to see in the village is the **Kihōin Shūshūkan** (喜宝院蒐集館; daily 9am–5pm; ¥300), a small museum with an attached gift shop. There are over two thousand items on display here, including old cigarette packets, rusting samurai swords, an ornate shrine and expressive festival masks. Punctuating the tiny landscaped garden a few blocks east of the museum is a concrete lookout tower, from which both Ishigaki and Iriomote can be seen. A nicer ocean scene is provided from the pier on the west side of the village – the best spot from which to view sunset. The star-sand beaches, **Kondoi** (コンドイビーチ) and **Hoshizuna** (星砂ビーチ), also known as **Kaiji** (カイジビーチ), are a short pedal south of here, also on the west side of the island.

Swimming is possible at both, but at low tide you'll have to wade a long way out. The best snorkelling spot is at **Misashi** (ミサシ), on the northern coast, where three rocky islets and their surrounding reefs provide a home to a multitude of colourful sea life.

Eating and drinking

The village offers a few **eating** options, but things can wind down early so be prepared. A mini-market next to the post office sells snacks and sundries until about 7pm.

Kanifu かにふ There's a mild South Seas atmosphere to the outer seating at this excellent restaurant, especially at the cute tropically-styled bar. *Gōya champuru*, *sōki soba* and local shrimp are the stars of the show. Daily except Thurs eve 11am–5pm, 6.30–10.30pm.

Shidamē しだめー館 The favoured drinking venue of visitors and locals alike, yet no slouches in the kitchen department either – try the taco rice or *sōki soba* (both ¥800). Daily 10am–11pm.

Takenoko 竹の子 Pleasing little *sobaya*, also known for its curry rice. Open some evenings until 9pm, and its outdoor tables are a good spot for a beer.

Iriomote-jima

Brooding darkly some 20km west of Ishigaki, **Iriomote-jima** (西表島) is an extraordinarily wild place for Japan. Rising sharply out of the ocean, some ninety percent of its uncharted, mountainous interior is covered with dense subtropical rainforest, much of it protected as the **Iriomote National Park**. Yaeyama rumour would have it that Iriomote often – or even perpetually – plays host to disaffected Japanese, living rough in the jungle. A more substantiated inhabitant, though equally elusive, is one of the world's rarest species, the *yamaneko* or **Iriomote lynx**, a nocturnal, cat-like animal. The island and its surrounding waters are also home to a splendid array of flora and coral reefs shimmering with tropical fish. There are also plenty of opportunities for snorkelling, diving, kayaking and hiking through the rainforest.

Although it's Okinawa's second-largest island, fewer than two thousand people live here, most of them along barely developed strips on the north and south coasts. Ferries from Ishigaki sail to two ports on the island: **ŌHARA** (大原) in the south and **UEHARA** (上原) in the north. The latter is the better place to head for since it's closer to Iriomote's main scenic attractions and offers the widest range of accommodation.

Arrival and local transport

Yaeyama Kankō and Anei Kankō both run several high-speed **ferries** from Ishigaki to Uehara (50min; ¥2000 one way, ¥3800 return) and Ōhara (45min; ¥1540 one way, ¥2930 return). Inclement conditions may force ferries to use Uehara – check with your guesthouse owner when you're on your way back to Ishigaki.

Iriomote's only main road runs along the coast from Ōhara via Funaura and Uehara to Shirahama in the west; all these villages are linked by infrequent public buses. To really explore the island you'll need to **rent a bike** or **car**; this can be arranged at both youth hostels (see p.762). Bring plenty of cash with you since there are no convenient exchange facilities.

Accommodation and eating

It's certainly worth **staying** at least one night on the island and it's best to opt for a deal that includes two meals, since **eating** options are thin on the ground. Those that do exist are clustered on the main road near Uehara ferry terminal – *Shimpachi*

Diving on Iriomote

Iriomote is a **divers' paradise**, with the Manta Way between the island's eastern coast and **Kohama-jima** being particularly famous for its shoals of manta rays; you're most likely to see them between April and June. The youth hostels and all minshuku can put you in touch with the island's several dive operations (see box, p.730, for more on diving). **Snorkelling** is particularly good at **Hoshizuna Beach** (星砂の浜), around 4km northwest of Funaura, where you'll also find a **campsite**, a decent restaurant and snorkelling gear for rent – all of which makes it popular. If you're looking to escape the crowds, head to **Funauki** (船浮), reached by three ferries a day (¥410) from **Shirahama** (白浜), at the far west end of the coastal road; the beach here, a short trek through the jungle, is one of the most beautiful in all of Japan.

Shokudō (新八食堂) does good, simple meals, while tropically-themed *Kake-tā* (かけたー) is good for pizza or cocktails (closed Wed & Thurs). There's also a small 24-hour supermarket in the area.

Coconut Village ココナッツビレッジ ⓣ0980/85-6045, ⓕ85-6308. On the northwestern outskirts of Uehara, this modern beachside complex has small tatami and Western-style rooms (with very low beds), a restaurant and a freshwater pool. ❺

Eco Village ⓣ0980/85-5115. As its name infers, this is an unobtrusive, low-rise establishment, very much in the Iriomote spirit of things – set away from the village, there's little to do but relax on a swing-chair, grab a bite at the on-site snack shack or sip a drink under the stars, before retreating to the cosy, pine-panelled rooms. ❼

Irumote-sō Youth Hostel いるもて荘ユースホステル ⓣ0980/85-6255. Without a doubt the best budget place to stay on the island, with a hilltop location that makes it a little hard to walk to from Uehara – no matter, since the friendly owners will pick you up. Serves excellent meals, has bikes and scooters for rent and lots of info on local diving companies. Dorm beds ¥3100.

Maruma-sō まるま荘 ⓣ0980/85-6156. One of Funaura's nicer minshuku, run by a friendly family. Features small tatami rooms, shared bathroom, coin-operated a/c and a spacious garden by the harbour with access to a sandy, but littered, cove. ❹

Midori-sō Youth Hostel みどり荘ユースホステル ⓣ0980/85-6526. An easy walk from Uehara ferry terminal, this spartan but clean hostel also has good-value minshuku accommodation for ¥4500 per person including two meals, and dorm beds (¥2500 per person). Can arrange transport hire and the full range of Iriomote adventure activities. ❸

Pension Hoshinosuna ペンション星砂 ⓣ0980/85-6448, ⓔbluehaven@soleil.ocn.ne.jp. Tastefully furnished Western-style rooms and spacious tatami rooms with attached bathrooms at this small beachside complex, with restaurant, shop and diving centre on hand. Also has a good camping ground (¥300 per pitch; tent rental for ¥525). ❺–❻

Uminchu-no-Ie 海人の家 ⓣ0980/85-6119, ⓕ84-8321. Simple Japanese-style accommodation in a large municipal building at Shirahama – useful if you want to get away from what constitutes crowds on Iriomote and spend time exploring the beautiful coastline here by kayak, which can be rented from the local store at ¥4000 per day. Rates include a breakfast of coffee and bread. ❹

Urauchi-gawa and the waterfalls

The vast majority of visitors to Iriomote-jima come only for the day, heading straight to the **Urauchi-gawa** (浦内川), a broad, Amazon-like river, where they hop on boat tours (¥1500; 3hr round trip including hike) to the trail up to the scenic waterfalls **Kampirē-no-taki** (カンピレーの滝) and **Mariudo-no-taki** (マリウドの滝). Boats make the 8km run from 9am to 4pm daily and it's best to get there early and catch the tour groups, since they won't depart with fewer than four passengers. The touristy nature of this excursion (even the elderly can easily negotiate the gentle 1.5km trail through the rainforest up to the falls) is undeniable, yet it's still enjoyable and offers several options for more adventurous trips. One is to hike some 15km across the island from the head of the Kampirē falls to the **Nakama-gawa** (仲間川), Iriomote's second-largest waterway, and Ōhara. This far from clear route takes at least six hours – get local advice before tackling it, be prepared to camp out, don't go alone and let the police know your plans (call ⓣ0980/85-6510). The other option is to paddle back from the falls in a **kayak**, a great way to view the rainforest at close quarters. Kayak trips can be arranged at the youth hostels or at the river trip departure point and cost around ¥8400 including lunch for a full day. To hire a kayak and paddle on your own, go to *Kōto Sharē Puraza* (ⓣ0980/85-6723), the café opposite where the tour buses stop for the Kampirē falls; they charge ¥3900 a day. If you're staying at *Irumote-sō Youth Hostel*, they organize a daily drop-off at the Urauchi-gawa and Hoshizuna beach (see opposite).

Pinaisāra-no-taki

Kayaking can also be combined with a trek up to **Pinaisāra-no-taki** (ピナイサーラの滝), the tallest waterfall in Okinawa, which you can clearly see from the Kaichūdōro bridge that spans the bay immediately south of Funaura (船浦). An excellent guide to arrange this with is Murata Susumu (ⓣ&ⓕ0980/85-6425), aka Hige-san, a wildlife photographer who runs a variety of eco-trips through his company Murata Shizenjuku (村田自然塾). At low tide you may well find yourself dragging your kayak across the shallows to the Hinai-gawa before paddling to the start of the trek. This will give you a chance to inspect the mangrove forests closely and see armies of purple soldier crabs scuttling across the sandbanks. On the climb to the head of the falls, keep a lookout for snakes and be prepared for leeches, especially in the wet season. At the foot of the trail you'll also pass many of the distinctive **sakishima suōnoki** trees, with huge, billowing buttress roots. You'll also notice lumps of coal sparkling in the ground – this was one of Iriomote's riches that Commodore Perry had his eye on when he forced the opening up of Japan in the mid-nineteenth century. The youth hostels can also provide details of hiking trails from Funaura to the falls if you don't fancy kayaking.

Yonaguni-jima

Some 127km northwest of Ishigaki and 2000km from Tokyo, **Yonaguni-jima** (与那国島) is the furthest west you can go and still be in Japan; on a clear day you can see Taiwan 111km away from Yonaguni's high point, **Mount Urabu**. It's accessible on daily **flights** (30min; ¥9400) and twice-weekly **ferries** (4hr; ¥3460) from Ishigaki.

Just 11km long, it won't take you long to tour this predominantly rural but hilly island. **SONAI** (祖納) on the north coast is the main community; ferries dock in its port and the **airport** is a couple of kilometres west. The best way to get around is by rented **bike or car**, which can be arranged in town or at the airport. A circuit of the island shouldn't take you more than half a day, although you'd be mad to pass up the chance to linger at some of the most deserted beaches in the Yaeyamas. Head first west towards the tiny port of **Kubura** (久部良) and out to **Irizaki** (西崎), where you'll find a simple monument marking Japan's westernmost point, atop sheer cliffs.

Much more interesting is what lies on the sea bed beneath. In 1986 local divers came across what looked like a giant rock-carved staircase, or possibly part of a pyramid, 80m long, 50m wide and 20m high. Researchers have flocked to what have been described as the **underwater ruins** (海底遺跡) ever since. Some claim the rocks are part of the legendary ancient civilization of Mu, an Asian Atlantis. Weather dictates whether diving is possible – when the wind's blowing from the south it's too dangerous. Another diving highlight here is the sight of schools of hammerhead sharks, particularly in the winter months.

More intriguing rock formations can be found above water on Yonaguni's east coast. **Gunkan-iwa** is said to resemble a battleship, although it actually looks more like a submarine rising to the surface. There's little debate over what the **Tachigami-iwa** outcrop resembles – it's worshipped by locals as a symbol of virility. On the nearby hillsides, wild Yonaguni horses roam.

Sonai has a handful of **hotels**, including the friendly *Hotel Irifune* (ホテル入船; Ⓣ0980/87-2311; ⑤); owner Aratake Kihachiro discovered the aforementioned ruins and runs glass-bottom boat tours, diving and fishing trips. *Guesthouse ADAN* (ゲストハウス阿檀; Ⓣ0980/87-2947, Ⓕ87-2957; ③) is cheap and cheerful, with internet access and bike, scooter and kayak hire.

Travel details

Ferries

Ishigaki-jima to: Hateruma-jima (6 daily; 1hr); Ōhara, Iriomote-jima (every 30min; 45min); Uehara, Iriomote-jima (hourly; 50min); Yonaguni-jima (2 weekly; 4hr 30min).

Naha to: Kagoshima (daily; 25hr); Kōbe (1–2 weekly; 42hr); Ōsaka (weekly; 41hr); Tokyo (1–2 weekly; 54hr); Zamami-jima (3 daily; 55min–2hr 15min).

Flights

Ishigaki to: Fukuoka (daily; 2hr); Kōbe (daily; 2hr 15min); Ōsaka Kansai (2 daily; 2hr 15min); Miyako (2 daily; 30min); Nagoya (daily; 2hr 40min); Naha (1–2 hourly; 1hr); Tokyo (daily; 3hr 15min); Yonaguni (2 daily; 30min).

Miyako to: Ōsaka Kansai (daily; 1hr 55min); Miyako (2 daily; 30min); Naha (hourly; 45min); Tokyo (2 daily; 2hr 35min).

Naha to: Fukuoka (16 daily; 1hr 40min); Hiroshima (2 daily; 1hr 40min); Hong Kong (2 weekly; 2hr 40min); Ishigaki (1–2 hourly; 1hr); Kagoshima (3 daily; 1hr 15min); Kōbe (8 daily; 1hr 50min); Kumamoto (daily; 1hr 35min); Matsuyama (daily; 1hr 35min); Miyako (hourly; 45min); Miyazaki (daily; 1hr 35min); Nagasaki (daily; 1hr 35min); Nagoya (8 daily; 2hr); Ōsaka Kansai (8 daily; 1hr 50min); Okayama (daily; 1hr 50min); Sendai (daily; 2hr 30min); Seoul (daily; 2hr 20min); Shanghai (daily; 2hr); Shizuoka (daily; 2hr 10min); Taipei (2 daily; 1hr 30min); Takamatsu (daily; 1hr 50min); Tokyo (1–3 hourly; 2hr 15min).

Contexts

Contexts

History

The Japanese are believed to have descended from immigrants from mainland Asia as well as Polynesians who, pre-10,000 BC, moved north along the east Asian coast. The earliest migrants, in what is now known as the **Jōmon** era (10,000 BC–300 BC), were gradually pushed north by succeeding groups, until today only a few remain, known as the **Ainu**, who live mainly in Hokkaidō (see p.288). The subsequent **Yayoi** era saw the development of wet-rice cultivation and the use of bronze and iron implements. Then came the **Kofun** era (300–710 AD), whose main legacy is many thousands of burial mounds, mainly in central and western Japan.

Much of this early history is the stuff of myth and legend, first recorded in the **Kojiki**, "Record of Ancient Matters", and the **Nihon-shoki**, "Chronicles of Japan", Japan's oldest surviving historical documents, completed in 712 AD and 720 AD respectively. Though they don't always agree, the accounts tell of a land peopled by semi-gods engaged in fabulous adventures.

According to traditional belief, Jimmu, great-great-grandson of the sun goddess Amaterasu, founded the imperial dynasty about 660 BC and died at well over 100 years of age. Historians, however, consider that Jimmu was, in fact, based on a local chieftain who probably lived about six hundred years later and who gave the name Yamato to what is now Japan.

Rise of the Fujiwara clan

Buddhism arrived in Japan via Korea in the mid-sixth century when the first of Japan's non-imperial ruling dynasties, the **Soga** clan, rose to power and adopted the religion. **Prince Shōtoku** was installed as heir apparent and regent to Empress Suiko around 592 AD. A zealous Buddhist and great patron of the arts and sciences, Shōtoku also fostered an exchange of scholars with China and Korea, framed a legal code and was responsible for introducing the Chinese calendar.

In 645 the Nakatomi clan staged a successful coup against the Soga, changed their name to **Fujiwara** and rose to become Japan's most influential and aristocratic family. In the late seventh century, Emperor Mommu chose a Fujiwara lady as his consort, starting a trend that continued until the reign of Emperor Taishō in 1921.

In 646, the Fujiwara introduced the **Taika**, or Great Reforms, reorganizing the government on Chinese lines in order to strengthen the throne. The Chinese system of land tenure and taxation was adopted, and an attempt was made to decentralize the government. In 701 further reforms saw the nationalization of

The major historical eras

Jōmon	10,000–300 BC	Momoyama	1573–1600
Yayoi	300 BC–300 AD	Edo (or Tokugawa)	1600–1868
Kofun	300–710	Meiji	1868–1912
Nara	710–794	Taishō	1912–1926
Heian	794–1185	Shōwa	1926–1989
Kamakura	1185–1333	Heisei	1989–present day
Muromachi	1333–1573		

land and the founding of a university to teach Chinese history and philosophy. Confucian principles, which espoused filial piety and the subordination of women, were encouraged. For a while it also became the custom to relocate the royal palace after the death of each emperor, until Japan's first permanent capital, **Nara**, was founded in 710.

The Heian era

In 784 the Fujiwara court distanced itself from the monks and priests in Nara who were meddling too much in politics by first moving to nearby Nagaoka, then to **Heian-kyō** (Capital of Peace), later known as **Kyoto**, in 794. From this base the Fujiwara steadily increased their grip on power, fostering a great blossoming of the arts. In 866 Fujiwara no Yoshifusa was the first non-royal to be appointed regent, to rule on behalf of the emperor, and his successors held this position virtually continuously for the next three hundred years. The clan's power reached its zenith under **Regent Fujiwara no Michinaga**, who held control for thirty years after 995 AD, partly by marrying his daughters to four successive emperors.

During the eleventh century, Buddhist monks were again meddling in secular affairs. The Fujiwara, whose lives were now dedicated to courtly pursuits, invited the militaristic **Minamoto** and **Taira** (also known as the Genji and Heike respectively) clans to act on their behalf. Using this opportunity to advance their own status, the two clans engaged in a struggle for power culminating in the **Genpei Wars** (1180–85).

The Taira initially gained the upper hand, under the leadership of Lord Kiyomori, whose great mistake was to spare the lives of the Minamoto brothers **Yoritomo** and **Yoshitsune**. This pair are the stuff of Japanese legend, with Yoritomo as the great statesman – despite an unpleasant degree of cruelty and paranoia – and Yoshitsune as the dashing young general. With Yoshitsune commanding the Minamoto fleet, the Taira were finally defeated at the **Battle of Dannoura** (1185), in the straits of Shimonoseki between Honshū and Kyūshū, in one of the most decisive moments of Japanese history.

Following this victory, Yoritomo feared his brother might stage a coup, and this suspicion sparked off a period of internecine strife that ended with Yoshitsune's death in 1189.

The Kamakura era

Yoritomo established his military-based *Bakufu*, or "tent government", at **Kamakura** (see p.203) styling himself Sei-i Tai Shogun, the "Barbarian-subduing Great General". Japan settled in to a period of **semi-feudalism**, with the peasants being allowed tenure of land in return for service to their local lord. After Yoritomo's death in 1199 his loyal lieutenant **Hōjō Tokimasa**, in partnership with Yoritomo's widow Hōjō Masako, took the helm, assuming the combined roles of military and civil governor, and ushering in the century-long era of the **Hōjō regents** – these, rather than the figurehead emperor or shogun, were the real power holders during this time.

In 1268 the great Mongol leader, **Kublai Khan**, sent six envoys to demand that Japan pay tribute to China. Japan's rejection provoked the Khan to invade in

1274, when the **Mongol army** landed at Hakata (north Kyūshū) but had to withdraw when a storm threatened their fleet. After the Japanese executed further envoys, in 1281 the Khan dispatched a 100,000-man army. The invaders gained a foothold and fought fiercely for seven weeks, but their fleet was again scattered by a typhoon. The grateful Japanese dubbed it the **kamikaze**, or "Divine Wind".

The Muromachi era

The war-torn economy and an ineffectual government led to the collapse of the Hōjō in 1333 to the forces of **emperor Go-Daigo**. After Go-Daigo's commander defeated the Hōjō, the Kamakura *Bakufu* had dispatched the warrior **Ashikaga Takauji** to bring Go-Daigo to heel. The wily Takauji initially switched allegiance to the emperor but later turned against him, forcing Go-Daigo to retreat to the mountains of Yoshino. Takauji set up a rival emperor in Kyoto and for sixty years Japan had two courts, until they were reconciled in 1392. By this time, the **Ashikaga Shogunate** had established its headquarters in Kyoto's **Muromachi** district, from where they ruled for more than two centuries.

Over the years, the Ashikaga, too, began to lose their grip on power. By the end of the fifteenth century central authority had all but disappeared. Festering inter-clan enmities culminated in the **Ōnin Wars** (1467–77), which took place mainly in and around Kyoto, and marked the start of a series of civil wars that lasted until the early seventeenth century.

In 1549, towards the end of the Muromachi era, the Portuguese missionary **Saint Francis Xavier** arrived on the shores of Kyūshū. Initially the **Christian** newcomers were treated with tolerance, partly out of curiosity, but mainly because they carried valuable new technology, including **firearms**. Japan's warlords were quick to master the new weapons and eventually developed tactical use of massed musketry unsurpassed even in Europe.

Reunification

The civil wars ended with the **reunification of Japan** under a triumvirate of generals of outstanding ability. The first, **Oda Nobunaga**, achieved dominance of the Kyoto region; however, in 1582, he was betrayed and forced to commit ritual suicide. **Toyotomi Hideyoshi**, who had risen from obscurity to be one of Nobunaga's most trusted generals, avenged Nobunaga's death and managed to outmanoeuvre all rivals with a shrewd mix of force and diplomacy. Success went to his head, however, and he embarked on costly excursions into Korea, which eventually had to be abandoned.

Shortly before his death in 1598, Hideyoshi persuaded **Tokugawa Ieyasu**, now an ally after a period of circumspect confrontation, to support the succession of his son **Hideyori**. This trust was misplaced. Five years after defeating the remaining western clans at the **Battle of Sekigahara** in 1600, Ieyasu seized power, and sacked Ōsaka castle, Hideyori's stronghold. The western clans retreated to their fiefdoms to brood on their grievances for the next 250 years, when they emerged to exact a sort of revenge against the Tokugawa Shogunate (see p.770).

The Tokugawa Shogunate

In 1590 Ieyasu made his capital in **Edo**, now Tokyo (see p.87), and set about guaranteeing the security of the **Tokugawa Shogunate**. The three Tokugawa-related clans were given estates in the most strategically important areas, followed by the lords who had fought on the Tokugawa side. Last came the "outside lords", whose loyalty was questionable; they were allocated fiefdoms in the remotest regions. To keep all these *daimyō* in check they were required to reside part of the year in Edo, thus forcing them into expensive, time-consuming journeys, and to surrender family hostages who lived permanently under the eyes of the authorities. A network of inspectors and spies was set up, and any significant rebuilding of local castles had to be reported.

As **Christianity** increasingly appeared to threaten state security, heavy restrictions were placed on all foreigners, and missionaries and Christian converts were persecuted. By 1639, the year of final exclusion of foreigners, an estimated 250,000 Japanese Christians had been executed, imprisoned or forced to apostatize. The final stand took place in 1637 at **Shimabara**, near Nagasaki, when a Christian-led rebel army was annihilated (see p.677). Thus began the period of *sakoku*, or the **closed country**, which lasted more or less continuously until 1853. The only exceptions to the edicts were Korean diplomats and a handful of Dutch and Chinese traders allowed to operate out of Nagasaki.

The long period of stability under the Tokugawa, interrupted only by a few peasant rebellions, brought steady **economic development**. By the late eighteenth century Edo had become the world's largest city, with a population of roughly one million. The arts flourished, especially during the Genroku Period (1688–1703), which saw the first mention of **ukiyo**, the "floating world" of fleeting pleasures. Artists churned out **woodblock prints** (*ukiyo-e*); **Hokusai** alone is said to have produced 35,000 paintings and illustrated 437 volumes (see p.786).

The arrival of the Black Ships

During Japan's period of seclusion, a small number of Westerners managed to breach the barriers, including **Engelbert Kaempfer**, a Dutchman who wrote the

The way of the warrior

The origins of the **samurai**, Japan's warrior caste, go back to the ninth century, when the feudal lords began to maintain regular forces. Gradually, they evolved into an elite group of hereditary warriors, their lives governed by an unwritten code of behaviour and unquestioning loyalty that came to be known as *bushidō*, **the way of the warrior**.

According to *bushidō*, the samurai and his family were expected to die willingly to protect the life and honour of their feudal lord. If they failed in this duty, or were about to be taken prisoner on a battlefield, then suicide was the only fitting response. The traditional method of **ritual suicide** was disembowelment with a sword or dagger (*seppuku*), though in later years an accomplice would stand by to cut off the victim's head. The samurai creed reached full bloom in the early Tokugawa era when class distinctions were officially delineated. The samurai were deemed "the masters of the four classes" – above farmers, artisans and merchants – and they alone were permitted to carry swords. They even had the right to kill any member of the lower orders for disrespectful behaviour, real or imagined.

During the more peaceful seventeenth and eighteenth centuries, many samurai found themselves out of work as their lords were dispossessed and fiefdoms redistributed. Many became **rōnin**, or masterless samurai, whose lives were romanticized in such films as *The Seven Samurai* (see p.807).

first European-language history of Japan in the late seventeenth century. Various British survey vessels and Russian envoys also visited Japan in the early nineteenth century, but the greatest pressure came from the **US**, whose trading and whaling routes passed to the south of the country.

In 1853 **Commodore Matthew Perry** of the US Navy arrived with a small fleet of "black ships" demanding that Japan open at least some ports to foreigners. Japan's ruling elite was thrown into turmoil. The shogunate was already fearful of foreign incursions following the British defeat of China in the Opium Wars. However, when the emperor demanded that the foreigners be rebuffed it quickly became clear that Japan's military was no longer up to the task.

There followed a decade of jockeying for power between the Japanese factions, and for influence by the foreign envoys. The first of these was the American **Townsend Harris** (see p.195), who managed to extract concessions in the form of the pioneering **Treaty of Commerce and Navigation** in 1858. This was followed by a flurry of similar agreements with other Western countries, which opened the **treaty ports** of Yokohama, Hakodate, Nagasaki and, later, Kōbe and Ōsaka to trade, forbade the Japanese to impose protective tariffs and allowed foreigners the right of residence and certain judicial rights in the enclaves. Opponents of such shameful appeasement by the shogunate took up the slogan "Revere the emperor! Expel the barbarians!". Other, less reactionary, factions could see that Japan was in no state to do this, and their only hope of remaining independent was to learn from the more powerful nations.

Eventually the great **western clans**, the Satsuma, Chōshū, Tosa and Hizen, previously rivals, combined under the banner of the **emperor** to exact revenge against the Tokugawa, whom they had seen as usurpers of the throne ever since Sekigahara (see p.769). Evidence of the shift in power came in 1863 when the emperor ordered Shogun Iemochi to Kyoto to explain his conciliatory actions – it was the first visit by a shogun to the imperial capital since 1634. To add to the humiliation, he could muster a mere three thousand retainers, compared with the three hundred thousand who accompanied Ieyasu to Kyoto on that earlier occasion.

In 1867 the fifteenth and final shogun, **Tokugawa Yoshinobu**, formally applied to the emperor to have imperial power restored. The shogunate was terminated and in December of the same year the **Imperial Restoration** was formally proclaimed and the 15-year-old Mutsuhito acceded to the throne, ushering in a period dubbed **Meiji** or "enlightened rule". In 1869, the young emperor shifted his court from Kyoto to Edo, and renamed it **Tokyo** (Eastern Capital).

The Meiji era

The reign of **Emperor Meiji**, as Mutsuhito was posthumously known, saw vast changes in Japan. A policy of **modernization**, termed *fukoku kyōhei* ("enrich the country, strengthen the military"), was adopted. Railways were built, compulsory education and military service introduced, the solar calendar adopted and the feudal fiefs and the class system abolished. Such rapid changes created resistance and in 1877 **Saigō Takamori**, a hero of the restoration, led an army of 40,000 in the **Satsuma Rebellion**, named after the area of Kyūshū in which it erupted (see p.712).

In the 1880s, even more changes were rubber-stamped by the ruling oligarchy of Meiji Restoration leaders, who imported thousands of foreign advisers for assistance. But as Japan adopted a Western-style constitution in 1889, drawn up by the emperor's trusted adviser **Itō Hirobumi**, the seeds of the country's later troubles were being sown.

The **Meiji Constitution** created a weak parliament (the Diet), the lower house of which less than two percent of the population were entitled to vote for. In effect, the military was still in charge, a situation enforced with the Imperial Rescript on Education in 1890, which enshrined almost as law loyalty to the emperor, family and state. Shinto, which emphasized emperor-worship, became the state religion, while Buddhism, associated too closely with the previous order, was disestablished.

Japan's rulers also began to copy the West's territorial ambitions. The island of Hokkaidō, previously left pretty much to the native Ainu, was actively colonized, partly to ward off a rival takeover by Russia. Territorial spats with an ailing China developed into the **Sino-Japanese War** in 1894, over the Chinese tributary state of Korea. The fighting lasted less than a year, with a treaty being signed in Shimonoseki in 1895 which granted Korea independence, and indemnities, economic concessions and territory to Japan, including Taiwan, then called Formosa.

This unexpected victory brought Japan into conflict with Russia who had her eye on China's Liaodong peninsula for a naval base at Port Arthur. After cordial relations with Britain were cemented in the 1902 Anglo-Japanese Alliance, Japan launched her navy on a successful rout of the Russian fleet in 1904. The land battles of the **Russo-Japanese War** were less decisive, but in a US-mediated treaty in 1905, Russia was forced to make many territorial concessions to Japan.

In 1909, the assassination of Itō Hirobumi, the newly appointed "resident general" of Korea, provided Japan with an excuse to fully annexe the country the following year. With the military in control, and a plot against the emperor's life uncovered in 1910, any domestic left-wing dissent was quashed.

The Taishō era

The sudden death of Emperor Meiji in 1912 ushered in the relatively brief **Taishō** (Great Righteousness) **era**. Meiji's son Yoshihito, the only surviving male out of his fourteen children, suffered hereditary mental illness and by 1921 was so incapacitated that his own son Hirohito was declared regent.

During **World War I** Japan allied itself with Britain. Despite gaining more territory in Asia after the war and being one of the "Big Five" at the Paris Peace Conference and a founder member of the League of Nations in 1920, Japan was frustrated by Australia, Britain and the US in its attempts to get a declaration of racial equality inserted as part of the Charter of the League. This snub, however, didn't preclude continued friendly relations between Japan and the West. In 1921 Crown Prince Hirohito was a guest of King George V at Buckingham Palace, while the following year the Prince of Wales spent a month touring Japan.

Levelling Yokohama and much of Tokyo, and leaving 140,000 dead or missing, the 1923 **Great Kantō Earthquake** was a significant blow, but the country was quickly back on its feet and celebrating the inauguration of **Emperor Hirohito** in 1926, who chose the name **Shōwa** (Enlightened Peace) for his reign.

The slide to war

Economic and political turmoil in the early 1930s provided the military with the opportunity it needed to seize full control. In 1931 the **Manchurian Incident** saw army officers cook up an excuse for attacking and occupying the Manchurian region of northern China. Japan installed **P'u Yi**, the last emperor of China's

Qing dynasty, as the head of their puppet state, Manchukuo, and responded to Western condemnation of its actions by pulling out of the League of Nations.

At home, the military increased its grip on power in the wake of **assassinations** in 1932 of both the prime minister and the former finance minister, and a confused, short-lived **coup** by 1400 dissident army officers in February 1936. **Rapid industrialization** also laid the foundations for some of the most famous Japanese firms of the twentieth century, including the automobile makers Mazda, Toyota and Nissan, the film company Fuji and the electronics giant Matsushita.

In 1936, Japan joined Nazi Germany and Fascist Italy in the **Anti-Comintern Pact**, and the following year launched a full-scale invasion of China. In December 1937, the infamous **Rape of Nanking** occurred when appalling atrocities and massacres were committed against hundreds of thousands of unarmed Chinese soldiers and civilians.

As **World War II** began in Europe, Japan initially held off attacking Allied colonies in the Far East, but when France and Holland fell to Germany their qualms disappeared. Sanctions were imposed by Britain and the US as Japan's army moved into Indo-China, threatening Malaya and the East Indies.

The Pacific War

On December 7, 1941, the Japanese launched a surprise attack on the US naval base at Hawaii's **Pearl Harbor**, starting the **Pacific War**. In rapid succession, the Philippines, Indonesia, Malaya and Burma fell to Japanese forces. However, the tide was stemmed in New Guinea and, in June 1942, the US Navy won a decisive victory at the **Battle of Midway** by sinking four Japanese aircraft carriers.

Although Japan had launched her campaign to secure the "Greater East Asia Co-Prosperity Sphere", in which she would free her neighbours from colonization and help them develop like the West, the brutal, racist and exploitative reality of Japanese occupation meant there was no support from these potential Southeast Asian allies. Nor was there a likelihood of military cooperation between Japan and Germany, who both eyed each other suspiciously despite their pact.

By 1944, with the US capture of the Pacific island of Saipan, Japan was heading for **defeat**. The country was now within range of US heavy bombers, but there was a determination to fight to the bitter end, as exemplified by suicidal kamikaze pilots and the defending forces on the islands of Iwō-jima and Okinawa who fought to the last man.

In March 1945, Tokyo was in ashes and 100,000 were dead following three days of fire bombings. The government insisted that the emperor system remain inviolate when they put down arms, but no such assurances were offered in July 1945 when the Allies called for Japan's unconditional surrender in the Potsdam Declaration. Japan failed to respond, providing the Allies with the excuse they needed to drop the **Atomic bomb** on **Hiroshima** on August 6. Two days later, the USSR declared war on Japan, and the next day, August 9, the second A-bomb exploded over **Nagasaki**.

With millions homeless and starving, and the country brought to its knees, it was a breathtaking understatement for Emperor Hirohito to broadcast, on August 15, 1945, that the war had "developed not necessarily to Japan's advantage". For his subjects, gathered at wireless sets around the country, the realization of defeat was tempered by their amazement at hearing, for the first time, the voice of a living god.

The American occupation

Having never been occupied by a foreign power, Japan little knew what to expect from the arrival of the "American Shogun" **General Douglas MacArthur**, designated the Supreme Commander of the Allied Forces (SCAP). Some five hundred soldiers committed suicide, but for the rest of the population the **Occupation** was a welcome relief from the privations of war and an opportunity to start again.

MacArthur wasted no time in instituting **political and social reform**. The country was demilitarized, the bureaucracy purged of military supporters and war trials held, resulting in seven hangings, including that of the ex-prime minister, Tōjō Hideki. The emperor, whose support for the new regime was seen as crucial, was spared although he had to publicly renounce his divinity to become a symbolic head of state.

In 1946 the Americans took a week to draft a **new constitution**, which, ironically, proclaimed that sovereignty resided in the Japanese people, and contained the unique provision renouncing war and "the threat or use of force as a means of settling international disputes". Land and educational reform followed.

The **peace treaty** signed in San Francisco on September 8, 1951, resolved all issues with the Allies, leaving only the USSR as a threatening communist force. The outbreak of the **Korean War** in 1950 gave a much needed boost to Japan's economy as the country became the main supplier of food and arms for the US forces.

The Occupation officially ended on April 28, 1952, but with the Korean War continuing and the **Treaty of Mutual Cooperation and Security** guaranteeing the US the right to maintain bases on Japanese soil, a strong American presence remained for many years to come. The island of Okinawa was, in fact, only returned to Japan in 1972.

The 1960s economic miracle

In 1955, in the face of rising left-wing antagonism to the continued security pact with the US, America's CIA provided funding for the right-wing Liberal and Democrat parties to join forces. The **Liberal Democratic Party** (LDP), a tight coalition of power-hungry factions, governed Japan uninterrupted for close on the next forty years, creating the stable political conditions for an incredible economic recovery. The term **Japan Inc** was coined for the close cooperation that developed between government, bureaucracy and business.

In 1959, **Crown Prince Akihito** married Shōda Michiko, a commoner he had met while playing tennis at the summer resort of Karuizawa. Five years later Japan joined the rich nations "club", the Organization for Economic Cooperation and Development, inaugurated the high-speed bullet train, or Shinkansen, and hosted the Summer Olympic Games.

During the 1960s Japanese **exports** grew twice as fast as world trade, while it protected its home markets by subjecting imports to quotas, a mass of regulations or outright bans. Yet the associated rapid industrialization physically scarred the country, and **pollution** wrecked lives. In 1971, Tokyo's metropolitan government officially declared that the capital's residents breathed polluted air, drank contaminated water and were "subjected to noise levels that strain the nerves".

By the 1970s, the ingrained **corruption** festering at the heart of Japanese politics was also becoming clear. The conservative LDP had continued to hold power mainly by entering into cosy financial relationships with supporters in industry and commerce. Prime Minister **Tanaka Kakuei**, a self-made politician from Niigata, had already attracted criticism for pushing through the needless construction of a Shinkansen line to his home town, when his abuse of party funds in the Upper House elections of July 1974 caused fellow LDP grandees to quit the Cabinet in protest. Tanaka rode the scandal out, but couldn't survive the bribery charges, brought in February 1976, in connection with the purchase of aircraft from America's Lockheed Corporation.

The bubble economy

A buzzword of the booming 1980s was **kokusaika** (internationalization), even if nobody seemed to know quite what it meant. At the same time as the Japanese were being urged to take a global view, the world was increasingly complaining about Japan's insular ways. The country's huge **balance of payments surplus** and restrictive trade practices set it at odds with the international community, and particularly the US. The tense situation wasn't eased as cash-rich Japanese companies snapped up American firms and assets, such as the Rockefeller Center in New York, and the trade surplus with the US totalled over $30 billion.

This overseas spending spree was made possible by what would later be known as the **bubble economy** – a period when low interest rates fuelled booming land prices and a runaway stock market. Construction, long the bedrock of the economy, was rampant. Despite the factional infighting within the LDP, the party clung on to power by providing voters with a continually rising standard of living and because of weak opposition parties. However, a succession of **scandal-prone prime ministers** slipped quickly in and out of office in the wake of bribery allegations and sexual shenanigans. When Emperor Hirohito died in January 1989, it wasn't just the Shōwa era coming to an end: the overheated bubble economy had also reached bursting point.

The new **Heisei** (Accomplished Peace) **era** and the 1990s kicked off with the coronation of Emperor Akihito. In 1993 Crown Prince Naruhito married Owada Masako, a high-flying career diplomat (see p.102 for more about the modern royal family). The same year a successful no-confidence motion forced Prime Minister Miyazawa Kiichi's shaky government into a hasty **general election**. Although the LDP actually gained one seat, the overall balance of power passed to a coalition of opposition parties, who formed the first non-LDP government in 38 years under leadership of the populist, reforming politician **Hosokawa Morihiro**.

The grim 1990s

Hopes of a new beginning for Japanese politics quickly faded as Hosokawa's rule lasted less than a year. A plan to double the hated consumption tax went down like a lead balloon, and when a story broke about Hosokawa's chequered past with regard to election funding, he was forced to stand down. His successor **Hata Tsutomu** saw the Socialists walk out on the coalition on his first day of office, and his premiership went down in history as the shortest since World War II, at just two months.

The Socialists, already decimated in numbers at the last election, did themselves no favours by siding with their old foes, the LDP, to form the next government. This cynical alliance put the LDP back in the control seat, just over a year since it had lost power, and forced new premier **Murayama Tomiichi**, a Socialist elder statesman, to have his party drop long-held pacifist policies (much to the disgust of voters).

The government gathered further ignominy following its botched response to the massive **Great Hanshin Earthquake** of January 1995, which devastated Kōbe. Offers of foreign help were initially rebuffed and the local *yakuza* further shamed the government by organizing food supplies to the thousands of homeless. The nation's self-confidence took a further battering less than a couple of months later when members of a religious cult, **AUM Shinrikyō**, killed twelve and poisoned 5500 in a nerve gas attack on the Tokyo subway.

In 1996, the LDP returned to full power, under the leadership of former tough-talking trade negotiator **Hashimoto Ryūtarō**, but economic woes continued. The official announcement of **recession** in June 1998, coupled with the plummeting value of the yen and rising unemployment, saw the LDP take a drubbing in the July 1998 upper-house **elections**. Hashimoto resigned and was replaced by the genial but lacklustre **Obuchi Keizō**. A major **nuclear accident** in September (see "Environmental Issues", p.798) caused pause for thought, but no cancellation of Japan's increased reliance on this form of energy.

LDP defeated

Much hope for positive change was placed on reform-minded **Koizumi Junichiro** who became prime minister in April 2001. **Exports** began to recover in 2003 and the stock market headed for the heights previously seen in the 1980s, helping Koizumi win two general elections for the LDP. However, when he stepped down as prime minister in 2006, Koizumi's reputation as a maverick reformer was undermined by the fact that he had ultimately been unable to push through many of the structural changes to Japan's system of government and economy. He'd also angered pacifists at home by deploying Self-Defence Force

Japanese–Korean relations

For centuries Japan has had close links with **Korea**, with a significant number of Japan's ruling class – including the imperial family – believed to have had Korean connections. Despite this, relations between the two countries have frequently been far from neighbourly. Toyotomi Hideyoshi (see p.769) led two unsuccessful invasions of the peninsula in the late sixteenth century before Japan annexed Korea in 1910. Japan's harsh colonial rule has impacted on relations ever since with its neighbour.

The successful co-hosting of the **2002 World Cup** and a Japanese taste for the country's soap operas, pop music and spicy food have helped mend relations with South Korea. There have also been several official apologies for Japan's colonial rule of the peninsula, the latest coming from PM Kan Naoto in August 2010, which also stated that various confiscated cultural artefacts will be returned to South Korea.

Japan's latest apologies were specifically directed at South Korea, rather than **North Korea** where relations remain decidedly frosty. In 2002, after decades of denials, North Korea came clean about how it had abducted thirteen Japanese citizens in the 1970s and 1980s and forced them to train North Korean spies in Japanese language and culture. Some of the kidnapped were eventually returned to Japan but others had died while in captivity. North Korea's nuclear weapons ambitions also don't help, especially as the rogue state keeps launching test missiles in Japan's direction.

troops in Iraq and – much to the ire of China and South Korea – continuing to visit Tokyo's controversial Yasakuni shrine (see p.103).

Koizumi's successors didn't fare much better and as Japan's economy was battered by the global financial crisis of 2008, voters signalled they had finally had their fill of the LDP's style of money politics. After a nearly unbroken run of 54 years in power, the party lost almost two-thirds of its seats in the Diet's lower house in the **general election of 2009**. It was replaced by the Democratic Party of Japan (DPJ) with Hatoyama Yukio as prime minister.

The euphoria over this major political change quickly evaporated in 2010 when a series of events dented national pride. The national airline **JAL** declared bankruptcy and **Toyota** was forced to recall millions of its cars from around the world in the light of possible product faults, calling into question the famed automobile maker's integrity. In the political arena, too, the DPJ fumbled and following more of the usual funding scandals and the breaking of a campaign promise to close a military base on the island of Okinawa (see p.742), Hatoyama was forced to resign. His replacement, Kan Naoto – Japan's fifth prime minister in three years – saw his party lose badly in the upper house elections in July 2010. Voters had been turned off by Kan's brave call for a sales tax hike to help deal with the nation's public debt, estimated to be twice the size of Japan's US$5 trillion economy. Kan raised the ire of right-wingers a month later when his government issued an apology to Korea on the centenary of Japan's annexation of their country (see opposite) and, along with his cabinet, refrained from visiting Yasukuni-jinja, the Tokyo shrine that honours the nation's war dead.

Religion

Japan's indigenous religion is Shinto, and all Japanese belong to it by default. About half the population are also practising Buddhists and around one million are Christian. Combining religions may seem odd, but a mixture of philosophy, politics and a bit of creative interpretation has, over time, enabled this to happen.

It has helped that Shinto does not possess one all-powerful deity, sacred scriptures or a particular philosophy or moral code. Followers live their lives according to the way or mind of the **kami** (gods), and the *kami* favour harmony and cooperation. Therefore, Shinto tolerates its worshippers following other religions, and they find it an easy step to combine Shinto's nature worship with the worship of an almighty deity, such as that in Christianity, or with the philosophical moral code of Buddhism.

Religious festivals are common and many Shinto customs are still manifest in everyday life, from marriage ceremonies to purifying building plots and new cars. Nevertheless, few Japanese today are aware of anything other than the basic tenets of either Shinto or Buddhism and many would not consider themselves "religious" as such.

Shinto

Shinto, or "the way of the gods", only received its name in the sixth century to distinguish it from the newly arrived Buddhism. Gods are felt to be present in natural phenomena – mountains, for example, or trees, waterfalls, strangely shaped rocks, even in sounds. But Shinto is more than just a nature-worshipping faith; it is an amalgam of attitudes, ideas and ways of doing things that, over two thousand years, has become an integral part of what it is to be Japanese.

Shinto shrines

Shinto shrines are called **jinja** (*kami*-dwelling), although you will also see the suffixes *-jingū* and *-gū*. These terms, and the *torii* gates (see opposite), are the easiest ways to distinguish between Shinto shrines and Buddhist temples. The shrine provides a dwelling for the *kami*, who are felt to be present in the surrounding nature, and it is also a place to serve and worship them. Though there are many

State Shinto

Throughout most of Japanese history, Shinto did not play a particularly important role in state politics. This all changed, however, after the Meiji Restoration of 1868 when Shinto was declared the national faith, largely to re-establish the cult of the emperor. Most Buddhist elements were removed from Shinto shrines and destroyed, and Buddhism was suppressed. **State Shinto** ushered in a period of **extreme nationalism** that lasted from around 1890 to 1945. During this period, Japan's mythological origins were taught as historical fact and people were encouraged to believe that all Japanese were descended from the imperial line. At the same time, the traditional values of *bushidō* (see p.770) were promoted as desirable personal qualities. After the war, Emperor Hirohito was forced to renounce his divinity, becoming a merely titular head of state, and the State branch of Shinto was abolished, returning freedom of religion to Japan.

styles of **shrine architecture**, they are traditionally built from unpainted cypress wood with a grass-thatch roof. The best examples of such traditional architecture are the Grand Shrine of Ise, Izumo Taisha (near Matsue) and Tokyo's Meiji-jingū. Later designs show Chinese or Korean influences, such as the use of red and white paint or other ornamentation.

The **torii** marks the gateway between the secular and the spiritual world. Traditionally, these were plain and simple wooden constructions consisting of two upright pillars and two crossbeams. Gradually various styles, such as the distinctive red paint, evolved on the same basic design until there were over twenty different types of *torii*. Nowadays, they are also made of stone, metal and concrete, in which case they tend to remain unpainted.

Inside the compound, you often find pairs of human or animal **statues** on the approach to the shrine building: austere dignitaries in ancient court costume laden with weapons are the traditional Japanese guardians, though you'll also find lion-dogs (*koma-inu*), or large, ferocious-looking *Niō* borrowed from Buddhist temples. Others may be animal-messengers of the *kami*, such as the fox-messenger of Inari, the deity of good harvests.

Somewhere in the compound you'll often see a **sacred tree**, denoted by a twisted straw rope, *shimenawa*, sporting zigzags of white paper tied around it. In the past these trees were believed to be the special abode of some *kami*. Now they're just an expression of divine consciousness which, like other aspects of the surrounding nature, helps to bring people's minds out of the mundane world and enter into that of the *kami*.

Finally, you come to the **shrine building** itself. At the entrance there's a slotted box for donations and a rope with a bell or gong at the top. Some say the bell is rung as a purification rite to ward off evil spirits, others that it's to attract the *kami*'s attention. You'll also notice another *shimenawa* delineating the *kami*'s sacred dwelling place. Inside each shrine there's an **inner chamber** containing the *shintai* (divine body). This is a sacred object which symbolizes the presence of the *kami* and is kept under lock and key – if ever seen, it loses its religious power.

A large shrine will also comprise many other buildings, such as subordinate shrines, an oratory, ablution pavilion, offering hall, shrine office and shop, priests' living quarters, treasure house and sometimes even a platform for sacred dances, a nō drama stage or a sumo arena. In some cases there will be no shrine building as such, but simply a *torii* and a straw rope around a tree or rock to indicate a *kami*'s dwelling place.

Visiting a shrine

When **visiting a shrine**, try to fulfil at least three of the four elements of worship. Of these, **purification** is perhaps the most important as it indicates respect for the *kami*. At the ablution pavilion (a water trough near the entrance), ladle some water over your fingertips and then pour a little into your cupped hand and rinse your mouth with it; afterwards, spit the water out into the gutter below. Now purified, proceed to the shrine itself and the **offering**. This normally consists of throwing a coin in the box – a five or fifty yen coin (the ones with holes in the middle) are considered luckiest – though a special service warrants a larger sum wrapped in formal paper. Depending on the occasion, food, drink, material goods or even sacred dances (*kagura*, performed by female shrine attendants) or sumo contests are offered to the *kami*.

The third element is **prayer**. Pull the rope to ring the bell, bow slightly once, then deeply twice, pray, bow deeply two more times, clap your hands twice at

Know your folk gods

Adding spice to the Japanese religious pot is a legion of folk gods, guardians and demons. The ones to have on your side are the **Seven Lucky Gods** (*Shichi Fuku-jin*), often seen sailing in a boat on New Year greetings cards to wish good fortune for the coming year. Of these, the best-loved are **Ebisu**, the god of prosperity, identified by his fishing rod and sea-bream; **Daikoku**, the god of wealth, who carries a treasure-sack over one shoulder and a lucky hammer; the squat **Fukurokuju**, god of longevity, marked by a bald, egg-shaped head; while the jovial god of happiness, **Hotei**, sports a generous belly and a beaming smile.

Characters to avoid, on the other hand, are the **oni**, a general term for demons and ogres, though *oni* aren't always bad. **Tengu** are mischievous mountain goblins with red faces and very long noses, while **kappa** are a bit like small trolls and live under bridges. If anything goes missing while you're hiking, you can probably blame one of these, as they both like to steal things. If it's your liver that's missing, however, it will definitely be a *kappa*; he likes to extract them from people's bodies through the anus, so watch out.

chest level and end with two last bows, deep and then slight. The final element of worship is the **sacred feast**, which usually only follows a special service or a festival. It sometimes takes the form of consuming the food or drink offered to the *kami* – once the *kami*'s had its symbolic share.

At the shrine shop you can buy charms (*omamori*) against all manner of ills, fortune papers (*omikuji*), which people then twist round tree branches to make them come true, and wooden votive tablets (*ema*) – write your wishes on the tablet and tie it up alongside the others.

All shrines have at least one annual **festival**, during which the *kami* is symbolically transferred from the inner chamber to an ornate palanquin or portable shrine, called a *mikoshi*. This is its temporary home while young men hurtle around the local area with it so that the *kami* can bless the homes of the faithful. The passion with which they run, turning it this way and that, jostling it up and down shouting "*wasshoi, wasshoi*", has to be seen to be believed, especially in rural towns where festivals are usually conducted with more gusto. All this frantic action is said to make the *kami* happy, and it is highly contagious: long after the palanquin has returned to the shrine the merriment continues with the help of copious amounts of alcohol.

Buddhism

Buddhism, which originated in India, was introduced to Japan from China and Korea in the mid-sixth century. As with many things, Japan adapted this import to suit its own culture and values. The Buddha was accepted as a *kami* and, over the years, certain religious aspects were dropped or played down, for example celibacy and the emphasis on private contemplation.

But Buddhism did not travel alone to Japan; it brought with it Chinese culture. Over the next two centuries, monks, artists and scholars went to China to study religion, art, music, literature and politics, all of which brought great advances to Japanese culture. As a result, Buddhism became embroiled in the **political struggles** of the Nara and Heian eras, when weak emperors used Buddhist and Chinese culture to enhance their own power and level of sophistication and to reduce the influence of their Shintoist rivals. Buddhist temples were often built next to Shinto shrines, and statues and regalia placed on Shinto altars to help raise the *kami* to the level of the Buddha. Eventually, some *kami* became the guardians of temples, while the Buddha was regarded as the prime spiritual being.

Up until the end of the twelfth century, Japanese Buddhism was largely restricted to a small, generally aristocratic minority. However, at this time the dominant sect, **Tendai**, split into various **new sects**, notably Jōdo, Jōdo Shinshū, Nichiren and Zen Buddhism. The first two – simple forms of the faith – enabled Buddhism to evolve from a religion of the elite to one which also appealed to the population en masse. The Nichiren sect had a more scholastic approach, while Zen's concern for ritual, form and practice attracted the samurai classes and had a great influence on Japan's traditional arts. Almost all contemporary Japanese Buddhism developed from these sects, which are still very much in existence today.

Buddhist temples and worship

As with Shinto shrines, **Buddhist temples** (called *-tera*, *-dera* or *-ji*) come in many different styles, depending on the sect and the date they were built, but the foremost architectural influences are Chinese and Korean. The temple's **main hall** (the *kon-dō* or *hon-dō*) is where you will find the principal image of the Buddha, and a table for offerings. Sometimes the entry **gate** (*San-mon*) is as imposing as the temple itself, consisting of a two-storey wooden structure with perhaps a pair of brightly coloured, fearsome guardians called *Niō*, or *Kongō Rikishi*. Despite their looks, *Niō* are actually quite good-natured – except to evil spirits.

Some temples also have a **pagoda** in their compound – they are Chinese versions of stupas, the Indian structures built to enshrine a relic of the Buddha, and historically used to be the main focus of Buddhist worship. Depending on the temple's size, you might also see other buildings such as a study hall (*kō-dō*), scripture or treasure houses and living quarters. Zen temples are also famous for their stunningly beautiful rock and landscape gardens, which are designed to aid meditation.

The most important occasion in Japan's Buddhist calendar is **Obon**, in mid-August, when spirits return to earth and families traditionally gather to welcome them back to the ancestral home. *O-higan*, which falls on the spring and autumn equinox (usually March 21 and Sept 23), is again a time to visit ancestors' graves. But probably the biggest celebration is **Shōgatsu** (New Year), though it's as much a Shinto event as a Buddhist one.

Christianity

Though churches can be found even in small rural towns, Christians represent less than one percent of Japan's population. The religion arrived in Japan with the Jesuit missionary **Saint Francis Xavier** in 1549 (see p.653) Initially, the local *daimyō* were eager to convert, largely in order to acquire firearms and other advanced European technologies, while the poor appreciated social programmes which helped raise their standard of living.

The port of **Nagasaki** soon became a centre of Jesuit missionary activity, from where Catholicism spread rapidly throughout Kyūshū. Converts were tolerated, but by the late sixteenth century the authorities considered that the Christian traders' increasing stranglehold on trade, coupled with a growing influence in secular affairs, was beginning to pose a threat. **Persecution** began in 1587. Suspected Christians were forced to trample on pictures of Christ or the Virgin Mary to prove their innocence. If they refused, they were tortured, burnt at the

Sōka Gakkai

Several **new religions** appeared in Japan during the nineteenth and twentieth centuries, many of them offshoots of Shinto or Nichiren Buddhism. The most successful has been **Sōka Gakkai** (Value Creation Society), founded in 1930 by schoolteacher Makiguchi Tsunesaburō, who emphasized the importance of educational philosophy alongside the day-to-day benefits of religion. With its proselytizing mission and broad appeal to people of all ages and classes, Sōka Gakkai International (Ⓦwww.sgi.org) now claims around twelve million members. The movement also endorses the political party New Kōmeitō (Ⓦwww.komei.or.jp).

stake or thrown into boiling sulphur; over three thousand local converts were martyred between 1597 and 1660.

Following the **Battle of Shimabara** of 1637 (see p.770), Christianity was forbidden in Japan up until the late nineteenth century. Amazingly, the religion endured and when foreign missionaries again appeared in Nagasaki in the mid-1860s, they were astonished to discover some 20,000 "hidden Christians". Since then, around 250 Japanese martyrs have either been recognized as saints or beatified by the Catholic Church, including Nagasaki's 26 martyrs (see p.671).

Japanese arts

One of the joys of visiting Japan is experiencing the ordinary ways in which the Japanese aesthetic enters into everyday life. The presentation of food, a window display or the simplest flower arrangement can convey, beyond the walls of any museum or gallery, the essential nature of Japanese art.

Periods of aristocratic rule, military supremacy and merchant wealth have all left their mark on Japanese arts, building on a rich legacy of religious art, folk traditions and the assimilated cultural influences of China and Korea. More recently, the West became a model for artists seeking to join the ranks of the avant-garde. Today Japanese artists both draw on traditional sources and take their place among international trends.

Spanning the centuries is a love of nature, respect for the highest standards of craftsmanship and the potential for finding beauty in the simplest of things. These qualities pervade the visual arts of Japan but are also reflected in aspects of the performing arts, where the actor's craft, costume and make-up combine with the stage setting to unique dramatic effect. The official designation of valued objects and individuals as **National Treasures** and **Living National Treasures** acknowledges the extent to which the arts and artists of Japan are revered.

The religious influence

Shinto and Buddhism, Japan's two core religions, have both made vital contributions to its arts. **Shinto's** influence is extremely subtle, but apparent in the Japanese love of simplicity, understatement and a deep affinity with the natural environment. The plain wooden surfaces of Shinto shrines, for example, together with their human

The way of the flower

Ikebana, or the art of flower arranging, has its roots in ancient Shinto rituals and Buddhist practice. The original emphasis was on creating flower displays that imitated their **natural state**. This gradually evolved into using just three leading sprays to represent heaven, earth and humankind, which are arranged to express the harmonious balance of these elements, with the use of empty space being as crucial as the sprays themselves. The container, setting and season influence the choice of materials, which can range from bare branches and withered leaves to fruits, moss and grass. The idea is to highlight the beauty of the materials and to evoke the essential characteristics of nature in shorthand form. As with so much Japanese art, the very act of creating the arrangement has a **spiritual** element. Focusing entirely on which materials to use, what "message" they carry and how best to bring this out, Zen Buddhists would say the arranger is "living the moment".

The art of ikebana reached its peak in the sixteenth century, largely on the coat-tails of the **tea ceremony** (see p.55) in which the only decoration in the room is an ikebana display or hanging scroll. As it became more widely practised, several distinct styles evolved, broadly divided into the self-explanatory *shōka* (living flowers), the formal *rikka* (standing flowers), *moribana* (heaped flowers), and the more naturalistic *nage-ire* (thrown in). Each of these is further subdivided into different schools, dominated nowadays by Ikenobō (Ⓦwww.ikenobo.jp), Ohara (Ⓦwww.ohararyu.or.jp) and Sōgetsu (Ⓦwww.sogetsu.or.jp). To find out more, contact Ikebana International (Ⓦwww.ikebanahq.org), an umbrella organization with branches in sixty countries.

scale, is reflected in a native approach to architecture in which buildings strive to be in harmony with their surroundings (for more about Shinto shrines, see p.778).

Some of Japan's earliest **Buddhist sculptures** can be found at Hōryū-ji near Nara (see p.472) and take their inspiration from Chinese and Korean sculpture of an earlier period. The temple's bronze Shaka (the Historic Buddha) Triad by Tori Bushii, a Korean–Chinese immigrant, dates back to 623 and reflects the stiff frontal poses, archaic smiles and waterfall drapery patterns of fourth-century Chinese sculpture. At the same time, Hōryū-ji's standing wooden Kudara Kannon, depicting the most compassionate of the Bodhisattvas, is delicately and sensitively carved to emphasize its spirituality.

During the early years of Buddhism in Japan and the periods of closest contact with China (the seventh to tenth centuries), Japanese styles of Buddhist art mimicked those current in China or from its recent past. However, a gradual process of assimilation took place in both painting and sculpture until during the Kamakura era (see p.768), when the adaptation of a distinctly Japanese model can be observed in Buddhist art.

The Heian era

In 898 the Japanese stopped sending embassies to the Chinese T'ang court, ending centuries of close relations with China. Gradually the cloistered and leisured lifestyle of the Heian era (794–1185) aristocracy spawned a uniquely Japanese cultural identity.

Court life in Heian Japan revolved around worldly pleasures and aesthetic pastimes, and the period is renowned for its artistic and cultural innovation. *Kana*, or the phonetic syllabary, was developed and employed in the composition of one of Japan's greatest literary masterpieces, **The Tale of Genji**, or *Genji Monogatari*. Lady Murasaki's portrayal of the Heian-court nobility eloquently described the artistic pursuits which dominated their daily life – poetry competitions, the arts of painting, calligraphy and gardening and the elaborate rituals of court dress.

A new painting format, the *emaki* or **picture scroll**, also evolved during the Heian era. *Emaki* depicted romances, legends and historical tales, of which the most famous is an illustrated edition of *The Tale of Genji*, published around 1130. The painting technique used, known as *Yamato-e*, employs flat blocks of colour with a strong linear focus and a unique boldness of style. The **decorative arts** reached a similarly high level of sophistication. Inlaid lacquerware, using the *maki-e* technique (sprinkling the surface with gold or silver powder) and finely crafted bronze mirrors employed surface designs to equally dramatic effect.

The lavishness of Heian taste is reflected in **Buddhist painting and sculpture** of this period. New sects of Buddhism gave rise to the diagrammatic mandalas, schematic depictions of the Buddhist universe, while religious sculpture became more graceful and sensual, with gilded, delicately featured deities marking the transition to an aristocratic form of Buddhist art.

Samurai culture

The establishment of the Kamakura Shogunate in 1185 (see p.768) generated an alternative artistic taste more in keeping with the simplicity, discipline and rigour of the military lifestyle. This new realism made itself felt in the portrait painting and picture scrolls of the **Kamakura era** (1185–1333), most graphically in the *Handbook on Hungry Ghosts*, now in Tokyo's National Museum. Highly individualized portraits of military figures and Zen masters became popular. Kamakura sculpture similarly combined a high degree of realism with a dynamic energy. The two giant guardian figures at Nara's Tōdai-ji, fashioned by the sculptors Unkei and Kaikei in 1203, are outstanding examples of this vigorous new style.

However, samurai culture had a more direct impact on the development of the decorative arts. By the Edo era (1600–1868), Edo and Ōsaka had become leading centres of **sword-making**, where swordsmiths were noted for their skill in forging and for the meticulousness of finish which they applied to the blades. Through the peaceful years of the Edo era, however, sword fittings gradually came to be more decorative than functional.

The arts of Zen

With the spread of **Zen Buddhism** in the thirteenth century, Japanese arts acquired a new focus. Meditation is at the centre of Zen practice and many Zen art forms can be seen as vehicles for inward reflection or as visualizations of the sudden and spontaneous nature of enlightenment.

Monochromatic **ink painting**, known as *suiboku-ga* or *sumi-e*, portrayed meditative landscapes and other subjects in a variety of formats including screens, hanging scrolls and hand-scrolls, with a free and expressive style of brushwork that was both speedily and skilfully rendered. *Haboku*, or "flung-ink" landscapes, took this technique to its logical extreme by building up (barely) recognizable imagery from the arbitrary patterns formed by wet ink splashed onto highly absorbent paper. **Sesshū** (1420–1506), a Zen priest, was Japan's foremost practitioner of this technique.

Zen **calligraphy** similarly can be so expressively rendered as to be almost unreadable except to the practised eye. One of the most striking examples, by the monk Ryōkan Daigu (1757–1831), is a hanging scroll with the intertwined symbols for heaven and earth. These qualities of abstraction and suggestion were also applied to the design of **Zen gardens**, while meditation techniques spawned the highly ritualized and almost mesmeric **tea ceremony** (see p.55).

The Momoyama and Edo eras

Japanese art was most opulent during the **Momoyama era** (1573–1600). The scale of feudal architecture created a new demand for decorative **screen paintings**, which were placed on walls, sliding doors (*fusuma*) and folding screens (*byōbu*). From the late sixteenth century, the Kyoto-based **Kanō School** of artists came to dominate official taste. Subjects were mainly drawn from nature and from history and legend, while the extensive use of gold leaf added a shimmering brightness to the dark interior spaces of the great Momoyama castles, palaces and temples. Kanō Eitoku and his grandson, Kanō Tan'yū, were the school's most famous exponents and their works can still be seen in Kyoto's Daitoku-ji and Nijō-jō.

During the **Edo-era** (1600–1868) the arts flourished under the patronage of a newly wealthy merchant class. Artists such as Tawaraya Sōtatsu and Ogata Kōrin stand out for reviving aspects of the *Yamato-e* tradition and injecting new decorative life into Japanese painting. Sōtatsu's famous golden screen paintings based on *The Tale of Genji* dramatically adapt the subject matter and style of Heian-era *emaki*

Pictures of the Floating World

During the Edo era the lively entertainment districts of Edo, Ōsaka and Kyoto, with their brothels, teahouses and kabuki theatres, provided inspiration for artists. This new genre of painting, **ukiyo-e**, or "pictures of the floating world", devoted itself to the hedonistic pastimes of the new rich. By the early eighteenth century, *ukiyo-e* were most commonly produced as hand-coloured woodblock prints which became more sophisticated in their subtle use of line and colour as mass-printing techniques developed.

Late eighteenth-century artists such as Harunobu, Utamaro and Sharaku portrayed famous beauties of the day and kabuki actors in dramatic poses. Explicitly erotic prints known as *shunga* (spring pictures) were also big sellers, as were humorous scenes of daily life (*manga*), the forerunners of today's comics. **Hokusai** (1760–1849), perhaps the most internationally famous *ukiyo-e* artist, was originally known for his *manga*, but went on to create one of the most enduring images of Japan, "The Great Wave", as part of his series *Thirty-Six Views of Mount Fuji*. Followed by the equally popular *Fifty-Three Stages of the Tōkaidō*, by Hiroshige (1797–1858), these later landscape prints were instantly popular at a time when travel was both difficult and restricted.

to this larger format. Kōrin's most noted works include the "Irises" screens at Tokyo's Nezu Museum (p.130).

The **decorative arts** reached new heights of elegance and craftsmanship. Varieties of Imari- and Kutani-ware **porcelain** were made in large quantities for domestic consumption and later for export. Inlaid **lacquerware** was executed in bold and simple designs. Honami Kōetsu was a leading lacquer artist of the period, as well as a celebrated painter and calligrapher. One of Kōetsu's most famous lacquer works, an inkstone box in the Tokyo National Museum, reflects these combined talents with its inlaid-lead bridge and silver calligraphy forming integral parts of the overall design.

Western influences

The period of **modernization and westernization** which followed the fall of the Tokugawa Shogunate in 1867 transformed the face of Japanese visual arts. The opening of the treaty ports furnished a new subject matter for woodblock print artists who produced marvellous portraits of Westerners in Yokohama and other ports. The opening of the first railway, spinning factory and many other advances were also recorded for posterity.

In the early years of the Meiji era (1868–1912), traditional Japanese and Chinese styles of painting were rejected in favour of Western styles and techniques. Artists such as Kuroda Seiki and Fujishima Takeji studied in Paris and returned to become leaders of **Western-style painting** (*Yōga*) in Japan. Realism, Impressionism and other Western art movements were directly transplanted to the Tokyo art scene. More conservative painters, such as Yokoyama Taikan, worked to establish *Nihon-ga*, a modern style of Japanese painting, drawing on a mixture of Chinese, Japanese and Western techniques.

Western influence on the arts expanded greatly in the Taishō era (1912–26) with **sculpture**, as well as painting, closely following current trends. In the postwar period, Japanese artists looked again to Europe and America but more selectively took their inspiration from a range of avant-garde developments in the West.

Mingei: the folk craft tradition

Japanese **folk crafts**, *mingei*, delight in the simplicity and utilitarian aspects of ordinary everyday objects. *Mingei* really is "people's art", the works of unknown craftsmen from all regions of Japan that are revered for their natural and unpretentious qualities.

While Japanese folk crafts flourished during the Edo era, the mass production techniques of the machine age led to a fall in the quality of textiles, ceramics, lacquer and other craft forms. The art critic and philosopher Yanagi Sōetsu (1889–1961) worked from the 1920s to stem this tide and to preserve the craft products of the pre-industrial age. Yanagi established the **Mingei-kan**, or Japanese Folk Crafts Museum, in Tokyo in 1936. But the revival of the *mingei* tradition also celebrated works by living artist-craftsmen as well as regional differences in style and technique. The potters Hamada Shōji, Kawai Kanjirō and the Englishman Bernard Leach were most famously associated with the Mingei movement, as was the woodblock artist, Munakata Shiko, and the textile designer Kiesuke Serizawa.

A wide range of traditional handicrafts, including pottery, lacquerware, wood, bamboo and handmade paper products, is still being produced today all over Japan. *Yūzen*-style kimono dyeing and *kumihimo* braid craft are associated with Kyoto; *shuri* weaving techniques with Okinawa; *Hakata ningyō*, or earthenware dolls, with Fukuoka; and Kumano brushes with Hiroshima.

Contemporary visual art

Visual art in Japan today blends Japanese and international currents, which at best interact to create innovative new styles. A prime example of such vigorous cross-fertilization is the development of **manga** (see *Manga & anime* colour section) as a sophisticated, internationally popular art form in which sources of tradition can no longer be identified purely with the East or the West.

The international success of pop artists such as **Nara Yoshitomo** and **Murakami Takashi** has shaped the world's perception of Japanese contemporary art during the last decade. The works of **Matsuura Hiroyuki** and **Nishizawa Chiharu** are also much in demand at international art fairs and auctions. Matsuura, a one-time manga character model maker, now produces ambiguous but dynamic canvases that have been described as "manga as fine art". Nishizawa's work uses the elevated point of view of traditional Japanese painting, but portrays the uneasy emptiness of modern life. **Ito Zon** is known for his delicate drawings, embroideries and video works that explore nature. The mystical paintings of **Yamaguchi Akira** are rooted in traditional Asian aesthetics and display a masterful technique.

Performing arts

The traditional theatre arts of **nō** (sometimes written Noh in English), **bunraku** and kabuki evolved in the context of broader cultural developments during different periods of Japan's history. The plays of each art form often draw on similar plots but their presentation couldn't be more different.

Nō

The oldest – and most difficult to appreciate – type of Japanese theatre is **nō**. This form of masked drama has its roots in sacred Shinto dances, but was

Rising art stars

Up-and-coming Japanese visual artists include **Tabaimo** who creates really interesting installations involving video animation that reflect modern life, and the Damien Hirst-influenced **Kohei Nawa** (Ⓦwww.kohei-nawa.net). The art collective **Chim Pom** who took part in the 2007 Venice Biennale is also very active, sometimes with a lot of controversy and media attention, such as for their video of a young girl spewing up pink vomit. **Miyanaga Aiko** (Ⓦwww.aiko-m.com) does 3D work and installations, while Odani Motohiko does large, gothic sculptures. Also worth looking out for are **Teppei Kaneuji** (Ⓦteppeikaneuji.com) and **Aoyama Satoru**, both of whose gallery and museum shows have been modestly successful in the past few years.

formalized six hundred years ago under the patronage of the Ashikaga shoguns and the aesthetic influence of Zen. The bare wooden stage with its painted backdrop of an ancient pine tree, the actors' stylized robes and the fixed expressions of the finely crafted masks create an atmosphere that is both understated and refined. The dramatic contrasts of stillness and sudden rushes of movement, and of periods of silence punctuated by sound, conjure up the essence of the Zen aesthetic.

The actor's skill lies in transcending the conventions of archaic language, mask and formalized costume to convey the dramatic tensions inherent in the play. Dance elements and musical effects aid directly in this process and draw on the folk entertainment tradition from which nō is derived.

The comic **kyōgen** interludes in a nō programme provide light relief. As in the main drama, *kyōgen* performers are all male and assume a variety of roles, some of which are completely independent of the nō play, while others comment on the development of the main story. The language used is colloquial (though of sixteenth-century origin) and, compared with the esoteric poetry of nō, far more accessible to a contemporary audience.

Kabuki

Colourful, exuberant and full of larger-than-life characters, **kabuki** is a highly stylized theatrical form which delights in flamboyant gestures and elaborate costumes, make-up and staging effects. While the language may still be incomprehensible, the plots themselves deal with easily understandable, often tragic themes of love and betrayal, commonly taken from famous historical episodes.

Kabuki originated in the early 1600s as rather risqué dances performed by all-female troupes. The shogun eventually banned women because of kabuki's association with prostitution, but their replacement – young men – was no more successful and in the end kabuki actors were predominantly older men, some of whom specialize in female roles (*onnagata*). Kabuki developed as a more serious form of theatre in the late sixteenth century when it was cultivated chiefly by the merchant class. It gave theatrical expression to the vitality of city life and to the class tensions between samurai, merchants and peasants that inform the plots of so many plays. To learn more about kabuki go to Ⓦwww.kabuki21.com.

Bunraku

Japan's puppet theatre, **bunraku**, developed out of the *jōruri* storytelling tradition, in which travelling minstrels recited popular tales of famous heroes and legends, accompanied by the *biwa* (Japanese lute) or *shamisen* (three-stringed guitar). Adapted to the stage in the early seventeenth century, *bunraku* made use of stylized puppets, one-half to one-third the size of humans, to enact the various roles. The great Ōsaka playwright **Chikamatsu Monzaemon** (1653–1724), often referred to as "the Shakespeare of Japan", is responsible for around one hundred *bunraku* plays, many of which are still performed today.

Puppets are worked by three operators while a chanter, using a varied vocal range, tells the story to the accompaniment of *shamisen* music. The main puppeteer is in full view of the audience and uses his left hand to manipulate the face and head, with his right controlling the puppet's right arm. One assistant operates the left arm while another moves the puppet's legs. The skill of the puppeteers – the result of lengthy apprenticeships – contributes to the high degree of realism in the performance, and the stylized movements can result in great drama. Indeed, kabuki actors employ some puppet-like gestures from *bunraku* to enhance and enliven their own acting techniques. To learn more about *bunraku* go to ⓦwww.bunraku.or.jp.

Contemporary theatre

Contemporary Japanese theatre ranges from the all-female musical reviews of **Takarazuka** (see p.497) to the abstract and improvisational dance form of **butō** (or Butoh) which draws on the traditions of kabuki and nō as well as contemporary American dancers such as Martha Graham. Though it remains a marginal art form in Japan, *butō*'s haunting beauty has found greater appreciation in Europe and America.

In the 1970s **Hideki Noda** became one of the most prominent figures in Japanese contemporary theatre and has since been involved in projects ranging from new kabuki writing and working with his theatre group, Noda Map (ⓦwww.nodamap.com), to forays into opera. The director **Ninagawa Yukio** has also won a considerable following both inside and outside Japan for his traditional Japanese plays and productions of Shakespeare that bridge the theatrical conventions of East and West. Members of the **Setagaya Public Theatre** have also collaborated with foreign producers on international productions such as a stage adaptation of Haruki Murakami's collection of short stories, *The Elephant Vanishes*.

There are hundreds of other theatre groups throughout Japan creating original works. One of the most acclaimed and active both locally and abroad is **chelftisch** (ⓦchelfitsch.net/en), the baby of **Okada Toshiki**. The work of auteur/director Tanino Kurou, a specialist in the theatre of the absurd, is also worth looking out for. A good **blog** to find out more about the local theatre scene is ⓦtokyostages.wordpress.com.

Online resources for theatre

KIE (Kateigaho International Edition) ⓦint.kateigaho.com. This biannual magazine covers the range of Japanese arts and culture.

Japan Cultural Profile ⓦwww.culturalprofiles.net/japan. Comprehensive overview of Japanese arts and culture from nō to contemporary dance. Also has a wonderful database of artists, venues, festivals and more.

The Performing Arts Network ⓦwww.performingarts.jp. Presents the broad range of Japanese performing arts, with a focus on groups and artists active on the international scene.

The Virtual Museum of Japanese Arts ⓦweb-japan.org/museum/menu.html. Useful overview of traditional Japanese arts and culture from the Ministry of Foreign Affairs.

Music

The arrival of eighty Korean musicians in 453 AD and the introduction of Buddhism in the mid-sixth century are key early events in the history of Japanese music. **Gagaku** (court orchestral music) and religious music survive from this period, and Buddhist chanting, **shōmyō**, can still be heard in temples today.

Similar to a chamber orchestra, *gagaku* ensembles include as many as twenty instruments, with flutes, oboes, zithers, lutes, gongs and drums. *Gagaku* is now played only as **bugaku** (dance music) or **kangen** (instrumental music), typically at the imperial court and at a few Shinto shrines and Buddhist temples. Unlike Western classical music, themes aren't stated and repeated. Instead, the rhythms are based on breathing and the result is a form that sounds sometimes discordant, sometimes meditative.

Distinctive musical styles also developed for the principal theatrical arts: Nō (p.787), *bunraku* (p.788) and kabuki (p.788). The sparse music of **nō** features solo singers, small choruses and an instrumental ensemble of *fue* (bamboo flute), two hourglass drums and a barrel drum. The **shamisen** (three-string lute) was added to the flute and drums for *bunraku*, leading to a more lively and popular musical style.

In the seventeenth and eighteenth centuries, during Japan's period of isolation from the outside world, instruments like the *koto* (a kind of zither) continued to develop repertoire, as did the *shakuhachi* bamboo flute. The *nagauta shamisen* style for kabuki theatre also developed at this time, as did the *sankyoku*, the typical instrumental ensemble of the age – *koto*, *shamisen*, *shakuhachi* and *kokyu* (a bowed fiddle).

Min'yō – regional folk music

Each region of Japan has its own style of **min'yō** (folk music), the most famous being the instrumental *shamisen* style from Tsugaru in Tōhoku. Kinoshita Shin'ichi has earned the nickname "the man with the divine hands" for his pioneering Tsugaru *shamisen* playing that marries the traditional northern *shamisen* style of fast plucking with jazz and rock. Kinoshita played a major part in the *shin-min'yo* (new *min'yō*) wave led by singer Takio Ito, well known for his passionate singing style and willingness to experiment. Since the millennium, Tsugaru *shamisen* has been experiencing a boom in popularity, with the **Yoshida Brothers** (ⓦwww.domo.com/yoshidabrothers) and **Agatsuma Hiromitsu** (ⓦagatsuma.tv/index.html) stand-out performers.

Traditional **drumming** from Sado-ga-shima (see p.280) has now become famous internationally. **Za Ondekoza** (ⓦwww.ondekoza.com), the original group of drummers, and its off-shoot, **Kodō** (ⓦwww.kodo.or.jp), are capable of playing very powerful, theatrical gigs with just the various Japanese drums (from the big *daiko* to small hand-drums).

At Japan's northern extremity is the island of Hokkaidō, home to the indigenous Ainu. Their traditional music and instruments, including the skinny string instrument the *tonkori* and the *mukkuri* (Jew's harp), have been taken up by **Oki Kano**, a half-Ainu musician. Together with his Oki Dub Ainu Band (ⓦwww.tonkori.com), Oki has released several toe-tapping and soulful albums and has played at international music festivals including WOMAD in the UK.

Enka

Described as *Nihonjin no kokoro,* the soul of the Japanese, **enka** (from *enzetsu*, meaning public speech, and *ka*, meaning a song) are songs about lost love, homesickness or simply drowning the sorrows of a broken heart with sake. Over one hundred years old, and still enormously popular, *enka* originally was a form of political dissent, disseminated by song sheets. However, in the early twentieth century it became the first style to truly synthesize Western scales and Japanese modes. Shimpei Nakayama and Koga Masao were the trailblazing composers. Koga's first hit in 1931, *Kage Wo Shitaite* ("Longing For Your Memory"), remains a much-loved classic.

It's difficult to escape *enka.* Television specials pump it out, and you'll hear it in restaurants and bars. And, of course, it received a major boost with the invention of karaoke, which helped to spread the genre's popularity both with younger Japanese and foreigners.

The classic image is of *enka* queen **Hibari Misora** (see box below) decked out in a kimono, tears streaming down her face as she sobs through Koga's *Kanashi Sake* ("Sad Sake"), with typically understated backing and single-line guitar. **Harumi Miyako** is also famed for her growling attack and the song *Sayonara*. Many *enka* stars have long careers, and veterans like Kitajima Suburō are still going strong today, as are Mori Shin'ichi, Yashiro Aki, Kobayashi Sachiko and Itsuki Hiroshi. More recent stars are Hikawa Kiyoshi, known as the prince of *enka*, and Pittsburgh native **Jero**, aka Jerome Charles White Jr, whose hip-hop attire gives a contemporary spin to the genre.

Rock & pop classics

By the late 1960s, musicians were starting to create **Japanese-language rock**. Seminal band **Happy End** were pioneers. Led by composer Hosono Haruomi (later a founding member of Yellow Magic Orchestra) and lyricist Matsumoto Takashi, the band meshed folk-rock with Japanese lyrics about love and politics. Their song *Kaze Wo Atsumete* featured on the soundtrack for the film *Lost in Translation*.

Okinawan musician **Kina Shoukichi** and his band **Champloose** (the name comes from the name of a traditional Okinawan stir-fry) gained acclaim in the 1970s, particularly with his song *Haisai Oji-san* ("Hey, Man"), which became so famous that it is used today as a drill song for high-school baseball games. **Southern All Stars** (Ⓦwww.jvcmusic.co.jp/sas), whose way of singing Japanese as if it were English helped them to become Japan's biggest-selling band in the late 1980s, were another influential group; they're still going strong.

Beautiful Skylark

A musical icon and the undisputed queen of *enka* is **Hibari Misora** ("beautiful skylark"). Born Kazue Kato, she made her debut as a singer in 1946, at the tender age of 9, and became an instant hit for her ability to memorize long poems and mimic adult singers. Her powerful, sobbing *kobushi* vocal technique created a highly charged atmosphere, but she was also talented enough to cover jazz, *min'yō,* Latin, chanson and torch songs in the thousand recordings and 166 films she made before her untimely death at 52 in 1989. See Ⓦwww.misorahibari.com for more information on this Japanese musical legend.

The Avant-Garde

The best-known practitioners of Japan's **avant-garde** music scene are Ōsakan "noise band" **Boredoms** (Ⓦwww.boredoms.jp), but others like **Haco** (herself once the leader of an influential 1980s post-punk outfit, After Dinner) and **Yamamoto Sei'ichi** continue to push back the boundaries of musical improvisation, and many members of this wide-ranging community regularly perform overseas, especially in Europe. The **Improvised Music from Japan** website (Ⓦwww.japanimprov.com) has extensive biographies and details.

Yellow Magic Orchestra (YMO; Ⓦwww.ymo.org), formed in 1978 by Hosono Haruomi, Sakamoto Ryuchi and Takahashi Yukihiro, were heavily influenced by German technopop band Kraftwerk. Having gone their own ways in the mid-1980s – Sakamoto, in particular having a highly successful international career, both as a soloist and as an Oscar-winning film-score composer – the trio reformed in 2007 and still play together today.

The roots boom

The growing popularity of **world music** has had a significant effect in Japan. **Reggae**, for example, was considered "underground" for years, but is now part of the mainstream, as is ska following the success of the **Tokyo Ska Paradise Orchestra** (Ⓦwww.tokyoska.net/index.html). **Latin** music has also had a big effect, propelling salsa band **Orquesta de la Luz** (Ⓦlaluz.jp) to the top of the Billboard Latin chart in the early 1990s.

The Boom (Ⓦwww.theboom.jp), led by Miyazawa Kazufumi, helped to spawn the Okinawan music boom (see opposite) in 1993 with their single *Shima Uta* ("Island Songs"). In the mid-1990s they experimented with Brazilian music, opening up a new generation's ears to the South American melodies. In 2006 Miyazawa formed a new band **Ganga Zumba**, with Brazilians Marcos Suzano and Fernando Moura, again playing a mix of Brazilian- and Latin-inspired pop.

The most significant development of the 1980s, however, was the rise of **roots-influenced** bands and singers such as **Shang Shang Typhoon** (Ⓦwww.shangshang.jp/shang.html), Rinken Band, Nenes and Daiku Tetsuhiro. Inspiration came from both within Japan (Okinawa and local popular culture) and outside (World Music).

Foremost among the 1990s wave of bands plundering global music styles was **Soul Flower Union** (SFU), a seven-member outfit from Ōsaka led by Nakagawa Takashi. SFU also have an appealing alter ego, **Soul Flower Mononoke Summit** (SFMU), where the band blends acoustic guitars, Okinawan and *chindon* (street) music, which advertises products or shops, with drums and various brass instruments. Recent work has included gigs with the respected Irish musician and producer Donal Lunny who is married to SFU member Itami Hideko.

Contemporary sounds

Among teenagers and young adults across Asia it's **J-pop** (Japanese pop) that shifts the largest number of units. **Hamasaki Ayumi** (Ⓦwww.avexnet.or.jp/ayu) commonly known as Ayu, is J-pop's ruling empress. **SMAP**, formed in 1991, has

The sound of the deep, deep south

Music has been integral to **Okinawa**'s culture and social life for centuries; it's said that peasants carried their musical instruments into the rice fields, ready for a jam session after work. The **folk tradition** is very much alive: in some villages *umui* (religious songs) are still sung at festivals to honour ancestors; work songs that reflect communal agriculture techniques can still be heard; and various kinds of group and circle dances, some performed exclusively by women, can be found in the smaller islands.

Popular entertainment is known by the general term *zo odori* (common dance), though everyone calls these songs **shima uta** (island songs). The best-known style, one no wedding would be complete without, is called *katcharsee*. Set to lively rhythms laid down by the *sanshin*, which plays both melody and rhythm, and various drums, the dance is performed with the upper body motionless and the lower body swaying sensuously, accompanied by graceful hand movements that echo similar dances in Thailand and Indonesia.

The Asian connection can be clearly seen in the history of the *sanshin*. This three-stringed lute began life in China as the long-necked *sanxian* and was introduced to Okinawa around 1392. Local materials were quickly exhausted so that Thai snakeskin was used for the soundbox and Filipino hardwood for the shorter neck of the altered instrument, which became known as the *sanshin*. Once introduced to mainland Japan, the *sanshin* became bigger, produced a harder sound and was renamed the *shamisen*, one of the quintessential Japanese instruments.

A more recent influence on Okinawan music has come via the US military presence. Local musicians started to copy American pop styles in the 1950s, sometimes mixing in folk music. One major star whose music developed in this way was **Kina Shoukichi** who formed the band Champloose (see p.791) while still at high school, thus opening the way for a new generation of Okinawan rockers, including ex-band members **Nagama Takao**, famous for his fast-action *sanshin* playing, and **Hirayasu Takashi**.

Another legendary Okinawan musician is **Sadao China**, who records his own solo *min'yō*, as well as reggae-rock with an Okinawan flavour. As a producer, China brought the all-female group **Nenes** to international fame; the original four band members have since played with Ry Cooder and Michael Nyman among others. China has a club, *Shima Uta Live House*, in Ginowan, which is one of the best places in the islands to see Okinawan roots music.

graduated from Japan's premier boy band to simply its top band. SMAP member **Kimura Takuya** is as big a star as you can get, his celebrity bolstered by many acting roles on TV and in films. More appealing to goths, glam-rock and cyberpunk fans are the so-called **Visual kei**, bands such as Dir en Grey, X and Luna Sea.

Hip hop and **rap** have been enthusiastically adopted by musicians and spin-masters such as DJ Krush (aka Ishi Hideaki; ⓦwww.sus81.jp/djkrush), the duo **m-flo** (ⓦm-flo.com) and rock band **Dragon Ash** (ⓦwww.dragonash.co.jp). Techno DJs **Ken Ishii** and **Ishino Takkyu** (of Denki Groove fame) and electronica outfits such as **Ryukyu Underground** (ⓦwww.ryukyu-underground.wwma.net), who mix up the sounds of Okinawa with dub beats and the occasional lounge-style tempo, are also finding an audience outside Japan.

Indie bands and singers are increasingly popular. One of the most successful has been the band **HY** (ⓦwww.hymode.net), hailing from Okinawa. **Ringo Sheena**'s 2003 *Karuki, Zamen, Kuri no Hana* ("Chlorine, Semen, Chestnut Flowers") is an impressive concept album embracing everything from big-band swing to traditional *koto*, *shamisen* and flute music. Sheena has since gone on to form the band Tokyo

Internet resources for Japanese music

CD Japan (Ⓦwww.cdjapan.co.jp) Online shop offering comprehensive selection of CDs, DVDs and other collectables released in Japan.

Far Side Music (Ⓦwww.farsidemusic.com) A good place to buy CDs and DVDs, and for further explorations into Japanese and Okinawan music.

NEC Navigates Japan's Classical Music Artists (Ⓦjapansclassic.com) Promoting not only top local musicians specializing in Western classical music but also those skilled at traditional Japanese instruments and forms.

Jihen, before going solo again to score the music for the period drama film *Sakuran*. She's also collaborated with explosive jazz combo **Soil & "Pimp" Sessions** (Ⓦwww.jvcmusic.co.jp/soilpimp) which is gaining international attention.

Out-and-out rock continues to have a following: check out the angsty blues-rock of **Yura Yura Teikoku** (Ⓦmesh-key.com/yura.html) and the alt-rock of **Pillows** (Ⓦwww.pillows.jp).

If you want to hear work by some of the artists mentioned above, the *Rough Guide to the Music of Japan* (World Music Network; Ⓦwww.worldmusic.net) offers a fine introduction to the nation's music scene.

The Environment

In the words of one of Japan's leading environmental activists, Yamashita Hirofumi, "Japan's postwar development has had a disastrous impact on the natural environment." Despite this, nature continues to play a pivotal role in Japanese life. Spectacular areas of unspoilt natural beauty remain and there's a growing awareness of the need to safeguard them, including from the government (see p.8). Japan also stands guilty of over-packaging products and wasteful use of disposable chopsticks, but at the same time levels of recycling of items such as plastic, paper and metal cans are admirably high.

Fauna and flora

Generally speaking, the fauna and flora of the Japanese archipelago can be divided into three categories: the Southeast Asiatic tropical zone, the Korean and Chinese temperate zone and the Siberian subarctic zone.

The **Southeast Asiatic tropical zone** extends from Taiwan up into the Ryūkyū island chain (Okinawa). Wildlife typically associated with this zone includes the flying fox, crested serpent eagle, variable lizard and butterflies of the Danaidae family. Animals that belong to the **Korean and Chinese temperate zone** inhabit the deciduous forests of Honshū, Shikoku and Kyūshū, the most common of which are the racoon dog, sika deer and mandarin duck. If you're lucky, you'll see the rarer yellow marten, badger and flying squirrel, while in the seas around central Honshū you may also spot sea lions and fur seals. The **Siberian subarctic zone** covers the coniferous forests of Hokkaidō, inhabited by the brown bear, rabbit-like pika, hazel grouse, common lizard, arctic hare and nine-spined stickleback, among other species.

In addition, the archipelago contains a number of **endemic species** such as the Japanese macaque, Japanese dormouse, copper pheasant, giant salamander, Pryer's woodpecker and Amami spiny mouse, all of which are now relatively rare. Japan is also home to a number of "living fossils", animals whose characteristics differ

Last chance to see...

According to the Mammalogical Society of Japan (Ⓦwww.mammalogy.jp), over half of the country's **endangered animals** are close to extinction. Examples include the Iriomote wild cat, endemic to Iriomote-jima (p.761), of which probably fewer than one hundred remain, the short-tailed albatross and the Japanese otter of Shikoku, both of which were once thought to be extinct.

Conservation efforts come in the form of breeding and feeding programmes, habitat improvement and research projects. In an example of Russo–Japanese cooperation, researchers from both countries attached transmitters to fourteen sea eagles and tracked them by satellite to discover their migratory routes and feeding grounds. Unfortunately, however, many such conservation programmes fall far short of their goals, largely due to an ineffective government system.

One programme that has been successful has been that to protect the **red-crowned** or **Japanese crane** (*tancho* in Japanese). This magnificent tall-standing bird, highly celebrated in Japan for its grace and beauty and as a symbol of longevity, has benefited from volunteer-based feeding programmes and other conservation measures in its home territory of eastern Hokkaidō (see p.325).

from more developed species, such as the critically endangered Amami rabbit and Iriomote wild cat (both native to the Ryūkyū Islands), the frilled shark and the horseshoe crab of Sagami Bay, off Kamakura.

You don't need to get off the beaten track to encounter wildlife in Japan. In urban areas **racoon dogs** (*tanuki*) come out at night to forage for food. These dogs are an integral part of Japanese folklore and are believed to have supernatural powers and cause all sorts of mischief; they are always depicted as big-bellied, with huge testicles and a bottle of sake. Foxes, too, are widespread and were believed to possess people – fox (or *Inari*) shrines are found across the country.

Monkeys are also common in some areas, such as Wakinosawa and Shiga Kōgen, while **wild boar** occasionally make an appearance in outer urban areas, though fortunately these forbidding-looking creatures avoid human contact and are generally heard but not seen. Kites, cranes, herons, cormorants and migratory seagulls can often be seen around lakes and rivers, while the steamy summer brings an onslaught of insects, none more so than the **cicada** (*semi*), whose singing provides a constant background thrum.

Marine life

Japan's seas and rivers contain roughly three thousand species of fish. The waters around the Ryūkyū Islands are home to subtropical anemone fish, parrot fish, wrass and spiny lobster as well as numerous species of shark, turtle and whale. The ocean south of Shikoku and Honshū teems with life, from loggerhead turtles and butterfly fish to dugongs and porpoises, while the colder waters around Hokkaidō bring with them some of the larger whale species – humpback, grey and blue whale – from the Bering Sea and north Pacific.

Ocean currents play a crucial role in this diversity. Warm water flowing round Taiwan and up through the Ryūkyū island chain splits into two on reaching the island of Kyūshū. The branch flowing north into the Sea of Japan, between Japan and China, is known as the Tsushima-shio, while the Kuro-shio or "Black current" follows the more easterly route. Bearing down from the north, hitting Hokkaidō's northern and eastern shores, comes the cold, nutrient-rich Oya-shio or Kuril current. Where it meets the Kuro-shio off northeastern Honshū, abundant plankton and the mingling of cold- and warm-water species create one of the richest fishing grounds in the entire world.

Forests

Forests of beech, silver fir, broad-leaf evergreens and mangroves once carpeted Japan. However, the postwar economic boom and in particular the massive increase in construction and the rampant building of golf courses, led to the decimation of many of these natural forests. While nearly 67 percent of Japan is still forested, about half of this comprises commercial plantations of quick-growing Japanese cedar and cypress. Not only do these contain a fraction of the biodiversity found in natural forests, but when cheaper timber flooded in from Southeast Asia, Canada and South America in the 1970s and local demand slumped, a large proportion of Japan's domestic plantations were left unused and untended.

As a result, Japan has come precariously close to losing some of its most spectacular areas of natural forest. The old-growth **beech forests** – stands of ancient

The national parks

The growing popularity of recreational activities such as mountaineering in the early twentieth century provided the spur for the creation of Japan's first **national parks** (*kokuritsu-kōen*) in 1931, now under control of the **Ministry of Environment** (Ⓦwww.env.go.jp). There are 29 national parks, covering around 5.4 percent of Japan's land mass, and 55 quasi-national parks (*kokutei-kōen*; 3.6 percent), which between them receive over 900 million visitors each year. In addition, prefectural natural parks cover a further 5.4 percent of Japan. While for the most part national parks are thought of in terms of recreation, their establishment has been a lifesaver for ecological preservation. Below are details of some of the most important.

Akan National Park, Hokkaidō (p.329). Contains three vast volcanic craters surrounded by dense forests of silver fir. Lake Akan is home to the unique *marimo* weedballs, which float beneath the surface of the lake on sunny days.

Aso-Kujū National Park, Kyūshū (p.686). Includes the world's largest volcano crater (90km in circumference), part of which is still active.

Chichibu-Tama-Kai National Park, Honshū. Only three hours west of Tokyo, this is a haven for city dwellers. Its forested hills, gorges and valleys give rise to the Tama river that flows through Tokyo.

Iriomote National Park, Okinawa (p.761). Features lush, virgin jungle, cascading waterfalls, mangroves, white beaches and Japan's largest coral reef, with spectacular underwater life. The dense jungle, which has served to resist human encroachment, is home to the rare Iriomote wild cat.

Kirishima-Yaku National Park. Includes both the Kirishima mountain range (p.706) and the island of Yakushima (p.720), a UNESCO World Heritage Site protected for its primary and old-growth forests.

Kushiro-Shitsugen National Park, Hokkaidō (p.333). Kushiro's protected wetlands are of massive ecological importance, and include breeding grounds of red-crowned cranes.

Rikuchū-Kaigan National Park, Honshū. Comprises a narrow strip of Japan's northeast coast, famous for its stretch of white trachyte quartz sand known as Jōdogahama, or Paradise Beach, and wealth of birdlife. Black-tailed gulls and petrels, among other species, nest on the rugged cliffs.

Shiretoko National Park, Hokkaidō (p.327). Another UNESCO World Heritage Site, and utterly wild; it's home to brown bears, Blakiston's fish-owls and Steller's sea eagles.

trees, but not necessarily untouched virgin forest – of the Shirakami Mountains in northwest Honshū, for example, came under direct threat in the 1980s from a government proposal to build a logging road right through them. Citizens' groups, together with the Nature Conservation Society of Japan (NCSJ), mounted a huge campaign to demonstrate the forest's immeasurable ecological and national value. The government reconsidered the plan and the forest is now designated a UNESCO World Heritage Site.

Another successful campaign was that launched by the world-famous animator Miyazaki Hayao to save from development a 1500-square-metre patch of land adjacent to the Fuchi no Mori forest on the border of Tokyo and Saitama prefecture. This forest, near where Miyazaki grew up, was the inspiration for the locations of his much-loved film *My Neighbour Totoro*. For more details see Ⓦwww.totoro.or.jp. Also notable is the creation in 2002 by British-born, Japan-based naturalist CW Nicol of the 296,070-square-metre CW Afan Woodland Trust, in Kurohime, Nagano prefecture (Ⓦwww.afan.or.jp).

Environmental Issues

Japan is forging ahead with measures to improve its environmental performance (see p.8). The gradual shift from heavy to hi-tech industry has led to apparently cleaner rivers and air; anecdotal evidence points to an increase in birdlife and statistics show that Mount Fuji is visible more often these days from Tokyo. However, although there have been successes down the years, there remains a litany of **environmental issues** blotting Japan's environmental scorecard.

Waste and recycling

In 2009 Japan's Ministry of Environment announced plans to reduce the country's total waste from a staggering 52 million tons a year (as measured in 2007) to about 50 million tons in 2012, and to raise the waste recycling rate from 20 to 25 percent. It also aims to reduce the total amount of waste generation by raising awareness and promoting a charging system for waste disposal services.

Despite such moves, working out exactly what to do with all the waste remains a logistical nightmare. Burning it releases poisonous dioxins, while recycling and other measures to cut waste also have their problems: illegal dumping in the countryside, for example, has increased since people now have to pay for the disposal of large items. A common "solution" is to use garbage for land reclamation and landfill, sometimes with disastrous results.

One bright spark has been the launch of the **Mottainai campaign** (Ⓦmottainai.info/english). The campaign, backed by the Mainichi newspapers and the Itochu Corporation, aims to cut all types of waste by reducing consumption and recycling.

Nuclear power

With hardly any natural resources of its own, Japan has long been reliant on fossil fuel imports to meet its energy needs. Government tax incentives and subsidies supporting the use of solar power mean that Japan is now a world leader in photovoltaic production. It is also beginning to develop – albeit slowly – wind power, biomass and other renewable energies. However, the main area of investment remains in nuclear power. According to the Federation of Electric Power Companies of Japan (FEPC; Ⓦwww.japannuclear.com) its 55 nuclear reactors, including the world's biggest nuclear plant, near Kariwa on the western Sea of Japan coast, meet around a third of the country's electricity needs. The plan is to increase this to sixty percent by 2050.

Environmentalists are extremely worried about this strategy, particularly given the string of serious **accidents** in the industry. Revelations over the years of cases of serious malpractice, including incidents leading to "uncontrolled criticality" and faked records of inspections, haven't inspired public confidence. The government is taking steps to improve safety measures and tighten up monitoring, but public opposition continues to grow in the light of these accidents and cover-ups. One major ongoing campaign is that to stop the building of a nuclear reprocessing plant in Rokkasho in northeast Aomori prefecture (Ⓦstop-rokkasho.org).

An additional worry is the age of the reactors (seventeen of which have been in operation for at least thirty years) and whether they can withstand a major earthquake. In 2007, a 6.8 scale earthquake caused a fire and "small" radioactive leakage at the Kariwa plant, which is located near a major fault line. Though the reactors

Lake Biwa's Blues

In the late 1960s water quality of **Lake Biwa**, Japan's largest lake, near Kyoto, began to deteriorate rapidly under the combined onslaught of population pressure, lack of adequate wastewater treatment and overuse of agro-chemicals. From 1977 onwards, annual outbreaks of "freshwater red tide" (a discoloration of the water caused by the blooming of algae which thrives in water with abnormally high nutrient levels and kills animal life by depriving it of oxygen) indicated exactly how sick the lake was.

In response, a group of local women launched the **Soap Movement**, calling on people to boycott phosphate-containing detergents, which were a major polluter, and putting pressure on the prefectural authorities to act. In 1979 the local authorities passed a law setting stricter limits on phosphorous and nitrogen in waste water, and, for the first time in Japan, prohibiting the use of detergents containing phosphates. The movement quickly spread nationwide and nowadays no detergents containing phosphates are manufactured or sold in Japan.

Despite the success of the Soap Movement, Lake Biwa's problems are far from over. Water quality improved temporarily in the early 1980s, but has continued to deteriorate ever since. A conservation plan for the lake and its catchment area was set up in 2000, with the aim of restoring water quality to late-1950s levels by 2050. At the same time, invasive species of black bass and bluegill fish introduced to the lake are now causing havoc with its natural ecosystem.

shut down automatically during the quake, the incident revived concerns about the ultimate wisdom of Japan's nuclear programme. Nevertheless, the government remains strongly committed to nuclear power and several new reactors are currently under construction.

Pollution

The Minamata tragedy of the 1950s, in which a Kyūshū community suffered the devastating effects of organic mercury poisoning, was a landmark case that brought to public attention the hazards of industrial pollution. Half a century later, **chemical pollution** – from agriculture and domestic use, as well as the industrial sector – remains a serious problem; one of the issues raised in the Oscar-winning documentary *The Cove* (see p.800) is about the off-the-scale toxicity levels of some types of seafood.

Citizens' movements have been active in tackling issues related to **air pollution** from factories, power plants and national highways, helping victims to win important lawsuits or reach out-of-court settlements against local authorities and industrial corporations. In November 2000, for example, the Nagoya District Court ordered the state and ten enterprises to pay a total of nearly 300 million yen in compensation to pollution victims and ordered that emissions along a stretch of national highway should be substantially reduced. The government subsequently imposed stricter emission limits and is gradually replacing its own transport fleets with "green" vehicles and working towards phasing out diesel buses and trucks in general.

A related issue is the widespread habit of drivers to keep their engines running – for the air-conditioning or heating – even when parked or in long traffic queues. You'll often see taxis parked up, for example, engine running and the driver sound asleep inside. Despite a number of public awareness campaigns, the message is slow getting across and, though some prefectures have even introduced "anti-idling" laws, there is little enforcement.

The Cove

The Oscar-winning documentary **The Cove** (ⓦwww.thecovemovie.com) created much controversy in Japan. Hidden cameras were used to film the carnage involved in the annual dolphin hunt that takes place out of Taiji. Whales and dolphins have been hunted from this fishing town on the Kii Pennisula for 400 years. It remains a lucrative trade as sales of live bottlenose dolphins to aquariums and dolphin meat account for around $1 million of the town's annual fishing economy. Director Louie Psihoyos has said that he will donate all profits from the film's screenings in Japan to Taiji's fishermen, if they stop the dolphin hunt and switch to whale-watching or other sustainable enterprises.

Apart from the dolphin slaughter, *The Cove* also documents the scarily high levels of mercury contamination in the meat of dolphins and other cetaceans such as whales (dolphin is sometimes sold labelled as whale meat). This pollution warning is critical for a nation with a marine food culture. But, as Jun Morikawa points out in his book *Whaling in Japan: Power, Politics and Diplomacy*, it is something that is largely going unheeded due to lack of exposure in the Japanese media. For more information about the issues covered in the documentary and what you can do, see ⓦwww.savejapandolphins.org and www.takepart.com/thecove.

Whaling

The Japanese have traditionally caught whale for oil and meat, and the country continues to catch hundreds of these mammals a year, despite an international ban, exploiting a loophole which allows a quota for "scientific research". Japan argues the research provides essential data on populations, feeding habits and distribution to allow the mammals to be properly monitored. Indeed, it now claims that populations of minke, humpback and some other whale species have recovered sufficiently to support managed commercial whaling. In 2005 it started hunting endangered fin whale for the first time and in 2006 added the vulnerable humpback to its target, which now stands at a total of nearly 1300 whales a year.

All the major political parties support whaling and it is often presented as a matter of national pride to preserve Japanese cultural identity in the face of Western, particularly American, imperialism. Opponents of whaling, on the other hand, accuse Japan of buying the votes of developing countries in order to overturn the 1986 ban imposed by the International Whaling Commission (IWC).

Ironically, less than thirty percent of the Japanese public are in favour of whaling; some surveys put the figure as low as ten percent. Consumption of whale meat, or *kujira*, has declined markedly since 1986 and the only way the government can now get rid of the meat its scientific fleet brings home is to sell it at highly subsidized prices. Even then, as revealed by Jun Morikawa in his book *Whaling in Japan: Power, Politics and Diplomacy*, a third of this meat remains unsold.

Scientists have also begun voicing their concerns over the high levels of toxins found in dolphin and whale meat available in Japanese stores (see *The Cove* box, above). At the same time, interest in whale-watching has been on the increase and it is becoming abundantly clear there's more money to be made from whales through tourism than from killing them. For more information on whaling see the site of the **Whale and Dolphin Conservation Society** (ⓦwww.wdcs.org).

Over-fishing

To offset problems caused by **over-fishing**, the Japanese fishing fleet has been cut by a quarter in recent years and increasingly strict quotas are being imposed. This has not, however, stopped the import of fish into Japan from developing countries which, for their own economic reasons, are less concerned about protecting fish stocks.

Of particular concern is the **bluefin tuna** (*hon-maguro*), which is prized for sashimi and sushi, particularly the *toro* (the fatty belly meat). It's estimated that Japan consumes around eighty percent of the world's total bluefin tuna catch. At the same time, bluefin populations are decreasing at an alarming rate in the face of increasing demand worldwide. Conservationists argue that curbing Japanese consumption is a key to preventing total collapse. Japan's case was not helped when it admitted to exceeding its quota of southern bluefin (6000 tons), which lives in the southern hemisphere, by around 1800 tons in 2005. The **Commission for the Conservation of Southern Bluefin Tuna** (ⓦwww.ccsbt.org) says the figure is probably much higher if you also include fish caught by other countries over and above their quotas and sold in Japan. As a punishment, Japan's quota was halved to 3000 tons a year until 2011.

At the consumer's end, the rocketing price of bluefin tuna should put the breaks on consumption. Conservation bodies are also starting to mount awareness campaigns, encouraging people to opt for yellowfin tuna and other environmentally sustainable species instead.

Sustainable forestry

Japan has long been the world's largest consumer of tropical timber and the activities of Japanese paper and timber companies in the old-growth and primary forests

Environmental contacts and resources

Bicycle for Everyone's Earth ⓦwww.beejapan.org. Promotes environmental awareness and green living through direct action, including an annual bike tour from Hokkaidō to Kyūshū.

Earth Embassy ⓦwww.earthembassy.org. Promoting environmentally sustainable lifestyles, Earth Embassy runs a guesthouse and café (see p.187), and an organic farm, and develops environmentally friendly technologies at its centre, run by international volunteers, near Mt Fuji.

Friends of the Earth Japan ⓦwww.foejapan.org. Local branch of the international environmental organization.

Green Action ⓦwww.greenaction-japan.org. Working for a nuclear-free Japan.

Greenpeace Japan ⓦwww.greenpeace.or.jp. Local branch of the worldwide campaigning organization.

Jambo International ⓦwww.jambointernational.com. Works towards improving the natural environment and organizes weekly hikes around Tokyo.

Japan Ecotourism Society ⓦwww.ecotourism.gr.jp. Provides a forum for people involved in ecotourism and promotes good practice.

Japan Environmental Exchange ⓦwww.jeeeco.org. Disseminates information on environmental issues and organizes international exchanges.

Japan for Sustainability ⓦwww.japanfs.org. Information service for sustainability projects nationwide.

Japanese NGO Center for International Cooperation (JANIC) ⓦwww.janic.org. Provides a rundown of NGOs working in Japan.

Nature Conservation Society of Japan ⓦwww.nacsj.or.jp. NGO working in general environmental conservation.

Wild Bird Society of Japan ⓦwww.wbsj.org. Concerned with monitoring and protecting Japan's wild bird populations.

WWF Japan ⓦwww.wwf.or.jp. Local branch of World Wide Fund for Nature.

(those subjected to only minimal human disturbance) of neighbouring countries is a huge concern for environmentalists worldwide. Much of the timber is now imported in the form of plywood, which is used in the construction industry to make moulds for pouring concrete, used a couple of times and then incinerated. Since the early 1990s, rainforest protection groups in Japan and abroad have had some success in persuading construction companies and local authorities to reduce their use of tropical wood.

Excessive packaging and disposable wooden chopsticks (*waribashi*) are other incredibly wasteful uses of resources. While "my chopsticks" awareness drives are having some impact in getting people to carry their own chopsticks with them, Japan still gets through a staggering 130 million *waribashi* daily, accounting for over 400,000 cubic metres of timber a year.

The role of Japanese companies in the Australian woodchip industry has also caused much criticism, both at home and abroad. One such company operates a wood-chipping mill that is fed by old-growth eucalyptus trees at a rate of several football fields a day under a twenty-year licence granted by the Australian government. Various Australian environmental groups, including Chipstop (Ⓦwww.chipstop.forests.org.au) and The Wilderness Society (Ⓦwww.wilderness.org.au), have joined forces with the Japan Tropical Forest Action Network (JATAN; Ⓦwww.jca.apc.org/jatan), among others, to petition the Australian government and the Japanese paper industry to use woodchips from sustainable sources instead. Again, the campaign seems to be paying off: due to public pressure, Japanese companies are increasingly sourcing woodchips from sustainable forests.

Film

Japan got its first taste of cinema at Kōbe's Shinko Club in 1896 – and since then, as in many other creative endeavours, the country has excelled at making films, producing many internationally recognized directors including Kurosawa Akira, Ozu Yasujirō, Itami Jūzō, Kitano Takeshi and Miyazaki Hayao. For more information, **Midnight Eye** (®www.midnighteye.com) provides an excellent introduction to the wealth of Japanese cinema, as does film scholar Donald Richie's book *A Hundred Years of Japanese Films*.

Pre-World War II

From the advent of cinema in Japan, theatrical embellishments were considered a vital part of the experience; one theatre had a mock-up of a valley in front of the screen, complete with fish-filled ponds, rocks and fan-generated breeze, to increase the sense of realism. Additionally, the story and dialogue were acted out to the audience by a *benshi* (narrator). Thus when "talkies" arrived in Japan they were less of a sensation because sound had long been part of the film experience.

The **1930s** were the boom years for early Japanese cinema with some five hundred features being churned out a year, second only in production to the United States. One of the era's top directors, though he didn't gain international recognition until the mid-1950s, was **Mizoguchi Kenji** (1898–1956). His initial speciality was melodramas based in Meiji-era Japan, but he is best known in the West for his later lyrical medieval samurai dramas, such as *Ugetsu Monogatari* (1954). During the 1920s and 1930s, however, Mizoguchi also turned his hand to detective, expressionist, war, ghost and comedy films.

As Japan fell deeper into the ugliness of nationalism and war, Mizoguchi embraced traditional concepts of stylized beauty in films such as 1939's *The Story of the Last Chrysanthemums* (*Zangiku Monogatari*). Also honing his reputation during the pre-World War II period was director **Ozu Yasujirō**, whose *Tokyo Story* (see p.807) from 1954 is a classic.

The 1950s and 1960s

World War II and its immediate aftermath put the dampers on Japan's cinematic ambitions, but in 1950, the local industry produced **Kurosawa Akira**'s brilliant *Rashōmon* (see p.807) which subsequently won a Golden Lion at the following year's Venice Film Festival and an honorary Oscar. A string of Kurosawa-directed classics followed, including *The Seven Samurai* (1954; see p.807), *Throne of Blood* (*Kumonosu-jō*; 1957) based on *Macbeth*, *Yōjimbō* (1961; see p.808) and *Ran* (1985; see p.807).

The 1950s also saw the birth of one of Japan's best-known cinema icons, **Godzilla** – or *Gojira* as he was known on initial release in 1954. Despite the monster being killed off in the grand finale, the film's success led to an American release, with added footage, in 1956, under the title *Godzilla, King of the Monsters*. Over the next four decades in 28 movies Godzilla survived to do battle with, among others, King Kong, giant shrimps, cockroaches and moths, and a smog monster.

Tora-san

Although hardly known outside of Japan, the country's most beloved – and financially successful – series of films are those featuring **Tora-san**, or Kuruma Torajirō, a loveable itinerant peddler from Tokyo's Shitamachi. The series began with *Otoko wa Tsurai Yo* (*It's Tough Being a Man*) in 1969 and the lead character was played by Atsumi Kiyoshi in 48 films up until the actor's death in 1996. The format of the films is invariably the same, with Tora-san chasing after his latest love, or "Madonna", in various scenic areas of Japan, before returning to his exasperated family.

Highly romanticized, violent **yakuza** flicks were also popular in the 1960s. These *ninkyō eiga* (chivalry films) often played like modern-day samurai sagas, the tough, fair *yakuza* being driven by a code of loyalty or honour. One of the major actors to emerge from these films is Takakura Ken, who has since starred in Western films including Ridley Scott's *Black Rain*. Try to check out the cult classics *Branded to Kill* (*Koroshi no Rakuin*) and *Tokyo Drifter* (*Tokyo Nagaremono*) by maverick director **Suzuki Seijun**, whose visual style and nihilistic cool was an inspiration to Kitano Takeshi and Quentin Tarantino among others.

The 1970s and 1980s

In 1976 *In the Realm of the Senses* (see p.807) by rebel filmmaker **Ōshima Nagisa** created an international stir with its explicit sex scenes and violent content. Ōshima fought against Japan's censors, who demanded cuts, but ultimately lost. This was all the more galling for the director, whose film gathered critical plaudits abroad, but remained unseen in its full version at home, because at the same time major Japanese studios were making money from increasingly violent films and soft-core porn, called *roman poruno*.

By the **late 1970s**, Japanese cinema was in the doldrums. Entrance fees at the cinema were the highest in the world (they're still relatively expensive), leaving the public less willing to sample offbeat local films when they could see sure-fire Hollywood hits instead. Ōshima turned in the prisoner-of-war drama *Merry Christmas Mr Lawrence* in 1983 and the decidedly quirky *Max Mon Amour* (1986), in which Charlotte Rampling takes a chimp as a lover, before retiring from directing to build his reputation as a TV pundit. Instead of investing money at home, Japanese companies, like Sony, went on a spending spree in Hollywood, buying up major American studios and film rights, thus securing access to lucrative video releases.

Flying the flag for the local industry was **Itami Jūzō**, an actor who turned director with the mildly satirical *The Funeral* (see p.808) in 1984. His follow-up, *Tampopo* (1986; see p.808), a comedy set against the background of Japan's gourmet boom, was an international hit, as was his *A Taxing Woman* (*Marusa no Onna*) in 1988. The female star of Itami's films, which poke gentle fun at Japanese behaviour and society, was his wife, the comic actress Miyamoto Nobuko.

The 1990s

Itami Jūzō's 1992 satire *The Gentle Art of Japanese Extortion* (*Minbō-no-Onna*), which sent up the *yakuza*, led to the director suffering a knife attack by mob thugs. Undaunted, he recovered and went on to direct more challenging

Anime on the big screen

In 1958, Toei produced Japan's first full-length full-colour animated feature *Hakujaden* (released as *Tale of the White Panda* in the US) and went on to make a series of increasingly sophisticated films, culminating in *Little Norse Prince* (*Taiyō no Ōji Horusu no Daibōken*) in 1968. This was the directorial debut of Takahata Isao who in 1985 teamed up with Miyazaki Hayao to form **Studio Ghibli** (Ⓦwww.ghibli.jp), the most successful of Japanese animation companies.

During the 1960s, TV anime came to fore with **Tezuka Osamu**'s *Tetsuwan Atomu* series, more popularly known as *Astro Boy*, a success both at home and abroad. Tezuka's *Kimba the White Lion* and Tatsuo Yoshida's *Mach Go Go Go* (*Speed Racer* in the US) were other hit TV series from this era, while in the 1970s it was space-based adventures, such as *Space Battleship Yamato* (*Star Blazers*) and *Kagaku Ninja tai Gatchaman* (*Battle of the Planets*), that had kids glued to the gogglebox.

By the 1980s ambitious artists were pushing the boundaries of the genre into cinema-scale works with higher production values such as Ōtomo Katsuhiro's dark sci-fi fantasy **Akira** (see p.809). Miyazaki Hayao was also making his name, initially with his ecological man vs nature fantasy adventure *Nausicaä of the Valley of Wind* (1984), then with Studio Ghibli smashes such as *My Neighbour Totoro* (see p.809), *Princess Mononoke* (see p.809) and the Oscar-winning **Spirited Away** (see p.809). Miyazaki's latest effort, *Ponyo*, a kids' film with elements of *The Little Mermaid* tale, played on international screens in 2009, while in 2010 Studio Ghibli released *Karigurashi no Arrietty*, based on Mary Norton's children's book *The Borrowers*.

Among other cinema anime directors to watch out for are: **Kon Satoshi**, whose film include the Hitchcockian psychological drama *Perfect Blue* (1997), *Tokyo Godfathers* (see p.809), and *Paprika* (2006), a visually splendid tale about the search for a stolen device that allows physical access to people's dreams; **Oshii Mamoru**, who has the seminal *Ghost in the Shell* (see p.809) and *The Sky Crawlers* (2008) to his credit; and **Hosada Mamoru**, whose *The Girl Who Leapt Through Time* (*Toki o Kakeru Shōjo*; 2006) and *Summer Wars* (2009) have both garnered rave reviews. For an in-depth look at the medium, read *The Rough Guide to Anime*.

comedies, such as *Daibyōnin* (1993), about the way cancer is treated in Japanese hospitals, and *Sūpā-no-Onna* (1995), which revealed the shady practices of supermarkets. Itami committed suicide in 1997, prior to the publication of an exposé of his love life in a scandal magazine, leaving the field clear for **Takeshi Kitano** (see p.806) to emerge as Japan's new cinema darling.

Kurosawa received a lifetime achievement Academy Award in 1990, the same year as he teamed up with George Lucas and Steven Spielberg to make the semi-autobiographical *Yume* (*Dreams*). His anti-war film *Rhapsody in August* (*Hachigatsu-no-Kyōshikyoku*; 1991), however, attracted criticism abroad for its somewhat one-sided treatment of the subject. Referred to respectfully as "Sensei" (teacher) by all in the industry, Kurosawa's final film before his death, aged 88, on September 6, 1998, was the low-key drama *Mādadayo* (1993) about an elderly academic.

Meanwhile, the prolific **Kurosawa Kiyoshi** had begun to make waves with quirky genre pictures, such as *The Excitement of the Do-Re-Mi-Fa Girls* (1985), *The Serpent Path* (1998) and its sequel *Eyes of the Spider* (1998). Tsukamoto Shin'ya had an art-house hit with the sci-fi horror film *Tetsuo* about a man turning into a machine, a story inspired by the acclaimed anime *Akira* (see p.809). A much bigger hit, with both local and international audiences, was *Shall We Dance?*, a charming ballroom dancing comedy-drama which swept up all thirteen of Japan's Academy Awards in 1996.

Beat Takeshi

Comedian, actor, director, writer, painter and video game designer – is there anything that **Kitano Takeshi** (ⓦwww.kitanotakeshi.com) can't do? Known locally as Beat Takeshi after his old comedy double act, the Two Beats, Kitano, who was born in Tokyo in 1947, first came to international attention for his role as a brutal camp sergeant in Ōshima's *Merry Christmas Mr Lawrence*. His directorial debut *Violent Cop* (1989) saw him star as a police officer in the *Dirty Harry* mould. His next film, *Boiling Point (3-4 x 10 Gatsu)*, was an equally bloody outing, but it was his more reflective and comic *Sonatine* (see p.808), about a gang war in sunny Okinawa, that had foreign critics hailing him as Japan's Quentin Tarantino.

Kitano survived a near-fatal motorbike accident in 1994, and triumphed with *Hanabi* (see p.808), which scooped up a Golden Lion at the Venice Festival in 1997. In *Dolls* (2002) he collaborated with fashion designer Yohji Yamamoto in a visually ravishing but glacially slow film based on the plots of *bunraku* puppet plays. Far more fun is *Zatoichi* (see p.808) which saw a bleached blonde Kitano play the blind swordsman of the title. Recent titles – *Achilles and the Tortoise* (*Akiresu to Kami*; 2008) about the life-long struggles of a talentless painter, and *Kantoku Banzai!* (2007), concerning a director tying to escape his image as a maker of gangster films – both contain autobiographical elements. His 2010 opus *Outrage* sees him returning to the *yakuza* power struggle themes of this earlier hits. For another side of Kitano, read *Boy*, an English translation, published by Vertical, of a trio of captivating short stories about adolescence.

The new millennium

While Kitano continues to be one of Japan's most internationally popular filmmakers, other directors are coming to the fore. Master of the gleeful splatterfest is the prolific **Miike Takashi**, who has jumped around from the stylized gangster violence of *Ichi the Killer* (see p.808) to the sci-fi action of his *Dead or Alive* trilogy, via the musical horror comedy of *The Happiness of the Katakuris*. In 2009 his *Yatterman*, based on a popular cartoon series from the 1970s, was a local hit.

Reinterpreting the horror genre has been **Nakata Hideo** whose *Ring* (1998) and paranormal chiller *Dark Water* (2002) were both remade in English in Hollywood before Nakata himself went West in 2005 to direct his English-language debut *The Ring Two*, a new sequel to the Hollywood version of *Ring*. Fans will want to compare it to Nakata's original – and different – Japanese sequel *Ring 2* (1999). This trend of English-language remakes and new versions has continued with Takashi Shimizu's *Ju-on: The Grudge* (2000) and *Ju-on: The Grudge Two* (2003).

A decade into the new millennium, Japan's film industry is thriving and in top creative form. In his 80s, Suzuki Seijun made a wonderful and surprising comeback in 2006 with the fairy-tale musical *Princess Racoon*. In 2007, *The Mourning Forest* scooped up the Grand Prix at Cannes for director Naomi Kawase, a decade after her debut film *Moe no Suzaku* had scored a prize at the same festival. Also scoring at Cannes and other awards ceremonies was Kurosawa Kiyoshi's satirical drama *Tokyo Sonata* (see p.809). And in 2009 Takita Yōjirō's *Departures* (see p.808) took top honours as best foreign language film at the Oscars.

Films to look out for

Japanese classics

Black Rain (Imamura Shohei; 1989). Not to be confused with the US *yakuza* flick, this serious drama traces the strains put on family life in a country village after the atomic bomb is dropped on Hiroshima.

Godzilla, King of the Monsters (1956). Originally released two years earlier in Japan as *Gojira*, the giant mutant lizard, born after a US hydrogen bomb test in the Bikini Atoll, was such a hit that previously cut scenes were added for the American market. Raymond Burr plays the journalist telling in flashback the event that led to Godzilla running amok in Tokyo.

In the Realm of the Senses (*Ai-no-Corrida*; Ōshima Nagisa; 1976). Based on the true story of servant girl Sada Abe and her intensely violent sexual relationship with her master Kichi – who ends up dead and minus his penis.

Kagemusha (Kurosawa Akira; 1980). Nominated for an Academy Award and co-winner of the Grand Prize at Cannes, Kurosawa showed he was still on form with this sweeping historical epic. A poor actor is recruited to impersonate a powerful warlord who has inconveniently died mid-campaign.

Ran (Kurosawa Akira; 1985). This much-lauded, loose adaptation of *King Lear* is a true epic, with thousands of extras and giant battle scenes. The daughters become sons, although the Regan and Goneril characters survive in the form of the gleefully vengeful wives Lady Kaede and Lady Sue.

Rashōmon (Kurosawa Akira; 1950). The film that established Kurosawa's reputation in the West. A notorious bandit, the wife he perhaps rapes, the man he perhaps murders and the woodcutter who perhaps witnesses the events each tell their different story of what happened in the woods. Fascinatingly open-ended narrative and a memorable performance by Mifune Toshirō as the restless bandit make this a must-see film.

The Seven Samurai (*Shichinin-no-Samurai*; Kurosawa Akira; 1954). A small village in sixteenth-century Japan is fed up with being raided each year by bandits so it hires a band of samurai warriors for protection. Kurosawa's entertaining period drama was later remade in Hollywood as *The Magnificent Seven*.

Tokyo Story (*Tōkyō Monogatari*; Ozu Yasujirō; 1954). An elderly couple travel to Tokyo to visit their children and grandchildren. The only person who has any time for them is Noriko, the widow of their son who was killed in the war. On their return, the mother falls ill and dies. Ozu's themes of loneliness and the breakdown of tradition are grim, but his simple approach and the sincerity of the acting make the film a genuine classic.

Twenty Four Eyes (*Nijūshi-no-Hitomi*; Kinoshita Keisuke; 1954). This four-hankie weepy is one of Japan's most-loved films. Events leading up to, during and after World War II are seen through the eyes of a first-grade female teacher (a luminous performance by Takahime Hideko), on the island of Shōdo-shima. The twelve cute children in Ōishi-san's class make up the 24 eyes.

When a Woman Ascends the Stairs (*Onna ga Kaidan o agaru toki*; Naruse Mikio; 1960). In Japan Naruse ranks alongside Kurosawa and Ozu as one of the country's great film directors. This film, about an ageing hostess in a Ginza bar, is from the latter end of his career and has a splendid central performance by Takamine Hideko.

Yōjimbō (Kurosawa Akira; 1961). Mifune Toshirō stars in one of Kurosawa's best-known samurai sagas as a *rōnin* who arrives in a dusty town, is greeted by a dog carrying a human hand and discovers he's walked in on a bloody feud.

Itami Jūzō and Kitano Takeshi

Hanabi (Kitano Takeshi; 1997). Venice Festival winner with Kitano directing himself as a detective pushed to breaking point by a stake-out that goes wrong, a seriously ill wife and outstanding loans to the *yakuza*. Kitano also painted the artwork that appears in the film.

The Funeral (*Osōshiki;* Itami Jūzō; 1984). Itami's directorial debut is a wry comedy about a grieving family bumbling their way through the obscure conventions of a proper Japanese funeral. The young couple learn the "rules" by watching a video and the Buddhist priest turns up in a white Rolls-Royce.

Sonatine (Kitano Takeshi; 1993). One of Kitano's most accomplished films; he plays a tired gangster, hightailing it to the sunny isles of Okinawa and getting mixed up in mob feuds, before it all turns nasty on the beach.

Tampopo (Itami Jūzō; 1985). Tampopo, the proprietress of a noodle bar, is taught how to prepare the perfect ramen, in this comedy about Japan's gourmet boom. From the old woman squishing fruit in a supermarket to the gangster and his moll passing a raw egg sexily between their mouths, this is a film packed with memorable scenes.

Zatoichi (Kitano Takeshi; 2003). A classic of Japanese TV remade with an assured, modern touch by Kitano, who also stars as the eponymous hero, a blind master swordsman whom you really don't want to tangle with. The film's finale has the cast doing a tap-dancing number in *geta* (wooden sandals).

Contemporary Japanese cinema

Campaign (*Senkyo*; Soda Kazuhiro; 2007). Fly-on-the-wall style documentary following a novice LDP candidate on the campaign trail during the Kawasaki municipal elections. A brilliant, ironic insight on Japanese politics and society.

Dark Water (*Honogurai Mizu no Soko Kara*; Nakata Hideo; 2002). Stylish tale of everyday terror told by the new master of the genre. Yoshimi is going through a messy, emotionally distressing divorce when she moves with her daughter into a creepy apartment. Water starts dripping through the ceiling and things get worse from there.

Departures (*Okuribito*; Takita Yōjirō; 2008). Oscar-winning drama about an out-of-work cellist who winds up working at a funeral parlour in his hometown in Yamagata prefecture. Because of the nature of this taboo profession he at first keeps his new job secret from his family and friends.

Ichi the Killer (Miike Takashi; 2001). Stand by for graphic depictions of bodies sliced in half in this *yakuza* tale set in Tokyo's Kabukichō, as told by the *enfant terrible* of Japanese cinema. Not for the squeamish.

Kamikaze Taxi (Masato Harada; 1995). A gangster flick with a twist; it also deals with the issue of ethnic Japanese returning to Japan from South America and being discriminated against as foreigners. Watch out for Yakusho Kōji in a very different role from his ballroom-dancing salaryman in *Shall We Dance?*

The Mourning Forest (*Mogari-no-Mori*; Naomi Kawase; 2007). This Cannes film festival prize winner is a moving tale of a caretaker at a retirement home and one of the residents, both struggling with bereavement, who make a road trip into the forests around Nara.

Ōsaka Story (Nakata Toichi; 1994). Nakata Toichi ticks off many difficult contemporary issues in his film, which follows the homecoming of a gay, Korean–Japanese film student to his Ōsaka-based family. His staunchly Korean father expects him to take over the business and get married, but the son has other ideas.

Ring (Nakata Hideo; 1998). Remade in Hollywood, this is the original and far superior spine-chiller about a videotape that kills everyone who sees it exactly one week after viewing.

Shall We Dance? (Suo Masayuki; 1996). At turns touching and hilarious, *Shall We Dance?* features Yakusho Kōji playing a quietly frustrated middle-aged salaryman whose spark returns when he takes up ballroom dancing. He has to keep it secret from his family and work colleagues, though, because of the social stigma attached.

Tokyo Sonata (Kurosawa Kiyoshi; 2008). When a father decides not to tell his family he's lost his job as a salaryman it has all kinds of repercussions. A bleak, satirical drama reflective of contemporary Japanese society.

Essential anime

Akira (Ōtomo Katsuhiro; 1988). Dynamic action sequences drive forward this nihilistic sci-fi fantasy about biker gangs, terrorists, government plots and a telekinetic teenager mutating in Tokyo, 2019.

Ghost in the Shell (*Kokaku Kidōtai*; Oshii Mamoru; 1995). A sophisticated sci-fi thriller that's director Mamoru Oshii's finest work, together with its sequel *Innocence* and the fascinating TV series it spawned.

Only Yesterday (*Omohide Poroporo*; Takahata Isao; 1988). Beautifully realized, Isao Takahata-directed film about a woman, on a life-changing vacation in the countryside, recalling the childhood episodes that shaped her personality.

My Neighbour Totoro (*Tonari no Totoro*; Miyazaki Hayao; 1988). Charming kids' fable set in 1950s Japan about two little girls with a sick mother who make friends with the mythical creatures of the forest, including the giant cuddly character of the title.

Tokyo Godfathers (Kon Satoshi; 2003). This heart-warming Christmas fairy tale of redemption for three tramps and the baby they discover in the trash is pure anime magic.

Princess Mononoke (*Mononoke Hime*; Miyazaki Hayao; 1997). Exciting period drama set in medieval Japan has an ecological message about saving the earth's resources.

Spirited Away (*Sen to Chihiro no Kamikaskushi*; Miyazaki Hayao; 2001). Oscar-winning Japanese *Alice in Wonderland*-style adventure. When her parents take a wrong turn into a mysteriously deserted theme park,

Chihiro finds she has to negotiate her way around the strange creatures she meets at a huge bathhouse before finding a way home.

Foreign films featuring Japan

Babel (Alejandro González Iñárritu; 2006). The talented Mexican director's world-spanning vision captures the essence of contemporary Tokyo. There's a particularly beautiful sequence filmed at Shibuya club *Womb*. Oscar-nominated Kikuchi Rinko as the mute Chieko and her father, played by veteran actor Yakusho Kōji, are outstanding.

Black Rain (Ridley Scott; 1989). Gruff Michael Douglas and younger sidekick Andy Garcia team up with stoic Ōsaka policeman, played by Takakura Ken, to deal with the *yakuza*.

The Last Samurai (Edward Zwick; 2003). Tom Cruise, Billy Connolly and some of Japan's top acting talent star in this tale of a US Civil War vet who comes to train the Emperor Meiji's troops in modern warfare, but finds much to learn himself in the samurai code of honour.

Letters from Iwo-jima (Clint Eastwood; 2006). Experience the bloody battle for the island of Iwo-jima at the end of World War II from the point of view of two Japanese soldiers played by Ken Watanabe and Ninomiya Kazunari.

Lost in Translation (Sofia Coppola; 2003). Memorable performances from Bill Murray and Scarlett Johansson in this stylish comedy-drama set in and around Shinjuku's *Park Hyatt* hotel. Brilliantly captures what it's like to be a *gaijin* adrift in Tokyo.

Memoirs of a Geisha (Rob Marshall; 2005). Epic-scale film which gallops through Arthur Golden's bestselling tale of the trials and tribulations of apprentice geisha Sayuri, played here by Chinese actor Zhang Ziyi, wearing uncommonly blue contact lenses. Gong Li chews up the scenery as her arch rival and Ken Watanabe, Hollywood's pin-up Japanese actor *de jour*, also puts in an appearance as Sayuri's saviour, the Chairman.

Mishima (Paul Schrader; 1985). Art-house take on the bizarre and fascinating life of Japan's contemporary literary giant Mishima Yukio, who committed ritual suicide after leading a failed military coup in 1970.

You Only Live Twice (Lewis Gilbert; 1967). Sean Connery's fifth outing as 007 has Bondo-san grappling with arch-enemy Blofeld and sundry Oriental villains in Tokyo and the countryside.

Books

The one thing the world is not short of is books about Japan; the following selection includes ones that provide a deeper understanding of what is lazily assumed to be one of the world's most enigmatic countries. As throughout this guide, for Japanese names we have given the family name first. This may not always be the order in which it is printed on the English translation.

The following publishers specialize in English language books on Japan, as well as translations of Japanese works: Kodansha (ⓦwww.kodansha-intl.com); Charles E. Tuttle (ⓦwww.tuttlepublishing.com); Stonebridge Press (ⓦwww.stonebridge.com); and Vertical (ⓦwww.vertical-inc.com), which publishes not only great manga titles but also a series of fiction and non-fiction titles by lesser-known (outside of Japan) talents.

History

Ian Buruma *Inventing Japan*. Focusing on the period 1853 to 1964, during which Japan went from a feudal, isolated state to a powerhouse of the modern world economy. Buruma's *The Wages of Guilt* also skilfully explains how and why Germany and Japan have come to terms so differently with their roles in World War II.

John Dower *Embracing Defeat: Japan in the Aftermath of World War II*. Accessible look by a Pulitzer Prize winner at the impact of the American occupation on Japan. First-person accounts and snappy writing bring the book alive.

John Hersey *Hiroshima*. Classic account of the devastation and suffering wrought by the first A-bomb to be used in war.

George Hicks *The Comfort Women*. The story of one of the more shameful episodes of World War II, when the Japanese forced women to become sex slaves (euphemistically known as "comfort women") for the army.

Giles Milton *Samurai William*. Will Adams was one of a handful of shipwrecked sailors who arrived in Japan in 1600 and went on to become adviser to the shogun and the only foreigner ever to be made a samurai. Milton tells the tale with gusto.

Oliver Statler *Japanese Inn* and *Japanese Pilgrimage*. In the first book, a ryokan on the Tōkaidō road provides the focus for an entertaining account of over four hundred years of Japanese history. In *Japanese Pilgrimage*, Statler applies his talents to bringing alive the history of the 88-temple hike around Shikoku.

Richard Storry *A History of Modern Japan*. Ideal primer for basics and themes of Japanese history.

Richard Tames *A Traveller's History of Japan*. This clearly written and succinct volume romps through Japan's history and provides useful cultural descriptions and essays.

Business, economics and politics

Alex Kerr *Dogs and Demons*. A scathing and thought-provoking attack on Japan's economic, environmental and social policies of the past decades, by someone who first came to Japan as a child in the 1960s and has been fascinated by it ever since. Also worth reading is his earlier book *Lost Japan*.

Laura J Kriska *Accidental Office Lady*. Kriska's account of her two years working in Japan as a trainee for Honda in the late 1980s is particularly good for its gender perspective on Japanese corporate life.

Robert M. March *Working for a Japanese Company*. One of the best studies on what it's really like inside Japan's corporate powerhouses by an Aussie management consultant.

Miyamoto Masao *Straitjacket Society*. As the subtitle hints, this "insider's irreverent view of bureaucratic Japan" is quite an eye-opener. Unsurprisingly, Miyamoto was fired from the Ministry of Health and Welfare, but his book sold over 400,000 copies.

Niall Murtagh *The Blue-eyed Salaryman*. Anyone who has ever worked for a Japanese company will find much to identify with in this honest, witty account by an Irish computer programmer, who became a salaryman for Mitsubishi.

Jacob M. Schlesinger *Shadow Shoguns*. Cracking crash course in Japan's political scene, scandals and all, from *Wall Street Journal* reporter Schlesinger, who spent five years at the newspaper's Tokyo bureau.

Karel Van Wolferen *The Enigma of Japanese Power*. A weighty, thought-provoking tome, but one worth wading through. This is the standard text on the triad of Japan's bureaucracy, politicians and business.

Traditional arts, architecture and gardens

Liza Dalby *Geisha*. In the 1970s, anthropologist Dalby immersed herself in the fast-disappearing world of the geisha. This is the fascinating account of her experience and those of her teachers and fellow pupils. *Kimono*, her history of that most Japanese of garments, is also worth a look.

Thomas F. Judge and Tomita Hiroyuki *Edo Craftsmen*. Beautifully produced portraits of some of Shitamachi's traditional craftsmen, who can still be found working in the backstreets of Tokyo. A timely insight into a disappearing world.

Joan Stanley-Baker *Japanese Art*. Highly readable introduction to the broad range of Japan's artistic traditions (though excluding theatre and music), tracing their development from prehistoric to modern times.

Itoh Teiji *The Gardens of Japan*. Splendid photos of all Japan's great historical gardens, including many not generally open to the public, as well as contemporary examples.

Nakagawa Takeshi *The Japanese House*. Comprehensively illustrated book, which takes the reader step by step through the various elements of the traditional Japanese home, and is the essential manual on vernacular architecture.

Culture and society

Ruth Benedict *The Chrysanthemum and the Sword*. This classic study of the hierarchical order of Japanese society, first published in 1946, remains relevant for its intriguing insight into the psychology of a nation that had just suffered defeat in World War II.

Ian Buruma *A Japanese Mirror* and *The Missionary and the Libertine*. The first book is an intelligent, erudite examination of Japan's popular culture, while *The Missionary and the Libertine* collects together a range of essays including pieces on Japan-bashing,

Hiroshima, Pearl Harbor, the authors Mishima Yukio and Tanizaki Junichirō and the film director Ōshima Nagisa.

Veronica Chambers *Kickboxing Geishas*. Based on interviews with a broad cross section of women, from Hokkaidō DJs to top executives, Chambers argues that modern Japanese women are not the submissive characters so often portrayed in the media, but in fact a strong force for change. A sympathetic and insightful book.

Lesley Downer *The Brothers*. The Tsutsumi family saga of wealth, illegitimacy and the fabled hatred of the two half-brothers is turned into a gripping read by Downer. Also look out for *On the Narrow Road to the Deep North*, her book following in the footsteps of the poet Bashō, and *Madame Sadayakko* about one of Japan's most celebrated geisha.

Jake Adelstein *Tokyo Vice*. With forensic thoroughness and gallows humour Adelstein documents his unsentimental education in crime reporting for the *Yomiuri Shimbun*, Japan's top selling newspaper. His main scoop is about three *yakuza* heavyweights who sneaked into the US, with FBI approval, to get liver transplants. A true crime classic.

Bruce S. Feiler *Learning to Bow*. An enlightening and entertaining read, especially for anyone contemplating teaching English in Japan. This book recounts the experiences of a young American on the JET programme, plonked into a high school in rural Tochigi-ken.

Edward Fowler *San'ya Blues*. Fowler's experiences living and working among the casual labourers of Tokyo's San'ya district make fascinating reading. He reveals the dark underbelly of Japan's economic miracle and blows apart a few myths and misconceptions on the way.

Robin Gerster *Legless in Ginza*. A funny and spot-on account of the writer's two-year residence at Japan's most prestigious university, Tokyo's Todai. Gerster writes with a larrikin Aussie verve and notices things that many other expat commentators ignore.

Jeff Kingston *Japan's Quiet Transformation*. A bit heavy going at times, but Kingston provides a valuable counterpoint to the normal doom-laden portrayal of post-bubble Japan, arguing that subtle but important social, economic and political shifts are changing the country.

John K. Nelson *A Year in the Life of a Shinto Shrine*. Fascinating insight into Japan's native animist religion based on this American ethnologist's research at Suwa-jinja in Nagasaki. Amid all the detail, Nelson also catches gossipy asides such as a trainee priest being told to be "careful not to fart during the ritual".

Saga Junichi *Confessions of a Yakuza*. This life story of a former *yakuza* boss, beautifully retold by a doctor whose clinic he just happened to walk into, gives a rare insight into a secret world. Saga also wrote the award-winning *Memories of Silk and Straw*, a collection of reminiscences about village life in pre-modern Japan.

David Suzuki and Oiwa Keibo *The Japan We Never Knew*. Canadian scientist, broadcaster and writer Suzuki teamed up with half-Japanese anthropologist Oiwa to tour the country and interview an extraordinary range of people, from the Ainu of Hokkaidō to descendants of the "untouchable" caste, the Burakumin. The result is an excellent riposte to the idea of a monocultural, conformist Japan.

Tendo Shoko *Yakuza Moon*. The daughter of a *yakuza*, Tendo's lived her teens in a blur of violence, sex and drugs. By age 15 she was in a detention centre, and then gradually pulled her life together to write this searing account of life in the underclass of Japanese society.

Robert Twigger *Angry White Pyjamas*. The subtitle "An Oxford poet trains with the Tokyo riot police"

Japan through an American's eyes

Donald Richie has been writing intelligently about Japanese culture ever since he first arrived in the country back in 1947 to work as a typist for the US occupying forces. Richie is best known as a scholar of Japanese cinema, but among his forty odd books it's his essay collections – *Public People, Private People*, *A Lateral View* and *Partial Views* – that set a standard other expat commentators can only aspire to. *Public People* is a series of sketches of famous and unknown Japanese, including profiles of novelist Mishima Yukio and the actor Mifune Toshiro. In *A Lateral View* and *Partial Views*, Richie tackles Tokyo style, avant-garde theatre, *pachinko*, the Japanese kiss and the Zen rock garden at Kyoto's Ryōan-ji temple, among many other things.

His subtle, elegiac travelogue *The Inland Sea*, first published in 1971, captures the timeless beauty of the island-studded waterway and is a must read. In *Tokyo*, Richie captures the essence of the city he has lived in for more than fifty years. Naturally, he also serves as editor on *Lafcadio Hearn's Japan*, which includes sections from the classic *Glimpses of Unfamiliar Japan*, among Hearn's other works (see p.582). For an overview of the immense Richie *ouevre,* dip into *The Donald Richie Reader: 50 Years of Writing on Japan* or his *Japan Journals 1947–2004*.

gives you the gist. Twigger provides an intense forensic account of the daily trials, humiliations and triumphs of becoming a master of *aikido*.

Robert Whiting *Got to Have Wa*. Whiting's third book on baseball and Japan follows the often hilarious exploits of US baseball players in Japan. In the process it reveals much about Japanese society. His *The Meaning of Ichiro* turns the tables by focusing on the experiences of Ichiro Suzuki, a top baseball star who now plays for the Seattle Mariners.

Robert Whiting *Tokyo Underworld*. This well-researched tale follows the ups and downs of Nick Zapapetti, a larger-than-life Italian American who arrived with the occupying forces in 1945 and stayed on to become "the king of Roppongi" and Tokyo's Mafia boss. In the process, Whiting also charts the history of the *yakuza* in postwar Japan.

Pop culture

Apart from the following, also read *The Rough Guide to Anime* by Simon Richmond and *The Rough Guide to Manga* by Jason Yadao.

Peter Carey *Wrong About Japan*. The Booker-prize winning Australian author treats his anime-obsessed 12-year-old son to a trip to Tokyo, and thoughtfully arranges interviews with such luminaries as Yoshiyuki Tomino and Hayao Miyazaki. Carey's befuddled opinions about anime's cultural impact will strike a chord with many other parents wondering about their offsprings' obsession.

Roland Kelts *JapanAmerica*. Highly accessible, personalized account of how Japanese pop culture and in particular manga and anime has become such a huge success in the US. Kelts, half-Japanese, half-American and living in both countries, makes many intelligent observations and digs up some fascinating tales.

Mark Schilling *The Encyclopedia of Japanese Pop Culture*. Although it's getting dated, Schilling's book remains an indispensable, spot-on guide to late-twentieth-century Japan. Schilling also authored *The Yakuza Movie Book*.

Frederik L. Schodt *Dreamland Japan: Writings on Modern Manga*. A series of entertaining and informative essays on the art of Japanese comic books, profiling the top publications, artists, animated films and English-language manga. Also read Schodt's *The Astro Boy Essays* for great insight into the life and times of Astro Boy's creator Tezuka Osamu.

Food and drink

Shirley Booth *Food of Japan*. More than a series of recipes, this nicely illustrated book gives lots of background detail and history of Japanese food.

Philip Harper *The Insider's Guide to Sake*. Handy pocket-sized guide that will tell you most of what you need to know about Japanese rice wine, from an English writer who brews his own sake near Nara. The listing of over one hundred different sakes, plus their labels, is very useful.

Kurihara Harumi *Harumi's Japanese Cooking*. Japan's Martha Stewart offers an easy to follow and down-to-earth approach to preparing typical dishes that Japanese eat at home.

Mark Robinson *Izakaya: The Japanese Pub Cookbook*. A beautifully illustrated celebration of some of the author's favourite Tokyo-based *izakaya*, with over 60 recipes for their rustic food.

Yukari Sakamoto *Food Sake Tokyo*. Packed with evocative photos and useful information on local food and drink, this guide to the best places to buy, eat and imbibe, is an indispensable guide to the capital's culinary treasures.

Robb Satterwhite *What's What in Japanese Restaurants*. Written by a Tokyo-based epicure, this handy guide covers all the types of Japanese food and drink you're likely to encounter, and the menus annotated with Japanese characters are particularly useful.

Travel writing

Isabella Bird *Unbeaten Tracks in Japan*. After a brief stop in Meiji-era Tokyo, intrepid Victorian adventurer Bird is determined to reach parts of Japan not trampled by tourists. She heads north to Hokkaidō, taking the time to make acute, vivid observations along the way.

Alan Booth *The Roads to Sata* and *Looking for the Lost*. Two classics by one of the most insightful and entertaining modern writers on Japan, whose talents were tragically cut short by his death in 1993. The first book sees Booth, an avid long-distance walker, hike (with the aid of many a beer) from the far north of Hokkaidō to the southern tip of Kyūshū, while *Looking for the Lost*, a trio of walking tales, is by turns hilarious and heartbreakingly poignant.

Josie Drew *A Ride in the Neon Sun*. At nearly seven hundred pages, this isn't a book to pop in your panniers, but full of useful tips for anyone planning to tour Japan by bike. Drew has subsequently put out an equally entertaining sequel, *The Sun in My Eyes*.

Will Ferguson *Hokkaido Highway Blues*. Humorist Ferguson decides to hitch from one end of Japan to the other, with the aim of travelling with the Japanese, not among them. He succeeds (despite everyone telling him – even those who stop to pick him up – that Japanese never stop for hitch-hikers), and in the process turns out a great book of travel writing about the country. Funny and ultimately moving.

Pico Iyer *The Lady and the Monk*. Devoted to a year Iyer spent studying

Zen Buddhism and dallying with a married woman in Kyoto, who subsequently became his life partner. It's a rose-tinted, dreamy view of Japan, which he has since followed up, in a more realistic way, with his excellent and thought-provoking *The Global Soul*.

Karin Muller *Japanland*. Documentary filmmaker and travel writer Muller heads to Japan in search of *wa* – the Japanese concept of harmony. The interesting cast of characters she meets in the year she spends there – part of the time living just south of Tokyo, the other travelling, including to Kyoto, Shikoku and northern Honshū – is what makes this book rise above similar efforts.

Guides and reference books

Diane Durston *Old Kyoto* and *Kyoto: Seven Paths to the Heart of the City* (Mitsumura Suko Shoin). Few people can get under the skin of this enigmatic city as well as Diane Durston. In the former she seeks out the best traditional craft shops, restaurants and ryokan, while in the latter she explores seven neighbourhoods where Kyoto's special magic still survives.

Ed Readicker-Henderson *The Traveller's Guide to Japanese Pilgrimages*. A practical guide to Japan's top three pilgrim routes: Hiei-zan (near Kyoto); the 33 Kannon of Saigoku (a broad sweep from the Kii peninsula to Lake Biwa); and following the steps of Kōbō Daishi round Shikoku's 88 temples.

Mary Sutherland and Dorothy Britton *National Parks of Japan*. With gorgeous photos and a thoroughly researched text, this inspirational book is the essential guide to all 28 of Japan's national parks, covering wildlife, plants, and natural and cultural history.

Marc Treib and Ron Herman *A Guide to the Gardens of Kyoto*. Handy, pocket-sized guide to more than fifty of the city's gardens, with concise historical details and step-by-step descriptions of each garden.

Classic literature

Kawabata Yasunari *Snow Country*, *The Izu Dancer* and other titles. Japan's first Nobel Prize winner for fiction writes intense tales of passion – usually about a sophisticated urban man falling for a simple country girl.

Matsuo Bashō *The Narrow Road to the Deep North*. The seventeenth-century haiku poetry master chronicles his journey through northern Japan, pausing to compose his thoughts along the way.

Murasaki Shikibu *The Tale of Genji*. Claimed as the world's first novel, this lyrical epic about the lives and loves of a nobleman was spun by a lady of the Heian court around 1000 AD.

Natsume Sōseki *Botchan*, *Kokoro* and *I am a Cat*. In his comic novel *Botchan*, Sōseki draws on his own experiences as an English teacher in turn-of-the-twentieth-century Matsuyama. The three volumes of *I am a Cat* see the humurist adopting a wry feline point of view on the world. *Kokoro* – about an ageing *sensei* (teacher) trying to come to terms with the modern era – is considered his best book.

Sei Shōnagon *The Pillow Book*. Fascinating insight into the daily life and artful thoughts of a tenth-century noblewoman.

Tanizaki Jun'ichirō *Some Prefer Nettles* and *The Makioka Sisters*. One of the great stylists of Japanese prose, Tanizaki's finest book is often considered to be *Some Prefer Nettles*, about a romantic liaison between a Japanese man and a Eurasian woman. However, there's an epic sweep to *The Makioka Sisters*, which documents the decline of a wealthy merchant family in Ōsaka.

Contemporary fiction

Alfred Birnbaum ed. *Monkey Brain Sushi*. A good introduction to modern Japanese prose, with eleven often quirky short stories by contemporary authors.

Van C. Gessel and Tomone Matsumoto (ed.) *The Shōwa Anthology*. This collection of short stories is essential reading if you want to get up to speed with the best in contemporary Japanese fiction. The anthology covers the Shōwa era (1926–89) and includes a number of stories not previously translated into English.

Ishiguro Kazuo *An Artist of the Floating World* and *A Pale View of the Hills*. Nagasaki-born author who's lived in Britain since 1960. *A Pale View of the Hills*, his first novel, is a haunting tale set in Nagasaki which unravels the vaguely expressed horrors of the atomic bombing against the backdrop of a dislocated postwar society. *An Artist of the Floating World* takes a look at the rise of Japanese militarism in the twentieth century through the eyes of an ageing painter.

Natsuo Kirino *Out*. Four women working in a bentō factory just outside Tokyo discover that committing murder is both easier and much more complicated than they could ever have imagined, in this dark, superior thriller that mines a very dark seam of Japan's underbelly. Follow-up books include *Grotesque*, about the deaths of two Tokyo prostitutes, and *Real World*, a grim thriller about alienated Japanese teenagers.

Mishima Yukio *After the Banquet*, *Confessions of Mask*, *Forbidden Colours*, *The Sea of Fertility*. Novelist Mishima sealed his notoriety by committing ritual suicide after leading a failed military coup in 1970. He left behind a

Haruki Murakami

One of Japan's most entertaining and translated contemporary writers, **Haruki Murakami** has been hailed as a postwar successor to the great novelists Mishima, Kawabata and Tanizaki, and talked of as a future Nobel laureate.

Many of Murakami's books are set in Tokyo, drawing on his time studying at Waseda University in the early 1970s and running a jazz bar, a place that became a haunt for literary types and, no doubt, provided inspiration for his jazz-bar-running hero in the bittersweet novella *South of the Border, West of the Sun*. A good introduction to Murakami is *Norwegian Wood*, a book in two volumes about the tender coming-of-age love story of two students, which has sold over five million copies.

Considered among his best works are *The Wind-Up Bird Chronicle*, a hefty yet dazzling cocktail of mystery, war reportage and philosophy, and the surreal *Kafka on the Shore*, a murder story in which cats talk to people and fish rain from the sky. *After Dark*, set in the dead of Tokyo night, has all the usual Murakami trademark flourishes from quirky characters to metaphysical speculation.

Overseas fans are eagerly awaiting the English translation of his latest mega-opus *1Q84*, a complex tale of cults and assassins set in 1984 that unravels over more than 1000 pages.

For a wonderful insight into what makes this publicity-shy author tick, read his brief memoir about running marathons and writing, *What I Talk About When I Talk About Running*.

highly respectable, if at times melodramatic, body of literature, including some of Japan's finest postwar novels.

Murakami Ryū *Almost Transparent Blue*, *Sixty-nine*, *Coin Locker Babies*. Murakami burst onto Japan's literary scene in the mid-1980s with *Almost Transparent Blue*, a hip tale of student life mixing reality and fantasy. *Sixty-nine* is his semi-autobiographical account of a 17-year-old stirred by the rebellious passions of the late 1960s, set in Sasebo, Kyūshū. *Coin Locker Babies* is his most ambitious work, spinning a revenger's tragedy about the lives of two boys dumped in adjacent coin lockers as babies.

Ōe Kenzaburō *Nip the Buds, Shoot the Kids*, *A Personal Matter* and *A Healing Family*. Winner of Japan's second Nobel Prize for literature in 1994, Ōe is a writer who aims, in his own words, to "push back the rising tide of conformity". *Nip the Buds*, his first full-length novel, published in 1958, is a tale of lost innocence concerning fifteen reformatory school boys evacuated in wartime to a remote mountain village and left to fend for themselves when a threatening plague frightens away the villagers. *A Personal Matter* sees Ōe tackling the trauma of his handicapped son Hikari's birth, while *A Healing Family* catches up with Hikari thirty years later, documenting his trials and triumphs.

Japan in foreign fiction

Alan Brown *Audrey Hepburn's Neck*. Beneath this rib-tickling, acutely observed tale of a young guy from the sticks adrift in big-city Tokyo, Brown weaves several important themes, including the continuing impact of World War II and the confused relationships between the Japanese and *gaijin*.

James Clavell *Shogun*. Blockbuster fictionalized account of Englishman Will Adams' life in seventeenth-century Japan as an adviser to Shogun Tokugawa Ieyasu.

William Gibson *Idoru*. Love in the age of the computer chip. Cyberpunk novelist Gibson's sci-fi vision of Tokyo's hi-tech future – a world of non-intrusive DNA checks at airports and computerized pop icons (the *idoru* of the title) – rings disturbingly true. The hip thriller *Pattern Recognition* is also partly set in Tokyo.

Arthur Golden *Memoirs of a Geisha*. Rags to riches potboiler following the progress of Chiyo from her humble beginnings in a Japanese fishing village through training as a geisha in Kyoto to setting up her own teahouse in New York. Full of accurate details and colourful characters – impressively so, given that Golden has spent so little time in Japan itself.

David Mitchell *Ghostwritten*, *number9dream* and *The Thousand Autumns of Jacob De Zoet*. Mitchell lived in Japan for several years, a fact that is reflected in three of his novels. *Ghostwritten* is a dazzling collection of interlocked short stories, a couple based in Japan. *number9dream* conjures up a postmodern Japan of computer hackers, video games, gangsters and violence. His latest, *The Thousand Autumns of Jacob De Zoet*, is a fascinating historical novel focusing on life on Nagasaki's island enclave of Dejima – the only place Europeans were allowed to live in Japan during the Tokugawa era.

David Pearce *Tokyo Year Zero* and *Occupied City*. The first two instalments in Pearce's crime trilogy set in Tokyo immediately after the end of World War II. Peace's novels impress with their attention to detail, complex plots and compelling characters.

Language

Language

Japanese

Picking up a few words of Japanese is not difficult. Pronunciation is simple and standard and there are few exceptions to the straightforward grammar rules. With a just a little effort you should be able to read the words spelled out in *hiragana* and *katakana*, Japanese phonetic characters, even if you can't understand them. And any time spent learning Japanese will be amply rewarded by delighted locals, who'll always politely comment on your fine linguistic ability.

That said, it does take a very great effort to master Japanese. The primary stumbling block is the thousands of **kanji** characters (Chinese ideograms) that need to be memorized, most of which have at least two pronunciations, depending on the sentence and their combination with other characters. Also tricky is the language's multiple levels of **politeness**, married with different sets of words used by men and women, as well as different **dialects** to deal with, involving whole new vocabularies.

Japanese characters

Japanese is written in a combination of three systems. To be able to read a newspaper, you'll need to know around two thousand *kanji*, much more difficult than it sounds, since what each one means varies with its context.

The easier writing systems to pick up are the phonetic syllabaries, **hiragana** and **katakana**. Both have 46 regular characters (see box, p.822) and can be learned within a couple of weeks. *Hiragana* is used for Japanese words, while *katakana*, with the squarer characters, is used mainly for "loan words" borrowed from other languages (especially English) and technical names. **Rōmaji** (see p.823), the roman script used to spell out Japanese words, is also used in advertisements and magazines.

The first five letters in *hiragana* and *katakana* (**a**, **i**, **u**, **e**, **o**) are the vowel sounds (see Pronunciation, p.823). The remainder are a combination of a consonant and a vowel (eg **ka**, **ki**, **ku**, **ke**, **ko**), with the exception of **n**, the only consonant that exists on its own. While *hiragana* provides an exact phonetic reading of all Japanese words, *katakana* does not do the same for foreign loan words. Often words are abbreviated, hence television becomes *terebi* and sexual harassment *sekuhara*. Sometimes, they become almost unrecognizable, as with *kakuteru* (cocktail).

Traditionally, Japanese is written in vertical columns and read right to left. However, the Western way of writing from left to right, horizontally from top to bottom is increasingly common. In the media and on signs you'll see a mixture of the two ways of writing.

Hiragana and Katakana

Hiragana and *katakana* are two phonetic syllabaries represented by the characters shown below. *Katakana*, the squarer characters in the first table, are used for writing foreign "loan words". The rounder characters in the bottom table, *hiragana*, are used for Japanese words, in combination with, or as substitutes for, *kanji*.

Katakana

a	ア	i	イ	u	ウ	e	エ	o	オ
ka	カ	ki	キ	ku	ク	ke	ケ	ko	コ
sa	サ	shi	シ	su	ス	se	セ	so	ソ
ta	タ	chi	チ	tsu	ツ	te	テ	to	ト
na	ナ	ni	ニ	nu	ヌ	ne	ネ	no	ノ
ha	ハ	hi	ヒ	fu	フ	he	ヘ	ho	ホ
ma	マ	mi	ミ	mu	ム	me	メ	mo	モ
ya	ヤ			yu	ユ			yo	ヨ
ra	ラ	ri	リ	ru	ル	re	レ	ro	ロ
wa	ワ							wo	ヲ
n	ン								

Hiragana

a	あ	i	い	u	う	e	え	o	お
ka	か	ki	き	ku	く	ke	け	ko	こ
sa	さ	shi	し	su	す	se	せ	so	そ
ta	た	chi	ち	tsu	つ	te	て	to	と
na	な	ni	に	nu	ぬ	ne	ね	no	の
ha	は	hi	ひ	fu	ふ	he	へ	ho	ほ
ma	ま	mi	み	mu	む	me	め	mo	も
ya	や			yu	ゆ			yo	よ
ra	ら	ri	り	ru	る	re	れ	ro	ろ
wa	わ							wo	を
n	ん								

Grammar

In Japanese **verbs** do not change according to the person or number, so that *ikimasu* can mean "I go", "he/she/it goes", or "we/they go". **Pronouns** are usually omitted, since it's generally clear from the context who or what the speaker is referring to. There are no **definite articles**, and **nouns** stay the same whether they refer to singular or plural words.

Compared to English grammar, Japanese **sentences** are structured back to front. An English-speaker would say "I am going to Tokyo" which in Japanese would translate directly as "Tokyo to going". Placing the sound "*ka*" at the end of a verb indicates a **question**, hence *Tokyo e ikimasu-ka* means "Are you going to Tokyo?" There are also levels of **politeness** to contend with, which alter the way the verb is conjugated, and sometimes change the word entirely. Stick to the polite *-masu* form of verbs and you should be fine.

Japanese: A Rough Guide Phrasebook includes essential phrases and expressions and a dictionary section and menu reader. The phonetic translations in this phrasebook are rendered slightly differently from the standard way *rōmaji* is written in this book, as an aid to pronunciation.

Pronunciation

Japanese words in this book have been transliterated into the standard Hepburn system of romanization, called **rōmaji**. Pronunciation is as follows:

a as in r**a**ther
i as in macaron**i**, or **ee**
u as in p**u**t, or **oo**
e as in b**e**d; e is always pronounced, even at the end of a word
o as in n**o**t
ae as in the two separate sounds, **ah-eh**
ai as in Th**ai**
ei as in w**ei**ght
ie as in two separate sounds, **ee-eh**
ue as in two separate sounds, **oo-eh**
g, a hard sound as in **g**irl
s as in ma**ss** (never z)
y as in **y**et

A bar (macron) over a vowel or "ii" means that the vowel sound is twice as long as a vowel without a bar. Only where words are well known in English, such as Tokyo, Kyoto, judo and shogun, have we not used a bar to indicate long vowel sounds. Sometimes, vowel sounds are shortened or softened; for example, the verb *desu* sounds more like *des* when pronounced, and *sukiyaki* like *skiyaki*. Some syllables are also softened or hardened by the addition of a small ° or " above the character; for example, **ka** (か) becomes **ga** (が) and **ba** (ば) becomes **pa** (ぱ). Likewise a smaller case ya, yu or yo following a character alters its sound, such as **kya** (きゃ) and **kyu** (きゅ). All syllables are evenly stressed and pronounced in full. For example, Nagano is Na-ga-no, not Na-GA-no.

Useful words and phrases

Basics

Yes	hai	はい
No	iie/chigaimasu	いいえ／違います
OK	daijōbu/ōkē	大丈夫／オーケー
Please (offering something)	dōzo	どうぞ
Please (asking for something)	onegai shimasu	お願いします
Excuse me	sumimasen/shitsurei shimasu	すみません／失礼します
I'm sorry	gomen nasai/sumimasen	ごめんなさい／すみません
Thanks (informal)	dōmo	どうも
Thank you	arigatō	ありがとう
Thank you very much	dōmo arigatō gozaimasu	どうもありがとうございます
What?	nani?	なに

Japanese script in the guide

To help you find your way around, in the guide we've included **Japanese script** for all places covered, as well as sights, hotels, restaurants, cafés, bars and shops where there is no prominent English sign. Where the English name for a point of interest is very different from its Japanese name, we've also provided the *rōmaji* (see above), so you can pronounce the Japanese.

When?	itsu?	いつ
Where?	doko?	どこ
Who?	dare?	だれ
This	kore	これ
That	sore	それ
That (over there)	are	あれ
How many?	ikutsu?	いくつ
How much?	ikura?	いくら
I want (x)	Watashi wa (x) ga hoshii desu	私は(x)が欲しいです
I don't want (x)	Watashi wa (x) ga irimasen	私は(x)がいりません
Is it possible...?	...koto ga dekimasu ka	｡｡｡ことができますか
It is not possible	...koto ga dekimasen	｡｡｡ことができません
Is it...?	...desu ka	｡｡｡ですか
Can you please help me?	Tetsudatte kuremasen ka	手伝ってくれませんか
I don't speak Japanese	Nihongo wa hanashimasen	日本語は話せません
I don't read Japanese	Nihongo wa yomimasen	日本語は読めません
Can you speak English?	Eigo ga dekimasu ka	英語ができますか
Is there someone who can interpret?	Tsūyaku wa imasu ka	通訳はいますか
Could you please speak more slowly?	Motto yukkuri hanashite kuremasen ka	もっとゆっくり話してくれませんか
Please say that again	Mō ichido itte kuremasen ka	もう一度言ってくれませんか
I understand/I see	Wakarimasu/Naruhodo	わかります／なるほど
I don't understand	Wakarimasen	わかりません
What does this mean?	Kore wa dōiu imi desu ka	これはどういう意味ですか
How do you say (x) in Japanese?	Nihongo de (x) o nan-te yiimasu ka	日本語で(x)を何て言いますか
What's this called?	Kore wa nan-to iimasu ka	これは何と言いますか
How do you pronounce this character?	Kono kanji wa nan-te yomimasu ka	この漢字は何て読みますか
Please write in English/Japanese	Eigo/Nihongo de kaite kudasai	英語／日本語で書いてください

Personal pronouns

I	watashi	私
I (familiar, men only)	boku	ぼく
You	anata	あなた
You (familiar)	kimi	きみ
He	kare	彼
She	kanojo	彼女
We	watashi-tachi	私たち
You (plural)	anata-tachi	あなたたち
They (male/female)	karera/kanojo-tachi	彼ら／彼女たち
They (objects)	sorera	それら

Greetings and basic courtesies

Hello/Good day	Konnichiwa	今日は
Good morning	Ohayō gozaimasu	おはようございます
Good evening	Konbanwa	今晩は
Good night (when leaving)	Osaki ni	お先に
Good night (when going to bed)	Oyasuminasai	おやすみなさい
How are you?	O-genki desu ka	お元気ですか
I'm fine (informal)	Genki desu	元気です
I'm fine, thanks	Okagesama de	おかげさまで
How do you do/Nice to meet you	Hajimemashite	はじめまして
Don't mention it /You're welcome	Dō itashimashite	どういたしまして
I'm sorry	Gomen nasai	ごめんなさい
Just a minute please	Chotto matte kudasai	ちょっと待ってください
Goodbye	Sayonara	さよなら
Goodbye (informal)	Dewa mata/Jā ne	では又／じゃあね

Chitchat

What's your name?	Shitsurei desu ga o-namae wa	失礼ですがお名前は
My name is (x)	Watashi no namae wa (x) desu	私の名前は(x)
Where are you from?	O-kuni wa doko desu ka	お国はどこですか
Britain	Eikoku/Igirisu	イギリス
Ireland	Airurando	アイルランド
America	Amerika	アメリカ
Australia	Ōsutoraria	オーストラリア
Canada	Kanada	カナダ
France	Furansu	フランス
Germany	Doitsu	ドイツ
New Zealand	Nyū Jiirando	ニュージーランド
Japan	Nihon	日本
Outside Japan	Gaikoku	外国
How old are you?	O-ikutsu desu ka	おいくつですか
I am (age)	(age) sai desu	(age) 才です
Are you married?	Kekkon shite imasu ka	結婚していますか
I am married/not married	Kekkon shite imasu/imasen	結婚しています／いません
Do you like...?	...suki desu ka	...好きですか
I do like	...suki desu	...好きです
I don't like	...suki dewa arimasen	...好きではありません
What's your job?	O-shigoto wa nan desu ka	お仕事は何ですか
I'm a student	Gakusei desu	学生です
I'm a teacher	Sensei desu	先生です

I work for a company	Kaishain desu	会社員です
I'm a tourist	Kankō kyaku desu	観光客です
Really?	Hontō	本当
That's a shame	Zannen desu	残念です
It can't be helped (informal)	Shikata ga nai/shō ga nai	仕方がない／しょうがない

Numbers

There are special ways of **counting** different things in Japanese. The most common first translation is used when counting time and quantities and measurements, with added qualifiers such as minutes (*pun/fun*) or yen (*en*). The second translations are sometimes used for counting objects. From ten, there is only one set of numbers. For four, seven and nine, alternatives to the first translation are used in some circumstances.

Zero	zero			0
One	ichi	hitotsu	一	ひとつ
Two	ni	futatsu	二	ふたつ
Three	san	mittsu	三	みっつ
Four	yon/shi	yottsu	四	よっつ
Five	go	itsutsu	五	いつつ
Six	roku	muttsu	六	むっつ
Seven	shichi/nana	nanatsu	七	ななつ
Eight	hachi	yattsu	八	やっつ
Nine	ku/kyū	kokonotsu	九	ここのつ
Ten	jū	tō	十	とう
Eleven	jū-ichi		十一	
Twelve	jū-ni		十二	
Twenty	ni-jū		二十	
Twenty-one	ni-jū-ichi		二十一	
Thirty	san-jū		三十	
One hundred	hyaku		百	
Two hundred	ni-hyaku		二百	
Thousand	sen		千	
Ten thousand	ichi-man		一万	
One hundred thousand	jū-man		十万	
One million	hyaku-man		百万	
One hundred million	ichi-oku		一億	

Time and dates

Now	ima	今
Today	kyō	今日
Morning	asa	朝
Evening	yūgata	夕方
Night	yoru	夜
Tomorrow	ashita	明日
The day after tomorrow	asatte	あさって

Yesterday	kinō	昨日
Week	shū	週
Month	gatsu	月
Year	nen/toshi	年
Monday	Getsuyōbi	月曜日
Tuesday	Kayōbi	火曜日
Wednesday	Suiyōbi	水曜日
Thursday	Mokuyōbi	木曜日
Friday	Kin'yōbi	金曜日
Saturday	Doyōbi	土曜日
Sunday	Nichiyōbi	日曜日
What time is it?	Ima nan-ji desu ka	今何時ですか
It's 10 o'clock	Jū-ji desu	十時です
...10.20	Jū-ji ni-juppun	十時二十分
...10.30	Jū-ji han	十時半
10.50	Jū-ichi-ji juppun mae	十一時十分前
AM	gozen	午前
PM	gogo	午後
January	Ichigatsu	一月
February	Nigatsu	二月
March	Sangatsu	三月
April	Shigatsu	四月
May	Gogatsu	五月
June	Rokugatsu	六月
July	Shichigatsu	七月
August	Hachigatsu	八月
September	Kugatsu	九月
October	Jūgatsu	十月
November	Jūichigatsu	十一月
December	Jūnigatsu	十二月
1st (day)	tsuitachi	一日
2nd (day)	futsuka	二日
3rd (day)	mikka	三日
4th (day)	yokka	四日
5th (day)	itsuka	五日
6th (day)	muika	六日
7th (day)	nanoka	七日
8th (day)	yōka	八日
9th (day)	kokonoka	九日
10th (day)	tōka	十日
11th (day)	jū-ichi-nichi	十一日
12th (day)	jū-ni-nichi	十二日
20th (day)	hatsuka	二十日

21st (day)	ni-jū-ichi nichi	二十一日
30th (day)	san-jū-nichi	三十日

Getting around

Aeroplane	hikōki	飛行機
Airport	kūkō	空港
Bus	basu	バス
Long-distance bus	chōkyori basu	長距離バス
Bus stop	basu tei	バス停
Train	densha	電車
Station	eki	駅
Subway	chikatetsu	地下鉄
Ferry	ferii	フェリー
Left-luggage office	ichiji azukarijo	一時預かり所
Coin locker	koin rokkā	コインロッカー
Ticket office	kippu uriba	切符売り場
Ticket	kippu	切符
One-way	kata-michi	片道
Return	ōfuku	往復
Non-smoking seat	kin'en seki	禁煙席
Window seat	mado-gawa no seki	窓側の席
Platform	hōmu	ホーム
Bicycle	jitensha	自転車
Taxi	takushii	タクシー
Map	chizu	地図
Where is (x)?	(x) wa doko desu ka	(x)はどこですか
Straight ahead	massugu	まっすぐ
In front of	mae	前
Right	migi	右
Left	hidari	左
North	kita	北
South	minami	南
East	higashi	東
West	nishi	西
Entrance	iriguchi	入口
Exit	deguchi/-guchi	出口／–口
Highway	kaidō	街道
Street	tōri/dōri/michi	通り／道

Places

Temple	otera/-dera/-ji/-in	お寺／–寺／–院
Shrine	jinja/jingū/-gū/-taisha	神社／神宮／–宮／–大社
Castle	-jō	城
Park	kōen	公園
River	kawa/gawa	川

Bridge	hashi/bashi	橋
Museum	hakubutsukan	博物館
Art gallery	bijutsukan	美術館
Garden	niwa/teien/-en	庭／庭園／−園
Island	shima/-jima/-tō	島
Slope	saka/-zaka	坂
Hill	oka	丘
Mountain	yama/-san/-take	山／岳
Hot spring spa	onsen	温泉
Lake	-ko	湖
Bay	-wan	湾
Peninsula	hantō	半島
Cape	misaki/saki	岬
Sea	umi/kai/nada	海／灘
Gorge	kyō	峡
Plateau	kōgen	高原
Prefecture	-ken/-fu	県／府
Ward	-ku	区
Shop	mise/-ten/-ya	店／屋

Accommodation

Hotel	hoteru	ホテル
Traditional-style inn	ryokan	旅館
Guesthouse	minshuku	民宿
Youth hostel	yūsu hosuteru	ユースホステル
Single room	shinguru rūmu	シングルルーム
Double room	daburu rūmu	ダブルルーム
Twin room	tsuin rūmu	ツインルーム
Dormitory	kyōdō/ōbeya	共同／大部屋
Japanese-style room	washitsu	和室
Western-style room	yōshitsu	洋室
Western-style bed	beddo	ベッド
Bath	o-furo	お風呂

Do you have any vacancies?	Kūshitsu wa arimasu ka	空室はありますか
I'd like to make a reservation	Yoyaku o shitai no desu ga	予約をしたいのですが
I have a reservation	Yoyaku shimashita	予約しました
I don't have a reservation	Yoyaku shimasen deshita	予約しませんでした
How much is it per person?	Hitori ikura desu ka	一人いくらですか
Does that include meals?	Shokuji wa tsuite imasu ka	食事はついていますか
I would like to stay one night/two nights	Hitoban/futaban tomaritai no desu ga	一晩／二晩泊まりたいのですが
I would like to see the room	Heya o misete kudasaimasen ka	部屋を見せてくださいませんか
Key	kagi	鍵
Passport	pasupōto	パスポート

Shopping, money and banks

Shop	mise/-ten/-ya	店／屋
How much is it?	Kore wa ikura desu ka	これはいくらですか
It's too expensive	Taka-sugimasu	高すぎます
Is there anything cheaper?	Mō sukoshi yasui mono wa arimasu ka	もう少し安いものはありますか
Do you accept credit cards?	Kurejitto kādo wa tsukaemasu ka	クレジットカードは使えますか
I'm just looking	Miru dake desu	見るだけです
Gift/souvenir	omiyage	お土産
Foreign exchange	gaikoku-kawase	外国為替
Bank	ginkō	銀行
Travellers' cheque	toraberāzu chekku	トラベラーズチェック

Internet, post and telephones

Internet	intāneto	インターネット
Post office	yūbinkyoku	郵便局
Envelope	fūtō	封筒
Letter	tegami	手紙
Postcard	hagaki	葉書
Stamp	kitte	切手
Airmail	kōkūbin	航空便
Surface mail	sarubin	サル便
Sea mail	funabin	船便
Telephone	denwa	電話
International telephone call	kokusai-denwa	国際電話
Reverse charge/collect call	korekuto-kōru	コレクトコール
Mobile phone	keitai-denwa	携帯電話
Fax	fakkusu	ファックス
Telephone card	terefon kādo	テレフォンカード
I would like to call (place)	(place) e denwa o kaketai no desu	(place) へ電話をかけたいのです
I would like to send a fax to (place)	(place) e fakkusu shitai no desu	(place) へファックスしたいのです

Health

Hospital	byōin	病院
Pharmacy	yakkyoku	薬局
Medicine	kusuri	薬
Doctor	isha	医者
Dentist	haisha	歯医者
Diarrhoea	geri	下痢
Fever	netsu	熱
Food poisoning	shoku chūdoku	食中毒
I'm ill	byōki desu	病気です
I've got a cold/flu	kaze o hikimashita	風邪を引きました
I'm allergic to (x)	(x) arerugii desu	(x) アレルギーです

Antibiotics	kōsei busshitsu	抗生物質
Antiseptic	shōdoku	消毒

Food and drink

Places to eat and drink

Bar	nomiya	飲み屋
Standing-only bar	tachinomiya	立ちのみ屋
Café/coffee shop	kissaten	喫茶店
Cafeteria	shokudō	食堂
Pub	pabu	パブ
Pub-style restaurant	izakaya	居酒屋
Restaurant	resutoran	レストラン
Restaurant specializing in charcoal-grilled foods	robatayaki	炉端焼
Street food stall	yatai	屋台

Ordering

Breakfast	asa-gohan	朝ご飯
Lunch	hiru-gohan	昼ご飯
Dinner	ban-gohan	晩ご飯
Boxed meal	bentō	弁当
Chopsticks	hashi	はし
Fork	fōku	フォーク
Knife	naifu	ナイフ
Spoon	supūn	スプーン
Set meal	teishoku	定食
Daily special set meal	higawari-teishoku	日替り定食
Menu	menyū	メニュー
Do you have an English menu?	eigo no menyū arimasu ka	英語のメニューありますか
How much is that?	ikura desu ka	いくらですか
I would like (a)…	(a) …o onegai shimasu	(a)をお願いします
May I have the bill?	okanjō o onegai shimasu	お勘定をお願いします

Staple foods

abura	oil	油
batā	butter	バター
gohan	rice	ご飯
koshō	pepper	こしょう
miso	fermented soyabean paste	味噌
ninniku	garlic	にんにく
nori	dried seaweed	のり
pan	bread	パン
satō	sugar	砂糖
shio	salt	塩

shōyu	soy sauce	しょうゆ
tamago	egg	卵
tōfu	bean curd tofu	豆腐

Fish and seafood dishes

aji	horse mackerel	あじ
awabi	abalone	あわび
ayu	sweet smelt	あゆ
buri	yellowtail	ぶり
chirashi-zushi	sushi topped with fish, egg and vegetables	ちらし寿司
ebi	prawn	えび
fugu	blowfish	ふぐ
ika	squid	いか
ise-ebi	lobster	伊勢海老
kai	shellfish	貝
kaki	oyster	かき
kani	crab	かに
maguro	tuna	まぐろ
maki-zushi	sushi rolled in crisp seaweed	まき寿司
nigiri-zushi	sushi mixed selection	にぎり寿司
nishin	herring	にしん
sakana	fish	魚
sashimi	raw fish	さしみ
sushi	sushi	寿司
tai	sea bream	たい
tako	octopus	たこ
tara	cod	たら
unagi	eel	うなぎ
uni	sea urchin	うに

Fruit

banana	banana	バナナ
budō	grapes	ぶどう
gurēpufurūtsu	grapefruit	グレープフルーツ
ichigo	strawberry	いちご
kaki	persimmon	柿
kudamono	fruit	果物
meron	melon	メロン
mikan	tangerine	みかん
momo	peach	桃
nashi	pear	なし
orenji	orange	オレンジ
painappuru	pineapple	パイナップル
remon	lemon	レモン
ringo	apple	りんご

suika	watermelon	すいか
ume	Japanese plum	うめ

Vegetables

daikon	radish	だいこん
karifurawā	cauliflower	カリフラワー
kinoko	mushroom	きのこ
kōn	sweetcorn	コーン
mame	beans	豆
moyashi	beansprouts	もやし
nasu	aubergine	なす
negi	leek	ねぎ
ninjin	carrot	にんじん
piiman	green pepper	ピーマン
poteto	potato	ポテト、じゃがいも
sarada	salad	サラダ
tamanegi	onion	たまねぎ
tomato	tomato	トマト
wasabi	green horseradish	わさび
yasai	vegetables	野菜

Meat and meat dishes

butaniku	pork	豚肉
gyūniku	beef	牛肉
kushiage	skewers of food dipped in breadcrumbs and deep-fried	串揚げ
nabe	stew including meat (or seafood), vegetables and noodles	鍋
niku	meat	肉
ramu	lamb	ラム
shabu-shabu	thin beef slices cooked in broth	しゃぶしゃぶ
sukiyaki	thin beef slices braised in a sauce	すきやき
tonkatsu	breaded, deep-fried slice of pork	とんかつ
toriniku	chicken	鶏肉
yakiniku	grilled meat	焼肉
yakitori	chicken, other meat and vegetables grilled on skewers	焼き鳥

Vegetarian and noodle dishes

gyōza	Chinese-style dumplings	ぎょうざ
kake-soba	soba in a hot soup	かけそば
oden	stewed chunks of vegetables and fish on skewers	おでん
rāmen	Chinese-style noodles	ラーメン
shōjin-ryōri	Buddhist-style vegetarian cuisine	精進料理
soba	thin buckwheat noodles	そば

udon	thick wheat noodles	うどん
yakisoba/udon	fried noodles	焼そば／うどん
zaru-soba/mori-soba	cold soba served with a dipping sauce	ざるそば／もりそば

Other dishes

chāhan	fried rice	チャーハン
Chūka-/Chūgoku-ryōri	Chinese food	中華／中国料理
donburi	rice topped with fish, meat or vegetable	どんぶり
Furansu-ryōri	French food	フランス料理
Itaria-ryōri	Italian food	イタリア料理
kaiseki-ryōri	Japanese haute cuisine	懐石料理
Kankoku-ryōri	Korean food	韓国料理
karē raisu	mild curry served with rice	カレーライス
mochi	pounded rice cakes	もち
mukokuseki-ryōri	"no-nationality" food	無国籍料理
nattō	pounded rice cakes	納豆
okonomiyaki	savoury pancakes	お好み焼き
onigiri	rice triangles wrapped in crisp seaweed	おにぎり
Tai-ryōri	Thai food	タイ料理
takoyaki	octopus in balls of batter	たこやき
tempura	lightly battered seafood and vegetables	天ぷら
teriyaki	meat, vegetable and fish cooked in soy sauce and sweet sake	照り焼き
washoku	Japanese-style food	和食
yōshoku	Western-style food	洋食

Drinks

biiru	beer	ビール
jūsu	fruit juice	ジュース
kōcha	black tea	紅茶
kōhii	coffee	コーヒー
macha	powdered green tea	抹茶
miruku	milk	ミルク
mizu	water	水
mizu-wari	whisky and water	水割り
sake/nihon-shu	sake (rice wine)	酒／日本酒
sencha	green tea	煎茶
shōchū	distilled liquor	焼酎
uisukii	whisky	ウイスキー
ūron-cha	Oolong tea	ウーロン茶
wain	wine	ワイン

Glossary

aikido A form of self-defence recognized as a sport.

ANA All Nippon Airways.

anime Japanese animation.

banzai Traditional cheer, meaning "10,000 years".

Bashō Sumo tournament.

Benten or **Benzai-ten** One of the most popular folk-goddesses, usually associated with water.

bodhisattva or **bosatsu** A Buddhist intermediary who has forsaken nirvana to work for the salvation of all humanity.

bunraku Traditional puppet theatre.

Butō or **Butoh** Highly expressive contemporary performance art.

cha-no-yu, **chadō** or **sadō** The tea ceremony. Ritual tea drinking raised to an art form.

-chō or **-machi** Subdivision of a city, smaller than a -ku.

-chōme Area of the city consisting of a few blocks.

daimyō Feudal lords.

Dainichi Nyorai or **Rushana Butsu** The Cosmic Buddha in whom all Buddhas are unified.

-dake Mountain peak, usually volcanic.

donjon Castle keep.

DPJ Democratic Party of Japan.

Edo Pre-1868 name for Tokyo.

ema Small wooden boards found at shrines, on which people write their wishes or thanks.

fusuma Paper-covered sliding doors, more substantial than shōji, used to separate rooms or for cupboards.

futon Padded quilt used for bedding.

gagaku Traditional Japanese music used for court ceremonies and religious rites.

gaijin Foreigner.

geisha Traditional female entertainer accomplished in the arts.

genkan Foyer or entrance hall of a house, ryokan and so forth, for changing from outdoor shoes into slippers.

genki Friendly, lively and/or healthy.

geta Traditional wooden sandals.

haiku Seventeen-syllable verse form, arranged in three lines of five, seven and five syllables.

hanami "Flower-viewing"; most commonly associated with spring outings to admire the cherry blossom.

-hashi or **-bashi** Bridge.

hiragana Phonetic script used for writing Japanese in combination with kanji.

ijinkan Western-style brick and clapboard houses.

ikebana Traditional art of flower arranging.

Inari Shinto god of harvests, often represented by his fox-messenger.

JAL Japan Airlines.

-ji Buddhist temple.

jigoku The word for Buddhist "hell", also applied to volcanic mud pools and steam vents.

-jinja or **-jingū** Shinto shrine.

Jizō Buddhist protector of children, travellers and the dead.

JNTO Japan National Tourist Organization.

-jō Castle.

JR Japan Railways.

kabuki Popular theatre of the Edo period.

kami Shinto deities residing in trees, rocks and other natural phenomena.

kamikaze The "Divine Wind" which saved Japan from the Mongol invaders (see p.769). During World War II the name was applied to Japan's suicide bombers.

kanji Japanese script derived from Chinese characters.

Kannon Buddhist goddess of mercy. A bodhisattva who appears in many different forms.

katakana Phonetic script used mainly for writing foreign words in Japanese.

-kawa or **-gawa** River.

-ken Prefecture. The principal administrative region, similar to a state or county.

kendo Japan's oldest martial art, using wooden staves, with its roots in samurai training exercises.

kimono Literally "clothes", though usually referring to women's traditional dress.

-ko Lake.

kōban Neighbourhood police box.

kōen or **gyoen** Public park.

Kōgen Plateau.

-ku Principal administrative division of the city, usually translated as "ward".

kura Traditional storehouse built with thick mud walls as protection against fire, for keeping produce and family treasures.

kyōgen Short, satirical plays, providing comic interludes in nō drama.

LDP Liberal Democratic Party.

-machi Town or area of a city.

maiko Apprentice geisha.

manga Japanese comics.

macha Powdered green tea used in the tea ceremony.

matsuri Festival.

Meiji Period named after Emperor Meiji (1868–1912), meaning "enlightened rule".

Meiji Restoration End of the Tokugawa Shogunate, when power was fully restored to the emperor.

mikoshi Portable shrine used in festivals.

minshuku Family-run lodgings which are cheaper than ryokan.

mon Gate, usually to a castle, temple or palace.

mura Village.

netsuke Small, intricately carved toggles for fastening the cords of cloth bags.

ningyō Japanese doll.

nō Highly stylized dance-drama, using masks and elaborate costumes.

noren Split curtain hanging in shop and restaurant doorways to indicate they're open.

notemburo Outdoor hot-spring pool, usually in natural surroundings.

obi Wide sash worn with kimono.

odori Traditional dances performed in the streets during the summer Obon festival.

onsen Hot spring, generally developed for bathing.

pachinko Vertical pinball machines.

pond-garden Classic form of garden design focused around a pond.

rōmaji System of transliterating Japanese words using the roman alphabet.

rōnin Masterless samurai.

rotemburo Outdoor hot-spring pool, often in the grounds of a ryokan.

ryokan Traditional Japanese inn.

salarymen Office-workers who keep Japan's companies and ministries ticking over.

samurai Warrior class who were retainers of the *daimyō*.

SDF (Self-Defence Forces) Japan's army, navy and airforce.

sensei Teacher.

sentō Neighbourhood public bath.

seppuku Ritual suicide by disembowelment, also referred to as *harakiri*.

Shaka Nyorai The Historical Buddha, Sakyamuni.

shamisen Traditional, three-stringed instrument played with a plectrum.

-shima or **-jima** Island.

Shinkansen Bullet train.

Shinto Japan's indigenous animist religion.

Shitamachi Old working-class districts of east Tokyo.

shogun Japan's military rulers before 1868, nominally subordinate to the emperor.

shōji Paper-covered sliding screens used to divide rooms or cover windows.

shukubō Temple lodgings.

sumi-e Ink paintings, traditionally using black ink.

sumo A form of heavyweight wrestling which evolved from ancient Shinto divination rites.

taiko Drums.

tatami Rice-straw matting, the traditional covering for floors.

tokonoma Alcove in a room where flowers or a scroll are displayed.

torii Gate to a Shinto shrine.

ukiyo-e Colourful woodblock prints.

waka Thirty-one-syllable poem, arranged in five lines of five, seven, five, seven and seven syllables.

washi Traditional handmade paper.

Yakushi Nyorai The Buddha in charge of physical and spiritual healing.

yakuza Professional criminal gangs, somewhat akin to the Mafia.

yamabushi Ascetic mountain priests.

yokuzuna Champion sumo wrestler.

yukata Loose cotton dressing gown.

Travel store

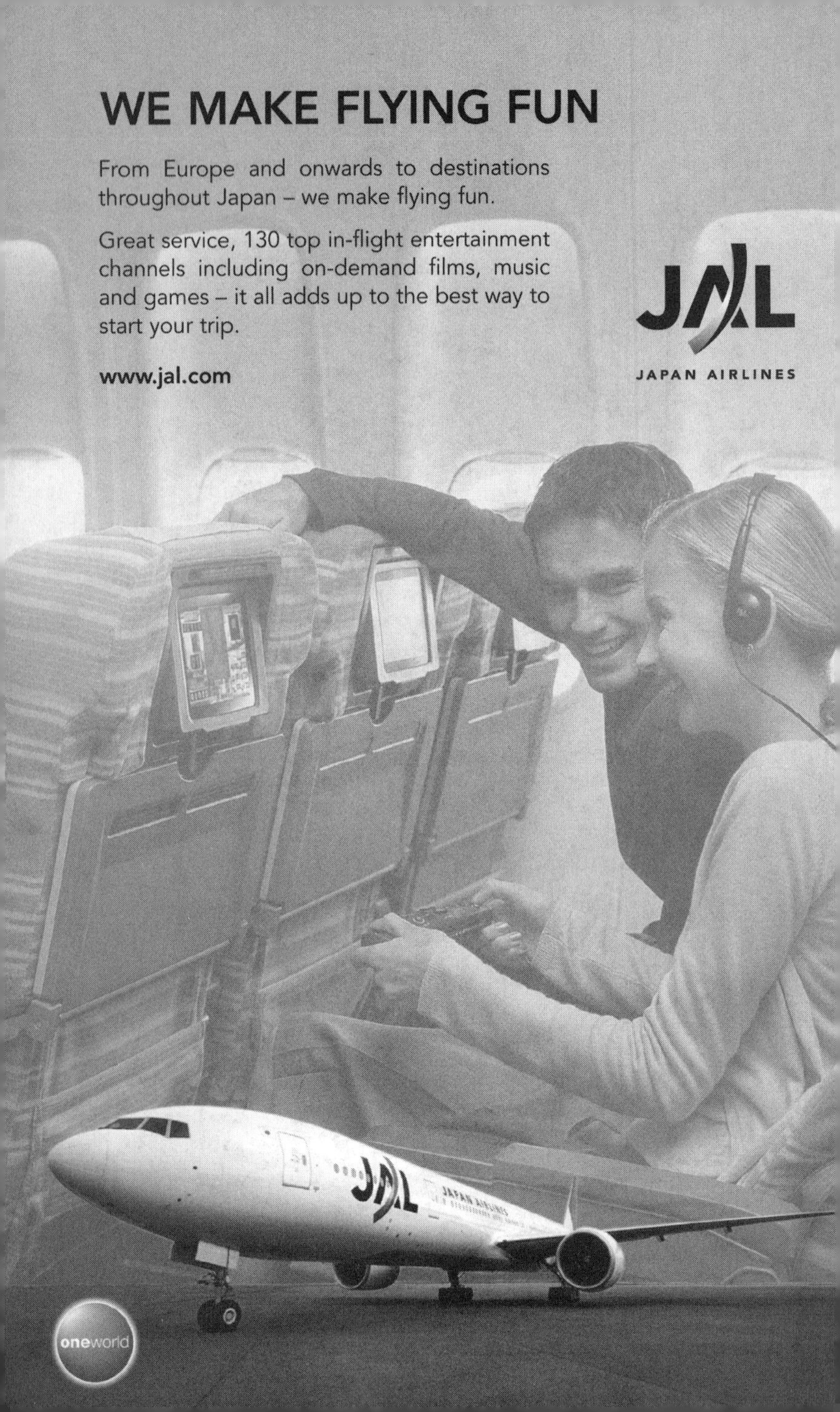
WE MAKE FLYING FUN
From Europe and onwards to destinations throughout Japan – we make flying fun.
Great service, 130 top in-flight entertainment channels including on-demand films, music and games – it all adds up to the best way to start your trip.
www.jal.com
JAL
JAPAN AIRLINES
oneworld

ROUGH GUIDES World Coverage

Travel

Andorra The Pyrenees, Pyrenees & Andorra Map, Spain
Antigua The Caribbean
Argentina Argentina, Argentina Map, Buenos Aires, South America on a Budget
Aruba The Caribbean
Australia Australia, Australia Map, East Coast Australia, Melbourne, Sydney, Tasmania
Austria Austria, Europe on a Budget, Vienna
Bahamas The Bahamas, The Caribbean
Barbados Barbados DIR, The Caribbean
Belgium Belgium & Luxembourg, Bruges DIR, Brussels, Brussels Map, Europe on a Budget
Belize Belize, Central America on a Budget, Guatemala & Belize Map
Benin West Africa
Bolivia Bolivia, South America on a Budget
Brazil Brazil, Rio, South America on a Budget
British Virgin Islands The Caribbean
Brunei Malaysia, Singapore & Brunei [1 title], Southeast Asia on a Budget
Bulgaria Bulgaria, Europe on a Budget
Burkina Faso West Africa
Cambodia Cambodia, Southeast Asia on a Budget, Vietnam, Laos & Cambodia Map [1 Map]
Cameroon West Africa
Canada Canada, Pacific Northwest, Toronto, Toronto Map, Vancouver
Cape Verde West Africa
Cayman Islands The Caribbean
Chile Chile, Chile Map, South America on a Budget
China Beijing, China, Hong Kong & Macau, Hong Kong & Macau DIR, Shanghai
Colombia South America on a Budget
Costa Rica Central America on a Budget, Costa Rica, Costa Rica & Panama Map
Croatia Croatia, Croatia Map, Europe on a Budget
Cuba Cuba, Cuba Map, The Caribbean, Havana
Cyprus Cyprus, Cyprus Map
Czech Republic The Czech Republic, Czech & Slovak Republics, Europe on a Budget, Prague, Prague DIR, Prague Map
Denmark Copenhagen, Denmark, Europe on a Budget, Scandinavia
Dominica The Caribbean
Dominican Republic Dominican Republic, The Caribbean
Ecuador Ecuador, South America on a Budget
Egypt Egypt, Egypt Map
El Salvador Central America on a Budget
England Britain, Camping in Britain, Devon & Cornwall, Dorset, Hampshire and The Isle of Wight [1 title], England, Europe on a Budget, The Lake District, London, London DIR, London Map, London Mini Guide, Walks In London & Southeast England
Estonia The Baltic States, Europe on a Budget
Fiji Fiji
Finland Europe on a Budget, Finland, Scandinavia
France Brittany & Normandy, Corsica, Corsica Map, The Dordogne & the Lot, Europe on a Budget, France, France Map, Languedoc & Roussillon, The Loire, Paris, Paris DIR, Paris Map, Paris Mini Guide, Provence & the Côte d'Azur, The Pyrenees, Pyrenees & Andorra Map
French Guiana South America on a Budget
Gambia The Gambia, West Africa
Germany Berlin, Berlin Map, Europe on a Budget, Germany, Germany Map
Ghana West Africa
Gibraltar Spain
Greece Athens Map, Crete, Crete Map, Europe on a Budget, Greece, Greece Map, Greek Islands, Ionian Islands
Guadeloupe The Caribbean
Guatemala Central America on a Budget, Guatemala, Guatemala & Belize Map
Guinea West Africa
Guinea-Bissau West Africa
Guyana South America on a Budget
Holland see The Netherlands
Honduras Central America on a Budget
Hungary Budapest, Europe on a Budget, Hungary
Iceland Iceland, Iceland Map
India Goa, India, India Map, Kerala, Rajasthan, Delhi & Agra [1 title], South India, South India Map
Indonesia Bali & Lombok, Southeast Asia on a Budget
Ireland Dublin DIR, Dublin Map, Europe on a Budget, Ireland, Ireland Map
Israel Jerusalem
Italy Europe on a Budget, Florence DIR, Florence & Siena Map, Florence & the best of Tuscany, Italy, The Italian Lakes, Naples & the Amalfi Coast, Rome, Rome DIR, Rome Map, Sardinia, Sicily, Sicily Map, Tuscany & Umbria, Tuscany Map, Venice, Venice DIR, Venice Map
Jamaica Jamaica, The Caribbean
Japan Japan, Tokyo
Jordan Jordan
Kenya Kenya, Kenya Map
Korea Korea
Laos Laos, Southeast Asia on a Budget, Vietnam, Laos & Cambodia Map [1 Map]
Latvia The Baltic States, Europe on a Budget
Lithuania The Baltic States, Europe on a Budget
Luxembourg Belgium & Luxembourg, Europe on a Budget
Malaysia Malaysia Map, Malaysia, Singapore & Brunei [1 title], Southeast Asia on a Budget
Mali West Africa
Malta Malta & Gozo DIR
Martinique The Caribbean
Mauritania West Africa
Mexico Baja California, Baja California, Cancún & Cozumel DIR, Mexico, Mexico Map, Yucatán, Yucatán Peninsula Map
Monaco France, Provence & the Côte d'Azur
Montenegro Montenegro
Morocco Europe on a Budget, Marrakesh DIR, Marrakesh Map, Morocco, Morocco Map,
Nepal Nepal
Netherlands Amsterdam, Amsterdam DIR, Amsterdam Map, Europe on a Budget, The Netherlands
Netherlands Antilles The Caribbean
New Zealand New Zealand, New Zealand Map

DIR: Rough Guide **DIRECTIONS** for short breaks

Nicaragua Central America on a Budget
Niger West Africa
Nigeria West Africa
Norway Europe on a Budget, Norway, Scandinavia
Panama Central America on a Budget, Costa Rica & Panama Map, Panama
Paraguay South America on a Budget
Peru Peru, Peru Map, South America on a Budget
Philippines The Philippines, Southeast Asia on a Budget,
Poland Europe on a Budget, Poland
Portugal Algarve DIR, The Algarve Map, Europe on a Budget, Lisbon DIR, Lisbon Map, Madeira DIR, Portugal, Portugal Map, Spain & Portugal Map
Puerto Rico The Caribbean, Puerto Rico
Romania Europe on a Budget, Romania
Russia Europe on a Budget, Moscow, St Petersburg
St Kitts & Nevis The Caribbean
St Lucia The Caribbean
St Vincent & the Grenadines The Caribbean
Scotland Britain, Camping in Britain, Edinburgh DIR, Europe on a Budget, Scotland, Scottish Highlands & Islands
Senegal West Africa
Serbia Montenegro Europe on a Budget
Sierra Leone West Africa
Singapore Malaysia, Singapore & Brunei [1 title], Singapore, Singapore DIR, Southeast Asia on a Budget
Slovakia Czech & Slovak Republics, Europe on a Budget
Slovenia Europe on a Budget, Slovenia
South Africa Cape Town & the Garden Route, South Africa, South Africa Map
Spain Andalucía, Andalucía Map, Barcelona, Barcelona DIR, Barcelona Map, Europe on a Budget, Ibiza & Formentera DIR, Gran Canaria DIR, Madrid DIR, Lanzarote & Fuerteventura DIR Madrid Map, Mallorca & Menorca, Mallorca DIR, Mallorca Map, The Pyrenees, Pyrenees & Andorra Map, Spain, Spain & Portugal Map, Tenerife & La Gomera DIR
Sri Lanka Sri Lanka, Sri Lanka Map
Suriname South America on a Budget
Sweden Europe on a Budget, Scandinavia, Sweden
Switzerland Europe on a Budget, Switzerland
Taiwan Taiwan
Tanzania Tanzania, Zanzibar
Thailand Bangkok, Southeast Asia on a Budget, Thailand, Thailand Map, Thailand Beaches & Islands
Togo West Africa
Trinidad & Tobago The Caribbean, Trinidad & Tobago
Tunisia Tunisia, Tunisia Map
Turkey Europe on a Budget, Istanbul, Turkey, Turkey Map
Turks and Caicos Islands The Bahamas, The Caribbean
United Arab Emirates Dubai DIR, Dubai & UAE Map [1 title]
United Kingdom Britain, Devon & Cornwall, Edinburgh DIR England, Europe on a Budget, The Lake District, London, London DIR, London Map, London Mini Guide, Scotland, Scottish Highlands & Islands, Wales, Walks In London & Southeast England
United States Alaska, Boston, California, California Map, Chicago, Colorado, Florida, Florida Map, The Grand Canyon, Hawaii, Los Angeles, Los Angeles Map, Los Angeles and Southern California, Maui DIR, Miami & South Florida, New England, New England Map, New Orleans & Cajun Country, New Orleans DIR, New York City, NYC DIR, NYC Map, New York City Mini Guide, Oregon & Washington, Orlando & Walt Disney World® DIR, San Francisco, San Francisco DIR, San Francisco Map, Seattle, Southwest USA, USA, Washington DC, Yellowstone & the Grand Tetons National Park, Yosemite National Park
Uruguay South America on a Budget
US Virgin Islands The Bahamas, The Caribbean
Venezuela South America on a Budget
Vietnam Southeast Asia on a Budget, Vietnam, Vietnam, Laos & Cambodia Map [1 Map],
Wales Britain, Camping in Britain, Europe on a Budget, Wales
First-Time Series FT Africa, FT Around the World, FT Asia, FT Europe, FT Latin America
Inspirational guides Earthbound, Clean Breaks, Make the Most of Your Time on Earth, Ultimate Adventures, World Party
Travel Specials Camping in Britain, Travel with Babies & Young Children, Walks in London & SE England

ROUGH GUIDES Don't Just Travel

Computers Cloud Computing, FWD this link, The Internet, iPhone, iPods & iTunes, Macs & OS X, Website Directory
Film & TV American Independent Film, British Cult Comedy, Comedy Movies, Cult Movies, Film, Film Musicals, Film Noir, Gangster Movies, Horror Movies, Sci-Fi Movies, Westerns
Lifestyle Babies & Toddlers, Brain Training, Food, Girl Stuff, Green Living, Happiness, Men's Health, Pregnancy & Birth, Running, Saving & Selling Online, Sex, Weddings
Music The Beatles, The Best Music You've Never Heard, Blues, Bob Dylan, Book of Playlists, Classical Music, Heavy Metal, Jimi Hendrix, Led Zeppelin, Nirvana, Opera, Pink Floyd, The Rolling Stones, Soul and R&B, Velvet Underground, World Music
Popular Culture Anime, Classic Novels, Conspiracy Theories, Crime Fiction, The Da Vinci Code, Graphic Novels, Hidden Treasures, His Dark Materials, Hitchhiker's Guide to the Galaxy, The Lost Symbol, Manga, Next Big Thing, Shakespeare, True Crime, Tutankhamun, Unexplained Phenomena, Videogames
Science The Brain, Climate Change, The Earth, Energy Crisis, Evolution, Future, Genes & Cloning, The Universe, Weather

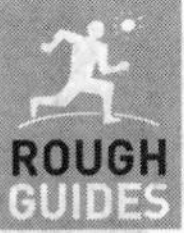

For more information go to www.roughguides.com

www.roughguides.com

nformation on over 25,000 destinations around the world

- **Read** Rough Guides' trusted travel info
- **Access** exclusive articles from Rough Guides authors
- **Update** yourself on new books, maps, CDs and other products
- **Enter** our competitions and win travel prizes
- **Share** ideas, journals, photos & travel advice with other users
- **Earn** points every time you contribute to the Rough Guide community and get rewards

NOTES

NOTES

NOTES

NOTES

NOTES

NOTES

Small print and Index

A Rough Guide to Rough Guides

Published in 1982, the first Rough Guide – to Greece – was a student scheme that became a publishing phenomenon. Mark Ellingham, a recent graduate in English from Bristol University, had been travelling in Greece the previous summer and couldn't find the right guidebook. With a small group of friends he wrote his own guide, combining a highly contemporary, journalistic style with a thoroughly practical approach to travellers' needs.

The immediate success of the book spawned a series that rapidly covered dozens of destinations. And, in addition to impecunious backpackers, Rough Guides soon acquired a much broader and older readership that relished the guides' wit and inquisitiveness as much as their enthusiastic, critical approach and value-for-money ethos.

These days, Rough Guides include recommendations from shoestring to luxury and cover more than 200 destinations around the globe, including almost every country in the Americas and Europe, more than half of Africa and most of Asia and Australasia. Our ever-growing team of authors and photographers is spread all over the world, particularly in Europe, the US and Australia.

In the early 1990s, Rough Guides branched out of travel, with the publication of Rough Guides to World Music, Classical Music and the Internet. All three have become benchmark titles in their fields, spearheading the publication of a wide range of books under the Rough Guide name.

Including the travel series, Rough Guides now number more than 350 titles, covering: phrasebooks, waterproof maps, music guides from Opera to Heavy Metal, reference works as diverse as Conspiracy Theories and Shakespeare, and popular culture books from iPods to Poker. Rough Guides also produce a series of more than 120 World Music CDs in partnership with World Music Network.

Visit www.roughguides.com to see our latest publications.

Rough Guide credits

Text editor: Emma Gibbs and Harry Wilson
Layout: Ajay Verma
Cartography: Rajesh Mishra
Picture editor: Jess Carter
Production: Rebecca Short
Proofreader: Jan McCann and Naori Priestly
Cover design: Nicole Newman, Dan May
Photographer: Martin Richardson
Editorial: **London** Andy Turner, Keith Drew, Edward Aves, Alice Park, Lucy White, Jo Kirby, James Smart, Natasha Foges, Róisín Cameron, James Rice, Emma Beatson, Kathryn Lane, Monica Woods, Mani Ramaswamy, Lucy Cowie, Alison Roberts, Lara Kavanagh, Eleanor Aldridge, Ian Blenkinsop, Joe Staines, Matthew Milton, Tracy Hopkins; **Delhi** Madhavi Singh, Jalpreen Kaur Chhatwal, Jubbi Francis
Design & Pictures: **London** Scott Stickland, Dan May, Diana Jarvis, Mark Thomas, Nicole Newman, Sarah Cummins, Emily Taylor; **Delhi** Umesh Aggarwal, Jessica Subramanian, Ankur Guha, Pradeep Thapliyal, Sachin Tanwar, Anita Singh, Nikhil Agarwal, Sachin Gupta
Production: Liz Cherry, Louise Daly, Erika Pepe
Cartography: **London** Ed Wright, Katie Lloyd-Jones; **Delhi** Rajesh Chhibber, Ashutosh Bharti, Animesh Pathak, Jasbir Sandhu, Swati Handoo, Deshpal Dabas, Lokamata Sahu
Online: **London** Faye Hellon, Jeanette Angell, Fergus Day, Justine Bright, Clare Bryson, Aine Fearon, Adrian Low, Ezgi Celebi; **Delhi** Amit Verma, Rahul Kumar, Narender Kumar, Ravi Yadav, Debojit Borah, Rakesh Kumar, Ganesh Sharma, Shisir Basumatari
Marketing & Publicity: **London** Liz Statham, Jess Carter, Vivienne Watton, Anna Paynton, Rachel Sprackett, Laura Vipond; **New York** Katy Ball; **Delhi** Aman Arora
Digital Travel Publisher: Peter Buckley
Reference Director: Andrew Lockett
Operations Assistant: Becky Doyle
Operations Manager: Helen Atkinson
Publishing Director (Travel): Clare Currie
Commercial Manager: Gino Magnotta
Managing Director: John Duhigg

Publishing information

This fifth edition published February 2011 by
Rough Guides Ltd,
80 Strand, London WC2R 0RL
11, Community Centre, Panchsheel Park, New Delhi 110017, India
Distributed by the Penguin Group
Penguin Books Ltd,
80 Strand, London WC2R 0RL
Penguin Group (USA)
375 Hudson Street, NY 10014, USA
Penguin Group (Australia)
250 Camberwell Road, Camberwell, Victoria 3124, Australia
Penguin Group (NZ)
67 Apollo Drive, Mairangi Bay, Auckland 1310, New Zealand
Rough Guides is represented in Canada by Tourmaline Editions Inc. 662 King Street West, Suite 304, Toronto, Ontario M5V 1M7
Cover concept by Peter Dyer.
Typeset in Bembo and Helvetica to an original design by Henry Iles.
Printed in Italy by L.E.G.O. S.p.A, Lavis (TN)

872pp includes index
A catalogue record for this book is available from the British Library
ISBN: 978-1-84836-615-2

1 3 5 7 9 8 6 4 2

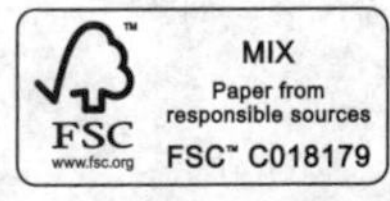

Help us update

We've gone to a lot of effort to ensure that the fifth edition of **The Rough Guide to Japan** is accurate and up-to-date. However, things change – places get "discovered", opening hours are notoriously fickle, restaurants and rooms raise prices or lower standards. If you feel we've got it wrong or left something out, we'd like to know, and if you can remember the address, the price, the hours, the phone number, so much the better.

Please send your comments with the subject line "**Rough Guide Japan Update**" to Ⓔmail @uk.roughguides.com. We'll credit all contributions and send a copy of the next edition (or any other Rough Guide if you prefer) for the very best emails.

Find more travel information, connect with fellow travellers and book your trip on Ⓦwww .roughguides.com

Acknowledgements

Sophie Branscombe Many thanks to Kylie at JNTO London, Helen and Mark at JAL, Simon for the gig – and the fire festival – and all the RG team. Thanks also to KC & Hideto for fun in the snow, Shirakami-kun and Paddy for a messy night out in Hiroshima, *Sumiyoshi Bed & Bicycle* for the welcome, and Dom & Yuri for saving the best *okonomiyaki* till last. Much gratitude, as always, to all my Kurayoshi pals and the Amakusa posse, and finally to Chris the Bish for keeping the home fires burning, and the kitchen-fitters at bay.

Rob Goss A very big thank you to: Sarah Joff and the team at JNTO London; Yoshimune Nakamura at the Nikkanren; Tanaka-san for a fascinating tour around Zuigan-ji in Matsushima; fellow Stones fan Daisuke Hagihara at *Shodoshima Olive Youth Hostel* for a great day exploring the island; the dancers at Awa Odori Kaikan for letting me on stage, and the audience for not laughing too much. A big *kampai* to everyone else who made traveling Shikoku and Tohoku such an unforgettable experience. Most of all though, love and thanks to Yoko and Arthur for putting up with my travels, and for making home the perfect place to come back to.

Simon Richmond Shout outs go to the following people: Kylie Clark and her colleagues at JNTO; Homma Yuko and Noriko Naito at TCVB; William Andrews from TAB; James Mutter and colleagues at Prince Hotels; Yoshimune Nakamura at the Japan Ryokan & Hotel Association; Minami Tomoko and colleagues at Hikari Home; Ed Yakumo and the folks at Mitsubishi Estates; Max Hodges and Joseph Tame; Patrick Galbraith; James Hadfield; super tour leader Tatsuya Yamazawa; the ever-errudite Giles Murray; friends Toshiko and Kenichi. In Hokkaido thanks to Saito Nobumichi, Scott Tovey, Chris Chan, Shouya Grigg, Stefan Stosik and Arudou Debito. Cheers also to Mark Hammond in Kanazawa, Matt Goldman (aka Madame Matty) and Evgeniy Podolskiy in Nagoya and Keiji Shimizu in Kyoto. This book would not exist without the hard work of my original co-author Jan, contributors Amy, Jean, Martin, Rob, Sally and Sophie and editors Emma and Harry. As ever it's dedicated to Tonny for patiently waiting for me at home and support along the way.

Jean Snow Thanks to my loving wife, for the patience and support, and to my editors, for helping to make me more readable.

Martin Zatko Thanks to the JTO for their assistance, the tourist information staff at Okinawa airport for their patience and kindness, Iriomote-jima and Taketomi-jima for rescuing me from a bitter winter, and the British Embassy staff in Tokyo for taking rare diplomatic pity on my soul by processing my new passport in record time. Thanks also to the wonderful people whom I had the fortune to meet on the way; their names would fill a book on their own, but special mentions to the power-ballad-loving Dutch trio (and bike-riding Brazilian) in Naha, as well as Chika Kimura in Kagoshima, who has since gone on to become a regular travel buddy.

Readers' letters

Thanks to all the readers who have taken the time to write in with comments and suggestions (and apologies if we've inadvertently omitted or misspelt anyone's name):

Melanie Dudley, Peter Fine, John Gorick, Zoe Hoida, Bernard Holley, Anna Langstone, Alexis Le-Quoc, André Manook, Adam Newman, Zeljko Novacic, Trina and Geoff Stickland, James Tartaglia, Adrienne Thunder, Bill Wang, Eleanor Wason

Photo credits

All photos © Rough Guides except the following:

Introduction

Floating torii at Itsukushima © Chris Pritchard/ iStockphoto
Commuters in Akihabara Electric Town © Tom Bonaventure/Getty Images
Fuji with Mt. Fuji in the background © Adina Tovy/Robert Harding World Imagery/Corbis
Bamboo forest © airportrait/ iStockphoto
Shinkansen © B.S.P.I./Corbis
Man and robot © Yoshikazu Tsuno © Yoshikazu Tsuno/AFP/Getty Images
Macaques in onsen © Andrew Evans/ iStockphoto
Geisha on metro © Jean_Baptiste Rabouan/ Hemis/Corbis
Monk statues © Paul Whitton/iStockphoto
Sushi restaurant © B.S.P.I./Corbis
Fuji TV headquarters © Gavin Hellier/Corbis

Things not to miss

01 Golden Temple © DAJ/Getty Images/amana images
02 Skiing, Niseko © Scott Markewitz/Getty Images
03 Fireworks © Photolibrary
05 Ice sculptures © Wolfgang Kaehler/Corbis
06 Buddha at Nara © Junko Kimura/Getty Images AsiaPac
07 Naoshima pumpkin © Washington Post/Getty Images
08 Hiroshima © Photolibrary
09 Koya-san © Ernst Haas/Getty Images
10 Kabuki © Koichi Kamoshida/Getty Images
11 Tsumago hotels © Kazuhiro Tomaru/Sebun Photo/Getty Images/Sebun
12 Earth Celebration © JNTO
13 Kaiseki-ryōri © Alberto Paredes/Alamy
14 Cedar tree roots © Karin Slade/Getty Images
15 Mount Fuji at sunrise © Mark Harris/Getty Images
16 Ryokan © Michael Freeman/Corbis
17 Awa Odori © Tokushima Prefecture/JNTO
18 Taketomi-jima © Photolibrary
19 Sumo © Photolibrary
20 Nikkō © Daryl Benson/Getty Images
21 Kamikochi © Photolibrary
22 Kumano Kodō © Everett Kennedy Brown/ Corbis
23 Onsen © Tohoku Color Agency/Getty Images/ Tohoku
24 Sake © Rudy Sulgan/Corbis
25 Himeji © Gavin Hellier/Getty Images
26 Golden Gai © T.Lehne/Lotuseaters/Alamy
27 Roppongi Art Night © Franck Robichon/Corbis
28 Kenroku-en © David Bartruff/Corbis
29 Ogimachi © Photolibrary

Manga & anime colour section

Man passing comics shop © Jochen Tack/Alamy
Sazai Hall of the Five-Hundred-Rakan Temple © Christie's Images/Corbis
Illustration on locker © B.S.P.I./Corbis
Howl's Moving Castle © The Kobal Collection
Stained glass © Jeremy Sutton-Hibert/Alamy
Akira poster © The Kobal Collection
Astro Boy © Jon Hicks/Corbis
Character mural © Alex Segre/Alamy
Tetsujin © Sankei/Getty Images
Manga Museum © Jean-Baptiste Rabouan/ Hemis/Corbis

Regional cuisine colour section

Traditional soba delivery © mikecranephotography .com/Alamy
Men eating ramen © Camelot/Getty Images
Noodle making © Tokushima Prefecture/JNTO
Hakodate crabs © Iain Masterton/Alamy
Mongolian mutton barbecue © Hokkaido Tourism Organization/JNTO
Okinawa market © Allison Emily Maletz/Getty Images
Shōchū bottle and cup © John Lander/Alamy

Festival fun colour section

Kumano Nachi Fire Festival © Sankei/Getty Images
Adult's Day © Tibor Bognar/Alamy
Cherry blossom viewing © Frank Kletschkus/ Alamy
Fireworks © Photolibrary
Sanja Matsuri © Photolibrary
Kanamara Matsuri © frank'n'focus/Alamy
Hadaka Matsuri © Alan Howden/Alamy

Black and whites

p.170 Buddha © Mangesh Ambetkar/ iStockphoto
p.226 Kinkasan © MIXA Co. Ltd./Photolibrary
p.284 Cable car © Yoshio Tomii Photo Studio/ Photolibrary
p.336 Matsumoto Castle © Katsuhiro Yamanashi/ Getty Images/Sebun
p.402 Manga Museum © Jean-Baptiste Rabouan/ Hemis/Corbis
p.478 Kumano Ancient Road © JNTO
p.526 Itsukushima Shrine © Junko Kimura/Getty Images AsiaPac
p.592 Oboke © DAJ/Getty Images/amana images
p.650 Food stalls © Tibor Bognar/Corbis
p.728 Whale sharks © Yuriko Nakao/Reuters/ Corbis

Index

Map entries are in colour.

C

D

E

F

L

M

N

INDEX

O

P

R

S

INDEX

U

V

W

Y

Z